MyManagementLab®: Improves Student Engagement Before, During, and After Class

Prep and Engagement

- **Personal Inventory** ... promote self-reflection and engagem... ...ect what they are learning to their pe... ...ong with a graphic display that sh... ...s will also have access to this graphic ...

- **NEW! VIDEO LIBR...** ...os that include easy-to-assign assessm... ...he ability for students to upload vid...

- **Decision-making si...** ...ce your students in the role of a key de... ...make, providing a variation of scenario... grade, as well as a deta... associated consequenc...

- **Video exercises – U...** Engaging videos that b... explore business topic... are learning in class. C... comprehension of the...

- **Learning Catalytic...** student engagement,... intelligence system he... critical-thinking skills...

- **Dynamic Study M...** ...ough adaptive learning, students get... ...g greater engagement, improvi... ...lso available on mobile devices.

Critical Thinking

turnitin

- **Writing Space – UPDATED with new commenting tabs, new prompts, and a new tool for students called Pearson Writer.** A single location to develop and assess concept mastery and critical thinking, the Writing Space offers assisted graded and create your own writing assignments, allowing you to exchange personalized feedbac...

Writing Space can also check students... ...y comparing it against the world's most accurate text compa...

...sonmylabandmastering.com

913SE

PEARSON

Organizational Behavior

Organizational Behavior

EDITION

17

GLOBAL EDITION

Stephen P. Robbins
—San Diego State University

Timothy A. Judge
—University of Notre Dame

PEARSON

Boston   Columbus   Indianapolis   New York   San Francisco   Amsterdam
Cape Town   Dubai   London   Madrid   Milan   Munich   Paris   Montreal   Toronto
Delhi   Mexico City   São Paulo   Sydney   Hong Kong   Seoul   Singapore   Taipei   Tokyo

Vice President, Business Publishing: Donna Battista
Editor-in-Chief: Stephanie Wall
Senior Acquisitions Editor: Kris Ellis-Levy
Development Editor: Elisa Adams
Editorial Assistant: Lauren Russell
Vice President, Product Marketing: Maggie Moylan
**Director of Marketing, Digital Services
   and Products:** Jeanette Koskinas
Executive Field Marketing Manager: Adam Goldstein
Field Marketing Manager: Lenny Ann Kucenski
Product Marketing Assistant: Jessica Quazza
Team Lead, Program Management: Ashley Santora
Program Manager: Sarah Holle
Team Lead, Project Management: Jeff Holcomb
Project Manager: Kelly Warsak
Project Manager, Global Edition: Sudipto Roy
Editorial Assistant, Global Edition: Alice Dazeley
Senior Project Editor, Global Edition: Daniel Luiz
Manager, Media Production, Global Edition: M. Vikram Kumar

**Senior Manufacturing Controller, Production,
   Global Edition:** Trudy Kimber
Operations Specialist: Carol Melville
Creative Director: Blair Brown
Art Director: Janet Slowik
**Vice President, Director of Digital Strategy and
   Assessment:** Paul Gentile
Manager of Learning Applications: Paul DeLuca
Digital Editor: Brian Surette
Director, Digital Studio: Sacha Laustsen
Digital Studio Manager: Diane Lombardo
Digital Studio Project Manager:
Monique Lawrence
Digital Studio Project Manager: Alana Coles
Digital Studio Project Manager: Robin Lazrus
**Full-Service Project Management, Composition,
   Interior Design:** Integra
Cover Photo: © Dudarev Mikhail/Shutterstock
Cover Designer: Lumina Datamatics Ltd.

Pearson Education Limited
Edinburgh Gate
Harlow
Essex CM20 2JE
England

and Associated Companies throughout the world

Visit us on the World Wide Web at:
www.pearsonglobaleditions.com

© Pearson Education Limited 2017

ISBN 10: 1-292-14630-3
ISBN 13: 978-1-292-14630-0

British Library Cataloguing-in-Publication Data
A catalogue record for this book is available from the British Library.

10 9 8 7 6 5 4 3 2
18 17

Typeset in New Baskerville ITC Pro Roman by Integra.
Printed and bound by Lego in Italy.

Brief Contents

4 | The Organization System

Contents

2 | The Individual

4   *Emotions and Moods* 138

5 *Personality and Values* 172

8 *Motivation: From Concepts to Applications* 280

3 The Group

9 *Foundations of Group Behavior* 312

10   *Understanding Work Teams* 348

11   *Communication* 380

12 *Leadership* 418

13 *Power and Politics* 458

14   *Conflict and Negotiation* 494

15   *Foundations of Organization Structure* 528

4 The Organization System

16 *Organizational Culture* 562

17 *Human Resource Policies and Practices* 598

18 *Organizational Change and Stress Management* 640

Appendix **Research in Organizational Behavior** 682

Comprehensive Cases 689

Stephen P. Robbins

Education

Ph.D., University of Arizona

Professional Experience

Academic Positions: Professor, San Diego State University, Southern Illinois University at Edwardsville, University of Baltimore, Concordia University in Montreal, and University of Nebraska at Omaha.

Research: Research interests have focused on conflict, power, and politics in organizations; behavioral decision making; and the development of effective interpersonal skills.

Books Published: World's best-selling author of textbooks in both management and organizational behavior. His books have sold more than 5 million copies and have been translated into 20 languages; editions have been adapted for Canada, Australia, South Africa, and India, such as these:

- *Essentials of Organizational Behavior,* 12th ed. (Prentice Hall, 2014)
- *Management,* 12th ed. with Mary Coulter (Prentice Hall, 2014)
- *Fundamentals of Human Resource Management,* 10th ed., with David DeCenzo (Wiley, 2010)
- *Prentice Hall's Self-Assessment Library 3.4* (Prentice Hall, 2010)
- *Fundamentals of Management,* 8th ed., with David DeCenzo and Mary Coulter (Prentice Hall, 2013)
- *Supervision Today!* 7th ed., with David DeCenzo and Robert Wolter (Prentice Hall, 2013)
- *Training in Interpersonal Skills: TIPS for Managing People at Work,* 6th ed., with Phillip Hunsaker (Prentice Hall, 2012)
- *Managing Today!* 2nd ed. (Prentice Hall, 2000)
- *Organization Theory,* 3rd ed. (Prentice Hall, 1990)
- *The Truth About Managing People,* 2nd ed. (Financial Times/Prentice Hall, 2008)
- *Decide and Conquer: Make Winning Decisions and Take Control of Your Life* (Financial Times/Prentice Hall, 2004).

Other Interests

In his "other life," Dr. Robbins actively participates in masters' track competition. After turning 50 in 1993, he won 18 national championships and 12 world titles. He is the current world record holder at 100 meters (12.37 seconds) and 200 meters (25.20 seconds) for men 65 and over.

Timothy A. Judge

Education

Ph.D., University of Illinois at Urbana-Champaign

Professional Experience

Academic Positions: Associate Dean for Faculty and Research, University of Notre Dame; Franklin D. Schurz Chair, Department of Management, Mendoza College of Business, University of Notre Dame; Concurrent Professor, Department of Psychology, University of Notre Dame; Visiting Distinguished Adjunct Professor of King Abdulaziz University, Saudi Arabia; Visiting Professor, Division of Psychology & Language Sciences, University College London; Matherly-McKethan Eminent Scholar in Management, Warrington College of Business Administration, University of Florida; Stanley M. Howe Professor in Leadership, Henry B. Tippie College of Business, University of Iowa; Associate Professor (with tenure), Department of Human Resource Studies, School of Industrial and Labor Relations, Cornell University; Lecturer, Charles University, Czech Republic, and Comenius University, Slovakia; Instructor, Industrial/Organizational Psychology, Department of Psychology, University of Illinois at Urbana-Champaign.

Research: Dr. Judge's primary research interests are in (1) personality, moods, and emotions; (2) job attitudes; (3) leadership and influence behaviors; and (4) careers (person–organization fit, career success). Dr. Judge has published more than 154 articles on these and other major topics in journals such as *Journal of Organizational Behavior, Personnel Psychology, Academy of Management Journal, Journal of Applied Psychology, European Journal of Personality*, and *European Journal of Work and Organizational Psychology*. He serves as Director of Research for Stay Metrics Corporation, linking his research with application in the trucking industry.

Fellowship: Dr. Judge is a fellow of the American Psychological Association, the Academy of Management, the Society for Industrial and Organizational Psychology, and the American Psychological Society.

Awards: In 1995, Dr. Judge received the Ernest J. McCormick Award for Distinguished Early Career Contributions from the Society for Industrial and Organizational Psychology. In 2001, he received the Larry L. Cummings Award for mid-career contributions from the Organizational Behavior Division of the Academy of Management. In 2007, he received the Professional Practice Award from the Institute of Industrial and Labor Relations, University of Illinois. In 2008, he received the University of Florida Doctoral Mentoring Award. And in 2012, he received the Editorial Board of the European Journal of Work and Organizational Psychology (EJWOP) best paper of the year award.

Other Books Published: H. G. Heneman III, T. A. Judge, and J. D. Kammeyer-Mueller, *Staffing Organizations*, 8th ed. (Mishawaka, IN: Pangloss Industries, 2015).

Other Interests

Although he cannot keep up (literally!) with Dr. Robbins' accomplishments on the track, Dr. Judge enjoys golf, cooking and baking, literature (he's a particular fan of Thomas Hardy and is a member of the Thomas Hardy Society), and keeping up with his three children, who range in age from adult to middle school.

Preface

Welcome to the seventeenth edition of *Organizational Behavior!* Long considered the standard for all organizational behavior textbooks, this edition continues its tradition of making current, relevant topics come alive for students. While maintaining its hallmark features—engaging writing style, cutting-edge content, and intuitive pedagogy—this edition has been significantly updated to reflect the most recent research and current business events within the field of organizational behavior worldwide. The seventeenth edition is one of the most contemporary revisions of *Organizational Behavior* we've undertaken, and while we've preserved the core relevant material, we're confident that this edition reflects the most important issues facing organizations, managers, and employees today with a balanced, discerning approach.

Key Changes to the Seventeenth Edition

- *NEW* Feature in every chapter! *Career OBjectives* in advice, question-and-answer format to help students think through issues they may face in the workforce today.
- *NEW Opening Vignette* in every chapter to bring current business trends and events to the forefront.
- *NEW* **key terms presented in bold** throughout the text (up to three new per chapter) highlight new vocabulary pertinent to today's study of organizational behavior.
- *NEW* **photos and captions** in every chapter link the chapter content to contemporary real-life worldwide situations to enhance the student's understanding of hands-on application of concepts.
- *NEW* These feature topics are either **completely new or substantially updated** within each chapter as applicable to reflect ongoing challenges in business worldwide and focus the student's attention on new topics:
  - *Learning Objectives* (in 15 chapters)
  - *Exhibits* (15 throughout the text)
  - *Myth or Science?* (8 of 18 total)
  - *An Ethical Choice* (10 of 18 total)
  - *Point/Counterpoint* (8 of 18 total)
- *NEW* The following end-of-chapter material is either **completely new or substantially revised and updated** for each chapter to bring the most contemporary thinking to the attention of students:
  - *Summary* (4 of 18 total)
  - *Implications for Managers* (11 of 18 total)
  - *Questions for Review* (in 16 chapters)
  - *Experiential Exercise* (12 of 18 total)
  - *Ethical Dilemma* (14 of 18 total)
  - *Case Incidents* (25 of 36 total)

MyManagementLab Suggested Activities

For the 17th edition the author is excited that Pearson's MyManagementLab has been integrated fully into the text. These new features are outlined below.

Making assessment activities available on line for students to complete before coming to class will allow you the professor more discussion time during the class to review areas that students are having difficulty in comprehending.

Learn It

Students can be assigned the Chapter Warm-Up before coming to class. Assigning these questions ahead of time will ensure that students are coming to class prepared.

Personal Inventory Assessments (PIA)

Students learn better when they can connect what they're learning to their personal experience. PIA (Personal Inventory Assessments) is a collection of online exercises designed to promote self-reflection and student engagement, enhancing their ability to connect with concepts taught in principles of management, organizational behavior, and human resource management classes. Assessments are assignable by instructors who can then track students completions. Student results include a written explanation along with a graphic display that shows how their results compare to the class as a whole. Instructors will also have access to this graphic representation of results to promote classroom discussion.

Watch It!

Recommends a video clip that can be assigned to students for outside classroom viewing or that can be watched in the classroom. The video corresponds to the chapter material and is accompanied by multiple choice questions that re-enforce the student's comprehension of the chapter content.

Try It!

Recommends a mini simulation that can be assigned to students as an outside classroom activity or it can be done in the classroom. As the students watch the simulation, they will be asked to make choices based on the scenario presented in the simulation. At the end of the simulation, the student will receive immediate feedback based on the answers they gave. These simulations re-enforce the concepts of the chapter and the students, comprehension of those concepts.

Talk About It

These are discussion questions that can be assigned as an activity within the classroom.

Assisted Graded Writing Questions

These are short essay questions that the students can complete as an assignment and submit to you the professor for grading.

Chapter Quiz

These are review questions that can be assigned to students to answer upon completion of the chapter, this gradeable activity allows you the professor to see if the students have comprehended the chapter's content.

Chapter-by-Chapter Changes

Chapter 1: What Is Organizational Behavior?

- New *Opening Vignette* (China's Prominent Business Leader Revives a Troubled Bank)
- New Feature! *Try It* (Simulation: What Is Management?)

- New research in The Importance of Interpersonal Skills
- New Feature! *Watch It (Herman Miller: Organizational Behavior)*
- Newly revised section: Management and Organizational Behavior
- Updated *Myth or Science?* (Management by Walking Around Is the Most Effective Management)
- New research in Big Data
- New section: Current Usage
- New section: New Trends
- New section: Limitations
- New research in Overseeing Movement of Jobs to Countries with Low-Cost Labor
- New research in Adapting to Differing Cultural and Regulatory Norms
- New major section: Workforce Demographics
- New research in Customer Service
- New major section: Social Media
- New research in Positive Work Environment
- New research in Ethical Behavior
- New Feature! *Career OBjectives* (What do I say about my termination?)
- Updated *OB Poll* (Percentage of Men and Women Working)
- New Feature! *Personal Inventory Assessment* (Multicultural Awareness Scale)
- New section in Withdrawal Behavior
- New international research in Productivity
- Revised *Questions for Review*
- New *Point/Counterpoint* (The Battle of the Texts)
- New *Experiential Exercise* (Managing the OB Way)
- New *Ethical Dilemma* (There's a Drone in Your Soup)
- Updated *Case Incident 1* (Apple Goes Global)
- New *Case Incident 2* (Big Data for Dummies)

Chapter 2: Diversity in Organizations

- Revised *Learning Objectives*
- New *Opening Vignette (*Exploiting a Loophole)
- Revised section: Demographic Characteristics
- Updated *OB Poll* (Gender Pay Gap: Narrowing but Still There)
- Updated *An Ethical Choice* (Affirmative Action for Unemployed Veterans)
- New major section: Stereotype Threat
- New Feature! *Personal Inventory Assessment* (Intercultural Sensitivity Scale)
- New research in Discrimination in the Workplace
- Updated *Myth or Science?* (Bald Is Better)
- New research and section in Age
- New international research in Sex
- New international research in Race and Ethnicity
- New international research in Disabilities
- New major section: Hidden Disabilities
- New international research in Religion
- New international research in Sexual Orientation and Gender Identity
- New Feature! *Career OBjectives* (Is it okay to be gay at work?)
- New Feature! *Watch It* (Verizon: Diversity)
- New research in Intellectual Abilities
- Major new section: Hidden Disabilities
- New international research in Physical Abilities
- New research in Diversity in Groups
- New Feature! *Try It* (Simulation: Human Resources and Diversity)
- Updated *Implications for Managers*

- New/updated *Point/Counterpoint* (Affirmative Action Programs Have Outlived Their Usefulness)
- Revised *Questions for Review*
- New *Experiential Exercise* (Differences)
- New/updated *Ethical Dilemma* (The 30% Club in Hong Kong Aims to Uphold Board Diversity)
- New *Case Incident 1* (Walking the Walk)
- New/updated *Case Incident 2* (The Encore Career)

Chapter 3: Attitudes and Job Satisfaction

- Revised *Learning Objectives*
- New *Opening Vignette* (Patching Together a Career)
- New Feature! *Watch It* (Gawker Media: Attitudes and Job Satisfaction)
- New *An Ethical Choice* (Office Talk)
- New *Exhibit 3-2* (Worst Jobs of 2014 for Job Satisfaction)
- New research in How Satisfied Are People in Their Jobs?
- New section: Job Conditions
- New section: Personality
- New Feature! *Personal Inventory Assessment* (Core Self-Evaluation [CSE] Scale)
- New *Exhibit 3-5* (Relationship Between Average Pay in Job and Job Satisfaction of Employees in That Job)
- New major section: Corporate Social Responsibility (CSR)
- New research in Organizational Citizenship Behavior (OCB)
- New section: Life Satisfaction
- New Feature! *Career OBjectives* (How can I make my job better?)
- New major section: Counterproductive Work Behavior (CWB)
- Revised *Implications for Managers*
- New/updated *Point/Counterpoint* (Employer-Employee Loyalty Is an Outdated Concept)
- Revised *Questions for Review*
- New *Experiential Exercise* (What Satisfies You about Your Dream Job?)
- New *Ethical Dilemma* (Because It's Worth It?)
- Updated *Case Incident 1* (The Pursuit of Happiness: Flexibility)
- Updated *Case Incident 2* (Job Crafting)

Chapter 4: Emotions and Moods

- Revised *Learning Objectives*
- New *Opening Vignette* (The Lasting Consequences of Our Emotions)
- New international research in The Basic Emotions
- Updated *Myth or Science?* (Smile, and the Work World Smiles with You)
- New research and discussion in Moral Emotions
- Updated *Exhibit 4-2* (The Structure of Mood)
- New international research in Experiencing Moods and Emotions
- New research in The Functions of Emotions
- New research in Do Emotions Make Us Ethical?
- New research in Time of the Day
- New research and discussion in Sleep
- New research and discussion in Emotional Labor
- New research and discussion in Emotional Intelligence
- Updated *An Ethical Choice* (Should Managers Use Emotional Intelligence [EI] Tests?)
- New section in Emotion Regulation Influences and Outcomes
- New section in Emotion Regulation Techniques
- New section: Ethics of Emotion Regulation

- New Feature! *Career OBjectives* (How do I turn down the volume on my screaming boss?)
- New research in Safety and Injury at Work
- Revised *Implications for Managers*
- New Feature! *Emotional Intelligence Assessment*
- Updated *Point/Counterpoint* (Sometimes Yelling Is for Everyone's Good)
- Revised *Questions for Review*
- New *Experiential Exercise* (The Happiness Test)
- New *Ethical Dilemma* (Data Mining Emotions)
- Updated *Case Incident 1* (Crybabies)
- New *Case Incident 2* (Tall Poppy Syndrome)

Chapter 5: Personality and Values

- Revised *Learning Objectives*
- New *Opening Vignette* (Secrets of a Successful Entrepreneur)
- New research in What is Personality?
- New international research and discussion in Measuring Personality
- New Feature! *Career OBjectives* (How do I ace the personality test?)
- New introduction in Personality Frameworks
- New section in The Myers-Briggs Type Indicator
- New research and discussion in The Big Five Personality Model
- New sections: Conscientiousness at Work, Emotional Stability at Work, Extraversion at Work, Openness at Work, and Agreeableness at Work
- New Feature! *Try It* (Simulation: Individual Behavior)
- New research in The Dark Triad
- New major section: Other Traits
- New/updated *Myth or Science?* (We Can Accurately Judge Individuals' Personalities a Few Seconds After Meeting Them)
- New research and discussion in Proactive Personality
- New research and discussion in Situation Strength Theory
- New Feature! *Watch It* (Honest Tea: Ethics—Company Mission and Values)
- Updated *An Ethical Choice* (Do You Have a Cheating Personality?)
- New international research in Person-Job Fit
- New research and discussion in Person-Organization Fit
- New major section: Other Dimensions of Fit
- New Feature! *Try It* (Simulation: Human Behavior)
- New discussion in Cultural Values
- Revised *Summary*
- Revised *Implications for Managers*
- *New Feature! Personality Inventory Assessment* (Personality Style Indicator)
- New/updated *Point/Counterpoint* (Millennials Are More Narcissistic Than Their Parents)
- Revised *Questions for Review*
- New *Experiential Exercise* (Your Best Self)
- Updated *Case Incident 2* (The Power of Quiet)

Chapter 6: Perception and Individual Decision Making

- Revised *Learning Objectives*
- New *Opening Vignette* (Is Palmer Luckey Lucky or Masterfully Creative?)
- New research and discussion in Perceiver
- New research and discussion in Target
- New research and discussion in Context

- New Feature! *Watch It* (Orpheus Group Casting: Social Perception and Attribution)
- New discussion and research in Person Perception: Making Judgments about Others
- New Feature! *Career OBjectives* (So what if I'm a few minutes late to work?)
- New research in Attribution Theory
- Updated discussion in Halo Effect
- New research and discussion in The Link Between Perception and Individual Decision Making
- New research in Escalation of Commitment
- New Feature! *Try It* (Simulation: Decision Making)
- New research in Gender
- New section: Nudging
- New international research and discussion in Three Ethical Decision Criteria
- New major section: Lying
- New research in Creative Behavior
- New sections created with new research and discussion: Intelligence and Creativity, Personality and Creativity, Expertise and Creativity, Ethics and Creativity
- New section in Creative Environment
- Revised *Implications for Managers*
- New Feature! *Personal Inventory Assessment* (How Creative Are You?)
- Revised *Point-Counterpoint* (Stereotypes Are Dying)
- Revised *Questions for Review*
- New *Experiential Exercise* (Good Liars and Bad Liars)
- New *Case Incident 1* (Too Much of a Good Thing)

Chapter 7: Motivation Concepts

- Revised *Learning Objectives*
- New *Opening Vignette* (Motivated Toward Corporate Social Responsibility)
- New Feature! *Watch It* (Motivation [TWZ Role Play])
- New research and discussion in Hierarchy of Needs Theory
- Updated *Exhibit 7-1* (Maslow's Hierarchy of Needs)
- New international research and discussion in McClelland's Theory of Needs
- New Feature! *Career OBjectives* (Why won't he take my advice?)
- New research and discussion in Self-Determination Theory
- New international research, discussion, and organization in Goal-Setting Theory
- New section: Goal-Setting and Ethics
- New research in Self-Efficacy Theory
- Updated *An Ethical Choice* (Motivated by Big Brother)
- New research and organization in Equity Theory/Organizational Justice
- New section: Ensuring Justice
- New section with international research and discussion: Culture and Justice
- New Feature! *Try It* (Simulation: Motivation)
- New Feature! *Personal Inventory Assessment* (Work Motivation Indicator)
- Revised *Questions for Review*
- New *Ethical Dilemma* (The New GPA)
- New *Case Incident 1* (The Demotivation of CEO Pay)
- New *Case Incident 2* (The Sleepiness Epidemic)

Chapter 8: Motivation: From Concepts to Applications

- New *Opening Vignette* (Motivated to Risk It All)
- Updated *Exhibit 8-1* (The Job Characteristics Model)

- New section, international research, and discussion in The Job Characteristics Model
- New research and discussion in Job Rotation
- New/updated *Myth or Science?* (Money Can't Buy Happiness)
- New section and research in Relational Job Design
- New Feature! *Personal Inventory Assessment* (Need for Team Building)
- New research in Flextime
- New research in Job Sharing
- New Feature! *Career OBjectives* (How can I get flextime?)
- New research and discussion in Telecommuting
- New international research and discussion in Employee Involvement and Participation
- New research in Participative Management
- New research in Representative Participation
- New section, research, and discussion in How to Pay: Rewarding Individual Employees Through Variable-Pay Programs
- New section, international research, and discussion in Piece-Rate Pay
- New research in Merit-Based Pay
- New international research in Bonuses
- New international research in Profit-Sharing Plans
- New research in Employee Stock Ownership Plans
- New/updated section: Evaluation of Variable Pay
- Updated *An Ethical Choice* (Sweatshops and Worker Safety)
- New section and international research in Flexible Benefits: Developing a Benefits Package
- New research in Employee Recognition Programs
- New Feature! *Watch It* (Zappos: Motivating Employees Through Company Culture)
- Revised *Questions for Review*
- New *Case Incident 2* (Pay Raises Every Day)

Chapter 9: Foundations of Group Behavior

- Revised *Learning Objectives*
- New *Opening Vignette* (Crushed by the Herd)
- New major section: Social Identity
- New section: Ingroups and Outgroups
- New section: Social Identity Threat
- New Feature! *Watch It* (Witness.org: Managing Groups & Teams)
- New section: Role Perception
- New section: Role Expectations
- New section: Role Conflict
- New section: Role Play and Assimilation
- New *Myth or Science?* (Gossip and Exclusion Are Toxic for Groups)
- New research in Group Property 2: Norms
- New section: Norms and Emotions
- New research in Norms and Conformity
- Updated *An Ethical Choice*
- New section: Norms and Behavior
- New major section: Positive Norms and Group Outcomes
- New section: Negative Norms and Group Outcomes
- New section: Norms and Culture
- New introduction in new section: Group Property 3: Status and Group Property 4: Size and Dynamics
- New research in Status and Norms

- New research in Status and Group Interaction
- New section: Group Status
- New research in Group Property 4: Size and Dynamics
- New introduction in Group Property 5: Cohesiveness and Group Property 6: Diversity
- New international research in Group Property 6: Diversity
- New Feature! *Personal Inventory Assessment* (Communicating Supportively)
- New international research in Effectiveness and Efficiency
- New Feature! *Career OBjectives* (Can I fudge the numbers and not take the blame?)
- Revised *Implications for Managers*
- Revised *Questions for Review*
- New *Case Incident 2* (Intragroup Trust and Survival)

Chapter 10: Understanding Work Teams

- New *Opening Vignette* (Teams That Play Together Stay Together)
- New research and discussion in Why Have Teams Become So Popular?
- New discussion in Problem-Solving Teams
- New research in Cross-Functional Teams
- New research in Virtual Teams
- New research and discussion in Multiteam Systems
- New Feature! *Watch It* (Teams [TWZ Role Play])
- New research and discussion in Creating Effective Teams
- Revised *Exhibit 10-3* (Team Effectiveness Model)
- New international research in Climate of Trust
- New research in Team Composition
- New research and discussion in Personality of Members
- New section: Cultural Differences
- New Feature! *Career OBjectives* (Is it wrong that I'd rather have guys on my team?)
- New research in Size of Teams
- New major section: Team Identity
- New major section: Team Cohesion
- New international research and discussion in Mental Models
- New international research and discussion in Conflict Levels
- New Feature! *Personal Inventory Assessment* (Team Development Behaviors)
- New Feature! *Try It* (Simulation: Teams)
- Revised *Implications for Managers*
- New *Ethical Dilemma* (The Sum of the Team Is Less Than Its Members)
- Updated *Case Incident 1* (Tongue-Tied in Teams)
- New *Case Incident 2* (Smart Teams and Dumb Teams)

Chapter 11: Communication

- Revised *Learning Objectives*
- New *Opening Vignette* (Curious Communication)
- New research and discussion in Functions of Communication
- New research in Downward Communication
- New section in Upward Communication
- New research and discussion in The Grapevine
- New Feature! *Watch It* (Communication [TWZ Role Play])
- New *Exhibit 11-4* (Dealing with Gossip and Rumors)
- New section in Oral Communication
- Major new section in Meetings
- Major new section in Videoconferencing and Conference Calling

- Major new section in Telephone
- New Feature! *Career OBjectives* (Isn't this too much to accommodate?)
- New research in Letters
- New major section in E-mail
- New research in Social Media Websites
- New section: Apps
- New research in Blogs
- New Feature! *Personal Inventory Assessment* (Communication Styles)
- Updated *Exhibit 11-7* (Information Richness and Communication Channels)
- New research in Choosing Communication Methods
- New Feature! *Try It* (Simulation: Communication)
- New research in Information Overload
- Revised *Questions for Review*
- New *Ethical Dilemma* (BYOD)
- Updated *Case Incident 1* (Organizational Leveraging of Social Media)

Chapter 12: Leadership

- Revised *Learning Objectives*
- New *Opening Vignette* (The Flamboyant Leadership of Jack Ma)
- New Feature! *Watch It* (Leadership [TWZ Role Play])
- New Feature! *Career OBjectives* (How can I get my boss to be a better leader?)
- New international research in Trait Theories
- New introduction in Contemporary Theories of Leadership
- New research in Leader-Member Exchange Theory
- New research in What Is Charismatic Leadership?
- New research in Transactional and Transformational Leadership
- New research in How Transformational Leadership Works
- New international research in Evaluation of Transformational Leadership
- New section Transformational versus Charismatic Leadership
- New Feature! *Personal Inventory Assessment* (Ethical Leadership Assessment)
- New introduction in Responsible Leadership
- New research in Servant Leadership
- New section: Trust and Culture
- New Feature! *Try It* (Simulation: Leadership)
- Revised *Summary*
- Revised *Implications for Managers*
- New *Questions for Review*
- New *Point-Counterpoint* (CEOs Start Early)
- New *Ethical Dilemma* (Smoking Success)
- New *Case Incident 1* (My Holiday the Virgin Way)
- New *Case Incident 2* (Leadership Traits)

Chapter 13: Power and Politics

- Revised *Learning Objectives*
- New *Opening Vignette* (Power in College Sports)
- New Feature! *Watch It* (Power and Political Behavior)
- New Learning Objectives and Questions
- New discussion in Power and Leadership
- Major new section: Social Network Analysis: A Tool for Assessing Resources
- New *Exhibit 13-1* (Sociogram)
- New international research and discussion in Sexual Harassment
- New research and discussion in Individual Factors
- New Feature! *Career OBjectives* (Should I become political?)
- New research and discussion in Organizational Factors
- New research in Impression Management

- New *An Ethical Choice* (How Much Should You Manage Interviewer Impressions?)
- New section: Interviews and IM
- New section: Performance Evaluations and IM
- New Feature! *Personal Inventory Assessment* (Gaining Power and Influence)
- Updated *Point/Counterpoint* (Everyone Wants Power)
- Revised *Questions for Review*
- New *Experiential Exercise* (Comparing Influence Tactics)
- Updated *Case Incident 2* (Barry's Peer Becomes His Boss)

Chapter 14: Conflict and Negotiation

- Revised *Learning Objectives*
- New *Opening Vignette* (A Change of Tune)
- New discussion and organization in A Definition of Conflict
- New international research in Personal Variables
- New research and discussion in Stage IV: Behavior
- New research in Functional Outcomes
- New Feature! *Watch It* (Gordon Law Group: Conflict and Negotiation)
- New international research and discussion in Managing Functional Conflict
- New research in Preparation and Planning
- New Feature! *Career OBjectives* (How can I get a better job?)
- New research and discussion in Personality Traits in Negotiations
- New research and discussion in Gender Differences in Negotiations
- New major section: Negotiating in a Social Context
- New research in Third-Party Negotiations
- Revised *Implications for Managers*
- New Feature! *Personal Inventory Assessment* (Strategies for Handling Conflict)
- Updated *Point-Counterpoint* (Pro Sports Strikes Are Caused by Greedy Owners)
- Revised *Questions for Review*
- New *Experiential Exercise* (A Negotiation Role-Play)
- New *Case Incident 1* (Disorderly Conduct)
- New *Case Incident 2* (Is More Cash Worth the Clash?)

Chapter 15: Foundations of Organization Structure

- New *Learning Objectives*
- New *Opening Vignette* (In the Flat Field)
- Revised *Exhibit 15-1* (Key Design Questions and Answers for Designing the Proper Organizational Structure)
- New section in Departmentalization
- New major section: Boundary Spanning
- New major section: The Functional Structure
- New major section: The Divisional Structure
- New design and discussion in Alternate Design Options
- New section: The Team Structure
- New Feature! *Career OBjectives* (What structure should I choose?)
- New section: The Circular Structure
- New Feature! *Personal Inventory Assessment* (Organizational Structure Assessment)
- New research in The Leaner Organization: Downsizing
- New research in Organizational Strategies
- New international research in Technology

- New major section: Institutions
- New Feature! *Try It* (Simulation: Organizational Structure)
- New Feature! *Watch It* (ZipCar: Organizational Structure)
- Revised *Questions for Review*
- New *Ethical Dilemma* (Post-Millennium Tensions in the Flexible Organization)
- New *Experiential Exercise* (The Sandwich Shop)

Chapter 16: Organizational Culture

- Revised *Learning Objectives*
- New *Opening Vignette* (Welcome to the Machine)
- New discussion on What Is Organizational Culture?
- New major section: Culture and Sustainability
- Updated research in Culture and Innovation
- New section: Strengthening Dysfunctions
- New section in Barriers to Acquisitions and Mergers
- New research in Socialization
- Revised *An Ethical Choice*
- New Feature! *Try It* (Simulation: Organizational Culture)
- New section introduction: Influencing an Organizational Culture
- New section topic: A Positive Culture
- New Feature! *Career OBjectives* (How do I learn to lead?)
- New section topic: The Global Context
- New international research in The Global Context
- New Feature! *Personal Inventory Assessment* (Comfort with Change Scale)
- Revised *Questions for Review*
- New *Experiential Exercise* (Greeting Newcomers)
- New *Ethical Dilemma* (Culture of Deceit)
- New *Case Incident 1* (The Place Makes the People)
- New *Case Incident 2* (Active Cultures)

Chapter 17: Human Resource Policies and Practices

- Revised *Learning Objectives*
- New *Opening Vignette* (Swedish Work-Life Balance Policy Thrives in China)
- Revised *Exhibit 17-1* (Model of Selection Process in Organizations)
- New Feature! *Career OBjectives* (How do I fire someone?)
- New research and discussion in Recruitment Practices
- New research in Written Tests
- New research and discussion in Interviews
- New research and discussion in Civility Training
- New international research and discussion in Evaluating Effectiveness
- New *Exhibit 17-2* (360-Degree Evaluations)
- New research in Providing Performance Feedback
- New Feature! *Try It* (Simulation: HR)
- New major section: Communicating HR Practices
- New research in Designing and Administering Benefit Programs
- Updated *An Ethical Choice* (HIV/AIDS and the Multinational Organization)
- New research in Drafting and Enforcing Employment Policies
- New *Myth or Science?* (The 24-Hour Workplace Is Harmful)
- New research in Managing Work–Life Conflicts
- Revised/updated *Exhibit 17-4* (Work–Life Initiatives)
- New Feature! *Watch It* (Patagonia: Human Resource Management)
- New *Summary*
- Revised *Implications for Managers*
- New Feature! *Personal Inventory Assessment* (Positive Practices Survey)

- New *Point/Counterpoint* (Employers Should Check Applicant Criminal Backgrounds)
- Revised *Questions for Review*
- New *Experiential Exercise* (Designing an Effective Structured Job Interview)
- New *Ethical Dilemma* (Are On-Demand Workers Really Employees?)
- New *Case Incident 1* (Who Are You?)

Chapter 18: Organizational Change and Stress Management

- Revised *Learning Objectives*
- New *Opening Vignette* (Supporting Change from the Bottom Up)
- New research in Change
- New discussion in Forces for Change
- New research and discussion in Planned Change
- New research in Resistance to Change
- New research in Develop Positive Relationships
- New discussion in Coercion
- New Feature! *Try It* (Simulation: Change)
- New major section: Managing Paradox
- New research in Stimulating a Culture of Innovation
- New international research in Sources of Innovation
- New research in Creating a Learning Organization
- New Feature! *Watch It* (East Haven Fire Department: Managing Stress)
- Updated *Exhibit 18-7* (Work Is the Biggest Stress for Most
- Updated *OB Poll* (Many Employees Feel Extreme Stress)
- New research and section in What Is Stress?
- Revised/Updated *Exhibit 18-8* (A Model of Stress)
- New Feature! *Career OBjectives* (How can I bring my team's overall stress level down?)
- New research in Organizational Factors
- New research in Personal Factors
- Updated *Myth or Science?* (When You're Working Hard, Sleep Is Optional)
- New research in Behavioral Symptoms
- New research in Organizational Approaches
- Revised *Summary*
- Revised *Implications for Managers*
- New Feature! *Personal Inventory Assessment* (Tolerance of Ambiguity Scale)
- New *Point/Counterpoint* (Companies Should Encourage Stress Reduction)
- New *Experiential Exercise* (Mindfulness at Work)
- New *Ethical Dilemma* (All Present and Accounted For)
- New *Case Incident 1* (Atos: Zero Email Program)

Instructor Resources

At the Instructor Resource Center, www.pearsonglobaleditions.com/Robbins, instructors can easily register to gain access to a variety of instructor resources available with this text in downloadable format. If assistance is needed, our dedicated technical support team is ready to help with the media supplements that accompany this text. Visit http://247.pearsoned.com for answers to frequently asked questions and toll-free user support phone numbers.

The following supplements are available with this text:

- **Instructor's Resource Manual**
- **Test Bank**
- **TestGen® Computerized Test Bank**
- **PowerPoint Presentation**

Acknowledgments

Getting this book into your hands was a team effort. It took faculty reviewers and a talented group of designers and production specialists, editorial personnel, and marketing and sales staff.

The seventeenth edition was peer reviewed by many experts in the field. Their comments, compliments, and suggestions have significantly improved the final product. The authors would also like to extend their sincerest thanks to the following instructors: Pam DeLotell, Kaplan University; Phil Roth, Clemson University; Jody Tolan, MBA, Lecturer, Management and Organization, University of Southern California Marshall School of Business; Holly A. Schroth, University of California, Berkeley; Jon C. Tomlinson, Ph.D., University of Northwestern Ohio; Andrew Johnson, Santa Clara University; Dr. Alan Goldman, Professor of Management, Faculty Director, W. P. Carey School of Business, Arizona State University West; Dr. Edward F. Lisoski, Angelo State University; E. Anne Christo-Baker, Purdue University North Central; and Dr. Josh Plaskoff, Kelley School of Business—IUPUI.

The authors wish to thank Lori Ehrman Tinkey of the University of Notre Dame and John Kammeyer-Mueller of the University of Minnesota for help with several key aspects of this revision.

We owe a debt of gratitude to all those at Pearson Education who have supported this text over the past 30 years and who have worked so hard on the development of this latest edition. On the development and editorial side, we want to thank Kris Ellis-Levy, Senior Acquisitions Editor; Ashley Santora, Program Manager Team Lead; Sarah Holle, Program Manager; and Elisa Adams, Development Editor. On the design and production side, Jeff Holcomb, Project Manager Team Lead, did an outstanding job, as did Kelly Warsak, Project Manager, and Nancy Moudry, Photo Development Editor. Last but not least, we would like to thank Lenny Ann Kucenski, Marketing Manager; Maggie Moylan, Director of Marketing; and their sales staff, who have been selling this text over its many editions. Thank you for the attention you've given to this text.

Pearson would like to thank the following people for their work on the Global Edition:

Contributors:

Caroline Akhras, *Notre Dame University*
Charbel Aoun, *Lebanese American University*
Iva Bimpli, *University of Leeds*
Lindos Daou, *Holy Spirit University of Kaslik*
Humphry Hung, *Hong Kong Polytechnic University*
Michele Kehoe, *National College of Ireland*
Linzi Kemp, *American University of Sharjah*
Jos Mesu, *Saxion University of Applied Science*
Stephanie Pougnet, *Ecole hôtelière de Lausanne*
Joseph C. Santora, *Ecole des Ponts Business School*
Cecile Schultz, *Tshwane University of Technology*
Matthias Spitzmuller, *The Stephen J.R. Smith School of Business*
Diane Sutherland
John Sutherland
Vimala Venugopal, *Taylor's University*
Randall Zindler, *Lancaster University*

Reviewers:

Evangelos Dedousis, *American University in Dubai*
Richard Jefferies, *University of the West of Scotland*
Lenka Klimplova, *Dalarna University and Masaryk University*
Anthony Lok, *Hong Kong Polytechnic University*
Riani Rachmawati, *Universitas Indonesia*

1

What Is Organizational Behavior?

LEARNING OBJECTIVES

After studying this chapter, you should be able to:

1-1 Demonstrate the importance of interpersonal skills in the workplace.

1-2 Define *organizational behavior (OB)*.

1-3 Show the value to OB of systematic study.

1-4 Identify the major behavioral science disciplines that contribute to OB.

1-5 Demonstrate why few absolutes apply to OB.

1-6 Identify managers' challenges and opportunities in applying OB concepts.

1-7 Compare the three levels of analysis in this text's OB model.

MyManagementLab®
⭐ **Chapter Warm Up**

If your professor has chosen to assign this, go to the Assignments section of **mymanagementlab.com** to complete the chapter warm up.

CHINA'S PROMINENT BUSINESS LEADER REVIVES A TROUBLED BANK

In January 2015, Hong Qi, Chairman of China Minsheng Banking Corporation, one of China's biggest private financial institutions, announced that he would serve as acting president after the then president, Mao Xiaofeng, resigned for personal reasons. There was speculation that Mao had been taken away to help with an investigation led by the Central Commission for Discipline Inspection, China's anti-corruption agency.

Mao's resignation came during a widespread crackdown on corruption by the central government that created great concern among senior government officials, private businessmen, and CEOs of state-owned enterprises in China. *People's Daily*, China's leading newspaper, warned that Minsheng Bank's employees needed to prepare to respond to a possible emergency as a result of the sudden change in top management. As the news broke out, the bank's share price dropped by more than 5 percent.

Hong Qi had been the president of the bank from 2009 to 2014. Mao Xiafeng, 42, with a master's degree from Harvard University, was appointed as President of the bank in 2014 to succeed Hong. Mao joined Minsheng in 2002 and worked as a vice president in charge of retail banking and corporate businesses for many years before being promoted to President. *The Beijing News* reported that Mao allegedly had very close financial relationships with some high officials of the Chinese Government.

In less than a month after Mao resigned, the Anbang Insurance Group, a major insurer in China, purchased about US$7.9 billion worth of Minsheng's shares from the secondary market. The purchase increased Anbang's stake to about 20 percent, which allowed it at least one seat on the bank's board. Anbang is a large investment and insurance conglomerate with more than US$157 billion in assets and a strong will to expand its financial business in the banking sector. Minsheng was thus at a sensitive and turbulent juncture, facing threats coming from both inside and outside.

But Hong Qi took up the challenge proactively. Holding a doctorate in economics from Renmin University, Hong was acclaimed as among China's best business leaders by Forbes China in 2013. He immediately mitigated the turmoil's effects by giving his assurance that Mao's resignation would not affect Minsheng's strategic development.

Many people see Hong as a passionate banker as well as an ethical business leader. At the Global Entrepreneur Summit 2011 held in Beijing, Hong stated publicly that commercial banks in China failed to provide sufficient financial support to the development of new industries and the modernization of agriculture in less developed provinces. He even openly admitted that he felt guilty about the fact that banks made exorbitant profits while corporations suffered financially.

China Minsheng Bank was founded in 1996 as one of the country's first privately owned financial institutions. Based in Beijing, the bank has thrived by lending to small entrepreneurs and businesses. However, China has recently kept tight control on the interest rates for loans in banks, which undermines the bank's ability to provide cheap loans to their small-scale customers.

Hong stated out that Minsheng would focus more on large customers, including strategic customers on the interbank market. The latest business plan calls for the bank to reduce small enterprises' loans to about 30 percent of Minsheng's revenues, down from 40 percent in 2014.

Hong also pledged to strengthen risk control and internal management over the next five years. Plans were formulated to accelerate disposal of non-performing loans in 2015 and to reinforce the bank's measures to cast out possible illegal linkage to government officials. All these cannot be done without the support of ethical leadership, effective communication and motivation of staff. Hong has remarked simply that they are doing their best. The share price of the bank eventually since stabilized.

Sources: Wu Hongyuran, Ling Huawei, and Yu Ning, "Minsheng Tries Weathering a Maelstrom," Caixin Online, http://english.caixin.com/2015-02-26/100785702.html; Russell Flannery, "China Minsheng Banking's Hong Qi Tops Forbes China's Best CEOs List," *Forbes*, http://www .forbes.com/sites/russellflannery/2013/07/02/china-minsheng-bankings-hong-qi-tops-forbes -chinas-best-ceo-list/; David Barboza, "President of China Minsheng Bank Steps Down," Dealbook, http://dealbook.nytimes.com/2015/01/31/president-of-china-minsheng-bank-steps-down/? _r=0; "Chinese Bank President 'Embarrassed' by Riches," China Real Time, http://blogs.wsj .com/chinarealtime/2011/12/02/chinese-bank-president-embarrassed-by-riches/.

The details of this story are at once disheartening and inspiring, reflecting the increasing complexity of organizational life. They also highlight several issues of interest to those of us seeking to understand organizational behavior, including motivation, ethics, emotions, personality, and culture. Throughout this text, you'll learn how we can systematically study all these elements.

The Importance of Interpersonal Skills

1-1 Demonstrate the importance of interpersonal skills in the workplace.

Until the late 1980s, business school curricula emphasized the technical aspects of management, focusing on economics, accounting, finance, and quantitative techniques. Course work in human behavior and people skills received relatively less attention. Since then, however, business schools have realized the significant role interpersonal skills play in determining a manager's effectiveness. In fact, a survey of over 2,100 CFOs across 20 industries indicated that a lack of interpersonal skills is the top reason why some employees fail to advance.[1]

Incorporating OB principles into the workplace can yield many important organizational outcomes. For one, companies known as good places to work—such as Genentech, the Boston Consulting Group, Qualcomm, McKinsey & Company, Procter & Gamble, Facebook, and Southwest Airlines[2]—have been found to generate superior financial performance.[3] Second, developing managers' interpersonal skills helps organizations attract and keep high-performing employees, which is important since outstanding employees are always in short supply and are costly to replace. Third, there are strong associations between the quality of workplace relationships and employee job satisfaction, stress, and turnover. One very large survey of hundreds of workplaces and more than 200,000 respondents showed that social relationships among coworkers and supervisors were strongly related to overall job satisfaction. Positive social relationships also were associated with lower stress at work and lower intentions

IBM Chief Executive Virginia Rometty has the interpersonal skills required to succeed in management. Communication and leadership skills distinguish managers such as Rometty, who rise to the top of their profession. Shown here at a meeting in Beijing, Rometty is an innovative leader capable of driving IBM's entrepreneurial culture.
Source: Li Tao/Xinhua Press/Corbis

to quit.[4] Further research indicates that employees who relate to their managers with supportive dialogue and proactivity find that their ideas are endorsed more often, which improves workplace satisfaction.[5] Fourth, increasing the OB element in organizations can foster social responsibility awareness. Accordingly, universities have begun to incorporate social entrepreneurship education into their curriculum in order to train future leaders to address social issues within their organizations.[6] This is especially important because there is a growing need for understanding the means and outcomes of corporate social responsibility, known as CSR.[7]

We understand that in today's competitive and demanding workplace, managers can't succeed on their technical skills alone. They also have to exhibit good people skills. This text has been written to help both managers and potential managers develop those people skills with the knowledge that understanding human behavior provides.

> ⊙ **TRY IT!**
> If your professor has assigned this, go to the Assignments section of **mymanagementlab.com** to complete the **Simulation: *What Is Management?***

Management and Organizational Behavior

1-2 Define *organizational behavior (OB)*.

manager   An individual who achieves goals through other people.

organization   A consciously coordinated social unit, composed of two or more people, that functions on a relatively continuous basis to achieve a common goal or set of goals.

planning   A process that includes defining goals, establishing strategy, and developing plans to coordinate activities.

organizing   Determining what tasks are to be done, who is to do them, how the tasks are to be grouped, who reports to whom, and where decisions are to be made.

leading   A function that includes motivating employees, directing others, selecting the most effective communication channels, and resolving conflicts.

controlling   Monitoring activities to ensure they are being accomplished as planned and correcting any significant deviations.

Let's begin by briefly defining the terms *manager* and *organization*. First, the defining characteristic of **managers** is that they get things done through other people. They make decisions, allocate resources, and direct the activities of others to attain goals. Managers are sometimes called *administrators*, especially in not-for-profit organizations. They do their work in an **organization**, which is a consciously coordinated social unit, composed of two or more people, that functions on a relatively continuous basis to achieve a common goal or set of goals. By this definition, manufacturing and service firms are organizations, and so are schools, hospitals, churches, military units, nonprofits, police departments, and local, state, and federal government agencies.

More than ever, a manager is someone placed into the position without management training or informed experience. According to a large-scale survey, more than 58 percent of managers reported they had not received any training and 25 percent admitted they were not ready to lead others when they were given the role.[8] Added to that challenge, the demands of the job have increased: the average manager has seven direct reports (five was once the norm), and has less management time to spend with them than before.[9] Considering that a Gallup poll found organizations chose the wrong candidate for management positions 82 percent of the time,[10] we conclude that the more you can learn about people and how to manage them, the better prepared you will be to be that right candidate. OB will help you get there. Let's start with identifying the manager's primary activities.

The work of managers can be condensed to four activities: **planning**, **organizing**, **leading**, and **controlling**. The **planning** function encompasses defining an organization's goals, establishing an overall strategy for achieving those goals, and developing a comprehensive set of plans to integrate and coordinate activities. Evidence indicates the need for planning increases the most as managers move from lower-level to mid-level management.[11]

When managers engage in designing their work unit's structure, they are **organizing**. The organizing function includes determining what tasks are to be done, who is to do them, how the tasks are to be grouped, who reports to whom, and where decisions are to be made.

Every organization contains people, and it is management's job to direct and coordinate those people. This is the **leading** function. When managers motivate employees, direct their activities, select the most effective communication channels, or resolve conflicts, they're engaging in leading.

To ensure things are going as they should, management must monitor the organization's performance and compare it with previously set goals. If there are any significant deviations, it is management's job to get the organization back on track. This monitoring, comparing, and potential correcting is the **controlling** function.

Management Roles

Henry Mintzberg, now a prominent management scholar, undertook a careful study of executives to determine what they did on their jobs early in his career. On the basis of his observations, Mintzberg concluded that managers perform 10 different, highly interrelated roles, or sets of behaviors, and serve a critical function in organizations.[12] As shown in Exhibit 1-1, these 10 roles are primarily (1) interpersonal, (2) informational, or (3) decisional. Although much has changed in the world of work since Mintzberg developed this model, research indicates the roles have changed very little.[13]

Interpersonal Roles   All managers are required to perform duties that are ceremonial and symbolic in nature. For instance, when the president of a college hands out diplomas at commencement or a factory supervisor gives a group of high school students a tour of the plant, they are acting in a *figurehead* role. Another key interpersonal role all managers have is a *leadership* role.

Exhibit **1-1**	Minztberg's Managerial Roles
Role	**Description**
Interpersonal	
Figurehead	Symbolic head; required to perform a number of routine duties of a legal or social nature
Leader	Responsible for the motivation and direction of employees
Liaison	Maintains a network of outside contacts who provide favors and information
Informational	
Monitor	Receives a wide variety of information; serves as nerve center of internal and external information of the organization
Disseminator	Transmits information received from outsiders or from other employees to members of the organization
Spokesperson	Transmits information to outsiders on organization's plans, policies, actions, and results; serves as expert on organization's industry
Decisional	
Entrepreneur	Searches organization and its environment for opportunities and initiates projects to bring about change
Disturbance handler	Responsible for corrective action when organization faces important, unexpected disturbances
Resource allocator	Makes or approves significant organizational decisions
Negotiator	Responsible for representing the organization at major negotiations

Source: Mintzberg, Henry, *The Nature of Managerial Work*, 1st Ed., © 1973, pp. 92–93. Reprinted and Electronically reproduced by permission of Pearson Education, Inc., New York, NY.

This role includes hiring, training, motivating, and disciplining employees. The third role within the interpersonal grouping is the *liaison* role, or contacting and fostering relationships with others who provide valuable information. The sales manager who obtains information from the quality-control manager in his own company has an internal liaison relationship. When that sales manager has contact with other sales executives through a marketing trade association, he has external liaison relationships.

Informational Roles   All managers, to some degree, collect information from outside organizations and institutions, typically by scanning the news media and talking with other people to learn of changes in the public's tastes, what competitors may be planning, and the like. Mintzberg called this the *monitor* role. Managers also act as a conduit to transmit information to organizational members. This is the *disseminator* role. In addition, managers perform a *spokesperson* role when they represent the organization to outsiders.

Decisional Roles   Mintzberg identified four roles that require making choices. In the *entrepreneur* role, managers initiate and oversee new projects that will improve their organization's performance. As *disturbance handlers*, managers take corrective action in response to unforeseen problems. As *resource allocators*, managers are responsible for allocating human, physical, and monetary resources. Finally, managers perform a *negotiator* role, in which they discuss issues and bargain with other units (internal or external) to gain advantages for their own unit.

Management Skills

Still another way of considering what managers do is to look at the skills or competencies they need to achieve their goals. Researchers have identified a number of skills that differentiate effective from ineffective managers.[14] Each of these skills is important, and all are needed to become a well-rounded and effective manager.

technical skills   The ability to apply specialized knowledge or expertise.

Technical Skills   **Technical skills** encompass the ability to apply specialized knowledge or expertise. When you think of the skills of professionals such as civil engineers or oral surgeons, you typically focus on the technical skills they have learned through extensive formal education. Of course, professionals don't have a monopoly on technical skills, and not all technical skills have to be learned in schools or other formal training programs. All jobs require some specialized expertise, and many people develop their technical skills on the job.

human skills   The ability to work with, understand, and motivate other people, both individually and in groups.

Human Skills   The ability to understand, communicate with, motivate, and support other people, both individually and in groups, defines **human skills**. Many people may be technically proficient but poor listeners, unable to understand the needs of others, or weak at managing conflicts. Because managers get things done through other people, they must have good human skills.

conceptual skills   The mental ability to analyze and diagnose complex situations.

Conceptual Skills   Managers must have the mental ability to analyze and diagnose complex situations. These tasks require **conceptual skills**. Decision making, for instance, requires managers to identify problems, develop alternative solutions to correct those problems, evaluate those alternative solutions, and select the best one. After they have selected a course of action, managers must be able to organize a plan of action and then execute it. The ability to integrate new ideas with existing processes and innovate on the job are also crucial conceptual skills for today's managers.

Effective versus Successful Managerial Activities

Fred Luthans and his associates looked at what managers do from a somewhat different perspective.[15] They asked, "Do managers who move up most quickly in an organization do the same activities and with the same emphasis as managers who do the best job?" You might think the answer is yes, but that's not always the case.

Luthans and his associates studied more than 450 managers. All engaged in four managerial activities:

1. **Traditional management.** Decision making, planning, and controlling.
2. **Communication.** Exchanging routine information and processing paperwork.
3. **Human resource management.** Motivating, disciplining, managing conflict, staffing, and training.
4. **Networking.** Socializing, politicking, and interacting with outsiders.

The "average" manager spent 32 percent of his or her time in traditional management activities, 29 percent communicating, 20 percent in human resource management activities, and 19 percent networking. However, the time and effort different *individual* managers spent on those activities varied a great deal. As shown in Exhibit 1-2, among managers who were *successful* (defined in terms of speed of promotion within their organization), networking made the largest relative contribution to success, and human resource management activities made the least relative contribution. Among *effective* managers (defined in terms of quantity and quality of their performance and the satisfaction and commitment of employees), communication made the largest relative contribution and networking the least. Other studies in Australia, Israel, Italy, Japan, and the United States confirm the link between networking, social relationships, and success within an organization.[16] The connection between communication and effective managers is also clear. Managers who explain their decisions and seek information from colleagues and employees—even if the information turns out to be negative—are the most effective.[17]

This research offers important insights. *Successful* (in terms of promotion) managers give almost the opposite emphases to traditional management, communication, human resource management, and networking as do *effective*

When you see this icon, Global OB issues are being discussed in the paragraph.

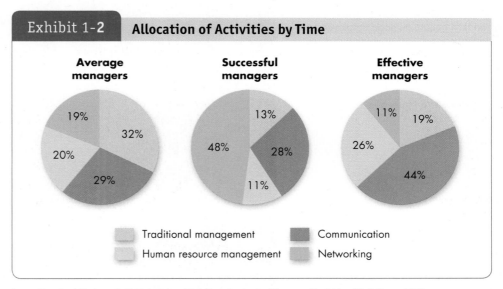

Exhibit 1-2   Allocation of Activities by Time

Source: Based on F. Luthans, R. M. Hodgetts, and S. A. Rosenkrantz, *Real Managers* (Cambridge, MA: Ballinger, 1988).

managers. This finding challenges the historical assumption that promotions are based on performance, and it illustrates the importance of networking and political skills in getting ahead in organizations.

Now that we've established what managers do, we need to study how best to do these things. **Organizational behavior (OB)** is a field of study that investigates the impact individuals, groups, and structure have on behavior within organizations, for the purpose of applying such knowledge toward improving an organization's effectiveness. That's a mouthful, so let's break it down.

OB is a field of study, meaning that it is a distinct area of expertise with a common body of knowledge. What does it study? It studies three determinants of behavior in organizations: individuals, groups, and structure. In addition, OB applies the knowledge gained about individuals, groups, and the effect of structure on behavior in order to make organizations work more effectively.

To sum up our definition, OB is the study of what people do in an organization and the way their behavior affects the organization's performance. Because OB is concerned specifically with employment-related situations, it examines behavior in the context of job satisfaction, absenteeism, employment turnover, productivity, human performance, and management. Although debate exists about the relative importance of each, OB includes these core topics:

- Motivation
- Leader behavior and power
- Interpersonal communication
- Group structure and processes
- Attitude development and perception
- Change processes
- Conflict and negotiation
- Work design[18]

organizational behavior (OB) A field of study that investigates the impact individuals, groups, and structure have on behavior within organizations, for the purpose of applying such knowledge toward improving an organization's effectiveness.

⭐ **WATCH IT!**

If your professor has assigned this, go to the Assignments section of **mymanagementlab.com** to complete the video exercise titled *Herman Miller: Organizational Behavior*.

Internet retailer Zappos.com understands how organizational behavior affects an organization's performance. The firm maintains good employee relationships by offering generous benefits, extensive training, and a positive work environment in which employees are encouraged "to create fun and a little weirdness."
Source: Ronda Churchill/Bloomberg/Getty Images

Complementing Intuition with Systematic Study

1-3 Show the value to OB of systematic study.

systematic study Looking at relationships, attempting to attribute causes and effects, and drawing conclusions based on scientific evidence.

evidence-based management (EBM) The basing of managerial decisions on the best available scientific evidence.

intuition An instinctive feeling not necessarily supported by research.

Whether you've explicitly thought about it before or not, you've been "reading" people almost all your life by watching their actions and interpreting what you see, or by trying to predict what people might do under different conditions. The casual approach to reading others can often lead to erroneous predictions, but using a systematic approach can improve your accuracy.

Underlying the systematic approach in this text is the belief that behavior is not random. Rather, we can identify fundamental consistencies underlying the behavior of all individuals and modify them to reflect individual differences.

These fundamental consistencies are very important. Why? Because they allow predictability. Behavior is generally predictable, and the *systematic study* of behavior is a means to making reasonably accurate predictions. When we use the term **systematic study**, we mean looking at relationships, attempting to attribute causes and effects, and basing our conclusions on scientific evidence—that is, on data gathered under controlled conditions and measured and interpreted in a rigorous manner.

Evidence-based management (EBM) complements systematic study by basing managerial decisions on the best available scientific evidence. For example, we want doctors to make decisions about patient care based on the latest available evidence, and EBM argues that managers should do the same, thinking more scientifically about management problems. A manager might pose a question, search for the best available evidence, and apply the relevant information to the question or case at hand. You might wonder what manager would not base decisions on evidence, but the vast majority of management decisions are still made "on the fly," with little to no systematic study of available evidence.[19]

Systematic study and EBM add to **intuition**, or those "gut feelings" about what makes others (and ourselves) "tick." Of course, the things you have come to believe in an unsystematic way are not necessarily incorrect. Jack Welch (former CEO of General Electric) noted, "The trick, of course, is to know when to go with your gut." But if we make *all* decisions with intuition or gut instinct, we're likely working with incomplete information—like making an investment decision with only half the data about the potential for risk and reward.

Relying on intuition is made worse because we tend to overestimate the accuracy of what we think we know. Surveys of human resource managers have also shown that many managers hold "commonsense" opinions regarding effective management that have been flatly refuted by empirical evidence.

We find a similar problem in chasing the business and popular media for management wisdom. The business press tends to be dominated by fads. As a writer for *The New Yorker* put it, "Every few years, new companies succeed, and they are scrutinized for the underlying truths they might reveal. But often there is no underlying truth; the companies just happened to be in the right place at the right time."[20] Although we try to avoid it, we might also fall into this trap. It's not that the business press stories are all wrong; it's that without a systematic approach, it's hard to separate the wheat from the chaff.

Big Data

Data has been used to evaluate behavior since at least 1749, when the word "statistic" was coined to mean a "description of the state."[21] Statistics back then were used for purposes of governance, but since the data collection methods

Management by Walking Around Is the Most Effective Management

This is mostly a myth, but with a caveat. Management by walking around (MBWA) is an organizational principle made famous with the 1982 publication of *In Search of Excellence* and based upon a 1970s initiative by Hewlett-Packard—in other words, it's a dinosaur. Years of research indicate that effective management practices are not built around MBWA. But the idea of requiring managers at all levels of the organization to wander around their departments to observe, converse, and hear from employees continues as a common business practice.

Many companies expecting managers and executives to do regular "floor time" have claimed benefits from increased employee engagement to deeper management understanding of company issues. A recent three-year study also suggested that a modified form of MBWA may significantly improve safety in organizations as employees become more mindful of following regulatory procedures when supervisors observe and monitor them frequently.

While MBWA sounds helpful, its limitations suggest that modern practices focused on building trust and relationships are more effective for management. Limitations include available hours, focus, and application.

1. **Available hours.** Managers are charged with planning, organizing, coordinating, and controlling, yet even CEOs—the managers who should be the most in control of their time—report spending 53 percent of their average 55-hour workweek in time-wasting meetings.
2. **Focus.** MBWA turns management's focus toward the concerns of employees. This is good, but only to a degree. As noted by Jeff Weiner, CEO of LinkedIn, "Part of the key to time management is carving out time to think, as opposed to constantly reacting. And during that thinking time, you're not only thinking strategically, thinking proactively, thinking longer-term, but you're literally thinking about what is urgent versus important." Weiner and other CEOs argue that meetings distract them from their purpose.
3. **Application.** The principle behind MBWA is that the more managers know their employees, the more effective those managers will be. This is not always (or even often) true. As we'll learn in Chapter 6, knowing something (or thinking we know it) should not always lead us to act on *only* that information because our internal decision making is subjective. We need objective data to make the most effective management decisions.

Based on the need for managers to dedicate their efforts to administering and growing businesses, and given the proven effectiveness of objective performance measures, it seems the time for MBWA is gone. Yet there is that one caveat: managers should know their employees well. As Rick Russell, CEO of Greer Laboratories, says, "Fostering close ties with your lieutenants is the stuff that gets results. You have to rally the troops. You can't do it from a memo." Management should therefore not substitute walking around for true management.

Sources: G. Luria and I. Morag, "Safety Management by Walking Around (SMBWA): A Safety Intervention Program Based on Both Peer and Manager Participation," *Accident Analysis and Prevention* (March 2012): 248–57; J. S. Lublin, "Managers Need to Make Time for Face Time," *The Wall Street Journal* (March 17, 2015), http://www.wsj.com/articles/managers-need-to-make-time-for-face-time-1426624214; and R. E. Silverman, "Where's the Boss? Trapped in a Meeting," *The Wall Street Journal* (February 14, 2012), B1, B9.

were clumsy and simplistic, so were the conclusions. "Big data"—the extensive use of statistical compilation and analysis—didn't become possible until computers were sophisticated enough to both store and manipulate large amounts of information. Let's look at the roots of the application of big data for business, which originated in the marketing department of online retailers.

Background It's difficult to believe now, but not long ago companies treated online shopping as a virtual point-of-sale experience: shoppers browsed websites anonymously, and sellers tracked sales data only on what customers bought. Gradually, though, online retailers began to track and act upon information about customer preferences that was uniquely available through the Internet shopping experience, information that was far superior to data gathered in simple store transactions. This enabled them to create more targeted marketing strategies than ever before. The bookselling industry is a case in point: Before online selling, brick-and-mortar bookstores could collect data about book sales only to create projections about consumer interests and trends. With the advent of Amazon, suddenly a vast array of information about consumer preferences became available for tracking: what customers bought, what they looked at, how they navigated the site, and what they were influenced by (such as promotions, reviews, and page presentation). The challenge for Amazon then was to identify which statistics were *persistent,* giving relatively constant outcomes over time, and *predictive,* showing steady causality between certain inputs and outcomes. The company used these statistics to develop algorithms to forecast which books customers would like to read next. Amazon then could base its wholesale purchase decisions on the feedback customers provided, both through these passive collection methods and through solicited recommendations for upcoming titles.

Current Usage   No matter how many terabytes of data firms can collect or from how many sources, the reasons for data analytics include: *predicting* any event, from a book purchase to a spacesuit malfunction; detecting how much *risk* is incurred at any time, from the risk of a fire to that of a loan default; and *preventing* catastrophes large and small, from a plane crash to an overstock of product.[22] With big data, U.S. defense contractor BAE Systems protects itself from cyber-attacks, San Francisco's Bank of the West uses customer data to create tiered pricing systems, and London's Graze.com analyzes customers' preferences to select snack samples to send with their orders.[23]

Naturally, big data has been used by technology companies like Google and Facebook, who rely on advertising dollars for revenue and thus need to predict user behavior. Companies like Netflix and Uber similarly use big data to predict where and when customers may want to use their virtual services, although their revenue comes from subscribers to their services. Insurance firms predict behavior to assess risks, such as the chance of traffic accidents, in order to set customer premiums. Even museums like the Solomon R. Guggenheim Museum in New York, the Dallas Museum of Art, and the Minneapolis Institute of Arts analyze data from transmitters, kiosks, and surveys to cater to their paying guests.[24]

Online retailers like eBay and Amazon that market tangible products through online platforms also rely on big data to predict what will sell. For organizations like Nielson Holdings, which tracks television and radio watching, the results of data analyses *are* the product they sell. Still other organizations collect big data but do not directly use it. These are often organizations whose primary business is not online. Kroger, a U.S. grocery store chain, electronically collects information from 55 million customers who have loyalty cards and sells the data to vendors who stock Kroger's shelves.[25] Sometimes even technology companies simply sell their data; Twitter sells 500 million tweets a day to four data assimilation companies.[26]

New Trends   While accessibility to data increases organizations' ability to predict human behavioral trends, the use of big data for understanding, helping, and managing people is relatively new but holds promise. In fact, research on 10,000 workers in China, Germany, India, the United Kingdom, and the United States indicated that employees expect the next transformation in the way people work will rely more on technological advancements than on any other factor, such as demographic changes.[27]

It is good news for the future of business that researchers, the media, and company leaders have identified the potential of data-driven management and decision making. A manager who uses data to define objectives, develop theories of causality, and test those theories can determine which employee activities are relevant to the objectives.[28] Big data has implications for correcting management assumptions and increasing positive performance outcomes. Increasingly, it is applied toward making effective decisions (Chapter 6) and managing human resources (HR; Chapter 17). It is quite possible that the best use of big data in managing people will come from organizational behavior and psychology research, where it might even help employees with mental illnesses monitor and change their behavior.[29]

Limitations   As technological capabilities for handling big data have increased, so have issues of privacy. This is particularly true when data collection includes surveillance instruments. For instance, an experiment in Brooklyn, New York, has been designed to improve the quality of life for residents, but the researchers will collect intensive data from infrared cameras, sensors, and smartphone Wi-Fi signals.[30] Through similar methods of surveillance monitoring, a bank call center and a pharmaceutical company found that employees were more productive with more social interaction, so they changed their break time policies so more people took breaks together. They then saw sales increase and turnover decrease. Bread Winners Café in Dallas, Texas, constantly monitors all employees in the restaurant through surveillance and uses the data to promote or discipline its servers.[31]

These big data tactics and others might yield results—and research indicates that, in fact, electronic performance monitoring does increase task performance and citizenship behavior (helping behaviors towards others), at least in the short term.[32] But critics point out that after Frederick Taylor introduced surveillance analytics in 1911 to increase productivity through monitoring and feedback controls, his management control techniques were surpassed by Alfred Sloan's greater success with management outcomes, achieved by providing meaningful work to employees.[33] This brings up a larger concern: What do people think about big data when *they* are the source of the data? Organizations using big data run the risk of offending the very people they are trying to influence: employees and customers. As Alderman Bob Fioretti said about the 65 sensors installed on Chicago's streets, "This type of invasion is a very slippery slope."[34]

We must keep in mind that big data will always be limited in predicting behavior, curtailing risk, and preventing catastrophes. In contrast to the replicable results we can obtain in the sciences through big data analytics, human behavior is often capricious and predicated on innumerable variables. Otherwise, our decision making would have been taken over by artificial intelligence by now! But that will never be a worthy goal.[35] Management is more than the sum of data.

Therefore, we are not advising you to throw intuition out the window. In dealing with people, leaders often rely on hunches, and sometimes the outcomes are excellent. At other times, human tendencies get in the way. Alex Pentland, a celebrated MIT data scientist, proposes a new science termed *social physics*, which is based on improving the way ideas and behaviors travel. Studies on social physics would lead to subtler forms of data collection and analysis than some of the more intrusive surveillance methods mentioned previously, while still intending to inform managers on how to help employees focus their energies.[36] The prudent use of big data, along with an understanding of human behavioral tendencies, can contribute to sound decision making and ease natural biases. What we are advising is to use evidence as much as possible to inform your intuition and experience. That is the promise of OB.

Disciplines That Contribute to the OB Field

1-4 Identify the major behavioral science disciplines that contribute to OB.

OB is an applied behavioral science built on contributions from a number of behavioral disciplines, mainly psychology and social psychology, sociology, and anthropology. Psychology's contributions have been principally at the individual or micro level of analysis, while the other disciplines have contributed to our understanding of macro concepts such as group processes and organization. Exhibit 1-3 is an overview of the major contributions to the study of organizational behavior.

Psychology

psychology   The science that seeks to measure, explain, and sometimes change the behavior of humans and other animals.

Psychology seeks to measure, explain, and sometimes change the behavior of humans and other animals. Contributors to the knowledge of OB are learning theorists, personality theorists, counseling psychologists and, most important, industrial and organizational psychologists.

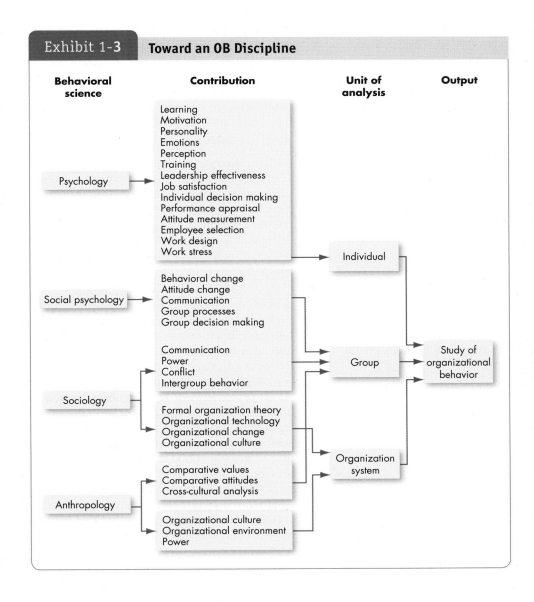

Exhibit 1-3   **Toward an OB Discipline**

Behavioral science	Contribution	Unit of analysis	Output
Psychology	Learning, Motivation, Personality, Emotions, Perception, Training, Leadership effectiveness, Job satisfaction, Individual decision making, Performance appraisal, Attitude measurement, Employee selection, Work design, Work stress	Individual	Study of organizational behavior
Social psychology	Behavioral change, Attitude change, Communication, Group processes, Group decision making	Group	
Sociology	Communication, Power, Conflict, Intergroup behavior		
	Formal organization theory, Organizational technology, Organizational change, Organizational culture	Organization system	
Anthropology	Comparative values, Comparative attitudes, Cross-cultural analysis		
	Organizational culture, Organizational environment, Power		

Early industrial/organizational psychologists studied the problems of fatigue, boredom, and other working conditions that could impede efficient work performance. More recently, their contributions have expanded to include learning, perception, personality, emotions, training, leadership effectiveness, needs and motivational forces, job satisfaction, decision-making processes, performance appraisals, attitude measurement, employee-selection techniques, work design, and job stress.

Social Psychology

social psychology An area of psychology that blends concepts from psychology and sociology to focus on the influence of people on one another.

Social psychology, generally considered a branch of psychology, blends concepts from both psychology and sociology to focus on people's influence on one another. One major study area is *change*—how to implement it and how to reduce barriers to its acceptance. Social psychologists also contribute to measuring, understanding, and changing attitudes; identifying communication patterns; and building trust. Finally, they have made important contributions to our study of group behavior, power, and conflict.

Sociology

sociology The study of people in relation to their social environment or culture.

While psychology focuses on the individual, **sociology** studies people in relation to their social environment or culture. Sociologists have contributed to OB through their study of group behaviors in organizations, particularly formal and complex organizations. Perhaps most important, sociologists have studied organizational culture, formal organization theory and structure, organizational technology, communications, power, and conflict.

Anthropology

anthropology The study of societies to learn about human beings and their activities.

Anthropology is the study of societies to learn about human beings and their activities. Anthropologists' work on cultures and environments has helped us understand differences in fundamental values, attitudes, and behavior among people in different countries and within different organizations. Much of our current understanding of organizational culture, organizational climate, and differences among national cultures is a result of the work of anthropologists or those using their methods.

There Are Few Absolutes in OB

1-5 Demonstrate why few absolutes apply to OB.

Laws in the physical sciences—chemistry, astronomy, physics—are consistent and apply in a wide range of situations. They allow scientists to generalize about the pull of gravity or to be confident about sending astronauts into space to repair satellites. Human beings are complex, and few, if any, simple and universal principles explain organizational behavior. Because we are not alike, our ability to make simple, accurate, and sweeping generalizations about ourselves is limited. Two people often act very differently in the same situation, and the same person's behavior changes in different situations. For example, not everyone is motivated by money, and people may behave differently at a religious service than they do at a party.

That doesn't mean, of course, that we can't offer reasonably accurate explanations of human behavior or make valid predictions. It does mean that OB concepts must reflect situational, or contingency, conditions. We can say x leads to y, but only under conditions specified in z—the **contingency variables**. The science of OB was developed by applying general concepts to a particular situation, person, or group. For example, OB scholars would avoid stating

contingency variables Situational factors: variables that moderate the relationship between two or more variables.

that everyone likes complex and challenging work (a general concept). Why? Because not everyone wants a challenging job. Some people prefer routine over varied work, or simple over complex tasks. A job attractive to one person may not be to another; its appeal is contingent on the person who holds it. Often, we'll find both general effects (money does have some ability to motivate most of us) and contingencies (some of us are more motivated by money than others, and some situations are more about money than others). We'll best understand OB when we realize how both (general effects, and the contingencies that affect them) often guide behavior.

Challenges and Opportunities for OB

1-6 Identify managers' challenges and opportunities in applying OB concepts.

Understanding organizational behavior has never been more important for managers. Take a quick look at the dramatic changes in organizations. The typical employee is getting older; the workforce is becoming increasingly diverse; and global competition requires employees to become more flexible and cope with rapid change.

As a result of these changes and others, employment options have adapted to include new opportunities for workers. Exhibit 1-4 details some of the types of options individuals may find offered to them by organizations or for which they would like to negotiate. Under each heading in the exhibit, you will find a grouping of options from which to choose—or combine. For instance, at one point in your career you may find yourself employed full time in an office in a localized, nonunion setting with a salary and bonus compensation package, while at another point you may wish to negotiate for a flextime, virtual

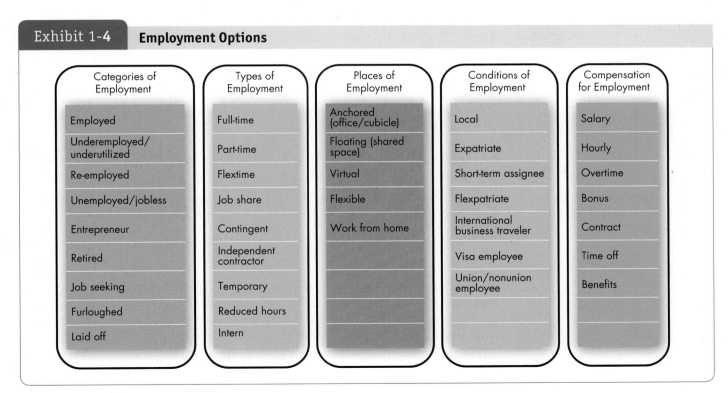

Exhibit 1-4   Employment Options

Categories of Employment	Types of Employment	Places of Employment	Conditions of Employment	Compensation for Employment
Employed	Full-time	Anchored (office/cubicle)	Local	Salary
Underemployed/ underutilized	Part-time	Floating (shared space)	Expatriate	Hourly
Re-employed	Flextime	Virtual	Short-term assignee	Overtime
Unemployed/jobless	Job share	Flexible	Flexpatriate	Bonus
Entrepreneur	Contingent	Work from home	International business traveler	Contract
Retired	Independent contractor		Visa employee	Time off
Job seeking	Temporary		Union/nonunion employee	Benefits
Furloughed	Reduced hours			
Laid off	Intern			

Sources: J. R. Anderson Jr., et al., "Action Items: 42 Trends Affecting Benefits, Compensation, Training, Staffing and Technology," *HR Magazine* (January 2013) p. 33; M. Dewhurst, B. Hancock, and D. Ellsworth, "Redesigning Knowledge Work," *Harvard Business Review* (January–February 2013), pp. 58–64; E. Frauenheim, "Creating a New Contingent Culture," *Workforce Management* (August 2012), pp. 34–39; N. Koeppen, "State Job Aid Takes Pressure off Germany," *The Wall Street Journal* (February 1, 2013), p. A8; and M. A. Shaffer, M. L. Kraimer, Y.-P. Chen, and M. C. Bolino, "Choices, Challenges, and Career Consequences of Global Work Experiences: A Review and Future Agenda," *Journal of Management* (July 2012), pp. 1282–1327.

position and choose to work from overseas for a combination of salary and extra paid time off.

In short, today's challenges bring opportunities for managers to use OB concepts. In this section, we review some of the most critical issues confronting managers for which OB offers solutions—or at least meaningful insights toward solutions.

Economic Pressures

When the U.S. economy plunged into a deep and prolonged recession in 2008, virtually all other large economies around the world followed suit. Layoffs and job losses were widespread, and those who survived the ax were often asked to accept pay cuts. When times are bad, as they were during the recession, managers are on the front lines with employees who are asked to make do with less, who worry about their futures, and who sometimes must be fired. The difference between good and bad management can be the difference between profit and loss or, ultimately, between business survival and failure.

Managing employees well when times are tough is just as hard as when times are good, if not harder. In good times, understanding how to reward, satisfy, and retain employees is at a premium. In bad times, issues like stress, decision making, and coping come to the forefront.

Continuing Globalization

Organizations are no longer constrained by national borders. Samsung, the largest South Korean business conglomerate, sells most of its products to organizations in other countries, Burger King is owned by a Brazilian firm, and McDonald's sells hamburgers in more than 118 countries on six continents. Even what is arguably the U.S. company with the strongest U.S. identity—Apple—employs twice as many workers outside the United States as it does inside the country. And all major automobile makers now manufacture cars outside their borders; Honda builds cars in Ohio, Ford in Brazil, Volkswagen in Mexico, and both Mercedes and BMW in the United States and South Africa.

The world has become a global village. In the process, the manager's job has changed. Effective managers will anticipate and adapt their approaches to the global issues we discuss next.

Increased Foreign Assignments   You are increasingly likely to find yourself in a foreign assignment—transferred to your employer's operating division or subsidiary in another country. Once there, you'll have to manage a workforce very different in needs, aspirations, and attitudes from those you are used to back home. To be effective, you will need to understand everything you can about your new location's culture and workforce—and demonstrate your cultural sensitivity—before introducing alternate practices.

Working with People from Different Cultures   Even in your own country, you'll find yourself working with bosses, peers, and other employees born and raised in different cultures. What motivates you may not motivate them. Or your communication style may be straightforward and open, which others may find uncomfortable and threatening. To work effectively with people from different cultures, you need to understand how their culture and background have shaped them and how to adapt your management style to fit any differences.

Overseeing Movement of Jobs to Countries with Low-Cost Labor   It is increasingly difficult for managers in advanced nations, where the minimum wage

Guy Woolaert, senior vice president and chief technical and innovation officer of the Coca-Cola Company, has worked effectively with people from many cultures. He learned from his 20 years of assignments abroad in Europe, the Pacific, and other geographic regions how to adapt his management style to reflect the values of different countries.
Source: Robin Nelson/ZUMA Press/Newscom

can be as high as \$16.88 an hour, to compete against firms that rely on workers from developing nations where labor is available for as little as nine cents an hour.[37] In a global economy, jobs tend to flow where lower costs give businesses a comparative advantage, though labor groups, politicians, and local community leaders see the exporting of jobs as undermining the job market at home. Managers face the difficult task of balancing the interests of their organizations with their responsibilities to the communities in which they operate.

Adapting to Differing Cultural and Regulatory Norms   To be effective, managers need to know the cultural norms of the workforce in each country where they do business. For instance, in some countries a large percentage of the workforce enjoys long holidays. There will be country and local regulations to consider, too. Managers of subsidiaries abroad need to be aware of the unique financial and legal regulations applying to "guest companies" or else risk violating them. Violations can have implications for their operations in that country and also for political relations between countries. Managers also need to be cognizant of differences in regulations for competitors in that country; many times, understanding the laws can lead to success or failure. For example, knowing local banking laws allowed one multinational firm—the Bank of China—to seize control of a storied (and very valuable) London building, Grosvenor House, from under the nose of the owner, the Indian hotel group Sahara. Management at Sahara contends that the loan default that led to the seizure was a misunderstanding regarding one of their other properties in New York.[38] Globalization can get complicated.

Workforce Demographics

The workforce has always adapted to variations in economies, longevity and birth rates, socioeconomic conditions, and other changes that have widespread impact. People adapt to survive, and OB studies the way those adaptations

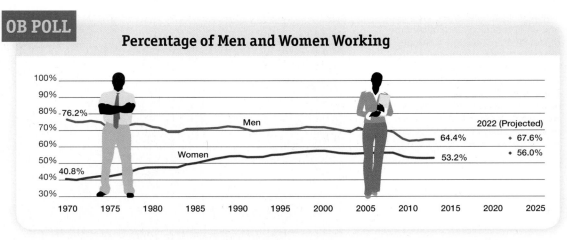

OB POLL

Percentage of Men and Women Working

Sources: U.S. Bureau of Labor Statistics, "Women in the Labor Force: A Datebook" (2014), www.bls.gov/opub/reports/cps/women-in-the-labor-force-a-databook-2014.pdf; and U.S. Bureau of Labor Statistics, "Economic News Release," (2013), http://www.bls.gov/news.release/ecopro.t02.htm.

affect individuals' behavior. For instance, even though the 2008 global recession ended years ago, some trends from those years are continuing: some people who have been long unemployed have left the workforce,[39] while others have cobbled together several part-time jobs[40] or settled for on-demand work.[41] Further options that have been particularly popular for younger educated workers have included obtaining specialized industry training after college,[42] accepting full-time jobs that are lower-level,[43] and starting their own companies.[44] As students of OB, we can investigate what factors lead employees to make various choices and how their experiences affect their perceptions of their workplaces. In turn, this can help us predict organizational outcomes.

Longevity and birth rates have also changed the dynamics in organizations; global longevity rates have increased six years in a very short time (since 1990),[45] while birth rates are decreasing for many developed countries, trends that together indicate a lasting shift toward an older workforce. OB research will help explain what this means for attitudes, organizational culture, leadership, structure, and communication. Finally, socioeconomic shifts have a profound effect on workforce demographics. The days when women stayed home because it was expected are just a memory in some cultures, while in others, women face significant barriers to entry into the workforce (see OB Poll). We are interested in how these women fare in the workplace, and how their conditions can be improved. This is just one illustration of how cultural and socioeconomic changes affect the workplace, but it is one of many. We will discuss how OB can provide understanding and insight on workforce issues throughout this text.

✪ PERSONAL INVENTORY ASSESSMENTS

Multicultural Awareness Scale

Any study of organizational behavior (OB) starts with knowledge of yourself. As one step, take this PIA to determine your multicultural awareness.

A Whole Foods Market customer learns how to grind flour with the help of the store's cooking coach, whose job is to provide information about cooking ingredients, methods, and techniques. Cooking coaches embody the best of the retailer's customer-responsive culture of serving people with competency, efficiency, knowledge, and flair.

Source: Evy Mages/The Washington Post/Getty Images

Workforce Diversity

workforce diversity The concept that organizations are becoming more heterogeneous in terms of gender, age, race, ethnicity, sexual orientation, and other characteristics.

One of the most important challenges for organizations is **workforce diversity**, a trend by which organizations are becoming more heterogeneous in terms of employees' gender, age, race, ethnicity, sexual orientation, and other characteristics. Managing this diversity is a global concern. Though we have more to say about it in the next chapter, suffice it to say here that diversity presents great opportunities and poses challenging questions for managers and employees. How can we leverage differences within groups for competitive advantage? Should we treat all employees alike? Should we recognize individual and cultural differences? What are the legal requirements in each country? Does increasing diversity even matter?

Customer Service

Service employees include technical support representatives, fast-food workers, sales clerks, nurses, automobile repair technicians, consultants, financial planners, and flight attendants. The shared characteristic of their jobs is substantial interaction with an organization's customers. OB can help managers increase the success of these interactions by showing how employee attitudes and behavior influence customer satisfaction.

Many an organization has failed because its employees failed to please customers. Management needs to create a customer-responsive culture. OB can provide considerable guidance in helping managers create such cultures—in which employees establish rapport with customers, put customers at ease, show genuine interest, and are sensitive to a customer's individual situation.[46]

People Skills

As you proceed through the chapters of this text, we'll present relevant concepts and theories that can help you explain and predict the behavior of people at work. You'll also gain insights into specific people skills you can use on the job. For instance, you'll learn ways to design motivating jobs, techniques for improving your management skills, and how to create more effective teams.

Networked Organizations

Networked organizations allow people to communicate and work together even though they may be thousands of miles apart. Independent contractors can telecommute via computer and change employers as the demand for their services changes. Software programmers, graphic designers, systems analysts, technical writers, photo researchers, book and media editors, and medical transcribers are just a few examples of people who can work from home or other non-office locations.

The manager's job is different in a networked organization. Motivating and leading people and making collaborative decisions online require different techniques than when individuals are physically present in a single location. As more employees do their jobs by linking to others through networks, managers must develop new skills. OB can provide valuable insights to help hone those skills.

Social Media

As we will discuss in Chapter 11, social media in the business world is here to stay. Despite its pervasiveness, many organizations continue to struggle with employees' use of social media in the workplace. In February 2015, a Texas pizzeria fired an employee before she showed up for her first day of work after she tweeted unflattering comments about her future job. In December 2014, Nordstrom fired an Oregon employee who had posted a personal Facebook comment seeming to advocate violence against white police officers.[47] These examples show that social media is a difficult issue for today's manager, presenting both a challenge and an opportunity for OB. For instance, how much should HR look into a candidate's social media presence? Should a hiring manager read the candidate's Twitter feeds, or just do a quick perusal of her Facebook profile? We will discuss this issue later in the text.

Once employees are on the job, many organizations have policies about accessing social media at work—when, where, and for what purposes. But what about the impact of social media on employee well-being? One recent study found that subjects who woke up in a positive mood and then accessed Facebook frequently found their mood decreased during the day. Moreover, subjects who checked Facebook frequently over a two-week period reported a decreased level of satisfaction with their lives.[48] Managers—and OB—are trying to increase employee satisfaction, and therefore improve and enhance positive organizational outcomes. We will discuss these issues further in Chapters 3 and 4.

Employee Well-Being at Work

The typical employee in the 1960s or 1970s showed up at a specified workplace Monday through Friday and worked for clearly defined 8- or 9-hour chunks of time. That's no longer true for a large segment of today's workforce, since the definition of the workplace has expanded to include anywhere a laptop or smartphone can go. However, even if employees work flexible hours at home or from half a continent away, managers need to consider their well-being at work.

One of the biggest challenges to maintaining employee well-being is the new reality that many workers never get away from the virtual workplace. And while communication technology allows many technical and professional employees to do their work at home, in their cars, or on the beach in Tahiti, it also means many feel like they're not part of a team. "The sense of belonging is very challenging for virtual workers, who seem to be all alone out in cyberland," said Ellen Raineri of Kaplan University.[49] Another challenge is that organizations are asking employees to put in longer hours. According to one study, one in four employees shows signs of burnout, and two in three report high stress levels and fatigue.[50] This may actually be an underestimate because workers report maintaining "always on" access for their managers through e-mail and texting. Finally, employee well-being is challenged by heavy outside commitments. Millions of single-parent employees and employees with dependent parents face significant challenges in balancing work and family responsibilities, for instance.

As a result of their increased responsibilities in and out of the workplace, employees want jobs that give them flexibility in their work schedules so they can better manage work–life conflicts.[51] In fact, 56 percent of men and women in a recent study reported that work–life balance was their definition of career success, more than money, recognition, and autonomy.[52] Most college and university students say attaining balance between personal life and work is a primary career goal; they want a life as well as a job. Organizations that don't help their people achieve work–life balance will find it increasingly difficult to attract and retain the most capable and motivated individuals.

As you'll see in later chapters, the field of OB offers a number of suggestions to guide managers in designing workplaces and jobs that can help employees deal with work–life conflicts.

Positive Work Environment

positive organizational scholarship
An area of OB research that concerns how organizations develop human strengths, foster vitality and resilience, and unlock potential.

A real growth area in OB research is **positive organizational scholarship** (also called *positive organizational behavior*), which studies how organizations develop human strengths, foster vitality and resilience, and unlock potential. Researchers in this area say too much of OB research and management practice has been targeted toward identifying what's wrong with organizations and their employees. In response, they try to study what's *good* about them.[53] Some key

Twitter employees rave about their company's culture, which creates a positive work environment where smart and friendly colleagues learn; share values, ideas, and information; and work together to help the company grow and succeed. At Twitter's San Francisco headquarters, employees like Jenna Sampson, community relations manager, enjoy free meals, yoga classes, and a rooftop garden.
Source: Noah Berger/Reuters

subjects in positive OB research are engagement, hope, optimism, and resilience in the face of strain. Researchers hope to help practitioners create positive work environments for employees.

Positive organizational scholars have studied a concept called "reflected best-self"—asking employees to think about when they were at their "personal best" in order to understand how to exploit their strengths. The idea is that we all have things at which we are unusually good, yet we too often focus on addressing our limitations and too rarely think about how to exploit our strengths.[54]

Although positive organizational scholarship does not deny the value of the negative (such as critical feedback), it does challenge researchers to look at OB through a new lens and pushes organizations to exploit employees' strengths rather than dwell on their limitations. One aspect of a positive work environment is the organization's culture, the topic of Chapter 16. Organizational culture influences employee behavior so strongly that organizations have begun to employ a culture officer to shape and preserve the company's personality.[55]

Ethical Behavior

In an organizational world characterized by cutbacks, expectations of increasing productivity, and tough competition, it's not surprising many employees feel pressured to cut corners, break rules, and engage in other questionable practices.

ethical dilemmas and ethical choices   Situations in which individuals are required to define right and wrong conduct.

Increasingly they face **ethical dilemmas and ethical choices**, in which they are required to identify right and wrong conduct. Should they "blow the whistle" if they uncover illegal activities in their company? Do they follow orders with which they don't personally agree? Do they "play politics" to advance their career?

What constitutes good ethical behavior has never been clearly defined and, in recent years, the line differentiating right from wrong has blurred. We see people all around us engaging in unethical practices—elected officials pad expense accounts or take bribes; corporate executives inflate profits to cash in lucrative stock options; and university administrators look the other way when winning coaches encourage scholarship athletes to take easy courses or even, in the recent case of the University of North Carolina-Chapel Hill, sham courses with fake grades.[56] When caught, people give excuses such as "Everyone does it" or "You have to seize every advantage."

Determining the ethically correct way to behave is especially difficult for both managers and employees in a global economy because different cultures have different perspectives on certain ethical issues.[57] The definition of fair treatment of employees in an economic downturn varies considerably across cultures, for instance. As we'll see in Chapter 2, perceptions of religious, ethnic, and gender diversity also differ across countries.

Today's manager must create an ethically healthy climate for employees in which they can do their work productively with minimal ambiguity about right and wrong behaviors. Companies that promote a strong ethical mission, encourage employees to behave with integrity, and provide strong leadership can influence employee decisions to behave ethically.[58] Classroom training sessions in ethics have also proven helpful in maintaining a higher level of awareness of the implications of employee choices as long as the training sessions are given on an ongoing basis.[59] In upcoming chapters, we'll discuss the actions managers can take to create an ethically healthy climate and help employees sort through ambiguous situations.

Vacation Deficit Disorder

Do you work to live, or live to work? Those of us who think it's a choice might be wrong. Almost a third of 1,000 respondents in a study by Kelton Research cited workload as a reason for not using allotted vacation days. Consider Ken Waltz, a director for Alexian Brothers Health System. He has 500 hours (approximately 3 months) in banked time off and no plans to spend it. "You're on call 24/7 and these days, you'd better step up or step out," he says, referring to today's leaner workforce. "It's not just me—it's upper management.... It's everybody."

Many people feel pressure, spoken or unspoken, to work through their vacation days. Employers expect workers to do more with less, putting pressure on workers to use all available resources—chiefly their time—to meet manager expectations. In today's economy there is always a ready line of replacement workers, and many employees will do everything possible to stay in their manager's good graces.

The issue of vacation time is an ethical choice for the employer and, moreover, for the employee. Many organizations have "use it or lose it" policies whereby employees forfeit the paid time off they've accrued for the year if they haven't used it. When employees forfeit vacation, the risk of burnout increases. Skipping vacation time can wear you down emotionally, leading to exhaustion, negative feelings about your work, and a reduced feeling of accomplishment. You may find you are absent more often, contemplate leaving your job, and grow less likely to want to help anyone (including your managers). Even though these are negative consequences for your employer as well as for you personally, often the employee must take charge of the situation. Here are some ways you can maintain your well-being and productivity:

1. **Recognize your feelings.** We solve few problems without first recognizing them. According to a recent study by ComPsych involving 2,000 employees, two in three identified high levels of stress, out-of-control feelings, and extreme fatigue.
2. **Identify your tendency for burnout.** Research on 2,089 employees found that burnout is especially acute for newcomers and job changers. Burnout symptoms should level off after 2 years, but each individual experiences stress differently.
3. **Talk about your stressors.** Thomas Donohoe, a researcher on work–life balance, recommends talking with trusted friends or family. On the job, appropriately discussing your stress factors can help you reduce job overload.
4. **Build in high physical activity.** Research found an increase in job burnout (and depression) was strongest for employees who did not engage in regular physical activity, while it was almost negligible for employees who did engage in regular high physical activity.
5. **Take brief breaks throughout your day.** For office employees, the current expert suggestion is to spend at least 1 to 2 minutes of every hour standing up to combat the effects of all-day sitting. Donohoe also suggests snack breaks, walks, or short naps to recharge.
6. **Take your vacation!** Studies suggest that recovery from stress can happen only if employees are (a) physically away from work and (b) not occupied by work-related duties. That means telling your manager that you will log off your e-mail accounts and shut off your phone for the duration of the vacation.

It is not always easy to look beyond the next deadline. But to maximize your long-term productivity and avoid stress, burnout, and illness—all of which are ultimately harmful to employer aims and employee careers alike—you should not succumb to vacation deficit disorder. Educate your managers. Your employer should thank you for it.

Sources: B. B. Dunford, A. J. Shipp, R. W. Boss, I. Angermeier, and A. D. Boss, "Is Burnout Static or Dynamic? A Career Transition Perspective of Employee Burnout Trajectories," *Journal of Applied Psychology* 97, no. 3 (2012): 637–50; E. J. Hirst, "Burnout on the Rise," *Chicago Tribune,* October 29, 2012, 3-1, 3-4; B. M. Rubin, "Rough Economy Means No Vacation," *Chicago Tribune,* September 3, 2012, 4; and S. Toker and M. Biron, "Job Burnout and Depression: Unraveling Their Temporal Relationship and Considering the Role of Physical Activity," *Journal of Applied Psychology* 97, no. 3 (2012): 699–710.

Coming Attractions: Developing an OB Model

7 Compare the three levels of analysis in this text's OB model.

We conclude this chapter by presenting a general model that defines the field of OB and stakes out its parameters, concepts, and relationships. By studying the model, you will have a good picture of how the topics in this text can inform your approach to management issues and opportunities.

An Overview

model An abstraction of reality, a simplified representation of some real-world phenomenon.

A **model** is an abstraction of reality, a simplified representation of some real-world phenomenon. Exhibit 1-5 presents the skeleton of our OB model. It proposes three types of variables (inputs, processes, and outcomes) at three levels of analysis (individual, group, and organizational). In the chapters to follow, we will proceed from the individual level (Chapters 2 through 8) to group behavior (Chapters 9 through 14) to the organizational system (Chapters 15 through 18). The model illustrates that inputs lead to processes, which lead to outcomes; we will discuss interrelationships at each level of analysis. Notice that the model also shows that outcomes can influence inputs in the future, which highlights the broad-reaching effect OB initiatives can have on an organization's future.

Inputs

input Variables that lead to processes.

Inputs are the variables like personality, group structure, and organizational culture that lead to processes. These variables set the stage for what will occur in an organization later. Many are determined in advance of the employment relationship. For example, individual diversity characteristics, personality, and values are shaped by a combination of an individual's genetic inheritance and childhood environment. Group structure, roles, and team responsibilities are

Exhibit 1-5 **A Basic OB Model**

Inputs	Processes	Outcomes
Individual Level • Diversity • Personality • Values	**Individual Level** • Emotions and moods • Motivation • Perception • Decision making	**Individual Level** • Attitudes and stress • Task performance • Citizenship behavior • Withdrawal behavior
Group Level • Group structure • Group roles • Team responsibilities	**Group Level** • Communication • Leadership • Power and politics • Conflict and negotiation	**Group Level** • Group cohesion • Group functioning
Organizational Level • Structure • Culture	**Organizational Level** • Human resource management • Change practices	**Organizational Level** • Productivity • Survival

typically assigned immediately before or after a group is formed. Finally, organizational structure and culture are usually the result of years of development and change as the organization adapts to its environment and builds up customs and norms.

Processes

processes Actions that individuals, groups, and organizations engage in as a result of inputs and that lead to certain outcomes.

If inputs are like the nouns in OB, processes are like verbs. **Processes** are actions that individuals, groups, and organizations engage in as a result of inputs and that lead to certain outcomes. At the individual level, processes include emotions and moods, motivation, perception, and decision making. At the group level, they include communication, leadership, power and politics, and conflict and negotiation. Finally, at the organizational level, processes include human resource management and change practices.

Outcomes

outcomes Key factors that are affected by some other variables.

Outcomes are the key variables that you want to explain or predict, and that are affected by some other variables. What are the primary outcomes in OB? Scholars have emphasized individual-level outcomes, such as attitudes and stress, task performance, citizenship behavior, and withdrawal behavior. At the group level, cohesion and functioning are the dependent variables. Finally, at the organizational level, we look at overall productivity and survival. Because these outcomes will be covered in all the chapters, we'll briefly discuss each here so you can understand what the goal of OB will be.

stress An unpleasant psychological process that occurs in response to environmental pressures.

Attitudes and Stress   Employee attitudes are the evaluations employees make, ranging from positive to negative, about objects, people, or events. For example, the statement "I really think my job is great" is a positive job attitude, and "My job is boring and tedious" is a negative job attitude. **Stress** is an unpleasant psychological process that occurs in response to environmental pressures.

Some people might think influencing employee attitudes and stress is purely soft stuff and not the business of serious managers, but as we will show, attitudes often have behavioral consequences that directly relate to organizational effectiveness. The belief that satisfied employees are more productive than dissatisfied employees has been a basic tenet among managers for years, though only now has research begun to support it. Ample evidence shows that employees who are more satisfied and treated fairly are more willing to engage in the above-and-beyond citizenship behavior so vital in the contemporary business environment.

task performance The combination of effectiveness and efficiency at doing core job tasks.

Task Performance   The combination of effectiveness and efficiency at doing your core job tasks is a reflection of your level of **task performance**. If we think about the job of a factory worker, task performance could be measured by the number and quality of products produced in an hour. The task performance of a teacher would be the level of education that students obtain. The task performance of consultants might be the timeliness and quality of the presentations they offer to the client. All these types of performance relate to the core duties and responsibilities of a job and are often directly related to the functions listed on a formal job description.

Obviously task performance is the most important human output contributing to organizational effectiveness, so in every chapter we devote considerable time to detailing how task performance is affected by the topic in question.

Organizational Citizenship Behavior (OCB)   The discretionary behavior that is not part of an employee's formal job requirements, and that contributes to the

These employees of W. L. Gore & Associates engage in good citizenship behavior, one of the primary individual-level outcomes in organizational behavior. Working in teams, these employees perform beyond expectations in helping each other, recognizing their peers, and doing more than their usual job responsibilities.
Source: PRNewsFoto/W. L. Gore & Associates, Inc/ AP images

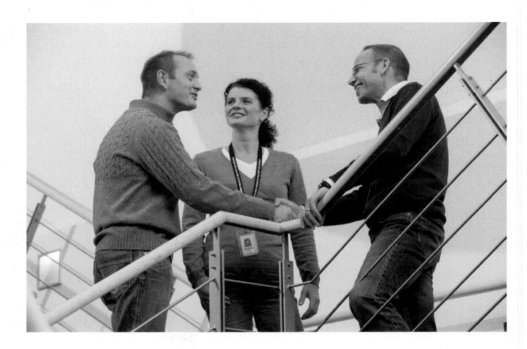

organizational citizenship behavior (OCB) Discretionary behavior that contributes to the psychological and social environment of the workplace.

psychological and social environment of the workplace, is called **organizational citizenship behavior (OCB)**, or simply citizenship behavior. Successful organizations have employees who will do more than their usual job duties—who will provide performance *beyond* expectations. In today's dynamic workplace, where tasks are increasingly performed by teams and flexibility is critical, employees who engage in "good citizenship" behaviors help others on their team, volunteer for extra work, avoid unnecessary conflicts, respect the spirit as well as the letter of rules and regulations, and gracefully tolerate occasional work-related impositions and nuisances.

Organizations want and need employees who will do things that aren't in any job description. Evidence indicates organizations that have such employees outperform those that don't. As a result, OB is concerned with citizenship behavior as an outcome variable.

withdrawal behavior The set of actions employees take to separate themselves from the organization.

Withdrawal Behavior We've already mentioned behavior that goes above and beyond task requirements, but what about behavior that in some way is below task requirements? **Withdrawal behavior** is the set of actions that employees take to separate themselves from the organization. There are many forms of withdrawal, ranging from showing up late or failing to attend meetings to absenteeism and turnover.

Employee withdrawal can have a very negative effect on an organization. The cost of employee turnover alone has been estimated to run into the thousands of dollars, even for entry-level positions. Absenteeism also costs organizations significant amounts of money and time every year. For instance, a recent survey found the average direct cost to U.S. employers of unscheduled absences is 8.7 percent of payroll.[60] And in Sweden, an average of 10 percent of the country's workforce is on sick leave at any given time.[61]

It's obviously difficult for an organization to operate smoothly and attain its objectives if employees fail to report to their jobs. The workflow is disrupted, and important decisions may be delayed. In organizations that rely heavily on assembly-line production, absenteeism can be considerably more than a disruption; it can drastically reduce the quality of output or even shut down the

What do I say about my termination?

I got fired! When prospective employers find out, they'll never hire me. Is there anything I can say to turn this around?

— *Matt*

Dear Matt:

Under this dark cloud, there are some silver linings: 1) firing, or involuntary termination, happens to just about everyone at least once in a career; and 2) there is a worldwide job shortage of skilled workers. You might be amazed to know that historically, individuals have changed jobs an average of 11 times over their early careers (from age 18 to 44). In fact, you can probably expect to stay in a job for less than three years, which means you'll have a lot of jobs in your lifetime.

Therefore, you shouldn't feel hopeless; you are likely to find your next job soon. ManpowerGroup's recent survey of over 37,000 employers in 42 countries found that 36 percent of organizations have talent shortages, the highest percentage in 7 years.

Still, we know you are worried about how to present the facts of your involuntary termination to prospective employers. If you give a truthful, brief account of the reason for your termination, you can position yourself well. Here are some additional suggestions:

- *Remember your soft skills count; in fact, they top the lists of employer requirements for all industries.* According to Chuck Knebl, a communications manager for the job placement company WorkOne, use your résumé and cover letter, interviews, and thank-you notes to showcase your communication skills. Employers report they are also looking for a teamwork attitude, positivity, personal responsibility, and punctuality, so use every opportunity to demonstrate these traits.
- *Although your soft skills count, don't forget your technical skills; employers agree they are equally important.* Knebl advises you to use your résumé to list your technical abilities and be prepared to elaborate upon request. Need some more skills? Job training has been shown to be helpful and can sometimes be free through colleges and unemployment offices.
- *Emphasize your ongoing training and education, especially as they relate to new technology; top performers are known to be continuous learners.* Also, if you've kept up with recent trends in social media, show it, but don't go on about your friend's tweet to Rihanna.

Best wishes for your success!

Sources: Bureau of Labor Statistics, United States Department of Labor, Employment Projections, http://www.bls.gov/emp/ep_chart_001.htm; G. Jones, "How the Best Get Better and Better," *Harvard Business Review* (June 2008): 123–27; ManpowerGroup, "The Talent Shortage Continues/2014," http://www.manpowergroup.com/wps/wcm/connect/0b882c15-38bf-41f3-8882-44c33d0e2952/2014_Talent_Shortage_WP_US2.pdf?MOD=AJPERES; J. Meister, "Job Hopping Is the 'New Normal' for Millennials: Three Ways to Prevent a Human Resource Nightmare," *Forbes* (August 14, 2012), http://www.forbes.com/sites/jeannemeister/2012/08/14/job-hopping-is-the-new-normal-for-millennials-three-ways-to-prevent-a-human-resource-nightmare/; and N. Schulz, "Hard Unemployment Truths about 'Soft' Skills," *The Wall Street Journal*, September 19, 2012, A15.

The opinions provided here are of the managers and authors only and do not necessarily reflect those of their organizations. The authors or managers are not responsible for any errors or omissions, or for the results obtained from the use of this information. In no event will the authors or managers, or their related partnerships or corporations thereof, be liable to you or anyone else for any decision made or action taken in reliance on the opinions provided here.

facility. Levels of absenteeism beyond the normal range have a direct impact on any organization's effectiveness and efficiency. A high rate of turnover can also disrupt the efficient running of an organization when knowledgeable and experienced personnel leave and replacements must be found to assume positions of responsibility. Research indicates that, in general, turnover is significantly harmful for organizational performance.[62]

All organizations have some turnover, of course. Turnover rates vary greatly by country and, in part, reflect the economy of that country. The U.S. national turnover rate in 2014 averaged about 40 percent; often the average is around 3 percent per month.[63] Is this good or bad? To answer that question, we need to know why there is turnover. Turnover includes voluntary terminations by the employee (quitting), involuntary terminations by the employer without cause (layoffs and discharges), and other separations including involuntary terminations with cause (firing). The yearly average for quitting in 2014 was about 20 percent; layoffs and discharges averaged about 14 percent; and other separations averaged about 4 percent for the year. Therefore, about half the turnover was due to employees quitting their jobs, about 35 percent was due to layoffs and discharges, and the remainder was for other reasons including firings.

While high turnover often impairs an organization's ability to achieve its goals, quitting is not all bad. In fact, U.S. Federal Reserve Chairwoman Janet Yellen has discussed the positive aspect of turnover for the economy: People quit because they are optimistic about their outside prospects.[64] Moreover, if the "right" people are leaving—the poorer performers—quits can actually be positive for an organization. They can create opportunities to replace under-performing individuals with others who have higher skills or motivation, open up increased opportunities for promotions, and bring new and fresh ideas to the organization. In today's changing world of work, reasonable levels of employee-initiated turnover improve organizational flexibility and employee independence, and they can lessen the need for management-initiated layoffs. Thus, while it is reasonable to conclude that high turnover often indicates high employee withdrawal (and thus has a negative effect on organizational performance), zero turnover is not necessarily the goal; and it's also important for organizations to assess which employees are leaving, and why.

So why do employees withdraw from work through counterproductive behaviors or quitting? As we will show later in the text, reasons include negative job attitudes, emotions, moods, and negative interactions with coworkers and supervisors.

group cohesion The extent to which members of a group support and validate one another while at work.

Group Cohesion   Although many outcomes in our model can be conceptualized as individual-level phenomena, some relate to the way groups operate. **Group cohesion** is the extent to which members of a group support and validate one another at work. In other words, a cohesive group is one that sticks together. When employees trust one another, seek common goals, and work together to achieve these common ends, the group is cohesive; when employees are divided among themselves in terms of what they want to achieve and have little loyalty to one another, the group is not cohesive.

There is ample evidence showing that cohesive groups are more effective.[65] These results are found both for groups studied in highly controlled laboratory settings and for work teams observed in field settings. This fits with our intuitive sense that people tend to work harder in groups that have a common purpose. Companies attempt to increase cohesion in a variety of ways, ranging from brief icebreaker sessions to social events like picnics, parties, and outdoor adventure-team retreats. Throughout the text we assess whether these specific efforts are likely to result in increases in group cohesiveness. We'll also consider ways that picking the right people to be on the team in the first place might be an effective way to enhance cohesion.

group functioning The quantity and quality of a group's work output.

Group Functioning   In the same way that positive job attitudes can be associated with higher levels of task performance, group cohesion should lead to positive group functioning. **Group functioning** refers to the quantity and quality of a group's work output. In the same way that the performance of a sports team is more than the sum of individual players' performance, group functioning in work organizations is more than the sum of individual task performances.

What does it mean to say that a group is functioning effectively? In some organizations, an effective group is one that stays focused on a core task and achieves its ends as specified. Other organizations look for teams that are able to work together collaboratively to provide excellent customer service. Still others put more of a premium on group creativity and the flexibility to adapt to changing situations. In each case, different types of activities will be required to get the most from the team.

productivity   The combination of the effectiveness and efficiency of an organization.

effectiveness   The degree to which an organization meets the needs of its clientele or customers.

efficiency   The degree to which an organization can achieve its ends at a low cost.

organizational survival   The degree to which an organization is able to exist and grow over the long term.

Productivity   The highest level of analysis in OB is the organization as a whole. An organization is productive if it achieves its goals by transforming inputs into outputs at the lowest cost. Thus **productivity** requires both **effectiveness** and **efficiency**.

A hospital is *effective* when it successfully meets the needs of its clientele. It is *efficient* when it can do so at a low cost. If a hospital manages to achieve higher output from its present staff by reducing the average number of days a patient is confined to bed or increasing the number of staff–patient contacts per day, we say the hospital has gained productive efficiency. A business firm is effective when it attains its sales or market share goals, but its productivity also depends on achieving those goals efficiently. Popular measures of organizational efficiency include return on investment, profit per dollar of sales, and output per hour of labor.

Service organizations must include customer needs and requirements in assessing their effectiveness. Why? Because a clear chain of cause and effect runs from employee attitudes and behavior to customer attitudes and profitability. For example, a recent study of six hotels in China indicated that negative employee attitudes decreased customer satisfaction and ultimately harmed the organization's profitability.[66]

Survival   The final outcome we will consider is **organizational survival**, which is simply evidence that the organization is able to exist and grow over the long term. The survival of an organization depends not just on how productive the organization is, but also on how well it fits with its environment. A company that is very productively making goods and services of little value to the market is unlikely to survive for long, so survival also relies on perceiving the market successfully, making good decisions about how and when to pursue opportunities, and successfully managing change to adapt to new business conditions.

Having reviewed the input, process, and outcome model, we're going to change the figure up a little bit by grouping topics together based on whether we study them at the individual, group, or organizational level. As you can see in Exhibit 1-6, we will deal with inputs, processes, and outcomes at all three

Exhibit 1-6   **The Plan of the Text**

The Individual

Inputs
- Diversity in Organizations (Ch. 2)
- Personality and Values (Ch. 5)

Processes
- Emotions and moods (Ch. 4)
- Motivation (Ch. 7 and 8)
- Perception and decision making (Ch. 6)

Outcomes
- Attitudes (Ch. 3) and stress (Ch. 18)
- Task performance (all)
- Citizenship behavior (all)
- Withdrawal behavior (all)

The Group

Inputs
- Group structure (Ch. 9 & 10)
- Group roles (Ch. 9 & 10)
- Team responsibilities (Ch. 9 & 10)

Processes
- Communication (Ch. 11)
- Leadership (Ch. 12)
- Power and politics (Ch. 13)
- Conflict and negotiation (Ch. 14)

Outcomes
- Group cohesion (Ch. 9 & 10)
- Group functioning (Ch. 9 & 10)

The Organization

Inputs
- Structure (Ch. 15)
- Culture (Ch. 16)

Processes
- Human resource management (Ch. 17)
- Change practices (Ch. 18)

Outcomes
- Productivity (all)
- Survival (all)

levels of analysis, but we group the chapters as shown here to correspond with the typical ways research has been done in these areas. For example, it is easier to understand one unified presentation about how personality leads to motivation, which leads to performance, than to jump around levels of analysis. Because each level builds on the one that precedes it, after going through them in sequence you will have a good idea of how the human side of organizations functions.

Summary

Managers need to develop their interpersonal, or people, skills to be effective in their jobs. Organizational behavior (OB) investigates the impact that individuals, groups, and structure have on behavior within an organization, and it applies that knowledge to make organizations work more effectively.

Implications for Managers

- Resist the inclination to rely on generalizations; some provide valid insights into human behavior, but many are erroneous. Get to know the person, and understand the context.
- Use metrics rather than hunches to explain cause-and-effect relationships.
- Work on your interpersonal skills to increase your leadership potential.
- Improve your technical skills and conceptual skills through training and staying current with OB trends like big data.
- OB can improve your employees' work quality and productivity by showing you how to empower your employees, design and implement change programs, improve customer service, and help your employees balance work–life conflicts.

The Battle of the Texts

POINT

Walk into your nearest major bookstore and you'll see shelves of management books whose titles tell us the topics we apparently need to know about:

- *The Secret* (Berrett-Koehler, 2014)
- *Turn the Ship Around!* (Portfolio, 2013)
- *The Way You Do Anything Is the Way You Do Everything* (Wiley, 2014)
- *Leadership Safari* (Best Seller, 2014)
- *Business Is a Baby* (Amazon Digital Services, 2014)
- *Think Like a Freak* (William Morrow, 2014)
- *Spiraling Upward* (Amazon Digital Services, 2015)
- *Refire! Don't Retire* (Berrett-Koehler, 2015)
- *Top Dog* (Amazon Digital Services, 2015)

Popular books on organizational behavior often have cute titles and are fun to read, but they make the job of managing people seem like it's just a matter of having a good slogan and five easy steps. If you dig into the texts, you'll find that most are based on the author's opinions rather than substantive research. Most become popular, in part, because people largely agree with the opinions they are reading and enjoy the author's writing style. Often, the writers are presentation speakers or consultants whose real business is in delivering ideas to you. When the author is a veteran from the business world, it is doubtful that one person's experience translates into an effective management practice for everyone. Even when the authors are numbers-oriented, as are the "Freak" authors Steven Levitt and Stephen Dubner, their conclusions for management are not management-research based. So why do we base our own management philosophies on these books when, with a little effort, we can access knowledge produced by thousands of scientific studies on human behavior in organizations?

Organizational behavior is a complex subject. Few if any simple statements about human behavior are generalizable to all people in all situations. Would you try to apply leadership insights you got from a book about *Star Wars* or *Breaking Bad* to managing software engineers in the twenty-first century? Surely not. Neither should we try to apply leadership insights that aren't based on research about the type of workplaces in which we function.

COUNTERPOINT

People want to know about management—the good, the bad, and the ugly. People who have experience or high interest write about the topics that interest readers, and publishers put out the best of these texts. When books become popular, we know people are learning from them and finding good results by applying the author's management ideas. It's a good process. Texts like these can provide people with the secrets to management that others have worked out through experience. Isn't it better to learn about management from people in the trenches, as opposed to the latest obscure references from academia? Many of the most important insights we gain in life aren't necessarily the product of careful empirical research studies.

"Fluffy" management guides sometimes do get published, and once in a while they become popular. But do they outnumber the esoteric research studies published in scholarly journal articles every year? Far from it; sometimes it seems that for every popular business text, there are thousands of scholarly journal articles. Many of these articles can hardly be read by individuals in the workplace—they are buried in academic libraries, riddled with strange acronyms and "insider" terms, and light on practical application. Often they apply to specific management scenarios, so they are even less generalizable. For example, a few recent management and OB studies were published in 2015 with the following titles:

- *Transferring Management Practices to China: A Bourdieusian Critique of Ethnocentricity*
- *Cross-Cultural Perceptions of Clan Control in Korean Multi-national Companies: A Conceptual Investigation of Employees' Fairness Monitoring Based on Cultural Values*
- *The Resistible Rise of Bayesian Thinking in Management: Historical Lessons from Decision Analysis*
- *A Model of Rhetorical Legitimation: The Structure of Communication and Cognition Underlying Institutional Maintenance and Change*

We don't mean to poke fun at these studies, but our point is that all ways of creating knowledge can be criticized. If business books can sometimes be "fluffy," academic articles can be esoteric and even less relevant. Popular books can add to our understanding of how people work and how to best manage them; we shouldn't assume they are not of value. And while there is no one right way to learn the science and art of managing people in organizations, the most enlightened managers gather insights from multiple sources: their own experience, research findings, observations of others, and, yes, the popular business press. Authors and academics have an important role to play, and it isn't fair to condemn business books with catchy titles.

CHAPTER REVIEW

MyManagementLab

Go to **mymanagementlab.com** to complete the problems marked with this icon. ⭐

QUESTIONS FOR REVIEW

1-1 What is the importance of interpersonal skills in the workplace?

1-2 What is the definition of organizational behavior (OB)?

1-3 How does systematic study contribute to our understanding of OB?

1-4 What are the major behavioral science disciplines that contribute to OB?

1-5 Why are there so few absolutes in OB?

1-6 What are the challenges and opportunities for managers in using OB concepts?

1-7 What are the three levels of analysis in our OB model?

EXPERIENTIAL EXERCISE   Managing the OB Way

Divide the class into groups of approximately four members each. Each group should consider the following scenario:

You will assume the role of a special committee of district managers at a large pharmaceutical company. Your committee will be meeting to discuss some problems. The process set up by the company is as follows:

1. Each committee member should first review the problem privately and formulate independent ideas for what might be done.
2. At the start of the meeting, each member should spend one minute addressing the group.

During the meeting, the committee must reach a consensus on both the *best solution* and *supporting rationale* to each problem. How this is done is entirely up to the committee members, but you must come up with a *consensus decision* and not a majority opinion achieved by voting.

Here is the problem your committee is to consider:

The company has no specific policy regarding facial hair. Tom, a pharmaceutical sales rep with a little more than a year's experience and an average (but declining) sales record, has grown a very long and ragged beard that detracts significantly from his appearance. His hobby is playing bass in an amateur bluegrass

band, and he feels that a ragged beard is an important part of the act. Tom says his beard is a personal fashion statement that has to do with his individual freedom.

There have been numerous complaints about Tom's appearance from both doctors and pharmacists. The manager has talked to him on many occasions about the impact his appearance could have on his sales. Nevertheless, Tom still has the beard.

The manager is concerned about Tom's decreasing sales as well as the professional image of the sales force in the medical community. Tom says his sales decrease has nothing to do with his beard. However, sales in the other territories in the district are significantly better than they were last year.

When the groups have reached their consensus decisions, the following questions will serve for class discussion:

1-8. What do you think are the concerns for the company regarding Tom's facial hair? Should they care about his appearance?

1-9. What was your group's consensus decision regarding the issue with Tom's facial hair?

1-10. Let's say Tom told you he thinks the beard is part of his personal religion that he is forming. Do you think that announcement would change how you talk to Tom about the issue?

ETHICAL DILEMMA There's a Drone in Your Soup

It is the year 2020, and drones are everywhere. Alibaba quadcopters have been delivering special ginger tea to customers in Beijing, Shanghai, and Guangzhou for years; Amazon's octocopters finally deliver packages in most major cities within 30 minutes without knocking down pedestrians; and college students everywhere welcome late-night nachos from Taco Bell Tacocopters. Indoor drones are still in the pioneering phase—backyard enthusiasts are building tiny versions, but no large-scale commercial efforts have been put toward indoor utility drones. That's all about to change.

You work for a multinational technology corporation on a sprawling, 25-acre headquarters campus, with offices in 2 million square feet of interior space in one large building and four additional smaller (but still large) buildings. The official Head of Interior Spaces is your boss; you're the leader of the Consideration of New Things team. In a meeting with your team, your boss says, "I've just heard from my friend at Right To Drones Too (R2D2) that his group has perfected their inside drone. It's small and light but can carry up to 10 pounds. It includes a camera, a speaker, and a recorder."

Your team expresses surprise; no one even knew an inside utility drone was under development, and governments worldwide are still haggling over regulations for drones. Your boss goes on enthusiastically, "I've seen the little drones, and I think you'll be impressed—not only can they scoot across the quad, but they can fetch things off tables, grab me a latté, attend meetings for me, check over your shoulders to see what you're working on … anything!

They're really accurate, agile, and super quiet, so you'll barely even know they're around. My friend wants us to have the first 100 drones here for free, and he's willing to send them over tomorrow! I figure we can hand them out randomly, although of course we'll each have one."

Your boss sits back, smiling and expecting applause. You glance at your team members and are relieved to see doubt and hesitation on their faces.

"Sounds, uh, great," you reply. "But how about the team takes the afternoon to set the ground rules?"

Questions

1-11. How might the R2D2 drones influence employee behavior? Do you think they will cause people to act more or less ethically? Why?

1-12. Who should get the drones initially? How can you justify your decision ethically? What restrictions for use should these people be given, and how do you think employees, both those who get drones and those who don't, will react to this change?

1-13. How will your organization deal with sabotage or misuse of the drones? The value of an R2D2 drone is $2,500.

1-14. Many organizations already use electronic monitoring of employees, including sifting through website usage and e-mail correspondence, often without the employees' direct knowledge. In what ways might drone monitoring be better or worse for employees than covert electronic monitoring of Web or e-mail activity?

CASE INCIDENT 1 Apple Goes Global

It wasn't long ago that products from Apple, perhaps the most recognizable name in electronics manufacturing around the world, were made entirely in America. This is not the case anymore. Now, almost all of the approximately 70 million iPhones, 30 million iPads, and 59 million other Apple products sold yearly are manufactured overseas. This change represents more than 20,000 jobs directly lost by U.S. workers, not to mention more than 700,000 other jobs given to foreign companies in Asia, Europe, and elsewhere. The loss is not temporary. As the late Steven P. Jobs, Apple's iconic co-founder, told President Obama, "Those jobs aren't coming back."

At first glance, the transfer of jobs from one workforce to another would seem to hinge on a difference in wages, but Apple shows this is an oversimplification. In fact, some say paying U.S. wages would add only $65 to each iPhone's expense, while Apple's profits average hundreds of dollars per phone. Rather, and of more concern, Apple's leaders

believe the intrinsic characteristics of the labor force available to them in China—which they identify as flexibility, diligence, and industrial skills—are superior to those of the U.S. labor force. Apple executives tell of shorter lead times and faster manufacturing processes in China that are becoming the stuff of company legend. "The speed and flexibility is breathtaking," one executive said. "There's no American plant that can match that." Another said, "We shouldn't be criticized for using Chinese workers. The U.S. has stopped producing people with the skills we need."

Because Apple is one of the most imitated companies in the world, this perception of an overseas advantage might suggest that the U.S. workforce needs to be better led, better trained, more effectively managed, and more motivated to be proactive and flexible. If U.S. (and western European) workers are less motivated and less adaptable, it's hard to imagine that does not spell trouble for the future of the American workforce. Perhaps, though, Apple's switch from "100 percent Made in the U.S.A." to "10 percent Made in the U.S.A." represents the natural growth pattern of a company going global. At this point, the iPhone is largely designed in the United States (where Apple has 43,000 employees); parts are made in South Korea, Taiwan, Singapore, Malaysia, Japan, Europe, and elsewhere; and products are assembled in China. The future of at least 247 suppliers worldwide depends on Apple's approximately $30.1 billion in orders per quarter. And we can't forget that Apple posted $16.1 billion in revenue from China in the first quarter of 2015, up 70 percent from the first quarter of 2014, perhaps in part because its manufacturing in China builds support for the brand there.

As maker of some of the most cutting-edge, revered products in the electronics marketplace, perhaps Apple serves not as a failure of one country to hold onto a company completely, but as one of the best examples of global ingenuity.

Questions

1-15. What are the pros and cons for local and overseas labor forces of Apple's going global? What are the potential political implications for country relationships?

1-16. As a U.S. corporation, does Apple and its management have a moral obligation to provide jobs for U.S. employees first? If this is the case, then does this put international employees at a distinct disadvantage?

1-17. Is it possible for U.S. managers to organize, motivate, and ensure quality in their Chinese manufacturing facilities?

Sources: B. X. Chen, "IPhone Sales in China Bolster Apple Earnings," *The New York Times* (January 27, 2015), http://www.nytimes.com/2015/01/28/technology/apple-quarterly-earnings.html?_r=0; C. Duhigg and K. Bradsher, "How U.S. Lost Out on iPhone Work," *The New York Times,* January 22, 2013, A1, A22–A23; H. Gao, "How the Apple Confrontation Divides China," *The Atlantic* (April 8, 2013), www.theatlantic.com/china/archive/2013/04/how-the-apple-confrontation-divides-china/274764/; and A. Satariano, "Apple Slowdown Threatens $30 Billion Global Supplier Web," *Bloomberg,* www.bloomberg.com/news/2013-04-18/apple-slowdown-threatens-30-billion-global-supplier-web-tech.html.

CASE INCIDENT 2 Big Data for Dummies

Do you need big data? Maybe the question is better phrased as: Can you afford not to use big data? The age of big data is here, and to ignore its benefits is to run the risk of missed opportunities.

Organizations using big data are quickly reaping rewards, as a survey of 2,022 managers worldwide indicated recently. In fact, 71 percent of respondents agreed that organizations using big data will gain a "huge competitive advantage." These managers also saw the need for big data: 58 percent responded that they never, rarely, or only sometimes have enough data to make key business decisions. Furthermore, they've witnessed the benefits: 67 percent agreed that big data has helped their organization to innovate. So why did only 28 percent find that their access to useful data significantly increased in a year?

According to Amy Braverman, a principal statistician who analyzes NASA's spacecraft data, the problem is in interpreting the new kinds and volumes of data we are able to collect. "This opportunistic data collection is leading to entirely new kinds of data that aren't well suited to the existing statistical and data-mining methodologies," she said. IT and business leaders agree: in a recent survey, "determining how to get value" was identified as the number 1 challenge of big data.

With strong need combating the high hurdle for usability, how should a company get started using big data? The quick answer seems to be to hire talent. But not just anyone will do. Here are some points to ponder when hiring data professionals:

1. **Look for candidates with a strong educational background in analytics/statistics.** You want someone who knows more than you do about handling copious amounts of data.
2. **The ideal candidates will have specific experience in your industry or a related industry.** "When you have all those Ph.D.s in a room, magic doesn't necessarily happen because they may not have the business capability," said Andy Rusnak, a senior executive at Ernst & Young.
3. **Search for potential candidates from industry leader organizations that are more advanced in big data.**
4. **Communication skills are a must.** Look for a candidate "who can translate Ph.D. to English," says SAP Chief Data Scientist David Ginsberg. He adds, "Those are the hardest people to find."
5. **Find candidates with a proven record of finding useful information from a mess of data, including data from questionable sources.** You want someone who is analytical *and* discerning.
6. **Look for people who can think in 8- to 10-week periods, not just long term.** Most data projects have a short-term focus.

7. **Test candidates' expertise on real problems.** Netflix's Director of Algorithms asks candidates, "You have this data that comes from our users. How can you use it to solve this particular problem?"

Questions

1-18. Let's say you work in a metropolitan city for a large department store chain and your manager puts you in charge of a team to find out whether keeping the store open an hour longer each day would increase profits. What data might be available to your decision-making process? What data would be important to your decision?

⭐1-19. What kinds of data might we want in OB applications?

1-20. As Braverman notes, one problem with big data is making sense of the information. How might a better understanding of psychology help you sift through all this data?

Sources: M. Taes, "If I Could Have More Data...," *The Wall Street Journal,* March 24, 2014, R5; S. Thurm, "It's a Whole New Data Game," *The Wall Street Journal,* February 10, 2015, R6; and J. Willhite, "Getting Started in 'Big Data'," *The Wall Street Journal,* February 4, 2014, B7.

MyManagementLab

Go to **mymanagementlab.com** for the following Assisted-graded writing questions:

1-21. Now that you've read the chapter and Case Incident 1, if you were an Apple manager whose employees were losing their jobs to overseas workers, what would you advise your teams to do in order to find re-employment in their professions? What types of training—basic, technical, interpersonal, problem-solving—would you recommend?

1-22. In relation to Case Incident 2, why do you think it is important to have educated, experienced statisticians on any team that is using big data for decision making? What might be the consequences of hiring someone with less experience?

1-23. **MyManagementLab Only** – comprehensive writing assignment for this chapter.

ENDNOTES

[1] "Survey: Few CFOs Plan to Invest in Interpersonal Skills Development for Their Teams," Accountemps press release, June 19, 2013, http://accountemps.rhi.mediaroom.com/2013-06-19-Survey-Few-CFOs-Plan-to-Invest-in-Interpersonal-Skills-Development-for-Their-Teams.

[2] K. Dill, "The 20 Best Places to Work in 2015," *Forbes*, December 10, 2014, http://www.forbes.com/sites/kathryndill/2014/12/10/the-best-places-to-work-in-2015/.

[3] I. S. Fulmer, B. Gerhart, and K. S. Scott, "Are the 100 Best Better? An Empirical Investigation of the Relationship between Being a 'Great Place to Work' and Firm Performance," *Personnel Psychology*, Winter 2003, 965–93.

[4] S. E. Humphrey, J. D. Nahrgang, and F. P. Morgeson, "Integrating Motivational, Social, and Contextual Work Design Features: A Meta-Analytic Summary and Theoretical Extension of the Work Design Literature," *Journal of Applied Psychology* 92, no. 5 (2007): 1332–56.

[5] E. R. Burris, "The Risks and Rewards of Speaking Up: Managerial Responses to Employee Voice," *Academy of Management Journal* 55, no. 4 (2012): 851–75.

[6] T. L. Miller, C. L. Wesley II, and D. E. Williams, "Educating the Minds of Caring Hearts: Comparing the Views of Practitioners and Educators on the Importance of Social Entrepreneurship Competencies," *Academy of Management Learning & Education* 2, no. 3 (2012): 349–70.

[7] H. Aguinis and A. Glavas, "What We Don't Know about Corporate Social Responsibility: A Review and Research Agenda," *Journal of Management*, July 2012, 932–68.

[8] D. Meinert, "Background on Bosses," *HR Magazine*, August 2014, 29.

[9] Ibid.

[10] Ibid.

[11] A. I. Kraut, P. R. Pedigo, D. D. McKenna, and M. D. Dunnette, "The Role of the Manager: What's Really Important in Different Management Jobs," *Academy of Management Executive* 19, no. 4 (2005): 122–29.

[12] C. Matheson, "Understanding the Policy Process: The Work of Henry Mintzberg," *Public Administration Review* 69 (2009): 1148–61; S. Segal, "A Heideggerian Perspective on the Relationship between Mintzberg's Distinction between Engaged and Disconnected Management: The Role of Uncertainty in Management," *Journal of Business Ethics* 103 (2011): 469–83; H. Mintzberg, "Productivity is Killing American Enterprise," *Harvard Business Review* 85 (2007): 25; and H. Mintzberg, "Rebuilding Companies as Communities," *Harvard Business Review* 87 (2009): 140–43.

[13] Ibid.

[14] D. Bartram, "The Great Eight Competencies: A Criterion-Centric Approach to Validation," *Journal of Applied Psychology* 90, no. 6 (2005): 1185–1203; and S. E. Scullen, M. K. Mount, and T. A. Judge, "Evidence of the Construct Validity of Developmental Ratings of Managerial Performance," *Journal of Applied Psychology* 88, no. 1 (2003): 50–66.

[15] For the original study, see F. Luthans, "Successful vs. Effective Real Managers," *Academy of Management Executive*, May 1988, 127–32. A great deal of research has been built by Fred Luthans and others from this study. See, for example, F. Shipper and J. Davy, "A Model and Investigation of Managerial Skills, Employees' Attitudes, and Managerial Performance," *Leadership Quarterly* 13 (2002): 95–120.

[16] P. Wu, M. Foo, and D. B. Turban, "The Role of Personality in Relationship Closeness, Developer Assistance, and Career Success," *Journal of Vocational Behavior* 73, no. 3 (2008): 440–48; and A. M. Konrad, R. Kashlak, I. Yoshioka, R. Waryszak, and N. Toren, "What Do Managers Like to Do? A Five-Country Study," *Group & Organization Management*, December 2001, 401–33.

[17] L. Dragoni, H. Park, J. Soltis, and S. Forte-Trammell, "Show and Tell: How Supervisors Facilitate Leader Development Among Transitioning Leaders," *Journal of Applied Psychology* 99, no. 1 (2014): 66-86.

[18] For a review of what one researcher believes *should* be included in organizational behavior, based on survey data, see J. B. Miner, "The Rated Importance, Scientific Validity, and Practical Usefulness of Organizational Behavior Theories: A Quantitative Review," *Academy of Management Learning & Education*, September 2003, 250–68.

[19] D. M. Rousseau, *The Oxford Handbook of Evidence-Based Management (Oxford Library of Psychology)* (New York: Oxford University Press, 2014).

[20] J. Surowiecki, "The Fatal-Flaw Myth," *The New Yorker*, July 31, 2006, 25.

[21] Z. Karabell, "Everyone Has a Data Point," *The Wall Street Journal*, February 19, 2014, A11.

[22] E. Morozov, "Every Little Byte Counts," *The New York Times Book Review*, May 18, 2014, 23.

[23] M. Taves, "If I Could Have More Data…," *The Wall Street Journal*, March 24, 2014, R5.

[24] E. Gamerman, "When the Art is Watching You," *The Wall Street Journal*, December 12, 2014, D1–D2.

[25] V. Monga, "What Is All That Data Worth?" *The Wall Street Journal*, October 13, 2014, B3, B6.

[26] E. Dwoskin and Y. Koh, "Twitter Pushes Deeper into Data," *The Wall Street Journal*, April 16, 2014, B2.

[27] "What Will Transform the Way People Work?" *HR Magazine*, December 2014, 16.

[28] N. Bloom, R. Sadun, and J. Van Reenan, "How Three Essential Practices Can Address Even the Most Complex Global Practices," *Harvard Business Review*, November 2012, 77–82.

[29] C. Cole, "Changing Neurobiology with Behavior," Association for Psychological Science *Observer* 27, no. 6 (2014): 29–32.

[30] E. Dwoskin, "Big Data Knows When You Turn off the Lights," *The Wall Street Journal*, October 21, 2014, B1–B2.

[31] S. Lohr, "Unblinking Eyes Track Employees," *The New York Times*, June 22, 2014, 1, 15.

[32] D. B. Bhave, "The Invisible Eye? Electronic Performance Monitoring and Employee Job Performance," *Personnel Psychology* 67 (2003): 605–35.

[33] R. Karlgaard, "Danger Lurking: Taylor's Ghost," *Forbes*, May 26, 2014, 34.

[34] E. Dwoskin, "Big Data Knows When You Turn off the Lights."

[35] W. Isaacson, "Of Man and Machine," *The Wall Street Journal*, September 27–28, 2015, C1–C2.

[36] V. Morozov, "Every Little Byte Counts."

[37] J. Farrar, "U.S. Minimum Wage—Compare It to the Rest of the World," (January 29, 2014), Worldcrunch, http://www.worldcrunch.com/eyes-on-the-u.s./u.s.-minimum-wage-compare-it-to-the-rest-of-world/state-of-the-union-minimum-wage-workers-labor/c5s14866/#.VQBdd_nF9uk, accessed March 11, 2015.

[38] C. Karmin and S. Chaturvedi, "Grosvenor House Is Seized," *The Wall Street Journal*, March 4, 2015, C8.

[39] V. McGrane, "The Downside of Lower Unemployment," *The Wall Street Journal*, February 3, 2014, A2.

[40] A. Lowrey, "Long Out of Work, and Running Out of Options," *The New York Times*, April 4, 2014, B1, B4.

[41] L. Weber and R. E. Silverman, "On-Demand Workers: 'We Are Not Robots,'" *The Wall Street Journal*, January 28, 2015, B1, B7.

[42] C. Porter and M. Korn, "Can This Online Course Get Me a Job?" *The Wall Street Journal*, March 4, 2014, B7.

[43] D. Belkin and M. Peters, "For New Grads, Path to a Career is Bumpy," *The Wall Street Journal*, May 24–25, 2014, A5.

[44] N. Kitsantonis, "A Hands-On Approach to the Greek Economy," *The New York Times*, March 25, 2014, B3.

[45] G. Naik, "Global Life Expectancy Rises by Six Years," *The Wall Street Journal*, December 18, 2014, A10.

[46] I. O. Karpen, "Service-Dominant Orientation: Measurement and Impact on Performance Outcomes," *Journal of Retailing* 91, no. 1 (2015): 89–108.

[47] J. Greenwald, "Tips for Dealing with Employees Whose Social Media Posts Reflect Badly on Your Company," *Forbes*, March 6, 2015, www.forbes.com/sites/entrepreneursorganization/2015/03/06/

tips-for-dealing-with-employees-whose-social-media-posts-reflect-badly-on-your-company/.

[48]E. Jaffe, "Using Technology to Scale the Scientific Mountain," *Association for Psychological Science Observer* 27, no. 6 (2014): 17–19.

[49]N. Fallon, "No Face Time? No Problem: How to Keep Virtual Workers Engaged," *Business News Daily*, October 2, 2014, http://www.businessnewsdaily.com/7228-engaging-remote-employees.html.

[50]E. J. Hirst, "Burnout on the Rise," *Chicago Tribune*, October 19, 2012, http://articles.chicagotribune.com/2012-10-29/business/ct-biz-1029-employee-burnout-20121029_1_employee-burnout-herbert-freudenberger-employee-stress.

[51]S. Shellenbarger, "Single and off the Fast Track," *The Wall Street Journal*, May 23, 2012, D1, D3.

[52]M. Mithel, "What Women Want," *Business Today*, March 8, 2013, http://businesstoday.intoday.in/story/careers-work-life-balance-women/1/193135.html.

[53]F. Luthans and C. M. Youssef, "Emerging Positive Organizational Behavior," *Journal of Management*, June 2007, 321–49; C. M. Youssef and F. Luthans, "Positive Organizational Behavior in the Workplace: The Impact of Hope, Optimism, and Resilience," *Journal of Management* 33, no. 5 (2007): 774–800; and J. E. Dutton and S. Sonenshein, "Positive Organizational Scholarship," in C. Cooper and J. Barling (eds.), *Encyclo-pedia of Positive Psychology* (Thousand Oaks, CA: Sage, 2007).

[54]L. M. Roberts, G. Spreitzer, J. Dutton, R. Quinn, E. Heaphy, and B. Barker, "How to Play to Your Strengths," *Harvard Business Review*, January 2005, 1–6; and L. M. Roberts, J. E. Dutton, G. M. Spreitzer, E. D. Heaphy, and R. E. Quinn, "Composing the Reflected Best Self-Portrait: Becoming Extraordinary in Work Organizations," *Academy of Management Review* 30, no. 4 (2005): 712–36.

[55]"Five Jobs That Won't Exist in 10 Years… And One New Title You'll Start to See," *HR Magazine*, February 2014, 16.

[56]Editorial Board, "NCAA Should Punish the University of North Carolina for Cheating Scandal," *Chicago Tribune*, November 7, 2014, http://www.chicagotribune.com/news/opinion/editorials/ct-north-carolina-sports-scandal-edit-1108-20141107-story.html, accessed March 11, 2015.

[57]W. Bailey and A. Spicer, "When Does National Identity Matter? Convergence and Divergence in International Business Ethics," *Academy of Management Journal* 50, no. 6 (2007): 1462–80; and A. B. Oumlil and J. L. Balloun, "Ethical Decision-Making Differences between American and Moroccan Managers," *Journal of Business Ethics* 84, no. 4 (2009): 457–78.

[58]D. M. Mayer, M. Kuenzi, R. Greenbaum, M. Bardes, and R. Salvador, "How Low Does Ethical Leadership Flow? Test of a Trickle-Down Model," *Organizational Behavior and Human Decision Processes* 108, no. 1 (2009): 1–13; and A. Ardichvili, J. A. Mitchell, and D. Jondle, "Characteristics of Ethical Business Cultures," *Journal of Business Ethics* 85, no. 4 (2009): 445–51.

[59]D. Meinert, "Managers' Influence," *HR Magazine*, April 2014, 25.

[60]"Unplanned Absence Costs Organizations 8.7 Percent of Payroll, Mercer/Kronos Study" (June 28, 2010), www.mercer.com/press-releases/1383785.

[61]W. Hoge, "Sweden's Cradle-to-Grave Welfare Starts to Get Ill," *International Herald Tribune*, September 25, 2002, 8.

[62]T.-Y. Park and J. D. Shaw, "Turnover Rates and Organizational Performance: A Meta-Analysis," *Journal of Applied Psychology* 98 (2013): 268–309.

[63]"Job Openings and Labor Turnover Survey/2014 Revised," www.bls.gov, http://www.bls.gov/jlt/revisiontables.htm, accessed March 13, 2015.

[64]N. Shah, "Good Sign for Jobs: Less Caution, More Quitting," *The Wall Street Journal*, February 10, 2014, A2.

[65]M. Casey-Campbell and M. L. Martens, "Sticking It All Together: A Critical Assessment of the Group Cohesion-Performance Literature," *International Journal of Management Reviews* 11 (2008): 223–46.

[66]X. Zhao and A. S. Mattila, "Examining the Spillover Effect of Frontline Employees' Work-Family Conflict on Their Affective Work Attitudes and Customer Satisfaction," *International Journal of Hospitality Management*, June 2013, 310–15.

2 Diversity in Organizations

2-1 Describe the two major forms of workplace diversity.

2-4 Explain how other differentiating characteristics factor into OB.

2-2 Demonstrate how workplace discrimination undermines organizational effectiveness.

2-5 Demonstrate the relevance of intellectual and physical abilities to OB.

2-3 Describe how the key biographical characteristics are relevant to OB.

2-6 Describe how organizations manage diversity effectively.

MyManagementLab®
⭐ **Chapter Warm Up**

If your professor has chosen to assign this, go to the Assignments section of **mymanagementlab.com** to complete the chapter warm up.

EXPLOITING A LOOPHOLE

Welcome to Atalissa, Iowa, a quintessential small town of 311 people— and a nasty secret. If you've seen this picture before, you are probably aware that what happened in this converted schoolhouse is the basis of the largest U.S. Equal Employment Opportunity Commission (EEOC) award in history.

The tale of the Atalissa bunkhouse begins in 1974, when Henry's Turkey Service of Texas rented the abandoned building near its Iowa processing plant to house its workers, a group of young, mentally disabled men taken from state institutions. At the time, the unregulated work-to-live arrangement that provided the men with an average of only $65 per month for full-time employment was completely legal. Why? A section of the Fair Labor Standards Act of 1938 allowed certified for-profit employers to pay less than minimum wage to workers with disabilities. Furthermore, the company legally deducted money from the men's meager earnings and their Social Security checks to cover room, board, and "extras" like medical care, since the workers didn't have health insurance or Medicaid. At the plant, the men were assigned the worst jobs of manually eviscerating 20,000 turkeys per day. The work was back-breaking and "too bloody," said Billy Penner, who awoke at 3 a.m. for decades to work alongside the hundreds of men who came and went from the bunkhouse.

Conditions in the bunkhouse were horrible, with no heat, covered windows and padlocked doors, cockroaches, and filth. Two "caretakers" doled out punishments that included standing with hands on a pole for hours and walking in circles while carrying heavy weights. Men were sometimes handcuffed to their beds overnight, denied bathroom breaks, kicked in the groin, and verbally abused. Men who ran away were caught and brought back.

Through the years, allegations about Henry's Turkey Service made their way into the legal system. They cited the poor treatment of workers; violation of the federal Migrant and Seasonal Worker Protection Act; harsh labor that killed an elderly, disabled worker; pay inequity; deplorable conditions; and fire hazards. However, the Iowa Department of Human Services, the U.S. Department of Labor, Iowa Workforce Development, and the Department of Inspections and Appeals dismissed most of the allegations without investigation. None of the departments ever questioned whether the indentured servitude was legal.

Finally, in 2009, a worker's sister alerted a newspaper reporter, and investigators rescued the 21 remaining men. A number of lawsuits followed, resulting in the largest verdict ever obtained by the EEOC and the largest verdict relating to the Americans with Disabilities Act, over $240 million (the business was worth only $4 million, though). No amount of money can restore the men to health or well-being. EEOC attorney Robert Canino referenced their "broken hearts, broken spirits, shattered dreams and, ultimately, their broken lives."

EEOC chairwoman Jacqueline Berrien said, "The verdict sends an important message that the conduct that occurred here is intolerable in this nation." But does it? After all, the people of Atalissa knew the men well. The workers attended Atalissa Zion Lutheran Church, sang in the choir, joined in town celebrations, and spent their money at the mini mart. Atalissa owned the bunkhouse Henry's Turkey rented; the men were known by the mayor and the sheriff. And the town claimed to love them. Carol O'Neill of the Atalissa Betterment Committee said, "Even though they were adult men, they were boys to us. They were like—our boys." Sadly, these men were not extended protection, and their rights were repeatedly ignored and dismissed. The Atalissa scandal serves as a reminder that true fairness is not just a warm feeling toward the disabled, but the ethical responsibility of us all.

Sources: Atalissa Population, https://suburbanstats.org/population/iowa/how-many-people-live-in-atalissa, accessed March 24, 2015; K. Allemeier, "How 21 Men Lived in Atalissa Bunkhouse," *The WCF Courier* (February 12, 2009), http://wcfcourier.com/news/local/how-men-lived-in-atalissa-bunkhouse/article_0d1867dc-c722-54f4-97e3-8b0d5e73e587.html; K. Bracken, "The 'Boys' in the Bunkhouse," *The New York Times* (March 9, 2014), http://www.nytimes.com/interactive/2014/03/09/us/the-boys-in-the-bunkhouse.html; C. Kauffman, "Jury: $240 Million for Atalissa Workers," *Des Moines Register* (May 1, 2013), http://archive.desmoinesregister.com/article/20130501/NEWS/305010095/Jury-240-million-Atalissa-workers; and C. Kauffman, "Witness: Disabled Workers Physically Abused," *Des Moines Register* (April 25, 2013), http://archive.desmoinesregister.com/article/20130425/NEWS/304240092/Witness-Disabled-workers-physically-abused.

The exploitation of the disabled men in the opening story is a tragic example of mistreating people for the ways in which they are different. Not only were the men abused by their supposed caretakers, but they also suffered workplace discrimination that kept them in debilitating roles without regard to their abilities and needs. In this chapter, we look at how organizations should work to maximize the potential contributions of a diverse workforce. Because each of us is different from others in myriad ways, we consider diversity in many different forms. We also show how individual differences in abilities affect employee behavior and effectiveness in organizations.

Diversity

2-1 Describe the two major forms of workplace diversity.

We are, each of us, unique. This is obvious enough, but managers sometimes forget they need to recognize and capitalize on individual differences to get the most from their employees. In this chapter, we'll learn how individual characteristics like age, gender, race, ethnicity, and abilities can influence employee performance. We'll also see how managers can develop awareness about these characteristics and manage a diverse workforce effectively. But first, let's take an overview perspective of the changing workforce.

Demographic Characteristics

The predominantly white, male managerial workforce of the past has given way to a gender-balanced, multiethnic workforce. For instance, in 1950 only 29.6 percent of the U.S. workforce was female,[1] but by 2014, women comprised 47 percent.[2] Both in the United States and internationally, women today are much more likely than before to be employed full time, have an advanced education, and earn wages comparable to those of men (see the OB Poll).[3] In addition, the earnings gap between whites and other racial and ethnic groups in the United States has decreased significantly, partially due to the rising number of minorities in the workforce. Hispanics will grow from 13 percent of the workforce in 2014 to 25.1 percent in 2044, blacks will increase from 12 to 12.7 percent, and

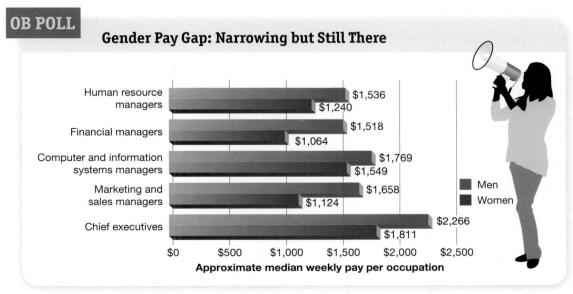

OB POLL

Gender Pay Gap: Narrowing but Still There

Human resource managers: $1,536 / $1,240
Financial managers: $1,518 / $1,064
Computer and information systems managers: $1,769 / $1,549
Marketing and sales managers: $1,658 / $1,124
Chief executives: $2,266 / $1,811

Men / Women

Approximate median weekly pay per occupation

Source: Bureau of Labor Statistics, http://www.bls.gov/opub/reports/cps/highlights-of-womens-earnings-in-2013.pdf.

Target store manager Jerald Bryant (center) motivating his team reflects demographic traits of today's workforce. By making diversity management a central part of its policies and practices, Target has created a gender-balanced, multiethnic, and inclusive workplace.
Sources: Lexington Herald-Leader/ZUMAPRESS/Alamy

Asians from 5 to 7.9 percent.[4] Workers over the age of 55 are an increasingly large portion of the workforce as well, both in the United States and globally. In the United States, the 55-and-older age group will increase from 19.5 percent of the labor force in 2010 to 25.2 percent by 2020.[5] Currently, in Australia there are more workers over age 55 than under age 25, and that shift is set to continue.[6] These changes are increasingly reflected in the makeup of managerial and professional jobs. These changes also mean organizations must make diversity management a central component of their policies and practices.

Levels of Diversity

Although much has been said about diversity in age, race, gender, ethnicity, religion, and disability status, experts now recognize that these demographic characteristics are just the tip of the iceberg.[7] Demographics mostly reflect **surface-level diversity**, not thoughts and feelings, and can lead employees to perceive one another through stereotypes and assumptions. However, evidence has shown that people are less concerned about demographic differences if they see themselves as sharing more important characteristics, such as personality and values, that represent **deep-level diversity**.[8]

To understand the difference between surface- and deep-level diversity, consider an example. Luis and Carol are managers who seem to have little in common. Luis is a young, recently hired male from a Spanish-speaking neighborhood in Miami with a business degree. Carol is an older woman from rural Kansas who started as a customer service trainee after high school and worked her way up the hierarchy. At first, these coworkers may notice their surface-level differences in education, ethnicity, regional background, and gender. However, as they get to know one another, they may find they are both deeply committed to their families, share a common way of thinking about important work problems, like to work collaboratively, and are interested in international assignments. These deep-level similarities can overshadow the more superficial differences between them, and research suggests they will work well together.

surface-level diversity Differences in easily perceived characteristics, such as gender, race, ethnicity, age, or disability, that do not necessarily reflect the ways people think or feel but that may activate certain stereotypes.

deep-level diversity Differences in values, personality, and work preferences that become progressively more important for determining similarity as people get to know one another better.

Affirmative Action for Unemployed Veterans

Unemployed veterans, take heart: Walmart wants YOU. In a historic move, the retailing giant vowed to hire any returning U.S. veteran who applied. As a result, the company hired more than 42,000 veterans by mid-2014 and expects that total to reach 100,000 by 2018. Other businesses have launched similar initiatives, such as the 100,000 Jobs Mission, which aimed to hire 100,000 veterans by 2020. The coalition, which originally included 11 companies, now consists of 190 companies from nearly every industry. As of 2015, 217,000 veterans had been hired, prompting the coalition to commit to hiring another 100,000 veterans. Is this an ethical choice all businesses should be emulating?

Few people would disagree that there is a need to address the plight of returning soldiers to America. Many veterans say employers don't want them. "There are a lot of companies that say they want veterans, but that conflicts with the unemployment numbers," claims Hakan Jackson, a former technician in the Air Force. He's right: Unemployment rates remain higher for veterans than civilians.

According to some veterans, the returning soldiers are not competitive enough in the marketplace. Erik Sewell, an Iraq war veteran, suggested the reason the veteran unemployment rate is poor is partly that vets often don't market their strengths well or showcase their transferable skills to potential employers. Bryson DeTrent, a 12-year veteran of the National Guard, observed that one of the key reasons some vets haven't found jobs is that they aren't working hard at it, preferring to collect unemployment instead. However, he has also found that companies are reluctant to hire veterans, especially National Guard members, fearing these employees may later be called to duty. Mental and emotional well-being are also a concern as employers may worry that veterans suffer from post-traumatic stress disorder (PTSD). Despite concerns, some managers report that veterans' work ethic, team outlook, and receptivity to training are greater than among the general populace.

Sometimes, affirmative action is needed to give an unfairly disadvantaged workforce segment an opportunity to succeed, whether it is done through percentage quotas, number quotas, or hiring all prospective employees from the desired groups. But any program risks including underqualified individuals from the target group while excluding qualified individuals from other workforce segments. This might mean hiring an underqualified veteran instead of a well-qualified civilian.

Resources are always scarce, and there are only so many jobs to go around. Managers must balance the ethics of affirmative action against the responsibility of strengthening their workforces for the good of their organizations.

Sources: "100,000 Jobs Mission Hires Over 200,000 Veterans," Veteran Jobs Mission press release (February 9, 2015), https://www.veteranjobsmission.com/press-releases/750; D. C. Baldridge and M. L. Swift, "Withholding Requests for Disability Accommodation: The Role of Individual Differences and Disability Attributes," *Journal of Management* (March 2013): 743–62; "Walmart Celebrates More Than 40,000 Hires in First Year of Veterans Commitment," Walmart Foundation press release (May 21, 2014), http://news.walmart.com/news-archive/2014/05/21/walmart-celebrates-more-than-40-000-hires-in-first-year-of-veterans-commitment; B. Yerbak and C. V. Jackson, "Battling to Get More Vets in the Work Force," *Chicago Tribune* (October 28, 2012), http://articles.chicagotribune.com/2012-10-28/business/ct-biz-1028-vets-20121028_1_train-veterans-unemployment-rate-war-zone; and "Veterans Unemployment Drops but Remains High," *HR Magazine,* February 2013, 16.

discrimination   Noting of a difference between things; often we refer to unfair discrimination, which means making judgments about individuals based on stereotypes regarding their demographic group.

Throughout this text, we will encounter differences between deep- and surface-level diversity in various contexts. Diversity is an important concept in OB since individual differences shape preferences for rewards, communication styles, reactions to leaders, negotiation styles, and many other aspects of behavior in organizations. Unfortunately, increased diversity may also mean increases in discriminatory practices, which we will discuss next.

Discrimination

2-2   Demonstrate how workplace discrimination undermines organizational effectiveness.

Although diversity presents many opportunities for organizations, diversity management includes working to eliminate unfair **discrimination**. To discriminate is to note a difference between things, which in itself isn't necessarily bad. Noticing one employee is more qualified is necessary for making hiring decisions;

stereotyping   Judging someone on the basis of our perception of the group to which that person belongs.

noticing another is taking on leadership responsibilities exceptionally well is necessary for making promotion decisions. Usually when we talk about discrimination, though, we mean allowing our behavior to be influenced by stereotypes about *groups* of people. **Stereotyping** is judging someone on the basis of our perception of the group to which that person belongs. To use a machine metaphor, you might think of stereotypes as the fuel that powers the discrimination engine. Stereotypes can be insidious not only because they may affect the perpetrators of discrimination, but also because they can affect how potential targets of discrimination see themselves.

Stereotype Threat

Let's say you are sitting in a restaurant, waiting for the blind date your coworker arranged to find you in the crowded room. How do you think your coworker described you to this person? Now consider how you would describe yourself to this new person if you'd talked on the phone before the date. What identifiable groups would you mention as a shorthand way for your date to know a bit about you so he or she could recognize you in the restaurant?

Chances are good that you'd mention your race, something about how you express your gender (such as the way you dress), how old you are, and maybe what you do for a living. You might also mention how tall you are if you are remarkably tall or short, and—if you're candid—you might mention something about your build (heavyset, petite, in between). Overall, you'd give cues to your blind date about characteristics that are *distinctive*, or stand out, about you. Interestingly, what you tell someone about yourself says a lot about what you think about yourself. Just as we stereotype others, we also stereotype ourselves.

stereotype threat   The degree to which we internally agree with the generally negative stereotyped perceptions of our groups.

Stereotype threat describes the degree to which we internally agree with the generally negative stereotyped perceptions of our groups. Along with that comes a fear of being judged when we are identified with the negative connotations of that group. This can happen when we are a minority in a situation. For instance, an older worker applying for a job in a predominately Millennial-age workforce may assume the interviewer thinks he is out of touch with current trends. What creates a stereotype threat is not whether the worker is or is not up to date with trends, but whether he internally agrees that older workers (the group he identifies with) are out of date (the stereotype).

People become their own worst enemies when they feel a stereotype threat. Ironically, they may unconsciously exaggerate the stereotype, like an older job applicant who talks about aging, rambles during the conversation, and discloses too much.[9] Second, they may over-identify with the stereotype. For example, studies of unemployed and underemployed workers have suggested they experience the stereotyped identity of nonworkers as lazy and aimless. Even when re-employed, they often retain the stereotype threat of their earlier status.[10] Third, people may over-compensate for the stereotype threat they feel. A Hispanic who tries to be as busy as possible at work and rushes conspicuously around the office may be attempting to overcome a stereotype threat of Hispanics as slower workers. This may happen even if the workplace has many ethnic minority employees, since minorities perceive stereotypes about each other.[11] Lastly, people may perform differently when reminded of their stereotyped group. For instance, older adults may not perform as well on memory tests when they are reminded beforehand of their older status, evoking stereotype threat.[12]

Stereotype threat has serious implications for the workplace. Employees who feel it may have lower performance, lower satisfaction, negative job attitudes, decreased engagement, decreased motivation, higher absenteeism, more health issues, and higher turnover intentions.[13] Thankfully, this is something we can combat in the workplace by treating employees as individuals, and not highlighting group differences. The following organizational changes can be successful in reducing stereotype threat: increasing awareness of how stereotypes may be perpetuated, reducing differential and preferential treatment through objective assessments, banning stereotyped practices and messages, confronting micro-aggressions against minority groups, and adopting transparent practices that signal the value of all employees.[14]

⭐ PERSONAL INVENTORY ASSESSMENTS

Intercultural Sensitivity Scale

Are you aware of intercultural dynamics? Take this PIA to assess your intercultural sensitivity.

Discrimination in the Workplace

To review, rather than looking at individual characteristics, unfair discrimination assumes everyone in a group is the same. This discrimination is often very harmful for employees, as we've just discussed, and for organizations.

Exhibit 2-1 provides definitions and examples of some forms of discrimination in organizations. Although many are prohibited by law and therefore are not a part of organizations' official policies, the practices persist. Tens of thousands of cases of employment discrimination are documented every year, and many more go unreported. Since discrimination has increasingly come under

Exhibit 2-1	**Forms of Discrimination**

Type of Discrimination	Definition	Examples from Organizations
Discriminatory policies or practices	Actions taken by representatives of the organization that deny equal opportunity to perform or unequal rewards for performance.	Older workers may be targeted for layoffs because they are highly paid and have lucrative benefits.
Sexual harassment	Unwanted sexual advances and other verbal or physical conduct of a sexual nature that create a hostile or offensive work environment.	Salespeople at one company went on company-paid visits to strip clubs, brought strippers into the office to celebrate promotions, and fostered pervasive sexual rumors.
Intimidation	Overt threats or bullying directed at members of specific groups of employees.	African-American employees at some companies have found nooses hanging over their work stations.
Mockery and insults	Jokes or negative stereotypes; sometimes the result of jokes taken too far.	Arab-Americans have been asked at work whether they were carrying bombs or were members of terrorist organizations.
Exclusion	Exclusion of certain people from job opportunities, social events, discussions, or informal mentoring; can occur unintentionally.	Many women in finance claim they are assigned to marginal job roles or are given light workloads that don't lead to promotion.
Incivility	Disrespectful treatment, including behaving in an aggressive manner, interrupting the person, or ignoring his or her opinions.	Female lawyers note that male attorneys frequently cut them off or do not adequately address their comments.

Sources: J. Levitz and P. Shishkin, "More Workers Cite Age Bias after Layoffs," *The Wall Street Journal,* March 11, 2009, D1–D2; W. M. Bulkeley, "A Data-Storage Titan Confronts Bias Claims," *The Wall Street Journal,* September 12, 2007, A1, A16; D. Walker, "Incident with Noose Stirs Old Memories," *McClatchy-Tribune Business News,* June 29, 2008; D. Solis, "Racial Horror Stories Keep EEOC Busy," *Knight-Ridder Tribune Business News,* July 30, 2005, 1; H. Ibish and A. Stewart, *Report on Hate Crimes and Discrimination against Arab Americans: The Post-September 11 Backlash, September 11, 2001–October 11, 2001* (Washington, DC: American-Arab Anti-Discrimination Committee, 2003); A. Raghavan, "Wall Street's Disappearing Women," *Forbes,* March 16, 2009, 72–78; and L. M. Cortina, "Unseen Injustice: Incivility as Modern Discrimination in Organizations," *Academy of Management Review* 33, no. 1 (2008): 55–75.

both legal scrutiny and social disapproval, most overt forms have faded, which may have resulted in an increase in more covert forms like incivility or exclusion, especially when leaders look the other way.[15]

As you can see, discrimination can occur in many ways, and its effects can vary depending on organizational context and the personal biases of employees. Some forms of discrimination like exclusion or incivility are especially hard to root out because they may occur simply because the actor isn't aware of the effects of his or her actions. Like stereotype threat, actual discrimination can lead to increased negative consequences for employers, including reduced productivity and organizational citizenship behavior (OCB), more conflict, increased turnover, and even increased risk-taking behavior.[16] Unfair discrimination also leaves qualified job candidates out of initial hiring and promotions. Thus, even if an employment discrimination lawsuit is never filed, a strong business case can be made for aggressively working to eliminate unfair discrimination.

Whether it is overt or covert, intentional or unintentional, discrimination is one of the primary factors that prevent diversity. On the other hand, recognizing diversity opportunities can lead to an effective diversity management program and ultimately to a better organization. *Diversity* is a broad term, and the phrase *workplace diversity* can refer to any characteristic that makes people different from one another. The following section covers some important surface-level characteristics that differentiate members of the workforce.

Biographical Characteristics

2-3 Describe how the key biographical characteristics are relevant to OB.

biographical characteristics Personal characteristics—such as age, gender, race, and length of tenure—that are objective and easily obtained from personnel records. These characteristics are representative of surface-level diversity.

Biographical characteristics such as age, gender, race, and disability are some of the most obvious ways employees differ. Let's begin by looking at factors that are easily definable and readily available—data that can be obtained, for the most part, from an employee's human resources (HR) file. Variations in surface-level characteristics may be the basis for discrimination against classes of employees, so it is worth knowing how related they actually are to work outcomes. As a general rule, many biographical differences are not important to actual work outcomes, and far more variation occurs *within* groups sharing biographical characteristics than between them.

Age

Age in the workforce is likely to be an issue of increasing importance during the next decade for many reasons. For one, the workforce is aging worldwide in most developed countries;[17] by projections, 93 percent of the growth in the labor force from 2006 to 2016 will have come from workers over age 54.[18] In the United States, the proportion of the workforce age 55 and older is 22 percent and increasing,[19] and legislation has, for all intents and purposes, outlawed mandatory retirement. Moreover, the United States and Australia, among other countries, have laws directly against age discrimination.[20] Most workers today no longer have to retire at age 70, and 62 percent of workers age 45 to 60 plan to delay retirement.[21]

The stereotypes of older workers as being behind the times, grumpy, and inflexible are changing. Managers often see a number of positive qualities older workers bring to their jobs, such as experience, judgment, a strong work ethic, and commitment to quality. The Public Utilities Board, the water agency of Singapore, reports that 27 percent of its workforce is over age 55 because older workers bring workforce stability.[22] And industries like health care, education, government, and nonprofits often welcome older workers.[23] But older workers are still perceived as less adaptable and less motivated to learn new technology.[24]

Myth or Science?

Bald Is Better

Surprisingly, it appears true that bald is better for men in the workplace. A recent study showed that observers believe a male's shaved head indicates greater masculinity, dominance, and leadership potential than longer or thinning hair. Thinning hair was perceived as the least powerful look, and other studies have agreed that male-pattern baldness (when some hair remains) is not considered advantageous. Why is this?

In some respects, the reported youthful advantage of a shaved head is counterintuitive. Because we have more hair when we are young, and contemporary culture considers youthfulness a desirable characteristic in the workplace (if you doubt this, see the discussions on aging in this chapter), it would make more sense for a hairless head to be a distinct disadvantage. Yet the media is loaded with images of powerful men with shaved heads—military

heroes, winning athletes, and action heroes. No wonder study participants declared that the men with shaved heads were an inch taller and 13 percent stronger than the same men with hair.

A bald head has become the hallmark of some important business leaders, notably Jeff Bezos of Amazon, Lloyd Blankfein of Goldman Sachs, Marc Andreessen of Netscape, and "Shark Tank" investor Daymond John. Men who shave their heads report it can give them a business advantage, whether or not it makes them look younger (which is debatable). According to psychologist Caroline Keating, just as older silver-back gorillas are "typically the powerful actors in their social groups," so it is in the office, where baldness may "signal who is in charge and potentially dangerous." Research professor Michael Cunningham agrees, adding that baldness "is nature's way of telling the rest of the world you are a

survivor." Men with shaved heads convey aggressiveness, competitiveness, and independence, he adds. Will you join the 13 percent of men who shave their heads? Though we don't wish to advocate head-shaving for this reason, it does demonstrate how biased we continue to be in judging people by superficial characteristics. Time will tell if this situation ever improves.

Sources: D. Baer, "People Are Psychologically Biased to See Bald Men as Dominant Leaders," *Business Insider* (February 13, 2015), http://www.businessinsider.com/bald-men-signals-dominance-2015-2; J. Misener, "Men with Shaved Heads Appear More Dominant, Study Finds," *The Huffington Post* (October 1, 2012), www.huffingtonpost.com/2012/10/01/bald-men-dominant-shaved-heads-study_n_1930489.html; A. E. Mannes, "Shorn Scalps and Perceptions of Male Dominance," *Social Psychological and Personality Science*, (2012), doi: 10.1177/1948550612449490; and R. E. Silverman, "Bald Is Powerful," *The Wall Street Journal* (October 3, 2012), B1, B6.

When organizations seek individuals who are open to change and training, the perceived negatives associated with age clearly hinder the initial hiring of older workers and increase the likelihood they will be let go during cutbacks.

Now let's take a look at the evidence. What effect does age actually have on turnover, absenteeism, productivity, and satisfaction? Regarding turnover, the older you are, the less likely you are to quit your job.[25] As workers get older, they have fewer alternate job opportunities because their skills have become more specialized. Within organizations, older workers' longer tenure tends to provide them with higher wages, longer paid vacations, and benefits that may bind them to their employers.

It may seem likely that age is positively correlated to absenteeism, but this isn't true. Most studies show that older employees have lower rates of avoidable absence versus younger employees.[26] Furthermore, older workers do not have more psychological problems or day-to-day physical health problems than younger workers.[27]

The majority of studies have shown "virtually no relationship between age and job performance," according to Director Harvey Sterns of the Institute for Life-Span Development and Gerontology.[28] Indeed, some studies indicate that older adults perform better. In Munich, a 4-year study of 3,800 Mercedes-Benz workers found that "the older workers seemed to know better how to avoid severe errors," said Matthias Weiss, the academic coordinator of the study.[29] Related to performance, there is a conception that creativity lessens as people age. Researcher David Galenson, who studied the ages of peak creativity, found

At Tofutti, maker of dairy-free products, older employees are an integral part of the workforce. Tofutti's CEO David Mintz values the experience, work ethic, maturity, enthusiasm, knowledge, and skills that older workers bring to their jobs. He says older employees have fewer absences, make fewer mistakes, are better at solving problems, and are willing to work more hours.

Sources: Julio Cortez/AP images

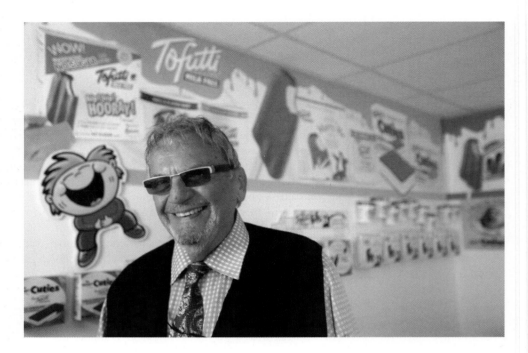

that people who create through experimentation do "their greatest work in their 40s, 50s, and 60s. These artists rely on wisdom, which increases with age."[30]

What about age and satisfaction? Regarding life satisfaction, which we will discuss further in later chapters, there is a cultural assumption that older people are more prone to depression and loneliness. Actually, a study of adults ages 18 to 94 found that positive moods increased with age. "Contrary to the popular view that youth is the best time of life, the peak of emotional life may not occur until well into the seventh decade," researcher Laura Carstensen said.[31]

Regarding job satisfaction, an important topic in Chapter 3, a review of more than 800 studies found that older workers tend to be more satisfied with their work, report better relationships with coworkers, and are more committed to their organizations.[32] Other studies, however, have found that job satisfaction increases up to middle age, at which point it begins to drop off. When we separate the results by job type, though, we find that satisfaction tends to continually increase among professionals as they age, whereas among nonprofessionals it falls during middle age and then rises again in the later years.

In sum, we can see that the surface-level characteristic of an employee's age is an unfounded basis for discrimination, and that an age-diverse workforce is a benefit to an organization.

Sex

Few issues initiate more debates, misconceptions, and unsupported opinions than whether women perform as well on jobs as men.

The best place to begin to consider this is with the recognition that few, if any, differences between men and women affect job performance.[33] Though men may have slightly higher math ability and women slightly higher verbal ability, the differences are fairly small, and there are no consistent male–female differences in problem-solving ability, analytical skills, or learning ability.[34] One meta-analysis of job performance studies found that women scored slightly higher than men on performance measures.[35] A separate meta-analysis of 95 leadership studies indicated that women and men are rated equally effective as leaders.[36]

Yet biases and stereotypes persist. In the hiring realm, managers are influenced by gender bias when selecting candidates for certain positions.[37] For instance, men are preferred in hiring decisions for male-dominated occupations, particularly when men are doing the hiring.[38] Once on the job, men and women may be offered a similar number of developmental experiences, but females are less likely to be assigned challenging positions by men, assignments that could help them achieve higher organizational positions.[39] Moreover, men are more likely to be chosen for leadership roles even though men and women are equally effective leaders. A study of 20 organizations in Spain, for example, suggested that men are generally selected for leadership roles that require handling organizational crises.[40] According to Naomi Sutherland, senior partner in diversity at recruiter Korn Ferry, "Consciously or subconsciously, companies are still hesitant to take the risk on someone who looks different from their standard leadership profile."[41]

Sex discrimination has a pervasive negative impact. Notably, women still earn less money than men for the same positions,[42] even in traditionally female roles.[43] In a recent experiment, experienced managers allocated 71 percent of the fictional pay raise funds for male employees, leaving only 29 percent for females.[44] Working mothers also face "maternal wall bias," meaning they often are not considered for new positions after they have children, and both men and women experience discrimination for their family caregiving roles.[45] Women who receive fewer challenging assignments and development opportunities from biased managers tend to curtail their management aspirations.[46] Research continues to underline that sex discrimination is detrimental to organizational performance.[47]

We've seen that there are many misconceptions and contradictions about male and female workers. Thankfully, many countries have laws against sex discrimination including Australia, the United Kingdom, and the United States. Other countries, such as Belgium, France, Norway, and Spain are seeking gender diversity through laws to increase the percentage of women on boards of directors.[48] Gender biases and gender discrimination are still serious issues, but there are indications that the situation is improving.

Race and Ethnicity

Race is a controversial issue in society and in organizations. We define *race* as the heritage people use to identify themselves; *ethnicity* is the additional set of cultural characteristics that often overlaps with race. Typically, we associate race with biology and ethnicity with culture, but there is a history of self-identifying for both classifications. Laws against race and ethnic discrimination are in effect in many countries, including Australia, the United Kingdom, and the United States.[49]

Race and ethnicity have been studied as they relate to employment outcomes such as hiring decisions, performance evaluations, pay, and workplace discrimination. Individuals may slightly favor colleagues of their own race in performance evaluations, promotion decisions, and pay raises, although such differences are not found consistently, especially when highly structured methods of decision making are employed.[50] Also, some industries have remained less racially diverse than others. For instance, U.S. advertising and media organizations suffer from a lack of racial diversity in their management ranks even though their client base is increasingly ethnically diverse.[51]

Finally, members of racial and ethnic minorities report higher levels of discrimination in the workplace.[52] African Americans generally fare worse than whites in employment decisions (a finding that may not apply outside the United States). They receive lower ratings in employment interviews, lower job performance ratings, less pay, and fewer promotions.[53] Lastly, while this does not necessarily prove overt racial discrimination, African Americans are often discriminated against even in controlled experiments. For example, one study of low-wage jobs found that African American applicants with no criminal history received fewer job offers than did white applicants with criminal records.[54]

As we discussed before, discrimination—for any reason—leads to increased turnover, which is detrimental to organizational performance. While better representation of all racial groups in organizations remains a goal, an individual of minority status is much less likely to leave the organization if there is a feeling of inclusiveness, known as a **positive diversity climate**.[55] A positive climate for diversity can also lead to increased sales, suggesting there are organizational performance gains associated with reducing racial and ethnic discrimination.[56]

How do we move beyond the destructiveness of discrimination? The answer is in understanding one another's viewpoint. Evidence suggests that some people find interacting with other racial groups uncomfortable unless there are clear behavioral scripts to guide their behavior,[57] so creating diverse work groups focused on mutual goals could be helpful, along with developing a positive diversity climate.

positive diversity climate In an organization, an environment of inclusiveness and an acceptance of diversity.

Disabilities

Workplace policies, both official and circumstantial, regarding individuals with physical or mental disabilities vary from country to country. Countries such as Australia, the United States, the United Kingdom, and Japan have specific laws to protect individuals with disabilities.[58] These laws have resulted in greater acceptance and accommodation of people with physical or mental impairments. In the United States, for instance, the representation of individuals with disabilities in the workforce rapidly increased with the passage of the Americans with Disabilities Act (ADA, 1990).[59] According to the ADA, employers are required to make reasonable accommodations so their workplaces will be accessible to individuals with physical or mental disabilities.

The U.S. Equal Employment Opportunity Commission (EEOC), the federal agency responsible for enforcing employment discrimination laws, classifies a person as *disabled* who has any physical or mental impairment that substantially limits one or more major life activities. One of the most controversial aspects of the ADA is the provision that requires employers to make reasonable accommodations for people with psychiatric disabilities.[60] Examples of recognized disabilities include missing limbs, seizure disorder, Down syndrome, deafness, schizophrenia, alcoholism, diabetes, depression, and chronic back pain. These conditions share almost no common features, so there's no specific definition about how each condition is related to employment.

The impact of disabilities on employment outcomes has been explored from a variety of perspectives. On one hand, when disability status is randomly manipulated among hypothetical candidates, disabled individuals are rated as having superior personal qualities like dependability.[61] Another review suggested that workers with disabilities receive higher performance evaluations. However, individuals with disabilities tend to encounter lower performance expectations and are less likely to be hired.[62] Mental disabilities may impair performance more than physical disabilities: Individuals with such common mental health issues as depression and anxiety are significantly more likely to be absent from work.[63]

The elimination of discrimination against the disabled workforce has long been problematic. In Europe, for instance, policies to motivate employers have failed to boost the workforce participation rate for workers with disabilities, and outright quota systems in Germany, France, and Poland have backfired.[64]

Employees with disabilities are valuable assets at the Anne-Sophie Hotel in Germany, where they use their talents and abilities in performing kitchen and service jobs. Posing here with Chef Serkan Guezelcoban (in blue shoes) at the hotel's Handicap restaurant are some of the 18 disabled employees who work side by side with other employees of the hotel's 39-member staff.

Sources: Thomas Kienzle/EPA/Landov

However, the recognition of the talents and abilities of individuals with disabilities has made a positive impact. In addition, technology and workplace advancements have greatly increased the scope of available jobs for those with all types of disabilities. Managers need to be attuned to the true requirements of each job and match the skills of the individual to them, providing accommodations when needed. But what happens when employees do not disclose their disabilities? Let's discuss this next.

Hidden Disabilities

As we mentioned earlier, disabilities include observable characteristics like missing limbs, illnesses that require a person to use a wheelchair, and blindness. Other disabilities may not be obvious, at least at first. Unless an individual decides to disclose a disability that isn't easily observable, it can remain hidden at the discretion of the employee. These are called *hidden disabilities* (or invisible disabilities). Hidden, or invisible, disabilities generally fall under the categories of sensory disabilities (for example, impaired hearing), autoimmune disorders (like rheumatoid arthritis), chronic illness or pain (like carpal tunnel syndrome), cognitive or learning impairments (like ADHD), sleep disorders (like insomnia), and psychological challenges (like PTSD).[65]

As a result of recent changes to the Americans with Disabilities Act Amendments Act of 2008 (ADAAA), U.S. organizations must accommodate employees with a very broad range of impairments. However, employees must disclose their conditions to their employers in order to be eligible for workplace accommodations and employment protection. Since many employees do not want to disclose their invisible disabilities, they are prevented from getting the workplace accommodations they need in order to thrive in their jobs. Research indicates that individuals with hidden disabilities are afraid of being stigmatized or ostracized if they disclose their disabilities to others in the workplace, and they believe their managers will think they are less capable of strong job performance.[66]

In some ways, a hidden disability is not truly invisible. For example, a person with undisclosed autism will still exhibit the behaviors characteristic of the condition, such as difficulty with verbal communication and lack of adaptability.[67] You may observe behaviors that lead you to suspect an individual has a hidden disability. Unfortunately, you may attribute the behavior to other causes—for instance, you may incorrectly ascribe the slow, slurred speech of a coworker to an alcohol problem rather than to the long-term effects of a stroke.

As for the employee, research suggests that disclosure helps all—the individual, others, and organizations. Disclosure may increase the job satisfaction and well-being of the individual, help others understand and assist the individual to succeed in the workplace, and allow the organization to accommodate the situation to achieve top performance.[68]

Other Differentiating Characteristics

2-4 Explain how other differentiating characteristics factor into OB.

The last set of characteristics we'll look at includes tenure, religion, sexual orientation and gender identity, and cultural identity. These characteristics illustrate deep-level differences that provide opportunities for workplace diversity, as long as discrimination can be overcome.

Tenure

Except for gender and racial differences, few issues are more subject to misconceptions and speculations than the impact of seniority and *tenure,* meaning time spent in a job, organization, or field.

Extensive reviews have been conducted of the seniority–productivity relationship.[69] If we define *seniority* as time on a particular job, the evidence demonstrates a positive relationship between seniority and job productivity. So tenure, expressed as work experience, appears to be a good predictor of employee productivity, though there is some evidence that the relationship is not linear: differences in tenure are more important to job performance for relatively new or inexperienced employees than among those who have been on the job longer. To use an NFL analogy, a second-year quarterback has more of an edge over a rookie than a 10th-year quarterback has over one in his 9th year.

Religion

Not only do religious and nonreligious people question each other's belief systems; often people of different religious faiths conflict. There are few—if any—countries in which religion is a nonissue in the workplace. For this reason, employers are prohibited by law from discriminating against employees based on religion in many countries, including Australia, the United Kingdom, and the United States.[70]

Islam is one of the most popular religions in the world, and it is the majority religion in many countries. However, in the United States, Muslims are a minority group that is growing. There are nearly 3 million Muslims in the United States, and the number is predicted to double by 2030, when they will represent 1.7 percent of the population, according to the Pew Research Center. At that point, there will be as many Muslims in the United States as there are Jews and Episcopalians.[71] Despite these numbers, there is evidence that people are discriminated against for their Islamic faith even in studies. For instance, U.S. job applicants in Muslim-identified religious attire who applied for hypothetical retail jobs had shorter, more interpersonally negative interviews than applicants who did not wear Muslim-identified attire.[72]

Faith can be an employment issue wherever religious beliefs prohibit or encourage certain behaviors. The behavioral expectations can be informal, such as employees leaving work early on Christmas Eve. Or they may be systemic, such as the Monday to Friday workweek, which accommodates a Christian tradition of not working on Sundays and a Jewish tradition of not working on Saturdays. Religious individuals may also believe they have an obligation to express their beliefs in the workplace, and those who do not share those beliefs may object.

Religious discrimination has been a growing source of discrimination claims in the United States, partially because the issues are complex. Recently, Samantha Elauf, who was turned down for employment because she wears a hijab, a black head scarf, sued for religious discrimination. "I learned I was not hired by Abercrombie because I wear a head scarf, which is a symbol of modesty in my Muslim faith," she said. She was not aware of the organization's rule against head coverings and did not mention her reason for the scarf. Should employers be required to deduce why applicants dress as they do and then protect them? Even the Supreme Court is not certain.[73]

Sexual Orientation and Gender Identity

While much has changed, the full acceptance and accommodation of lesbian, gay, bisexual, and transgender (LGBT) employees remains a work in progress. In the United States, a Harvard University study sent fictitious but realistic résumés to 1,700 actual entry-level job openings. The applications were identical with one exception: Half mentioned involvement in gay organizations during college, and the other half did not. The applications without the mention received 60 percent more callbacks than the ones with it.[74]

Perhaps as a result of perceived discrimination, many LGBT employees do not disclose their status. For example, John Browne, former CEO of BP, hid his sexual orientation until he was 59, when the press threatened to disclose that he was gay. Fearing the story would result in turmoil for the company, he resigned. Browne wrote recently, "Since my outing in 2007, many societies around the world have done more to embrace people who are lesbian, gay, bisexual, or transgender. But the business world has a long way to go."[75]

U.S. federal law does not prohibit discrimination against employees based on sexual orientation, though 29 states and more than 160 municipalities do. For states and municipalities that protect against discrimination based on sexual orientation, roughly as many claims are filed for sexual orientation discrimination as for sex and race discrimination.[76] Some other countries are more progressive: for instance, Australia has laws against discriminating on the basis of sexual preference, and the United Kingdom has similar laws regarding sexual orientation.[77] However, the distinctions in these laws may not be broad enough—researchers have acknowledged a new acronym, QUILTBAG, to describe individuals who are queer/questioning, undecided, intersex, lesbian, transgender, bisexual, asexual, or gay.[78]

As a first step in the United States, the federal government has prohibited discrimination against *government* employees based on sexual orientation. The EEOC recently held that sex-stereotyping against lesbian, gay, and bisexual individuals represents gender discrimination enforceable under the Civil Rights Act of 1964.[79] Also, pending federal legislation against discrimination based on sexual orientation—the Employment Non-Discrimination Act (ENDA)—passed the Senate but is not yet law.[80]

Even in the absence of federal legislation, many organizations have implemented policies and procedures that cover sexual orientation. IBM, once famous for requiring all employees to wear white shirts and ties, has changed its ultra-conservative environment. Former vice president Ted Childs said, "IBM ensures that people who are gay, lesbian, bisexual or transgender feel safe, welcomed and valued within the global walls of our business…. The contributions that are made by [gay and transgender] IBMers accrue directly to our bottom line and ensure the success of our business."[81]

IBM is not alone. Surveys indicate that more than 90 percent of the Fortune 500 have policies that cover sexual orientation. As for gender identity, companies are increasingly adopting policies to govern the way their organizations treat transgender employees. In 2001, only eight companies in the Fortune 500 had policies on gender identity. That number is now more than 250.

However, among the Fortune 1,000, some noteworthy companies do not currently have domestic-partner benefits or nondiscrimination clauses for LGBT employees, including ExxonMobil, currently number 2 in the *Fortune* rankings

---

Is it okay to be gay at work?

I'm gay, but no one at my workplace knows it. How much should I be willing to tell? I want to be sure to have a shot at the big positions in the firm.

— *Ryan*

Dear Ryan:

Unfortunately, you are right to be concerned. Here are some suggestions:

- *Look for an inclusive company culture.* Apple CEO Tim Cook said, "I've had the good fortune to work at a company that loves creativity and innovation and knows it can only flourish when you embrace people's differences. Not everyone is so lucky." Recent research has focused on discovering new methods to counteract a discrimination culture in the United States, the United Kingdom, and Australia.

- *Choose your moral ground.* Do you feel you have a responsibility to "come out" to help effect social change? Do you have a right to keep your private life private? The balance is a private decision. A recent study by the U.S. Human Rights Campaign indicated that only half of LGBT employees nationwide disclose their status.

- *Consider your future in top management.* Corporate-level leaders are urged to be open with peers and employees. As Ernst & Young global vice chairperson Beth Brooke said about her decades of staying closeted, the pressure to be "authentic" adds stress if you are keeping your gay status a secret.

- *Weigh your options.* The word from people at the top who are gay (some who have come out and others who have not) is mixed. Brooke said, "Life really did get better" after she announced her status in a company-sponsored video. Mark Stephanz, a vice chairman at Bank of America Merrill Lynch, agreed, remarking that "most people still deal with you the same way they always do." Yet Deena Fidas, deputy director for the largest LGBT civil rights group in the United States, reported that being gay in the workplace is still "far from being a 'nonissue'."

- *Be aware of international and national laws.* Sadly, some nations and states are intolerant. You will need to study the laws to be sure you will be safe from repercussions when you reveal your status.

So, think about your decision from both an ethical and a self-interested point of view. Your timing depends not only on what you think are your ethical responsibilities, but also on your context—where you work, the culture of your organization, and the support of the people within it. Thankfully, globalization is ensuring that the world becomes increasingly accepting and fair.

Good luck in your career!

Sources: M. D. Birtel, "'Treating' Prejudice: An Exposure-Therapy Approach to Reducing Negative Reactions Toward Stigmatized Groups," *Psychological Science* (November 2012): 1379–86; L. Cooper and J. Raspanti, "The Cost of the Closet and the Rewards of Inclusion," Human Rights Campaign report (May 2014), http://hrc-assets.s3-website-us-east-1.amazonaws.com//files/assets/resources/Cost_of_the_Closet_May2014.pdf; N. Rumens and J. Broomfield, "Gay Men in the Police: Identity Disclosure and Management Issues," *Human Resource Management Journal* (July 2012): 283–98; and A. M Ryan and J. L. Wessel, "Sexual Orientation Harassment in the Workplace: When Do Observers Intervene?" *Journal of Organizational Behavior* (May 2012): 488–509.

of the largest U.S. companies.[82] Some companies claim they do not need to provide LGBT benefits for religious reasons. Recently, the U.S. Supreme Court allowed that Hobby Lobby, a retail arts and crafts chain, does not need to provide contraception insurance coverage due to the religious objections of its founding family, and many fear this ruling will pave the way for overt LGBT discrimination by organizations.[83] Moreover, some organizations that claim to be inclusive don't live up to the claim. For example, a recent study of five social cooperatives in Italy indicated that these so-called inclusive organizations actually expect individuals to remain quiet about their status.[84]

Thus, while times have certainly changed, sexual orientation and gender identity remain individual differences that organizations must address in eliminating discrimination and promoting diversity.

Cultural Identity

We have seen that people sometimes define themselves in terms of race and ethnicity. Many people carry a strong *cultural identity* as well, a link with the culture of family ancestry or youth that lasts a lifetime, no matter where the individual may live in the world. People choose their cultural identity, and they also choose how closely they observe the norms of that culture. Cultural norms influence the workplace, sometimes resulting in clashes. Organizations must adapt.

Workplace practices that coincided with the norms of a person's cultural identity were commonplace years ago, when societies were less mobile. People looked for work near familial homes and organizations established holidays, observances, practices, and customs that suited the majority. Organizations were generally not expected to accommodate each individual's preferences.

Thanks to global integration and changing labor markets, today's organizations do well to understand and respect the cultural identities of their employees, both as groups and as individuals. A U.S. company looking to do business in, say, Latin America, needs to understand that employees in those cultures expect long summer holidays. A company that requires employees to work during this culturally established break will meet strong resistance.

An organization seeking to be sensitive to the cultural identities of its employees should look beyond accommodating its majority groups and instead create as much of an individualized approach to practices and norms as possible. Often, managers can provide the bridge of workplace flexibility to meet both organizational goals and individual needs.

> **✪ WATCH IT!**
> If your professor has assigned this, go to the Assignments section of **mymanagementlab.com** to complete the video exercise titled *Verizon: Diversity*.

Ability

2-5 Demonstrate the relevance of intellectual and physical abilities to OB.

Contrary to what we were taught in grade school, we weren't all created equal in our abilities. For example, regardless of how motivated you are, you may not be able to act as well as Jennifer Lawrence, play basketball as well as LeBron James, or write as well as Stephen King. Of course, all of us have strengths and weaknesses that make us relatively superior or inferior to others in performing certain tasks or activities. From management's standpoint, the challenge is to understand the differences to increase the likelihood that a given employee will perform the job well.

ability   An individual's capacity to perform the various tasks in a job.

What does *ability* mean? As we use the term, **ability** is an individual's current capacity to perform the various tasks in a job. Overall abilities are essentially made up of two sets of factors: intellectual and physical.

Intellectual Abilities

intellectual abilities   The capacity to do mental activities—thinking, reasoning, and problem solving.

Intellectual abilities are abilities needed to perform mental activities—thinking, reasoning, and problem solving. Most societies place a high value on intelligence, and for good reason. Smart people generally earn more money and attain higher levels of education. They are also more likely to emerge as leaders of groups. However, assessing and measuring intellectual ability are not always simple. People aren't consistently capable of correctly assessing their own cognitive ability.[85] IQ tests are designed to ascertain a person's general intellectual abilities, but the origins, influence factors, and testing of intelligence quotient (IQ) are controversial.[86] So, too, are popular college admission tests, such as the SAT and ACT, and graduate admission tests in business (GMAT), law (LSAT), and medicine (MCAT). The firms that produce these tests don't claim they assess intelligence, but experts know they do.[87]

The seven most frequently cited dimensions making up intellectual abilities are number aptitude, verbal comprehension, perceptual speed, inductive reasoning, deductive reasoning, spatial visualization, and memory.[88] Exhibit 2-2 describes these dimensions.

general mental ability (GMA)   An overall factor of intelligence, as suggested by the positive correlations among specific intellectual ability dimensions.

Intelligence dimensions are positively correlated, so if you score high on verbal comprehension, for example, you're more likely to also score high on spatial visualization. The correlations aren't perfect, meaning people do have specific abilities that predict important work-related outcomes when considered individually.[89] However, they are high enough that researchers also recognize a general factor of intelligence, **general mental ability (GMA)**. Evidence supports the idea that the structures and measures of intellectual abilities generalize across cultures. Someone in Venezuela or Sudan, for instance, does not have a different set of mental abilities than a U.S. or Czech individual. There is some evidence that IQ scores vary to some degree across

Exhibit 2-2	Dimensions of Intellectual Ability	
Dimension	**Description**	**Job Example**
Number aptitude	Ability to do speedy and accurate arithmetic	Accountant: Computing the sales tax on a set of items
Verbal comprehension	Ability to understand what is read or heard and the relationship of words to each other	Plant manager: Following corporate policies on hiring
Perceptual speed	Ability to identify visual similarities and differences quickly and accurately	Fire investigator: Identifying clues to support a charge of arson
Inductive reasoning	Ability to identify a logical sequence in a problem and then solve the problem	Market researcher: Forecasting demand for a product in the next time period
Deductive reasoning	Ability to use logic and assess the implications of an argument	Supervisor: Choosing between two different suggestions offered by employees
Spatial visualization	Ability to imagine how an object would look if its position in space were changed	Interior decorator: Redecorating an office
Memory	Ability to retain and recall past experiences	Salesperson: Remembering the names of customers

cultures, but those differences become much smaller when we take into account educational and economic differences.[90]

Jobs differ in the demands they place on intellectual abilities. Research consistently indicates a correspondence between cognitive ability and task performance.[91] Where employee tasks are highly routine and there are few or no opportunities to exercise discretion, a high IQ is not as important to performing well. However, that does not mean people with high IQs cannot have an impact on traditionally less complex jobs.

It might surprise you that the intelligence test most widely used in hiring decisions takes only 12 minutes to complete. It's the Wonderlic Cognitive Ability Test. There are different forms of the test, but each has 50 questions and the same general construct. Here are two questions to try:

- When rope is selling at $0.10 a foot, how many feet can you buy for $0.60?
- Assume the first two statements are true. Is the final one:
    1. True.
    2. False.
    3. Not certain.
        a. The boy plays baseball.
        b. All baseball players wear hats.
        c. The boy wears a hat.

The Wonderlic measures both speed (almost nobody has time to answer every question) and power (the questions get harder as you go along), so the average score is quite low—about 21 of 50. Because the Wonderlic is able to provide valid information cheaply (for $5 to $10 per applicant), many organizations use it in hiring decisions, including Publix supermarkets, Manpower staffing systems, British Petroleum (BP), and Dish satellite systems.[92] Most of these companies don't give up other hiring tools, such as application forms or interviews. Rather, they add the Wonderlic for its ability to provide valid data on applicants' intelligence levels.

While intelligence is a big help in performing a job well, it doesn't make people happier or more satisfied with their jobs. Why not? Although intelligent people perform better and tend to have more interesting jobs, they are also more critical when evaluating their job conditions. Thus, smart people have it better, but they also expect more.[93]

Physical Abilities

physical abilities The capacity to do tasks that demand stamina, dexterity, strength, and similar characteristics.

Though the changing nature of work suggests intellectual abilities are increasingly important for many jobs, **physical abilities** have been and will remain valuable. Research on hundreds of jobs has identified nine basic abilities needed in the performance of physical tasks.[94] These are described in Exhibit 2-3. High employee performance is likely to be achieved when the extent to which a job requires each of the nine abilities matches the abilities of employees in that job.

In sum, organizations are increasingly aware that an optimally productive workforce includes all types of people and does not automatically exclude anyone on the basis of personal characteristics. The potential benefits of diversity are enormous for forward-thinking managers. For example, a pilot program of software company SAP in Germany, India, and Ireland has found that employees with autism perform excellently in precision-oriented tasks like debugging software.[95] Of course, integrating diverse people into an optimally productive workforce takes skill. We will discuss how to bring the talents of a diverse workforce together in the next section.

Exhibit 2-3	Nine Basic Physical Abilities

Strength Factors

1. Dynamic strength	Ability to exert muscular force repeatedly or continuously over time
2. Trunk strength	Ability to exert muscular strength using the trunk (particularly abdominal) muscles
3. Static strength	Ability to exert force against external objects
4. Explosive strength	Ability to expend a maximum of energy in one or a series of explosive acts

Flexibility Factors

5. Extent flexibility	Ability to move the trunk and back muscles as far as possible
6. Dynamic flexibility	Ability to make rapid, repeated flexing movements

Other Factors

7. Body coordination	Ability to coordinate the simultaneous actions of different parts of the body
8. Balance	Ability to maintain equilibrium despite forces pulling off balance
9. Stamina	Ability to continue maximum effort requiring prolonged effort over time

Implementing Diversity Management Strategies

2-6 Describe how organizations manage diversity effectively.

diversity management The process and programs by which managers make everyone more aware of and sensitive to the needs and differences of others.

Having discussed a variety of ways in which people differ, we now look at how a manager can and should manage these differences. **Diversity management** makes everyone more aware of and sensitive to the needs and differences of others. This definition highlights the fact that diversity programs include and are meant for everyone. Diversity is much more likely to be successful when we see it as everyone's business than when we believe it helps only certain groups of employees.

Attracting, Selecting, Developing, and Retaining Diverse Employees

One method of enhancing workforce diversity is to target recruitment messages to specific demographic groups that are underrepresented in the workforce. This means placing advertisements in publications geared toward those groups; pairing with colleges, universities, and other institutions with significant numbers of underrepresented minorities, as Microsoft is doing to encourage women into technology studies;[96] and forming partnerships with associations like the Society of Women Engineers or the National Minority Supplier Development Council.

Research has shown that women and minorities have greater interest in employers that make special efforts to highlight a commitment to diversity in their recruiting materials. Diversity advertisements that fail to show women and minorities in positions of organizational leadership send a negative message about the diversity climate at an organization.[97] Of course, to show the pictures, organizations must actually have diversity in their management ranks

Developing the talents of women is a strategic diversity imperative for business success at Nissan Motor Company in Japan. Attracted by Nissan's commitment to equality for women in the workplace and to developing their careers, Li Ning of China decided to join the company after graduating from Tokyo University.
Sources: Franck Robichon/EPA/Newscom

Some companies have been actively working toward recruiting less-represented groups. Etsy, an online retailer, hosts engineering classes and provides grants for aspiring women coders, and then hires the best.[98] McKinsey & Co., Bain & Co., Boston Consulting Group, and Goldman Sachs have similarly been actively recruiting women who left the workforce to start families by offering phase-in programs and other benefits.[99]

The selection process is one of the most important places to apply diversity efforts. Managers who hire need to value fairness and objectivity in selecting employees and focus on the productive potential of new recruits. When managers use a well-defined protocol for assessing applicant talent and the organization clearly prioritizes nondiscrimination policies, qualifications become far more important in determining who gets hired than demographic characteristics.[100]

Individuals who are demographically different from their coworkers may be more likely to feel low commitment and to leave, but a positive diversity climate can aid retention. Many diversity training programs are available to employers, and research efforts are focusing on identifying the most effective initiatives. It seems that the best programs are inclusive in both their design and implementation.[101] A positive diversity climate should be the goal since all workers appear to prefer an organization that values diversity.

Diversity in Groups

Most contemporary workplaces require extensive work in group settings. When people work in groups, they need to establish a common way of looking at and accomplishing the major tasks, and they need to communicate with one another often. If they feel little sense of membership and cohesion in their groups, all group attributes are likely to suffer.

In some cases, diversity in traits can hurt team performance, whereas in others it can facilitate performance.[102] Whether diverse or homogeneous teams are more effective depends on the characteristic of interest. Demographic diversity (in gender, race, and ethnicity) does not appear to either help or hurt team performance in general, although racial diversity in management groups may increase organizational performance in the right conditions.[103]

Teams of individuals who are highly intelligent, conscientious, and interested in working in team settings are more effective. Thus, diversity on these variables is likely to be a bad thing—it makes little sense to try to form teams that mix in members who are lower in intelligence or conscientiousness, and who are uninterested in teamwork. In other cases, diversity can be a strength. Groups of individuals with different types of expertise and education are more effective than homogeneous groups. Similarly, a group made entirely of assertive people who want to be in charge, or a group whose members all prefer to follow the lead of others, will be less effective than a group that mixes leaders and followers.

Regardless of the composition of the group, differences can be leveraged to achieve superior performance. The most important factor is to emphasize the similarities among members.[104] Managers who emphasize higher-order goals and values in their leadership style are more effective in managing diverse teams.[105]

Effective Diversity Programs

Organizations use a variety of diversity programs in recruiting and selection policies, as well as training and development practices. Effective, comprehensive workforce programs encouraging diversity have three distinct components. First, they teach managers about the legal framework for equal employment opportunity and encourage fair treatment of all people regardless of their demographic characteristics. Second, they teach managers how a diverse workforce will be better able to serve a diverse market of customers and clients. Third, they foster personal development practices that bring out the skills and abilities of all workers, acknowledging how differences in perspective can be a valuable way to improve performance for everyone.[106]

Most negative reactions to employment discrimination are based on the idea that discriminatory treatment is unfair. Regardless of race or gender, people are generally in favor of diversity-oriented programs, including affirmative action

Employees of Grow Financial Credit Union in Tampa, Florida, enjoy a lunch-hour program on women executives and their careers sponsored by the firm's diversity committee. Reflecting Grow's diverse employee mix, the diversity programs foster the skills, abilities, personal development, and performance of all employees.
Sources: Cherie Diez/ZUMA Press/Newscom

programs (AAP), to increase the representation of minority groups and ensure everyone a fair opportunity to show their skills and abilities.

Organizational leaders should examine their workforce to determine whether target groups have been underutilized. If groups of employees are not proportionally represented in top management, managers should look for any hidden barriers to advancement. Managers can often improve recruiting practices, make selection systems more transparent, and provide training for those employees who have not had adequate exposure to diversity material in the past. The organization should also clearly communicate its policies to employees so they can understand how and why certain practices are followed. Communications should focus as much as possible on qualifications and job performance; emphasizing certain groups as needing more assistance could backfire.

Finally, research indicates a tailored approach will be needed for international organizations. For instance, a case study of the multinational Finnish company TRANSCO found it was possible to develop a consistent global philosophy for diversity management. However, differences in legal and cultural factors across nations forced the company to develop unique policies to match the cultural and legal frameworks of each country in which it operated.[107]

> ✪ **TRY IT!**
> If your professor has assigned this, go to the Assignments section of **mymanagementlab.com** to complete the **Simulation: *Human Resources and Diversity***.

Summary

This chapter looked at diversity from many perspectives. We paid particular attention to three variables—biographical characteristics, abilities, and diversity programs. Diversity management must be an ongoing commitment that crosses all levels of the organization. Policies to improve the climate for diversity can be effective, and diversity management can be learned.

Implications for Managers

- Understand your organization's anti-discrimination policies thoroughly and share them with all employees.
- Assess and challenge your stereotype beliefs to increase your objectivity.
- Look beyond readily observable biographical characteristics and consider the individual's capabilities before making management decisions; remain open and encouraging for individuals to disclose any hidden disabilities.
- Fully evaluate what accommodations a person with disabilities will need and then fine-tune a job to that person's abilities.
- Seek to understand and respect the unique biographical characteristics of each individual; a fair but individualistic approach yields the best performance.

Affirmative Action Programs Have Outlived Their Usefulness

POINT

U.S. Supreme Court Justice Sonia Sotomayor is arguably the court's strongest supporter of affirmative action...in theory. In a recent case upholding the Michigan ban on affirmative action for underrepresented races in state university admission practices, Justice Sotomayor refused to use the term. "Affirmative action," she said, has the connotation of "intentional preferential treatment based on race alone." Yes, it does. Isn't that the point?

Affirmative action programs (AAP) were needed to get the process of workplace diversity started, but that was all a long time ago. The practice, now outlawed in Arizona, California, Florida, Michigan, Nebraska, New Hampshire, Oklahoma, and Washington, raises the percentage of minority individuals but does not create a positive diversity climate. Here's why:

- *Affirmative action lowers the standards for everyone by shifting the criteria for hiring from experience, education, and abilities to quotas based on race or other non-performance attributes.* Performance standards for the organization are then effectively lowered. Groups not helped by the initiative will be resentful, which can lead to workplace discrimination. Individuals "helped" into the organization also suffer from perceptions of low self-competence ("I don't know if I would have made it here if not for AAP") and stereotype threat ("I'm afraid others can't see me as competent because I was let in by the AAP").

- *Research indicates that minorities are not helped by AAP in pursuing higher education.* In fact, a large-scale study showed that minority law students who attended schools best matched to their LSAT scores performed better than those who went to higher-ranked schools than their scores would warrant without affirmative action.

- *Some of the world's AAPs have resulted in strife.* For example, Sri Lanka has suffered from civil wars partially caused by affirmative action that further polarized the Tamils and Shinalese. In Africa, the quota system to help blacks created a climate of race entitlement and marginalization of Indians. In fact, most countries have struggled with issues arising from affirmative action policies.

Affirmative action has outlived its usefulness in creating diversity, and it's time to create true equality by focusing on merit-based achievements.

COUNTERPOINT

Affirmative action was enacted to ensure equality, and it's still needed today. When the United States was considering the issue for black minorities back in 1965, President Lyndon B. Johnson said, "You do not take a person who, for years, has been hobbled by chains and liberate him, bring him up to the starting line of a race and then say, 'You are free to compete with all the others,' and still justly believe that you have been completely fair." Dr. Martin Luther agreed that, in order to create equal opportunity, proactive measures are needed as long as some people remain at a disadvantage. Therefore, what we should be asking is: are minority groups faring as well as majority groups in the United States? No, not by any indicator.

South Africa has affirmative action for blacks through the Equal Employment Act; China has "preferential policies" that require ethnic minorities and women be appointed to top government positions; Israel has a class-based affirmative action policy to promote women, Arabs, blacks, and people with disabilities; India has a policy of reservation, a form of affirmative action, for under-represented castes; Sri Lanka has the Standardization affirmative action policy to help those in areas with lower rates of education; Malaysia's New Economic Policy (NEP) provides advantage for the majority group, the Malays, who have lower income; Brazil, Finland, France, New Zealand, and Romania have education AAPs; Germany's Basic Law has AAPs for women and those with handicaps; Russia has quotas for women and ethnic minorities; and Canada's Employment Equity Act provides affirmative action to women, the disabled, aboriginal people, and visible minorities.

To be certain, fairness is in the eye of the beholder. Affirmative action provides opportunity, but then it is up to the individual to meet the expectations of schools or employers. As blogger Berneta Haynes wrote, "I'm not ashamed to admit that without affirmative action, I'm not certain I would be on the precipice of the law career that I'm at right now. As an African-American woman from a poor family, I have little doubt that affirmative action helped me get into college, earn a degree, and enroll in law school."

If we change anything about affirmative action, we should expand the program until the achievements of underserved groups fully match those of long-overprivileged groups.

Sources: D. Desilver, "Supreme Court Says States Can Ban Affirmative Action: 8 Already Have," Pew Research Center *Thinktank* (April 22, 2014), http://www.pewresearch.org/fact-tank/2014/04/22/supreme-court-says-states-can-ban-affirmative-action-8-already-have/; B. Haynes, "Affirmative Action Helped Me," *Inside Higher Ed* (March 12, 2013), www.insidehighered.com/views/2013/03/12/affirmative-action-helped-me-and-benefits-society-essay; D. Leonhardt, "Rethinking Affirmative Action," *The New York Times* (October 13, 2012), www.nytimes.com/2012/10/14/sunday-review/rethinking-affirmative-action.html?pagewanted=all; L. M. Leslie, D. M. Mayer, and D. A. Kravitz, "The Stigma of Affirmative Action: A Stereotyping-Based Theory and Meta-Analytic Test of the Consequences for Performance," *Academy of Management Journal* 57, no. 4 (2014): 964–89; and B. Zimmer, "Affirmative Action's Hazy Definitions," *The Wall Street Journal* (April 26–27, 2014), C4. With help from Wikipedia.

CHAPTER REVIEW

MyManagementLab

Go to **mymanagementlab.com** to complete the problems marked with this icon.

QUESTIONS FOR REVIEW

2-1 What are the two major forms of workplace diversity?

2-2 How does workplace discrimination undermine organizational effectiveness?

2-3 How are the key biographical characteristics relevant to OB?

2-4 How do other differentiating characteristics factor into OB?

2-5 What are the relevant points of intellectual and physical abilities to organizational behavior?

2-6 How can organizations manage diversity effectively?

EXPERIENTIAL EXERCISE Differences

The instructor randomly assigns the class into groups of four. It is important that group membership is truly randomly decided, not done by seating, friendships, or preferences. Without discussion, each group member first answers the following question on paper:

> **2-7.** How diverse is your group, on a scale of 1–10, where 1 = very dissimilar and 10 = very similar?

Putting that paper away, each person shares with the group his or her answers to the following questions:

- *What games/toys did you like to play with when you were young?*
- *What do you consider to be your most sacred value (and why)?*
- *Are you spiritual at all?*
- *Tell us a little about your family.*
- *Where's your favorite place on earth and why?*

Each group member then answers the following question on paper:

> **2-8.** How diverse is your group, on a scale of 1–10, where 1 = very dissimilar and 10 = very similar?

After groups calculate the average ratings from before and after the discussion, they will share with the class the difference between their averages and answer the following questions:

> **2-9.** Did your personal rating increase after the discussion time? Did your group's average ratings increase after the discussion time?
>
> **2-10.** Do you think that if you had more time for discussion, your group's average rating would increase?
>
> **2-11.** What do you see as the role of surface-level diversity and deep-level diversity in a group's acceptance of individual differences?

ETHICAL DILEMMA The 30% Club in Hong Kong Aims to Uphold Board Diversity

It seems obvious that women are significantly underrepresented on the boards of Hong Kong companies. According to the 2015 Women on Boards' Report, published by Community Business, out of 655 board directors of blue-chip companies in Hong Kong, only 73 of them are women, representing only 11 percent. The corresponding percentage of female directors in the United States is 19 percent.

Fern Ngai, CEO of Community Business, believes that there are still cultural and structural barriers that bar women from key decision-making positions. Although

Germany just passed a law in 2015 requiring public companies to give 30 percent of board seats to women, Ngai does not believe in mandatory quotas for female directors. She claims that what really matters is the shift in mindset to seek greater gender diversity.

Is there a large enough supply of board-ready women to serve as directors? As a matter of fact, 33 percent of senior management positions are held by women in Hong Kong—the third-highest in the Asia Pacific region. These female senior managers will have the potential to become directors.

This is why the 30% Club Hong Kong has been formed. It is an outreach arm of The Women's Foundation, one of Hong Kong's leading non-profit-making organizations dedicated to the advancement of women's social status. The purpose of the Club is to raise awareness among business leaders of the importance of gender diversity through empirical research, community programs, as well as advocacy. The target is to increase the percentage of female directors to at least 30 percent. The club has been endorsed by the Equal Opportunities Commission of Hong Kong.

However, changing the dominance of male directors in Hong Kong is not easy. According to Jenny To, Talent Management and Communications Director at Pernod Ricard Asia in Hong Kong, the main challenge is to change the mindset of existing board members to accept diversity.

A spokesperson for the 30% Club said that companies with more women on their boards perform better than those with fewer women directors. This is supported by the Credit Suisse Research Institute's report in 2013 that the net income growth of firms with women directors averaged 14 percent from 2007 to 2012, compared with only 10 percent for companies with no female board members. Wendy Yung, Executive Director of Hysan Development Company, notes out that directors from a diverse background could bring more collective insight and enrich constructive board decision-making.

Progression of board diversity remains hopeful and the 30 percent Club will continue to support sustainable business-led voluntary change to improve the current gender imbalance on corporate boards.

Questions

2-12. Given that women participate in the labor force in roughly the same proportion as men, why do you think women occupy so few seats on boards of directors?

2-13. Do you agree with the quotas established in many countries? Why or why not?

2-14. Beyond legal remedies, what do you think can be done to increase women's representation on boards of directors?

Sources: 30% Club HK, "Introduction to the 30% Club Hong Kong," http://30percentclub.org.hk/media/pdfs/Introduction-to-the-30-percent-club.pdf; "More Women Needed on Board," South China Morning Post, http://www.scmp.com/article/996437/more-women-needed-board; 30% Club HK, Office Web site, http://30percentclub.org.hk/; PricewaterhouseCoopers, http://"Annual Corporate Directors Survey: The Gender Edition," May 2015, http://www.pwc.com/us/en/corporate-governance/publications/assets/pwc-acds-2014-the-gender-edition.pdf; Grant Thornton, "Corporate Governance Review," 2012, http://www.grant-thornton.co.uk/Global/Publication_pdf/Corporate_Governance_Review_2012.pdf; Chartered Secretaries, "Diversity on the Boards of Hong Kong Main Board Listed Companies," https://www.hkics.org.hk/media/publication/attachment/PUBLICATION_A_2333_Board%20Diversity_Full%20Report.pdf; Hong Kong Exchanges and Clearing Limited, Consultation Paper: Board Diversity, September 2012, https://www.hkex.com.hk/eng/newsconsul/mktconsul/Documents/cp201209.pdf; George W. Russell, "Balancing the Boards," http://app1.hkicpa.org.hk/APLUS/2013/03/pdf/14-19-Diversity.pdf; Luo Weiteng, "More Women Board Directors Fuels Company Growth in HK," *China Daily,* http://www.chinadaily.com.cn/hkedition/2015-03/04/content_19714310.htm; Claire Cain Miller, "Women on Boards: Where the U.S. Ranks," *The New York Times,* www.nytimes.com/2015/03/11/upshot/women-on-boards-where-the-us-ranks.html?_r=0.

CASE INCIDENT 1   Walking the Walk

Do you want to work for Google? In some ways, who wouldn't? Sunny California, fabulous campus, free organic meals, perks galore…oh, and challenging work with some of the brightest minds in the field. By all accounts, Google is a class act, a symbol of modernization.

Does Google want you to work for it? Ah, that is the question. Eric Schmidt, a former Google CEO, and Jonathan Rosenberg, a former Google senior product manager, say Google searches for a certain type of person: a "smart creative." They say smart creatives are "a new kind of animal"—and the secret ingredient to Google's success.

Do you think you are a smart creative? Are you an impatient, outspoken, risk taker who is easily bored? Do you change jobs frequently? Are you intellectually flexible? Do you have technical know-how, business knowledge, and creativity? Do you think analytically? According to Schmidt and Rosenberg, answering yes to these questions makes you a smart creative. As you can see, being a smart creative is not all positive. But it will get you hired at Google.

One last question: Are you male or female? Google may be a symbol of the modernization of the work*place*, but perhaps not of the work*force*. The Google workforce, with 48,600 individuals, is a man's world—70 percent male overall. On the technical side, a full 83 percent of the engineering employees are male. In the management ranks, 79 percent of the managers are male. On the executive level, only three of the company's 36 executives are women.

Google officials say they are aware of the lack of diversity, but that their diversity initiatives have failed. However, others report that sexist comments go unchecked and there is a frat-house atmosphere. In fact, an interviewer at an all-company presentation insultingly teased a man and woman who shared an office, asking them, "Which one of you does the dishes?"

Thankfully, Google has begun to put its smart creatives to work on new thoughts about diversity. With the help of social psychology research, the company sent all employees through training on unconscious bias—our reflexive tendency to be biased toward our own groups—to force people to consider their racist and sexist mindsets. So far, the training seems to be making a bigger difference than former initia-

tives, but the firm has a long way to go. Laszlo Bock, Google's top HR executive, said, "Suddenly you go from being completely oblivious to going, 'Oh my god, it's everywhere.'"

Critics are skeptical that Google and other large technology firms will ever count women in their ranks in numbers that reflect the population, though research continues to indicate that men and women are highly similar employees. Once Google has achieved greater diversity than it currently has, perhaps its executives can begin to work on the pay differentials: a recent Harvard study indicated that women computer scientists receive 89 percent of the pay men earn for the same jobs.

Questions

⭐ **2-15.** Does this article change your perception of Google as an employer? How?

2-16. Would you agree that although Google helps to modernize the workplace in other companies, its own workforce is old-fashioned?

2-17. Why are older employees often neglected or discriminated against?

Sources: S. Goldenberg, "Exposing Hidden Bias at Google," *The New York Times,* September 25, 2014, B1, B9; S. Lohr, "The Google Formula for Success," *The New York Times,* September 29, 2014, B8; N. Wingfield, "Microsoft Chief Backpedals on Women's Pay," *The New York Times,* October 10, 2014, B7–B8; and E. Zell, Z. Krizan, and S. R. Teeter, "Evaluating Gender Similarities and Differences Using Metasynthesis," *American Psychologist* 70 (2015): 10–20.

CASE INCIDENT 2 The Encore Career

Over the past century, the average age of the workforce has increased as medical science has continued to enhance longevity and vitality. As we discussed in this chapter, many individuals will work past the previously established ages of retirement, and the fastest-growing segment of the workforce is individuals over the age of 55.

Unfortunately, older workers face a variety of discriminatory attitudes in the workplace. Researchers scanned more than 100 publications on age discrimination to determine what types of age stereotypes were most prevalent across studies. They found that stereotypes inferred that older workers are lower performers. Research, on the other hand, indicates they are not, and organizations are realizing the benefits of this needed employee group.

Dale Sweere, HR director for engineering firm Stanley Consultants, is one of the growing number of management professionals actively recruiting the older workforce. Sweere says older workers "typically hit the ground running much quicker and they fit into the organization well." They bring to the job a higher skill level earned through years of experience, remember an industry's history, and know the aging customer base.

Tell that to the older worker who is unemployed. Older workers have long been sought by government contractors, financial firms, and consultants, according to Cornelia Gamlem, president of consulting firm GEMS Group Ltd., and she actively recruits them. However, the U.S. Bureau of Labor Statistics reports that the average job search for an unemployed worker over age 55 is 56 weeks, versus 38 weeks for the rest of the unemployed population.

Enter the encore career, a.k.a. unretirement. Increasingly, older workers who aren't finding fulfilling positions are seeking to opt out of traditional roles. After long careers in the workforce, an increasing number are embracing flexible, work-from-home options such as customer service positions. For instance, Olga Howard, 71, signed on as an independent contractor for 25–30 hours per week with Arise Virtual Solutions, handling questions for a financial software company after her long-term career ended. Others are starting up new businesses. Chris Farrell, author of *Unretirement,* said, "Older people are starting businesses more than any other age group." Others funnel into nonprofit organizations, where the pay may not equal the individual's previous earning power, but the mission is strong. "They need the money and the meaning," said Encore.org CEO Marc Freedman. Still others are gaining additional education, such as Japan's "silver entrepreneurs," who have benefited from the country's tax credits for training older workers.

Individuals who embark on a second-act career often report they are very fulfilled. However, the loss of workers from their longstanding careers may be undesirable. "In this knowledge economy, the retention of older workers gives employers a competitive edge by allowing them to continue to tap a generation of knowledge and skill," said Mark Schmit, executive director of the Society for Human Resource Management (SHRM) Foundation. "New think-

ing by HR professionals and employers will be required to recruit and retain them. Otherwise, organizations' greatest asset will walk out the door."

Questions

2-18. What changes in employment relationships are likely to occur as the population ages?

⭐ 2-19. Do you think increasing age diversity will create new challenges for managers? What types of challenges do you expect will be most profound?

2-20. How can organizations cope with differences related to age discrimination in the workplace? How can older employees help?

Sources: N. Eberstadt and M. W. Hodin, "America Needs to Rethink 'Retirement," *The Wall Street Journal,* March 11, 2014, A15; S. Giegerich, "Older Job-Seekers Must Take Charge, Adapt," *Chicago Tribune,* September 10, 2012, 2–3; R. J. Grossman, "Encore!" *HR Magazine,* July 2014, 27–31; T. Lytle, "Benefits for Older Workers," *HR Magazine,* March 2012, 53–58; G. Norman, "Second Acts After 65," *The Wall Street Journal,* September 24, 2014, A13; D. Stipp, "The Anti-Aging Revolution," *Fortune,* June 14, 2010, 124–30; R. A. Posthuma and M. A. Campion, "Age Stereotypes in the Workplace: Common Stereotypes, Moderators, and Future Research Directions," *Journal of Management* 35 (2009): 158–88; and P. Sullivan, "Older, They Turn a Phone Into a Job," *The New York Times,* March 25, 2014, F3.

MyManagementLab

Go to **mymanagementlab.com** for the following Assisted-graded writing questions:

2-21. In relation to this chapter's Ethical Dilemma, one recent study found no link between female representation on boards of directors and these companies' corporate sustainability or environmental policies. The study's author expressed surprise at the findings. Do the findings surprise you? Why or why not?

2-22. Now that you've read the chapter and Case Incident 2, do you think organizations should work harder to retain and hire older workers? Why or why not?

2-23. **MyManagementLab Only** – comprehensive writing assignment for this chapter.

ENDNOTES

[1] M. Toossi, "A Century of Change: The U.S. Labor Force, 1950–2050," *Bureau of Labor Statistics,* May 2002, www.bls.gov/opub/2002/05/art2full.pdf.

[2] U.S. Census Bureau, DataFerrett, *Current Population Survey,* December 2014; S. Ricker, "The Changing Face of U.S. Jobs," CareerBuilder, March 26, 2015, www.thehiringsite.careerbuilder.com/2015/03/26/9-findings-diversity-americas-workforce.

[3] L. Colley, "Not Codgers in Cardigans! Female Workforce Participation and Ageing Public Services," *Gender Work and Organization,* May 2013, 327–48; and M. DiNatale and S. Boraas, "The Labor Force Experience of Women from Generation X," *Monthly Labor Review,* March 2002, 1–15.

[4] W. H. Frey, *Diversity Explosion* (Washington, DC: Brookings Institution Press, 2014).

[5] M. Toossi, "Labor Force Projections to 2020: A More Slowly Growing Workforce," *Bureau of Labor Statistics,* January 2012, www.bls.gov/opub/mlr/2012/01/art3full.pdf.

[6] C. T. Kulik, "Spotlight on the Context: How a Stereotype Threat Framework Might Help Organizations to Attract and Retain Older Workers," *Industrial and Organizational Psychology* 7, no. 3 (2014): 456–61.

[7] A. H. Eagly and J. L. Chin, "Are Memberships in Race, Ethnicity, and Gender Categories Merely Surface Characteristics?" *American Psychologist* 65 (2010): 934–35.

[8] W. J. Casper, J. H. Wayne, and J. G. Manegold, "Who Will We Recruit? Targeting Deep- and Surface-Level Diversity with Human

Resource Policy Advertising," *Human Resource Management* 52, no. 3 (2013): 311–32.

[9] C. T. Kulik, "Spotlight on the Context: How a Stereotype Framework Might Help Organizations to Attract and Retain Older Workers."

[10] R. Melloy and S. Liu, "Nontraditional Employment History: A Less Obvious Source of Stereotype Threat," *Industrial and Organizational Psychology* 7, no. 3 (2014): 461–66.

[11] E. J. Kenny and R. B. Briner, "Stereotype Threat and Minority Ethnic Employees: What Should Our Research Priorities Be?" *Industrial and Organizational Psychology* 7, no. 3 (2014): 425–29.

[12] C. T. Kulik, "Spotlight on the Context: How a Stereotype Threat Might Help Organizations to Attract and Retain Older Workers."

[13] J. H. Carlson and J. D. Seacat, "Multiple Threat: Overweight/Obese Women in the

Workforce," and B. J. Casad and S. M. Merritt, "The Importance of Stereotype Threat Mechanisms in Workplace Outcomes," *Industrial and Organizational Psychology* 7, no. 3 (2014): 413–18.

[14] G. Czukor and M. Bayazit, "Casting a Wide Net? Performance Deficit, Priming, and Subjective Performance Evaluation in Organizational Stereotype Threat Research," *Industrial and Organizational Psychology* 7, no. 3 (2014): 409–12; K. S. Jones and N. C. Carpenter, "Toward a Sociocultural Psychological Approach to Examining Stereotype Threat in the Workplace," *Industrial and Organizational Psychology* 7, no. 3 (2014): 429–32; and C. T. Kulik, "Spotlight on the Context: How a Stereotype Threat Framework Might Help Organizations to Attract and Retain Older Workers."

[15] L. M. Cortina, "Unseen Injustice: Incivility as Modern Discrimination in Organizations," *Academy of Management Review* 33, no. 1 (2008): 55–75; and C. M. Harold and B. C. Holtz, "The Effects of Passive Leadership on Workplace Incivility," *Journal of Organizational Behavior*, January 2015, 16–38.

[16] J. P. Jamieson, K. Koslov, M. K. Nock, and W. B. Mendes, "Experiencing Discrimination Increases Risk Taking," *Psychological Science* 24, no. 2 (2012): 131–39.

[17] C. T. Kulik, S. Ryan, S. Harper, and G. George, "Aging Populations and Management," *Academy of Management Journal* 57, no. 4 (2014): 929–35.

[18] T. Lytle, "Benefits for Older Workers," *HR Magazine*, March 2012, 53–58.

[19] A. Tergesen, "Why Everything You Know about Aging is Probably Wrong," *The Wall Street Journal*, December 1, 2014, B1–B2.

[20] L. Turner and A. Suflas, "Global Diversity—One Program Won't Fit All," *HR Magazine*, May 2014, 59–61.

[21] L. Weber, "Americans Rip Up Retirement Plans," *The Wall Street Journal*, January 31, 2013, http://online.wsj.com/article/SB1000 14241278873239261045782762417414480 64.html.

[22] M. Chand and R. L. Tung, "The Aging of the World's Population and Its Effects on Global Business," *Academy of Management Perspectives* 28, no. 4 (2014): 409–29.

[23] S. Shellenbarger, "Work & Family Mailbox," *The Wall Street Journal*, January 29, 2014, D2.

[24] N. E. Wolfson, T. M. Cavanaugh, and K. Kraiger, "Older Adults and Technology-Based Instruction: Optimizing Learning Outcomes and Transfer," *Academy of Management Learning & Education* 13, no. 1 (2014): 26-44.

[25] T. W. H. Ng and D. C. Feldman, "Re-examining the Relationship between Age and Voluntary Turnover," *Journal of Vocational Behavior* 74 (2009): 283–94.

[26] T. W. H. Ng and D. C. Feldman, "The Relationship of Age to Ten Dimensions of Job Performance," *Journal of Applied Psychology* 93 (2008): 392–423.

[27] T. W. H. Ng and D. C. Feldman, "Evaluating Six Common Stereotypes about Older Workers with Meta-Analytical Data," *Personnel Psychology* 65 (2012): 821–58.

[28] A. Tergesen, "Why Everything You Know about Aging Is Probably Wrong."

[29] Ibid.

[30] Ibid.

[31] Ibid.

[32] T. W. H. Ng and D. C. Feldman, "The Relationship of Age with Job Attitudes: A Meta-Analysis," *Personnel Psychology* 63 (2010): 677–718.

[33] E. Zell, Z. Krizan, and S. R. Teeter, "Evaluating Gender Similarities and Differences Using Metasynthesis," *American Psychologist* 70, no. 1 (2015): 10–20.

[34] J. B. Allendorfer et al., "Females and Males Are Highly Similar in Language Performance and Cortical Activation Patterns During Verb Generation," *Cortex* 48, no. 9 (2012): 1218–33; and A. Ardilla, M. Rosselli, E. Matute, and O. Inozemtseva, "Gender Differences in Cognitive Development," *Developmental Psychology* 47, no. 4 (2011): 984–90.

[35] P. L. Roth, K. L. Purvis, and P. Bobko, "A Meta-Analysis of Gender Group Differences for Measures of Job Performance in Field Studies," *Journal of Management*, March 2012, 719–39.

[36] S. C. Paustian-Underdahl, L. S. Walker, and D. J. Woehr, "Gender and Perceptions of Leadership Effectiveness: A Meta-Analysis of Contextual Moderators," *Journal of Applied Psychology* 99, no. 6 (2014): 1129–45.

[37] R. E. Silverman, "Study Suggests Fix for Gender Bias on the Job," *The Wall Street Journal*, January 9, 2013, D4.

[38] A. J. Koch, S. D. D'Mello, and P. R. Sackett, "A Meta-Analysis of Gender Stereotypes and Bias in Experimental Simulations of Employment Decision Making," *Journal of Applied Psychology* 100, no. 1 (2015): 128–61.

[39] E. B. King et al., "Benevolent Sexism at Work: Gender Differences in the Distribution of Challenging Developmental Experiences," *Journal of Management*, November 2012, 1835–66.

[40] L. Gartzia, M. K. Ryan, N. Balluerka, and A. Aritzeta, "Think Crisis-Think Female: Further Evidence," *European Journal of Work and Organizational Psychology* 21, no. 4 (2014): 603–28.

[41] P. Wechsler, "58 women CFOs in the Fortune 500: Is This progress?" *Fortune*, February 24, 2015, http://fortune.com/2015/02/24/58-women-cfos-in-the-fortune-500-is-this-progress/.

[42] A. Damast, "She Works Hard for Less Money," *Bloomberg Businessweek*, December 24, 2012–January 6, 2013, 31–32.

[43] B. Casselman, "Male Nurses Earn More," *The Wall Street Journal*, February 26, 2013, A2.

[44] M. A. Belliveau, "Engendering Inequity? How Social Accounts Create vs. Merely Explain Unfavorable Pay Outcomes for Women," *Organization Science*, July–August 2012, 1154–74.

[45] A. J. C. Cuddy, "Increasingly, Juries are Taking the Side of Women Who Face Workplace Discrimination," *Harvard Business Review*, September 2012, 95–100.

[46] J. M. Hoobler, G. Lemmon, and S. J. Wayne, "Women's Managerial Aspirations: An Organizational Development Perspective," *Journal of Management* 40, no. 3 (2014): 703–30.

[47] J. I. Hancock, D. G. Allen, F. A. Bosco, K. R. McDaniel, and C. A. Pierce, "Meta-Analytic Review of Employee Turnover as a Predictor of Firm Performance," *Journal of Management*, March 2013, 573–603.

[48] L. Turner and A. Suflas, "Global Diversity—One Program Won't Fit All."

[49] Ibid.

[50] G. N. Powell and D. A. Butterfield, "Exploring the Influence of Decision Makers' Race and Gender on Actual Promotions to Top Management," *Personnel Psychology* 55, no. 2 (2002): 397–428.

[51] T. Vega, "With Diversity Still Lacking, Industry Focuses on Retention," *The New York Times*, September 4, 2012, B3.

[52] D. R. Avery, P. F. McKay, and D. C. Wilson "What Are the Odds? How Demographic Similarity Affects the Prevalence of Perceived Employment Discrimination," *Journal of Applied Psychology* 93 (2008): 235–49.

[53] J. M. Sacco, C. R. Scheu, A. M. Ryan, and N. Schmitt, "An Investigation of Race and Sex Similarity Effects in Interviews: A Multilevel Approach to Relational Demography," *Journal of Applied Psychology* 88, no. 5 (2003): 852–65; and P. F. McKay and M. A. McDaniel, "A Reexamination of Black-White Mean Differences in Work Performance: More Data, More Moderators," *Journal of Applied Psychology* 91, no. 3 (2006): 538–54.

[54] S. Mullainathan, "The Measuring Sticks of Racial Bias," *The New York Times*, January 4, 2015, 6.

[55] B. R. Ragins, J. A. Gonzalez, K. Ehrhardt, and R. Singh, "Crossing the Threshold: The Spillover of Community Racial Diversity and Diversity Climate to the Workplace," *Personnel Psychology* 65 (2012): 755–87.

[56] P. F. McKay, D. R. Avery, and M. A. Morris, "Mean Racial-Ethnic Differences in Employee Sales Performance: The Moderating Role of Diversity Climate," *Personnel Psychology* 61, no. 2 (2008): 349–74.

[57] D. R. Avery, J. A. Richeson, M R. Hebl, and N. Ambady, "It Does Not Have to Be Uncomfortable: The Role of Behavioral Scripts in Black-White Interracial Interactions," *Journal of Applied Psychology* 94 (2009): 1382–93.

[58] L. Turner and A. Suflas, "Global Diversity—One Program Won't Fit All."

[59] Information on the Americans with Disabilities Act can be found on their website at www.ada.gov, accessed July 28, 2015.

[60] S. G. Goldberg, M. B. Killeen, and B. O'Day, "The Disclosure Conundrum: How People with Psychiatric Disabilities Navigate Employment," *Psychology, Public Policy, and Law* 11, no. 3 (2005): 463–500; and M. L. Ellison, Z. Russinova, K. L. MacDonald-Wilson, and A. Lyass, "Patterns and Correlates of Workplace Disclosure among Professionals and Managers with Psychiatric Conditions," *Journal of Vocational Rehabilitation* 18, no. 1 (2003): 3–13.

[61] B. S. Bell and K. J. Klein, "Effect of Disability, Gender, and Job Level on Ratings of Job Applicants," *Rehabilitation Psychology* 46, no. 3 (2001): 229–46; and E. Louvet, "Social Judgment Toward Job Applicants with Disabilities: Perception of Personal Qualities and Competences," *Rehabilitation Psychology* 52, no. 3 (2007): 297–303.

[62] L. R. Ren, R. L. Paetzold, and A. Colella, "A Meta-Analysis of Experimental Studies on the Effects of Disability on Human Resource Judgments," *Human Resource Management Review* 18, no. 3 (2008): 191–203.

[63] S. Almond and A. Healey, "Mental Health and Absence from Work: New Evidence from the UK Quarterly Labour Force Survey," *Work, Employment, and Society* 17, no. 4 (2003): 731–42.

[64] P. T. J. H. Nelissen, K. Vornholt, G. M. C. Van Ruitenbeek, U. R. Hulsheger, and S. Uitdewilligen, "Disclosure or Nondisclosure—Is This the Question?" *Industrial and Organizational Psychology* 7 (2014): 231–35.

[65] A. M. Santuzzi, P. R. Waltz, and L. M. Finkelstein, "Invisible Disabilities: Unique Challenges for Employees and Organizations," *Industrial and Organizational Psychology* 7 (2014): 204–19.

[66] Ibid.

[67] R. A. Schriber, R. W. Robins, and M. Solomon, "Personality and Self-Insight in Individuals with Autism Spectrum Disorder," *Journal of Personality and Social Psychology* 106, no. 1 (2014): 112–30.

[68] C. L. Nittrouer, R. C. E. Trump, K. R. O'Brien, and M. Hebl, "Stand Up and Be Counted: In the Long Run, Disclosing Helps All," *Industrial and Organizational Psychology* 7 (2014): 235–41.

[69] T. W. H. Ng and D. C. Feldman, "Organizational Tenure and Job Performance," *Journal of Management* 36 (2010): 1220–50.

[70] L. Turner and A. Suflas, "Global Diversity—One Program Won't Fit All."

[71] T. Audi, "A New Mosque Rises in Anchorage," *The Wall Street Journal*, August 15, 2014, A5.

[72] E. B. King and A. S. Ahmad, "An Experimental Field Study of Interpersonal Discrimination Toward Muslim Job Applicants," *Personnel Psychology* 63 (2010): 881–906.

[73] A. Liptak, "In a Case of Religious Dress, Justices Explore the Obligations of Employers," *The New York Times* (February 25, 2015), http://www.nytimes.com/2015/02/26/us/in-a-case-of-religious-dress-justices-explore-the-obligations-of-employers.html?ref=topics&_r=2.

[74] A. Tilcsik, "Pride and Prejudice: Employment Discrimination against Openly Gay Men in the United States," *American Journal of Sociology* 117 (2011): 586–626.

[75] J. Browne, "What One CEO Learned by Being Outed," *The Wall Street Journal*, June 7–8, 2014, C3.

[76] "Facts about Discrimination in Federal Government Employment Based on Marital Status, Political Affiliation, Status as a Parent, Sexual Orientation, or Transgender (Gender Identity) Status," U.S. Equal Employment Opportunity Commission (2013), www.eeoc.gov/federal/otherprotections.cfm.

[77] L. Turner and A. Suflas, "Global Diversity—One Program Won't Fit All."

[78] V. Priola, D. Lasio, S. De Simone, and F. Serri, "The Sound of Silence: Lesbian, Gay, Bisexual, and Transgender Discrimination in 'Inclusive Organizations'," *British Journal of Management* 25 (2012): 488–502.

[79] "Sex-Based Discrimination," U.S. Equal Employment Opportunity Commission 2013, www.eeoc.gov/laws/types/sex.cfm.

[80] M. Keisling, "No Longer at Zero: An Update on ENDA," *Huffington Post*, March 13, 2013, www.huffingtonpost.com/mara-keisling/no-longer-at-zero-an-upda_b_2861885.html; and J. Pike, "One-Year Anniversary of Senate ENDA Passage," Human Rights Campaign, November 7, 2014, http://www.hrc.org/blog/entry/one-year-anniversary-of-senate-enda-passage), accessed March 26, 2015.

[81] C. Burns, "The Costly Business of Discrimination," *Center for American Progress*, March 2012, www.scribd.com/doc/81214767/The-Costly-Business-of-Discrimination.

[82] *HRC Corporate Equality Index*, 2015, http://hrc-assets.s3-website-us-east-1.amazonaws.com//files/documents/CEI-2015-rev.pdf#__utma=149406063.1562509373.1426273478.1426273478.1426273478.1&__utmb=149406063.1.10.1426273478&__utmc=149406063&__utmx=-&__utmz=149406063.1426273478.1.1.utmcsr=google|utmccn=(organic)|utmcmd=organic|utmctr=(not%20provided)&__utmv=-&__utmk=167575230".

[83] P. Levy, "Does the Hobby Lobby Decision Threaten Gay Rights?" *Newsweek*, July 9, 2014, http://www.newsweek.com/does-hobby-lobby-decision-threaten-gay-rights-258098.

[84] V. Priola, D. Lasio, S. De Simone, and F. Serri, "The Sound of Silence: Lesbian, Gay, Bisexual, and Transgender Discrimination in 'Inclusive Organizations'."

[85] P. A. Freund and N. Kasten, "How Smart Do You Think You Are? A Meta-Analysis of the Validity of Self-Estimates of Cognitive Ability," *Psychological Bulletin* 138 (2012): 296–321.

[86] R. E. Nisbett et al., "Intelligence: New Findings and Theoretical Developments," *American Psychologist*, February–March 2012, 130–59.

[87] L. S. Gottfredson, "The Challenge and Promise of Cognitive Career Assessment," *Journal of Career Assessment* 11, no. 2 (2003), pp. 115–135.

[88] M. D. Dunnette and E. A. Fleishman (eds.), *Human Performance and Productivity: Human Capability Assessment* (New York and London: Psychology Press/Taylor & Francis Group, 2014).

[89] J. W. B. Lang, M. Kersting, U. R. Hülscheger, and J. Lang, "General Mental Ability, Narrower Cognitive Abilities, and Job Performance: The Perspective of the Nested-Factors Model of Cognitive Abilities" *Personnel Psychology* 63 (2010): 595–640.

[90] N. Barber, "Educational and Ecological Correlates of IQ: A Cross-National Investigation," *Intelligence*, May–June 2005, 273–84.

[91] M. E. Beier and F. L. Oswald, "Is Cognitive Ability a Liability? A Critique and Future Research Agenda on Skilled Performance," *Journal of Experimental Psychology: Applied* 18 (2012): 331–45.

[92] "What Companies Will Make You Take a Wonderlic Test?" Beat the Wonderlic, December 31, 2014, http://www.beatthewonderlic.com/blog/2014/12/31/what-companies-will-make-you-take-a-wonderlic-test.

[93] Y. Ganzach, "Intelligence and Job Satisfaction," *Academy of Management Journal* 41, no. 5 (1998): 526–39; and Y. Ganzach, "Intelligence, Education, and Facets of Job Satisfaction," *Work and Occupations* 30, no. 1 (2003): 97–122.

[94] J. J. Caughron, M. D. Mumford, and E. A. Fleishman, "The Fleishman Job Analysis Survey: Development, Validation, and Applications," in M. A. Wilson, W. Bennett Jr., S. G. Gibson, and G. M. Alliger (eds.), *The Handbook of Work Analysis: Methods, Systems, Applications and Science of Work Measurement in Organizations* (New York: Routledge/Taylor & Francis Group, 2012); and P. D. Converse, F. L. Oswald, M. A. Gillespie, K. A. Field, and E. B. Bizot, "Matching Individuals to Occupations Using Abilities and the O*Net: Issues and an Application in Career Guidance," *Personnel Psychology*, Summer 2004, 451–87.

[95] S. S. Wang, "Companies Find Autism Can Be a Job Skill," *The Wall Street Journal*, March 28, 2014, B1–B2.

[96] N. Wingfield, "Microsoft Chief Backpedals on Women's Pay," *The Wall Street Journal*, October 10, 2014, B1, B7.

[97] D. R. Avery, "Reactions to Diversity in Recruitment Advertising: Are the Differences Black and White?" *Journal of Applied Psychology* 88, no. 4 (2003): 672–79; P. F. McKay and D. R. Avery, "What Has Race Got to Do with It? Unraveling the Role of Racioethnicity in Job Seekers' Reactions to Site Visits," *Personnel Psychology* 59, no. 2 (2006): 395–429; and D. R. Avery and P. F. McKay, "Target Practice: An Organizational Impression Management Approach to Attracting Minority and Female Job Applicants," *Personnel Psychology* 59, no. 1 (2006): 157–87.

[98] A. Overholt, "More Women Coders," *Fortune*, February 25, 2013, 14.

[99] L. Kwoh, "McKinsey Tries to Recruit Mothers Who Left the Fold," *The Wall Street Journal*, February 20, 2013, B1, B7.

[100] M. R. Buckley, K. A. Jackson, M. C. Bolino, J. G. Veres, and H. S. Field, "The Influence of Relational Demography on Panel Interview Ratings: A Field Experiment," *Personnel Psychology* 60 (2007): 627–46; J. M. Sacco, C. R. Scheu, A. M. Ryan, and N. Schmitt, "An Investigation of Race and Sex Similarity Effects in Interviews: A Multilevel Approach to Relational Demography," *Journal of Applied Psychology* 88 (2003): 852–65; and J. C. Ziegert and P. J. Hanges, "Employment Discrimination: The Role of Implicit Attitudes, Motivation, and a Climate for Racial Bias," *Journal of Applied Psychology* 90 (2005): 553–62.

[101] K. Bezrukova, K. A. Jehn, and C. S. Spell, "Reviewing Diversity Training: Where We Have Been and Where We Should Go," *Academy of Management Learning & Education* 2 (2012): 207–27.

[102] S. T. Bell, "Deep-Level Composition Variables as Predictors of Team Performance: A Meta–Analysis," *Journal of Applied Psychology* 92, no. 3 (2007): 595–615; S. K. Horwitz and I. B. Horwitz, "The Effects of Team Diversity on Team Outcomes: A Meta-Analytic Review of Team Demography," *Journal of Management* 33, no. 6 (2007): 987–1015; G. L. Stewart, "A Meta-Analytic Review of Relationships between Team Design Features and Team Performance," *Journal of Management* 32, no. 1 (2006): 29–54; and A. Joshi and H. Roh, "The Role of Context in Work Team Diversity Research: A Meta-Analytic Review," *Academy of Management Journal* 52, no. 3 (2009): 599–627.

[103] G. Andrevski, O. C. Richard, J. D. Shaw, and W. J. Ferrier, "Racial Diversity and Firm Performance: The Mediating Role of Competitive Intensity," *Journal of Management* 40, no. 3 (2014): 820–44.

[104] A. C. Homan, J. R. Hollenbeck, S. E. Humphrey, D. Van Knippenberg, D. R. Ilgen, and G. A. Van Kleef, "Facing Differences with an Open Mind: Openness to Experience, Salience of Intragroup Differences, and Performance of Diverse Work Groups," *Academy of Management Journal* 51, no. 6 (2008): 1204–22.

[105] E. Kearney and D. Gebert, "Managing Diversity and Enhancing Team Outcomes: The Promise of Transformational Leadership," *Journal of Applied Psychology* 94, no. 1 (2009): 77–89.

[106] C. L. Holladay and M. A. Quiñones, "The Influence of Training Focus and Trainer Characteristics on Diversity Training Effectiveness," *Academy of Management Learning and Education* 7, no. 3 (2008): 343–54; and R. Anand and M. Winters, "A Retrospective View of Corporate Diversity Training from 1964 to the Present," *Academy of Management Learning and Education* 7, no. 3 (2008): 356–72.

[107] A. Sippola and A. Smale, "The Global Integration of Diversity Management: A Longitudinal Case Study," *International Journal of Human Resource Management* 18, no. 11 (2007): 1895–1916.

3 Attitudes and Job Satisfaction

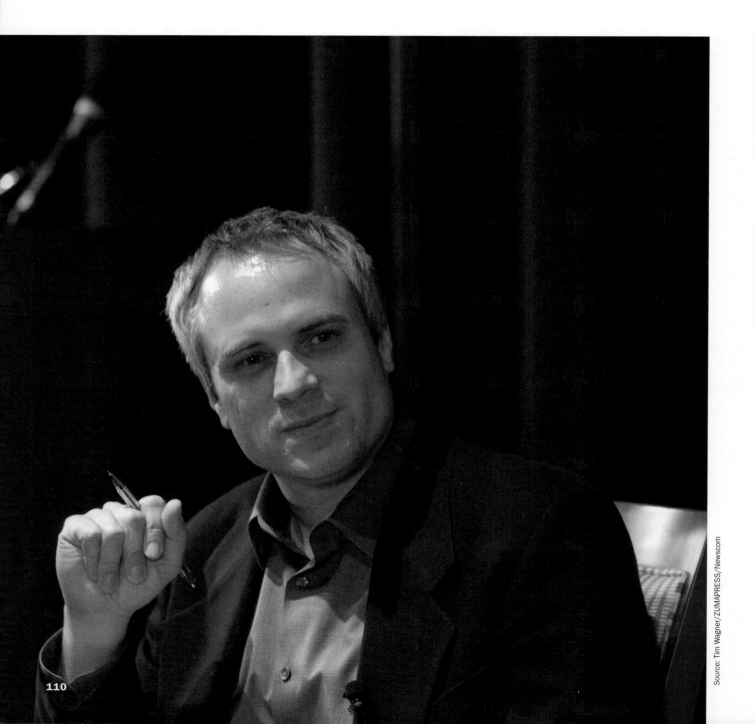

LEARNING OBJECTIVES

After studying this chapter, you should be able to:

3-1 Contrast the three components of an attitude.

3-2 Summarize the relationship between attitudes and behavior.

3-3 Compare the major job attitudes.

3-4 Define *job satisfaction*.

3-5 Summarize the main causes of job satisfaction.

3-6 Identify three outcomes of job satisfaction.

3-7 Identify four employee responses to job dissatisfaction.

MyManagementLab®
⭐ **Chapter Warm Up**

If your professor has chosen to assign this, go to the Assignments section of **mymanagementlab.com** to complete the chapter warm up.

PATCHING TOGETHER A CAREER

In today's temp economy, there are self-employed, part-time, contract, micro-entrepreneur, temporary, and freelance workers. One example is Brad Stone of *Bloomberg Businessweek*, pictured here, who worked as a micro-entrepreneur through task-brokerage firms TaskRabbit, Postmates, and Cherry. These may seem like dream jobs–quick paychecks, work-when-you-want-to hours, and ultra-flexibility. But how satisfied with their jobs are people who have these arrangements?

It depends on your expectations, it seems. Recent research in Canada studied the concept of work congruence, or the match between the number of hours a person wants to work and the number of hours the person is offered work. The study found that as work congruence increased, especially when the number of hours increased for individuals who wanted more hours, job satisfaction increased.

Finding a job where the hours fit your wishes seems like an obvious key to a satisfying job, but it's not the whole story. For one thing, some contingent workers get enough hours, but in the form of unpaid overtime—meaning extra time they put into the job, but for which they receive no pay. Unpaid overtime is common in many countries. According to a study of 4,530 workers in 735 workplaces in Britain, part-timers—who were 27 percent of the workforce—worked almost 10 unpaid overtime hours per week, particularly in professional/managerial jobs. The study also found that part-timers who worked unpaid overtime were more likely to lose their job satisfaction, be absent, and quit than full-time workers who worked extra hours without additional pay.

In the United States, where contingent workers make up 20 percent of the workforce, job satisfaction suffers from a lack of paid hours. Many contingent workers say they cannot reliably find enough paid hours to support themselves and they feel insecure as a result. Professor Arne Kallenberg acknowledged, "Work has become much more insecure, much more precarious."

One large study in China found that job insecurity is strongly negatively related to job satisfaction, meaning the more insecure you are about your work situation, the less satisfied in your job you are likely to be. As a help, the U.S. Affordable Care Act has provided a measure of security for millions of people not covered by an employer's medical insurance plan, and some workforce brokerage-type firms like TaskRabbit are offering their "micro-entrepreneurs" benefits such as a guaranteed hourly wage. "If we want people to feel comfortable moving from job to job in a very flexible, decentralized economy, they need to have some basic protections that allow them to do that," said Jacob Hacker, a Yale political scientist.

While benefits are helpful, some scholars argue that for millions of contingent workers, security, and thus job satisfaction, will come only from work congruency—the availability of jobs and schedules that provide enough paid hours to meet workers' needs. Stone agrees. "My three-day haul won't feed my family," he observed in counting his roughly $67/day earnings as a micro-entrepreneur. Freelance worker Heather Burdette, who has been piecing together a career since 2008, had to declare bankruptcy in 2005. "I'm actually more secure right now," she said, "because I understand that the bottom can fall out at any time."

Sources: N. Conway and J. Sturges, "Investigating Unpaid Overtime Working among the Part-Time Workforce," *British Journal of Management* 25 (2014): 755–71; B. Y. Lee, J. Wang, and J. Weststar, "Work Hour Congruence: The Effect on Job Satisfaction and Absenteeism," *International Journal of Human Resource Management* 26, no. 5 (2015): 657–75; B. Stone, "My Life as a Task Rabbit," *Bloomberg Businessweek* (September 13, 2012), www.businessweek .com/articles/2012-09-13/my-life-as-a-taskrabbit#p1; L. Weber, "For Digital Temps, a Safety Net Emerges," *The Wall Street Journal,* July 30, 2014, B7; and I. U. Zeytinoglu, M. Denton, S. Davies, A. Baumann, J. Blythe, and L. Boos, "Retaining Nurses in their Employing Hospitals and in the Profession: Effects of Job Preference, Unpaid Overtime, Importance of Earnings and Stress," *Health Policy* 79, no. 1 (2006): 57–72.

It's almost a truism to say that a job that fits you is one that satisfies you. As the vignette shows, however, what makes a satisfying job is a bit more complex. What factors besides work schedule compatibility and job security affect job attitudes?[1] Does having a satisfying job really matter? Before we tackle these important questions, it's important to define what we mean by attitudes generally, and job attitudes in particular.

Attitudes

3-1 Contrast the three components of an attitude.

attitudes Evaluative statements or judgments concerning objects, people, or events.

cognitive component The opinion or belief segment of an attitude.

affective component The emotional or feeling segment of an attitude.

behavioral component An intention to behave in a certain way toward someone or something.

Attitudes are evaluative statements—either favorable or unfavorable—about objects, people, or events. They reflect how we feel about something. When you say "I like my job," you are expressing your attitude about your work.

Attitudes are complex. If you ask people about their attitude toward religion, Lady Gaga, or an organization, you may get a simple response, but the underlying reasons are probably complicated. To fully understand attitudes, we must consider their fundamental properties or components.

Typically, researchers assume attitudes have three components: cognition, affect, and behavior.[2] The statement "My pay is low" is a **cognitive component** of an attitude—a description of or belief in the way things are. It sets the stage for the more critical part of an attitude—its **affective component**. Affect is the emotional or feeling segment of an attitude reflected in the statement, "I am angry over how little I'm paid." Affect can lead to behavioral outcomes. The **behavioral component** of an attitude describes an intention to behave a certain way toward someone or something—as in, "I'm going to look for another job that pays better."

Viewing attitudes as having three components—cognition, affect, and behavior—helps understand their complexity and the potential relationship between attitudes and behavior. For example, imagine you realized that someone treated you unfairly. Aren't you likely to have feelings about that, occurring virtually instantaneously with the realization? Thus, cognition and affect are intertwined.

Exhibit 3-1 illustrates how the three components of an attitude are related. In this example, an employee didn't get a promotion he thought he deserved.

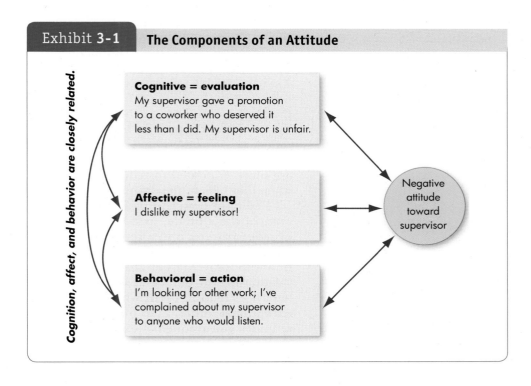

Exhibit 3-1   The Components of an Attitude

Cognition, affect, and behavior are closely related.

Cognitive = evaluation
My supervisor gave a promotion to a coworker who deserved it less than I did. My supervisor is unfair.

Affective = feeling
I dislike my supervisor!

Behavioral = action
I'm looking for other work; I've complained about my supervisor to anyone who would listen.

Negative attitude toward supervisor

His attitude toward his supervisor is illustrated as follows: The employee thought he deserved the promotion (cognition), he strongly dislikes his supervisor (affect), and he has complained and taken action (behavior). Although we often think cognition causes affect, which then causes behavior, in reality these components are difficult to separate.

In organizations, attitudes are important for their behavioral component. If workers believe, for example, that managers, auditors, and engineers are in a conspiracy to make employees work harder for less money, we should try to understand how this attitude formed, how it impacts job behavior, and how it might be changed.

Attitudes and Behavior

3-2   Summarize the relationship between attitudes and behavior.

Early research on attitudes assumed they were causally related to behavior—that is, the attitudes people hold determine what they do. However, one researcher—Leon Festinger—argued that attitudes *follow* behavior. Other researchers have agreed that attitudes predict future behavior.[3]

Did you ever notice how people change what they say so it doesn't contradict what they do? Perhaps a friend of yours consistently argued that her apartment complex was better than yours until another friend in your complex asked her to move in with him; once she moved to your complex, you noticed her attitude toward her former apartment became more critical. Cases of attitude following behavior illustrate the effects of **cognitive dissonance**,[4] contradictions individuals might perceive between their attitudes and their behavior.

cognitive dissonance Any incompatibility between two or more attitudes or between behavior and attitudes.

People seek consistency among their attitudes, and between their attitudes and their behavior.[5] Any form of inconsistency is uncomfortable, and individuals will therefore attempt to reduce it. People seek a stable state, which is a minimum of dissonance. When there is a dissonance, people will alter either the attitudes or the behavior, or they will develop a rationalization for the discrepancy. Recent research found, for instance, that the attitudes of employees who had emotionally challenging work events improved after they talked about their experiences with coworkers. Social sharing helped these workers adjust their attitudes to behavioral expectations.[6]

No individual can avoid dissonance. You know texting while walking is unsafe, but you do it anyway and hope nothing bad happens. Or you give someone advice you have trouble following yourself. The desire to reduce dissonance depends on three factors, including the *importance* of the elements creating dissonance and the degree of *influence* we believe we have over the elements. The third factor is the *rewards* of dissonance; high rewards accompanying high dissonance tend to reduce tension inherent in the dissonance (dissonance is less distressing if accompanied by something good, such as a higher pay raise than expected). Individuals are more motivated to reduce dissonance when the attitudes are important or when they believe the dissonance is due to something they can control.

The most powerful moderators of the attitudes relationship are the *importance* of the attitude, its *correspondence to behavior,* its *accessibility,* the presence of *social pressures,* and whether a person has *direct experience* with the attitude.[7] Important attitudes reflect our fundamental values, self-interest, or identification with individuals or groups we value. These attitudes tend to show a strong relationship to our behavior. However, discrepancies between attitudes and behaviors tend to occur when social pressures to behave in certain ways hold exceptional power, as in most organizations. You're more likely to remember attitudes you frequently express, and attitudes that our memories can easily access are more likely to predict our behavior. The attitude–behavior relationship is also likely to be much stronger if an attitude refers to something with which we have direct personal experience.

Westin Hotels strives for consistency between employee attitudes and behavior through a global wellness program to help employees improve their health. Shown here is Westin's executive chef, Frank Tujague, whose cooking demonstrations give employees direct experience with healthy ingredients and cooking techniques.

Source: Diane Bondareff/AP Images

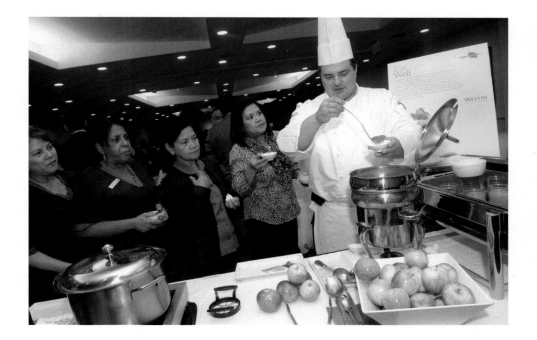

Office Talk

You are peacefully at work in your cubicle when your coworker invades your space, sitting on your desk and nearly overturning your coffee. As she talks about the morning meeting, do you: a) stop what you're doing and listen; or b) explain that you're in the middle of a project and ask to talk some other time?

Your answer may reflect your attitude toward office talk, but it should be guided by whether your participation is ethical. Sometimes, office conversations can help employees to process information and find solutions to problems. Other times, office talk can be damaging to everyone. Consider the scenario from two perspectives: oversharing and venting.

More than 60 percent of 514 professional employees recently surveyed indicated they encounter individuals who frequently share too much about themselves. Some are self-centered, narcissistic, and "think you want to know all the details of their lives," according to psychologist Alan Hilfer.

Despite the drawbacks, oversharers can be strong contributors. Billy Bauer, director of marketing for manufacturer Royce Leather, is an oversharer who boasts about his latest sales—which may push other employees to work harder. Oversharers can also contribute to teamwork when they share personal stories related to organizational goals, according to a Harvard Business Review article.

Now let's look at this the other way. According to Yale Professor Amy Wrzesniewski, organization-lovers are often "the first people to become offended" when they think the organization is making wrong decisions. They can become emotional, challenging, and outspoken about their views. If they are not heard, they can increase their venting or withdraw.

Yet organization-lovers can be top-performing employees: they are often highly engaged, inspiring, and strong team players who are more likely to work harder than others. Venting their frustrations helps restore a positive attitude to keep them high performing. Research indicates that venting to coworkers can also build camaraderie.

Since guidelines for acceptable office conversation are almost nonexistent in the contemporary age of openness, personalization, and transparency, you must decide what kinds of office talk are ethical and productive. Knowing who is approaching you for conversation, why they are approaching you, what they may talk about, and how you may keep the discussion productive and ethical can help you choose whether to engage or excuse yourself.

Sources: S. Shellenbarger, "Office Oversharers: Don't Tell Us about Last Night," *The Wall Street Journal,* June 25, 2014, D2; A. S. McCance, C. D. Nye, L. Wang, K. S. Jones, and C. Chiu, "Alleviating the Burden of Emotional Labor: The Role of Social Sharing," *Journal of Management* (February 2013): 392–415; and S. Shellenbarger, "When It Comes to Work, Can You Care too Much?" *The Wall Street Journal,* April 30, 2014, D3.

Job Attitudes

We have thousands of attitudes, but OB focuses on a very limited number that form positive or negative evaluations employees hold about their work environments. Much of the research has looked at three attitudes: job satisfaction, job involvement, and organizational commitment.[8] Other important attitudes include perceived organizational support and employee engagement.

Job Satisfaction and Job Involvement

job satisfaction   A positive feeling about one's job resulting from an evaluation of its characteristics.

When people speak of employee attitudes, they usually mean **job satisfaction**, a positive feeling about a job resulting from an evaluation of its characteristics. A person with high job satisfaction holds positive feelings about the work, while a person with low satisfaction holds negative feelings. Because OB researchers give job satisfaction high importance, we'll review this attitude in detail later.

job involvement   The degree to which a person identifies with a job, actively participates in it, and considers performance important to self-worth.

psychological empowerment   Employees' belief in the degree to which they affect their work environment, their competence, the meaningfulness of their job, and their perceived autonomy in their work.

Related to job satisfaction is **job involvement**, the degree to which people identify psychologically with their jobs and consider their perceived performance levels important to their self-worth.[9] Employees with high job involvement strongly identify with and really care about the kind of work they do. Another closely related concept is **psychological empowerment**, or employees' beliefs in: the degree to which they influence their work environment, their competencies, the meaningfulness of their job, and their perceived autonomy.[10]

Research suggests that empowerment initiatives need to be tailored to desired behavioral outcomes. Research in Singapore found that good leaders empower their employees by fostering their self-perception of competence—through involving them in decisions, making them feel their work is important, and giving them discretion to "do their own thing."[11]

Organizational Commitment

organizational commitment   The degree to which an employee identifies with a particular organization and its goals and wishes to maintain membership in the organization.

An employee with **organizational commitment** identifies with a particular organization and its goals and wishes to remain a member. Emotional attachment to an organization and belief in its values is the "gold standard" for employee commitment.[12]

Employees who are committed will be less likely to engage in work withdrawal even if they are dissatisfied because they have a sense of organizational loyalty or attachment.[13] Even if employees are not currently happy with their work, they are willing to make sacrifices for the organization if they are committed enough.

Perceived Organizational Support

perceived organizational support (POS)   The degree to which employees believe an organization values their contribution and cares about their well-being.

Perceived organizational support (POS) is the degree to which employees believe the organization values their contributions and cares about their well-being. An excellent example is R&D engineer John Greene, whose POS is sky-high because when he was diagnosed with leukemia, CEO Marc Benioff and 350 fellow Salesforce.com employees covered all his medical expenses and stayed in touch with him throughout his recovery. No doubt stories like this are part of the reason Salesforce.com was number 8 of *Fortune*'s 100 Best Companies to Work For in 2015.[14]

People perceive their organizations as supportive when rewards are deemed fair, when employees have a voice in decisions, and when they see

power distance The degree to which people in a country accept that power in institutions and organizations is distributed unequally.

employee engagement An individual's involvement with, satisfaction with, and enthusiasm for the work he or she does.

their supervisors as supportive.[15] POS is a predictor, but there are some cultural influences. POS is important in countries where the **power distance**, the degree to which people in a country accept that power in institutions and organizations is distributed unequally, is lower. In low power-distance countries like the United States, people are more likely to view work as an exchange than as a moral obligation, so employees look for reasons to feel supported by their organizations. In high power-distance countries like China, employee POS perceptions are not as deeply based on demonstrations of fairness, support, and encouragement.

Employee Engagement

Employee engagement is an individual's involvement with, satisfaction with, and enthusiasm for the work he or she does. To evaluate engagement, we might ask employees whether they have access to resources and opportunities to learn new skills, whether they feel their work is important and meaningful, and whether interactions with coworkers and supervisors are rewarding.[16] Highly engaged employees have a passion for their work and feel a deep connection to their companies; disengaged employees have essentially checked out, putting time but not energy or attention into their work. Engagement becomes a real concern for most organizations because surveys indicate that few employees—between 17 percent and 29 percent—are highly engaged by their work.

Engagement levels determine many measurable outcomes. A study of nearly 8,000 business units in 36 companies found that units whose employees reported high-average levels of engagement achieved higher levels of customer satisfaction, were more productive, brought in higher profits, and experienced lower levels of turnover and accidents than at other business units.[17] Molson Coors, for example, found engaged employees were five times less likely to have safety incidents, and when an accident did occur it was much less serious and less costly for the engaged employee than for a disengaged one ($63 per

Employees waving to guests at Hong Kong Disneyland are committed to the company and its goal of giving visitors a magical and memorable experience. Through careful hiring and extensive training, Disney ensures that employees identify with its priority of pleasing customers by serving them as special guests.

Source: Matt Stroshane/UPPA/ZUMAPRESS/Newscom

incident versus $392). Caterpillar set out to increase employee engagement and recorded a resulting 80 percent drop in grievances and a 34 percent increase in highly satisfied customers.[18]

Such promising findings have earned employee engagement a following in many business organizations and management consulting firms. However, the concept generates active debate about its usefulness, partly because of the difficulty of identifying what creates job engagement. The two top reasons for job engagement that participants in one study gave recently were (1) having a good manager they enjoy working for and (2) feeling appreciated by their supervisor. However, most of their other reasons didn't relate to the job engagement construct.[19] Another study in Australia found that emotional intelligence is linked to employee engagement.[20] Other research suggested that engagement fluctuates partially due to daily challenges and demands.[21]

One review of the job engagement literature concluded, "The meaning of employee engagement is ambiguous among both academic researchers and among practitioners who use it in conversations with clients." Another reviewer called engagement "an umbrella term for whatever one wants it to be."[22] Research has set out to identify the dimensions of employee engagement, but the debate is far from settled. For now, we can see that job engagement, in its various incarnations, yields important organizational outcomes.

Are These Job Attitudes Really All That Distinct?

You might wonder whether job attitudes are really distinct. If people feel deeply engaged by their jobs (high job involvement), isn't it probable they like it, too (high job satisfaction)? Won't people who think their organization is supportive (high perceived organizational support) also feel committed to it (strong organizational commitment)? Evidence suggests these attitudes *are* highly related, perhaps to a confusing degree.

There is some distinctiveness among attitudes, but they overlap greatly for various reasons, including the employee's personality. Generally, if you know someone's level of job satisfaction, you know most of what you need to know about how that person sees the organization. Next, we will consider the implications of job satisfaction and then job dissatisfaction.

Job Satisfaction

3-4   Define *job satisfaction*.

We have already discussed job satisfaction briefly. Now let's dissect the concept more carefully. How do we measure job satisfaction? What causes an employee to have a high level of job satisfaction? How do satisfied employees affect an organization? Before you answer, a look at the list of worst jobs for job satisfaction (Exhibit 3-2) may give you some indications. You may be surprised that they are not all low-paid jobs.

Measuring Job Satisfaction

Our definition of job satisfaction—a positive feeling about a job resulting from an evaluation of its characteristics—is broad. Yet that breadth is appropriate. A job is more than just shuffling papers, writing programming code, waiting on customers, or driving a truck. Jobs require interacting with coworkers and bosses, following organizational rules and policies, determining the power structure, meeting performance standards, living with less-than-ideal working conditions, adapting to new technology, and so forth. An employee's assessment

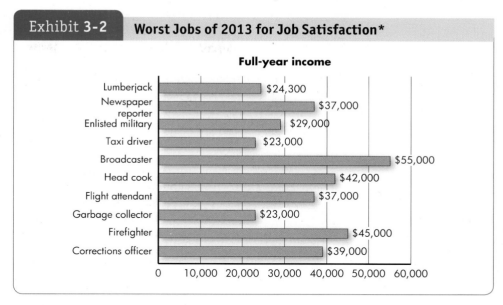

Exhibit 3-2   **Worst Jobs of 2013 for Job Satisfaction***

Full-year income

Job	Income
Lumberjack	$24,300
Newspaper reporter	$37,000
Enlisted military	$29,000
Taxi driver	$23,000
Broadcaster	$55,000
Head cook	$42,000
Flight attendant	$37,000
Garbage collector	$23,000
Firefighter	$45,000
Corrections officer	$39,000

*Based on physical demands, work environment, income, stress, and hiring outlook.

Source: CareerCast.com (2014), http://www.careercast.com/jobs-rated/worst-jobs-2014.

of satisfaction with the job is thus a complex summation of many discrete elements. How, then, do we measure it?

Two approaches are popular. The single global rating is a response to one question, such as "All things considered, how satisfied are you with your job?" Respondents circle a number between 1 and 5 on a scale from "highly satisfied" to "highly dissatisfied." The second method, the summation of job facets, is more sophisticated. It identifies key elements in a job such as the type of work, skills needed, supervision, present pay, promotion opportunities, culture, and relationships with coworkers. Respondents rate these on a standardized scale, and researchers add the ratings to create an overall job satisfaction score.

Is one of these approaches superior? Intuitively, summing up responses to a number of job factors seems likely to achieve a more accurate evaluation of job satisfaction. Research, however, doesn't support the intuition.[23] This is one of those rare instances in which simplicity seems to work as well as complexity, making one method essentially as valid as the other. Both methods can be helpful. The single global rating method isn't very time consuming, while the summation of job facets helps managers zero in on problems and deal with them faster and more accurately.

How Satisfied Are People in Their Jobs?

Are most people satisfied with their jobs? You may want to consider the OB Poll before you answer. Job satisfaction levels can remain quite consistent over time. For instance, U.S. average job satisfaction levels were consistently high from 1972 to 2006.[24] However, economic conditions tend to influence job satisfaction rates. In late 2007, the economic contraction precipitated a drop-off in job satisfaction; the lowest point was in 2010, when 42.6 percent of U.S. workers reported satisfaction with their jobs.[25] Approximately 47.7 percent of U.S. workers reported satisfaction with their jobs in 2014,[26] but the rebound was still far off

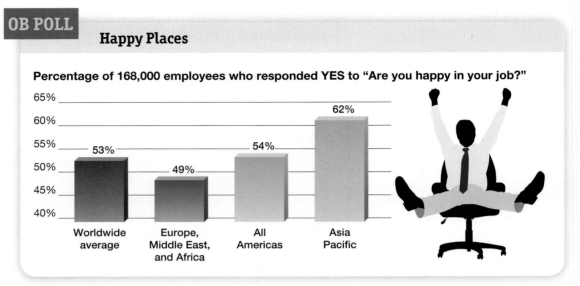

OB POLL

Happy Places

Percentage of 168,000 employees who responded YES to "Are you happy in your job?"

Sources: Statista (2013), http://www.statista.com/statistics/224508/employee-job-satisfaction-worldwide/; Kelly Services Group (2012), http://www.kellyocg.com/uploadedFiles/Content/Knowledge/Kelly_Global_Workforce_Index_Content/Acquisition%20and%20Retention%20 in%20the%20War%20for%20Talent%20Report.pdf.

the 1987 level of 61.1 percent.[27] Job satisfaction rates tend to vary in different cultures worldwide, and of course there are always competing measurements that offer alternative viewpoints.

The facets of job satisfaction levels can vary widely. As shown in Exhibit 3-3, people have typically been more satisfied with their jobs overall, the work itself, and their supervisors and coworkers than they have been with their pay and promotion opportunities.

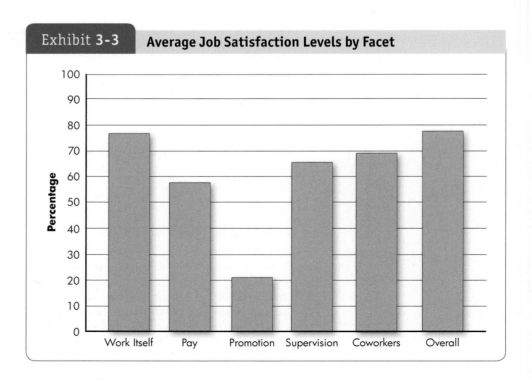

| Exhibit 3-3 | **Average Job Satisfaction Levels by Facet** |

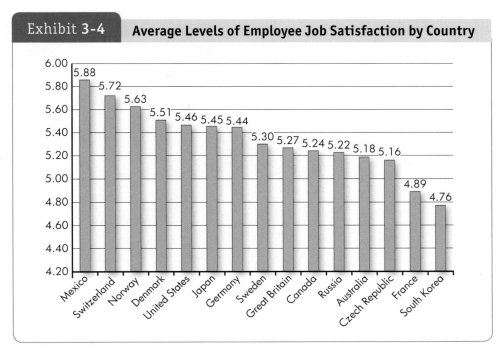

Exhibit 3-4 | Average Levels of Employee Job Satisfaction by Country

Source: Based on J. H. Westover, "The Impact of Comparative State-Directed Development on Working Conditions and Employee Satisfaction," *Journal of Management & Organization* (July 2012): 537–54.

There are some cultural differences in job satisfaction. Exhibit 3-4 provides the results of a global study of job satisfaction levels of workers in 15 countries, with the highest levels in Mexico and Switzerland. Do employees in these cultures have better jobs? Or are they simply more positive (and less self-critical)? Conversely, the lowest score in the study was for South Korea. Autonomy is low in South Korean culture, and businesses tend to be rigidly hierarchical in structure. Does this make for low job satisfaction?[28] It is difficult to discern all the factors influencing the scores, but considering how businesses are responding to changes brought on by globalization may give us clues.

What Causes Job Satisfaction?

3-5 Summarize the main causes of job satisfaction.

Think about the best job you've ever had. What made it great? The reasons can differ greatly. Let's discuss some characteristics that likely influence job satisfaction, starting with job conditions.

Job Conditions

Generally, interesting jobs that provide training, variety, independence, and control satisfy most employees. Interdependence, feedback, social support, and interaction with coworkers outside the workplace are also strongly related to job satisfaction, even after accounting for characteristics of the work itself.[29] As you may have guessed, managers also play a big role in employees' job satisfaction. Employees who feel empowered by their leaders experience higher job satisfaction, one study of a large Hong Kong telecommunications corporation found.[30] Research in Israel suggested that a manager's attentiveness, responsiveness, and support increase the employee's job satisfaction.[31]

Employee engagement is high at Baptist Health of South Florida, where employees share a serious commitment to patient care and are passionate about the work they do. Looking at an EKG readout, hospital employees Yaima Millan and Marvin Rosete feel their work is meaningful and can make a difference in patients' lives.
Source: Wilfredo Lee/AP Images

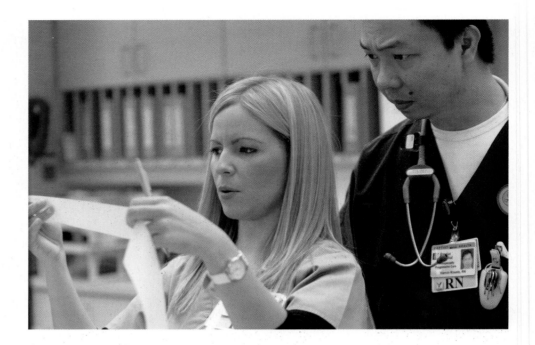

Thus, job conditions—especially the intrinsic nature of the work itself, social interactions, and supervision—are important predictors of job satisfaction. Although each is important, and although their relative value will vary across employees, the intrinsic nature of the work is most important.[32]

Personality

core self-evaluation (CSE) Believing in one's inner worth and basic competence.

As important as job conditions are to job satisfaction, personality also plays an important role. People who have positive **core self-evaluations (CSEs)**—who believe in their inner worth and basic competence—are more satisfied with their jobs than people with negative CSEs. Additionally, in the context of career commitment, CSE influences job satisfaction as people with high levels of both CSE and career commitment may realize particularly high job satisfaction.[33]

⭐ **PERSONAL INVENTORY ASSESSMENTS**   PERSONAL INVENTORY ASSESSMENT

Core Self Evaluation (CSE) Scale

In this chapter, you were introduced to the concept of core self-evaluation (CSE). You probably have a general awareness of your CSE, or how you candidly view your capabilities. This PIA can provide you with further insight.

Pay

You've probably noticed that pay comes up often when people discuss job satisfaction. Pay does correlate with job satisfaction and overall happiness for many people, but the effect can be smaller once an individual reaches a standard level of comfortable living. Take a look at Exhibit 3-5. It shows the relationship between the average pay for a job and the average level of job satisfaction. As you can see, there isn't much of a relationship there. Money does

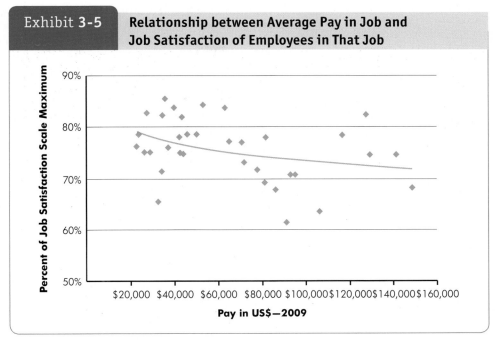

Exhibit **3-5**   **Relationship between Average Pay in Job and Job Satisfaction of Employees in That Job**

Source: T. A. Judge, R. F. Piccolo, N. P. Podsakoff, J. C. Shaw, and B. L. Rich, "The Relationship between Pay and Job Satisfaction: A Meta-Analysis of the Literature," *Journal of Vocational Behavior* 77, no. 2 (2010): 157–67.

motivate people, as we will discover in Chapter 6. But what motivates us is not necessarily the same as what makes us happy.

Corporate Social Responsibility (CSR)

Would you be as happy to work for an organization with a stated social welfare mission as one without? An organization's commitment to **corporate social responsibility (CSR)**, or its self-regulated actions to benefit society or the environment beyond what is required by law, increasingly affects employee job satisfaction. Organizations practice CSR in a number of ways, including environmental sustainability initiatives, nonprofit work, and charitable giving.

CSR is good for the planet and good for people. Employees whose personal values fit with the organization's CSR mission are often more satisfied. In fact, of 59 large and small organizations recently surveyed, 86 percent reported they have happier employees as a result of their CSR programs.[34]

The relationship between CSR and job satisfaction is particularly strong for Millennials. "The next generation of employees is seeking out employers that are focused on the triple bottom line: people, planet, and revenue," said Susan Cooney, founder of philanthropy firm Givelocity.[35] CSR allows workers to serve a higher purpose or contribute to a mission. According to researcher Amy Wrzesniewski, people who view their work as part of a higher purpose often realize higher job satisfaction.[36] However, an organization's CSR efforts must be well governed and its initiatives must be sustainable for long-term job satisfaction benefits.[37]

Although the link between CSR and job satisfaction is strengthening, not all employees find value in CSR.[38] Therefore, organizations need to address a few issues in order to be most effective. First, not all projects are equally meaningful for every person's job satisfaction, yet participation for all employees is

corporate social responsibility (CSR) An organization's self-regulated actions to benefit society or the environment beyond what is required by law.

sometimes expected. For instance, Lisa Dewey, a partner at one of the world's largest law firms, said, "All DLA Piper attorneys and staff are encouraged to participate in the firm's pro bono and volunteer projects."[39] Requiring these activities may decrease overall job satisfaction for those who do not wish to volunteer their time but are required to do so.

Second, some organizations require employees to contribute in a prescribed manner. For instance, consulting firm entreQuest's CEO, Joe Mechlinksi, requires employees to participate in "Give Back Days" by serving in a soup kitchen, building a Habitat for Humanity house, or mentoring children. These choices may not fit every individual's vision of CSR. Furthermore, pressuring people to go "above and beyond" in ways that are not natural for them can burn them out for future CSR projects[40] and lower their job satisfaction, particularly when CSR projects provide direct benefits to the organization (such as positive press coverage).[41] People want CSR to be genuine and authentic.

Third, CSR measures can seem disconnected from the employee's actual work,[42] providing no increase to job satisfaction. After watching consulting firm KPMG's "over the top" video that boasted of involvement in the election of Nelson Mandela and the end of Apartheid, the launch of the first space station by NASA, and the freedom of U.S. hostages in Iran, one anonymous employee questioned his employment. "If I want to really make a change," he said, "why would I sit here?"[43]

In sum, CSR is a needed, positive trend of accountability and serving. It can also significantly contribute to increased employee job satisfaction when managed well.

Outcomes of Job Satisfaction

3-6 Identify three outcomes of job satisfaction.

Having discussed some of the causes of job satisfaction, we now turn to some specific outcomes.

Job Performance

As several studies have concluded, happy workers are more likely to be productive workers. Some researchers used to believe the relationship between job satisfaction and job performance was a myth, but a review of 300 studies suggested the correlation is quite robust.[44] Individuals with higher job satisfaction perform better, and organizations with more satisfied employees tend to be more effective than those with fewer.

Organizational Citizenship Behavior (OCB)

It seems logical that job satisfaction should be a major determinant of an employee's organizational citizenship behavior (known as OCB or citizenship behavior, see Chapter 1).[45] OCBs include people talking positively about their organizations, helping others, and going beyond the normal expectations of their jobs. Evidence suggests job satisfaction *is* moderately correlated with OCB; people who are more satisfied with their jobs are more likely to engage in citizenship behavior.[46]

Why does job satisfaction lead to OCB? One reason is trust. Research in 18 countries suggests that managers reciprocate employees' OCB with trusting behaviors of their own.[47] Individuals who feel their coworkers support them are also more likely to engage in helpful behaviors than those who have antagonistic coworker relationships.[48] Personality matters, too. Individuals with certain personality traits (agreeableness and conscientiousness, see Chapter 5) are more

Service firms like Air Canada understand that satisfied employees increase customer satisfaction and loyalty. As frontline employees who have regular customer contact, the airline's ticket agents are friendly, upbeat, and responsive while greeting passengers and helping them with luggage check-in and seat assignments.

Source: Aaron Harris/Bloomberg/Getty Images

satisfied with their work, which in turn leads them to engage in more OCB.[49] Finally, individuals who receive positive feedback on their OCB from their peers are more likely to continue their citizenship activities.[50]

Customer Satisfaction

Because service organization managers should be concerned with pleasing customers, it's reasonable to ask whether employee satisfaction is related to positive customer outcomes. For frontline employees who have regular customer contact, the answer is "yes." Satisfied employees appear to increase customer satisfaction and loyalty.[51]

A number of companies are acting on this evidence. Online shoe retailer Zappos is so committed to finding customer service employees who are satisfied with the job that it offers a $2,000 bribe to quit the company after training, figuring the least satisfied will take the cash and go.[52] Zappos employees are empowered to "create fun and a little weirdness" to ensure that customers are satisfied, and it works: of the company's more than 24 million customers, 75 percent are repeat buyers. Therefore, for Zappos, employee satisfaction has a direct effect on customer satisfaction.

Life Satisfaction

Until now, we've treated job satisfaction as if it were separate from life satisfaction, but they may be more related than you think.[53] Research in Europe indicated that job satisfaction is positively correlated with life satisfaction, and your attitudes and experiences in life spill over into your job approaches and experiences.[54] Furthermore, life satisfaction decreases when people become unemployed, according to research in Germany, and not just because of the loss of income.[55] For most individuals, work is an important part of life, and therefore it makes sense that our overall happiness depends in no small part on our happiness in our work (our job satisfaction).

How can I make my job better?

Honestly, I hate my job. But there are reasons I should stay: this is my first job out of college, it pays pretty well, and it will establish my career. Is there any hope, or am I doomed until I quit?

— *Taylor*

Dear Taylor:

You're not doomed! You can work on your attitude to either improve your experience or find a positive perspective. In other words, if you can turn "I hate my job" into "this is what I'm doing to make my situation better," your job satisfaction is likely to improve. Try this:

- *Write down everything you hate about your job, but wait until you have a few days off so you can get a more objective viewpoint.* Be specific. Keep asking yourself why, as in, "Why do I dislike my office mate?" Also, consider your history: was the job always a problem, or perhaps circumstances have changed?
- *Now write down everything you like about the job.* Again, be specific. Think about the environment, the people, and the work separately. Find something positive, even if it's just the coffee in the break room.

- *Compare your lists for clues about your attitude and job satisfaction.* Look for mentions of the work or the people. Job satisfaction is generally more strongly related to how interesting your work is than it is to other factors. People, especially your supervisor, are important to your attitude toward work as well.
- *Read your lists aloud to a few trusted friends (you don't want to rant about your boss with your coworker).* Ask them to help process your grievances. Are there deal-breakers like harassment?
- *Decide whether you can talk with your manager about this.* According to Roy L. Cohen, author of *The Wall Street Professional's Survival Guide*, "consider whether how you're being treated is unique to you or shared by your colleagues." If everyone has the same problem, especially if the problem is the boss, you probably shouldn't approach your manager. But changes can be made in most situations.

Based on the sources of your grievances and your ability to make changes

in the workplace, you may choose to address the issues, or develop skills for your next job. Meanwhile, don't sabotage yourself with sloppy performance and complaints. Instead, look for positive reinforcement, join a professional organization, or volunteer. Happy employees are healthier. You deserve to be one of them.

_____

Sources: "Employee Engagement," *Workforce Management* (February 2013): 19; A. Hurst, "Being 'Good' Isn't the Only Way to Go," *The New York Times*, April 20, 2014, 4; R. E. Silverman, "Work as Labor or Love?" *The Wall Street Journal*, October 18, 2012, D3; H. J. Smith, T. F. Pettigrew, G. M. Pippin, and S. Bialosiewicz, "Relative Deprivation: A Theoretical and Meta-Analytic Review," *Personality and Social Psychology Review* 16 (2012): 203–32; and A. Tugend, "Survival Skills for a Job You Detest," *The Wall Street Journal*, April 7, 2012, B5.

The Impact of Job Dissatisfaction

3-7 Identify four employee responses to job dissatisfaction.

What happens when employees dislike their jobs? One theoretical model—the exit–voice–loyalty–neglect framework—is helpful for understanding the consequences of dissatisfaction. Exhibit 3-6 illustrates employees' four responses to job dissatisfaction, which differ along two dimensions: constructive/destructive and active/passive. The responses are as follows:[56]

exit   Dissatisfaction expressed through behavior directed toward leaving the organization.

- **Exit**.   *The exit response* directs behavior toward leaving the organization, including looking for a new position or resigning. To measure the effects of this response to dissatisfaction, researchers study individual terminations and *collective turnover*, the total loss to the organization of employee knowledge, skills, abilities, and other characteristics.[57]

voice   Dissatisfaction expressed through active and constructive attempts to improve conditions.

- **Voice**.   *The voice response* includes actively and constructively attempting to improve conditions, including suggesting improvements, discussing problems with superiors, and undertaking union activity.

Exhibit **3-6**   **Responses to Dissatisfaction**

	Constructive	Destructive
Active	VOICE	EXIT
Passive	LOYALTY	NEGLECT

loyalty   Dissatisfaction expressed by passively waiting for conditions to improve.

neglect   Dissatisfaction expressed through allowing conditions to worsen.

- **Loyalty.**   *The loyalty response* means passively but optimistically waiting for conditions to improve, including speaking up for the organization in the face of external criticism and trusting the organization and its management to "do the right thing."
- **Neglect.**   *The neglect response* passively allows conditions to worsen and includes chronic absenteeism or lateness, reduced effort, and an increased error rate.

Exit and neglect behaviors are linked to performance variables such as productivity, absenteeism, and turnover. But this model expands employee responses to include voice and loyalty—constructive behaviors that allow individuals to tolerate unpleasant situations or improve working conditions.

The model helps us understand various situations. For instance, union members often express dissatisfaction through the grievance procedure or formal contract negotiations. These voice mechanisms allow them to continue in their jobs while acting to improve the situation.

As helpful as this framework is, it's quite general. We will next address counterproductive work behavior, a behavioral response to job dissatisfaction.

Counterproductive Work Behavior (CWB)

counterproductive work behavior (CWB)   Actions that actively damage the organization, including stealing, behaving aggressively toward coworkers, or being late or absent.

Substance abuse, stealing at work, undue socializing, gossiping, absenteeism, and tardiness are examples of behaviors that are destructive to organizations. They are indicators of a broader syndrome called **counterproductive work behavior (CWB)**, also termed deviant behavior in the workplace, or simply employee withdrawal (see Chapter 1).[58] Like other behaviors we have discussed, CWB doesn't just happen—the behaviors often follow negative and sometimes longstanding attitudes. Therefore, if we can identify the predictors of CWB, we may lessen the probability of its effects.

Generally, job dissatisfaction predicts CWB. People who are not satisfied with their work become frustrated, which lowers their performance[59] and makes them more likely to commit CWB.[60] Other research suggests that, in addition to vocational misfit (being in the wrong line of work), lack of fit with the organization (working in the wrong kind of organizational culture) also predicts CWBs.[61] Our immediate social environment also matters. One German study suggests that we are influenced toward CWB by the norms of our immediate work environment, such that individuals in teams with high absenteeism are more likely to be absent themselves.[62] CWB can, furthermore, be a response to abusive supervision from managers, which then increases the abuse, starting a vicious cycle.[63]

One important point about CWB is that dissatisfied employees often choose one or more of these specific behaviors due to idiosyncratic factors. One worker might quit. Another might use work time to surf the Internet or take work supplies home for personal use. In short, workers who don't like their jobs "get even" in various ways. Because those ways can be quite creative, controlling only one behavior with policies and punishments leaves the root cause untouched. Employers should seek to correct the source of the problem—the dissatisfaction—rather than try to control the different responses.

According to U.K. research, sometimes CWB is an emotional reaction to perceived unfairness, a way to try to restore an employee's sense of equity exchange.[64] It therefore has complex ethical implications. For example, is someone who takes a box of markers home from the office for his children acting ethically? Some people consider this stealing. Others may want to look at moderating factors such as the employee's contribution to the organization before they decide. Does the person generously give extra time and effort to the organization, with little thanks or compensation? If so, they might see CWB behavior as part of an attempt to "even the score."

As a manager, you can take steps to mitigate CWB. You can poll employee attitudes, for instance, and identify areas for workplace improvement. If there is no vocational fit, the employee will not be fulfilled,[65] so you can screen for that. Tailoring tasks so a person's abilities and values can be exercised should increase job satisfaction and reduce CWB.[66] Furthermore, creating strong teams, integrating supervisors with them, providing formalized team policies, and introducing team-based incentives may help lower the CWB "contagion" that lowers the standards of the group.[67]

Absenteeism   We find a consistent negative relationship between satisfaction and absenteeism, but the relationship is moderate to weak.[68] Generally, when numerous alternative jobs are available, dissatisfied employees have high absence rates, but when there are few alternatives, dissatisfied employees have the same (low) rate of absence as satisfied employees.[69] Organizations that provide liberal sick leave benefits are encouraging all their employees—including those who are highly satisfied—to take days off. You can find work satisfying yet still want to enjoy a 3-day weekend if those days come free with no penalties.

Turnover   The relationship between job satisfaction and turnover is stronger than between satisfaction and absenteeism.[70] Overall, a pattern of lowered job satisfaction is the best predictor of intent to leave. Turnover has a workplace environment connection too. If the climate within an employee's immediate workplace is one of low job satisfaction leading to turnover, there will be a contagion effect. This suggests managers consider the job satisfaction (and turnover) patterns of coworkers when assigning workers to a new area.[71]

The satisfaction–turnover relationship is affected by alternative job prospects. If an employee accepts an unsolicited job offer, job dissatisfaction was less predictive of turnover because the employee more likely left in response to "pull" (the lure of the other job) than "push" (the unattractiveness of the

Happy Workers Means Happy Profits

There are exceptions, of course, but this statement is basically true. A glance at *Fortune*'s Best Companies to Work For list, where companies are chosen by the happiness inducements they provide, reveals recognizable profit leaders: Google, SAS, Edward Jones, and REI, to name a few. However, all happiness is not created equal.

An employee who is happy because her coworker did most of the work on her team's project isn't necessarily going to work harder, for instance. Some happiness-inducers also seem unrelated to profit increases, such as Google's bowling alley and Irish pub, Facebook's free chocolate lunches, and Salesforce.com's off-the-charts parties. Traditional benefits programs also don't necessarily yield higher job satisfaction, productivity, and profits. Research indicates employees highly value paid time off, a retirement plan such as a 401(k),

and lower health premiums. But many companies offer these benefits and are nowhere near the Fortune 500 organizations in profits.

It turns out that the value of keeping happiness in the profit equation may be felt in the level of employee engagement. As Julie Gebauer, a managing director for consulting firm Towers Watson, said, "It's not just about making them happy—that's not a business issue. Engagement is." Job engagement "represents employees' commitment...and the level of discretionary effort they are willing to put forth at work," wrote Jack in the Box's Executive VP Mark Blankenship. Happy employees with higher job engagement are willing to work hard, make customers happy, and stay with the company—three factors that affect the bottom line in a big way. Conversely, a review of 300 studies revealed that turnover rates re-

sulting from poor attitudes or low engagement led to poorer organizational performance.

So the moral of the story seems to be this: treat others as we want to be treated in the workplace. It's just good business.

Sources: M. H. Blankenship, "Happier Employees + Happier Customers = More Profit," *HR Magazine,* July 2012, 36–38; A. Edmans, "The Link between Job Satisfaction and Firm Value, with Implications for Corporate Social Responsibility," *Academy of Management Perspectives* (November 2012): 1–19; "Getting Them to Stay," *Workforce Management* (February 2013): 19; J. K. Harter et al., "Causal Impact of Employee Work Perceptions on the Bottom Line of Organizations," *Perspectives on Psychological Science* (July 2010): 378–89; T.-Y. Park and J. D. Shaw, "Turnover Rates and Organizational Performance: A Meta-Analysis," *Journal of Applied Psychology* (March 2013): 268–309; and J. Waggoner, "Do Happy Workers Mean Higher Profit?" *USA Today,* February 20, 2013, B1–B2.

current job). Similarly, job dissatisfaction is more likely to translate into turnover when other employment opportunities are plentiful. Furthermore, when employees have high "human capital" (high education, high ability), job dissatisfaction is more likely to translate into turnover because they have, or perceive, many available alternatives.[72]

There are some factors that help break the dissatisfaction–turnover relationship. Employees' embeddedness—connections to the job and community—can help lower the probability of turnover, particularly in collectivist (group-oriented) cultures.[73] Embedded employees seem less likely to want to consider alternative job prospects.

Managers Often "Don't Get It"

Given the evidence we've just reviewed, it should come as no surprise that job satisfaction can affect the bottom line. One study by a management consulting firm separated large organizations into those with high morale (more than 70 percent of employees expressed overall job satisfaction) and medium or low morale (fewer than 70 percent). The stock prices of companies in the high-morale group grew 19.4 percent, compared with 10 percent for the medium- or low-morale group. Despite these results, many managers are unconcerned about employee job satisfaction. Others overestimate how satisfied employees are, so they don't think there's a problem when there is. In one study of 262 large employers, 86 percent of senior managers believed their organizations treated employees well, but only 55 percent of employees agreed. Another study found 55 percent of managers thought morale was good in their organization, compared to only 38 percent of employees.[74]

Regular surveys can reduce gaps between what managers *think* employees feel and what they *really* feel. A gap in understanding can affect the bottom line in small franchise sites as well as in large companies. As manager of a KFC restaurant in Houston, Jonathan McDaniel surveyed his employees every 3 months. Some results led him to make changes, such as giving employees greater say about which workdays they had off. However, McDaniel believed the process itself was valuable. "They really love giving their opinions," he said. "That's the most important part of it—that they have a voice and that they're heard." Surveys are no panacea, but if job attitudes are as important as we believe, organizations need to use every reasonable method find out how they can be improved.[75]

Summary

Managers should be interested in their employees' attitudes because attitudes influence behavior and indicate potential problems. Creating a satisfied workforce is hardly a guarantee of successful organizational performance, but evidence strongly suggests managers' efforts to improve employee attitudes will likely result in positive outcomes, including greater organizational effectiveness, higher customer satisfaction, and increased profits.

Implications for Managers

- Of the major job attitudes—job satisfaction, job involvement, organizational commitment, perceived organizational support (POS), and employee engagement—remember that an employee's job satisfaction level is the best single predictor of behavior.
- Pay attention to your employees' job satisfaction levels as determinants of their performance, turnover, absenteeism, and withdrawal behaviors.
- Measure employee job attitudes objectively and at regular intervals in order to determine how employees are reacting to their work.
- To raise employee satisfaction, evaluate the fit between the employee's work interests and the intrinsic parts of the job; then create work that is challenging and interesting to the individual.
- Consider the fact that high pay alone is unlikely to create a satisfying work environment.

Employer–Employee Loyalty Is an Outdated Concept

POINT

The word *loyalty* is horribly outdated. Long gone are the days when an employer would keep an employee for life, as are the days when an employee would want to work for a single company for an entire career.

Professor Linda Gratton says, "Loyalty is dead—killed off through shortening contracts, outsourcing, automation, and multiple careers. Faced with what could be 50 years of work, who honestly wants to spend that much time with one company? Serial monogamy is the order of the day." Many employers agree; only 59 percent of employers report feeling loyal to their employees, while a mere 32 percent believe their employees are loyal to them.

The loyalty on each side of the equation is weak. For the most part, this is warranted—why retain employees who are subpar performers? It's only a matter of the employer handling the loyalty of employees with respect. Admittedly, some breaches happen. For example, Renault ended the 31-year career of employee Michel Balthazard (and two others) on false charges of espionage. When the wrongness of the charges became public, Renault halfheartedly offered the employees their jobs back and a lame apology: "Renault thanks them for the quality of their work at the group and wishes them every success in the future."

As for employees' loyalty to their employers, that is worth little nowadays. One manager with Deloitte says the current employee attitude is, "I'm leaving, I had a great experience, and I'm taking that with me." There just isn't an expectation of loyalty. In fact, only 9 percent of recent college graduates would stay with an employer for more than a year if they didn't like the job, research indicated. But there is nothing wrong with this. A "loyal" employee who stays with the organization but isn't satisfied with the job can do a lot of damage. At best, this person will be less productive. At worst, he or she can engage in years' worth of damaging CWB. For the worker, staying with an organization forever—no matter what—can limit career and income prospects.

The sooner we see the employment experience for what it is (mostly transactional, mostly short- to medium-term), the better off we'll be. The workplace is no place for fantasies of loyalty.

COUNTERPOINT

Agreed: the word *loyalty* is outdated when it refers to employers and employees. But the basic concept is valid in the workplace. We now just measure loyalty with finer measurements such as *organizational trust* and *organizational commitment*. There certainly are employers and employees who show little loyalty to each other, but that isn't the norm.

Says management guru Tom Peters, "Bottom line: loyalty matters. A lot. Yesterday. Today. Tomorrow." University of Michigan's Dave Ulrich says, "Leaders who encourage loyalty want employees who are not only committed to and engaged in their work but who also find meaning from it." Commitment. Engagement. Trust. These are some of the building blocks of loyalty.

It is true that the employer–employee relationship has changed. For example, (largely) gone are the days when employers provided guaranteed payout pensions to which employees contribute nothing. But is that such a bad thing? Many employers have helped employees take charge of their own retirement plans.

Moreover, it's not that loyalty is dead, but rather that employers are loyal to a different kind of employee. True, employers no longer refuse to fire a long-tenured but incompetent employee, which is a good thing. These employees can bring down everyone's productivity and morale. Furthermore, in a globalized world where customer options are plentiful, organizations with "deadwood"—people who don't contribute—will not be competitive enough to survive. Companies are instead loyal to employees who do their jobs well, and that is as it should be.

In short, employees become loyal—trusting, engaged, and committed—when organizations and their people act decently. Employers with superior managers who empower their employees obtain high levels of this kind of loyalty. A true reciprocal relationship is a stronger business model than employees staying with an organization for years in exchange for an organization's caretaking. Bonds of trust and loyalty rest on the relationships of individuals. Workplace psychologist Binna Kandola observes, "Workplaces may have changed but loyalty is not dead—the bonds between people are too strong."

Sources: "If You Started a Job and You Didn't Like It, How Long Would You Stay?" *USA Today,* June 11, 2012, 1B; O. Gough and S. Arkani, "The Impact of the Shifting Pensions Landscape on the Psychological Contract," *Personnel Review* 40, no. 2 (2011): 173-84; "Loyalty Gap Widens," *USA Today,* May 16, 2012, 1B; P. Korkki, "The Shifting Definition of Worker Loyalty," *The New York Times,* April 24, 2011, BU8; I. Macsinga, C. Sulea, P. Sarbescu, and C. Dumitru, "Engaged, Committed and Helpful Employees: The Role of Psychological Empowerment," *Journal of Psychology* 19, no. 3, 263-76; M. Top, M. Akdere, and M. Tarcan, "Examining Transformational Leadership, Job Satisfaction, Organizational Commitment and Organizational Trust in Turkish Hospitals: Public Servants versus Private Sector Employees," *International Journal of Human Resource Management* 26, no. 9 (2015): 1259-82; and "Is Workplace Loyalty an Outmoded Concept?" *Financial Times,* March 8, 2011, www.ft.com/, accessed July 29, 2015.

CHAPTER REVIEW

QUESTIONS FOR REVIEW

3-1 What are the three components of attitudes?

3-2 Does behavior always follow from attitudes?

3-3 What are the major job attitudes?

3-4 How do we measure job satisfaction?

3-5 What causes job satisfaction?

3-6 What are the three outcomes of job satisfaction?

3-7 How do employees respond to job satisfaction?

EXPERIENTIAL EXERCISE   What Satisfies You about Your Dream Job?

Each class member is to write the job title of his or her ideal first job out of college on a small piece of paper. The class then breaks into random teams of five to six people each and completes the following steps:

1. List the top three characteristics each of the members wants from their first job out of college (the aspects that would make them satisfied in the job). Everyone should contribute, and identical ideas should be recorded as often as they occur.
2. Each team should identify whether each job characteristic is an intrinsic satisfier (like working with others, or the job itself) or an extrinsic one (like pay or benefits) by marking an "I" or "E" next to it.
3. Tally the I's and E's and write them in descending order. For instance, if pay was mentioned by all the team members, it goes at the top of the list under "E."

The class can then reassemble to share their findings and discuss the following questions.

Questions

3-8. Is there a consensus in the class about which list is longer (intrinsic or extrinsic)? If so, why do you think one list is longer than the other?

3-9. Is there a consensus about the top three intrinsic or extrinsic characteristics? What do you think explains whether there is or not?

3-10. Looking at your individual dream job title, how likely do you think your job is to match the characteristics generated by the class? How likely do you think your job is to match your top three characteristics?

ETHICAL DILEMMA   Because It's Worth It?

If you work at L'Oréal, the company's meals, gym, massage service, concierge service, day-nursery, and around three months' salary in profit-sharing schemes may seem a good reason to be very satisfied with your job. Indeed, L'Oréal is among the most sought-after companies to work for, with 1 million applications every year. The 2015 *Universum* survey, which is conducted yearly in 12 European countries from a sample of 168,000 undergraduate business school students, ranked L'Oréal as the second most preferred employer in Europe.

Innovative recruiting tools such as REVEAL, Brandstorm, and Talentube support L'Oréal's reputation as an employer of choice by raising youngsters' positive attitudes toward its

brands. According to Bocco Chen, Recruitment and Integration Manager at L'Oréal Hong Kong, what makes Brandstorm an efficient assessing tool is that competing teams of students from renowned business schools and universities play the role of a brand manager by analyzing market trends and creating product packaging so that they experience real work situations at L'Oréal and can connect with their potential future jobs. In France, 90 percent of all new recruits at L'Oréal were interns, the reasoning being that internships serve to build future employees' organizational commitment. Before taking up any managerial position, new recruits are all sent on the road for six to twelve months to stack products on shelves at 5AM in supermarkets. It is an ordeal. Candidates are reportedly thrown in at the deep end and forced to learn on their own. The job allows little time for socialization outside the organization. Being part of L'Oréal has been described as "cult-like." In-the-field initiations serve as filters. You must be highly engaged by your job even if you feel a lack of organizational support, or you will be seen as weak—and the weakest do not last.

Everyone has key objectives and accountabilities. To ensure that employees will be devoted to their job and perform up to its standards, L'Oréal has five Development and Learning Centers worldwide. Each Oréalien has personalized access to learning modules that enable them to meet the needs of each function. To track and promote the most talented Oréaliens, L'Oréal has a sharp management and performance appraisal process. Managers with strong potential who have completed several successful projects will be promoted every two or three years.

Indeed, at L'Oréal, careers can be built quicker than elsewhere, but you have to first survive several challenges. Managers can be intransigent with employees who are dissatisfied with their jobs and also underperform, for staff satisfaction surveys at L'Oréal show these employees often exhibit behaviors that demotivate their colleagues. Twice a year, the L'Oréal international brand directors present their launch campaigns. Through this presentation and several others, top managers aim to spread a so-called "healthy worry" among Oréaliens. They also make and break many careers. One Oréalien said that she understood what humiliation really meant when she saw a colleague publically fired during one such meeting. And yet, to her, "L'Oréal is worth it."

Questions

3-11. What positive and negative outcomes can L'Oréal expect from its Oréaliens' devotion? To what extent do you think employers should require their employees to be totally devoted to their company?

3-12. How would you react if one of your peers were humiliated and then fired by your common supervisor during a meeting?

3-13. How can companies satisfy their employees? Should companies offer their employees the best work conditions or the most challenging responsibilities?

Sources: H.J. Hong and Y.L. Doz, "L'Oréal Masters Multiculturalism," *Harvard Business Review*, June 2013; B. Iyer and T.H. Davenport, "Reverse Engineering Google's Innovation Machine," *Harvard Business Review*, April 2008; E. Botta, "L'Oréal, la machine à fabriquer des cracks," *Management*, November 2010; M. Durin-Valois, "Il était une fois… L'Oréal," *Le Figaro Magazine*, August 2009; loreal.com; glassdoor.com; universumglobal.com.

CASE INCIDENT 1 The Pursuit of Happiness: Flexibility

The management team at Learner's Edge, an online continuing education company, decided to adopt a ROWE (results-only work environment) policy, developed by Best Buy employees and summarized in its slogan, "Work whenever you want, wherever you want, as long as the work gets done." Kyle Pederson was one of only three Learner's Edge employees who showed up the first day of the ROWE experiment. And the second day, and the third.

"For almost a month, everyone cleared out," Pederson said. "It was just me, my co-founder and our executive director all wondering, 'What on earth have we done?'"

Clearly, employees were testing the outer limits of workplace flexibility. Thankfully, it paid off. Learner's Edge reported "better work, higher productivity" after the initial phase of the program. It seems employees knew the ways they work best. In fact, some of Pederson's employees have returned to the office, while others gather at Starbucks or over dinner…whatever gets the work done.

Suntell president and COO, Veronica Wooten, whose risk-management software firm adopted the ROWE program a few years ago, is also a fan of the flexible workplace. "We made the transition, and started letting go and letting people make their own decisions," Wooten said. As a result of workplace flexibility, the company's customer base increased 20 percent, meetings were reduced by 50 percent, and expenses decreased 12 percent (Wooten used the savings to give everyone a raise).

It seems that everyone should be happy with this ultimate degree of job flexibility. Employees worldwide do seem to increasingly value flexible work environments, with roughly two of three workers of all ages wanting to work from home, at least occasionally. However, the benefit may not be as great for some people. In a recent study, 62 percent of respondents believed that Gen X individuals benefit most from flexibility arrangements, 35 percent believed Gen Y individuals benefit most, and only 3 percent believed baby boomers benefit most.

Research correlates job satisfaction most strongly with the nature of the work itself, not the location where it is performed. Thus, while as employees we say we want flexibility, what actually makes us satisfied is often something else. Then there are the costs of such work arrangements. Employers such as Yahoo!'s Marissa Mayer have thought that flexible workers become detached from the organization, communicate less, are less available, and lose the benefits of teamwork. Employees have concerns about long periods of working away from the office: Will out of sight mean out of mind to their employers?

For ROWE or any flexible arrangement to work, organizations need to create clear job descriptions, set attainable goals, and rely on strong metrics to indicate productivity. Managers need to foster close connections and communicate meaningfully to keep flexible workers engaged in the company, its culture, and its processes. Most importantly, employees need to get the work done, no matter where and when they do it.

Questions

⭐ **3-14.** Do you think only certain individuals are attracted to flexible work arrangements? Why or why not?

3-15. How might flexible work place more pressure on managers to organize their employees?

3-16. How might flexible work affect a company's bottom line?

Sources: "The 2015 Workplace Flexibility Study," WorkplaceTrends (February 3, 2015), https://workplacetrends.com/the-2015-workplace-flexibility-study/; L. Belkin, "Is ROWE the Future of Work? Or an Unworkable Fantasy?" *The Huffington Post Business* (April 17, 2013), www.huffingtonpost.com/2013/04/15/rowe-future-work_n_3084426.html; R. R. Hastings, "Full Engagement Lacking Around World," *Society for Human Resources Management* (January 3, 2011), www.shrm.org/hrdisciplines/employeerelations/articles/Pages/FullEngagementLacking.aspx; A. McGrory-Dixon, "Workplace Flexibility, Equity Important for Millennials," *Benefits Pro* (April 19, 2013), www.benefitspro.com/2013/04/19/workplace-flexibility-equity-important-for-millenn; and F. Origo and L. Pagani, "Workplace Flexibility and Job Satisfaction: Some Evidence from Europe," *International Journal of Manpower* 29 (2008): 539–66.

CASE INCIDENT 2 Job Crafting

Consider for a moment a midlevel manager, Fatima, who seems to be doing well. She's consistently making her required benchmarks and goals, she has built successful relationships with colleagues, and senior management has identified her as having "high potential." But she isn't satisfied in her job. She'd be interested in understanding how her organization can use social media in marketing efforts at all levels of the organization, for example, but her job doesn't allow her to work on this. She wants to quit and find something that better suits her passions, but in her economic situation this may not be an option. So she has decided to proactively reconfigure her current job.

Fatima is part of a movement toward job "crafting," which is the process of deliberately reorganizing your job so that it better fits your motives, strengths, and passions. So how did Fatima craft her job? She first noticed that she was spending too much of her time monitoring her team's performance and answering questions, and not enough time working on the creative projects that inspire her. She then considered how to modify her relationship with the team so that her activities incorporated her passion for social media strategies, with the team's activities more centered on developing new marketing. She also identified members of her team who might be able to help her implement her new strategies and directed her

interactions with these individuals toward her new goals. As a result, not only did her engagement in her work increase, but she also developed new ideas that were recognized and advanced within the organization. In sum, she found that by actively and creatively examining her work, she was able to shape her job into one that is truly satisfying.

As you may have noted, Fatima exhibited a proactive personality—she was eager to develop her own options and find her own resources. Proactive individuals are often self-empowered and are, therefore, more likely to seek workable solutions when they are not satisfied. Research leads us to believe Fatima will be successful in her customized job and that she will experience increased well-being. To the extent possible, then, all employees should feel encouraged to be proactive in creating their best work situations.

Questions

3-17. Fatima chose to remain in her old job rather than looking for a new one elsewhere. What are her constraints?

3-18. Fatima is described as having a proactive personality. What does this mean and what is the pre-requisite for it?

3-19. Are there any potential drawbacks to the job crafting approach? If so, how can they be minimized?

Sources: A. B. Bakker, M. Tims, and D. Derks, "Proactive Personality and Job Performance: The Role of Job Crafting and Work Engagement," *Human Relations* (October 2012): 1359–78; A. Wrzesniewski, J. M. Berg, and J. E. Dutton, "Turn the Job You Have into the Job You Want," *Harvard Business Review* (June 2010): 114–17; A. Wrzesniewski and J. E. Dutton, "Crafting a Job: Revisioning Employees as Active Crafters of Their Work," *Academy of Management Review* 26 (2010): 179–201; and G. R. Slemp and D. A. Vella-Brodrick, "Optimising Employee Mental Health: The Relationship between Intrinsic Need Satisfaction, Job Crafting, and Employee Well-Being," *Journal of Happiness Studies* 15, no. 4 (2014): 957–77.

MyManagementLab

Go to **mymanagementlab.com** for the following Assisted-graded writing questions:

3-20. How can you measure job satisfaction? How can job satisfaction impact your organization?

3-21. In consideration of Case Incident 2, some contend that job crafting sounds good in principle but is not necessarily practical for every job. What types of jobs are probably not good candidates for job crafting activities?

3-22. MyManagementLab Only—comprehensive writing assignment for this chapter.

ENDNOTES

[1]A. Gengler, "Chained to Your Desk No More," *CNNMoney*, April 2014, 53.

[2]A. Barsky, S. A. Kaplan, and D. J. Beal, "Just Feelings? The Role of Affect in the Formation of Organizational Fairness Judgments," *Journal of Management*, January 2011, 248–79; J. A. Mikels, S. J. Maglio, A. E. Reed, and L. J. Kaplowitz, "Should I Go with My Gut? Investigating the Benefits of Emotion-Focused Decision Making," *Emotion*, August 2011, 743–53; and A. J. Rojas Tejada, O. M. Lozano Rojas, M. Navas Luque, and P. J. Pérez Moreno, "Prejudiced Attitude Measurement Using the Rasch Scale Model," *Psychological Reports*, October 2011, 553–72.

[3]See L. S. Glasman and D. Ablarracín, "Forming Attitudes That Predict Future Behavior: A Meta-Analysis of the Attitude-Behavior Relation," *Psychological Bulletin*, September 2006, 778–822.

[4]Y. L. Liu and C.-J. Keng, "Cognitive Dissonance, Social Comparison, and Disseminating Untruthful or Negative Truthful EWOM Messages," *Social Behavior and Personality* 24, no. 6 (2014): 979–94.

[5]See, for instance, L. R. Fabrigar, R. E. Petty, S. M. Smith, and S. L. Crites, "Understanding Knowledge Effects on Attitude-Behavior Consistency: The Role of Relevance, Complexity, and Amount of Knowledge," *Journal of Personality and Social Psychology* 90, no. 4 (2006): 556–77; and D. J. Schleicher, J. D. Watt, and G. J. Greguras, "Reexamining the Job Satisfaction-Performance Relationship: The Complexity of Attitudes," *Journal of Applied Psychology* 89, no. 1 (2004): 165–77.

[6]A. S. McCance, C. D. Nye, L. Wang, K. S. Jones, and C. Chiu, "Alleviating the Burden of Emotional Labor: The Role of Social Sharing," *Journal of Management*, February 2013, 392–415.

[7]Ibid.

[8]D. P. Moynihan and S. K. Pandey, "Finding Workable Levers over Work Motivation: Comparing Job Satisfaction, Job Involvement, and Organizational Commitment," *Administration & Society* 39, no. 7 (2007): 803–32.

[9]S. Zhang, "Impact of Job Involvement on Organizational Citizenship Behaviors in China," *Journal of Business Ethics* 120 (2014): 165–74.

[10]G. Chen and R. J. Klimoski, "The Impact of Expectations on Newcomer Performance in Teams as Mediated by Work Characteristics, Social Exchanges, and Empowerment," *Academy of Management Journal* 46, no. 5 (2003): 591–607; A. Ergeneli, G. Saglam, and S. Metin, "Psychological Empowerment and Its Relationship to Trust in Immediate Managers," *Journal of Business Research*, January 2007, 41–49; and S. E. Seibert, S. R. Silver, and W. A. Randolph, "Taking Empowerment to the Next Level: A Multiple-Level Model of Empowerment, Performance, and Satisfaction," *Academy of Management Journal* 47, no. 3 (2004): 332–49.

[11]B. J. Avolio, W. Zhu, W. Koh, and P. Bhatia, "Transformational Leadership and Organizational Commitment: Mediating Role of Psychological Empowerment and Moderating Role of Structural Distance," *Journal of Organizational Behavior* 25, no. 8 (2004): 951–68.

[12]O. N. Solinger, W. van Olffen, and R. A. Roe, "Beyond the Three-Component Model of Organizational Commitment," *Journal of Applied Psychology* 93 (2008): 70–83.

[13]J. P. Hausknecht, N. J. Hiller, and R. J. Vance, "Work-Unit Absenteeism: Effects of Satisfaction, Commitment, Labor Market Conditions, and Time," *Academy of Management Journal* 51 (2008): 1223–45.

[14]"100 Best Companies to Work For," *Fortune*, February 2015, www.fortune.com/best-companies/, accessed March 16, 2015.

[15]L. Rhoades, R. Eisenberger, and S. Armeli, "Affective Commitment to the Organization: The Contribution of Perceived Organizational Support," *Journal of Applied Psychology* 86, no. 5 (2001): 825–36.

[16]B. L. Rich, J. A. Lepine, and E. R. Crawford, "Job Engagement: Antecedents and Effects on Job Performance," *Academy of Management Journal* 53 (2010): 617–35.

[17]J. K. Harter, F. L. Schmidt, and T. L. Hayes, "Business-Unit-Level Relationship between Employee Satisfaction, Employee Engagement, and Business Outcomes: A Meta-Analysis," *Journal of Applied Psychology* 87, no. 2 (2002): 268–79.

[18]N. R. Lockwood, *Leveraging Employee Engagement for Competitive Advantage* (Alexandria, VA: Society for Human Resource Management, 2007); and R. J. Vance, *Employee Engagement and Commitment* (Alexandria, VA: Society for Human Resource Management, 2006).

[19]"Employee Engagement," *Workforce Management*, February 2013, 19; and "The Cornerstone OnDemand, 2013, U.S. Employee Report," *Cornerstone OnDemand*, 2013, www.cornerstoneondemand.com/resources/research/survey-2013.

[20]Y. Brunetto, S. T. T. Teo, K. Shacklock, and R. Farr-Wharton, "Emotional Intelligence, Job Satisfaction, Well-being and Engagement: Explaining Organisational Commitment and Turnover Intentions in Policing," *Human Resource Management Journal*, 2012, 428–41.

[21]P. Petrou, E. Demerouti, M. C. W. Peeters, W. B. Schaufeli, and Jørn Hetland, "Crafting a Job on a Daily Basis: Contextual Correlates and the Link to Work Engagement," *Journal of Organizational Behavior*, November 2012, 1120–41.

[22]W. H. Macey and B. Schneider, "The Meaning of Employee Engagement," *Industrial and Organizational Psychology* 1 (2008): 3–30; and A. Saks, "The Meaning and Bleeding of Employee Engagement: How Muddy Is the Water?" *Industrial and Organizational Psychology* 1 (2008): 40–43.

[23]C. L. Dolbier, J. A. Webster, K. T. McCalister, M. W. Mallon, and M. A. Steinhardt, "Reliability and Validity of a Single-Item Measure of Job Satisfaction," *American Journal of Health Promotion*, January–February 2005, 194–98.

[24]N. A. Bowling, M. R. Hoepf, D. M. LaHuis, and L. R. Lepisto, "Mean Job Satisfaction Levels over Time: Are Things Bad and Getting Worse?" *The Industrial-Organizational Psychologist*, April 2013, 57–64.

[25]L. Weber, "U.S. Workers Can't Get No (Job) Satisfaction," *The Wall Street Journal*, June 18, 2014, http://blogs.wsj.com/atwork/2014/06/18/u-s-workers-cant-get-no-job-satisfaction/.

[26]"Job Satisfaction: 2014 Edition," The Conference Board, https://www.conference-board.org/topics/publicationdetail.cfm?publicationid=2785.

[27]L. Weber, "U.S. Workers Can't Get No (Job) Satisfaction."

[28]World Business Culture, "Doing Business in South Korea," www.worldbusinessculture.com/Business-in-South-Korea.html, accessed July 29, 2015.

[29]S. E. Humphrey, J. D. Nahrgang, and F. P. Morgeson, "Integrating Motivational, Social, and Contextual Work Design Features: A Meta-Analytic Summary and Theoretical Extension of the Work Design Literature," *Journal of Applied Psychology* 92, no. 5 (2007): 1332–56; and D. S. Chiaburu and D. A. Harrison, "Do Peers Make the Place? Conceptual Synthesis and Meta-Analysis of Coworker Effect on Perceptions, Attitudes, OCBs, and Performance," *Journal of Applied Psychology* 93, no. 5 (2008): 1082–103.

[30]K. H. Fong and E. Snape, "Empowering Leadership, Psychological Empowerment and Employee Outcomes: Testing a Multi-Level Mediating Model," *British Journal of Management* 26 (2015): 126–38.

[31]S. Ronen, M. Mikulincer, "Predicting Employees' Satisfaction and Burnout from Managers' Attachment and Caregiving Orientations," *European Journal of Work and Organizational Psychology* 21, no. 6 (2012): 828–49.

[32]A. Calvo-Salguero, J.-M. Salinas Martinez-de-Lecea, and A.-M. Carrasco-Gonzalez, "Work-Family and Family-Work Conflict: Does Intrinsic-Extrinsic Satisfaction Mediate the Prediction of General Job Satisfaction?" *The Journal of Psychology* 145, no. 5 (2011): 435–61.

[33]J. Zhang, Q. Wu, D. Miao, X. Yan, and J. Peng, "The Impact of Core Self-Evaluations on Job Satisfaction: The Mediator Role of Career Commitment," *Social Indicators Research* 116, no. 3 (2014): 809–22.

[34]D. Thorpe, "Why CSR? The Benefits of Corporate Social Responsibility Will Move You to Act," *Forbes* (May 18, 2013), http://www.forbes.com/sites/devinthorpe/2013/05/18/why-csr-the-benefits-of-corporate-social-responsibility-will-move-you-to-act/.

[35]N. Fallon, "What Is Corporate Responsibility?" *Business News Daily* (December 22, 2014), http://www.businessnewsdaily.com/4679-corporate-social-responsibility.html.

[36]R. Feintzeig, "I Don't Have a Job. I Have a Higher Calling," *The Wall Street Journal*, February 25, 2015, B1, B4.

[37]See I. Filatotchev and C. Nakajima, "Corporate Governance, Responsible Managerial Behavior, and Corporate Social Responsibility: Organizational Efficiency versus Organizational Legitimacy?" *The Academy of Management Perspectives* 28, no. 3 (2014): 289–306.

[38]A. Hurst, "Being 'Good' Isn't the Only Way to Go," *The New York Times*, April 20, 2014, 4.

[39]D. Thorpe, "Why CSR? The Benefits of Corporate Social Responsibility Will Move You to Act."

[40]M. C. Bolino, H.-H. Hsiung, J. Harvey, and J. A. LePine, "'Well, I'm Tired of Tryin'! Organizational Citizenship Behavior and Citizenship Fatigue," *Journal of Applied Psychology* 100, no. 1 (2015): 56–74.

[41]G. E. Newman and D. M. Cain, "Tainted Altruism: When Doing Some Good Is Evaluated as Doing Worse Than Doing No Good at All," *Psychological Science* 25, no. 3 (2014): 648–55.

[42]Ibid.

[43]Ibid.

[44]T. A. Judge, C. J. Thoresen, J. E. Bono, and G. K. Patton, "The Job Satisfaction–Job Performance Relationship: A Qualitative and Quantitative Review," *Psychological Bulletin*, May 2001, 376–407.

[45]See P. M. Podsakoff, S. B. MacKenzie, J. B. Paine, and D. G. Bachrach, "Organizational Citizenship Behaviors: A Critical Review of the Theoretical and Empirical Literature and Suggestions for Future Research," *Journal of Management* 26, no. 3 (2000): 513–63.

[46]B. J. Hoffman, C. A. Blair, J. P. Maeriac, and D. J. Woehr, "Expanding the Criterion Domain? A Quantitative Review of the OCB Literature," *Journal of Applied Psychology* 92, no. 2 (2007): 555–66.

[47]B. B. Reiche et al., "Why Do Managers Engage in Trustworthy Behavior? A Multilevel Cross-Cultural Study in 18 Countries," *Personnel Psychology* 67 (2014): 61–98.

[48]D. S. Chiaburu and D. A. Harrison, "Do Peers Make the Place? Conceptual Synthesis and Meta-Analysis of Coworker Effect on Perceptions, Attitudes, OCBs, and Performance," *Journal of Applied Psychology* 93, no. 5 (2008): 1082–103.

[49]R. Ilies, I. S. Fulmer, M. Spitzmuller, and M. D. Johnson, "Personality and Citizenship Behavior: The Mediating Role of Job Satisfaction," *Journal of Applied Psychology* 94 (2009): 945–59.

[50]G. L. Lemoine, C. K. Parsons, and S. Kansara, "Above and Beyond, Again and Again: Self-Regulation in the Aftermath of Organizational Citizenship Behaviors," *Journal of Applied Psychology* 100, no. 1 (2015): 40–55.

[51]C. Vandenberghe, K. Bentein, R. Michon, J. Chebat, M. Tremblay, and J. Fils, "An Examination of the Role of Perceived Support and Employee Commitment in Employee-Customer Encounters," *Journal of Applied Psychology* 92, no. 4 (2007): 1177–87; and M. Schulte, C. Ostroff, S. Shmulyian, and A. Kinicki, "Organizational Climate Configurations: Relationships to Collective Attitudes, Customer Satisfaction, and Financial Performance," *Journal of Applied Psychology* 94 (2009): 618–34.

[52]B. Taylor, "Why Amazon Is Copying Zappos and Paying Employees to Quit," *Harvard Business Review*, April 14, 2014, https://hbr.org/2014/04/why-amazon-is-copying-zappos-and-paying-employees-to-quit/.

[53]J. Barling, E. K. Kelloway, and R. D. Iverson, "High-Quality Work, Job Satisfaction, and Occupational Injuries," *Journal of Applied Psychology* 88, no. 2 (2003): 276–83; and F. W. Bond and D. Bunce, "The Role of Acceptance and Job Control in Mental Health, Job Satisfaction, and Work Performance," *Journal of Applied Psychology* 88, no. 6 (2003): 1057–67.

[54]Y. Georgellis and T. Lange, "Traditional versus Secular Values and the Job-Life Satisfaction Relationship across Europe," *British Journal of Management* 23 (2012): 437–54.

[55]O. Stavrova, T. Schlosser, and A. Baumert, "Life Satisfaction and Job-Seeking Behavior of the Unemployed: The Effect of Individual Differences in Justice Sensitivity," *Applied Psychology: An International Review* 64, no. 4 (2014): 643–70.

[56]J. Zhou and J. M. George, "When Job Dissatisfaction Leads to Creativity: Encouraging the Expression of Voice," *Academy of Management Journal*, August 2001, 682–96; J. B. Olson-Buchanan and W. R. Boswell, "The Role of Employee Loyalty and Formality in Voicing Discontent," *Journal of Applied Psychology*, December 2002, 1167–74; and A. Davis-Blake, J. P. Broschak, and E. George, "Happy Together? How Using Nonstandard Workers Affects Exit, Voice, and Loyalty among Standard Employees," *Academy of Management Journal* 46, no. 4 (2003): 475–85.

[57]A. J. Nyberg and R. E. Ployhart, "Context-Emergent Turnover (CET) Theory: A Theory of Collective Turnover," *Academy of Management Review* 38 (2013): 109–31.

[58]P. E. Spector, S. Fox, L. M. Penney, K. Bruursema, A. Goh, and S. Kessler, "The Dimensionality of Counterproductivity: Are All Counterproductive Behaviors Created Equal?" *Journal of Vocational Behavior* 68, no. 3 (2006): 446–60; and D. S. Chiaburu and D. A. Harrison, "Do Peers Make the Place? Conceptual Synthesis and Meta-Analysis of Coworker Effect on Perceptions, Attitudes, OCBs, and Performance," *Journal of Applied Psychology* 93, no. 5 (2008): 1082–103.

[59]P. A. O'Keefe, "Liking Work Really Does Matter," *The New York Times*, September 7, 2014, 12.

[60]D. Iliescu, D. Ispas, C. Sulea, and A. Ilie, "Vocational Fit and Counterproductive Work Behaviors: A Self-Regulation Perspective," *Journal of Applied Psychology* 100, no. 1 (2015): 21–39.

[61]A. S. Gabriel, J. M. Diefendorff, M. M. Chandler, C. M. M. Pradco, and G. J. Greguras, "The Dynamic Relationships of Work Affect and Job Satisfaction with Perceptions of Fit," *Personnel Psychology* 67 (2014): 389–420.

[62]S. Diestel, J. Wegge, and K.-H. Schmidt, "The Impact of Social Context on the Relationship between Individual Job Satisfaction and Absenteeism: The Roles of Different Foci of Job Satisfaction and Work-Unit Absenteeism," *Academy of Management Journal* 57, no. 2 (2014): 353–82.

[63]H. Lian, D. L. Ferris, R. Morrison, and D. J. Brown, "Blame It on the Supervisor or the Subordinate? Reciprocal Relations between Abusive Supervision and Organizational Deviance," *Journal of Applied Psychology* 99, no. 4 (2014): 651–64.

[64]T. A. Beauregard, "Fairness Perceptions of Work-Life Balance Initiatives; Effects on Counterproductive Work Behavior," *British Journal of Management* 25 (2014): 772–89.

[65]D. Iliescu, D. Ispas, C. Sulea, and A. Ilie, "Vocational Fit and Counterproductive Work Behaviors: A Self-Regulation Perspective."

[66]A. S. Gabriel, J. M. Diefendorff, M. M. Chandler, C. M. M. Pradco, and G. J. Greguras, "The Dynamic Relationships of Work Affect and Job Satisfaction with Perceptions of Fit."

[67]S. Diestel, J. Wegge, and K.-H. Schmidt, "The Impact of Social Context on the Relationship between Individual Job Satisfaction and Absenteeism: The Roles of Different Foci of Job Satisfaction and Work-Unit Absenteeism."

[68]J. F. Ybema, P. G. W. Smulders, and P. M. Bongers, "Antecedents and Consequences of Employee Absenteeism: A Longitudinal Perspective on the Role of Job Satisfaction and Burnout," *European Journal of Work and Organizational Psychology* 19 (2010): 102–24.

[69]J. P. Hausknecht, N. J. Hiller, and R. J. Vance, "Work-Unit Absenteeism: Effects of Satisfaction, Commitment, Labor Market Conditions, and Time," *Academy of Management Journal* 51, no. 6 (2008): 1123–245.

[70]G. Chen, R. E. Ployhart, H. C. Thomas, N. Anderson, and P. D. Bliese, "The Power of Momentum: A New Model of Dynamic Relationships between Job Satisfaction Change and Turnover Intentions," *Academy of Management Journal*, February 2011, 159–81; and R. W. Griffeth, P. W. Hom, and S. Gaertner, "A Meta-Analysis of Antecedents and Correlates of Employee Turnover: Update, Moderator Tests, and Research Implications for the Next Millennium," *Journal of Management* 26, no. 3 (2000): 479.

[71]D. Liu, T. R. Mitchell, T. W. Lee, B. C. Holtom, and T. R. Hinkin, "When Employees Are Out of Step with Coworkers: How Job Satisfaction Trajectory and Dispersion Influence Individual- and Unit-Level Voluntary Turnover," *Academy of Management Journal* 55, no. 6 (2012): 1360–80.

[72]T. H. Lee, B. Gerhart, I. Weller, and C. O. Trevor, "Understanding Voluntary Turnover: Path-Specific Job Satisfaction Effects and the Importance of Unsolicited Job Offers," *Academy of Management Journal* 51, no. 4 (2008): 651–71.

[73]K. Jiang, D. Liu, P. F. McKay, T. W. Lee, and T. R. Mitchell, "When and How Is Job Embeddedness Predictive of Turnover? A Meta-Analytic Investigation," *Journal of Applied Psychology* 97 (2012): 1077–96.

[74]K. Holland, "Inside the Minds of Your Employees," *The New York Times,* January 28, 2007, B1; "Study Sees Link between Morale and Stock Price," *Workforce Management,* February 27, 2006, 15; and "The Workplace as a Solar System," *The New York Times,* October 28, 2006, B5.

[75]E. White, "How Surveying Workers Can Pay Off," *The Wall Street Journal,* June 18, 2007, B3.

Emotions and Moods

LEARNING OBJECTIVES

After studying this chapter, you should be able to:

4-1	Differentiate between emotions and moods.	**4-5**	Describe emotional intelligence.
4-2	Identify the sources of emotions and moods.	**4-6**	Identify strategies for emotion regulation.
4-3	Show the impact emotional labor has on employees.	**4-7**	Apply concepts about emotions and moods to specific OB issues.
4-4	Describe affective events theory.		

MyManagementLab®
⭐ **Chapter Warm Up**

If your professor has chosen to assign this, go to the Assignments section of **mymanagementlab.com** to complete the chapter warm up.

THE LASTING CONSEQUENCES OF OUR EMOTIONS

Nelson Mandela was an iconic leader who is famous for remaining cool under extreme pressure. He is known for his grace, self-awareness, composure, passion, a big sense of humour, and the ability to encourage others. Richard Branson, his long-time friend and Chairman of the Virgin Group, has said that he relied on Mandela's example during the pressures of the Virgin Atlantic deal and especially admired Mandela's ability to stay positive and focused and avoid harboring feelings of resentment.

Sheryl Sandberg, Chief Operating Officer of Facebook and author of *Lean In: Women, Work and the Will to Lead*, is another example of someone who remains cool under pressure, is excellent at engaging with colleagues, and is very open with her emotions. In her book she challenges the stereotypes of gender and leadership behaviors. She believes that deeper relationships are built when one shares one's emotions, and values striving for authenticity rather than perfection. She suggests that emotions related to compassion and sensitivity, which may have held some women back, could make them more natural leaders in the future.

These examples show attributes of leaders who have a high level of emotional intelligence in how they face long term challenges, and how they react and relate to others along the way. Of course, not all displays of emotions lead to positive outcomes, as was the case involving Cho Hyun-ah in the first-class cabin of a flight bound for Seoul in December 2014. Ms. Cho, daughter of the Chairman of Korean Air Lines Co., was Chief Executive of a hotel network, a leisure development company, and a travel service company as well as a board director of Korean Air. The incident began when she was served an unopened bag of macadamia nuts. She told the flight attendant that she should have been asked if she wanted it. Ms. Cho is reported to have screamed at the flight attendant, and the argument escalated to the point that she demanded that the flight attendant be removed from the aircraft, delaying the flight. Investigations from aviation authorities ensued, and as the plane had broken procedures, there was talk of a 10-year jail term. There was also an outcry among South Koreans about the economic power of large family-owned businesses and the way the rich behave. The media dubbed the incident "nut rage." Ms. Cho's televised public apology was very quiet and in a posture of humility. Looking downward in front of the cameras and press, she resigned from her position with the company.

Emotions can have an impact across roles, business sectors, political boundaries, genders, and economic backgrounds of the individual and groups. Positive or negative emotions can have long-lasting consequences that may affect many more people than just the person on the receiving end.

Sources: "Nelson Mandela Biography," *Leadership Lime*, http://www.leadershiplime.com/nelson-mandela-biography.html; Caroline Fairchild, "Richard Branson Remembers Nelson Mandela," *Fortune*, http://fortune.com/2013/12/06/richard-branson-remembers-nelson-mandela/; "Sheryl Sandberg: The HBR Interview," *Harvard Business Review*, https://hbr.org/2013/03/sheryl-sandberg-the-hbr-interv, accessed December 14, 2015; S. Sandberg, *Lean In: Women, Work, and the Will to Lead* (Knopf Doubleday Publishing Group, 2013); In-Soo Nam, "Korean Air Executive Resigns after Nutty Flight Delay," *The Wall Street Journal*, http://www.wsj.com/articles/korean-air-executive-resigns-after-delaying-flight-over-nut-service-1418125386; "Former Korean Air Executive Apologises for 'Nut Rage'," *BBC News*, http://www.bbc.com/news/world-asia-30444228; "Nut Rage Incident Wiped Out All of Korean Air Heiress Cho Hyun Ah's Hard Work," *The Straits Times*, The http://www.straitstimes.com/asia/nut-rage-incident-wiped-out-all-of-korean-air-heiress-cho-hyun-ahs-hard-work; B.R., "Nuts!," *The Economist*, http://www.economist.com/blogs/gulliver/2014/12/korean-air-and-flight-delays.

As the escalation over an unopened bag of macadamia nuts illustrates, emotions can greatly influence decision making, even sparking conflict with potentially disastrous consequences. In truth, we cannot set aside our emotions, but we can acknowledge and work with them. And not all emotions have negative influences on us.

Given the obvious role emotions play in our lives, it might surprise you that, until recently, the field of OB has not given the topic of emotions much attention. Why? Generally, because emotions in the workplace were historically thought to be detrimental to performance. Although managers knew emotions were an inseparable part of everyday life, they tried to create organizations that were emotion-free. Researchers tended to focus on strong negative emotions—especially anger—that interfered with an employee's ability to work effectively.

Thankfully, this type of thinking is changing. Certainly some emotions, particularly exhibited at the wrong time, can hinder performance. Other emotions are neutral, and some are constructive. Employees bring their emotions to work every day, so no study of OB would be comprehensive without considering their role in workplace behavior.

What Are Emotions and Moods?

4-1   Differentiate between emotions and moods.

affect   A broad range of feelings that people experience.

emotions   Intense feelings that are directed at someone or something.

moods   Feelings that tend to be less intense than emotions and that lack a contextual stimulus.

In our analysis, we'll need three terms that are closely intertwined: *affect, emotions,* and *moods.* **Affect** is a generic term that covers a broad range of feelings, including both emotions and moods.[1] **Emotions** are intense feelings directed at someone or something.[2] **Moods** are less intense feelings than emotions and often arise without a specific event acting as a stimulus.[3] Exhibit 4-1 shows the relationships among affect, emotions, and moods.

First, as the exhibit shows, *affect* is a broad term that encompasses emotions and moods. Second, there are differences between emotions and moods. Emotions are more likely to be caused by a specific event and are more fleeting than moods. Also, some researchers speculate that emotions may be more action-oriented—they may lead us to some immediate action—while moods may be more cognitive, meaning they may cause us to think or brood for a while.[4]

Affect, emotions, and moods are separable in theory; in practice the distinction isn't always defined. When we review the OB topics on emotions and moods, you may see more information about emotions in one area and moods in another. This is simply the state of the research. Let's start with a review of the basic emotions.

The Basic Emotions

How many emotions are there? There are dozens, including anger, contempt, enthusiasm, envy, fear, frustration, disappointment, embarrassment, disgust, happiness, hate, hope, jealousy, joy, love, pride, surprise, and sadness. Numerous researchers have tried to limit them to a fundamental set.[5] Other scholars argue that it makes no sense to think in terms of "basic" emotions, because even emotions we rarely experience, such as shock, can have a powerful effect on us.[6]

Psychologists have tried to identify basic emotions by studying how we express them. Facial expressions have proved difficult to interpret.[7] One problem is that some emotions are too complex to be easily represented on our faces. Second, a

---

Exhibit 4-1   Affect, Emotions, and Moods

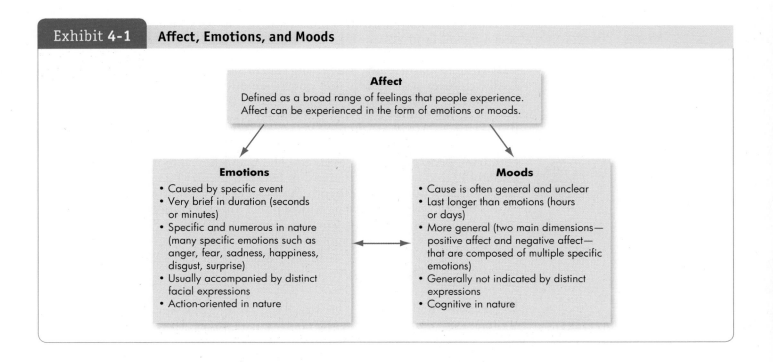

Affect
Defined as a broad range of feelings that people experience. Affect can be experienced in the form of emotions or moods.

Emotions
- Caused by specific event
- Very brief in duration (seconds or minutes)
- Specific and numerous in nature (many specific emotions such as anger, fear, sadness, happiness, disgust, surprise)
- Usually accompanied by distinct facial expressions
- Action-oriented in nature

Moods
- Cause is often general and unclear
- Last longer than emotions (hours or days)
- More general (two main dimensions—positive affect and negative affect—that are composed of multiple specific emotions)
- Generally not indicated by distinct expressions
- Cognitive in nature

Smile, and the Work World Smiles with You

It is true that a smile is not always an emotional expression. Smiles are used as social currency in most organizations to create a positive atmosphere, and a smile usually evokes an unconscious reflexive return smile. However, anyone who has ever smiled at an angry manager knows this doesn't always work. In truth, the giving and withholding of smiles is often an unconscious power play of office politics.

Research on the "boss effect" suggests that the amount of power and status a person feels over another person dictates who will smile. Subordinates generally smile more often than their bosses smile back at them. This may happen in part because workers are increasingly expected to show expressions of happiness with their jobs. However, the relationship is complex and varies by national culture: in one study, Chinese workers reflexively smiled only at bosses who had the power to give them negative job evaluations, while

U.S. participants smiled most to managers perceived to have higher social power. Other researchers found that when individuals felt powerful, they usually didn't return even a high-ranking individual's smile. Conversely, when people felt powerless, they returned everyone's smiles. Thus, "Your feelings about power and status seem to dictate how much you are willing to return a smile to another person," cognitive neuroscientist Evan Carr affirmed.

The science of smiling transcends the expression of emotion. While an angry manager may not smile back, a happy manager might not either, according to the "boss effect" research. "The relationship of what we show on our face and how we feel is a very loose one," said Arvid Kappas, a professor of emotion research at Jacobs University Bremen in Germany. This suggests that, when we want to display positive emotions to others, we should do more than smile, as service representatives

do when they try to create happy moods in their customers with excited voice pitch, encouraging gestures, and energetic body movement.

The science of smiling is an area of current research, but it is clear already that knowing about the "boss effect" suggests many practical applications. For one, managers and employees can be made more aware of ingrained tendencies toward others and, through careful self-observation, change their habits. Comprehensive displays of positive emotion using voice inflection, gestures, and word choice may also be more helpful in building good business relationships than the simple smile.

Sources: R. L. Hotz, "Too Important to Smile Back: The 'Boss Effect'," *The Wall Street Journal,* October 16, 2012, D2; P. Jaskunas, "The Tyranny of the Forced Smile," *The New York Times,* February 15, 2015, 14; and E. Kim and D. J. Yoon, "Why Does Service with a Smile Make Employees Happy? A Social Interaction Model," *Journal of Applied Psychology* 97 (2012): 1059–67.

recent study suggested that people do not interpret emotions from vocalizations (such as sighs or screams) the same way across cultures. While vocalizations conveyed meaning in all cultures, the specific emotions people perceived varied. For example, Himba participants (from northwestern Namibia) did not agree with Western participants that crying meant sadness or a growl meant anger.[8] Lastly, cultures have norms that govern emotional expression, so the way we *experience* an emotion isn't always the same as the way we *show* it. For example, people in the Middle East and the United States recognize a smile as indicating happiness, but in the Middle East a smile is also often interpreted as a sign of sexual attraction, so women have learned not to smile at men. In collectivist countries, people are more likely to believe another's emotional displays have something to do with the relationship between them, while people in individualistic cultures don't think others' emotional expressions are directed at them.

It's unlikely psychologists or philosophers will ever completely agree on a set of basic emotions, or even on whether there is such a thing. Still, many researchers agree on six universal emotions—anger, fear, sadness, happiness, disgust, and surprise.[9] We sometimes mistake happiness for surprise, but rarely do we confuse happiness and disgust.

Moral Emotions

We may tend to think our internal emotions are innate. For instance, if someone jumped out at you from behind a door, wouldn't you feel surprised? Maybe you would, but you may also feel any of the other five universal emotions—anger, fear, sadness, happiness, or disgust—depending on the circumstance. Our experiences of emotions are closely tied to our interpretations of events.

moral emotions Emotions that have moral implications.

Researchers have been studying what are called **moral emotions**; that is, emotions that have moral implications because of our instant judgment of the situation that evokes them. Examples of moral emotions include sympathy for the suffering of others, guilt about our own immoral behavior, anger about injustice done to others, and contempt for those who behave unethically.

Another example is the disgust we feel about violations of moral norms, called *moral disgust*. Moral disgust is different from disgust. Say you stepped in cow dung by mistake—you might feel disgusted by it, but not moral disgust—you probably wouldn't make a moral judgment. In contrast, say you watched a video of a police officer making a sexist or racist slur. You might feel disgusted in a different way because it offends your sense of right and wrong. In fact, you might feel a variety of emotions based on your moral judgment of the situation.[10]

Interestingly, research indicates that our responses to moral emotions differ from our responses to other emotions.[11] When we feel moral anger, for instance, we may be more likely to confront the situation that causes it than when we just feel angry. However, we cannot assume our emotional reactions to events on a moral level will be the same as someone else's. Moral emotions are learned, usually in childhood,[12] and thus they are not universal like innate emotions. Because morality is a construct that differs between cultures, so do moral emotions. Therefore, we need to be aware of the moral aspects of situations that trigger our emotions and make certain we understand the context before we act, especially in the workplace.

You can think about this research in your own life to see how moral emotions operate. Consider the earthquakes that struck China in 2014. When you heard about the disaster, did you feel emotionally upset about the suffering of others, or did you make more of a rational calculation about their unfortunate situation? Consider a time when you have done something that hurt someone else. Did you feel angry or upset with yourself? Or think about a time when you have seen someone else treated unfairly. Did you feel contempt for the person acting unfairly, or did you engage in a cool, rational calculation of the justice of the situation? Most people who think about these situations have some sense of an emotional stirring that might prompt them to engage in ethical actions like donating money to help others, apologizing and attempting to make amends, or intervening on behalf of those who have been mistreated. In sum, we can conclude that people who are behaving ethically are at least partially making decisions based on their emotions and feelings.

Emotions can be fleeting, but moods can endure…for quite a while. In order to understand the impact of emotions and moods in organizations, we next classify the many distinct emotions into broader mood categories.

The Basic Moods: Positive and Negative Affect

As a first step toward studying the effect of moods and emotions in the workplace, we will classify emotions into two categories: positive and negative. Positive emotions—such as joy and gratitude—express a favorable evaluation or feeling. Negative emotions—such as anger and guilt—express the opposite. Keep in mind that emotions can't be neutral. Being neutral is being nonemotional.[13]

When we group emotions into positive and negative categories, they become *mood states* because we are now looking at them more generally instead of isolating one particular emotion. In Exhibit 4-2, excited is a pure marker of high positive affect, while boredom is a pure marker of low positive affect. Nervous is a pure marker of high negative affect; relaxed is a pure marker of low negative affect. Finally, some emotions—such as contentment and sadness—are in

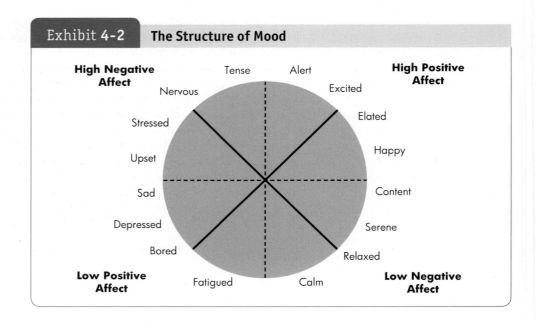

Exhibit 4-2   **The Structure of Mood**

High Negative Affect — Tense — Alert — High Positive Affect

Nervous, Excited, Elated, Stressed, Upset, Happy, Sad, Content, Depressed, Serene, Bored, Relaxed

Low Positive Affect — Fatigued — Calm — Low Negative Affect

positive affect   A mood dimension that consists of specific positive emotions such as excitement, enthusiasm, and elation at the high end.

negative affect   A mood dimension that consists of emotions such as nervousness, stress, and anxiety at the high end.

positivity offset   The tendency of most individuals to experience a mildly positive mood at zero input (when nothing in particular is going on).

between. You'll notice this model does not include all emotions. Some, such as surprise, don't fit well because they're not as clearly positive or negative.

So, we can think of **positive affect** as a mood dimension consisting of positive emotions such as excitement, enthusiasm, and elation at the high end (high positive affect). **Negative affect** is a mood dimension consisting of nervousness, stress, and anxiety at the high end (high negative affect). While we rarely experience both positive and negative affect at the same time, over time people do differ in how much they experience each. Some people (we might call them emotional or intense) may experience quite a bit of high positive and high negative affect over, say, a week's time. Others (we might call them unemotional or phlegmatic) experience little of either. And still others may experience one much more predominately than the other.

Experiencing Moods and Emotions

As if it weren't complex enough to consider the many distinct emotions and moods a person might identify, the reality is that we all experience moods and emotions differently. For most people, positive moods are somewhat more common than negative moods. Indeed, research finds a **positivity offset**, meaning that at zero input (when nothing in particular is going on), most individuals experience a mildly positive mood.[14] This appears to be true for employees in a wide range of job settings. For example, one study of customer-service representatives in a British call center revealed that people reported experiencing positive moods 58 percent of the time despite the stressful environment.[15] Another research finding is that negative emotions lead to negative moods. Perhaps this happens because people think about events that created strong negative emotions five times as long as they do about events that created strong positive ones.[16]

Does the degree to which people experience positive and negative emotions vary across cultures? Yes (see the OB Poll). The reason is not that people of different cultures are inherently different: People in most cultures appear to experience certain positive and negative emotions, and people interpret them in much the same way worldwide. We all view negative emotions such as hate, terror, and rage as dangerous and destructive, and we desire positive emotions such as joy, love, and happiness. However, an individual's experience of emotions appears to be culturally shaped. Some cultures value certain emotions

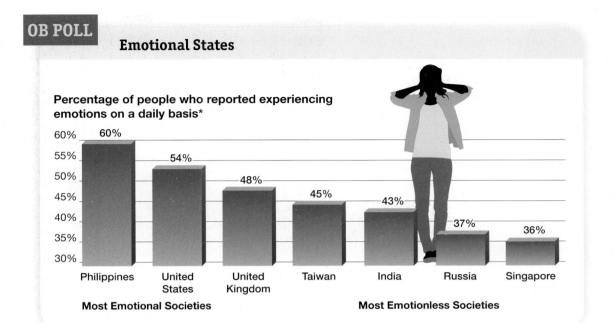

OB POLL

Emotional States

Percentage of people who reported experiencing emotions on a daily basis*

Philippines	60%
United States	54%
United Kingdom	48%
Taiwan	45%
India	43%
Russia	37%
Singapore	36%

Most Emotional Societies   **Most Emotionless Societies**

*Respondents in 150+ countries worldwide over two years were asked whether they experienced five positive (well-rested, treated with respect, enjoyment, smiling and laughing, learning or doing something interesting) and five negative emotions (anger, stress, sadness, physical pain, worry) daily.
Source: J. Clifton, "Singapore Ranks as Least Emotional Country in the World," Gallup (November 21, 2012), http://www.gallup.com/poll/158882/singapore-ranks-least-emotional-country-world.aspx.

more than others, which leads individuals to change their perspective on experiencing these emotions.

There is much to be learned in exploring the value differences. Some cultures embrace negative emotions, such as Japan and Russia, while others emphasize positive emotions and expressions, such as Mexico and Brazil.[17] There may also be a difference in the value of negative emotions between collectivist and individualist countries. The difference may be the reason negative emotions are less detrimental to the health of Japanese than Americans.[18] For example, the Chinese consider negative emotions—while not always pleasant—as potentially more useful and constructive than do people in the United States.

The Chinese may be right: Research has suggested that negative affect can have benefits. Visualizing the worst-case scenario often allows people to accept present circumstances and cope, for instance.[19] Negative affect may also allow managers to think more critically and fairly.[20]

Now that we've identified the basic emotions, the basic moods, and our experience of them, let's explore the function of emotions and moods, particularly in the workplace.

The Function of Emotions

In some ways, emotions are a mystery. What function do they serve? As we discussed, organizational behaviorists have been finding that emotions can be critical to an effectively functioning workplace. For example, happy employees demonstrate higher performance and organizational citizenship behavior (OCB), fewer CWBs, and less turnover, particularly when they feel supported by their organizations in their effort to do well in their jobs.[21] Gratefulness and awe have been shown to positively predict OCB,[22] which in turn increases trust and emotional expressions of concern.[23] Let's discuss two critical areas—rationality and ethicality—in which emotions can enhance performance.

Do Emotions Make Us Irrational?   How often have you heard someone say, "Oh, you're just being emotional"? You might have been offended. Observations like

By studying brain injuries, such as the injury experienced by Phineas Gage, whose skull is illustrated here, researchers discovered an important link between emotions and rational thinking. They learned that our emotions provide us with valuable information that helps our thinking process.
Source: BSIP/Science Source

this suggest that rationality and emotion are in conflict, and by exhibiting emotion, you are acting irrationally. The perceived association between the two is so strong that some researchers argue displaying emotions such as sadness to the point of crying is so toxic to a career that we should leave the room rather than allow others to witness it.[24] This perspective suggests the demonstration or even experience of emotions can make us seem weak, brittle, or irrational. However, this is wrong. Our emotions actually make our thinking more rational. Why? Because our emotions provide important information about how we understand the world around us and they help guide our behaviors. For instance, individuals in a negative mood may be better able to discern truthful from accurate information than are people in a happy mood.[25]

Consider Phineas Gage, a railroad worker in Vermont. One September day in 1848, a 3-foot, 7-inch iron bar propelled by an explosive charge flew into his lower-left jaw and out through the top of his skull. Remarkably, Gage survived his injury, was able to read and speak, and performed well above average on cognitive ability tests. However, he completely lost his ability to experience emotion, which eventually took away his ability to reason. After the accident, he often behaved erratically and against his self-interests. He drifted from job to job, eventually joining a circus. In commenting on Gage's condition, one expert noted, "Reason may not be as pure as most of us think it is or wish it were…emotions and feelings may not be intruders in the bastion of reason at all: they may be enmeshed in its networks, for worse *and* for better."[26]

Do Emotions Make Us Ethical?   A growing body of research has begun to examine the relationship between emotions and moral attitudes.[27] It was previously believed that, like decision making in general, most ethical decision making was based on higher-order cognitive processes, but the research on moral emotions increasingly questions this perspective. Numerous studies suggest that moral judgments are largely based on feelings rather than on cognition, even though we tend to see our moral boundaries as logical and reasonable, not as emotional.

To some degree, our beliefs are actually shaped by our groups, which influence our perceptions of others, resulting in unconscious responses and a feeling that our shared emotions are "right." Unfortunately, this feeling sometimes allows us to justify purely emotional reactions as rationally "ethical."[28] We also tend to judge outgroup members (anyone who is not in our group) more harshly for moral transgressions than ingroup members, even when we are trying to be objective.[29] In addition, perhaps to restore an emotional sense of fair play, we are more likely to spitefully want outgroup members to be punished.[30]

When we can identify the sources of emotions and moods, we are better able to predict behavior and manage people well. Let's explore that topic next.

Sources of Emotions and Moods

4-2   Identify the sources of emotions and moods.

Have you ever said, "I got up on the wrong side of the bed today?" Have you ever snapped at a coworker or family member for no reason? If you have, you probably wonder where those emotions and moods originated. Here we discuss some of the primary influences.

Personality

Moods and emotions have a personality trait component, meaning that some people have built-in tendencies to experience certain moods and emotions more frequently than others do. People also experience the same emotions with different intensities; the degree to which they experience them is called

affect intensity Individual differences in the strength with which individuals experience their emotions.

their **affect intensity**.[31] Affectively intense people experience both positive and negative emotions more deeply: when they're sad, they're really sad, and when they're happy, they're really happy.

Time of Day

Moods vary by the time of day. However, research suggests most of us actually follow the same pattern. Levels of positive affect tend to peak in the late morning (10 a.m.–noon) and then remain at that level until early evening (around 7 p.m.).[32] Starting about 12 hours after waking, positive affect begins to drop until midnight, and then, for those who remain awake, the drop accelerates until positive mood picks up again after sunrise.[33] As for negative affect, most research suggests it fluctuates less than positive affect,[34] but the general trend is for it to increase over the course of a day, so that it is lowest early in the morning and highest late in the evening.[35]

A fascinating study assessed moods by analyzing millions of Twitter messages from across the globe.[36] The researchers noted the presence of words connoting positive affect (happy, enthused, excited) and negative (sad, angry, anxious) affect. You can see the trends they observed in the positive affect part of Exhibit 4-3. Daily fluctuations in mood followed a similar pattern in most countries. These results are comparable to what we reported above from previous research. A major difference, though, happens in the evening. Whereas most research suggests that positive affect tends to drop after 7 p.m., this study suggests that it *increases* before the midnight decline. We'll have to wait for further research to see which description is accurate. The negative affect trends in this study were more consistent with past research, showing that negative affect is lowest in the morning and tends to increase over the course of the day and evening.

You may wonder what happens for people who work the third shift at night. When our internal circadian process is out of line with our waking hours, our moods and well-being are likely to be negatively affected. However, researchers studying how the body's inner clock can be adjusted have found that governing our exposure to light may allow us to shift our circadian rhythms.[37] Thus, by manipulating light and darkness, someone who is awake at night might have a similar mood cycle to someone who sleeps at night.

Day of the Week

Are people in their best moods on the weekends? In most cultures that is true—for example, U.S. adults tend to experience their highest positive affect on Friday, Saturday, and Sunday, and their lowest on Monday.[38] As shown in Exhibit 4-4, again based on the study of Twitter messages, that tends to be true in several other cultures as well. For Germans and Chinese, positive affect is highest from Friday to Sunday and lowest on Monday. This isn't the case in all cultures, however. As the exhibit shows, in Japan positive affect is higher on Monday than on either Friday or Saturday.

As for negative affect, Monday is the highest negative-affect day across most cultures. However, in some countries, negative affect is lower on Friday and Saturday than on Sunday. It may be that while Sunday is enjoyable as a day off (and thus we have higher positive affect), we also get a bit stressed about the week ahead (which is why negative affect is higher).

Weather

When do you think you would be in a better mood—when it's 70 degrees and sunny, or on a gloomy, cold, rainy day? Many people believe their mood is tied to the weather. However, a fairly large and detailed body of evidence suggests weather has

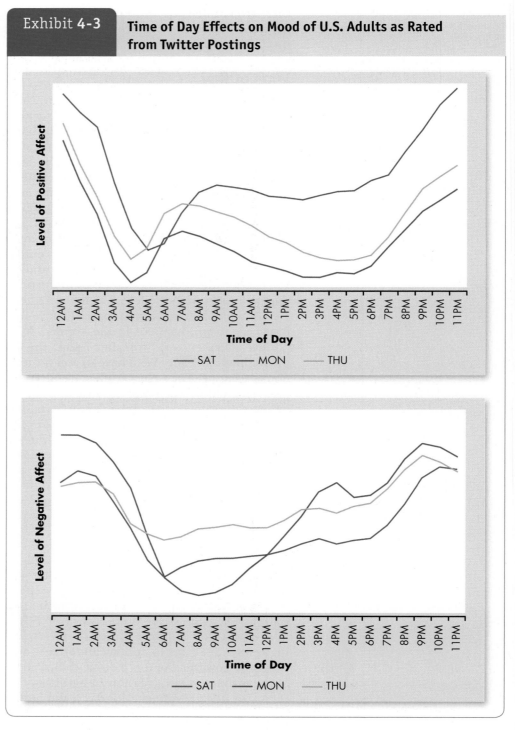

Exhibit 4-3   Time of Day Effects on Mood of U.S. Adults as Rated from Twitter Postings

Note: Based on analysis of U.S. Twitter postings and coding of words that represent positive feelings (delight, enthusiasm) and negative feelings (fear, guilt). Lines represent percent of total words in Twitter post that convey these moods.

Sources: Based on S. A. Golder and M. W. Macy, "Diurnal and Seasonal Mood Vary with Work, Sleep, and Daylength Across Diverse Cultures," *Science* 333 (2011): 1878–81; A. Elejalde-Ruiz, "Seize the Day," *Chicago Tribune,* September 5, 2012, downloaded June 20, 2013 from http://articles.chicagotribune.com/.

illusory correlation The tendency of people to associate two events when in reality there is no connection.

little effect on mood, at least for most people.[39] One expert concluded, "Contrary to the prevailing cultural view, these data indicate that people do not report a better mood on bright and sunny days (or, conversely, a worse mood on dark and rainy days)."[40] **Illusory correlation**, which occurs when we associate two events that

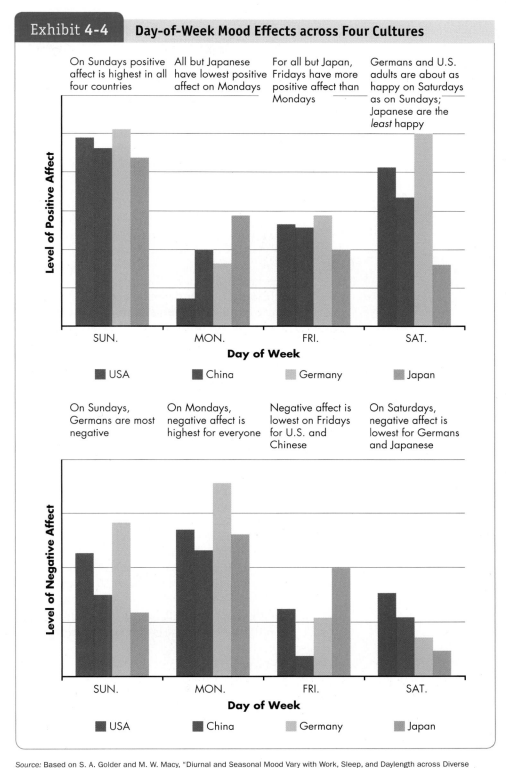

Exhibit 4-4   Day-of-Week Mood Effects across Four Cultures

On Sundays positive affect is highest in all four countries

All but Japanese have lowest positive affect on Mondays

For all but Japan, Fridays have more positive affect than Mondays

Germans and U.S. adults are about as happy on Saturdays as on Sundays; Japanese are the *least* happy

On Sundays, Germans are most negative

On Mondays, negative affect is highest for everyone

Negative affect is lowest on Fridays for U.S. and Chinese

On Saturdays, negative affect is lowest for Germans and Japanese

Source: Based on S. A. Golder and M. W. Macy, "Diurnal and Seasonal Mood Vary with Work, Sleep, and Daylength across Diverse Cultures," *Science* 333 (2011): 1878–81; A. Elejalde-Ruiz, "Seize the Day," *Chicago Tribune,* September 5, 2012, downloaded June 20, 2013 from http://articles.chicagotribune.com/.

in reality have no connection, explains why people tend to *think* weather influences them. For example, employees may be more productive on bad weather days, a study in Japan and the United States recently indicated, but not because of mood—instead, the worse weather removed some work distractions.[41]

Stress

As you might imagine, stressful events at work (a nasty e-mail, impending deadline, loss of a big sale, reprimand from the boss, etc.) negatively affect moods. The effects of stress also build over time. As the authors of one study note, "A constant diet of even low-level stressful events has the potential to cause workers to experience gradually increasing levels of strain over time."[42] Mounting levels of stress can worsen our moods, as we experience more negative emotions. Although sometimes we thrive on it, most of us find stress usually takes a toll on our mood. In fact, when situations are overly emotionally charged and stressful, we have a natural response to disengage, to literally look away.[43]

Social Activities

Do you tend to be happiest when out with friends? For most people, social activities increase a positive mood and have little effect on a negative mood. But do people in positive moods seek out social interactions, or do social interactions cause people to be in good moods? It seems both are true,[44] though the *type* of social activity does matter. Activities that are physical (skiing or hiking with friends), informal (going to a party), or epicurean (eating with others) are more strongly associated with increases in positive mood than events that are formal (attending a meeting) or sedentary (watching TV with friends).[45]

Sleep

U.S. adults report sleeping less than adults a generation ago.[46] According to researchers and public health specialists, a large portion of the U.S. workforce suffers from sleep deprivation: 41 million workers sleep less than 6 hours per night. Sleep quality affects moods and decision making, and increased fatigue puts workers at risk of disease, injury, and depression.[47] Poor or reduced sleep also makes it difficult to control emotions. Even one bad night's sleep makes us more angry and risk-prone,[48] possibly because poor sleep impairs job satisfaction[49] and makes us less able to make ethical judgments.[50]

On the positive side, increased regular sleep enhances creativity, performance, and career success. University of California-San Diego researchers calculated that for employees who do not sleep enough, "a one-hour increase in long-run average sleep increases wages by 16 percent, equivalent to more than a year of schooling."[51] Other researchers are trying to reduce how much sleep is needed for high functioning through drug therapy, hoping to find "something better than caffeine," said Ying-Hui Fu of the University of California-San Francisco.[52]

Exercise

You often hear people should exercise to improve their mood. Does "sweat therapy" really work? It appears so. Research consistently shows exercise enhances peoples' positive moods.[53] While not terribly strong overall, the effects are strongest for those who are depressed.

Age

Do young people experience more extreme positive emotions (so-called youthful exuberance) than older people? Surprisingly, no. One study of people ages 18 to 94 revealed that negative emotions occur less as people get older. Periods of highly positive moods lasted longer for the study's older participants, and bad moods faded more quickly.[54]

Staples believes that exercise increases positive moods and results in happier, healthier, and more productive employees. At company headquarters, the office supply retailer offers employees onsite strength training and cardiovascular conditioning classes during their lunch hour, including a "truck push" (shown here), military crawls, and other boot-camp-type activities.

Source: Boston Globe/Getty Images

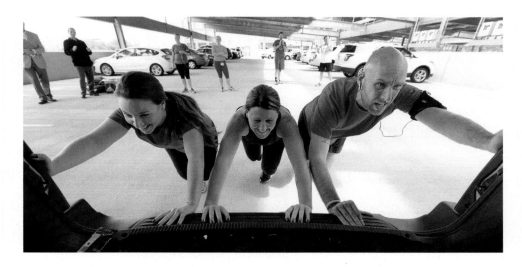

Sex

Many believe women are more emotional than men. Is there any truth to this? Evidence does confirm women experience emotions more intensely, tend to "hold onto" emotions longer than men, and display more frequent expressions of both positive and negative emotions, except anger.[55] Evidence from a study of participants from 37 different countries found that men consistently reported higher levels of powerful emotions like anger, whereas women reported more powerless emotions like sadness and fear. Thus, there are some sex differences in the experience and expression of emotions.[56]

People also tend to attribute men's and women's emotions in ways that might be based on stereotypes of typical emotional reactions. One study showed that when viewing pictures of faces, participants interpreted the women's emotional expressions as being dispositional (related to personality), whereas the men's expressions were interpreted as situational.[57] For example, a picture of a sad woman led observers to believe she had an emotional personality, whereas a picture of sadness in a man was more likely to be attributed to having a bad day. Another study showed that participants were quicker to detect angry expressions on male faces and happy expressions on female faces; neutral faces in men were attributed as more angry and neutral faces in women were interpreted as happy.[58]

It might seem by now that we all—leaders, managers, and employees alike—operate as unwitting slaves to our emotions and moods. On an internal experiential level, this may be true. Yet we know from our workplace experiences that people aren't expressing every brief emotion that flits through their consciousness. Let's put together what we've learned about emotions and moods with workplace coping strategies, beginning with emotional labor.

Emotional Labor

4-3 Show the impact emotional labor has on employees.

If you've ever had a job in retail, sales, or waited on tables in a restaurant, you know the importance of projecting a friendly demeanor and smiling. Even though there were days when you didn't feel cheerful, you knew management expected you to be upbeat when dealing with customers, so you faked it.

Every employee expends physical and mental labor by putting body and mind, respectively, into the job. But jobs also require **emotional labor**, an employee's expression of organizationally desired emotions during interpersonal transactions at work. Emotional labor is a key component of effective job

emotional labor   A situation in which an employee expresses organizationally desired emotions during interpersonal transactions at work.

Employees of Apple's store in Manhattan, New York, greet customers with enthusiasm and excitement as they exit the store after buying an iPhone 6 on its first day of sales. Employees' smiles and high fives are expressions of emotional labor that Apple requires and considers appropriate for their jobs.
Source: Adrees Latif/Reuters/Landov

felt emotions   An individual's actual emotions.

displayed emotions   Emotions that are organizationally required and considered appropriate in a given job.

surface acting   Hiding one's inner feelings and forgoing emotional expressions in response to display rules.

deep acting   Trying to modify one's true inner feelings based on display rules.

performance. We expect flight attendants to be cheerful, funeral directors to be sad, and doctors emotionally neutral. At the least, your managers expect you to be courteous, not hostile, in your interactions with coworkers.

The way we experience an emotion is obviously not always the same as the way we show it. To analyze emotional labor, we divide emotions into *felt* or *displayed emotions.*[59] **Felt emotions** are our actual emotions. In contrast, **displayed emotions** are those the organization requires workers to show and considers appropriate in a given job. They're not innate; they're learned, and they may or may not coincide with felt emotions. For instance, research suggests that in U.S. workplaces, it is expected that employees should typically display positive emotions like happiness and excitement and suppress negative emotions like fear, anger, disgust, and contempt.[60]

Effective managers have learned to look serious when they give an employee a negative performance evaluation, and to look calm when they are berated by their bosses, because the organization expects these displays. Of course, there are no display rules for many workplace situations. Does your employer dictate what emotions you display when you are, say, heading out for lunch? Probably not. Many workplaces have explicit display rules, but usually only for interactions that matter, particularly between employees and customers. Regarding employee and customer interactions, you might expect that the more an employer dictates salespeople's emotional displays, the higher the sales. Actually, employees under very high or very low display rules do not perform as well in sales situations as employees who have moderate display rules and a high degree of discretion in their roles.[61] Displaying fake emotions requires us to suppress real ones. **Surface acting** is hiding inner feelings and emotional expressions in response to display rules. A worker who smiles at a customer even when he doesn't feel like it is surface acting. **Deep acting** is trying to modify our true inner feelings based on display rules. Surface acting deals with *displayed* emotions, and deep acting deals with *felt* emotions.

Displaying emotions we don't really feel can be exhausting. Surface acting is associated with increased stress and decreased job satisfaction.[62] Surface acting on a daily basis can also lead to emotional exhaustion at home, work-family conflict, and insomnia.[63] On the other hand, deep acting has a positive relationship with job satisfaction and job performance.[64] We also experience less emotional exhaustion with deep acting.

emotional dissonance Inconsistencies between the emotions people feel and the emotions they project.

When employees have to project one emotion *while feeling another*, this disparity is called **emotional dissonance**. Bottled-up feelings of frustration, anger, and resentment can lead to emotional exhaustion. Long-term emotional dissonance is a predictor for job burnout, declines in job performance, and lower job satisfaction.[65]

mindfulness Objectively and deliberately evaluating the emotional situation in the moment.

It is important to counteract the effects of emotional labor and emotional dissonance. Research in the Netherlands and Belgium indicated that while surface acting is stressful to employees, **mindfulness**—objectively and deliberately evaluating our emotional situation in the moment—was negatively correlated with emotional exhaustion and positively affected job satisfaction.[66] Mindfulness is one of several emotion regulation techniques that we will discuss later in this text. Beyond emotion regulation, employees who engage in surface displays should be given a chance to relax and recharge. For example, a study that looked at how cheerleading instructors spent their breaks from teaching found those who used the time to rest and relax were more effective after their breaks than those who did chores during their breaks.[67] Lastly, employees who can depersonalize or standardize their work interactions that require emotional labor may be able to successfully carry on their acting while thinking of other tasks, thus bypassing the emotional impact.[68]

The concept of emotional labor makes intuitive and organizational sense. Affective events theory, discussed in the next section, fits a job's emotional labor requirements into a construct with implications for work events, emotional reactions, job satisfaction, and job performance.

Affective Events Theory

4-4 Describe affective events theory.

affective events theory (AET) A model that suggests that workplace events cause emotional reactions on the part of employees, which then influence workplace attitudes and behaviors.

We've seen that emotions and moods are an important part of our personal and work lives. But how do they influence our job performance and satisfaction? **Affective events theory (AET)** proposes that employees react emotionally to things that happen to them at work, and this reaction influences their job performance and satisfaction.[69] Say you just found out your company is downsizing. You might experience a variety of negative emotions, causing you to worry that you'll lose your job. Because it is out of your hands, you feel insecure and fearful, and spend much of your time worrying rather than working. Needless to say, your job satisfaction will also be down.

Work events trigger positive or negative emotional reactions, to which employees' personalities and moods predispose them to respond with greater or lesser intensity.[70] People who score low on emotional stability are more likely to react strongly to negative events, and our emotional response to a given event can change depending on mood. Finally, emotions influence a number of performance and satisfaction variables, such as OCB, organizational commitment, level of effort, intention to quit, and workplace deviance.

In sum, AET offers two important messages.[71] First, emotions provide valuable insights into how workplace events influence employee performance and satisfaction. Second, employees and managers shouldn't ignore emotions or the events that cause them, even when they appear minor, because they accumulate. Emotional intelligence is another framework that helps us understand the impact of emotions on job performance, so we will look at that next.

Emotional Intelligence

4-5 Describe emotional intelligence.

As the CEO of an international talent company, Terrie Upshur-Lupberger was at a career pinnacle. So why was she resentful and unhappy? A close friend observed, "Terrie, you were out on the skinny branch—you know, the one that breaks easily in a strong wind. You were so busy and overwhelmed and out of touch with your own values, cares, and guiding beliefs that you failed to pay attention to the branch that was about to break."[72] According to Upshur-Lupberger, she had failed to notice that her moods constantly swung toward frustration and exhaustion. Her job satisfaction, productivity, relationships, and results suffered. Worst, she was too busy to realize the deficiencies until she was completely depleted.[73] She said, "I learned that, as a leader, you either pay attention to and manage the moods (including your own) in the organization, or…you ignore them and pay the price." Upshur-Lupberger learned the value of emotional intelligence.

emotional intelligence (EI) The ability to detect and to manage emotional cues and information.

Emotional intelligence (EI) is a person's ability to (1) perceive emotions in the self and others, (2) understand the meaning of these emotions, and (3) regulate his or her own emotions accordingly, as shown in Exhibit 4-5. People who know their own emotions and are good at reading emotional cues—for instance, knowing why they're angry and how to express themselves without violating norms—are most likely to be effective.[74]

Several studies suggest EI plays an important role in job performance. One study that used functional magnetic resonance imaging (fMRI) technology found that executive MBA students who performed best on a strategic decision-making task were more likely to incorporate emotion centers of the brain into their choice process.[75] One simulation study showed that students who were good at identifying and distinguishing among their own feelings were able to make more profitable investment decisions.[76] For an overall perspective, research studied 11 U.S. presidents—from Franklin Roosevelt to Bill Clinton—and evaluated them on six qualities: communication, organization, political skill, vision, cognitive style, and emotional intelligence. The key quality that differentiated the successful (such as Roosevelt, Kennedy, and Reagan) from the unsuccessful (such as Johnson, Carter, and Nixon) was emotional intelligence.[77]

Although the field is progressing in its understanding of EI, many questions have not been answered. One relates to proving what EI may predict. For example, while evidence indicates that EI has some correlation with job performance, the correlation isn't high, and it is explained to a large degree by traits such as emotional stability. A second question is about the reliability of EI testing. For example, part of the reason EI has only a modest correlation with job effectiveness is that it is hard to measure—mostly it is measured with self-report inventories, which of course are often far from objective!

Exhibit 4-5   A Cascading Model of Emotional Intelligence

Conscientiousness	→	Perceive Emotions in Self and Others
Cognitive	→	Understand the Meaning of Emotions
Emotional Stability	→	Regulate Emotions

Should Managers Use Emotional Intelligence (EI) Tests?

As we discussed in this chapter, the concept of emotional intelligence has raised some debate. One of the questions for managers is whether to use EI tests in the selection process. Here are some ethical considerations:

- *There is no commonly accepted test.* For instance, researchers have recently used the Mayer–Salovey–Caruso Emotional Intelligence Test (MSCEIT), the Trait Emotional Intelligence Questionnaire, and the Situational Judgment Test of Emotional Intelligence (SJT of EI) in studies. Researchers feel EI tests may need to be culturally specific because emotional displays vary by culture; thus, the interpretation of emotional cues differs. For example, a recent study comparing the emotional intelligence scores for Indian and North American executives using the Emotional Competence Inventory (ECI-2) test found the results similar but not the same, suggesting the need for modification.
- *Applicants may react negatively to taking an EI test in general, or to parts of it.* The face recognition test, for example, may seem culturally biased to some if the subject photos

are not diverse. Also, participants who score high on EI tests tend to consider them fair; applicants who score lower may not perceive the tests to be fair and can thus view the hiring organizations unfavorably—even if they score well on other assessments.

- *EI tests may not be predictive of performance for all types of jobs.* In a study of 600 Romanian participants, results indicated that EI was valid for salespeople, public servants, and CEOs of public hospitals, but these were all roles requiring significant social interaction. EI tests may need to be tailored for each position category or not be used when the position description does not warrant.
- *It remains somewhat unclear what EI tests are actually measuring.* They may reflect personality or intelligence, in which case other measures might be better. Also, mixed EI tests may predict job performance, but many of these tests include personality constructs and measures of general mental ability.
- *There is not enough research on how emotional intelligence affects, for instance, counterproductive work behavior (CWB).* It may not be prudent to test and select applicants

who are rated high on EI when we aren't yet certain that everything about EI leads to desired workplace outcomes.

These concerns suggest EI tests should be avoided in hiring decisions. However, because research has indicated that emotional intelligence does predict job performance to some degree, managers should not be too hasty to dismiss them altogether. Rather, those wishing to use EI in hiring decisions should be aware of these issues to make informed and ethical decisions about not only whom to hire, but how.

Sources: D. Iliescu, A. Ilie, D. Ispas, and A. Ion, "Emotional Intelligence in Personnel Selection: Applicant Reactions, Criterion, and Incremental Validity," *International Journal of Selection and Assessment* (September 2012): 347–58; D. L. Joseph, J. Jin, D. A. Newman, and E. H. O'Boyle, "Why Does Self-Reported Emotional Intelligence Predict Job Performance? A Meta-Analytic Investigation of Mixed EI," *Journal of Applied Psychology* 100, no. 2 (2015): 298–342; "R. Sharma, "Measuring Social and Emotional Intelligence Competencies in the Indian Context," *Cross Cultural Management* 19 (2012): 30–47; and S. Sharma, M. Gangopadhyay, E. Austin, and M. K. Mandal, "Development and Validation of a Situational Judgment Test of Emotional Intelligence," *International Journal of Selection and Assessment* (March 2013): 57–73.

All questions aside, EI is wildly popular among consulting firms and in the popular press, and it has accumulated some support in the research literature. Love it or hate it, one thing is for sure—EI is here to stay. So might be our next topic, emotion regulation, which is increasingly studied as an independent concept.[78]

✪ PERSONAL INVENTORY ASSESSMENTS

Emotional Intelligence Assessment

Have you always been able to "read" others well? Do people say you seem to have "the right thing to say" for every occasion? Complete this PIA to determine your emotional intelligence (EI).

Emotion Regulation

4-6 Identify strategies for emotion regulation.

Have you ever tried to cheer yourself up when you're feeling down, or calm yourself when you're feeling angry? If so, you have engaged in *emotion regulation*. The central idea behind emotion regulation is to identify and modify the emotions you feel. Recent research suggests that emotion management ability is a strong predictor of task performance for some jobs and for OCB.[79] Therefore, in our study of OB, we are interested in *whether* and *how* emotion regulation should be used in the workplace. We begin by identifying which individuals might naturally employ it.

Emotion Regulation Influences and Outcomes

As you might suspect, not everyone is equally good at regulating emotions. Individuals who are higher in the personality trait of neuroticism have more trouble doing so and often find their moods are beyond their ability to control. Individuals who have lower levels of self-esteem are also less likely to try to improve their sad moods, perhaps because they are less likely than others to feel they deserve to be in a good mood.[80]

The workplace environment has an effect on an individual's tendency to employ emotion regulation. In general, diversity in work groups increases the likelihood that you will regulate your emotions. For example, younger employees are likely to regulate their emotions when their work groups include older members.[81] Racial diversity also has an effect: if diversity is low, the minority will engage in emotion regulation, perhaps to "fit in" with the majority race as much as possible; if diversity is high and many different races are represented, the majority race will employ emotion regulation, perhaps to integrate themselves with the whole group.[82] These findings suggest a beneficial outcome of diversity—it may cause us to regulate our emotions more consciously and effectively.

While regulating your emotions might seem beneficial, research suggests there is a downside to trying to change the way you feel. Changing your emotions takes effort, and as we noted when discussing emotional labor, this effort can be exhausting. Sometimes attempts to change an emotion actually make the emotion stronger; for example, trying to talk yourself out of being afraid can make you focus more on what scares you, which makes you more afraid.[83] From another perspective, research suggests that avoiding negative emotional experiences is less likely to lead to positive moods than does seeking out positive emotional experiences.[84] For example, you're more likely to experience a positive mood if you have a pleasant conversation with a friend than if you avoid an unpleasant conversation with a hostile coworker.

Emotion Regulation Techniques

Researchers of emotion regulation often study the strategies people employ to change their emotions. One technique we have discussed in this chapter is surface acting, or literally "putting on a face" of appropriate response to a given situation. Surface acting doesn't change the emotions, though, so the regulation effect is minimal, and the result of daily surface acting leads to exhaustion and fewer OCBs.[85] Perhaps due to the costs of creatively expressing what we don't feel, individuals who vary their surface-acting response may have lower job satisfaction and higher levels of work withdrawal than those who consistently give the same responses.[86]

Deep acting, another technique we have covered, is less psychologically costly than surface acting because the employee is actually trying to experience the emotion. Emotion regulation through deep acting can have a positive

New employees of the ward office in the city of Daejeon, South Korea, practice smiling during their training on how to be kind public employees. The strategy of surface acting, or "putting on a face," is an appropriate technique the employees learn for modifying their emotions that helps them create positive interactions with customers.

Source: Yonhap News/YNA/Newscom

impact on work outcomes. For example, a recent study in the Netherlands and Germany found that individuals in service jobs earned significantly more direct pay (tips) after they received training in deep acting.[87]

One technique of emotion regulation is *emotional suppression,* or suppressing initial emotional responses to situations. This response seems to facilitate practical thinking in the short term. However, it appears to be helpful only when a strongly negative event would illicit a distressed emotional reaction in a crisis situation.[88] For example, a soldier in battle may suppress initial emotional distress after a shooting and thus be able to make clearer decisions about how to proceed. A portfolio manager might suppress an emotional reaction to a sudden drop in the value of a stock and therefore be able to clearly decide how to plan. Suppression used in crisis situations appears to help an individual recover from the event emotionally, while suppression used as an everyday emotion regulation technique can take a toll on mental ability, emotional ability, health, and relationships.[89]

Thus, unless we're truly in a crisis situation, acknowledging rather than suppressing our emotional responses to situations, and re-evaluating events after they occur, yield the best outcomes.[90] *Cognitive reappraisal,* or reframing our outlook on an emotional situation, is one way to effectively regulate emotions.[91] Cognitive reappraisal ability seems to be the most helpful to individuals in situations where they cannot control the sources of stress.[92] A recent study illustrates the potentially powerful effect of this technique. Israeli participants who were shown anger-inducing information about the Israeli-Palestinian conflict after they were primed to reappraise the situation showed more inclination toward conciliation and less inclination toward aggressive tactics against Palestinians than the control group, not only immediately after the study but up to 5 months later. This result suggests that cognitive reappraisal may allow people to change their emotional responses, even when the subject matter is as highly emotionally charged as the Israeli-Palestinian conflict.[93] Mindfulness also has been shown to increase the ability to shape our behavioral responses to emotions.[94] When people become non-judgmentally aware of the emotions they are experiencing, they are better able to look at situations separately from their emotions.

Another technique with potential for emotion regulation is *social sharing*, or venting. Research shows that the open expression of emotions can help individuals to regulate their emotions, as opposed to keeping emotions "bottled up." Social sharing can reduce anger reactions when people can talk about the facts of a bad situation, their feelings about the situation, or any positive aspects of the situation.[95] Caution must be exercised, though, because expressing your frustration affects other people. In fact, whether venting emotions helps the "venter" feel better depends very much upon the listener's response. If the listener doesn't respond (many refuse to respond to venting), the venter actually feels worse. If the listener responds with expressions of support or validation, the venter feels better. Therefore, if we are going to vent to a coworker, we need to choose someone who will respond sympathetically. Venting to the perceived offender rarely improves things and can result in heightening the negative emotions.[96]

While emotion regulation techniques can help us cope with difficult workplace situations, research indicates that the effect varies. For example, a recent study in Taiwan found that all participants who worked for abusive supervisors reported emotional exhaustion and work withdrawal tendencies, but to different degrees based on the emotion regulation strategies they employed. Employees who used suppression techniques suffered greater emotional exhaustion and work withdrawal than employees who used cognitive reappraisal. This suggests that more research on the application of techniques needs to be done to help employees increase their coping skills.[97]

Thus, while there is much promise in emotion regulation techniques, the best route to a positive workplace is to recruit positive-minded individuals and train leaders to manage their moods, job attitudes, and performance.[98] The best leaders manage emotions as much as they do tasks and activities. The best employees can use their knowledge of emotion regulation to decide when to speak up and how to express themselves effectively.[99]

Ethics of Emotion Regulation

Emotion regulation has important ethical implications. On one end of the continuum, some people might argue that controlling your emotions is unethical because it requires a degree of acting. On the other end, other people might argue that all emotions should be controlled so you can take a dispassionate perspective. Both arguments—and all arguments in between—have ethical pros and cons you will have to decide for yourself. Consider the reasons for emotion regulation and the outcomes. Are you regulating your emotions so you don't react inappropriately, or are you regulating your emotions so no one knows what you are thinking? Finally, consider this: you may be able to "fake it 'til you make it." Recent research has found that acting like you are in a good mood might *put* you in a good mood. In one study, a group of participants was asked to hold only an efficient conversation with a barista serving them at Starbucks, while another group was asked to act happy. The happy actors reported later that they were in much better moods.[100]

Now that we have studied the role of emotions and moods in organizational behavior, let's consider the opportunities for more specific applications that our understanding provides.

☼ WATCH IT!

If your professor has assigned this, go to the Assignments section of **mymanagementlab.com** to complete the video exercise titled *East Haven Fire Department: Emotions and Moods*.

OB Applications of Emotions and Moods

4-7 Apply concepts about emotions and moods to specific OB issues.

Our understanding of emotions and moods can affect many aspects of organizational behavior including the selection process, decision making, creativity, motivation, leadership, negotiation, customer service, job attitudes, deviant workplace behavior, and safety. Let's think through each of these.

Selection

One implication from the evidence on EI is that employers should consider it a factor in hiring employees, especially for jobs that demand a high degree of social interaction. In fact, more employers *are* starting to use EI measures to hire people. For example, a study of U.S. Air Force recruiters showed that top-performing recruiters exhibited high levels of EI. Using these findings, the Air Force revamped its selection criteria. A follow-up investigation found hires who had high EI scores were 2.6 times more successful than those who didn't.

Decision Making

Moods and emotions have effects on decision making that managers should understand. Positive emotions and moods seem to help people make sound decisions. Positive emotions also enhance problem-solving skills, so positive people find better solutions.[101]

OB researchers continue to debate the role of negative emotions and moods in decision making. One recent study suggested that people who are saddened by events may make the same decisions as before, while people who are angered by events might make stronger (though not necessarily better) choices than before.[102] Another study found that participants made choices reflecting more originality in a negative mood.[103] Still other research indicated that individuals in a negative mood may take higher risks than when in a positive mood.[104] Taken together, these and other studies suggest negative (and positive) emotions impact decision making, but that there are other variables which require further research.[105]

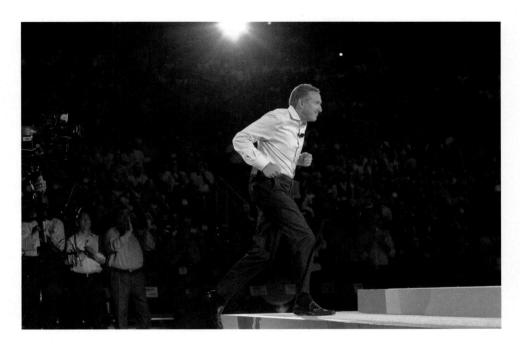

A leader of high emotional intelligence, Starbucks CEO Howard Schultz bounds on stage before addressing 10,000 Starbucks managers at the firm's Global Leadership Conference. Schultz's optimism, excitement, and enthusiasm energize employees and motivate them to accept his vision of the company's future.
Source: F. Carter Smith/Bloomberg/Getty Images

Creativity

As we see throughout this text, one goal of leadership is to maximize employee productivity through creativity. Creativity is influenced by emotions and moods, but there are two schools of thought on the relationship. Much research suggests that people in good moods tend to be more creative than people in bad moods.[106] People in good moods produce more ideas and more options, and others think their ideas are original.[107] It seems that people experiencing positive moods or emotions are more flexible and open in their thinking, which may explain why they're more creative.[108] Supervisors should actively try to keep employees happy because doing so creates more good moods (employees like their leaders to encourage them and provide positive feedback on a job well done), which in turn leads people to be more creative.[109]

Some researchers, however, do not believe a positive mood makes people more creative. They argue that when people are in positive moods, they may relax ("If I'm in a good mood, things must be going okay, and I don't need to think of new ideas") and not engage in the critical thinking necessary for some forms of creativity.[110] Individuals who worry more may perform better on creative tasks than those who are less neurotic.

Determining which perspective is correct may lie in thinking of moods somewhat differently. Rather than looking at positive or negative affect, it's possible to conceptualize moods as active feelings like anger, fear, or elation and contrast these with deactivating moods like sorrow, depression, or serenity. All the activating moods, whether positive *or* negative, seem to lead to more creativity, whereas deactivating moods lead to less.[111] We discussed earlier that other factors such as fatigue may boost creativity. A study of 428 students found they performed best on a creative problem-solving task when they were fatigued, suggesting that tiredness may free the mind to consider novel solutions.[112]

Motivation

Several studies have highlighted the importance of moods and emotions on motivation. One study asked two groups of people to solve word puzzles. The first group saw a funny video clip intended to put them in a good mood first. The other group was not shown the clip and started working on the puzzles right away. The positive-mood group reported higher expectations of being able to solve the puzzles, worked harder at them, and did solve more as a result.[113] Another study looked at the moods of insurance sales agents in Taiwan.[114] Agents in a good mood were found to be more helpful toward their coworkers and also felt better about themselves. These factors in turn led to superior performance in the form of higher sales and better supervisor reports of performance.

Giving people performance feedback—whether real or fake—influences their mood, which then influences their motivation.[115] A cycle can be created in which positive moods cause people to be more creative, leading to positive feedback from those observing their work. The feedback further reinforces the positive mood, which makes people perform even better, and so on. Overall, the findings suggest a manager may enhance employee motivation—and performance—by encouraging good moods.

Leadership

Research indicates that putting people in a good mood makes good sense. Leaders who focus on inspirational goals generate greater optimism, cooperation, and enthusiasm in employees, leading to more positive social interactions with coworkers and customers.[116] A study with Taiwanese military participants indicates that by sharing emotions, transformational leaders inspire positive emotions in their followers that lead to higher task performance.[117]

Leaders are perceived as more effective when they share positive emotions, and followers are more creative in a positive emotional environment. What about when leaders are sad? Research found that leader displays of sadness increased the analytic performance of followers, perhaps because followers attended more closely to tasks to help the leaders.[118]

Corporate executives know emotional content is critical for employees to buy into their vision of the company's future and accept change. When higher-ups offer new visions, especially with vague or distant goals, it is often difficult for employees to accept the changes they'll bring. By arousing emotions and linking them to an appealing vision, leaders may help managers and employees alike to accept change and feel connected to the new plan.

Negotiation

Have you considered the potential of using emotions and moods to enhance your negotiation skills? Several studies suggest that a negotiator who feigns anger has an advantage over an opponent. Why? Because when a negotiator shows anger, the opponent concludes the negotiator has conceded all he or she can and so gives in.[119] However, anger should be used selectively in negotiation: angry negotiators who have less information or less power than their opponents have significantly worse outcomes.[120]

As in the use of any emotion, context matters. Displaying a negative emotion (such as anger) can be effective, but feeling bad about your performance appears to impair future negotiations. Individuals who do poorly in negotiation experience negative emotions, develop negative perceptions of their counterparts, and are less willing to share information or be cooperative in future negotiations.[121]

Altogether, the best negotiators are probably those who remain emotionally detached. One study of people who suffered damage to the emotional centers of their brains suggested that unemotional people may be the best negotiators because they're not likely to overcorrect when faced with negative outcomes.[122]

Customer Service

Workers' emotional states influence the level of customer service they give, which in turn influences levels of repeat business and customer satisfaction.[123] This result is primarily due to **emotional contagion**—the "catching" of emotions from others.[124] When someone experiences positive emotions and laughs and smiles at you, you tend to respond positively. Of course, the opposite is true as well.

Studies indicate a matching effect between employee and customer emotions. In the employee-to-customer direction, research finds that customers who catch the positive moods or emotions of employees shop longer. In the other direction, when an employee feels unfairly treated by a customer, it's harder for him to display the positive emotions his organization expects.[125] High-quality customer service makes demands on employees because it often puts them in a state of emotional dissonance, which can be damaging to the employee and the organization. Managers can interrupt negative contagion by fostering positive moods.

Job Attitudes

There is good news and bad news about the relationship between moods and job attitudes, in that both are affected by work and home events. Ever hear the advice "Never take your work home with you," meaning you should forget about work once you go home? That's easier said than done. The good news is that it appears a positive mood at work can spill over to your off-work hours, and a negative mood at work can be restored to a positive mood after a break. Several studies have shown people who had a good day at work tend to be in a better mood at home that evening, and vice versa.[126] Other research has found

emotional contagion The process by which peoples' emotions are caused by the emotions of others.

How do I turn down the volume on my screaming boss?

My boss is a yeller. One time, he kicked my chair and yelled for me to get out of the office just because I'd forgotten to tell him that lunch had been delivered. His rage makes me so mad I want to yell back, but I don't because it isn't professional. Is there a way to get him to think before he fumes?

— *Leslie*

Dear Leslie:

We feel for you! Actually, your internal anger response is perfectly normal. Almost everyone has an emotional reaction to screaming and other situations of workplace incivility like swearing and rude behavior, and a majority of employees react somehow. For example, 66 percent of participants in a recent study reported their performance declined when they were the recipients of incivility, and 25 percent admitted they took their frustration out on customers. Another study found that verbal aggression reduces victims' working memory, making even simple instructions difficult to follow. So you're right to want to strategize how to calm the situation

since it hurts you, your coworkers, and the company.

The good news is that you can work on your reactions to de-escalate an episode. Experts suggest empathizing with your boss (often we find if we try to understand where someone is coming from, it helps us deal with the emotions more effectively), apologizing if you've done something wrong, and not talking back (incivility is never cured by payment in kind). Find situations where you can laugh over mutual frustrations and don't take his outbursts personally.

The bad news is that you probably can't change his emotional response to incidents, but you may be able to help him see the error of his ways by modeling better behavior. Of course, there are situations in which you cannot and should not tolerate uncivil behavior (such as when you are being threatened or when the behavior becomes truly abusive). In those cases, you may need to deal with the situation more directly by first calmly confronting your boss or, if that fails, seeing someone in human resources.

But short of that breaking point, our experience and the research suggest that your best response is not to respond outwardly but rather to rethink the way you are responding inwardly.

As the British poster says, "Keep calm and carry on!"

Sources: C. Porath and C. Pearson, "The Price of Incivility," *Harvard Business Review* (January–February 2013): 114–21; A. Rafaeli et al., "When Customers Exhibit Verbal Aggression, Employees Pay Cognitive Costs," *Journal of Applied Psychology* (September 2012): 931–50; S. Shellenbarger, "'It's Not My Fault!' A Better Response to Criticism at Work," *The Wall Street Journal*, June 18, 2014, D1, D4; and S. Shellenbarger, "When the Boss Is a Screamer," *The Wall Street Journal*, August 15, 2012, D1, D2.

that although people do emotionally take their work home with them, by the next day the effect is usually gone.[127] The bad news is that the moods of your household may interfere with yours. As you might expect, one study found if one member of a couple was in a negative mood during the workday, the negative mood spilled over to the spouse at night.[128] Thus, the relationship between moods and job attitudes is reciprocal—the way our workday goes colors our moods, but our moods also affect the way we see our jobs.

Deviant Workplace Behaviors

Anyone who has spent much time in an organization realizes people can behave in ways that violate established norms and threaten the organization, its members, or both. As we saw in Chapter 1, these actions are called counterproductive work behaviors (CWB).[129] They can be traced to negative emotions and can take many forms. People who feel negative emotions are more likely than others to engage in short-term deviant behavior at work, such as gossiping or surfing the Internet,[130] though negative emotions can also lead to more serious forms of CWB.

For instance, envy is an emotion that occurs when you resent someone for having something you don't have but strongly desire—such as a better work assignment, larger office, or higher salary. It can lead to malicious deviant behaviors. An envious employee could undermine other employees and take all the credit for things others accomplished. Angry people look for other people to blame for their bad mood, interpret other people's behavior as hostile, and have trouble considering others' points of view.[131] It's also not hard to see how these thought processes can lead directly to verbal or physical aggression.

A recent study in Pakistan found that anger correlated with more aggressive CWBs such as abuse against others and production deviance, while sadness did not. Interestingly, neither anger nor sadness predicted workplace withdrawal, which suggests that managers need to take employee expressions of anger seriously; employees may stay with an organization and continue to act aggressively toward others.[132] Once aggression starts, it's likely that other people will become angry and aggressive, so the stage is set for a serious escalation of negative behavior. Managers therefore need to stay connected with their employees to gauge emotions and emotional intensity levels.

Safety and Injury at Work

Research relating negative affectivity to increased injuries at work suggests employers might improve health and safety (and reduce costs) by ensuring workers aren't engaged in potentially dangerous activities when they're in a bad mood. Bad moods can contribute to injury at work in several ways.[133] Individuals in negative moods tend to be more anxious, which can make them less able to cope effectively with hazards. A person who is always fearful will be more pessimistic about the effectiveness of safety precautions because she feels she'll just get hurt anyway, or she might panic or freeze up when confronted with a threatening situation. Negative moods also make people more distractable, and distractions can obviously lead to careless behaviors.

Selecting positive team members can contribute toward a positive work environment because positive moods transmit from team member to team member. One study of 130 leaders and their followers found that leaders who are charismatic transfer their positive emotions to their followers through a contagion effect.[134] It makes sense, then, to choose team members predisposed to positive moods.

Summary

Emotions and moods are similar in that both are affective in nature. But they're also different—moods are more general and less contextual than emotions. The time of day, stressful events, and sleep patterns are some of the factors that influence emotions and moods. OB research on emotional labor, affective events theory, emotional intelligence, and emotion regulation helps us understand how people deal with emotions. Emotions and moods have proven relevant for virtually every OB topic we study, with implications for managerial practices.

Implications for Managers

- Recognize that emotions are a natural part of the workplace and good management does not mean creating an emotion-free environment.
- To foster effective decision making, creativity, and motivation in employees, model positive emotions and moods as much as is authentically possible.
- Provide positive feedback to increase the positivity of employees. Of course, it also helps to hire people who are predisposed to positive moods.
- In the service sector, encourage positive displays of emotion, which make customers feel more positive and thus improve customer service interactions and negotiations.
- Understand the role of emotions and moods to significantly improve your ability to explain and predict your coworkers' and others' behavior.

Sometimes Yelling Is for Everyone's Good

POINT

Anger is discussed throughout this chapter for a reason: It's an important emotion. There are benefits to expressing anger. For one, research indicates that only employees who are committed to their organizations tend to express their anger, and generally only to leaders who created the situation. This type of expression of anger could lead to positive organizational change. Second, suppressed anger can lower job satisfaction and lead to a feeling of hopelessness that things will improve.

Even with these findings, we hear a lot about not responding emotionally to work challenges. Work cultures teach us to avoid showing any anger at all, lest we be seen as poor workers or, worse, unprofessional or even deviant or violent. While, of course, there *are* times when the expression of anger is harmful or unprofessional, we've taken this view so far that we now teach people to suppress perfectly normal emotions, and to ignore the effectiveness of some emotional expression.

Emerging research shows that suppressing anger takes a terrible internal toll on individuals. One Stanford University study found, for example, that when individuals were asked to wear a poker face during the showing of a movie clip depicting the atomic bombings of Japan during World War II, they were much more stressed in conversations after the video. Other research shows that college students who suppress emotions like anger have more trouble making friends and are more likely to be depressed, and that employees who suppress anger feel more stressed by work.

For the good of organizations and their employees, we should encourage people not to hold back their emotions, but to share them constructively.

COUNTERPOINT

Yes, anger is a common emotion. But it's also a toxic one for the giver and the receiver. Angry outbursts can compromise the heart and contribute to diabetes, among other ill effects. The experience of another's anger and its close correlate, hostility, is also linked to many counterproductive behaviors in organizations. The Bureau of Labor Statistics estimates that 16 percent of fatal workplace injuries result from workplace violence. That is why many organizations have developed counteractive techniques—to blunt the harmful effects of anger in the workplace.

To reduce outcomes, many companies develop policies that govern conduct such as yelling, shouting profanities, and making hostile gestures. Others institute anger management programs. For example, one organization conducted mandatory in-house workshops that showed individuals how to deal with conflicts in the workplace before they boil over. The director who instituted the training said it "gave people specific tools for opening a dialogue to work things out." MTS Systems, a Minnesota engineering firm, engages an outside consulting company to conduct anger management programs for its organization. Typically, MTS consultants hold an 8-hour seminar that discusses sources of anger, conflict resolution techniques, and organizational policies. This is followed by one-on-one sessions with individual employees that focus on cognitive behavioral techniques to manage their anger. The outside trainer charges around $10,000 for the seminar and one-on-one sessions. The financial cost, though, is worth it for the emotional benefits the participants receive. "You want people to get better at communicating with each other," says MTS manager Karen Borre.

In the end, everyone wins when organizations seek to diminish both the experience and the expression of anger at work. The work environment becomes less threatening and stressful to employees and customers. Employees are likely to feel safer, and the angry employee is often helped as well.

Sources: B. Carey, "The Benefits of Blowing Your Top," *The New York Times,* July 6, 2010, D1; R. Y. Cheung and I. J. Park, "Anger Suppression, Interdependent Self-Construal, and Depression among Asian American and European American College Students," *Cultural Diversity and Ethnic Minority Psychology* 16, no. 4 (2010): 517–25; D. Geddes and L. T. Stickney, "The Trouble with Sanctions: Organizational Responses to Deviant Anger Displays at Work," *Human Relations* 64, no. 2 (2011): 201–30; J. Fairley, "Taking Control of Anger Management," *Workforce Management* (October 2010): 10; L. T. Stickney and D. Geddes, "Positive, Proactive, and Committed: The Surprising Connection Between Good Citizens and Expressed (vs. Suppressed) Anger at Work," *Negotiation and Conflict Management Research* 7, no. 4 (November 2014): 243–64; and J. Whalen, "Angry Outbursts Really Do Hurt Your Health, Doctors Find," *The Wall Street Journal,* March 24, 2015, D1, D4.

CHAPTER REVIEW

> ## MyManagementLab
> Go to **mymanagementlab.com** to complete the problems marked with this icon.

QUESTIONS FOR REVIEW

4-1 How are emotions different from moods?

4-2 What are the sources of emotions and moods?

4-3 What impact does emotional labor have on employees?

4-4 What is affective events theory?

4-5 What is emotional intelligence?

4-6 What are some strategies for emotion regulation?

4-7 How do you apply concepts about emotions and moods to specific OB issues?

EXPERIENTIAL EXERCISE The Happiness Test

Class members begin by taking out a piece of paper and recording the appropriate answer for themselves next to each of the words below.

Indicate to what extent you have felt this way during the past week, using a scale of 1 to 5 where:

1 = very slightly   2 = a little   3 = moderately   4 = quite a bit   5 = extremely or not at all

Items:

__interested	__irritable	__distressed	__alert	__excited
__ashamed	__upset	__inspired	__strong	__nervous
__guilty	__determined	__scared	__attentive	__hostile
__jittery	__enthusiastic	__active	__proud	__afraid

Next, class members write two to three sentences about a memory of the time they were the happiest over the last year. Students should consider: What made you happy? What did the happiness feel like? What did the event make you think about? How long did the feeling of happiness last? Students may then take a few minutes to talk with others about their memories.

Turning over the paper with the happiness ratings, class members now rate themselves a second time on the items above, using the scale. When this is complete, the class is ready to discuss the following questions:

4-8. Looking over your initial ratings, how happy do your responses indicate you've been in the last week? Was this a usual week for you?

4-9. Comparing your two ratings, did the second set change? Did your ratings go up or down? Why do you think they would change?

4-10. The items in the rating represent the PANAS (Positive and Negative Affect Scale). The PANAS happiness scale has been shown to be a strong indicator of happiness. Do you think the test accurately measured your happiness? Why or why not?

ETHICAL DILEMMA Data Mining Emotions

Did anyone ever tell you that you wear your heart on your sleeve? It's a popular expression, but obviously no one is looking at your sleeve to read your emotions. Instead, we tend to study a person's facial expressions to "read" their emotions. Most of us think we're rather good at reading faces, but we couldn't say exactly how we make our interpretations, and we don't know whether they are accurate. But what if we could use technology to know how another person is feeling? Would it be ethical to do so in the workplace and then act on our findings?

Thankfully, technology is not quite ready to do this. Face reading is a complex science. Paul Eckman, a noted psychologist, may be the best human face reader in the world. He has been studying the interpretation of emotions for over 40 years and developed a catalog of over 5,000 muscle movements and their emotional content. His work even spawned a television series called *Lie to Me*, in which the main characters analyzed microexpressions—expressions that occur in the fraction of a second—to assist in corporate and governmental investigations. Using Eckman's Facial Coding System, technology firms like Emotient Inc. have been developing algorithms to match microexpressions to emotions. These organizations are currently looking for patterns of microexpressions that might predict behavior.

Honda, P&G, Coca-Cola, and Unilever have tried the technology to identify the reactions to new products, with mixed results. For one thing, since expressions can change instantly, it is challenging to discern which emotions prevail. A person watching a commercial, for instance, may smile, furrow his brow, and raise his eyebrows all in the space of 30 seconds, indicating expressiveness, confusion, and surprise in turn. Second, it is difficult to know whether a person will act upon these fleeting emotions. Third, the technology might misinterpret the underlying emotions or their causes.

The potential applications of this technology to the workplace include surveillance, gauging reactions to organization announcements, and lie detection. Cameras could be in every meeting room, hallway, and even on employees' computer screens. Emotion monitoring could be an announced event—say, every Monday from 8 to 9 a.m.—or random. Monitoring could be conducted with or without the knowledge of employees; for instance, data on the emotional reactions of every employee in an organizational announcement meeting could be read and interpreted through a camera on the wall.

So far, the most reliable workplace application seems to be using the technology to capture inconsistencies (lying). Even the pioneer of facial emotion recognition, Ekman, said, "I can't control usage [of his technology]. I can only be certain that what I'm providing is at least an accurate depiction of when someone is concealing emotion."

For each usage, there is an ethical consideration and a responsibility, particularly if a manager is going to act on the findings or infer the employee's future behavior. The fact that the technology has not yet fully evolved for workplace application allows time for ethical guidelines to be developed. Foremost among the ethical concerns is privacy. "I can see few things more invasive than trying to record someone's emotions in a database," said privacy advocate Ginger McCall. Concerns about ethical usage are also highly important if managers use the technology to make decisions about employees. For example, what if a manager learns from the software that an employee is unhappy and thus decides to look for a work reassignment for the employee, when actually the employee is unhappy about his spouse? Former U.S. counterterrorism detective Charles Lieberman advises, "Recognize [the technology's] limitations—it can lead you in the right direction but is not definitive."

Questions

4-11. What do you think are the best workplace applications for emotion reading technology?

4-12. One corporation has already developed algorithms to match micro-expressions to emotions. What are the likely underlying implications?

4-13. Assuming you could become better at detecting the real emotions of others from facial expressions, do you think it would help your career? Why or why not?

Sources: Paul Ekman profile, Being Human, http://www.beinghuman.org/mind/paul-ekman, accessed April 17, 2015; E. Dwoskin and E. M. Rusli, "The Technology That Unmasks Your Hidden Emotions," *The Wall Street Journal*, January 29, 2015, B1, B8; and D. Matsumoto and H. S. Hwang, "Reading Facial Expressions of Emotion," Psychological Science Agenda, May 2011, http://www.apa.org/science/about/psa/2011/05/facial-expressions.aspx.

CASE INCIDENT 1   Crybabies

As this chapter has shown, emotions are an inevitable part of people's behavior at work. At the same time, people may not feel comfortable expressing *all* emotions at work. The reason might be that business culture and etiquette remain poorly suited to handling overt emotional displays. The question is: Can organizations become more intelligent about emotional management? Is it ever appropriate to yell, laugh, or cry at work?

Some people are skeptical about the virtues of emotional displays in the workplace. Emotions are automatic, physiological responses to the environment, and as such, they can be difficult to control appropriately. One 22-year-old customer service representative named Laura, who

was the subject of a case study, noted that fear and anger were routinely used as methods to control employees at her workplace, and the employees deeply resented this manipulation and wanted to act out. In another case, the chairman of a major television network made a practice of screaming at employees whenever anything went wrong, leading to hurt feelings and a lack of loyalty to the organization. Like Laura, workers at this organization were hesitant to show their true reactions to these emotional outbursts for fear of being branded as "weak" or "ineffectual." Research indicated that while employees who could regulate their emotions would refrain from acting on their anger, employees who were low in self-regulation and didn't think the boss would do anything were likely to retaliate.

It might seem like these individuals worked in highly emotional workplaces, but in fact only a narrow range of emotions was deemed acceptable at work. Anger appears to be more acceptable than sadness in many organizations, despite the serious maladaptive consequences. Many people find their negative reaction to hearing an angry outburst lasts, making it difficult for them to concentrate at work.

Organizations that recognize and work with emotions effectively may be more creative, satisfying, and productive. For example, Laura noted that if she were able to express her hurt feelings without fear, she would have been much more satisfied with her work. In other words, the problem with Laura's organization was not that emotions were displayed, but that emotional displays were handled poorly. Others note that the use of emotional knowledge—like the ability to read and understand the reactions of others—is crucial for workers, ranging from salespeople and customer service agents all the way to managers and executives. One survey even found that

88 percent of workers felt that being sensitive to the emotions of others is an asset. Management consultant Erika Anderson notes, "Crying at work is transformative and can open the door to change." The question then is: Can organizations take specific steps to become better at allowing emotional displays without opening a Pandora's box of outbursts?

Questions

⭐ **4-14.** Do you think the strategic use and display of emotions serve to protect employees, or does covering your true emotions at work lead to more problems than it solves?

4-15. Have you ever worked where the free expression of emotion was part of the management style? Describe the advantages and disadvantages of this approach from your experience.

4-16. Research shows that the acts of coworkers (37 percent) and management (22 percent) cause more negative emotions for employees than do acts of customers (7 percent). What can Laura's company do to change its emotional climate?

Sources: E. Bernstein, "Why People Have Big Explosions for Very Small Reasons," *The Wall Street Journal,* October 16, 2012, D1, D2; A. Kreamer, "Go Ahead—Cry at Work," *Time,* April 4, 2010, www.time.com; J. S. Lerner and K. Shonk, "How Anger Poisons Decision Making," *Harvard Business Review* (September 2010): 26; H. Lian, D. J. Brown, D. L. Ferris, L. H. Liang, L. M. Keeping, and R. Morrison, "Abusive Supervision and Retaliation: A Self-Control Framework," *Academy of Management Journal* 57, no. 1 (2014): 116–39; S. Shellenbarger, "When the Boss Is a Screamer," *The Wall Street Journal,* August 15, 2012, D1–D2; and J. Perrone and M. H. Vickers, "Emotions as Strategic Game in a Hostile Workplace: An Exemplar Case," *Employee Responsibilities and Rights Journal* 16, no. 3 (2004): 167–78.

CASE INCIDENT 2   Tall Poppy Syndrome

". . . the tall poppy syndrome, where the successful are cut down to the same size as everyone else, quick smart. You're not supposed to stand out for intelligence, achievement, or, worst of all, wealth."
— Peter Hartcher

You may be wondering what poppies have to do with the workplace. It's a reasonable question. The allegory behind tall poppy syndrome goes back centuries, but the emotions of envy and resentment toward strong performers—and the desire to "cut them down to size"—are timeless. So is the reality—evidence indicates that individuals whose performance and status rises above the rest (the tall poppies) sometimes find their careers are decapitated by jealous coworkers (the shorter poppies) who undermine their efforts. Tall poppies are more likely to be victimized by group members, and group members are often pleased if a tall poppy is "brought down" by outsiders.

Tall poppy syndrome seems to be motivated by the observer's personality traits, emotions, and perception of justice. When individuals believe the high achiever is

undeserving of his or her status, or conversely when individuals believe they deserve a higher status than they've been given (called relative deprivation), resentment and envy are heightened. The degree of tall poppy syndrome also seems to relate to the traits of the people who judge their coworkers. People who have lower self-esteem and who do not value power and achievement tend to think high performers are undeserving and should fall. Finally, the general likability of the achiever seems to influence the emotions of observers. If achievers are popular, part of the in-group, work hard, and exhibit high moral character, observers are less likely to feel resentful and wish them ill.

Tall poppy syndrome may be universal, but there are cultural differences. Research has shown that in collectivistic societies like Japan, students in a study were more inclined to cut down a high performer because they resented distinguishing one person more than the rest of the group. In contrast, students from the individualistic

United States were more likely to reward high achievers than were Australian students because the Americans did not feel the same degree of envy.

To the extent that it cuts down those with legitimate achievements, there is nothing good about tall poppy syndrome when high performers are victimized and work performance is limited to a common denominator. Both the high performer and the organization can employ some countermeasures aimed at lessening the emotional reactions of observers. For one, high performers can demonstrate humbleness and humility. This may allow them to boost the performance of coworkers, who then no longer feel resentful of their success. Second, managers can increase work group identity for the coworkers, so they see the success of one individual as the success of the group, rather than as an injustice.

Questions

✪ **4-17.** Have you observed tall poppy syndrome in your workplace or school? Which traits seemed to bother the observers the most?

4-18. In what specific ways do you think high performers can mitigate feelings of envy and resentment? Give examples.

4-19. In what ways do you think managers can foster a group attitude toward success?

Sources: P. Hartcher, "Voters Now at Ease with Rich Pickings," *The Sydney Morning Herald* (July 30, 2013), http://www.smh.com.au/federal-politics/federal-election-2013/voters-now-at-ease-with-rich-pickings-20130729-2quvp.html; N. T. Feather, "Analyzing Relative Deprivation in Relation to Deservingness, Entitlement and Resentment," *Social Justice Research* 28 (2015): 7–26; E. Kim and T. M. Glomb, "Victimization of High Performers: The Roles of Envy and Work Group Identification," *Journal of Applied Psychology* 99, no. 4 (2014): 619–34; and K. Van Valkenburgh, *Investigating Tall Poppy Syndrome in United States Financial Institutions: An Attitude and Values Perspective*, doctoral dissertation, Alliant International University (2013), publication number 3595388.

MyManagementLab

Go to **mymanagementlab.com** for the following Assisted-graded writing questions:

4-20. State and describe the potential efforts that an organization or managers may make to increase the positive emotional states of their employees.

4-21. Concerning Case Incident 2, have you ever been a tall poppy? If so, what reactions from others did you get, and were there consequences for you? If not, why not?

4-22. MyManagementLab Only – comprehensive writing assignment for this chapter.

ENDNOTES

[1]S. G. Barsade and D. E. Gibson, "Why Does Affect Matter in Organizations?" *Academy of Management Perspectives* February, 2007, 36–59.

[2]emotion. Oxford Advanced Learner's Dictionary, http://www.oxforddictionaries.com/us/definition/american_english/emotion, retrieved July 31, 2015.

[3]mood. *The American Heritage Medical Dictionary* (2007), retrieved April 27, 2015 from http://medical-dictionary.thefreedictionary.com/mood.

[4]mood. *Farlex Partner Medical Dictionary* (2012), retrieved April 27, 2015, from http://medical-dictionary.thefreedictionary.com/mood.

[5]See, for example, J. L. Tracy and R. W. Robins, "Emerging Insights into the Nature and Function of Pride," *Current Directions in Psychological Science* 16, no. 3 (2007): 147–50.

[6]R. C. Solomon, "Back to Basics: On the Very Idea of 'Basic Emotions,'" *Journal for the Theory of Social Behaviour* 32, no. 2 (June 2002): 115–44.

[7]P. Ekman, *Emotions Revealed: Recognizing Faces and Feelings to Improve Communication and Emotional Life* (New York: Times Books/Henry Holt and Co., 2003).

[8]M. Gendron, D. Roberson, J. M. van der Vyver, and L. F. Barrett, "Cultural Relativity of Perceiving Emotion from Vocalizations," *Psychological Science* 25, no. 4 (2014): 911–20.

[9]See, for instance, J. Wegge, R. van Dick, G. K. Fisher, et al., "A Test of Basic Assumptions of Affective Events Theory (AET) In Call Center Work," *British Journal of Management* 17, no. 3 (2006): 237–254; and H. M. Weiss and D. J. Beal, "Reflections on Affective Events Theory," in N. M. Ashkanasy, W. J. Zerbe, and C. E. J. Hartel (Eds.), *Effect of Affect in Organizational Settings*, 2005, 1–21.

[10]P. S. Russell and R. Giner-Sorolla, "Bodily Moral Disgust: What It Is, How It Is Different from Anger, and Why It Is an Unreasoned Emotion," *Psychological Bulletin* 139, no. 2 (2013): 328–51.

[11]H. A. Chapman and A. K. Anderson, "Things Rank and Gross in Nature: A Review and Synthesis of Moral Disgust," *Psychological Bulletin* 139, no. 2 (2013): 300–27.

[12]T. Krennenauer, J. B. Asendorpf, and G. Nunner-Winkler, "Moral Emotion Attributions and Personality Traits As Long-Term Predictors of Antisocial Conduct in Early Adulthood: Findings from a 20-Year Longitudinal Study," *International Journal of Behavioral Development*, May 2013, 192–201.

[13]A. Ben-Ze'ev, *The Subtlety of Emotions* (Cambridge, MA: MIT Press, 2000), 94.

[14]T. A. Ito and J. T. Cacioppo, "Variations on a Human Universal: Individual Differences in Positivity Offset and Negativity Bias," *Cognition and Emotion* 19, no. 1 (2005): 1–26.

[15]D. Holman, "Call Centres," in D. Holman, T. D. Wall, C. Clegg, P. Sparrow, and A. Howard (eds.), *The Essentials of the New Work Place: A Guide to the Human Impact of Modern Working Practices* (Chichester, UK: Wiley, 2005), 111–32.

[16]Ben-Ze'ev, *The Subtlety of Emotions*.

[17]S. D. Pressman, M. W. Gallagher, S. J. Lopez, and B. Campos, "Incorporating Culture Into the Study of Affect and Health," *Psychological Science* 25, no. 12 (2014): 2281–83.

[18]K. B. Curhan, T. Simms, H. R. Markus, ... C. D. Ryff, "Just How Bad Negative Affect Is for Your Health Depends on Culture," *Psychological Science* 25, no. 12 (2014): 2277–80.

[19]O. Burkeman, "The Power of Negative Thinking," *The New York Times*, August 5, 2012, 9.

[20]E. Jaffe, "Positively Negative," *Association for Psychological Science*, November 2012, 13–17.

[21]D. Xanthopoulou, A. B. Bakker, E. Demerouti, and W. B. Schaufeli, "A Diary Study on the Happy Worker: How Job Resources Relate to Positive Emotions and Personal Resources," *European Journal of Work and Organizational Psychology* 21, no. 4 (2012): 489–517.

[22]J. R. Spence, D. J. Brown, L. M. Keeping, and H. Lian, "Helpful Today, but Not Tomorrow? Feeling Grateful as a Predictor of Daily Organizational Citizenship Behaviors," *Personnel Psychology* 67 (2014): 705–38.

[23]E. Bernstein, "Feeling Awesome: Studies Find an Emotion Has Myriad Benefits," *The Wall Street Journal*, February 24, 2015, D3.

[24]L. M. Poverny and S. Picascia, "There Is No Crying in Business," Womensmedia.com, October 20, 2009, www.womensmedia.com/new/Crying-at-Work.shtml.

[25]M.-A. Reinhard and N. Schwartz, "The Influence of Affective States on the Process of Lie Detection," *Journal of Experimental Psychology* 18 (2012): 377–89.

[26]K. D. McCaul and A. B. Mullens, "Affect, Thought and Self-Protective Health Behavior: The Case of Worry and Cancer Screening." In J. Suls and K. A. Wallston (eds.), *Social Psychological Foundations of Health and Illness* (Malden, MA: Blackwell, 2003): 161.

[27]J. Haidt, "The New Synthesis in Moral Psychology," *Science* 316 (May 18, 2007): 998, 1002; I. E. de Hooge, R. M. A. Nelissen, S. M. Breugelmans, and M. Zeelenberg, "What Is Moral about Guilt? Acting 'Prosocially' at the Disadvantage of Others," *Journal of Personality and Social Psychology* 100 (2011): 462–73; and C. A. Hutcherson and J. J. Gross, "The Moral Emotions: A Social-Functionalist Account of Anger, Disgust, and Contempt," *Journal of Personality and Social Psychology* 100 (2011): 719–37.

[28]T. Jacobs, "My Morals Are Better Than Yours," *Miller-McCune.com*, March/April 2012, 68–69.

[29]A. Gopnik, "Even Children Get More Outraged at 'Them' and 'Us'," *The Wall Street Journal*, August 30–31, 2014, C2.

[30]N. Angier, "Spite Is Good. Spite Works," *The Wall Street Journal*, April 1, 2014, D1, D3.

[31]D. C. Rubin, R. M. Hoyle, and M. R. Leary, "Differential Predictability of Four Dimensions of Affect Intensity," *Cognition and Emotion* 26 (2012): 25–41.

[32]D. Watson, *Mood and Temperament* (New York: Guilford Press, 2000).

[33]B. P. Hasler, M. S. Mehl, R. R. Bootzin, and S. Vazire, "Preliminary Evidence of Diurnal Rhythms in Everyday Behaviors Associated with Positive Affect," *Journal of Research in Personality* 42 (2008): 1537–46.

[34]Watson, *Mood and Temperament*.

[35]A. A. Stone, J. E. Schwartz, D. Schkade, N. Schwarz, A. Krueger, and D. Kahneman, "A Population Approach to the Study of Emotion: Diurnal Rhythms of a Working Day Examined with the Day Reconstruction Method," *Emotion* 6 (2006): 139–49.

[36]S. A. Golder and M. W. Macy, "Diurnal and Seasonal Mood Vary with Work, Sleep, and Daylength across Diverse Cultures," *Science* 333, (2011): 1878–81.

[37]G. D. Block, "Fixes for Our Out-of Sync Body Clocks," *The Wall Street Journal*, August 16–17, 2014, C3.

[38]S. A. Golder and M. W. Macy, "Diurnal and Seasonal Mood Vary with Work, Sleep, and Daylength across Diverse Cultures."

[39]J. J. A. Denissen, L. Butalid, L. Penke, and M. A. G. van Aken, "The Effects of Weather on Daily Mood: A Multilevel Approach," *Emotion* 8, no. 5 (2008): 662–67; M. C. Keller, B. L. Fredrickson, O. Ybarra, S. Côté, K. Johnson, J. Mikels, A. Conway, and T. Wagner, "A Warm Heart and a Clear Head: The Contingent Effects of Weather on Mood and Cognition," *Psychological Science* 16 (2005): 724–31; and Watson, *Mood and Temperament*.

[40]Watson, *Mood and Temperament*, 100.

[41]J. J. Lee, F. Gino, and B. R. Staats, "Rainmakers: Why Bad Weather Means Good Productivity," *Journal of Applied Psychology* 99, no. 3 (2014): 504–13.

[42]J. A. Fuller, J. M. Stanton, G. G. Fisher, C. Spitzmüller, S. S. Russell, and P. C. Smith, "A Lengthy Look at the Daily Grind: Time Series Analysis of Events, Mood, Stress, and Satisfaction," *Journal of Applied Psychology* 88, no. 6 (December 2003): 1019–33.

[43]G. Schaffer, "What's Good, When, and Why?" *Association for Psychological Science*, November 2012, 27–29.

[44]A. M. Isen, "Positive Affect as a Source of Human Strength," in L. G. Aspinwall and U. Staudinger (eds.), *The Psychology of Human Strengths* (Washington, DC: American Psychological Association, 2003), 179–95.

[45]Watson, *Mood and Temperament*.

[46]*Sleep in America Poll* (Washington, DC: National Sleep Foundation, 2005), www.kintera.org/atf/cf/%7Bf6bf2668-a1b4-4fe8-8d1a-a5d39340d9cb%7D/2005_summary_of_findings.pdf.

[47]D. Meinert, "Sleepless in Seattle ... and Cincinnati and Syracuse," *HR Magazine*, October 2012, 55–57.

[48]E. Bernstein, "Changing the Clocks Wasn't Good for Your Relationships," *The Wall Street Journal*, March 10, 2015, D1, D2.

[49]B. A. Scott and T. A. Judge, "Insomnia, Emotions, and Job Satisfaction: A Multilevel Study," *Journal of Management* 32, no. 5 (2006): 622–45.

[50]E. Bernstein, "Changing the Clocks Wasn't Good for Your Relationships."

[51]B. Arends, "To Sleep, Perchance to Earn," *The Wall Street Journal*, September 20–21, 2014, B8.

[52]S. Reddy, "Husband and Wife Scientists Troll Genetics for Clues to Restful Shut Eye for All," *The Wall Street Journal*, June 10, 2014, D1, D2.

[53]P. R. Giacobbi, H. A. Hausenblas, and N. Frye, "A Naturalistic Assessment of the Relationship between Personality, Daily Life Events, Leisure-Time Exercise, and Mood," *Psychology of Sport & Exercise* 6, no. 1 (January 2005): 67–81.

[54]L. L. Carstensen, M. Pasupathi, M. Ulrich, and J. R. Nesselroade, "Emotional Experience in Everyday Life across the Adult Life Span," *Journal of Personality and Social Psychology* 79, no. 4 (2000): 644–55.

[55]M. G. Gard and A. M. Kring, "Sex Differences in the Time Course of Emotion," *Emotion* 7, no. 2 (2007): 429–37; and M. Jakupcak, K. Salters, K. L. Gratz, and L. Roemer, "Masculinity and Emotionality: An Investigation of Men's Primary and Secondary Emotional Responding," *Sex Roles* 49 (2003): 111–20.

[56]A. H. Fischer, P. M. Rodriguez Mosquera, A. E. M. van Vianen, and A. S. R. Manstead, "Gender and Culture Differences in Emotion," *Emotion* 4 (2004): 84–87.

[57]L. F. Barrett and E. Bliss-Moreau, "She's Emotional. He's Having a Bad Day: Attributional Explanations for Emotion Stereotypes," *Emotion* 9 (2009): 649–58.

[58]D. V. Becker, D. T. Kenrick, S. L. Neuberg, K. C. Blackwell, and D. M. Smith, "The Confounded Nature of Angry Men and Happy Women," *Journal of Personality and Social Psychology* 92 (2007): 179–90.

[59]M. W. Kramer and J. A. Hess, "Communication Rules for the Display of Emotions in Organizational Settings," *Management Communication Quarterly* August 2002, 66–80; and J. M. Diefendorff and E. M. Richard, "Antecedents and Consequences of Emotional Display Rule Perceptions," *Journal of Applied Psychology* April 2003, 284–94.

[60]J. M. Diefendorff and G. J. Greguras, "Contextualizing Emotional Display Rules: Examining the Roles of Targets and Discrete Emotions in Shaping Display Rule Perceptions," *Journal of Management* 35 (2009): 880–98.

[61]P. S. Christoforou and B. E. Ashforth, "Revisiting the Debate on the Relationships between Display Rules and Performance: Considering the Explicitness of Display Rules," *Journal of Applied Psychology* 100, no. 1 (2015): 249–61.

[62]J. D. Kammeyer-Mueller, A. L. Rubenstein, D. M. Long, M. A. Odio, B. R. Buckman, Y. Zhang, and M. D. K. Halvorsen-Ganepola, "A Meta-Analytic Structural Model of Dispositionally Affectivity and Emotional Labor," *Personnel Psychology* 66 (2013): 47–90.

[63]D. T. Wagner, C. M. Barnes, and B. A. Scott, "Driving It Home: How Workplace Emotional Labor Harms Employee Home Life," *Personnel Psychology* 67 (2014): 487–516.

[64]J. D. Kammeyer-Mueller, A. L. Rubenstein, D. M. Long, M. A. Odio, B. R. Buckman, Y. Zhang, and M. D. K. Halvorsen-Ganepola,

"A Meta-Analytic Structural Model of Dispositionally Affectivity and Emotional Labor."

[65] A. A. Grandey, "When 'The Show Must Go On,'" *Academy of Management Journal* 46 (2003): 86–96.

[66] U. R. Hulsheger, H. J. E. Alberts, A. Feinholdt, and J. W. B. Lang, "Benefits of Mindfulness at Work: The Role of Mindfulness in Emotion Regulation, Emotional Exhaustion, and Job Satisfaction," *Journal of Applied Psychology* 98, no. 2 (2013): 310–25.

[67] J. P. Trougakos, D. J. Beal, S. G. Green, and H. M. Weiss, "Making the Break Count: An Episodic Examination of Recovery Activities, Emotional Experiences, and Positive Affective Displays," *Academy of Management Journal* 51 (2008): 131–46.

[68] K. L. Wang and M. Groth, "Buffering the Negative Effects of Employee Surface Acting: The Moderating Role of Employee-Customer Relationship Strength and Personalized Services," *Journal of Applied Psychology* 99, no. 2 (2014): 341–50.

[69] H. Guenter, I. J. H. van Emmerik, and B. Schreurs, "The Negative Effects of Delays in Information Exchange: Looking at Workplace Relationships from an Affective Events Perspective," *Human Resource Management Review* 24, no. 4 (December 2014): 283–98; and F. K. Matta, H. T. Erol-Korkmaz, R. E. Johnson, and P. Biçaksiz, "Significant Work Events and Counterproductive Work Behavior: The Role of Fairness, Emotions, and Emotion Regulation," *Journal of Organizational Behavior* 35, no. 7 (2014): 920–44.

[70] C. D. Fisher, A. Minbashian, N. Beckmann, and R. E. Wood, "Task Appraisals, Emotions, and Performance Goal Orientations," *Journal of Applied Psychology* 98, no. 2 (2013): 364–73.

[71] N. M. Ashkanasy, C. E. J. Hartel, and C. S. Daus, "Diversity and Emotion: The New Frontiers in Organizational Behavior Research," *Journal of Management* 28, no. 3 (2002): 324.

[72] T. Upshur-Lupberger, "Watch Your Mood: A Leadership Lesson," *The Huffington Post*, April 22, 2015, http://www.huffingtonpost.com/terrie-upshurlupberger/watch-your-mood-a-leaders_b_7108648.html.

[73] D. R. Caruso, J. D. Mayer, and P. Salovey, "Emotional Intelligence and Emotional Leadership," in R. E. Riggio, S. E. Murphy, and F. J. Pirozzolo (eds.), *Multiple Intelligences and Leadership* (Mahwah, NJ: Lawrence Erlbaum, 2002), 70; O. J. Sheldon, D. Dunning, and D. R. Ames, "Emotionally Unskilled, Unaware, and Uninterested in Learning More: Reactions to Feedback about Deficits in Emotional Intelligence," *Journal of Applied Psychology* 99, no. 1 (2014): 125–37.

[74] P. Salovey and D. Grewal, "The Science of Emotional Intelligence," *Current Directions in Psychological Science* 14, no. 6 (2005): 281–85; and D. Geddes and R. R. Callister, "Crossing the Line(s): A Dual Threshold Model of Anger in Organizations," *Academy of Management Review* 32, no. 3 (2007): 721–46.

[75] R. Gilkey, R. Caceda, and C. Kilts, "When Emotional Reasoning Trumps IQ," *Harvard Business Review*, September 2010, 27.

[76] M. Seo and L. F. Barrett, "Being Emotional During Decision Making—Good or Bad? An Empirical Investigation," *Academy of Management Journal* 50, no. 4 (2007): 923–40.

[77] F. I. Greenstein, *The Presidential Difference: Leadership Style from FDR to Clinton* (Princeton, NJ: Princeton University Press, 2001).

[78] S. L. Koole, "The Psychology of Emotion Regulation: An Integrative Review," *Cognition and Emotion* 23 (2009): 4–41; H. A. Wadlinger and D. M. Isaacowitz, "Fixing Our Focus: Training Attention to Regulate Emotion," *Personality and Social Psychology Review* 15 (2011): 75–102.

[79] D. H. Kluemper, T. DeGroot, and S. Choi, "Emotion Management Ability: Predicting Task Performance, Citizenship, and Deviance," *Journal of Management*, May 2013, 878–905.

[80] J. V. Wood, S. A. Heimpel, L. A. Manwell, and E. J. Whittington, "This Mood Is Familiar and I Don't Deserve to Feel Better Anyway: Mechanisms Underlying Self-Esteem Differences in Motivation to Repair Sad Moods," *Journal of Personality and Social Psychology* 96 (2009): 363–80.

[81] E. Kim, D. P. Bhave, and T. M. Glomb, "Emotion Regulation in Workgroups: The Roles of Demographic Diversity and Relational Work Context," *Personnel Psychology*, Autumn 2013, 613–44.

[82] Ibid.

[83] S. L. Koole, "The Psychology of Emotion Regulation: An Integrative Review," *Cognition and Emotion* 23 (2009): 4–41.

[84] L. K. Barber, P. G. Bagsby, and D. C. Munz, "Affect Regulation Strategies for Promoting (or Preventing) Flourishing Emotional Health," *Personality and Individual Differences* 49 (2010): 663–66.

[85] J. P. Trougakos, D. J. Beal, B. H. Cheng, I. Hideg, and D. Zweig, "Too Drained to Help: A Resource Depletion Perspective on Daily Interpersonal Citizenship Behaviors," *Journal of Applied Psychology* 100, no. 1 (2015): 227–36.

[86] B. A. Scott, C. M. Barnes, and D. T. Wagner, "Chameleonic or Consistent? A Multilevel Investigation of Emotional Labor Variability and Self-Monitoring," *Academy of Management Journal* 55, no. 4 (2012): 905–26.

[87] U. R. Hülsheger, J. W. B. Lang, A. F. Schewe, and F. R. H. Zijlstra, "When Regulating Emotions at Work Pays Off: A Diary and an Intervention Study on Emotion Regulation and Customer Tips in Service Jobs," *Journal of Applied Psychology*, March 2015, 263–77.

[88] J. L. Jooa and G. Francesca, "Poker-Faced Morality: Concealing Emotions Leads to Utilitarian Decision Making," *Organizational Behavior and Human Decision Processes* 126 (January 2015): 49–64.

[89] Ibid.

[90] T. L. Webb, E. Miles, and P. Sheeran, "Dealing with Feeling: A Meta-Analysis of the Effectiveness of Strategies Derived from the Process Model of Emotion Regulation," *Psychological Bulletin* 138, no. 4 (2012): 775–808; S. Srivastava, M. Tamir, K. M. McGonigal, O. P. John, and J. J. Gross, "The Social Costs of Emotional Suppression: A Prospective Study of the Transition to College," *Journal of Personality and Social Psychology* 96 (2009): 883–97; Y. Liu, L. M. Prati, P. L. Perrewé, and R. A. Brymer, "Individual Differences in Emotion Regulation, Emotional Experiences at Work, and Work-Related Outcomes: A Two-Study Investigation," *Journal of Applied Social Psychology* 40 (2010): 1515–38; and H. A. Wadlinger and D. M. Isaacowitz, "Fixing our Focus: Training Attention to Regulate Emotion," *Personality and Social Psychology Review* 15 (2011): 75–102.

[91] J. J. Gross, E. Halperin, and R. Porat, "Emotion Regulation in Intractable Conflicts," *Current Directions in Psychological Science* 22, no. 6 (2013): 423–29.

[92] A. S. Troy, A. J. Shallcross, and I. B. Mauss, "A Person-by-Person Situation Approach to Emotion Regulation: Cognitive Reappraisal Can Either Help or Hurt, Depending on the Context," *Psychological Science* 24, no. 12 (2013): 2505–14.

[93] E. Halperin, R. Porat, M. Tamir, and J. J. Gross, "Can Emotion Regulation Change Political Attitudes in Intractable Conflicts? From the Laboratory to the Field," *Psychological Science*, January 2013, 106–11.

[94] R. Teper, Z. V. Segal, and M. Inzlicht, "Inside the Mindful Mind: How Mindfulness Enhances Emotion Regulation through Improvements in Executive Control," *Current Directions in Psychological Science* 22, no. 6 (2013): 449–54.

[95] A. S. McCance, C. D. Nye, L. Wang, K. S. Jones, and C. Chiu, "Alleviating the Burden of Emotional Labor: The Role of Social Sharing," *Journal of Management* 39, no. 2 (2013): 392–415.

[96] F. Nils and B. Rimé, "Beyond the Myth of Venting: Social Sharing Modes Determine the Benefits of Emotional Disclosure," *European Journal of Social Psychology* 42 (2012): 672–81; and J. D. Parlamis, "Venting as Emotion Regulation: The Influence of Venting Responses and Respondent Identity on Anger and Emotional Tone," *International Journal of Conflict Management* 23 (2012): 77–96.

[97] S.-C. S. Chi and S.-G. Liang, "When Do Subordinates' Emotion-Regulation Strategies Matter? Abusive Supervision, Subordinates' Emotional Exhaustion, and Work Withdrawal," *Leadership Quarterly*, February 2013, 125–37.

[98] R. H. Humphrey, "How Do Leaders Use Emotional Labor?" *Journal of Organizational Behavior* July 2012, 740–44.

[99] A. M. Grant, "Rocking the Boat but Keeping It Steady: The Role of Emotion Regulation in Employee Voice," *Academy of Management Journal* 56, no. 6 (2013): 1703–23.

[100] S. Reddy, "Walk This Way: Acting Happy Can Make It So," *The Wall Street Journal*, November 18, 2014, D3.

[101] See A. M. Isen, "Positive Affect and Decision Making," in M. Lewis and J. M. Haviland-Jones (eds.), *Handbook of Emotions*, 2nd ed. (New York: Guilford, 2000), 261–77.

[102]N. Nunez, K. Schweitzer, C. A. Chai, and B. Myers, "Negative Emotions Felt During Trial: The Effect of Fear, Anger, and Sadness on Juror Decision Making," *Applied Cognitive Psychology* 29, no. 2 (2015): 200–9.

[103]S. N. Mohanty and D. Suar, "Decision Making Under Uncertainty and Information Processing in Positive and Negative Mood States," *Psychological Reports* 115, no. 1 (2014): 91–105.

[104]S.-C. Chuang and H.-M. Lin, "The Effect of Induced Positive and Negative Emotion and Openness-to-Feeling in Student's Consumer Decision Making," *Journal of Business and Psychology* 22, no. 1 (2007): 65–78.

[105]D. van Knippenberg, H. J. M. Kooij-de Bode, and W. P. van Ginkel, "The Interactive Effects of Mood and Trait Negative Affect in Group Decision Making," *Organization Science* 21, no. 3 (2010): 731–44.

[106]S. Lyubomirsky, L. King, and E. Diener, "The Benefits of Frequent Positive Affect: Does Happiness Lead to Success?" *Psychological Bulletin* 131, no. 6 (2005): 803–55; and M. Baas, C. K. W. De Dreu, and B. A. Nijstad, "A Meta-Analysis of 25 Years of Mood-Creativity Research: Hedonic Tone, Activation, or Regulatory Focus," *Psychological Bulletin* 134 (2008): 779–806.

[107]M. J. Grawitch, D. C. Munz, and E. K. Elliott, "Promoting Creativity in Temporary Problem-Solving Groups: The Effects of Positive Mood and Autonomy in Problem Definition on Idea-Generating Performance," *Group Dynamics* 7, no. 3 (September 2003): 200–13.

[108]S. Lyubomirsky, L. King, and E. Diener, "The Benefits of Frequent Positive Affect: Does Happiness Lead to Success?" *Psychological Bulletin* 131, no. 6 (2005): 803–55.

[109]N. Madjar, G. R. Oldham, and M. G. Pratt, "There's No Place Like Home? The Contributions of Work and Nonwork Creativity Support to Employees' Creative Performance," *Academy of Management Journal* 45, no. 4 (2002): 757–67.

[110]J. M. George and J. Zhou, "Understanding When Bad Moods Foster Creativity and Good Ones Don't: The Role of Context and Clarity of Feelings," *Journal of Applied Psychology* 87, no. 4 (August 2002): 687–97; and J. P. Forgas and J. M. George, "Affective Influences on Judgments and Behavior in Organizations: An Information Processing Perspective," *Organizational Behavior and Human Decision Processes* 86, no. 1 (2001): 3–34.

[111]C. K. W. De Dreu, M. Baas, and B. A. Nijstad, "Hedonic Tone and Activation Level in the Mood-Creativity Link: Toward a Dual Pathway to Creativity Model," *Journal of Personality and Social Psychology* 94, no. 5 (2008): 739–56; J. M. George and J. Zhou, "Dual Tuning in a Supportive Context: Joint Contributions of Positive Mood, Negative Mood, and Supervisory Behaviors to Employee Creativity," *Academy of Management Journal* 50, no. 3 (2007): 605–22.

[112]M. B. Wieth and R. T. Zacks, "Time of Day Effects on Problem Solving: When the Nonoptimal Is Optimal," *Thinking & Reasoning* 17 (2011): 387–401.

[113]A. Erez and A. M. Isen, "The Influence of Positive Affect on the Components of Expectancy Motivation," *Journal of Applied Psychology* 87, no. 6 (2002): 1055–67.

[114]W. Tsai, C.-C. Chen, and H. Liu, "Test of a Model Linking Employee Positive Moods and Task Performance," *Journal of Applied Psychology* 92, no. 6 (2007): 1570–83.

[115]R. Ilies and T. A. Judge, "Goal Regulation across Time: The Effect of Feedback and Affect," *Journal of Applied Psychology* 90, no. 3 (May 2005): 453–67.

[116]J. E. Bono, H. J. Foldes, G. Vinson, and J. P. Muros, "Workplace Emotions: The Role of Supervision and Leadership," *Journal of Applied Psychology* 92, no. 5 (2007): 1357–67.

[117]S. G. Liang and S.-C. S. Chi, "Transformational Leadership and Follower Task Performance: The Role of Susceptibility to Positive Emotions and Follower Positive Emotions," *Journal of Business and Psychology*, March 2013, 17–29.

[118]V. A. Visser, D. van Knippenberg, G. van Kleef, and B. Wisse, "How Leader Displays of Happiness and Sadness Influence Follower Performance: Emotional Contagion and Creative versus Analytical Performance," *Leadership Quarterly*, February 2013, 172–88.

[119]G. A. Van Kleef, C. K. W. De Dreu, and A. S. R. Manstead, "The Interpersonal Effects of Emotions in Negotiations: A Motivated Information Processing Approach," *Journal of Personality and Social Psychology* 87, no. 4 (2004): 510–28; and G. A. Van Kleef, C. K. W. De Dreu, and A. S. R. Manstead, "The Interpersonal Effects of Anger and Happiness in Negotiations," *Journal of Personality and Social Psychology* 86, no. 1 (2004): 57–76.

[120]E. van Dijk, G. A. Van Kleef, W. Steinel, and I. van Beest, "A Social Functional Approach to Emotions in Bargaining: When Communicating Anger Pays and When It Backfires," *Journal of Personality and Social Psychology* 94, no. 4 (2008): 600–14.

[121]K. M. O'Connor and J. A. Arnold, "Distributive Spirals: Negotiation Impasses and the Moderating Role of Disputant Self-Efficacy," *Organizational Behavior and Human Decision Processes* 84, no. 1 (2001): 148–76.

[122]B. Shiv, G. Loewenstein, A. Bechara, H. Damasio, and A. R. Damasio, "Investment Behavior and the Negative Side of Emotion," *Psychological Science* 16, no. 6 (2005): 435–39.

[123]W.-C. Tsai and Y.-M. Huang, "Mechanisms Linking Employee Affective Delivery and Customer Behavioral Intentions," *Journal of Applied Psychology*, October 2002, 1001–08.

[124]See P. B. Barker and A. A. Grandey, "Service with a Smile and Encounter Satisfaction: Emotional Contagion and Appraisal Mechanisms," *Academy of Management Journal* 49, no. 6 (2006): 1229–38; and S. D. Pugh, "Service with a Smile: Emotional Contagion in the Service Encounter," *Academy of Management Journal*, October 2001, 1018–27.

[125]D. E. Rupp and S. Spencer, "When Customers Lash Out: The Effects of Customer Interactional Injustice on Emotional Labor and the Mediating Role of Emotions, *Journal of Applied Psychology* 91, no. 4 (2006): 971–78; and Tsai and Huang, "Mechanisms Linking Employee Affective Delivery and Customer Behavioral Intentions."

[126]R. Ilies and T. A. Judge, "Understanding the Dynamic Relationships among Personality, Mood, and Job Satisfaction: A Field Experience Sampling Study," *Organizational Behavior and Human Decision Processes* 89 (2002): 1119–39.

[127]T. A. Judge and R. Ilies, "Affect and Job Satisfaction: A Study of Their Relationship at Work and at Home," *Journal of Applied Psychology* 89 (2004): 661–73.

[128]Z. Song, M. Foo, and M. A. Uy, "Mood Spillover and Crossover among Dual-Earner Couples: A Cell Phone Event Sampling Study," *Journal of Applied Psychology* 93, no. 2 (2008): 443–52.

[129]See R. J. Bennett and S. L. Robinson, "Development of a Measure of Workplace Deviance," *Journal of Applied Psychology*, June 2000, 349–60; see also P. R. Sackett and C. J. DeVore, "Counterproductive Behaviors at Work," in N. Anderson, D. S. Ones, H. K. Sinangil, and C. Viswesvaran (eds.), *Handbook of Industrial, Work & Organizational Psychology*, vol. 1 (Thousand Oaks, CA: Sage, 2001), 145–64.

[130]K. Lee and N. J. Allen, "Organizational Citizenship Behavior and Workplace Deviance: The Role of Affect and Cognition," *Journal of Applied Psychology* 87, no 1 (2002): 131–42; T. A. Judge, B. A. Scott, and R. Ilies, "Hostility, Job Attitudes, and Workplace Deviance: Test of a Multilevel Mode," *Journal of Applied Psychology* 91, no. 1 (2006): 126–38; and S. Kaplan, J. C. Bradley, J. N. Luchman, and D. Haynes, "On the Role of Positive and Negative Affectivity in Job Performance: A Meta-Analytic Investigation," *Journal of Applied Psychology* 94, no. 1 (2009): 152–76.

[131]S. C. Douglas, C. Kiewitz, M. Martinko, P. Harvey, Y. Kim, and J. U. Chun, "Cognitions, Emotions, and Evaluations: An Elaboration Likelihood Model for Workplace Aggression," *Academy of Management Review* 33, no. 2 (2008): 425–51.

[132]A. K Khan, S. Ouratulain, and J. R. Crawshaw, "The Mediating Role of Discrete Emotions in the Relationship between Injustice and Counterproductive Work Behaviors: A Study in Pakistan," *Journal of Business and Psychology*, March 2013, 49–61.

[133]Kaplan, Bradley, Luchman, and Haynes, "On the Role of Positive and Negative Affectivity in Job Performance: A Meta-Analytic Investigation"; and J. Maiti, "Design for Worksystem Safety Using Employees' Perception about Safety," *Work—A Journal of Prevention Assessment & Rehabilitation* 41 (2012): 3117–22.

[134]J. E. Bono and R. Ilies, "Charisma, Positive Emotions and Mood Contagion," *The Leadership Quarterly* 17, no. 4 (2006): 317–34.

5

Personality and Values

LEARNING OBJECTIVES

After studying this chapter, you should be able to:

5-1 Describe personality, the way it is measured, and the factors that shape it.

5-2 Describe the strengths and weaknesses of the Myers-Briggs Type Indicator (MBTI) personality framework and the Big Five model.

5-3 Discuss how the concepts of core self-evaluation (CSE), self-monitoring, and proactive personality contribute to the understanding of personality.

5-4 Describe how the situation affects whether personality predicts behavior.

5-5 Contrast terminal and instrumental values.

5-6 Describe the differences between person–job fit and person–organization fit.

5-7 Compare Hofstede's five value dimensions and the GLOBE framework.

 MyManagementLab®

⭐ **Chapter Warm Up**

If your professor has chosen to assign this, go to the Assignments section of **mymanagementlab.com** to complete the chapter warm up.

SECRETS OF A SUCCESSFUL ENTREPRENEUR

How does someone become a successful entrepreneur? Some say it's a process of elimination—when people find through trial and error that there is no job that fits them, they create their own; and the more trial and error, the more likely the person will become successful. Others say success comes from a lengthy process of nurturing and mentoring. Still others say it's about having the right stuff—the right personality.

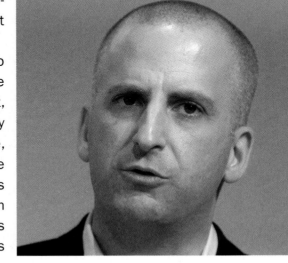

CEO Mark Josephson (shown here) of Bitly, the leading Web link shortening service, would say his success is from all the above: personality, nurturing/mentoring, and experience. First, his entrepreneurial tendencies were apparent from an early age. "I'm competitive, and I want to win. I want us to do more, and I want to push. I find that if you don't ask for more, you're never going to get it." Second, Josephson was nurtured by his father, a successful entrepreneur. "I learned from watching him that you're always working as an entrepreneur. My dad always told us that it doesn't matter who you work for and who signs your check; you work for yourself. That resonated with me."

Third, Josephson learned from personal experience. After holding a number of different jobs, a coach asked him what was most satisfying. He realized, "I was the happiest and most successful and most fulfilled when I was building a team and selling the vision and the passion and the dream. And

I love growing a business and succeeding as a team. Seeing your numbers go up is just incredibly addicting."

Research has found that experience, mentoring, and local social environmental factors can support entrepreneurial tendencies. However, the strongest case can be made for an entrepreneurial personality type. For example, one large study in the United Kingdom, Germany, and the United States indicated entrepreneurs can be categorized by high extraversion, conscientiousness, and openness, and low agreeableness and neuroticism. Another study of female entrepreneurs in Malaysia suggested individuals who rated high on a need to achieve, self-empowerment, and risk-taking are more likely to be successful. Further research in Germany, the Czech Republic, Italy, and Switzerland suggested creative individuals who are adept at overcoming obstacles are more successful at entrepreneurial innovation. Entrepreneurs also have a confident personality. Winston Churchill once said, "Success is the ability to go from one failure to another with no loss of enthusiasm."

Josephson has the personality, nurturing, and experience to succeed. He offers this advice to others who want to capitalize on their entrepreneurial personalities: "In your 20s, work harder than anybody else and put yourself in a position where you're close to the business. Find a mentor within a smaller company, where you can learn the business and work really hard and where your growth is capped only by how good you are and how hard you work." Of course, the most important thing is to discover for yourself, as did Josephson, whether you have the personality of an entrepreneur. While a recent survey revealed that two-thirds of individuals across 38 nations believed entrepreneurs are made, not born, research—and profiles of entrepreneurs like Mark Josephson—suggest there's more to it.

Sources: Bitly.com official website; A. Bryant, "Mark Josephson of Bitly, on Leading with a Compass," *The New York Times*, May 1, 2014, B2; M. Obschonka, E. Schmitt-Rodermund, R. K. Silbereisen, S. D. Gosling, and J. Potter, "The Regional Distribution and Correlates of an Entrepreneurship-Prone Personality Profile in the United States, Germany, and the United Kingdom: A Socioecological Perspective," *Journal of Personality and Social Psychology* (2013): doi: 10.1037/a0032275; D. Olanoff, "Bitly CEO Peter Stern Steps Down from the URL Shortening and Analytics Company," *TC* (March 11, 2013), http://techcrunch.com/2013/03/11/bit-ly-ceo-peter-stern-steps-down-from-the-url-shortening-and-analytics-company/; L. Liyen, T. K. Sin, and J. Kuppusamy, "Effects of Personality Traits on Entrepreneurial Success: A Study on Malaysian Women Entrepreneurs," *Creating Global Competitive Economies: A 360-Degree Approach* (2011): 1–4, 18–23; M. Lukes, "Entrepreneurs as Innovators: A Multi-Country Study on Entrepreneurs' Innovative Behavior," *Prague Economic Papers* 22, 1 (2013): 72–84; M. H. Nierhoff, "Twitter Link Shortening Analysis—Bitly Is the Clear Market Leader," *Quintly* (September 8, 2014), https://www.quintly.com/blog/2014/09/twitter-link-shortening-analysis-bit-ly-clear-market-leader/; J. Rampton, "5 Personality Traits of an Entrepreneur," *Forbes* (April 14, 2014), http://www.forbes.com/sites/johnrampton/2014/04/14/5-personality-traits-of-an-entrepreneur/; and S. Van Anden, "Are True Entrepreneurs Born and Not Made?" *CNBC* (November 18, 2014), http://www.cnbc.com/id/102196386.

As you can see from our opening story, personality plays a major role in Mark Josephson's entrepreneurial success. Personality is indeed a strong factor for many life and work outcomes. We will explain traits such as extraversion, conscientiousness, openness, agreeableness, and neuroticism—the most defined traits—that were discussed in the story. We'll also review frameworks that describe an individual's personality and tendencies.

Personality

5-1 Describe personality, the way it is measured, and the factors that shape it.

Why are some people quiet and passive, while others are loud and aggressive? Are certain personality types better adapted than others for certain jobs? Before we can answer these questions, we need to address a more basic one: What is personality?

What Is Personality?

When we speak of someone's personality, we use many adjectives to describe how they act and seem to think; in fact, participants in a recent study used 624 distinct adjectives to describe people they knew.[1] As organizational behaviorists, however, we organize personality characteristics by overall traits, describing the growth and development of a person's personality.

personality The sum total of ways in which an individual reacts to and interacts with others.

Defining Personality   For our purposes, think of **personality** as the sum of ways in which an individual reacts to and interacts with others. We most often describe personality in terms of the measurable traits a person exhibits.

Measuring Personality   Personality assessments have been increasingly used in diverse organizational settings. In fact, eight of the top 10 U.S. private companies and 57 percent of all large U.S. companies use them,[2] including Xerox, McDonald's, and Lowe's,[3] and schools such as DePaul University have begun to use personality tests in their admissions process.[4] Personality tests are useful in hiring decisions and help managers forecast who is best for a job.[5]

The most common means of measuring personality is through self-report surveys in which individuals evaluate themselves on a series of factors, such as "I worry a lot about the future." In general, when people know their personality scores are going to be used for hiring decisions, they rate themselves as about half a standard deviation more conscientious and emotionally stable than if they are taking the test to learn more about themselves.[6] Another problem is accuracy; a candidate who is in a bad mood when taking the survey may have inaccurate scores.

Research indicates our culture influences the way we rate ourselves. People in individualistic countries trend toward self-enhancement, while people in collectivist countries like Taiwan, China, and South Korea trend toward self-diminishment. Self-enhancement does not appear to harm a person's career in individualistic countries, but it does in collectivist countries, where humility is valued. Interestingly, underrating (self-diminishment) may harm a person's career in both collectivistic and individualistic communities.[7]

Observer-ratings surveys provide an independent assessment of personality. Here, a coworker or another observer does the rating. Though the results of self-reports and observer-ratings surveys are strongly correlated, research suggests observer-ratings surveys predict job success more than self-ratings alone.[8] However, each can tell us something unique about an individual's behavior, so a combination of self-reports and observer reports predicts performance better than any one type of information. The implication is clear: Use both observer

How do I ace the personality test?

I just landed a second-round interview with a great company, and I'm super excited. And super nervous because I've read a few articles about how more and more companies are using personality testing. Do you have tips for how I can put my best foot forward?

— *Lauren*

Dear Lauren:
Congratulations! It's natural for you to want to understand the tests your prospective employer uses. You've probably deduced that it's possible to respond in a favorable manner. For example, if a statement says, "I am always prepared," you know that employers are looking for an applicant who agrees with this statement. You might think responding in the most favorable way possible increases your chances of getting hired, and you might be right.

There are a few caveats, however. First, some companies build in "lie scales" that flag individuals who respond to statements in an extremely favorable manner. It's not always easy to detect them, but clues usually appear across a number of items. If you respond in the most favorable way to a long list of items, then, you might pop up on the lie scale.

Second, high scores on every trait are not desirable for every kind of job. Some employers might be more interested in low scores on a particular trait or pay more attention to a total profile that would be hard to "game." For example, agreeableness is not a good predictor of job performance for jobs that are competitive in nature (sales, coach, trader).

Third, there is an ethical perspective you should consider. How are you going to feel once you are in the organization if you have not represented yourself correctly in the hiring process? What is your general attitude toward lying? How are you going to make sure your behavior fits the traits you tried to portray?

Finally, perhaps you should look at the assessment differently. The organization—and you—should be looking for a good match. If you are not a good match and are hired, you are likely to be unsuccessful, and miserable in the process.

However, if you have a good, honest match, you can arrive for your first day confident and ready for success.

In the end, you might increase your chances of getting hired by responding to a personality test in a favorable manner. However, we still think honesty is the best policy—for you and for your future employer!

Sources: M. N. Bing, H. K. Davison, and J. Smothers, "Item-Level Frame-of-Reference Effects in Personality Testing: An Investigation of Incremental Validity in an Organizational Setting," *International Journal of Selection and Assessment* 22, no. 2 (2014): 165–78; P. R. Sackett and P. T. Walmsley, "Which Personality Attributes Are Most Important in the Workplace?" *Perspectives on Psychological Science* 9, no. 5 (2014): 538–51; and L. Weber, "To Get a Job, New Hires are Put to the Test," *The Wall Street Journal*, April 15, 2015, A1, A10.

The opinions provided here are of the authors only. The authors are not responsible for any errors or omissions, or for the results obtained from the use of this information. In no event will the authors or their related partnerships or corporations thereof, be liable to you or anyone else for any decision made or action taken in reliance on the opinions provided here.

ratings and self-report ratings of personality when making important employment decisions.

Personality Determinants   An early debate centered on whether an individual's personality is the result of heredity or environment. Personality appears to be a result of both; however, research tends to support the importance of heredity over environment.

heredity   Factors determined at conception; one's biological, physiological, and inherent psychological makeup.

Heredity refers to factors determined at conception. Physical stature, facial features, gender, temperament, muscle composition and reflexes, energy level, and biological rhythms are either completely or substantially influenced by parentage—by your biological parents' biological, physiological, and inherent psychological makeup. The heredity approach argues that the ultimate explanation of an individual's personality is the molecular structure of the genes, located on the chromosomes.

This is not to suggest that personality never changes. People's scores on dependability tend to increase over time, as when young adults start families and establish careers. However, strong individual differences in dependability remain; everyone tends to change by about the same amount, so their rank

Energetic, charismatic, decisive, ambitious, adaptable, courageous, and industrious are personality traits used to describe Richard Branson, chairman of Virgin Group. These traits helped Branson, shown here promoting Virgin Trains, build one of the most recognized and respected global brands in travel, entertainment, and lifestyle.
Source: Rex Features/AP Images

order stays roughly the same.[9] Furthermore, personality is more changeable in adolescence and more stable among adults.[10]

Early work on personality tried to identify and label enduring characteristics that describe an individual's behavior, including shy, aggressive, submissive, lazy, ambitious, loyal, and timid. When someone exhibits these characteristics in a large number of situations and they are relatively enduring over time, we call them **personality traits**.[11] The more consistent the characteristic over time, and the more frequently it occurs in diverse situations, the more important the trait is in describing the individual.

personality traits Enduring characteristics that describe an individual's behavior.

✪ **PERSONAL INVENTORY ASSESSMENTS**   PERSONAL INVENTORY ASSESSMENT

Personality Style Indicator

What's your personality? You've probably been wondering as you read this chapter. Take this PIA to obtain some indications of your personality style.

Personality Frameworks

5-2 Describe the strengths and weaknesses of the Myers-Briggs Type Indicator (MBTI) personality framework and the Big Five model.

Throughout history, people have sought to understand what makes individuals behave in myriad ways. Many of our behaviors stem from our personalities, so understanding the components of personality helps us predict behavior. Important theoretical frameworks and assessment tools help us categorize and study the dimensions of personality.

The most widely used and best known personality frameworks are the Myers-Briggs Type Indicator (MBTI) and the Big Five Personality Model. Both describe a person's total personality through exploration of the facets of personality. Other frameworks, such as the Dark Triad, explain certain aspects, but not the total, of an individual's personality. We discuss each below, but let's begin with the dominant frameworks.

Myers-Briggs Type Indicator (MBTI)
A personality test that taps four characteristics and classifies people into one of 16 personality types.

The Myers-Briggs Type Indicator

The **Myers-Briggs Type Indicator (MBTI)** is the most widely used personality-assessment instrument in the world.[12] It is a 100-question personality test that asks people how they usually feel or act in situations. Respondents are classified as extraverted or introverted (E or I), sensing or intuitive (S or N), thinking or feeling (T or F), and judging or perceiving (J or P):

* *Extraverted (E) versus Introverted (I).* Extraverted individuals are outgoing, sociable, and assertive. Introverts are quiet and shy.
* *Sensing (S) versus Intuitive (N).* Sensing types are practical and prefer routine and order, and they focus on details. Intuitives rely on unconscious processes and look at the "big picture."
* *Thinking (T) versus Feeling (F).* Thinking types use reason and logic to handle problems. Feeling types rely on their personal values and emotions.
* *Judging (J) versus Perceiving (P).* Judging types want control and prefer order and structure. Perceiving types are flexible and spontaneous.

The MBTI describes personality types by identifying one trait from each of the four pairs. For example, Introverted/Intuitive/Thinking/Judging people (INTJs) are visionaries with original minds and great drive. They are skeptical, critical, independent, determined, and often stubborn. ENFJs are natural teachers and leaders. They are relational, motivational, intuitive, idealistic, ethical, and kind. ESTJs are organizers. They are realistic, logical, analytical, and decisive, perfect for business or mechanics. The ENTP type is innovative, individualistic, versatile, and attracted to entrepreneurial ideas. This person tends to be resourceful in solving challenging problems but may neglect routine assignments.

According to the Myers & Briggs Foundation, introverts account for over 50 percent of the E/I responses in the U.S. population. Indeed, two of the three most common MBTI types are introverts: ISFJ and ISTJ. ISFJs are nurturing and responsible, and ISTJs are dutiful and logical. The least common types are INFJ (insightful and protective) and ENTJ (focused and decisive).[13]

The MBTI is used in a variety of organizational settings. It is taken by over 2.5 million people each year and 89 of the Fortune 100 companies use it.[14] Evidence is mixed about its validity as a measure of personality; however, most is against it.[15] As Professor Dan Ariely noted about MBTI results, "Next time, just look at the horoscope. It is just as valid and takes less time."[16]

One problem with the MBTI is that the model forces a person into one type or another; that is, you're either introverted or extraverted. There is no in-between. Another problem is with the reliability of the measure: When people retake the assessment, they often receive different results. An additional problem is in the difficulty of interpretation. There are levels of importance for each of the MBTI facets, and separate meanings for certain combinations of facets, all of which require trained interpretation that can leave room for error. Finally, results from the MBTI tend to be unrelated to job performance. The MBTI can thus be a valuable tool for increasing self-awareness and providing career guidance, but because results tend to be unrelated to job performance, managers should consider using the Big Five Personality Model, discussed next, as the personality selection test for job candidates instead.

The Big Five Personality Model

Big Five Model   A personality assessment model that taps five basic dimensions.

The MBTI may lack strong supporting evidence, but an impressive body of research supports the **Big Five Model**, which proposes that five basic dimensions underlie all others and encompass most of the significant variation in human personality.[17] Test scores of these traits do a very good job of predicting how people behave in a variety of real-life situations[18] and remain relatively stable for an individual over time, with some daily variations.[19] These are the Big Five factors:

conscientiousness A personality dimension that describes someone who is responsible, dependable, persistent, and organized.

- *Conscientiousness.* The **conscientiousness** dimension is a measure of reliability. A highly conscientious person is responsible, organized, dependable, and persistent. Those who score low on this dimension are easily distracted, disorganized, and unreliable.

emotional stability A personality dimension that characterizes someone as calm, self-confident, and secure (positive) versus nervous, depressed, and insecure (negative).

- *Emotional stability.* The **emotional stability** dimension taps a person's ability to withstand stress. People with emotional stability tend to be calm, self-confident, and secure. High scorers are more likely to be positive and optimistic and experience fewer negative emotions; they are generally happier than low scorers. Emotional stability is sometimes discussed as its converse, neuroticism. Low scorers (those with high neuroticism) are hypervigilant and vulnerable to the physical and psychological effects of stress. Those with high neuroticism tend to be nervous, anxious, depressed, and insecure.

extraversion A personality dimension describing someone who is sociable, gregarious, and assertive.

- *Extraversion.* The **extraversion** dimension captures our comfort level with relationships. Extraverts tend to be gregarious, assertive, and sociable. They are generally happier and are often ambitious.[20] They experience more positive emotions than do introverts, and they more freely express these feelings. On the other hand, introverts (low extraversion) tend to be more thoughtful, reserved, timid, and quiet.

openness to experience A personality dimension that characterizes someone in terms of imagination, sensitivity, and curiosity.

- *Openness to experience.* The **openness to experience** dimension addresses the range of interests and fascination with novelty. Open people are creative, curious, and artistically sensitive. Those at the low end of the category are conventional and find comfort in the familiar.

agreeableness A personality dimension that describes someone who is good natured, cooperative, and trusting.

- *Agreeableness.* The **agreeableness** dimension refers to an individual's propensity to defer to others. Agreeable people are cooperative, warm, and trusting. You might expect agreeable people to be happier than disagreeable people. They are, but only slightly. When people choose organizational team members, agreeable individuals are usually their first choice. In contrast, people who score low on agreeableness are cold and antagonistic.

General Motors CEO Mary Barra is unusual in that she appears to score high on all of the Big Five personality dimensions. Her unique combination of traits has helped her become the first female CEO of a major global automaker.
Source: Michael Buholzer/Photoshot/Newscom

How Do the Big Five Traits Predict Behavior at Work?   There are many relationships between the Big Five personality dimensions and job performance,[21] and we are learning more about them every day. Let's explore one trait at a time, beginning with the strongest predictor of job performance—conscientiousness.

Conscientiousness at Work   As researchers recently stated, "Personal attributes related to conscientiousness and agreeableness are important for success across many jobs, spanning across low to high levels of job complexity, training, and experience."[22] Employees who score higher in conscientiousness develop higher levels of job knowledge, probably because highly conscientious people learn more (conscientiousness may be related to GPA),[23] and these levels correspond with higher levels of job performance. Conscientious people are also more able to maintain their job performance when faced with abusive supervision, according to a recent study in India.[24]

Conscientiousness is important to overall organizational success. As Exhibit 5-1 shows, a study of the personality scores of 313 CEO candidates in private equity companies (of whom 225 were hired) found conscientiousness— in the form of persistence, attention to detail, and setting high standards—was more important to success than other traits.

Like any trait, conscientiousness has pitfalls. Highly conscientious individuals can prioritize work over family, resulting in more conflict between their work and family roles (termed work-family conflict).[25] They may also become too focused on their own work to help others in the organization,[26] and they don't adapt well to changing contexts. Furthermore, conscientious people may have trouble learning complex skills early in a training process because their focus is on performing well rather than on learning. Finally, they are often less creative, especially artistically.[27]

Conscientiousness is the best predictor of job performance. However, the other Big Five traits are also related to aspects of performance and have other implications for work and for life. Exhibit 5-2 summarizes.

Emotional Stability at Work   Of the Big Five traits, emotional stability is most strongly related to life satisfaction, job satisfaction, and low stress levels. People with high emotional stability can adapt to unexpected or changing demands in the workplace.[28] At the other end of the spectrum, neurotic individuals, who may be unable to cope with these demands, may experience burnout.[29] These people also tend to experience work-family conflict, which can affect work outcomes.[30]

Extraversion at Work   Extraverts perform better in jobs with significant interpersonal interaction. They are socially dominant, "take charge" people who are usually more assertive than introverts.[31] Extraversion is a relatively strong

Exhibit 5-1	Traits That Matter Most to Business Success at Buyout Companies

Most Important	Less Important
Persistence	Strong oral communication
Attention to detail	Teamwork
Efficiency	Flexibility/adaptability
Analytical skills	Enthusiasm
Setting high standards	Listening skills

Exhibit 5-2 — Model of How Big Five Traits Influence OB Criteria

BIG FIVE TRAITS	WHY IS IT RELEVANT?	WHAT DOES IT AFFECT?
Emotional stability	• Less negative thinking and fewer negative emotions • Less hypervigilant	• Higher job and life satisfaction • Lower stress levels
Extraversion	• Better interpersonal skills • Greater social dominance • More emotionally expressive	• Higher performance • Enhanced leadership • Higher job and life satisfaction
Openness	• Increased learning • More creative • More flexible and autonomous	• Training performance • Enhanced leadership • More adaptable to change
Agreeableness	• Better liked • More compliant and conforming	• Higher performance • Lower levels of deviant behavior
Conscientiousness	• Greater effort and persistence • More drive and discipline • Better organized and planning	• Higher performance • Enhanced leadership • Greater longevity

predictor of leadership emergence in groups. Some negatives are that extra-verts are more impulsive than introverts, more likely to be absent from work, and may be more likely than introverts to lie during job interviews.[32]

Openness at Work   Open people are more likely to be effective leaders—and more comfortable with ambiguity. They cope better with organizational change and are more adaptable. While openness isn't related to initial performance on a job, individuals higher in openness are less susceptible to a decline in performance over a longer time period.[33] Open people also experience less work-family conflict.[34]

Agreeableness at Work   Agreeable individuals are better liked than disagreeable people; they tend to do better in interpersonally-oriented jobs such as customer service. They're more compliant and rule abiding, less likely to get into accidents, and more satisfied in their jobs. They also contribute to organizational performance by engaging in organizational citizenship behavior (OCB).[35] Disagreeable people, on the other hand, are more likely to engage in counterproductive work behaviors (CWBs), as are people low in conscientiousness.[36] Low agreeableness also predicts involvement in work accidents.[37] Lastly, agreeableness is associated with lower levels of career success (especially earnings), per haps because highly agreeable people consider themselves less marketable and are less willing to assert themselves.[38]

   In general, the Big Five personality factors appear in almost all cross-cultural studies,[39] including China, Israel, Germany, Japan, Spain, Nigeria, Norway,

Pakistan, and the United States. However, a study of illiterate indigenous people in Bolivia suggested the Big Five framework may be less applicable when studying the personalities of small, remote groups.[40]

> ## ✪ TRY IT!
> If your professor has assigned this, go to the Assignments section of **mymanagementlab.com** to complete the **Simulation:** *Individual Behavior*.

Research indicates the Big Five traits have the most verifiable links to important organizational outcomes, but they are not the only traits a person exhibits, nor the only ones with OB implications. Let's discuss some other traits, known collectively as the Dark Triad.

The Dark Triad

With the exception of neuroticism, the Big Five traits are what we call socially desirable, meaning we would be glad to score high on them. Researchers have found three other socially *undesirable* traits, which we all have in varying degrees, are also relevant to organizational behavior: Machiavellianism, narcissism, and psychopathy. Owing to their negative nature, researchers have labeled these the **Dark Triad**—though they do not always occur together.[41]

The Dark Triad may sound sinister, but these traits are not clinical pathologies hindering everyday functioning. They might be expressed particularly strongly when an individual is under stress and unable to moderate any inappropriate responses. Sustained high levels of dark personality traits can cause individuals to derail their careers and personal lives.[42]

Dark Triad   A constellation of negative personality traits consisting of Machiavellianism, narcissism, and psychopathy.

Machiavellianism   Hao is a young bank manager in Shanghai. He's received three promotions in the past 4 years and makes no apologies for the aggressive tactics he's used. "My name means clever, and that's what I am—I do whatever I have to do to get ahead," he says. Hao would be termed Machiavellian.

The personality characteristic of **Machiavellianism** (often abbreviated *Mach*) is named after Niccolo Machiavelli, who wrote in the sixteenth century on how to gain and use power. An individual high in Machiavellianism is pragmatic, maintains emotional distance, and believes ends can justify means. "If it works, use it" is consistent with a high-Mach perspective. High Machs manipulate more, win more, are persuaded less by others, but persuade others more than do low Machs.[43] They are more likely to act aggressively and engage in CWBs as well. Surprisingly, Machiavellianism does not significantly predict overall job performance.[44] High-Mach employees, by manipulating others to their advantage, win in the short term at a job, but they lose those gains in the long term because they are not well liked.

Machiavellianism   The degree to which an individual is pragmatic, maintains emotional distance, and believes that ends can justify means.

Machiavellianism tendencies may have ethical implications. One study showed high-Mach job seekers were less positively affected by the knowledge that an organization engaged in a high level of corporate social responsibility (CSR),[45] suggesting that high-Mach people may care less about sustainability issues. Another study found Machs' ethical leadership behaviors were less likely to translate into followers' work engagement because followers see through these behaviors and realize it is a case of surface acting.[46]

Narcissism   Sabrina likes to be the center of attention. She often looks at herself in the mirror, has extravagant dreams about her future, and considers herself a person of many talents. Sabrina is a narcissist. The trait is named for the

OB POLL

Does Business School Make You Narcissistic?

Average levels of narcissism by college major and gender

Source: Based on J. W. Westerman, J. Z. Bergman, S. M. Bergman, and J. P. Daly, "Are Universities Creating Millennial Narcissistic Employees? An Empirical Examination of Narcissism in Business Students and Its Implications," *Journal of Management Education* 36 (2012), 5–32.

narcissism The tendency to be arrogant, have a grandiose sense of self-importance, require excessive admiration, and have a sense of entitlement.

Greek myth of Narcissus, a youth so vain and proud he fell in love with his own image. In psychology, **narcissism** describes a person who has a grandiose sense of self-importance, requires excessive admiration, and is arrogant. Narcissists often have fantasies of grand success, a tendency to exploit situations and people, a sense of entitlement, and a lack of empathy.[47] However, narcissists can be hypersensitive and fragile people.[48] They also may experience more anger.[49]

While narcissism seems to have little relationship to job effectiveness or OCB,[50] it is one of the largest predictors of increased CWB in individualistic cultures—but not in collectivist cultures that discourage self-promotion.[51] Narcissists commonly think they are overqualified for their positions.[52] When they receive feedback about their performance, they often tune out information that conflicts with their positive self-perception, but they will work harder if rewards are offered.[53]

On the bright side, narcissists may be more charismatic than others.[54] They also might be found in business more often than in other fields (see OB Poll). They are more likely to be chosen for leadership positions, and medium ratings of narcissism (neither extremely high nor extremely low) are positively correlated with leadership effectiveness.[55] Some evidence suggests that narcissists are more adaptable and make better business decisions than others when the issue is complex.[56] Furthermore, a study of Norwegian bank employees found those scoring high on narcissism enjoyed their work more.[57]

Special attention has been paid to narcissistic CEOs who make more acquisitions, pay higher premiums for those acquisitions, respond less clearly to objective measures of performance, and respond to media praise by making even more acquisitions.[58] Research using data compiled over 100 years has shown that narcissistic CEOs of baseball organizations generate higher levels of manager turnover, although members of external organizations see them as more influential.[59]

Narcissism and its effects are not confined to CEOs or celebrities. Like the effects of Machiavellianism, those of narcissism vary by context, but are evident in all areas of life.

psychopathy The tendency for a lack of concern for others and a lack of guilt or remorse when actions cause harm.

Psychopathy Psychopathy is part of the Dark Triad, but in organizational behavior, it does not connote clinical mental illness. In the OB context, **psychopathy** is defined as a lack of concern for others, and a lack of guilt or remorse when actions cause harm.[60] Measures of psychopathy attempt to assess the motivation to comply with social norms, impulsivity, willingness to use deceit to obtain desired ends, and disregard, that is, lack of empathic concern for others.

The literature is not consistent about whether psychopathy is important to work behavior. One review found little correlation between measures of psychopathy and job performance or CWB. Another found antisocial personality, which is closely related to psychopathy, was positively related to advancement in the organization but unrelated to other aspects of career success and effectiveness.[61] Still other research suggests psychopathy is related to the use of hard influence tactics (threats, manipulation) and bullying work behavior (physical or verbal threatening).[62] The cunning displayed by people who score high on psychopathy may thus help them gain power in an organization but keep them from using it toward healthy ends for themselves or their organizations.

Other Traits   The Dark Triad is a helpful framework for studying the three dominant dark-side traits in current personality research, and researchers are exploring other traits as well. One emerging framework incorporates five additional aberrant compound traits based on the Big Five. First, *antisocial* people are indifferent and callous toward others. They use their extraversion to charm people, but they may be prone to violent CWBs and risky decision making. Second, *borderline* people have low self-esteem and high uncertainty. They are unpredictable in their interactions at work, are inefficient, and may have low job satisfaction. Their low self-esteem can lead to clinical depression.[63] Third, *schizotypal* individuals are eccentric and disorganized. In the workplace, they can be highly creative, although they are susceptible to work stress. Fourth, *obsessive-compulsive* people are perfectionists and can be stubborn, yet they attend to details, carry a strong work ethic, and may be motivated by achievement. Fifth, *avoidant* individuals feel inadequate and hate criticism. They can function only in environments requiring little interaction.[64]

Personality traits have both positive and negative aspects. The degree of each trait—the Big Five, the Dark Triad, and others—in a person, and the combination of traits, matter a great deal to organizational outcomes. It would be easy to make quick management decisions based on our observations, but it is important to keep discussions on personality in perspective and to consider other theories.

Other Personality Attributes Relevant to OB

5-3 Discuss how the concepts of core self-evaluation (CSE), self-monitoring, and proactive personality contribute to the understanding of personality.

As we've discussed, studies of traits have much to offer to the field of OB. Now we'll look at other attributes that are powerful predictors of behavior in organizations: core self-evaluations, self-monitoring, and proactive personality.

Core Self-Evaluations (CSEs)

core self-evaluation (CSE)   Bottom-line conclusions individuals have about their capabilities, competence, and worth as a person.

Core self-evaluations (CSEs) are bottom-line conclusions individuals have about their capabilities, competence, and worth as a person. People who have positive CSEs like themselves and see themselves as effective and in control of their environment. Those with negative CSEs tend to dislike themselves, question their capabilities, and view themselves as powerless over their environment.[65] Recall we discussed in Chapter 3 that CSEs relate to job satisfaction because people who are positive on this trait see more challenge in their jobs and actually attain more complex jobs.

Blake Mycoskie, founder of TOMS Shoes, is confident, capable, and effective. His high core self-evaluations enabled him to realize his dream of a company that uses profits to give shoes to children in need.
Source: Donato Sardella/Getty Images

People with positive CSEs perform better than others because they set more ambitious goals, are more committed to their goals, and persist longer in attempting to reach them. People who have high CSEs provide better customer service, are more popular coworkers, and may have careers that begin on better footing and ascend more rapidly over time.[66] They perform especially well if they feel their work provides meaning and is helpful to others.[67] Therefore, people with high CSEs may thrive in organizations with high corporate social responsibility (CSR).

Self-Monitoring

Zoe is always in trouble at work. Although she's competent, hardworking, and productive, she receives average ratings in performance reviews, and seems to have made a career out of irritating her bosses. Zoe's problem is that she's politically inept and unable to adjust her behavior to fit changing situations. As she said, "I'm true to myself. I don't remake myself to please others." Zoe is a low self-monitor.

self-monitoring A personality trait that measures an individual's ability to adjust his or her behavior to external, situational factors.

Self-monitoring describes an individual's ability to adjust behavior to external, situational factors.[68] High self-monitors show considerable adaptability in adjusting their behavior to external situational factors. They are highly sensitive to external cues and can behave differently in varying situations, sometimes presenting striking contradictions between their public personae and their private selves. Low self-monitors like Zoe can't disguise themselves in that way. They tend to display their true dispositions and attitudes in every situation; hence, there is high behavioral consistency between who they are and what they do.

Evidence indicates high self-monitors pay closer attention to the behavior of others and are more capable of conforming than are low self-monitors.[69] High self-monitor employees show less commitment to their organizations, but receive better performance ratings and are more likely to emerge as leaders.[70] High self-monitor managers tend to be more mobile in their careers, receive

We Can Accurately Judge Individuals' Personalities a Few Seconds after Meeting Them

Surprisingly, this statement appears to be true.

Research indicates that individuals can accurately appraise others' personalities only a few seconds after first meeting them, or sometimes even from a photo. This "zero acquaintance" approach shows that regardless of the way in which people first meet someone, whether in person or online, their first judgments about the other's personality have validity. In one study, for example, individuals were asked to introduce themselves in, on average, 7.4 seconds. Observers' ratings of those individuals' extraversion were significantly correlated with the individuals' self-reported extraversion. Other research suggests personalities can be surmised from online profiles at zero acquaintance as well. One study even found that participants were able to determine the personality traits of individuals at the ends of the trait spectrum from viewing only photos.

Some traits, such as extraversion, are easier to perceive than others upon initial acquaintance, but less obvious traits like self-esteem are also often judged fairly accurately by others. Even being forced to make intuitive, quick judgments rather than deliberate evaluations does not seem to undermine the accuracy of the appraisals.

Situations make a difference in the accuracy of the judgments for some personality traits. For example, although neuroticism is perhaps the most difficult trait to detect accurately, a recent study found neuroticism could be judged much more accurately when the situation made the individual react nervously. This makes sense when you consider that some situations activate or draw out a trait much more readily than others. Almost everybody looks calm when they're about to fall asleep!

The moderate accuracy of "thin slices" helps to explain the moderate validity of employment interviews, which we discuss in Chapter 17. Specifically, research shows that interviewers make up their minds about candidates within 2 minutes of first meeting them. While this is hardly an ideal way to make important employment decisions, the research on personality shows these judgments do have some level of validity. It is important to keep in mind, however, that though we can ascertain people's personalities quickly, we should still keep an open mind and suspend judgment. There is always more to people than first meets the eye.

Sources: A. Beer, "Comparative Personality Judgments: Replication and Extension of Robust Findings in Personality Perception Using an Alternative Method," *Journal of Personality Assessment* 96, no. 6 (2014): 610–18; S. Hirschmueller, B. Egloff, S. C. Schmukle, S. Nestler, and M. D. Back, "Accurate Judgments of Neuroticism at Zero Acquaintance: A Question of Relevance," *Journal of Personality* 83, no. 2 (2015): 221–28; S. Hirschmüller, B. Egloff, S. Nestler, and D. Mitja, "The Dual Lens Model: A Comprehensive Framework for Understanding Self–Other Agreement of Personality Judgments at Zero Acquaintance," *Journal of Personality and Social Psychology* 104 (2013): 335–53; and J. M. Stopfer, B. Egloff, S. Nestler, and M. D. Back, "Personality Expression and Impression Formation in Online Social Networks: An Integrative Approach to Understanding the Processes of Accuracy, Impression Management, and Meta-Accuracy," *European Journal of Personality* 28 (2014): 73–94.

more promotions (both internal and cross-organizational), and are more likely to occupy central positions in organizations.[71]

Proactive Personality

proactive personality People who identify opportunities, show initiative, take action, and persevere until meaningful change occurs.

Did you ever notice that some people actively take the initiative to improve their current circumstances or create new ones? These are proactive personalities.[72] Those with a **proactive personality** identify opportunities, show initiative, take action, and persevere until meaningful change occurs, compared to others who generally react to situations. Proactive individuals have many desirable behaviors that organizations covet. They have higher levels of job performance[73] and do not need much oversight.[74] They are receptive to changes in job demands and thrive when they can informally tailor their jobs to their strengths. Proactive individuals often achieve career success.[75]

Proactive personality may be important for work teams. One study of 95 R&D teams in 33 Chinese companies revealed that teams with high-average levels of proactive personality were more innovative.[76] Proactive individuals are also more likely to exchange information with others in a team, which builds trust relationships.[77] Like other traits, proactive personality is affected by the context. One study of bank branch teams in China found that if a team's leader was not proactive, the benefits of the team's proactivity became dormant or, worse, was suppressed by the leader.[78] In terms of pitfalls, one study of 231 Flemish unemployed individuals found that proactive individuals abandoned their job searches sooner. It may be that proactivity includes stepping back in the face of failure.[79]

In short, while proactive personality may be important to individual and team performance, it has downsides, and its effectiveness may depend on the context. Do you think personality changes in different situations? Let's explore this possibility.

Personality and Situations

5-4 Describe how the situation affects whether personality predicts behavior.

Earlier we discussed how research shows heredity is more important than the environment in developing our personalities. The environment is not irrelevant, though. Some personality traits, such as the Big Five, tend to be effective in almost any environment or situation. For example, research indicates conscientiousness is helpful to the performance of most jobs, and extraversion is related to emergence as a leader in most situations. However, we are learning that the effect of particular traits on organizational behavior depends on the situation. Two theoretical frameworks, situation strength and trait activation, help explain how this works.

Situation Strength Theory

Imagine you are in a meeting with your department. How likely are you to walk out, shout at someone, or turn your back on everyone? Probably highly unlikely. Now imagine working from home. You might work in your pajamas, listen to loud music, or take a catnap.

situation strength theory A theory indicating that the way personality translates into behavior depends on the strength of the situation.

Situation strength theory proposes that the way personality translates into behavior depends on the strength of the situation. By *situation strength*, we mean the degree to which norms, cues, or standards dictate appropriate behavior. Strong situations show us what the right behavior is, pressure us to exhibit it, and discourage the wrong behavior. In weak situations, conversely, "anything goes," and thus we are freer to express our personality in behavior. Thus, personality traits better predict behavior in weak situations than in strong ones.

Researchers have analyzed situation strength in organizations in terms of four elements:[80]

1. **Clarity,** or the degree to which cues about work duties and responsibilities are available and clear. Jobs high in clarity produce strong situations because individuals can readily determine what to do. For example, the job of janitor probably provides higher clarity about each task than the job of nanny.
2. **Consistency,** or the extent to which cues regarding work duties and responsibilities are compatible with one another. Jobs with high consistency represent strong situations because all the cues point toward the same desired behavior. The job of acute care nurse, for example, probably has higher consistency than the job of manager.
3. **Constraints,** or the extent to which individuals' freedom to decide or act is limited by forces outside their control. Jobs with many constraints represent strong situations because an individual has limited individual discretion. Bank examiner, for example, is probably a job with stronger constraints than forest ranger.
4. **Consequences,** or the degree to which decisions or actions have important implications for the organization or its members, clients, supplies, and so on. Jobs with important consequences represent strong situations because the environment is probably heavily structured to guard against mistakes. A surgeon's job, for example, has higher consequences than a foreign-language teacher's.

Some researchers have speculated organizations are, by definition, strong situations because they impose rules, norms, and standards that govern behavior. These constraints are usually appropriate. For example, we would not want an employee to feel free to engage in sexual harassment, follow questionable accounting procedures, or come to work only when the mood strikes.

Beyond the basics, though, it is not always desirable for organizations to create strong situations for their employees for a number of reasons. First, the elements of situation strength are often determined by organization rules and guidelines, which adds some objectivity to them. However, the perception of these rules influences how the person will respond to the situation's strength. For instance, a person who is usually self-directed may view step-by-step instructions (high clarity) for a simple task as a lack of faith in his ability. Another person who is a rule-follower might appreciate the detailed instructions. Their responses (and work attitudes) will reflect their perception of the situation.[81]

Second, jobs with myriad rules and tightly controlled processes can be dull or demotivating. Imagine that all work was executed with an assembly-line approach. Some people may prefer the routine, but many prefer having some variety and freedom. Third, strong situations might suppress the creativity, initiative, and discretion prized by some organizational cultures. One recent study, for example, found that in weak organizational situations, employees were more likely to behave proactively in accordance with their values.[82] Finally, work is increasingly complex and interrelated globally. Creating strong rules to govern diverse systems might be not only difficult but also unwise. In sum, managers need to recognize the role of situation strength in the workplace and find the appropriate balance.

Trait Activation Theory

trait activation theory (TAT) A theory that predicts that some situations, events, or interventions "activate" a trait more than others.

Another important theoretical framework toward understanding personality and situations is **trait activation theory (TAT)**. TAT predicts that some situations, events, or interventions "activate" a trait more than others. Using TAT, we can foresee which jobs suit certain personalities. For example, a commission-based compensation plan would likely activate individual differences because extraverts are more reward-sensitive, than, say, open people. Conversely, in jobs that encourage creativity, differences in openness may better predict desired behavior than differences in extraversion. See Exhibit 5-3 for specific examples.

TAT also applies to personality tendencies. For example, a recent study found people learning online responded differently when their behavior was being electronically monitored. Those who had a high fear of failure had higher apprehension from the monitoring than others and learned significantly less. In this case, a feature of the environment (electronic monitoring) activated a trait (fear of failing), and the combination of the two meant lowered job performance.[83] TAT can also work in a positive way. One study found that, in a supportive environment, everyone behaved prosocially, but in a harsh environment, only people with prosocial tendencies exhibited them.[84]

Together, situation strength and trait activation theories show that the debate over nature versus nurture might best be framed as nature *and* nurture. Not only does each affect behavior, but they interact with one another. Put another way, personality and the situation both affect work behavior, but when the situation is right, the power of personality to predict behavior is even higher.

Having discussed personality traits, we now turn to values. Values are often very specific and describe belief systems rather than behavioral tendencies. Some beliefs or values reflect a person's personality, but we don't always act consistently with our values.

Exhibit 5-3	Trait Activation Theory: Jobs in Which Certain Big Five Traits Are More Relevant				
Detail Orientation Required	Social Skills Required	Competitive Work	Innovation Required	Dealing with Angry People	Time Pressure (Deadlines)
Jobs scoring high (the traits listed here should predict behavior in these jobs)					
Air traffic controller	Clergy	Coach/scout	Actor	Correctional officer	Broadcast news analyst
Accountant	Therapist	Financial manager	Systems analyst	Telemarketer	Editor
Legal secretary	Concierge	Sales representative	Advertising writer	Flight attendant	Airline pilot
Jobs scoring low (the traits listed here should not predict behavior in these jobs)					
Forester	Software engineer	Postal clerk	Court reporter	Composer	Skincare specialist
Masseuse	Pump operator	Historian	Archivist	Biologist	Mathematician
Model	Broadcast technician	Nuclear reactor operator	Medical technician	Statistician	Fitness trainer
Jobs that score high activate these traits (make them more relevant to predicting behavior)					
Conscientiousness (+)	Extraversion (+) Agreeableness (+)	Extraversion (+) Agreeableness (–)	Openness (+)	Extraversion (+) Agreeableness (+) Neuroticism (–)	Conscientiousness (+) Neuroticism (–)

Note: A plus (+) sign means individuals who score high on this trait should do better in this job. A minus (–) sign means individuals who score low on this trait should do better in this job.

Values

5-5   Contrast terminal and instrumental values.

values   Basic convictions that a specific mode of conduct or end-state of existence is personally or socially preferable to an opposite or converse mode of conduct or end-state of existence.

value system   A hierarchy based on a ranking of an individual's values in terms of their intensity.

Is capital punishment right or wrong? Is a desire for power good or bad? The answers to these questions are value-laden.

Values represent basic convictions that "a specific mode of conduct or end-state of existence is personally or socially preferable to an opposite or converse mode of conduct or end-state of existence."[85] Values contain a judgmental element because they carry an individual's ideas about what is right, good, or desirable. They have both content and intensity attributes. The content attribute says a mode of conduct or end-state of existence is *important*. The intensity attribute specifies *how important* it is. When we rank values in terms of intensity, we obtain that person's **value system**. We all have a hierarchy of values according to the relative importance we assign to values such as freedom, pleasure, self-respect, honesty, obedience, and equality.

Values tend to be relatively stable and enduring.[86] Many of the values we hold are established in our early years—by parents, teachers, friends, and others. If we question our values, they may change, but more often they are reinforced. There is also evidence linking personality to values, implying our values may be partly determined by genetically transmitted traits.[87] Open people, for example, may be more politically liberal, whereas conscientious people may place a greater value on safe and ethical conduct. To explore the topic further, we will discuss the importance and organization of values first.

The Importance and Organization of Values

Values lay the foundation for understanding attitudes and motivation, and they influence our perceptions. We enter an organization with preconceived notions of what "ought" and "ought not" to be. These notions contain our interpretations of right and wrong and our preferences for certain behaviors or outcomes. Regardless of whether they clarify or bias our judgment, our values influence our attitudes and behaviors at work.

While values can sometimes augment decision making, at times they can cloud objectivity and rationality.[88] Suppose you enter an organization with the view that allocating pay on the basis of performance is right, while allocating pay on the basis of seniority is wrong. How will you react if you find the organization you've just joined rewards seniority and not performance? You're likely to be disappointed—this can lead to job dissatisfaction and a decision not to exert a high level of effort because "It's probably not going to lead to more money anyway." Would your attitudes and behavior be different if your values aligned with the organization's pay policies? Most likely.

> ✪ **WATCH IT!**
>
> If your professor has assigned this, go to the Assignments section of **mymanagementlab.com** to complete the video exercise titled *Honest Tea: Ethics—Company Mission and Values*.

Terminal versus Instrumental Values

terminal values Desirable end-states of existence; the goals a person would like to achieve during his or her lifetime.

instrumental values Preferable modes of behavior or means of achieving one's terminal values.

How can we organize values? One researcher—Milton Rokeach—argued that we can separate them into two categories. One set, called **terminal values**, refers to desirable end-states. These are the goals a person would like to achieve during a lifetime. The other set, called **instrumental values**, refers to preferable modes of behavior, or means of achieving the terminal values. Some examples of terminal values are prosperity and economic success, freedom, health and well-being, world peace, and meaning in life. Examples of instrumental values are autonomy and self-reliance, personal discipline, kindness, and goal-orientation. Each of us places value on both the ends (terminal values) and the means (instrumental values). A balance between the two is important, as well as an understanding of how to strike this balance.

Generational Values

Researchers have integrated several analyses of work values into groups that attempt to capture the shared views of different cohorts or generations in the U.S. workforce.[89] You will surely be familiar with the labels, some of which are used internationally. It is important to remember that while categories are helpful, they represent trends ... not the beliefs of individuals.

Exhibit 5-4 segments employees by the era during which they entered the workforce. Because most people start work between the ages of 18 and 23, the eras also correlate closely with employee age.

Exhibit 5-4	Dominant Work Values in Today's Workforce		
Cohort	**Entered the Workforce**	**Approximate Current Age**	**Dominant Work Values**
Boomers	1965–1985	50s to 70s	Success, achievement, ambition, dislike of authority; loyalty to career
Xers	1985–2000	Mid-30s to 50s	Work-life balance, team-oriented, dislike of rules; loyalty to relationships
Millennials	2000 to present	To mid-30s	Confident, financial success, self-reliant but team-oriented; loyalty to both self and relationships

Do You Have a Cheating Personality?

Stories of widespread cheating have been on the rise, leading many experts to conclude that the incidence of cheating is increasing. Recently a major cheating scandal was uncovered at Harvard University, where more than 125 students were found to be involved in an organized cheating scheme.

Like most complex behaviors, cheating in school, at work, and in life is a product of the person and the situation. As for the person, research reveals certain traits are related to the tendency to cheat, including high levels of narcissism, low levels of conscientiousness and agreeableness, and high levels of competitiveness.

As for the situation, cheating increases when it is easier to cheat (such as on take-home exams), when there is greater pressure to cheat, and when clear standards are lacking or are not reinforced (such as when an organization's sexual harassment policy is not communicated to employees). How can this research help inform you as a student and employee?

1. **Recognize situations that are more likely to provoke pressures to cheat.** Being explicit and open with yourself about your response to pressure should keep you from succumbing to a moral blind spot, in which you engage in behavior without considering its ethical undertones. Remember that technological advancements in the detection of cheating increase the probability of getting caught.

2. **If you score high on certain traits that predispose you to cheat, this does not mean you are destined to cheat.** However, you should realize that you may be more susceptible and therefore need to avoid certain environments, especially unethical ones.

Sources: M. J. Cooper, and C. Pullig, "I'm Number One! Does Narcissism Impair Ethical Judgment Even for the Highly Religious?" *Journal of Business Ethics* 112 (2013): 167–76; H. E. Hershfield, T. R. Cohen, and L. Thompson, "Short Horizons and Tempting Situations: Lack of Continuity to our Future Selves Leads to Unethical Decision Making and Behavior," *Organizational Behavior and Human Decision Processes* 117 (2012): 298–310; C. H. Hsiao, "Impact of Ethical and Affective Variables on Cheating: Comparison of Undergraduate Students with and without Jobs," *Higher Education* 69, no. 1 (2015): 55–77; M. Carmichael, "Secret E-mail Searches on Harvard Cheating Scandal Broader Than Initially Described," *Boston Globe* (April 2, 2013), www.boston.com/metrodesk/2013/04/02/secret-mail-searches-harvard-cheating-scandal-broader-than-initially-described/MgzOmc8hSk3IgWGjxLwsJP/story.html; P. E. Mudrack, J. M. Bloodgood, and W. H. Turnley, "Some Ethical Implications of Individual Competitiveness," *Journal of Business Ethics* 108 (2012): 347–59; and R. Pérez-Peña, "Studies Find More Students Cheating, with High Achievers No Exception," *The New York Times,* September 8, 2012, A13.

Though it is fascinating to think about generational values, remember these classifications lack solid research support. Early research was plagued by methodological problems that made it difficult to assess whether differences actually exist. Reviews suggest many of the generalizations are either overblown or incorrect.[90] Differences across generations often do not support popular conceptions of how generations differ. For example, the value placed on leisure has increased over generations from the baby boomers to the Millennials and work centrality has declined, but research did not find that Millennials had more altruistic work values.[91] Generational classifications may help us understand our own and other generations better, but we must also appreciate their limits.

Linking an Individual's Personality and Values to the Workplace

5-6 Describe the differences between person–job fit and person–organization fit.

Thirty years ago, organizations were concerned with personality in order to match individuals to specific jobs. That concern has expanded to include how well the individual's personality *and* values match the organization. Why? Because managers today are less interested in an applicant's ability to perform a *specific* job than with his or her *flexibility* to meet changing situations and maintain commitment to the organization. Still, one of the first types of fit managers look for is person–job fit.

Person–Job Fit

personality–job fit theory   A theory that identifies six personality types and proposes that the fit between personality type and occupational environment determines satisfaction and turnover.

The effort to match job requirements with personality characteristics is described by John Holland's **personality–job fit theory**, one of the more proven theories in use internationally.[92] The Vocational Preference Inventory questionnaire contains 160 occupational titles. Respondents indicate which they like or dislike, and their answers form personality profiles. Holland presented six personality types and proposed that satisfaction and the propensity to leave a position depend on how well individuals match their personalities to a job. Exhibit 5-5 describes the six types, their personality characteristics, and examples of the congruent occupations for each.

There are cultural implications for person–job fit that speak to workers' expectations that jobs will be tailored. In individualistic countries where workers expect to be heard and respected by management, increasing person–job fit by tailoring the job to the person increases the individual's job satisfaction. However, in collectivistic countries, person–job fit is a weaker predictor of job satisfaction because people do not expect to have a job tailored to them, so they value person–job fit efforts less. Therefore, managers in collectivistic cultures should not violate cultural norms by designing jobs for individuals; rather they should seek people who will likely thrive in jobs that have already been structured.[93]

Person–Organization Fit

person–organization fit   A theory that people are attracted to and selected by organizations that match their values, and leave when there is not compatibility.

We've noted that researchers have looked at matching people to organizations and jobs. If an organization has a dynamic and changing environment and needs employees able to readily change tasks and move easily between teams, it's more important that employees' personalities fit with the overall organization's culture than with the characteristics of any specific job.

Person–organization fit essentially means people are attracted to and selected by organizations that match their values, and they leave organizations that are not compatible with their personalities.[94] Using the Big Five terminology, for instance, we could expect that extraverts fit well with aggressive and team-oriented cultures, people high on agreeableness match up better with a supportive organizational climate, and highly open people fit better

---

| Exhibit 5-5 | Holland's Typology of Personality and Congruent Occupations |

Type	Personality Characteristics	Congruent Occupations
Realistic: Prefers physical activities that require skill, strength, and coordination	Shy, genuine, persistent, stable, conforming, practical	Mechanic, drill press operator, assembly-line worker, farmer
Investigative: Prefers activities that involve thinking, organizing, and understanding	Analytical, original, curious, independent	Biologist, economist, mathematician, news reporter
Social: Prefers activities that involve helping and developing others	Sociable, friendly, cooperative, understanding	Social worker, teacher, counselor, clinical psychologist
Conventional: Prefers rule-regulated, orderly, and unambiguous activities	Conforming, efficient, practical, unimaginative, inflexible	Accountant, corporate manager, bank teller, file clerk
Enterprising: Prefers verbal activities in which there are opportunities to influence others and attain power	Self-confident, ambitious, energetic, domineering	Lawyer, real estate agent, public relations specialist, small business manager
Artistic: Prefers ambiguous and unsystematic activities that allow creative expression	Imaginative, disorderly, idealistic, emotional, impractical	Painter, musician, writer, interior decorator

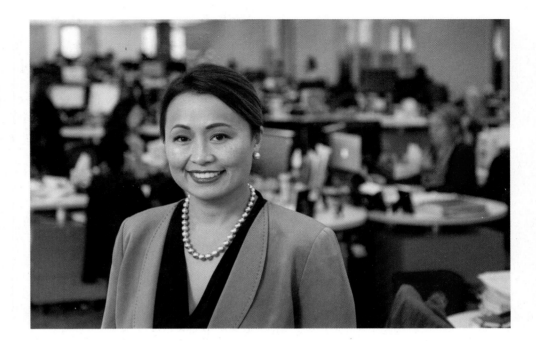

Person–organization fit is important to Sheila Marcelo, founder and CEO of Care.com, an online sitter and care service. Marcelo seeks to hire employees who share the company's culture of helping others and who are passionate about working on projects that achieve Care.com's mission of improving the lives of families and caregivers.

Source: Kelvin Ma/Bloomberg/Getty Images

in organizations that emphasize innovation rather than standardization.[95] Following these guidelines when hiring should yield employees who fit better with the organization's culture, which should, in turn, result in higher employee satisfaction and reduced turnover. Research on person–organization fit has also looked at whether people's values match the organization's culture. A match predicts job satisfaction, commitment to the organization, and low turnover.[96]

It is more important than ever for organizations to manage their image online since job seekers view company websites as part of their pre-application process. Applicants want to see a user-friendly website that provides information about company philosophies and policies. For example, Millennials in particular may react positively when they perceive an organization is committed to work-life balance. The website is so important to the development of perceived person–organization fit that improvements to its style (usability) and substance (policies) can lead to more applicants.[97]

Other Dimensions of Fit

Although person–job fit and person–organization fit are considered the most salient dimensions for workplace outcomes, other avenues of fit are worth examining. These include *person–group fit* and *person–supervisor fit*. Person–group fit is important in team settings, where the dynamics of team interactions significantly affect work outcomes. Person–supervisor fit has become an important area of research since poor fit in this dimension can lead to lower job satisfaction and reduced performance.

All dimensions of fit are sometimes broadly referred to as person–environment fit. Each dimension can predict work attitudes, which are partially based on culture. A recent meta-analysis of person–environment fit in East Asia, Europe, and North America suggested the dimensions of person–organization and person–job fit are the strongest predictors of positive work attitudes and performance in North America. These dimensions are important to a lesser degree in Europe, and they are the least important in East Asia.[98]

Cultural Values

5-7 Compare Hofstede's five value dimensions and the GLOBE framework.

Unlike personality, which is largely genetically determined, values are learned. They are passed down through generations and vary by cultures. As researchers have sought to understand cultural value differences, two important frameworks that have emerged are from Geert Hofstede and the GLOBE studies.

Hofstede's Framework

One of the most widely referenced approaches for analyzing variations among cultures was done in the late 1970s by Geert Hofstede.[99] Hofstede surveyed more than 116,000 IBM employees in 40 countries about their work-related values and found managers and employees varied on five value dimensions of national culture:

power distance A national culture attribute that describes the extent to which a society accepts that power in institutions and organizations is distributed unequally.

individualism A national culture attribute that describes the degree to which people prefer to act as individuals rather than as members of groups.

collectivism A national culture attribute that describes a tight social framework in which people expect others in groups of which they are a part to look after them and protect them.

masculinity A national culture attribute that describes the extent to which the culture favors traditional masculine work roles of achievement, power, and control. Societal values are characterized by assertiveness and materialism.

femininity A national culture attribute that indicates little differentiation between male and female roles; a high rating indicates that women are treated as the equals of men in all aspects of the society.

uncertainty avoidance A national culture attribute that describes the extent to which a society feels threatened by uncertain and ambiguous situations and tries to avoid them.

long-term orientation A national culture attribute that emphasizes the future, thrift, and persistence.

short-term orientation A national culture attribute that emphasizes the present and accepts change.

- *Power distance.* **Power distance** describes the degree to which people in a country accept that power in institutions and organizations is distributed unequally. A high rating on power distance means large inequalities of power and wealth exist and are tolerated in the culture, as in a class or caste system that discourages upward mobility. A low power distance rating characterizes societies that stress equality and opportunity.
- *Individualism versus collectivism.* **Individualism** is the degree to which people prefer to act as individuals rather than as members of groups and believe in an individual's rights above all else. **Collectivism** emphasizes a tight social framework in which people expect others in groups of which they are a part to look after them and protect them.
- *Masculinity versus femininity.* Hofstede's construct of **masculinity** is the degree to which the culture favors traditional masculine roles such as achievement, power, and control, as opposed to viewing men and women as equals. A high masculinity rating indicates the culture has separate roles for men and women, with men dominating the society. A high **femininity** rating means the culture sees little differentiation between male and female roles and treats women as the equals of men in all respects.
- *Uncertainty avoidance.* The degree to which people in a country prefer structured over unstructured situations defines their **uncertainty avoidance**. In cultures scoring high on uncertainty avoidance, people have increased anxiety about uncertainty and ambiguity and use laws and controls to reduce uncertainty. People in cultures low on uncertainty avoidance are more accepting of ambiguity, are less rule oriented, take more risks, and more readily accept change.
- *Long-term versus short-term orientation.* This typology measures a society's devotion to traditional values. People in a culture with **long-term orientation** look to the future and value thrift, persistence, and tradition. In a **short-term orientation**, people value the here and now; they also accept change more readily and don't see commitments as impediments to change.

How do different countries score on Hofstede's dimensions? Exhibit 5-6 shows the ratings of the countries for which data are available. For example, power distance is higher in Malaysia than in any other country. The United States is very individualistic; in fact, it's the most individualistic nation of all (closely followed by Australia and Great Britain). Guatemala is the most collectivistic nation. The country with the highest masculinity rank by far is Japan, and

Exhibit 5-6	Hofstede's Cultural Values by Nation

Country	Power Distance		Individualism versus Collectivism		Masculinity versus Femininity		Uncertainty Avoidance		Long- versus Short-Term Orientation	
	Index	Rank	Index	Rank	Index	Rank	Index	Rank	Index	Rank
Argentina	49	35–36	46	22–23	56	20–21	86	10–15		
Australia	36	41	90	2	61	16	51	37	31	22–24
Austria	11	53	55	18	79	2	70	24–25	31	22–24
Belgium	65	20	75	8	54	22	94	5–6	38	18
Brazil	69	14	38	26–27	49	27	76	21–22	65	6
Canada	39	39	80	4–5	52	24	48	41–42	23	30
Chile	63	24–25	23	38	28	46	86	10–15		
Colombia	67	17	13	49	64	11–12	80	20		
Costa Rica	35	42–44	15	46	21	48–49	86	10–15		
Denmark	18	51	74	9	16	50	23	51	46	10
Ecuador	78	8–9	8	52	63	13–14	67	28		
El Salvador	66	18–19	19	42	40	40	94	5–6		
Finland	33	46	63	17	26	47	59	31–32	41	14
France	68	15–16	71	10–11	43	35–36	86	10–15	39	17
Germany	35	42–44	67	15	66	9–10	65	29	31	22–24
Great Britain	35	42–44	89	3	66	9–10	35	47–48	25	28–29
Greece	60	27–28	35	30	57	18–19	112	1		
Guatemala	95	2–3	6	53	37	43	101	3		
Hong Kong	68	15–16	25	37	57	18–19	29	49–50	96	2
India	77	10–11	48	21	56	20–21	40	45	61	7
Indonesia	78	8–9	14	47–48	46	30–31	48	41–42		
Iran	58	29–30	41	24	43	35–36	59	31–32		
Ireland	28	49	70	12	68	7–8	35	47–48	43	13
Israel	13	52	54	19	47	29	81	19		
Italy	50	34	76	7	70	4–5	75	23	34	19
Jamaica	45	37	39	25	68	7–8	13	52		
Japan	54	33	46	22–23	95	1	92	7	80	4
Korea (South)	60	27–28	18	43	39	41	85	16–17	75	5
Malaysia	104	1	26	36	50	25–26	36	46		
Mexico	81	5–6	30	32	69	6	82	18		
The Netherlands	38	40	80	4–5	14	51	53	35	44	11–12
New Zealand	22	50	79	6	58	17	49	39–40	30	25–26
Norway	31	47–48	69	13	8	52	50	38	44	11–12
Pakistan	55	32	14	47–48	50	25–26	70	24–25	0	34
Panama	95	2–3	11	51	44	34	86	10–15		
Peru	64	21–23	16	45	42	37–38	87	9		
Philippines	94	4	32	31	64	11–12	44	44	19	31–32
Portugal	63	24–25	27	33–35	31	45	104	2	30	25–26
Singapore	74	13	20	39–41	48	28	8	53	48	9
South Africa	49	35–36	65	16	63	13–14	49	39–40		
Spain	57	31	51	20	42	37–38	86	10–15	19	31–32
Sweden	31	47–48	71	10–11	5	53	29	49–50	33	20
Switzerland	34	45	68	14	70	4–5	58	33	40	15–16
Taiwan	58	29–30	17	44	45	32–33	69	26	87	3
Thailand	64	21–23	20	39–41	34	44	64	30	56	8
Turkey	66	18–19	37	28	45	32–33	85	16–17		
United States	40	38	91	1	62	15	46	43	29	27
Uruguay	61	26	36	29	38	42	100	4		
Venezuela	81	5–6	12	50	73	3	76	21–22		
Yugoslavia	76	12	27	33–35	21	48–49	88	8		
Regions:										
Arab countries	80	7	38	26–27	53	23	68	27		
East Africa	64	21–23	27	33–35	41	39	52	36	25	28–29
West Africa	77	10–11	20	39–41	46	30–31	54	34	16	33

Scores range from 0 = extremely low on dimension to 100 = extremely high.

Note: 1 = highest rank. LTO ranks: 1 = China; 15–16 = Bangladesh; 21 = Poland; 34 = lowest.

Source: Geert Hofstede, Gert Jan Hofstede, Michael Minkov, "Cultures and Organizations, Software of the Mind", Third Revised Edition, McGrawHill 2010, ISBN 0-07-166418-1. © Geert Hofstede B.V. quoted with permission.

According to Hofstede's framework, many Asian countries have a strong collectivist culture that fosters a team-based approach to work. These employees in a department store outlet in Busan, South Korea, are likely to consider the success of their team as more important than personal success on the job.
Source: Yonhap News/YNA/Newscom

the country with the highest femininity rank is Sweden. Greece scores the highest in uncertainty avoidance, while Singapore scores the lowest. Hong Kong has one of the longest-term orientations; Pakistan has the shortest-term orientation.

Research across 598 studies with more than 200,000 respondents has investigated the relationship of Hofstede's cultural values and a variety of organizational criteria at both the individual and national level of analysis.[100] Overall, the five original culture dimensions were found to be equally strong predictors of relevant outcomes. The researchers also found measuring individual scores resulted in much better predictions of most outcomes than assigning all people in a country the same cultural values. In sum, this research suggests Hofstede's framework may be a valuable way of thinking about differences among people, but we should be cautious about assuming all people from a country have the same values.

The GLOBE Framework

Begun in 1993, the Global Leadership and Organizational Behavior Effectiveness (GLOBE) research program is an ongoing cross-cultural investigation of leadership and national culture. Using data from 825 organizations in 62 countries, the GLOBE team identified nine dimensions on which national cultures differ.[101] Some dimensions—such as power distance, individualism/collectivism, uncertainty avoidance, gender differentiation (similar to masculinity versus femininity), and future orientation (similar to long-term versus short-term orientation)—resemble the Hofstede dimensions. The main difference is that the GLOBE framework added dimensions, such as humane orientation (the degree to which a society rewards individuals for being altruistic, generous, and kind to others) and performance orientation (the degree to which a society encourages and rewards group members for performance improvement and excellence).

Comparison of Hofstede's Framework and the GLOBE Framework

Which framework is better, Hofstede's or the GLOBE? That's hard to say, and each has its supporters. We give more emphasis to Hofstede's dimensions here because they have stood the test of time and the GLOBE study confirmed them. For example, a review of the organizational commitment literature shows both the Hofstede and GLOBE individualism/collectivism dimensions operated similarly. Specifically, both frameworks showed organizational commitment tends to be lower in individualistic countries.[102] Both frameworks have a great deal in common, and each has something to offer.

Summary

Personality matters to organizational behavior. It does not explain all behavior, but it sets the stage. Emerging theory and research reveal how personality matters more in some situations than others. The Big Five has been a particularly important advancement, though the Dark Triad and other traits matter as well. Every trait has advantages and disadvantages for work behavior, and there is no perfect constellation of traits that is ideal in every situation. Personality can help you to understand why people (including yourself!) act, think, and feel the way we do, and the astute manager can put that understanding to use by taking care to place employees in situations that best fit their personalities.

Values often underlie and explain attitudes, behaviors, and perceptions. Values tend to vary internationally along dimensions that can predict organizational outcomes; however, an individual may or may not hold values that are consistent with the values of the national culture.

Implications for Managers

- Consider screening job candidates for conscientiousness—and the other Big Five traits, depending on the criteria your organization finds most important. Other aspects, such as core self-evaluation or narcissism, may be relevant in certain situations.
- Although the MBTI has faults, you can use it in training and development to help employees better understand each other, open up communication in workgroups, and possibly reduce conflicts.
- Evaluate jobs, workgroups, and your organization to determine the optimal personality fit.
- Take into account situational factors when evaluating observable personality traits, and lower the situation strength to better ascertain personality characteristics.
- The more you consider people's different cultures, the better you will be able to determine their work behavior and create a positive organizational climate that performs well.

Millennials Are More Narcissistic Than Their Parents

POINT

Millennials have some great virtues: as a group, they are technologically savvy, socially tolerant, and engaged. They value their quality of life as equal to their career, seeking a balance between home and work. In these ways, Millennials surpass their baby boomer parents, who are less technologically adept, less tolerant, more localized, and who have a history of striving to get ahead at all costs. However, Millennials have a big Achilles' heel—they are more narcissistic.

Several large-scale, longitudinal studies found Millennials are more likely than baby boomers to have seemingly inflated views of themselves, and psychologists have found narcissism has been growing since the early 1980s. More Millennials rate themselves as above average on attributes such as academic ability, leadership, public speaking ability, and writing ability. Millennials are also more likely to agree they would be "very good" spouses (56 percent, compared to 37 percent among 1980 graduates), parents (54 percent; 36 percent for 1980 graduates), and workers (65 percent; 49 percent for 1980 graduates).

Cliff Zukin, a senior faculty fellow at Rutgers University, believes the reason is in the childhood upbringing of Millennials. "This is the most affirmed generation in history," he said. "They were raised believing they could do anything they wanted to, and that they have skills and talents to bring to a job setting." Jean M. Twenge, author of *Generation Me*, agrees. "People were not saying, 'Believe in yourself' and 'You are special' in the '60s."

Narcissism is bad for society, and particularly bad for the work place. "[Narcissists] tend to be very self-absorbed; they value fun in their personal and their work life," one administrator said. "I can't expect them to work on one project for any amount of time without getting bored."

COUNTERPOINT

Wasn't "The Me Generation" generations ago? Honestly, every generation thinks they are better than the ones that come after! "You can find complaints [about the younger generation] in Greek literature, in the Bible," Professor Cappelli of the Wharton School observed. "There's no evidence Millennials are different. They're just younger." While Millennials are the 20-somethings of today, what *is* universally true is that young people share certain characteristics...*because* they are young.

A recent study shows the similarity between how Millennials and baby boomers thought about themselves at the same stage of life. As college freshmen, 71 percent of Millennials thought they were above average academically, and 63 percent of baby boomers thought the same thing when they were college freshmen. Similarly, 77 percent of Millennials believed they were above average in the drive to achieve, versus 68 percent for baby boomers. In other words, "Every generation is Generation Me."

In some ways, Millennials may be less narcissistic than baby boomers today. As one manager observed, "[Millennials] don't have that line between work and home that used to exist, so they're doing Facebook for the company at night, on Saturday or Sunday. We get incredible productivity out of them." Millennials also may be more altruistic. For example, 29 percent of Millennials believe individuals have a responsibility to remain involved in issues and causes for the good of all, while only 24 percent of baby boomers feel the same level of responsibility.

Rather than comparing different generations, it is more accurate to compare people at one life stage with others at the same life stage. Research supports that people in their 20s tend to be more narcissistic than people in their 50s. Since Millennials are in their 20s, and many of their parents are in their 50s, Millennials are no more narcissistic than baby boomers were in their youth.

Sources: J. M. Twenge, W. K. Campbell, and E. C. Freeman, "Generational Differences in Young Adults' Life Goals, Concern for Others, and Civic Orientation, 1966–2009," *Journal of Personality and Social Psychology* 102 (2012): 1045–62; M. Hartman, "Millennials at Work: Young and Callow, Like Their Parents," *The New York Times,* March 25, 2014, F4; J. Jin and J. Rounds, "Stability and Change in Work Values: A Meta-Analysis of Longitudinal Studies," *Journal of Vocational Behavior* 80 (2012): 326–39; C. Lourosa-Ricardo, "How America Gives," *The Wall Street Journal,* December 15, 2014, R3; "Millennials Rule," *The New York Times Education Life,* April 12, 2015, 4; G. Ruffenach, "A Generational Gap: Giving to Charity," *The Wall Street Journal,* January 20, 2015, R4; and S. W. Lester, R. L. Standifer, N. J. Schultz, and J. M. Windsor, "Actual versus Perceived Generational Differences at Work: An Empirical Examination," *Journal of Leadership & Organizational Studies* 19 (2012): 341–54.

CHAPTER REVIEW

MyManagementLab

Go to **mymanagementlab.com** to complete the problems marked with this icon. ✪

QUESTIONS FOR REVIEW

5-1 What is personality? How do we typically measure it? What factors determine personality?

5-2 What are the strengths and weaknesses of the Myers-Briggs Type Indicator (MBTI) and the Big Five personality model?

5-3 How do the concepts of core self-evaluation (CSE), self-monitoring, and proactive personality help us to understand personality?

5-4 How does the situation or environment affect the degree to which personality predicts behavior?

5-5 What is the difference between terminal and instrumental values?

5-6 What are the differences between person–job fit and person–organization fit?

5-7 How do Hofstede's five value dimensions and the GLOBE framework differ?

EXPERIENTIAL EXERCISE Your Best Self

The object of this game is to end up with the labels that best represent each person's values. The following rows represent 11 rounds of play. Break the class into groups of four students (if the number of students is not divisible by four, then we suggest three). Play begins with the person in the group whose name comes first in alphabetical order. That student picks one of the values in round one that represents him- or herself, crosses it off this list, and writes it down on a piece of paper. Values can be used by only one person at a time. Moving clockwise, the next person does the same, and so forth for round one until all the values have been taken.

For round two, the first player can either add a second value from the round two row, or take a value from one of the other players by adding it to his or her list while the other player crosses off the value. The player whose value has been taken selects two new values from the one and two rows. Play proceeds clockwise.

The rest of the rounds continue the same way, with a new row available for each round. At the end of the rounds, students rank the importance to them of the values they have accumulated.

1. Freedom	Integrity	Spirituality	Respect
2. Loyalty	Achievement	Fidelity	Exploration
3. Affection	Challenge	Serenity	Justice
4. Charity	Discipline	Security	Mastery
5. Prudence	Diversity	Kindness	Duty
6. Wisdom	Inspiration	Harmony	Joy
7. Depth	Compassion	Excellence	Tolerance
8. Honesty	Success	Growth	Modesty
9. Courage	Dedication	Empathy	Openness
10. Faith	Service	Playfulness	Learning
11. Discovery	Independence	Humor	Understanding

Questions for class discussion:

5-8. What are your top three values? How well do they represent you? Did you feel pressure to choose values that might seem most socially acceptable?

5-9. Is there a value you would claim for yourself that is not on the list?

5-10. It is often argued that values are meaningful only when they conflict and we have to choose between them. Do you think that was one of the objectives of this game? Do you agree with the premise?

ETHICAL DILEMMA   Personal Values and Ethics in the Workplace

Sipho Dlamini was born in a small rural village in Swaziland. He spent his childhood years looking after his family's livestock. The community upheld high values, such as honesty and respect, but the people were desperately poor. He realized that he would have to go to South Africa and apply for a job at a gold mine.

As a young man Sipho left his village in the mountains and took on the difficult job of getting to South Africa. He went in search of one of his distant family members who was working for a gold mine near Johannesburg. He managed to find his relative, who was engaged as a personnel assistant. Sipho's relative managed to find him a job as a general mine worker and accommodation in one of the mine hostels. Sipho was dedicated to his work, and time passed quickly. Every month, he forwarded most of his wages to his family in Swaziland.

One day Sipho's family member called him into his office and informed him that he was due for promotion. He also told Sipho that he would be required to pay him R500.00 (about $60) for his "efforts." This arrangement seemed strange to Sipho since he knew that it was not in line with company procedures. When Sipho asked about this, the personnel assistant replied that he had the authority to do so and that Sipho would not be promoted if

he did not pay the R500.00. Sipho returned to his room and wrestled in his mind that night with the options before him. He had grown up with strong personal values that included honesty and hard work, but his family needed the extra income. What was he to do?

After a restless night, he returned the next day to the personnel assistant's office and handed him the R500.00. He was immediately promoted, but he returned to his room with a troubled mind. A few weeks later, the personnel assistant was reported and investigated for fraudulent behavior. He was suspended from work, and the investigation revealed all his corrupt activities. The record he had kept on all employees who paid bribes to him was also found. All employees on this list were called in and charged with fraud. Sipho's name was on the list, and he was found guilty and dismissed from the service of the company along with all the others.

Questions

5-11. What should Sipho have done differently?

5-12. In what way could the mine management have provided support to him prior to his wrongful act?

5-13. How would you have acted had you been in a similar situation?

Sources: S. Collins, "Millennials Take On the Workforce," *SHIFT Magazine* (May 3, 2011), May 12, 2011, www.smudailymustang.com; and R. Wartzman, "Generation Mobility," *Los Angeles Times* (July 16, 2010), downloaded May 12, 2011, from www.dailytidings.com/.

CASE INCIDENT 1   On the Costs of Being Nice

Agreeable people tend to be kinder and more accommodating in social situations, which you might think could add to their success in life. However, one downside of agreeableness is potentially lower earnings. Research has shown the answer to this and other puzzles; some of them may surprise you.

First, and perhaps most obvious, agreeable individuals are less adept at a type of negotiation called distributive bargaining. As we discuss in Chapter 14, distributive bargaining is less about creating win–win solutions and more about claiming as large a share of the pie as possible. Because salary negotiations are generally distributive, agreeable individuals often negotiate lower salaries for themselves than they might otherwise get.

Second, agreeable individuals may choose to work in industries or occupations that earn lower salaries, such

as the "caring" industries of education and health care. Agreeable individuals are also attracted to jobs both in the public sector and in nonprofit organizations. Third, the earnings of agreeable individuals also may be reduced by their lower drive to emerge as leaders and by their tendency to engage in lower degrees of proactive task behaviors, such as coming up with ways to increase organizational effectiveness.

While being agreeable certainly doesn't appear to help your paycheck, it does provide other benefits. Agreeable individuals are better liked at work, more likely to help others at work, and generally happier at work and in life.

Nice guys and gals may finish last in terms of earnings, but wages do not define a happy life, and on that front, agreeable individuals have the advantage.

Questions

⭐ **5-14.** Do you think employers must choose between agreeable employees and top performers? Why or why not?

5-15. Research seems to suggest that agreeable individuals make fairly poor managers and decision makers. Why might this be the case? What are the implications for organizations? How does this affect their earning potential?

5-16. Agreeable individuals tend to be attracted to specific types of occupations and follow different career paths. What has research indicated in this respect? What are the implications and where are you more likely to find agreeable employees?

Sources: T. A. Judge, B. A. Livingston, and C. Hurst, "Do Nice Guys—and Gals—Really Finish Last? The Joint Effects of Sex and Agreeableness on Income," *Journal of Personality and Social Psychology* 102 (2012): 390–407; J. B. Bernerth, S. G. Taylor, H. J. Walker, and D. S. Whitman, "An Empirical Investigation of Dispositional Antecedents and Performance-Related Outcomes of Credit Scores," *Journal of Applied Psychology* 97 (2012): 469–78; J. Carpenter, D. Doverspike, and R. F. Miguel, "Public Service Motivation as a Predictor of Attraction to the Public Sector," *Journal of Vocational Behavior* 80 (2012): 509–23; and A. Neal, G. Yeo, A. Koy, and T. Xiao, "Predicting the Form and Direction of Work Role Performance from the Big 5 Model of Personality Traits," *Journal of Organizational Behavior* 33 (2012): 175–92.

CASE INCIDENT 2 The Power of Quiet

If someone labeled you an "introvert" how would it make you feel?

Judging from research on social desirability, most of us would prefer to be labeled extraverts. Normal distributions being what they are, however, half the world is more introverted than average. Earlier in the chapter we discussed the upside of introversion, but in many ways, it's an extravert's world. So says Susan Cain in her bestselling book *Quiet.*

Cain makes three arguments:

1. **We see ourselves as extraverts.** Introversion is generally seen as undesirable, partly because extraverts like being in charge and are more apt to shape environments to fit their wishes. "Many of the most important institutions of contemporary life are designed for those who enjoy group projects and high levels of stimulation."
2. **Introversion is driven underground.** Thanks to social norms and structures, introverts often are forced to be "closet introverts"—acting according to an extraverted ideal, even if that is not their personality at heart. Think about it. If someone comments, "You're awfully quiet," they nearly always assume an underlying problem, as if not being quiet is the norm.
3. **Extraversion is not all it's cracked up to be.** Because introversion is suppressed, we cause the introverts of the world distress and fail to capitalize on the many virtues of introversion. We may overlook the quiet, thoughtful introvert when choosing a leader, we may quell creativity by doing most of our work in groups, and we may mistake appearance for reality ("Don't mistake assertiveness or eloquence for good ideas," Cain writes). Society may unwittingly push people to take risks more than is warranted, to act before they think, and to focus on short-term rewards above all else. Introverts prefer quiet conditions to concentrate on difficult tasks.

Cain is not anti-extravert. She simply thinks we should encourage people to be who they truly are, and that means valuing extraversion *and* introversion. Research indicates happy introverts are every bit as happy as happy extraverts. Cain concludes, "The next time you see a person with a composed face and soft voice, remember that inside her mind she might be solving an equation, composing a sonnet, designing a hat. She might, that is, be deploying the powers of quiet."

Questions

5-17. Would you classify yourself as introverted or extraverted? How would people who know you describe you?

⭐ **5-18.** Would you prefer to be more introverted, or more extraverted, than you are? Why?

5-19. Do you agree with Cain's arguments? Why or why not?

Source: Based on S. Cain, *Quiet: The Power of Introverts in a World That Can't Stop Talking* (New York: Random House/Broadway Paperbacks, 2013); G. Belojevic; V. Slepcevic, and B. Jakovljevic, "Mental Performance in Noise: The Role of Introversion," *Journal of Environmental Psychology* 21, no. 2 (2001): 209–13; and P. Hills and M. Argyle, "Happiness, Introversion-Extraversion and Happy Introverts," *Personality and Individual Differences* 30, no. 4 (2001): 595–608.

MyManagementLab

Go to **mymanagementlab.com** for the following Assisted-graded writing questions:

5-20. What do you feel are the pros and cons of extraversion and introversion for your work life? Can you increase desirable traits?

5-21. In your opinion, what are the desired personalities that an employer would seek in a potential candidate?

5-22. MyManagementLab Only – comprehensive writing assignment for this chapter.

ENDNOTES

[1] D. Leising, J. Scharloth, O. Lohse, and D. Wood, "What Types of Terms Do People Use When Describing an Individual's Personality?" *Psychological Science* 25, no. 9 (2014): 1787–94.

[2] L. Weber, "To Get a Job, New Hires Are Put to the Test," *The Wall Street Journal*, April 15, 2015, A1, A10.

[3] L. Weber and E. Dwoskin, "As Personality Tests Multiply, Employers Are Split," *The Wall Street Journal*, September 30, 2014, A1, A10.

[4] D. Belkin, "Colleges Put the Emphasis on Personality," *The Wall Street Journal*, January 9, 2015, A3.

[5] K. I. van der Zee, J. N. Zaal, and J. Piekstra, "Validation of the Multicultural Personality Questionnaire in the Context of Personnel Selection," *European Journal of Personality* 17, Supl. 1 (2003): S77–S100.

[6] S. A. Birkeland, T. M. Manson, J. L. Kisamore, M. T. Brannick, and M. A. Smith, "A Meta-Analytic Investigation of Job Applicant Faking on Personality Measures," *International Journal of Selection and Assessment* 14, no. 14 (2006): 317–35.

[7] K. L. Cullen, W. A. Gentry, and F. J. Yammamarino, "Biased Self-Perception Tendencies: Self-Enhancement/Self-Diminishment and Leader Derailment in Individualistic and Collectivistic Cultures," *Applied Psychology: An International Review* 64, no. 1 (2015): 161–207.

[8] D. H. Kluemper, B. D. McLarty, and M. N. Bing, "Acquaintance Ratings of the Big Five Personality Traits: Incremental Validity Beyond and Interactive Effects with Self-Reports in the Prediction of Workplace Deviance," *Journal of Applied Psychology* 100, no. 1 (2015): 237–48; I. Oh, G. Wang, and M. K. Mount, "Validity of Observer Ratings of the Five-Factor Model of Personality Traits: A Meta-Analysis," *Journal of Applied Psychology* 96, no. 4 (2011): 762–73.

[9] S. Srivastava, O. P. John, and S. D. Gosling, "Development of Personality in Early and Middle Adulthood: Set Like Plaster or Persistent Change?" *Journal of Personality and Social Psychology* 84, no. 5 (2003): 1041–53; and B. W. Roberts, K. E. Walton, and W. Viechtbauer, "Patterns of Mean-Level Change in Personality Traits across the Life Course: A Meta-Analysis of Longitudinal Studies," *Psychological Bulletin* 132, no. 1 (2006): 1–25.

[10] S. E. Hampson and L. R. Goldberg, "A First Large Cohort Study of Personality Trait Stability Over the 40 Years between Elementary School and Midlife," *Journal of Personality and Social Psychology* 91, no. 4 (2006): 763–79.

[11] L. R. James and M. D. Mazerolle, *Personality in Work Organizations* (Thousand Oaks, CA: Sage, 2002); and B. W. Roberts and D. Mroczek, "Personality Trait Change in Adulthood," *Current Directions in Psychological Science* 17, no. 1 (2008): 31–35.

[12] R. B. Kennedy and D. A. Kennedy, "Using the Myers-Briggs Type Indicator in Career Counseling," *Journal of Employment Counseling* 41, no. 1 (2004): 38–44.

[13] The Myers & Briggs Foundation, "How Frequent Is My Type?" http://www.myersbriggs .org/my-mbti-personality-type/my-mbti-results/how-frequent-is-my-type.asp, accessed April 24, 2015.

[14] A. Grant, "Goodbye to MBTI, the Fad That Won't Die," *Huffington Post*, (September 17, 2013), http://www.huffingtonpost .com/adam-grant/goodbye-to-mbti-the-fad-t_b_3947014.html.

[15] See, for instance, D. J. Pittenger, "Cautionary Comments Regarding the Myers-Briggs Type Indicator," *Consulting Psychology Journal: Practice and Research* 57, no. 3 (2005): 10–221; L. Bess and R. J. Harvey, "Bimodal Score Distributions and the Myers-Briggs Type Indicator: Fact or Artifact?" *Journal of Personality Assessment* 78, no. 1 (2002): 176–86; R. M. Capraro and M. M. Capraro, "Myers-Briggs Type Indicator Score Reliability across Studies: A Meta-Analytic Reliability Generalization Study," *Educational & Psychological Measurement* 62, no. 4 (2002): 590–602; and R. C. Arnau, B. A. Green, D. H. Rosen, D. H. Gleaves, and J. G. Melancon, "Are Jungian Preferences Really Categorical? An Empirical Investigation Using Taxometric Analysis," *Personality & Individual Differences* 34, no. 2 (2003): 233–51.

[16] D. Ariely, "When Lame Pick-Up Lines Actually Work," *The Wall Street Journal*, July 19–20, 2014, C12.

[17] See, for example, Oh, Wang, and Mount, "Validity of Observer Ratings of the Five-Factor Model of Personality Traits: A Meta-Analysis"; and M. R. Barrick and M. K. Mount, "Yes, Personality Matters: Moving On to More Important Matters," *Human Performance* 18, no. 4 (2005): 359–72.

[18] W. Fleeson and P. Gallagher, "The Implications of Big Five Standing for the Distribution of Trait Manifestation in Behavior: Fifteen Experience-Sampling Studies and a Meta-Analysis," *Journal of Personality and Social Psychology* 97, no. 6 (2009): 1097–114.

[19] T. A. Judge, L. S. Simon, C. Hurst, and K. Kelley, "What I Experienced Yesterday Is Who I Am Today: Relationship of Work Motivations and Behaviors to Within-Individual Variation in the Five-Factor Model of Personality," *Journal of Applied Psychology* 99, no. 2 (2014): 199–221.

[20] R. D. Zimmerman, W. R. Boswell, A. J. Shipp, B. B. Dunford, and J. W. Boudreau, "Explaining the Pathways between Approach-Avoidance Personality Traits and Employees' Job Search Behavior," *Journal of Management* 38, no. 5 (2012): 1450–75.

[21] See, for instance, I. Oh and C. M. Berry, "The Five-Factor Model of Personality and Managerial Performance: Validity Gains through the Use of 360 Degree Performance Ratings," *Journal of Applied Psychology* 94, no. 6 (2009): 1498–513; J. Hogan and B. Holland, "Using Theory to Evaluate Personality and Job-Performance Relations: A Socioanalytic Perspective," *Journal of Applied Psychology* 88, no. 1 (2003): 100–12; and M. R. Barrick and M. K. Mount, "Select on Conscientiousness and Emotional Stability," in E. A. Locke (ed.), *Handbook of Principles of Organizational Behavior* (Malden, MA: Blackwell, 2004), 15–28.

[22] P. R. Sackett and P. T. Walmsley, "Which Personality Attributes Are Most Important in the Workplace?" *Perspectives on Psychological Science* 9, no. 5 (2014): 538–51.

[23] A. E. Poropat, "A Meta-Analysis of the Five-Factor Model of Personality and Academic Performance," *Psychological Bulletin* 135, no. 2 (2009): 322–38.

[24] A. K. Nandkeolyar, J. A. Shaffer, A. Li, S. Ekkirala, and J. Bagger, "Surviving an Abusive Supervisor: The Joint Roles of Conscientiousness and Coping Strategies," *Journal of Applied Psychology* 99, no. 1 (2014): 138–50.

[25] B. Wille, F. De Fruyt, and M. Feys, "Big Five Traits and Intrinsic Success in the New Career Era: A 15-Year Longitudinal Study on Employability and Work-Family Conflict," *Applied Psychology: An International Review* 62, no. 1 (2013): 124–56.

[26] M. K. Shoss, K. Callison, and L. A. Witt, "The Effects of Other-Oriented Perfectionism and Conscientiousness on Helping at Work," *Applied Psychology: An International Review* 64, no. 1 (2015): 233–51.

[27] C. Robert and Y. H. Cheung, "An Examination of the Relationship between Conscientiousness and Group Performance on a Creative Task," *Journal of Research in Personality* 44, no. 2 (2010): 222–31; and M. Batey, T. Chamorro-Premuzic, and A. Furnham, "Individual Differences in Ideational Behavior. Can the Big Five and Psychometric Intelligence Predict Creativity Scores?" *Creativity Research Journal* 22, no. 1 (2010): 90–97.

[28] J. L. Huang, A. M. Ryan, K. L. Zabel, and A. Palmer, "Personality and Adaptive Performance at Work: A Meta-Analytic Investigation," *Journal of Applied Psychology* 99, no. 1 (2014): 162–79.

[29] R. D. Zimmerman, W. R. Boswell, A. J. Shipp, B. B. Dunford, and J. W. Boudreau, "Explaining the Pathways between Approach-Avoidance Personality Traits and Employees' Job Search Behavior," *Journal of Management* 38, no. 5 (2012): 1450–75.

[30] B. Wille, F. De Fruyt, and M. Feys, "Big Five Traits and Intrinsic Success in the New Career Era: A 15-Year Longitudinal Study on Employability and Work-Family Conflict."

[31] R. J. Foti and M. A. Hauenstein, "Pattern and Variable Approaches in Leadership Emergence and Effectiveness," *Journal of Applied Psychology* 92, no. 2 (2007): 347–55.

[32] B. Weiss, and R. S. Feldman, "Looking Good and Lying to Do It: Deception as an Impression Management Strategy in Job Interviews," *Journal of Applied Social Psychology* 36, no. 4 (2006): 1070–86.

[33] A. Minbashian, J. Earl, and J. E. H. Bright, "Openness to Experience as a Predictor of Job Performance Trajectories," *Applied Psychology: An International Review* 62, no. 1 (2013): 1–12.

[34] B. Wille, F. De Fruyt, and M. Feys, "Big Five Traits and Intrinsic Success in the New Career Era: A 15-Year Longitudinal Study on Employability and Work-Family Conflict."

[35] R. Ilies, I. S. Fulmer, M. Spitzmuller, and M. D. Johnson, "Personality and Citizenship Behavior: The Mediating Role of Job Satisfaction," *Journal of Applied Psychology* 94, no. 4 (2009): 945–59.

[36] D. H. Kluemper, B. D. McLarty, and M. N. Bing, "Acquaintance Ratings of the Big Five Personality Traits: Incremental Validity Beyond and Interactive Effects with Self-Reports in the Prediction of Workplace Deviance," *Journal of Applied Psychology* 100, no. 1 (2015): 237–48.

[37] S. Clarke and I. Robertson, "An Examination of the Role of Personality in Accidents Using Meta-Analysis," *Applied Psychology: An International Review* 57, no. 1 (2008): 94–108.

[38] B. Wille, F. De Fruyt, and M. Feys, "Big Five Traits and Intrinsic Success in the New Career Era: A 15-Year Longitudinal Study on Employability and Work-Family Conflict."

[39] See, for instance, S. Yamagata, A. Suzuki, J. Ando, Y. Ono, K. Yutaka, N. Kijima, et al., "Is the Genetic Structure of Human Personality Universal? A Cross-Cultural Twin Study from North America, Europe, and Asia," *Journal of Personality and Social Psychology* 90, no. 6 (2006): 987–98; and R. R. McCrae, P. T. Costa Jr., T. A. Martin, V. E. Oryol, A. A. Rukavishnikov, I. G. Senin, et al., "Consensual Validation of Personality Traits across Cultures," *Journal of Research in Personality* 38, no. 2 (2004): 179–201.

[40] M. Gurven, C. von Ruden, M. Massenkoff, H. Kaplan, and M. L. Vie, "How Universal Is the Big Five? Testing the Five-Factor Model of Personality Variation among Forager-Farmers in the Bolivian Amazon," *Journal of Personality and Social Psychology* 104, no. 2 (2013): 354–70.

[41] J. F. Rauthmann, "The Dark Triad and Interpersonal Perception: Similarities and Differences in the Social Consequences of Narcissism, Machiavellianism, and Psychopathy," *Social Psychological and Personality Science* 3 (2012): 487–96.

[42] P. D. Harms and S. M. Spain, "Beyond the Bright Side: Dark Personality at Work," *Applied Psychology: An International Review* 64, no. 1 (2015): 15–24.

[43] P. K. Jonason, S. Slomski, and J. Partyka, "The Dark Triad at Work: How Toxic Employees Get Their Way," *Personality and Individual Differences* 52 (2012): 449–53.

[44] E. H. O'Boyle, D. R. Forsyth, G. C. Banks, and M. A. McDaniel, "A Meta-Analysis of the Dark Triad and Work Behavior: A Social Exchange Perspective," *Journal of Applied Psychology* 97 (2012): 557–79.

[45] L. Zhang, and M. A. Gowan, "Corporate Social Responsibility, Applicants' Individual Traits, and Organizational Attraction: A Person–Organization Fit Perspective," *Journal of Business and Psychology* 27 (2012): 345–62.

[46] D. N. Hartog and F. D. Belschak, "Work Engagement and Machiavellianism in the Ethical Leadership Process," *Journal of Business Ethics* 107 (2012): 35–47.

[47] E. Grijalva and P. D. Harms, "Narcissism: An Integrative Synthesis and Dominance Complementary Model" *The Academy of Management Perspectives* 28, no. 2 (2014): 108–27.

[48] D. C. Maynard, E. M. Brondolo, C. E. Connelly, and C. E. Sauer, "I'm Too Good for This Job: Narcissism's Role in the Experience of Overqualification," *Applied Psychology: An International Review* 64, no. 1 (2015): 208–32.

[49] E. Grijalva and P. D. Harms, "Narcissism: An Integrative Synthesis and Dominance Complementary Model."

[50] B. J. Brummel and K. N. Parker, "Obligation and Entitlement in Society and the Workplace," *Applied Psychology: An International Review* 64, no. 1 (2015): 127–60.

[51] E. Grijalva and D. A. Newman, "Narcissism and Counterproductive Work Behavior (CWB): Meta-Analysis and Consideration of Collectivist Culture, Big Five Personality, and Narcissism's Facet Structure," *Applied Psychology: An International Review* 2015, 93–126.

[52] D. C. Maynard, E. M. Brondolo, C. E. Connelly, and C. E. Sauer, "I'm Too Good for This Job: Narcissism's Role in the Experience of Overqualification."

[53] E. Grijalva and P. D. Harms, "Narcissism: An Integrative Synthesis and Dominance Complementary Model."

[54] J. J. Sosik, J. U. Chun, and W. Zhu, "Hang On to Your Ego: The Moderating Role of Leader Narcissism on Relationships between Leader Charisma and Follower Psychological Empowerment and Moral Identity," *Journal of Business Ethics*, February 12, 2013, and B. M. Galvin, D. A. Waldman, and P. Balthazard, "Visionary Communication Qualities as Mediators of the Relationship between Narcissism and Attributions of Leader Charisma," *Personnel Psychology* 63, no. 3 (2010): 509–37.

[55] D. Meinert, "Narcissistic Bosses Aren't All Bad, Study Finds," *HR Magazine*, March 2014, 18.

[56] K. A. Byrne and D. A. Worthy, "Do Narcissists Make Better Decisions? An Investigation of Narcissism and Dynamic Decision-Making Performance," *Personality and Individual Differences*, July 2013, 112–17.

[57] C. Andreassen, H. Ursin, H. Eriksen, S. Pallesen, "The Relationship of Narcissism with Workaholism, Work Engagement, and Professional Position," *Social Behavior and Personality* 40, no. 6 (2012): 881–90.

[58] A. Chatterjee and D. C. Hambrick, "Executive Personality, Capability Cues, and Risk Taking: How Narcissistic CEOs React to Their Successes and Stumbles," *Administrative Science Quarterly* 56 (2011): 202–37.

[59] C. J. Resick, D. S. Whitman, S. M. Weingarden, and N. J. Hiller, "The Bright-Side and Dark-Side of CEO Personality: Examining Core Self-Evaluations, Narcissism, Transformational Leadership, and Strategic Influence," *Journal of Applied Psychology* 94, no. 6 (2009): 1365–81.

[60] O'Boyle, Forsyth, Banks, and McDaniel, "A Meta-Analysis of the Dark Triad and Work Behavior: A Social Exchange Perspective," 558.

[61] B. Wille, F. De Fruyt, and B. De Clercq, "Expanding and Reconceptualizing Aberrant Personality at Work: Validity of Five-Factor Model Aberrant Personality Tendencies to Predict Career Outcomes," *Personnel Psychology* 66 (2013): 173–223.

[62] P. K. Jonason, S. Slomski, and J. Partyka, "The Dark Triad at Work: How Toxic

Employees Get Their Way," *Personality and Individual Differences* 52 (2012): 449–53; and H. M. Baughman, S. Dearing, E. Giammarco, and P. A. Vernon, "Relationships between Bullying Behaviours and the Dark Triad: A Study with Adults," *Personality and Individual Differences* 52 (2012): 571–75.

[63] U. Orth and R. W. Robins, "Understanding the Link between Low Self-Esteem and Depression," *Current Directions in Psychological Science* 22, no. 6 (2013): 455–60.

[64] B. Wille, F. De Fruyt, and B. De Clercq, "Expanding and Reconceptualizing Aberrant Personality at Work: Validity of Five-Factor Model Aberrant Personality Tendencies to Predict Career Outcomes," *Personnel Psychology* 66 (2013): 173–223.

[65] T. A. Judge and J. E. Bono, "A Rose by Any Other Name ... Are Self-Esteem, Generalized Self-Efficacy, Neuroticism, and Locus of Control Indicators of a Common Construct?" in B. W. Roberts and R. Hogan (eds.), *Personality Psychology in the Workplace* (Washington, DC: American Psychological Association, 2001), 93–118.

[66] A. N. Salvaggio, B. Schneider, L. H. Nishi, D. M. Mayer, A. Ramesh, and J. S. Lyon, "Manager Personality, Manager Service Quality Orientation, and Service Climate: Test of a Model," *Journal of Applied Psychology* 92, no. 6 (2007): 1741–50; B. A. Scott and T. A. Judge, "The Popularity Contest at Work: Who Wins, Why, and What Do They Receive?" *Journal of Applied Psychology* 94, no. 1 (2009): 20–33; and T. A. Judge and C. Hurst, "How the Rich (and Happy) Get Richer (and Happier): Relationship of Core Self-Evaluations to Trajectories in Attaining Work Success," *Journal of Applied Psychology* 93, no. 4 (2008): 849–63.

[67] A. M. Grant and A. Wrzesniewksi, "I Won't Let You Down ... or Will I? Core Self-Evaluations, Other-Orientation, Anticipated Guilt and Gratitude, and Job Performance," *Journal of Applied Psychology* 95, no. 1 (2010): 108–21.

[68] L. Parks-Leduc, M. W. Pattie, F. Pargas, and R. G. Eliason, "Self-Monitoring as an Aggregate Construct: Relationships with Personality and Values," *Personality and Individual Differences* 58 (2014): 3–8.

[69] F. J. Flynn and D. R. Ames, "What's Good for the Goose May Not Be as Good for the Gander: The Benefits of Self-Monitoring for Men and Women in Task Groups and Dyadic Conflicts," *Journal of Applied Psychology* 91, no. 2 (2006): 272–81; and Snyder, *Public Appearances/Private Realities.*

[70] D. V. Day, D. J. Shleicher, A. L. Unckless, and N. J. Hiller, "Self-Monitoring Personality at Work: A Meta-Analytic Investigation of Construct Validity," *Journal of Applied Psychology* 87, no. 2 (2002): 390–401.

[71] H. Oh and M. Kilduff, "The Ripple Effect of Personality on Social Structure: Self-Monitoring Origins of Network Brokerage," *Journal of Applied Psychology* 93, no. 5 (2008): 1155–64; and A. Mehra, M. Kilduff, and D. J. Brass, "The Social Networks of High and Low Self-Monitors: Implications for Workplace Performance," *Administrative Science Quarterly* 46, no. 1 (2001): 121–46.

[72] P.-Y. Liao, "The Role of Self-Concept in the Mechanism Linking Proactive Personality to Employee Work Outcomes," *Applied Psychology-An International Review* 64, no. 2 (2015): 421–43.

[73] K. Tornau and M. Frese, "Construct Cleanup in Proactivity Research: A Meta-Analysis on the Nomological Net of Work-Related Proactivity Concepts and Their Incremental Values," *Applied Psychology: An International Review* 62, no. 1 (2013): 44–96.

[74] W.-D. Li, D. Fay, M. Frese, P. D. Harms, and X. Y. Gao, "Reciprocal Relationship between Proactive Personality and Work Characteristics: A Latent Change Score Approach," *Journal of Applied Psychology* 99, no. 5 (2014): 948–65.

[75] P. D. Converse, Patrick J. Pathak, A. M. DePaul-Haddock, T. Gotlib, and M. Merbedone, "Controlling Your Environment and Yourself: Implications for Career Success," *Journal of Vocational Behavior* 80 (2012): 148–59.

[76] G. Chen, J. Farh, E. M. Campbell-Bush, Z. Wu, and X. Wu, "Teams as Innovative Systems: Multilevel Motivational Antecedents of Innovation in R&D Teams," *Journal of Applied Psychology*, 98 (2013): 1018–27.

[77] Y. Gong, S.-Y. Cheung, M. Wang, and J.-C. Huang, "Unfolding the Proactive Process for Creativity: Integration of the Employee Proactivity, Information Exchange, and Psychological Safety Perspectives," *Journal of Management* 38, no. 5 (2012): 1611–33.

[78] Z. Zhang, M. Wang, and S. Junqi, "Leader-Follower Congruence in Proactive Personality and Work Outcomes: The Mediating Role of Leader-Member Exchange," *Academy of Management Journal* 55 (2012): 111–30.

[79] G. Van Hoye and H. Lootens, "Coping with Unemployment: Personality, Role Demands, and Time Structure," *Journal of Vocational Behavior* 82 (2013): 85–95.

[80] R. D. Meyer, R. S. Dalal, and R. Hermida, "A Review and Synthesis of Situational Strength in the Organizational Sciences," *Journal of Management* 36 (2010): 121–40.

[81] R. D. Meyer, R. S. Dalal, I. J. Jose, R. Hermida, T. R. Chen, R. P. Vega ... V. P. Khare, "Measuring Job-Related Situational Strength and Assessing Its Interactive Effects with Personality on Voluntary Work Behavior," *Journal of Management* 40, no. 4 (2014): 1010–41.

[82] A. M. Grant and N. P. Rothbard, "When in Doubt, Seize the Day? Security Values, Prosocial Values, and Proactivity Under Ambiguity," *Journal of Applied Psychology*, 2013.

[83] A. M. Watson, T. F. Thompson, J. V. Rudolph, T. J. Whelan, T. S. Behrend, et al., "When Big Brother Is Watching: Goal Orientation Shapes Reactions to Electronic Monitoring During Online Training," *Journal of Applied Psychology*, 98 (2013): 642–57.

[84] Y. Kim, L. Van Dyne, D. Kamdar, and R. E. Johnson, "Why and When Do Motives Matter? An Integrative Model of Motives, Role Cognitions, and Social Support as Predictors of OCB," *Organizational Behavior and Human Decision Processes*, 121 (2013): 231–45.

[85] G. R. Maio, J. M. Olson, M. M. Bernard, and M. A. Luke, "Ideologies, Values, Attitudes, and Behavior," in J. Delamater (ed.), *Handbook of Social Psychology* (New York: Springer, 2003), 283–308.

[86] See, for instance, A. Bardi, J. A. Lee, N. Hofmann-Towfigh, and G. Soutar, "The Structure of Intraindividual Value Change," *Journal of Personality and Social Psychology* 97, no. 5 (2009): 913–29.

[87] S. Roccas, L. Sagiv, S. H. Schwartz, and A. Knafo, "The Big Five Personality Factors and Personal Values," *Personality and Social Psychology Bulletin* 28, no. 6 (2002): 789–801.

[88] B. C. Holtz and C. M. Harold, "Interpersonal Justice and Deviance: The Moderating Effects of Interpersonal Justice Values and Justice Orientation," *Journal of Management*, February 2013, 339–65.

[89] See, for example, N. R. Lockwood, F. R. Cepero, and S. Williams, *The Multigenerational Workforce* (Alexandria, VA: Society for Human Resource Management, 2009).

[90] E. Parry and P. Urwin, "Generational Differences in Work Values: A Review of Theory and Evidence," *International Journal of Management Reviews* 13, no. 1 (2011): 79–96.

[91] J. M. Twenge, S. M. Campbell, B. J. Hoffman, and C. E. Lance, "Generational Differences in Work Values: Leisure and Extrinsic Values Increasing, Social and Intrinsic Values Decreasing," *Journal of Management* 36, no. 5 (2010): 1117–42.

[92] B. J. Dik, S. R. Strife, and J.-I. C. Hansen, "The Flip Side of Holland Type Congruence: Incongruence and Job Satisfaction," *Career Development Quarterly* 58, no. 4 (2010): 352–58; A. Rezaei, A. Qorbanpoor, T. A. Gatab, and A. Rezaei, "Comparative Research for Personality Types of Guilan University Physical Exercise and Counseling Students Based on Holland Theory," *Procedia-Social and Behavioral Sciences* 30 (2011): 2032–36; and D. L. Ohler and E. M. Levinson, "Using Holland's Theory in Employment Counseling: Focus on Service Occupations," *Journal of Employment Counseling* 49, no. 4 (2012): 148–59.

[93] Y. Lee and J. Antonakis, "When Preference Is Not Satisfied but the Individual Is: How Power Distance Moderates Person-Job Fit," *Journal of Management* 40, no. 3 (2014): 641–57.

[94] See W. Arthur Jr., S. T. Bell, A. J. Villado, and D. Doverspike, "The Use of Person-Organization Fit in Employment Decision-Making: An Assessment of Its Criterion-Related Validity," *Journal of Applied Psychology* 91, no. 4 (2006): 786–801; and J. R. Edwards, D. M. Cable, I. O. Williamson, L. S. Lambert, and A. J. Shipp, "The Phenomenology of Fit: Linking the Person and Environment to the Subjective Experience of Person–Environment Fit," *Journal of Applied Psychology* 91, no. 4 (2006): 802–27.

[95] A. Leung and S. Chaturvedi, "Linking the Fits, Fitting the Links: Connecting Different Types of PO Fit to Attitudinal Outcomes," *Journal of Vocational Behavior*, October 2011, 391–402.

[96] M. L. Verquer, T. A. Beehr, and S. E. Wagner, "A Meta-Analysis of Relations between Person–Organization Fit and Work Attitudes," *Journal of Vocational Behavior* 63, no. 3 (2003): 473–89; and J. C. Carr, A. W. Pearson, M. J. Vest, and S. L. Boyar, "Prior Occupational Experience, Anticipatory Socialization, and Employee Retention, *Journal of Management* 32, no. 32 (2006): 343–59.

[97] K. H. Ehrhart, D. M. Mayer, and J. C. Ziegert, "Web-based Recruitment in the Millennial Generation: Work-Life Balance, Website Usability, and Organizational Attraction," *European Journal of Work and Organizational Psychology* 21, no. 6 (2012): 850–74.

[98] I.-S. Oh, R. P. Guay, K. Kim, C. M. Harold, J. H. Lee, C.-G. Heo, and K-H. Shin, "Fit Happens Globally: A Meta-Analytic Comparison of the Relationships of Person-Environment Fit Dimensions with Work Attitudes and Performance across East Asia, Europe, and North America," *Personnel Psychology* 67 (2014): 99–152.

[99] See The Hofstede Centre, www.geert-hofstede.com.

[100] V. Taras, B. L. Kirkman, and P. Steel, "Examining the Impact of Culture's Consequences: A Three-Decade, Multilevel, Meta-Analytic Review of Hofstede's Cultural Value Dimensions," *Journal of Applied Psychology* 95, no. 5 (2010): 405–39.

[101] M. Javidan and R. J. House, "Cultural Acumen for the Global Manager: Lessons from Project GLOBE," *Organizational Dynamics* 29, no. 4 (2001): 289–305; and R. J. House, P. J. Hanges, M. Javidan, and P. W. Dorfman (eds.), *Leadership, Culture, and Organizations: The GLOBE Study of 62 Societies* (Thousand Oaks, CA: Sage, 2004).

[102] J. P. Meyer, D. J. Stanley, T. A. Jackson, K. J. McInnis, E. R. Maltin, et al., "Affective, Normative, and Continuance Commitment Levels across Cultures: A Meta-Analysis," *Journal of Vocational Behavior* 80 (2012): 225–45.

6

Perception and Individual Decision Making

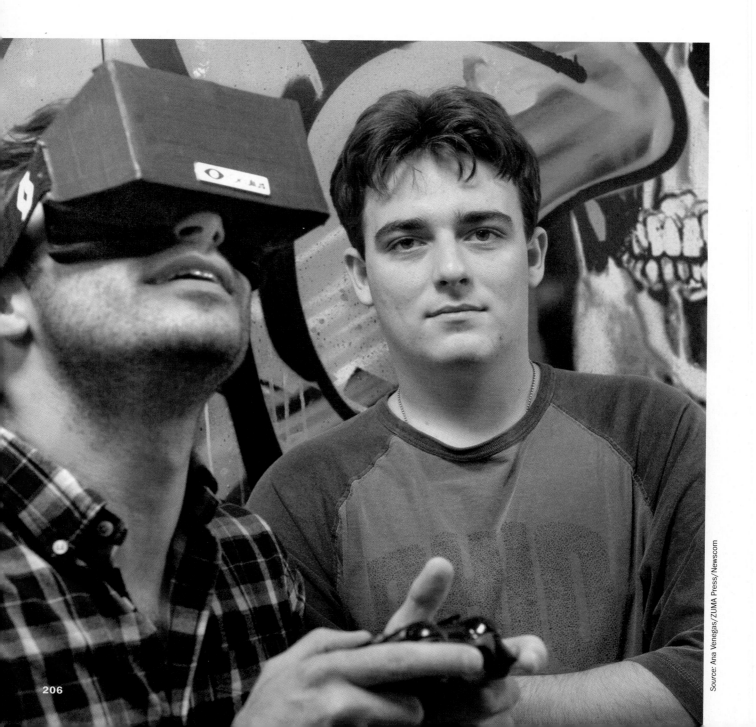

LEARNING OBJECTIVES

After studying this chapter, you should be able to:

6-1 Explain the factors that influence perception.

6-2 Describe attribution theory.

6-3 Explain the link between perception and decision making.

6-4 Contrast the rational model of decision making with bounded rationality and intuition.

6-5 Explain how individual differences and organizational constraints affect decision making.

6-6 Contrast the three ethical decision criteria.

6-7 Describe the three-stage model of creativity.

MyManagementLab®
⭐ **Chapter Warm Up**

If your professor has chosen to assign this, go to the Assignments section of **mymanagementlab.com** to complete the chapter warm up.

IS PALMER LUCKEY LUCKY OR MASTERFULLY CREATIVE?

What would you do if you were 22 years old and Mark Zuckerberg said your invention was "the coolest thing I've ever seen"—and then bought your company for $2.3 billion? Palmer Luckey, inventor of the Oculus Rift virtual reality headset (pictured on the right), first went shopping for another recent innovation, the Tesla car. And then he got to work at Facebook so his invention could be sold to consumers in 2016.

Luckey follows in the footsteps of fellow backyard innovators Zuckerberg and Apple's Steve Jobs, dropping out of college to tinker in a garage with an idea that just might revolutionize the world. His virtual reality headset may have an impact in architecture, education, business, medicine, psychology, and any field where putting people in a virtual situation they believe is real can help. Imagine an architect walking through her new building before it exists and a student physician performing open-heart surgery without risk to a real patient. Think of all the errors that could be reduced if we could virtually live through the consequences of some of our decisions before enacting them. How could one young man make all these sci-fi scenarios possible when scores of others have failed for decades? A close look at Luckey's life may reveal some clues to understanding an individual's creativity variables.

Luckey was imaginative with technology in his early life; in his teens, he built computers and video game consoles. As a home-schooled kid, he also loved learning on his own "about electronics, engineering, how the world ticks." He set his sights on fame. "Ever since I was 15 I've tried to act and talk as if I was a public figure, because I was sure that I would be one day and wanted to be prepared," he said. Then the movie *The Matrix,* about virtual reality, sparked his imagination. Although the film was science fiction, Luckey saw potential in optimizing the virtual reality experience. He used his imagination and his income from repairing iPhones to build a prototype virtual reality headset. "It wasn't very good," he admitted. But instead of quitting, Luckey worked harder and soon realized a breakthrough, a headset that tricked the visual cortex into interpreting the images as real. He quickly broadcast his success and used crowdfunding to raise capital, aiming for $250,000 to build a few hundred units. Instead, he raised $2.4 million and attracted the attention of venture capital firm Andreessen Horowitz, which invested $75 million in his idea. Facebook bought the company 2 years later.

Luckey is not modest about his success. "I brought [the virtual reality experience] back from the dead," he said. He identifies with innovation heroes and seeks the spotlight. "If you look at who most people respect now, they don't idolize politicians, they idolize these people founding companies, the self-made entrepreneurs," he observed. Luckey reads and replies to all his fan mail and is the public face of Oculus Rift. Yet he claims he is now after something bigger than his own fame—a technology that changes the world. "This isn't about me, it's about something much, much bigger—bigger than perhaps any of us."

This look at Luckey's life may show one winning formula for individual creativity: a longstanding, focused interest; openness to learning new things; a knowledge-seeking attitude; a degree of narcissism manifested in a desire for renown and a belief in your own capabilities; perseverance; willingness to work hard; and enough extraversion to reach out for help and support. As Luckey's buddy and CEO Brendan Iribe (pictured on the left) said, "Maybe his name is Luckey for a reason."

Sources: T. Clark, "How Palmer Luckey Created Oculus Rift," *The Smithsonian,* November 2014, http://www.smithsonianmag.com/innovation/how-palmer-luckey-created-oculus-rift-180953049/?no-ist=&page=1; J. Ensor, "Oculus Rift's Palmer Luckey: 'I Brought Virtual Reality from the Dead," *The Telegraph,* January 2, 2015, http://www.telegraph.co.uk/technology/11309013/Oculus-Rifts-Palmer-Luckey-I-brought-virtual-reality-back-from-the-dead.html; and J. Vilaga, "100 Most Creative People in Business 2014," *Fast Company,* 2014, http://www.fastcompany.com/3029369/most-creative-people-2014/palmer-luckey.

The case of Palmer Luckey illustrates how important—and perhaps rare—an individual's creativity can be to an industry. As we will see later in the chapter, the creativity of individuals can lead to breakthroughs in innovation. To better understand what influences us and our organizations, we start at the roots of our thought processes: our perceptions and the way they affect our decision making.

What Is Perception?

6-1 Explain the factors that influence perception.

perception A process by which individuals organize and interpret their sensory impressions in order to give meaning to their environment.

Perception is a process by which we organize and interpret sensory impressions in order to give meaning to our environment. What we perceive can be substantially different from objective reality. For example, all employees in a firm may view it as a great place to work—favorable working conditions, interesting job assignments, good pay, excellent benefits, understanding and responsible management—but, as most of us know, it's very unusual to find agreement universal opinion.

Why is perception important in the study of OB? Simply because people's behavior is based on their perception of what reality is, not on reality itself. *The world as it is perceived is the world that is behaviorally important.* In other words, our perception becomes the reality from which we act. To understand what all of us have in common in our interpretations of reality, we need to begin with the factors that influence our perceptions.

Factors That Influence Perception

A number of factors shape and sometimes distort perception. These factors can reside in the *perceiver*, the object or *target* being perceived, or the *situation* in which the perception is made (see Exhibit 6-1).

Perceiver   When you look at a target, your interpretation of what you see is influenced by your personal characteristics—attitudes, personality, motives, interests, past experiences, and expectations. In some ways, we hear what we

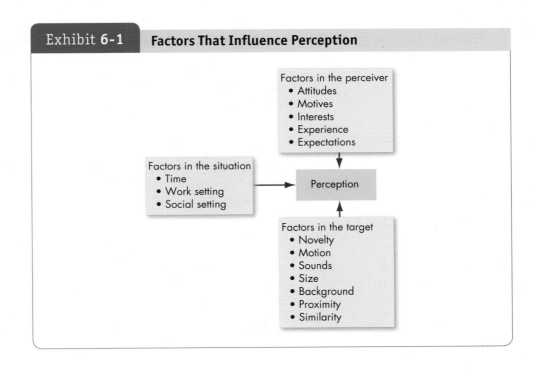

Exhibit 6-1   **Factors That Influence Perception**

want to hear[1] and we see what we want to see—not because it's the truth, but because it conforms to our thinking. For instance, recent research indicated that supervisors perceived employees who started work earlier in the day as more conscientious and therefore as higher performers; however, supervisors who were night owls *themselves* were less likely to make that erroneous assumption.[2] Some perceptions created by attitudes like these can be counteracted by objective evaluation, but others can be insidious. Consider, for instance, observer perceptions of a recent shooting in New York. There were two eyewitnesses—one said a police officer chased and shot a fleeing man; the other said a handcuffed man lying on the ground was shot. Neither perceived the situation correctly: The man was actually attempting to attack a police officer with a hammer when he was shot by another officer.[3]

Target   The characteristics of the target also affect what we perceive. Because we don't look at targets in isolation, the relationship of a target to its background influences perception, as does our tendency to group close things and similar things together. We can perceive women, men, whites, African Americans, Asians, or members of any other group that has clearly distinguishable characteristics as alike in other, unrelated ways as well. Often, these assumptions are harmful, as when people who have criminal records are prejudged in the workplace even when it is known they were wrongly arrested.[4] Sometimes differences can work in our favor, though, such as when we are drawn to targets that are different from what we expect. For instance, in a recent study participants respected a professor wearing a T-shirt and sneakers in the classroom more than the same professor dressed traditionally. The professor stood out from the norm for the classroom setting and was therefore perceived as an individualist.[5]

Context   Context matters too. The time at which we see an object or event can influence our attention, as can location, light, heat, or situational factors. For instance, at a club on Saturday night you may not notice someone "decked out." Yet that same person so attired for your Monday morning management class would certainly catch your attention. Neither the perceiver nor the target has changed between Saturday night and Monday morning, but the situation is different.

People are usually not aware of the factors that influence their view of reality. In fact, people are not even that perceptive about their *own* abilities.[6] Thankfully, awareness and objective measures can reduce our perception distortions. For instance, when people are asked to ponder specific aspects of their ability, they become more realistic in their self-perceptions.[7] Let's next consider *how* we make perceptions of others.

✪ **WATCH IT!**

If your professor has assigned this, go to the Assignments section of **mymanagementlab.com** to complete the video exercise titled *Orpheus Group Casting: Social Perception and Attribution*.

Person Perception: Making Judgments About Others

6-2 Explain attribution theory.

The perception concepts most relevant to OB include *person perceptions,* or the perceptions people form about each other. Many of our perceptions of others are formed by first impressions and small cues that have little supporting evidence. This is particularly troublesome—but common—when we infer another person's morality. Research indicates we form our strongest impressions based on what we perceive about another's moral character, but our initial information about this can be sketchy and unfounded.[8] Let's unravel some of our other human tendencies that interfere with correct person perception, beginning with the evidence behind attribution theory.

Attribution Theory

Nonliving objects such as desks, machines, and buildings are subject to the laws of nature, but they have no beliefs, motives, or intentions. People do. When we observe people, we attempt to explain their behavior. Our perception and judgment of a person's actions are influenced by the assumptions we make about that person's state of mind.

attribution theory tries to explain the ways we judge people differently, depending on the meaning we attribute to a behavior.[9] For instance, consider what you think when people smile at you. Do you think they are cooperative, exploitative, or competitive? We assign meaning to smiles and other expressions in many different ways.[10]

Attribution theory suggests that when we observe an individual's behavior, we attempt to determine whether it was internally or externally caused. That determination depends largely on three factors: (1) distinctiveness, (2) consensus, and (3) consistency. Let's clarify the differences between internal and external causation, and then we'll discuss the determining factors.

Internally caused behaviors are those an observer believes to be under the personal behavioral control of another individual. *Externally* caused behavior is what we imagine the situation forced the individual to do. If an employee is late for work, you might attribute that to his overnight partying and subsequent oversleeping. This is an internal attribution. But if you attribute his lateness to a traffic snarl, you are making an external attribution.

Now let's discuss the three determining factors. *Distinctiveness* refers to whether an individual displays different behaviors in different situations. Is the employee who arrives late today also one who regularly "blows off" other kinds of commitments? What we want to know is whether this behavior is unusual. If it is, we are likely to give it an external attribution. If it's not, we will probably judge the behavior to be internal.

If everyone who faces a similar situation responds in the same way, we can say the behavior shows *consensus*. The behavior of our tardy employee meets this criterion if all employees who took the same route were also late. From an attribution perspective, if consensus is high, you would probably give an external attribution to the employee's tardiness, whereas if other employees who took the same route made it to work on time, you would attribute his lateness to an internal cause.

Finally, an observer looks for *consistency* in a person's actions. Does the person respond the same way over time? Coming in 10 minutes late for work is not perceived the same for an employee who hasn't been late for several months as for an employee who is late three times a week. The more consistent the behavior, the more we are inclined to attribute it to internal causes.

Exhibit 6-2 summarizes the key elements in attribution theory. It tells us, for instance, that if an employee, Katelyn, generally performs at about the same level on related tasks as she does on her current task (low distinctiveness), other employees frequently perform differently—better or worse—than Katelyn on that task (low consensus), and Katelyn's performance on this current task is consistent over time (high consistency), anyone judging Katelyn's work will likely hold her primarily responsible for her task performance (internal attribution).

attribution theory An attempt to determine whether an individual's behavior is internally or externally caused.

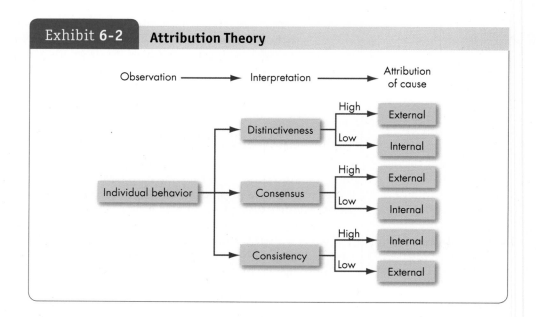

Exhibit 6-2   Attribution Theory

Observation ⟶ Interpretation ⟶ Attribution of cause

Errors or biases distort attributions. When we make judgments about the behavior of other people, we tend to underestimate the influence of external factors and overestimate the influence of internal or personal factors.[11] This **fundamental attribution error** can explain why a sales manager attributes the poor performance of her sales agents to laziness rather than to a competitor's innovative product line. Individuals and organizations tend to attribute their own successes to internal factors such as ability or effort, while blaming failure on external factors such as bad luck or difficult coworkers. People tend to attribute ambiguous information as relatively flattering, accept positive feedback, and reject negative feedback. This is called **self-serving bias**.[12]

The evidence on cultural differences in perception is mixed, but most suggests there are differences across cultures in the attributions people make.[13] In one study, Asian managers were more likely to blame institutions or whole organizations when things went wrong, whereas Western observers believed individual managers should get blame or praise.[14] That probably explains why U.S. newspapers feature the names of individual executives when firms do poorly, whereas Asian media report the firm as a whole has failed. This tendency to make group-based attributions also explains why individuals from Asian cultures, which are more collectivistic in orientation, are more likely to use group stereotypes.[15]

Self-serving biases may be less common in East Asian cultures, but evidence suggests they still operate there.[16] Studies indicate Chinese managers assess blame for mistakes using the same distinctiveness, consensus, and consistency cues Western managers use.[17] They also become angry and punish those deemed responsible for failure, a reaction shown in many studies of Western managers. It may just take more evidence for Asian managers to conclude someone else should be blamed.

The concept of attribution theory significantly advances our understanding of people perception by helping us identify why we draw certain conclusions from people's behavior. Having introduced person perception, let's consider the common shortcuts we use to simplify our processing of others' behavior.

So what if I'm a few minutes late to work?

I'm often late to work; something always comes up at the last minute. But my boss is such a jerk about it! He's threatening to install a time clock. This is so insulting—I'm in management, I'm a professional, I'm on salary, and I do the work! Please tell me how to talk some sense into him.

—*Renée*

Dear Renée,

This issue seems to be very frustrating to you, and we'd like to help you eliminate that dissatisfaction. Let's start by analyzing why you and your boss think differently on the issue. You and he certainly perceive of the situation differently—he sees your lateness as a violation, and you see it as a natural occurrence. In many other jobs, precise timing may not be expected, valued, or needed. Perhaps your boss is trying to highlight the value he places on punctuality. Or maybe he sees your lateness as unethical behavior that cheats your organization of your valuable work time.

According to Ann Tenbrunsel, Director of the Institute for Ethical Business Worldwide, the way we look at our decisions changes our perception of our

behaviors. You view your tardiness as something that just happens, not part of a decision process. What if you looked at your tardiness as a daily ethical decision? Your organization has a start time to which you agreed as a condition of your employment, so coming in late is a deviation from the standard. There *are* actions you can take throughout your early morning that control your arrival time. So, by this model, your behavior is unethical.

Your situation is not uncommon; we all have moral blind spots, or situations with ethical ramifications we don't see. Also, as we said earlier, other organizations may not care about your arrival time, so it's not always an ethical situation. But for situations where ethics are in play, research indicates punishment doesn't work. Reframing the decisions so we see the ethical implications does work. Try these steps to gain insight:

* *Look at the motives for your decisions during your morning routine.* Can you see where you make choices?
* *Consider your past actions.* When you think back about your early morning decisions, do you find yourself

justifying your delays? Justification signals that our decisions might be suspect.

* *Look at the facts.* How do the reasons for your past delays reflect attitudes you have unconsciously acted on?

If you can see the ethical aspect of your daily lateness, you can work to meet the expectation. Think briefly about the ethics of your morning choices when you first wake up, and you'll be much more likely to be on time.

Sources: C. Moore and A. E. Tenbrunsel, "'Just Think About It'? Cognitive Complexity and Moral Choice," *Organizational Behavior and Human Decision Processes* 123, no. 2 (2014): 138–49; A. Tenbrunsel, Ethical Systems, www.ethicalsystems.org/content/ann-tenbrunsel, accessed May 7, 2015; Review and podcast of *Blind Spots: Why We Fail to Do What's Right and What to Do about It*, May 4, 2015, http://press.princeton.edu/titles/9390.html, accessed May 7, 2015.

The opinions provided here are of the authors only. The authors are not responsible for any errors or omissions, or for the results obtained from the use of this information. In no event will the authors or their related partnerships or corporations thereof, be liable to you or anyone else for any decision made or action taken in reliance on the opinions provided here.

Common Shortcuts in Judging Others

Shortcuts for judging others often allow us to make accurate perceptions rapidly and provide valid data for making predictions. However, they can and do sometimes result in significant distortions.

Selective Perception   Any characteristic that makes a person, an object, or an event stand out will increase the probability we will perceive it. Why? Because it is impossible for us to assimilate everything we see; we can take in only certain stimuli. Thus, you are more likely to notice cars like your own, and your boss may reprimand some people and not others doing the same thing. Because we can't observe everything going on around us, we use **selective perception**. But we don't choose randomly: We select according to our interests, background, experience, and attitudes. Seeing what we want to see, we sometimes draw unwarranted conclusions from an ambiguous situation.

selective perception The tendency to selectively interpret what one sees on the basis of one's interests, background, experience, and attitudes.

Halo Effect   When we draw an impression about an individual on the basis of a single characteristic, such as intelligence, sociability, or appearance,

halo effect   The tendency to draw a general impression about an individual on the basis of a single characteristic.

contrast effect   Evaluation of a person's characteristics that is affected by comparisons with other people recently encountered who rank higher or lower on the same characteristics.

stereotyping   Judging someone on the basis of one's perception of the group to which that person belongs.

a **halo effect** is operating.[18] The halo effect is easy to demonstrate. If you knew someone was, say, gregarious, what else would you infer? You probably wouldn't say the person was introverted, right? You might assume the person was loud, happy, or quick-witted, when in fact gregarious does not include those other attributes. As managers, we need to be careful not to draw inferences from small clues.

Contrast Effects   An old adage among entertainers is "Never follow an act that has kids or animals in it." Why? Audiences love children and animals so much that you'll look bad in comparison. This example demonstrates how the **contrast effect** can distort perceptions. We don't evaluate a person in isolation. Our reaction is influenced by other people we have recently encountered.

In a series of job interviews, for instance, a candidate is likely to receive a more favorable evaluation if preceded by mediocre applicants and a less favorable evaluation if preceded by strong applicants. Thus, interviewers can make distortions in any given candidate's evaluation as a result of his place in the interview schedule.

Stereotyping   When we judge someone on the basis of our perception of the group to which he or she belongs, we are **stereotyping**.[19]

We deal with the unmanageable number of stimuli of our complex world by using stereotypes or shortcuts called *heuristics* to make decisions quickly. For example, it does make sense to assume that Allison from finance will be able to help you figure out a forecasting problem. The challenge occurs when we generalize inaccurately or too much. Stereotypes can be deeply ingrained and powerful enough to influence life-and-death decisions. One study, controlling for a wide array of factors (such as aggravating or mitigating circumstances), showed that the degree to which black defendants in murder trials looked "stereotypically black" essentially doubled their odds of receiving a death sentence if convicted.[20] Another study found that students tended to assign higher scores

Nurse Li Hongfei, who works at No. 4 People's Hospital in Shenyang, China, experiences negative stereotyping based on his gender. Like Li, male nurses in many countries report that gender stereotyping generalizes inaccurately that nursing is a profession for only women because men lack the patience, empathy, and compassion required to succeed as a nurse.
Source: Zhang Wenkui Xinhua News Agency/Newscom

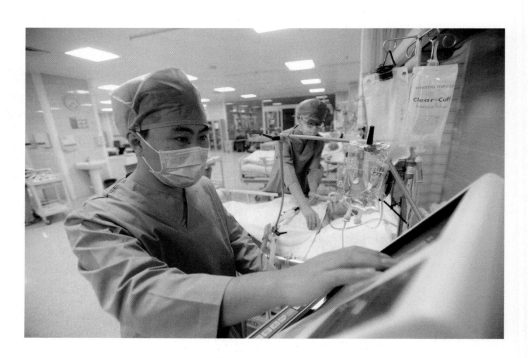

for leadership potential and effective leadership to whites than to minorities, supporting the stereotype of whites as better leaders.[21]

One problem with stereotypes is that they *are* widespread generalizations, though they may not contain a shred of truth when applied to a particular person or situation. We have to monitor ourselves to make sure we're not unfairly applying a stereotype in our evaluations and decisions. Stereotypes are an example of the warning, "The more useful, the more danger from misuse."

It should be obvious by now that our perceptions, many of which are near-instantaneous and without conscious deliberation, color our outlook. Sometimes they have little impact on anyone, but more often our perceptions greatly influence our decisions. The first step toward increasing the effectiveness of organizational decision making is to understand the perception process on an individualized level, discussed next.

Specific Applications of Shortcuts in Organizations

People in organizations are always judging each other. Managers must appraise their employees' performances. We evaluate how much effort our coworkers are putting into their jobs. Team members immediately "size up" a new person. In many cases, our judgments have important consequences for the organization. Let's look at the most obvious applications.

Employment Interview   Few people are hired without an interview. But interviewers make perceptual judgments that are often inaccurate[22] and draw early impressions that quickly become entrenched. Research shows we form impressions of others within a tenth of a second, based on our first glance.[23] Most interviewers' decisions change very little after the first 4 or 5 minutes of an interview. As a result, information elicited early in the interview carries greater weight than does information elicited later, and a "good applicant" is probably characterized more by the absence of unfavorable characteristics than by the presence of favorable ones. Our individual intuition about a job candidate is not reliable in predicting job performance, so collecting input from multiple independent evaluators can be predictive.[24]

Performance Expectations   People attempt to validate their perceptions of reality even when these perceptions are faulty.[25] The terms **self-fulfilling prophecy** and *Pygmalion effect* describe how an individual's behavior is determined by others' expectations. If a manager expects big things from her people, they're not likely to let her down. Similarly, if she expects only minimal performance, they'll likely meet those low expectations. Expectations become reality. The self-fulfilling prophecy has been found to affect the performance of students, soldiers, and even accountants.[26]

self-fulfilling prophecy   A situation in which a person inaccurately perceives a second person, and the resulting expectations cause the second person to behave in ways consistent with the original perception.

Performance Evaluations   We'll discuss performance evaluations in Chapter 17, but note that they very much depend on the perceptual process.[27] An employee's future is closely tied to his or her appraisal—promotion, pay raises, and continuation of employment are among the outcomes. Although the appraisal can be objective (for example, a salesperson is appraised on how many dollars of sales he generates in his territory), many jobs are evaluated subjectively. Subjective evaluations, though often necessary, are problematic because of the errors we've discussed—selective perception, contrast effects, halo effects, and so on. Sometimes performance ratings say as much about the evaluator as they do about the employee!

Myth or Science?

All Stereotypes Are Negative

This statement is false. Positive stereotypes exist as much as negative ones.

A study of Princeton University students shows, for example, that even today we believe Germans are better workers, Italians and African Americans are more loyal, Jews and Chinese are more intelligent, and Japanese and English are more courteous. What is surprising is that positive stereotypes are not always positive.

We may be more likely to "choke" (fail to perform) when we identify with positive stereotypes because they induce pressure to perform at the stereotypical level. For example, men are commonly believed to have higher math ability than women. One study shows that when this stereotype is activated before men take a math test, their performance on the test actually goes down. Another study found that the belief that white men are better at science and math than women or minorities caused white men to leave science, technology, engineering, and math majors. Finally, a study used basketball to illustrate the complexity of stereotypes. Researchers provided evidence to one group of undergradu-ates that whites were better free throw shooters than blacks. Another group was provided evidence that blacks were better free throw shooters than whites. A third group was given no stereotypic information. The undergraduates in all three groups then shot free throws while observers watched. The people who performed the worst were those in the negative stereotype condition (black undergraduates who were told whites were better and white under-graduates who were told blacks were better). However, the positive stereo-type group (black undergraduates who were told blacks were better and white undergraduates who were told whites were better) also did not perform well. The best performance was turned in by those in the group without stereotypic information.

"Choking" is not the only negative thing about positive stereotypes. Research revealed that when women or Asian Americans heard positive stereo-types about themselves ("women are nurturing"; "Asians are good at math"), they felt depersonalized and reacted negatively to the individual express-ing the positive stereotype. Another study showed that positive stereotypes about African Americans actually solidi-fied negative stereotypes because any stereotype tends to reinforce group-based differences, whether positive or negative.

Stereotypes are understandable. To function, we need shortcuts. This short-cut, however, runs both ways. Because stereotypes are socially learned, we need to be vigilant about not accepting or propagating them among our cowork-ers and peers.

Sources: A. C. Kay, M. V. Day, M. P. Zanna, and A. D. Nussbaum, "The Insidious (and Ironic) Effects of Positive Stereotypes," *Journal of Experimental Social Psychology* 49 (2013): 287–91; J. O. Sly and S. Cheryan, "When Compliments Fail to Flatter: American Individualism and Responses to Positive Ste-reotypes," *Journal of Personality and Social Psychology* 104 (2013): 87–102; M. J. Tagler, "Choking under the Pressure of a Positive Stereotype: Gender Identification and Self-Consciousness Moderate Men's Math Test Performance," *Journal of Social Psychology* 152 (2012): 401–16; M. A. Beasley and M. J. Fischer, "Why They Leave: The Impact of Stereotype Threat on the Attrition of Wom-en and Minorities from Science, Math and Engineering Majors," *Social Psychology of Education* 15 (2012): 427–48; and A. Krendl, I. Gainsburg, and N. Ambady, "The Effects of Stereotypes and Observer Pressure on Athletic Performance," *Journal of Sport & Exercise Psychology* 34 (2012): 3–15.

The Link Between Perception and Individual Decision Making

6-3 Explain the link between perception and decision making.

decisions   Choices made from among two or more alternatives.

problem   A discrepancy between the current state of affairs and some desired state.

Individuals make **decisions**, choices from among two or more alternatives. Ideally, decision making would be an objective process, but the way individuals make decisions and the quality of their choices are largely influenced by their perceptions. Individual decision making is an important factor of behavior at all levels of an organization.

Decision making occurs as a reaction to a **problem**. That is, a discrepancy exists between the current state of affairs and some desired state, requiring us to consider alternative courses of action. If your car breaks down and you rely on it to get to work, you have a problem that requires a decision on your part.[28] Unfortunately, most problems don't come neatly labeled. One person's *problem* is another person's *satisfactory state of affairs*. One manager may view her division's 2 percent decline in quarterly sales to be a serious problem requiring immediate action on her part. Her counterpart in another division, who also had a 2 percent sales decrease, might consider it quite acceptable. So awareness that a problem exists and that a decision might or might not be needed is a perceptual issue.

Every decision requires us to interpret and evaluate information. We typically receive data from multiple sources that we need to screen, process, and interpret. Which data are relevant to the decision, and which are not? Our perceptions will answer that question. We also need to develop alternatives and evaluate their strengths and weaknesses. Again, our perceptual process will affect the outcome. Finally, we have to consider how our perceptions of the situation influence our decisions. For instance, how good are you at saying no? Research indicates that we perceive that saying no is uncomfortable, and often after saying no we will feel obligated to say yes to subsequent requests. In fact, people are so uncomfortable saying no that they may agree to unethical acts. When student participants in a study asked 108 strangers to write "pickle" in library books, half of them did it![29]

Decision Making in Organizations

6-4   Contrast the rational model of decision making with bounded rationality and intuition.

Business schools train students to follow rational decision-making models. While such rationalistic models have merit, they don't always describe how people make decisions. OB improves the way we make decisions in organizations by addressing the decision-making errors people commit in addition to the perception errors we've discussed. First, we describe some decision-making constructs, and then outline a few of the most common errors.

The Rational Model, Bounded Rationality, and Intuition

In OB, there are generally accepted constructs of decision making each of us employs to make determinations: rational decision making, bounded rationality, and intuition. Though their processes make sense, they may not lead to the most accurate (or best) decisions. More importantly, there are times when one strategy may lead to a better outcome than another in a given situation.

rational   Characterized by making consistent, value-maximizing choices within specified constraints.

rational decision-making model   A decision-making model that describes how individuals should behave in order to maximize some outcome.

Rational Decision Making   We often think the best decision maker is **rational** and makes consistent, value-maximizing choices within specified constraints.[30] Rational decisions follow a six-step **rational decision-making model**[31] (see Exhibit 6-3).

The rational decision-making model assumes the decision maker has complete information, is able to identify all relevant options in an unbiased manner, and chooses the option with the highest utility.[32] In reality,

Exhibit 6-3	Steps in the Rational Decision-Making Model

1. Define the problem.
2. Identify the decision criteria.
3. Allocate weights to the criteria.
4. Develop the alternatives.
5. Evaluate the alternatives.
6. Select the best alternative.

Nintendo president Satoru Iwata (right) and DeNA president Isao Moriyasu operated within the confines of bounded rationality in deciding to form an alliance to develop and operate new game applications for mobile devices. The alliance brings Nintendo's games and characters to the mobile user market and strengthens DeNA's mobile gaming business.
Source: Akio Kon/Bloomberg/Getty Images

though, most decisions don't follow the rational model; people are usually content to find an acceptable or reasonable solution to a problem rather than an optimal one. We tend to limit our choices to the neighborhood of the problem's symptom and the current alternative at hand. As one expert in decision making put it, "Most significant decisions are made by judgment, rather than by a defined prescriptive model."[33] People are remarkably unaware of making suboptimal decisions.[34]

Bounded Rationality   Often, we don't follow the rational decision-making model for a reason: Our limited information-processing capability makes it impossible to assimilate all the information necessary to optimize, even if the information is readily obtainable.[35] Many problems don't have an optimal solution because they are too complicated to fit the rational decision-making model, so people *satisfice;* they seek solutions that are satisfactory and sufficient. We tend to reduce complex problems to a level we can readily understand.

Because the human mind cannot formulate and solve complex problems with full rationality, we operate within the confines of **bounded rationality**. We construct simplified models that extract the essential features from problems without capturing all their complexity. We can then behave rationally within the limits of the simple model.

How does bounded rationality work for the typical individual? Once we've identified a problem, we begin to search for criteria and alternatives. The criteria are unlikely to be exhaustive. We identify alternatives that are highly visible and that usually represent familiar criteria and tried-and-true solutions. Next, we begin reviewing the alternatives, focusing on choices that differ little from the current state until we identify one that is "good enough"—that meets an acceptable level of performance. Thus ends our search. Therefore, the solution represents a satisficing choice—the first *acceptable* one we encounter—rather than an optimal one.

bounded rationality   A process of making decisions by constructing simplified models that extract the essential features from problems without capturing all their complexity.

Satisficing is not always bad—a simple process may frequently be more sensible than the traditional rational decision-making model.[36] To use the rational model, you need to gather a great deal of information about all the options, compute applicable weights, and then calculate values across a huge number of criteria. All these processes can cost time, energy, and money. If there are many unknown weights and preferences, the fully rational model may not be any more accurate than a best guess. Sometimes a fast-and-frugal process of solving problems might be your best option.

intuitive decision making
An unconscious process created out of distilled experience.

Intuition   Perhaps the least rational way of making decisions is **intuitive decision making**, an unconscious process created from distilled experience.[37] Intuitive decision making occurs outside conscious thought; relies on holistic associations, or links between disparate pieces of information; is fast; and is *affectively charged*, meaning it engages the emotions.[38] While intuition isn't rational, it isn't necessarily wrong. Nor does it always contradict rational analysis; the two can complement each other.

Does intuition help effective decision making? Researchers are divided, but most experts are skeptical, in part because intuition is hard to measure and analyze. Probably the best advice from one expert is: "Intuition can be very useful as a way of setting up a hypothesis but is unacceptable as 'proof.'" Use hunches derived from your experience to speculate, yes, but always make sure to test those hunches with objective data and rational, dispassionate analysis.[39]

As you can see, the more we use objective processes for decision making, the more likely we are to correct some of the problems with our perceptual process. Just as there are biases and errors in the perception process, it stands to reason there are identifiable biases and errors in our decision making, which we will outline next.

Common Biases and Errors in Decision Making

Decision makers engage in bounded rationality, but they also allow systematic biases and errors to creep into their judgments.[40] To minimize effort and avoid trade-offs, people tend to rely too heavily on experience, impulses, gut feelings,

Intuition plays an important role in the investment buying decisions of Warren Buffett, chairman and CEO of Berkshire Hathaway. Buffett begins exploring investment alternatives by using his intuition as a guide in selecting a firm he understands and finds interesting before he starts analyzing the firm, its industry, and its valuation.
Source: Xinhua/Alamy

| Exhibit 6-4 | Reducing Biases and Errors |

Focus on Goals. Without goals, you can't be rational, you don't know what information you need, you don't know which information is relevant and which is irrelevant, you'll find it difficult to choose between alternatives, and you're far more likely to experience regret over the choices you make. Clear goals make decision making easier and help you eliminate options that are inconsistent with your interests.

Look for Information That Disconfirms Your Beliefs. One of the most effective means for counteracting overconfidence and the confirmation and hindsight biases is to actively look for information that contradicts your beliefs and assumptions. When we overtly consider various ways we could be wrong, we challenge our tendencies to think we're smarter than we actually are.

Don't Try to Create Meaning out of Random Events. The educated mind has been trained to look for cause-and-effect relationships. When something happens, we ask why. And when we can't find reasons, we often invent them. You have to accept that there are events in life that are outside your control. Ask yourself if patterns can be meaningfully explained or whether they are merely coincidence. Don't attempt to create meaning out of coincidence.

Increase Your Options. No matter how many options you've identified, your final choice can be no better than the best of the option set you've selected. This argues for increasing your decision alternatives and for using creativity in developing a wide range of diverse choices. The more alternatives you can generate, and the more diverse those alternatives, the greater your chance of finding an outstanding one.

Source: S. P. Robbins, *Decide & Conquer: Making Winning Decisions and Taking Control of Your Life* (Upper Saddle River, NJ: Financial Times/Prentice Hall, 2004), 164–68.

and convenient rules of thumb. Shortcuts can distort rationality. Following are the most common biases in decision making. Exhibit 6-4 provides some suggestions for how to avoid falling into these biases and errors.

Overconfidence Bias   We tend to be overconfident about our abilities and the abilities of others; also, we are usually not aware of this bias.[41] For example, when people say they're 90 percent confident about the range a certain number might take, their estimated ranges contain the correct answer only about 50 percent of the time—and experts are no more accurate in setting up confidence intervals than are novices.[42]

Individuals whose intellectual and interpersonal abilities are *weakest* are most likely to overestimate their performance and ability.[43] There's also a negative relationship between entrepreneurs' optimism and performance of their new ventures: the more optimistic, the less successful.[44] The tendency to be too confident about their ideas might keep some from planning how to avoid problems that arise.

Investor overconfidence operates in a variety of ways.[45] Finance professor Terrance Odean says, "People think they know more than they do, and it costs them." Investors, especially novices, overestimate not just their skill in processing information, but also the quality of the information. Most investors will do only as well as or just slightly better than the market.

anchoring bias   A tendency to fixate on initial information, from which one then fails to adequately adjust for subsequent information.

Anchoring Bias   **Anchoring bias** is a tendency to fixate on initial information and fail to adequately adjust for subsequent information.[46] As we discussed earlier in the chapter in relationship to employment interviews, the mind appears to give a disproportionate amount of emphasis to the first information it receives. Anchors are widely used by people in professions in which persuasion skills are important—advertising, management, politics, real estate, and law.

Any time a negotiation takes place, so does anchoring. When a prospective employer asks how much you made in your prior job, your answer typically anchors the employer's offer. (Remember this when you negotiate your salary, but set the anchor only as high as you truthfully can.) The more precise your anchor, the smaller the adjustment. Some research suggests people think of making an adjustment after an anchor is set as rounding off a number: If you suggest a salary of $55,000, your boss will consider $50,000 to $60,000 a reasonable range for negotiation, but if you mention $55,650, your boss is more likely to consider $55,000 to $56,000 the range of likely values.[47]

Confirmation Bias   The rational decision-making process assumes we objectively gather information. But we don't. We *selectively* gather it. **Confirmation bias** represents a case of selective perception: we seek out information that reaffirms our past choices, and we discount information that contradicts them.[48] We also tend to accept at face value information that confirms our preconceived views, while we are skeptical of information that challenges them. We even tend to seek sources most likely to tell us what we want to hear, and we give too much weight to supporting information and too little to contradictory. Fortunately, those who feel there is a strong need to be accurate in making a decision are less prone to confirmation bias.

Availability Bias   More people fear flying more than driving in a car. But if flying on a commercial airline were as dangerous as driving, the equivalent of two 747s filled to capacity would crash every week, killing all aboard. Because the media give more attention to air accidents, we tend to overstate the risk of flying and understate the risk of driving.

Availability bias is our tendency to base judgments on readily available information. A combination of readily available information and our previous direct experience with similar information has a particularly strong impact on our decision making. Also, events that evoke emotions, are particularly vivid, or are more recent tend to be more available in our memory, leading us to overestimate the chances of unlikely events such as being in an airplane crash, suffering complications from medical treatment, or getting fired.[49] Availability bias can also explain why managers give more weight in performance appraisals to recent employee behaviors than to behaviors of 6 or 9 months earlier.[50]

Escalation of Commitment   Another distortion that creeps into decisions is a tendency to escalate commitment, often for increasingly nonrational reasons.[51] **Escalation of commitment** refers to our staying with a decision even if there is clear evidence it's wrong. Consider a friend who has been dating someone for several years. Although he admits things aren't going too well, he says he is still going to marry her. His justification: "I have a lot invested in the relationship!"

When is escalation most likely to occur? Evidence indicates it occurs when individuals view themselves as responsible for the outcome. The fear of personal failure even biases the way we search for and evaluate information so that we choose only information that supports our dedication. It doesn't appear to matter whether we chose the failing course of action or it was assigned to us—we feel responsible and escalate in either case. Also, the sharing of decision authority—such as when others review the choice we made—can lead to higher escalation.[52]

We usually think of escalation of commitment as ungrounded. However, persistence in the face of failure is responsible for a great many of history's greatest feats, the building of the Pyramids, the Great Wall of China, the Panama Canal, and the Empire State Building among them. Researchers suggest a balanced

confirmation bias   The tendency to seek out information that reaffirms past choices and to discount information that contradicts past judgments.

availability bias   The tendency for people to base their judgments on information that is readily available to them.

escalation of commitment   An increased commitment to a previous decision in spite of negative information.

approach includes frequent evaluation of the spent costs and whether the next step is worth the anticipated costs.[53] What we want to combat is thus the tendency to *automatically* escalate commitment.

Randomness Error   Most of us like to think we have some control over our world. Our tendency to believe we can predict the outcome of random events is the **randomness error**.

randomness error   The tendency of individuals to believe that they can predict the outcome of random events.

Decision making suffers when we try to create meaning in random events, particularly when we turn imaginary patterns into superstitions.[54] These can be completely contrived ("I never make important decisions on Friday the 13th") or they can evolve from a reinforced past pattern of behavior (Tiger Woods often wears a red shirt during a golf tournament's final round because he won many junior tournaments wearing red shirts). Decisions based on random occurrences can handicap us when they affect our judgment or bias our major decisions.

Risk Aversion   Mathematically speaking, we should find a 50–50 flip of the coin for $100 to be worth as much as a sure promise of $50. After all, the expected value of the gamble over a number of trials is $50. However, nearly everyone but committed gamblers would rather have the sure thing than a risky prospect.[55] For many people, a 50–50 flip of a coin even for $200 might not be worth as much as a sure promise of $50, even though the gamble is mathematically worth twice as much! This tendency to prefer a sure thing over a risky outcome is **risk aversion**.

risk aversion   The tendency to prefer a sure gain of a moderate amount over a riskier outcome, even if the riskier outcome might have a higher expected payoff.

Risk aversion has important implications. For example, to offset the inherent risk employees accept in a commission-based wage, companies may pay commissioned employees considerably more than they do those on straight salaries. Second, risk-averse employees will stick with the established way of doing their jobs rather than take a chance on innovative methods. Continuing with a strategy that has worked in the past minimizes risk, but it will lead to stagnation. Third, ambitious people with power that can be taken away (most managers) appear to be especially risk averse, perhaps because they don't want to gamble with everything they've worked so hard to achieve.[56] CEOs at risk of termination are exceptionally risk averse, even when a riskier investment strategy is in their firms' best interests.[57]

Risk preference is sometimes reversed: People take chances when trying to prevent a negative outcome.[58] They may thus risk losing a lot of money at trial rather than settle for less out of court. Stressful situations can make risk preferences stronger. People under stress will more likely engage in risk-seeking behavior to avoid negative outcomes, and risk-averse behavior in seeking positive outcomes.[59]

Hindsight Bias   **Hindsight bias** is the tendency to believe falsely, after the outcome is known, that we would have accurately predicted it.[60] When we have feedback on the outcome, we seem good at concluding it was obvious.

hindsight bias   The tendency to believe falsely, after an outcome of an event is actually known, that one would have accurately predicted that outcome.

For instance, the original home video rental industry, renting movies at brick-and-mortar stores, collapsed as online distribution outlets ate away at the market.[61] Some have suggested that if rental companies like Blockbuster had leveraged their brand to offer online streaming and kiosks, they could have avoided failure. While that seems obvious now in hindsight, tempting us to think we would have predicted it, many experts failed to predict industry trends in advance. Though criticisms of decision makers may have merit, as Malcolm Gladwell, author of *Blink* and *The Tipping Point*, writes, "What is clear in hindsight is rarely clear before the fact."[62]

We are all susceptible to biases like hindsight bias, but are we all susceptible to the same degree? It is not likely. Our individual differences play a significant role in our decision-making processes, while our organizations constrain the range of our available decision choices.

> ## ✪ TRY IT!
> If your professor has assigned this, go to the Assignments section of **mymanagementlab.com** to complete the **Simulation: *Decision Making*.**

Influences on Decision Making: Individual Differences and Organizational Constraints

6-5 Explain how individual differences and organizational constraints affect decision making.

We turn here to factors that influence the way people make decisions and the degree to which they are susceptible to errors and biases. We discuss individual differences and then organizational constraints.

Individual Differences

As we discussed, decision making in practice is characterized by bounded rationality, common biases and errors, and the use of intuition. Individual differences such as personality also create deviations from the rational model.

Personality   Research suggests personality influences our decisions. Let's look at conscientiousness and self-esteem.

Specific facets of conscientiousness—particularly achievement-striving and dutifulness—may affect escalation of commitment.[63] First, achievement-oriented people hate to fail, so they escalate their commitment, hoping to forestall failure. Dutiful people, however, are more inclined to do what they see as best for the organization, so they are less likely to escalate their commitment. Second, achievement-striving individuals appear more susceptible to hindsight bias,[64] perhaps because they have a need to justify their actions. We don't have evidence yet on whether dutiful people are immune to this bias.

Self-esteem, or a general self-perception of being good enough, is a rather stable trait. People with high self-esteem are strongly motivated to maintain it, so they use the self-serving bias to preserve it. They blame others for their failures while taking credit for successes.[65]

Gender   Who makes better decisions, men or women? It depends on the situation. When the situation isn't stressful, decision making by men and women is about equal in quality. In stressful situations, it appears that men become more egocentric and make more risky decisions, while women become more empathetic and their decision making improves.[66] Research on rumination, or reflecting at length, offers further insights into gender differences in decision making.[67] Women spend more time than men analyzing the past, present, and future. They're more likely to overanalyze problems before making a decision and to rehash a decision once made. This can make problems harder to solve, increase regret over past decisions, and increase depression. Women are nearly twice as likely as men to develop depression,[68] but why women ruminate more than men is not clear. However, the gender difference seems to lessen with age. Differences are largest during young adulthood and smallest after age 65, when both men and women ruminate the least.[69]

Mental Ability   We know people with higher levels of mental ability are able to process information more quickly, solve problems more accurately, and learn faster, so you might expect them to be less susceptible to common decision errors. However, mental ability appears to help people avoid only some of them.[70] Smart people are just as likely to fall prey to anchoring, overconfidence, and escalation of commitment, probably because being smart doesn't alert you to the possibility you're too confident or emotionally defensive. It's not that intelligence never matters. Once warned about decision-making errors, more intelligent people learn more quickly to avoid them.

Cultural Differences   The rational model makes no acknowledgment of cultural differences, nor does the bulk of OB research literature on decision making. But Indonesians, for instance, don't necessarily make decisions the same way Australians do. Therefore, we need to recognize that the cultural background of a decision maker can significantly influence the selection of problems, the depth of analysis, the importance placed on logic and rationality, and whether organizational decisions should be made autocratically by an individual manager or collectively in groups.[71]

Cultures differ in time orientation, the value they place on rationality, their belief in the ability of people to solve problems, and their preference for collective decision making. First, differences in time orientation help us understand, for instance, why managers in Egypt make decisions at a much slower and more deliberate pace than their U.S. counterparts. Second, while rationality is valued in North America, that's not true elsewhere. A North American manager might make a decision intuitively but know it's important to appear to proceed in a rational fashion because rationality is highly valued in the West. In countries such as Iran, where rationality is not paramount to other factors, efforts to appear rational are not necessary.

Third, some cultures emphasize solving problems, while others focus on accepting situations as they are. The United States falls in the first category; Thailand and Indonesia are examples of the second. Because problem-solving managers believe they can and should change situations to their benefit, U.S. managers might identify a problem long before their Thai or Indonesian counterparts would choose to recognize it as such. Fourth, decision making in Japan is much more group-oriented than in the United States. The Japanese value conformity and cooperation, so before Japanese CEOs make an important decision, they collect a large amount of information to use in consensus-forming group decisions.

Nudging   Anyone who has ever seen a commercial knows about nudging. Commercials are one of the most outright forms of an organization's attempt to influence our perceptions of a product and our decision to acquire that product. Nudging has also been used positively in the development of corporate social responsibility (CSR) initiatives to change people's expectations for organizations.[72] People differ in their susceptibility to suggestion, but it is probably fair to say we are all receptive to nudging to some degree.

OB researchers are on the leading edge of figuring out how organizations can nudge individuals into better decision making.[73] Nudging uses psychology to circumvent our natural negative tendencies. In organizations, nudging usually involves strategic placement of facts and resources that subtly suggest a better decision. For instance, organizations that automatically enroll employees in retirement plans have greater participation than those whose employees choose from many options, including not to enroll.[74]

Organizational Constraints

Organizations can constrain decision makers, creating deviations from the rational model. For instance, managers shape decisions to reflect the organization's performance evaluation and reward systems, to comply with formal regulations, and to meet organizationally imposed time constraints. Precedents can also limit decisions.

Performance Evaluation Systems Managers are influenced by the criteria on which they are evaluated. If a division manager believes the manufacturing plants under his responsibility are operating best when he hears nothing negative, the plant managers will spend a good part of their time ensuring that negative information doesn't reach him.

Reward Systems The organization's reward systems influence decision makers by suggesting which choices have better personal payoffs. If the organization rewards risk aversion, managers are more likely to make conservative decisions. For instance, for over half a century (the 1930s through the mid-1980s), General Motors consistently gave promotions and bonuses to managers who kept a low profile and avoided controversy. These executives became adept at dodging tough issues and passing controversial decisions on to committees, which harmed the organization over time.

Formal Regulations David, a shift manager at a Taco Bell restaurant in San Antonio, Texas, describes constraints he faces on his job: "I've got rules and regulations covering almost every decision I make—from how to make a burrito to how often I need to clean the restrooms. My job doesn't come with much freedom of choice." David's situation is not unique. All but the smallest organizations create rules and policies to program decisions and get individuals to act in the intended manner. In doing so, they limit decision choices.

Manager Kely Guardado (center) prepares hamburgers alongside employees at a Five Guys Burger and Fries restaurant. Decision choices of Five Guys crew members are limited because workers are required to follow rules and regulations for food preparation that meet the firm's high standards of quality, safety, and service.
Source: Yuri Gripas/Reuters

System-Imposed Time Constraints   Almost all important decisions come with explicit deadlines. For example, a report on new-product development may have to be ready for executive committee review by the first of the month. Such conditions often make it difficult, if not impossible, for managers to gather all information before making a final choice.

Historical Precedents   Decisions aren't made in a vacuum; they have context. Individual decisions are points in a stream of choices; those made in the past are like ghosts that haunt and constrain current choices. It's common knowledge that the largest determinant of the size of any given year's budget is last year's budget. Choices made today are largely a result of choices made over the years.

What About Ethics in Decision Making?

6-6   Contrast the three ethical decision criteria.

Ethical considerations should be important to all organizational decision making. In this section, we present three ways to frame decisions ethically and then address the important issue of the effect of lying on decision making.

Three Ethical Decision Criteria

utilitarianism   A system in which decisions are made to provide the greatest good for the greatest number.

The first ethical yardstick is **utilitarianism**, which proposes making decisions solely on the basis of their *outcomes,* ideally to provide the greatest good for the greatest number.[75] This view dominates business decision making and is consistent with goals such as efficiency, productivity, and high profits. Keep in mind that utilitarianism is not always as objective as it sounds. A recent study indicated that the ethicality of utilitarianism is influenced in ways we don't realize. Participants were given a moral dilemma: The weight of five people bends a footbridge so it is low to some train tracks. A train is about to hit the bridge. The choice is to let all five people perish, or push the one heavy man off the bridge to save four people. In the United States, South Korea, France, and Israel, 20 percent of respondents chose to push the man off the bridge, in Spain, 18 percent, and in Korea, none. These might speak to cultural utilitarian values, but a minor change, asking people to answer in a non-native language they knew, caused more participants to push the man overboard: in one group, 33 percent pushed the man, and in another group 44 percent did.[76] The emotional distance of answering in a non-native language thus seemed to foster a utilitarian viewpoint. It appears that even our view of what we consider pragmatic is changeable.

Another ethical criterion is to make decisions consistent with fundamental liberties and privileges, as set forth in documents such as the U.S. Bill of Rights. An emphasis on *rights* in decision making means respecting and protecting the basic rights of individuals, such as the right to privacy, free speech, and due process. This criterion protects **whistle-blowers**[77] when they reveal an organization's unethical practices to the press or government agencies, using their right to free speech.

whistle-blowers   Individuals who report unethical practices by their employer to outsiders.

A third criterion is to impose and enforce rules fairly and impartially to ensure *justice* or an equitable distribution of benefits and costs.[78] Justice perspectives are sometimes used to justify paying people the same wage for a given job regardless of performance differences and using seniority as the primary determinant in layoff decisions.

Decision makers, particularly in for-profit organizations, feel comfortable with utilitarianism. The "best interests" of the organization and its stockholders can justify a lot of questionable actions, such as large layoffs. But many critics feel this perspective needs to change. Public concern about individual rights and social justice suggests managers should develop ethical standards based on nonutilitarian criteria. This presents a challenge because satisfying individual rights and social justice creates far more ambiguities than utilitarian effects on efficiency and profits. However, while raising prices, selling products with questionable effects on consumer health, closing down inefficient plants, laying off large numbers of employees, and moving production overseas to cut costs can be justified in utilitarian terms, there may no longer be a single measure by which good decisions are judged.

This is where corporate social responsibility (CSR) comes in to affect a positive change. As we can see by looking at utilitarian ideals, organizations are not motivated to respond equitably when they are looking only at a balance sheet. However, public pressure on organizations to behave responsibly has meant sustainability issues now affect the bottom line: Consumers increasingly choose to purchase goods and services from organizations with effective CSR initiatives, high performers are attracted to work at CSR organizations, governments offer incentives to organizations for sustainability efforts, and so forth. CSR is now beginning to make good business sense, folding ethics into utilitarian computations.

behavioral ethics Analyzing how people actually behave when confronted with ethical dilemmas.

Increasingly, researchers are turning to **behavioral ethics**—an area of study that analyzes how people behave when confronted with ethical dilemmas. Their research tells us that while ethical standards exist collectively in societies and organizations, and individually in the form of personal ethics, we do not always follow ethical standards promoted by our organizations, and we sometimes violate our own standards. Our ethical behavior varies widely from one situation to the next.

How might we increase ethical decision making in organizations? First, sociologist James Q. Wilson promulgated the *broken windows theory*—the idea that decayed and disorderly urban environments may facilitate criminal behavior because they signal antisocial norms. Although controversial, the theory does fit with behavioral ethics research showing that seemingly superficial aspects of the environment—such as lighting, outward displays of wealth and status, and cleanliness—can affect ethical behavior in organizations.[79] Managers must first realize that ethical behavior can be affected by signals; for example, if signs of status and money are everywhere, an employee may perceive those, rather than ethical standards, to be of the highest importance. Second, managers should encourage conversations about moral issues; they may serve as a reminder and increase ethical decision making. One study found that simply asking business school students to think of an ethical situation had powerful effects when they were making ethical choices later.[80] Finally, we should be aware of our own moral "blind spots"—the tendency to see ourselves as more moral than we are and others as less moral than they are. An environment that encourages open discussions and does not penalize people for coming forward is key to overcoming blind spots and increasing the ethicality of decision making.[81]

Behavioral ethics research stresses the importance of culture to ethical decision making. There are few global standards for ethical decision making,[82] as contrasts between Asia and the West illustrate. What is ethical in one culture may be unethical in another. For example, because bribery is more common in countries such as China, a Canadian working in China might face a dilemma: Should I pay a bribe to secure business if it is an accepted part of that country's culture? Although some companies, such as

IBM, explicitly address this issue, many do not. Without sensitivity to cultural differences as part of the definition of ethical conduct, organizations may encourage unethical conduct without even knowing it.

Lying

Are you a liar? Many of us would not like to be labeled as a liar. But if a liar is merely someone who lies, we are all liars. We lie to ourselves, and we lie to others. We lie consciously and unconsciously. We tell big lies and create small deceptions. Lying is one of the top unethical activities we may indulge in daily, and it undermines all efforts toward sound decision making.

The truth is that one of the reasons we lie is because lying is difficult for others to detect. In more than 200 studies, individuals correctly identified people who were lying only 47 percent of the time, which is less than random picking.[83] This seems to be true no matter what lie-detection technique is employed. For example, one technique police officers use is based on the theory that people look up and to the right when they lie. Unfortunately, researchers who tested the technique could not substantiate the underlying theory.[84]

Another technique is to study a person's body language, but researchers found that the probability of detecting lying based solely on body language was less than a random guess. Psychologist Maria Hartwig observed, "The common-sense notion that liars betray themselves through body language appears to be little more than a cultural fiction."[85] Still another technique is to study facial expressions. Here again, many researchers could not support the technique with evidence. Research professor Nicholas Epley concluded, "Reading people's expressions can give you a little information, but you can get so much more just by talking to them."[86]

What about our words? Liars may indeed give verbal cues, but which cues apply to which people is a matter of debate. Whether liars tell better stories, or conversely give fewer details, is not certain. Law enforcers analyze an individual's words, looking for emphatic or repeated phrases to indicate lying. Detecting lies from our written words is even trickier since there are fewer cues. However, that doesn't stop lie-detection speculation for written communications. Some say that in e-mail messages, liars omit personal pronouns, use noncommittal expressions, change tenses, skip topics, provide too much detail, or add qualifying statements.[87] Yet a person who regularly does those things when writing may not be lying.

The best hope for lie detection is to read a combination of cues unique to the person. Perhaps it is true that a mother can sometimes tell when her child is lying, for instance, because the mother knows how the child changes his behavior when he's stressed. Thus, although we may feel that our lying is "written all over our face," as Epley says, "The mind comes through the mouth."[88] Lie detection is also easier if the person is a bad liar without a lot of experience. According to Tyler Cohen Wood of the Defense Intelligence Agency's Science and Technology Directorate, "The majority of people prefer to tell the truth. That's why when they are lying, the truth is going to leak out."[89] Finally, research indicates that while we do not consciously discern lying in others, we are able to sense on some level when lying is happening.[90]

Lying is deadly to decision making, whether we sense the lies or not. Managers—and organizations—simply cannot make good decisions when facts are misrepresented and people give false motives for their behaviors. Lying is a big ethical problem as well. From an organizational perspective, using fancy lie-detection techniques and entrapping liars when possible yield unreliable results.[91] The most lasting solution comes from organizational behavior, which studies ways to prevent lying by working with our natural propensities to create environments non-conducive to lying.

Choosing to Lie

Mark Twain wrote, "The wise thing is for us diligently to train ourselves to lie thoughtfully." Not everyone agrees that lying is wrong. But we probably agree that people do lie, including each of us, to varying degrees. And most of us probably agree that if we lied less, organizations and society would be better off. So how might that be done? Research conducted by behavioral scientists suggests some steps to recovery.

1. **Stop lying to ourselves.** We lie to ourselves about how much we lie. Specifically, many studies reveal that we deem ourselves much less likely to lie than we judge others to be. At a collective level, this is impossible—everyone can't be below above average in their propensity to lie. So step 1 is to admit the truth: We underestimate the degree to which we lie, we overestimate our morality compared to that of others, and we tend to engage in "moral hypocrisy"—we think we're more moral than we are.

2. **Trust, but verify.** Lying is learned at a very young age. When a toy was placed out of view, an experimenter told young children not to look at the toy and went out of sight. More than 80 percent of the children looked at the toy. When asked whether they had looked, 25 percent of 2½-year-olds lied, compared to 90 percent of 4-year-olds. Why do we learn to lie? Because we often get away with it. Negotiation research shows that we are more likely to lie in the future when our lies have succeeded or gone undetected in the past. Managers need to eliminate situations in which lying is available to employees.

3. **Reward honesty.** "The most difficult thing is to recognize that sometimes we too are blinded by our own incentives," writes author Dan Ariely, "because we don't see how our conflicts of interest work on us." So if we want more honesty, we have to provide greater incentives for the truth, and more disincentives for lying and cheating.

Sources: Based on D. Ariely, *The Honest Truth about Dishonesty: How We Lie to Everyone—and Especially Ourselves* (New York: Harper, 2012); K. Canavan, "Even Nice People Cheat Sometimes," *The Wall Street Journal,* August 8, 2012, 4B; M. H. Bazerman and Ann E. Tenbrunsel, *Blind Spots: Why We Fail to Do What's Right and What to Do about It* (Princeton, NJ: Princeton University Press, 2012); A. D. Evans and K. Lee, "Emergence of Lying in Very Young Children," *Developmental Psychology* (2013); and L. Zhou, Y. Sung, and D. Zhang, "Deception Performance in Online Group Negotiation and Decision Making: The Effects of Deception Experience and Deception Skill," *Group Decision and Negotiation* 22 (2013): 153–72.

Creativity, Creative Decision Making, and Innovation in Organizations

6-7 Describe the three-stage model of creativity.

creativity The ability to produce novel and useful ideas.

three-stage model of creativity The proposition that creativity involves three stages: causes (creative potential and creative environment), creative behavior, and creative outcomes (innovation).

problem formulation The stage of creative behavior that involves identifying a problem or opportunity requiring a solution that is as yet unknown.

Models will often improve our decisions, but a decision maker also needs **creativity**, the ability to produce novel and useful ideas. Novel ideas are different from what's been done before but which are appropriate for the problem.

Creativity allows the decision maker to fully appraise and understand problems, including seeing problems others can't see. Although all aspects of organizational behavior are complex, that is especially true for creativity. To simplify, Exhibit 6-5 provides a **three-stage model of creativity** in organizations. The core of the model is *creative behavior,* which has both *causes* (predictors of creative behavior) and *effects* (outcomes of creative behavior). In this section, we discuss the three stages of creativity, starting with the center, creative behavior.

Creative Behavior

Creative behavior occurs in four steps, each of which leads to the next[92]:

1. **Problem formulation.** Any act of creativity begins with a problem that the behavior is designed to solve. Thus, **problem formulation** is the stage

Exhibit 6-5	Three-Stage Model of Creativity in Organizations

Causes of creative behavior

Creative potential	Creative environment

⬇

Creative behavior

Problem formulation ⇨ Information gathering ⇨ Idea generation ⇨ Idea evaluation

⬇

Creative outcomes (Innovation)

Novelty	Usefulness

of creative behavior in which we identify a problem or opportunity that requires a solution as yet unknown. For example, Marshall Carbee and John Bennett founded Eco Safety Products after discovering that even paints declared safe by the Environmental Protection Agency (EPA) emitted hazardous chemical compounds. Thus, Eco's development of artist-safe soy-based paint began with identifying a safety problem with paints currently on the market.[93]

2. **Information gathering.** Given a problem, the solution is rarely directly at hand. We need time to learn more and to process that learning. Thus, **information gathering** is the stage of creative behavior when knowledge is sought and possible solutions to a problem incubate in an individual's mind. Information gathering leads us to identifying innovation opportunities.[94] Niklas Laninge of Hoa's Tool Shop, a Stockholm-based company that helps organizations become more innovative, argues that creative information gathering means thinking beyond usual routines and comfort zones. For example, have lunch with someone outside your field to discuss the problem. "It's so easy, and you're forced to speak about your business and the things that you want to accomplish in new terms. You can't use buzz-words because people don't know what you mean," Laninge says.[95]

3. **Idea generation.** **Idea generation** is the process of creative behavior in which we develop possible solutions to a problem from relevant information and knowledge. Sometimes we do this alone, when tricks like taking a walk[96] and doodling[97] can jumpstart the process. Increasingly, though, idea generation is collaborative. For example, when NASA engineers developed the idea for landing a spacecraft on Mars, they did so collaboratively. Before coming up with the Curiosity—an SUV-sized rover that lands on Mars from a sky crane—the team spent 3 days scribbling potential ideas on whiteboards.[98]

4. **Idea evaluation.** Finally, it's time to choose from the ideas we have generated. Thus, **idea evaluation** is the process of creative behavior in which we evaluate potential solutions to identify the best one. Sometimes the method of choosing can be innovative. When Dallas Mavericks owner Mark Cuban was unhappy with the team's uniforms, he asked fans to help design and choose the best uniform. Cuban said, "What's the best way to come up with creative ideas? You ask for them. So we are going to crowd source the design and colors of our uniforms."[99] Generally, you want those who evaluate ideas to be different from those who generate them, to eliminate the obvious biases.

information gathering The stage of creative behavior when possible solutions to a problem incubate in an individual's mind.

idea generation The process of creative behavior that involves developing possible solutions to a problem from relevant information and knowledge.

idea evaluation The process of creative behavior involving the evaluation of potential solutions to problems to identify the best one.

Causes of Creative Behavior

Having defined creative behavior, the main stage in the three-stage model, we now look back to the causes of creativity: creative potential and creative environment.

Creative Potential   Is there such a thing as a creative personality? Indeed. While creative genius is rare—whether in science (Stephen Hawking), performing arts (Martha Graham), or business (Steve Jobs)—most people have some of the characteristics shared by exceptionally creative people. The more of these characteristics we have, the higher our creative potential. Innovation is one of the top organizational goals for leaders (see OB Poll). Consider these facets of potential:

1. **Intelligence and Creativity**   Intelligence is related to creativity. Smart people are more creative because they are better at solving complex problems. However, intelligent individuals may also be more creative because they have greater "working memory," that is, they can recall more information related to the task at hand.[100] Along the same lines, recent research in the Netherlands indicates that an individual's high need for cognition (desire to learn) is correlated with greater creativity.[101]

2. **Personality and Creativity**   The Big Five personality trait of openness to experience (see Chapter 5) correlates with creativity, probably because open individuals are less conformist in action and more divergent in thinking.[102] Other traits of creative people include proactive personality, self-confidence, risk taking, tolerance for ambiguity, and perseverance.[103] Hope, self-efficacy (belief in your capabilities), and positive affect also predict an individual's creativity.[104] Furthermore, research in China suggests that people with high core self-evaluations are better able than others to maintain creativity in negative situations.[105] Perhaps counterintuitively, some research supports the "mad genius" theory that some people with mental illness are wildly creative partially due to their psychopathology; history certainly provides examples, such as Vincent Van Gogh, John Forbes Nash, and

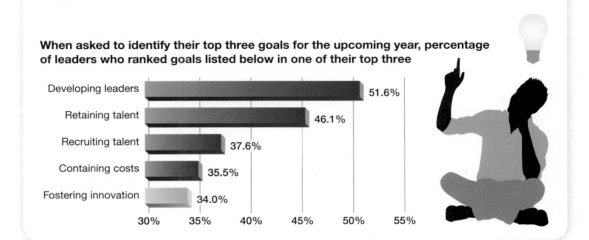

OB POLL

Is Innovation More Talk than Show?

When asked to identify their top three goals for the upcoming year, percentage of leaders who ranked goals listed below in one of their top three

Goal	Percentage
Developing leaders	51.6%
Retaining talent	46.1%
Recruiting talent	37.6%
Containing costs	35.5%
Fostering innovation	34.0%

Source: Based on T. Henneman, "Bright Ideas," *Workforce Management* (January 2013), 18–25.

others. However, the converse isn't true—people who are creative may have less psychopathology as a group than the general population.[106]

3. **Expertise and Creativity** *Expertise* is the foundation for all creative work and thus is the single most important predictor of creative potential. Film writer, producer, and director Quentin Tarantino spent his youth working in a video rental store, where he built up an encyclopedic knowledge of movies. The potential for creativity is enhanced when individuals have abilities, knowledge, proficiencies, and similar expertise to their field of endeavor. For instance, you wouldn't expect someone with minimal knowledge of programming to be very creative as a software engineer. The expertise of others is important, too. People with larger social networks have greater exposure to diverse ideas and informal access to the expertise and resources of others.[107]

4. **Ethics and Creativity** Although creativity is linked to many desirable individual characteristics, it is not correlated with ethicality. People who cheat may actually be more creative than those who behave ethically, according to recent research. It may be that dishonesty and creativity can both stem from a rule-breaking desire.[108]

★ PERSONAL INVENTORY ASSESSMENTS

How Creative Are You?

Everyone is innovative, to some degree. Take this PIA to find out if you are wildly or mildly creative.

Creative Environment Most of us have creative potential we can learn to apply, but as important as creative potential is, by itself it is not enough. We need to be in an environment where creative potential can be realized. What environmental factors affect whether creative potential translates into creative behaviors?

First and perhaps most important is *motivation.* If you aren't motivated to be creative, it is unlikely you will be. Intrinsic motivation, or the desire to work on something because it's interesting, exciting, satisfying, and challenging (discussed in more detail in the next chapter), correlates fairly strongly with creative outcomes.[109]

It is also valuable to work in an environment that rewards and recognizes creative work. A study of health care teams found that team creativity translated into innovation only when the climate actively supported innovation.[110] The organization should foster the free flow of ideas, including providing fair and constructive judgment. Freedom from excessive rules encourages creativity; employees should have the freedom to decide what work is to be done and how to do it. One study in China revealed that both structural empowerment (in which the structure of the work unit allows sufficient employee freedom) and psychological empowerment (which lets the individual feel personally enabled to decide) were related to employee creativity.[111] However, research in Slovenia found that creating a competitive climate where achievement at any cost is valued will stymie creativity.[112]

You may be wondering about the link between organizational resources and creativity. While it is said that "necessity is the mother of invention," recent research indicates that creativity can be inspired by an abundance of resources as well. It appears that managers greatly affect the outcomes. They may be able to heighten innovation when resources are limited by encouraging employees to find resources for their novel ideas, and by giving direct attention to appropriate tools when resources are plentiful.[113] Managers also serve an important bridge role for knowledge transfer. When managers link teams to additional information and resources, radical creativity (introducing creative ideas that break the status quo) is more likely.[114] The weaker ties between team members and manager networks may actually have more impact on creativity than the direct, stronger ties that team members have with their own networks, because the weaker sources provide more divergent thinking.[115]

What is the role of culture? A recent nation-level study suggests that countries scoring high on Hofstede's culture dimension of individuality (see Chapter 5) are more creative.[116] Western countries like the United States, Italy, and Belgium score high on individuality, and South American and eastern countries like China, Colombia, and Pakistan score low. Does this mean Western cultures are more creative? Some evidence suggests this is true. One study compared the creative projects of German and Chinese college students, some of whom were studying in their homeland, and some of whom were studying abroad. An independent panel of Chinese and German judges determined that the German students were most creative and that Asian German students were more creative than domestic Chinese students. This suggested the German culture was more creative.[117] However, even if some cultures are more creative on average, there is always strong variation within cultures. Put another way, there are millions of Chinese more creative than their U.S. counterparts.

Good leadership matters to creativity too. One study of more than 100 teams working in a large bank revealed that when the leader behaved in a punitive, unsupportive manner, the teams were less creative.[118] On the other hand, when leaders are encouraging in tone, run their units in a transparent fashion, and encourage the development of their employees, the individuals they supervise are more creative.[119]

As we will learn in Chapter 10, more work today is being done in teams, and many people believe diversity will increase team creativity. Past research has suggested that diverse teams are not more creative. More recently, however, one study of Dutch teams revealed that when team members were explicitly asked to understand and consider the point of view of the other team members (an exercise called perspective-taking), diverse teams *were* more creative than those with less diversity.[120] Leadership might make the difference. One study of 68 Chinese teams reported that diversity was positively related to team creativity only when the team's leader was inspirational and instilled members with confidence.[121]

There are other worthwhile findings regarding creativity. One study in a multinational drug company found that teams from diverse business functions were more creative when they shared knowledge of each other's areas of expertise.[122] However, if team members have a similar background, creativity may be heightened only when the members are sharing specific, detailed information,[123] since general information may be dismissed by members with the same expertise. As you might expect, newcomers to a team can be a rich source of creative ideas, although they are unfortunately often expected to contribute less early on.[124] Putting individuals who are resistant to change into teams that are supportive of change can increase total creativity,[125] perhaps because of the group's positive influence. Collectively, these studies show that diverse teams *can* be more creative, especially if they are intentionally led.

Creative Outcomes (Innovation)

The final stage in our model of creativity is the outcome. Creative behavior does not always produce an innovative outcome. An employee might generate a creative idea and never share it. Management might reject a creative solution.

Teams might squelch creative behaviors by isolating those who propose different ideas. One study showed that most people have a bias against accepting creative ideas because ideas create uncertainty. When people feel uncertain, their ability to see any idea as creative is blocked.[126]

We can define *creative outcomes* as ideas or solutions judged to be novel and useful by relevant stakeholders. Novelty itself does not generate a creative outcome if it isn't useful. Thus, "off-the-wall" solutions are creative only if they help solve the problem. The usefulness of the solution might be self-evident (the iPad), or it might be considered successful by only the stakeholders initially.[127]

An organization may harvest many creative ideas from its employees and call itself innovative. However, as one expert stated, "Ideas are useless unless used." Soft skills help translate ideas into results. One researcher found that in a large agribusiness company, creative ideas were most likely to be implemented when an individual was motivated to translate the idea into practice—and had strong networking ability.[128] These studies highlight an important fact: Creative ideas do not implement themselves; translating them into creative outcomes is a social process that requires utilizing other concepts addressed in this text, including power and politics, leadership, and motivation.

Summary

Individuals base their behavior not on the way their external environment actually is, but rather on the way they see it or believe it to be. An understanding of the way people make decisions can help us explain and predict behavior, but few important decisions are simple or unambiguous enough for the rational model's assumptions to apply. We find individuals looking for solutions that satisfice rather than optimize, injecting biases and prejudices into the decision process, and relying on intuition. Managers should encourage creativity in employees and teams to create a route to innovative decision making.

Implications for Managers

- Behavior follows perception, so to influence behavior at work, assess how people perceive their work. Often behaviors we find puzzling can be explained by understanding the initiating perceptions.
- Make better decisions by recognizing perceptual biases and decision-making errors we tend to commit. Learning about these problems doesn't always prevent us from making mistakes, but it does help.
- Adjust your decision-making approach to the national culture you're operating in and to the criteria your organization values. If you're in a country that doesn't value rationality, don't feel compelled to follow the decision-making model or to try to make your decisions appear rational. Adjust your decision approach to ensure compatibility with the organizational culture.
- Combine rational analysis with intuition. These are not conflicting approaches to decision making. By using both, you can actually improve your decision-making effectiveness.
- Try to enhance your creativity. Actively look for novel solutions to problems, attempt to see problems in new ways, use analogies, and hire creative talent. Try to remove work and organizational barriers that might impede creativity.

Stereotypes Are Dying

POINT

I n the *Myth or Science?* feature in this chapter, we discussed the harmful effects of stereotypes, even positive ones. Fortunately, stereotypes are dying a slow but inexorable death. Whether they are about women, racial or ethnic minorities, or those of minority sexual orientations, each passing year brings evidence that stereotypes are losing their hold—thanks to the progress of society, but also thanks to younger individuals replacing older ones in the workforce. Younger people are less likely to endorse stereotypes across the board.

In the 1930s, when asked whether African Americans were "superstitious," 84 percent agreed; 75 percent endorsed a stereotype that African Americans were "lazy." Thankfully, those stereotypes are nearly gone. Results vary by study, but today between 0 and 10 percent of individuals agree with those stereotypes. These results show that racism still exists, but they also show it is waning.

Even when people endorse stereotypes, their consensus has weakened dramatically over time. For example, if forced to choose 10 adjectives to describe a group of people, at one time people converged on a few (often incorrect) traits. Today, the lists will vary dramatically by person.

There is another factor at play here: the media. Media reports are not a good source of scientific information, yet to listen to them, you'd think stereotypes were as alive as ever. Fortunately, that's not the case, but when stereotypes fade, it's not newsworthy. Someday soon, stereotypic thinking will be as retrograde as outright acts of racism or sexism. We should count ourselves lucky to live in societies and work in organizations where such thinking and behavior are viewed quite negatively.

COUNTERPOINT

U nfortunately, stereotypes are alive and well. We may have just become better at hiding them. People conceal negative stereotypes in favor of emphasizing positive ones, especially when communicating publicly (to a casual acquaintance) rather than privately (to a close friend). When someone communicates a negative stereotype, listeners think less of the communicator, *even when they agree*. Research shows that people do not communicate their negative stereotypes to others because they know that expressing stereotypes may make them look bad.

We cannot assume that unspoken stereotypes are benign. A prejudice unexpressed is no less a prejudice. Negative stereotypes don't magically reverse themselves over time. Thankfully, positive stereotypes help to balance out the equation a little bit, and negative stereotypes can change when they are openly refuted. For example, nearly half (48.9 percent) of individuals describe Italians as "passionate"— and that has remained stable over time—whereas only 1.5 percent now describe them as "cowardly"—which declined greatly over time.

The decline of a few negative stereotypes may seem like progress, but it's less than it seems. All stereotypes are undesirable, positive stereotypes beget negative ones, and the negative ones haven't gone away; they've just been driven underground. We can only really hope to eliminate stereotypes by addressing them openly. When such prejudices are concealed, they are harder to change.

Time and the entrance of younger individuals into society and organizations have not eliminated or necessarily even reduced stereotypes. Ironically, even the assertion that younger workers are less likely to hold stereotypes than older ones relies on a stereotype (that older people are more likely to be prejudiced)!

Sources: J. L. Skorinko and S. A. Sinclair, "Perspective Taking Can Increase Stereotyping: The Role of Apparent Stereotype Confirmation," *Journal of Experimental Social Psychology* 49 (2013): 10–18; and H. B. Bergsieker, L. M. Leslie, V. S. Constantine, and S. T. Fiske, "Stereotyping by Omission: Eliminate the Negative, Accentuate the Positive," *Journal of Personality and Social Psychology* 102 (2012): 1214–38.

CHAPTER REVIEW

MyManagementLab

Go to **mymanagementlab.com** to complete the problems marked with this icon. ⬤

QUESTIONS FOR REVIEW

6-1 What are the factors that influence our perception?

6-2 What is attribution theory?

6-3 What is the link between perception and decision making?

6-4 How is the rational model of decision making different from bounded rationality and intuition?

6-5 How do individual differences and organizational constraints influence decision making?

6-6 What are the three ethical decision criteria, and how do they differ?

6-7 What are the parts of the three-stage model of creativity?

EXPERIENTIAL EXERCISE   Good Liars and Bad Liars

Break the class into groups of three (this exercise can be adjusted for groups of four). Have each student write down four statements about themselves—three should be truths, and one should be a lie. The lie should not be obvious; each student's objective is to sell the lie as a truth along with the actual truths.

Going around the circle, each student states the truths and the lie. The group may ask a maximum of two follow-up questions for each statement. Then the group votes on each of the statements: truth or lie? The student can finally reveal the lie after everyone has voted.

After everyone in the circle has taken a turn, the group answers the following questions:

6-8. How many of the lies were detected? Were they easy or difficult to detect?

6-9. What made you think a statement was a lie: was it the probability of the statement itself, or the delivery by the student?

6-10. Do you think it is possible to be a good liar? What factors would a good liar have to control in order to pass off a lie as truth?

ETHICAL DILEMMA   Max's Burger: The Dollar Value of Ethics

In July 2011, Nassar Group, a well-diversified conglomerate operating in Dubai, bought the rights to manage Max's Burger's network of franchised outlets in Dubai. Max's Burger is an emerging American fast-food chain with franchised outlets across the globe. The move was a personal project of Houssam Nassar, the Group's managing director and a businessman with an excellent reputation.

Dubai's fast-food market is overwhelmed with franchised restaurants. Meat quality at Max's Burger, however, was lower than the standards set by franchisors. This was all about to change, because Nassar did not intend to jeopardize his reputation and image. Accordingly, as the new operator of Max's Burger outlets, he issued a directive instructing the warehouse manager to decline any frozen meat shipment that did not comply with the franchisor's set standards.

A few weeks after Nassar Group took over the management of Max's Burger, a frozen meat shipment was delivered to the Max's Burger main warehouse. Upon measuring the temperature of the meat, the warehouse manager found that it was a few degrees outside acceptable limits. In terms of governmental regulations, a couple of degrees' difference in temperature would present no risk to customers' health; however, such a difference could have a minimal effect on the taste and texture of the meat.

Prior to the change of management, and for many years before, the warehouse manager had no second thoughts about accepting such a shipment: no food poisoning claim was ever filed against Max's Burger, and taste inconsistencies never bothered anyone enough to complain. Further, the company supplying the meat to Max's Burger is owned by a relative of the warehouse manager.

With the new directive in place, however, the warehouse manager was unsure about his decision. Even though he knew that Nassar would have no way of finding out that the received meat was noncompliant, he wasn't as sure about his decision this time around.

Questions

6-11. Does the decision to accept or refuse the frozen meat shipment call for ethical or legal considerations? Why?

6-12. Identify the stakeholders who will be influenced by the decision to accept or refuse the frozen meat shipment.

6-13. What type of decision-making framework would you advise the warehouse manager to adopt in order to help him reach an optimal decision? How will your suggestion help?

Sources: "The Dollar Value of Ethics!", Charbel Aoun, Instructor and AVP for Human Resources, Lebanese American University, Beirut - Lebanon. The case was adapted to provide materials for class discussions. The author does not intend to illustrate either effective or ineffective handling of a situation. To protect confidentiality, the author may have disguised certain names and other identifying information without jeopardizing the fundamentals of the case.

CASE INCIDENT 1 Too Much of a Good Thing

Have you created an e-portfolio for job applications? If you attend the University of Massachusetts, the University of South Florida, Stanford, Marquette, or Westminster College, where e-portfolios are expected, you probably have developed one. E-portfolios—digitized dossiers of presentations, projects, writing samples, and other work—are used by over 50 percent of students looking for jobs or internships. Putting together an e-portfolio is "a learning experience, linked to a career opportunity," said Associate Professor Tim Shea, who oversees a business school's mandatory e-portfolio program.

Proponents contend that e-portfolios don't replace résumés, they enhance them. "You can write on a résumé that you did an internship somewhere, but if I can see the projects that you worked on, it gives me a more rounded view of the candidate," said Greg Haller, president of the western U.S. region for Verizon Wireless. Student Inga Zakradze agrees, saying the e-portfolio gives "a better feel for me as a well-rounded student." And in a recent Association of American Colleges and Universities survey, 83 percent of respondents believed an e-portfolio would be useful.

With all this affirmation, you might think an e-portfolio is critical to obtaining a job, but that would be a misperception. Other than Haller, opinions seem divided: schools like students to make e-portfolios, but employers don't want them. One of the reasons is technological—HR screening software doesn't allow for links to websites where e-portfolios would be stored. Portfolio hubs Pathbrite and thePortfolium have tried to get around this problem, but they have yet to obtain a single corporate contract. Another reason is information overload—managers don't have time to read through, say, your travel log from a semester at sea. Third, many companies don't believe e-portfolios are value-added. "They are typically not a factor in our screening process," said Enterprise talent acquisition VP Marie Artim. Stuart Silverman, a university dean, acknowledged the possibility. "Whether or not the prospective employer looked at it, or weighed it, who knows."

Proponents of e-portfolios, primarily from the education sector, believe there is value in them beyond job seeking. Kerri Shaffer Carter, a university director of e-portfolios, says, "We don't draw a sharp distinction between the portfolio as a learning process and the portfolio as an employment tool, since the self-awareness that comes out of that process ultimately prepares the student for the workplace." Just don't expect all that hard work to land you a job.

Questions

6-14. How might the misperception about the importance of having an e-portfolio have begun?

✪ **6-15.** What are the reasons you would decide to use an e-portfolio?

6-16. What do you think would be the best way to deliver an e-portfolio to a prospective employer?

Sources: "Global Digital Positioning Systems: E-Portfolios in a Digital Age," 2015 Forum on Digital Learning and E-Portfolios, January 24, 2015, Association of American Colleges and Universities, https://www.aacu.org/meetings/annualmeeting/AM15/eportfolioforum; M. Korn, "Giant Resumes Fail to Impress," *The Wall Street Journal,* February 6, 2014, B7; G. Lorenzo and J. Ittelson, "An Overview of E-Portfolios," Educause Learning Initiative, July 2005, https://net.educause.edu/ir/library/pdf/eli3001.pdf, accessed May 7, 2015.

CASE INCIDENT 2 The Youngest Billionaire

Picture this. The billionaire owner and founder stands in the conference room trying on bras while the CEO stands behind her, adjusting the straps. The floor is littered with underwear. The owner takes off one bra and puts on another. Five executives in the conference room barely blink.

Welcome to Sara Blakely's company, Spanx. In just a few years, Spanx became to slimming underwear what Jello is to gelatin and Kleenex is to facial tissue: So dominant that its name is synonymous with the industry.

At 44, Blakely is one of the youngest billionaires in the world. Like many stories of entrepreneurial success, hers is part gritty determination, part inspiration, and part circumstance. The grit was easy to see early on. As a child growing up in Clearwater Beach, Florida, she lured friends into doing her chores by setting up a competition. At 16, Blakely was so intent on success that she listened to self-help guru Wayne Dyer's recordings incessantly. Friends refused to ride in her car. "No! She's going to make us listen to that motivational crap!" Blakely recalls they said.

After twice failing to get into law school, Blakely started her first business in 1990, running a kids' club at the Clearwater Beach Hilton. It worked until the Hilton's general manager found out. Later, while working full-time in sales, Blakely began learning how to start a more viable business. Her inspiration for Spanx came while she was cold-calling customers as a sales manager for an office supply company. She hated pantyhose. "It's Florida, it's hot, I'm carrying copy machines," she noted.

At the Georgia Tech library, Blakely researched every pantyhose patent ever filed. She wrote her patent application by following a textbook she read in Barnes & Noble.

Then she worked on marketing, manufacturing, and financing, treating each as its own project. After numerous rejections, she finally found mill owners in North Carolina willing to finance the manufacturing. "At the end of the day, the guy ended up just wanting to help me," Blakely said. "He didn't even believe in the idea."

For a time, Blakely relied on stores like Neiman Marcus to set up her table and on word of mouth to get the news out to the public. Her big break came when she sent samples to Oprah Winfrey's stylist. Harpo Productions called to say that Winfrey would name Spanx her favorite product of the year and warned Blakely to get her website ready. She didn't have a website.

Billions of dollars in sales later, Blakely has no plans to slow down. Spanx is sold in 55 countries, and Blakely wants to double international sales. She says: "The biggest risk in life is not risking. Every risk you take in life is in direct proportion to the reward. If I'm afraid of something, it's the next thing I have to go do. That's just the way I've been."

Questions

6-17. How much of Blakely's success is due to her personality and effort and how much to serendipity (being in the right place at the right time)? Does attribution theory help you answer this question? Why or why not?

6-18. What evidence is there in the case to suggest that Blakeley is not risk-averse?

⭐ 6-19. Use the three-stage model of creativity to analyze Blakely's decision making. What can you learn from her story that might help you be more creative in the future?

Sources: Based on J. Mulkerrins, "All Spanx to Sara," Daily Mail, April 6, 2013, downloaded May 7, 2013, from www.dailymail.co.uk/home/; C. O'Connor, "American Booty," Forbes, March 26, 2012, 172–78; and R. Tulshyan, "Spanx's Sara Blakely: Turning $5,000 into $1 Billion with Panties," CNN.com, December 5, 2012, http://www.cnn.com/2012/12/04/business/sara-blakely-spanx-underwear/.

MyManagementLab

Go to **mymanagementlab.com** for the following Assisted-graded writing questions:

6-20. In relation to Case Incident 1, how do you think more employers' dim view of e-portfolios can be changed?

6-21. Consider Case Incident 2, the chapter-opening story, and the chapter. Do you think creativity is "born" (inherent in the individual) or "made" (a product of opportunity and reinforcement)? Compare what we know of the lives of Palmer Luckey and Sara Blakely with those of other creative individuals you know personally.

6-22. MyManagementLab Only – comprehensive writing assignment for this chapter.

ENDNOTES

[1] E. Bernstein, "'Honey, You Never Said…,'" *The Wall Street Journal*, March 24, 2015, D1, D4.

[2] K. C. Yam, R. Fehr, and C. M. Barnes, "Morning Employees Are Perceived as Better Employees: Employees' Start Times Influence Supervisor Performance Ratings," *Journal of Applied Psychology* 99, no. 6 (2014): 1288–99.

[3] J. Dwyer, "Witness Accounts in Midtown Hammer Attack Show the Power of False Memory," *The New York Times,* May 14, 2015, http://www.nytimes.com/2015/05/15/nyregion/witness-accounts-in-midtown-hammer-attack-show-the-power-of-false-memory.html?_r=1.

[4] G. Fields and J. R. Emshwiller, "Long after Arrests, Records Live On," *The Wall Street Journal,* December 26, 2014, A1, A10.

[5] S. S. Wang, "The Science of Standing Out," *The Wall Street Journal,* March 18, 2014, D1, D4.

[6] E. Zell and Z. Krizan, "Do People Have Insight into Their Abilities? A Metasynthesis," *Perspectives on Psychological Science* 9, no. 2 (2014): 111–25.

[7] E. Demerouti, D. Xanthopoulou, I. Tsaousis, and A. B. Bakker, "Disentangling Task and Contextual Performance," *Journal of Personnel Psychology* 13, no. 2 (2014): 59–69.

[8] G. P. Goodwin, J. Piazza, and P. Rozin, "Moral Character Predominates in Person Perception and Evaluation," *Journal of Personality and Social Psychology* 106, no. 1 (2014): 148–68.

[9] P. Harvey, K. Madison, M. Martinko, T. R. Crook, and T. A. Crook, "Attribution Theory in the Organizational Sciences: The Road Traveled and the Path Ahead," *The Academy of Management Perspectives* 28, no. 2 (2014): 128–46; and M. J. Martinko, P. Harvey, and M. T. Dasborough, "Attribution Theory in the Organizational Sciences: A Case of Unrealized Potential," *Journal of Organizational Behavior* 32, no. 1 (2011): 144–49.

[10] C. M. de Melo, P. J. Carnevale, S. J. Read, and J. Gratch, "Reading People's Minds from Emotion Expressions in Interdependent Decision Making," *Journal of Personality and Social Psychology* 106, no. 1 (2014): 73–88.

[11] J. M. Moran, E. Jolly, and J. P. Mitchell, "Spontaneous Mentalizing Predicts the Fundamental Attribution Error," *Journal of Cognitive Neuroscience* 26, no. 3 (2014): 569–76; and D. R. Stadler, "Competing Roles for the Subfactors of Need for Closure in Committing the Fundamental Attribution Error," *Personality and Individual Differences* 47, no. 7 (2009): 701–05.

[12] See, for instance, N. Epley and D. Dunning, "Feeling 'Holier Than Thou': Are Self-Serving Assessments Produced by Errors in Self or Social Prediction?" *Journal of Personality and Social Psychology* 76, no. 6 (2000): 861–75;

M. Goerke, J. Moller, S. Schulz-Hardt, U. Napiersky, and D. Frey, "'It's Not My Fault—But Only I Can Change It': Counterfactual and Prefactual Thoughts of Managers," *Journal of Applied Psychology* 89, no. 2 (2004): 279–92; and E. G. Hepper, R. H. Gramzow, and C. Sedikides, "Individual Differences in Self-Enhancement and Self-Protection Strategies: An Integrative Analysis," *Journal of Personality* 78, no. 2 (2010): 781–814.

[13] See, for instance, A. H. Mezulis, L. Y. Abramson, J. S. Hyde, and B. L. Hankin, "Is There a Universal Positivity Bias in Attributions: A Meta-Analytic Review of Individual, Developmental, and Cultural Differences in the Self-Serving Attributional Bias," *Psychological Bulletin* 130, no. 5 (2004): 711–47; C. F. Falk, S. J. Heine, M. Yuki, and K. Takemura, "Why Do Westerners Self-Enhance More Than East Asians?" *European Journal of Personality* 23, no. 3 (2009): 183–203; and F. F. T. Chiang and T. A. Birtch, "Examining the Perceived Causes of Successful Employee Performance: An East–West Comparison," *International Journal of Human Resource Management* 18, no. 2 (2007): 232–48.

[14] R. Friedman, W. Liu, C. C. Chen, and S.-C. S. Chi, "Causal Attribution for Interfirm Contract Violation: A Comparative Study of Chinese and American Commercial Arbitrators," *Journal of Applied Psychology* 92, no. 3 (2007): 856–64.

[15] J. Spencer-Rodgers, M. J. Williams, D. L. Hamilton, K. Peng, and L. Wang, "Culture and Group Perception: Dispositional and Stereotypic Inferences about Novel and National Groups," *Journal of Personality and Social Psychology* 93, no. 4 (2007): 525–43.

[16] J. D. Brown, "Across the (Not So) Great Divide: Cultural Similarities in Self-Evaluative Processes," *Social and Personality Psychology Compass* 4, no. 5 (2010): 318–30.

[17] A. Zhang, C. Reyna, Z. Qian, and G. Yu, "Interpersonal Attributions of Responsibility in the Chinese Workplace: A Test of Western Models in a Collectivistic Context," *Journal of Applied Social Psychology* 38, no. 9 (2008): 2361–77; and A. Zhang, F. Xia, and C. Li, "The Antecedents of Help Giving in Chinese Culture: Attribution, Judgment of Responsibility, Expectation Change and the Reaction of Affect," *Social Behavior and Personality* 35, no. 1 (2007): 135–42.

[18] See P. Rosenzweig, *The Halo Effect* (New York: The Free Press, 2007); I. Dennis, "Halo Effects in Grading Student Projects," *Journal of Applied Psychology* 92, no. 4 (2007): 1169–76; C. E. Naquin and R. O. Tynan, "The Team Halo Effect: Why Teams Are Not Blamed for Their Failures," *Journal of Applied Psychology* 88, no. 2 (2003): 332–40; and T. M. Bechger,

G. Maris, and Y. P. Hsiao, "Detecting Halo Effects in Performance-Based Evaluations," *Applied Psychological Measurement* 34, no. 8 (2010): 607–19.

[19] J. K. Clark, K. C. Thiem, J. Barden, J. O'Rourke Stuart, and A. T. Evans, "Stereotype Validation: The Effects of Activating Negative Stereotypes after Intellectual Performance," *Journal of Personality and Social Psychology* 108, no. 4 (2015): 531–52.

[20] J. L. Eberhardt, P. G. Davies, V. J. Purdic-Vaughns, and S. L. Johnson, "Looking Deathworthy: Perceived Stereotypicality of Black Defendants Predicts Capital-Sentencing Outcomes," *Psychological Science* 17, no. 5 (2006): 383–86.

[21] A. S. Rosette, G. J. Leonardelli, and K. W. Phillips, "The White Standard: Racial Bias in Leader Categorization," *Journal of Applied Psychology* 93, no. 4 (2008): 758–77.

[22] H. G. Heneman III, T. A. Judge, and J. D. Kammeyer-Mueller, *Staffing Organizations* (Middleton, WI: Mendota House, 2012).

[23] J. Willis and A. Todorov, "First Impressions: Making Up Your Mind after a 100ms Exposure to a Face," *Psychological Science* 17, no. 7 (2006): 592–98.

[24] N. Eisenkraft, "Accurate by Way of Aggregation: Should You Trust Your Intuition-Based First Impressions?" *Journal of Experimental Social Psychology* (March 2013): 277–79.

[25] See, for example, G. Natanovich and D. Eden, "Pygmalion Effects among Outreach Supervisors and Tutors: Extending Sex Generalizability," *Journal of Applied Psychology* 93, no. 6 (2008): 1382–89.

[26] D. B. McNatt and T. A. Judge, "Boundary Conditions of the Galatea Effect: A Field Experiment and Constructive Replication," *Academy of Management Journal* (August 2004): 550–65; and X. M. Bezuijen, P. T. van den Berg, K. van Dam, and H. Thierry, "Pygmalion and Employee Learning: The Role of Leader Behaviors," *Journal of Management* 35, (2009): 1248–67.

[27] See, for example, K. F. E. Wong and J. Y. Y. Kwong, "Effects of Rater Goals on Rating Patterns: Evidence from an Experimental Field Study," *Journal of Applied Psychology* 92, no. 2 (2007): 577–85; and S. E. DeVoe and S. S. Iyengar, "Managers' Theories of Subordinates: A Cross-Cultural Examination of Manager Perceptions of Motivation and Appraisal of Performance," *Organizational Behavior and Human Decision Processes* (January 2004): 47–61.

[28] D. A. Hofmann, "Overcoming the Obstacles to Cross-Functional Decision Making: Laying the Groundwork for Collaborative Problem Solving," *Organizational Dynamics* 44, no. 1 (2015): 17–25.

[29] E. Bernstein, "The Right Answer is 'No,'" *The Wall Street Journal*, March 11, 2014, D1–D2.

[30]E. Shafir and R. A. LeBoeuf, "Rationality," *Annual Review of Psychology* 53 (2002): 491–517.

[31]For a review of the rational decision-making model, see M. H. Bazerman and D. A. Moore, *Judgment in Managerial Decision Making*, 7th ed. (Hoboken, New Jersey: Wiley, 2008).

[32]J. G. March, *A Primer on Decision Making* (New York: The Free Press, 2009); and D. Hardman and C. Harries, "How Rational Are We?" *Psychologist* (February 2002): 76–79.

[33]Bazerman and Moore, *Judgment in Managerial Decision Making*.

[34]J. E. Russo, K. A. Carlson, and M. G. Meloy, "Choosing an Inferior Alternative," *Psychological Science* 17, no. 10 (2006): 899–904.

[35]N. Halevy and E. Y. Chou, "How Decisions Happen: Focal Points and Blind Spots in Interdependent Decision Making," *Journal of Personality and Social Psychology* 106, no. 3 (2014): 398–417; D. Kahneman, "Maps of Bounded Rationality: Psychology for Behavioral Economics," *The American Economic Review* 93, no. 5 (2003): 1449–75; and J. Zhang, C. K. Hsee, and Z. Xiao, "The Majority Rule in Individual Decision Making," *Organizational Behavior and Human Decision Processes* 99 (2006): 102–11.

[36]G. Gigerenzer, "Why Heuristics Work," *Perspectives on Psychological Science* 3, no. 1 (2008): 20–29; and A. K. Shah and D. M. Oppenheimer, "Heuristics Made Easy: An Effort-Reduction Framework," *Psychological Bulletin* 134, no. 2 (2008): 207–22.

[37]See A. W. Kruglanski and G. Gigerenzer, "Intuitive and Deliberate Judgments Are Based on Common Principles," *Psychological Review* 118 (2011): 97–109.

[38]E. Dane and M. G. Pratt, "Exploring Intuition and Its Role in Managerial Decision Making," *Academy of Management Review* 32, no. 1 (2007): 33–54; and J. A. Hicks, D. C. Cicero, J. Trent, C. M. Burton, and L. A. King, "Positive Affect, Intuition, and Feelings of Meaning," *Journal of Personality and Social Psychology* 98 (2010): 967–79.

[39]C. Akinci and E. Sadler-Smith, "Intuition in Management Research: A Historical Review," *International Journal of Management Reviews* 14 (2012): 104–22.

[40]S. P. Robbins, *Decide & Conquer: Making Winning Decisions and Taking Control of Your Life* (Upper Saddle River, NJ: Financial Times/ Prentice Hall, 2004), 13.

[41]S. Ludwig and J. Nafziger, "Beliefs about Overconfidence," *Theory and Decision* (April 2011): 475–500.

[42]C. R. M. McKenzie, M. J. Liersch, and I. Yaniv, "Overconfidence in Interval Estimates: What Does Expertise Buy You," *Organizational Behavior and Human Decision Processes* 107 (2008): 179–91.

[43]R. P. Larrick, K. A. Burson, and J. B. Soll, "Social Comparison and Confidence: When Thinking You're Better Than Average Predicts Overconfidence (and When It Does Not)," *Organizational Behavior and Human Decision Processes* 102 (2007): 76–94.

[44]K. M. Hmieleski and R. A. Baron, "Entrepreneurs' Optimism and New Venture Performance: A Social Cognitive Perspective," *Academy of Management Journal* 52, no. 3 (2009): 473–88.

[45]R. Frick and A. K. Smith, "Overconfidence Game," *Kiplinger's Personal Finance* 64, no. 3 (2010): 23.

[46]See, for instance, J. P. Simmons, R. A. LeBoeuf, and L. D. Nelson, "The Effect of Accuracy Motivation on Anchoring and Adjustment: Do People Adjust from Their Provided Anchors?" *Journal of Personality and Social Psychology* 99 (2010): 917–32.

[47]C. Janiszewski and D. Uy, "Precision of the Anchor Influences the Amount of Adjustment," *Psychological Science* 19, no. 2 (2008): 121–27.

[48]See E. Jonas, S. Schultz-Hardt, D. Frey, and N. Thelen, "Confirmation Bias in Sequential Information Search after Preliminary Decisions," *Journal of Personality and Social Psychology* (April 2001): 557–71; and W. Hart, D. Albarracín, A. H. Eagly, I. Brechan, M. Lindberg, and L. Merrill, "Feeling Validated versus Being Correct: A Meta-Analysis of Selective Exposure to Information," *Psychological Bulletin* 135 (2009): 555–88.

[49]T. Pachur, R. Hertwig, and F. Steinmann, "How Do People Judge Risks: Availability Heuristic, Affect Heuristic, or Both?" *Journal of Experimental Psychology: Applied* 18 (2012): 314–30.

[50]G. Morgenson, "Debt Watchdogs: Tamed or Caught Napping?" *The New York Times*, December 7, 2009, 1, 32.

[51]B. M. Staw, "The Escalation of Commitment to a Course of Action," *Academy of Management Review* (October 1981): 577–87.

[52]D. J. Sleesman, D. E. Conlon, G. McNamara, and J. E. Miles, "Cleaning Up the Big Muddy: A Meta-Analytic Review of the Determinants of Escalation of Commitment," *Academy of Management Journal* 55 (2012): 541–62.

[53]H. Drummond, "Escalation of Commitment: When to Stay the Course?" *The Academy of Management Perspectives* 28, no. 4 (2014): 430–46.

[54]See, for instance, A. James and A. Wells, "Death Beliefs, Superstitious Beliefs and Health Anxiety," *British Journal of Clinical Psychology* (March 2002): 43–53; and U. Hahn and P. A. Warren, "Perceptions of Randomness: Why Three Heads Are Better Than One," *Psychological Review* 116 (2009): 454–61.

[55]See, for example, D. J. Keys and B. Schwartz, "Leaky Rationality: How Research on Behavioral Decision Making Challenges Normative Standards of Rationality," *Psychological Science* 2, no. 2 (2007): 162–80; and U. Simonsohn, "Direct Risk Aversion: Evidence from Risky Prospects Valued below Their Worst Outcome," *Psychological Science* 20, no. 6 (2009): 686–92.

[56]J. K. Maner, M. T. Gailliot, D. A. Butz, and B. M. Peruche, "Power, Risk, and the Status Quo: Does Power Promote Riskier or More Conservative Decision Making?" *Personality and Social Psychology Bulletin* 33, no. 4 (2007): 451–62.

[57]A. Chakraborty, S. Sheikh, and N. Subramanian, "Termination Risk and Managerial Risk Taking," *Journal of Corporate Finance* 13 (2007): 170–88.

[58]P. Bryant and R. Dunford, "The Influence of Regulatory Focus on Risky Decision-Making," *Applied Psychology: An International Review* 57, no. 2 (2008): 335–59.

[59]A. J. Porcelli and M. R. Delgado, "Acute Stress Modulates Risk Taking in Financial Decision Making," *Psychological Science* 20, no. 3 (2009): 278–83.

[60]R. L. Guilbault, F. B. Bryant, J. H. Brockway, and E. J. Posavac, "A Meta-Analysis of Research on Hindsight Bias," *Basic and Applied Social Psychology* (September 2004): 103–17; and L. Werth, F. Strack, and J. Foerster, "Certainty and Uncertainty: The Two Faces of the Hindsight Bias," *Organizational Behavior and Human Decision Processes* (March 2002): 323–41.

[61]J. Bell, "The Final Cut?" *Oregon Business* 33, no. 5 (2010): 27.

[62]E. Dash and J. Creswell, "Citigroup Pays for a Rush to Risk," *The New York Times*, November 20, 2008, 1, 28; S. Pulliam, S. Ng, and R. Smith, "Merrill Upped Ante as Boom in Mortgage Bonds Fizzled," *The Wall Street Journal*, April 16, 2008, A1, A14; and M. Gladwell, "Connecting the Dots," *The New Yorker*, March 10, 2003.

[63]H. Moon, J. R. Hollenbeck, S. E. Humphrey, and B. Maue, "The Tripartite Model of Neuroticism and the Suppression of Depression and Anxiety within an Escalation of Commitment Dilemma," *Journal of Personality* 71 (2003): 347–68; and H. Moon, "The Two Faces of Conscientiousness: Duty and Achievement Striving in Escalation of Commitment Dilemmas," *Journal of Applied Psychology* 86 (2001): 535–40.

[64]J. Musch, "Personality Differences in Hindsight Bias," *Memory* 11 (2003): 473–89.

[65]M. D. Coleman, "Emotion and the Self-Serving Bias," *Current Psychology* (December 2011): 345–54.

[66]T. Huston, "Are Women Better Decision Makers?" *The New York Times*, October 19, 2014, 9.

[67]A. Borders and K. A. Hennebry, "Angry Rumination Moderates the Association between Perceived Ethnic Discrimination and Risky Behaviors," *Personality and Individual Differences* 79 (2015): 81–86; and J. S. Hyde, A. H. Mezulis, and L. Y. Abramson, "The ABCs of Depression: Integrating Affective,

Biological, and Cognitive Models to Explain the Emergence of the Gender Difference in Depression," *Psychological Review* 115, no. 2 (2008): 291–313.

[68]H. Connery and K. M. Davidson, "A Survey of Attitudes to Depression in the General Public: A Comparison of Age and Gender Differences," *Journal of Mental Health* 15, no. 2 (April 2006): 179–89.

[69]M. Elias, "Thinking It Over, and Over, and Over," *USA Today*, February 6, 2003, 10D.

[70]K. E. Stanovich and R. F. West, "On the Relative Independence of Thinking Biases and Cognitive Ability," *Journal of Personality and Social Psychology* 94, no. 4 (2008): 672–95.

[71]N. J. Adler, *International Dimensions of Organizational Behavior*, 4th ed. (Cincinnati, OH: South-Western Publishing, 2002), 182–89.

[72]B. Burrough, "How Big Business Can Take the High Road," *The New York Times*, March 9, 2014, 10.

[73]A. Lukits, "Podcasts Send Shoppers to Omega-3s," *The Wall Street Journal*, December 9, 2014, D2.

[74]E. DeAngelis, "Coaxing Better Behavior," *Monitor on Psychology* (December 2014): 62–67.

[75]K. V. Kortenkamp and C. F. Moore, "Ethics under Uncertainty: The Morality and Appropriateness of Utilitarianism When Outcomes Are Uncertain," *American Journal of Psychology* 127, no. 3 (2014): 367–82.

[76]A. Lukits, "Hello and Bonjour to Moral Dilemmas," *The Wall Street Journal*, May 13, 2014, D4.

[77]J. Hollings, "Let the Story Go: The Role of Emotion in the Decision-Making Process of the Reluctant, Vulnerable Witness or Whistle-Blower," *Journal of Business Ethics* 114, no. 3 (2013): 501–12.

[78]D. E. Rupp, P. M. Wright, S. Aryee, and Y. Luo, "Organizational Justice, Behavioral Ethics, and Corporate Social Responsibility: Finally the Three Shall Merge," *Management and Organization Review* 11 (2015): 15–24.

[79]L. L. Shu and F. Gino, "Sweeping Dishonesty under the Rug: How Unethical Actions Lead to Forgetting of Moral Rules," *Journal of Personality and Social Psychology* 102 (2012): 1164–77.

[80]B. C. Gunia, L. Wang, L. Huang, J. Wang, and J. K. Murnighan, "Contemplation and Conversation: Subtle Influences on Moral Decision Making," *Academy of Management Journal* 55 (2012): 13–33.

[81]R. F. West, R. J. Meserve, and K. E. Stanovich, "Cognitive Sophistication Does Not Attenuate the Bias Blind Spot," *Journal of Personality and Social Psychology* 103 (2012): 506–19.

[82]J. B. Cullen, K. P. Parboteeah, and M. Hoegl, "Cross-National Differences in Managers' Willingness to Justify Ethically Suspect Behaviors: A Test of Institutional Anomie Theory," *Academy of Management Journal* (June 2004): 411–21.

[83]N. Klein and H. Zhou, "Their Pants Aren't on Fire," *The New York Times*, March 25, 2014, D3.

[84]Ibid.

[85]Ibid.

[86]Ibid.

[87]E. Bernstein, "Lie Detection for Your Email," *The Wall Street Journal*, May 20, 2014, D1.

[88]N. Klein and H. Zhou, "Their Pants Aren't on Fire."

[89]E. Bernstein, "Lie Detection for Your Email."

[90]L. ten Brinke, D. Simson, and D. R. Carney, "Some Evidence for Unconscious Lie Detection," *Psychological Science* 25, no. 5 (2014): 1098–105.

[91]S. D. Levitt and S. J. Dubner, "Traponomics," *The Wall Street Journal*, May 10–11 2014, C1, C2.

[92]N. Anderson, K. Potocnik, and J. Zhou, "Innovation and Creativity in Organizations: A State-of-the-Science Review, Prospective Commentary, and Guiding Framework," *Journal of Management* 40, no. 5 (2014): 1297–333.

[93]"Is Your Art Killing You?" Investorideas.com, May 13, 2013, www.investorideas.com/news/2013/renewable-energy/05134.asp.

[94]M. M. Gielnik, A.-C. Kramer, B. Kappel, and M. Frese, "Antecedents of Business Opportunity Identification and Innovation: Investigating the Interplay of Information Processing and Information Acquisition," *Applied Psychology: An International Review* 63, no. 2 (2014): 344–81.

[95]G. Anderson, "Three Tips to Foster Creativity at Your Startup," *ArcticStartup*, May 8, 2013, downloaded May 14, 2013, from http://www.arcticstartup.com/.

[96]G. Reynolds, "Want a Good Idea? Take a Walk," *The New York Times*, May 6, 2014, D6.

[97]S. Shellenbarger, "The Power of the Doodle: Improve Your Focus and Memory," *The Wall Street Journal*, July 30, 2014, D1, D3.

[98]E. Millar, "How Do Finnish Kids Excel without Rote Learning and Standardized Testing?" *The Globe and Mail*, May 9, 2013, downloaded May 12, 2015, from www.theglobeandmail.com/.

[99]Z. Harper, "Mark Cuban Wants You to Design the New Dallas Mavericks Uniforms," CBSSports.com, May 13, 2013, http://sports.yahoo.com/blogs/nba-ball-dont-lie/mark-cuban-wants-designs-dallas-mavericks-uniforms-214849952.html.

[100]C. K. W. De Dreu, B. A. Nijstad, M. Baas, I. Wolsink, and M. Roskes, "Working Memory Benefits Creative Insight, Musical Improvisation, and Original Ideation through Maintained Task-Focused Attention," *Personality and Social Psychology Bulletin* 38 (2012): 656–69.

[101]C.-H. Wu, S. K. Parker, and J. P. J. de Jong, "Need for Cognition as an Antecedent of Individual Innovation Behavior," *Journal of Management* 40, no. 6 (2014): 1511–34.

[102]S. M. Wechsler, C. Vendramini, and T. Oakland, "Thinking and Creative Styles: A Validity Study," *Creativity Research Journal* 24 (April 2012): 235–42.

[103]Y. Gong, S. Cheung, M. Wang, and J. Huang, "Unfolding the Proactive Processes for Creativity: Integration of the Employee Proactivity, Information Exchange, and Psychological Safety Perspectives," *Journal of Management* 38 (2012): 1611–33.

[104]A. Rego, F. Sousa, C. Marques, and M. P. E. Cunha, "Retail Employees' Self-Efficacy and Hope Predicting Their Positive Affect and Creativity," *European Journal of Work and Organizational Psychology* 21, no. 6 (2012): 923–45.

[105]H. Zhang, H. K. Kwan, X. Zhang, and L.-Z. Wu, "High Core Self-Evaluators Maintain Creativity: A Motivational Model of Abusive Supervision," *Journal of Management* 40, no. 4 (2012): 1151–74.

[106]D. K. Simonton, "The Mad-Genius Paradox: Can Creative People Be More Mentally Healthy But Highly Creative People More Mentally Ill?" *Perspectives on Psychological Science* 9, no. 5 (2014): 470–80.

[107]C. Wang, S. Rodan, M. Fruin, and X. Xu, "Knowledge Networks, Collaboration Networks, and Exploratory Innovation," *Academy of Management Journal* 57, no. 2 (2014): 484–514.

[108]F. Gino and S. S. Wiltermuth, "Evil Genius? Dishonesty Can Lead to Greater Creativity," *Psychological Science* 25, no. 4 (2014): 973–81.

[109]S. N. de Jesus, C. L. Rus, W. Lens, and S. Imaginário, "Intrinsic Motivation and Creativity Related to Product: A Meta-Analysis of the Studies Published between 1990–2010," *Creativity Research Journal* 25 (2013): 80–84.

[110]A. Somech and A. Drach-Zahavy, "Translating Team Creativity to Innovation Implementation: The Role of Team Composition and Climate for Innovation," *Journal of Management* 39 (2013): 684–708.

[111]L. Sun, Z. Zhang, J. Qi, and Z. X. Chen, "Empowerment and Creativity: A Cross-Level Investigation," *Leadership Quarterly* 23 (2012): 55–65.

[112]M. Cerne, C. G. L. Nerstad, A. Dysvik, and M. Skerlavaj, "What Goes around Comes around: Knowledge Hiding, Perceived Motivational Climate, and Creativity," *Academy of Management Journal* 57, no. 1 (2014): 172–92.

[113]S. Sonnenshein, "How Organizations Foster the Creative Use of Resources," *Academy of Management Journal* 57, no. 3 (2014): 814–48.

[114]V. Venkataramani, A. W. Richter, and R. Clarke, "Creative Benefits from Well-Connected Leaders: Leader Social Network Ties as Facilitators of Employee Radical Creativity," *Journal of Applied Psychology* 99, no. 5 (2014): 966–75.

[115]J. E. Perry-Smith, "Social Network Ties beyond Nonredundancy: An Experimental Investigation of the Effect of Knowledge Content and Tie Strength on Creativity," *Journal of Applied Psychology* 99, no. 5 (2014): 831–46.

[116]T. Rinne, D. G. Steel, and J. Fairweather, "The Role of Hofstede's Individualism in National-Level Creativity," *Creativity Research Journal* 25 (2013): 129–36.

[117]X. Yi, W. Hu, H. Scheithauer, and W. Niu, "Cultural and Bilingual Influences on Artistic Creativity Performances: Comparison of German and Chinese Students," *Creativity Research Journal* 25 (2013): 97–108.

[118]D. Liu, H. Liao, and R. Loi, "The Dark Side of Leadership: A Three-Level Investigation of the Cascading Effect of Abusive Supervision on Employee Creativity," *Academy of Management Journal* 55 (2012): 1187–212.

[119]J. B. Avey, F. L. Richmond, and D. R. Nixon, "Leader Positivity and Follower Creativity: An Experimental Analysis," *Journal of Creative Behavior* 46 (2012): 99–118; and

A. Rego, Arménio, F. Sousa, C. Marques, and M. E. Cunha, "Authentic Leadership Promoting Employees' Psychological Capital and Creativity," *Journal of Business Research* 65 (2012): 429–37.

[120]I. J. Hoever, D. van Knippenberg, W. P. van Ginkel, and H. G. Barkema, "Fostering Team Creativity: Perspective Taking as Key to Unlocking Diversity's Potential," *Journal of Applied Psychology* 97 (2012): 982–96.

[121]S. J. Shin, T. Kim, J. Lee, and L. Bian, "Cognitive Team Diversity and Individual Team Member Creativity: A Cross-Level Interaction," *Academy of Management Journal* 55 (2012): 197–212.

[122]A. W. Richter, G. Hirst, D. van Knippenberg, and M. Baer, "Creative Self-Efficacy and Individual Creativity in Team Contexts: Cross-Level Interactions with Team Informational Resources," *Journal of Applied Psychology* 97 (2012): 1282–90.

[123]X. Huang, JJ P.-A. Hsieh, and W. He, "Expertise Dissimilarity and Creativity: The Contingent Roles of Tacit and Explicit

Knowledge Sharing," *Journal of Applied Psychology* 99, no. 5 (2014): 816–30.

[124]T. B. Harris, N. Li, W. R. Boswell, X.-A. Zhang, and Z. Xie, "Getting What's New from Newcomers: Empowering Leadership, Creativity, and Adjustment in the Socialization Context," *Personnel Psychology* 67 (2014): 567–604.

[125]A. H. Y. Hon, M. Bloom, and J. M. Crant, "Overcoming Resistance to Change and Enhancing Creative Performance," *Journal of Management* 40, no. 3 (2014): 919–41.

[126]J. S. Mueller, S. Melwani, and J. A. Goncalo, "The Bias against Creativity: Why People Desire but Reject Creative Ideas," *Psychological Science* 23 (2012): 13–17.

[127]T. Montag, C. P. Maertz, and M. Baer, "A Critical Analysis of the Workplace Creativity Criterion Space," *Journal of Management* 38 (2012): 1362–86.

[128]M. Baer, "Putting Creativity to Work: The Implementation of Creative Ideas in Organizations," *Academy of Management Journal* 55 (2012): 1102–19.

7

Motivation Concepts

LEARNING OBJECTIVES

After studying this chapter, you should be able to:

7-1 Describe the three key elements of motivation.

7-2 Compare the early theories of motivation.

7-3 Contrast the elements of self-determination theory and goal-setting theory.

7-4 Demonstrate the differences among self-efficacy theory, reinforcement theory, equity theory, and expectancy theory.

7-5 Identify the implications of employee job engagement for managers.

7-6 Describe how the contemporary theories of motivation complement one another.

MyManagementLab®

⭐ **Chapter Warm Up**

If your professor has chosen to assign this, go to the Assignments section of **mymanagementlab.com** to complete the chapter warm up.

MOTIVATED TOWARD CORPORATE SOCIAL RESPONSIBILITY

As organizations face increasing public pressure for sustainability, corporate social responsibility (CSR) has become a major part of most CEOs' agendas. The motivation for these CEOs is clear: the media, customers, employees, and governments herald sustainability initiatives like GE's Ecomagination, which pioneers technology efficiency, and philanthropy programs like Richard Branson's Re*Generation, which supports homeless youth. But how does an organization motivate employees for huge and ongoing volunteer efforts like Lowe's Heroes, shown in the picture, which helps rebuild homes after disasters and revitalize communities?

According to research in the United Kingdom, a good portion of employees may already be motivated toward CSR work. Some employees are motivated by a sense of reciprocity, giving back to the communities in which they live or aiding organizations from which they've previously benefited. An example is Lowe's Hero James Jackson, who helped revitalize an Indianapolis park. "I'm so thrilled to have been a part of this transformational journey for the JV Hill Park," he said. "The community has new life again, which impacts so many youth for years to come." Other employees are motivated by the opportunity to socialize with people within the organization and community, while still others want to develop business networks for future use. Many seem to like exercising the networks they already have, drawing upon their contacts for CSR projects. And most like to use volunteering opportunities to learn more. For example, one study participant who has been mentoring students in business said, "It's nice to meet other people in Derby and around, see how they do things, get tips and lots of business information."

How do organizations influence their employees to volunteer? Research suggests that half the organizations in Canada actively encourage employee volunteering. As a result, fully one-quarter of all the volunteer work in the country is done by employee volunteers. The study found that the availability of organizational support—use of work time, paid time to volunteer, facility space, organizational resources—was critical to employee CSR motivation. Such support was correlated with an increase in annual volunteer hours, particularly among women. Furthermore, support yielded higher participation for almost all types of organizational volunteer CSR activities.

However, the study found employees age 35 and older, with less education than a high school diploma, or who were married, received less support. The reasons for these differences are not known. Women also received less support than men when it came to flexible hours and time off needed for volunteering. It also seems that women might make fewer requests for support. Although these findings are from just one study, the message is clear: Organizations may increase their overall CSR contributions by clearly offering tangible support for *everyone,* along with opportunities to serve.

One final employee motivator is the intrinsic reward from working with your organization's team to accomplish a worthy project. After a tough day cleaning up in the aftermath of the 2014 tornado in Tupelo, Mississippi, Tad Agoglia of the First Response Team of America told the Lowe's Heroes team, "You guys, your attitudes, [you do] just anything and everything to get it done, just do it, you really took your time to help this family, and it meant a lot. So this was a great day, and you guys made it a great day. Thank you."

Sources: Lowe's in the Community, May 5, 2015, http://Lowesinthecommunity.Tumblr.Com/Post/118215046887/The-Week-Leading-Up-To-The-Final-Four; F. Macphail and P. Bowles, "Corporate Social Responsibility as Support for Employee Volunteers: Impacts, Gender Puzzles and Policy Implications in Canada," *Journal of Business Ethics* 84 (2009): 405–16; and J. N. Muthuri, D. Matten, and J. Moon, "Employee Volunteering and Social Capital: Contributions to Corporate Social Responsibility," *British Journal of Management* 20 (2009): 75–89.

As we read in the opening story, employees don't always volunteer just because it's a good thing to do; they have to be motivated. A significant part of their motivation comes from an internal desire to contribute, but organizations can also play an important role by encouraging and enabling them. Motivating employees—to volunteer *and* to work—is one of the most important and challenging aspects of management. As we will see, there is no shortage of advice about how to do it.

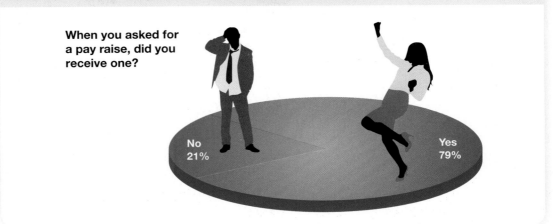

Note: Survey of 3,900 executives from 31 countries.

Source: Based on Accenture, "The Path Forward" (2012), http://www.accenture.com/SiteCollectionDocuments/PDF/Accenture-IWD-Research-Deck-2012-FINAL.pdf#zoom=50, 36.

Motivation is one of the most frequently researched topics in organizational behavior (OB).[1] In one survey, 69 percent of workers reported wasting time at work every day, and nearly a quarter said they waste between 30 and 60 minutes each day. How? Usually by surfing the Internet (checking the news and visiting social network sites) and chatting with coworkers.[2] So, though times change, the problem of motivating a workforce stays the same.

In this chapter, we'll review the basics of motivation, assess motivation theories, and provide an integrative model that fits theories together. But first, take a look at the potential that a little motivation to ask for a raise can yield, shown in the OB Poll.

Motivation and Early Theories

7-1 Describe the three key elements of motivation.

Some individuals seem driven to succeed. The same young student who struggles to read a textbook for more than 20 minutes may devour a *Harry Potter* book in a day. The difference is the situation. As we analyze the concept of motivation, keep in mind that the level of motivation varies both between individuals and within individuals at different times.

We define **motivation** as the processes that account for an individual's *intensity*, *direction*, and *persistence* of effort toward attaining a goal.[3] While general motivation is concerned with effort toward *any* goal, we'll narrow the focus to *organizational* goals.

Intensity describes how hard a person tries. This is the element most of us focus on when we talk about motivation. However, high intensity is unlikely to lead to favorable job-performance outcomes unless the effort is channeled in a *direction* that benefits the organization. Therefore, we consider the quality of effort as well as its intensity. Effort directed toward, and consistent with, the organization's goals is the kind of effort we should be seeking. Finally, motivation has a *persistence* dimension. This measures how long a person can maintain effort. Motivated individuals stay with a task long enough to achieve their goals.

motivation The processes that account for an individual's intensity, direction, and persistence of effort toward attaining a goal.

Early Theories of Motivation

7-2 Compare the early theories of motivation.

Three theories of employee motivation formulated during the 1950s are probably the best known. Although they are now of questionable validity (as we'll discuss), they represent a foundation, and practicing managers still use their terminology.

Hierarchy of Needs Theory

hierarchy of needs Abraham Maslow's hierarchy of five needs—physiological, safety, social, esteem, and self-actualization—in which, as each need is substantially satisfied, the next need becomes dominant.

The best-known theory of motivation is Abraham Maslow's **hierarchy of needs**,[4] which hypothesizes that within every human being there is a hierarchy of five needs. Recently, a sixth need has been proposed for a highest level—intrinsic values—which is said to have originated from Maslow, but it has yet to gain widespread acceptance.[5] The original five needs are:

1. **Physiological.** Includes hunger, thirst, shelter, sex, and other bodily needs.
2. **Safety-security.** Security and protection from physical and emotional harm.
3. **Social-belongingness.** Affection, belongingness, acceptance, and friendship.
4. **Esteem.** Internal factors such as self-respect, autonomy, and achievement, and external factors such as status, recognition, and attention.
5. **Self-actualization.** Drive to become what we are capable of becoming; includes growth, achieving our potential, and self-fulfillment.

According to Maslow, as each need becomes substantially satisfied, the next one becomes dominant. So if you want to motivate someone, you need to understand what level of the hierarchy that person is currently on and focus on satisfying needs at or above that level. We depict the hierarchy as a pyramid in Exhibit 7-1 since this is its best-known presentation, but Maslow referred to the needs only in terms of levels.

Maslow's theory has received long-standing wide recognition, particularly among practicing managers. It is intuitively logical and easy to understand, and some research has validated it.[6] Unfortunately, however, most research does not, especially when the theory is applied to diverse cultures,[7] with the possible exception of physiological needs.[8] But old theories, especially intuitively

| Exhibit 7-1 | Maslow's Hierarchy of Needs |

Self-actualization
Esteem
Social-belongingness
Safety-security
Physiological

Source: H. Skelsey, "Maslow's Hierarchy of Needs—the Sixth Level," *Psychologist* (2014): 982–83.

logical ones, die hard. It is thus important to be aware of the prevailing public acceptance of the hierarchy when discussing motivation.

Two-Factor Theory

two-factor theory A theory that relates intrinsic factors to job satisfaction and associates extrinsic factors with dissatisfaction. Also called motivation-hygiene theory.

Believing an individual's relationship to work is basic, and that the attitude toward work can determine success or failure, psychologist Frederick Herzberg wondered, "What do people want from their jobs?" He asked people to describe, in detail, situations in which they felt exceptionally *good* or *bad* about their jobs. The responses differed significantly and led Hertzberg to his **two-factor theory** (also called *motivation-hygiene theory*, but this term is not used much today).[9]

As shown in Exhibit 7-2, intrinsic factors such as advancement, recognition, responsibility, and achievement seem related to job satisfaction. Respondents who felt good about their work tended to attribute these factors to their situations, while dissatisfied respondents tended to cite extrinsic factors, such as supervision, pay, company policies, and work conditions.

To Herzberg, the data suggest that the opposite of satisfaction is not dissatisfaction, as was traditionally believed. Removing dissatisfying characteristics from a job does not necessarily make the job satisfying. Herzberg proposed a dual continuum: The opposite of "satisfaction" is "no satisfaction," and the opposite of "dissatisfaction" is "no dissatisfaction" (see Exhibit 7-3).

hygiene factors Factors—such as company policy and administration, supervision, and salary—that, when adequate in a job, placate workers. When these factors are adequate, people will not be dissatisfied.

Under two-factor theory, the factors that lead to job satisfaction are separate and distinct from those that lead to job dissatisfaction. Therefore, managers who seek to eliminate factors that can create job dissatisfaction may bring about peace, but not necessarily motivation. They will be placating rather than motivating their workers. Conditions such as quality of supervision, pay, company policies, physical work conditions, relationships with others, and job security are **hygiene factors**. When they're adequate, people will not be dissatisfied; neither

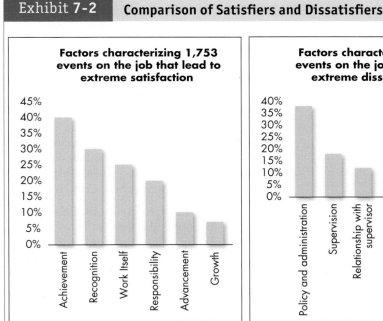

Exhibit 7-2   Comparison of Satisfiers and Dissatisfiers

Exhibit 7-3   Contrasting View of Satisfaction and Dissatisfaction

will they be satisfied. If we want to *motivate* people on their jobs, we should emphasize factors associated with the work itself or with outcomes directly derived from it, such as promotional opportunities, personal growth opportunities, recognition, responsibility, and achievement. These are the characteristics people find intrinsically rewarding.

The two-factor theory has not been well supported in research. Criticisms center on Herzberg's original methodology and his assumptions, such as the statement that satisfaction is strongly related to productivity. Subsequent research has also shown that if hygiene and motivational factors are equally important to a person, both are capable of motivating.

Regardless of the criticisms, Herzberg's theory has been quite influential and currently is very much in use in research in Asia.[10] Few managers worldwide are unfamiliar with its recommendations.

McClelland's Theory of Needs

You have one beanbag and five targets set up in front of you, each farther away than the last. Target A sits almost within arm's reach. If you hit it, you get $2. Target B is a bit farther out and pays $4, but only about 80 percent of the people who try can hit it. Target C pays $8, and about half the people who try can hit it. Very few people can hit Target D, but the payoff is $16 for those who do. Finally, Target E pays $32, but it's almost impossible to achieve. Which would you try for? If you selected C, you're likely to be a high achiever. Why? Read on.

McClelland's theory of needs was developed by David McClelland and his associates.[11] As opposed to, say, Maslow's hierarchy, these needs are more like motivating factors than strict needs for survival. There are three:

- *Need for achievement (nAch)* is the drive to excel, to achieve in relationship to a set of standards.
- *Need for power (nPow)* is the need to make others behave in a way they would not have otherwise.
- *Need for affiliation (nAff)* is the desire for friendly and close interpersonal relationships.

McClelland and subsequent researchers focused most of their attention on nAch. High achievers perform best when they perceive their probability of success as 0.5—that is, a 50–50 chance. They dislike gambling with high odds because they get no achievement satisfaction from success that comes by pure chance. Similarly, they dislike low odds (high probability of success) because

McClelland's theory of needs A theory that states achievement, power, and affiliation are three important needs that help explain motivation.

need for achievement (nAch) The drive to excel, to achieve in relationship to a set of standards, and to strive to succeed.

need for power (nPow) The need to make others behave in a way in which they would not have behaved otherwise.

need for affiliation (nAff) The desire for friendly and close interpersonal relationships.

then there is no challenge to their skills. They like to set goals that require stretching themselves a little.

Relying on an extensive amount of research, we can predict some relationships between achievement need and job performance. First, when jobs have a high degree of personal responsibility, feedback, and an intermediate degree of risk, high achievers are strongly motivated. Second, a high need to achieve does not necessarily make someone a good manager, especially in large organizations. People with a high achievement need are interested in how well they do personally, and not in influencing others to do well. Third, needs for affiliation and power tend to be closely related to managerial success. The best managers may be high in their need for power and low in their need for affiliation.[12]

The view that a high achievement need acts as an internal motivator presupposes two cultural characteristics—willingness to accept a moderate degree of risk (which excludes countries with strong uncertainty-avoidance characteristics), and concern with performance (which applies to countries with strong achievement characteristics). This combination is found in Anglo-American countries such as the United States, Canada, and Great Britain, and much less in Chile and Portugal.

McClelland's theory has research support, particularly cross-culturally (when cultural dimensions including power distance are taken into account).[13] The concept of the need for achievement has received a great deal of research attention and acceptance in a wide array of fields, including organizational behavior, psychology, and general business.[14] Therefore, in this text we utilize the concept descriptively. The need for power also has research support, but it may be more familiar to people in broad terms than in relation to the original definition.[15] We will discuss power much more in Chapter 13. The need for affiliation is well established and accepted in research. Although it may seem like an updated version of Maslow's social need, it is actually quite separate. Many people take for granted the idea that human beings have a drive toward relationships, so none of us may completely lack this motivation. However, recent research of Cameroonian and German adults suggests we may be

Entrepreneur Fred DeLuca is a high achiever motivated by work that demands a high degree of personal responsibility. He co-founded a Subway sandwich shop in 1965 at the age of 17 to help finance his college education and grew the company into the world's largest fast-food franchise with almost 44,000 shops in more than 100 countries.
Source: Geoff Caddick/AP Images

Why won't he take my advice?

The new guy in the office is nice enough, but he's straight out of college, and I have 20 years of experience in the field. I'd like to help him out, but he won't take it no matter how I approach him. Is there anything I can do to motivate him to accept my advice? He badly needs a few pointers.

—James

Dear James:

It's great that you want to help, and surely you have wisdom to offer. But let's start with this: When is the last time you took someone else's advice? Chances are it's easier for you to remember the last time you *didn't* take someone's advice than when you did. That's because we want success on our own terms, and we don't like the idea that a ready answer was out there all along (and we missed it). "When somebody says, 'You should do something,' the subtext is: 'You're an idiot for not already doing it,'" said psychologist Alan Goldberg. "Nobody takes advice under those conditions." So under what conditions *do* people take advice?

There are two parts to the motivation equation for advice: what your coworker wants to hear, and how you can approach him. For the first part, keep this rule in mind: He wants to hear that whatever decisions he's made are brilliant. If he hears anything different from that, he's likely to tune you out or keep talking until you come over to his side.

For the second part, your coworker's motivation to accept and, more importantly, act on advice has a lot to do with how you approach him. Are you likely to "impart your wisdom to the younger generation?" Anything like "I wish I had known this when I was just starting out like you" advice will likely have him thinking you (and your advice) are out of date. Are you going to give "if I were you, I would do this" advice? He may resent your intrusion. According to research, what is most likely to work is a gentle suggestion, phrased as a request. Ravi Dhar, a director at Yale, said, "Interrogatives have less reactance and may be more effective." You might say, for instance, "Would you consider trying out this idea?"

Take heart, the problem isn't that we don't like advice—we do, as long as we seek it. According to research, we are more motivated toward advice when we are facing important decisions, so good timing may work in your favor. When he does ask, you may suggest that he writes down the parameters of his choices and his interpretations of the ethics of each decision. Researcher Dan Ariely has found that we are much more motivated to make morally right decisions when we've considered the moral implications in a forthright manner. In this way, your coworker may motivate himself to make the right decisions.

Keep trying!

_____

Sources: D. Ariely, "What Price for the Soul of a Stranger?" *The Wall Street Journal,* May 10–11, 2014, C12; J. Queenan, "A Word to the Wise," *The Wall Street Journal,* February 8–9, 2014, C1–C2; and S. Reddy, "The Trick to Getting People to Take the Stairs? Just Ask," *The Wall Street Journal,* February 17, 2015, R4.

The opinions provided here are of the managers and authors only and do not necessarily reflect those of their organizations. The authors or managers are not responsible for any errors or omissions, or for the results obtained from the use of this information. In no event will the authors or managers, or their related partnerships or corporations thereof, be liable to you or anyone else for any decision made or action taken in reliance on the opinions provided here.

constrained by our personalities to the extent that we are high in neuroticism. Agreeableness supports our pursuit of affiliation, while extraversion has no significant effect.[16]

The degree to which we have each of the three needs is difficult to measure, and therefore the theory is difficult to put into practice. It is more common to find situations in which managers aware of these motivational drivers label employees based on observations made over time. Therefore, the concepts are helpful, but not often used objectively.

Contemporary Theories of Motivation

7-3   Contrast the elements of self-determination theory and goal-setting theory.

Contemporary theories of motivation have one thing in common: Each has a reasonable degree of valid supporting documentation. We call them "contemporary theories" because they represent the latest thinking in explaining employee motivation. This doesn't mean they are unquestionably right.

Self-Determination Theory

"It's strange," said Marcia. "I started work at the Humane Society as a volunteer. I put in 15 hours a week helping people adopt pets. And I loved coming to work. Then, 3 months ago, they hired me full-time at $11 an hour. I'm doing the same work I did before. But I'm not finding it as much fun."

Does Marcia's reaction seem counterintuitive? There's an explanation for it. It's called **self-determination theory**, which proposes that people prefer to feel they have control over their actions, so anything that makes a previously enjoyed task feel more like an obligation than a freely chosen activity will undermine motivation.[17] The theory is widely used in psychology, management, education, and medical research.

self-determination theory A theory of motivation that is concerned with the beneficial effects of intrinsic motivation and the harmful effects of extrinsic motivation.

Much research on self-determination theory in OB has focused on **cognitive evaluation theory**, a complementary theory hypothesizing that extrinsic rewards will reduce intrinsic interest in a task. When people are paid for work, it feels less like something they *want* to do and more like something they *have* to do. Self-determination theory proposes that in addition to being driven by a need for autonomy, people seek ways to achieve competence and make positive connections with others. Its major implications relate to work rewards.

cognitive evaluation theory A version of self-determination theory that holds that allocating extrinsic rewards for behavior that had been previously intrinsically rewarding tends to decrease the overall level of motivation if the rewards are seen as controlling.

What does self-determination theory suggest about providing rewards? It suggests that some caution in the use of extrinsic rewards to motivate is wise, and that pursuing goals from intrinsic motives (such as a strong interest in the work itself) is more sustaining to human motivation than are extrinsic rewards. Similarly, cognitive evaluation theory suggests that providing extrinsic incentives may, in many cases, undermine intrinsic motivation. For example, if a computer programmer values writing code because she likes to solve problems, a bonus for writing a certain number of lines of code every day could feel coercive, and her intrinsic motivation would suffer. She may or may not increase her number of lines of code per day in response to the extrinsic motivator. In support, a recent meta-analysis confirms that intrinsic motivation contributes to the quality of work, while incentives contribute to the quantity of work. Although intrinsic motivation predicts performance whether or not there are incentives, it may be less of a predictor when incentives are tied to performance directly (such as with monetary bonuses) rather than indirectly.[18]

self-concordance The degree to which people's reasons for pursuing goals are consistent with their interests and core values.

A more recent outgrowth of self-determination theory is **self-concordance**, which considers how strongly people's reasons for pursuing goals are consistent with their interests and core values. OB research suggests that people who pursue work goals for intrinsic reasons are more satisfied with their jobs, feel they fit into their organizations better, and may perform better.[19] Across cultures, if individuals pursue goals because of intrinsic interest, they are more likely to attain goals, are happier when they do, and are happy even if they do not.[20] Why? Because the process of striving toward goals is fun whether or not the goal is achieved. Recent research reveals that when people do not enjoy their work for intrinsic reasons, those who work because they feel obligated to do so can still perform acceptably, though they experience higher levels of strain as a result.[21] In contrast, people who pursue goals for extrinsic reasons (money, status, or other benefits) are less likely to attain goals and less happy even when they do. Why? Because the goals are less meaningful to them.[22]

What does all this mean? For individuals, it means you should choose your job for reasons other than extrinsic rewards. For organizations, it means managers should provide intrinsic as well as extrinsic incentives. Managers need to make the work interesting, provide recognition, and support employee growth and development. Employees who feel that what they do is within their control and a result of free choice are likely to be more motivated by their work and committed to their employers.[23]

Helping Others and Being a Good Citizen Is Good for Your Career

We might think we should motivate employees to display organizational citizenship behavior (OCB), and that helping others would benefit their careers. We would probably also believe our own OCB will yield us career benefits. Surprisingly, there is some evidence that these assumptions are false, at least in certain organizations. Why?

In some organizations, employees are evaluated more on *how* their work gets done than on how much. If they possess the requisite knowledge and skills, or if they demonstrate the right behaviors on the job (for example, always greeting customers with a smile), they are determined by management to be motivated, "good" performers. In these situations, OCBs are considered as the next higher level of good employee behavior. Employees' careers thus benefit as a result of their helpfulness toward coworkers.

However, in other organizations, employees are evaluated more on *what* gets done. Here, employees are determined to be "good" performers if they meet objective goals such as billing clients a certain number of hours or reaching a certain sales volume. When managers overlook employee OCB, frown on helpful behaviors, or create an overly competitive organizational culture, employees become unmotivated to continue their helpful actions. Those who still engage in OCB can find their career progress is slowed when they take time away from core tasks to be helpful.

The upshot? There may be a trade-off between being a good performer and being a good citizen. In organizations that focus more on behaviors, following your motivation to be a good citizen can help to accomplish your career goals. However, in organizations that focus more on objective outcomes, you may need to consider the cost of your good deeds.

_____

Sources: D. M. Bergeron, "The Potential Paradox of Organizational Citizenship Behavior: Good Citizens at What Cost?" *Academy of Management Review* 32, no. 4 (2007); and D. M. Bergeron, A. J. Shipp, B. Rosen, and S. A. Furst, "Organizational Citizenship Behavior and Career Outcomes: The Cost of Being a Good Citizen," *Journal of Management* 39, no. 4 (2013): 958–84.

Goal-Setting Theory

goal-setting theory A theory that says that specific and difficult goals, with feedback, lead to higher performance.

You've likely heard the sentiment a number of times: "Just do your best. That's all anyone can ask." But what does "do your best" mean? Do we ever know whether we've achieved that vague goal? Research on **goal-setting theory**, proposed by Edwin Locke, reveals the impressive effects of goal specificity, challenge, and feedback on performance. Under the theory, intentions to work toward a goal are considered a major source of work motivation.[24]

Goal-setting theory is well supported. Evidence strongly suggests that *specific* goals increase performance; that *difficult* goals, when accepted, result in higher performance than do easy goals; and that *feedback* leads to higher performance than does nonfeedback.[25] Why? First, specificity itself seems to act as an internal stimulus. When a trucker commits to making 12 round-trip hauls between Toronto and New York each week, this intention gives him a specific objective to attain. All things being equal, he will outperform a counterpart with no goals or the generalized goal "do your best."

Second, if factors such as acceptance of goals are held constant, the more difficult the goal, the higher the level of performance. Of course, it's logical to assume easier goals are more likely to be accepted. But once a hard task has been accepted, we can expect the employee to exert a high level of effort to try to achieve it.

Third, people do better when they get feedback on how well they are progressing toward their goals because it helps identify discrepancies between what they have done and what they want to do next—that is, feedback guides behavior. But all feedback is not equally potent. Self-generated feedback—with which

Co-founders Anthony Thomson, left, and Vernon Hill launched the Metro Bank in London in 2010 with the goal of adding 200 new branches and capturing 10 percent of London's banking market. This challenging goal motivates employees to exert a high level of effort in giving customers exceptionally convenient, flexible, and friendly—including pet-friendly—service.
Source: Toby Melville/Reuters

employees are able to monitor their own progress or receive feedback from the task process itself—is more powerful than externally generated feedback.[26]

If employees can participate in the setting of their own goals, will they try harder? The evidence is mixed. In some studies, participatively set goals yielded superior performance; in others, individuals performed best when assigned goals by their boss. One study in China found, for instance, that participative team goal setting improved team outcomes.[27] Another study found that participation results in more achievable goals for individuals.[28] Without participation, the individual pursuing the goal needs to clearly understand its purpose and importance.[29]

Three personal factors influence the goals–performance relationship: *goal commitment, task characteristics,* and *national culture.*

Goal Commitment   Goal-setting theory assumes an individual is committed to the goal and determined not to lower or abandon it. The individual (1) believes he or she can achieve the goal and (2) wants to achieve it.[30] Goal commitment is most likely to occur when goals are made public, when the individual has an internal locus of control, when the goals are self-set rather than assigned, and when they are based at least partially on individual ability.[31]

Task Characteristics   Goals themselves seem to affect performance more strongly when tasks are simple rather than complex, well learned rather than novel, independent rather than interdependent, and on the high end of achievable.[32] On interdependent tasks, group goals are preferable. Paradoxically, goal abandonment following an initial failure is more likely for individuals who self-affirm their core values, possibly because they more strongly internalize the implications of failure than others.[33]

National Culture   Setting specific, difficult, individual goals may have different effects in different cultures. In collectivistic and high-power-distance cultures, achievable moderate goals can be more motivating than difficult ones.[34] Finally, assigned goals appear to generate greater goal commitment in high than in low power-distance cultures.[35] However, research has not shown that group-based goals are more effective in collectivist than in individualist cultures. More research is needed to assess how goal constructs might differ across cultures.

Although goal-setting has positive outcomes, it's not unequivocally beneficial. For example, some goals may be *too* effective.[36] When learning something is important, goals related to performance undermine adaptation and creativity because people become too focused on outcomes and ignore the learning process. Nor are all goals equally effective. For rote tasks with quantifiable standards of productivity, goals that reward quantity can be highly motivating. For other jobs that require complex thinking and personal investment, goals and rewards for quantity may not be effective.[37] Finally, individuals may fail to give up on an unattainable goal even when it might be beneficial to do so.

Research has found that people differ in the way they regulate their thoughts and behaviors during goal pursuit. Generally, people fall into one of two categories, though they could belong to both. Those with a **promotion focus** strive for advancement and accomplishment and approach conditions that move them closer toward desired goals. This concept is similar to the approach side of the approach-avoidance framework discussed in Chapter 5. Those with a **prevention focus** strive to fulfill duties and obligations and avoid conditions that pull them away from desired goals. Aspects of this concept are similar to the avoidance side of the approach-avoidance framework. Although you would be right in noting that both strategies are in the service of goal accomplishment, the manner in which they get there is quite different. As an example, consider studying for an exam. You could engage in promotion-focused activities such as reading class materials, or you could engage in prevention-focused activities such as refraining from doing things that would get in the way of studying, such as playing video games.

You may ask, "Which is the better strategy?" Well, the answer depends on the outcome you are striving for. While a promotion (but not a prevention) focus is related to higher levels of task performance, citizenship behavior, and innovation, a prevention (but not a promotion) focus is related to safety performance. Ideally, it's probably best to be both promotion *and* prevention oriented.[38] Keep in mind a person's job satisfaction will be more heavily impacted by low success when that person has an avoidance (prevention) outlook,[39] so set achievable goals, remove distractions, and provide structure for these individuals.[40]

Implementing Goal-Setting How do managers make goal-setting theory operational? That's often left up to the individual. Some managers set aggressive performance targets—what General Electric called "stretch goals." Some leaders, such as Procter & Gamble's former CEO Robert McDonald and Best Buy's CEO Hubert Joly, are known for their demanding performance goals. But many managers don't set goals. When asked whether their jobs had clearly defined goals, a minority of survey respondents said yes.[41]

A more systematic way to utilize goal-setting is with **management by objectives (MBO)**, an initiative most popular in the 1970s but still used today. MBO emphasizes participatively set goals that are tangible, verifiable, and measurable. As in Exhibit 7-4, the organization's overall objectives are translated into specific cascading objectives for each level (divisional, departmental, individual). But because lower-unit managers jointly participate in setting their own goals, MBO works from the bottom up as well as from the top down. The result is a hierarchy that links objectives at one level to those at the next. For the individual employee, MBO provides specific personal performance objectives.

promotion focus A self-regulation strategy that involves striving for goals through advancement and accomplishment.

prevention focus A self-regulation strategy that involves striving for goals by fulfilling duties and obligations.

management by objectives (MBO) A program that encompasses specific goals, participatively set, for an explicit time period, with feedback on goal progress.

Exhibit 7-4   Cascading of Objectives

Four ingredients are common to MBO programs: goal specificity, participation in decision making (including the setting of goals or objectives), an explicit time period, and performance feedback.[42] Many elements in MBO programs match the propositions of goal-setting theory.

You'll find MBO programs in many business, health care, educational, government, and nonprofit organizations.[43] A version of MBO, called Management by Objectives and Results (MBOR), has been used for 30 years in the governments of Denmark, Norway, and Sweden.[44] However, the popularity of these programs does not mean they always work.[45] When MBO fails, the culprits tend to be unrealistic expectations, lack of commitment by top management, and inability or unwillingness to allocate rewards based on goal accomplishment.

Goal-Setting and Ethics   The relationship between goal-setting and ethics is quite complex: If we emphasize the attainment of goals, what is the cost? The answer is probably found in the standards we set for goal achievement. For example, when money is tied to goal attainment, we may focus on getting the money and become willing to compromise ourselves ethically. If we are instead primed with thoughts about how we are spending our time when we are pursuing the goal, we are more likely to act more ethically.[46] However, this result is limited to thoughts about how we are spending our time. If we are put under time pressure and worry about that, thoughts about time turn against us. Time pressure often increases as we are nearing a goal, which can tempt us to act unethically to achieve it.[47] Specifically, we may forego mastering tasks and adopt avoidance techniques so we don't look bad,[48] both of which can incline us toward unethical choices.

Other Contemporary Theories of Motivation

7-4   Demonstrate the differences among self-efficacy theory, reinforcement theory, equity theory, and expectancy theory.

Self-determination theory and goal-setting theory are well supported contemporary theories of motivation. But they are far from the only noteworthy OB theories on the subject. Self-efficacy, reinforcement, equity/organizational justice, and expectancy theories reveal different aspects of our motivational processes and tendencies. We begin with the concept of self-efficacy.

Self-Efficacy Theory

self-efficacy theory An individual's belief that he or she is capable of performing a task.

Self-efficacy theory, also known as *social cognitive theory* or *social learning theory*, refers to an individual's belief that he or she is capable of performing a task.[49] The higher your self-efficacy, the more confidence you have in your ability to succeed. So, in difficult situations, people with low self-efficacy are more likely to lessen their effort or give up altogether, while those with high self-efficacy will try harder to master the challenge.[50] Self-efficacy can create a positive spiral in which those with high efficacy become more engaged in their tasks and then, in turn, increase performance, which increases efficacy further.[51] One recent study introduced a further explanation, in that self-efficacy was associated with a higher level of focused attention, which led to increased task performance.[52]

Feedback influences self-efficacy; individuals high in self-efficacy seem to respond to negative feedback with increased effort and motivation, while those low in self-efficacy are likely to lessen their effort after negative feedback.[53] Changes in self-efficacy over time are related to changes in creative performance as well.[54] How can managers help their employees achieve high levels of self-efficacy? By bringing goal-setting theory and self-efficacy theory together.

Goal-setting theory and self-efficacy theory don't compete; they complement each other. As Exhibit 7-5 shows, employees whose managers set difficult goals for them will have a higher level of self-efficacy and set higher goals for their own performance. Why? Setting difficult goals for people communicates your confidence in them.

Increasing Self-Efficacy in Yourself   The researcher who developed self-efficacy theory, Albert Bandura, proposes four ways self-efficacy can be increased:[55]

1. Enactive mastery.
2. Vicarious modeling.
3. Verbal persuasion.
4. Arousal.

Exhibit 7-5   Joint Effects of Goals and Self-Efficacy on Performance

Source: Based on E. A. Locke and G. P. Latham, "Building a Practically Useful Theory of Goal Setting and Task Motivation: A 35-Year Odyssey," *American Psychologist* (September 2002): 705–17.

The most important source of increasing self-efficacy is *enactive mastery*—that is, gaining relevant experience with the task or job. If you've been able to do the job successfully in the past, you're more confident you can do it in the future.

The second source is *vicarious modeling*—becoming more confident because you see someone else doing the task. If your friend quits smoking, it increases your confidence that you can quit, too. Vicarious modeling is most effective when you see yourself as similar to the person you are observing. Watching Tiger Woods play a difficult golf shot might not increase your confidence in being able to play the shot yourself, but if you watch a golfer with a handicap similar to yours, it's persuasive.

The third source is *verbal persuasion:* we become more confident when someone convinces us we have the skills necessary to be successful. Motivational speakers use this tactic.

Finally, *arousal* increases self-efficacy. Arousal leads to an energized state, so we get "psyched up," feel up to the task, and perform better. But if the task requires a steady, lower-key perspective (say, carefully editing a manuscript), arousal may in fact hurt performance even as it increases self-efficacy because we might hurry through the task.

Intelligence and personality are absent from Bandura's list, but they too can increase self-efficacy.[56] People who are intelligent, conscientious, and emotionally stable are so much more likely to have high self-efficacy that some researchers argue self-efficacy is less important than prior research would suggest.[57] They believe it is partially a by-product in a smart person with a confident personality.

Influencing Self-Efficacy in Others   The best way for a manager to use verbal persuasion is through the *Pygmalion effect,* a term based on a Greek myth about a sculptor (Pygmalion) who fell in love with a statue he carved. The Pygmalion effect is a form of *self-fulfilling prophecy* in which believing something can make it true. Here, it is often used to describe "that what one person expects of another can come to serve a self-fulfilling prophecy."[58] An example should make this clear. In studies, teachers were told their students had very high IQ scores when, in fact, they spanned a range from high to low. Consistent with the Pygmalion effect, the teachers spent more time with the students they *thought* were smart, gave them more challenging assignments, and expected more of them—all of which led to higher student self-efficacy and better achievement outcomes.[59] This strategy has been used in the workplace too, with replicable results and enhanced effects when leader-subordinate relationships are strong.[60]

Training programs often make use of enactive mastery by having people practice and build their skills. In fact, one reason training works is that it increases self-efficacy, particularly when the training is interactive and feedback is given after training.[61] Individuals with higher levels of self-efficacy also appear to reap more benefits from training programs and are more likely to use their training on the job.[62]

Reinforcement Theory

reinforcement theory   A theory that says that behavior is a function of its consequences.

Goal-setting is a cognitive approach, proposing that an individual's purposes direct his or her action. **Reinforcement theory**, in contrast, takes a behavioristic view, arguing that reinforcement conditions behavior. The two theories are clearly philosophically at odds. Reinforcement theorists see behavior as environmentally caused. You need not be concerned, they would argue, with internal cognitive events; what controls behavior are reinforcers—any consequences that, when they immediately follow responses, increase the probability that the behavior will be repeated.

An Ethical Choice

Motivated by Big Brother

Technology is a great thing. The Internet provides us with instant access to an abundance of information, and smartphones allow us to stay easily connected with others through e-mail, texting, tweeting, and conversation. Yet that ease of connectivity has also given employees the sinking feeling they are being watched...and they are right. But is it ethical?

Some companies are using technology to track their employees' activities, and some of this tracking is done in the name of science. For example, Bank of America Corp. wanted to learn whether face-to-face interaction made a difference to the productivity of its call-center teams, so it asked around 100 workers to wear badges for a few weeks that tracked their whereabouts. Discovering that the most productive workers interacted most frequently with others, the company scheduled work breaks for groups rather than individually. This is a

nice outcome, but how did the monitoring affect the behavior and motivation of the workers?

Other companies track employees to ensure they are hard at work, which risks completely demotivating some. Accurate Biometrics, for example, uses computer monitoring to oversee its telecommuters. Says Timothy Daniels, VP of operations, looking at websites his employees have visited "enables us to keep a watchful eye without being overinvasive." Currently, around 70 percent of organizations monitor their employees.

Practically speaking, managers may not want to adopt technologies that demotivate their employees through micromanagement. Perhaps more importantly, though, how can they use monitoring technology ethically in workplace applications? First and foremost, employees should be informed their activities will be tracked. Second,

the purpose of tracking should be made clear to employees. Are workers being monitored to learn something that might help them and the organization as a whole? Or are they being monitored to ensure they never slack off? Finally, it should be made clear which behaviors are inappropriate. Taking a legitimate work break is different from spending hours on a social networking site. These guidelines should increase the likelihood that monitoring programs are accepted and perceived to be fair.

Sources: S. Shellenbarger, "Working from Home without Slacking Off," *The Wall Street Journal,* July 13–15, 2012, 29; R. Richmond, "3 Tips for Legally and Ethically Monitoring Employees Online," *Entrepreneur,* May 31, 2012, http://www.entrepreneur.com/article/223686; and R. E. Silverman, "Tracking Sensors Invade the Workplace," *The Wall Street Journal,* March 7, 2003, www.wsj.com.

Reinforcement theory ignores the inner state of the individual and concentrates solely on what happens when he or she takes some action. Because it does not concern itself with what initiates behavior, it is not, strictly speaking, a theory of motivation. But it does provide a powerful means of analyzing what controls behavior, and this is why we typically consider it in discussions of motivation.[63]

Operant Conditioning/Behaviorism and Reinforcement   *Operant conditioning theory,* probably the most relevant component of reinforcement theory for management, argues that people learn to behave to get something they want or to avoid something they don't want. Unlike reflexive or unlearned behavior, operant behavior is influenced by the reinforcement or lack of reinforcement brought about by consequences. Reinforcement strengthens a behavior and increases the likelihood it will be repeated.[64]

B. F. Skinner, one of the most prominent advocates of operant conditioning, demonstrated that people will most likely engage in desired behaviors if they are positively reinforced for doing so; rewards are most effective if they immediately follow the desired response; and behavior that is not rewarded, or is punished, is less likely to be repeated. The concept of operant conditioning was part of Skinner's broader concept of **behaviorism**, which argues that behavior follows stimuli in a relatively unthinking manner. Skinner's form of radical behaviorism rejects feelings, thoughts, and other states of mind as causes of behavior. In short, people learn to associate stimulus and response, but their conscious awareness of this association is irrelevant.[65]

behaviorism   A theory that argues that behavior follows stimuli in a relatively unthinking manner.

You can see illustrations of operant conditioning everywhere. For instance, a commissioned salesperson wanting to earn a sizable income finds doing so is contingent on generating high sales in his territory, so he sells as much as possible. Of course, the linkage can also teach individuals to engage in behaviors that work against the best interests of the organization. Assume your boss says if you work overtime during the next 3-week busy season you'll be compensated for it at your next performance appraisal. However, when performance-appraisal time comes, you are given no positive reinforcement for your overtime work. The next time your boss asks you to work overtime, what will you do? You'll probably decline!

Social-Learning Theory and Reinforcement Individuals can learn by being told or by observing what happens to other people, as well as through direct experience. Much of what we have learned comes from watching models—parents, teachers, peers, film and television performers, bosses, and so forth. The view that we can learn through both observation and direct experience is called **social-learning theory**.[66]

Although social-learning theory is an extension of operant conditioning—that is, it assumes behavior is a function of consequences—it also acknowledges the effects of observational learning and perception. People respond to the way they perceive and define consequences, not to the objective consequences themselves.

Models are central to the social-learning viewpoint. Four processes determine their influence on an individual:

1. **Attentional processes.** People learn from a model only when they recognize and pay attention to its critical features. We tend to be most influenced by models that are attractive, repeatedly available, important to us, or similar to us (in our estimation).
2. **Retention processes.** A model's influence depends on how well the individual remembers the model's action after the model is no longer readily available.

social-learning theory The view that we can learn through both observation and direct experience.

At Thai Takenaka, a leading construction firm in Thailand, experienced employees teach younger workers construction management skills, building techniques, and the basics of craftsmanship through training by "looking, touching, and realization." This social learning view helps employees succeed in meeting the firm's high standards of quality and efficiency.
Source: Kyodo/Newscom

3. **Motor reproduction processes.** After a person has seen a new behavior by observing the model, watching must be converted to doing. This process demonstrates that the individual can perform the modeled activities.
4. **Reinforcement processes.** Individuals are motivated to exhibit the modeled behavior if positive incentives or rewards are provided. Positively reinforced behaviors are given more attention, learned better, and performed more often.

Equity Theory/Organizational Justice

Ainsley is a student working toward a bachelor's degree in finance. In order to gain some work experience and increase her marketability, she has accepted a summer internship in the finance department at a pharmaceutical company. She is quite pleased at the pay: $15 an hour is more than other students in her cohort receive for their summer internships. At work she meets Josh, a recent graduate working as a middle manager in the same finance department. Josh makes $30 an hour.

On the job, Ainsley is a go-getter. She's engaged, satisfied, and always seems willing to help others. Josh is the opposite. He often seems disinterested in his job and entertains thoughts about quitting. When pressed one day about why he is unhappy, Josh cites his pay as the main reason. Specifically, he tells Ainsley that, compared to managers at other pharmaceutical companies, he makes much less. "It isn't fair," he complains. "I work just as hard as they do, yet I don't make as much. Maybe I should go work for the competition."

How could someone making $30 an hour be less satisfied with his pay than someone making $15 an hour and be less motivated as a result? The answer lies in **equity theory** and, more broadly, in principles of organizational justice. According to equity theory, employees compare what they get from their job (their "Outcomes," such as pay, promotions, recognition, or a bigger office) to what they put into it (their "Inputs," such as effort, experience, and education). They take the ratio of their outcomes to their inputs and compare it to the ratio of others, usually someone similar like a coworker or someone doing the same job. This is shown in Exhibit 7-6. If we believe our ratio is equal to those with whom we compare ourselves, a state of equity exists and we perceive our situation as fair.

Based on equity theory, employees who perceive inequity will make one of six choices:[67]

1. **Change inputs** (exert less effort if underpaid or more if overpaid).
2. **Change outcomes** (individuals paid on a piece-rate basis can increase their pay by producing a higher quantity of units of lower quality).

equity theory A theory that says that individuals compare their job inputs and outcomes with those of others and then respond to eliminate any inequities.

Exhibit 7-6	**Equity Theory**

Ratio Comparisons*	Perception
$\dfrac{O}{I_A} < \dfrac{O}{I_B}$	Inequity due to being underrewarded
$\dfrac{O}{I_A} = \dfrac{O}{I_B}$	Equity
$\dfrac{O}{I_A} > \dfrac{O}{I_B}$	Inequity due to being overrewarded

*Where $\dfrac{O}{I_A}$ represents the employee and $\dfrac{O}{I_B}$ represents relevant others

3. **Distort perceptions of self** ("I used to think I worked at a moderate pace, but now I realize I work a lot harder than everyone else").
4. **Distort perceptions of others** ("Mike's job isn't as desirable as I thought").
5. **Choose a different referent** ("I may not make as much as my brother-in-law, but I'm doing a lot better than my Dad did when he was my age").
6. **Leave the field** (quit the job).

Equity theory has support from some researchers, but not from all.[68] There are some concerns with the propositions. First, inequities created by overpayment do not seem to significantly affect behavior in most work situations. So don't expect an employee who feels overpaid to give back part of his salary or put in more hours to make up for the inequity. Although individuals may sometimes perceive that they are overrewarded, they restore equity by rationalizing their situation ("I'm worth it because I work harder than everyone else"). Second, not everyone is equally equity-sensitive, for various reasons, including feelings of entitlement.[69] Others actually prefer outcome–input ratios lower than the referent comparisons. Predictions from equity theory are not likely to be very accurate about these "benevolent types."[70]

Although equity theory's propositions have not all held up, the hypothesis served as an important precursor to the study of **organizational justice**, or more simply fairness, in the workplace.[71] Organizational justice is concerned more broadly with how employees feel authorities and decision-makers at work treat them. For the most part, employees evaluate how fairly they are treated, as shown in Exhibit 7-7.

organizational justice An overall perception of what is fair in the workplace, composed of distributive, procedural, informational, and interpersonal justice.

distributive justice Perceived fairness of the amount and allocation of rewards among individuals.

Distributive Justice   **Distributive justice** is concerned with the fairness of the outcomes, such as pay and recognition that employees receive. Outcomes can

Exhibit 7-7   Model of Organizational Justice

Distributive Justice
Definition: perceived fairness of outcome
Example: I got the pay raise I deserved.

Procedural Justice
Definition: perceived fairness of process used to determine outcome
Example: I had input into the process used to give raises and was given a good explanation of why I received the raise I did.

Interactional Justice
Definition: perceived degree to which one is treated with dignity and respect
Example: When telling me about my raise, my supervisor was very nice and complimentary.

Organizational Justice
Definition: overall perception of what is fair in the workplace
Example: I think this is a fair place to work.

be allocated in many ways. For example, we could distribute raises equally among employees, or we could base them on which employees need money the most. However, as we discussed about equity theory, employees tend to perceive their outcomes are fairest when they are distributed equitably.

Does the same logic apply to teams? At first glance, it would seem that distributing rewards equally among team members is best for boosting morale and teamwork—that way, no one is favored more than another. A study of U.S. National Hockey League teams suggests otherwise. Differentiating the pay of team members on the basis of their inputs (how well they performed in games) attracted better players to the team, made it more likely they would stay, and increased team performance.[72]

The way we have described things so far, it would seem that individuals gauge distributive justice and equity in a rational, calculative way as they compare their outcome–input ratios to those of others. But the experience of justice, and especially of injustice, is often not so cold and calculated. Instead, people base distributive judgments on a feeling or an emotional reaction to the way they think they are being treated relative to others, and their reactions are often "hot" and emotional rather than cool and rational.[73]

Procedural Justice   Although employees care a lot about *what* outcomes are distributed (distributive justice), they also care about *how* they are distributed. While distributive justice looks at *what* outcomes are allocated, **procedural justice** examines *how*.[74] For one, employees perceive that procedures are fairer when they are given a say in the decision-making process. Having direct influence over how decisions or made, or at the very least being able to present our opinion to decision makers, creates a sense of control and makes us feel empowered (we discuss empowerment more in the next chapter). Employees also perceive that procedures are fairer when decision makers follow several "rules." These include making decisions in a consistent manner (across people and over time), avoiding bias (not favoring one group or person over another), using accurate information, considering the groups or people their decisions affect, acting ethically, and remaining open to appeals or correction.

procedural justice The perceived fairness of the process used to determine the distribution of rewards.

As part of its "Putting Employees First" belief, The Container Store involves employees in the decision-making process by empowering them to make decisions that directly affect how they work. This contributes to a sense of procedural justice for employees like Krysy Winden, shown here, and can result in higher job satisfaction and trust.
Source: Richard Sennott/ZUMAPRESS/Newscom

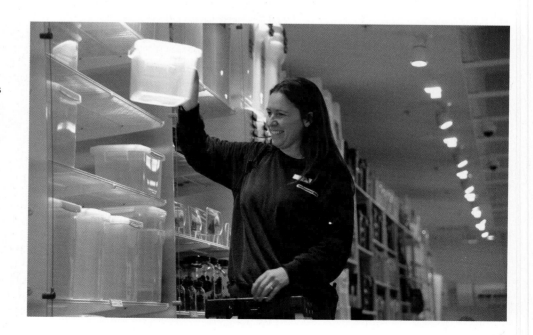

If outcomes are favorable and individuals get what they want, they care less about the process, so procedural justice doesn't matter as much when distributions are perceived to be fair. It's when outcomes are unfavorable that people pay close attention to the process. If the process is judged to be fair, then employees are more accepting of unfavorable outcomes.[75]

Why is this the case? It's likely that employees believe fair procedures, which often have long-lasting effects, will eventually result in a fair outcome, even if the immediate outcome is unfair. Think about it. If you are hoping for a raise and your manager informs you that you did not receive one, you'll probably want to know how raises were determined. If it turns out your manager allocated raises based on merit and you were simply outperformed by a coworker, then you're more likely to accept your manager's decision than if raises were based on favoritism. Of course, if you get the raise in the first place, then you'll be less concerned with how the decision was made.

Informational Justice   Beyond outcomes and procedures, research has shown that employees care about two other types of fairness that have to do with the way they are treated during interactions with others. The first type is **informational justice**, which reflects whether managers provide employees with explanations for key decisions and keep them informed of important organizational matters. The more detailed and candid managers are with employees, the more fairly treated those employees feel.

Though it may seem obvious that managers should be honest with their employees and not keep them in the dark about organizational matters, many managers are hesitant to share information. This is especially the case with bad news, which is uncomfortable for both the manager delivering it and the employee receiving it. Explanations for bad news are beneficial when they take the form of excuses after the fact ("I know this is bad, and I wanted to give you the office, but it wasn't my decision") rather than justifications ("I decided to give the office to Sam, but having it isn't a big deal").[76]

Interpersonal Justice   The second type of justice relevant to interactions between managers and employees is **interpersonal justice**, which reflects whether employees are treated with dignity and respect. Compared to the other forms of justice we've discussed, interpersonal justice is unique in that it can occur in everyday interactions between managers and employees.[77] This quality allows managers to take advantage of (or miss out on) opportunities to make their employees feel fairly treated. Many managers may view treating employees politely and respectfully as too "soft," choosing more aggressive tactics out of a belief that doing so will be more motivating. Although displays of negative emotions such as anger may be motivating in some cases,[78] managers sometimes take this too far. Consider former Rutgers University men's basketball coach Mike Rice who was caught on video verbally and even physically abusing players and was subsequently fired.[79]

Justice Outcomes   After all this talk about types of justice, how much does justice really matter to employees? A great deal, as it turns out. When employees feel fairly treated, they respond in a number of positive ways. All the types of justice discussed in this section have been linked to higher levels of task performance and citizenship behaviors such as helping coworkers, as well as lower levels of counterproductive behaviors such as shirking job duties. Distributive and procedural justice are more strongly associated with task performance, while informational and interpersonal justice are more strongly associated with citizenship behavior. Even more physiological

informational justice   The degree to which employees are provided truthful explanations for decisions.

interpersonal justice   The degree to which employees are treated with dignity and respect.

outcomes, such as how well employees sleep and the state of their health, have been linked to fair treatment.[80]

Why does justice have these positive effects? Fair treatment enhances commitment to the organization and makes employees feel it cares about their well-being. In addition, employees who feel fairly treated trust their supervisors more, which reduces uncertainty and fear of being exploited by the organization. Finally, fair treatment elicits positive emotions, which in turn prompts behaviors like citizenship.[81]

Despite all attempts to enhance fairness, perceived injustices are still likely to occur. Fairness is often subjective; what one person sees as unfair, another may see as perfectly appropriate. In general, people see allocations or procedures favoring themselves as fair.[82] So, when addressing perceived injustices, managers need to focus their actions on the source of the problem. In addition, if employees feel they have been treated unjustly, having opportunities to express their frustration has been shown to reduce their desire for retribution.[83]

Ensuring Justice   How can an organization affect the justice perceptions and rule adherence of its managers? This depends upon the motivation of each manager. Some managers are likely to calculate justice by their degree of adherence to the justice rules of the organization. These managers will try to gain greater subordinate compliance with behavioral expectations, create an identity of being fair to their employees, or establish norms of fairness. Other managers may be motivated in justice decisions by their emotions. When they have a high positive affect and/or a low negative affect, these managers are most likely to act fairly.

It might be tempting for organizations to adopt strong justice guidelines in attempts to mandate managerial behavior, but this isn't likely to be universally effective. In cases where managers have more rules and less discretion, those who calculate justice are more likely to act fairly, but managers whose justice behavior follows from their affect may act more fairly when they have greater discretion.[84]

Culture and Justice   Across nations, the same basic principles of procedural justice are respected in that workers around the world prefer rewards based on performance and skills over rewards based on seniority.[85] However, inputs and outcomes are valued differently in various cultures.[86]

We may think of justice differences in terms of Hofstede's cultural dimensions (see Chapter 5). One large-scale study of over 190,000 employees in 32 countries and regions suggested that justice perceptions are most important to people in countries with individualistic, feminine, uncertainty avoidance, and low power-distance values.[87] Organizations can tailor programs to meet these justice expectations. For example, in countries that are highest in individualism, such as Australia and the United States, competitive pay plans and rewards for superior individual performance will enhance feelings of justice. In countries dominated by uncertainty avoidance, such as France, fixed pay compensation and employee participation may help employees feel more secure. The dominant dimension in Sweden is femininity, so relational concerns are considered important. Swedish organizations may therefore want to provide work-life balance initiatives and social recognition. Austria, in contrast, has a strong low power-distance value. Ethical concerns may be foremost to individuals in perceiving justice in Austrian organizations, so it will be important for organizations to justify inequality between leaders and workers and provide symbols of ethical leadership.

We can also look at other cultural factors. Some cultures emphasize status over individual achievement as a basis for allocating resources. Materialistic cultures are more likely to see cash compensation and rewards as the most relevant

Exhibit 7-8   **Expectancy Theory**

Individual effort → ① → Individual performance → ② → Organizational rewards → ③ → Personal goals

① Effort–performance relationship
② Performance–reward relationship
③ Rewards–personal goals relationship

outcomes of work, whereas relational cultures will see social rewards and status as important outcomes. International managers must consider the cultural preferences of each group of employees when determining what is "fair" in different contexts.

Expectancy Theory

expectancy theory   A theory that says that the strength of a tendency to act in a certain way depends on the strength of an expectation that the act will be followed by a given outcome and on the attractiveness of that outcome to the individual.

One of the most widely accepted explanations of motivation is Victor Vroom's **expectancy theory**.[88] Although it has critics, most evidence supports the theory.[89]

Expectancy theory argues that the strength of our tendency to act a certain way depends on the strength of our expectation of a given outcome and its attractiveness. In practical terms, employees will be motivated to exert a high level of effort when they believe that it will lead to a good performance appraisal, that a good appraisal will lead to organizational rewards such as salary increases and/or intrinsic rewards, and that the rewards will satisfy their personal goals. The theory, therefore, focuses on three relationships (see Exhibit 7-8):

1. **Effort–performance relationship.**   The probability perceived by the individual that exerting a given amount of effort will lead to performance.
2. **Performance–reward relationship.**   The degree to which the individual believes performing at a particular level will lead to the attainment of a desired outcome.

The performance–reward relationship is strong at Mary Kay Cosmetics, which offers a rewards and recognition program based on the achievement of personal goals set by each salesperson. The women shown here in China pose before a pink sedan, one of many rewards that motivate Mary Kay's independent sales force.
Source: China Photos/Getty Images

3. **Rewards–personal goals relationship.** The degree to which organizational rewards satisfy an individual's personal goals or needs and the attractiveness of those potential rewards for the individual.[90]

Expectancy theory helps explain why a lot of workers aren't motivated on their jobs and do only the minimum necessary to get by. Let's frame the theory's three relationships as questions employees need to answer in the affirmative if their motivation is to be maximized.

First, *if I give maximum effort, will it be recognized in my performance appraisal?* For many employees, the answer is "no." Why? Their skill level may be deficient, which means no matter how hard they try, they're not likely to be high performers. Or the organization's performance appraisal system may be designed to assess non-performance factors such as loyalty, initiative, or courage, which means more effort won't necessarily result in a higher evaluation. Another possibility is that employees, rightly or wrongly, perceive the boss doesn't like them. As a result, they expect a poor appraisal, regardless of effort. These examples suggest that people will be motivated only if they perceive a link between their effort and their performance.

Second, *if I get a good performance appraisal, will it lead to organizational rewards?* Many organizations reward things besides performance. When pay is based on factors such as having seniority, being cooperative, or "kissing up" to the boss, employees are likely to see the performance–reward relationship as weak and demotivating.

Finally, *if I'm rewarded, are the rewards attractive to me?* The employee works hard in the hope of getting a promotion but gets a pay raise instead. Or the employee wants a more interesting and challenging job but receives only a few words of praise. Unfortunately, many managers are limited in the rewards they can distribute, which makes it difficult to tailor rewards to individual employee needs. Some managers incorrectly assume all employees want the same thing, thus overlooking the motivational effects of differentiating rewards. In these cases, employee motivation is submaximized.

As a vivid example of how expectancy theory can work, consider stock analysts. They make their living trying to forecast a stock's future price; the accuracy of their buy, sell, or hold recommendations is what keeps them in work or gets them fired. But the dynamics are not simple. Analysts place few sell ratings on stocks, although in a steady market, by definition, as many stocks are falling as are rising. Expectancy theory provides an explanation: Analysts who place a sell rating on a company's stock have to balance the benefits they receive by being accurate against the risks they run by drawing that company's ire. What are these risks? They include public rebuke, professional blackballing, and exclusion from information. When analysts place a buy rating on a stock, they face no such trade-off because, obviously, companies love it when analysts recommend that investors buy their stock. So the incentive structure suggests the expected outcome of buy ratings is higher than the expected outcome of sell ratings, and that's why buy ratings vastly outnumber sell ratings.[91]

✪ PERSONAL INVENTORY ASSESSMENTS

Work Motivation Indicator

Do you find that some jobs motivate you more than others? Take this PIA to determine your work motivation.

Job Engagement

7-5 Identify the implications of employee job engagement for managers.

job engagement The investment of an employee's physical, cognitive, and emotional energies into job performance.

When Joseph reports to his job as a hospital nurse, it seems that everything else in his life goes away, and he becomes completely absorbed in what he is doing. His emotions, thoughts, and behavior are all directed toward patient care. In fact, he can get so caught up in his work that he isn't even aware of how long he's been there. As a result of this total commitment, he is more effective in providing patient care and feels uplifted by his time at work.

Joseph has a high level of **job engagement**, the investment of an employee's physical, cognitive, and emotional energies into job performance.[92] Practicing managers and scholars have become interested in facilitating job engagement, believing factors deeper than liking a job or finding it interesting drives performance. Studies attempt to measure this deeper level of commitment.

The Gallup organization has been studying the extent to which employee engagement is linked to positive work outcomes for millions of employees over the past 30 years.[93] They have found there are far more engaged employees in highly successful organizations than in average ones, and groups with more engaged employees have higher levels of productivity, fewer safety incidents, and lower turnover. Academic studies have also found positive outcomes. For instance, one review found higher levels of engagement were associated with task performance and citizenship behavior.[94]

What makes people more likely to be engaged in their jobs? One key is the degree to which an employee believes it is meaningful to engage in work. This is partially determined by job characteristics and access to sufficient resources to work effectively.[95] Another factor is a match between the individual's values and those of the organization.[96] Leadership behaviors that inspire workers to a greater sense of mission also increase employee engagement.[97]

One of the critiques of the concept of engagement is that the construct is partially redundant with job attitudes like satisfaction or stress.[98] However, engagement questionnaires usually assess motivation and absorption in a task, quite unlike job satisfaction questionnaires. Engagement may also predict important work outcomes better than traditional job attitudes.[99] Other critics note there may be a "dark side" to engagement, as evidenced by positive relationships between engagement and work–family conflict.[100] It is possible individuals might grow so engaged in their work roles that family responsibilities become an unwelcome intrusion. Also, an overly high level of engagement can lead to a loss of perspective and, ultimately, burnout. Further research exploring how engagement relates to these negative outcomes may help clarify whether some highly engaged employees might be getting "too much of a good thing."

> ✪ **TRY IT!**
> If your professor has assigned this, go to the Assignments section of **mymanagementlab.com** to complete the **Simulation: *Motivation***.

Integrating Contemporary Theories of Motivation

7-6 Describe how the contemporary theories of motivation complement one another.

Our job might be simpler if, after presenting a half dozen theories, we could say only one was found valid. But many of the theories in this chapter are complementary. We now tie them together to help you understand their interrelationships.

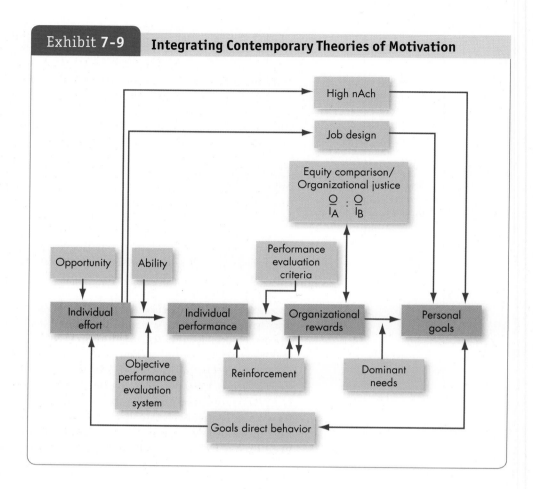

Exhibit **7-9** **Integrating Contemporary Theories of Motivation**

Exhibit 7-9 integrates much of what we know about motivation. Its basic foundation is the expectancy model that was shown in Exhibit 7-8. Let's walk through Exhibit 7-9. (We will look at job design closely in Chapter 8.)

We begin by explicitly recognizing that opportunities can either aid or hinder individual effort. The individual effort box on the left also has another arrow leading into it, from the person's goals. Consistent with goal-setting theory, the goals–effort loop is meant to remind us that goals direct behavior.

Expectancy theory predicts employees will exert a high level of effort if they perceive a strong relationship between effort and performance, performance and reward, and rewards and satisfaction of personal goals. Each of these relationships is, in turn, influenced by other factors. For effort to lead to good performance, the individual must have the ability to perform and perceive the performance appraisal system as fair and objective. The performance–reward relationship will be strong if the individual perceives that performance (rather than seniority, personal favorites, or other criteria) is rewarded. If cognitive evaluation theory were fully valid in the actual workplace, we would predict that basing rewards on performance should decrease the individual's intrinsic motivation. The final link in expectancy theory is the rewards–goals relationship. Motivation is high if the rewards for high performance satisfy the dominant needs consistent with individual goals.

A closer look at Exhibit 7-9 also reveals that the model considers achievement motivation, job design, reinforcement, and equity theories/organizational justice. A high achiever is not motivated by an organization's assessment of performance or organizational rewards, hence the jump from effort to personal goals for those with a high nAch. Remember, high achievers are internally driven as long as their jobs provide them with personal responsibility, feedback, and moderate risks. They are not concerned with the effort–performance, performance–reward, or rewards–goal linkages.

Reinforcement theory enters the model by recognizing that the organization's rewards reinforce the individual's performance. If employees see a reward system as "paying off" for good performance, the rewards will reinforce and encourage good performance. Rewards also play a key part in organizational justice research. Individuals will judge the favorability of their outcomes (for example, their pay) relative to what others receive but also with respect to how they are treated: When people are disappointed in their rewards, they are likely to be sensitive to the perceived fairness of the procedures used and the consideration given to them by their supervisors.

Summary

The motivation theories in this chapter differ in their predictive strength. Maslow's hierarchy, two-factor theory, and McClelland's theory focus on needs. Self-determination theory and related theories have merits to consider. Goal-setting theory can be helpful but does not cover absenteeism, turnover, or job satisfaction. Self-efficacy theory contributes to our understanding of personal motivation. Reinforcement theory can also be helpful, but not regarding employee satisfaction or the decision to quit. Equity theory provided the spark for research on organizational justice. Expectancy theory can be helpful, but assumes employees have few constraints on decision making, and this limits its applicability. Job engagement goes a long way toward explaining employee commitment.

Implications for Managers

- Make sure extrinsic rewards for employees are not viewed as coercive, but instead provide information about competence and relatedness.
- Consider goal-setting theory: Clear and difficult goals often lead to higher levels of employee productivity.
- Consider reinforcement theory regarding quality and quantity of work, persistence of effort, absenteeism, tardiness, and accident rates.
- Consult equity theory to help understand productivity, satisfaction, absence, and turnover variables.
- Expectancy theory offers a powerful explanation of performance variables such as employee productivity, absenteeism, and turnover.

Goals Get You to Where You Want to Be

POINT

Of course this is a true statement. Goal-setting theory is one of the best-supported theories in the motivation literature. Study after study has consistently shown the benefits of goals. Want to excel on a test, lose a certain amount of weight, secure a job with a particular income level, or improve your golf game? If you want to be a high performer, merely set a specific, difficult goal and let nature take its course. That goal will dominate your attention, cause you to focus, and make you try harder.

All too often, people are told by others to simply "do their best." Could anything be more vague? What does "do your best" actually mean? Maybe you feel that your "best" on one day is to muster a grade of 50 percent on an exam, while your "best" on another day is an 80. But if you were given a more difficult goal—say, to score a 95 on the exam—and you were committed to that goal, you would ultimately perform better.

Edwin Locke and Gary Latham, the researchers best known for goal-setting theory, put it best when they said: "The effects of goal setting are very reliable." In short, goal-setting theory is among the most valid and practical theories of motivation in organizational psychology.

COUNTERPOINT

Sure, a lot of research has shown the benefits of goal-setting, but those studies ignore the harm that's often done. For one, how often have you set a "stretch" goal, only to see yourself later fail? Goals create anxiety and worry about reaching them, and they often create unrealistic expectations as well. Imagine those who set a goal to earn a promotion in a certain period of time (a specific, difficult goal), only to find themselves laid off once a recession hit. Or how about those who envision a retirement of leisure yet are forced to take on a part-time job or delay retirement altogether in order to continue making ends meet. When too many influential factors are out of our control, our difficult goals become impossible.

Or, consider this: Goals can lead to unethical behavior and poorer performance. How many reports have you heard over the years about teachers who "fudged" students' test scores in order to achieve educational standards? Another example: When Ken O'Brian, as a professional quarterback for the New York Jets, was penalized for every interception he threw, he achieved his goal of fewer interceptions quite easily—by refusing to throw the ball even when he should have.

In addition to this anecdotal evidence, research has directly linked goal-setting to cheating. We should heed the warning of Professor Maurice E. Schweitzer—"Goal-setting is like a powerful medication"—before blindly accepting that specific, difficult goal.

Sources: E. A. Locke and G. P. Latham, "Building a Practically Useful Theory of Goal Setting and Task Motivation," American Psychologist 57 (2002): 705–71; A. Tugend, "Expert's Advice to the Goal-Oriented: Don't Overdo It," The New York Times, October 6, 2012, B5; and C. Richards, "Letting Go of Long-Term Goals," The New York Times, August 4, 2012.

CHAPTER REVIEW

MyManagementLab

Go to **mymanagementlab.com** to complete the problems marked with this icon.

QUESTIONS FOR REVIEW

7-1 What are the three key elements of motivation?

7-2 What are some early theories of motivation? How applicable are they today?

7-3 What are the similarities and differences between self-determination theory and goal-setting theory?

7-4 What are the key principles of self-efficacy theory, reinforcement theory, equity theory, and expectancy theory?

7-5 Why is employee job engagement important to managers?

7-6 How do the contemporary theories of motivation compare to one another?

EXPERIENTIAL EXERCISE Organizational Justice Task

Break the class into groups of three or four.

7-7. Each person should recall an instance in which he or she was (a) treated especially fairly and (b) treated especially unfairly. Work-related instances are preferable, but nonwork examples are fine too. What do the stories have in common?

7-8. Spend several minutes discussing whether the instance was more distributive, procedural, informational, or interpersonal in nature. What

was the source of the fair/unfair treatment? How did you feel, and how did you respond?

7-9. Each group should develop a set of recommendations for handling the unfair situations in a fairer manner. Select a leader for your group who will briefly summarize the unfair instances, along with the group's recommendations for handling them better. The discussion should reflect the four types of justice discussed in this chapter (distributive, procedural, informational, and interpersonal).

ETHICAL DILEMMA The New GPA

In the college classroom, is an A the new B? Grade inflation is of particular concern in graduate programs, where it is not uncommon for 75 percent of grades to be As. In fact, the most frequent grade given in U.S. universities is an A, by 43 percent. This percentage has risen from 30 percent 20 years ago, representing a significant increase. And at Harvard, the average grade is an A-. While this may sound like a great place to be, there is a powerful downside to grade inflation. If an A- is the new class average, the crowding of grades at the top end of the scale can sap away the student's motivation to work hard. Organizations also have a tougher time of evaluating candidates'

transcripts if grades are inflated, which means they must rely more on results of standardized tests, often ones that were taken in high school, that may not reflect a student's current or best capabilities. Professors too may be less motivated to accurately assess and teach students through strong grading feedback that would help students learn.

There is no easy solution to the phenomenon of grade inflation. In a culture where "everyone does it," schools that take a stand against grade inflation produce students with potentially lower grades—but no less education—than their peers. These students may not be able to stand out in the increasingly competitive job market even when they are equally prepared. Over time, their schools will not be able to boast of the accomplishments of their graduates in terms of grades and employment placements. No longer will these schools look as attractive to potential students, so enrollment and thus revenue will suffer, endangering the institution's ability to teach. Therefore, eliminating grade inflation poses powerful disincentives, and few if any colleges have successfully tried it. There is much more motivation for organizations, schools, professors, and students to continue grade inflation practices, even though they may be wrong.

Questions

7-10. How could you manage an engineered downgrade to C as an average?

7-11. If an employer can no longer distinguish between candidates on the basis of grades, how can they distinguish between them?

7-12. State funding of many schools has decreased dramatically over the years, increasing the pressure on administrators to generate revenue through tuition increases and other means. How might this pressure create ethical tensions among the need to generate revenue, student retention, and grading?

Sources: A. Ellin, "Failure Is Not an Option," *The New York Times,* April 15, 2012, 13–14; A. Massoia, "The New Normal: The Problem of Grade Inflation in American Schools," *The Huffington Post,* January 12, 2015, http://www.huffingtonpost.com/angelina-massoia/the-new-normal-the-proble_b_6146236 .html15; and S. Slavov, "How to Fix College Grade Inflation," *US News,* December 26, 2013, http:// www.usnews.com/opinion/blogs/economic-intelligence/2013/12/26/why-college-grade-inflation-is-a-real-problem-and-how-to-fix-it.

CASE INCIDENT 1   The Demotivation of CEO Pay

Quick: How much did your CEO get paid this year? What did any CEO get paid? You may not know the exact amounts, but you probably think the answer is, "Too much money." According to research from 40 countries that probed the thoughts of CEOs, cabinet ministers, and unskilled employees, we all think leaders should be paid less. Beyond that, we are clueless.

Where we err can be calculated by an organization's pay ratio, or the ratio between CEO pay and average worker pay. In the United States, for example, the average S&P 500 CEO is paid 354 times what the lowest-ranking employee makes, for a ratio of 354:1 (eight times greater than in the 1950s). Yet, U.S. participants in the study estimated that the ratio between CEOs and unskilled workers was only 30:1! Americans are not alone in making this gross underestimate: Participants from Germany, for instance, estimated a ratio of around 18:1 when the actual is closer to 151:1.

In general, people worldwide are unhappy with—and demotivated by—their perception of inequity, even when their estimates of the ratios are far below the reality. Taking the German example further, the ideal ratio of CEO pay to unskilled workers as judged by study participants was around 7:1. To put it all together, then, people think the ratio should be 7:1, believe it is 18:1, and don't realize it is actually 151:1. For all the countries worldwide in the study, the estimated ratios were above the ideal ratios, meaning participants universally thought CEOs are overpaid.

How does this affect the average worker's motivation? It appears that the less a person earns, the less satisfied the person is with the pay gap. Yet virtually everyone in the study wanted greater equality. The ideal ratio, they indicated, should be between 5:1 and 4:1, whereas they thought it was between 10:1 and 8:1. They believed skilled employees should earn more money than unskilled individuals, but that the gap between them should be smaller.

No one in the United States would likely think the 354:1 ratio is going to dip to the ideal of 7:1 soon, although some changes in that direction have been suggested. Other countries have tried to be more progressive. The Social Democratic Party in Switzerland proposed a ceiling for the ratio of 12:1, but putting a cap into law was considered too extreme by voters. No countries have yet been able to successfully impose a maximum ratio.

Therefore, the job of restoring justice perceptions has fallen to CEOs themselves. Many CEOs, such as Mark Zuckerberg of Facebook and Larry Page of Google, have taken $1 annual salaries, though they still earn substantial compensation by exercising their stock options. In one extreme recent example, Gravity CEO Dan Price cut his salary by $1 million to $70,000, using the money to give significant raises to the payment processing firm's employees. Price said he expects to "see more of this." In addition, shareholders of some companies, such as Verizon, are playing a greater role in setting CEO compensation by reducing awards when the company underperforms.

Questions

7-13. What do you think is the ideal ratio? Why might the ideal vary from country to country?

7-14. How does the executive compensation issue relate to equity theory? How should we determine what is a "fair" level of pay for top executives?

⭐ **7-15.** The study found that participants thought performance should be essential or very important in deciding pay. What might be the positive motivational consequences for average employees if CEO pay is tied to performance?

Sources: J. Ewing, "Swiss Voters Decisively Reject a Measure to Put Limits on Executive Pay," *The New York Times*, November 24, 2013, http://www.nytimes.com/2013/11/25/business/swiss-reject-measure-to-curb-executive-pay.html?_r=0; C. Isidore, "Gravity Payments CEO Takes 90% Pay Cut to Give Workers Huge Raise," *CNN Money*, April 15, 2015, http://money.cnn.com/2015/04/14/news/companies/ceo-pay-cuts-pay-increases/; S. Kiatpongsan and M. I. Norton, "How Much (More) Should CEOs Make? A Universal Desire for More Equal Pay," *Perspectives on Psychological Science* 9, no. 6 (2014): 587–93; A. Kleinman, "Mark Zuckerberg $1 Salary Puts Him in Elite Group of $1 CEOs," *The Huffington Post*, April 29, 2013, www.huffingtonpost.com; and G. Morgenson, "If Shareholders Say 'Enough Already,' the Board May Listen," *The New York Times*, April 6, 2013, www.newyorktimes.com.

CASE INCIDENT 2   The Sleepiness Epidemic

Ronit Rogosziniski, a financial planner, loses sleep because of her 5 a.m. wake-up call, so she sneaks to her car for a quick lunchtime snooze each day. She is not alone, as evidenced by the comments on Wall Street Oasis, a website frequented by investment bankers who blog about their travails. Should the legions of secret nappers be blessed or cursed by their organizations for this behavior? Research suggests they should be encouraged.

Sleep is a problem, or rather, lack of *quality* zzz's is a costly organizational problem we can no longer overlook. Sleepiness, a technical term in this case that denotes a true physiological pressure for sleep, lowers performance and increases accidents, injuries, and unethical behavior. One survey found that 29 percent of respondents slept on the job, 12 percent were late to work, 4 percent left work early, and 2 percent did not go to work due to sleepiness. While sleepiness affects 33 percent of the U.S. population, the clinical extreme, excessive daytime sleepiness (EDS), is fully debilitating to an additional 11 percent.

In a vicious cycle where the effects of sleepiness affect the organization, which leads to longer work hours and thus more sleepiness, the reason for the sleepiness epidemic seems to be the modern workplace. Full-time employees have been getting less sleep over the past 30 years as a direct result of longer work days, putting them more at risk for sleep disorders. Sleepiness directly decreases attention span, memory, information processing, affect, and emotion regulation capabilities. Research on sleep deprivation has found that tired workers experience higher levels of back pain, heart disease, depression, work withdrawal, and job dissatisfaction. All these outcomes have significant implications for organizational effectiveness and costs.

Sleepiness may account for $14 billion of medical expenses, up to $69 billion for auto accidents, and up to $24 billion in workplace accidents in the United States annually.

Although being around bright light and loud sounds, standing, eating, and practicing good posture can reduce sleepiness temporarily, there is only one lasting cure: more hours of good-quality sleep. Some companies are encouraging napping at work as a solution to the problem, and one survey of 600 companies revealed that 6 percent had dedicated nap rooms. In addition, in a poll of 1,508 workers conducted by the National Sleep Foundation, 34 percent said they were allowed to nap at work. These policies may be a good start, but they are only Band-Aid approaches since more and better sleep is what's needed. Researchers suggest that organizations should consider flexible working hours and greater autonomy to allow employees to maximize their productive waking hours. Given the high costs of sleepiness, it's time for them to take the problem much more seriously.

Questions

7-16. Should organizations be concerned about the sleepiness of their employees? What factors influencing sleep might be more or less under the control of an organization?

7-17. How might sleep deprivation demonstrate aspects of expectancy theory? How might the incorporation of "nap rooms" for sleep-deprived employees demonstrate aspects of equity theory?

7-18. Sleep deprivation can be extremely hazardous to health. What are the key health issues and how should an organization seek to manage the problems that arise from sleep deprivation?

Sources: C. Delo, "Why Companies Are Cozying up to Napping at Work," *CNN*, August 18, 2011, www .management.fortune.cnn.com; H. M. Mullins, J. M. Cortina, C. L. Drake, and R. S. Dalal, "Sleepiness at Work: A Review and Framework of How the Physiology of Sleepiness Impacts the Workplace," *Journal of Applied Psychology* 99, no. 6 (2014): 1096–112; and D. Wescott, "Do Not Disturb," *Bloomberg Businessweek*, April 23–29, 2012, 90.

MyManagementLab

Go to **mymanagementlab.com** for the following Assisted-graded writing questions:

7-19. In regard to the Ethical Dilemma, do you believe your school has experienced grade inflation? Do you think schools like yours should endeavor to curtail grade inflation? What are the pros and cons for you as a student?

7-20. In considering Case Incident 1, do you think the government has a legitimate role in controlling executive compensation? How might aspects of justice (distributive, procedural, and informational) inform this debate?

7-21. MyManagementLab Only – comprehensive writing assignment for this chapter.

ENDNOTES

[1]See, for example, G. P. Latham and C. C. Pinder, "Work Motivation Theory and Research at the Dawn of the Twenty-First Century," *Annual Review of Psychology* 56 (2005): 485–516; and C. C. Pinder, *Work Motivation in Organizational Behavior*, 2nd ed. (London, UK: Psychology Press, 2008).

[2]"The 2013 Wasting Time at Work Survey: Everything You've Always Wanted to Know about Wasting Time in the Office," Salary. com, 2013, www.salary.com.

[3]See, for instance, Pinder, *Work Motivation in Organizational Behavior*.

[4]R. J. Taormina and J. H. Gao, "Maslow and the Motivation Hierarchy: Measuring Satisfaction of the Needs," *American Journal of Psychology* 126, no. 2 (2013): 155–57.

[5]H. Skelsey, "Maslow's Hierarchy of Needs—The Sixth Level," *Psychologist* (2014): 982–83.

[6]Ibid.

[7]S. H. Mousavi and H. Dargahi, "Ethnic Differences and Motivation Based on Maslow's Theory on Iranian Employees," *Iranian Journal of Public Health* 42, no. 5 (2013): 516–21.

[8]D. Lester, "Measuring Maslow's Hierarchy of Needs," *Psychological Reports* 113, no. 1 (2013): 127–29.

[9]J.-K. Lee and J.-G. Choi, "Testing the Applicability of the Herzberg's Motivation-Hygiene Theory to the Hotel Industry," *Korean Journal of Business Administration* (2012): 2091–111.

[10]See, for instance, C.-S. Park and K.-S. Ko, "A Study on Factors of Job Satisfaction of Caregivers in Home Care Facilities Based on Herzberg's Motivation-Hygiene Theory," *Church Social Work* (2012): 123–58; and "Study on the Important Factors for Non-Commissioned Officer's Job Satisfaction in R.O.K. Army Based on Herzberg's Two Factor Theory," *Journal of*

Korean Public Police and Security Studies (2012): 217–38.

[11]H. van Emmerick, W. L. Gardner, H. Wendt, et al., "Associations of Culture and Personality with McClelland's Motives: A Cross-Cultural Study of Managers in 24 Countries," *Group and Organization Management* 35, no. 3 (2010): 329–67.

[12]D. G. Winter, "The Motivational Dimensions of Leadership: Power, Achievement, and Affiliation," in R. E. Riggio, S. E. Murphy, and F. J. Pirozzolo (eds.), *Multiple Intelligences and Leadership* (Mahwah, NJ: Lawrence Erlbaum, 2002), 119–38.

[13]H. van Emmerick, W. L. Gardner, H. Wendt, et al., "Associations of Culture and Personality with McClelland's Motives: A Cross-Cultural Study of Managers in 24 Countries."

[14]See, for instance, "F. Yang, J. E. Ramsay, O. C. Schultheiss, and J. S. Pang, "Need for Achievement Moderates the Effect of Motive-Relevant Challenge on Salivary Cortisol Changes," *Motivation and Emotion* (2015): 321–34; M. S. Khan, R. J. Breitnecker, and E. J. Schwarz, "Adding Fuel to the Fire: Need for Achievement Diversity and Relationship Conflict in Entrepreneurial Teams," *Management Decision* 53, no. 1 (2015): 75–79; M. G. Koellner and O. C. Schultheiss, "Meta-Analytic Evidence of Low Convergence between Implicit and Explicit Measures of the Needs for Achievement, Affiliation, and Power," *Frontiers in Psychology* 5 (2014): article 826; and T. Bipp and K. van Dam, "Extending Hierarchical Achievement Motivation Models: The Role of Motivational Needs for Achievement Goals and Academic Performance," *Personality and Individual Differences* 64 (2014): 157–62.

[15]M. G. Koellner and O. C. Schultheiss, "Meta-Analytic Evidence of Low Convergence between Implicit and Explicit Measures of the Needs for Achievement, Affiliation, and Power."

[16]J. Hofer, H. Busch, and C. Schneider, "The Effect of Motive-Trait Interaction on Satisfaction of the Implicit Need for Affiliation among German and Cameroonian Adults," *Journal of Personality* 83, no. 2 (2015): 167–78.

[17]E. Deci and R. Ryan (eds.), *Handbook of Self-Determination Research* (Rochester, NY: University of Rochester Press, 2002); R. Ryan and E. Deci, "Self-Determination Theory and the Facilitation of Intrinsic Motivation, Social Development, and Well-Being," *American Psychologist* 55, no. 1 (2000): 68–78; and M. Gagné and E. L. Deci, "Self-Determination Theory and Work Motivation," *Journal of Organizational Behavior* 26, no. 4 (2005): 331–62.

[18]C. P. Cerasoli, J. M. Nicklin, and M. T. Ford, "Intrinsic Motivation and Extrinsic Incentives Jointly Predict Performance: A 40-Year Meta-Analysis," *Psychological Bulletin* 140, no. 4 (2014): 980–1008.

[19]J. E. Bono and T. A. Judge, "Self-Concordance at Work: Toward Understanding the Motivational Effects of Transformational Leaders," *Academy of Management Journal* 46, no. 5 (2003): 554–71.

[20]K. M. Sheldon, A. J. Elliot, and R. M. Ryan, "Self-Concordance and Subjective Well-being in Four Cultures," *Journal of Cross-Cultural Psychology* 35, no. 2 (2004): 209–23.

[21]L. M. Graves, M. N. Ruderman, P. J. Ohlott, and Todd J. Webber, "Driven to Work and Enjoyment of Work: Effects on Managers' Outcomes," *Journal of Management* 38, no. 5 (2012): 1655–80.

[22]K. M. Sheldon, A. J. Elliot, and R. M. Ryan, "Self-Concordance and Subjective Well-Being in Four Cultures," *Journal of Cross-Cultural Psychology* 35, no. 2 (2004): 209–23.

[23]J. P. Meyer, T. E. Becker, and C. Vandenberghe, "Employee Commitment and Motivation: A Conceptual Analysis and Integrative Model," *Journal of Applied Psychology* 89, no. 6 (2004): 991–1007.

[24]E. A. Locke and G. P. Latham, "New Directions in Goal-Setting Theory," *Current Directions in Psychological Science* 15, no. 5 (2006): 265–68.

[25]Ibid.

[26]C. Gabelica, P. Van den Bossche, M. Segers, and W. Gijselaersa, "Feedback, a Powerful Lever in Teams: A Review," *Educational Research Review* (June 2012): 123–44.

[27]J. Lee and F. Wei, "The Mediating Effect of Psychological Empowerment on the Relationship between Participative Goal Setting and Team Outcomes—A Study in China," *International Journal of Human Resource Management* 22, no. 2 (2011): 279–95.

[28]S. W. Anderson, H. C. Dekker, and K. L. Sedatole, "An Empirical Examination of Goals and Performance-to-Goal Following the Introduction of an Incentive Bonus Plan with Participative Goal Setting," *Management Science* 56, no. 1 (2010): 90–109.

[29]T. S. Bateman and B. Bruce, "Masters of the Long Haul: Pursuing Long-Term Work Goals," *Journal of Organizational Behavior* (October 2012): 984–1006.

[30]Ibid.

[31]J. E. Bono and A. E. Colbert, "Understanding Responses to Multi-Source Feedback: The Role of Core Self-Evaluations," *Personnel Psychology* 58, no. 1 (2005): 171–203; and S. A. Jeffrey, A. Schulz, and A. Webb, "The Performance Effects of an Ability-Based Approach to Goal Assignment," *Journal of Organizational Behavior Management* 32 (2012): 221–41.

[32]T. Tammemagi, D. O'Hora, and K. A. Maglieri, "The Effects of a Goal Setting Intervention on Productivity and Persistence in an Analogue Work Task," *Journal of Organizational Behavior Management* (March 1, 2013): 31–54.

[33]K. D. Vohs, J. K. Park, and B. J. Schmeichel, "Self-Affirmation Can Enable Goal Disengagement," *Journal of Personality and Social Psychology* 104, no. 1 (2013): 14–27.

[34]D. F. Crown, "The Use of Group and Group-centric Individual Goals for Culturally Heterogeneous and Homogeneous Task Groups: An Assessment of European Work Teams," *Small Group Research* 38, no. 4 (2007): 489–508; and J. Kurman, "Self-Regulation Strategies in Achievement Settings: Culture and Gender Differences," *Journal of Cross-Cultural Psychology* 32, no. 4 (2001): 491–503.

[35]C. Sue-Chan and M. Ong, "Goal Assignment and Performance: Assessing the Mediating Roles of Goal Commitment and Self-Efficacy and the Moderating Role of Power Distance,"

Organizational Behavior and Human Decision Processes 89, no. 2 (2002): 1140–61.

[36]L. D. Ordóñez, M. E. Schweitzer, A. D. Galinsky, and M. H. Bazerman, "Goals Gone Wild: The Systematic Side Effects of Overprescribing Goal Setting," *Academy of Management Perspectives* 23, no. 1 (2009): 6–16; and E. A. Locke and G. P. Latham, "Has Goal Setting Gone Wild, or Have Its Attackers Abandoned Good Scholarship?" *Academy of Management Perspectives* 23, no. 1 (2009): 17–23.

[37]C. P. Cerasoli, J. M. Nicklin, and M. T. Ford, "Intrinsic Motivation and Extrinsic Incentives Jointly Predict Performance: A 40-Year Meta-Analysis."

[38]K. Lanaj, C. D. Chang, and R. E. Johnson, "Regulatory Focus and Work-Related Outcomes: A Review and Meta-Analysis," *Psychological Bulletin* 138, no. 5 (2012): 998–1034.

[39]D. L. Ferris, R. E. Johnson, C. C. Rosen, E. Djurdjevic, C.-H. Chang, and J. A. Tan, "When Is Success Not Satisfying? Integrating Regulatory Focus and Approach/Avoidance Motivation Theories to Explain the Relation between Core Self-Evaluation and Job Satisfaction," *Journal of Applied Psychology* 98, no. 2 (2013): 342–53.

[40]M. Roskes, A. J. Elliot, and C. K. W. De Dreu, "Why Is Avoidance Motivation Problematic, and What Can Be Done about It?" *Current Directions in Psychological Science* 23, no. 2 (2014): 133–38.

[41]"KEYGroup Survey Finds Nearly Half of All Employees Have No Set Performance Goals," *IPMA-HR Bulletin* (March 10, 2006): 1; S. Hamm, "SAP Dangles a Big, Fat Carrot," *BusinessWeek* (May 22, 2006): 67–68; and "P&G CEO Wields High Expectations but No Whip," *USA Today*, February 19, 2007, 3B.

[42]See, for instance, F. Ceresia, "A Model of Goal Dynamics in Organizations: Goal Setting, Goal Commitment, Training, and Management by Objectives," *Proceedings of 2009 Conference on Systems Science, Management Science & System Dynamics* 1 (2009): 37–46; and H. Levinson, "Management by Whose Objectives?" *Harvard Business Review* 81, no. 1 (2003): 107–16.

[43]See, for example, E. Lindberg and T. L. Wilson, "Management by Objectives: The Swedish Experience in Upper Secondary Schools," *Journal of Educational Administration* 49, no. 1 (2011): 62–75; and A. C. Spaulding, L. D. Gamm, and J. M. Griffith, "Studer Unplugged: Identifying Underlying Managerial Concepts," *Hospital Topics* 88, no. 1 (2010): 1–9.

[44]M. B. Kristiansen, "Management by Objectives and Results in the Nordic Countries: Continuity and Change, Differences and Similarities," *Public Performance and Management Review* 38, no. 3 (2015): 542–69.

[45]See, for instance, M. Tanikawa, "Fujitsu Decides to Backtrack on Performance-Based Pay," *New York Times*, March 22, 2001, W1; and W. F. Roth, "Is Management by Objectives Obsolete?" *Global Business and Organizational Excellence* 28 (May/June 2009): 36–43.

[46]F. Gino and C. Mogilner, "Time, Money, and Morality," *Psychological Science* 25, no. 2 (2014): 414–21.

[47]V. Lopez-Kidwell, T. J. Grosser, B. R. Dineen, and S. P. Borgatti, "What Matters When: A Multistage Model and Empirical Examination of Job Search Effort," *Academy of Management Journal* 56, no. 6 (2012): 1655–78.

[48]J. W. Beck and A. M. Schmidt, "State-Level Goal Orientations as Mediators of the Relationship between Time Pressure and Performance: A Longitudinal Study," *Journal of Applied Psychology* 98, no. 2 (2013): 354–63.

[49]J. R. Themanson and P. J. Rosen, "Examining the Relationships between Self-Efficacy, Task-Relevant Attentional Control, and Task Performance: Evidence from Event-Related Brain Potentials," *British Journal of Psychology* 106, no. 2 (2015): 253–71.

[50]A. Bandura, "Cultivate Self-Efficacy for Personal and Organizational Effectiveness," in E. Locke (ed.), *Handbook of Principles of Organizational Behavior* (Malden, MA: Blackwell, 2004), 120–36; and M. Ventura, M. Salanova, and S. Llorens, "Professional Self-Efficacy as a Predictor of Burnout and Engagement: The Role of Challenge and Hindrance Demands," *Journal of Psychology* 149, no. 3 (2015): 277–302.

[51]M. Salanova, S. Llorens, and W. B. Schaufeli, "Yes I Can, I Feel Good, and I Just Do It! On Gain Cycles and Spirals of Efficacy Beliefs, Affect, and Engagement," *Applied Psychology* 60, no. 2 (2011): 255–85.

[52]J. R. Themanson and P. J. Rosen, "Examining the Relationships between Self-Efficacy, Task-Relevant Attentional Control, and Task Performance: Evidence from Event-Related Brain Potentials."

[53]A. P. Tolli and A. M. Schmidt, "The Role of Feedback, Causal Attributions, and Self-Efficacy in Goal Revision," *Journal of Applied Psychology* 93, no. 3 (2008): 692–701.

[54]P. Tierney and S. M. Farmer, "Creative Self-Efficacy Development and Creative Performance Over Time," *Journal of Applied Psychology* 96, no. 2 (2011): 277–93.

[55]S. L. Anderson and N. E. Betz, "Sources of Social Self-Efficacy Expectations: Their Measurement and Relation to Career Development," *Journal of Vocational Behavior* 58, no. 1 (2001): 98–117; M. Ben-Ami, J. Hornik, D. Eden, et al., "Boosting Consumers' Self-Efficacy by Repositioning the Self," *European Journal of Marketing* 48 (2014): 1914–38; L. De Grez and D. Van Lindt, "Students' Gains in Entrepreneurial Self-Efficacy: A Comparison of 'Learning-by-Doing' versus Lecture-Based Courses," *Proceedings of the 8th European Conference on Innovation and Entrepreneurship* (2013): 198–203; and K. S. Hendricks, "Changes in Self-Efficacy Beliefs over Time: Contextual Influences of Gender, Rank-Based Placement, and Social Support in a Competitive Orchestra Environment," *Psychology of Music* 42, no. 3 (2014): 347–65.

[56]T. A. Judge, C. L. Jackson, J. C. Shaw, B. Scott, and B. L. Rich, "Self-Efficacy and Work-Related Performance: The Integral Role of Individual Differences," *Journal of Applied Psychology* 92, no. 1 (2007): 107–27.

[57]Ibid.

[58]A. M. Paul, "How to Use the 'Pygmalion' Effect," *Time*, April 1, 2013, http://ideas.time.com/2013/04/01/how-to-use-the-pygmalion-effect/.

[59]A. Friedrich, B. Flunger, B. Nagengast, K. Jonkmann, and U. Trautwein, "Pygmalion Effects in the Classroom: Teacher Expectancy Effects on Students' Math Achievement," *Contemporary Educational Psychology* 41 (2015): 1–12.

[60]L. Karakowsky, N. DeGama, and K. McBey, "Facilitating the Pygmalion Effect: The Overlooked Role of Subordinate Perceptions of the Leader," *Journal of Occupational and Organizational Psychology* 85, no. 4 (2012): 579–99; and P. Whiteley, T. Sy, and S. K. Johnson, "Leaders' Conceptions of Followers: Implications for Naturally Occurring Pygmalion Effects," *Leadership Quarterly* 23, no. 5 (2012): 822–34.

[61]A. Gegenfurtner, C. Quesada-Pallares, and M. Knogler, "Digital Simulation-Based Training: A Meta-Analysis," *British Journal of Educational Technology* 45, no. 6 (2014): 1097–114.

[62]E. C. Dierdorff, E. A. Surface, and K. G. Brown, "Frame-of-Reference Training Effectiveness: Effects of Goal Orientation and Self-Efficacy on Affective, Cognitive, Skill-Based, and Transfer Outcomes," *Journal of Applied Psychology* 95, no. 6 (2010): 1181–91; and R. Grossman and E. Salas, "The Transfer of Training: What Really Matters," *International Journal of Training and Development* 15, no. 2 (2011): 103–20.

[63]K. M. Eddington, C. Majestic, and P. J. Silvia, "Contrasting Regulatory Focus and Reinforcement Sensitivity: A Daily Diary Study of Goal Pursuit and Emotion," *Personality and Individual Differences* (August 2012): 335–40.

[64]X. Zhu and M. Tian, "On the Incentive System for Chinese Local Governments' Work of Environmental Protection from the Perspective of Skinner's Reinforcement Theory," *Proceedings of the 2013 International Conference on Public Administration* (2013): 271–77.

[65]M. J. Goddard, "Critical Psychiatry, Critical Psychology, and the Behaviorism of B. F. Skinner," *Review of General Psychology* 18, no. 3 (2014): 208–15.

[66]J. R. Brauer and C. R. Tittle, "Social Learning Theory and Human Reinforcement," *Sociological Spectrum* 32, no. 2 (2012): 157–77.

[67]C. Buzea, "Equity Theory Constructs in a Romanian Cultural Context," *Human Resource Development Quarterly* 25, no. 4 (2014): 421–39; A. W. Cappelen, T. Eichele, K. Hugdahl, K. Specht, and B. Tungodden, "Equity Theory and Fair Inequality: A Neuroeconomic Study," *Proceedings of the National Academy of Sciences in the United States of America* 111(2014): 15368–72; C. Maslach and M. P. Leiter, "Early

Predictors of Job Burnout and Engagement, *Journal of Applied Psychology* (May 2008): 498–512; and Q. Xiaoqing, K. Zhang, and Y. Xu, "Applicable Scope of Equity Theory and Reaction on Productivity under the Influence of Traditional Culture," 2014 2nd International Conference on Social Science and Health, Pt. 3 in *Advances in Education Research* 57 (2014): 365–69.

[68]J. Bai, "Analysis of Equity Theory in the Modern Enterprise Staff Motivation," *Proceedings of the 2012 International Conference on Management Innovation and Public Policy* (2012): 165–67; C. Buzea, "Equity Theory Constructs in a Romanian Cultural Context," *Human Resource Development Quarterly* 25, no. 4 (2014): 421–39; R. W. Griffeth and S. Gaertner, "A Role for Equity Theory in the Turnover Process: An Empirical Test," *Journal of Applied Social Psychology* 31, no. 5 (2001): 1017–37; and L. K. Scheer, N. Kumar, and J-B. E. M. Steenkamp, "Reactions to Perceived Inequity in U.S. and Dutch Interorganizational Relationships," *Academy of Management* 46, no. 3 (2003): 303–16.

[69]B. K. Miller, "Entitlement and Conscientiousness in the Prediction of Organizational Deviance," *Personality and Individual Differences* 82 (2015): 114–19; and H. J. R. Woodley and N. J. Allen, "The Dark Side of Equity Sensitivity," *Personality and Individual Differences* 67 (2014): 103–08.

[70]J. M. Jensen, P. C. Patel, and J. L. Raver, "Is It Better to Be Average? High and Low Performance as Predictors of Employee Victimization," *Journal of Applied Psychology* 99, no. 2 (2014): 296–309.

[71]See, for instance, J. A. Colquitt, D. E. Conlon, M. J. Wesson, C. O. L. H. Porter, and K.-Y. Ng, "Justice at the Millennium: A Meta-Analytic Review of the 25 Years of Organizational Justice Research," *Journal of Applied Psychology* 86, no. 3 (2001): 425–45; T. Simons and Q. Roberson, "Why Managers Should Care about Fairness: The Effects of Aggregate Justice Perceptions on Organizational Outcomes," *Journal of Applied Psychology* 88, no. 3 (2003): 432–43; and B. C. Holtz and C. M. Harold, "Fair Today, Fair Tomorrow? A Longitudinal Investigation of Overall Justice Perceptions," *Journal of Applied Psychology* 94, no. 5 (2009): 1185–99.

[72]C. O. Trevor, G. Reilly, and B. Gerhart, "Reconsidering Pay Dispersion's Effect on the Performance of Interdependent Work: Reconciling Sorting and Pay Inequality," *Academy of Management Journal* (June 2012): 585–610.

[73]See, for example, R. Cropanzano, J. H. Stein, and T. Nadisic, *Social Justice and the Experience of Emotion* (New York: Routledge/Taylor and Francis Group, 2011).

[74]A. Caza, M. W. McCarter, and G. B. Northcraft, "Performance Benefits of Reward Choice: A Procedural Justice Perspective," *Human Resource Management Journal* 25, no. 2 (2015): 184–99; R. E. Johnson, K. Lanaj, and

C. M. Barnes, "The Good and Bad of Being Fair: Effects of Procedural and Interpersonal Justice Behaviors on Regulatory Resources," *Journal of Applied Psychology* 99, no. 4 (2014): 635–50; and D. Liu, M. Hernandez, and L. Wang, "The Role of Leadership and Trust in Creating Structural Patterns of Team Procedural Justice: A Social Network Investigation," *Personnel Psychology* 67, no. 4 (2014): 801–45.

[75]H. He, W. Zhu, and X. Zheng, "Procedural Justice and Employee Engagement: Roles of Organizational Identification and Moral Identity Centrality," *Journal of Business Ethics* 122, no. 4 (2014): 681–95.

[76]J. C. Shaw, E. Wild, and J. A. Colquitt, "To Justify or Excuse? A Meta-Analytic Review of the Effects of Explanations," *Journal of Applied Psychology* 88, no. 3 (2003): 444–58.

[77]R. J. Bies, "Are Procedural and Interactional Justice Conceptually Distinct?" in J. Greenberg and J. A. Colquitt (eds.), *Handbook of Organizational Justice* (Mahwah, NJ: Erlbaum, 2005), 85–112; and B. A. Scott, J. A. Colquitt, and E. L. Paddock, "An Actor-Focused Model of Justice Rule Adherence and Violation: The Role of Managerial Motives and Discretion," *Journal of Applied Psychology* 94, no. 3 (2009): 756–69.

[78]G. A. Van Kleef, A. C. Homan, B. Beersma, D. V. Knippenberg, B. V. Knippenberg, and F. Damen, "Searing Sentiment or Cold Calculation? The Effects of Leader Emotional Displays on Team Performance Depend on Follower Epistemic Motivation," *Academy of Management Journal* 52, no. 3 (2009): 562–80.

[79]"Rutgers Fires Mike Rice," ESPN, 2013, http://espn.go.com/sportsnation/post/_/id/9129245/rutgers-fires-mike-rice

[80]J. M. Robbins, M. T. Ford, and L. E. Tetrick, "Perceived Unfairness and Employee Health: A Meta-Analytic Integration," *Journal of Applied Psychology* 97, no. 2 (2012): 235–72.

[81]J. A. Colquitt, B. A. Scott, J. B. Rodell, D. M. Long, C. P. Zapata, D. E. Conlon, and M. J. Wesson, "Justice at the Millennium, A Decade Later: A Meta-Analytic Test of Social Exchange and Affect-Based Perspectives," *Journal of Applied Psychology* 98, no. 2 (2013): 199–236.

[82]K. Leung, K. Tong, and S. S. Ho, "Effects of Interactional Justice on Egocentric Bias in Resource Allocation Decisions," *Journal of Applied Psychology* 89, no. 3 (2004): 405–15; and L. Francis-Gladney, N. R. Manger, and R. B. Welker, "Does Outcome Favorability Affect Procedural Fairness as a Result of Self-Serving Attributions," *Journal of Applied Social Psychology* 40, no. 1 (2010): 182–94.

[83]L. J. Barclay and D. P. Skarlicki, "Healing the Wounds of Organizational Injustice: Examining the Benefits of Expressive Writing," *Journal of Applied Psychology* 94, no. 2 (2009): 511–23.

[84]This section is based on B. A. Scott, A. S. Garza, D. E. Conlon, and Y. J. Kim, "Why Do Managers Act Fairly in the First Place? A Daily Investigation of 'Hot' and 'Cold' Motives and Discretion," *Academy of Management Journal* 57, no. 6 (2014): 1571–91.

[85]F. F. T. Chiang and T. Birtch, "The Transferability of Management Practices: Examining Cross-National Differences in Reward Preferences," *Human Relations* 60, no. 9 (2007): 1293–330; and M. J. Gelfand, M. Erez, and Z. Aycan, "Cross-Cultural Organizational Behavior," *Annual Review of Psychology* 58 (2007): 479–514.

[86]M. C. Bolino and W. H. Turnley, "Old Faces, New Places: Equity Theory in Cross-Cultural Contexts," *Journal of Organizational Behavior* 29, no. 1 (2008): 29–50.

[87]R. Shao, D. E. Rupp, D. P. Skarlicki, and K. S. Jones, "Employee Justice across Cultures: A Meta-Analytic Review," *Journal of Management* 39, no. 1 (2013): 263–301.

[88]R. L. Purvis, T. J. Zagenczyck, and G. E. Mc-Cray, "What's in It for Me? Using Expectancy Theory and Climate to Explain Stakeholder Participation, Its Direction and Intensity," *International Journal of Project Management* 33, no. 1 (2015): 3–14.

[89]M. Renko, K. G. Koeck, and A. Bullough, "Expectancy Theory and Nascent Entrepreneurship," *Small Business Economics* 39, no. 3 (2012): 667–84; J. J. Donovan, "Work Motivation," in N. Anderson et al. (eds.), *Handbook of Industrial, Work & Organizational Psychology*, vol. 2 (Thousand Oaks, CA: Sage, 2001), 56–59; and G. Yu and J. Guo, "Research on Employee Motivation Mechanism in Modern Enterprises Based on Victor H. Vroom's Expectancy Theory," in G. Duysters, A. DeHoyos, and K. Kaminishi (eds.), *Proceedings of the 9th International Conference on Innovation and Management* (2012): 988–91.

[90]Vroom refers to these three variables as expectancy, instrumentality, and valence, respectively.

[91]J. Nocera, "The Anguish of Being an Analyst," *The New York Times,* March 4, 2006, B1, B12.

[92]H.-T. Chang, H.-M. Hsu, J.-W. Liou, and C.-T. Tsai, "Psychological Contracts and Innovative Behavior: A Moderated Path Analysis of Work Engagement and Job Resources," *Journal of Applied Social Psychology* 43, no. 10 (2013): 2021–135.

[93]See topics of employee engagement from Gallup on http://www.gallup.com/topic/employee_engagement.aspx, accessed May 28, 2015.

[94]M. S. Christian, A. S. Garza, and J. E. Slaughter, "Work Engagement: A Quantitative Review and Test of Its Relations with Task and Contextual Performance," *Personnel Psychology* 64, no. 1 (2011): 89–136.

[95]W. B. Schaufeli, A. B. Bakker, and W. van Rhenen, "How Changes in Job Demands and Resources Predict Burnout, Work Engagement, and Sickness Absenteeism," *Journal of Organizational Behavior* 30, no. 7 (2009): 893–917; E. R. Crawford, J. A. LePine, and B. L. Rich, "Linking Job Demands and Resources to Employee Engagement and Burnout: A Theoretical Extension and Meta-Analytic Test," *Journal of Applied Psychology* 95, no. 5 (2010): 834–48; and D. Xanthopoulou, A. B. Bakker, E. Demerouti, and W. B. Schaufeli, "Reciprocal Relationships between Job Resources, Personal Resources, and Work Engagement," *Journal of Vocational Behavior* 74, no. 3 (2009): 235–44.

[96]B. L. Rich, J. A. LePine, and E. R. Crawford, "Job Engagement: Antecedents and Effects on Job Performance," *Academy of Management Journal* 53, no. 3 (2010): 617–35.

[97]M. Tims, A. B. Bakker, and D. Xanthopoulou, "Do Transformational Leaders Enhance Their Followers' Daily Work Engagement?" *Leadership Quarterly* 22, no. 1 (2011): 121–31; and F. O. Walumbwa, P. Wang, H. Wang, J. Schaubroeck, and B. J. Avolio, "Psychological Processes Linking Authentic Leadership to Follower Behaviors," *Leadership Quarterly* 21, no. 5 (2010): 901–14.

[98]D. A. Newman and D. A. Harrison, "Been There, Bottled That: Are State and Behavioral Work Engagement New and Useful Construct 'Wines?'" *Industrial and Organizational Psychology* 1, no. 1 (2008): 31–35; and A. J. Wefald and R. G. Downey, "Job Engagement in Organizations: Fad, Fashion, or Folderol," *Journal of Organizational Behavior* 30, no. 1 (2009): 141–45.

[99]See, for example, Rich, LePine, and Crawford, "Job Engagement: Antecedents and Effects on Job Performance;" and Christian, Garza, and Slaughter, "Work Engagement: A Quantitative Review and Test of Its Relations with Task and Contextual Performance."

[100]J. M. George, "The Wider Context, Costs, and Benefits of Work Engagement," *European Journal of Work and Organizational Psychology* 20, no. 1 (2011): 53–59; and J. R. B. Halbesleben, J. Harvey, and M. C. Bolino, "Too Engaged? A Conservation of Resources View of the Relationship between Work Engagement and Work Interference with Family," *Journal of Applied Psychology* 94, no. 6 (2009): 1452–65.

8 Motivation: From Concepts to Applications

Source: Bruce Ackerman/Ocala Star-Banner/Landov

LEARNING OBJECTIVES

After studying this chapter, you should be able to:

8-1 Describe how the job characteristics model motivates by changing the work environment.

8-2 Compare the main ways jobs can be redesigned.

8-3 Explain how specific alternative work arrangements can motivate employees.

8-4 Describe how employee involvement measures can motivate employees.

8-5 Demonstrate how the different types of variable-pay programs can increase employee motivation.

8-6 Show how flexible benefits turn benefits into motivators.

8-7 Identify the motivational benefits of intrinsic rewards.

MyManagementLab®
⭐ **Chapter Warm Up**

If your professor has chosen to assign this, go to the Assignments section of **mymanagementlab.com** to complete the chapter warm up.

MOTIVATED TO RISK IT ALL

These days, Lee Farkas (seen here) is wearing the same outfit in every picture: a heavy cloth shirt with the bold orange stripes of a U.S. federal penitentiary. But it wasn't long ago that Farkas wore the expensive suits of a successful mortgage banker and posed with his private jet. "It's not a crime to have a plane," he said. True, unless you buy the plane using $38.5 million of personally misappropriated funds. Farkas and six others are responsible for a $2.9 billion fraud that collapsed two banks and created the sixth-largest U.S. bank failure ever. He is the most senior executive incarcerated as a result of the housing bubble debacle and, with his group of co-conspirators, owes $3.5 billion in restitution. Farkas is currently serving 30 years in the same prison as the infamous Bernie Madoff, who is serving a life term for bank fraud.

The motives for Farkas's crimes defy logic. By all accounts, he had the intelligence and savvy to live an honest rags-to-riches story: originally broke and with no experience in finance, he bought Taylor, Bean & Whitaker (TBW), a small mortgage firm, with $75,000 (he says it was $25,000) in borrowed funds and within a decade transformed it into one of the top mortgage lenders. Somehow this success wasn't enough for him, though, so he created and sold phony mortgages, siphoning the gains into his private accounts to fund a lavish lifestyle including houses, cars, and planes. When TBW accumulated a huge deficit as a result, Farkas enlisted Colonial Bank's Senior VP Catherine Kissick to help sell loans concurrently to multiple hedge funds and push the phony proceeds back into TBW's accounts. Soon both firms collapsed.

Why wasn't Farkas motivated to continue his earlier honest success? He seems to have felt he simply wasn't making enough money. "I wasn't the kind of guy they painted a picture of, big high-living," he said. "Among my peer group, I was a pauper." Farkas also felt entitled to the money he stole, for while he admits he did "things that were not really smart," he maintains his innocence. Farkas furthermore minimizes his role, saying it is "important to understand that I was a small-town businessman...with no political connections or power." Finally, he refuses to accept responsibility. District Court Judge Leonie Brinkema, who presided over the restitution ruling, commented that Farkas showed no remorse beyond sorrow over "getting caught." Indeed, Farkas said he was disbelieving when he was arrested. "I go 'ha ha, get away,'" he said. "Finally, they took these guns out."

For the love of money, Farkas was willing to risk it all—even freedom for the rest of his life. If he fails to have his sentence overturned, he will not be released until he is in his 80s. Farkas feels he already lives only "vicariously" through e-mail contact with family and friends. "You're not really alive in here, you're a zombie—just a body walking around, eating, sleeping and being yelled at," he complained. His motive for living now is to get out. His last conviction appeal failed, and if the next one fails too, he says, "Maybe I'll just fade away."

Sources: L. B. Farkas, "Lee B. Farkas Story," US vs Lee B. Farkas, www.leefarkas.com; P. Fitzgerald, "Bank of America Paid $315 to Settle with Banks over Ocala Losses," *The Wall Street Journal,* May 5, 2015, http://www.wsj.com/articles/bank-of-america-paid-315-million-to-settle-with-banks-over-ocala-losses-1430863619?tesla=y; J. Eaglesham, "A Prison Life: Ex-Banker Struggles," *The Wall Street Journal,* March 19, 2014, C1; and A Macias, "Someone You've Never Heard of, and He Feels Like a 'Zombie' in Prison," *Business Insider,* March 20, 2014, http://www.businessinsider.com/ex-mortgage-mogul-lee-farkus-2014-3.

As we can see in the ongoing saga of Lee Farkas, money can be an extremely powerful motivator. For most individuals, though, pay is not the only motivator. It is a central means of motivation, but what you're actually doing for the money matters, too. The process of motivating employees is complex, and people feel strongly about the implications of changes to their extrinsic or intrinsic benefits.

In Chapter 7, we focused on motivation theories. While it's important to understand the underlying concepts, it's also important to see how you can use them as a manager. In this chapter, we apply motivation concepts to practices, beginning with job design.

Motivating by Job Design: The Job Characteristics Model

8-1 Describe how the job characteristics model motivates by changing the work environment.

job design The way the elements in a job are organized.

job characteristics model (JCM) A model that proposes that any job can be described in terms of five core job dimensions: skill variety, task identity, task significance, autonomy, and feedback.

skill variety The degree to which a job requires a variety of different activities.

task identity The degree to which a job requires completion of a whole and identifiable piece of work.

task significance The degree to which a job has a substantial impact on the lives or work of other people.

autonomy The degree to which a job provides substantial freedom and discretion to the individual in scheduling the work and in determining the procedures to be used in carrying it out.

feedback The degree to which carrying out the work activities required by a job results in the individual obtaining direct and clear information about the effectiveness of his or her performance.

The way work is structured has a bigger impact on an individual's motivation than might first appear. **Job design** suggests that the way elements in a job are organized can influence employee effort, and the job characteristics model, discussed next, can serve as a framework to identify opportunities for changes to those elements.

The Job Characteristics Model

Developed by J. Richard Hackman and Greg Oldham, the **job characteristics model (JCM)** describes jobs in terms of five core job dimensions:[1]

1. **Skill variety** is the degree to which a job requires different activities using specialized skills and talents. The work of a garage owner-operator who does electrical repairs, rebuilds engines, does bodywork, and interacts with customers scores high on skill variety. The job of a body shop worker who sprays paint 8 hours a day scores low on this dimension.
2. **Task identity** is the degree to which a job requires completion of a whole and identifiable piece of work. A cabinetmaker who designs furniture, selects the wood, builds the objects, and finishes them has a job that scores high on task identity. A job scoring low on this dimension is operating a lathe solely to make table legs.
3. **Task significance** is the degree to which a job affects the lives or work of other people. The job of a nurse helping patients in a hospital intensive care unit scores high on task significance; sweeping floors in a hospital scores low.
4. **Autonomy** is the degree to which a job provides the worker freedom, independence, and discretion in scheduling work and determining the procedures for carrying it out. A sales manager who schedules his own work and tailors his sales approach for each customer without supervision has a highly autonomous job. An account representative who is required to follow a standardized sales script with potential customers has a job low on autonomy.
5. **Feedback** is the degree to which carrying out work activities generates direct and clear information about your own performance. A job with high feedback is testing and inspecting iPads. Installing components of iPads as they move down an assembly line provides low feedback.

Exhibit 8-1 presents the JCM. Note how the first three dimensions—skill variety, task identity, and task significance—combine to create meaningful work the employee will view as important, valuable, and worthwhile. Jobs with high autonomy give employees a feeling of personal responsibility for results; feedback will show them how effectively they are performing. The JCM proposes that individuals obtain internal rewards when they learn (knowledge of results in the model) that they personally have performed well (experienced responsibility) on a task they care about (experienced meaningfulness). The more these three psychological states are present, the greater will be employees' motivation, performance, and satisfaction, and the lower their absenteeism and likelihood of leaving. As Exhibit 8-1 indicates, individuals with a high growth need are more likely to experience the critical psychological states when their jobs are enriched—and respond to them more positively.

Much evidence supports the JCM concept that the presence of these job characteristics generates higher job satisfaction and organizational commitment through increased motivation.[2] In general, research concurs with the

| Exhibit 8-1 | The Job Characteristics Model |

Source: J. L. Pierce, I. Jussila, and A. Cummings, "Psychological Ownership within the Job Design Context: Revision of the Job Characteristics Model," *Journal of Organizational Behavior* 30, no. 4 (2009): 477–96.

theory behind the JCM, although studies have introduced potential modifiers. One study suggested that when employees were "other oriented" (concerned with the welfare of others at work), the relationship between intrinsic job characteristics and job satisfaction was weaker,[3] meaning that our job satisfaction comes less from these characteristics when we care about others. Another study proposed that the degree of psychological ownership we feel toward our work enhances our motivation, particularly if the feelings of ownership are shared among a work group.[4] Other research has explored the JCM in unique settings such as in virtual work situations, finding that if individuals work together online but not in person, their experience of meaningfulness, responsibility, and knowledge of results can suffer. Thankfully, managers can mitigate these for employees by consciously developing personal relationships with them and increasing their sense of task significance, autonomy, and feedback.[5]

We can combine the core dimensions of the JCM into a single predictive index, called the **motivating potential score (MPS)** and calculated as follows:

motivating potential score (MPS)
A predictive index that suggests the motivating potential in a job.

$$\text{MPS} = \frac{\text{Skill variety} + \text{Task identiy} + \text{Task Significance}}{3} \times \text{Autonomy} \times \text{Feedback}$$

To be high on motivating potential, jobs must be high on at least one of the three factors that lead to experienced meaningfulness and high on both autonomy and feedback. If jobs score high on motivating potential, the model predicts that motivation, performance, and satisfaction will improve, while absence and turnover will be reduced. But we can better calculate motivating potential by simply adding characteristics rather than using the formula. Think about your job. Do you have the opportunity to work on different tasks, or is your day routine? Are you able to work independently, or do you constantly have a supervisor or coworker looking over your shoulder? Your answers indicate your job's motivating potential.

A few studies have tested the JCM in different cultures, but the results aren't consistent. The fact that the model is relatively individualistic (it considers the relationship between the employee and his or her work) suggests job enrichment strategies may not have the same effects in collectivistic cultures as in individualistic cultures (such as the United States). Indeed, one study in Niger found that while the MPS was highly influenced by job dimensions, the correlations were different than the general data gathered from predominately individualist countries.[6] In contrast, another study suggested the degree to which jobs had intrinsic job motivators predicted job satisfaction and job involvement equally well for U.S., Japanese, and Hungarian employees.[7]

Job Redesign

8-2 Compare the main ways jobs can be redesigned.

"Every day was the same thing," Frank said. "Stand on that assembly line. Wait for an instrument panel to be moved into place. Unlock the mechanism and drop the panel into the Jeep Liberty as it moved by on the line. Then I plugged in the harnessing wires. I repeated that for eight hours a day. I don't care that they were paying me 24 dollars an hour. I was going crazy. Finally, I just said this isn't going to be the way I'm going to spend the rest of my life. My brain was turning to JELL-O. So I quit. Now I work in a print shop and I make less than 15 dollars an hour. But let me tell you, the work I do is really interesting. The job changes all the time, I'm continually learning new things, and the work really challenges me! I look forward every morning to going to work again."

The repetitive tasks in Frank's job at the Jeep plant provided little variety, autonomy, or motivation. In contrast, his job in the print shop is challenging and stimulating. From an organizational perspective, the failure of Frank's first employer to redesign his job into a more satisfying one led to increased turnover. Redesigning jobs therefore has important practical implications—reduced turnover and increased job satisfaction among them. Let's look at some ways to put the JCM into practice to make jobs more motivating.

Job Rotation

job rotation The periodic shifting of an employee from one task to another.

If employees suffer from over-routinization of their work, one alternative is **job rotation**, or the periodic shifting of an employee from one task to another with similar skill requirements at the same organizational level (also called *cross-training*). Manufacturers also use job rotation as needed to respond more flexibly to the volume of incoming orders. New managers are sometimes rotated through jobs, too, to help them get a picture of a whole organization.[8] For these reasons, job rotation can be applied in any setting where cross-training is feasible, from manufacturing floors to hospital wards. At Singapore Airlines, for instance, a ticket agent may temporarily take on the duties of a baggage handler, both to be cross-trained and get exposure to different aspects of the organization. Extensive job rotation is among the reasons Singapore Airlines is rated one of the best airlines in the world.[9]

The use of job rotation has been shown to increase job satisfaction and organizational commitment.[10] Additionally, international evidence from Italy, Britain, and Turkey shows that job rotation is associated with higher levels of organizational performance in manufacturing settings.[11] It reduces boredom, increases motivation, and helps employees understand how their work contributes to the organization. It may also increase safety and reduce repetitive-based work injuries, but this is currently a topic of much study and debate, with mixed findings.[12]

Job rotation does have drawbacks. Work that is done repeatedly may become habitual and routine, which makes decision making more automatic and efficient, but less thoughtfully considered. Second, training costs increase when each rotation necessitates a round of training. Third, moving a worker into

Money Can't Buy Happiness

Along with this clichéd statement, you've probably heard that money *does* buy happiness. Both may be true. Economist Richard Easterlin argued that once basic financial needs have been met, more money doesn't really do much to make a person happy. Researchers set the limit at around $75,000, recently prompting one CEO to give away all his earnings above that amount to his employees!

This is by no means the last word, nor a directive to be unhappy until you make $75,000 and no happier afterward. More recent research worldwide indicates the exact opposite: The more money, the better. The authors said, "If there is a satiation point, we are yet to reach it."

Given these mixed findings, the relationship between happiness and income is probably not direct. In fact, other research suggests your *level* of income is less important than *how* you spend it. Think about why you may be motivated by money. Do you envision the number of zeroes in your bank account increasing? Probably not. You're probably more motivated by what you can buy with the money than by the money itself. From research, we know:

- *Giving money away makes people happier than spending it on themselves.* In one study, students were given money and told to either give it away or spend it on themselves. Then the study asked people to give away their own money. Either way, people were happier giving away the money, even if the givers were relatively poor. What seems to matter is not the amount, but how much impact you think your donation will have on others.
- *People are happier when they spend money on experiences rather than products.* Research professor Thomas Gilovich says we think to ourselves, "I have a limited amount of money, and I can either go there, or I can have this. If I go there, it'll be great, but it'll be over in no time. If I buy this thing, at least I'll always have it. That is factually true, but not psychologically true. We adapt to our material goods."

- *People are happier when they buy time...but only if they use it well.* Outsource tasks when you can, for instance, and "think of it as 'windfall time' and use it to do something good," says researcher Elizabeth Dunn.

Saying that money brings more happiness when spent on our experiences (and the time to do them) may seem counterintuitive until we think about it closely. What did you think of your cell phone when you bought it compared to what you think of it now? Chances are you were interested and engaged when you bought it, but now it is an everyday object. For experiences, what did you think of your greatest vacation when you were on it, and what do you think of it now? Both the experience at the time and the recollection now may bring a smile to your face.

Sources: A. Blackman, "Can Money Buy Happiness?" *The Wall Street Journal,* November 10, 2014, R1, R2; D. Kurtzleben, "Finally: Proof That Money Buys Happiness (Sort Of)," *USNews.com,* April 29, 2013; and A. Novotney, "Money Can't Buy Happiness," *Monitor on Psychology* (July/August 2012): 24–26.

a new position reduces overall productivity for that role. Fourth, job rotation creates disruptions when members of the work group have to adjust to new employees. Finally, supervisors may have to spend more time answering questions and monitoring the work of recently rotated employees.

Relational Job Design

While redesigning jobs on the basis of job characteristics theory is likely to make work more intrinsically motivating, research is focusing on how to make jobs more prosocially motivating to people. In other words, how can managers design work so employees are motivated to promote the well-being of the organization's beneficiaries (customers, clients, patients, and employees)? This view, **relational job design**, shifts the spotlight from the employee to those whose lives are affected by the job that employee performs.[13] It also motivates individuals toward increased job performance.[14]

One way to make jobs more prosocially motivating is to better connect employees with the beneficiaries of their work by relating stories from customers who have found the company's products or services to be helpful. For example,

relational job design   Constructing jobs so employees see the positive difference they can make in the lives of others directly through their work.

Medical device maker Stryker provides opportunities for its employees to connect with people affected by their work. Shown here are its employees with endurance athlete Daren Wendell (center, in hat), who has an implanted titanium rod in his leg that Stryker produced.

Source: Diane Bondareff/Invsion for Stryker/AP Images

the medical device manufacturer Medtronic invites people to describe how its products have improved, or even saved, their lives and shares these stories with employees during annual meetings, providing the employees a powerful reminder of the impact of their work. For another example, researchers found that when university fundraisers briefly interacted with the undergraduates who would receive the scholarship money they raised, they persisted 42 percent longer than and raised nearly twice as much money as those who didn't interact with potential recipients.[15] The positive impact was apparent even when fundraisers met with just a single scholarship recipient.

Personal contact with beneficiaries may not always be necessary. One study found that radiologists who saw photographs of patients whose scans they were examining made more accurate diagnoses of their medical problems. Why? Seeing the photos made it more personal, which elicited feelings of empathy in the radiologists.[16]

Why do these connections have such positive consequences? Meeting beneficiaries firsthand—or even just seeing pictures of them—allows employees to see that their actions affect a real person and have tangible consequences. It makes customers or clients more memorable and emotionally vivid, which leads employees to consider the effects of their work actions more. Finally, connections allow employees to easily take the perspective of beneficiaries, which fosters higher levels of commitment.

You might be wondering whether connecting employees with the beneficiaries of their work is already covered by the idea of task significance in job characteristics theory. However, some differences make beneficiary contact unique. For one, many jobs might be perceived to be high in significance, yet employees in those jobs never meet the individuals affected by their work. Second, beneficiary contact seems to have a distinct relationship with prosocial behaviors such as helping others. For example, one study found that lifeguards who read stories about how their actions benefited swimmers were rated as more helpful by their bosses; this was not the case for lifeguards who read stories about the personal benefits of their work for themselves.[17] The upshot? There are many ways you can design jobs to be more motivating, and your choice should depend on the outcomes you'd like to achieve.

Relational job design, with its focus on prosocial motivation, is an especially salient topic for organizations with corporate social responsibility (CSR) initiatives. As we discussed in earlier chapters, CSR efforts often include invitations for employees to volunteer their time and effort, sometimes using the skills they gained on the job (like Home Depot employees when they help rebuild homes) but often not (such as when bank employees help rebuild homes with groups like Habitat for Humanity). In both cases, the employees may be able to interact with the beneficiaries of their efforts, and research indicates that corporate-sponsored volunteer programs enhanced in the JCM dimensions of meaningfulness and task significance motivate employees to volunteer.[18] But while this motivation for prosocial behavior is noteworthy, it is not the same as relational job design: for one, the CSR efforts are through volunteering (not on-the-job); and for another, the work they are providing is not usually the same work they do at their jobs (Home Depot workers do not build homes on the job). However, relational job design holds intriguing possibilities for CSR initiatives.

✪ PERSONAL INVENTORY ASSESSMENTS

Diagnosing the Need for Team Building

We might be tempted to think that assembling a group for a project is team building, but intentional team building is much different. Take this PIA to find out how to diagnose the need for planned team building.

Alternative Work Arrangements

8-3 Explain how specific alternative work arrangements can motivate employees.

As you surely know, there are many approaches toward motivating people, and we've discussed some of them. Another approach to motivation is to consider alternative work arrangements such as flextime, job sharing, and telecommuting. These are likely to be especially important for a diverse workforce of dual-earner couples, single parents, and employees caring for a sick or aging relative.

Flextime

Susan is the classic "morning person." Every day she rises at 5:00 A.M. sharp, full of energy. However, as she puts it, "I'm usually ready for bed right after the 7:00 P.M. news."

Susan's work schedule as a claims processor at The Hartford Financial Services Group is flexible. Her office opens at 6:00 A.M. and closes at 7:00 P.M., and she schedules her 8-hour day within this 13-hour period. Because she is a morning person whose 7-year-old son gets out of school at 3:00 p.m. every day, Susan opts to work from 6:00 A.M. to 3:00 P.M. "My work hours are perfect. I'm at the job when I'm mentally most alert, and I can be home to take care of my son after he gets out of school."

flextime   Flexible work hours.

Susan's schedule is an example of **flextime**, short for "flexible work time." Flextime employees must work a specific number of hours per week but may

PricewaterhouseCoopers provides flexible work options that allow employees to control how and when their work gets done. PwC employees like Global Mobility Process and Quality Managers Robin Croft and Shari Alatorre, shown here, may choose flexible work plans that include flextime, job sharing, and telecommuting.
Source: Eve Edelheit/Tampa Bay Times/ZUMAPRESS .com/Alamy

vary their hours of work within limits. As in Exhibit 8-2, each day consists of a common core, usually 6 hours, with a flexibility band surrounding it. The core may be 9:00 A.M. to 3:00 P.M., with the office actually opening at 6:00 A.M. and closing at 6:00 P.M. Employees must be at their jobs during the common core period, but they may accumulate their other 2 hours around that. Some flextime programs allow employees to accumulate extra hours and turn them into days off.

Flextime has become extremely popular. According to a recent survey, a majority (60 percent) of U.S. organizations offer some form of flextime.[19] This is not just a U.S. phenomenon, though. In Germany, for instance, 73 percent of businesses offer flextime, and such practices are becoming more widespread in Japan as well.[20] In Germany, Belgium, the Netherlands, and France, by law employers are not allowed to refuse an employee's request for either a part-time or a flexible work schedule as long as the request is reasonable, such as to care for an infant child.[21]

Claimed benefits of flextime include reduced absenteeism, increased productivity, reduced overtime expenses, reduced hostility toward management, reduced traffic congestion,[22] elimination of tardiness, and increased autonomy and responsibility for employees—any of which may increase employee job satisfaction.[23] But what is flextime's actual record?

Most of the evidence stacks up favorably. Perhaps most important from the organization's perspective, flextime increases profitability. Interestingly, though, this effect seems to occur only when flextime is promoted as a work–life balance strategy (not when it is for the organization's gain).[24] Flextime also tends to reduce absenteeism,[25] probably for several reasons. Employees can schedule their work hours to align with personal demands, reducing tardiness and absences, and they can work when they are most productive. Flextime can also help employees balance work and family lives; it is a popular criterion for judging how "family friendly" a workplace is.

Flextime's major drawback is that it's not applicable to every job or every worker. It works well for clerical tasks when an employee's interaction with people outside the department is limited, but it is not a viable option for receptionists

| Exhibit 8-2 | Possible Flextime Staff Schedules |

Schedule 1

Percent Time:	100% = 40 hours per week
Core Hours:	9:00 A.M.–5:00 P.M., Monday through Friday (1 hour lunch)
Work Start Time:	Between 8:00 A.M. and 9:00 A.M.
Work End Time:	Between 5:00 P.M. and 6:00 P.M.

Schedule 2

Percent Time:	100% = 40 hours per week
Work Hours:	8:00 A.M.–6:30 P.M., Monday through Thursday (1/2 hour lunch)
	Friday off
Work Start Time:	8:00 A.M.
Work End Time:	6:30 P.M.

Schedule 3

Percent Time:	90% = 36 hours per week
Work Hours:	8:30 A.M.–5:00 P.M., Monday through Thursday (1/2 hour lunch)
	8:00 A.M.–Noon Friday (no lunch)
Work Start Time:	8:30 A.M. (Monday–Thursday); 8:00 A.M. (Friday)
Work End Time:	5:00 P.M. (Monday–Thursday); Noon (Friday)

Schedule 4

Percent Time:	80% = 32 hours per week
Work Hours:	8:00 A.M.–6:00 P.M., Monday through Wednesday (1/2 hour lunch)
	8:00 A.M.–11:30 A.M. Thursday (no lunch)
	Friday off
Work Start Time:	Between 8:00 A.M. and 9:00 A.M.
Work End Time:	Between 5:00 P.M. and 6:00 P.M.

or salespeople in retail stores—anyone whose service job requires being at a workstation at predetermined times. It also appears that people who have a strong desire to separate their work and family lives are less apt to want flextime, so it's not a motivator for everyone.[26] Those who ask for it are often stigmatized, which can be avoided only if the majority of the organization's leaders adopt flexible hours to signal that flextime is acceptable.[27] And finally, research in the United Kingdom indicated that employees in organizations with flextime do not realize a reduction in their levels of stress, suggesting that this option may not truly improve work–life balance.[28] Since flextime is intuitively a worthwhile business practice, these findings suggest additional research is needed to determine the motivational aspects of flextime.

Job Sharing

job sharing An arrangement that allows two or more individuals to split a traditional 40-hour-a-week job.

Job sharing allows two or more individuals to split a traditional full-time job. One employee might perform the job from 8:00 A.M. to noon, perhaps, and the other from 1:00 P.M. to 5:00 P.M., or the two could work full but alternate days. For example, top Ford engineers Julie Levine and Julie Rocco engaged in a job-sharing program that allowed both of them to spend time with their families while redesigning the Explorer crossover. Typically, one of them would work late afternoons and evenings while the other worked mornings. They both agreed that the program worked well, although making it feasible required a great deal of time and preparation.[29]

Only 18 percent of U.S. organizations offered job sharing in 2014, a 29 percent decrease since 2008.[30] Reasons it is not more widely adopted include the difficulty of finding compatible partners to job share and the historically negative perceptions of individuals not completely committed to their jobs and employers. However, eliminating job sharing for these reasons might be short-sighted. Job sharing allows an organization to draw on the talents of more than one individual for a given job. It opens the opportunity to acquire skilled workers—for instance, parents with young children and retirees—who might not be available on a full-time basis. From the employee's perspective, job sharing can increase motivation and satisfaction.

An employer's decision to use job sharing is often based on economics and national policy. Two part-time employees sharing a job can be less expensive in terms of salary and benefits than one full-timer, but experts suggest this is not often the case because training, coordination, and administrative costs can be high. On the other hand, in the United States the Affordable Care Act may create a financial incentive for companies to increase job-sharing arrangements in order to avoid the requirement to provide health care to full-time employees.[31] Many German and Japanese[32] firms have been using job sharing—but for a very different reason. Germany's Kurzarbeit program, which is now close to 100 years old, kept employment levels from plummeting throughout the economic crisis by switching full-time workers to part-time job sharing work.[33]

Ideally, employers should consider each employee and job separately, seeking to match the skills, personality, and needs of the employee with the tasks required for the job, taking into account that individual's motivating factors.

Telecommuting

telecommuting Working from home at least 2 days a week on a computer that is linked to the employer's office.

It might be close to the ideal job for many people: no rush hour traffic, flexible hours, freedom to dress as you please, and few interruptions. **Telecommuting** refers to working at home—or anywhere else the employee chooses that is outside the workplace—at least 2 days a week on a computer linked to the employer's office.[34] (A closely related concept—working from a *virtual office*—describes working outside the workplace on a relatively permanent basis.) A sales manager working from home is telecommuting, but a sales manager working from her car on a business trip is not.

Telecommuting seems to mesh with the cultural transition to knowledge work (which often can be performed anywhere), and as the OB Poll on page 255 indicates, people with more education are more apt to work from home. However, telecommuting has been a popular topic lately not for its potential, but for its organizational acceptance, or lack thereof. Despite the benefits of telecommuting, large organizations such as Yahoo! and Best Buy have eliminated it.[35] Yahoo! CEO Marissa Mayer discussed how telecommuting may undermine corporate culture, noting, "People are more productive when they're alone, but they're more collaborative and innovative when they're together."[36]

While the movement away from telecommuting by some companies made headlines, it appears that for most organizations, it remains popular. Almost 50 percent of managers in Germany, the United Kingdom, and the United States are permitted telecommuting options. In developing countries, this percentage is between 10 and 20 percent.[37] Organizations that actively encourage telecommuting include Amazon, IBM, American Express,[38] Intel, Cisco Systems,[39] and

How can I get flextime?

My job is great, but I can't understand why management won't allow flextime. After all, I often work on a laptop in the office! I could just as easily be working on the same laptop at home without interruptions from my colleagues. I know I'd be more productive. How can I convince them to let me?

—Sophia

Dear Sophia:

We can't help but wonder two things: 1) is the ban on working from home a company policy, or your manager's policy; and 2) do you want flextime, or telecommuting? If you work for Yahoo!, for instance, you may not be able to convince anyone to let you work from home after CEO Marissa Mayer's very public decree against the policy. If the ban is your manager's policy—or even your division's policy—in an organization open to alternative work arrangements, you just may be able to get your way.

That leads us to the second question, about flextime versus telecommuting. If you want flextime as you stated and just want to work from home during some non-core hours (say, work in the office for 6 hours a day and work another 2 hours a day from home), your employer may be more likely to grant your wish than if you want to completely telecommute (work all your hours from home).

Research indicates that employees are most likely to be granted

work from home privileges as a result of a direct sympathetic relationship with their managers (not as a result of a company policy). Employees are also more likely to gain acceptance for partial than for full telecommuting (either flextime or by alternating days). It helps if you have a legitimate need to be home and if you do knowledge-based work. Jared Dalton, for instance, telecommutes 2 days a week as a manager for accounting firm Ernst & Young, and his wife Christina telecommutes on 2 different days, so they can oversee the care of their infant.

If it sounds like flextime depends on favoritism, you might be right. It's also, however, a reflection of the state of telecommuting: only 38 percent of U.S. organizations permit *some* of their employees to regularly work from home. To be one of the lucky few:

- *Check your organization's flexible options policies.*
- *Develop a plan for working from home to show your manager.* Include how many hours/week, which days/week, and where you will work, and explain how your manager can retain oversight of you.
- *Assemble evidence on your productivity.* Have you worked from home before? If so, show how much you achieved. You stated you would be more productive at home: How much more?

- *Outline your reasons for working from home.* Do you need to help care for an aging relative, for instance? Would working from home save you commuting time you could use for work?
- *Address management's concerns.* Research indicates the biggest ones are the possibility of abuse of the system and issues of fairness.
- *Consider your relationship with your manager.* Has he or she been supportive of you in the past? Is your manager approachable?

When you're ready, discuss your request with your manager. Remember, pitching the idea of telecommuting is the same as pitching any idea—you've got to think about what's in it for your employer, not for yourself.

Sources: "The 2015 Workplace Flexibility Study," *WorkplaceTrends.com,* February 3, 2015, https://workplacetrends.com/the-2015-workplace-flexibility-study/; T. S. Bernard, "For Workers, Less Flexible Companies," *The New York Times,* May 20, 2014, B1, B7; and C. C. Miller and L. Alderman, "The Flexibility Gap," *The New York Times,* December 14, 2014, 1, 5.

a number of U.S. government agencies.[40] Telecommuting is less practiced in China, but there, too, it is growing.[41]

What kinds of jobs lend themselves to telecommuting? Writers, attorneys, analysts, and employees who spend the majority of their time on computers or the telephone—including telemarketers, customer-service representatives, reservation agents, and product-support specialists—are candidates. As telecommuters, they can access information on their computers at home as easily as in the company's office.

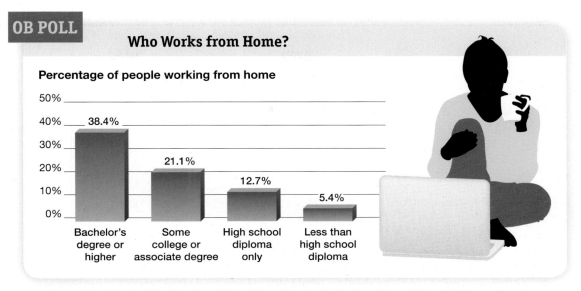

OB POLL

Who Works from Home?

Percentage of people working from home

Bachelor's degree or higher	38.4%
Some college or associate degree	21.1%
High school diploma only	12.7%
Less than high school diploma	5.4%

Source: Bureau of Labor Statistics, Table 6 from Economic News Release, "American Time Use Survey Summary," June 20, 2013, www.bls.gov/news .release/atus.t06.htm.

Telecommuting has several potential benefits. These include a larger labor pool from which to select (some people can/will only work by telecommuting), higher productivity, improved morale, and reduced office-space costs. A positive relationship exists between telecommuting and supervisor performance ratings, but a relationship between telecommuting and potentially lower turnover intentions has not been substantiated in research to date.[42] Beyond the benefits to organizations and their employees, telecommuting has potential benefits to society. One study estimated that if people in the United States telecommuted half the time, carbon emissions would be reduced by approximately 51 metric tons per year. Environmental savings could come about from lower office energy consumption, fewer traffic jams that emit greenhouse gasses, and a reduced need for road repairs.[43]

Telecommuting has several downsides too. The major one for management is less direct supervision. In today's team-focused workplace, telecommuting may also make it more difficult for managers to coordinate teamwork, and it can reduce knowledge transfer in organizations.[44] Managers are also challenged to handle the demotivation of office workers who feel they are unfairly denied the freedom of telecommuters.[45] Contrary to Mayer's conclusions for Yahoo!, research indicates that more creative tasks may actually be best suited for telecommuting, whereas dull repetitive tasks like data entry decrease motivation and thus performance for remote workers.[46]

From the employee's standpoint, telecommuting can increase feelings of isolation and reduce job satisfaction.[47] Research indicates it does not reduce work–family conflicts, perhaps because it often increases work hours beyond the contracted workweek.[48] Telecommuters are also vulnerable to the "out of sight, out of mind" effect: Employees who aren't at their desks, miss meetings, and don't share in day-to-day informal workplace interactions may be at a disadvantage when it comes to raises and promotions because they're perceived as not putting in the requisite "face-time."[49] As for a CSR benefit of reducing car emissions by allowing telecommuting, research indicates that employees actually drive over 45 miles more per day, due to increased personal trips, when they telecommute![50]

Telecommuting is a contemporary reality, particularly in the minds of employees. However, initial studies suggest they view it differently in different cultures. For example, in China and perhaps in other collectivist cultures, employees are more comfortable with telecommuting when they clearly know what is expected of them and can acknowledge their manager's superiority in their communications.[51] The success of telecommuting will always depend on the quality of communications in order to establish good, though remote, working relationships. Telecommuting certainly does appear to make sense given changes in technology, the nature of work, and preferences of younger workers. Yet as the Yahoo! experience shows, some leaders do not think those benefits outweigh the costs.

Employee Involvement and Participation

8-4 Describe how employee involvement measures can motivate employees.

employee involvement and participation (EIP) A participative process that uses the input of employees to increase employee commitment to organizational success.

Employee involvement and participation (EIP)[52] is a process that uses employees' input to increase their commitment to organizational success. If workers are engaged in decisions that increase their autonomy and control over their work lives, they will become more motivated, more committed to the organization, more productive, and more satisfied with their jobs. These benefits don't stop with individuals—when teams are given more control over their work, morale and performance increase as well.[53]

To be successful, EIP programs should be tailored to local and national norms.[54] A study of four countries, including India and the United States, confirmed the importance of modifying practices to reflect national culture.[55] While U.S. employees readily accepted EIP programs, managers in India who tried to empower their employees were rated low by those employees. These reactions are consistent with India's high power–distance culture, which accepts and expects differences in authority. The work culture in India may not be in as much transition as in China, in which some employees are becoming less high power–distance oriented. Chinese workers who were very accepting of traditional Chinese cultural values showed few benefits from participative decision making. However, Chinese workers who were less traditional were more satisfied and had higher performance ratings under participative management.[56] Another study conducted in China showed that involvement increased employees' thoughts and feelings of job security, enhancing their well-being.[57] These differences within China may well reflect the current transitional nature of that culture. For example, research in urban China indicated that some aspects of EIP programs, namely those that favor consultation and expression but not participation in decision making, yield higher job satisfaction.[58]

Examples of Employee Involvement Programs

Let's look at two major forms of employee involvement—participative management and representative participation—in more detail.

participative management A process in which subordinates share a significant degree of decision-making power with their immediate superiors.

Participative Management   Common to all **participative management** programs is joint decision making, in which subordinates share a significant degree of decision-making power with their immediate superiors. This sharing can occur either formally through, say, briefings or surveys, or informally through daily consultations, as a way to enhance motivation through trust and commitment.[59] Participative management has, at times, been considered a panacea for poor morale and low productivity. In reality, for participative management to be effective, followers must have trust and confidence in their leaders. Leaders should avoid coercive techniques and instead stress the organizational consequences of decision making to their followers.[60]

Studies of the participation–performance relationship have yielded mixed findings.[61] Organizations that institute participative management may realize higher stock returns, lower turnover rates, and higher labor productivity, although these effects are typically not large.[62] Research at the individual level indicates participation typically has only a modest influence on employee productivity, motivation, and job satisfaction. This doesn't mean participative management isn't beneficial. However, it is not a sure means for improving performance.

representative participation   A system in which workers participate in organizational decision making through a small group of representative employees.

Representative Participation   Most countries in western Europe require companies to practice **representative participation**. Representative participation redistributes power within an organization, putting labor's interests on a more equal footing with the interests of management and stockholders by including a small group of employees as participants in decision making. In the United Kingdom, Ireland, Australia, and New Zealand, representative participation was originally the only EIP program, formed to allow employee representatives to discuss issues outside union agreements, and the representatives were all from the union. However, representative groups are now increasingly a mix of union and nonunion, or separate from the union arrangement.[63]

The two most common forms of representation are works councils and board representatives. Works councils are groups of nominated or elected employees who must be consulted when management makes decisions about employees. Board representatives are employees who sit on a company's board of directors and represent employees' interests.

The influence of representative participation on working employees seems to be mixed, but generally an employee would need to feel his or her interests are well represented and make a difference to the organization in order for motivation to increase. Thus representative participation as a motivational tool is surpassed by more direct participation methods.

In sum, EIP programs clearly have the potential to increase employees' intrinsic motivation. The opportunity to make and implement decisions—and

Bernd Osterloh, chairman of Volkswagen's works councils, speaks to production line workers at company headquarters in Wolfsburg, Germany. VW includes employees in decision making by allowing them to participate in discussions about work rules, the company's finances and business plans, and workplace productivity and safety.
Source: Fabian Bimmer/Reuters

then see them work out—can contribute to all desirable organizational outcomes. And giving employees control over key decisions, along with ensuring that their interests are represented, can enhance feelings of procedural justice. But, like any other initiatives, EIP programs must be carefully designed.

Using Rewards to Motivate Employees

8-5 Demonstrate how the different types of variable-pay programs can increase employee motivation.

As we saw in Chapter 3, pay is not the only factor driving job satisfaction. However, it does motivate people, and companies often underestimate its importance. One study found that while 45 percent of employers thought pay was a key factor in losing top talent, 71 percent of top performers called it a top reason.[64]

Given that pay is so important, will the organization lead, match, or lag the market in pay? How will individual contributions be recognized? In this section, we consider (1) what to pay employees (decided by establishing a pay structure), and (2) how to pay individual employees (decided through variable-pay plans).

What to Pay: Establishing a Pay Structure

There are many ways to pay employees. The process of initially setting pay levels entails balancing *internal equity*—the worth of the job to the organization (usually established through a technical process called job evaluation), and *external equity*—the competitiveness of an organization's pay relative to pay in its industry (usually established through pay surveys). Obviously, the best pay system reflects what the job is worth while also staying competitive relative to the labor market.

Some organizations prefer to pay above the market, while some may lag the market because they can't afford to pay market rates, or they are willing to bear the costs of paying below market (namely, higher turnover as people are lured to better-paying jobs). Some companies that have realized impressive gains in income and profit margins have done so in part by holding down employee wages; they include Comcast, Walt Disney, McDonald's, and AT&T.[65]

Pay more, and you may get better-qualified, more highly motivated employees who will stay with the organization longer. A study covering 126 large

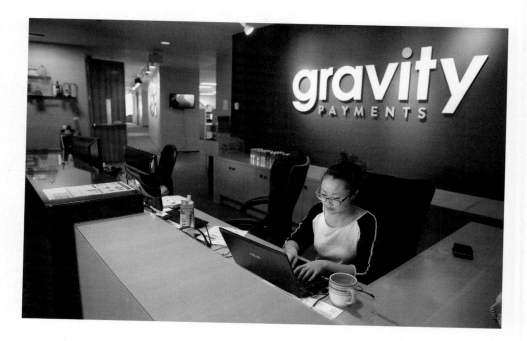

Cary Chin works at the front desk for Gravity Payments, a credit card processing firm in Seattle, where the cost of living is extremely high. Gravity's CEO Dan Price established a new pay structure for all employees of a $70,000 base salary to improve their quality of life and motivate them to work harder on achieving high customer satisfaction.

Source: Ted S. Warren/AP Images

organizations found employees who believed they were receiving a competitive pay level had higher morale and were more productive, and customers were more satisfied as well.[66] But pay is often the highest single operating cost for an organization, which means paying too much can make the organization's products or services too expensive. It's a strategic decision an organization must make, with clear trade-offs.

In the case of Walmart, it appears that its strategic decision on pay did not work. While annual growth in U.S. stores slowed to around 1 percent in 2011, one of Walmart's larger competitors, Costco, grew around 8 percent. The average worker at Costco made approximately $45,000, compared to approximately $17,500 for the average worker at Walmart-owned Sam's Club. Costco's strategy was that it will get more if it pays more—and higher wages resulted in increased employee productivity and reduced turnover. Given the recent Walmart decision to increase worker wages throughout the organization, perhaps its executives agree.[67]

How to Pay: Rewarding Individual Employees through Variable-Pay Programs

"Why should I put any extra effort into this job?" asked Anne, a fourth-grade elementary schoolteacher in Denver, Colorado. "I can excel or I can do the bare minimum. It makes no difference. I get paid the same. Why do anything above the minimum to get by?" Comments like Anne's have been voiced by schoolteachers for decades because pay increases were tied to seniority. Recently, however, a number of states have revamped their compensation systems to motivate teachers by linking pay to results in the classroom, and other states are considering such programs, admittedly with mixed results so far.[68] Many organizations, public and private, are moving away from pay based on seniority or credentials.

variable-pay program A pay plan that bases a portion of an employee's pay on some individual and/or organizational measure of performance.

Piece-rate, merit-based, bonus, profit-sharing, and employee stock ownership plans are all forms of a **variable-pay program** (also known as *pay-for-performance*), which bases a portion of an employee's pay on some individual and/or organizational measure of performance. The variable portion may be all or part of the paycheck, and it may be paid annually or upon attainment of benchmarks. It can also be either optional for the employee or an accepted condition of employment.[69] Variable-pay plans have long been used to compensate salespeople and executives, but the scope of variable-pay jobs has broadened.

Globally, around 80 percent of companies offer some form of variable-pay plan. In the United States, 91 percent of companies offer a variable-pay program.[70] In Latin America, more than 90 percent of companies offer some form of variable-pay plan. Latin American companies also have the highest percentage of total payroll allocated to variable pay, at nearly 18 percent. European and U.S. companies are lower, at about 12 percent.[71] When it comes to executive compensation, Asian companies are outpacing Western companies in their use of variable pay.[72]

Unfortunately, not all employees see a strong connection between pay and performance. The results of pay-for-performance plans are mixed; the context and receptivity of the individual to the plans play a large role. For instance, one study of 415 companies in South Korea suggested that group-based pay-for-performance plans may have a strong positive effect on organizational performance.[73] On the other hand, research in Canada indicated that variable-pay plans increase job satisfaction only if employee *effort* is rewarded as well as performance.[74] Finally, secrecy pays a role in the motivational success of variable-pay plans. Although in some government and not-for-profit agencies, pay amounts are either specifically or generally made public, most U.S. organizations encourage or require pay secrecy.[75] Is this good or bad? Unfortunately, it's bad: pay secrecy has a detrimental effect on job performance. Even worse, it adversely affects high performers more than other employees. It very likely increases employees' perception that pay is subjective, which can be demotivating. While individual pay amounts may not need to be broadcast to restore the balance, if general pay categories are made public and employees feel variable pay is linked objectively to their performance, the motivational effects of variable pay can be retained.[76]

The fluctuation in variable pay is what makes these programs attractive to management. It turns part of an organization's fixed labor costs into a variable cost, thus reducing expenses when performance declines. For example, when the U.S. economy encountered a recession in 2001 and again in 2008, companies with variable pay were able to reduce their labor costs much faster than others.[77] When pay is tied to performance, the employee's earnings also reflect their contributions rather than being a form of entitlement. Over time, low performers' pay stagnates, while high performers enjoy pay increases commensurate with their contributions.

Let's examine the different types of variable-pay programs in more detail.

piece-rate pay plan A pay plan in which workers are paid a fixed sum for each unit of production completed.

Piece-Rate Pay   The **piece-rate pay plan** has long been popular as a means of compensating production workers with a fixed sum for each unit of production completed, but it can be used in any organizational setting where the outputs are similar enough to be evaluated by quantity. A pure piece-rate plan provides no base salary and pays the employee only for what he or she produces. Ballpark workers selling peanuts and soda are frequently paid piece-rate. If they sell 40 bags of peanuts at $1 each for their earnings, their take is $40. The more peanuts they sell, the more they earn. Alternatively, piece-rate plans are sometimes distributed to sales teams, so a ballpark worker makes money on a portion of the total number of bags of peanuts sold by the group during a game.

Piece-rate plans are known to produce higher productivity and wages, so they can be attractive to organizations and motivating for workers.[78] In fact, one major Chinese university increased its piece-rate pay for articles by professors and realized 50 percent increased research productivity.[79] In the workplace, employees most likely to be motivated by piece-rate plans are managers and more tenured workers. Low-performing workers are generally not interested in piece-rate pay, for obvious reasons—they won't get paid much!

The chief concern of both individual and team piece-rate workers is financial risk. A recent experiment in Germany found that 68 percent of risk-averse individuals prefer an individual piece-rate system, and that lower performers prefer team piece-rate pay. Why? The authors suggested risk-averse and high-performing individuals would rather take their chances on pay based on what they can control (their own work) because they are concerned others will slack off in a team setting.[80] This is a valid concern, as we will discuss in the next chapter. Organizations, on the other hand, should verify that their piece-rate plans are indeed motivating to individuals. European research has suggested that when the pace of work is determined by uncontrollable outside factors such as customer requests, rather than internal factors such as coworkers, targets, and machines, a piece rate plan is not motivating.[81] Either way, managers must be mindful of the motivation for workers to decrease quality in order to increase their speed of output. They should also be aware that by rewarding volume, piece-rate plans increase the probability of workplace injuries.[82]

Thus, while piece-rate plans can be a powerful motivator in many organizational settings, an obvious limitation is that they're not feasible for many jobs. An emergency room (ER) doctor and nurse can earn significant salaries regardless of the number of patients they see or their patients' outcomes. Would it be better to pay them only if their patients fully recover? It seems unlikely that most would accept such a deal, and it might cause unanticipated consequences as well (such as ERs turning away patients with terminal diseases or life-threatening injuries). So, although incentives are motivating and relevant for some jobs, it is unrealistic to think they work universally.

merit-based pay plan   A pay plan based on performance appraisal ratings.

Merit-Based Pay   A **merit-based pay plan** pays for individual performance based on performance appraisal ratings. A main advantage is that high performers can get bigger raises. If designed correctly, merit-based plans let individuals perceive a strong relationship between their performance and their rewards.[83]

Most large organizations have merit pay plans, especially for salaried employees. Merit pay is slowly taking hold in the public sector. For example, most U.S. government employees are unionized, and the unions that represent them have usually demanded that pay raises be based solely on seniority. Claiming a new era of accountability, however, New Jersey Governor Chris Christie implemented merit pay for teachers. The Newark teachers union approved the plan, which included funding from Facebook CEO Mark Zuckerberg.[84] In another unusual move, New York City's public hospital system pays doctors based on how well they reduce costs, increase patient satisfaction, and improve the quality of care.[85]

A move away from merit pay, on the other hand, is coming from some organizations that don't feel it separates high and low performers enough. "There's a very strong belief and there's evidence and academic research that shows that variable pay does create focus among employees," said Ken Abosch, a compensation manager at human resource consulting firm Aon Hewitt. But when the annual review and raise are months away, the motivation of this reward for high performers diminishes. Even companies that have retained merit pay are rethinking the allocation.[86]

Although you might think a person's average level of performance is the key factor in merit pay decisions, the projected level of future performance also plays a role. One study found that National Basketball Association (NBA) players whose performance was on an upward trend were paid more than their average performance would have predicted. Managers of all organizations may unknowingly be basing merit pay decisions on how they *think* employees will perform, which may result in overly optimistic (or pessimistic) pay decisions.[87]

Despite their intuitive appeal, merit pay plans have several limitations. One is that they are typically based on an annual performance appraisal and thus are only as valid as the performance ratings, which are often subjective. This brings up issues of discrimination, as we discussed in Chapter 2. Research indicates that African American employees receive lower performance ratings than white employees, women's ratings are higher than men's, and there are demographic differences in the distribution of salary increases, even with all other factors equal.[88] Another limitation is that the pay-raise pool of available funds fluctuates on economic or other conditions that have little to do with individual performance. For instance, a colleague at a top university who performed very well in teaching and research was given a pay raise of $300. Why? Because the pay-raise pool was very small. Yet that amount is more of a cost-of-living increase than pay-for-performance. Lastly, unions typically resist merit pay plans. Relatively few teachers are covered by merit pay for this reason. Instead, seniority-based pay, which gives all employees the same raises, predominates.

The concept and intention of merit pay—that employees are paid for performance—is sound. For employee motivation purposes, however, merit pay should be only one part of a performance recognition program.

bonus   A pay plan that rewards employees for recent performance rather than historical performance.

Bonus   An annual **bonus** is a significant component of total compensation for many jobs. Once reserved for upper management, bonus plans are now routinely offered to employees in all levels of the organization. The incentive effects should be higher than those of merit pay because rather than paying for

Chinese Internet firm Tencent Holdings rewards employees with attractive incentives that include cash bonuses for lower-ranking employees. The young men shown here were among 5,000 employees who received a special bonus tucked in red envelopes and personally handed out by Tencent's CEO and co-founder Pony Ma.

Source: Keita Wen sz/Imaginechina via AP Images

previous performance now rolled into base pay, bonuses reward recent performance (merit pay is cumulative, but the increases are generally much smaller than bonus amounts). When times are bad, firms can cut bonuses to reduce compensation costs. Workers on Wall Street, for example, saw their average bonus drop by more than a third as their firms faced greater scrutiny.[89]

Bonus plans have a clear upside: they are motivating for workers. As an example, a recent study in India found that when a higher percentage of overall pay was reserved for the potential bonuses of managers and employees, productivity increased.[90] This example also highlights the downside of bonuses: They leave employees' pay more vulnerable to cuts. This is problematic especially when employees depend on bonuses or take them for granted. "People have begun to live as if bonuses were not bonuses at all but part of their expected annual income," said Jay Lorsch, a Harvard Business School professor. KeySpan Corp., a 9,700-employee utility company in New York, combined yearly bonuses with a smaller merit-pay raise. Elaine Weinstein, KeySpan's senior vice president of HR, credits the plan with changing the culture from "entitlement to meritocracy."[91]

The way bonuses and rewards are categorized also affects peoples' motivation. Although it is a bit manipulative, splitting rewards and bonuses into categories—even if the categories are meaningless—may increase motivation.[92] Why? Because people are more likely to feel they missed out on a reward if they don't receive one from each category, and then work harder to earn rewards from more categories.

profit-sharing plan An organization-wide program that distributes compensation based on some established formula designed around a company's profitability.

Profit-Sharing Plan A **profit-sharing plan** distributes compensation based on some established formula designed around a company's profitability. Compensation can be direct cash outlays or, particularly for top managers, allocations of stock options. When you read about executives like Mark Zuckerberg, who accepts an absurdly modest $1 salary, remember that many executives are granted generous stock options. In fact, Zuckerberg has made as much as $2.3 billion after cashing out some of his stock options.[93] Of course, the vast majority of profit-sharing plans are not so grand in scale. For example, Jacob Luke started his own lawn-mowing business at age 13. He employed his brother Isaiah and friend Marcel and paid them each 25 percent of the profits he made on each yard.

Studies generally support the idea that organizations with profit-sharing plans have higher levels of profitability than those without them.[94] These plans have also been linked to higher levels of employee commitment, especially in small organizations.[95] Profit-sharing at the organizational level appears to have positive impacts on employee attitudes; employees report a greater feeling of psychological ownership.[96] Recent research in Canada indicates that profit-sharing plans motivate individuals to higher job performance when they are used in combination with other pay-for-performance plans.[97] Obviously, profit sharing does not work when there is no reported profit per se, such as in non-profit organizations, or often in the public sector. However, profit sharing may make sense for many organizations, large or small.

employee stock ownership plan (ESOP) A company-established benefits plan in which employees acquire stock, often at below-market prices, as part of their benefits.

Employee Stock Ownership Plan An **employee stock ownership plan (ESOP)** is a company-established benefit plan in which employees acquire stock, often at below-market prices, as part of their benefits. Research on ESOPs indicates they increase employee satisfaction and innovation.[98] ESOPs have the potential to increase job satisfaction only when employees psychologically experience ownership.[99] Even so, ESOPs may not inspire lower absenteeism or greater motivation,[100] perhaps because the employee's actual monetary benefit comes with cashing in the stock at a later date. Thus, employees need to be kept regularly informed of the status of the business and have the opportunity to positively influence it in order to feel motivated toward higher personal performance.[101]

ESOPs for top management can reduce unethical behavior. For instance, CEOs are less likely to manipulate firm earnings reports to make themselves

---

An Ethical Choice

Sweatshops and Worker Safety

Industrialized countries have come a long way in terms of worker safety and compensation. The number of worker-related injuries has decreased substantially over generations, and many employees earn better wages than in the past. Unfortunately, the same cannot be said for all parts of the world.

To keep costs down, many Western companies and their managers turn to suppliers in developing nations, where people have little choice but to work for low pay and no benefits, in top-down management structures without participative management opportunities or unions to represent them. Unregulated and even unsafe working conditions are common, especially in the garment industry. However, three recent accidents in Bangladesh are raising questions about the ethics of tolerating and supporting such conditions. In November 2012, a fire at the Tazreen Fashion factory that made low-cost garments for

several U.S. stores, including Walmart, killed 112 workers. In April 2013, the collapse of Rana Plaza, home to a number of garment factories, killed more than 1,100. And in May 2013, a fire at the Tung Hai Sweater Company killed 8 workers. An investigation of the Rana Plaza incident revealed that the building had been constructed without permits, using substandard materials. Although workers reported seeing and hearing cracks in the structure of the building, they were ordered back to work.

In response, some companies such as PVH, owner of Tommy Hilfiger and Calvin Klein, as well as Tchibo, a German retailer, have signed the legally binding "IndustriALL" proposal, which requires overseas manufacturers to conduct building and fire-safety inspections regularly and to make their findings public. However, many other companies have not signed, and none of the 15 companies whose clothing

was manufactured at the Rana Plaza plant donated to the International Labour Organization fund for survivors.

With the rise of CSR initiatives, what is the responsibility of organizations toward the working conditions of their subcontractors, at home or abroad? Professor Cindi Fukami asks, "Should [companies] outsource the production of these items made under conditions that wouldn't be approved of in the United States, but...are perfectly legal in the situation where they are [produced]?" There is clearly not an easy solution.

Sources: B. Kennedy, "The Bangladesh Factory Collapse One Year Later," CBS, April 23, 2014, http://www.cbsnews.com/news/the-bangladesh-factory-collapse-one-year-later/; J. O'Donnell and C. Macleod, "Latest Bangladesh Fire Puts New Pressure on Retailers," *USA Today,* May 9, 2013, www.usatoday.com; and T. Hayden, "Tom Hayden: Sweatshops Attract Western Investors," *USA Today,* May 17, 2013, www.usatoday.com.

look good in the short run when they have an ownership share.[102] Of course, not all companies want ESOPs, and they won't work in all situations, but they can be an important part of an organization's motivational strategy.

Evaluation of Variable Pay   Do variable-pay programs increase motivation and productivity? Generally yes, but that doesn't mean everyone is equally motivated by them.[103] Many organizations have more than one variable pay element in operation, such as an ESOP and bonuses, so managers should evaluate the effectiveness of the overall plan in terms of the employee motivation gained from each element separately and from all elements together. Managers should monitor their employees' performance-reward expectancy, since a combination of elements that makes employees feel that their greater performance will yield them greater rewards will be the most motivating.[104]

Using Benefits to Motivate Employees

8-6   Show how flexible benefits turn benefits into motivators.

Now that we have discussed what and how to pay employees, let's discuss two other motivating factors organizations must decide: (1) what benefits and choices to offer (such as flexible benefits), and (2) how to construct employee recognition programs. Like pay, benefits are both a provision and a motivator. Whereas organizations of yesteryear issued a standard package to every employee, contemporary leaders understand that each employee values benefits differently. A flexible program turns the benefits package into a motivational tool.

Flexible Benefits: Developing a Benefits Package

Todd E. is married and has three young children; his wife is at home full-time. His Citigroup colleague Allison M. is married too, but her husband has a high-paying job with the federal government, and they have no children. Todd is concerned about having a good medical plan and enough life insurance to support his family in case it's needed. In contrast, Allison's husband already has her medical needs covered on his plan, and life insurance is a low priority. Allison is more interested in extra vacation time and long-term financial benefits such as a tax-deferred savings plan.

A standardized benefits package would be unlikely to meet the needs of Todd and Allison well. Citigroup can, however, cover both sets of needs with flexible benefits.

flexible benefits   A benefits plan that allows each employee to put together a benefits package individually tailored to his or her own needs and situation.

Consistent with expectancy theory's thesis that organizational rewards should be linked to each employee's goals, **flexible benefits** individualize rewards by allowing each employee to choose the compensation package that best satisfies his or her current needs and situation. Flexible benefits can accommodate differences in employee needs based on age, marital status, partner's benefit status, and number and age of dependents.

Benefits in general can be a motivator for a person to go to work, and for a person to choose one organization over another. But are flexible benefits more motivating than traditional plans? It's difficult to tell. Some organizations that have moved to flexible plans report increased employee retention, job satisfaction, and productivity. However, flexible benefits may not substitute for higher salaries when it comes to motivation.[105] Furthermore, as more organizations worldwide adopt flexible benefits, the individual motivation they produce will likely decrease (the plans will be seen as a standard work provision). The downsides of flexible benefit plans may be obvious: They may be more costly to administrate, and identifying the motivational impact of different provisions is challenging.

Given the intuitive motivational appeal of flexible benefits, it may be surprising that their usage is not yet global. In China, only a limited percentage of companies offer flexible plans,[106] as in other Asian countries.[107] Almost all major corporations in the United States offer them, and a recent survey of 211 Canadian organizations found that 60 percent offer flexible benefits, up from 41 percent in 2005.[108] A similar survey of firms in the United Kingdom found that nearly all major organizations were offering flexible benefits programs, with options ranging from supplemental medical insurance to holiday trading (with coworkers), discounted bus travel, and child care assistance.[109]

Using Intrinsic Rewards to Motivate Employees

8-7 Identify the motivational benefits of intrinsic rewards.

We have discussed motivating employees through job design and by the extrinsic rewards of pay and benefits. On an organizational level, are those the only ways to motivate employees? Not at all! We would be remiss if we overlooked intrinsic rewards organizations can provide, such as employee recognition programs, discussed next.

Employee Recognition Programs

Laura makes $8.50 per hour working at her fast-food job in Pensacola, Florida, and the job isn't very challenging or interesting. Yet Laura talks enthusiastically about the job, her boss, and the company that employs her. "What I like is the fact that Guy [her supervisor] appreciates the effort I make. He compliments me regularly in front of the other people on my shift, and I've been chosen Employee of the Month twice in the past six months. Did you see my picture on that plaque on the wall?"

Organizations are increasingly realizing what Laura knows: Recognition programs and other ways of increasing an employee's intrinsic motivation work. An **employee recognition program** is a plan to encourage specific behaviors by formally appreciating specific employee contributions. Employee recognition programs range from a spontaneous and private thank-you to widely publicized formal programs in which the procedures for attaining recognition are clearly identified.

employee recognition program   A plan to encourage specific employee behaviors by formally appreciating specific employee contributions.

As companies and government organizations face tighter budgets, nonfinancial incentives become more attractive. Everett Clinic in Washington State uses a combination of local and centralized initiatives to encourage managers to recognize employees.[110] Employees and managers give "Hero Grams" and "Caught in the Act" cards to colleagues for exceptional accomplishments at work. Part of the incentive is simply to receive recognition, but there are also drawings for prizes based on the number of cards a person receives. Multinational corporations like Symantec Corporation, Intuit, and Panduit have also increased their use of recognition programs. Symantec claims it increased engagement 14 percent in less than a year due to the Applause recognition program administered by Globoforce, a corporation that implements employee recognition programs.[111] Centralized programs across multiple offices in different countries can help ensure that all employees, regardless of where they work, can be recognized for their contribution to the work environment.[112] Recognition programs are common in Canadian and Australian firms as well.[113]

A few years ago, 1,500 employees were surveyed in a variety of work settings to find out what they considered the most powerful workplace motivator. Their response? Recognition, recognition, and more recognition. Other research suggests financial incentives may be more motivating in the short term, but in the long run nonfinancial incentives work best.[114] Surprisingly, there is not a lot of research on the motivational outcomes or global usage of employee recognition programs. However, recent studies indicate that employee recognition programs are associated with self-esteem, self-efficacy, and job satisfaction,[115] and the broader outcomes from intrinsic motivation are well documented.

An obvious advantage of recognition programs is that they are inexpensive: praise is free![116] With or without financial rewards, they can be highly motivating to employees. Despite the increased popularity of such programs, though, critics argue they are highly susceptible to political manipulation by management. When applied to jobs for which performance factors are relatively objective, such as sales, recognition programs are likely to be perceived by employees as fair. In most jobs, however, performance criteria aren't self-evident, which allows managers to manipulate the system and recognize their favorites. Abuse can undermine the value of recognition programs and demoralize employees. Therefore, where formal recognition programs are used, care must be taken to ensure fairness. Where they are not, it is important to motivate employees by consistently recognizing their performance efforts.

✪ WATCH IT!

If your professor has assigned this, go to the Assignments section of **mymanagementlab.com** to complete the video exercise titled *Zappos: Motivating Employees Through Company Culture*.

Summary

As we've seen in the chapter, understanding what motivates individuals is ultimately key to organizational performance. Employees whose differences are recognized, who feel valued, and who have the opportunity to work in jobs tailored to their strengths and interests will be motivated to perform at the highest levels. Employee participation also can increase employee productivity, commitment to work goals, motivation, and job satisfaction. However, we cannot overlook the powerful role of organizational rewards in influencing motivation. Pay, benefits, and intrinsic rewards must be carefully and thoughtfully designed in order to enhance employee motivation toward positive organizational outcomes.

Implications for Managers

- Recognize individual differences. Spend the time necessary to understand what's important to each employee. Design jobs to align with individual needs and maximize their motivation potential.
- Use goals and feedback. You should give employees firm, specific goals, and they should get feedback on how well they are faring in pursuit of those goals.
- Allow employees to participate in decisions that affect them. Employees can contribute to setting work goals, choosing their own benefits packages, and solving productivity and quality problems.
- Link rewards to performance. Rewards should be contingent on performance, and employees must perceive the link between the two.
- Check the system for equity. Employees should perceive that individual effort and outcomes explain differences in pay and other rewards.

"Face-Time" Matters

POINT

Although allowing people to work from home is gaining popularity, telecommuting will only hurt firms and their employers. Sure, employees say they're happier when their organization allows them the flexibility to work wherever they choose, but who wouldn't like to hang around at home in their pajamas pretending to work? I know plenty of colleagues who say, with a wink, that they're taking off to "work from home" the rest of the day. Who knows whether they are really contributing?

The bigger problem is the lack of face-to-face interaction between employees. Studies have shown that great ideas are born through interdependence, not independence. It's during those informal interactions around the water cooler or during coffee breaks that some of the most creative ideas arise. If you take that away, you stifle the organization's creative potential.

Trust is another problem. Ever trust someone you haven't met? I didn't think so. Again, face-to-face interactions allow people to establish trusting relationships more quickly, which fosters smoother social interactions and allows the company to perform better.

But enough about employers. Employees also benefit when they are in the office. If you're out of sight, you're out of mind. Want that big raise or promotion? You're not going to get it if your supervisor doesn't even know who you are.

So think twice the next time you either want to leave the office early or not bother coming in at all, to "work from home."

COUNTERPOINT

Please. So-called face-time is overrated. If all managers do is reward employees who hang around the office the longest, they aren't being very good managers. Those who brag about the 80 hours they put in at the office (being sure to point out they were there on weekends) aren't necessarily the top performers. Being present is not the same thing as being efficient.

Besides, there are all sorts of benefits for employees and employers who take advantage of telecommuting practices. For one, it's seen as an attractive perk companies can offer. With so many dual-career earners, the flexibility to work from home on some days can go a long way toward achieving a better balance between work and family. That translates into better recruiting and better retention. In other words, you'll get and keep better employees if you offer the ability to work from home.

Plus, studies have shown that productivity is *higher*, not lower, when people work from home. This result is not limited to the United States. For example, one study found that Chinese call center employees who worked from home outproduced their "face-time" counterparts by 13 percent.

You say all these earth-shattering ideas would pour forth if people interacted. I say consider that one of the biggest workplace distractions is chatty coworkers. So, although I concede there are times when "face-time" is beneficial, the benefits of telecommuting far outweigh the drawbacks.

Sources: J. Surowiecki, "Face Time," *The New Yorker,* March 18, 2013, www.newyorker.com; and L. Taskin and F. Bridoux, "Telework: A Challenge to Knowledge Transfer in Organizations," *International Journal of Human Resource Management* 21, no. 13 (2010): 2503–20.

CHAPTER REVIEW

> ## MyManagementLab
> Go to **mymanagementlab.com** to complete the problems marked with this icon. ⭐

QUESTIONS FOR REVIEW

8-1 How does the job characteristics model motivate individuals?

8-2 What are the major ways that jobs can be redesigned?

8-3 What are the motivational benefits of the specific alternative work arrangements?

8-4 How can employee involvement measures motivate employees?

8-5 How can the different types of variable-pay programs increase employee motivation?

8-6 How can flexible benefits motivate employees?

8-7 What are the motivational benefits of intrinsic rewards?

EXPERIENTIAL EXERCISE Occupations and the Job Characteristics Model

Break the class into groups of three to five.

8-8. As a group, consider each of the five job characteristics (skill variety, task identity, task significance, autonomy, and feedback). Then, write down jobs that have high levels of each characteristic (if you can think of jobs that have high levels of multiple characteristics, note those as well). Do you think the jobs you identified are high or low paying? Why?

8-9. Next, write down jobs that have low levels of each characteristic (and if you can think of jobs that have low levels of multiple characteristics, note those as well.) Do you think the jobs you identified are high or low paying? Why?

8-10. For those jobs you identified as having low levels of job characteristics, come up with some strategies to increase them. Be specific in your recommendations. Discuss these with the class.

ETHICAL DILEMMA Inmates for Hire

We've all heard about how companies are using overseas workers to reduce labor costs, but the real cost savings for some jobs may lie with prison workers. Federal Prison Industries (FPI, also called UNICOR) is a company owned by the government that employs prison inmates. Like some overseas sweatshop workers, prisoners are paid exceptionally low rates of 23 cents to $1.15 an hour, receive no benefits for their work, and do not work in a participative management environment. The motivation for them to work hard is instead completely intrinsic: to learn trade skills and the value of work while they are incarcerated, in hopes that they will be more employable upon their release.

Although the organization is unable to supply workers to the private sector, federal agencies are required to purchase goods produced by its workers whenever FPI's bids are competitive. Steven Eisen, CFO of Tennier Industries, came face-to-face with FPI when his company lost a $45 million contract to manufacture clothing for the U.S. Defense Department. One hundred of Tennier's workers were laid off as a result. He argues it is wrong to give jobs to prison inmates at the expense of law-abiding citizens who may be struggling to find employment. "Our government screams, howls, and yells how the rest of the world is using prisoners or slave labor to manufacture items, and here we take the items right out of the mouths of people who need it," says Eisen.

Proponents of the program say it is beneficial to inmates, pointing to data from the Bureau of Prisons showing that inmates who work for FPI are 24 percent less likely to be incarcerated again and 14 percent more likely to be employed when released. Traci Billingsley, speaking for the Bureau of Prisons, states, "FPI supplies only a small fraction of the government's goods and services. FPI also helps support American jobs as it often partners with private American companies as a supplier."

Questions

8-11. Do you think it is fair for companies to have to compete against prison inmates for government work? Why or why not?

8-12. Michigan representative Bill Huizenga said, "If China did this—having their prisoners work at subpar wages in prisons—we would be screaming bloody murder." Do you agree or disagree with his statement? Why?

8-13. Do you think prisoner employees should have any benefits other workers have? Why or why not?

Sources: Based on D. Cardwell, "Competing with Prison Labor," *The New York Times,* March 15, 2012, 1, 4.

CASE INCIDENT 1   Motivation for Leisure

"When I have time I don't have money. When I have money I don't have time," says Glenn Kelman, Redfin CEO. He's not alone. While many workers find themselves faced with 60-, 70-, or 80-hour weeks (and sometimes more), others who are unemployed can find themselves with too much time on their hands. Take Dennis Lee, a sales associate working in Chicago whose girlfriend is unemployed. She has time to spare, but he says her unemployment makes it "financially impossible for me to support the both of us, even if we just go on a small trip, like, to Wisconsin and get a small hotel and stay for a couple of days."

Those who are employed and who may have the financial means to take a vacation often leave those vacation days on the table. The average U.S. worker gets 2.6 weeks of vacation a year, yet only 43 percent take that time. Although the reasons U.S. employees may not be motivated to take their vacation time vary from a sense of job insecurity to heavy employer workload demands, some companies now let employees trade vacation days for cash, essentially motivating them to sell the vacation hours they do not intend to use.

The challenge of taking leisure time does not seem to be a problem for many European countries. Take the French, who get 30 days of vacation and say they take all of them. In fact, if you work in the European Union and get sick on vacation, the European Court of Justice says you are entitled to take a make-up vacation.

Questions

8-14. What is the average number of vacation days per year in your country? Should companies allow their employees to trade vacation days for cash? Justify your answer

⭐ 8-15. Why do you think U.S. workers often do not take all their allotted vacation time, even if they may lose the benefit? Are these personal choices, or are they driven by society, or by organizational culture?

8-16. If many unemployed are spending around 2 hours/day looking for work as some research indicates, how would you evaluate the impact of unemployment on work motivation? How would you spend your days if unemployed?

Sources: P. Coy, "The Leisure Gap," *Bloomberg Businessweek* (July 23–29, 2012): 8–10; A. B. Krueger and A. I. Mueller, "Time Use, Emotional Well-Being, and Unemployment: Evidence from Longitudinal Data," *American Economic Review* (May 2012): 594–99; and L. Kwoh, "More Firms Offer Option to Swap Cash for Time," *The Wall Street Journal,* September 26, 2012, B6.

CASE INCIDENT 2   Pay Raises Every Day

How do you feel when you get a raise? Happy? Rewarded? Motivated to work harder for that next raise? The hope of an increase in pay, followed by a raise, can increase employee motivation. However, the effect may not last. In fact, the "warm fuzzies" from a raise last less than a month, according to a recent study. If raises are distributed annually, performance motivation can dip for many months in between evaluations.

Some organizations have tried to keep the motivation going by increasing the frequency of raises. Currently, only

about 5 percent of organizations give raises more than annually, but some larger employers like discount website retailer Zulily, Inc., assess pay quarterly. Zulily CEO Darrell Cavens would like to do so even more frequently. "If it wasn't a big burden, you'd almost want to work on it on a weekly basis," he said. That's because raises increase employee focus, happiness, engagement, and retention.

CEO Jeffrey Housenbold of online photo publisher Shutterfly, Inc., also advocates frequent pay assessments, but for a different reason. The company gives bonuses four times a year to supplement its biannual raise structure as part of a review of employee concerns. "You can resolve problems early versus letting them fester," he said. Another reason is to increase feedback. Phone app designer Solstice Mobile gives promotions and salary increases six times a year; with this structure, Kelly O'Reagan climbed from $10/hour to $47.50/hour in 4 years. The company's CEO, John Schwan, said that young workers are especially motivated by the near-constant feedback. O'Reagan said, "Seeing that increase was like, 'Wow, this is quite different than what I had ever dreamed of.'"

You might be wondering how organizations can keep the dollar increases to employees flowing. Organizations are wondering, too. One tactic is to start employees at a low pay rate. Ensilon, a marketing services company, has coupled low starting salaries with twice-yearly salary reviews. Initial job candidates are skeptical, but most of the new hires earn at least 20 percent more after 2 years than they would with a typical annual raise structure.

No one is saying frequent pay raises are cheap, or easy to administrate. Pay itself is a complex issue, and maintaining pay equity adds another level of difficulty. Frequent pay reviews are motivating, but only for the people receiving them—for the others, it's a struggle to stay engaged. If a person has a track record of raises and then pay levels off, it can feel like a loss of identity as a strong performer rather than a natural consequence of achieving a higher level of pay. The frustration can lead to lower performance and increased turnover for high performers. CEO Schwan acknowledged, "It's definitely a risk."

Questions

8-17. How can HR administer a complex pay structure that rewards pay increases on a regular basis?

8-18. Why are younger employees more likely to be motivated by very regular pay increases than older workers?

8-19. In some countries a national minimum wage or a "living wage" has been set by the government. What are the drawbacks of such an approach to dealing with low pay?

Sources: R. Feintzeig, "When the Annual Raise Isn't Enough," *The Wall Street Journal*, July 16, 2014, B1, B5; J. C. Marr and S. Thau, "Falling from Great (and Not-So-Great) Heights: How Initial Status Position Influences Performance after Status Loss," *Academy of Management Journal* 57, no. 1 (2014): 223–48; and "Pay Equity & Discrimination," IWPR, http://www.iwpr.org/initiatives/pay-equity-and-discrimination.

MyManagementLab

Go to **mymanagementlab.com** for the following Assisted-graded writing questions:

8-20. In regard to Case Incident 1, what cultural differences in collectivism/individualism might help predict motivation for the amount of vacation employees want to accrue and will take annually?

8-21. How would you design a bonus/reward program to avoid the problems mentioned in Case Incident 2?

8-22. MyManagementLab Only – comprehensive writing assignment for this chapter.

ENDNOTES

[1] C. B. Gibson, J. L. Gibbs, T. L. Stanko, P. Tesluk, and S. G. Cohen, "Including the 'I' in Virtuality and Modern Job Design: Extending the Job Characteristics Model to Include the Moderating Effect of Individual Experiences of Electronic Dependence and Copresence," *Organization Science* 22, no. 6 (2011): 1481–99.

[2] S. E. Humphrey, J. D. Nahrgang, and F. P. Morgeson, "Integrating Motivational, Social, and Contextual Work Design Features: A Meta-Analytic Summary and Theoretical Extension of the Work Design Literature," *Journal of Applied Psychology* 92, no. 5 (2007): 1332–56.

[3] B. M. Meglino and A. M. Korsgaard, "The Role of Other Orientation in Reactions to Job Characteristics," *Journal of Management* 33, no. 1 (2007): 57–83.

[4] J. L. Pierce, I. Jussila, and A. Cummings, "Psychological Ownership within the Job Design Context: Revision of the Job Characteristics Model," *Journal of Organizational Behavior* 30, no. 4 (2009): 477–96.

[5] C. B. Gibson, J. L. Gibbs, T. L. Stanko, P. Tesluk, and S. G. Cohen, "Including the 'I' in Virtuality and Modern Job Design: Extending the Job Characteristics Model to Include the Moderating Effect of Individual Experiences of Electronic Dependence and Copresence."

[6] B. M. Naba and L. Fan, "Employee Motivation and Satisfaction in Niger: An Application of the Job Characteristics Model." In A. de Hoyos, K. Kaminishi, and G. Duysters (eds.), *Proceedings of the 10th International Conference on Innovation and Management* (2013): 523–27.

[7]M. F. Peterson and S. A. Ruiz-Quintanilla, "Cultural Socialization as a Source of Intrinsic Work Motivation," *Group & Organization Management* 28, no. 2 (2003): 188–216.

[8]T. Silver, "Rotate Your Way to Higher Value," *Baseline* (March/April 2010): 12; and J. J. Salopek, "Coca-Cola Division Refreshes Its Talent with Diversity Push on Campus," *Workforce Management Online*, March 2011, www.workforce.com.

[9]Skytrax website review of Singapore Airlines, www.airlinequality.com/Airlines/SQ.htm, accessed May 31, 2013.

[10]S.-Y. Chen, W.-C. Wu, C.-S. Chang, and C.-T. Lin, "Job Rotation and Internal Marketing for Increased Job Satisfaction and Organisational Commitment in Hospital Nursing Staff," *Journal of Nursing Management* 23, no. 3 (2015): 297–306.

[11]A. Christini and D. Pozzoli, "Workplace Practices and Firm Performance in Manufacturing: A Comparative Study of Italy and Britain," *International Journal of Manpower* 31, no. 7 (2010): 818–42; and K. Kaymaz, "The Effects of Job Rotation Practices on Motivation: A Research on Managers in the Automotive Organizations," *Business and Economics Research Journal* 1, no. 3 (2010): 69–86.

[12]S.-H. Huang and Y.-C. Pan, "Ergonomic Job Rotation Strategy Based on an Automated RGB-D Anthropometric Measuring System," *Journal of Manufacturing Systems* 33, no. 4 (2014): 699–710; and P. C. Leider, J. S. Boschman, M. H. W. Frings-Dresen, et al., "Effects of Job Rotation on Musculoskeletal Complaints and Related Work Exposures: A Systematic Literature Review," *Ergonomics* 58, no. 1 (2015): 18–32.

[13]A. M. Grant, "Leading with Meaning: Beneficiary Contact, Prosocial Impact, and the Performance Effects of Transformational Leadership," *Academy of Management Journal* 55 (2012): 458–76; and A. M. Grant and S. K. Parker, "Redesigning Work Design Theories: The Rise of Relational and Proactive Perspectives," *Annals of the Academy of Management* 3, no. 1 (2009): 317–75.

[14]J. Devaro, "A Theoretical Analysis of Relational Job Design and Compensation," *Journal of Organizational Behavior* 31 (2010): 279–301.

[15]A. M. Grant, E. M. Campbell, G. Chen, K. Cottone, D. Lapedis, and K. Lee, "Impact and the Art of Motivation Maintenance: The Effects of Contact with Beneficiaries on Persistence Behavior," *Organizational Behavior and Human Decision Processes* 103, no. 1 (2007): 53–67.

[16]Y. N. Turner, I. Hadas-Halperin, and D. Raveh, "Patient Photos Spur Radiologist Empathy and Eye for Detail." Paper presented at the annual meeting of the Radiological Society of North America, November 2008.

[17]A. M. Grant, "The Significance of Task Significance: Job Performance Effects, Relational Mechanisms, and Boundary Conditions," *Journal of Applied Psychology* no. 93 (2008): 108–24.

[18]K. Pajo and L. Lee, "Corporate-Sponsored Volunteering: A Work Design Perspective," *Journal of Business Ethics* 99, no. 3 (2011): 467–82.

[19]K. Bal, "Does Flextime Penalize Night Owls?" *Human Resource Executive,* June 23, 2014, http://www.hreonline.com/HRE/view/story.jhtml?id=534357257.

[20]T. Kato, "Work and Family Practices in Japanese Firms: Their Scope, Nature, and Impact on Employee Turnover," *International Journal of Human Resource Management* 20, no. 2 (2009): 439–56; and P. Mourdoukoutas, "Why Do Women Fare Better in the German World of Work Than in the US?" *Forbes,* March 25, 2013, www.forbes.com/sites/panosmourdoukoutas/2013/03/25/why-do-women-fare-better-in-the-german-world-of-work-than-in-the-us/.

[21]R. Waring, "Sunday Dialogue: Flexible Work Hours," *The New York Times,* January 19, 2013, www.nytimes.com.

[22]S. Y. He, "Does Flextime Affect Choice of Departure Time for Morning Home-Based Commuting Trips? Evidence from Two Regions in California," *Transport Policy* 25 (2013): 210–21.

[23]S. Westcott, "Beyond Flextime: Trashing the Workweek," *Inc.* (August 2008): 30.

[24]B. Y. Lee and S. E. DeVoe, "Flextime and Profitability," *Industrial Relations* 51, no. 2 (2012): 298–316.

[25]See, for example, K. M. Shockley, and T. D. Allen, "When Flexibility Helps: Another Look at the Availability of Flexible Work Arrangements and Work–Family Conflict," *Journal of Vocational Behavior* 71, no. 3 (2007): 479–93; J. G. Grzywacz, D. S. Carlson, and S. Shulkin, "Schedule Flexibility and Stress: Linking Formal Flexible Arrangements and Perceived Flexibility to Employee Health," *Community, Work, and Family* 11, no. 2 (2008): 199–214; and L. A. McNall, A. D. Masuda, and J. M. Nicklin "Flexible Work Arrangements, Job Satisfaction, and Turnover Intentions: The Mediating Role of Work-to-Family Enrichment," *Journal of Psychology* 144, no. 1 (2010): 61–81.

[26]K. M. Shockley and T. D. Allen, "Investigating the Missing Link in Flexible Work Arrangement Utilization: An Individual Difference Perspective," *Journal of Vocational Behavior* 76, no. 1 (2010): 131–42.

[27]C. L. Munsch, C. L. Ridgeway, and J. C. Williams, "Pluralistic Ignorance and the Flexibility Bias: Understanding and Mitigating Flextime and Flexplace Bias at Work," *Work and Occupations* 41, no. 1 (2014): 40–62.

[28]D. Eldridge and T. M. Nisar, "Employee and Organizational Impacts of Flextime Work Arrangements," *Industrial Relations* 66, no. 2 (2011): 213–34.

[29]J. LaReau, "Ford's 2 Julies Share Devotion—and Job," *Automotive News* (October 25, 2010): 4.

[30]S. Adams, "Workers Have More Flextime, Less Real Flexibility, Study Shows," *Forbes,* May 2, 2014, http://www.forbes.com/sites/susanadams/2014/05/02/workers-have-more-flextime-less-real-flexibility-study-shows/.

[31]C. B. Mulligan, "What Job Sharing Brings," *Forbes,* May 8, 2013, http://economix.blogs.nytimes.com/2013/05/08/what-job-sharing-brings/; and "The Employer Mandate/Employer Penalty Delayed until 2015/2016," http://obamacarefacts.com/obamacare-employer-mandate/.

[32]L. Woellert, "U.S. Work Share Program Helps Employers Avoid Layoffs," *Bloomberg Businessweek,* January 24, 2013, www.businessweek.com/articles/2013-01-24/u-dot-s-dot-work-share-program-helps-employers-avoid-layoffs.

[33]P. R. Gregory, "Why Obama Cannot Match Germany's Jobs Miracle," *Forbes,* May 5, 2013, www.forbes.com/sites/paulroderickgregory/2013/05/05/why-obama-cannot-match-germanys-jobs-miracle/.

[34]See, for example, E. J. Hill, M. Ferris, and V. Martinson, "Does It Matter Where You Work? A Comparison of How Three Work Venues (Traditional Office, Virtual Office, and Home Office) Influence Aspects of Work and Personal/Family Life," *Journal of Vocational Behavior* 63, no. 2 (2003): 220–41; B. Williamson, "Managing Virtual Workers," *Bloomberg Businessweek,* July 16, 2009, www.businessweek.com; and B. A. Lautsch and E. E. Kossek, "Managing a Blended Workforce: Telecommuters and Non-Telecommuters," *Organizational Dynamics* 40, no. 1 (2010): 10–17.

[35]B. Belton, "Best Buy Copies Yahoo, Reins in Telecommuting," *USA Today,* March 6, 2013, www.usatoday.com.

[36]C. Tkaczyk, "Marissa Mayer Breaks Her Silence on Yahoo's Telecommuting Policy," *Fortune,* April 13, 2013, http://fortune.com/2013/04/19/marissa-mayer-breaks-her-silence-on-yahoos-telecommuting-policy/.

[37]D. Wilkie, "Has the Telecommuting Bubble Burst?" Society for Human Resource Management, June 1, 2015, http://www.shrm.org/publications/hrmagazine/editorialcontent/2015/0615/pages/0615-telecommuting.aspx.

[38]B. W. Reynolds, "100 Top Companies with Remote Jobs in 2015," *Flexjobs,* January 20, 2015, http://www.flexjobs.com/blog/post/100-top-companies-with-remote-jobs-in-2015.

[39]S. Florentine, "10 Most Telecommuting-Friendly Tech Companies," *CIO,* January 15, 2014, http://www.cio.com/article/2369810/telecommuting/136064-10-Most-Telecommuting-Friendly-Tech-Companies.html#slide11.

[40]See, for instance, M. Conlin, "The Easiest Commute of All," *BusinessWeek* (December 12, 2005): 78; S. Shellenbarger, "Telework Is on the Rise, but It Isn't Just Done from Home Anymore," *The Wall Street Journal,* January 23, 2001, B1; and E. O'Keefe, "Teleworking Grows but Still a Rarity," *The Washington Post,* February 22, 2011, B3.

[41]S. Raghuram and D. Fang, "Telecommuting and the Role of Supervisory Power in China," *Asia Pacific Journal of Management* 31, no. 2 (2014): 523–47.

[42]E. E. Kossek, B. A. Lautsch, and S. C. Eaton, "Telecommuting, Control, and Boundary Management: Correlates of Policy Use and Practice, Job Control, and Work-Family Effectiveness," *Journal of Vocational Behavior* 68, no. 2 (2006): 347–67.

[43]J. Kotkin, "Marissa Mayer's Misstep and the Unstoppable Rise of Telecommuting," *Forbes*, March 26, 2013.

[44]L. Taskin and F. Bridoux, "Telework: A Challenge to Knowledge Transfer in Organizations," *International Journal of Human Resource Management* 21, no. 13 (2010): 2503–20.

[45]S. M. B. Thatcher and J. Bagger, "Working in Pajamas: Telecommuting, Unfairness Sources, and Unfairness Perceptions," *Negotiation and Conflict Management Research* 4, no. 3 (2011): 248–76.

[46]E. G. Dutcher, "The Effects of Telecommuting on Productivity: An Experimental Examination. The Role of Dull and Creative Tasks," *Journal of Economic Behavior & Organization* 84, no. 1 (2014): 355–63.

[47]See, for example, P. Brotherton, "For Teleworkers, Less Is Definitely More," *T1D* 65 (March 2011): 29; and M. Virick, N. DaSilva, and K. Arrington, "Moderators of the Curvilinear Relation between Extent of Telecommuting and Job and Life Satisfaction: The Role of Performance Outcome Orientation and Worker Type," *Human Relations* 63, no. 1 (2010): 137–54.

[48]M. C. Noonan and J. L. Glass, "The Hard Truth about Telecommuting," *Monthly Labor Review* (2012): 1459–78.

[49]J. Welch and S. Welch, "The Importance of Being There," *BusinessWeek*, April 16, 2007, 92; Z. I. Barsness, K. A. Diekmann, and M. L. Seidel, "Motivation and Opportunity: The Role of Remote Work, Demographic Dissimilarity, and Social Network Centrality in Impression Management," *Academy of Management Journal* 48, no. 3 (2005): 401–19.

[50]P. Zhu and S. G. Mason, "The Impact of Telecommuting on Personal Vehicle Usage and Environmental Sustainability," *International Journal of Environmental Science and Technology* 11, no. 8 (2014): 2185–200.

[51]S. Raghuram and D. Fang, "Telecommuting and the Role of Supervisory Power in China."

[52]M. Marchington, "Analysing the Forces Shaping Employee Involvement and Participation (EIP) at Organisation Level in Liberal Market Economies (LMEs)," *Human Resource Management Journal* 25, no. 1 (2015): 1–18.

[53]See, for example, the literature on empowerment, such as D. P. Ashmos, D. Duchon, R. R. McDaniel Jr., and J. W. Huonker, "What a Mess! Participation as a Simple Managerial Rule to 'Complexify' Organizations," *Journal of Management Studies* 39, no. 2 (2002): 189–206; S. E. Seibert, S. R. Silver, and W. A. Randolph,

"Taking Empowerment to the Next Level: A Multiple-Level Model of Empowerment, Performance, and Satisfaction," *Academy of Management Journal* 47, no. 3 (2004): 332–49; M. M. Butts, R. J. Vandenberg, D. M. DeJoy, B. S. Schaffer, and M. G. Wilson, "Individual Reactions to High Involvement Work Processes: Investigating the Role of Empowerment and Perceived Organizational Support," *Journal of Occupational Health Psychology* 14, no. 2 (2009): 122–36; R. Park, E. Applebaum, and D. Kruse, "Employee Involvement and Group Incentives in Manufacturing Companies: A Multi-Level Analysis," *Human Resource Management Journal* 20, no. 3 (2010): 227–43; D. C. Jones, P. Kalmi, and A. Kauhanen, "How Does Employee Involvement Stack Up? The Effects of Human Resource Management Policies in a Retail Firm," *Industrial Relations* 49, no. 1 (2010): 1–21; and M. T. Maynard, L. L. Gilson, and J. E. Mathieu, "Empowerment—Fad or Fab? A Multilevel Review of the Past Two Decades of Research," *Journal of Management* 38, no. 4 (2012): 1231–81.

[54]See, for instance, A. Sagie and Z. Aycan, "A Cross-Cultural Analysis of Participative Decision-Making in Organizations," *Human Relations* 56, no. 4 (2003): 453–73; and J. Brockner, "Unpacking Country Effects: On the Need to Operationalize the Psychological Determinants of Cross-National Differences," in R. M. Kramer and B. M. Staw (eds.), *Research in Organizational Behavior*, vol. 25 (Oxford, UK: Elsevier, 2003), 336–40.

[55]C. Robert, T. M. Probst, J. J. Martocchio, R. Drasgow, and J. J. Lawler, "Empowerment and Continuous Improvement in the United States, Mexico, Poland, and India: Predicting Fit on the Basis of the Dimensions of Power Distance and Individualism," *Journal of Applied Psychology* 85, no. 5 (2000): 643–58.

[56]Z. X. Chen and S. Aryee, "Delegation and Employee Work Outcomes: An Examination of the Cultural Context of Mediating Processes in China," *Academy of Management Journal* 50, no. 1 (2007): 226–38.

[57]G. Huang, X. Niu, C. Lee, and S. J. Ashford, "Differentiating Cognitive and Affective Job Insecurity: Antecdents and Outcomes," *Journal of Organizational Behavior* 33, no. 6 (2012): 752–69.

[58]Z. Cheng, "The Effects of Employee Involvement and Participation on Subjective Wellbeing: Evidence from Urban China," *Social Indicators Research* 118, no. 2 (2014): 457–83.

[59]M. Marchington, "Analysing the Forces Shaping Employee Involvement and Participation (EIP) at Organisation Level in Liberal Market Economies (LMEs)."

[60]J. J. Caughron and M. D. Mumford, "Embedded Leadership: How Do a Leader's Superiors Impact Middle-Management Performance?" *Leadership Quarterly* (June 2012): 342–53.

[61]See, for instance, A. Pendleton and A. Robinson, "Employee Stock Ownership, Involvement, and Productivity: An Interaction-Based

Approach," *Industrial and Labor Relations Review* 64, no. 1 (2010): 3–29.

[62]D. K. Datta, J. P. Guthrie, and P. M. Wright, "Human Resource Management and Labor Productivity: Does Industry Matter? *Academy of Management Journal* 48, no. 1 (2005): 135–45; C. M. Riordan, R. J. Vandenberg, and H. A. Richardson, "Employee Involvement Climate and Organizational Effectiveness." *Human Resource Management* 44, no. 4 (2005): 471–88; and J. Kim, J. P. MacDuffie, and F. K. Pil, "Employee Voice and Organizational Performance: Team versus Representative Influence," *Human Relations* 63, no. 3 (2010): 371–94.

[63]M. Marchington, "Analysing the Forces Shaping Employee Involvement and Participation (EIP) at Organisation Level in Liberal Market Economies (LMEs)."

[64]E. White, "Opportunity Knocks, and It Pays a Lot Better," *The Wall Street Journal*, November 13, 2006, B3.

[65]D. A. McIntyre and S. Weigley, "8 companies That Most Owe Workers a Raise," *USA Today*, May 13, 2013, www.usatoday.com/story/money/business/2013/05/12/8-companies-that-most-owe-workers-a-raise/2144013/.

[66]M. Sabramony, N. Krause, J. Norton, and G. N. Burns "The Relationship between Human Resource Investments and Organizational Performance: A Firm-Level Examination of Equilibrium Theory," *Journal of Applied Psychology* 93, no. 4 (2008): 778–88.

[67]C. Isidore, "Walmart Ups Pay Well above Minimum Wage," CNN Money, February 19, 2015, http://money.cnn.com/2015/02/19/news/companies/walmart-wages/.

[68]See, for example, B. Martinez, "Teacher Bonuses Emerge in Newark," *The Wall Street Journal*, April 21, 2011, A15; K. Taylor, "Differing Results When Teacher Evaluations Are Tied to Test Scores," *The New York Times*, March 23, 2015, A16; and D. Weber, "Seminole Teachers to Get Bonuses Instead of Raises," *Orlando Sentinel*, January 19, 2011, www.orlandosentinel.com.

[69]See, for example, M. Damiani and A. Ricci, "Managers' Education and the Choice of Different Variable Pay Schemes: Evidence from Italian Firms," *European Management Journal* 32, no. 6 (2014): 891–902; and J. S. Heywood and U. Jirjahn, "Variable Pay, Industrial Relations and Foreign Ownership: Evidence from Germany," *British Journal of Industrial Relations* 52, no. 3 (2014): 521–52.

[70]S. Miller, "Variable Pay Spending Spikes to Record High," *Society for Human Resource Management*, September 2, 2014, http://www.shrm.org/hrdisciplines/compensation/articles/pages/variable-pay-high.aspx.

[71]S. Miller, "Companies Worldwide Rewarding Performance with Variable Pay," *Society for Human Resource Management*, March 1, 2010, www.shrm.org.

[72]S. Miller, "Asian Firms Offer More Variable Pay Than Western Firms," *Society for Human*

Resource Management, March 28, 2012, www .shrm.org.

[73]H. Kim, K. L. Sutton, and Y. Gong, "Group-Based Pay-for-Performance Plans and Firm Performance: The Moderating Role of Empowerment Practices," *Asia Pacific Journal of Management* (March 2013): 31–52.

[74]J. Cloutier, D. Morin, and S. Renaud, "How Does Variable Pay Relate to Pay Satisfaction among Canadian Workers?" *International Journal of Manpower* 34, no. 5 (2013): 465–85.

[75]E. Belogolovsky and P. A. Bamberger, "Signaling in Secret: Pay for Performance and the Incentive and Sorting Effects of Pay Secrecy," *Academy of Management Journal* 57, no. 6 (2014): 1706–33.

[76]Ibid.

[77]B. Wysocki Jr., "Chilling Reality Awaits Even the Employed," *The Wall Street Journal,* November 5, 2001, A1; and J. C. Kovac, "Sour Economy Presents Compensation Challenges," *Employee Benefit News,* July 1, 2008, 18.

[78]K. A. Bender, C. P. Green, and J. S. Heywood, "Piece Rates and Workplace Injury: Does Survey Evidence Support Adam Smith?" *Journal of Population Economics* 25, no. 2 (2012): 569–90.

[79]J. S. Heywood, X. Wei, and G. Ye, "Piece Rates for Professors," *Economics Letters* 113, no. 3 (2011): 285–87.

[80]A. Baker and V. Mertins, "Risk-Sorting and Preference for Team Piece Rates," *Journal of Economic Psychology* 34 (2013): 285–300.

[81]A. Clemens, "Pace of Work and Piece Rates," *Economics Letters* 115, no. 3 (2012): 477–79.

[82]K. A. Bender, C. P. Green, and J. S. Heywood, "Piece Rates and Workplace Injury: Does Survey Evidence Support Adam Smith?"

[83]S. L. Rynes, B. Gerhart, and L. Parks, "Personnel Psychology: Performance Evaluation and Pay for Performance," *Annual Review of Psychology* 56, no. 1 (2005): 571–600.

[84]K. Zernike, "Newark Teachers Approve a Contract with Merit Pay," *The New York Times,* November 14, 2012, www.nytimes.com/.

[85]"Paying Doctors for Performance," *The New York Times,* January 27, 2013, A16.

[86]S. Halzack, "Companies Look to Bonuses Instead of Salary Increases in an Uncertain Economy," *Washington Post,* November 6, 2012, http://articles.washingtonpost.com/.

[87]C. M. Barnes, J. Reb, and D. Ang, "More Than Just the Mean: Moving to a Dynamic View of Performance-Based Compensation," *Journal of Applied Psychology* 97, no. 3 (2012): 711–18.

[88]E. J. Castillo, "Gender, Race, and the New (Merit-Based) Employment Relationship," *Industrial Relations* 51, no. S1 (2012): 528–62.

[89]P. Furman, "Ouch! Top Honchos on Wall Street See Biggest Cuts to Bonuses," *New York Daily News,* February 18, 2013, www .nydailynews.com.

[90]N. Chun and S. Lee, "Bonus Compensation and Productivity: Evidence from Indian Manufacturing Plant-Level Data," *Journal of Productivity Analysis* 43, no. 1 (2015): 47–58.

[91]E. White, "Employers Increasingly Favor Bonuses to Raises," *The Wall Street Journal,* August 28, 2006, B3; and J. S. Lublin, "Boards Tie CEO Pay More Tightly to Performance," *The Wall Street Journal,* February 21, 2006, A1, A14.

[92]S. S. Wiltermuth and F. Gino, "'I'll Have One of Each': How Separating Rewards into (Meaningless) Categories Increases Motivation," *Journal of Personality and Social Psychology* (January 2013): 1–13.

[93]"Mark Zuckerberg Reaped $2.3 Billion on Facebook Stock Options," *Huffington Post,* April 26, 2013, www.huffingtonpost.com.

[94]D. D'Art and T. Turner, "Profit Sharing, Firm Performance, and Union Influence in Selected European Countries," *Personnel Review* 33, no. 3 (2004): 335–50; and D. Kruse, R. Freeman, and J. Blasi, *Shared Capitalism at Work: Employee Ownership, Profit and Gain Sharing, and Broad-Based Stock Options* (Chicago: University of Chicago Press, 2010).

[95]A. Bayo-Moriones and M. Larraza-Kintana, "Profit-Sharing Plans and Affective Commitment: Does the Context Matter?" *Human Resource Management* 48, no. 2 (2009): 207–26.

[96]N. Chi and T. Han, "Exploring the Linkages between Formal Ownership and Psychological Ownership for the Organization: The Mediating Role of Organizational Justice," *Journal of Occupational and Organizational Psychology* 81, no. 4 (2008): 691–711.

[97]J. H. Han, K. M. Barol, and S. Kim, "Tightening Up the Performance-Pay Linkage: Roles of Contingent Reward Leadership and Profit-Sharing in the Cross-Level Influence of Individual Pay-for-Performance," *Journal of Applied Psychology* 100, no. 2 (2015): 417–30.

[98]R. P. Garrett, "Does Employee Ownership Increase Innovation?" *New England Journal of Entrepreneurship* 13, no. 2, (2010): 37–46.

[99]D. McCarthy, E. Reeves, and T. Turner, "Can Employee Share-Ownership Improve Employee Attitudes and Behaviour?" *Employee Relations* 32, no. 4 (2010): 382–95.

[100]A. Pendleton, "Shared Capitalism at Work: Employee Ownership, Profit and Gain Sharing, and Broad-Based Stock Options," *Industrial & Labor Relations Review* 64, no. 3 (2011): 621–22.

[101]A. Pendleton and A. Robinson, "Employee Stock Ownership, Involvement, and Productivity: An Interaction-Based Approach," *Industrial and Labor Relations Review* 64, no. 1 (2010): 3–29.

[102]X. Zhang, K. M. Bartol, K. G. Smith, M. D. Pfarrer, and D. M. Khanin, "CEOs on the Edge: Earnings Manipulation and Stock-Based Incentive Misalignment," *Academy of Management Journal* 51, no. 2 (2008): 241–58.

[103]C. B. Cadsby, F. Song, and F. Tapon, "Sorting and Incentive Effects of Pay for Performance: An Experimental Investigation," *Academy of Management Journal* 50, no. 2 (2007): 387–405.

[104]J. H. Han, K. M. Barol, and S. Kim, "Tightening Up the Performance-Pay Linkage: Roles of Contingent Reward Leadership and Profit-Sharing in the Cross-Level Influence of Individual Pay-for-Performance."

[105]Z. Lin, J. Kellly, and L. Trenberth, "Antecedents and Consequences of the Introduction of Flexible Benefit Plans in China," *The International Journal of Human Resource Management* vol. 22, no. 5 (2011): 1128–45.

[106]Ibid.

[107]R. C. Koo, "Global Added Value of Flexible Benefits," *Benefits Quarterly* 27, no. 4 (2011): 17–20.

[108]P. Stephens, "Flex Plans Gain in Popularity," *CA Magazine,* January/February 2010, 10.

[109]D. Lovewell, "Flexible Benefits: Benefits on Offer," *Employee Benefits,* March 2010, S15.

[110]L. Shepherd, "Special Report on Rewards and Recognition: Getting Personal," *Workforce Management,* September 2010, 24–29.

[111]www.globoforce.come/our-clients, accessed June 4, 2015.

[112]L. Shepherd, "On Recognition, Multinationals Think Globally," *Workforce Management,* September 2010, 26.

[113]R. J. Long and J. L. Shields, "From Pay to Praise? Non-Case Employee Recognition in Canadian and Australian Firms," *International Journal of Human Resource Management* 21, no. 8 (2010): 1145–72.

[114]S. E. Markham, K. D. Scott, and G. H. McKee, "Recognizing Good Attendance: A Longitudinal, Quasi-Experimental Field Study," *Personnel Psychology* 55, no. 3 (2002): 641; and S. J. Peterson and F. Luthans, "The Impact of Financial and Nonfinancial Incentives on Business Unit Outcomes over Time," *Journal of Applied Psychology* 91, no. 1 (2006): 156–65.

[115]C. Xu and C. Liang, "The Mechanisms Underlying an Employee Recognition Program," in L. Hale and J. Zhang (eds.), *Proceedings of the International Conference on Public Human Resource Management and Innovation* (2013): 28–35.

[116]A. D. Stajkovic and F. Luthans, "Differential Effects of Incentive Motivators on Work Performance," *Academy of Management Journal* 4, no. 3 (2001): 587. See also F. Luthans and A. D. Stajkovic, "Provide Recognition for Performance Improvement," in E. A. Locke (ed.), *Handbook of Principles of Organizational Behavior* (Malden, MA: Blackwell, 2004), 166–80.

9 Foundations of Group Behavior

Source: Handout/Reuters

LEARNING OBJECTIVES

After studying this chapter, you should be able to:

9-1 Distinguish between the different types of groups.

9-2 Describe the punctuated-equilibrium model of group development.

9-3 Show how role requirements change in different situations.

9-4 Demonstrate how norms exert influence on an individual's behavior.

9-5 Show how status and size differences affect group performance.

9-6 Describe how issues of cohesiveness and diversity can be integrated for group effectiveness.

9-7 Contrast the strengths and weaknesses of group decision making.

MyManagementLab®
⭐ **Chapter Warm Up**

If your professor has chosen to assign this, go to the Assignments section of **mymanagementlab.com** to complete the chapter warm up.

CRUSHED BY THE HERD

Answer quickly: If you were an employee of this car's manufacturer and could have prevented the accident that killed two people and injured a third, would you?

No doubt you answered "yes" automatically, but if we took a few minutes to think about it, we might have to honestly answer "maybe." When we are members of groups as powerful as those in General Motors (GM), it can be very difficult to predict our behavior. Our perceptions of right and wrong can become skewed, making even straightforward ethical decisions like this one confusing.

Courtland Kelley of GM (which made the Chevrolet Cobalt in the photo) learned firsthand the pressures groups can exert on an individual. As the leader of GM's U.S. safety inspection program, he expected his workgroups to act upon the serious safety flaws he found in the vehicle. Instead, "Group after group and committee after committee within GM that reviewed the issue failed to take action or acted too slowly," a later report noted. Kelley's colleague, auditor William McAleer, agreed that management refused to acknowledge safety issues with vehicles. "Any time you had a problem, you ran into resistance," he said. "Nobody owns [the] defect. And the plant can say, 'It was working when it left here.' And the supplier can say, 'My part was good.' It relieves everybody of responsibility."

When Kelley pushed harder to have the Cobalt's faulty ignition switch addressed, management actively discouraged his efforts. The group ordered him to stay quiet about defects and rename them as mere convenience issues. At one point, his direct supervisor forbade him to share data on serious defects with McAleer and threatened to transfer him to a lesser position on the outskirts of town, while the management group tried to stifle the information. Kelley said, "I heard them have many discussions about not wanting to notify the government, not putting voice mails out to dealers, because the government could get them" and learn of the defects.

When Kelley couldn't be silenced, the group pressured him into toning down the wording in his reports and shuffled him into less responsible jobs. McAleer, who suffered similar circumstances until he was laid off in 2004, observed, "The system acts as if raising a safety issue internally were an act of corporate treason." Kelley landed off the organization chart in a "special assignment job," where he was told to "come up with charts, predict warranty for the vehicle, but not find every problem that GM might have." McAleer said of Kelley, "He still has a job—he doesn't have a career. He has no possibility of promotion." Kelley was not fired likely only because he brought lawsuits against GM.

On the positive side, Kelley's efforts have doubtlessly saved lives. After 13 deaths and 54 crashes, 2,084,000 Cobalts were recalled, as were almost 70,000 other vehicles with defects he found. From this standpoint, the battle he fought and his years in a "GM purgatory" job have been worth it. "I felt morally responsible to fix a problem that I found in a vehicle," he said of his work on the Chevy Trailblazer. However, his heroic efforts have cost him many court battles, and he has developed chest pains, panic attacks, depression, and insomnia. "I clearly saw him age drastically," his doctor, Van Alstine, said. "You just knew he was under a tremendous amount of stress. . . . It shook him to the core."

Sources: G. Gutierrez and R. Gardella, "'Willful Ignorance' Ex-Auditor Blasts GM for Cutting Safety Program," *NBC News,* July 9, 2014, http://www.nbcnews.com/storyline/gm-recall/willful-ignorance-ex-auditor-blasts-gm-cutting-safety-program-n152311; T. Higgins and N. Summers, "If Only They Had Listened," *Bloomberg Businessweek,* June 2014, 48–53; and S. McEachern, "General Motors 'Whistleblower' Was Told to Back Off after Finding Safety Flaws," *GM Authority,* June 19, 2014, http://gmauthority.com/blog/2014/06/general-motors-whistleblower-was-told-to-back-off-after-finding-safety-flaws/.

The story of Courtland Kelley's attempts to counter the effects of group pressure provides us with a powerful example of the ways groups can (mis)behave. Even though Kelley resisted for all the right ethical reasons, sometimes countering group pressure can mean costly consequences for the individual, as he found.

Groups have their place—and their pitfalls. Some groups can exert a powerful positive influence, and others can be tragically negative. The objectives of this chapter and Chapter 10 are to familiarize you with group and team concepts, provide you with a foundation for understanding how groups and teams work, and show you how to create effective working units. Let's begin by defining a *group*.

Defining and Classifying Groups

9-1

Distinguish between the different types of groups.

group Two or more individuals, interacting and interdependent, who have come together to achieve particular objectives.

formal group A designated workgroup defined by an organization's structure.

informal group A group that is neither formally structured nor organizationally determined; such a group appears in response to the need for social contact.

In organizational behavior, a **group** is two or more individuals, interacting and interdependent, who have come together to achieve particular objectives. Groups can be either formal or informal. A **formal group** is defined by the organization's structure, with designated work assignments and established tasks. In formal groups, the behaviors team members should engage in are stipulated by and directed toward organizational goals. The six members of an airline flight crew are a formal group, for example. In contrast, an **informal group** is neither formally structured nor organizationally determined. Informal groups in the work environment meet the need for social contact. Three employees from different departments who regularly have lunch or coffee together are an informal group. These types of interactions among individuals, though informal, deeply affect their behavior and performance.

Social Identity

social identity theory Perspective that considers when and why individuals consider themselves members of groups.

People often feel strongly about their groups partly because, as research indicates, shared experiences amplify our perception of events.[1] Also, according to research in Australia, sharing painful experiences, in particular, increases our felt bond and trust with others.[2] Why do people form groups, and why do they feel so strongly about them? Consider the celebrations that follow when a sports team wins a national championship. The winner's supporters are elated, and sales of team-related shirts, jackets, and hats skyrocket. Fans of the losing team feel dejected, even embarrassed. Why? Even though fans have little to do with the actual performance of the sports team, their self-image can be wrapped up in their identification with the group. Our tendency to personally invest in the accomplishments of a group is the territory of **social identity theory**.

Jeffrey Webster, director of human resources at a Nissan plant in Mississippi, also serves as the director of the plant's gospel choir. Choir members are a diverse group of employees who identify with each other as they all share a love of singing and performing for fellow workers, company executives, state officials, and community events.
Source: Rogelio V. Solis/AP Images

Social identity theory proposes that people have emotional reactions to the failure or success of their group because their self-esteem gets tied to whatever happens to the group.[3] When your group does well, you bask in reflected glory, and your own self-esteem rises. When your group does poorly, you might feel bad about yourself, or you might reject that part of your identity like "fair-weather fans." Furthermore, if your group is devalued and disrespected, your social identity might feel threatened, and you might endorse deviant behaviors to "get even" and restore your group's standing.[4] Social identities can even lead people to experience pleasure as a result of seeing another group suffer. We often see these feelings of *schadenfreude* in the joy fans experience when a hated team loses.[5]

People develop many identities through the course of their lives. You might define yourself in terms of the organization you work for, the city you live in, your profession, your religious background, your ethnicity, and/or your gender. Over time, some groups you belong to may become more significant to you than others. A U.S. expatriate working in Rome might be very aware of being from the United States, for instance, but doesn't give national identity a second thought when transferring from Tulsa to Tucson.[6] We may thus pick and choose which of our social identities are salient to the situation, or we may find that our social identities are in conflict, such as the identities of business leader and parent.[7]

Our social identities help us understand who we are and where we fit in with other people, and research indicates they bring us better health and lower levels of depression because we become less likely to attribute negative situations to internal or insurmountable reasons.[8] However, to experience these good outcomes, we need to feel our social identities are positive.[9]

Until now, we've discussed social identities primarily in a cultural context. However, the identity we may feel with respect to our organization is only one aspect of our work-related identities (see OB Poll). Within our organizations and workgroups, we can develop many identities through: (1) *relational* identification, when we connect with others because of our roles, and (2) *collective* identification, when we connect with the aggregate characteristics of our groups.

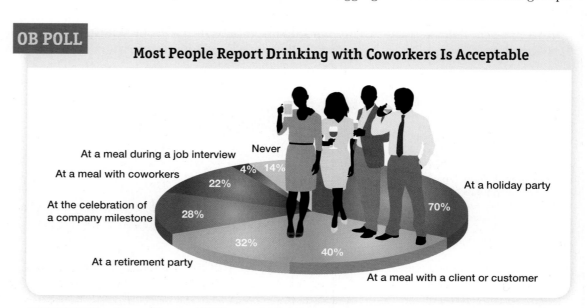

OB POLL

Most People Report Drinking with Coworkers Is Acceptable

At a meal during a job interview — 4%
Never — 14%
At a meal with coworkers — 22%
At the celebration of a company milestone — 28%
At a retirement party — 32%
At a meal with a client or customer — 40%
At a holiday party — 70%

Note: Society for Human Resources Management (SHRM) survey of 501 individuals and how drinking is viewed in their organization at a range of work-related activities.

Source: Based on S. M. Heathfield, "To Drink or Not to Drink: Does Alcohol Drinking Mix Safely with Work Events?" *About.com Guide,* 2013, http://humanresources.about.com/od/networking/qt/drink_i3.htm.

Often, our identification with our workgroups is stronger than with our organizations, but both are important to positive outcomes in attitudes and behaviors. Additionally, if we have low identification in relation to the group, there may be increased among by group members. If we have low identification with our organizations, we may experience decreased satisfaction and engage in fewer organizational citizenship behaviors (OCBs).[10]

Ingroups and Outgroups

ingroup favoritism Perspective in which we see members of our ingroup as better than other people, and people not in our group as all the same.

outgroup The inverse of an ingroup, which can mean everyone outside the group, but more usually an identified other group.

Ingroup favoritism occurs when we see members of our group as better than other people, and people not in our group as all the same. Recent research suggests that people with low openness and/or low agreeableness are more susceptible to ingroup favoritism.[11]

Whenever there is an ingroup, there is by necessity an **outgroup**, which is sometimes everyone else, but is usually an identified group known by the ingroup's members. For example, if my ingroup is the Republican party in U.S. politics, my outgroup might be anyone in the world who is not a Republican, but it's more likely to be the other U.S. political parties, or perhaps just Democrats.

When there are ingroups and outgroups, there is often animosity between them. One of the most powerful sources of ingroup–outgroup feelings is the practice of religion, even in the workplace. One global study, for instance, found that when groups became heavily steeped in religious rituals and discussions, they became especially discriminatory toward outgroups and aggressive if the outgroups had more resources.[12] Consider an example from another study of a U.K. Muslim organization that supported Al-Qaeda and identified moderate U.K. Muslims as its outgroup. The Al-Qaeda ingroup was not neutral toward the moderate outgroup; instead, the ingroup denounced the moderates, denigrating them as deviant and threatening outward aggression.[13]

Social Identity Threat

Ingroups and outgroups pave the way for *social identity threat*, which is akin to stereotype threat (see Chapter 6). With social identity threat, individuals believe they will be personally negatively evaluated due to their association with a devalued group, and they may lose confidence and performance effectiveness. One study found, for example, that when subjects from high and low socioeconomic backgrounds took a high-pressure math test, the low-status subjects who felt social identity threat could be as confident as the high-status subjects only when they were first deliberately encouraged about their abilities.[14]

Stages of Group Development

> ✪ **WATCH IT!**
> If your professor has assigned this, go to the Assignments section of **mymanagementlab.com** to complete the video exercise titled *Witness.org: Managing Groups & Teams*.

9-2 Describe the punctuated-equilibrium model of group development.

Temporary groups with finite deadlines pass through a unique sequencing of actions (or inaction): (1) Their first meeting sets the group's direction, (2) the first phase of group activity is one of inertia and thus slower progress, (3) a transition takes place exactly when the group has used up half its allotted time, (4) this transition initiates major changes, (5) a second phase of inertia follows the transition, and (6) the group's last meeting is characterized by markedly

Exhibit **9-1**   **The Punctuated-Equilibrium Model**

punctuated-equilibrium model A set of phases that temporary groups go through that involves transitions between inertia and activity.

accelerated activity.[15] This pattern, called the **punctuated-equilibrium model**, is shown in Exhibit 9-1.

Let's discuss each stage of the model. At the first meeting, the group's general purpose and direction is established, and then a framework of behavioral patterns and assumptions through which the group will approach its project emerges, sometimes in the first few seconds of the group's existence. Once set, the group's direction is solidified and is unlikely to be reexamined throughout the first half of its life. This is a period of inertia—the group tends to stand still or become locked into a fixed course of action even if it gains new insights that challenge initial patterns and assumptions.

One of the most interesting discoveries in studies was that groups experienced a transition precisely halfway between the first meeting and the official deadline—whether members spent an hour on their project or 6 months. The midpoint appears to work like an alarm clock, heightening members' awareness that their time is limited and they need to get moving. This transition ends phase 1 and is characterized by a concentrated burst of changes, dropping of old patterns, and adoption of new perspectives. The transition sets a revised direction for phase 2, a new equilibrium or period of inertia in which the group executes plans created during the transition period.

The group's last meeting is characterized by a final burst of activity to finish its work. In summary, the punctuated-equilibrium model characterizes groups as exhibiting long periods of inertia interspersed with brief revolutionary changes triggered primarily by members' awareness of time and deadlines. This is not the only model of group stages by far, but it is a dominant theory with strong support. Keep in mind, however, that this model doesn't apply to all groups but is suited to the finite quality of temporary task groups working under a time deadline.[16]

Group Property 1: Roles

9-3 Show how role requirements change in different situations.

Workgroups shape members' behavior, and they also help explain individual behavior as well as the performance of the group itself. Some defining group properties are *roles, norms, status, size, cohesiveness, and diversity*. We'll discuss each in the sections that follow. Let's begin with the first group property, roles.

Shakespeare said, "All the world's a stage, and all the men and women merely players." Using the same metaphor, all group members are actors, each playing

role   A set of expected behavior patterns attributed to someone occupying a given position in a social unit.

a **role**, a set of expected behavior patterns attributed to someone occupying a given position in a social unit. We are required to play a number of diverse roles, both on and off our jobs. As we'll see, one of the tasks in understanding behavior is grasping the role a person is currently playing.

Bill is a plant manager with EMM Industries, a large electrical equipment manufacturer in Phoenix. He fulfills a number of roles—employee, member of middle management, and electrical engineer. Off the job, Bill holds more roles: husband, father, Catholic, tennis player, member of the Thunderbird Country Club, and president of his homeowners' association. Many of these roles are compatible; some create conflicts. How does Bill's religious commitment influence his managerial decisions regarding layoffs, expense padding, and provision of accurate information to government agencies? A recent offer of promotion requires Bill to relocate, yet his family wants to stay in Phoenix. Can the role demands of his job be reconciled with the demands of his husband and father roles?

Different groups impose different role requirements on individuals. Like Bill, we all play a number of roles, and our behavior varies with each. But how do we know each role's requirements? We draw upon our role perceptions to frame our ideas of appropriate behaviors, and learn the expectations of our groups.

Role Perception

role perception   An individual's view of how he or she is supposed to act in a given situation.

Our view of how we're supposed to act in a given situation is a **role perception**. We get role perceptions from stimuli all around us—for example, friends, books, films, and television, as when we form an impression of politicians from *House of Cards*. Apprenticeship programs allow beginners to watch an expert so they can learn to act as they should.

Role Expectations

role expectations   How others believe a person should act in a given situation.

Role expectations are the way others believe you should act in a given context. A U.S. federal judge is viewed as having propriety and dignity, while a football coach is seen as aggressive, dynamic, and inspiring to the players.

psychological contract   An unwritten agreement that sets out what management expects from an employee and vice versa.

In the workplace, we look at role expectations through the perspective of the **psychological contract**: an unwritten agreement that exists between employees and employers. This agreement sets out mutual expectations.[17] Management

Les Hatton, manager of a Recreational Equipment, Inc., store in Manhattan, pumps up employees before the store's grand opening. Part of the psychological contract between REI and its employees is the expectation that salespeople will display enthusiasm and generate excitement while welcoming and serving customers.
Source: Matt Payton/AP Images

is expected to treat employees justly, provide acceptable working conditions, clearly communicate what is a fair day's work, and give feedback on how well an employee is doing. Employees are expected to demonstrate a good attitude, follow directions, and show loyalty to the organization.

What happens if management is derelict in its part of the bargain? We can expect negative effects on employee performance and satisfaction. One study among restaurant managers found that violations of the psychological contract were related to greater intentions to quit, while another study of a variety of different industries found psychological contracts were associated with lower levels of productivity, higher levels of theft, and greater work withdrawal.[18]

There is evidence that perceptions of psychological contracts vary across cultures. In France, where people are individualistic and power is more asymmetric, contracts are perceived as self-interested yet favoring the more powerful party. In Canada, where people are individualistic but power is more symmetric, contracts are perceived as self-interested yet focused on balanced reciprocity. In China, where people are collectivistic and power is more asymmetric, contracts are perceived as going beyond the work context into employees' lives. And in Norway, where people are collectivistic but power is more symmetric, contracts are perceived as more relational and based on trust.[19]

Role Conflict

role conflict   A situation in which an individual is confronted by divergent role expectations.

interrole conflict   A situation in which the expectations of an individual's different, separate groups are in opposition.

When compliance with one role requirement may make it difficult to comply with another, the result is **role conflict**.[20] At the extreme, two or more role expectations may be contradictory. For example, if as a manager you were to provide a performance evaluation of a person you mentored, your roles as evaluator and mentor may conflict. Similarly, we can experience **interrole conflict**[21] when the expectations of our different, separate groups are in opposition. An example can be found in work–family conflict, which Bill experiences when expectations placed on him as a husband and father differ from those placed on him as an executive with EMM Industries. Bill's wife and children want to remain in Phoenix, while EMM expects its employees to be responsive to the company's needs and requirements. Although it might be in Bill's financial and career interests to accept a relocation, the conflict centers on choosing between family and work role expectations. Indeed, a great deal of research demonstrates that work–family conflict is one of the most significant sources of stress for most employees.[22]

Within organizations, most employees are simultaneously in occupations, workgroups, divisions, and demographic groups, and these identities can conflict when the expectations of one clash with the expectations of another.[23] During mergers and acquisitions, employees can be torn between their identities as members of their original organization and of the new parent company.[24] Multinational organizations also have been shown to lead to dual identification—with the local division and with the international organization.[25]

Role Play and Assimilation

The degree to which we comply with our role perceptions and expectations—even when we don't agree with them initially—can be surprising. One of the most illuminating role and identity experiments was done a number of years ago by psychologist Philip Zimbardo and his associates.[26] They created a "prison" in the basement of the Stanford psychology building; hired emotionally stable, physically healthy, law-abiding students who scored "normal average" on personality tests; randomly assigned them the role of either "guard" or "prisoner"; and established some basic rules.

It took little time for the "prisoners" to accept the authority positions of the "guards" and for the mock guards to adjust to their new authority roles. Consistent with social identity theory, the guards came to see the prisoners as a negative outgroup, and they developed stereotypes about the "typical" prisoner personality type. After the guards crushed a rebellion attempt on the second day, the prisoners became increasingly passive. Whatever the guards "dished out," the prisoners took. The prisoners actually began to believe and act like they were inferior and powerless. Every guard, at some time during the simulation, engaged in abusive, authoritative behavior. One said, "I was surprised at myself. . . . I made them call each other names and clean the toilets out with their bare hands. I practically considered the prisoners cattle, and I kept thinking: 'I have to watch out for them in case they try something.'" Surprisingly, during the entire experiment—even after days of abuse—not one prisoner said, "Stop this. I'm a student like you. This is just an experiment!" The researchers had to end the study after only 6 days because of the participants' pathological reactions.

What can we conclude from this study? Like the rest of us, the participants had learned stereotyped conceptions of guard and prisoner roles from the mass media and their own personal experiences in power and powerless relationships gained at home (parent–child), in school (teacher–student), and in other situations. This background allowed them easily and rapidly to assume roles and, with a vague notion of the social identity of their roles and no prior personality pathology or training for the parts they were playing, to execute extreme forms of behavior consistent with those roles.

Myth or Science?

Gossip and Exclusion Are Toxic for Groups

This is not necessarily true. But it's certainly counterintuitive, so let's explore the conditions.

What is gossip? Most of us might say gossip is talking about others, sharing rumors, and speculating about others' behaviors; gossip affects a person's reputation. We might also say gossip is malicious, but according to researchers, it can serve positive social functions, too. Prosocial gossip can expose behavior that exploits other people, which can lead to positive changes. For example, if Julie tells Chris that Alex is bullying Summer, then Chris has learned about Alex's poor behavior through gossiping. Chris might refuse to partner with Alex on a work project, which might limit Alex's opportunities with the organization, preventing him from bullying more people. Alternatively, as the gossip spreads, Alex might feel exposed for his behavior and conform to group expectations against bullying behavior. In fact,

according to research, Alex is likely to cooperate with the group in response to the gossip, and others hearing and spreading the gossip are likely also to cooperate by not acting on their impulses toward bad behavior.

What about excluding Alex? There are two types of exclusion in the workplace: leaving someone out of a group, and ostracizing an individual. Both lead to the same end—the person isn't part of the group—but while simply leaving someone out of a group might not send a message of exclusion, ostracism certainly does. Ostracism is more of a felt punishment than gossip since it is more direct. Research indicates that ostracized individuals cooperate to a greater degree when they are around the group to show a willingness to conform, hoping to be invited back into the group.

Can gossip and ostracism work together? Yes, according to a recent study. When subjects were given an

opportunity to gossip about the work of another subject, that subject cooperated more than before; when the opportunity to gossip was paired with the ability to ostracize, that subject cooperated to a much greater degree.

Thus, gossip and exclusion may provide groups with benefits, at least when the gossip is confined to truthful work-related discussion, when the opportunity still exists to rejoin the group with full standing, and when the group norms are positive.

───────

Sources: M. Cikara and J. J. Van Bavel, "The Neuroscience of Intergroup Relations: An Integrative Review," *Perspectives on Psychological Science* 9, no. 3 (2014): 245–74; M. Feinberg, R. Willer, and M. Schultz, "Gossip and Ostracism Promote Cooperation in Groups," *Psychological Science* 25, no. 3 (2014): 656–64; and I. H. Smith, K. Aquino, S. Koleva, and J. Graham, "The Moral Ties That Bind...Even to Out-Groups: The Interactive Effect of Moral Identity and the Binding Moral Foundations," *Psychological Science* (2014): 1554–62.

A follow-up reality television show was conducted by the BBC.[27] The BBC results were dramatically different from those of the Stanford experiment, partially because the show used a less intense simulated prison setting. The "guards" were far more careful in their behavior, limiting their aggressive treatment of "prisoners" and expressing concerns about how their actions might be perceived. In short, they did not fully take on their authority roles, possibly because they knew their behavior was being observed by millions of viewers. These results suggest that less intense situations evoke less extreme behavior, and abuse of roles can be limited when people are made conscious of their behavior.

Group Property 2: Norms

9-4 Demonstrate how norms exert influence on an individual's behavior.

norms Acceptable standards of behavior within a group that are shared by the group's members.

Did you ever notice that golfers don't speak while their partners are putting? Why not? The answer is norms.

All groups have established **norms**—acceptable standards of behavior shared by members that express what they ought and ought not to do under certain circumstances. It's not enough for group leaders to share their opinions—even if members adopt the leaders' views, the effect may last only 3 days![28] When agreed to by the group, norms influence behavior with a minimum of external controls. Different groups, communities, and societies have different norms, but they all have them.[29] Let's discuss the levels of influence norms can exert over us, starting with our emotions.

Norms and Emotions

Have you ever noticed how the emotions of one member of your family, especially strong emotions, can influence the emotions of the other members? A family can be a highly normative group. So can a task group whose members work together on a daily basis, because frequent communication can increase the power of norms. A recent study found that, in a task group, individuals' emotions influenced the group's emotions and vice versa. This may not be surprising, but researchers also found that norms dictated the *experience* of emotions for the individuals and for the groups—in other words, people grew to interpret their shared emotions in the same way.[30] As we discovered in Chapters 5 and 6, our emotions and moods can shape our perspective, so the normative effect of groups can powerfully influence group attitudes and outcomes.

Norms and Conformity

conformity The adjustment of one's behavior to align with the norms of the group.

As a member of a group, you desire acceptance by the group. Thus, you are susceptible to conforming to group norms. Considerable evidence suggests that groups can place strong pressures on individual members to change their attitudes and behaviors to match the group's standard.[31] The impact that group pressures for **conformity** can have on an individual member's judgment was demonstrated in studies by Solomon Asch and others.[32] Asch made up groups of seven or eight people who were asked to compare two cards. One card had one line, and the other had three lines of varying length, one of which was identical to the line on the one-line card, as Exhibit 9-2 shows. The difference in line length was obvious; in fact, under ordinary conditions, subjects were incorrect less than 1 percent of the time in announcing which of the three lines matched the single line.

The experiment began with sets of matching exercises. Everyone gave the right answers. On the third set, however, the first subject, who was part of the

Exhibit **9-2**   **Examples of Cards Used in Asch's Study**

research team, gave an obviously wrong answer—for example, saying "C" in Exhibit 9-2. The next subject, also on the research team, gave the same wrong answer, and so forth. Now the dilemma confronting the subject, who didn't know any of the subjects were on the research team, was this: publicly state a perception that differed from the announced position of the others, or give an incorrect answer that agreed with the others.

The results over many experiments showed 75 percent of subjects gave at least one answer that conformed—that they knew was wrong but was consistent with the replies of other group members—and the average conformer gave wrong answers 37 percent of the time. This suggests that we feel the pressure toward conformity with group norms. Other recent research with moral decision

An Ethical Choice

Using Peer Pressure as an Influence Tactic

We've all experienced peer pressure, and it can be hard to behave differently from your friends and coworkers. As more work in organizations is performed in groups and teams, the possibilities and pitfalls of such pressure have become an increasingly important ethical issue for managers.

Peer pressure can be a positive force in some ways. In groups where high effort and performance are the norms, peer pressure from coworkers, whether direct or indirect, can encourage high performance from those not meeting expectations. A group with a norm toward behaving ethically could also use peer pressure to minimize negative behavior. Thus, peer pressure can promote all sorts of good behaviors, from donating to charity to volunteering at the local soup kitchen.

However, peer pressure can also be destructive. It can create a feeling of exclusion in those who do not go along with group norms and can be very stressful and hurtful for those who don't see eye-to-eye with the rest of the group. Peer pressure itself can be an unethical practice that unduly influences workers' behavior and thoughts. And while groups might pressure others into good behavior, they can just as easily sway them to bad behavior.

Should you use group peer pressure? As a leader, you may need to. One survey found that only 6 percent of leaders reported being able to successfully influence their employees on their own. Peer pressure hastens a group toward consensus, and levels of peer pressure predict how much the leader can control the group. If you use peer pressure to encourage

individuals to work toward team goals and behave consistently with organizational values, it can enhance ethical performance. But your behavior should emphasize acceptance and rewarding of positive behavior, rather than rejection and exclusion, as a means of getting everyone to behave consistently in the group.

Sources: E. Estrada and E. Vargas-Estrada, "How Peer Pressure Shapes Consensus, Leadership, and Innovations in Social Groups," *Scientific Reports* 3 (2013), article number 2905; A. Verghese, "The Healing Power of Peer Pressure," *Newsweek,* March 14, 2011, www.newsweek.com; J. Meer, "Brother, Can You Spare a Dime? Peer Pressure in Charitable Solicitation," *Journal of Public Economics* 95, no. 7–8 (2011): 926–41; and L. Potter, "Lack Influence at Work? Why Most Leaders Struggle to Lead Positive Change," *Yahoo,* May 14, 2013, http://finance.yahoo.com/news/lack-influence-why-most-leaders-121500672.html.

making indicated an even stronger effect of conformity when subjects found the nonconforming ideas not just incorrect but objectionable.[33] Does that mean we are mere robots? Certainly not. The flip side of the 37 percent of conforming responses is the 63 percent of independent responses, and 95 percent gave the correct (nonconforming) response at least once. Therefore, we feel the pressure to conform, but it is not a perfect predictor of what we will do. Furthermore, we don't tend to like the pressure. Asch wrote, "Those who participated in this challenging experiment agreed nearly without exception that independence was preferable to conformity."[34]

Do individuals conform to the pressures of all groups to which they belong? Obviously not, because people belong to many groups, and their norms vary and sometimes are contradictory. People conform to their **reference groups**, in which a person is aware of other members, defines himself or herself as a member or would like to be a member, and feels group members are significant to him or her. The implication, then, is that all groups do not impose equal conformity pressures on their members.

reference groups Important groups to which individuals belong or hope to belong and with whose norms individuals are likely to conform.

Norms and Behavior

Norms can cover any aspect of group behavior.[35] As we've mentioned, norms in the workplace significantly influence employee behavior. This may seem intuitive, but full appreciation of the influence of norms on worker behavior did not occur until the Hawthorne Studies conducted between 1924 and 1932 at the Western Electric Company's Hawthorne Works in Chicago.[36]

In the studies, the researchers first examined the relationship between the physical environment and productivity. As they increased the light level for the experimental group of workers, output rose for that unit and the control group. But as they dropped the light level, productivity continued to increase. In fact, productivity in the experimental group decreased only when the light intensity

From studies of employees at the Western Electric Company's Hawthorne Works in Chicago, researchers gained valuable insights into how individual behavior is influenced by group norms. They also learned that money was less of a factor in determining worker output than were group standards, sentiments, and security.
Source: Hawthorne Museum of Morton College

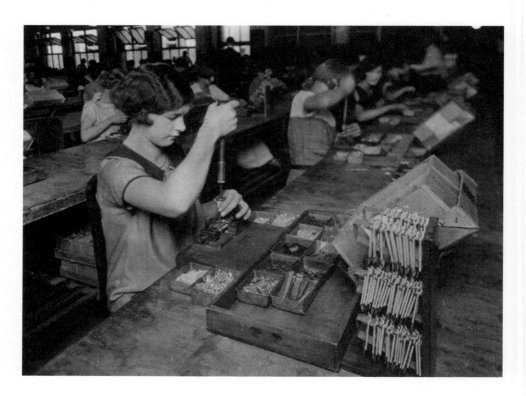

had been reduced to that of moonlight, leading researchers to believe that group dynamics, rather than the environment, influenced behavior.

The researchers next isolated a small group of women assembling telephones so their behavior could be more carefully observed. Over the next several years, this small group's output increased steadily, and the number of personal and sick absences was approximately one-third of that in the regular production department. It became evident this group's performance was significantly influenced by its "special" status. The members thought they were in an elite group, and that management showed concern about their interests by engaging in experimentation. In essence, workers in both the illumination and assembly experiments were really reacting to the increased attention they received.

A wage incentive plan was then introduced in the bank wiring observation room. The most important finding was that employees did not individually maximize their output. Rather, their role performance became controlled by a group norm. Members were afraid that if they significantly increased their output, the unit incentive rate might be cut, the expected daily output might be increased, layoffs might occur, or slower workers might be reprimanded. So the group established its idea of a fair output—neither too much nor too little. Members helped each other ensure their reports were nearly level, and the norms the group established included a number of behavioral "don'ts." *Don't* be a rate-buster, turning out too much work. *Don't* be a chiseler, turning out too little work. *Don't* squeal on any of your peers. The group enforced its norms with name-calling, ridicule, and even punches to the upper arms of violators. It thus operated well below its capability, using norms that were tightly established and strongly enforced.

Positive Norms and Group Outcomes

One goal of every organization with corporate social responsibility (CSR) initiatives is for its values to hold normative sway over employees. After all, if employees aligned their thinking with positive norms, these norms would become stronger and the probability of positive impact would grow exponentially. We might expect the same outcomes from political correctness (PC) norms. But what *is* the effect of strong positive norms on group outcomes? The popular thinking is that to increase creativity in groups, for instance, norms should be loosened. However, research on gender-diverse groups indicates that strong PC norms increase group creativity. Why? Clear expectations about male-female interactions reduce uncertainty about group expectations,[37] which allows the members to more easily express their creative ideas without combatting stereotype norms.

Positive group norms may well beget positive outcomes, but only if other factors are present, too. For instance, in a recent study a high level of group extraversion predicted helping behaviors more strongly when there were positive cooperation norms.[38] As powerful as norms can be, though, not everyone is equally susceptible to positive group norms. Individual personalities factor in, too, as well as the level of a person's social identity with the group. Also, a recent study in Germany indicated that the more satisfied people were with their groups, the more closely they followed group norms.[39]

Negative Norms and Group Outcomes

LeBron is frustrated by a coworker who constantly spreads malicious and unsubstantiated rumors about him. Lindsay is tired of a member of her workgroup who, when confronted with a problem, takes out his frustration by yelling and screaming at her and other members. And Mi-Cha recently quit her job as a dental hygienist after being sexually harassed by her employer.

deviant workplace behavior Voluntary behavior that violates significant organizational norms and, in so doing, threatens the well-being of the organization or its members. Also called antisocial behavior or workplace incivility.

What do these illustrations have in common? They represent employees exposed to acts of deviant workplace behavior.[40] As we discussed in Chapter 3, counterproductive work behavior (CWB) or **deviant workplace behavior** (also called *antisocial behavior* or *workplace incivility*) is voluntary behavior that violates significant organizational norms and, in so doing, threatens the well-being of the organization or its members. Exhibit 9-3 provides a typology of deviant workplace behaviors, with examples of each.

Few organizations will admit to creating or condoning conditions that encourage and maintain deviant behaviors. Yet they exist. For one, as we discussed before, a workgroup can become characterized by positive or negative attributes. When those attributes are negative, such as when a workgroup is high in psychopathy and aggression, the characteristics of deceit, amorality, and intent to harm others are pronounced.[41] Second, employees have been reporting an increase in rudeness and disregard toward others by bosses and coworkers in recent years. Workplace incivility, like many other deviant behaviors, has many negative outcomes for the victims.[42] Nearly half of employees who have suffered this incivility say it has led them to think about changing jobs; 12 percent actually quit because of it.[43] Also, a study of nearly 1,500 respondents found that in addition to increasing turnover intentions, incivility at work increased reports of psychological stress and physical illness.[44] Third, research suggests that a lack of sleep, which is often caused by heightened work demands and which hinders a person's ability to regulate emotions and behaviors, can lead to deviant behavior. As organizations have tried to do more with less, pushing their employees to work extra hours, they may indirectly be facilitating deviant behavior.[45]

Like norms in general, employees' antisocial actions are shaped by the group context within which they work. Evidence demonstrates deviant workplace behavior is likely to flourish where it's supported by group norms.[46] For example, workers who socialize either at or outside work with people who are frequently absent from work are more likely to be absent themselves.[47] Thus when deviant workplace norms surface, employee cooperation, commitment, and motivation are likely to suffer.

Exhibit 9-3   Typology of Deviant Workplace Behavior

Category	Examples
Production	Leaving early Intentionally working slowly Wasting resources
Property	Sabotage Lying about hours worked Stealing from the organization
Political	Showing favoritism Gossiping and spreading rumors Blaming coworkers
Personal aggression	Sexual harassment Verbal abuse Stealing from coworkers

Sources: S. H. Appelbaum, G. D. Iaconi, and A. Matousek, "Positive and Negative Deviant Workplace Behaviors: Causes, Impacts, and Solutions," *Corporate Governance* 7, no. 5 (2007): 586–98; and R. W. Griffin, and A. O'Leary-Kelly, *The Dark Side of Organizational Behavior* (New York: Wiley, 2004).

What are the consequences of workplace deviance for groups? Some research suggests a chain reaction occurs in groups with high levels of dysfunctional behavior.[48] The process begins with negative behaviors like shirking, undermining coworkers, or being generally uncooperative. As a result of these behaviors, the group collectively starts to have negative moods. These negative moods then result in poor coordination of effort and lower levels of group performance.

Norms and Culture

Do people in collectivist cultures have different norms than people in individualist cultures? Of course they do. But did you know that our orientation may be changed, even after years of living in one society? In a recent experiment, an organizational role-playing exercise was given to a neutral group of subjects; the exercise stressed either collectivist or individualist norms. Subjects were then given a task of their personal choice or were assigned one by an ingroup or outgroup person. When the individualist-primed subjects were allowed personal choice of the task, or the collectivist-primed subjects were assigned the task by an ingroup person, they became more highly motivated.[49]

Group Property 3: Status, and Group Property 4: Size and Dynamics

9-5 Show how status and size differences affect group performance.

We've discussed how the roles we play and the norms we internalize tend to dictate our behavior in groups. However, those are not the only two factors that influence who we are in a group and how the group functions. Have you ever noticed how groups tend to stratify into higher- and lower-status members? Sometimes the status of members reflects their status outside the group setting, but not always. Also, status often varies between groups of different sizes. Let's examine how these factors affect a workgroup's efficacy.

Group Property 3: Status

status A socially defined position or rank given to groups or group members by others.

Status—a socially defined position or rank given to groups or group members by others—permeates every society. Even the smallest group will show differences in member status over time. Status is a significant motivator and has major behavioral consequences when individuals perceive a disparity between what they believe their status is and what others perceive it to be.

status characteristics theory
A theory that states that differences in status characteristics create status hierarchies within groups.

What Determines Status?   According to **status characteristics theory**, status tends to derive from one of three sources:[50]

1. **The power a person wields over others**. Because they likely control the group's resources, people who control group outcomes tend to be perceived as high status.
2. **A person's ability to contribute to a group's goals**. People whose contributions are critical to the group's success tend to have high status.
3. **An individual's personal characteristics**. Someone whose personal characteristics are positively valued by the group (good looks, intelligence, money, or a friendly personality) typically has higher status than someone with fewer valued attributes.

Status and Norms   Status has some interesting effects on the power of norms and pressures to conform. High-status individuals may be more likely to deviate from norms when they have low identification (social identity) with the

Aaron Rodgers has high status as the quarterback of the Green Bay Packers football team. His status derives from his ability to contribute to his team's success in winning games. Rodgers's teammates and coaches value his character, leadership skills, expertise in calling plays, and ability to accurately throw touchdown passes on the move.
Source: Matt Ludtke/AP Images

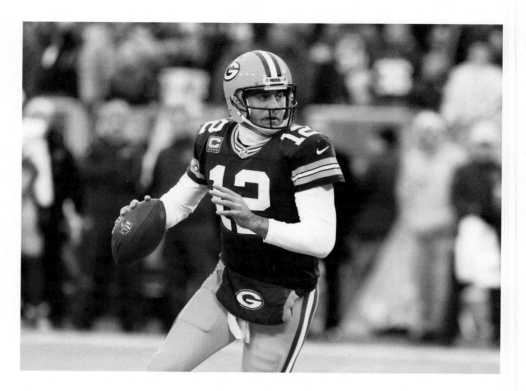

group.[51] They also eschew pressure from lower-ranking members of other groups. For instance, physicians actively resist administrative decisions made by lower-ranking medical insurance company employees.[52] High-status people are also better able to resist conformity pressures than their lower-status peers. An individual who is highly valued by a group but doesn't need or care about the group's social rewards is particularly able to disregard conformity norms.[53] In general, bringing high-status members into a group may improve performance, but only up to a point, perhaps because these members may introduce counter-productive norms.[54]

Status and Group Interaction   People tend to become more assertive when they seek to attain higher status in a group.[55] They speak out more often, criticize more, state more commands, and interrupt others more often. Lower-status members tend to participate less actively in group discussions; when they possess expertise and insights that could aid the group, failure to fully utilize these members reduces the group's overall performance. But that doesn't mean a group of only high-status individuals would be preferable. Adding *some* high-status individuals to a group of mid-status individuals may be advantageous because group performance suffers when too many high-status people are in the mix.[56]

Status Inequity   It is important for group members to believe the status hierarchy is equitable. Perceived inequity creates disequilibrium, which inspires various types of corrective behaviors. Hierarchical groups can lead to resentment among those at the lower end of the status continuum. Large differences in status within groups are also associated with poorer individual performance, lower health, and higher intentions for the lower-status members to leave the group.[57]

Groups generally agree within themselves on status criteria; hence, there is usually high concurrence on group rankings of individuals. Business executives may use personal income or the growth rate of their companies as determinants of status. Government bureaucrats may use the size of their budgets, and blue-collar workers may use their years of seniority. Managers who occupy central positions in their social networks are typically seen as higher in status by their subordinates, and this position actually translates into greater influence over the group's functioning.[58]

Groups generally form an informal status order based on ranking and command of needed resources.[59] Individuals can find themselves in conflicts when they move between groups whose status criteria are different, or when they join groups whose members have heterogeneous backgrounds. Cultures also differ in their criteria for conferring status upon individuals. When groups are heterogeneous, status differences may initiate conflict as the group attempts to reconcile the separate hierarchies. As we'll see in Chapter 10, this can be a problem when management creates teams of employees from varied functions.

Status and Stigmatization   Although it's clear that your own status affects the way people perceive you, the status of people with whom you are affiliated can also affect others' views of you. Studies have shown that people who are stigmatized can "infect" others with their stigma. This "stigma by association" effect can result in negative opinions and evaluations of the person affiliated with the stigmatized individual, even if the association is brief and purely coincidental. Of course, many of the foundations of cultural status differences have no merit in the first place. For example, men interviewing for a job were viewed as less qualified when they were sitting next to an obese woman in a waiting room. Another study looking at the effects of being associated with an overweight person found that even when onlookers were told the target person and the overweight person were unrelated, the target person was still devalued.[60]

Group Status   Early in life, we acquire an "us and them" mentality.[61] You may have correctly surmised that if you are in an outgroup, your group is of lower status in the eyes of the associated ingroup's members. Culturally, sometimes ingroups represent the dominant forces in a society and are given high status, which can create discrimination against their outgroups. Low-status groups, perhaps in response to this discrimination, are likely to leverage ingroup favoritism to compete for higher status.[62] When high-status groups then feel the discrimination from low-status groups, they may increase their bias against the outgroups.[63] With each cycle, the groups become more polarized.

Group Property 4: Size and Dynamics

Does the size of a group affect the group's overall behavior? Yes, but the effect depends on what dependent variables we examine. Groups with a dozen or more members are good for gaining diverse input. If the goal is fact-finding or idea-generating, then, larger groups should be more effective. Smaller groups of about seven members are better at doing something productive.

social loafing   The tendency for individuals to expend less effort when working collectively than when working individually.

One of the most important findings about the size of a group concerns **social loafing**, the tendency for individuals to expend less effort when working collectively than when alone.[64] Social loafing directly challenges the assumption that the productivity of the group as a whole should at least equal the sum of the productivity of the individuals in it, no matter what the group size.

What causes social loafing? It may be a belief that others in the group are not carrying their fair share. If you see others as lazy or inept, you can reestablish equity by reducing your effort. But simply failing to contribute may not be enough for someone to be labeled a "free rider." Instead, the group must believe the social loafer is acting in an exploitive manner (benefitting at the expense of other team members).[65] Another explanation for social loafing is the diffusion of responsibility. Because group results cannot be attributed to any single person, the relationship between an individual's input and the group's output is clouded. Individuals may then be tempted to become free riders and coast on the group's efforts.

The implications for OB are significant. When managers use collective work situations, they must also be able to identify individual efforts. Furthermore, greater performance diversity creates greater social loafing the longer a group is together, which decreases satisfaction and performance.[66]

Social loafing appears to have a Western bias. It's consistent with individualist cultures, such as the United States and Canada, that are dominated by self-interest. It is *not* consistent with collectivist societies, in which individuals are motivated by group goals. For example, in studies comparing U.S. employees with employees from China and Israel (both collectivist societies), the Chinese and Israelis showed no propensity to engage in social loafing and actually performed better in a group than alone.

Research indicates that the stronger an individual's work ethic is, the less likely that person is to engage in social loafing.[67] Also, the greater the level of conscientiousness and agreeableness in a group, the more likely that performance will remain high whether there is social loafing or not.[68] There are ways to prevent social loafing: (1) set group goals, so the group has a common purpose to strive toward; (2) increase intergroup competition, which focuses on the shared group outcome; (3) engage in peer evaluations; (4) select members who have high motivation and prefer to work in groups; and (5) base group rewards in part on each member's unique contributions.[69] Recent research indicates that social loafing can be counteracted by publicly posting individual performance ratings for group members, too.[70] Although no magic bullet will prevent social loafing, these steps should help minimize its effect.

Young employees of Alibaba's Tmall online shopping site celebrate their group's achievement of increasing the volume of sales orders during China's "Singles Day" shopping event. Although social loafing is consistent with individualistic cultures, in collectivist societies such as China, employees are motivated by group goals and perform better in groups than they do by working individually.
Source: Han Chuanhao Xinhua News Agency/Newscom

Group Property 5: Cohesiveness, and Group Property 6: Diversity

9-6 Describe how issues of cohesiveness and diversity can be integrated for group effectiveness.

For a group to be highly functioning, it must act cohesively as a unit, but not because all the group members think and act alike. In some ways, the properties of cohesiveness and diversity need to be valued way back at the tacit establishment of roles and norms—will the group be inclusive of all its members, regardless of differences in backgrounds? Let's discuss the importance of group cohesiveness first.

Group Property 5: Cohesiveness

cohesiveness The degree to which group members are attracted to each other and are motivated to stay in the group.

Groups differ in their **cohesiveness**—the degree to which members are attracted to each other and motivated to stay in the group. Some workgroups are cohesive because the members have spent a great deal of time together, the group's small size or purpose facilitates high interaction, or external threats have brought members close together.

Cohesiveness affects group productivity. Studies consistently show that the relationship between cohesiveness and productivity depends on the group's performance-related norms.[71] If norms for quality, output, and cooperation with outsiders are high, a cohesive group will be more productive than a less cohesive group. But if cohesiveness is high and performance norms are low, productivity will be low. If cohesiveness is low and performance norms are high, productivity increases, but less than in the high-cohesiveness/high-norms situation. When cohesiveness and performance-related norms are both low, productivity tends to fall into the low-to-moderate range. These conclusions are summarized in Exhibit 9-4.

What can you do to encourage group cohesiveness? (1) Make the group smaller, (2) encourage agreement with group goals, (3) increase the time members spend together, (4) increase the group's status and the perceived difficulty of attaining membership, (5) stimulate competition with other groups, (6) give rewards to the group rather than to individual members, and (7) physically isolate the group.[72]

Group Property 6: Diversity

diversity The extent to which members of a group are similar to, or different from, one another.

The final property of groups we consider is **diversity** in the group's membership, or the degree to which members of the group are similar to, or different from, one another. Overall, studies identify both costs and benefits from group diversity.

Exhibit 9-4   **Relationship Between Group Cohesiveness, Performance Norms, and Productivity**

		Cohesiveness	
		High	Low
Performance Norms	High	High productivity	Moderate productivity
	Low	Low productivity	Moderate to low productivity

Diversity appears to increase group conflict, especially in the early stages of a group's tenure; this often lowers group morale and raises dropout rates. One study compared groups that were culturally diverse and homogeneous (composed of people from the same country). On a wilderness survival test, the groups performed equally well, but the members from the diverse groups were less satisfied with their groups, were less cohesive, and had more conflict.[73] Another study examined the effect of differences in tenure on the performance of 67 engineering research and development groups.[74] When most people had roughly the same level of tenure, performance was high, but as tenure diversity increased, performance dropped off. There was an important qualifier: Higher levels of tenure diversity were not related to lower performance for groups when there were effective team-oriented human resources (HR) practices. More specifically, groups in which members' values or opinions differ tend to experience more conflict, but leaders who can get the group to focus on the task at hand and encourage group learning are able to reduce these conflicts and enhance discussion of group issues.[75] Gender diversity can also be a challenge to a group, but if inclusiveness is stressed, group conflict and dissatisfaction are lowered.[76]

You may have correctly surmised that the type of group diversity matters. Surface-level diversity—in observable characteristics such as national origin, race, and gender—alerts people to possible deep-level diversity—in underlying attitudes, values, and opinions. One researcher argues, "The mere presence of diversity you can see, such as a person's race or gender, actually cues a team that there's likely to be differences of opinion."[77] Surface-level diversity may subconsciously cue team members to be more open-minded in their views.[78] For example, two studies of MBA student groups found surface-level diversity led to greater openness. The effects of deep-level diversity are less understood. Research in Korea indicates that putting people with a high need for *power* with those with a low need for power can reduce unproductive group competition, whereas putting individuals with a similar need for *achievement* may increase task performance.[79]

Although differences can lead to conflict, they also provide an opportunity to solve problems in unique ways. One study of jury behavior found diverse juries were more likely to deliberate longer, share more information, and make fewer factual errors when discussing evidence. Altogether, the impact of diversity on groups is mixed. It is difficult to be in a diverse group in the short term. However, if members can weather their differences, over time diversity may help them be more open-minded and creative and to do better. But even positive effects are unlikely to be especially strong. As one review stated, "The business case (in terms of demonstrable financial results) for diversity remains hard to support based on the extant research."[80] Yet, other researchers argue that we shouldn't overlook the effects of homogeneity, many of which can be detrimental.[81]

⭐ PERSONAL INVENTORY ASSESSMENTS

Communicating Supportively

Are you a supportive person? Take this PIA to find out if you communicate supportively.

faultlines The perceived divisions that split groups into two or more subgroups based on individual differences such as sex, race, age, work experience, and education.

One possible side effect in diverse teams—especially those that are diverse in terms of surface-level characteristics—is **faultlines**, or perceived divisions that split groups into two or more subgroups based on individual differences such as sex, race, age, work experience, and education.

For example, let's say group A is composed of three men and three women. The three men have approximately the same amount of work experience and backgrounds in marketing. The three women have about the same amount of work experience and backgrounds in finance. Group B has three men and three women, but they all differ in terms of their experience and backgrounds. Two of the men are experienced, while the other is new. One of the women has worked at the company for several years, while the other two are new. In addition, two of the men and one woman in group B have backgrounds in marketing, while the other man and the remaining two women have backgrounds in finance. It is thus likely that a faultline will result in subgroups of males and females in group A but not in group B, based on the differentiating characteristics.

Research on faultlines has shown that splits are generally detrimental to group functioning and performance. Subgroups may compete with each other, which takes time away from core tasks and harms group performance. Groups that have subgroups learn more slowly, make more risky decisions, are less creative, and experience higher levels of conflict. Subgroups may not trust each other. Finally, satisfaction with subgroups is generally high, but the overall group's satisfaction is lower when faultlines are present.[82]

Are faultlines ever a good thing? One study suggested that faultlines based on differences in skill, knowledge, and expertise could be beneficial when the groups were in organizational cultures that strongly emphasized results. Why? A results-driven culture focuses people's attention on what's important to the company rather than on problems arising from subgroups.[83] Another study showed that problems stemming from strong faultlines based on gender and educational major were counteracted when their roles were cross-cut and the group as a whole was given a common goal to strive for. Together, these strategies force collaboration between members of subgroups and focus their efforts on accomplishing a goal that transcends the boundary imposed by the faultline.[84]

Overall, although research on faultlines suggests that diversity in groups is potentially a double-edged sword, recent work indicates they can be strategically employed to improve performance.

Group Decision Making

9-7 Contrast the strengths and weaknesses of group decision making.

The belief—characterized by juries—that two heads are better than one has long been accepted as a basic component of the U.S. legal system and those of many other countries. Many decisions in organizations are made by groups, teams, or committees. We'll discuss the advantages of group decision making, along with the unique challenges group dynamics bring to the decision-making process. Finally, we'll offer some techniques for maximizing the group decision-making opportunity.

Groups versus the Individual

Decision-making groups may be widely used in organizations, but are group decisions preferable to those made by an individual alone? The answer depends on a number of factors. Let's begin by looking at the strengths and weaknesses of group decision making.

Strengths of Group Decision Making   Groups generate *more complete information and knowledge*. By aggregating the resources of several individuals, groups bring more input as well as heterogeneity into the decision process. They offer *increased diversity of views*. This opens up the opportunity to consider more approaches and alternatives. Finally, groups lead to increased *acceptance of a solution*. Group members who participate in making a decision are more likely to enthusiastically support and encourage others to accept it later.

Weaknesses of Group Decision Making   Group decisions are time-consuming because groups typically take more time to reach a solution. There are *conformity pressures*. The desire by group members to be accepted and considered an asset to the group can squash any overt disagreement. Group discussion can be *dominated by one or a few members*. If they're low- and medium-ability members, the group's overall effectiveness will suffer. Finally, group decisions suffer from *ambiguous responsibility*. In an individual decision, it's clear who is accountable for the final outcome. In a group decision, the responsibility of any single member is diluted.

Effectiveness and Efficiency   Whether groups are more effective than individuals depends on how you define effectiveness. Group decisions are generally more *accurate* than the decisions of the average individual in a group, but less accurate than the judgments of the most accurate person.[85] In terms of *speed*, individuals are superior. If *creativity* is important, groups tend to be more effective. And if effectiveness means the degree of *acceptance* of achievable solutions, the nod again goes to the group.[86]

But we cannot consider effectiveness without also assessing efficiency. With few exceptions, group decision making consumes more work hours than having an individual tackle the same problem. The exceptions tend to be instances in which, to achieve comparable quantities of diverse input, the single decision maker must spend a great deal of time reviewing files and talking to other people. In deciding whether to use groups, then, managers must assess whether increases in effectiveness are more than enough to offset the reductions in efficiency.

In summary, groups are an excellent vehicle for performing many steps in the decision-making process and offer both breadth and depth of input for information gathering. If group members have diverse backgrounds, the alternatives generated should be more extensive and the analysis more critical. When the final solution is agreed on, there are more people in a group decision to support and implement it. These pluses, however, may be more than offset by the time consumed by group decisions, the internal conflicts they create, and the pressures they generate toward conformity. We must be careful to define the types of conflicts, however. Research in Korea indicates that group conflicts about tasks may increase group performance, while conflicts in relationships may decrease performance.[87] In some cases, therefore, we can expect individuals to make better decisions than groups.

Groupthink and Groupshift

Two by-products of group decision making, groupthink and groupshift, can affect a group's ability to appraise alternatives objectively and achieve high-quality solutions.

Groupthink relates to norms and describes situations in which group pressures for conformity deter the group from critically appraising unusual, minority, or unpopular views. Groupthink attacks many groups and can dramatically hinder their performance. **Groupshift** describes the way group members tend to exaggerate their initial positions when discussing a given set of alternatives to arrive at a solution. In some situations, caution dominates and there is a conservative shift, while in other situations groups tend toward a risky shift. Let's look at each phenomenon in detail.

groupthink   A phenomenon in which the norm for consensus overrides the realistic appraisal of alternative courses of action.

groupshift   A change between a group's decision and an individual decision that a member within the group would make; the shift can be toward either conservatism or greater risk but it generally is toward a more extreme version of the group's original position.

Can I fudge the numbers and not take the blame?

I've got a great workgroup, except for one thing: the others make me omit negative information about our group's success that I'm in charge of as the treasurer. They gang up on me, insult me, and threaten me, so in the end I report what they want. They say omitting the negative information is not really wrong, and it doesn't violate our organization's rules, but on my own I would report everything. I need to stay in the group or I'll lose my job. If we are called out on the numbers, can I just put the blame on the whole group?

— *Jean-Claude*

Dear Jean-Claude:

The short answer is that, since you are in a leadership role in the group, you may not have the option of blaming the others. Further, you may be held individually accountable as a leader for the outcomes of this situation.

Your dilemma is not unusual. Once we think of ourselves as part of a collective, we want to stay in the group and can become vulnerable to pressures to conform. The pressure you're getting from multiple members can make you aware that you're in the minority in the group, and taunting can make you feel like an outsider or lesser member; therefore threats to harm your group standing may feel powerful.

So you have a choice: Submit to the pressure and continue misrepresenting your group's success, or adhere to the responsibility you have as the treasurer and come clean. From an ethical standpoint, we hope you don't consider the first option an acceptable choice. To make a change, you may be able to use social identification to your advantage. Rather than challenging the group as a whole, try meeting with individual group members to build trust, talking to each as fellow members of a worthy group that can succeed without any ethical quandaries. Don't try to build a coalition; instead, build trust with individuals and change the climate of the group to value ethical behavior. Then the next time you need to report the numbers, you can call upon the group's increased ethical awareness to gain support for your leadership decisions.

Sources: M. Cikara and J. J. Van Bavel, "The Neuroscience of Intergroup Relations: An Integrative Review," *Perspectives on Psychological Science* 9, no. 3 (2014): 245–74; M. A. Korsgaard, H. H. Brower, and S. W. Lester, "It Isn't Always Mutual: A Critical Review of Dyadic Trust," *Journal of Management* 41, no. 1 (2015): 47–70; R. L. Priem and P. C. Nystrom, "Exploring the Dynamics of Workgroup Fracture: Common Ground, Trust-With-Trepidation, and Warranted Distrust," *Journal of Management* 40, no. 3 (2014): 674–795.

Groupthink   Groupthink appears closely aligned with the conclusions Solomon Asch drew in his experiments with a lone dissenter. Individuals who hold a position different from that of the dominant majority are under pressure to suppress, withhold, or modify their true feelings and beliefs. As members of a group, we find it more pleasant to be in agreement—to be a positive part of the group—than to be a disruptive force, even if disruption would improve effectiveness. Groups that are more focused on performance than learning are especially likely to fall victim to groupthink and to suppress the opinions of those who do not agree with the majority.[88]

Does groupthink attack all groups? No. It seems to occur most often when there is a clear group identity, when members hold a positive image of their group they want to protect, and when the group perceives a collective threat to its positive image.[89] One study showed that those influenced by groupthink were more confident about their course of action early on;[90] however, groups that believe too strongly in the correctness of their course of action are more likely to suppress dissent and encourage conformity than groups that are more skeptical about their course of action.

What can managers do to minimize groupthink?[91] First, they can monitor group size. People grow more intimidated and hesitant as group size increases, and although there is no magic number that will eliminate groupthink, individuals are likely to feel less personal responsibility when groups get larger than about 10 members. Managers should also encourage group leaders to play an impartial role. Leaders should actively seek input from all members and avoid expressing their own opinions, especially in the early stages of deliberation. In addition, managers should appoint one group member to play the role of devil's advocate, overtly challenging the majority position and offering divergent perspectives. Yet another suggestion is to use exercises that stimulate active discussion of diverse alternatives without threatening the group or intensifying identity protection. Have group members delay discussion of possible gains so they can first talk about the dangers or risks inherent in a decision. Requiring members to initially focus on the negatives of an alternative makes the group less likely to stifle dissenting views and more likely to gain an objective evaluation.

Groupshift or Group Polarization   There are differences between group decisions and the individual decisions of group members.[92] In groups, discussion leads members toward a more extreme view of the position they already held. Conservatives become more cautious, and more aggressive types take on more risk. We can view this group polarization as a special case of groupthink. The group's decision reflects the dominant decision-making norm—toward greater caution or more risk—that develops during discussion.

The shift toward polarization has several explanations.[93] It's been argued, for instance, that discussion makes the members more comfortable with each other and thus more willing to express extreme versions of their original positions. Another argument is that the group diffuses responsibility. Group decisions free any single member from accountability for the group's final choice, so a more extreme position can be taken. It's also likely that people take extreme positions because they want to demonstrate how different they are from the outgroup.[94] People on the fringes of political or social movements take on ever-more-extreme positions just to prove they are really committed to the cause, whereas those who are more cautious tend to take moderate positions to demonstrate how reasonable they are.

So how should you use the findings on groupshift? Recognize that group decisions exaggerate the initial position of individual members, that the shift has been shown more often to be toward greater risk, and that which way a group will shift is a function of the members' pre-discussion inclinations.

We now turn to the techniques by which groups make decisions. These reduce some of the dysfunctional aspects of group decision making.

Group Decision-Making Techniques

interacting groups   Typical groups in which members interact with each other face to face.

The most common form of group decision making takes place in **interacting groups**. Members meet face to face and rely on both verbal and nonverbal interaction to communicate. But as our discussion of groupthink demonstrated, interacting groups often censor themselves and pressure individual members toward conformity of opinion. Brainstorming and the nominal group technique can reduce problems inherent in the traditional interacting group.

brainstorming   An idea-generation process that specifically encourages any and all alternatives while withholding any criticism of those alternatives.

Brainstorming   **Brainstorming** can overcome the pressures for conformity that dampen creativity[95] by encouraging any and all alternatives while withholding criticism. In a typical brainstorming session, a half-dozen to a dozen people sit around a table. The group leader states the problem in a clear manner so all participants understand. Members then freewheel as many alternatives as they can in a given length of time. To encourage members to "think the unusual," no criticism is allowed, even of the most bizarre suggestions, and all ideas are recorded for later discussion and analysis.

| Exhibit 9-5 | Evaluating Group Effectiveness |

Effectiveness Criteria	Type of Group		
	Interacting	Brainstorming	Nominal
Number and quality of ideas	Low	Moderate	High
Social pressure	High	Low	Moderate
Money costs	Low	Low	Low
Speed	Moderate	Moderate	Moderate
Task orientation	Low	High	High
Potential for interpersonal conflict	High	Low	Moderate
Commitment to solution	High	Not applicable	Moderate
Development of group cohesiveness	High	High	Moderate

Brainstorming may indeed generate ideas—but not in a very efficient manner. Research consistently shows individuals working alone generate more ideas than a group in a brainstorming session. One reason for this is "production blocking." When people are generating ideas in a group, many are talking at once, which blocks individuals' thought process and eventually impedes the sharing of ideas.[96]

nominal group technique A group decision-making method in which individual members meet face to face to pool their judgments in a systematic but independent fashion.

Nominal Group Technique   The **nominal group technique** may be more effective. This technique restricts discussion and interpersonal communication during the decision-making process. Group members are all physically present, as in a traditional meeting, but they operate independently. Specifically, a problem is presented and then the group takes the following steps:

1. **Before any discussion takes place,** each member independently writes down ideas about the problem.
2. **After this silent period,** each member presents one idea to the group. No discussion takes place until all ideas have been presented and recorded.
3. **The group discusses the ideas** for clarity and evaluates them.
4. **Each group member silently and independently rank-orders** the ideas. The idea with the highest aggregate ranking determines the final decision.

The chief advantage of the nominal group technique is that it permits a group to meet formally but does not restrict independent thinking. Research generally shows nominal groups outperform brainstorming groups.[97]

Each of the group-decision techniques has its own set of strengths and weaknesses. The choice depends on the criteria you want to emphasize and the cost–benefit trade-off. As Exhibit 9-5 indicates, an interacting group is good for achieving commitment to a solution, brainstorming develops group cohesiveness, and the nominal group technique is an inexpensive means for generating a large number of ideas.

Summary

We can draw several implications from our discussion of groups. First, norms control behavior by establishing standards of right and wrong. Second, status inequities create frustration and can adversely influence productivity and willingness to remain with an organization. Third, the impact of size on a group's performance depends on the type of task. Fourth, cohesiveness may influence a group's level of productivity, depending on the group's performance-related norms. Fifth, diversity appears to have a mixed impact on group performance, with some studies suggesting that diversity can help performance and others suggesting the opposite. Sixth, role conflict is associated with job-induced tension and job dissatisfaction.[98] Groups can be carefully managed toward positive organizational outcomes and optimal decision-making. The next chapter will explore several of these conclusions in greater depth.

Implications for Managers

- Recognize that groups can dramatically affect individual behavior in organizations, to either positive or negative effect. Therefore, pay special attention to roles, norms, and cohesion—to understand how these are operating within a group is to understand how the group is likely to behave.
- To decrease the possibility of deviant workplace activities, ensure that group norms do not support antisocial behavior.
- Pay attention to the status aspect of groups. Because lower-status people tend to participate less in group discussions, groups with high status differences are likely to inhibit input from lower-status members and reduce their potential.
- Use larger groups for fact-finding activities and smaller groups for action-taking tasks. With larger groups, provide measures of individual performance.
- To increase employee satisfaction, make certain people perceive their job roles accurately.

People Are More Creative When They Work Alone

POINT

I know groups are all the rage. Businesses are knocking down walls and cubicles to create more open, "collaborative" environments. Students in universities are constantly working on group projects, and even young children are learning in small groups.

I also know *why* groups are all the rage. Work, they say, has become too complex for individuals to perform alone. Groups are better at brainstorming and coming up with creative solutions to complicated problems. Groups also produce higher levels of commitment and satisfaction—so long as group members develop feelings of cohesiveness and trust one another.

But for every group that comes up with a creative solution, I'll show you twice as many individuals who would come up with a better solution had they only been left alone. Consider creative geniuses like DaVinci, Newton, and Picasso. Or more recently, Steve Wozniak, the co-founder of Apple Computer. All were introverts who toiled by themselves. According to Wozniak, "I'm going to give you some advice that might be hard to take. That advice is: Work alone ... not on a committee. Not on a team."

But enough anecdotal evidence. Research has also shown that groups can kill creativity. One study found that computer programmers at companies that give them privacy and freedom from interruptions outperformed their counterparts at companies that forced more openness and collaboration. Or consider Adrian Furnham, an organizational psychologist whose research led him to conclude that "business people must be insane to use brainstorming groups." People slack off in groups, and they're afraid to communicate any ideas that might make them sound dumb. These problems don't exist when people work alone.

So heed Picasso's advice: "Without great solitude, no serious work is possible."

COUNTERPOINT

I'll grant you there are circumstances in which groups can hinder creative progress, but if the right conditions are put in place, groups are simply much better at coming up with novel solutions to problems than are individuals. Using strategies such as the nominal group technique, brainstorming, and ensuring that individuals do not evaluate others' ideas until all have been generated are just a few ways you can set up groups for creative success.

The fact of the matter is that problems *are* too complex these days for individuals to effectively perform alone. Consider the Rovers launched by NASA to roam around Mars collecting data. An accomplishment like that is made possible only by a group, not a lone individual. Steve Wozniak's collaboration with Steve Jobs is what really made Apple sail as a company. And could you assemble a car all by yourself?

In addition, the most influential research is conducted by groups of academics, rather than individuals. Indeed, if you look at recent Nobel Prize winners in areas such as economics, physics, and chemistry, the majority have been won by academics who collaborated on the research.

So if you want creativity (and who doesn't?), two heads are in fact better than one.

Sources: S. Cain, "The Rise of the New Groupthink," *The New York Times,* January 15, 2012, 1, 6; and C. Faure, "Beyond Brainstorming: Effects of Different Group Procedures on Selection of Ideas and Satisfaction with the Process," *Journal of Creative Behavior* 38 (2004): 13–34.

CHAPTER REVIEW

MyManagementLab

Go to **mymanagementlab.com** to complete the problems marked with this icon. ⭐

QUESTIONS FOR REVIEW

9-1 What are the different types of groups?

9-2 What are the key components of the punctuated-equilibrium model?

9-3 How do role requirements change in different situations?

9-4 How do group norms influence an individual's behavior?

9-5 How do status and size differences affect group performance?

9-6 How can cohesiveness and diversity support group effectiveness?

9-7 What are the strengths and weaknesses of group (versus individual) decision making?

EXPERIENTIAL EXERCISE   Surviving the Wild: Join a Group or Go It Alone?

You are a member of a hiking party. After reaching base camp on the first day, you decide to take a quick sunset hike by yourself. After a few exhilarating miles, you decide to return to camp. On your way back, you realize you are lost. You shout for help, to no avail. It is now dark. And getting cold.

Your Task

Without communicating with anyone else in your group, read the following scenarios and choose the best answer. Keep track of your answers on a sheet of paper. You have 10 minutes to answer the 10 questions.

9-8. The first thing you decide to do is to build a fire. However, you have no matches, so you use the bow-and-drill method. What is the bow-and-drill method?
   a. A dry, soft stick is rubbed between the hands against a board of supple green wood.
   b. A soft green stick is rubbed between the hands against a hardwood board.
   c. A straight stick of wood is quickly rubbed back and forth against a dead tree.
   d. Two sticks (one being the bow, the other the drill) are struck to create a spark.

9-9. It occurs to you that you can also use the fire as a distress signal. How do you form the international distress signal with fire?
   a. 2 fires
   b. 4 fires in a square

   c. 4 fires in a cross
   d. 3 fires in a line

9-10. You are very thirsty. You go to a nearby stream and collect some water in the small metal cup you have in your backpack. How long should you boil the water?
   a. 15 minutes
   b. A few seconds
   c. 1 minute
   d. It depends on the altitude.

9-11. You are very hungry, so you decide to eat what appear to be edible berries. When performing the universal edibility test, what should you do?
   a. Do not eat for 2 hours before the test.
   b. If the plant stings your lip, confirm the sting by holding it under your tongue for 15 minutes.
   c. If nothing bad has happened 2 hours after digestion, eat half a cup of the plant and wait again.
   d. Separate the plant into its basic components and eat each component, one at a time.

9-12. Next, you decide to build a shelter for the evening. In selecting a site, what do you *not* have to consider?
   a. It must contain material to make the type of shelter you need.
   b. It must be free of insects, reptiles, and poisonous plants.

c. It must be large enough and level enough for you to lie down comfortably.

d. It must be on a hill so you can signal rescuers and keep an eye on your surroundings.

9-13. In the shelter, you notice a spider. You heard from a fellow hiker that black widow spiders populate the area. How do you identify a black widow spider?

a. Its head and abdomen are black; its thorax is red.

b. It is attracted to light.

c. It runs away from light.

d. It is dark with a red or orange marking on the female's abdomen.

9-14. After getting some sleep, you notice that the night sky has cleared, so you decide to try to find your way back to base camp. You believe you can use the North Star for navigation. How do you locate the North Star?

a. Hold your right hand up as far as you can and look between your index and middle fingers.

b. Find Sirius and look 60 degrees above it and to the right.

c. Look for the Big Dipper and follow the line created by its cup end.

d. Follow the line of Orion's belt.

9-15. You come across a fast-moving stream. What is the best way to cross it?

a. Find a spot downstream from a sandbar, where the water will be calmer.

b. Build a bridge.

c. Find a rocky area, because the water will be shallow and you will have hand- and footholds.

d. Find a level stretch where it breaks into a few channels.

9-16. After walking for about an hour, you feel several spiders in your clothes. You don't feel any pain, but you know some spider bites are painless. Which of these spider bites is painless?

a. Black widow

b. Brown recluse

c. Wolf spider

d. Harvestman (daddy longlegs)

9-17. You decide to eat some insects. Which insects should you avoid?

a. Adults that sting or bite

b. Caterpillars and insects that have a pungent odor

c. Hairy or brightly colored ones

d. All the above

Group Task

Next, break into groups of five or six people. Once the group comes to an agreement for what to do in each situation, write your decision on the same sheet of paper you used for your individual answers.

Scoring Your Answers

Your instructor will provide you with the correct answers, which are based on expert judgments in these situations. Once you have received the answers, calculate (A) your individual score; (B) your group's score; (C) the average individual score in the group; and (D) the best individual score in the group. Write these down and consult with your group to ensure they are accurate.

A. Your individual score _____

B. Your group's score _____

C. Average individual score in group _____

D. Best individual score in group _____

Discussion Questions

9-18. How did your group (B) perform relative to yourself (A)?

9-19. How did your group (B) perform relative to the average individual score in the group (C)?

9-20. How did your group (B) perform relative to the best individual score in the group (D)?

9-21. Compare your results with those of other groups. Did some groups do a better job of outperforming individuals than others?

9-22. What do these results tell you about the effectiveness of group decision making?

9-23. What can groups do to make group decision making more effective?

9-24. What circumstances might cause a group to perform worse than its best individual?

ETHICAL DILEMMA   It's Obvious, They're Chinese.

The antithesis of social loafing was brought into sharp focus back in 2009 when Shanghai became the first Chinese region to enter the Programme for International Student Assessment (PISA). In its first entry year, Shanghai came top in mathematics, science, and reading by a considerable margin. PISA looks at the attainments of 15-year-

olds and by 2012 (the latest data set available), Shanghai had cemented their position as the top performing student groups.

This is an incredible achievement for a region of just 23.9 million people. Preconceived visions of Chinese students suggest they learn from rote, but in fact this is not the case. In terms of memorization, the Shanghai students performed less well than those from the United Kingdom. So what is it that sets the Shanghai students apart from most of the rest of the world?

A typical Chinese 15-year-old has eight 40-minute classes each day. Despite this heavy workload, the teacher-led sessions, according to observers, are performed with total pupil concentration even though classes can be up to 60 in strength. Age-old Chinese folktales recount the successes of those who show diligence and hard work. Concepts such as being gifted or talented have far less currency than simply working hard. For generations, Chinese students have worked hard to achieve good grades in their gaokao examinations. These are the key to university entrance.

The combination of hard work and high stake examinations mean that an average Chinese 15-year-old does 3 hours of homework every night. There is no time for social loafing; individual and cultural motivators drive the students forward.

Questions

9-25. Why does social loafing cause ethical dilemmas? What is it about social loafing that makes it difficult to cope with on a one-to-one basis if one your colleagues does it?

9-26. Social loafing is exposed in performance appraisals and other methods of assessing productivity and output. How should it be handled when it is exposed?

9-27. Most Chinese 15-year-olds spurn television, social media, and console gaming. On the other hand, many of the students do not excel in creative thinking or problem-solving. To what extent might this be an issue compared to other societies that might focus on these aspects?

Source: National Center for Education Statistics, Program for International Student Assessment, http://nces.ed.gov/surveys/pisa/index.asp, accessed January 23, 2014; "Shanghai Population 2015," WPR, http://worldpopulationreview.com/world-cities/shanghai-population/.

CASE INCIDENT 1 The Calamities of Consensus

When it is time for groups to reach a decision, many turn to consensus. Consensus, a situation of agreement, seems like a good idea. To achieve consensus, groups must cooperate and collaborate, which ultimately will produce higher levels of camaraderie and trust. In addition, if everyone agrees, the prevailing wisdom says everyone will be more committed to the decision.

However, the need for consensus can sometimes be detrimental to group functioning. Consider the "fiscal cliff" faced by the U.S. government toward the end of 2012. The White House and Congress needed to reach a deal that would reduce the swelling budget deficit. However, many Republicans and Democrats stuck to their party lines, refusing to compromise. Many viewed the end product that achieved consensus as a less-than-optimal solution. The public gave Congress an approval rating of only 13 percent, expressing frustration with the lack of compromise, but the group may not have been able to function well partly because of the need for consensus in the face of partisanship.

If consensus is reached, does that mean the decision is the right one? Critics of consensus-based methods argue that any decisions ultimately reached are inferior to decisions using other methods such as voting or having team members provide input to their leader, who then makes the final decision. Critics also argue that because of pressures to conform, groupthink is much more likely, and decisions reached through consensus are simply those everyone dislikes the least.

Questions

9-28. Is consensus a good way for groups to make decisions? Why or why not?

✪ **9-29.** Can you think of a time when a group of which you were a part relied on consensus? How do you think the decision turned out?

9-30. Martin Luther King Jr. once proclaimed, "A genuine leader is not a seeker of consensus but a modeler of consensus." What do you think he meant by that statement? Do you agree with it? Why or why not?

Sources: D. Leonhardt, "When the Crowd Isn't Wise," *The New York Times*, July 8, 2012, SR BW 4; and K. Jensen, "Consensus Is Poison! Who's with Me?" *Forbes*, May 20, 2013, downloaded on May 30, 2013, from www.forbes.com.

CASE INCIDENT 2   Intragroup Trust and Survival

When 10 British Army soldiers on a 10-day training exercise descended into Low's Gully, a narrow chasm that cuts through Mt. Kinabalu in Borneo, each knew "the golden rule for such expeditions—never split up." Yet, the fittest three struggled out of the jungle with a concussion, malaria, and infected wounds 19 days later; two more terribly ill soldiers found a village the next day; and the remaining five emaciated and injured men were rescued from a cave by a helicopter on day 33. What happened?

On a surface level, the near-tragic fracturing of the group began with a logical division of labor, according to the training's initiators, Lieutenant Colonel Neill and Major Foster:

> Because the group would be one of mixed abilities, and the young British and NCOs [non-commissioned officers] were likely to be fitter and more experienced than the Hong Kong soldiers, the team would work in two halves on the harder phases of the descent. The British, taking advantage of Mayfield's expertise (in rock climbing), would set up ropes on the difficult sections, while he [Neill] and Foster would concentrate on bringing the Hong Kong soldiers down. Every now and then the recce (reconnaissance) party would report back, and the expedition would go on down in one unit until another reconnaissance party became necessary.

The men reported that from then on, perilous climbing conditions, debilitating sickness, and monsoon rains permanently divided the group. A review board found differently, blaming Neill's and Foster's leadership and their decision to take some less-experienced soldiers on the exercise.

No rulings were made about the near-catastrophic decision to divide the group, but closer inquiries show that this temporary workgroup of diverse members who were not previously acquainted started out with a high level of intragroup trust that dissolved over time. The resulting faultlines, based on members' similarities and differences and the establishment of ad hoc leaders, may have been inevitable.

Initially, all group members shared the common ground of soldier training, clear roles, and volunteer commitment to the mission. When the leaders ignored the soldiers' concerns about the severity of conditions, lack of preparation, and low level of communication, however, trust issues divided the group into subgroups. The initial reconnaissance party established common ground and trust that allowed them to complete the mission and reach safety, even though they divided yet again. Meanwhile, the main group that stayed with the leaders in the cave under conditions of active distrust fractured further.

We will never know whether it would have been better to keep the group together. However, we do know that this small group of soldiers trained to stay together for survival fractured into at least four subgroups because they didn't trust their leaders or their group, endangering all their lives.

Questions

9-31. The review board blamed Neill and Foster. Was this a fair conclusion? Where should blame be apportioned under the circumstances?

9-32. Discuss the group properties presented in this chapter and use them to evaluate the failure of this group.

9-33. When the exercise was designed, Neill created a buddy system based on similarity of soldiers' backgrounds (rank, unit, age, fitness, skills level). The first group out of the jungle were assigned buddies and one other: two lance corporals and one corporal from the same unit (regular army); ages 24–26 with good fitness levels; all top roping and abseiling (TR&A) instructors. The second group out were assigned buddies: a sergeant and a lance corporal from the same unit (elite regular army); ages 25 and 37; good fitness levels; both with Commando Brigade skills. The group left in the cave split into: a lieutenant colonel and a major (buddies); one from the regular army and one from the part time territorial army; ages 46 and 54; fair fitness level; one TR&A and one ski instructor. The second faction was the three from the Hong Kong unit—a lance corporal and two privates, all from the Hong Kong unit; ages 24–32; fair to good fitness levels; one with jungle training and two novices. Would you have set up the buddy system Neill did? Why or why not, and if not, what would you have changed?

Sources: M. A. Korsgaard, H. H. Brower, and S. W. Lester, "It Isn't Always Mutual: A Critical Review of Dyadic Trust," *Journal of Management* 41, no. 1 (2014): 47–70; R. L. Priem and P. C. Nystrom, "Exploring the Dynamics of Workgroup Fracture: Common Ground, Trust-with-Trepidation, and Warranted Distrust," *Journal of Management* 40, no. 3 (2014): 764–95; and "The Call of Malaysia's 'Conquerable' Mount Kinabalu," *BBC,* June 5, 2015, http://www.bbc.com/news/world-asia-33020356.

MyManagementLab

Go to **mymanagementlab.com** for the following Assisted-graded writing questions:

9-34. Considering Case Incident 1, what are some ways groups can improve the effectiveness of consensus methods to make decisions?

9-35. After reading Case Incident 2, do you feel subgroups are good or bad? Why or why not? What might be the alternative?

9-36. MyManagementLab Only – comprehensive writing assignment for this chapter.

ENDNOTES

[1]E. J. Boothby, M. S. Clark, and J. A. Bargh, "Shared Experiences are Amplified," *Psychological Science* 25, no. 12 (2014): 2209–16.

[2]B. Bastien, J. Jetten, and L. J. Ferris, "Pain as Social Glue: Shared Pain Increases Cooperation," *Psychological Science* 25, no. 11 (2014): 2079–85.

[3]N. Karelaia and L. Guillen, "Me, a Woman and a Leader: Positive Social Identity and Identity Conflict," *Organizational Behavior and Human Decision Processes* 125, no. 2 (2014): 204–19.

[4]P. Belmi, R. C. Barragan, M. A. Neale, and G. L. Cohen, "Threats to Social Identity Can Trigger Social Deviance," *Personality and Social Psychological Bulletin* 41, no. 4 (2015): 467–84.

[5]H. Takahashi, M. Kato, M. Matsuura, D. Mobbs, T. Suhara, and Y. Okubo, "When Your Gain Is My Pain and Your Pain Is My Gain: Neural Correlates of Envy and Schadenfreude," *Science* 323, no. 5916 (2009): 937–39; and C. W. Leach, R. Spears, N. R. Branscombe, and B. Doosje, "Malicious Pleasure: Schadenfreude at the Suffering of Another Group," *Journal of Personality and Social Psychology* 84, no. 5 (2003): 932–43.

[6]O. Yakushko, M. M. Davidson, and E. N. Williams, "Identity Salience Model: A Paradigm for Integrating Multiple Identities in Clinical Practice," *Psychotherapy* 46, no. 2 (2009): 180–92; and S. M. Toh and A. S. Denisi, "Host Country Nationals as Socializing Agents: A Social Identity Approach," *Journal of Organizational Behavior* 28, no. 3 (2007): 281–301.

[7]N. Karelaia and L. Guillen, "Me, a Woman and a Leader: Positive Social Identity and Identity Conflict."

[8]T. Cruwys, E. I. South, K. H. Greenaway, and S. A. Haslam, "Social Identity Reduces Depression by Fostering Positive Attributions," *Social Psychological and Personality Science* 6, no. 1 (2015): 65–74.

[9]T. Schmader, K. Block, and B. Lickel, "Social Identity Threat in Response to Stereotypic Film Portrayals: Effects on Self-Conscious Emotion and Implicit Ingroup Attitudes," *Journal of Social Issues* 71, no. 1 (2015): 54–72.

[10]S. Zhang, G. Chen, X.-P. Chen, D. Liu, and M. D. Johnson, "Relational versus Collective Identification within Workgroups: Conceptualization, Measurement Development, and Nomological Network Building," *Journal of Management* 40, no. 6 (2014): 1700–31.

[11]G. J. Lewis and T. C. Bates, "Common Heritable Effects Underpin Concerns over Norm Maintenance and In-Group Favoritism: Evidence from Genetic Analyses of Right-Wing Authoritarianism and Traditionalism," *Journal of Personality* 82, no. 4 (2014): 297–309.

[12]S. L. Neuberg, C. M. Warner, S. A. Mistler, A. Berlin, E. D. Hill, J. D. Johnson, J. Schober, et al., "Religion and Intergroup Conflict: Findings from the Global Group Relations Project," *Psychological Science* 25, no. 1 (2014): 198–206.

[13]W. M. L. Finlay, "Denunciation and the Construction of Norms in Group Conflict: Examples from and Al-Qaeda-Supporting Group," *British Journal of Social Psychology* 53, no. 4 (2014): 691–710.

[14]T. C. Dennehy, A. Ben-Zeev, and N. Tanigawa, "'Be Prepared': An Implemental Mindset for Alleviating Social-Identity Threat," *British Journal of Social Psychology* 53 (2014): 585–94.

[15]M. J. Garfield and A. R. Denis, "Toward an Integrated Model of Group Development: Disruption of Routines by Technology-Induced Change," *Journal of Management Information Systems* 29, no. 3 (2012): 43–86; M. J. Waller, J. M. Conte, C. B. Gibson, and M. A. Carpenter, "The Effect of Individual Perceptions of Deadlines on Team Performance," *Academy of Management Review* (October 2001): 586–600; and A. Chang, P. Bordia, and J. Duck, "Punctuated Equilibrium and Linear Progression: Toward a New Understanding of Group Development," *Academy of Management Journal* (February 2003): 106–17.

[16]M. M. Kazmer, "Disengaging from a Distributed Research Project: Refining a Model of Group Departures," *Journal of the American Society for Information Science and Technology* (April 2010): 758–71.

[17]K. Giese and A. Thiel, "The Psychological Contract in Chinese-African Informal Labor Relations," *International Journal of Human Resource Management* 26, no. 14 (2015): 1807–26; L. Sels, M. Janssens, and I. Van den Brande, "Assessing the Nature of Psychological Contracts: A Validation of Six Dimensions," *Journal of Organizational Behavior* (June 2004): 461–88; and C. Hui, C. Lee, and D. M. Rousseau, "Psychological Contract and Organizational Citizenship Behavior in China: Investigating Generalizability and Instrumentality," *Journal of Applied Psychology* (April 2004): 311–21.

[18]M. D. Collins, "The Effect of Psychological Contract Fulfillment on Manager Turnover Intentions and Its Role as a Mediator in a Casual, Limited-Service Restaurant Environment," *International Journal of Hospitality Management* 29, no. 4 (2010): 736–42; J. M. Jensen, R. A. Opland, and A. M. Ryan, "Psychological Contracts and Counterproductive Work Behaviors: Employee Responses to Transactional and Relational Breach," *Journal of Business and Psychology* 25, no. 4 (2010): 555–68.

[19]D. C. Thomas, S. R. Fitzimmons, E. C. Ravlin, K. Y. Au, B. Z. Ekelund, and C. Barzantny, "Psychological Contracts across Cultures," *Organization Studies* 31 (2010): 1437–58.

[20]K. S. Wilson and H. M. Baumann, "Capturing a More Complete View of Employees' Lives outside of Work: The Introduction and Development of New Interrole Conflict Constructs," *Personnel Psychology* 68, no. 2 (2015): 235–82.

[21]Ibid.

[22]See, for example, F. T. Amstad, L L. Meier, U. Fasel, A. Elfering, and N. K. Semmer, "A Meta-Analysis of Work-Family Conflict and Various Outcomes with a Special Emphasis on Cross-Domain Versus Matching-Domain Relations," *Journal of Occupational Health Psychology* 16, no. 2 (2011): 151–69.

[23]K. S. Wilson and H. M. Baumann, "Capturing a More Complete View of Employees' Lives outside of Work: The Introduction and Development of New Interrole Conflict Constructs."

[24]D. Vora and T. Kostova. "A Model of Dual Organizational Identification in the Context of the Multinational Enterprise," *Journal of Organizational Behavior* 28 (2007): 327–50.

[25]C. Reade, "Dual Identification in Multinational Corporations: Local Managers and Their Psychological Attachment

to the Subsidiary versus the Global Organization," *International Journal of Human Resource Management,* 12, no. 3 (2001): 405–24.

[26]S. Drury, S. A. Hutchens, D. E. Shuttlesworth, and C. L. White, "Philip G. Zimbardo on His Career and the Stanford Prison Experiment's 40th Anniversary," *History of Psychology* 15, no. 2 (2012): 161–70; and S. A. Haslam and S. D. Reicher, "Contesting the 'Nature' of Conformity: What Milgram and Zimbardo's Studies Really Show," *Plos Biology* 10, no. 11 (2012): e1001426.

[27]S. A. Haslam and S. Reicher, "Stressing the Group: Social Identity and the Unfolding Dynamics of Responses to Stress," *Journal of Applied Psychology* 91, no. 5 (2006): 1037–52; S. Reicher and S. A. Haslam, "Rethinking the Psychology of Tyranny: The BBC Prison Study," *British Journal of Social Psychology* 45, no. 1 (2006): 1–40; and P. G. Zimbardo, "On Rethinking the Psychology of Tyranny: The BBC Prison Study," *British Journal of Social Psychology* 45, no. 1 (2006): 47–53.

[28]Y. Huang, K. M. Kendrick, and R. Yu, "Conformity to the Opinions of Other People Lasts for No More Than 3 Days," *Psychological Science* 25, no. 7 (2014): 1388–93.

[29]M. S. Hagger, P. Rentzelas, and N. K. D. Chatzisrantis, "Effects of Individualist and Collectivist Group Norms and Choice on Intrinsic Motivation," *Motivation and Emotion* 38, no. 2 (2014): 215–23; and M. G. Ehrhart and S. E. Naumann, "Organizational Citizenship Behavior in Work Groups: A Group Norms Approach," *Journal of Applied Psychology* (December 2004): 960–74.

[30]E. Delvaux, N. Vanbeselaere, and B. Mesquita, "Dynamic Interplay between Norms and Experiences of Anger and Gratitude in Groups," *Small Group Research* 46, no. 3 (2015): 300–23.

[31]R. B. Cialdini and N. J. Goldstein, "Social Influence: Compliance and Conformity," *Annual Review of Psychology* 55 (2004): 591–621.

[32]P. Kundu and D. D. Cummins, "Morality and Conformity: The Asch Paradigm Applied to Moral Decisions," *Social Influence* 8, no. 4 (2013): 268–79.

[33]Ibid.

[34]R. A. Griggs, "The Disappearance of Independence in Textbook Coverage of Asch's Social Pressure Experiments," *Teaching of Psychology* 42, no. 2 (2015): 137–42.

[35]S. Sansfacon and C. E. Amiot, "The Impact of Group Norms and Behavioral Congruence on the Internalization of an Illegal Downloading Behavior," *Group Dynamics-Theory Research and Practice* 18, no. 2 (2014): 174–88; and L. Rosh, L. R. Offermann, and R. Van Diest, "Too Close for Comfort? Distinguishing between Team Intimacy and Team Cohesion," *Human Resource Management Review* (June 2012): 116–27.

[36]J. S. Hassard, "Rethinking the Hawthorne Studies: The Western Electric Research in Its Social, Political, and Historical Context," *Human Relations* 65, no. 11 (2012): 1431–61.

[37]J. A. Goncalo, J. A. Chatman, M. M. Duguid, and J. A. Kennedy, "Creativity from Constraint? How the Political Correctness Norm Influences Creativity in Mixed-Sex Work Groups," *Administrative Science Quarterly* 60, no. 1 (2015): 1–30.

[38]E. Gonzalez-Mule, D. S. DeGeest, B. W. McCormick, et al., "Can We Get Some Cooperation Around Here? The Mediating Role of Group Norms on the Relationship between Team Personality and Individual Helping Behaviors," *Journal of Applied Psychology* 99, no. 5 (2014): 988–99.

[39]T. Masson and I. Fritsche, "Adherence to Climate Change-Related Ingroup Norms: Do Dimensions of Group Identification Matter?" *European Journal of Social Psychology* 44, no. 5 (2014): 455–65.

[40]See R. J. Bennett and S. L. Robinson, "The Past, Present, and Future of Workplace Deviance," in J. Greenberg (ed.), *Organizational Behavior: The State of the Science,* 2nd ed. (Mahwah, NJ: Erlbaum, 2003), 237–71; and C. M. Berry, D. S. Ones, and P. R. Sackett, "Interpersonal Deviance, Organizational Deviance, and Their Common Correlates: A Review and Meta-Analysis," *Journal of Applied Psychology* 92, no. 2 (2007): 410–24.

[41]M. A. Baysinger, K. T. Scherer, and J. M. LeBreton, "Exploring the Disruptive Effects of Psychopathy and Aggression on Group Processes and Group Effectiveness," *Journal of Applied Psychology* 99, no. 1 (2014): 48–65.

[42]T. C. Reich and M. S. Hershcovis, "Observing Workplace Incivility," Journal of Applied Psychology 100, no. 1 (2015): 203–15; and Z. E. Zhou, Y. Yan, X. X. Che, and L. L. Meier, "Effect of Workplace Incivility on End-of-Work Negative Affect: Examining Individual and Organizational Moderators in a Daily Diary Study," *Journal of Occupational Health Psychology* 20, no. 1 (2015): 117–30.

[43]See C. Pearson, L. M. Andersson, and C. L. Porath, "Workplace Incivility," in S. Fox and P. E. Spector (eds.), *Counterproductive Work Behavior: Investigations of Actors and Targets* (Washington, DC: American Psychological Association, 2005), 177–200.

[44]S. Lim, L. M. Cortina, and V. J. Magley, "Personal and Workgroup Incivility: Impact on Work and Health Outcomes," *Journal of Applied Psychology* 93, no. 1 (2008): 95–107.

[45]M. S. Christian and A. P. J. Ellis, "Examining the Effects of Sleep Deprivation on Workplace Deviance: A Self-Regulatory Perspective," *Academy of Management Journal* 54, no. 5 (2011): 913–34.

[46]Robinson and O'Leary-Kelly, "Monkey See, Monkey Do"; and T. M. Glomb and H. Liao, "Interpersonal Aggression in Workgroups: Social Influence, Reciprocal, and Individual

Effects," *Academy of Management Journal* 46 (2003): 486–96.

[47]P. Bamberger and M. Biron, "Group Norms and Excessive Absenteeism: The Role of Peer Referent Others," *Organizational Behavior and Human Decision Processes* 103, no. 2 (2007): 179–96; and A. Väänänen, N. Tordera, M. Kivimäki, A. Kouvonen, J. Pentti, A. Linna, and J. Vahtera, "The Role of Work Group in Individual Sickness Absence Behavior," *Journal of Health & Human Behavior* 49, no. 4 (2008): 452–67.

[48]M. S. Cole, F. Walter, and H. Bruch, "Affective Mechanisms Linking Dysfunctional Behavior to Performance in Work Teams: A Moderated Mediation Study," *Journal of Applied Psychology* 93, no. 5 (2008): 945–58.

[49]M. S. Hagger, P. Rentzelas, and N. K. D. Chatzisrantis, "Effects of Individualist and Collectivist Group Norms and Choice on Intrinsic Motivation."

[50]J. Dippong and W. Kalkhoff, "Predicting Performance Expectations from Affective Impressions: Linking Affect Control Theory and Status Characteristics Theory," *Social Science Research* 50 (2015): 1–14; and A. E. Randel, L. Chay-Hoon, and P. C. Earley, "It's Not Just about Differences: An Integration of Role Identity Theory and Status Characteristics Theory," in M. C. T. Hunt (ed.), *Research on Managing Groups and Teams* (2005), 23–42.

[51]A. E. Randel, L. Chay-Hoon, and P. C. Earley, "It's Not Just about Differences: An Integration of Role Identity Theory and Status Characteristics Theory."

[52]R. R. Callister and J. A. Wall Jr., "Conflict across Organizational Boundaries: Managed Care Organizations versus Health Care Providers," *Journal of Applied Psychology* 86, no. 4 (2001): 754–63; and P. Chattopadhyay, W. H. Glick, and G. P. Huber, "Organizational Actions in Response to Threats and Opportunities," *Academy of Management Journal* 44, no. 5 (2001): 937–55.

[53]P. F. Hewlin, "Wearing the Cloak: Antecedents and Consequences of Creating Facades of Conformity," *Journal of Applied Psychology* 94, no. 3 (2009): 727–41.

[54]B. Groysberg, J. T. Polzer, and H. A. Elfenbein, "Too Many Cooks Spoil the Broth: How High-Status Individuals Decrease Group Effectiveness," *Organization Science* (May–June 2011): 722–37.

[55]C. Bendersky and N. P. Shah, "The Cost of Status Enhancement: Performance Effects of Individuals' Status Mobility in Task Groups," *Organization Science* 23, no. 2 (2012): 308–22.

[56]B. Groysberg, J. T. Polzer, and H. A. Elfenbein, "Too Many Cooks Spoil the Broth: How High-Status Individuals Decrease Group Effectiveness," Organization Science 22, no. 3 (2011): 722–37.

[57]A. M. Christie and J. Barling, "Beyond Status: Relating Status Inequality to Performance and Health in Teams," *Journal of Applied Psychology* 95, no. 5 (2010): 920–34; and

L. H. Nishii and D. M. Mayer, "Do Inclusive Leaders Help to Reduce Turnover in Diverse Groups? The Moderating Role of Leader-Member Exchange in the Diversity to Turnover Relationship," *Journal of Applied Psychology* 94, no. 6 (2009): 1412–26.

[58]V. Venkataramani, S. G. Green, and D. J. Schleicher, "Well-Connected Leaders: The Impact of Leaders' Social Network Ties on LMX and Members' Work Attitudes," *Journal of Applied Psychology* 95, no. 6 (2010): 1071–84.

[59]H. van Dijk and M. L. van Engen, "A Status Perspective on the Consequences of Work Group Diversity," *Journal of Occupational and Organizational Psychology* (June 2013): 223–41.

[60]Based on J. B. Pryor, G. D. Reeder, and A. E. Monroe, "The Infection of Bad Company: Stigma by Association," *Journal of Personality and Social Psychology.* 102, no. 2 (2012): 224–41; E. Goffman, *Stigma: Notes on the Management of Spoiled Identity* (Touchstone Digital, 2009); and M. R. Hebl, and L. M. Mannix, "The Weight of Obesity in Evaluating Others: A Mere Proximity Effect," *Personality and Social Psychology Bulletin* 29 (2003): 28–38.

[61]M. Cikara and J. J. Van Bavel, "The Neuroscience of Intergroup Relations: An Integrative Review," *Perspectives on Psychological Science* 9, no. 3 (2014): 245–74.

[62]M. Rubin, C. Badea, and J. Jetten, "Low Status Groups Show In-Group Favoritism to Compensate for Their Low Status and Compete for Higher Status," *Group Processes & Intergroup Relations* 17, no. 5 (2014): 563–76.

[63]C. L. Wilkins, J. D. Wellman, L. G. Babbitt, N. R. Toosi, and K. D. Schad, "You Can Win but I Can't Lose: Bias against High-Status Groups Increases Their Zero-Sum Beliefs about Discrimination," *Journal of Experimental Social Psychology* 57 (2014): 1–14.

[64]R. B. Lount, Jr. and S. L. Wilk, "Working Harder or Hardly Working? Posting Performance Eliminates Social Loafing and Promotes Social Laboring in Workgroups," *Management Science* 60, no. 5 (2014): 1098–106; S. M. Murphy, S. J. Wayne, R. C. Liden, and B. Erdogan, "Understanding Social Loafing: The Role of Justice Perceptions and Exchange Relationships," *Human Relations* (January 2003): 61–84; and R. C. Liden, S. J. Wayne, R. A. Jaworski, and N. Bennett, "Social Loafing: A Field Investigation," *Journal of Management* (April 2004): 285–304.

[65]A. W. Delton, L. Cosmides, M. Guemo, T. E. Robertson, and J. Tooby, "The Psychosemantics of Free Riding: Dissecting the Architecture of a Moral Concept," *Journal of Personality and Social Psychology* 102, no. 6 (2012): 1252–70.

[66]C. Rubino, D. R. Avery, S. D. Volpone, et al., "Does Teaming Obscure Low Performance? Exploring the Temporal Effects of Team Performance Diversity," *Human Performance* 27, no. 5 (2014): 416–34.

[67]D. L. Smrt and S. J. Karau, "Protestant Work Ethic Moderates Social Loafing," *Group Dynamics-Theory Research and Practice* (September 2011): 267–74.

[68]M. C. Schippers, "Social Loafing Tendencies and Team Performance: The Compensating Effect of Agreeableness and Conscientiousness," *Academy of Management Learning & Education* 13, no. 1 (2014): 62–81.

[69]A. Gunnthorsdottir and A. Rapoport, "Embedding Social Dilemmas in Intergroup Competition Reduces Free-Riding," *Organizational Behavior and Human Decision Processes* 101 (2006): 184–99; and E. M. Stark, J. D. Shaw, and M. K. Duffy, "Preference for Group Work, Winning Orientation, and Social Loafing Behavior in Groups," *Group and Organization Management* 32, no. 6 (2007): 699–723.

[70]R. B. Lount, Jr. and S. L. Wilk, "Working Harder or Hardly Working? Posting Performance Eliminates Social Loafing and Promotes Social Laboring in Workgroups."

[71]A. Gunnthorsdottir and A. Rapoport, "Embedding Social Dilemmas in Intergroup Competition Reduces Free-Riding;" and E. M. Stark, J. D. Shaw, and M. K. Duffy, "Preference for Group Work, Winning Orientation, and Social Loafing Behavior in Groups."

[72]L. L. Greer, "Group Cohesion: Then and Now," *Small Group Research* (December 2012): 655–61.

[73]D. S. Staples and L. Zhao, "The Effects of Cultural Diversity in Virtual Teams Versus Face-to-Face Teams," *Group Decision and Negotiation* (July 2006): 389–406.

[74]N. Chi, Y. Huang, and S. Lin, "A Double-Edged Sword? Exploring the Curvilinear Relationship between Organizational Tenure Diversity and Team Innovation: The Moderating Role of Team-Oriented HR Practices," *Group and Organization Management* 34, no. 6 (2009): 698–726.

[75]K. J. Klein, A. P. Knight, J. C. Ziegert, B. C. Lim, and J. L. Saltz, "When Team Members' Values Differ: The Moderating Role of Team Leadership," *Organizational Behavior and Human Decision Processes* 114, no. 1 (2011): 25–36; and G. Park and R. P. DeShon, "A Multilevel Model of Minority Opinion Expression and Team Decision-Making Effectiveness," *Journal of Applied Psychology* 95, no. 5 (2010): 824–33.

[76]J. S. Chun and J. N. Choi, "Members' Needs, Intragroup Conflict, and Group Performance," *Journal of Applied Psychology* 99, no. 3 (2014): 437–50.

[77]M. Rigoglioso, "Diverse Backgrounds and Personalities Can Strengthen Groups," *Stanford Knowledgebase*, August 15, 2006, www.stanford.edu/group/knowledgebase/.

[78]K. W. Phillips and D. L. Loyd, "When Surface and Deep-Level Diversity Collide: The Effects on Dissenting Group Members," *Organizational Behavior and Human Decision Processes* 99 (2006): 143–60; and S. R. Sommers, "On Racial Diversity and Group Decision Making: Identifying Multiple Effects of Racial Composition on Jury Deliberations," *Journal of Personality and Social Psychology* (April 2006): 597–612.

[79]J. S. Chun and J. N. Choi, "Members' Needs, Intragroup Conflict, and Group Performance."

[80]E. Mannix and M. A. Neale, "What Differences Make a Difference? The Promise and Reality of Diverse Teams in Organizations," *Psychological Science in the Public Interest* (October 2005): 31–55.

[81]E. P. Apfelbaum, K. W. Phillips, and J. A. Richeson, "Rethinking the Baseline in Diversity Research: Should We Be Explaining the Effects of Homogeneity?" *Perspectives on Psychological Science* 9, no. 3 (2014): 235–44.

[82]See M. B. Thatcher and P. C. Patel, "Group Faultlines: A Review, Integration, and Guide to Future Research," *Journal of Management* 38, no. 4 (2012): 969–1009.

[83]K. Bezrukova, S. M. B. Thatcher, K. A. Jehn, and C. S. Spell, "The Effects of Alignments: Examining Group Faultlines, Organizational Cultures, and Performance," *Journal of Applied Psychology* 97, no. 1 (2012): 77–92.

[84]R. Rico, M. Sanchez-Manzanares, M. Antino, and D. Lau, "Bridging Team Faultlines by Combining Task Role Assignment and Goal Structure Strategies," *Journal of Applied Psychology* 97, no. 2 (2012): 407–20.

[85]B. L. Bonner, S. D. Sillito, and M. R. Baumann, "Collective Estimation: Accuracy, Expertise, and Extroversion as Sources of Intra-Group Influence," *Organizational*

Behavior and Human Decision Processes 103 (2007): 121–33.

[86]J. E. Kammer, W. Gaissmaier, T. Reimer, and C. C. Schermuly, "The Adaptive Use of Recognition in Group Decision Making," *Cognitive Science* 38, no. 5 (2014): 911–42.

[87]J. S. Chun and J. N. Choi, "Members' Needs, Intragroup Conflict, and Group Performance."

[88]G. Park and R. P. DeShon, "A Multilevel Model of Minority Opinion Expression and Team Decision-Making Effectiveness," *Journal of Applied Psychology* 95, no. 5 (2010): 824–33.

[89]R. Benabou, "Groupthink: Collective Delusions in Organizations and Markets," *Review of Economic Studies* (April 2013): 429–62.

[90]J. A. Goncalo, E. Polman, and C. Maslach, "Can Confidence Come Too Soon? Collective Efficacy, Conflict, and Group Performance over Time," *Organizational Behavior and Human Decision Processes* 113, no. 1 (2010): 13–24.

[91]See N. Richardson Ahlfinger and J. K. Esser, "Testing the Groupthink Model: Effects of Promotional Leadership and Conformity Predisposition," *Social Behavior & Personality* 29, no. 1 (2001): 31–41; and S. Schultz-Hardt, F. C. Brodbeck, A. Mojzisch, R. Kerschreiter, and D. Frey, "Group Decision Making in Hidden Profile Situations: Dissent as a Facilitator for Decision Quality," *Journal of Personality and Social Psychology* 91, no. 6 (2006): 1080–93.

[92]See I. Yaniv, "Group Diversity and Decision Quality: Amplification and Attenuation of the Framing Effect," *International Journal of Forecasting* (January–March 2011): 41–49.

[93]M. P. Brady and S. Y. Wu, "The Aggregation of Preferences in Groups: Identity, Responsibility, and Polarization," *Journal of Economic Psychology* 31, no. 6 (2010): 950–63.

[94]Z. Krizan and R. S. Baron, "Group Polarization and Choice-Dilemmas: How Important Is Self-Categorization?" *European Journal of Social Psychology* 37, no. 1 (2007): 191–201.

[95]See R. P. McGlynn, D. McGurk, V. S. Effland, N. L. Johll, and D. J. Harding, "Brainstorming and Task Performance in Groups Constrained by Evidence," *Organizational Behavior and Human Decision Processes* (January 2004): 75–87; and R. C. Litchfield, "Brainstorming Reconsidered: A Goal-Based View," *Academy of Management Review* 33, no. 3 (2008): 649–68.

[96]N. L. Kerr and R. S. Tindale, "Group Performance and Decision-Making," *Annual Review of Psychology* 55 (2004): 623–55.

[97]C. Faure, "Beyond Brainstorming: Effects of Different Group Procedures on Selection of Ideas and Satisfaction with the Process," *Journal of Creative Behavior* 38 (2004): 13–34.

[98]P. L. Perrewe, K. L. Zellars, G. R. Ferris, A. M. Rossi, C. J. Kacmar, and D. A. Ralston, "Neutralizing Job Stressors: Political Skill as an Antidote to the Dysfunctional Consequences of Role Conflict," *Academy of Management Journal* (February 2004): 141–52.

10 Understanding Work Teams

LEARNING OBJECTIVES

After studying this chapter, you should be able to:

10-1 Analyze the continued popularity of teams in organizations.

10-2 Contrast groups and teams.

10-3 Contrast the five types of team arrangements.

10-4 Identify the characteristics of effective teams.

10-5 Explain how organizations can create team players.

10-6 Decide when to use individuals instead of teams.

MyManagementLab®

⭐ **Chapter Warm Up**

If your professor has chosen to assign this, go to the Assignments section of **mymanagementlab.com** to complete the chapter warm up.

TEAMS THAT PLAY TOGETHER STAY TOGETHER

At SmugMug, an online photo sharing company, every day is a photo opportunity. If you're hired there, you might be expected to enjoy photography, have extensive Web knowledge, and be willing to work in teams. You might even be expected to become a subject in photos the organization posts. But would you anticipate having to crawl through muddy trenches under barbed wire with your team as these employees have? They've just finished the hard-core 10–12-mile obstacle course experience provided by Tough Mudder, an organization that creates physical challenges for organizational teams like those at SmugMug.

The mission of Tough Mudder is simple: solidify teams through a shared experience. Co-founder Chris MacAskill said, "You get muddy and tired and beat up. It is like the Marines and boot camp. The more athletic help the less athletic because you want to finish together as a team. At the end, you are arm in arm, and there are big smiles and high-fives." Tough Mudder events like the one pictured here teach values like mental grit by providing fun, success, and thrills. It seems to work, according to Lynn Gruber of *Fortune*, who remarked, "The teamwork and camaraderie out there was amazing." To date, the organization boasts a track record of over 100 events, 1.5 million participants, 4,000 Tough Mudder tattoos, and a 95 percent participation rate.

Is Tough Mudding not your cup of tea? Then perhaps you should consider employment at Grid Connect Inc., a software firm in Illinois. The game there is ping pong, and "Everybody plays, nobody can opt out. You can take your frustrations out playing ping pong. When you aren't playing, you can root for the underdogs," said founder and CEO Mike Justice. He is the trophy holder and his father is the official scorekeeper, but still, he says, the organization's tournaments enhance team building for his employees. "It's a real confidence booster. It was one of the best things we ever did for morale."

Perhaps old-fashioned athletic leagues are more your thing? Most companies have leagues for organized sports, which may or may not enhance their work teams. At Offerpop, a social-marketing firm, "The sports teams help to make everyone more comfortable with each other," said CEO Wendell Landsford, although he says the real team building happens during postgame drinks. Jerry Schranz of public-relations agency Beckerman personally learned an important job skill while captain of the softball team. He observed, "It is very difficult to give up the ball as a starting pitcher, where you think that no one can pitch as well as you. It was something I had to learn to do: delegate to others and let it unfold."

For all the good that intentional team-building recreation can do, note that programs such as Tough Mudder's may be more successful than off-hours sports leagues. John Pinkham of PAN Communications Inc. was in charge of the Boston PR firm's casual soccer team. He said, "Turns out the fun league we signed up for was super competitive, with ex-college players and Europeans who kicked the ball faster than I thought was possible." In response, losers either tried to out-strategize the perpetual winners or quit. Those that stayed tried to have fun no matter the score. Pinkham said, "I think everyone was glad they played, and it brought us more together as colleagues and friends—just maybe not as teammates."

Sources: B. Haislip, "Play Ball!" *The Wall Street Journal,* June 12, 2014, R4; M. L. Shuffler, D. DiazGranados, and E. Salas, "There's a Science for That: Team Development Interventions in Organizations," *Current Directions in Psychological Science* 20, no. 6 (2011): 365–72; and *Tough Mudder* website, www.toughmudder.com, accessed June 23, 2015.

Do teams that play together stay together, as the opening discussion suggests? There is definitely an upside to shared experiences, as we will find in this chapter. There may also be something about unique, unexpected challenges that bring teams together, as Tough Mudder claims. We are, however, cautioned to consider the effects of these "play" exercises, including possible discrimination against employees who are disabled or physically unfit. We will consider more types of team-building strategies, and teams in general, in this chapter.

Why Have Teams Become So Popular?

10-1 Analyze the continued popularity of teams in organizations.

Why are teams popular? In short, because we believe they are effective. "A team of people happily committed to the project and to one another will outperform a brilliant individual every time," writes *Forbes* publisher Rich Karlgaard.[1] In some ways, he's right. Teams can sometimes achieve feats an individual could never accomplish.[2] Teams are more flexible and responsive to changing events than traditional departments or other forms of permanent groupings. They can quickly assemble, deploy, refocus, and disband. They are an effective means to democratize organizations and increase employee involvement. And finally, research indicates that our involvement in teams positively shapes the way we think as individuals, introducing a collaborative mindset about even our personal decision making.[3]

The fact that organizations have embraced teamwork doesn't necessarily mean teams are always effective. Team members, as humans, can be swayed by fads and herd mentality that can lead them astray from the best decisions. What conditions affect their potential? How do members work together? Do we even like teams? Maybe not, according to the OB Poll. To answer these questions, let's first distinguish between groups and teams.

Differences Between Groups and Teams

10-2 Contrast groups and teams.

workgroup A group that interacts primarily to share information and to make decisions to help each group member perform within his or her area of responsibility.

Groups and teams are not the same thing. In Chapter 9, we defined a *group* as two or more individuals, interacting and interdependent, who work together to achieve particular objectives. A **workgroup** is a group that interacts primarily to share information and make decisions to help each member perform within his or her area of responsibility.

Workgroups have no need or opportunity to engage in collective work with joint effort, so the group's performance is merely the summation of each member's individual contribution. There is no positive synergy that would create an overall level of performance greater than the sum of the inputs. A workgroup

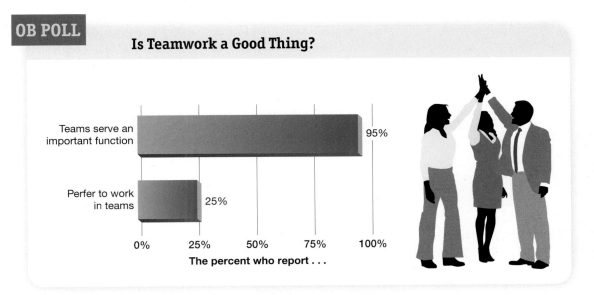

OB POLL

Is Teamwork a Good Thing?

Teams serve an important function — 95%

Perfer to work in teams — 25%

The percent who report . . .

Source: "University of Phoenix Survey Reveals Nearly Seven-in-Ten Workers Have Been Part of Dysfunctional Teams," downloaded on June 9, 2013, from www.prnewswire.com

Exhibit 10-1   **Comparing Workgroups and Work Teams**

Workgroups		Work Teams
Share information	←— Goal —→	Collective performance
Neutral (sometimes negative)	←— Synergy —→	Positive
Individual	←— Accountability —→	Individual and mutual
Random and varied	←— Skills —→	Complementary

work team   A group whose individual efforts result in performance that is greater than the sum of the individual inputs.

is a collection of individuals doing their work, albeit with interaction and/or dependency.

A **work team**, on the other hand, generates positive synergy through coordination. The individual efforts result in a level of performance greater than the sum of the individual inputs.

In both workgroups and work teams, there are often behavioral expectations of members, collective normalization efforts, active group dynamics, and some level of decision making (even if just informally about the scope of membership). Both may generate ideas, pool resources, or coordinate logistics such as work schedules; for the workgroup, however, this effort will be limited to information-gathering for decision makers outside the group.

Whereas we can think of a work team as a subset of a workgroup, the team is constructed to be purposeful (symbiotic) in its member interaction. The distinction between a workgroup and a work team should be kept even when the terms are mentioned interchangeably in differing contexts. Exhibit 10-1 highlights the differences between them.

The definitions help clarify why organizations structure work processes by teams. Management is looking for positive synergy that will create increased performance. The extensive use of teams creates the *potential* for an organization to generate greater outputs with no increase in employee headcount. Notice, however, that we said *potential*. There is nothing magical that ensures the achievement of positive synergy in the creation of teams. Merely calling a *group* a *team* doesn't automatically improve its performance. As we show later, effective teams have certain common characteristics. If management hopes to gain increases in organizational performance through the use of teams, their teams must possess these characteristics.

Types of Teams

10-3   Contrast the five types of team arrangements.

Teams can make products, provide services, negotiate deals, coordinate projects, offer advice, and make decisions.[4] In this section, first we describe four common types of teams in organizations: *problem-solving teams, self-managed work teams, cross-functional teams,* and *virtual teams* (see Exhibit 10-2). Then we will discuss *multiteam systems,* which utilize a "team of teams" and are becoming increasingly widespread as work increases in complexity.

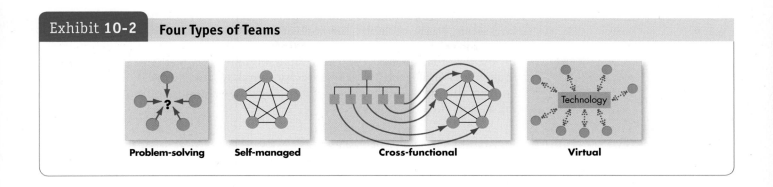

Exhibit **10-2**   **Four Types of Teams**

Problem-solving   Self-managed   Cross-functional   Virtual

Problem-Solving Teams

Quality-control teams have been in use for many years. Originally seen most often in manufacturing plants, these were permanent teams that generally met at a regular time, sometimes weekly or daily, to address quality standards and any problems with the products made. Also, the medical field in particular has recently implemented quality teams to improve their services in patient care. **Problem-solving teams** like these rarely have the authority to unilaterally implement their suggestions, but if their recommendations are paired with implementation processes, some significant improvements can be realized.

Self-Managed Work Teams

As we discussed, problem-solving teams only make recommendations. Some organizations have gone further and created teams that also implement solutions and take responsibility for outcomes.

Self-managed work teams are groups of employees (typically 10 to 15 in number) who perform highly related or interdependent jobs; these teams take on some supervisory responsibilities.[5] Typically, the responsibilities include planning and scheduling work, assigning tasks to members, making operating decisions, taking action on problems, and working with suppliers and customers. Fully self-managed work teams even select their own members who evaluate each other's performance. When these teams are established, former supervisory positions take on decreased importance and are sometimes eliminated.

Research results on the effectiveness of self-managed work teams have not been uniformly positive. Some research indicates that self-managed teams may be more or less effective based on the degree to which team-promoting behaviors are rewarded. For example, one study of 45 self-managing teams found that when team members perceived that economic rewards such as pay were dependent on input from their teammates, performance improved for both individuals and the team as a whole.[6]

A second area of research focus has been the impact of conflict on self-managed work team effectiveness. Some research indicates that self-managed teams are not effective when there is conflict. When disputes arise, members often stop cooperating and power struggles ensue, which lead to lower group performance.[7] However, other research indicates that when members feel confident they can speak up without being embarrassed, rejected, or punished by other team members—in other words, when they feel psychologically safe—conflict can be beneficial and boost team performance.[8]

Thirdly, research has explored the effect of self-managed work teams on member behavior. Here again the findings are mixed. Although individuals on teams report higher levels of job satisfaction than other individuals, stud-

problem-solving teams Groups of 5 to 12 employees from the same department who meet for a few hours each week to discuss ways of improving quality, efficiency, and the work environment.

self-managed work teams Groups of 10 to 15 people who take on responsibilities of their former supervisors.

ies indicate they sometimes have higher absenteeism and turnover rates. One large-scale study of labor productivity in British establishments found that although using teams improved individual (and overall) labor productivity, no evidence supported the claim that self-managed teams performed better than traditional teams with less decision-making authority.[9] On the whole, it appears that for self-managing teams to be advantageous, a number of facilitating factors must be in place.

Cross-Functional Teams

Starbucks created a team of individuals from production, global PR, global communications, and U.S. marketing to develop the Via brand of instant coffee. The team's suggestions resulted in a product that would be cost-effective to produce and distribute, and that was marketed with a tightly integrated, multifaceted strategy.[10] This example illustrates the use of **cross-functional teams**, made up of employees from about the same hierarchical level but different work areas who come together to accomplish a task.

Cross-functional teams are an effective means of allowing people from diverse areas within or even between organizations to exchange information, develop new ideas, solve problems, and coordinate complex projects. However, due to the high need for coordination, cross-functional teams are not simple to manage. First, it makes sense for power shifts to occur as different expertise is needed because the members are at roughly the same level in the organization, which creates leadership ambiguity. A climate of trust thus needs to be developed before shifts can happen without undue conflict.[11] Second, the early stages of development are often long, since members need to learn to work with higher levels of diversity and complexity. Third, it takes time to build trust and teamwork, especially among people with different experiences and perspectives.

cross-functional teams Employees from about the same hierarchical level, but from different work areas, who come together to accomplish a task.

Harley-Davidson Motor Company uses cross-functional teams at all levels of its organization in creating new products, such as its first electric motorcycle, shown here. From product conception to launch, cross-functional teams include Harley employees from product planning, engineering, design, marketing, manufacturing, and purchasing.
Source: Justin Lane/EPA/Newscom

Organizations have used horizontal, boundary-spanning teams for decades, and we would be hard-pressed to find a large organization or product launch that did not use them. Major automobile manufacturers—Toyota, Honda, Nissan, BMW, GM, Ford, and Chrysler—currently use this form of team to coordinate complex projects, as do other industries. For example, Cisco relies on specific cross-functional teams to identify and capitalize on new trends in several areas of the software market. Its teams are the equivalent of social-networking groups that collaborate in real time to identify new business opportunities in the field and then implement them from the bottom up.[12]

In sum, the strength of traditional cross-functional teams is the collaborative effort of individuals with diverse skills from a variety of disciplines. When the unique perspectives of these members are considered, these teams can be very effective.

Virtual Teams

virtual teams Teams that use computer technology to tie together physically dispersed members in order to achieve a common goal.

The teams described in the preceding section do their work face-to-face, whereas **virtual teams** use computer technology to unite physically dispersed members and achieve a common goal.[13] They collaborate online—using communication links such as wide-area networks, corporate social media, videoconferencing, and e-mail—whether members are nearby or continents apart. Nearly all teams do at least some of their work remotely.

Virtual teams should be managed differently than face-to-face teams in an office, partially because virtual team members may not interact along traditional hierarchical patterns. Because of the complexity of interactions, research indicates that shared leadership of virtual teams may significantly enhance team performance, although the concept is still in development.[14] For virtual teams to be effective, management should ensure that (1) trust is established among members (one inflammatory remark in an e-mail can severely undermine team trust), (2) progress is monitored closely (so the team doesn't lose sight of its goals and no team member "disappears"), and (3) the efforts and products of the team are publicized throughout the organization (so the team does not become invisible).[15]

It would be a mistake to think virtual teams are an easy substitute for face-to-face teams. While the geographical reach and immediacy of online communication make virtual teams a natural development, managers must make certain this type of team is the optimal choice for the desired outcome and then maintain an oversight role throughout the collaboration.

Multiteam Systems

multiteam system A collection of two or more interdependent teams that share a superordinate goal; a team of teams.

The types of teams we've described so far are typically smaller, standalone teams, though their activities relate to the broader objectives of the organization. As tasks become more complex, teams often grow in size. Increases in team size are accompanied by higher coordination demands, creating a tipping point at which the addition of another member does more harm than good. To solve this problem, organizations use **multiteam systems**, collections of two or more interdependent teams that share a superordinate goal. In other words, multiteam systems are a "team of teams."[16]

To picture a multiteam system, imagine the coordination of response needed after a major car accident. There is the emergency medical services team, which responds first and transports the injured to the hospital. An emergency room team then takes over, providing medical care, followed by a recovery team. Although the emergency services team, emergency room team, and recovery

The Size of Your Meeting's Carbon Footprint

Despite being in different countries, or even on different continents, many teams in geographically dispersed locations communicate without regularly meeting face-to-face, and may never meet each other in person. Although the merits of face-to-face versus electronic communication have been debated, there may be a strong *ethical* argument for virtual teams.

Keeping team members where they are, as opposed to having them travel every time they need to meet, may be in line with corporate social responsibility (CSR) initiatives. A very large proportion of airline, rail, and car transport is for business purposes and contributes greatly to global carbon dioxide emissions. When teams are able to meet virtually rather than face-to-face, they dramatically reduce their carbon footprint.

In a globally connected world, how might you minimize your organization's environmental impact from business travel? Several tips might get you started thinking about ways that virtual teams can be harnessed for greater sustainability:

1. **Encourage all team members to think about whether a face-to-face meeting is really necessary.** Try to utilize alternative communication methods whenever possible.
2. **Communicate as much as possible through virtual means.** This includes e-mail, telephone calls, and video-conferencing.
3. **When traveling to team meetings, choose the most environmentally responsible travel methods possible.** Also, check the environmental profile of hotels before booking rooms.
4. **If the environmental savings are not enough motivation to reduce travel, consider the financial savings.** According to one survey, businesses spend about 8 to 12 percent of their entire budget on travel. Communicating electronically can therefore result in two benefits: (1) it's cheaper and (2) it's good for the environment.

Sources: P. Tilstone, "Cut Carbon...and Bills," *Director*, May 2009, 54; L. C. Latimer, "6 Strategies for Sustainable Business Travel," *Greenbiz*, February 11, 2011, www.greenbiz.com; and F. Gebhart, "Travel Takes a Big Bite out of Corporate Expenses," *Travel Market Report*, May 30, 2013, downloaded June 9, 2013, from www.travelmarketreport.com.

---

team are technically independent, their activities are interdependent, and the success of one depends on the success of the others. Why? Because they all share the higher goal of saving lives.

Some factors that make smaller, more traditional teams effective do not necessarily apply to multiteam systems and can even hinder their performance. One study showed that multiteam systems performed better when they had "boundary spanners" whose jobs were to coordinate with members of the other subteams. This reduced the need for some team member communication, which was helpful because it reduced coordination demands.[17] Leadership of multiteam systems is also much different than for standalone teams. While leadership of all teams affects team performance, a multiteam leader must both facilitate coordination between teams and lead each team. Research indicated teams that received more attention and engagement from the organization's leaders felt more empowered, which made them more effective as they sought to solve their own problems.[18]

In general, a multiteam system is the best choice either when a team has become too large to be effective, or when teams with distinct functions need to be highly coordinated.

✪ WATCH IT!

If your professor has assigned this, go to the Assignments section of **mymanagementlab.com** to complete the video exercise titled *Teams (TWZ Role Play)*.

Creating Effective Teams

10-4 Identify the characteristics of effective teams.

Teams are often created deliberately but sometimes evolve organically. Take the rise of team "hives" over the past 5 years, for an organic example. Freelancing is typically the solo work of people who are highly specialized in their fields and can provide expertise to organizations on a short-term basis. The difficulty is for the freelancers to effectively market themselves to organizations, and for organizations to find freelancers who fit their needs. To bridge this gap, freelancers form teams with other freelancers from complementary specialties to present a cohesive working unit—a hive—to clients. This team-based approach has proven very successful.[19]

Many people have tried to identify factors related to team effectiveness. To help, some studies have organized what was once a large list of characteristics into a relatively focused model.[20] Exhibit 10-3 summarizes what we currently know about what makes teams effective. As you'll see, it builds on many of the group concepts introduced in Chapter 9.

In considering the team effectiveness model, keep in mind two points. First, teams differ in form and structure. The model attempts to generalize across all varieties of teams but avoids rigidly applying its predictions to all teams.[21] Use it as a guide. Second, the model assumes teamwork is preferable to individual work. Creating "effective" teams when individuals can do the job better is like perfectly solving the wrong problem. Third, let's consider what *team effectiveness* means in this model. Typically, team effectiveness includes objective measures

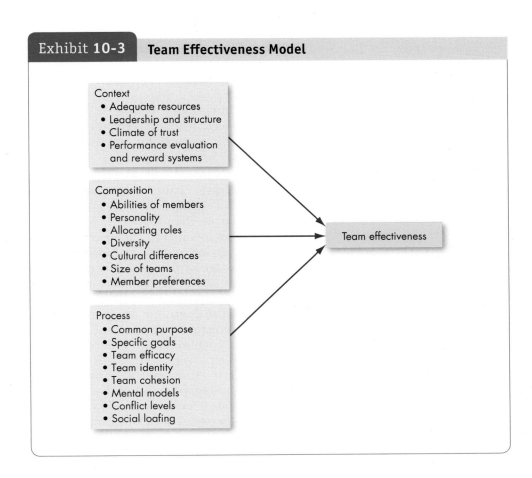

Exhibit 10-3 Team Effectiveness Model

Context
- Adequate resources
- Leadership and structure
- Climate of trust
- Performance evaluation and reward systems

Composition
- Abilities of members
- Personality
- Allocating roles
- Diversity
- Cultural differences
- Size of teams
- Member preferences

Process
- Common purpose
- Specific goals
- Team efficacy
- Team identity
- Team cohesion
- Mental models
- Conflict levels
- Social loafing

Team effectiveness

of the team's productivity, managers' ratings of the team's performance, and aggregate measures of member satisfaction.

We can organize the key components of effective teams into three general categories. First are the resources and other *contextual* influences that make teams effective. The second relates to the team's *composition*. Finally, *process* variables are events within the team that influence effectiveness. We will explore each of these components next.

Team Context: What Factors Determine Whether Teams Are Successful?

The four contextual factors most significantly related to team performance are adequate resources, effective leadership, a climate of trust, and a performance evaluation and reward system that reflects team contributions.

Adequate Resources   Teams are part of a larger organization system; every work team relies on resources outside the group to sustain it. A scarcity of resources directly reduces the ability of a team to perform its job effectively and achieve its goals. As one study concluded after looking at 13 factors related to group performance, "perhaps one of the most important characteristics of an effective work group is the support the group receives from the organization."[22] This support includes timely information, proper equipment, adequate staffing, encouragement, and administrative assistance.

Leadership and Structure   Teams can't function if they can't agree on who is to do what and ensure all members share the workload. Agreeing on the specifics of work and how they fit together to integrate individual skills requires leadership and structure, either from management or from team members themselves. In self-managed teams, members absorb many of the duties typically assumed by managers. A manager's job then becomes managing *outside* (rather than inside) the team.

As we mentioned before, leadership is especially important in multiteam systems. Here, leaders need to delegate responsibility to teams and play the role of facilitator, making sure the teams work together rather than against one another.[23]

Climate of Trust   Trust is the foundation of leadership; it allows a team to accept and commit to the leader's goals and decisions. Members of effective teams exhibit trust in their leaders.[24] They also trust each other. Interpersonal trust among team members facilitates cooperation, reduces the need to monitor each other's behavior, and bonds individuals through the belief that members won't take advantage of them. Members are more likely to take risks and expose vulnerabilities when they can trust others on their team. The overall level of trust in a team is important, but the way trust is dispersed among team members also matters. Trust levels that are asymmetric and imbalanced between team members can mitigate the performance advantages of a high overall level of trust—in such cases, coalitions form that often undermine the team as a whole.[25]

Trust is a perception that can be vulnerable to shifting conditions in a team environment. Also, trust is not unequivocally desirable. For instance, recent research in Singapore found that, in high-trust teams, individuals are less likely to claim and defend personal ownership of their ideas, but individuals who do still claim personal ownership are rated as lower contributors *by team members.*[26] This "punishment" by the team may reflect resentments that create negative relationships, increased conflicts, and reduced performance.

Performance Evaluation and Reward System   Individual performance evaluations and incentives may interfere with the development of high-performance teams. So, in addition to evaluating and rewarding employees for their individual contributions, management should utilize hybrid performance systems that incorporate an individual member component to recognize individual contributions and a group reward to recognize positive team outcomes.[27] Group-based appraisals, profit-sharing, small-group incentives, and other system modifications can reinforce team effort and commitment.

Team Composition

Maria Contreras-Sweet, head of the U.S. Small Business Administration, said, "When I'm building a team, I'm looking for people who are resourceful. I need people who are flexible, and I really need people who are discreet.... Discreetness also speaks to integrity."[28] These are good qualities, but not all that we should consider when staffing teams. The team composition category includes variables that relate to how teams should be staffed: the abilities and personalities of team members, allocation of roles, diversity, cultural differences, size of the team, and members' preferences for teamwork. As you can expect, opinions vary widely about the type of members leaders want on their teams.

Abilities of Members   It's true we occasionally read about an athletic team of mediocre players who, because of excellent coaching, determination, and precision teamwork, beat a far more talented group. But such cases make the news precisely because they are unusual. A team's performance depends in part on the knowledge, skills, and abilities of individual members.[29] Abilities set limits on what members can do and how effectively they will perform on a team.

Research reveals insights into team composition and performance. First, when solving a complex problem such as reengineering an assembly line, high-ability teams—composed of mostly intelligent members—do better than lower-ability teams. High-ability teams are also more adaptable to changing situations; they can more effectively apply existing knowledge to new problems.

Members of a research team at the innovation lab of Swiss bank UBS are testing digital, virtual reality, and other new technologies to attract a young generation of investors and to help current clients visualize complex investment portfolios. Team members have the technical expertise and skills needed to function as a high-ability team.
Source: Arnd Wiegmann/Reuters

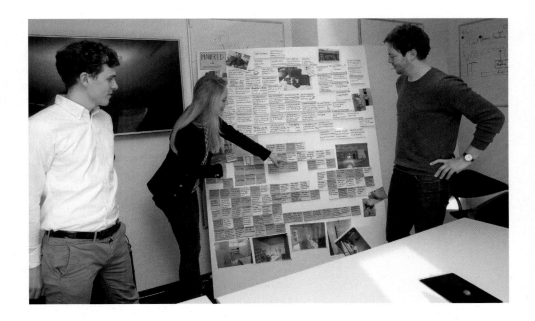

Myth or Science?

Team Members Who Are "Hot" Should Make the Play

Before we tell you whether this statement is true or false, we need to take a step back and ask: "Can individuals go on 'hot' streaks?" In teams, and especially in sports, we often hear about players who are on a streak and have the "hot hand." Basketball player LeBron James scores five baskets in a row, golfer Rory McIlroy makes three birdies in a row for the European Ryder Cup team, and tennis player Serena Williams hits four aces in a row during a doubles match with her sister Venus. Most people (around 90 percent) believe LeBron, Rory, and Serena score well because they are on a hot streak, performing above their average.

Although people *believe* in the hot hand, the scores tell the story. About half the relevant studies have shown that the hot hand is possible, while the remaining half show it is not. But perception can influence reality, so perhaps the more important question is whether belief in the hot hand affects teams' strategies. One study of volleyball players showed that coaches and players allocate more balls to players who are believed to have the hot hand. Is this a good strategy? If the hot player's performance is actually lower than her teammates', then giving her more balls to hit will hurt the team because the better players aren't getting enough chances to hit, while she gets more chances to perform.

Considering the research to date, then, the opening statement appears to be false.

Sources: M. Raab, B. Gula, and G. Gigerenzer, "The Hot Hand Exists in Volleyball and Is Used for Allocation Decisions," *Journal of Experimental Psychology: Applied* 18, no. 1 (2012): 81–94; T Gilovich, R. Vallone, and A. Tversky, "The Hot Hand in Basketball: On the Misperception of Random Sequences," *Cognitive Psychology* 17 (1985): 295–314; and M. Bar-Eli, S. Avugos, and M. Raab, "Twenty Years of 'Hot Hand' Research: The Hot Hand Phenomenon: Review and Critique," *Psychology, Sport, and Exercise* 7 (2006): 525–53.

Finally, the ability of the team's leader matters. Smart team leaders help less intelligent team members when they struggle with a task. A less intelligent leader can, conversely, neutralize the effect of a high-ability team.[30]

Personality of Members   We demonstrated in Chapter 5 that personality significantly influences individual behavior. Some dimensions identified in the Big Five personality model are particularly relevant to team effectiveness.[31] Conscientiousness is especially important to teams. Conscientious people are good at backing up other team members and sensing when their support is truly needed. Conscientious teams also have other advantages—one study found that behavioral tendencies such as organization, achievement orientation, and endurance were all related to higher levels of team performance.[32]

Team composition can be based on individual personalities to good effect. Suppose an organization needs to create 20 teams of 4 people each and has 40 highly conscientious people and 40 who score low on conscientiousness. Would the organization be better off (1) forming 10 teams of highly conscientious people and 10 teams of members low on conscientiousness, or (2) "seeding" each team with 2 people who scored high and 2 who scored low on conscientiousness? Perhaps surprisingly, evidence suggests option 1 is the best choice; performance across the teams will be higher if the organization forms 10 highly conscientious teams and 10 teams low in conscientiousness. The reason is that a team with varying conscientiousness levels will not work to the peak performance of its highly conscientious members. Instead, a group normalization dynamic (or simple resentment) will complicate interactions and force the highly conscientious members to lower their expectations, thus reducing the group's performance.[33]

What about the other traits? Teams with a high level of openness to experience tend to perform better, and research indicates that constructive task conflict *enhances* the effect. Open team members communicate better with one another and throw out more ideas, which makes teams composed of open people more creative and innovative.[34] Task conflict also enhances performance for teams with high levels of emotional stability.[35] It's not so much that the conflict itself improves performance for these teams, but that teams characterized by openness and emotional stability are able to handle conflict and leverage it to improve performance. The minimum level of team member agreeableness matters, too: teams do worse when they have one or more highly disagreeable members, and a wide span in individual levels of agreeableness can lower productivity. Research is not clear on the outcomes of extraversion, but a recent study indicated that a high mean level of extraversion in a team can increase the level of helping behaviors, particularly in a climate of cooperation.[36] Thus the personality traits of individuals are as important to teams as the overall personality characteristics of the team.

Allocation of Roles   Teams have different needs, and members should be selected to ensure all the various roles are filled. A study of 778 major league baseball teams over a 21-year period highlights the importance of assigning roles appropriately.[37] As you might expect, teams with more experienced and skilled members performed better. However, the experience and skill of those in core roles who handled more of the workflow of the team, and were central to all work processes (in this case, pitchers and catchers), were especially vital. In other words, put your most able, experienced, and conscientious workers in the most central roles in a team.

We can identify nine potential team roles (see Exhibit 10-4). Successful work teams have selected people to play all these roles based on their skills and preferences.[38] (On many teams, individuals will play multiple roles.) To increase the

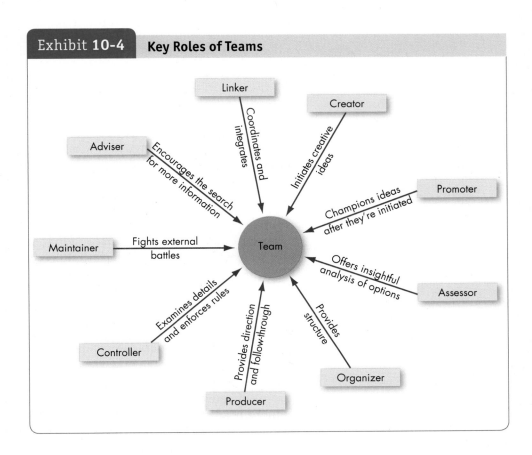

Exhibit 10-4   Key Roles of Teams

likelihood team members will work well together, managers need to understand the individual strengths each person can bring to a team, select members with their strengths in mind, and allocate work assignments that fit with members' preferred styles.

Diversity of Members   In Chapter 9, we discussed the effect of diversity on groups. How does *team* diversity affect *team* performance? The degree to which members of a work unit (group, team, or department) share a common demographic attribute, such as age, sex, race, educational level, or length of service in the organization, is the subject of **organizational demography**. Organizational demography suggests that attributes such as age or the date of joining should help predict turnover. The logic goes like this: Turnover will be greater among those with dissimilar experiences because communication is more difficult and conflict is more likely. Increased conflict makes membership less attractive, so employees are more likely to quit. Similarly, the losers of a conflict are more apt to leave voluntarily or be forced out.[39] The conclusion is that diversity negatively affects team performance.

Many of us hold the optimistic view that diversity should be a good thing—diverse teams should benefit from differing perspectives. Two meta-analytic reviews show, however, that demographic diversity is essentially unrelated to team performance, while a third review suggests that race and gender diversity are actually negatively related to team performance.[40] Other research findings are mixed. One qualifier is that gender and ethnic diversity have more negative effects in occupations dominated by white or male employees, but in more demographically balanced occupations, diversity is less of a problem. Diversity in function, education, and expertise are positively related to team performance, but these effects are small and depend on the situation.

Proper leadership can improve the performance of diverse teams.[41] For example, one study of 68 teams in China found that teams diverse in knowledge, skills, and ways of approaching problems were more creative, but only when their leaders were transformational (see Chapter 12 for definition) and inspiring.[42]

Cultural Differences   We have discussed research on team diversity regarding a number of differences. But what about cultural differences? Evidence indicates cultural diversity interferes with team processes, at least in the short term,[43] but let's dig a little deeper: what about differences in cultural status? Though it's debatable, people with higher cultural status are usually in the majority or ruling race group of their nations. Researchers in the United Kingdom found that cultural status differences affected team performance, whereby individuals in teams with more high cultural-status members than low cultural-status members realized improved performance...for *every* member.[44] This suggests not that diverse teams should be filled with individuals who have high cultural status in their countries, but that we should be aware of how people identify with their cultural status even in diverse group settings.

In general, cultural diversity seems to be an asset for tasks that call for a variety of viewpoints. But culturally heterogeneous teams have more difficulty learning to work with each other and solving problems. The good news is that these difficulties seem to dissipate with time.

Size of Teams   Most experts agree that keeping teams small is key to improving group effectiveness.[45] Amazon CEO Jeff Bezos uses the "two-pizza" rule, saying, "If it takes more than two pizzas to feed the team, the team is too big."[46] Psychologist George Miller claimed "the magical number [is] seven, plus or

organizational demography   The degree to which members of a work unit share a common demographic attribute, such as age, sex, race, educational level, or length of service in an organization, and the impact of this attribute on turnover.

Is it wrong that I'd rather have guys on my team?

Please don't call me sexist; women are great colleagues and equally effective managers, but I'd rather have men on my team. It's more relaxing for me, and for the other guys I think, because we naturally understand each other and can talk freely. The teams with all men that I've been in have all been very productive.

—*Jorge*

Dear Jorge,

With all the talk currently focused on gender diversity in organizations, your viewpoint is refreshingly honest. And your preferences are not uncommon. Researchers who studied 8 years of employee surveys from a large U.S. organization found that individuals were happier on teams mainly of their own gender, whereas those on diverse teams reported less happiness, trust, and cooperation. Researcher Sara Fisher Ellison noted, "People are more comfortable around other people who are like them."

In some ways, the preference for our own gender in teams is an ugly truth. After all, if there hadn't been gender diversity initiatives and protections, a majority of professional positions may still be closed to women in masculine cultures like Japan, Austria, and Venezuela (see Hofstede's cultural values in Chapter 5). The value system in many countries has fortunately changed, with increased recognition of team diversity's potential for higher morale, trust, and satisfaction. Notice that these are *values*, as opposed to the reported *reality* from the paragraph above. Ellison concluded that there is a "mismatch between the kind of workplace people think they would like and the actual workplace that would make them happier."

Don't think this is your ticket to male-only teams, though. Happiness aside, this study found that diverse teams realized significantly greater revenues, productivity, and performance. Other research in Spain indicated that gender-diverse teams realize novel solutions and radical innovation at a greater rate. Still other research suggested that gender-diverse teams perform better than male-dominated ones in sales and profits. The contextual climate is key, though. One meta-analysis found that gender equality and collectivism were important conditions for task performance in diverse teams; a Danish study indicated that diverse top management teams realized higher financial performance only when the structure supported cross-functional team work; and a study in South Korea indicated that cooperative group norms can lower the negative effects of gender diversity.

What all this means for you is that, while you may naturally prefer to work with men, it's not good for business.

You would be better off putting your efforts into creating an egalitarian atmosphere and choosing your teammates based on what they can contribute to your team.

Sources: C. Diaz-Garcia, A. Gonzalez-Moreno, and F. Jose Saez-Martinez, "Gender Diversity within R&D Teams: Its Impact on Radicalness of Innovation," *Innovation-Management Policy & Practice* 15, no. 2 (2013): 149–60; S. Hoogedoorn, H. Oosterbeek, and M. van Praag, "The Impact of Gender Diversity on the Performance of Business Teams: Evidence from a Field Experiment," *Management Science* 59, no. 7 (2013): 1514–28; N. Opstrup and A. R. Villadsen, "The Right Mix? Gender Diversity in Top Management Teams and Financial Performance," *Public Administration Review*, 2015, 291–301; M. Schneid, R. Isidor, C. Li, et al., "The Influence of Cultural Context on the Relationship between Gender Diversity and Team Performance: A Meta-Analysis," *International Journal of Human Resource Management* 26, no. 6 (2015): 733–56; J. Y. Seong and D.-S. Hong, "Gender Diversity: How Can We Facilitate Its Positive Effects on Teams?" *Social Behavior and Personality* 41, no. 3 (2013): 497–508; and R. E. Silverman, "Do Men and Women Like Working Together?" *The Wall Street Journal*, December 16, 2014, D2.

minus two," as the ideal team size.[47] Author and *Forbes* publisher Rich Karlgaard writes, "Bigger teams almost never correlate with a greater chance of success" because the potential connections between people grow exponentially as team size increases, complicating communications.[48]

Generally speaking, the most effective teams have five to nine members. Experts suggest using the smallest number of people who can do the task. Unfortunately, managers often err by making teams too large. It may require only four or five members to develop an array of views and skills, while coordination problems can increase as team members are added. When teams have excess members, cohesiveness and mutual accountability decline, social loafing

A Japanese nurse (left) served on a seven-member medical team formed by the International Committee of the Red Cross and deployed to the Philippines after a typhoon hit Mindanoa Island. The small team of health care workers had the capacity to respond quickly and effectively in providing patients with emergency medical care.
Source: Kyodo/AP Images

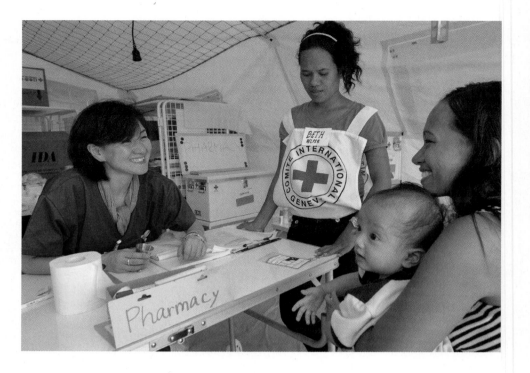

increases, and people communicate less. Members of large teams have trouble coordinating with one another, especially under time pressure. When a natural working unit is larger and you want a team effort, consider breaking the group into subteams.[49]

Member Preferences   Not every employee is a team player. Given the option, many employees will select themselves *out* of team participation. When people who prefer to work alone are required to team up, there is a direct threat to the team's morale and to individual member satisfaction.[50] This suggests that, when selecting team members, managers should consider individual preferences along with abilities, personalities, and skills. High-performing teams are likely to be composed of people who prefer working as part of a group.

Team Processes

The final category related to team effectiveness includes process variables such as member commitment to a common purpose, establishment of specific team goals, team efficacy, team identity, team cohesion, mental models, a managed level of conflict, and minimized social loafing. These will be especially important in larger teams and in teams that are highly interdependent.[51]

Why are processes important to team effectiveness? Teams should create outputs greater than the sum of their inputs. Exhibit 10-5 illustrates how group processes can have an impact on a group's actual effectiveness.[52] Teams are often used in research laboratories because they can draw on the diverse skills of various individuals to produce more meaningful research than researchers working independently—that is, they produce positive synergy, and their process gains exceed their process losses.

Common Plan and Purpose   Effective teams begin by analyzing the team's mission, developing goals to achieve that mission, and creating strategies for achieving the goals. Teams that consistently perform better have a clear sense of

Exhibit **10-5**   **Effects of Group Processes**

Potential group effectiveness + Process gains − Process losses = Actual group effectiveness

what needs to be done and how.[53] This sounds obvious, but many teams ignore this fundamental process.

Members of successful teams put a tremendous amount of time and effort into discussing, shaping, and agreeing on a purpose that belongs to them collectively and individually. This common purpose, when accepted by the team, becomes what GPS is to a ship captain: It provides direction and guidance under any conditions. Like a ship following the wrong course, teams that don't have good planning skills are doomed, executing the wrong plan.[54] Teams should agree on whether their purpose is to learn about and master a task or simply to perform the task; evidence suggests that differing perspectives on learning versus performance lead to lower levels of team performance overall.[55]

reflexivity A team characteristic of reflecting on and adjusting the master plan when necessary.

Effective teams show **reflexivity**, meaning they reflect on and adjust their purpose when necessary. A team must have a good plan, but it needs to be willing and able to adapt when conditions call for it.[56] Interestingly, some evidence suggests that teams high in reflexivity are better able to adapt to conflicting plans and goals among team members.[57]

Specific Goals   Successful teams translate their common purpose into specific, measurable, and realistic performance goals. Specific goals facilitate clear communication. They help teams maintain their focus on getting results.

Consistent with the research on individual goals, team goals should be challenging. Difficult but achievable goals raise team performance on those criteria for which they're set. So, for instance, goals for quantity tend to increase quantity, goals for accuracy increase accuracy, and so on.[58]

team efficacy A team's collective belief that they can succeed at their tasks.

Team Efficacy   Effective teams have confidence in themselves; they believe they can succeed. We call this **team efficacy**.[59] Teams that have been successful raise their beliefs about future success, which, in turn, motivates them to work harder. In addition, teams that have a shared knowledge of individual capabilities can strengthen the link between team members' self-efficacy and their individual creativity because members can more effectively solicit informed opinions from their teammates.[60] What can management do to increase team efficacy? Two options are helping the team achieve small successes that build confidence, and providing training to improve members' technical and interpersonal skills. The greater the abilities of team members, the more likely the team will develop confidence and the ability to deliver on that confidence.

Team Identity   In Chapter 9, we discussed the important role of social identity in people's lives. When people connect emotionally with the groups they're in, they are more likely to invest in their relationship with those groups. It's the same with teams. For example, research with soldiers in the Netherlands indicated that individuals who felt included and respected by team members became more willing to work hard for their teams, even though as soldiers they were already called upon to be dedicated to their units. Therefore, by recognizing individuals' specific skills and abilities, as well as creating a climate of

team identity A team member's affinity for and sense of belongingness to his or her team.

respect and inclusion, leaders and members can foster positive **team identity** and improved team outcomes.[61]

Organizational identity is important, too. Rarely do teams operate in a vacuum—more often teams interact with other teams, requiring interteam coordination. Individuals with a positive team identity but without a positive organizational identity can become fixed to their teams and unwilling to coordinate with other teams within the organization.[62]

Team Cohesion

team cohesion A situation when team members are emotionally attached to one another and motivated toward the team because of their attachment.

Have you ever been a member of a team that really "gelled," one in which team members felt connected? The term **team cohesion** means members are emotionally attached to one another and motivated toward the team because of their attachment. Team cohesion is a useful tool to predict team outcomes. For example, a large study in China recently indicated that if team cohesion is high and tasks are complex, costly investments in promotions, rewards, training, and so forth yield greater profitable team creativity. Teams with low cohesion and simple tasks, on the other hand, are not likely to respond to incentives with greater creativity.[63]

Team cohesion is a strong predictor of team performance such that when cohesion is harmed, performance may be, too. Negative relationships are one driver of reduced cohesion. To mitigate this effect, teams can foster high levels of interdependence and high-quality interpersonal interactions.

Mental Models

mental models Team members' knowledge and beliefs about how the work gets done by the team.

Effective teams share accurate **mental models**—organized mental representations of the key elements within a team's environment that team members share.[64] (If team mission and goals pertain to *what* a team needs to be effective, mental models pertain to *how* a team does its work.) If team members have the wrong mental models, which is particularly likely in teams under acute stress, their performance suffers.[65] One review of 65 independent studies found that teams with shared mental models engaged in more frequent interactions with one another, were more motivated, had more positive attitudes toward their work, and had higher levels of objectively-rated performance.[66] If team

Product Hunt founder Ryan Hoover (on computer) and his entrepreneurial team are highly cohesive. The company describes itself as a "tight-knit team" whose members share a love of new tech products, care about people, and are passionate about building communities that celebrate tech creations.

Source: LiPo Ching/Bay Area News Group/TNS/Landov

members have different ideas about how to do things, however, the team will fight over methods rather than focus on what needs to be done.[67]

Individuals who normally function in *action teams*—teams with specialists engaged in intense, interdependent, and unpredictable tasks—are likely to share mental models. Even though they are often under acute stress, their performance levels can be high because the stress has been normalized through the expected context. These action teams have learned that the best way to share mental models is to voice them. An anesthetic team in a hospital is one example of an action team with shared mental models. For example, research in Switzerland found that anesthetic teams communicated two distinct types of messages while in an operation: vocally monitoring each others' performance (not to criticize but to keep a vocal record of events), and "talking to the room" (announcements to everyone such as "Patient's blood pressure is dropping"). The study found that high- and low-performing teams communicated in these ways equally often; what mattered to performance was the sequencing of the communication to maintain a shared mental model. High-performing teams followed up monitoring dialogue with assistance and instructions, and talking-to-the-room dialogue with further team dialogue.[68] The message seems simple: to maintain shared mental models, share conversation about what is happening while the team is in operation!

Conflict Levels   Conflict has a complex relationship with team performance, and it's not necessarily bad. *Relationship conflicts*—those based on interpersonal incompatibility, tension, and animosity toward others—are almost always dysfunctional. However, when teams are performing nonroutine activities, disagreements about task content—called *task conflicts*—stimulate discussion, promote critical assessment of problems and options, and can lead to better team decisions. According to one study conducted in China, moderate levels of task conflict during the initial phases of team performance were positively related to team creativity, but both very low and very high levels of task conflict were negatively related to team performance.[69] In other words, both too much and too little disagreement about how a team should initially perform a creative task can inhibit performance.

The way conflicts are resolved can make the difference between effective and ineffective teams. A study of ongoing comments made by 37 autonomous work groups showed that effective teams resolved conflicts by explicitly discussing the issues, whereas ineffective teams had unresolved conflicts that were focused more on personalities and the way things were said.[70]

Which teams are more likely to have conflicts than others? It's not a simple answer. While we may presume that diversity increases conflicts, the answer is likely to be much more subtle than that. For example, recent research in Spain found that when individual team members varied greatly in their perceptions of organizational support, task conflict increased, communication decreased, and ultimately team performance suffered.[71] If the researchers had instead compared only the average level of organizational support given to the team, rather than how members perceived the support, they would have missed the correct causal links. Thus we need to be careful not to overgeneralize.

Social Loafing   As we noted earlier, individuals can engage in social loafing and coast on the group's effort when their particular contributions (or lack thereof) can't be identified. Effective teams undermine this tendency by making members individually and jointly accountable for the team's purpose, goals, and approach.[72] Therefore, members should be clear on what they are individually and jointly responsible for on the team.

Turning Individuals into Team Players

10-5 Explain how organizations can create team players.

We've made a case for the value and growing popularity of teams. But many people are not inherently team players, and many organizations have historically nurtured individual accomplishments. Teams often fit well in countries that score high on collectivism, but what if an organization wants to introduce teams into a work population of individuals born and raised in an individualistic society?

Here are options for managers trying to turn individuals into team players.

Selecting: Hiring Team Players

Some people already possess the interpersonal skills to be effective team players. When hiring team members, be sure candidates can fulfill their team roles as well as technical requirements.[73]

Creating teams often means resisting the urge to hire the best talent no matter what. For example, the New York Knicks professional basketball team pays Carmelo Anthony well because he scores a lot of points for his team; but statistics show he takes more shots than other highly paid players in the league, which means fewer shots for his teammates.[74]

As a final consideration, personal traits appear to make some people better candidates for working in diverse teams. Teams made of members who like to work through difficult mental puzzles also seem more effective and able to capitalize on the multiple points of view that arise from diversity in age and education.[75]

Training: Creating Team Players

Training specialists conduct exercises that allow employees to experience the satisfaction teamwork can provide. Workshops help employees improve their problem-solving, communication, negotiation, conflict-management, and coaching skills. L'Oréal, for example, found that successful sales teams required much more than a staff of high-ability salespeople. "What we didn't account for was that many members of our top team in sales had been promoted because they had excellent technical and executional skills," said L'Oréal's senior VP David Waldock. As a result of introducing purposeful team training, Waldock says, "We are no longer a team just on paper, working independently. We have a real group dynamic now, and it's a good one."[76] An effective team doesn't develop overnight—it takes time.

Rewarding: Providing Incentives to Be a Good Team Player

A traditional organization's reward system must be reworked to encourage cooperative efforts rather than competitive ones.[77] Hallmark Cards Inc. added to its basic individual-incentive system an annual bonus based on the achievement of team goals. Whole Foods directs most of its performance-based rewards toward team performance. As a result, teams select new members carefully so they will

New engineering employees of India's Tata Consultancy Services work in teams to construct paper boats during a team-building exercise at the firm's training center. Creating team players is essential to the success of TCS as employees must collaborate and work cohesively in providing IT consulting services and business solutions for global clients.

Source: Namas Bhojani/Bloomberg via Getty Images

contribute to team effectiveness (and, thus, team bonuses).[78] It is usually best to set a cooperative tone as soon as possible in the life of a team. As we already noted, teams that switch from competitive to cooperative do not immediately share information, and they still tend to make rushed, poor-quality decisions.[79] Apparently, the low trust typical of the competitive group will not be readily replaced by high trust with a quick change in reward systems.

Promotions, pay raises, and other forms of recognition should be given to individuals who work effectively as team members by training new colleagues, sharing information, helping resolve team conflicts, and mastering needed new skills. This doesn't mean individual contributions should be ignored; rather, they should be balanced with selfless contributions to the team.

Finally, don't forget the intrinsic rewards, such as camaraderie, that employees can receive from teamwork. It's exciting to be part of a successful team. The opportunity for personal development of self and teammates can be a very satisfying and rewarding experience.

✪ **TRY IT!**

If your professor has assigned this, go to the Assignments section of **mymanagementlab.com** to complete the **Simulation:** *Teams*.

Beware! Teams Aren't Always the Answer

10-6 Decide when to use individuals instead of teams.

Teamwork takes more time and often more resources than individual work. Teams have increased communication demands, conflicts to manage, and meetings to run. So, the benefits of using teams have to exceed the costs, and that's not always possible.[80]

How do you know whether the work of your group would be better done in teams? You can apply three tests.[81] First, can the work be done better by more than one person? Good indicators are the complexity of the work and the need for different perspectives. Simple tasks that don't require diverse input are probably better left to individuals. Second, does the work create a common purpose or set of goals for the people in the group that is more than the aggregate of individual goals? Many service departments of new-vehicle dealers have introduced teams that link customer-service people, mechanics, parts specialists, and sales representatives. Such teams can better manage collective responsibility for ensuring customer needs are properly met.

The final test is to determine whether the members of the group are interdependent. Using teams makes sense when there is interdependence among tasks—the success of the whole depends on the success of each one, *and* the success of each one depends on the success of the others. Soccer, for instance, is an obvious *team* sport. Success requires a great deal of coordination among interdependent players. Conversely, except possibly for relays, swim teams are not really teams. They're groups of individuals performing individually, whose total performance is merely the aggregate summation of their individual performances.

Summary

Few trends have influenced jobs as much as the massive movement of teams into the workplace. Working on teams requires employees to cooperate with others, share information, confront differences, and sublimate personal interests for the greater good of the team. Understanding the distinctions between problem-solving, self-managed, cross-functional, and virtual teams as well as multiteam systems helps determine the appropriate applications for team-based work. Concepts such as reflexivity, team efficacy, team identity, team cohesion, and mental models bring to light important issues relating to team context, composition, and processes. For teams to function optimally, careful attention must be given to hiring, creating, and rewarding team players. Still, effective organizations recognize that teams are not always the best method for getting the work done efficiently. Careful discernment and an understanding of organizational behavior are needed.

Implications for Managers

- Effective teams have adequate resources, effective leadership, a climate of trust, and a performance evaluation and reward system that reflects team contributions. These teams have individuals with technical expertise, and the right traits and skills.
- Effective teams tend to be small. They have members who fill role demands and who prefer to be part of a group.
- Effective teams have members who believe in the team's capabilities, are committed to a common plan and purpose, and have an accurate shared mental model of what is to be accomplished.
- Select individuals who have the interpersonal skills to be effective team players, provide training to develop teamwork skills, and reward individuals for cooperative efforts.
- Do not assume that teams are always needed. When tasks will not benefit from interdependency, individuals may be the better choice.

To Get the Most Out of Teams, Empower Them

POINT

If you want high-performing teams with members who like each other and their jobs, here's a simple solution: Remove the leash tied to them by management and let them make their own decisions. In other words, empower them. This trend started a long time ago, when organizations realized that creating layers of bureaucracy thwarts innovation, slows progress to a trickle, and merely provides hoops for people to jump through in order to get anything done.

You can empower teams in two ways. One way is structurally, by transferring decision making from managers to team members and giving teams the official power to develop their own strategies. The other way is psychologically, by enhancing team members' beliefs that they have more authority, even though legitimate authority still rests with the organization's leaders. Structural empowerment leads to heightened feelings of psychological empowerment, giving teams (and organizations) the best of both worlds.

Research suggests empowered teams benefit in a number of ways. Members are more motivated. They exhibit higher levels of commitment to the team and the organization. And they perform much better. Empowerment sends a signal to the team that it is trusted and doesn't have to be constantly micromanaged by upper leadership. And when teams get the freedom to make their own choices, they accept more responsibility for and take ownership of both the good and the bad.

Granted, that responsibility also means empowered teams must take the initiative to foster their ongoing learning and development, but teams entrusted with the authority to guide their own destiny do just that. So, do yourself (and your company) a favor and make sure that teams, rather than needless layers of middle managers, are the ones making the decisions that count.

COUNTERPOINT

Empowerment can do some good in certain circumstances, but it's certainly not a cure-all.

Yes, organizations have become flatter over the past several decades, paving the way for decision-making authority to seep into lower levels of the organization. But consider that many teams are "empowered" simply because the management ranks have been so thinned that there is no one left to make the key calls. Empowerment is then just an excuse to ask teams to take on more responsibility without an accompanying increase in tangible benefits like pay.

In addition, the organization's leadership already has a good idea of what it would like its teams (and individual employees) to accomplish. If managers leave teams to their own devices, how likely is it that those teams will always choose what the manager wanted? Even if the manager offers suggestions about how the team might proceed, empowered teams can easily ignore that advice. Instead, they need direction on what goals to pursue and how to pursue them. That's what effective leadership is all about.

When decision-making authority is distributed among team members, each member's role is less clear, and members lack a leader to whom they can go for advice. And finally, when teams are self-managed, they become like silos, disconnected from the rest of the organization and its mission. Simply handing people authority is no guarantee they will use it effectively. So, leave the power to make decisions in the hands of those who were assigned leadership roles. After all, they got to be leaders for a reason, and they can best guide the team to stay focused and perform at top levels to maximize organizational outcomes.

Sources: S. I. Tannenbaum, J. Mathieu, E. Salas, and D. Cohen, "Teams Are Changing: Are Research and Practice Evolving Fast Enough?" Industrial and Organizational Psychology 5 (2012): 2–24; and R. Ashkenas, "How to Empower Your Team for Non-Negotiable Results," Forbes, April 24, 2013, downloaded June 10, 2013, from www.forbes.com.

CHAPTER REVIEW

QUESTIONS FOR REVIEW

10-1 How do you explain the growing popularity of teams in organizations?

10-2 What is the difference between a group and a team?

10-3 What are the five types of team arrangements?

10-4 What conditions or context factors determine whether teams are effective?

10-5 How can organizations create team players?

10-6 When is work performed by individuals preferred over work performed by teams?

EXPERIENTIAL EXERCISE   Composing the "Perfect" Team

Break into teams of four to five. Assume you work for a company that redesigns existing products to improve them, from computer keyboards to bicycle helmets to toothbrushes. As a result, creativity is a key factor in whether your company succeeds in developing a product that is marketable.

You need to staff a new team of 5 individuals, and you have a pool of 20 to choose from. For each person, you have information about the following characteristics: intelligence, work experience, conscientiousness, agreeableness, neuroticism, openness to experience, and extraversion.

Answer the following questions as a team:

10-7. If you could form your perfect team for this context, what would it look like? In other words, what characteristics would you choose for each of the five members—a lot of work experience or a little; high, moderate, or low conscientiousness; and so on? Why?

10-8. How, if at all, would your choices change if the task required teams to make quick decisions that were not necessarily the most creative? Why?

10-9. Each member of your group should describe his or her ideal team member—one hypothetical person you'd most like to work with in this context (use the same criteria as in question 10-7). As a group, compare your responses. Does every person's ideal member share the same characteristics, or are there differences? If you could, would you compose a team entirely of your ideal individuals? Why or why not?

ETHICAL DILEMMA   The Sum of the Team Is Less Than Its Members

Of the billions of tons of carbon let loose into the world's atmosphere each year, China is responsible for 21 percent, mostly due to its growth in manufacturing. And due to the billions of tons of wastewater and sewage released into rivers and lakes by Chinese chemical firms every year, 300 million of its citizens do not have clean drinking water. Clearly, these ethical breaches represent the failure not of one individual but of scores of teams: to be exact, top management teams in organizations throughout the country. Does that mean the leaders of China's companies are all unethical? Surely not.

To increase corporate social responsibility (CSR), we need to understand the team dynamics that lead to unethical decision making. First, we examine the context. As a major emerging country, China witnessed unprecedented growth in industry that has brought opportunities for corporate profits, better salaries, and better access to services for its citizens. Millions have been able to pull themselves and their families out of poverty. Few would argue that providing jobs and services isn't a highly ethical pursuit. However, top management teams now face pressure to sustain growth at any cost. The top management team of Rongping Chemical Company made the tragic decision to cut costs and increase profits by dumping untreated chlorine into rivers, raising the level of chromium-6—a tasteless, odorless compound that causes ulcers and cancers—to over 20 times national standards. Other organizations, like Luliang Chemical Company, have done the same, endangering the health of the same citizens it helps with jobs and opportunities.

Some observers have been shocked that top management teams in a country with collectivist values, which stress a group-oriented outlook, would make decisions that don't consider everyone affected by them. One recent study indicated that the problem is competing ethical principles: duty to others v. duty to society. As management teams faced financial dissatisfaction about their firm's performance, environmental ethics and CSR actions decreased, suggesting the teams were feeling pressure from their organization's stakeholders and becoming less concerned about the environment. They may also have rationalized that providing jobs was for the greater societal good and believed that violating stakeholder expectations would cost them their own place on the management team. However, the study found that on an individual level, when a person's sense of collectivist values increased, environmental ethics also increased, suggesting that the top managers did favor CSR initiatives, but other concerns predominated in the team settings. We may conclude that these teams are likely hindering the progress of environmental awareness. When teams feel pressured to meet certain (sometimes narrow) metrics, there may be more unethical team decisions than individual members would make on their own.

Questions

10-10. Do you think you could be convinced to let your organization dump chemicals such as chromium-6 into the water supply? Why or why not?

10-11. Why might top management teams be more likely to make unethical decisions than their individual members would make?

10-12. The cases of Rongping and Luliang are far from isolated incidents. You may remember the case of Pacific Gas & Electric (PG&E), which dumped chromium-6 into the water supply in Hinckley, California, as recounted in the movie *Erin Brockovich*. That case resulted in a $333 million award, the largest settlement ever in a direct-action lawsuit, to help the town's 2,000 residents. In contrast, when 1,721 villagers brought suit against Rongping (more plaintiffs than ever in China, to date), the court ordered the company to pay only a total compensation of $105,000 for damage to the land. And the Chinese environmental group Friends of Nature filed the country's first-ever public-interest lawsuit, which shut down Rongping's plant in a village, but did not offer monetary restitution for the villagers. How might these outcomes affect the ethical decisions of top management teams in the future?

Sources: "Eight Cases That Mattered," *ChinaDialogue,* https://www.chinadialogue.net/article/show/single/en/4429-Eight-cases-that-mattered, accessed June 22, 2015; "Facts about Chromium," Environmental Protection Agency, http://www.epa.gov/region7/pdf/national_beef_leathers-prime_tanning_chromiumVI_Fact_Sheet.pdf, accessed June 22, 2015; EJOLT Team at School of Geography and China Centre, University of Oxford, "Heavy Metal Pollution in Quijing, Yunnan, China," *Environmental Justice Atlas,* February 25, 2015; S. Thau, R. Derfler-Rozin, M. Pitesa, M. S. Mitchell, and M. M. Pillutla, "Unethical for the Sake of the Group: Risk of Social Exclusion and Pro-Group Unethical Behavior," *Journal of Applied Psychology* 100, no. 1 (2015): 98–113; J. Steinberg, "Hinckley: No Hollywood Ending for Erin Brockovich's Tainted Town," *San Jose Mercury News,* July 7, 2013, http://www.mercurynews.com/ci_23649050/hinkley-no-hollywood-ending-erin-brockovichs-tainted-town; and X. Wang and M. N. Young, "Does Collectivism Affect Environmental Ethics? A Multi-Level Study of Top Management Teams from Chemical Firms in China," *Journal of Business Ethics* 122, no. 3 (2014): 387–94.

CASE INCIDENT 1   Tongue-Tied in Teams

Thirty-one-year-old Robert Murphy has the best intentions to participate in team meetings, but when it's "game time," he chokes. An online marketing representative, Robert cannot be criticized for lack of preparation. After being invited to a business meeting with six of his coworkers and his supervisor, Robert began doing his research on the meeting's subject matter. He compiled notes and arranged them neatly. As soon as the meeting began, however, "I just sat there like a lump, fixated on the fact that I was quiet." The entire meeting passed without Robert contributing a word.

Robert is certainly not the first person to fail to speak up during meetings, and he won't be the last. While some silent employees may not have any new ideas to contribute, the highly intelligent also freeze. One study found that if we believe our peers are smarter, we experience anxiety that temporarily blocks our ability to think effectively. In other words, worrying about what the group thinks of you makes you dumber. The study also found the effect was worse for women, perhaps because they can be more socially attuned to what others may think.

In other cases, failing to speak up may be attributed to personality. While the extraverted tend to be assertive and assured in group settings, the more introverted prefer to collect their thoughts before speaking—if they speak at all. But again, even those who are extraverted can remain quiet, especially when they feel they cannot contribute.

You may be wondering whether it is important for everyone to speak up. Collaboration (the word comes from "laboring together" in Latin) is at the heart of organizational transformation, so yes, the more participation, the more likely the collaboration will result in higher trust, increased productivity, and enhanced creativity. Furthermore, collaboration works best when individuals know their ideas are taken seriously.

The message from research is clear: give free speech a try!

Questions

10-13. Why are extroverts more likely to speak in a meeting than introverts? Do they have better things to say?

10-14. Is it really important that everyone has input in meetings?

10-15. Do you feel that your peers are quicker and smarter than you? Does this mean you fail to contribute to discussions? How can you reverse this?

Sources: E. Bernstein, "Speaking Up Is Hard to Do: Researchers Explain Why," *The Wall Street Journal,* February 7, 2012, D1; M. Kashtan, "Want Teamwork? Promote Free Speech," *The New York Times,* April 13, 2014, 8; and H. Leroy et al., "Behavioral Integrity for Safety, Priority of Safety, Psychological Safety, and Patient Safety: A Team-Level Study," *Journal of Applied Psychology* (November 2012): 1273–81.

CASE INCIDENT 2   Smart Teams and Dumb Teams

In this chapter, we've identified how some of the characteristics we use to describe individuals also can describe teams. For example, individuals can be high in the trait of openness, as can a team. Along the same lines, have you noticed that some teams seem to be smart, while others seem, um, dumb? This characteristic has nothing to do with the average IQ of the team members but instead reflects the functionality of the whole team. Teams that are synergistic excel in logical analysis, brainstorming, coordination, planning, and moral reasoning. And teams that are dumb? Think of long unproductive meetings, social loafing, and interpersonal conflicts.

You might be remembering a few teams you've witnessed that are in the dumb category, but we hope you can think of a few that excelled. Smart teams tend to be smart in everything—for any task, they will find a workable solution. But what makes them smart? Researchers in an MIT study grouped 697 subjects into teams of 2–5 members to solve tasks, looking for the characteristics of smart teams (they weren't all smart). The findings were:

1. **Smart teams did not allow individual members to dominate**. Instead, there were more equal contributions from members than in other teams.
2. **Smart teams had more members who were able to read minds**. Just kidding. But the members were able to read complicated emotions by looking into the eyes of others. There is a test for this ability called Reading the Mind in the Eyes.
3. **Smart teams had more women**. It's not that smart teams had more gender equality; these teams simply had more women. This result might be partly due to the fact that more women scored higher in the Reading the Mind in the Eyes test.

The researchers recently replicated the study using 68 teams and again found that some teams were smarter than others. This study added a new angle to the research: How would teams working in person differ from teams working online? Surprisingly, there was little difference: All smart teams had more equal member communication (and plenty of it) and were good at emotion reading. When the online collaborators could not see each other, they practiced Theory of Mind, remembering and reacting to the emotional cues they were able to detect through any mode of communication. Theory of Mind is related to emotional intelligence (EI), which we discussed in Chapter 4.

When we have the opportunity to hand-pick team members, we can look for those who listen as much as they speak, express empathy, and remember what others tell them about themselves. For teams to which we are assigned, we can seek these attributes in others and help guide the team toward its best self. As for IQ? Here's the good news: Recent research indicates that our membership in a team actually makes us smarter decision-makers as individuals!

Questions

10-16. From your experiences in teams, do you agree with the researchers' findings on the characteristics of smart teams? Why or why not?

10-17. On the highly functioning teams in which you've been a member, what other characteristics might have contributed to success?

⭐ **10-18.** The authors who suggested that membership in a team makes us smarter found that teams were more rational and quicker at finding solutions to difficult probability problems and reasoning tasks than were individuals. However, after participation in the study, team members were much better at decision making on their own, even up to 5 weeks later. Do you think this spillover effect would happen equally for people in smart teams and dumb teams? Why or why not?

Source: E. E. F. Bradford, I. Jentzsch, and J.-C. Gomez, "From Self to Cognition: Theory of Mind Mechanisms and Their Relation to Executive Functioning," *Cognition* 138 (2015): 21–34; B. Maciejovsky, M. Sutter, D. V. Budescu, et al., "Teams Make You Smarter: How Exposure to Teams Improves Individual Decisions in Probability and Reasoning Tasks," *Management Science* 59, no. 6 (2013): 1255–70; and A. Woolley, T. W. Malone, and C. Chabris, "Why Some Teams Are Smarter Than Others," *The New York Times*, January 18, 2015, 5.

MyManagementLab

Go to **mymanagementlab.com** for the following Assisted-graded writing questions:

10-19. Regarding Case Incident 1, do you think it's necessary for everyone to speak up in a team? Why or why not?

10-20. In reference to Case Incident 2, do you think you can read emotions from people's eyes enough to react well to them in teams? Why or why not? There are Reading the Mind from the Eyes tests online if you want to test your skill.

10-21. MyManagementLab Only – comprehensive writing assignment for this chapter.

ENDNOTES

[1] R. Karlgaard, "Think (Really!) Small," *Forbes*, April 13, 2015, 32.

[2] J. C. Gorman, "Team Coordination and Dynamics: Two Central Issues," *Current Directions in Psychological Science* 23, no. 5 (2014): 355–60.

[3] Ibid.

[4] J. Mathieu, M. T. Maynard, T. Rapp, and L. Gilson, "Team Effectiveness 1997–2007: A Review of Recent Advancements and a Glimpse into the Future," *Journal of Management* 34, no. 3 (2008): 410–76.

[5] See, for example, A. Erez, J. A. LePine, and H. Elms, "Effects of Rotated Leadership and Peer Evaluation on the Functioning and Effectiveness of Self-Managed Teams: A Quasi-experiment," *Personnel Psychology* (Winter 2002): 929–48.

[6] G. L. Stewart, S. H. Courtright, and M. R. Barrick, "Peer-Based Control in Self-Managing Teams: Linking Rational and Normative Influence with Individual and Group Performance," *Journal of Applied Psychology* 97, no. 2 (2012): 435–47.

[7] C. W. Langfred, "The Downside of Self-Management: A Longitudinal Study of the Effects of Conflict on Trust, Autonomy, and Task Interdependence in Self-Managing Teams," *Academy of Management Journal* 50, no. 4 (2007): 885–900.

[8] B. H. Bradley, B. E. Postlethwaite, A. C. Klotz, M. R. Hamdani, and K. G. Brown, "Reaping the Benefits of Task Conflict in Teams: The Critical Role of Team Psychological Safety Climate," *Journal of Applied Psychology*, 97, no. 1 (2012): 151–58.

[9] J. Devaro, "The Effects of Self-Managed and Closely Managed Teams on Labor Productivity and Product Quality: An Empirical Analysis of a Cross-Section of Establishments," *Industrial Relations* 47, no. 4 (2008): 659–98.

[10] A. Shah, "Starbucks Strives for Instant Gratification with Via Launch," *PRWeek* (December 2009): 15.

[11] F. Aime, S. Humphrey, D. S. DeRue, and J. B. Paul, "The Riddle of Heterarchy: Power Transitions in Cross-Functional Teams," *Academy of Management Journal* 57, no. 2 (2014): 327–52.

[12] B. Freyer and T. A. Stewart, "Cisco Sees the Future," *Harvard Business Review* (November 2008): 73–79.

[13] See, for example, L. L. Martins, L. L. Gilson, and M. T. Maynard, "Virtual Teams: What Do We Know and Where Do We Go from Here?" *Journal of Management* (November 2004): 805–35; and B. Leonard, "Managing Virtual Teams," *HRMagazine*, June 2011, 39–42.

[14] J. E. Hoch and S. W. J. Kozlowski, "Leading Virtual Teams: Hierarchical Leadership, Structural Supports, and Shared Team Leadership," *Journal of Applied Psychology* 99, no. 3 (2014): 390–403.

[15] A. Malhotra, A. Majchrzak, and B. Rosen, "Leading Virtual Teams," *Academy of Management Perspectives* (February 2007): 60–70; and J. M. Wilson, S. S. Straus, and B. McEvily, "All in Due Time: The Development of Trust in Computer-Mediated and Face-to-Face Teams," *Organizational Behavior and Human Decision Processes* 19 (2006): 16–33.

[16] P. Balkundi and D. A. Harrison, "Ties, Leaders, and Time in Teams: Strong Inference about Network Structure's Effects on Team Viability and Performance," *Academy of Management Journal* 49, no. 1 (2006): 49–68; G. Chen, B. L. Kirkman, R. Kanfer, D. Allen, and B. Rosen, "A Multilevel Study of Leadership, Empowerment, and Performance in Teams," *Journal of Applied Psychology* 92, no. 2 (2007): 331–46; L. A. DeChurch and M. A. Marks, "Leadership in Multiteam Systems," *Journal of Applied Psychology* 91, no. 2 (2006): 311–29; A. Srivastava, K. M. Bartol, and E. A. Locke, "Empowering Leadership in Management Teams: Effects on Knowledge Sharing, Efficacy, and Performance," *Academy of Management Journal* 49, no. 6 (2006): 1239–51; and J. E. Mathieu, K. K. Gilson, and T. M. Ruddy, "Empowerment and Team Effectiveness: An Empirical Test of an Integrated Model," *Journal of Applied Psychology* 91, no. 1 (2006): 97–108.

[17] R. B. Davison, J. R. Hollenbeck, C. M. Barnes, D. J. Sleesman, and D. R. Ilgen, "Coordinated Action in Multiteam Systems," *Journal of Applied Psychology* 97, no. 4 (2012): 808–24.

[18] M. M. Luciano, J. E. Mathieu, and T. M. Ruddy, "Leading Multiple Teams: Average and Relative External Leadership Influences on Team Empowerment and Effectiveness," *Journal of Applied Psychology* 99, no. 2 (2014): 322–31.

[19] R. Greenwald, "Freelancing Alone—But Together," *The Wall Street Journal*, February 3, 2014, R5.

[20] V. Gonzalez-Roma and A. Hernandez, "Climate Uniformity: Its Influence on Team Communication Quality, Task Conflict, and Team Performance," *Journal of Applied Psychology* 99, no. 6 (2014): 1042–58; C. F. Peralta, P. N. Lopes, L. L. Gilson, P. R. Lourenco, and L. Pais, "Innovation Processes and Team Effectiveness: The Role of Goal Clarity and Commitment, and Team Affective Tone," *Journal of Occupational and Organizational Psychology* 88, no. 1 (2015): 80–107; L. Thompson, *Making the Team* (Upper Saddle River, NJ: Prentice Hall, 2000), 18–33; and J. R. Hackman, *Leading Teams: Setting the Stage for Great Performance* (Boston: Harvard Business School Press, 2002).

[21] See G. L. Stewart and M. R. Barrick, "Team Structure and Performance: Assessing the Mediating Role of Intrateam Process and the Moderating Role of Task Type," *Academy of Management Journal* (April 2000): 135–48.

[22] Hyatt and Ruddy, "An Examination of the Relationship between Work Group Characteristics and Performance," 577.

[23] P. Balkundi and D. A. Harrison, "Ties, Leaders, and Time in Teams: Strong Inference about Network Structure's Effects on Team Viability and Performance," *Academy of Management Journal* 49, no. 1 (2006): 49–68; G. Chen, B. L. Kirkman, R. Kanfer, D. Allen, and B. Rosen, "A Multilevel Study of Leadership, Empowerment, and Performance in Teams," *Journal of Applied Psychology* 92, no. 2 (2007): 331–46; L. A. DeChurch and M. A. Marks, "Leadership in Multiteam Systems," *Journal of Applied Psychology* 91, no. 2 (2006): 311–29; A. Srivastava, K. M. Bartol, and E. A. Locke, "Empowering Leadership in Management Teams: Effects on Knowledge Sharing, Efficacy, and Performance," *Academy of Management Journal* 49, no. 6 (2006): 1239–51; and J. E. Mathieu, K. K. Gilson, and T. M. Ruddy, "Empowerment and Team Effectiveness: An Empirical Test of an Integrated Model," *Journal of Applied Psychology* 91, no. 1 (2006): 97–108.

[24] K. T. Dirks, "Trust in Leadership and Team Performance: Evidence from NCAA Basketball," *Journal of Applied Psychology* (December 2000): 1004–12; M. Williams, "In Whom We Trust: Group Membership as an Affective Context for Trust Development," *Academy of Management Review* (July 2001): 377–96; and J. Schaubroeck, S. S. K. Lam, and A. C. Peng, "Cognition-Based and Affect-Based Trust as Mediators of Leader Behavior Influences on Team Performance," *Journal of Applied Psychology*, Online First Publication (February 7, 2011), doi: 10.1037/a0022625.

[25] B. A. De Jong and K. T. Dirks, "Beyond Shared Perceptions of Trust and Monitoring in Teams: Implications of Asymmetry and

Dissensus," *Journal of Applied Psychology* 97, no. 2 (2012): 391–406.

[26]G. Brown, C. Crossley, and S. L. Robinson, "Psychological Ownership, Territorial Behavior, and Being Perceived as a Team Contributor: The Critical Role of Trust in the Work Environment," *Personnel Psychology* 67 (2014): 463–85.

[27]See F. Aime, C. J. Meyer, and S. E. Humphrey, "Legitimacy of Team Rewards: Analyzing Legitimacy as a Condition for the Effectiveness of Team Incentive Designs," *Journal of Business Research* 63, no. 1 (2010): 60–66; and P. A. Bamberger and R. Levi, "Team-Based Reward Allocation Structures and the Helping Behaviors of Outcome-Interdependent Team Members," *Journal of Managerial Psychology* 24, no. 4 (2009): 300–27; and M. J. Pearsall, M. S. Christian, and A. P. J. Ellis, "Motivating Interdependent Teams: Individual Rewards, Shared Rewards, or Something in Between?" *Journal of Applied Psychology* 95, no. 1 (2010): 183–91.

[28]A. Bryant, "Taking Your Skills with You," *The New York Times*, May 31, 2015, 2.

[29]R. R. Hirschfeld, M. H. Jordan, H. S. Feild, W. F. Giles, and A. A. Armenakis, "Becoming Team Players: Team Members' Mastery of Teamwork Knowledge as a Predictor of Team Task Proficiency and Observed Teamwork Effectiveness," *Journal of Applied Psychology* 91, no. 2 (2006): 467–74; and K. R. Randall, C. J. Resick, and L. A. DeChurch, "Building Team Adaptive Capacity: The Roles of Sensegiving and Team Composition," *Journal of Applied Psychology* 96, no. 3 (2011): 525–40.

[30]H. Moon, J. R. Hollenbeck, and S. E. Humphrey, "Asymmetric Adaptability: Dynamic Team Structures as One-Way Streets," *Academy of Management Journal* 47, no. 5 (October 2004): 681–95; A. P. J. Ellis, J. R. Hollenbeck, and D. R. Ilgen, "Team Learning: Collectively Connecting the Dots," *Journal of Applied Psychology* 88, no. 5 (October 2003): 821–35; C. L. Jackson and J. A. LePine, "Peer Responses to a Team's Weakest Link: A Test and Extension of LePine and Van Dyne's Model," *Journal of Applied Psychology* 88, no. 3 (June 2003): 459–75; and J. A. LePine, "Team Adaptation and Postchange Performance: Effects of Team Composition in Terms of Members' Cognitive Ability and Personality," *Journal of Applied Psychology* 88, no. 1 (February 2003): 27–39.

[31]C. C. Cogliser, W. L. Gardner, M. B. Gavin, and J. C. Broberg, "Big Five Personality Factors and Leader Emergence in Virtual Teams: Relationships with Team Trustworthiness,

Member Performance Contributions, and Team Performance," *Group & Organization Management* 37, no. 6 (2012): 752–84; and "Deep-Level Composition Variables as Predictors of Team Performance: A Meta-Analysis," *Journal of Applied Psychology* 92, no. 3 (2007): 595–615.

[32]T. A. O'Neill and N. J. Allen, "Personality and the Prediction of Team Performance," *European Journal of Personality* 25, no. 1 (2011): 31–42.

[33]S. E. Humphrey, J. R. Hollenbeck, C. J. Meyer, and D. R. Ilgen, "Personality Configurations in Self-Managed Teams: A Natural Experiment on the Effects of Maximizing and Minimizing Variance in Traits," *Journal of Applied Psychology* 41, no. 7 (2011): 1701–32.

[34]Ellis, Hollenbeck, and Ilgen, "Team Learning"; C. O. L. H. Porter, J. R. Hollenbeck, and D. R. Ilgen, "Backing Up Behaviors in Teams: The Role of Personality and Legitimacy of Need," *Journal of Applied Psychology* 88, no. 3 (June 2003): 391–403; and J. A. Colquitt, J. R. Hollenbeck, and D. R. Ilgen, "Computer-Assisted Communication and Team Decision-Making Performance: The Moderating Effect of Openness to Experience," *Journal of Applied Psychology* 87, no. 2 (April 2002): 402–10.

[35]B. H. Bradley, B. E. Postlewaite, and K. G. Brown, "Ready to Rumble: How Team Personality Composition and Task Conflict Interact to Improve Performance," *Journal of Applied Psychology* 98, no. 2 (2013): 385–92.

[36]E. Gonzalez-Mule, D. S. DeGeest, B. W. McCormick, J. Y. Seong, and K. G. Brown, "Can We Get Some Cooperation around Here? The Mediating Role of Group Norms on the Relationship between Team Personality and Individual Helping Behaviors," *Journal of Applied Psychology* 99, no. 5 (2014): 988–99.

[37]S. E. Humphrey, F. P. Morgeson, and M. J. Mannor, "Developing a Theory of the Strategic Core of Teams: A Role Composition Model of Team Performance," *Journal of Applied Psychology* 94, no. 1 (2009): 48–61.

[38]C. Margerison and D. McCann, *Team Management: Practical New Approaches* (London: Mercury Books, 2000).

[39]A. Joshi, "The Influence of Organizational Demography on the External Networking Behavior of Teams," *Academy of Management Review* (July 2006): 583–95.

[40]A. Joshi and H. Roh, "The Role of Context in Work Team Diversity Research: A Meta-Analytic Review," *Academy of Management Journal* 52, no. 3 (2009): 599–627; S. K. Horwitz and I. B. Horwitz, "The Effects of Team Diversity

on Team Outcomes: A Meta-Analytic Review of Team Demography," *Journal of Management* 33, no. 6 (2007): 987–1015; and S. T. Bell, A. J. Villado, M. A. Lukasik, L. Belau, and A. L. Briggs, "Getting Specific about Demographic Diversity Variable and Team Performance Relationships: A Meta-Analysis," *Journal of Management* 37, no. 3 (2011): 709–43.

[41]S. J. Shin and J. Zhou, "When Is Educational Specialization Heterogeneity Related to Creativity in Research and Development Teams? Transformational Leadership as a Moderator," *Journal of Applied Psychology* 92, no. 6 (2007): 1709–21; and K. J. Klein, A. P. Knight, J. C. Ziegert, B. C. Lim, and J. L. Saltz, "When Team Members' Values Differ: The Moderating Role of Team Leadership," *Organizational Behavior and Human Decision Processes* 114, no. 1 (2011): 25–36.

[42]S. J. Shin, T. Kim, J. Lee, and L. Bian, "Cognitive Team Diversity and Individual Team Member Creativity: A Cross-Level Interaction," *Academy of Management Journal* 55, no. 1 (2012): 197–212.

[43]S. Mohammed and L. C. Angell, "Surface- and Deep-Level Diversity in Workgroups: Examining the Moderating Effects of Team Orientation and Team Process on Relationship Conflict," *Journal of Organizational Behavior* (December 2004): 1015–39.

[44]Y. F. Guillaume, D. van Knippenberg, and F. C. Brodebeck, "Nothing Succeeds Like Moderation: A Social Self-Regulation Perspective on Cultural Dissimilarity and Performance," *Academy of Management Journal* 57, no. 5 (2014): 1284–308.

[45]D. Coutu, "Why Teams Don't Work" *Harvard Business Review* (May 2009): 99–105. The evidence in this section is described in Thompson, *Making the Team*, pp. 65–67. See also L. A. Curral, R. H. Forrester, and J. F. Dawson, "It's What You Do and the Way That You Do It: Team Task, Team Size, and Innovation-Related Group Processes," *European Journal of Work & Organizational Psychology* 10, no. 2 (June 2001): 187–204; R. C. Liden, S. J. Wayne, and R. A. Jaworski, "Social Loafing: A Field Investigation," *Journal of Management* 30, no. 2 (2004): 285–304.

[46]R. Karlgaard, "Think (Really!) Small."

[47]Ibid.

[48]Ibid.

[49]"Is Your Team Too Big? Too Small? What's the Right Number? *Knowledge@Wharton*, June 14, 2006, 1–5; see also A. M. Carton and J. N. Cummings, "A Theory of Subgroups in Work Teams," *Academy of Management Review* 37, no. 3 (2012): 441–70.

[50]Hyatt and Ruddy, "An Examination of the Relationship between Work Group Characteristics and Performance"; J. D. Shaw, M. K. Duffy, and E. M. Stark, "Interdependence and Preference for Group Work: Main and Congruence Effects on the Satisfaction and Performance of Group Members," *Journal of Management* 26, no. 2 (2000): 259–79; and S. A. Kiffin-Peterson and J. L. Cordery, "Trust, Individualism, and Job Characteristics of Employee Preference for Teamwork," *International Journal of Human Resource Management* (February 2003): 93–116.

[51]J. A. LePine, R. F. Piccolo, C. L. Jackson, J. E. Mathieu, and J. R. Saul, "A Meta-Analysis of Teamwork Processes: Tests of a Multidimensional Model and Relationships with Team Effectiveness Criteria," *Personnel Psychology* 61 (2008): 273–307.

[52]J. F. Dovidio, "Bridging Intragroup Processes and Intergroup Relations: Needing the Twain to Meet," *British Journal of Social Psychology* 52, no. 1 (2013): 1–24; and J. Zhou, J. Dovidio, and E. Wang, "How Affectively-Based and Cognitively-Based Attitudes Drive Intergroup Behaviours: The Moderating Role of Affective-Cognitive Consistency," *Plos One* 8, no. 11 (2013): article e82150.

[53]J. A. LePine, R. F. Piccolo, C. L. Jackson, J. E. Mathieu, and J. R. Saul, "A Meta-Analysis of Teamwork Processes: Tests of a Multidimensional Model and Relationships with Team Effectiveness Criteria"; and J. E. Mathieu and T. L. Rapp, "Laying the Foundation for Successful Team Performance Trajectories: The Roles of Team Charters and Performance Strategies," *Journal of Applied Psychology* 94, no. 1 (2009): 90–103.

[54]J. E. Mathieu and W. Schulze, "The Influence of Team Knowledge and Formal Plans on Episodic Team Process–Performance Relationships," *Academy of Management Journal* 49, no. 3 (2006): 605–19.

[55]A. N. Pieterse, D. van Knippenberg, and W. P. van Ginkel, "Diversity in Goal Orientation, Team Reflexivity, and Team Performance," *Organizational Behavior and Human Decision Processes* 114, no. 2 (2011): 153–64.

[56]A. Gurtner, F. Tschan, N. K. Semmer, and C. Nagele, "Getting Groups to Develop Good Strategies: Effects of Reflexivity Interventions on Team Process, Team Performance, and Shared Mental Models," *Organizational Behavior and Human Decision Processes* 102 (2007): 127–42; M. C. Schippers, D. N. Den Hartog, and P. L. Koopman, "Reflexivity in Teams: A Measure and Correlates," *Applied Psychology: An International Review* 56, no. 2 (2007): 189–211; and C. S. Burke, K. C. Stagl, E. Salas, L. Pierce, and D. Kendall, "Understanding Team Adaptation: A Conceptual Analysis and Model," *Journal of Applied Psychology* 91, no. 6 (2006): 1189–207.

[57]A. N. Pieterse, D. van Knippenberg, and W. P. van Ginkel, "Diversity in Goal Orientation, Team Reflexivity, and Team Performance," *Organizational Behavior and Human Decision Processes* 114, no. 2 (2011): 153–64.

[58]See R. P. DeShon, S. W. J. Kozlowski, A. M. Schmidt, K. R. Milner, and D. Wiechmann, "A Multiple-Goal, Multilevel Model of Feedback Effects on the Regulation of Individual and Team Performance," *Journal of Applied Psychology* (December 2004): 1035–56.

[59]K. Tasa, S. Taggar, and G. H. Seijts, "The Development of Collective Efficacy in Teams: A Multilevel and Longitudinal Perspective," *Journal of Applied Psychology* 92, no. 1 (2007): 17–27; D. I. Jung and J. J. Sosik, "Group Potency and Collective Efficacy: Examining Their Predictive Validity, Level of Analysis, and Effects of Performance Feedback on Future Group Performance," *Group & Organization Management* (September 2003): 366–91; and R. R. Hirschfeld and J. B. Bernerth, "Mental Efficacy and Physical Efficacy at the Team Level: Inputs and Outcomes among Newly Formed Action Teams," *Journal of Applied Psychology* 93, no. 6 (2008): 1429–37.

[60]A. W. Richter, G. Hirst, D. van Knippenberg, and M. Baer, "Creative Self-Efficacy and Individual Creativity in Team Contexts: Cross-Level Interactions with Team Informational Resources," *Journal of Applied Psychology* 97, no. 6 (2012): 1282–90.

[61]N. Ellemers, E. Sleebos, D. Stam, and D. de Gilder, "Feeling Included and Valued: How Perceived Respect Affects Positive Team Identity and Willingness to Invest in the Team," *British Journal of Management* 24 (2013): 21–37.

[62]T. A. De Vries, F. Walter, G. S. Van Der Vegt, and P. J. M. D. Essens, "Antecedents of Individuals' Interteam Coordination: Broad Functional Experiences as a Mixed Blessing," *Academy of Management Journal* 57, no. 5 (2014): 1334–59.

[63]S. Chang, L. Jia, R. Takeuchi, and Y. Cai, "Do High-Commitment Work Systems Affect Creativity? A Multilevel Combinational Approach to Employee Creativity," *Journal of Applied Psychology* 99, no. 4 (2014): 665–80.

[64]S. Mohammed, L. Ferzandi, and K. Hamilton, "Metaphor No More: A 15-Year Review of the Team Mental Model Construct," *Journal of Management* 36, no. 4 (2010): 876–910.

[65]A. P. J. Ellis, "System Breakdown: The Role of Mental Models and Transactive Memory on the Relationships between Acute Stress and Team Performance," *Academy of Management Journal* 49, no. 3 (2006): 576–89.

[66]L. A. DeChurch and J. R. Mesmer-Magnus, "The Cognitive Underpinnings of Effective Teamwork: A Meta-Analysis," *Journal of Applied Psychology* 95, no. 1 (2010): 32–53.

[67]S. W. J. Kozlowski and D. R. Ilgen, "Enhancing the Effectiveness of Work Groups and Teams," *Psychological Science in the Public Interest* (December 2006): 77–124; and B. D. Edwards, E. A. Day, W. Arthur Jr., and S. T. Bell, "Relationships among Team Ability Composition, Team Mental Models, and Team Performance," *Journal of Applied Psychology* 91, no. 3 (2006): 727–36.

[68]M. Kolbe, G. Grote, M. J. Waller, J. Wacker, B. Grande, and D. R. Spahn, "Monitoring and Talking to the Room: Autochthonous Coordination Patterns in Team Interaction and Performance," *Journal of Applied Psychology* 99, no. 6 (2014): 1254–67.

[69]J. Farh, C. Lee, and C. I. C. Farh, "Task Conflict and Team Creativity: A Question of How Much and When," *Journal of Applied Psychology* 95, no. 6 (2010): 1173–80.

[70]K. J. Behfar, R. S. Peterson, E. A. Mannix, and W. M. K. Trochim, "The Critical Role of Conflict Resolution in Teams: A Close Look at the Links between Conflict Type, Conflict Management Strategies, and Team Outcomes," *Journal of Applied Psychology* 93, no. 1 (2008): 170–88.

[71]V. Gonzalez-Roma and A. Hernandez, "Climate Uniformity: Its Influence on Team Communication Quality, Task Conflict, and Team Performance," *Journal of Applied Psychology* 99, no. 6 (2014): 1042–58.

[72]K. H. Price, D. A. Harrison, and J. H. Gavin, "Withholding Inputs in Team Contexts: Member Composition, Interaction Processes, Evaluation Structure, and Social Loafing," *Journal of Applied Psychology* 91, no. 6 (2006): 1375–84.

[73]G. Hertel, U. Konradt, and K. Voss, "Competencies for Virtual Teamwork: Development and Validation of a Web-Based Selection Tool for Members of Distributed Teams," *European Journal of Work and Organizational Psychology* 15, no. 4 (2006): 477–504.

[74]T. V. Riper, "The NBA's Most Overpaid Players," *Forbes*, April 5, 2013, http://www.forbes.com/sites/tomvanriper/2013/04/05/the-nbas-most-overpaid-players/.

[75]E. Kearney, D. Gebert, and S. C. Voelpel, "When and How Diversity Benefits Teams: The Importance of Team Members' Need for Cognition," *Academy of Management Journal* 52, no. 3 (2009): 581–98.

[76]H. M. Guttman, "The New High-Performance Player," *The Hollywood Reporter*, October 27, 2008, www.hollywoodreporter.com.

[77]C.-H. Chuang, S. Chen, and C.-W. Chuang, "Human Resource Management Practices and Organizational Social Capital: The Role of Industrial Characteristics," *Journal of Business Research* (May 2013): 678–87; and L. Prusak and D. Cohen, "How to Invest in Social Capital," *Harvard Business Review* (June 2001): 86–93.

[78]T. Erickson and L. Gratton, "What It Means to Work Here," *BusinessWeek*, January 10, 2008, www.businessweek.com.

[79]M. D. Johnson, J. R. Hollenbeck, S. E. Humphrey, D. R. Ilgen, D. Jundt, and C. J. Meyer, "Cutthroat Cooperation: Asymmetrical Adaptation to Changes in Team Reward Structures," *Academy of Management Journal* 49, no. 1 (2006): 103–19.

[80]C. E. Naquin and R. O. Tynan, "The Team Halo Effect: Why Teams Are Not Blamed for Their Failures," *Journal of Applied Psychology* (April 2003): 332–40.

[81]E. R. Crawford and J. A. Lepine, "A Configural Theory of Team Processes: Accounting for the Structure of Taskwork and Teamwork," *Academy of Management Review* (January 2013): 32–48.

11 Communication

LEARNING OBJECTIVES

After studying this chapter, you should be able to:

11-1 Describe the functions and process of communication.

11-2 Contrast downward, upward, and lateral communication through small-group networks and the grapevine.

11-3 Contrast oral, written, and nonverbal communication.

11-4 Describe how channel richness underlies the choice of communication method.

11-5 Differentiate between automatic and controlled processing of persuasive messages.

11-6 Identify common barriers to effective communication.

11-7 Discuss how to overcome the potential problems of cross-cultural communication.

MyManagementLab®
⭐ **Chapter Warm Up**

If your professor has chosen to assign this, go to the Assignments section of **mymanagementlab.com** to complete the chapter warm up.

CURIOUS COMMUNICATION

He's the producer of the hit TV show *Empire* and some of the hallmark movies of our time: *A Beautiful Mind, Apollo 13, Frost/Nixon,* and *Splash.* He is co-founder of Imagine Entertainment, an innovative, successful organization that has generated over $13.5 billion in revenues worldwide. With an Academy Award and three decades of industry accomplishments, what more does Brian Grazer need to know? Plenty, he claims. On a web page called grazeriscurious .com and in a book titled *The Curious Mind: The Secret to a Bigger Life,* 63-year-old Grazer (pictured here) gives credit for his success to his "curiosity conversations"—deliberate conversations with anyone who has something to share.

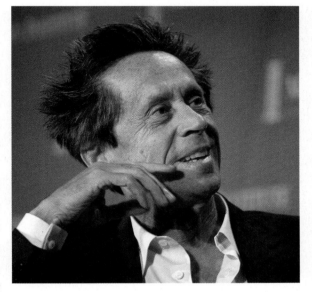

"For 35 years, I've been tracking down people about whom I was curious and asking if I could sit down with them for an hour," Grazer explained recently. "I've had as few as a dozen 'curiosity conversations' in a year, but sometimes I've done them as often as once a week. I was so serious about the curiosity conversations that I often spent a year or more trying to get together with particular people. I would spend hours calling, writing letters, cajoling, befriending assistants."

Who were these people worth hours of effort to meet once for an hour? In the beginning when Grazer was just a deliveryman, they were people he met while hand-delivering a law firm's documents to its Warner Bros. clients. After he landed his first job as a producer, he approached famous directors and actors—at least one a day—who walked by his office. Soon, he reached out to leaders from every walk of life...but not from the entertainment industry, and not with an idea for a movie. Just for the sake of satisfying his curiosity, Grazer met with leaders at the top of their careers including: U.S. president George W. Bush, Cuban president Fidel Castro, astronomer Carl Sagan, medical researcher Jonas Salk, writer Isaac Asimov, "the father of the hydrogen bomb" Edward Teller, investment banker Herbert A. Allen, Mexican business magnate Carlos Slim, astronaut Jim Lovell, Chilean activist Verónica de Negri, and famous lawyers Johnnie Cochran, F. Lee Bailey, and Gerry Spence.

Grazer said there are no rules for these conversations, no script. However, he has learned to prepare. After a disastrous meeting with Isaac and Janet Asimov in which Mrs. Asimov walked out after claiming she wasn't versed enough in her husband's work to continue the conversation, Grazer learned to research first, have a plan, and study the art of communication. He said, "You have to enter the psyche pretty quickly of the person you're talking to, to kind of know what matters to them. And if you know what matters to them, you're learning more, and you're living through their mind and process."

In addition to knowledge on many subjects, what has Grazer learned for business from over 600 curiosity conversations? How to interpret facial cues, to put the most challenging communications first in the day, and, most of all, to talk with people in person. "I really do Google a lot," he said, "but I really find that these personal meetings are more valuable because...there's so much more information through body language and eye contact and nuance." He found that one of the most important management tools is targeted communication through inquiry. "Asking questions elicits information, of course," he observed. "Asking questions creates the space for people to raise issues they are worried about that a boss, or colleagues, may not know about. Asking questions means people have to make their case for the way they want a decision to go." He discovered how people's communication predicts their behavior. "I like it when people at Imagine ask me questions, but here's the simplest and most powerful reason: If they ask the question, then they almost always listen to the answer," he wrote. "People are more likely to consider a piece of advice, or a flat-out instruction, if they've asked for it in the first place." Lastly, Grazer's curiosity conversations have sparked limitless creativity. He said, "You can never know how the dots will connect; how opportunities will come alive when you never knew they existed."

Sources: B. Grazer and C. Fishman, "Behind the Mind, and Out-of-This-World Hair, of Legendary Hollywood Producer Brian Grazer," *Vanity Fair,* March 2015, http://www.vanityfair.com/hollywood/2015/02/brian-grazer-hair-autobiography; B. Grazer and C. Fishman, "Movie Producer Brian Grazer Explains How Asking the Right Questions Will Make You a Better Boss," *Fast Company,* April 17, 2015, http://www.fastcompany.com/3044264/the-big-idea/the-man-of-many-questions; D. McNary, "Ron Howard-Brian Grazer's Imagine Entertainment Promotes Michael Rosenberg," *Variety,* November 26, 2013, http://variety.com/2013/film/news/ron-howard-brian-grazers-imagine-entertainment-promotes-michael-rosenberg-1200888431/; D. Miller, "Brain Grazer on the Benefits of a Curious Mind, #SXSW 2015 Recap," *Entrepreneur,* March 16, 2015; and A. Wolfe, "Brian Grazer," *The Wall Street Journal,* April 11–12, 2015, C17.

As Brian Grazer found, good communication makes organizations successful. Communication is powerful: no group or organization can exist without sharing meaning among its members. In this chapter, we'll analyze communication and ways we can make it more effective.

communication The transfer and the understanding of meaning.

Communication must include both the *transfer* and the *understanding* of meaning. Communicating is more than merely imparting meaning; that meaning must also be understood. It is only thus that we can convey information and ideas. In perfect communication, if it existed, a thought would be transmitted so the receiver understood the same mental picture the sender intended. Though it sounds elementary, perfect communication is never achieved in practice, for reasons we shall see.

Functions of Communication

11-1 Describe the functions and process of communication.

Communication serves five major functions within a group or organization: management, feedback, emotional sharing, persuasion, and information exchange.[1]

Communication acts to *manage* member behavior in several ways. Organizations have authority hierarchies and formal guidelines employees are required to follow. When employees follow their job descriptions or comply with company policies, communication performs a management function. Informal communication controls behavior too. When workgroups tease or harass a member who produces too much (and makes the rest of the members look bad), they are informally communicating, and managing, the member's behavior.

Communication creates *feedback* by clarifying to employees what they must do, how well they are doing it, and how they can improve their performance. We saw this operating in goal-setting theory in Chapter 7. Formation of goals, feedback on progress, and reward for desired behavior all require communication and stimulate motivation.

The workgroup is a primary source of social interaction for many employees. Communication within the group is a fundamental mechanism by which members show satisfaction and frustration. Communication, therefore, provides for the *emotional sharing* of feelings and fulfillment of social needs. For example, after a white police officer shot an unarmed black man in Ferguson, Missouri in 2015, software engineer Carl Jones wanted to process his feelings through talking with his coworkers at his corporation. As a second example, Starbucks had baristas write "Race Together" on coffee cups to start conversations about race relations. In both cases, the initial communications were awkward—so awkward that Starbucks pulled the campaign—but Jones and others have forged solid relationships from their emotional sharing.[2]

Like emotional sharing, *persuasion* can be good or bad depending on if, say, a leader is trying to persuade a workgroup to believe in the organization's commitment to corporate social responsibility (CSR) or to, conversely, persuade the workgroup to break the law to meet an organizational goal. These may be extreme examples, but it's important to remember that persuasion can benefit or harm an organization.

The final function of communication is *information exchange* to facilitate decision making. Communication provides the information individuals and groups need to make decisions by transmitting the data needed to identify and evaluate choices.

Almost every communication interaction that takes place in a group or organization performs one or more of these functions, and none of the five is more important than the others. To perform effectively, groups need to maintain some control over members, provide feedback to stimulate members to perform, allow emotional expression, monitor the persuasive efforts of individuals, and encourage information exchange.

Before communication can take place it needs a purpose, a message to be conveyed between a sender and a receiver. The sender encodes the message (converts it to a symbolic form) and passes it through a medium (channel) to the receiver, who decodes it. The result is a transfer of meaning from one person to another.[3]

communication process The steps between a source and a receiver that result in the transfer and understanding of meaning.

Exhibit 11-1 depicts this **communication process**. The key parts of this model are (1) the sender, (2) encoding, (3) the message, (4) the channel, (5) decoding, (6) the receiver, (7) noise, and (8) feedback.

The *sender* initiates a message by encoding a thought. The *message* is the actual physical product of the sender's *encoding*. When we speak, the speech is the message. When we write, the writing is the message. When we gesture, the movements of our arms and the expressions on our faces are the message. The *channel* is the medium through which the message travels. The sender selects it, determining whether to use a formal or informal channel. **Formal channels** are established by the organization and transmit messages related to the professional activities of members. They traditionally follow the authority chain within the organization. Other forms of messages, such as personal or social, follow **informal channels**, which are spontaneous and subject to individual choice.[4] The *receiver* is the person(s) to whom the message is directed, who must first translate the symbols into understandable form. This step is the *decoding* of the message. *Noise* represents communication barriers that distort the clarity of the message, such as perceptual problems, information overload, semantic difficulties, or cultural differences. The final link in the communication process is a feedback loop. *Feedback* is the check on how successful we have been in transferring our messages as originally intended. It determines whether understanding has been achieved.

formal channels Communication channels established by an organization to transmit messages related to the professional activities of members.

informal channels Communication channels that are created spontaneously and that emerge as responses to individual choices.

Exhibit 11-1   The Communication Process

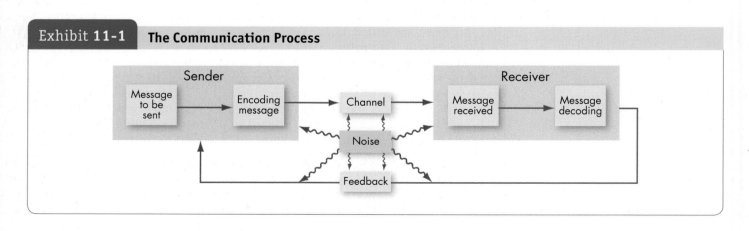

Direction of Communication

11-2 Contrast downward, upward, and lateral communication through small-group networks and the grapevine.

Communication can flow vertically or laterally, through formal small-group networks or the informal grapevine. We subdivide the vertical dimension into downward and upward directions.[5]

Downward Communication

Communication that flows from one level of a group or organization to a lower level is *downward communication*. Group leaders and managers use it to assign goals, provide job instructions, explain policies and procedures, point out problems that need attention, and offer feedback.

In downward communication, managers must explain the reasons *why* a decision was made. Although this may seem like common sense, many managers feel they are too busy to explain things or that explanations will raise too many questions. Evidence clearly indicates, though, that explanations increase employee commitment and the support of decisions.[6] Managers might think that sending a message one time is enough to get through to lower-level employees, but research suggests managerial communications must be repeated several times and through a variety of different media to be truly effective.[7]

Another problem in downward communication is its one-way nature; generally, managers inform employees but rarely solicit their advice or opinions. Research revealed that nearly two-thirds of employees said their boss rarely or never asks their advice. The study noted, "Organizations are always striving for higher employee engagement, but evidence indicates they unnecessarily create fundamental mistakes. People need to be respected and listened to." The way advice is solicited also matters. Employees will not provide input, even when conditions are favorable, if doing so seems against their best interests.[8]

In downward communication, the delivery mode and the context of the information exchange are of high importance. We will talk more about communication methods later, but consider the ultimate downward communication: the performance review. Alan Buckelew, CEO of Carnival Cruise Lines, says, "A review is probably the one time when you want to be physically present." Samsonite CEO agrees: "A conference call cannot substitute for face-to-face interactions." Automated performance reviews have allowed managers to review their subordinates without discussions, which is efficient but misses critical opportunities for growth, motivation, and relationship-building.[9] In general, employees subjected to less than direct, personalized communication are less likely to understand the intentions of the message correctly.

The best communicators explain the reasons behind their downward communications but also solicit communication from the employees they supervise. That leads us to the next direction: upward communication.

Upward Communication

Upward communication flows to a higher level in the group or organization. It's used to provide feedback to higher-ups, inform them of progress toward goals, and relay current problems. Upward communication keeps managers aware of how employees feel about their jobs, coworkers, and the organization in general. Managers also rely on upward communication for ideas on how conditions can be improved.

Given that most managers' job responsibilities have expanded, upward communication is increasingly difficult because managers can be overwhelmed and easily distracted. To engage in effective upward communication, try to communicate in short summaries rather than long explanations, sup-

Burger King improved lateral communication among its executives by eliminating their closed-door offices and organizing their desks in an open-space setting. Shown here, from left, are executives Jonathan Fitzpatrick, Jose Tomas, and Daniel Schwartz communicating in their new work area at company headquarters in Miami.

Source: C.W. Griffin/MCT/Newscom

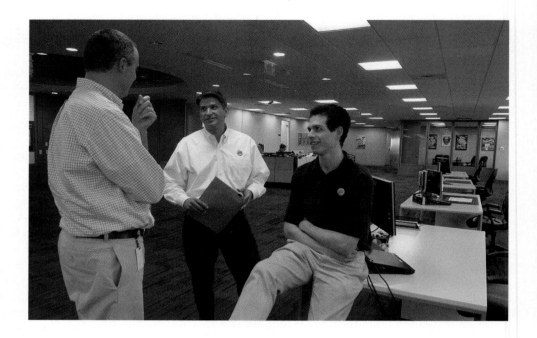

port your summaries with actionable items, and prepare an agenda to make sure you use your boss's attention well.[10] And watch what you say, especially if you are communicating something to your manager that will be unwelcome. If you're turning down an assignment, for example, be sure to project a "can do" attitude while asking advice about your workload dilemma or inexperience with the assignment.[11] Your delivery can be as important as the content of your communication.

Lateral Communication

When communication occurs between members of the same workgroup, members at the same level in separate workgroups, or any other horizontally equivalent workers, we describe it as *lateral communication.*

Lateral communication saves time and facilitates coordination. Some lateral relationships are formally sanctioned. More often, they are informally created to short-circuit the vertical hierarchy and expedite action. So from management's viewpoint, lateral communications can be good or bad. Because strictly adhering to the formal vertical structure for all communications can be inefficient, lateral communication occurring with management's knowledge and support can be beneficial. But dysfunctional conflict can result when formal vertical channels are breached, when members go above or around their superiors, or when bosses find actions have been taken or decisions made without their knowledge.

Formal Small-Group Networks

Formal organizational networks can be complicated, including hundreds of people and a half-dozen or more hierarchical levels. We've condensed these networks into three common small groups of five people each (see Exhibit 11-2): chain, wheel, and all-channel.

The *chain* rigidly follows the formal chain of command; this network approximates the communication channels you might find in a rigid three-level organization. The *wheel* relies on a central figure to act as the conduit for all group communication; it simulates the communication network you might find

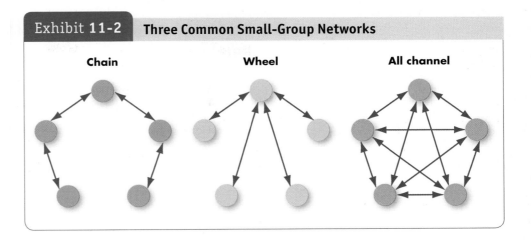

Exhibit 11-2   Three Common Small-Group Networks

Chain   Wheel   All channel

on a team with a strong leader. The *all-channel* network permits group members to actively communicate with each other; it's most often characterized by self-managed teams, in which group members are free to contribute and no one person takes on a leadership role. Many organizations today like to consider themselves all-channel, meaning that anyone can communicate with anyone (but sometimes they shouldn't).

As Exhibit 11-3 demonstrates, the effectiveness of each network is determined by the dependent variable that concerns you. The structure of the wheel facilitates the emergence of a leader, the all-channel network is best if you desire high member satisfaction, and the chain is best if accuracy is most important. Exhibit 11-3 leads us to the conclusion that no single network will be best for all occasions.

The Grapevine

The informal communication network in a group or organization is called the **grapevine**.[12] Although rumors and gossip transmitted through the grapevine may be informal, it's still an important source of information for employees and candidates. Grapevine or word-of-mouth information from peers about a company has important effects on whether job applicants join an organization,[13] even over and above informal ratings on websites like Glassdoor.

The grapevine is an important part of any group or organization communication network. It serves employees' needs: small talk creates a sense of closeness and friendship among those who share information, although research suggests it often does so at the expense of those in the outgroup.[14] It also gives managers a feel for the morale of their organization, identifies issues employees consider important, and helps them tap into employee anxieties. Evidence indicates that

grapevine An organization's informal communication network.

Exhibit 11-3   Small-Group Networks and Effective Criteria

Criteria	Networks		
	Chain	*Wheel*	*All-Channel*
Speed	Moderate	Fast	Fast
Accuracy	High	High	Moderate
Emergence of a leader	Moderate	High	None
Member satisfaction	Moderate	Low	High

> **Exhibit 11-4**   **Dealing with Gossip and Rumors**
>
> 1. **Share** the information you have, and the information you don't—where there is good formal communication with much information, there is no need for rumors. When you don't know information that others are seeking, discuss when you will know and follow up.
> 2. **Explain,** explain, explain. As a manager, discuss what decisions are made and why they were made, as well as the plan going forward.
> 3. **Respond** to rumors noncommittally, and then verify for yourself the truths you can. Make certain to gather all sides of the story.
> 4. **Invite** employees to discuss their concerns, ideas, suggestions, thoughts, and feelings about organizational matters. Help them frame their thoughts into more objective viewpoints.

managers can study the gossip driven largely by employee social networks to learn more about how positive and negative information is flowing through the organization.[15] Managers can furthermore identify influencers (highly networked people trusted by their coworkers[16]) by noting which individuals are small talkers (those who regularly communicate about insignificant, unrelated issues). Small talkers tend to be influencers. One study found that social talkers are so influential that they were significantly more likely to retain their jobs during layoffs.[17] Thus, while the grapevine may not be sanctioned or controlled by the organization, it can be understood and leveraged a bit.

Could managers entirely eliminate the gossip and rumors common to the grapevine if they so chose? No. Should they want to? Maybe not; in addition to the opportunities for managers to learn from the grapevine, some forms of gossip provide prosocial motivation for employees to help each other achieve organizational goals.[18] What managers should do is minimize the negative consequences of rumors by limiting their range and impact. Exhibit 11-4 offers a few practical suggestions.

> **✪ WATCH IT!**
> If your professor has assigned this, go to the Assignments section of **mymanagementlab.com** to complete the video exercise titled **Communication (TWZ Role Play)**.

Modes of Communication

11-3 Contrast oral, written, and nonverbal communication.

How do group members transfer meaning among each other? They rely on oral, written, and nonverbal communication. This much is obvious, but as we will discuss, the choice between modes can greatly enhance or detract from the way the perceiver reacts to the message. Certain modes are highly preferred for specific types of communication. We will cover the latest thinking and practical application.

Oral Communication

A primary means of conveying messages is oral communication. Speeches, formal one-on-one and group discussions, and the informal rumor mill or grapevine are popular forms of oral communication.

The advantages of oral communication are speed, feedback, and exchange. We can convey a verbal message and receive a response in minimal time. As one professional put it, "Face-to-face communication on a consistent basis is still the best way to get information to and from employees."[19] If the receiver is unsure of the message, rapid feedback allows the sender to quickly detect and correct it. The feedback we receive includes information and emotional content; however, we should acknowledge that we are usually bad listeners. Researchers indicate that we are prone to "listener burnout" in which we tune the other person out and rush to offer advice. "Good listeners overcome their natural inclination to fix the other's problems and to keep the conversation brief," said Professor Graham Bodie. Active listening—in which we remove distractions, lean in, make eye contact, paraphrase, and encourage the talker to continue[20]—helps us learn more and build trust if we are genuine and not judgmental.[21] The exchange given through oral communication has social, cultural, and emotional components. Cultural social exchange, in which we purposefully share social exchanges that transcend cultural boundaries, can build trust, cooperation, and agreement between individuals and teams.[22]

One major disadvantage of oral communication surfaces whenever a message has to pass through a number of people: the more people, the greater the potential distortion. If you've ever played the game "Telephone," you know the problem. Each person interprets the message in his or her own way. The message's content, when it reaches its destination, is often very different from the original, even when we think the message is simple and straightforward. Therefore, oral communication "chains" are generally more of a liability than an effective tool in organizations. Let's discuss some popular oral communication applications in specific.

Meetings   Meetings can be formal or informal, include two or more people, and take place in almost any venue. Although 11 million meetings take place in the United States daily, some people hate them. So we try to make them more effective: Amazon CEO Jeff Bezos begins meetings with 30 minutes of everyone silently reading his report to them, Twitter and Apple have meetings only on Mondays, BuzzFeed has 2 no-meeting days per week, and some organizations limit the duration of meetings.[23]

Framing even our casual business interactions as meetings helps us stay focused on progress. Every meeting is an opportunity to "get stuff done," as BetterWorks CEO Kris Duggan said, and to "sparkle." He noted, "You may be an expert in your field, but if you don't communicate well, or if you don't get people excited, or you're not passionate or enthusiastic, that's going to be a hindrance."[24] Other stumbling blocks to effective meetings are overuse of jargon[25] and qualifiers that undermine your words (for example, phrases like "to be perfectly honest" or "to tell the truth" imply that you aren't truthful the other 99 percent of the time!).[26]

Good interpersonal communication is key to making meetings effective. Some experts recommend using humor as an ice breaker; public relations firm Peppercomm even offers stand-up comedy workshops to help businesses teach people how to use humor.[27] But what if you don't have a voice in meetings? We don't mean someone who is speaking or hearing disabled, as we discuss in Career OBjectives. *Voice* refers to the ability to contribute words of value to the meeting.[28] By definition, voice challenges the status quo, supports others' viewpoints, adds constructively, or is defensive/destructive.[29] As you can see, voice refers to the input and reactions of a person within the meeting and the lack of voice creates a barrier to input (when no one is speaking, few people want to be the first to break the silence). A person without voice

Al Lieb (in blue shirt) is co-founder and CEO of ClearSlide, Inc., a maker of cloud-based communications software for sales teams. Shown here leading a staff meeting at company headquarters in San Francisco, Lieb believes meetings keep employees focused on ClearSlide's fast-paced growth and increasing customer base.
Source: John Green/Bay Area News Group/MCT/Landov

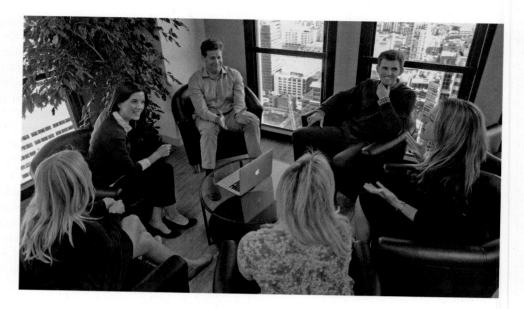

may have nothing to say, but research indicates that women in particular don't speak up in meetings even when they are in leadership positions, suggesting that certain group dynamics inhibit equal participation.[30] Without equitable participation, the benefits of meetings are questionable.

Videoconferencing and Conference Calling   *Videoconferencing* permits employees and clients to conduct real-time meetings with people at different locations. Live audio and video images let us see, hear, and talk with each other without being physically in the same location. *Conference calling* is generally limited to telephone exchanges where some people may gather around one speaker phone, and others call in through a secure line. There may be some shared files or videos everyone can see on their computers. Both modes are used selectively, according to the application.

Peter Quirk, an information technology director with EMC Corporation, uses videoconferencing to hold monthly meetings of employees at various locations while saving travel expenses and time. He notes it's important to deliberately stimulate questions and involve all participants in this forum to avoid having someone who is on the call but disengaged, a common problem. Other leaders wish they had that problem; instead, they have to mediate between callers who talk over one another, and address those who make too much noise. Erica Pearce, a sales executive, told one conference caller, "If you're vacuuming, I appreciate that, and you're welcome to come to my house afterward. But you need to be on mute."[31]

You might assume people prefer videoconferencing to conference calling since video offers a more "live" experience, but 65 percent of all remote meetings are done via audio only. For reasons not clearly understood besides some people's reluctance to be on camera, the time people spend on audio-only calls may be growing almost 10 percent per year.[32] To address the pitfalls of videoconferencing and conference calls, experts offer the following suggestions:

1. **Set more explicit agendas and firmer rules than for face-to-face meetings.**
2. **Have callers begin by introducing themselves, their roles in the project, and what they are looking for in the meeting.** They should also state their names each time they speak.
3. **Leaders should talk 40 percent of the time and listen 60 percent of the time.**

4. **Distribute discussion questions before the meeting, and note the responses of each participant during the meeting.**

5. **Assign a moderator for the meeting (not the leader) and a secretary (again, not the leader).**

6. **Understand people's preferences for videoconferencing versus conference calling before the meeting and make sure everyone understands the technology.** "I cannot tell you how many times I've heard people say, 'I don't know what's wrong with my webcam, so I'm just going to be here in voice'" when they might just prefer conference calling, said Laura Stack, author of *Execution Is the Strategy.*[33]

Telephone   The telephone has been around so long that we can overlook its efficiency as a mode of communication. Communication by telephone is fast, effective, and less ambiguous than e-mail. However, telephone messages can be easily overlooked, and a lack of functions has made the phone difficult to use

Isn't this disability too much to accommodate?

I thought it was a good, responsible move when my manager hired a guy who is hearing-impaired...but now I'm not so sure. We do okay in communicating with him, mostly thanks to e-mail and texting. None of us knows sign language but sometimes we spell out words with our hands. The problem is that the guy makes a LOT of inappropriate noises—farts, burps, coughs, moans, you name it. Isn't this too much to put up with?

— *Jackie*

Dear Jackie:

In short: No. Workplace accommodation means more than simply tolerating a disabled worker's presence. Perhaps you might consider this from your deaf coworker's point of view (by the way, "deaf" is the preferred term, according to the National Association of the Deaf):

· *How are the communication conditions for him to work?* Are you being sure to include him in discussions by, say, assigning one of you to write down the important points for him and ask his opinions in meetings? Search for "10 Annoying Habits of Hearing

People" online to get a glimpse of his perspective.

· *Do you know what he thinks about your "hand spelling?"* You may not know that American Sign Language (ASL) is not simply English. Your coworker probably doesn't appreciate your "pigeon" sign language and may be offended by your attempts, but he would likely appreciate an effort for the group to learn some ASL and/or use a translator. There are apps and online translators where you can type in a phrase and see someone sign your words on the screen, for instance. Similarly, new technology from MotionSavvy translates signs into written speech.

· *It seems you might be attributing emotions to your coworker when he makes noises, emotions he may not feel.* Do you think he is uncaring about his listening coworkers? It's much more likely that he simply doesn't realize he is making noises or thinks they are quieter than they are. Consider what it's like when you are in a loud room; you're probably less aware of your sounds than when you're in a quiet room where everyone can react.

If you can get past the barrier of thinking about how he should accommodate himself to your environment and instead show him how your group is willing to work to communicate with him, you may begin to develop an understanding of one another. Then, and only then, it would make sense to approach the noise problem respectfully and kindly, with a non-offensive one-on-one. But before you do, search the Internet for tips on communicating with the deaf, and show him some respect.

C. Swinbourne, "The 10 Annoying Habits of Hearing People," *The Huffington Post,* September 17, 2013, http://www.huffingtonpost.com/charlie-swinbourne/the-10-annoying-habits-of_b_3618327.html; National Association of the Deaf website, www.nad.org, accessed June 30, 2015; and R. Walker, "An Office Distraction," *The New York Times,* March 22, 2015, 8.

The opinions provided here are of the managers and authors only and do not necessarily reflect those of their organizations. The authors or managers are not responsible for any errors or omissions, or for the results obtained from the use of this information. In no event will the authors or managers, or their related partnerships or corporations thereof, be liable to you or anyone else for any decision made or action taken in reliance on the opinions provided here.

without electronic follow up. Recently, however, a number of software options have come to the rescue to make phoning more versatile. Switch uses the computer to dial phone numbers, and users can change telephones during calls and view document exchanges. Voice allows people to use a single phone number that's linked to multiple phones. Talko's app provides a forum for voice memos, texts, and photos. And Twilio offers businesses cheaper calling and automatic text messages. Supporters say these methods increase business communication capabilities beyond e-mail. "How many times have you been on a giant e-mail thread that's not making any progress?" asked the founder of Switch. With these tools, he said, "You've distilled all the waste out of the phone conversation, and what's left are these really important times when you need to talk to someone in real time, and get some emotion and back-and-forth."[34]

Written Communication

Written communication includes letters, e-mail, instant messaging, organizational periodicals, and any other method that conveys written words or symbols. Written business communication today is usually conducted via letters, Power-Point, e-mail, instant messaging, text messaging, social media, apps, and blogs. We are all familiar with these methods, but let's consider the unique current business communication applications of them.

Letters   With all the technology available, why would anyone write and send a letter? Of all the forms of written communication, letter writing is the oldest—and the most enduring. Letter writing can be used to great effect in business, adding a personal touch to a communication or, alternately, creating a lasting document to signal an official communication. Interestingly, research indicates that when we write by hand, the content is much more memorable to us than when we type.[35]

PowerPoint   PowerPoint and other slide formats like Prezi can be an excellent mode of communication because slide-generating software combines words with visual elements to engage the reader and help explain complex ideas. PowerPoint is often used in conjunction with oral presentations, but its appeal is so intuitive that it can serve as a primary mode of communication. It is not without its detractors, however, who argue that it is too impersonal, disengaging, and frequently hard to follow.

E-Mail   The growth of e-mail since its inception nearly 50 years ago has been spectacular, and its use is so pervasive it's hard to imagine life without it. There are more than 3.1 billion active e-mail accounts worldwide, and corporate employees average 105 e-mails each day.[36] Exhibit 11-5 shows the time managers and professionals spend daily on various tasks. Many managers report they spend too much time on e-mail. Do you?

The business benefits of e-mail messages are obvious: they can be quickly and cheaply written, edited, sent, and stored. E-mail is not without cost, however. In fact, according to e-mail software company Messagemind, corporations lose $650 billion each year from time spent processing unnecessary e-mails.[37] One study also indicated that people focus longer on tasks and are less stressed when they are cut off from checking e-mail.[38]

Despite the costs, e-mail is likely here to stay, and is "often the first impression that others get of you," according to executive coach and etiquette expert Jaqueline Whitmore.[39] Still, even seasoned e-mail aficionados struggle with striking the proper tone in their communications.

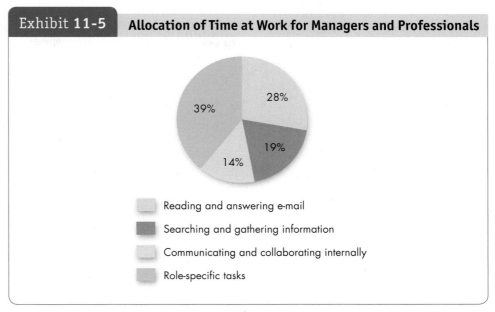

Exhibit **11-5**   **Allocation of Time at Work for Managers and Professionals**

- Reading and answering e-mail
- Searching and gathering information
- Communicating and collaborating internally
- Role-specific tasks

Source: Based on M. Chui et al., "The Social Economy: Unlocking Value and Productivity through Social Technologies," McKinsey & Company, July 2012, http://www.mckinsey.com/insights/high_tech_telecoms_internet/the_social_economy.

Whitmore offers the following advice:

1. **Don't skip the subject line, but make it short and topic-related.**
2. **Give a greeting/salutation.** "Dear" and "hello" are good starting points. In later exchanges, "hi" may be appropriate. Use the person's name. "Err on the side of being more formal" in your greeting and the body of the e-mail, Whitmore advises. Same for your closing; "Best regards" is more formal.
3. **Keep sentences, paragraphs, and thoughts short.** Use bullet points when possible.
4. **However, don't be curt.** "No one can see your facial expressions or hear your tone of voice, so the only way they're gauging your emotions is the tone that you use in that e-mail," she said.
5. **Don't use text language.** "Even if you've just graduated from college and you're now out in the workforce," Whitmore observed, "remember that a lot of your clients may be baby boomers. It's important for you to stay professional."
6. **Check your spelling.** Check it again.
7. **When people write back, reply within 24 hours.** "Even if you don't have an answer for someone, reply anyway," she said.[40]

Instant Messaging   Like e-mail, instant messaging (IM) is usually done via computer. There are distinct pros and cons to IM, but mostly negatives for business interactions. If you are present when the IM comes in, you can respond in real time to engage in online typed dialogue, but the conversation will not be saved for later reference. If you miss the incoming IM, you may be alerted when you next log on that a person tried to reach you, which may be long after a response was needed.

Text Messaging   Text messaging maybe a little bit better than IM but has many of the same pitfalls in business usage. The guidelines for the business use of texting are still evolving, but experts continually caution that business text language should be as formal as any other business communication. The level of informality and abbreviations we use in personal text messages is usually not advisable at work.[41]

OB POLL

Do You Use Social-Networking Sites to Research Job Candidates?

No, but soon
37%

No
52%

Yes
11%

Note: CareerBuilder survey of over 2,000 hiring professionals.

Source: Based on CareerBuilder at http://www.careerbuilder.com/JobPoster/Resources/page.aspx?pagever=2012SocialMedia&template=none.

Social Media Websites Nowhere has online communication been more transformed than in the rise of social networks like Facebook and LinkedIn, and business is taking advantage of the opportunities these social media present. Many organizations have developed their own in-house social networking applications, known as *enterprise social software,* and most have their own Facebook pages and Twitter feeds.[42] Social networking has become a tool for prospective employees, hiring managers, employees, and human resource divisions (see OB Poll).

Facebook has more than 1.44 billion active users per month,[43] and it's important to remember in business that users can send messages to other users either by posting on their walls (public), sending messages, or setting up chats (private). They can also communicate with multiple other users ("friends") by posting status updates, videos, and photos. Some of the modes of communication may be appropriate for business application (such as an organization's Facebook page) but many are not. Research has found that none of the world's 50 most profitable companies' CEOs are using Facebook.[44] This represents a dramatic shift from 2010, when these CEOs were using Facebook, LinkedIn, and Twitter quite equally. Leslie Gaines-Ross, who represents the study, observed, "I think that CEOs are identifying which platform really works for them."[45] Privacy remains a high concern for many Facebook users, and some regions of the world do not have access to it.[46]

Unlike many social media venues, LinkedIn was created as an online business network and now has 187 million active users per month.[47] User profiles on the site are like virtual résumés. Communication is sometimes limited to endorsements of others' skills and establishment of business connections, though direct private communication is available and users can form and belong to groups. LinkedIn is used increasingly by top CEOs and is the top popular network for them (22 percent of the top 50 companies' CEOs use LinkedIn).[48]

Twitter is a hybrid social networking service for users to post "micro-blog" entries of 140 characters to their subscribers about any topic, including work. Twitter has 236 million active users monthly on average[49] and is growing as a business venue. While only 10 percent of the top companies' CEOs are on Twitter,[50] some have many followers, such as Richard Branson of Virgin Group, who has 5.99 million. As former Medtronic CEO Bill George noted, "Can you think of a more cost-effective way of getting to your customers and employees?"[51] Having many followers can be an advantage to a firm or a manager, but a huge liability when posts (tweets) are badly written or negative.

Apps   LinkedIn and Twitter are two of the most widely used social media platforms for businesses, but they are not the only ones. Apps—easily accessed mobile-friendly platforms—are increasingly the forum of choice for the public. Some websites have apps, while other apps exist without corresponding websites. One of the biggest apps is WhatsApp, at 450 million active monthly users. Apps are most popular in regions where mobile phone usage is primary.[52] Asia has the world's largest number of social media users, and apps have a big part of that through Line (Japan), WeChat (China), and Kakao (South Korea).[53]

Blogs   A *blog* (short for web log) is a website about a single person or company. Experts see blogging as a business necessity for organizations, so it should not be overlooked as a vital form of communication to employees and customers, who can post feedback if they choose.[54] However, outdated blogs look bad to employees, customers, and the public, so new ones must be continually added to maintain relevancy.

Myth or Science?

Today, Writing Skills Are More Important Than Speaking Skills

Never before have the writing skills of managers and employees been more on display. Whether we are tapping on a keyboard or a screen, this communication with others is often unedited. (Thank goodness for spellcheck.) With all the written communication methods we currently employ, it would be easy to think upper management values writing skills over speaking skills. However, evidence suggests this is not the case.

As we discussed in Chapter 1, soft skills matter most to employers, regardless of industry. According to Nick Schultz of the American Enterprise Institute, "Considerable evidence suggests that many employers would be happy just to find applicants who have the sort of 'soft' skills that used to be almost taken for granted." Though soft skills refer to all interpersonal skills evident through speaking and writing, they are most on display in one-on-one discussions, interviews, meetings, and presentations. The ability to speak well, particularly English, has become a job prerequisite for many multinational corporations.

The good news is that speaking ability—knowledge of when to speak, how to speak, how to sound, what to say—can be improved through training. According to leadership coach and author Kristi Hedges, most people can train on their own and do not need formal presentation classes. You can make significant improvements by researching speaking techniques, watching videos of practice sessions, and practicing new techniques in meetings. If learning to speak a foreign language fluently is a problem, full immersion courses and overseas assignments can be helpful if they are an option, as well as listening to and mimicking television and radio broadcasts in the other language. Speaking well hinges on clarity and sincerity of expression.

Therefore, while it is a mistake to believe writing skills have become more important than speaking skills, we can all make significant improvements in our verbal communications relatively quickly.

Sources: R. J. Aldrick and J. Kasuku, "Escaping from American Intelligence: Culture, Ethnocentrism and the Anglosphere," *International Affairs,* September 2012, 1009–28; K. Hedges, "Confessions of a Former Public Speaking Trainer: Don't Waste Your Money," *Forbes,* April 19, 2012, www.forbes.com/sites/work-in-progress/2012/04/19/public-speaking-trainer-confesses-dont-waste-your-money-on-this/; and N. Schultz, "Hard Unemployment Truths about 'Soft' Skills," *The Wall Street Journal,* September 20, 2012, A15.

Others   Flickr, Pinterest, Google+, YouTube, Wikis, Jive, Socialtext, and Social Cast are just a few of the many public and industry-specific platforms, with new ones launching daily. Some are designed for only one type of posting: YouTube accepts only videos, for instance, and Flickr only videos and images. Other sites have a particular culture, such as Pinterest's informal posts sharing recipes or decorating tips. The business applications have not been fully realized yet, but soon there will probably be at least one social media site tailored to every type of business communication.

Nonverbal Communication

Every time we deliver a verbal message, we also impart an unspoken message.[55] Sometimes the nonverbal component may stand alone as a powerful message of our business communication. No discussion of communication would thus be complete without consideration of *nonverbal communication*—which includes body movements, the intonations or emphasis we give to words, facial expressions, and the physical distance between the sender and receiver.

We could argue that every *body movement* has meaning, and no movement is accidental (though some are unconscious). We act out our state of being with nonverbal body language. For example, we smile to project trustworthiness, uncross our arms to appear approachable, and stand to signal authority.[56]

Body language can convey status, level of engagement, and emotional state.[57] Body language adds to, and often complicates, verbal communication. In fact, studies indicate that people read much more about another's attitude and emotions from their nonverbal cues than their words! If nonverbal cues conflict with the speaker's verbal message, the cues are sometimes more likely to be believed by the listener.[58]

If you read the minutes of a meeting, you wouldn't grasp the impact of what was said the same way as if you had been there or could see the meeting on video. Why not? There is no record of nonverbal communication, and the emphasis given to words or phrases is missing. Both make the meaning clear. Exhibit 11-6 illustrates how *intonations* can change the meaning of a message. *Facial expressions* also convey meaning. Facial expressions, along with intonations, can show arrogance, aggressiveness, fear, shyness, and other characteristics.

Physical distance also has meaning. What is considered proper spacing between people largely depends on cultural norms. For example, a business-like distance in some European countries feels intimate in many parts of

Exhibit 11-6	Intonations: It's the Way You Say It!

Change your tone and you change your meaning:

Placement of the Emphasis	What It Means
Why don't I take **you** to dinner tonight?	I was going to take someone else.
Why don't **I** take you to dinner tonight?	Instead of the guy you were going with.
Why **don't** I take you to dinner tonight?	I'm trying to find a reason why I **shouldn't** take you.
Why don't I take you to dinner tonight?	Do you have a problem with me?
Why don't I **take** you to dinner tonight?	Instead of going on your own.
Why don't I take you to **dinner** tonight?	Instead of lunch tomorrow.
Why don't I take you to dinner **tonight**?	Not tomorrow night.

Source: Reproduced in A. Huczynski and D. Buchanan, *Organizational Behavior*, 4th ed. (Essex, UK: Pearson Education, 2001), 194.

North America. If someone stands closer to you than is considered appropriate, it may indicate aggressiveness or sexual interest; if farther away, it may signal disinterest or displeasure with what is being said.

★ PERSONAL INVENTORY ASSESSMENTS

Communication Styles

What is your preferred communication style? Take this PIA to learn more about our communication styles.

Choice of Communication Channel

11-4 Describe how channel richness underlies the choice of communication method.

Now that we've discussed various modes of business communication, why do people choose one channel of communication over another? A model of media richness helps explain channel selection among managers.[59]

Channel Richness

Channels differ in their capacity to convey information. Some are *rich* in that they can (1) handle multiple cues simultaneously, (2) facilitate rapid feedback, and (3) be very personal. Others are *lean* in that they score low on these factors. As Exhibit 11-7 illustrates, face-to-face conversation scores highest in **channel richness** because it transmits the most information per communication episode—multiple information cues (words, postures, facial expressions, gestures, intonations), immediate feedback (both verbal and nonverbal), and the personal touch of being present. Impersonal written media such as formal reports and bulletins rate lowest in richness.

In sum, rich channels give us the chance to observe. The unconscious aspects of communication help us understand the full meaning of a message. When these aspects are missing, we must look for other clues to deduce the sender's emotions and attitudes.

channel richness The amount of information that can be transmitted during a communication episode.

Exhibit 11-7   Information Richness and Communication Channels

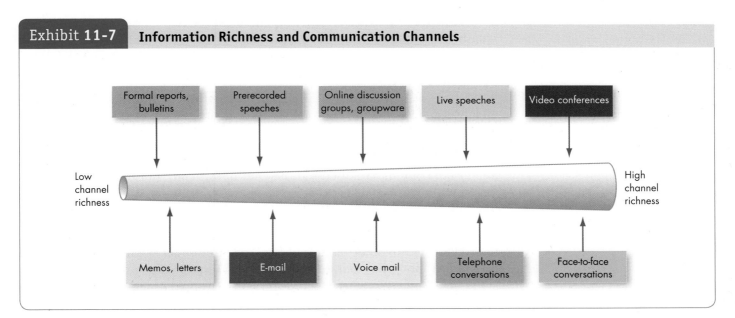

Sources: Reproduced from R. L. Daft and R. A. Noe, *Organizational Behavior* (Fort Worth, TX: Harcourt, 2001), 311.

Choosing Communication Methods

The choice of channel depends on whether the message is routine. Routine messages tend to be straightforward and have minimal ambiguity; channels low in richness can carry them efficiently. Nonroutine communications are likely to be complicated and have the potential for misunderstanding. Managers can communicate them effectively only by selecting rich channels.

Channel richness is a helpful framework for choosing your mode of communication. It is not always easy to know when to choose oral rather than written communication, for instance. Experts say oral communication or "face time" with coworkers, clients, and upper management is key to success. However, if you seek out the CEO just to say hello, you may be remembered as an annoyance rather than a star, and signing up for every meeting on the calendar to increase your face time is counterproductive to getting the work of the organization done. Your communication choice is worth a moment's thought: Is the message you need to communicate better suited to a discussion, or a diagram? Let's explore some decision points.

Whenever you need to gauge the receiver's receptivity, *oral communication* is usually the better choice. The marketing plan for a new product, for instance, may need to be worked out with clients in person, so you can see their reactions to each idea you propose. Also consider the receiver's preferred mode of communication; some individuals focus on content better in written form and others prefer discussion. For example, if your manager requests a meeting with you, you may not want to ask for an e-mail exchange instead. The pace of your work environment matters, too. A fast-paced workplace may thrive on pop-by meetings, while a deadline-heavy team project may progress faster with scheduled Skype videoconferences.

Much of what we communicate face-to-face is in the delivery, so also consider your speaking skills when choosing your communication method. Research indicates the sound of your voice is twice as important as what you are saying. A good speaking voice—clear, moderated—can be a help to your career, while loud, questioning, irritating, immature, falsetto, breathy, or monotone voice tones can hinder you. If your voice is problematic, your work teams can help you raise your awareness so you can make changes, or you may benefit from the help of a voice coach.[60]

Written communication is generally the most reliable mode for complex and lengthy communications, and it can be the most efficient method for short messages when, for instance, a two-sentence text can take the place of a 10-minute phone call. But keep in mind that written communication can be limited in its emotional expression.

Choose written communication when you want the information to be tangible, verifiable, and "on the record." People are usually forced to think more thoroughly about what they want to convey in a written message than in a spoken one, so your written communications can be well thought out, logical, and clear. But be aware that, as with oral communication, your delivery is just as important as the content. We discussed the level of formality, but note that managers report grammar mistakes and lack of business formality is unprofessional...and unacceptable. "People get passionate about grammar," corporate writing instructor and author Jack Appleman noted, and one study found that 45 percent of employers were adding training programs to teach grammar and communication skills. On the other hand, some experts argue that the use of social media jargon and abbreviations is good for business. Overall, for your professional success, know your audience when possible, and use good grammar.

Letters are used in business primarily for networking purposes and when signatures need to be authentic. A handwritten thank-you note is never a

To enhance her personal office visits with patients, pediatric physician Dr. Natasha Burgert communicates with them through e-mail, texting, and her blog. Written communication enables her to share reliable and timely medical information with patients' families so they can provide better care for their children.
Source: Orlin Wagner/AP Images

wrong choice for an applicant to send after an employment interview, for instance, and handwritten envelopes often are put right on the receiver's desk unopened by administrative staff. Although electronic written communication provides authentication by indicating the sender and date/time sent, a handwritten signature is still preferred and sometimes required for letters and contracts.

In general, you should respond to *instant messages* only when they are professional and initiate them only when you know they will be welcome. Remember that your conversation will not be stored for later reference.

There are significant gains and challenges from *text messaging* in business settings. Texts are cheap to send and receive, and the willingness to be available for quick communications from clients and managers is conducive to good business. However, some users—and managers—view text messaging as intrusive and distracting. The rules of business etiquette are not yet established, resulting in offenses ranging from texts sent at unreasonable hours to serial texting in bursts of short messages that keep receivers' phones buzzing annoyingly. Such a continual presence can also make it hard for employees to concentrate and stay focused. Consider these recent research findings from a survey of professionals:

- *84 percent think it's inappropriate to write texts or e-mails during formal meetings*
- *75 percent think it's inappropriate to read texts or e-mails during formal meetings*
- *66 percent think it's inappropriate to write texts or e-mails during any meetings*
- *At least 22 percent think it's inappropriate to use phones during any meetings*[61]

As you can see, it is best to severely limit personal text messages during office hours and be cautious in using texting for business purposes. You should discuss using texting for business with people before you text them for the first time, set up general availability ground rules, and take your cues about when to text from the other person. For longer messages, it is better to use e-mail; even though the receiver still might scroll through the message on a smartphone, the option of viewing—and saving—your message on a computer is preferable.

On the corporate level, the returns on using *social media* are mixed. Some of the most spectacular gains are in the sales arena, both business-to-public and business-to-business. For instance, one sales representative for virtual-meetings company PGi landed his fastest sale ever by instantly connecting with a potential client after TweetDeck alerted him that a CEO was tweeting his frustration about web conferencing.[62] Companies are also developing their own internal social networking platforms to encourage employees to collaborate and to improve training, reporting a 300 percent annual increase in corporate network activity.

Some organizations have policies governing the use of social media, but many don't. It is difficult for management to control the content employees post; even well-intentioned employees post comments that could be construed as harmful to their organization's reputation or that reveal confidential or sensitive information. Software that mines social media sites can check up on a job applicant, and the growing field of digital forensics helps investigate potential problems with current employees, but cybersleuthing can be time-consuming and expensive.[63] And acting upon violations of an organization's social media policy is tricky. Thus, if you want to use social media for business purposes, make certain you are connected with all levels of management engaged in the effort. And if you would like to mention your business in your personal social media, communicate with your organization about what you would like to do, and what you think the potential return for the company may be. Use discretion about which personal social media platforms and *apps* are acceptable for business communication. Finally, make sure you know your company's social media policies about corporate confidentiality and your company's view on your privacy.[64]

As an individual, you may choose to post a *blog* on your own blog page, or you may choose to comment on another person's blog. Both options are more public than you may think, and your words are easily reachable by your name via search engines like Google. If others in the company happen to read a critical or negative blog entry or post, there is nothing to keep them from sharing that information with management. You could be dismissed as a result.

It's important to be alert to *nonverbal* aspects of communication and look for these cues as well as the literal meaning of a sender's words. You should particularly be aware of contradictions between the messages. Someone who frequently glances at her wristwatch is giving the message that she would prefer to terminate the conversation no matter what she actually says, for instance. We misinform others when we express one message verbally, such as trust, but nonverbally communicate a contradictory message that reads, "I don't have confidence in you."

Information Security

Security is a huge concern for nearly all organizations with private or proprietary information about clients, customers, and employees. Organizations worry about the security of electronic information they seek to protect such as hospital patient data, physical information they still keep in file cabinets, and information they entrust their employees with knowing. Most companies actively monitor employee Internet use and e-mail records, and some even use video surveillance and record phone conversations. Necessary though they may be, such practices can seem invasive to employees. An organization can relieve employee concerns by engaging them in the creation of information-security policies and giving them some control over how their personal information is used.[65]

An Ethical Choice

Using Employees in Organizational Social Media Strategy

Social media are good for business communication, but their use is an ethical minefield for employers and employees. In a study of 24 industries in 115 countries, 63 percent of managers believed social media will be important to their businesses in 3 years. Research suggests that social media use may be an indicator of an organization's profitability. Companies at the forefront include McDonald's, IBM, Salesforce, SAP, and Yammer. Social media can turn customers into fans through increased and personalized communication, and quick and appropriate responses to customers' communication can turn those fans—and employees—into spokespeople for the brand. The key is forming emotional bonds or capitalizing on current relationships to spread the good word about the company to potential clients.

Social media sites pose a host of business ethical concerns. Employees with a huge online presence who use social media for both personal and company promotion (known as co-branded employees) become a liability if they leak corporate information, present a bad image, or leave the company. There are also ethical concerns about employees' privacy and right to free speech: If an employee who monitors the company Twitter feed, and wins a customer over, later tweets from her personal account, "Score for us: another happy customer," that may present no concern. But she would hurt the company if she lost the customer and tweeted, "Epic fail: we blew it again."

Other employer tasks with few tested ethical guidelines include ensuring employees make proper use of company time, compensating them for time they spend promoting the company through their personal social media connection, clarifying who should own personal devices used for company promotion, setting limits on company expectations of employees' promotion efforts, dealing with permissions/attributions, and clearing any legal hurdles.

Experts advise organizations to draft social media policies that reflect their company ethics rather than seek to "cover all the bases" of potential liabilities. While an organization could require job applicants to share their online passwords, for instance, this may violate trust and personal privacy rules. Policies that define ethical expectations for employee online behavior, discuss monitoring, define consequences for nonconformance, and explain the logic of the guidelines will be the most effective. Even still, the National Labor Relations Board (NLRB) finds many corporate policies aimed at the ethics of social media usage violate the National Labor Relations Act. A good social media policy can affirm the ethical expectations of the corporation and improve its organizational culture.

Sources: S. F. Gale, "Policies Must Score a Mutual Like," *Workforce Management,* August 2012, 18; B. Giamanco and K. Gregoire, "Tweet Me, Friend Me, Make Me Buy," *Harvard Business Review,* July–August 2012, 88–93; D. Kiron, D. Palmer, A. N Phillips, and N. Kruschwitz, "What Managers Really Think about Social Business," *MIT Sloan Management Review,* Summer 2012, 51–60; X. Luo, J. Zhang, and W. Duan, "Social Media and Firm Equity Value," *Information Systems Research,* March 2013, 146–63; C. M. Sashi, "Customer Engagement, Buyer-Seller Relationships, and Social Media," *Management Decision* 50 (2012): 253–72; and A. Smith, "NLRB Finds Social Media Policies Unlawful," *HR Magazine,* August 2012, 18.

✪ **TRY IT!**

If your professor has assigned this, go to the Assignments section of **mymanagementlab.com** to complete the **Simulation:** *Communication.*

Persuasive Communication

11-5

Differentiate between automatic and controlled processing of persuasive messages.

We've discussed a number of methods for communication up to this point. Now we turn our attention to one of the functions of communication—persuasion—and the features that might make messages more or less persuasive to an audience.

Automatic and Controlled Processing

To understand the process of persuasion, it is useful to consider two different ways we process information.[66] Think about the last time you bought a can of soda. Did you carefully research brands, or did you reach for the can that had the most appealing advertising? If we're honest, we'll admit glitzy ads and catchy slogans have an influence on our choices as consumers. We often rely on **automatic processing**, a relatively superficial consideration of evidence and information making use of heuristics like those we discussed in Chapter 6. Automatic processing takes little time and low effort, so it makes sense to use it for processing persuasive messages related to topics you don't care much about. The disadvantage is that it lets us be easily fooled by a variety of tricks, like a cute jingle or glamorous photo.

Now consider the last time you chose a place to live. You probably sourced experts who knew something about the area, gathered information about prices, and considered the costs and benefits of renting versus buying. You were engaging in more effortful **controlled processing**, a detailed consideration of evidence and information relying on facts, figures, and logic. Controlled processing requires effort and energy, but it's harder to fool someone who has taken the time and effort to engage in it. So what makes someone engage in either shallow or deep processing? Let's explore how we might determine what types of processing an audience will use.

Interest Level   One of the best predictors of whether people will use an automatic or controlled process for reacting to a persuasive message is their level of interest in it.[67] Interest levels reflect the impact a decision is going to have on your life. When people are very interested in the outcome of a decision, they're more likely to process information carefully. That's probably why people look for so much more information when deciding about something important (like where to live) than something relatively unimportant (like which soda to drink).

Prior Knowledge   People who are well informed about a subject area are more likely to use controlled processing strategies. They have already thought through various arguments for or against a specific course of action, and therefore won't readily change their position unless very good, thoughtful reasons are provided. On the other hand, people who are poorly informed about a topic can change their minds more readily, even in the face of fairly superficial arguments presented without a great deal of evidence. A better-informed audience is likely to be much harder to persuade.

Personality   Do you always read at least five reviews of a movie before deciding whether to see it? Perhaps you even research films by the same stars and director. If so, you are probably high in **need for cognition**, a personality trait of individuals who are most likely to be persuaded by evidence and facts.[68] Those who are lower in their need for cognition are more likely to use automatic processing strategies, relying on intuition and emotion to guide their evaluation of persuasive messages.

Message Characteristics   Another factor that influences whether people use an automatic or controlled processing strategy is the characteristics of the message itself. Messages provided through relatively lean communication channels, with little opportunity for users to interact with the content of the message, encourage automatic processing. Conversely, messages provided through richer communication channels encourage more deliberative processing.

automatic processing   A relatively superficial consideration of evidence and information making use of heuristics.

controlled processing   A detailed consideration of evidence and information relying on facts, figures, and logic.

need for cognition   A personality trait of individuals depicting the ongoing desire to think and learn.

Managers of Germany's construction firm Hochtief relied on controlled processing during a meeting when they presented rational arguments about a takeover bid by another firm. Fearing that a takeover would put their jobs at risk, Hochtief employees had a high level of interest in learning about managers' plans to prevent it.
Source: Bernd Thissen/dpa/picture-alliance/Newscom

Choosing the Message   The most important implication is to match your persuasive message to the type of processing your audience is likely to use. When the audience is not interested in a persuasive message topic, when they are poorly informed, when they are low in need for cognition, and when information is transmitted through relatively lean channels, they'll be more likely to use automatic processing. In these cases, use messages that are more emotionally laden and associate positive images with your preferred outcome. On the other hand, when the audience is interested in a topic, when they are high in need for cognition, or when the information is transmitted through rich channels, then it is a better idea to focus on rational arguments and evidence to make your case.

Barriers to Effective Communication

11-6 Identify common barriers to effective communication.

A number of barriers can slow or distort effective communication, barriers that we need to recognize and reduce. In this section, we highlight the most important.

Filtering

filtering A sender's manipulation of information so that it will be seen more favorably by the receiver.

Filtering refers to a sender's purposely manipulating information so the receiver will see it more favorably. A manager who tells his boss what he feels the boss wants to hear is filtering information.

The more vertical levels in the organization's hierarchy, the more opportunities there are for filtering. But some filtering will occur wherever there are status differences. Factors such as fear of conveying bad news and the desire to please the boss often lead employees to tell their superiors what they think they want to hear, thus distorting upward communications.

Selective Perception

Selective perception is important because the receivers in the communication process selectively see and hear based on their needs, motivations, experience, backgrounds, and other personal characteristics. Receivers also project their interests and expectations into communications as they decode them. For example, an employment interviewer who expects a female job applicant to put her family ahead of her career is likely to see that characteristic in all female applicants, regardless of whether any of the women actually feel that way. As we said in Chapter 6, we don't see reality; we interpret what we see and call it reality.

Information Overload

information overload A condition in which information inflow exceeds an individual's processing capacity.

Individuals have a finite capacity for processing data. When the information we have to work with exceeds our processing capacity, the result is **information overload**. We've seen in this text that dealing with it has become a huge challenge for individuals and for organizations. It's a challenge you can manage—to some degree—by following the steps outlined earlier in this chapter.

What happens when individuals have more information than they can sort and use? They tend to select, ignore, pass over, or forget it. Or they may put off further processing until the overload situation ends. In any case, lost information and less effective communication results, making it all the more important to deal well with overload.

More generally, as an Intel study shows, it may make sense to connect to technology less frequently, to, in the words of one article, "avoid letting the drumbeat of digital missives constantly shake up and reorder to-do lists." One radical way is to limit the number of devices you access. For example, Coors Brewing executive Frits van Paasschen jettisoned his desktop computer in favor of mobile devices only, and Eli Lilly & Co. moved its sales teams from laptops plus other devices to just iPads. Both these moves have resulted in increased productivity.[69]

As information technology and immediate communication have become a more prevalent component of modern organizational life, more employees find they are never able to get offline. For example, some business travelers were disappointed when airlines began offering wireless Internet connections in flight because they could no longer use their travel time as a rare opportunity to relax without a constant barrage of organizational communications. The negative impacts of these communication devices can spill over into employees' personal lives as well. Both workers and their spouses relate the use of electronic communication technologies outside work to higher levels of work–life conflict.[70] Employees must balance the need for constant communication with their personal need for breaks from work, or they risk burnout from being on call 24 hours a day.

Emotions

You may interpret the same message differently when you're angry or distraught than when you're happy. For example, individuals in positive moods are more confident about their opinions after reading a persuasive message, so well-designed arguments have a stronger impact on their opinions.[71] People in negative moods are more likely to scrutinize messages in greater detail, whereas those in positive moods tend to accept communications at face value.[72] Extreme emotions such as jubilation or depression are most likely to hinder effective communication. In such instances, we are most prone to disregard our rational and objective thinking processes and substitute emotional judgments.

Language

Even when we're communicating in the same language, words mean different things to different people. Age and context are two of the biggest factors that influence such differences. For example, when business consultant Michael Schiller asked his 15-year-old daughter where she was going with friends, he

Communication barriers exist between these call center employees in Manila, Philippines, and their U.S. and Canadian customers even though they all communicate in English. Training in pronunciation, intonation, vocabulary, and grammar helps employees to get messages across effectively to their customers.
Source: Dondi Tawatao/Getty Images

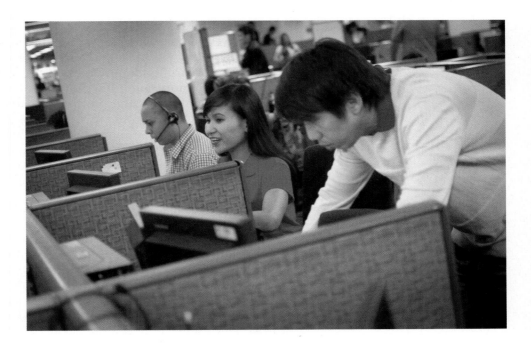

said, "You need to recognize your ARAs and measure against them." Schiller said that in response, his daughter "looked at him like he was from outer space." (ARA stands for accountability, responsibility, and authority.) Those new to corporate lingo may find acronyms such as ARA, words such as *deliverables* (verifiable outcomes of a project), and phrases such as *get the low-hanging fruit* (deal with the easiest parts first) bewildering, in the same way parents may be mystified by teen slang.[73]

Our use of language is far from uniform. If we knew how each of us modifies the language, we could minimize communication difficulties, but we usually don't know. Senders tend to incorrectly assume the words and terms they use mean the same to the receivers as to them.

Silence

It's easy to ignore silence or lack of communication because it is defined by the absence of information. This is often a mistake—silence itself can be the message to communicate non-interest or inability to deal with a topic. Silence can also be a simple outcome of information overload, or a delaying period for considering a response. For whatever reasons, research suggests using silence and withholding communication are common and problematic.[74] One survey found that more than 85 percent of managers reported remaining silent about at least one issue of significant concern.[75] The impact of silence can be organizationally detrimental. Employee silence can mean managers lack information about ongoing operational problems; management silence can leave employees bewildered. Silence regarding discrimination, harassment, corruption, and misconduct means top management cannot take action to eliminate problematic behavior.

Communication Apprehension

communication apprehension Undue tension and anxiety about oral communication, written communication, or both.

An estimated 5 to 20 percent of the population suffers debilitating **communication apprehension**, or social anxiety.[76] These people experience undue tension and anxiety in oral communication, written communication, or both.[77] They may find it extremely difficult to talk with others face-to-face or become extremely anxious when they have to use the phone, relying on memos or e-mails when a phone call would be faster and more appropriate.

Oral-communication apprehensives avoid situations, such as teaching, for which oral communication is a dominant requirement.[78] But almost all jobs require *some* oral communication. Of greater concern is evidence that high oral-communication apprehensives distort the communication demands of their jobs in order to minimize the need for communication. Be aware that some people severely limit their oral communication and rationalize their actions by telling themselves communicating isn't necessary for them to do their jobs effectively.

Lying

The final barrier to effective communication is outright misrepresentation of information, or lying. People differ in their definition of a lie. For example, is deliberately withholding information about a mistake a lie, or do you have to actively deny your role in the mistake to pass the threshold? While the definition of a lie befuddles ethicists and social scientists, there is no denying the prevalence of lying. People may tell one to two lies per day, with some individuals telling considerably more.[79] Compounded across a large organization, this is an enormous amount of deception happening every day. Evidence shows people are more comfortable lying over the phone than face-to-face, and more comfortable lying in e-mails than when they have to write with pen and paper.[80]

Can you detect liars? Research suggests most people are not very good at detecting deception in others.[81] The problem is there are no nonverbal or verbal cues unique to lying—averting your gaze, pausing, and shifting your posture can also be signals of nervousness, shyness, or doubt. Most people who lie take steps to guard against being detected, so they might look a person in the eye when lying because they know that direct eye contact is (incorrectly) assumed to be a sign of truthfulness. Finally, many lies are embedded in truths; liars usually give a somewhat true account with just enough details changed to avoid detection.

In sum, the frequency of lying and the difficulty in detecting liars makes this an especially strong barrier to effective communication.

Cultural Factors

11-7 Discuss how to overcome the potential problems of cross-cultural communication.

Effective communication is difficult under the best of conditions. Cross-cultural factors clearly create the potential for increased communication problems. A gesture that is well understood and acceptable in one culture can be meaningless or lewd in another. Unfortunately, only 18 percent of companies have documented strategies for communicating with employees across cultures, and only 31 percent require that corporate messages be customized for consumption in other cultures.

Cultural Barriers

There are a number of problems related to language difficulties in cross-cultural communications. First are *barriers caused by semantics*. Words mean different things to different people, particularly people from different national cultures. Some words don't translate between cultures. For instance, the Finnish word *sisu* means something akin to "guts" or "dogged persistence" but is essentially untranslatable into English. Similarly, capitalists in Russia may have difficulty communicating with British or Canadian counterparts because English terms such as *efficiency, free market,* and *regulation* have no direct Russian equivalents.

Second are *barriers caused by word connotations*. Words imply different things in different languages. Negotiations between U.S. and Japanese executives can be difficult because the Japanese word *hai* translates as "yes," but its connotation is "Yes, I'm listening" rather than "Yes, I agree."

Third are *barriers caused by tone differences*. In some cultures, language is formal; in others, it's informal. In some cultures, the tone changes depending on the context: People speak differently at home, in social situations, and at work. Using a personal, informal style when a more formal style is expected can be inappropriate.

Fourth are *differences in tolerance for conflict and methods for resolving conflicts*. People from individualist cultures tend to be more comfortable with direct conflict and will make the source of their disagreements overt. Collectivists are more likely to acknowledge conflict only implicitly and avoid emotionally charged disputes. They may attribute conflicts to the situation more than to the individuals and therefore may not require explicit apologies to repair relationships, whereas individualists prefer explicit statements accepting responsibility for conflicts and public apologies to restore relationships.

Cultural Context

high-context cultures   Cultures that rely heavily on nonverbal and subtle situational cues in communication.

low-context cultures   Cultures that rely heavily on words to convey meaning in communication.

Cultures tend to differ in the degree to which context influences the meaning individuals take from communication.[82] In **high-context cultures** such as China, Korea, Japan, and Vietnam, people rely heavily on nonverbal and subtle situational cues in communicating with others, and a person's official status, place in society, and reputation carry considerable weight. What is *not* said may be more significant than what *is* said. In contrast, people from Europe and North America reflect their **low-context cultures**. They rely essentially on spoken and written words to convey meaning; body language and formal titles are secondary (see Exhibit 11-8).

Contextual differences mean quite a lot in terms of communication. Communication in high-context cultures implies considerably more trust by both parties. What may appear to be casual and insignificant conversation in fact reflects the desire to build a relationship and create trust. Oral agreements imply strong commitments in high-context cultures. And who you are—your age, seniority, rank in the organization—is highly valued and heavily influences your credibility. Managers can therefore "make suggestions" rather than give orders. But in low-context cultures, enforceable contracts tend to be in

Exhibit 11-8   **High- versus Low-Context Cultures**

High context ↑
Chinese
Korean
Japanese
Vietnamese
Arab
Greek
Spanish
Italian
English
North American
Scandinavian
Swiss
German
Low context ↓

writing, precisely worded, and highly legalistic. Similarly, low-context cultures value directness. Managers are expected to be explicit and precise in conveying intended meaning.

A Cultural Guide

There is much to be gained from business intercultural communications. It is safe to assume every one of us has a different viewpoint that is culturally shaped. Because we do have differences, we have an opportunity to reach the most creative solutions possible with the help of others if we communicate effectively.

According to Fred Casmir, a leading expert in intercultural communication research, we often do not communicate well with people outside of our culture because we tend to generalize from only their cultural origin. This can be insensitive and potentially disastrous, especially when we make assumptions based on observable characteristics. Many of us have a richly varied ethnic background and would be offended if someone addressed us according to what culture our physical features might favor, for instance. Also, attempts to be culturally sensitive to another person are often based on stereotypes propagated by media. These stereotypes usually do not have a correct or current relevance.

Casmir noted that because there are far too many cultures for anyone to understand completely, and individuals interpret their own cultures differently, intercultural communication should be based on sensitivity and pursuit of common goals. He found the ideal condition is an ad hoc "third culture" a group can form when they seek to incorporate aspects of each member's cultural communication preferences. The norms this subculture establishes through appreciating individual differences create a common ground for effective communication. Intercultural groups that communicate effectively can be highly productive and innovative.

When communicating with people from a different culture, what can you do to reduce misinterpretations? Casmir and other experts offer the following suggestions:

1. **Know yourself.** Recognizing your own cultural identity and biases is critical to understanding the unique viewpoints of other people.
2. **Foster a climate of mutual respect, fairness, and democracy.** Clearly establish an environment of equality and mutual concern. This will be your "third culture" context for effective intercultural communication that transcends each person's cultural norms.
3. **State facts, not your interpretation.** Interpreting or evaluating what someone has said or done draws more on your own culture and background than on the observed situation. If you state only facts, you will have the opportunity to benefit from the other person's interpretation. Delay judgment until you've had sufficient time to observe and interpret the situation from the differing perspectives of all concerned.
4. **Consider the other person's viewpoint.** Before sending a message, put yourself in the recipient's shoes. What are his or her values, experiences, and frames of reference? What do you know about his or her education, upbringing, and background that can give you added insight? Try to see the people in the group as they really are first, and take a collaborative problem-solving approach whenever potential conflicts arise.
5. **Proactively maintain the identity of the group.** Like any culture, the establishment of a common-ground "third culture" for effective intercultural communication takes time and nurturing. Remind members of the group of your common goals, mutual respect, and need to adapt to individual communication preferences.[83]

Summary

You've probably discovered the link between communication and employee satisfaction in this chapter: the less uncertainty, the greater the satisfaction. Distortions, ambiguities, and incongruities between verbal and nonverbal messages all increase uncertainty and reduce satisfaction. Careful attention to the methods and modes for each communication better ensures that the message is properly interpreted by the receiver.

Implications for Managers

- Remember that your communication mode will partly determine your communication effectiveness.
- Obtain feedback to make certain your messages—however they are communicated—are understood.
- Remember that written communication creates more misunderstandings than oral communication; communicate with employees through in-person meetings when possible.
- Make sure you use communication strategies appropriate to your audience and the type of message you're sending.
- Keep in mind communication barriers such as gender and culture.

We Should Use Employees' Social Media Presence

POINT

Everyone uses social media. Well, almost everyone: A Pew Research Study found that the highest percentage of adults who use social networking sites was in Israel at 53 percent, followed by 50 percent in the United States, 43 percent in Russia and Great Britain, and 42 percent in Spain.

Business is social, and using employees' social contacts to increase business has always been a facet of marketing. Organizations that don't follow their employees' social media presence are missing an opportunity to expand their business and strengthen their workforce. For example, the Honda employee who once told 30 friends that Honda is best can now tell 300 Facebook friends and 500 Twitter followers about the latest model. Employees' savvy about social media can have a substantial positive effect on the bottom line.

Monitoring employees' social media presence can also strengthen the workforce by identifying the best talent. Managers can look for potential online celebrities—frequent bloggers and Twitter users with many followers—to approach for co-branding partnerships. Scrutiny can also help employers spot problems. For example, consider the employee who is fired one day and turns violent. A manager who had been monitoring the employee's social media posts may be able to detect warning signs. A human resources department monitoring employees' social media activity may be able to identify a substance abuse problem and provide help for the employee through the company's intervention policies.

A job candidate's social media presence provides one more input to hiring and retention decisions that many organizations already take advantage of. In reality, there is no difference between the employee and the person—they are one and the same, on or off working hours.

Employers that monitor social media can also identify employees who use their platforms to send out bad press or who leak proprietary information. For this reason, managers may someday be *required* to monitor employees' social media postings and to act upon infringements of company policies. Many do so already.

Managers should therefore develop enforceable social media policies and create a corporate infrastructure to regularly research and monitor social media activity. The potential increase in business and limit on liability is ample return for dedicating staff and work hours to building a successful social media program.

COUNTERPOINT

There is little to be gained and much to be lost when organizations follow candidates' and employees' presence on social media. Managers may be able to learn more about individuals through their online activity, and organizations may be able to catch some good press from employee postings, but the risk of liability for this intrusion on privacy is inescapable. Managers are ill-equipped to monitor, interpret, and act upon employees' social media postings, and few have any experience with relating the medium to business use.

Managers may also easily misinterpret information they find. Few companies have training programs for the proper use of social media; only 40 percent have social media policies of any kind. Those that do are skating on thin ice because monitoring policies can conflict with privacy regulations.

An employee's online image doesn't reveal much that is relevant to the job, certainly not enough to warrant the time and money a business would spend on monitoring. Most users view social media as a private, recreational venue, and their membership on Facebook and other sites should be regarded with the same respect as would membership in a club. In this light, monitoring employees' social media accounts is an unethical violation of their right to privacy.

Equal Employment Opportunity laws require companies to hire without respect to race, age, religion, national origin, or disability. But managers who check into candidates' social media postings often find out more than the candidate wanted to share, and then there is no way to keep that information from affecting the hiring decision. Searching through social media can, therefore, expose a company to a costly discrimination claim.

Using employees' personal social media presence as a marketing tool through company-supportive postings is unethical from many standpoints. First, it is unethical to expect employees to expand the company's client base through their personal contacts. Second, it is unreasonable to expect them to endorse the company after working hours. And the practice of asking employees for their social media passwords is an obvious intrusion into their personal lives.

In sum, people have a right to a professional and a private image. Unless the employee is offering to "friend" the company in a social media partnership, there is no question that employers should stay out of their personal business.

Sources: S. F. Gale, "Policies Must Score a Mutual Like," *Workforce Management,* August 2012; R. Huggins and S. Ward, "Countries with the Highest Percentage of Adults Who Use Social Networking Sites," *USA Today,* February 8, 2012, 1A; A. L. Kavanaugh et al., "Social Media Use by Government: From the Routine to the Critical," *Government Information Quarterly,* October 2012, 480–91; and S. Johnson, "Those Facebook Posts Could Cost You a Job," *San Jose Mercury News,* January 16, 2012, www.mercurynews.com/business/ci_19754451.

CHAPTER REVIEW

MyManagementLab

Go to **mymanagementlab.com** to complete the problems marked with this icon. ⭐

QUESTIONS FOR REVIEW

11-1 What are the functions and process of communication?

11-2 What are the communication differences between downward, upward, and lateral communication sent through small-group networks and the grapevine?

11-3 What are the methods of oral communication, written communication, and nonverbal communication?

11-4 How does channel richness underlie the choice of communication method?

11-5 What is the difference between automatic and controlled processing of persuasive messages?

11-6 What are some common barriers to effective communication?

11-7 How do you overcome the potential problems of cross-cultural communication?

EXPERIENTIAL EXERCISE An Absence of Nonverbal Communication

The class splits up into pairs (party A and party B).

11-8. Party A is to select a topic from the following list:
   a. Managing in the Middle East is significantly different from managing in North America.
   b. Employee turnover in an organization can be functional.
   c. Some conflict in an organization is good.
   d. Whistle-blowers do more harm than good for an organization.
   e. An employer has a responsibility to provide every employee with an interesting and challenging job.
   f. Everyone should register to vote.
   g. Organizations should require all employees to undergo regular drug tests.
   h. Individuals who majored in business or economics make better employees than those who majored in history or English.
   i. The place where you get your college degree is more important in determining your career success than what you learn while you're there.
   j. It's unethical for a manager to purposely distort communications to get a favorable outcome.

11-9. Party B is to choose a position on this topic (for example, arguing *against* the view "Some conflict in an organization is good"). Party A now must automatically take the opposite position.

The two parties debate their topic. The catch is that the individuals can only communicate verbally. They may *not* use gestures, facial movements, body movements, or any other nonverbal communication. It may help for each party to sit on their hands to remind them of their restrictions and to maintain an expressionless look.

11-10. After the debate is over, form groups of six to eight and discuss the following:
   a. How effective was communication during these debates?
   b. What barriers to communication existed?
   c. What purposes does nonverbal communication serve?
   d. Relate the lessons learned in this exercise to problems that might occur when communicating on the telephone or through e-mail.

ETHICAL DILEMMA BYOD

"What's your cell phone number? Good, I'll call you about the meeting." If you're like many people in the world who have used a smartphone for years, or one of the 1.3 billion people who bought one recently, chances are you've used it for work. In fact, your employer may have even invited—or asked—you to use your smartphone, tablet, or laptop in your job. Such is the bring-your-own-device (BYOD) trend, which started out of friendly convenience but now carries major ethical issues. For instance:

- *Did you know your employer can wipe your personal devices clean?* Remotely? With no warning? It happens, and not just at the 21 percent of organizations that erase devices when employees are terminated. Any time an organization has a privacy concern, it may wipe all devices clean to prevent a further breach of its cyber-defenses. Health-care consultant Michael Irvin lost his personal e-mail accounts, apps, music, contacts, and photos suddenly one day, leaving his multi-use iPhone "like it came straight from the factory." Another individual lost pictures of a relative who had died.

- *Is your device part of your employment contract, either explicitly or by understanding?* If so, who pays for the device? Well, you did, and you continue to pay for the service. If the device breaks, then…who pays for the replacement device? Can you lose your job if you can't afford the device and service?

- *Can you use your device for all work-related communications?* The cloud has brought opportunities for people to send classified work information anywhere, anytime. Organizations are concerned about what social media, collaboration, and file-sharing applications are in use, which is fair, but some policies can limit how you use your own device.

- *Once you use your personal device for work, where are the boundaries between work and home life?* Research indicates that intensive smartphone users, for instance, need to disengage in their off-hours to prevent work–home stress and burnout. Yet not everyone can do this even if they are allowed to; research indicated a significant proportion of smartphone users felt pressured to access their devices around the clock, whether or not that pressure was warranted.

The clear dilemma for employees is whether to acknowledge you own a smart device, and whether to offer its use for your employer's convenience. Put that way, it seems obvious to say no (why would you risk possibly later losing everything to a corporate swipe?), but the convenience of carrying one phone is for you as well. However, some people think it's just better to carry two phones—one for work, another for personal use. Attorney Luke Cocalis tried it and concluded, "It frankly keeps me saner."

Questions

11-11. Do you use your smartphone or other personal devices for work? If so, do you think this adds to your stress level or helps you by providing convenience?

11-12. Cocalis likes the two-phone lifestyle and says his boss has his personal phone number only for emergencies. But assistant talent manager Chloe Ifshin reports it doesn't work so well in practice. "I have friends who are clients and clients who are friends," she says, so work contacts end up on her personal phone and friends call her work phone. How does this consideration affect your thinking about BYOD?

11-13. Organizations are taking steps to protect themselves from what employees might be doing on their BYOD devices through allowing only approved computer programs and stricter policies, but no federal regulations protect employees from these. What ethical initiatives might organizations adopt to make this situation fair for everyone?

Sources: S. E. Ante, "Perilous Mix: Cloud, Devices from Home," *The Wall Street Journal,* February 20, 2014, B4; D. Derks and A. B. Bakker, "Smartphone Use, Work-Home Interference, and Burnout: A Diary Study on the Role of Recovery," *Applied Psychology: An International Review* 63, no. 3 (2014): 411–40; L. Duxbury, C. Higgins, R. Smart, and M. Stevenson, "Mobile Technology and Boundary Permeability," *British Journal of Management* 25 (2014): 570–88; E. Holmes, "When One Phone Isn't Enough," *The Wall Street Journal,* April 2, 2014, D1, D2; C. Mims, "2014: The Year of Living Vulnerably," *The Wall Street Journal,* December 22, 2014, B1, B2; L. Weber, "Leaving a Job? Better Watch Your Cellphone," *The Wall Street Journal,* January 22, 2014; and E. Yost, "Can an Employer Remotely Wipe an Employee's Cellphone?" *HR Magazine,* July 2014, 19.

CASE INCIDENT 1 Organizational Leveraging of Social Media

As you know, social media transformed the way we interact. The transparent, rapid-fire communication they make possible means people can spread information about companies more rapidly than ever.

Do organizations understand yet how to use social media effectively? Perhaps not. Only three of ten CEOs in the Fortune 500 have any presence on national social media sites. Many executives are wary of these new technologies because they cannot always control the outcomes of their communications. However, whether they are directly involved with social media or not, companies should recognize that messages are out there, so it behooves them to make their voices heard. Some experts even say social media tools improve productivity because they keep employees connected to their companies during nonoffice hours. And social media can be an important way to learn about emerging trends. For example, André Schneider, chairman of World Climate Ltd., uses feedback from LinkedIn discussion groups and Facebook friends to discover emerging trends and issues worldwide. Padmasree Warrior, former chief technology officer of Cisco, has used social media to refine her presentations before a test audience.

The first step in developing a social media strategy is establishing a brand for your communications after you define what you want your social media presence to express. Experts recommend that organizations first leverage their internal corporate networks to test their strategy in a medium that's easier to control. Most companies have the technology to use social media through their corporate websites and may use these platforms for communicating with employees and facilitating social networks for general information sharing. As social networking expert Soumitra Dutta of Cornell notes, "My advice is to build your audience slowly and be selective about your contacts."

Despite the potential advantages, companies also need to be aware of significant drawbacks for them. First, it's very difficult to control social media communications. Microsoft found this out when the professional blogger it hired spent more time promoting himself than getting positive information out about the company. Second, important intellectual capital might leak out. Companies need to establish strong policies and procedures to ensure that sensitive information about ongoing corporate strategies is not disseminated via social media. Finally, managers must be committed to monitoring motivation and interest beyond their initial forays into social media. A site that's rarely updated can send a very negative message about the organization's level of engagement with the world.

Questions

11-14. Are the drawbacks of the corporate leveraging of social media sufficient to make you think it's better for them to avoid certain media? If so, which media?

11-15. What features would you look for in a social media outlet? What types of information would you avoid making part of your social media strategy?

11-16. What do you think is the future direction of social media in business? How might emerging technologies change your forecast?

Sources: B. Acohido, "Social-Media Tools Boost Productivity," *USA Today,* August 13, 2012, 1B; H. Annabi and S. T. McGann, "Social Media as the Missing Links: Connecting Communities of Practice to Business Strategy," *Journal of Organizational Computing and Electronic Commerce* 23, no. 1–2 (2013): 56–83; S. Dutta, "What's Your Personal Social Media Strategy," *Harvard Business Review,* November 2010, 127–30; and G. Connors, "10 Social Media Commandments for Employers," *Workforce Management Online,* February 2010, www.workforce.com; and L. Kwoh and M. Korn, "140 Characters of Risk: CEOs on Twitter," *The Wall Street Journal,* September 26, 2012, B1, B8.

CASE INCIDENT 2 An Underwater Meeting

On Saturday October 17, 2009, democratically elected President Mohammad Nasheed of the Maldives invited his 13 officials to a cabinet meeting: the world's first underwater governmental meeting. The meeting "room" was in a lagoon off Girifushi, in the North Male atoll, and the ministers dove 20 feet (6 meters) to meet around a horseshoe-shaped table on the sea floor.

The Maldives, located southwest of Sri Lanka, is an Indian Ocean archipelago whose 1,192 islands stretch for 850 kilometers (530 miles). The Maldivian islands are on average only 2 meters (7 feet) above sea level, and they comprise the lowest-lying nation on the planet.

The meeting agenda highlighted how global warming was threatening the disappearance of the Maldives within a century. In 2007, data about this threat were confirmed by the United Nations Intergovernmental Panel on Climate Change, warning that a rise in sea levels of 18 to 59 centimeters (7 to 23 inches) by 2100 would be enough to make the Maldives virtually uninhabitable. The decision made at the meeting was to sign off on an agreement for carbon emission cuts: "We must unite in a global effort to halt further temperature rises." The meeting took place prior to the United Nations climate change conference in December in anticipation of the renegotiation of the Kyoto Protocol.

The safety of the ministers was well considered. They held a dress rehearsal the day before; coral on the reef was checked for harmful creatures and participants communicated via hand signals to indicate they were okay. Instead of dressing in business suits, though, the 14 government ministers donned scuba diving gear and

also wore name tags. Just as in every meeting, discussion took place, but here it was through writing on a special white board. The meeting was broadcast live on television. Inhabitants on Kuda Huvadhoo island built a sealed box, put their television in it, and, following their governments' lead, dove to the depths to view the underwater meeting—underwater.

Back on dry land, the cabinet ministers were to sign their wet suits for auctioning on the www.protectthemaldives.com Web site in a bid to raise money for protecting coral reefs. President Nasheed used the meeting venue as a publicity exercise to push for action so that his people can continue to live in the Maldives well into the future.

Questions

11-17. Identify the main function of the meeting.

11-18. Describe the communication process and distinguish between its formality and informality.

11-19. What is your opinion on the view that audiences prefer "live" presentations?

Sources: Based on: AFP, (October 17, 2009), "Maldives Officials Hold Underwater Meeting to Highlight Threat of Global Warming," *Gulf News,* p. 21, gulfnews.com/news/world/other-world/maldives-officialshold-underwater-meeting-to-highlight-threat-of-globalwarming-1.515739; AFP (October 16, 2009), accessed October 23, 2009; "Maldives Cabinet Rehearses Underwater Meeting," *Canwest* News Service, www.canada.com/technology/Maldives+cabinet+rehearses+underwater+meeting/2111098/story.html; O. Lang, (October 17, 2009), accessed October 23, 2009, "Maldives Leader in Climate Change Stunt," *BBC News,* accessed October 23, 2009 at news.bbc.co.uk/2/hi/south_asia/8312320.stm.

MyManagementLab

Go to **mymanagementlab.com** for the following Assisted-graded writing questions:

11-20. Based on Case Incident 1 and your chapter reading, how do you think social media might be used in business 5 years from now? Do you see the usage as growing or lessening, and why?

11-21. Considering Case Incident 2 and the chapter material, what are the positive aspects of PowerPoint as a communication method? One study found no difference in memory recall of listeners after presentations with (a) PowerPoint words only, (b) visual-only slides, (c) words and visual aids, and (d) no slides. How does this change your view of the usefulness of PowerPoint as a communication tool?

11-22. MyManagementLab Only – comprehensive writing assignment for this chapter.

ENDNOTES

[1]R. Wijn and K. van den Bos, "On the Social-Communicative Function of Justice: The Influence of Communication Goals and Personal Involvement on the Use of Justice Assertions," *Personality and Social Psychology Bulletin* 36, no. 2 (2010): 161–72.

[2]R. Swarns, "After Uneasy First Tries, Coworkers Find a Way to Talk about Race," *The New York Times,* March 23, 2015, A15.

[3]D. C. Barnlund, "A Transactional Model of Communication." In C. D. Mortenson (ed.), *Communication Theory* (New Brunswick, NJ: Transaction, 2008): 47–57; see K. Byron, "Carrying Too Heavy a Load? The Communication and Miscommunication of Emotion by E-mail," *Academy of Management Review* 33, no. 2 (2008): 309–27.

[4]A. Tenhiaelae and F. Salvador, "Looking inside Glitch Mitigation Capability: The Effect of Intraorganizational Communication Channels," *Decision Sciences* 45, no. 3 (2014): 437–66.

[5]S. Jhun, Z.-T. Bae, and S.-Y. Rhee, "Performance Change of Managers in Two Different Uses of Upward Feedback: A Longitudinal Study in Korea," International Journal of Human Resource Management 23, no. 20 (2012): 4246–64; and J. W. Smither and A. G. Walker, "Are the Characteristics of Narrative Comments Related to Improvement in Multirater Feedback Ratings over Time?" *Journal of Applied Psychology* 89, no. 3 (June 2004): 575–81.

[6]P. Dvorak, "How Understanding the 'Why' of Decisions Matters," *The Wall Street Journal,* March 19, 2007, B3.

[7]T. Neeley and P. Leonardi, "Effective Managers Say the Same Thing Twice (or More)," *Harvard Business Review,* May 2011, 38–39.

[8]H. A. Richardson and S. G. Taylor, "Understanding Input Events: A Model of Employees' Responses to Requests for Their Input," *Academy of Management Review* 37 (2012): 471–91.

[9]J. S. Lublin, "Managers Need to Make Time for Face Time," *The Wall Street Journal,* March 18, 2015, B6.

[10]E. Nichols, "Hyper-Speed Managers," *HR Magazine,* April 2007, 107–10.

[11]R. Walker, "Declining an Assignment, with Finesse," *The New York Times,* August 24, 2014, 8.

[12]See, for example, N. B. Kurland and L. H. Pelled, "Passing the Word: Toward a Model of Gossip and Power in the Workplace," *Academy of Management Review,* April 2000, 428–38; and

G. Michelson, A. van Iterson, and K. Waddington, "Gossip in Organizations: Contexts, Consequences, and Controversies," *Group and Organization Management* 35, no. 4 (2010): 371–90.

[13]G. Van Hoye and F. Lievens, "Tapping the Grapevine: A Closer Look at Word-of-Mouth as a Recruitment Source," *Journal of Applied Psychology* 94, no. 2 (2009): 341–52.

[14]J. K. Bosson, A. B. Johnson, K. Niederhoffer, and W. B. Swann Jr., "Interpersonal Chemistry through Negativity: Bonding by Sharing Negative Attitudes about Others," *Personal Relationships* 13 (2006): 135–50.

[15]T. J. Grosser, V. Lopez-Kidwell, and G. Labianca, "A Social Network Analysis of Positive and Negative Gossip in Organizational Life," *Group and Organization Management* 35, no. 2 (2010): 177–212.

[16]R. Feintzeig, "The Boss's Next Demand: Make Lots of Friends," *The Wall Street Journal,* February 12, 2014, B1, B6.

[17]R. E. Silverman, "A Victory for Small Office Talkers," *The Wall Street Journal,* October 28, 2014, D2.

[18]M. Feinberg, R. Willer, J. Stellar, and D. Keltner, "The Virtues of Gossip: Reputational Information Sharing as Prosocial Behavior," *Journal of Personality and Social Psychology* 102 (2012): 1015–30.

[19]L. Dulye, "Get Out of Your Office," *HR Magazine,* July 2006, 99–101.

[20]E. Bernstein, "How Well Are You Listening?" *The Wall Street Journal,* January 13, 2015, D1.

[21]S. Shellenbarger, "Work & Family Mailbox," *The Wall Street Journal,* July 30, 2014, D2.

[22]E. C. Ravlin, A.-K. Ward, and D. C. Thomas, "Exchanging Social Information across Cultural Boundaries," *Journal of Management* 40, no. 5 (2014): 1437–65.

[23]A. Kessler, "Let's Call off the Meeting and Get Back to Work," *The Wall Street Journal,* January 2, 2015, A13.

[24]A. Bryant, "Getting Stuff Done: It's a Goal, and a Rating System," *The New York Times,* March 9, 2013, www.nytimes.com/2013/03/10/business/kris-duggan-of-badgeville-on-the-getting-stuff-done-index.html?pagewanted=all&_r=0.

[25]J. Queenan, "Fire Away!—Military Metaphors," *The Wall Street Journal,* March 28–29, 2015, C11.

[26]E. Bernstein, "What Verbal Tics May Be Saying about Us," *The Wall Street Journal,* January 21, 2014, D3.

[27]M. Mihelich, "Bit by Bit: Stand-up Comedy as a Team-Building Exercise," *Workforce Management,* February 2013, 16; and "Comedy Experience," Peppercomm, http://peppercomm.com/services/comedy-experience, accessed July 1, 2015.

[28]A. Bryant, "Finding, and Owning, Their Voice," *The New York Times,* November 16, 2014, 6.

[29]T. D. Maynes and P. M. Podsakoff, "Speaking More Broadly: An Examination of the Nature, Antecedents, and Consequences of an Expanded Set of Employee Voice Behaviors," *Journal of Applied Psychology* 99, no. 1 (2014): 87–112.

[30]J. Lipman, "A Guide for Men," *The Wall Street Journal,* December 13–14, 2014, C1, C2.

[31]S. Shellenbarger, "Help! I'm on a Conference Call," *The Wall Street Journal,* February 26, 2014, D1, D2.

[32]Ibid.

[33]Ibid.

[34]S. Ovide, "Office Phone Calls Make a Comeback," *The Wall Street Journal,* March 13, 2015, B6.

[35]P. A. Mueller and D. M. Oppenheimer, "The Pen Is Mightier Than the Keyboard: Advantages of Longhand over Laptop Note Taking," *Psychological Science* 25, no. 6 (2014): 1159–68.

[36]N. Bilton, "Disruptions: Life's Too Short for So Much E-mail," *The New York Times,* July 8, 2012, http://bits.blogs.nytimes.com/2012/07/08/life%E2%80%99s-too-short-for-so-much-e-mail/.

[37]"Executive Summary," *Messagemind,* 2012, www.messagemind.com.

[38]G. J. Mark, S. Voida, and A. V. Cardello, "'A Pace Not Dictated by Electrons': An Empirical Study of Work without E-mail," *Proceedings of the SIGCHI Conference on Human Factors in Computing Systems,* 2012, 555–64.

[39]C. L.-L. Tan, "Mind Your E-mail Manners: No 'XOXO' or 'LOL' Allowed," *The Wall Street Journal,* April 21, 2015.

[40]Ibid.

[41]E. Bernstein, "The Miscommunicators," *The Wall Street Journal,* July 3, 2012, D1, D3.

[42]B. Roberts, "Social Media Gets Strategic," *HR Magazine,* October 2012, 30–38.

[43]"Number of Monthly Active Facebook Users Worldwide as of 1st Quarter 2015 (in Millions)," Statista/Facebook, http://www.statista.com/statistics/264810/number-of-monthly-active-facebook-users-worldwide/, accessed July 1, 2015.

[44]K. Wagner, "The World's Top CEOs Are Tweeting More, Facebooking Less," Re/Code, May 17, 2015, http://recode.net/2015/05/17/the-worlds-top-ceos-are-tweeting-more-facebooking-less/.

[45]Ibid.

[46]P. Mozur, J. Osawa, and N. Purnell, "Facebook and WhatsApp a Tough Sell in Asia," The Wall Street Journal, February 21, 2014, B4.

[47]C. Smith, "By the Numbers: 125+ Amazing LinkedIn Statistics," DMR, June 6, 2015, http://expandedramblings.com/index.php/by-the-numbers-a-few-important-linkedin-stats/.

[48]K. Wagner, "The World's Top CEOs Are Tweeting More, Facebooking Less."

[49]"Number of Monthly Active Twitter Users Worldwide from 1st Quarter 2010 to 1st Quarter 2015 (in Millions)," Statista/Twitter, http://www.statista.com/statistics/282087/number-of-monthly-active-twitter-users/, accessed July 1, 2015.

[50]K. Wagner, "The World's Top CEOs Are Tweeting More, Facebooking Less."

[51]L. Kwoh and M. Korn, "140 Characters of Risk: CEOs on Twitter," The Wall Street Journal, September 26, 2012, B1, B8.

[52]P. Mozur, J. Osawa, and N. Purnell, "Facebook and WhatsApp a Tough Sell in Asia."

[53]Ibid.

[54]O. Allen, "6 Stats You Should Know about Business Blogging in 2015," HubSpot Blogs, March 11, 2015, http://blog.hubspot.com/marketing/business-blogging-in-2015.

[55]L. Talley and S. Temple, "How Leaders Influence Followers through the Use of Nonverbal Communication," Leadership & Organizational Development Journal 36, no. 1 (2015): 69–80.

[56]C. K. Goman, "5 Body Language Tips to Increase Your Curb Appeal," Forbes, March 4, 2013, www.forbes.com/sites/carolkinseygoman/2013/03/14/5-body-language-tips-to-increase-your-curb-appeal/.

[57]A. Metallinou, A. Katsamanis, and S. Narayanan, "Tracking Continuous Emotional Trends of Participants During Affective Dyadic Interactions Using Body Language and Speech Information," Image and Vision Computing, February 2013, 137–52.

[58]J. Smith, "10 Nonverbal Cues That Convey Confidence at Work," Forbes, March 11, 2013, www.forbes.com/sites/jacquelynsmith/2013/03/11/10-nonverbal-cues-that-convey-confidence-at-work/.

[59]See L. K. Trevino, J. Webster, and E. W. Stein, "Making Connections: Complementary Influences on Communication Media Choices, Attitudes, and Use," Organization Science, March–April 2000, 163–82; and N. Kock, "The Psychobiological Model: Towards a New Theory of Computer-Mediated Communication Based on Darwinian Evolution," Organization Science 15, no. 3 (May–June 2004): 327–48.

[60]S. Shellenbarger, "Is This How You Really Talk?" The Wall Street Journal, April 24, 2013, D1, D3.

[61]K Kruse, "Why Successful People Never Bring Smartphones into Meetings," Forbes, December 26, 2013, http://www.forbes.com/sites/kevinkruse/2013/12/26/why-successful-people-never-bring-smartphones-into-meetings/.

[62]B. Giamanco and K. Gregoire, "Tweet Me, Friend Me, Make Me Buy," Harvard Business Review, July–August 2012, 88–93.

[63]T. Lytle, "Cybersleuthing," HR Magazine, January 2012, 55–57.

[64]J. Segal, "Widening Web of Social Media," HR Magazine, June 2012, 117–18.

[65]"At Many Companies, Hunt for Leakers Expands Arsenal of Monitoring Tactics," The Wall Street Journal, September 11, 2006, B1, B3; and B. J. Alge, G. A. Ballinger, S. Tangirala, and J. L. Oakley, "Information Privacy in Organizations: Empowering Creative and Extrarole Performance," Journal of Applied Psychology 91, No. 1 (2006): 221–32.

[66]R. E. Petty and P. Briñol, "Persuasion: From Single to Multiple to Metacognitive Processes," Perspectives on Psychological Science 3, no. 2 (2008): 137–47; F. A. White, M. A. Charles, and J. K. Nelson, "The Role of Persuasive Arguments in Changing Affirmative Action Attitudes and Expressed Behavior in Higher Education," Journal of Applied Psychology 93, no. 6 (2008): 1271–86.

[67]K. L. Blankenship and D. T. Wegener, "Opening the Mind to Close It: Considering a Message in Light of Important Values Increases Message Processing and Later Resistance to Change," Journal of Personality and Social Psychology 94, no. 2 (2008): 196–213.

[68]See, for example, Y. H. M. See, R. E. Petty, and L. R. Fabrigar, "Affective and Cognitive Meta-Bases of Attitudes: Unique Effects of Information Interest and Persuasion," Journal of Personality and Social Psychology 94, no. 6 (2008): 938–55; M. S. Key, J. E. Edlund, B. J. Sagarin, and G. Y. Bizer, "Individual Differences in Susceptibility to Mindlessness," Personality and Individual Differences 46, no. 3 (2009): 261–64 and M. Reinhard and M. Messner, "The Effects of Source Likeability and Need for Cognition on Advertising Effectiveness under Explicit Persuasion," Journal of Consumer Behavior 8, no. 4 (2009): 179–91.

[69]S. Norton, "A Post-PC CEO: No Desk, No Desktop," The Wall Street Journal, November 20, 2014, B5.

[70]D. Derks, D. van Duin, M. Tims, et al., "Smartphone Use and Work-Home Interference: The Moderating Role of Social Norms and Employee Work Engagement," Journal of Occupational and Organizational Psychology 88, no. 1 (2015): 155–77.

[71]P. Briñol, R. E. Petty, and J. Barden, "Happiness versus Sadness as a Determinant of Thought Confidence in Persuasion: A Self-Validation Analysis," Journal of Personality and Social Psychology 93, no. 5 (2007): 711–27.

[72]R. C. Sinclair, S. E. Moore, M. M. Mark, A. S. Soldat, and C. A. Lavis, "Incidental Moods, Source Likeability, and Persuasion: Liking Motivates Message Elaboration in Happy People," Cognition and Emotion 24, no. 6 (2010): 940–61; and V. Griskevicius, M. N. Shiota, and S. L. Neufeld, "Influence of Different Positive Emotions on Persuasion Processing: A Functional Evolutionary Approach," Emotion 10, no. 2 (2010): 190–206.

[73]J. Sandberg, "The Jargon Jumble: Kids Have 'Skeds,' Colleagues, 'Needs,'" The Wall Street Journal, October 24, 2006, http://online.wsj.com/article/SB116165746415401680.html.

[74]E. W. Morrison and F. J. Milliken, "Organizational Silence: A Barrier to Change and Development in a Pluralistic World," Academy of Management Review 25, no. 4 (2000): 706–25; and B. E. Ashforth and V. Anand, "The Normalization of Corruption in Organizations," Research in Organizational Behavior 25 (2003): 1–52.

[75]F. J. Milliken, E. W. Morrison, and P. F. Hewlin, "An Exploratory Study of Employee Silence: Issues That Employees Don't Communicate Upward and Why," Journal of Management Studies 40, no. 6 (2003): 1453–76.

[76]L. A. Withers, and L. L. Vernon, "To Err Is Human: Embarrassment, Attachment, and Communication Apprehension," Personality and Individual Differences 40, no. 1 (2006): 99–110.

[77]See, for instance, S. K. Opt and D. A. Loffredo, "Rethinking Communication Apprehension: A Myers-Briggs Perspective," Journal of Psychology, September 2000, 556–70; and B. D. Blume, G. F. Dreher, and T. T.

Baldwin, "Examining the Effects of Communication Apprehension within Assessment Centres," *Journal of Occupational and Organizational Psychology* 83, no. 3 (2010): 663–71.

[78]See, for example, T. L. Rodebaugh, "I Might Look OK, but I'm Still Doubtful, Anxious, and Avoidant: The Mixed Effects of Enhanced Video Feedback on Social Anxiety Symptoms," *Behaviour Research & Therapy* 42, no. 12 (December 2004): 1435–51.

[79]K. B. Serota, T. R. Levine, and F. J. Boster, "The Prevalence of Lying in America: Three Studies of Self-Reported Lies," *Human Communication Research* 36, no. 1. (2010): 2–25.

[80]DePaulo, Kashy, Kirkendol, Wyer, and Epstein, "Lying in Everyday Life"; and C. E. Naguin, T. R. Kurtzberg, and L. Y. Belkin, "The Finer Points of Lying Online: E-Mail versus Pen and Paper," *Journal of Applied Psychology* 95, no. 2 (2010): 387–94.

[81]A. Vrij, P. A. Granhag, and S. Porter, "Pitfalls and Opportunities in Nonverbal and Verbal Lie Detection," *Psychological Science in the Public Interest* 11, no. 3 (2010): 89–121.

[82]See E. T. Hall, *Beyond Culture* (Garden City, NY: Anchor Press/Doubleday, 1976); W. L. Adair, "Integrative Sequences and Negotiation Outcome in Same- and Mixed-Culture Negotiations," *International Journal of Conflict Management* 14, no. 3–4 (2003): 1359–92; W. L. Adair and J. M. Brett, "The Negotiation Dance: Time, Culture, and Behavioral Sequences in Negotiation," *Organization Science* 16, no. 1 (2005): 33–51; E. Giebels and P. J. Taylor, "Interaction Patterns in Crisis Negotiations: Persuasive Arguments and Cultural Differences," *Journal of Applied Psychology* 94, no. 1 (2009): 5–19; and M. G. Kittler, D. Rygl, and A. Mackinnon, "Beyond Culture or Beyond Control? Reviewing the Use of Hall's High-/Low-Context Concept," *International Journal of Cross-Cultural Management* 11, no. 1 (2011): 63–82.

[83]M. C. Hopson, T. Hart, and G. C. Bell, "Meeting in the Middle: Fred L. Casmir's Contributions to the Field of Intercultural Communication," *International Journal of Intercultural Relations,* November 2012, 789–97.

12 Leadership

LEARNING OBJECTIVES

After studying this chapter, you should be able to:

12-1 Summarize the conclusions of trait theories of leadership.

12-2 Identify the central tenets and main limitations of behavioral theories.

12-3 Contrast contingency theories of leadership.

12-4 Describe the contemporary theories of leadership and their relationship to foundational theories.

12-5 Discuss the roles of leaders in creating ethical organizations.

12-6 Describe how leaders can have a positive impact on their organizations through building trust and mentoring.

12-7 Identify the challenges to our understanding of leadership.

MyManagementLab®
★ Chapter Warm Up

If your professor has chosen to assign this, go to the Assignments section of **mymanagementlab.com** to complete the chapter warm up.

THE FLAMBOYANT LEADERSHIP OF JACK MA

Entrepreneur Jack Ma, pictured here, is at the top of his game. As the leader of China's largest online retailer and the richest man in China, Ma can afford to be a little unconventional, sometimes appearing in drag and belting out "I Love You, China" to an audience of 40,000 fans wearing devil-horned headbands and carrying glow-sticks. He can also afford to be a strategist, motivator, and ad hoc politician rather than a practical leader. He can even afford to know nothing about the technology that may make him one of the industry's richest people worldwide.

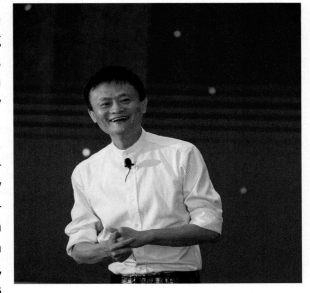

Ma had an unconventional start for an Internet billionaire. Originally an English teacher, he had no background in computers and didn't use the Internet until 1995, when he literally searched for "beer" in "China." The Chinese translation service he created shortly thereafter blossomed into the Alibaba Group in 1999. Now, 60 percent of packages shipped through China come from Alibaba via its websites Taobao Marketplace, AliExpress, and Tmall.com. The Chinese postal system has profited from the increase in shipments, as have countless manufacturers of goods sold through the websites. "He effectively represents millions of people who now depend on Alibaba for their livelihood," Ma's long-time friend Duncan Clark acknowledged.

More than fellow technology moguls Mark Zuckerberg of Facebook, the late Steve Jobs of Apple, and Bill Gates of Microsoft, the success of Ma's leadership seems to rest on his charisma, not techno-savvy. He uses his charm to tap into the heart of China's growing middle class with its penchant for spending rather than saving, hoping China will eventually rival the United States in consumer spending. According to McKinsey & Company, the probabilities are in his favor. Its report on China states, "The evolution of the middle class means that sophisticated and seasoned shoppers—those able and willing to...consider discretionary goods and not just basic necessities—will soon emerge as the dominant force."

Ma pictures himself as an artist and insists, "It's not about making money." He freely offers sometimes oblique advice such as, "Do not always learn from Bill Gates and Jack Ma. Learn from your neighbor." His charismatic messages carry a dose of poeticism, even when they are cryptic: "My philosophy is repair the roof while there is still sunshine. If the storm is coming, don't go up and repair the roof because you will be destroyed."

Fans and competitors agree, Ma is highly charismatic. Charismatic leaders inspire group identity in their employees who connect with the leader's emotional messages and vision, which Ma epitomizes. Alibaba employee Hao Wu said Ma's "pithy, witty, and audacious quotes are widely circulated, discussed, and memorized." During a conference, Ma "moved the room from laughter to awe and back like a master orchestra conductor." It seems Ma has Alibaba—and the world—in his spell.

Sources: T. B. Klich, "Why Alibaba's Jack Ma Sees Himself as an 'Artist,' and Maybe You Should, Too," *Entrepreneur,* June 13, 2015, www.entrepreneur.com/article/247287; P. J. Leithart, "Charismatic Leadership," *First Things,* September 23, 2014, www.first things.com/blogs/leithart/2014/09/charismatic-leadership; G. Weiss, "Who Knew? Charismatic Alibaba Founder Jack Ma Moonlights as a Singer," *Entrepreneur,* May 5, 2014, www.entrepreneur.com/article/233638; and A. Xenikou, "The Cognitive and Affective Components of Organisational Identification: The Role of Perceived Support Values and Charismatic Leadership," *Applied Psychology: An International Review* 63, no. 4 (2014): 567–88.

Charismatic leaders like Jack Ma possess a "special something" that sets them apart. However, theirs is not the only type of effective leadership. In this chapter, we'll look at all types of leaders, and what differentiates leaders from nonleaders. We'll present trait theories of leadership. Then, we'll discuss challenges to the meaning and importance of leadership. But before we begin, let's clarify what we mean by the term *leadership*.

We define **leadership** as the ability to influence a group toward the achievement of a vision or set of goals. But not all leaders are managers, nor are all

leadership   The ability to influence a group toward the achievement of a vision or set of goals.

managers leaders. Just because an organization provides its managers with certain formal rights is no assurance they will lead effectively. Leaders can emerge from within a group as well as by formal appointment. Nonsanctioned leadership—the ability to influence that arises outside the formal structure of the organization—is often as important, or more important, than formal influence.

Organizations need strong leadership *and* strong management for optimal effectiveness. We need leaders to challenge the status quo, create visions of the future, and inspire organizational members to achieve the visions. We need managers to formulate detailed plans, create efficient organizational structures, and oversee day-to-day operations.

✪ WATCH IT!

If your professor has assigned this, go to the Assignments section of **mymanagementlab.com** to complete the video exercise titled *Leadership (TWZ Role Play)*.

Trait Theories

12-1 Summarize the conclusions of trait theories of leadership.

trait theories of leadership   Theories that consider personal qualities and characteristics that differentiate leaders from nonleaders.

Throughout history, strong leaders have been described by their traits. Therefore, leadership research has long sought to identify the personality, social, physical, or intellectual attributes that differentiate leaders from nonleaders. **Trait theories of leadership** focus on personal qualities and characteristics. Leadership emergence and effectiveness are often evaluated separately vis-à-vis trait studies.

For personality, a comprehensive review of the leadership literature organized around the Big Five framework has found extraversion to be the most predictive trait of effective leadership.[1] However, extraversion sometimes relates more to the way leaders emerge than to their effectiveness. Sociable and dominant people are more likely to assert themselves in group situations, which can help extraverts be identified as leaders, but effective leaders are not domineering. One study found leaders who scored very high in assertiveness, a facet of extraversion, were less effective than those who were moderately high.[2] So although extraversion can predict effective leadership, the relationship may be due to unique facets of the trait.

Unlike agreeableness and emotional stability, which seem not to predict leadership, conscientiousness and openness to experience may predict leadership, especially leader effectiveness. For example, one recent study indicated that top management teams that were high in conscientiousness positively influenced organizational performance through their leadership.[3] Conscientiousness and extraversion are positively related to leaders' self-efficacy,[4] and people are more likely to follow someone who is confident he or she is going in the right direction, allowing these leaders to emerge.

In sum, leaders who like being around people and are able to assert themselves (extraverted), are disciplined and able to keep commitments they make (conscientious), and are creative and flexible (open) have an apparent advantage when it comes to leadership.

What about the Dark Side personality traits of Machiavellianism, narcissism, and psychopathy (see Chapter 5)? Research indicates they're not all bad for leadership. A study in Europe and the United States found that normative

As the CEO of Women's Bean Project, Tamra Ryan leads a team of professionals in managing the social enterprise that helps women earn a living while teaching them work and life skills. Her traits of extraversion, conscientiousness, confidence, and emotional stability contribute to her successful work.

Source: David Zalubowski/AP Images

(mid-range) scores on the Dark Side personality traits were optimal, while low (and high) scores were associated with ineffective leadership. Furthermore, the study suggested that high emotional stability may actually accentuate the ineffective behaviors.[5] However, higher scores on Dark Side traits and emotional stability can contribute to leadership emergence. Thankfully, both this study and other international research indicate that building self-awareness and self-regulation skills may be helpful for leaders to control the effects of their Dark Side traits.[6]

Another trait that may indicate effective leadership is emotional intelligence (EI), discussed in Chapter 4. A core component of EI is empathy. Empathetic leaders can sense others' needs, listen to what followers say (and don't say), and read the reactions of others. A leader who effectively displays and manages emotions will find it easier to influence the feelings of followers by expressing genuine sympathy and enthusiasm for good performance, and by showing irritation when employees fail to perform.[7] The link between EI and leadership effectiveness may be worth investigating in greater detail.[8] Research has also demonstrated that people high in EI are more likely to emerge as leaders, even after taking cognitive ability and personality into account.[9]

Based on the latest findings, we offer two conclusions. First, we can say that traits can predict leadership. Second, traits do a better job predicting the emergence of leaders and the appearance of leadership than distinguishing between effective and ineffective leaders.[10] The fact that an individual exhibits the right traits and others consider that person a leader does not necessarily mean he or she will be an effective one, successful at getting the group to achieve its goals.

Trait theories help us *predict* leadership, but they don't fully help us *explain* leadership. What do successful leaders do that makes them effective? Are different types of leader behaviors equally effective? Behavioral theories, discussed next, help us define the parameters of leadership.

Career **OB**jectives

How can I get my boss to be a better leader?

My boss is the CEO, and she's a gossipy, in-your-business oversharer. She's always asking our top management team personal questions and sharing information with anyone. The other day, I caught her e-mailing my colleague about my salary and career prospects! What should I do about her poor leadership?

— *Phil*

Dear Phil,

Nobody likes an oversharer! Perhaps your boss isn't aware of the impact of her behavior and thinks she is just being friendly. Assuming this is the case, you might be able to make her think first before sharing. If you're comfortable addressing her, you may suggest a private meeting to discuss your concerns. You should bring a list of the types of information she solicits and shares—with an example or two—and, if she's open to discussion, problem-solve with her about her habit. She may see that her "open book" approach is undermining her leadership effectiveness.

Another tactic might start with your researching the best privacy practices, laws, and business guidelines. Be sure to source your organization's HR handbook for any mentions of privacy expectations. Then in your meeting you could present your research findings.

With both direct approaches, you run the risk of offending your boss, which may very well happen if she becomes embarrassed. Moreover, she may defend her behavior if her oversharing is actually strategic gossip and not see the problem, which could have ramifications for what she then thinks and says about you!

These approaches still might be worth trying, but from what you've said about her, it's highly unlikely she will change her general behavior. Research indicates that her personal tendencies will prevail over time. It sounds like she is extraverted, for instance—you're not going to change that. She may be clever and manipulative, purposefully leveraging her information for personal gain without a concern for others (high-Machiavellian or narcissistic). In that case self-awareness can help, but her behavior won't change unless she is willing to practice self-regulation.

Perhaps most importantly, it doesn't seem that you like your boss.

This may be a real problem that you cannot surmount. How are you going to build a relationship of trust with her, trust that will be needed for you to continue to feel motivated and work hard? Unfortunately, if you cannot thrive in this environment, it may be best to move on.

Good luck for your best possible outcome!

Sources: A. E. Colbert, M. R. Barrick, and B. H. Bradley, "Personality and Leadership Composition in Top Management Teams: Implications for Organizational Effectiveness," *Personnel Psychology* 67 (2014): 351–87; R. B. Kaiser, J. M. LeBreton, and J. Hogan, "The Dark Side of Personality and Extreme Leader Behavior," *Applied Psychology: An International Review* 64, no. 1 (2015): 55–92; and R. Walker, "A Boss Who Shares Too Much," *The New York Times*, December 28, 2014, 7.

Behavioral Theories

12-2 Identify the central tenets and main limitations of behavioral theories.

behavioral theories of leadership Theories proposing that specific behaviors differentiate leaders from nonleaders.

initiating structure The extent to which a leader is likely to define and structure his or her role and those of subordinates in the search for goal attainment.

Trait research provides a basis for *selecting* the right people for leadership. **Behavioral theories of leadership**, in contrast, imply we can *train* people to be leaders.

The most comprehensive behavioral theories of leadership resulted from the Ohio State Studies,[11] which sought to identify independent dimensions of leader behavior. Beginning with more than a thousand dimensions, the studies narrowed the list to two that substantially accounted for most of the leadership behavior described by employees: *initiating structure* and *consideration*.

Initiating structure is the extent to which a leader is likely to define and structure his or her role and those of employees in the search for goal attainment. It includes behavior that attempts to organize work, work relationships, and goals. A leader high in initiating structure is someone who assigns followers particular tasks, sets definite standards of performance, and emphasizes deadlines.

Consideration is the extent to which a person's job relationships are characterized by mutual trust, respect for employees' ideas, and regard for their feelings. A leader high in consideration helps employees with personal problems, is friendly and approachable, treats all employees as equals, and expresses appreciation and support (people-oriented). Most of us want to work for considerate leaders—when asked to indicate what most motivated them at work, 66 percent of U.S. employees surveyed mentioned appreciation.[12]

consideration   The extent to which a leader is likely to have job relationships characterized by mutual trust, respect for subordinates' ideas, and regard for their feelings.

The results of behavioral theory studies have been mixed. However, one review found the followers of leaders high in consideration were more satisfied with their jobs, were more motivated, and had more respect for their leaders. Initiating structure was more strongly related to higher levels of group and organization productivity and more positive performance evaluations.

The reason for the mixed results from behavioral theory tests may lie partly in follower preferences, particularly cultural preferences. Research from the GLOBE program—a study of 18,000 leaders from 825 organizations in 62 countries, discussed in Chapter 5—suggested there are international differences in the preference for initiating structure and consideration.[13] The study found that leaders high in consideration succeeded best in countries where cultural values did not favor unilateral decision making, such as Brazil. As one Brazilian manager noted, "We do not prefer leaders who take self-governing decisions and act alone without engaging the group. That's part of who we are." A U.S. manager leading a team in Brazil would therefore need to be high in consideration—team-oriented, participative, and humane—to be effective. In contrast, the French have a more bureaucratic view of leaders and are less likely to expect them to be humane and considerate. A leader high in initiating structure (relatively task-oriented) will do best there and can make decisions in a relatively autocratic manner. A manager who scores high in consideration (people oriented) may find her style backfires in France. In other cultures, both dimensions may therefore be important—Chinese culture emphasizes being polite, considerate, and unselfish, but it has a high performance orientation. Thus, consideration and initiating structure may both be important for a manager to be effective in China.

Summary of Trait Theories and Behavioral Theories

In general, research indicates there is validity for both the trait and behavioral theories. Parts of each theory can help explain facets of leadership emergence and effectiveness. However, identifying the exact relationships is not a simple task. The first difficulty is in correctly identifying whether a trait or a behavior predicts a certain outcome. The second is in exploring which combinations of traits and behaviors yield certain outcomes. The third challenge is to determine the causality of traits to behaviors so that predictions toward desirable leadership outcomes can be made.

Leaders who have certain traits desirable to their positions and who display culturally appropriate initiating structure and consideration behaviors do appear to be more effective. Beyond that, the determinations are less clear. For example, perhaps you're wondering whether conscientious leaders (trait) are more likely to be structuring (behavior), and extraverted leaders (trait) to be considerate (behavior). Unfortunately, we are not sure there is a connection. Future research is needed.

As important as traits and behaviors are in identifying effective or ineffective leaders, they do not guarantee success. Some leaders may have the right traits or display the right behaviors and still fail. Context matters too, which has given rise to the contingency theories we discuss next.

Contingency Theories

12-3 Contrast contingency theories of leadership.

Some tough-minded leaders seem to gain a lot of admirers when they take over struggling companies and lead them out of crises. However, predicting leadership success is more complex than finding a few hero examples. Also, the leadership style that works in very bad times doesn't necessarily translate into long-term success. When researchers looked at situational influences, it appeared that under condition *a,* leadership style *x* would be appropriate, whereas style *y* was more suitable for condition *b,* and style *z* for condition *c.* But what *were* conditions *a, b,* and *c?* We next consider the Fiedler model, one approach to isolating situational variables.

The Fiedler Model

Fiedler contingency model The theory that effective groups depend on a proper match between a leader's style of interacting with subordinates and the degree to which the situation gives control and influence to the leader.

least preferred coworker (LPC) questionnaire An instrument that purports to measure whether a person is task or relationship oriented.

Fred Fiedler developed the first comprehensive contingency model for leadership.[14] The **Fiedler contingency model** proposes that group performance depends on the proper match between the leader's style and the degree to which the situation gives the leader control. With the model, the individual's leadership style is assumed to be permanent. The **least preferred coworker (LPC) questionnaire** identifies whether a person is *task-oriented* or *relationship-oriented* by asking respondents to think of all the coworkers they have ever had and describe the one they *least enjoyed* working with. If you describe this person in favorable terms (a high LPC score), you are relationship-oriented. If you see your least-preferred coworker in unfavorable terms (a low LPC score), you are primarily interested in productivity and are task-oriented.

After finding a score, a fit must be found between the organizational situation and the leader's style for there to be leadership effectiveness. We can assess the situation in terms of three contingency or situational dimensions:

leader–member relations The degree of confidence, trust, and respect subordinates have in their leader.

task structure The degree to which job assignments are procedurized.

position power Influence derived from one's formal structural position in the organization; includes power to hire, fire, discipline, promote, and give salary increases.

1. **Leader–member relations** is the degree of confidence, trust, and respect members have in their leader.
2. **Task structure** is the degree to which the job assignments are procedurized (that is, structured or unstructured).
3. **Position power** is the degree of influence a leader has over power variables such as hiring, firing, discipline, promotions, and salary increases.

According to the model, the higher the task structure becomes, the more procedures are added; and the stronger the position power, the more control the leader has. A very favorable situation (in which the leader has a great deal of control) might include a payroll manager who has the respect and confidence of his or her employees (good leader–member relations); activities that are clear and specific—such as wage computation, check writing, and report filing (high task structure); and considerable freedom to reward and punish employees (strong position power). The favorable situations are on the left side of the model in Exhibit 12-1. An unfavorable situation, to the right in the model, might be that of the disliked chairperson of a volunteer United Way fundraising team (low leader–member relations, low task structure, low position power). In this job, the leader has very little control.

| Exhibit 12-1 | Findings from the Fiedler Model |

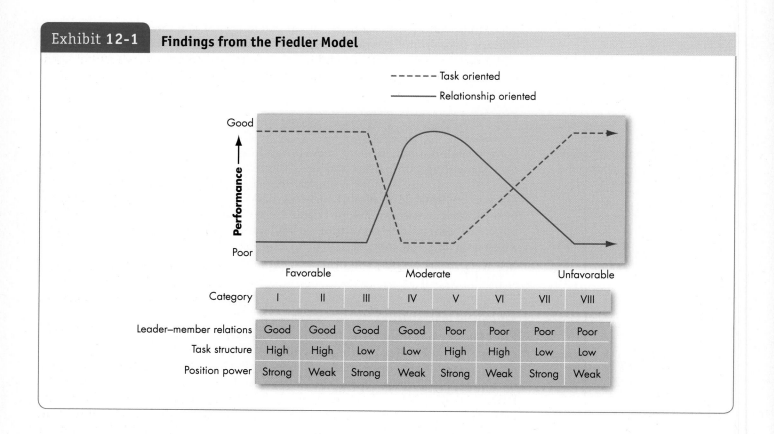

When faced with a category I, II, III, VII, or VIII situation, task-oriented leaders perform better. Relationship-oriented leaders (represented by the solid line), however, perform better in moderately favorable situations—categories IV, V, and VI.

Studies testing the overall validity of the Fiedler model were initially supportive, but the model hasn't been studied much in recent years. Therefore, while it provides some insights we should consider, its strict practical application is problematic.

Situational Leadership Theory

situational leadership theory (SLT)
A contingency theory that focuses on followers' readiness.

Situational leadership theory (SLT) focuses on the followers. It says successful leadership depends on selecting the right leadership style contingent on the followers' *readiness,* the extent to which followers are willing and able to accomplish a specific task. A leader should choose one of four behaviors depending on follower readiness.

If followers are *unable* and *unwilling* to do a task, the leader needs to give clear and specific directions; if they are *unable* but *willing,* the leader needs to display a high task orientation to compensate for followers' lack of ability, and high relationship orientation to get them to "buy into" the leader's desires. If followers are *able* but *unwilling,* the leader needs to use a supportive and participative style; if they are both *able* and *willing,* the leader doesn't need to do much.

SLT has intuitive appeal. It acknowledges the importance of followers and builds on the logic that leaders can compensate for followers' limited ability and motivation. Yet research efforts to test and support the theory have generally been disappointing.[15] Why? Possible explanations include internal ambiguities and inconsistencies in the model itself as well as problems with research methodology. So, despite its intuitive appeal and wide popularity, any endorsement must be cautious for now.

Path–Goal Theory

path-goal theory A theory that states that it is the leader's job to assist followers in attaining their goals and to provide the necessary direction and/or support to ensure that their goals are compatible with the overall objectives of the group or organization.

Developed by Robert House, **path–goal theory** extracts elements from the research on initiating structure and consideration, and on the expectancy theory of motivation.[16] Path–goal theory suggests it's the leader's job to provide followers with information, support, or other resources necessary to achieve goals. (The term *path–goal* implies effective leaders clarify followers' paths to their work goals and make the journey easier by reducing roadblocks.) The theory predicts:

- *Directive leadership yields greater employee satisfaction when tasks are ambiguous or stressful than when they are highly structured and well laid out.*
- *Supportive leadership results in high employee performance and satisfaction when employees are performing structured tasks.*
- *Directive leadership is likely to be perceived as redundant among employees with high ability or considerable experience.*

Of course, this is a simplification. The match between leadership style and situation can be individualistic and mercurial. Some tasks might be both stressful and highly structured, and employees may have high ability or experience in some tasks and not others. Other research has found that goal-focused leadership can lead to higher levels of emotional exhaustion for subordinates who are low in conscientiousness and emotional stability.[17] This suggests that leaders who set goals enable conscientious followers to achieve higher performance but may cause stress for workers who are low in conscientiousness.

Like SLT, path–goal theory has intuitive appeal, especially from a goal attainment perspective. Also like SLT, the theory can be only cautiously adopted for application, but it is a useful framework in examining the important role of leadership.[18]

Leader–Participation Model

leader-participation model A leadership theory that provides a set of rules to determine the form and amount of participative decision making in different situations.

The final contingency theory we cover argues that *the way* the leader makes decisions is as important as *what* he or she decides. The **leader–participation model** relates leadership behavior to subordinate participation in decision making.[19] Like path–goal theory, it says leader behavior must adjust to reflect the task structure (such as routine, non-routine, or in between), but it does not cover all leadership behaviors and is limited to recommending what types of decisions might be best made with subordinate participation. It lays the groundwork for the situations and leadership behaviors most likely to elicit acceptance from subordinates.

As one leadership scholar noted, "Leaders do not exist in a vacuum"; leadership is a symbiotic relationship between leaders and followers.[20] But the theories we've covered to this point assume leaders use a fairly homogeneous style with everyone in their work unit. Think about your experiences in groups. Did leaders often act very differently toward different people? It's common. Before we dig into differences between leaders, consider the OB Poll...and your own quest for leadership skills.

OB POLL

How Are You Developing Your Leadership Skills?

Reading leadership materials — 27%

Other activities, such as obtaining further education — 6%

Nothing

Attending conferences — 24%

Listening to mentor — 19%

Obtaining employee feedback — 24%

Note: Survey of 700 respondents.

Source: Based on J. Brox, "The Results Are In: How Do You Ensure You're Constantly Developing as a Leader?" May 14, 2013, http://www.refreshleadership.com/index.php/2013/05/results-ensure-youre-constantly-developing-leader/#more-4732.

Contemporary Theories of Leadership

12-4 Describe the contemporary theories of leadership and their relationship to foundational theories.

Leaders are important—to organizations, and to employees. The understanding of leadership is a constantly evolving science. Contemporary theories have been built upon the foundation we've just established to discover unique ways leaders emerge, influence, and guide their employees and organizations. Let's explore some of the leading current concepts, and look for aspects of the theories we've discussed already throughout.

Leader–Member Exchange (LMX) Theory

leader–member exchange (LMX) theory
A theory that supports leaders' creation of ingroups and outgroups; subordinates with ingroup status will have higher performance ratings, less turnover, and greater job satisfaction.

Think of a leader you know. Does this leader have favorites who make up an ingroup? If you answered "yes," you're acknowledging leader–member exchange theory.[21] **Leader–member exchange (LMX) theory** argues that, because of time pressures, leaders establish a special relationship with a small group of their followers. These individuals make up the ingroup—they are trusted, get a disproportionate amount of the leader's attention, and are more likely to receive special privileges. Other followers fall into the outgroup.

LMX theory proposes that early in the history of the interaction between a leader and a given follower, the leader implicitly categorizes the follower as an "in" or an "out"; that relationship becomes relatively stable over time. Leaders induce LMX by rewarding employees with whom they want a closer linkage and punishing those with whom they do not.[22] For the LMX relationship to remain intact, the leader and the follower must invest in the relationship.

Just how the leader chooses who falls into each category is unclear, but there is evidence ingroup members have demographic, attitude, and personality characteristics similar to those of their leader or a higher level of competence than outgroup members[23] (see Exhibit 12-2). Leaders and followers of the same gender tend to have closer (higher LMX) relationships than those of different genders.[24] Even though the leader does the choosing, the follower's characteristics drive the categorizing decision.

Exhibit 12-2   **Leader–Member Exchange Theory**

Research to test LMX theory has been generally supportive, with substantive evidence that leaders do differentiate among followers; these disparities are far from random; and followers with ingroup status receive higher performance ratings, engage in more helping or "citizenship" behaviors at work, and report greater satisfaction with their superior.[25]

One study conducted in Portugal and the United States found that LMX was associated strongly with followers' commitment to the organization when leaders were seen as embodying the values and identity of the organization.[26] Other research suggested that employees of leaders who provided family support (helped the employee achieve work–life balance) in the LMX relationship were more committed and performed better.[27] These findings shouldn't be surprising given our knowledge of self-fulfilling prophecy (see Chapter 6). Leaders invest resources with those they expect to perform best. Believing ingroup members are the most competent, leaders treat them as such and unwittingly fulfill their prophecy.

For all the positives the ingroup receives, research indicates that both the ingroup and the outgroup realize negative effects from LMX. For example, a study in Turkey demonstrated that when leaders differentiated strongly among their followers in terms of their relationships (some followers had very positive leader–member exchange, others very poor), employees from both groups responded with more negative work attitudes and higher levels of withdrawal behavior.[28] One study in China and the United States indicated that differential leadership treatment hurts team trust and perceptions of procedural justice, especially when the team members work closely together.[29] Other research indicated that, although ingroup team members showed increased performance, the team as a whole became uncoordinated in the LMX environment and overall performance suffered.[30] Close-knit teams may be able to help outgroup members to retain their confidence and self-efficacy by offering a supportive environment[31] at the cost of the relationship between employees and leaders.

Charismatic Leadership

Do you think leaders are born not made, or made not born? True, an individual may be literally born into a leadership position (think family heirs with surnames like Ford and Hilton), be endowed with a leadership position due to past accomplishments (like CEOs who worked their way up the organizational ranks), or be informally acknowledged as a leader (like a Twitter employee who knows everything because he was "there at the start"). But here we are talking

Nick Woodman, founder and CEO of digital camcorder company GoPro, is a charismatic leader: energetic, enthusiastic, optimistic, confident, and extraverted. Woodman's charisma inspires his employees to work toward GoPro's vision of enabling people to share their lives through photos and videos.
Source: Bloomberg/Getty Images

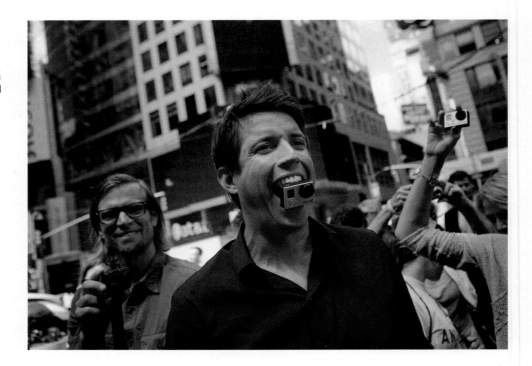

not about the inputs into leadership role attainment; rather, we are focused on what makes great leaders extraordinary. Two contemporary leadership theories—charismatic leadership and transformational leadership—share a common theme in the great leader debate: They view leaders as individuals who inspire followers through words, ideas, and behaviors.

What Is Charismatic Leadership?   Sociologist Max Weber defined *charisma* (from the Greek for "gift") as "a certain quality of an individual personality, by virtue of which he or she is set apart from ordinary people and treated as endowed with supernatural, superhuman, or at least specifically exceptional powers or qualities. These are not accessible to the ordinary person and are regarded as of divine origin or as exemplary, and on the basis of them the individual concerned is treated as a leader."[32]

The first researcher to consider charismatic leadership in terms of OB was Robert House. According to **charismatic leadership theory**, followers attribute heroic or extraordinary leadership abilities when they observe certain behaviors, and tend to give these leaders power.[33] A number of studies have attempted to identify the characteristics of charismatic leaders: They have a vision, are willing to take personal risks to achieve that vision, are sensitive to follower needs, and exhibit extraordinary behaviors[34] (see Exhibit 12-3). Recent research in Greece suggested that charismatic leadership increases follower organizational identification (commitment) by building a shared group identity among followers.[35] Other research indicates that charismatic leadership may predict follower job satisfaction.[36]

charismatic leadership theory
A leadership theory that states that followers make attributions of heroic or extraordinary leadership abilities when they observe certain behaviors.

Are Charismatic Leaders Born or Made?   Are charismatic leaders born with their qualities? Or can people actually learn to be charismatic leaders? Yes, and yes.

Individuals *are* born with traits that make them charismatic. In fact, studies of identical twins found they score similarly on charismatic leadership measures,

Exhibit 12-3	Key Characteristics of a Charismatic Leader

1. *Vision and articulation.* Has a vision—expressed as an idealized goal—that proposes a future better than the status quo; and is able to clarify the importance of the vision in terms that are understandable to others.

2. *Personal risk.* Willing to take on high personal risk, incur high costs, and engage in self-sacrifice to achieve the vision.

3. *Sensitivity to follower needs.* Perceptive of others' abilities and responsive to their needs and feelings.

4. *Unconventional behavior.* Engages in behaviors that are perceived as novel and counter to norms.

Source: Based on J. A. Conger and R. N. Kanungo, *Charismatic Leadership in Organizations* (Thousand Oaks, CA: Sage, 1998), 94.

even if they were raised in different households and never met. Personality is also related to charismatic leadership; charismatic leaders are likely to be extraverted, self-confident, and achievement oriented.[37] Consider the legendary qualities of U.S. presidents Barack Obama, Bill Clinton, and Ronald Reagan, and U.K. prime minister Margaret Thatcher, when they were in office: Whether you liked them or not, they are often compared because they all exhibited the qualities of charismatic leaders.

Research indicates that charismatic leadership is not only the province of world leaders—all of us can develop, within our own limitations, a more charismatic leadership style. If you stay active and central in your leadership roles, you will naturally communicate your vision for achieving goals to your followers, which increases the likelihood you will be seen as charismatic.[38] To further develop an aura of charisma, use your passion as a catalyst for generating enthusiasm. Speak in an animated voice, reinforce your message with eye contact and facial expressions, and gesture for emphasis. Bring out the potential in followers by tapping into their emotions, and create a bond that inspires them. Remember, enthusiasm is contagious!

How Charismatic Leaders Influence Followers   How do charismatic leaders actually influence followers? By articulating an appealing **vision**, a long-term strategy for attaining a goal by linking the present with a better future for the organization. Desirable visions fit the times and circumstances and reflect the uniqueness of the organization. Thus, followers are inspired not only by how passionately the leader communicates—there must be an underlying vision that appeals to followers as well.

A vision needs an accompanying **vision statement**, a formal articulation of an organization's vision or mission. Charismatic leaders may use vision statements to imprint on followers an overarching goal and purpose. These leaders also set a tone of cooperation and mutual support. They build followers' self-esteem and confidence with high performance expectations and the belief that followers can attain them. Through words and actions, the leader conveys a new set of values and sets an example for followers to imitate. Finally, the charismatic leader engages in emotion-inducing and often unconventional behavior to demonstrate courage and conviction about the vision.

Research indicates that charismatic leadership works as followers "catch" the emotions their leader is conveying.[39] One study found employees had a stronger sense of personal belonging at work when they had charismatic leaders, and increased their willingness to engage in helping and compliance-oriented behaviors.[40]

vision   A long-term strategy for attaining a goal or goals.

vision statement   A formal articulation of an organization's vision or mission.

Does Effective Charismatic Leadership Depend on the Situation?   Charismatic leadership has positive effects across many contexts. There are, however, characteristics of followers, and of the situation, that enhance or somewhat limit its effects.

One factor that enhances charismatic leadership is stress. People are especially receptive to charismatic leadership when they sense a crisis, when they are under stress, or when they fear for their lives. We may be more receptive to charismatic leadership under crises because we think bold leadership is needed. Some of it, however, may be more primal. When people are psychologically aroused, even in laboratory studies, they are more likely to respond to charismatic leaders.[41] This may explain why, when charismatic leaders surface, it's likely to be in politics or religion, during wartime, or when a business is in its infancy or facing a threatening crisis. For example, U.S. president Franklin D. Roosevelt offered a vision with charisma to get the United States out of the Great Depression in the 1930s. In 1997, when Apple Computer was floundering and lacking direction, the board persuaded charismatic co-founder Steve Jobs to return as interim CEO and restore the company to its innovative roots. Charismatic leaders are able to reduce stress for their employees, perhaps because they help make work seem more meaningful and interesting.[42]

You may wonder whether a situational factor limiting charisma is the person's level in the organization. Top executives create vision. We would think it is more difficult to utilize a person's charismatic leadership qualities in lower-level management jobs or to align his or her vision with specific top-management goals. However, while charismatic leadership may be more important in the upper echelons of organizations, it can be effective from a distance, or from close range.

Some personalities are especially susceptible to charismatic leadership.[43] For instance, an individual who lacks self-esteem and questions his or her self-worth is more likely to absorb a leader's direction rather than establish an individual way of leading or thinking. For these people, the situation may matter much less than the charismatic qualities of the leader.

The Dark Side of Charismatic Leadership   Unfortunately, charismatic leaders who are larger than life don't necessarily act in the best interests of their organizations.[44] Research has shown that individuals who are narcissistic are also higher in some behaviors associated with charismatic leadership.[45] Many charismatic—but corrupt—leaders have allowed their personal goals to override the goals of their organizations. Leaders at Enron, Tyco, WorldCom, and HealthSouth recklessly used organizational resources for their personal benefit and violated laws and ethics to inflate stock prices, and then cashed in millions of dollars in personal stock options. Some charismatic leaders—Hitler, for example—are all too successful at convincing their followers to pursue a disastrous vision. If charisma is power, then that power can be used for good—and for ill.

It's not that charismatic leadership isn't effective; overall, it is. But a charismatic leader isn't always the answer. Success depends, to some extent, on the situation and on the leader's vision, and on the organizational checks and balances in place to monitor the outcomes.

Transactional and Transformational Leadership

Charismatic leadership theory relies on leaders' ability to inspire followers to believe in them. In contrast, Fiedler's model, situational leadership theory, and path–goal theory describe **transactional leaders**, who guide their followers toward established goals by clarifying role and task requirements. A stream

transactional leaders   Leaders who guide or motivate their followers in the direction of established goals by clarifying role and task requirements.

Exhibit 12-4	Characteristics of Transactional and Transformational Leaders

Transactional Leader

Contingent Reward: Contracts exchange of rewards for effort, promises rewards for good performance, recognizes accomplishments.

Management by Exception (active): Watches and searches for deviations from rules and standards, takes corrective action.

Management by Exception (passive): Intervenes only if standards are not met.

Laissez-Faire: Abdicates responsibilities, avoids making decisions.

Transformational Leader

Idealized Influence: Provides vision and sense of mission, instills pride, gains respect and trust.

Inspirational Motivation: Communicates high expectations, uses symbols to focus efforts, expresses important purposes in simple ways.

Intellectual Stimulation: Promotes intelligence, rationality, and careful problem solving.

Individualized Consideration: Gives personal attention, treats each employee individually, coaches, advises.

Sources: Based on A. H. Eagly, M. C. Johannesen-Schmidt, and M. L. Van Engen, "Transformational, Transactional, and Laissez-faire Leadership Styles: A Meta-Analysis Comparing Women and Men," *Psychological Bulletin* 129, no. 4 (2003): 569–91; and T. A. Judge and J. E. Bono, "Five Factor Model of Personality and Transformational Leadership," *Journal of Applied Psychology* 85, no. 5 (2000): 751–65.

transformational leaders Leaders who inspire followers to transcend their own self-interests and who are capable of having a profound and extraordinary effect on followers.

of research has focused on differentiating transactional from **transformational leaders,**[46] who inspire followers to transcend their self-interests for the good of the organization. Transformational leaders can have an extraordinary effect on their followers, who respond with increased levels of commitment.[47] Richard Branson of the Virgin Group is a good example of a transformational leader. He pays attention to the concerns and needs of individual followers, changes followers' awareness of issues by helping them look at old problems in new ways, and excites and inspires followers to put forth extra effort to achieve group goals. Research suggests that transformational leaders are most effective when their followers are able to see the positive impact of their work through direct interaction with customers or other beneficiaries.[48] Exhibit 12-4 briefly identifies and defines characteristics that differentiate transactional from transformational leaders.

Transactional and transformational leadership complement each other; they aren't opposing approaches to getting things done.[49] The best leaders are transactional *and* transformational. Transformational leadership *builds on* transactional leadership and produces levels of follower effort and performance beyond what transactional leadership alone can do. But the reverse isn't true. If you are a good transactional leader but do not have transformational qualities, you'll likely only be a mediocre leader.

full range of leadership model A model that depicts seven management styles on a continuum: laissez-faire, management by exception, contingent reward leadership, individualized consideration, intellectual stimulation, inspirational motivation, and idealized influence.

Full Range of Leadership Model Exhibit 12-5 shows the **full range of leadership model**. Laissez-faire, which literally means "let it be" (do nothing), is the most passive and therefore least effective of leader behaviors.[50] Management by exception, in which leaders primarily "put out fires" when there are crisis exceptions to normal operating procedures, means they are often too late to be effective. Contingent reward leadership, which gives predetermined rewards for employee efforts, can be an effective style of leadership but will not get employees to go above and beyond the call of duty.

Top Leaders Feel the Most Stress

Leaders of corporations fight pressures from their boards, customers, managers, and employees. Wouldn't it stand to reason they are the most stressed people in their organizations? Apparently not. According to studies from Harvard University, the University of California–San Diego, and Stanford University, leadership brings a blissful relief from the stress felt by individuals who are not in managerial roles. Not only did leaders report less anxiety than nonleaders, but their cortisol (stress hormone) levels were also lower, indicating they biologically were less likely to register stress. Another study found that individuals in higher-status occupational groups registered less perceived stress and lower blood pressure readings than those in lower status occupations.

If you're thinking this is one more reason "it's better at the top," you may be right, if only partially. It is true that leaders appear to show fewer signs of stress by virtue of being leaders, regardless of higher income or longer job tenure. However, researchers found no "magic level" in an organization at which employees felt a reduction in stress levels.

One study indicated that stress reduction correlates with feelings of control. Leaders with more subordinates and greater power felt less stress than other individuals who knew they had less control over outcomes. Top leaders who control the resources of their corporations and have plenty of employees to carry out their directives therefore can fight stressors before they affect them.

Sources: M. Korn, "Top-Level Leaders Have Less Stress Than Others," *The Wall Street Journal,* October 3, 2012, B6; G. D. Sherman et al., "Leadership Is Associated with Lower Levels of Stress," *Proceedings of the National Academy of Sciences of the United States of America,* October 30, 2012, 17903–07; and E. Wiernik et al., "Occupational Status Moderates the Association between Current Perceived Stress and High Blood Pressure: Evidence from the IPC Cohort Study," *Hypertension,* March 2013, 571–77.

Exhibit **12-5**   **Full Range of Leadership Model**

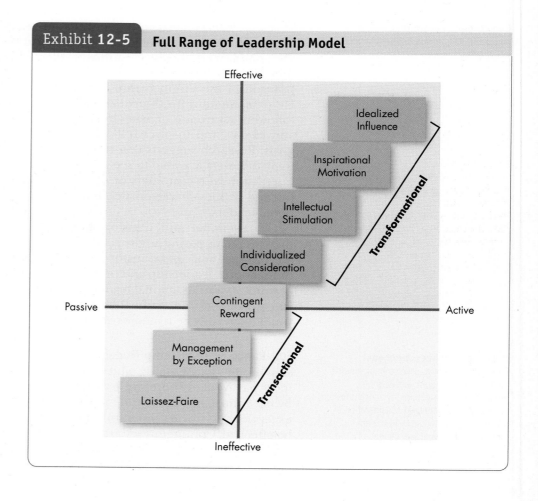

Only with the four remaining styles—all aspects of transformational leadership—are leaders able to motivate followers to perform above expectations and transcend their self-interest for the sake of the organization. Individualized consideration, intellectual stimulation, inspirational motivation, and idealized influence (known as the "four I's") all result in extra effort from workers, higher productivity, higher morale and satisfaction, higher organizational effectiveness, lower turnover, lower absenteeism, and greater organizational adaptability. Based on this model, leaders are generally most effective when they regularly use the four I's.

How Transformational Leadership Works   Organizations with transformational leaders generally have greater decentralization of responsibility, managers with more propensity to take risks, and compensation plans geared toward long-term results—all of which facilitate corporate entrepreneurship.[51] One study of information technology workers in China found empowering leadership behavior led to feelings of positive personal control among workers, which increased their creativity at work.[52] Other research in Germany found that transformational leadership positively influenced workers' creativity, but suggested leaders need to guard against dependent leader relationships, which lower employee creativity.[53]

Companies with transformational leaders often show greater agreement among top managers about the organization's goals, which yields superior organizational performance.[54] The Israeli military has seen similar results, showing that transformational leaders improve performance by building consensus among group members.[55]

Evaluation of Transformational Leadership   Transformational leadership has been supported at diverse job levels and occupations (school principals, teachers, marine commanders, ministers, presidents of MBA associations, military cadets, union shop stewards, sales reps). In general, organizations perform better when they have transformational leaders. For example, one study of R&D firms found teams whose project leaders scored high on transformational leadership

The transformational leadership of Netflix CEO Reed Hastings has helped the company grow from a small DVD rental service to an Internet streaming service with 53 million customers in 50 countries. Hastings encourages employees to take risks, empowers them to make decisions, and gives them the freedom and responsibility to create new ideas and products.
Source: TIBOUL/Maxppp/Landov

produced better-quality products as judged one year later and higher profits five years later.[56] A review of 117 studies testing transformational leadership found it was related to higher levels of individual follower performance, team performance, and organizational performance.[57]

The effect of transformational leadership on performance can vary by the situation. In general, transformational leadership has a greater impact on the bottom line in smaller, privately held firms than in more complex organizations.[58] Transformational leadership can also vary depending on whether work is evaluated at the team or the individual level.[59] Individual-focused transformational leadership is behavior that empowers individual followers to develop ideas, enhance their abilities, and increase self-efficacy. Team-focused transformational leadership emphasizes group goals, shared values and beliefs, and unified efforts. However, research in China suggested that, in team situations, the members' identification with the group could override the effects of transformational leadership.[60]

Just as vision helps explain how charismatic leadership works, it also explains part of the effect of transformational leadership. The GLOBE study links a number of elements of transformational leadership with effective leadership, regardless of country.[61] The GLOBE team concluded that "effective business leaders in any country are expected by their subordinates to provide a powerful and proactive vision to guide the company into the future, strong motivational skills to stimulate all employees to fulfill the vision, and excellent planning skills to assist in implementing the vision."[62]

Although vision is important in any culture, the way it is formed and communicated may need to be adapted. Transformational leadership may be more effective when leaders can directly interact with the workforce to make decisions than when they report to an external board of directors or deal with a complex bureaucratic structure. One study showed transformational leaders were more effective in improving group potency in teams higher in power distance and collectivism.[63] Transformational leaders also obtain higher levels of trust, which reduces stress for followers.[64]

Transformational leaders are more effective because they are creative, but also because they encourage those who follow them to be creative, too.[65] Creativity and empowerment are key to organizational success, and transformational leaders are able to increase follower self-efficacy, giving the group a "can do" spirit.[66] One study looking at employee creativity and transformational leadership found employees with transformational leaders had more confidence in their ability to be creative at work and realized higher levels of creative performance.[67] Empowered followers are more likely to pursue ambitious goals, agree on the strategic goals of the organization, and believe the goals they are pursuing are personally important.[68]

Transformational versus Transactional Leadership   We have seen that transformational leadership yields many desirable organizational outcomes. When comparing transformational leadership with transactional leadership, research indicates transformational leadership is more strongly correlated than transactional leadership with lower turnover rates, higher productivity, lower employee stress and burnout, and higher employee satisfaction.[69] However, transformational leadership theory is not perfect. The full range of leadership model shows a clear division between transactional and transformational leadership that may not fully exist in effective leadership. And contrary to the full range of leadership model, the four I's of transformational leadership are not always superior in effectiveness to transactional leadership; contingent reward leadership, in which leaders dole out rewards as certain goals are reached by employees, sometimes works as well as transformational leadership. More research is needed, but the general supportable conclusion is that transformational leadership is desirable and effective, given the right application.

Transformational versus Charismatic Leadership   In considering transformational and charismatic leadership, you surely noticed some commonalities. There are differences, too. Charismatic leadership places somewhat more emphasis on the way leaders communicate (are they passionate and dynamic?), while transformational leadership focuses more on what they are communicating (is it a compelling vision?). Still, the theories are more alike than different. At their heart, both focus on the leader's ability to inspire followers, and sometimes they do so in the same way. Because of this, some researchers believe the concepts are somewhat interchangeable.

✪ PERSONAL INVENTORY ASSESSMENTS

    PERSONAL INVENTORY ASSESSMENT

Ethical Leadership Assessment

If you've ever worked for someone who was an unethical leader, you know the importance of ethical leadership for positive outcomes. Take this PIA to explore ethical leadership further.

Responsible Leadership

12-5 Discuss the roles of leaders in creating ethical organizations.

Although theories have increased our understanding of effective leadership, they do not explicitly deal with the roles of ethics and trust, which some argue are essential to complete the picture. Here, we consider contemporary concepts that explicitly address the role of leaders in creating ethical organizations. These and the theories we discussed earlier are not mutually exclusive ideas (a transformational leader may also be a responsible one), but we could argue that leaders generally appear to be stronger in one category than another.

Authentic Leadership

SAP's Co-CEO Bill McDermott's motto is "Stay Hungry, Stay Humble," and he appears to practice what he preaches. Campbell Soup's CEO Denise Morrison decided to lower sodium in the company's soup products simply because it was the right thing to do. McDermott and Morrison appear to be good exemplars of authentic leadership.[70]

authentic leaders Leaders who know who they are, know what they believe in and value, and act on those values and beliefs openly and candidly. Their followers would consider them to be ethical people.

Authentic leadership focuses on the moral aspects of being a leader. **Authentic leaders** know who they are, know what they believe in, and act on those values and beliefs openly and candidly. Their followers consider them ethical people. The primary quality produced by authentic leadership is trust. Authentic leaders share information, encourage open communication, and stick to their ideals. The result: People come to have faith in them. Related to this behavior is the concept of humbleness, another characteristic of being authentic. Research indicates that leaders who model humility help followers to understand the growth process for their own development.[71]

Authentic leadership, especially when shared among top management team members, creates a positive energizing effect that heightens firm performance.[72] Transformational or charismatic leaders can have a vision and communicate it persuasively, but sometimes the vision is wrong (as in the case of Hitler), or the leader is more concerned with his or her own needs or pleasures, as were Dennis Kozlowski (ex-CEO of Tyco), Jeff Skilling (ex-CEO of Enron), and

Entrepreneur Grace Liu is an authentic leader. Shown here with her employees, Liu is co-founder and managing director of Asianera, a maker of hand-painted bone china. She built her successful business of high-quality porcelain and innovative design based on her strong personal core values of respecting each individual and operating with integrity.
Source: Tom Koene/ZUMApress/Newscom

Raj Rajaratnam (founder of the Galleon Group).[73] Authentic leaders do not exhibit these behaviors. They may also be more likely to promote corporate social responsibility (CSR).

Ethical Leadership

Leadership is not value-free. In assessing its effectiveness, we need to address the *means* a leader uses to achieve goals as well as the content of those goals. The role of the leader in creating the ethical expectations for all members is crucial.[74] Ethical top leadership influences not only direct followers, but all the way down the command structure as well, because top leaders create an ethical culture and expect lower-level leaders to behave along ethical guidelines.[75] Leaders rated as highly ethical tend to have followers who engage in more organizational citizenship behaviors (OCBs) and who are more willing to bring problems to the leaders' attention.[76] Research also found that ethical leadership reduced interpersonal conflicts.[77]

Ethical and authentic leadership intersect at a number of junctures. Leaders who treat their followers ethically and authentically—with fairness, especially by providing honest, frequent, and accurate information—are seen as more effective.[78] Transformational leadership has ethical implications since these leaders change the way followers think. Charisma, too, has an ethical component. Unethical leaders use their charisma to enhance power over followers, directed toward self-serving ends. To integrate ethical and charismatic leadership, scholars have advanced the idea of **socialized charismatic leadership**—conveying other-centered (not self-centered) values through leaders who model ethical conduct.[79] Charismatic leaders are able to bring employee values in line with their own values through their words and actions.[80]

Although every member of an organization is responsible for ethical behavior, many initiatives aimed at increasing organizational ethical behavior are focused on the leaders. Because top executives set the moral tone for

socialized charismatic leadership
A leadership concept that states that leaders convey values that are other-centered versus self-centered and who role-model ethical conduct.

an organization, they need to set high ethical standards, demonstrate them through their own behavior, and encourage and reward integrity in others while avoiding abuses of power. One research review found that role modeling by top leaders positively influenced managers throughout their organizations to behave ethically and fostered a climate that reinforced group-level ethical conduct. The findings suggest that organizations should invest in ethical leadership training programs, especially in industries with few ethical regulations. Leadership training programs that incorporate cultural values should be especially mandated for leaders who take foreign assignments or manage multicultural work teams.[81]

For ethical leadership to be effective, it is not enough for the leader to simply possess high moral character. After all, there is no universal standard for ethical behavior, and ethical norms vary by culture, by industry, and even sometimes within an organization. Leaders must be willing to express their ethical beliefs and persuade others to follow their standards. Followers must believe in both the leader and the overlying principles, even if they don't personally agree with every minor stance.

To convey their beliefs, leaders should learn to express their moral convictions in statements that reflect values shared with their organization's members. Leaders can build on this foundation of trust to show their character, enhance a sense of unity, and create buy-in from followers. The leader's message should announce high goals and express confidence that they can be reached.

Ethical leaders' statements are often positive messages, such as Winston Churchill's opening for his World War II victory speech: "This is your hour. This is not a victory of a party or of any class. It's a victory of the great British nation as a whole." An example of an ethical leader's negative message is this speech by Gandhi: "Even if all the United Nations opposes me, even if the whole of India forsakes me, I will say, 'You are wrong. India will wrench with nonviolence her liberty from unwilling hands.'" Positive and negative ethical leader statements

---

An Ethical Choice

Holding Leaders Ethically Accountable

No one thinks leaders shouldn't be accountable. Leaders must balance many and conflicting stakeholder demands. The first demand is for strong financial performance; leaders are probably terminated more often for missing this goal than for all other factors combined. Leaders balance the extreme pressure for financial performance with the desire most leaders have to act ethically, even when there is no formal accountability. Given those competing aims, ethical leadership may be underrewarded and depend solely on the leader's innate decency.

Ethical leadership is a relatively new area of research attention. Demonstrating fairness and social responsibility even run counter to many old-school models of leadership. Consider, for example, legendary management guru Peter Drucker's advice (1967): "It is the duty of the executive to remove ruthlessly anyone—and especially any manager—who consistently fails to perform with high distinction. To let such a man stay on corrupts the others." Modern ethical leadership guidelines say this cut-throat mindset fails to consider the moral implications of treating people as objects at an organization's disposal.

While few organizations still require "performance at all costs," financiers, shareholders, and boards have the reward power to teach leaders which outcomes to value. Ethical leadership resounds positively throughout all organizational levels, resulting in responsible and potentially highly profitable outcomes, but the ultimate ethical movement will come when shareholders—and leaders—show signs of balancing these accountabilities themselves.

Sources: T. E. Ricks, "What Ever Happened to Accountability?" *Harvard Business Review,* October 2012, 93–100; J. M. Schaubroeck et al., "Embedding Ethical Leadership within and across Organizational Levels," *Academy of Management Journal* 55 (2012): 1053–78; and J. Stouten, M. van Dijke, and D. De Cremer, "Ethical Leadership," *Journal of Personnel Psychology* 11 (2012): 1–6.

can be equally effective when they deliver clear, moral, inclusive, goal-setting statements with persuasiveness. In fact, they can set trends in motion to make the seemingly far-fetched become real.[82]

Servant Leadership

servant leadership A leadership style marked by going beyond the leader's own self-interest and instead focusing on opportunities to help followers grow and develop.

Scholars have recently considered ethical leadership from a new angle by examining **servant leadership**.[83] Servant leaders go beyond their self-interest and focus on opportunities to help followers grow and develop. Characteristic behaviors include listening, empathizing, persuading, accepting stewardship, and actively developing followers' potential. Because servant leadership focuses on serving the needs of others, research has focused on its outcomes for the well-being of followers. Perhaps not surprisingly, a study of 126 CEOs found that servant leadership is negatively correlated with the trait of narcissism.[84]

What are the effects of servant leadership? One study of 123 supervisors found it resulted in higher levels of commitment to the supervisor, self-efficacy, and perceptions of justice, which all were related to OCB.[85] This relationship between servant leadership and follower OCB appears to be stronger when followers are encouraged to focus on being dutiful and responsible.[86] Second, servant leadership increases team potency (a belief that your team has above-average skills and abilities), which in turn leads to higher levels of group performance.[87] Third, a study with a nationally representative sample found higher levels of citizenship were associated with a focus on growth and advancement, which in turn was associated with higher levels of creative performance.[88] Other research found that servant leadership and a resulting culture of serving increased employee job performance and creativity, while reducing turnover intentions.[89]

Servant leadership may be more prevalent and effective in certain cultures.[90] When asked to draw images of leaders, for example, U.S. subjects tended to draw them in front of the group, giving orders to followers. Singaporeans tended to draw leaders at the back of the group, acting more to gather a group's opinions together and then unify them from the rear. This suggests the East Asian prototype is more like a servant leader, which might mean servant leadership is more effective in these cultures.

Positive Leadership

12-6 Describe how leaders can have a positive impact on their organizations through building trust and mentoring.

In each of the theories we've discussed, you can see opportunities for the practice of good, bad, or mediocre leadership. Now let's think about the intentional development of positive leadership environments.

Trust

trust A positive expectation that another will not act opportunistically.

Trust is a psychological state that exists when you agree to make yourself vulnerable to another person because you have positive expectations about how things are going to turn out.[91] Although you aren't completely in control of the situation, you are willing to take a chance that the other person will come through for you. Trust is a primary attribute associated with leadership; breaking it can have serious adverse effects on a group's performance.[92]

Followers who trust a leader are confident their rights and interests will not be abused.[93] Transformational leaders, for example, create support for their ideas in part by arguing that their direction will be in everyone's best interests. People are unlikely to look up to or follow someone they perceive as dishonest or likely to take advantage of them. Thus, as you might expect, transformational leaders generate higher levels of trust from their followers, which in turn are related to higher levels of team confidence and, ultimately, higher levels of team performance.[94]

In a simple contractual exchange of goods and services, your employer is legally bound to pay you for fulfilling your job description. But today's rapid reorganizations, diffusion of responsibility, and collaborative team-based work mean employment relationships are not stable long-term contracts with explicit terms. Rather, they are based more on trusting relationships than ever before. You have to trust that if you show your supervisor a creative project you've been working on, he won't steal the credit behind your back. You have to trust that the extra work you've been doing will be recognized in your performance appraisal. In contemporary organizations, where work is less closely documented and specified, voluntary employee contribution based on trust is absolutely necessary. Only a trusted leader will be able to encourage employees to reach beyond themselves to a transformational goal.

The Outcomes of Trust   Trust between supervisors and employees has a number of specific advantages. Here are just a few from research:

- *Trust encourages taking risks.*   Whenever employees decide to deviate from the usual way of doing things, or to take their supervisor's word on a new direction, they are taking a risk. In both cases, a trusting relationship can facilitate that leap.
- *Trust facilitates information sharing.*   One big reason employees fail to express concerns at work is that they don't feel psychologically safe revealing their views. When managers demonstrate they will give employees' ideas a fair hearing and actively make changes, employees are more willing to speak out.[95]
- *Trusting groups are more effective.*   When a leader sets a trusting tone in a group, members are more willing to help each other and exert extra effort, which increases trust. Members of mistrusting groups tend to be suspicious of each other, constantly guard against exploitation, and restrict communication with others in the group. These actions tend to undermine and eventually destroy the group.
- *Trust enhances productivity.*   The bottom-line interest of companies appears to be positively influenced by trust. Employees who trust their supervisors tend to receive higher performance ratings, indicating higher productivity.[96] People respond to mistrust by concealing information and secretly pursuing their own interests.

Trust Development   What key characteristics lead us to believe a leader is trustworthy? Evidence has identified three: integrity, benevolence, and ability (see Exhibit 12-6).[97]

Integrity refers to honesty and truthfulness. When 570 white-collar employees were given a list of 28 attributes related to leadership, they rated honesty the most important by far.[98] Integrity also means maintaining consistency between what you do and say.

Benevolence means the trusted person has your interests at heart, even if your interests aren't necessarily in line with theirs. Caring and supportive behavior is part of the emotional bond between leaders and followers.

Ability encompasses an individual's technical and interpersonal knowledge and skills. You're unlikely to depend on someone whose abilities you don't believe in even if the person is highly principled and has the best intentions.

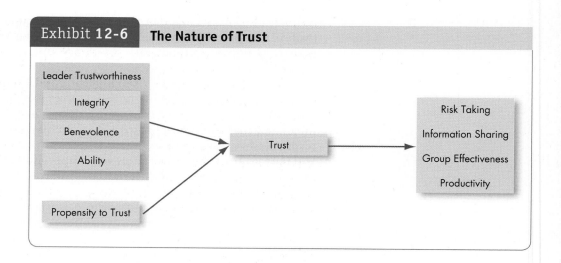

Exhibit 12-6   **The Nature of Trust**

Trust Propensity   Effective leadership is built on the trust of leaders and followers. **Trust propensity** refers to how likely a particular employee is to trust a leader. Some people are simply more likely to believe others can be trusted.[99] Those who carefully document every promise or conversation with their supervisors aren't very high in trust propensity, and they probably aren't going to take a leader's word for anything. Those who think most people are basically honest and forthright will be much more likely to seek evidence that their leaders have behaved in a trustworthy manner. Trust propensity is closely linked to the personality trait of agreeableness, and people with lower self-esteem are less likely to trust others.[100]

trust propensity How likely an employee is to trust a leader.

Trust and Culture   Does trust look the same in every culture? Using the basic definition of trust, certainly it does. However, in the work context, trust in an employment relationship may be built on very different perceptions from culture to culture. For example, a recent study in Taiwan indicated that employees responded to paternalistic leadership, when it is benevolent and ethical, with increased trust performance.[101] This positive response to paternalism may be unique to the collectivistic context where the Confucian values of hierarchy and relationship predominate. In individualistic societies, we might expect that paternalistic leadership will rankle many employees who prefer not to see themselves as part of a hierarchical family workgroup. Employees in individualist cultures may build trust along dimensions of leadership support and consistency instead, for instance.

The Role of Time   Time is the final component for building trust. We come to trust people by observing their behavior over a period of time.[102] To help, leaders need to demonstrate integrity, benevolence, and ability in situations where trust is important—say, where they could behave opportunistically or let employees down. Second, trust can be won in the ability domain by demonstrating competence. Third, research with 100 companies around the world suggests that leaders can build trust by shifting their communication style from top-down commands to ongoing organizational dialogue. Lastly, when leaders regularly create interpersonal conversations with their employees that are intimate, interactive, and inclusive and that intentionally follow an agenda, followers demonstrate trust with high levels of engagement.[103]

Regaining Trust   Managers who break the psychological contract with workers, demonstrating they aren't trustworthy leaders, will find employees are less satisfied and less committed, have a higher intent toward turnover, engage in less OCB, and have lower levels of task performance.[104] Leaders who betray trust are especially likely to be evaluated negatively by followers if there is already a low level of leader–member exchange.[105]

Once it has been violated, trust can be regained, but only in certain situations and depending on the type of violation.[106] If the cause is lack of ability, it's usually best to apologize and recognize you should have done better. When lack of integrity is the problem, apologies don't do much good. Regardless of the violation, saying nothing or refusing to confirm or deny guilt is never an effective strategy for regaining trust. Trust can be restored when we observe a consistent pattern of trustworthy behavior by the transgressor. However, if the transgressor used deception, trust never fully returns, not even after apologies, promises, or a consistent pattern of trustworthy actions.[107]

> ✪ **TRY IT!**
>
> If your professor has assigned this, go to the Assignments section of **mymanagementlab.com** to complete the **Simulation:** *Leadership*.

Mentoring

mentor A senior employee who sponsors and supports a less-experienced employee, called a protégé.

Leaders often take responsibility for developing future leaders. A **mentor** is a senior employee who sponsors and supports a less-experienced employee, a protégé. Successful mentors are good teachers. They present ideas clearly, listen well, and empathize with protégés' problems. Mentoring relationships serve career and psychosocial functions (see Exhibit 12-7).[108]

In formal mentoring relationships, protégé candidates are identified according to assessments of leadership potential, and then matched with leaders in corresponding organizational functions. Informal mentoring relationships develop when leaders identify a less experienced, lower-level employee who appears to have potential for future development.[109] The protégé is often tested with a particularly challenging assignment. If performance is acceptable, the mentor will develop the relationship. In both formal and informal mentoring, the goal is to show the protégé how the organization *really* works outside its formal structures and procedures.

Exhibit 12-7	Career and Psychological Functions of the Mentoring Relationship

Career Functions	Psychosocial Functions
• Lobbying to get the protégé challenging and visible assignments	• Counseling the protégé to bolster his or her self-confidence
• Coaching the protégé to help develop his or her skills and achieve work objectives	• Sharing personal experiences with the protégé
• Providing exposure to influential individuals within the organization	• Providing friendship and acceptance
• Protecting the protégé from possible risks to his or her reputation	• Acting as a role model
• Sponsoring the protégé by nominating him or her for potential advances or promotions	
• Acting as a sounding board for ideas the protégé might be hesitant to share with a direct supervisor	

Are all employees in an organization likely to participate in a mentoring relationship? Unfortunately, no.[110] However, research continues to indicate that employers should establish mentoring programs because they benefit both mentors and protégés. One study in Korea found that mentors achieved higher levels of transformational leadership as a result of the process, while organizational commitment and well-being increased for both mentors and protégés.[111]

Although begun with the best intentions, formal relationships are not as effective as informal ones,[112] perhaps due to poor planning, design, and communication. Mentors must see the relationship as beneficial to themselves and the protégé, and the protégé must have input into the relationship.[113] Formal mentoring programs are also most likely to succeed if they appropriately match the work style, needs, and skills of protégé and mentor.[114]

Mentors may be effective not because of the functions they provide, but because of the resources they can obtain; a mentor connected to a powerful network can build relationships that will help the protégé advance. Network ties, whether built through a mentor or not, are a significant predictor of career success.[115] If a mentor is not well connected or not a very strong performer, the best mentoring advice in the world will not be very beneficial.

You might assume mentoring is valuable for objective outcomes like compensation and job performance, but research suggests the gains are primarily psychological. Thus, while mentoring can have an impact on career success, it is not as much of a contributing factor as ability and personality. It may *feel* nice to have a mentor, but it doesn't appear that having a good mentor, or any mentor, is critical to your career. The mentor is a boost to your confidence.

Challenges to Our Understanding of Leadership

12-7 Identify the challenges to our understanding of leadership.

"In the 1500s, people ascribed all events they didn't understand to God. Why did the crops fail? God. Why did someone die? God. Now our all-purpose explanation is leadership."[116] This may be an astute observation from management consulting, but of course much of an organization's success or failure is due to factors outside the influence of leadership. Sometimes it's a matter of being in the right or wrong place at a given time. In this section, we present challenges to the accepted beliefs about the value of leadership.

Leadership as an Attribution

attribution theory of leadership
A leadership theory that says that leadership is merely an attribution that people make about other individuals.

As you may remember from Chapter 6, attribution theory examines how people try to make sense of cause-and-effect relationships. The **attribution theory of leadership** says leadership is merely an attribution people make about other individuals.[117] We attribute the following to leaders: intelligence, outgoing personality, strong verbal skills, aggressiveness, understanding, and industriousness.[118] At the organizational level, we tend, rightly or wrongly, to see leaders as responsible for both extremely negative and extremely positive performance.[119]

Perceptions of leaders by their followers strongly affect leaders' ability to be effective. First, one study of 128 major U.S. corporations found that whereas perceptions of CEO charisma did not lead to objectively better company performance, company performance did lead to perceptions of charisma.[120] Second, employee perceptions of leaders' behaviors are significant predictors of whether they blame the leader for failure, regardless of how the leader assesses him- or herself.[121] Third, a study of more than 3,000 employees from western Europe, the United States, and the Middle East found people who tended to "romanticize" leadership in general were more likely to believe their own leaders were transformational.[122]

We also make demographic assumptions about leaders. Respondents in a study assumed a leader described with no identifying racial information was white at a rate beyond the base rate of white employees in that company. Furthermore, where identical leadership situations are described but the leaders' race is manipulated, white leaders are rated as more effective than leaders of other racial groups.[123] One large-scale summary study (a meta-analysis) found that many individuals hold stereotypes of men as having more leader characteristics than women, although as you might expect, this tendency to equate leadership with masculinity has decreased over time.[124] Other data suggest women's perceived success as transformational leaders may be based on situations. Teams prefer male leaders when aggressively competing against other teams, but they prefer female leaders when the competition is within teams and calls for improving positive relationships within the group.[125]

Attribution theory suggests what's important is projecting the *appearance* of being a leader rather than focusing on *actual accomplishments*. Leader-wannabes who can shape the perception that they're smart, personable, verbally adept, aggressive, hardworking, and consistent in their style can increase the probability their bosses, colleagues, and employees will view them as effective leaders.

Substitutes for and Neutralizers of Leadership

substitutes Attributes, such as experience and training, that can replace the need for a leader's support or ability to create structure.

One theory of leadership suggests that in many situations, leaders' actions are irrelevant.[126] Experience and training are among the **substitutes** that can replace the need for a leader's support or ability to create structure. Organizations such as videogame producer Valve Corporation, Gore-Tex maker W. L. Gore, and collaboration-software firm GitHub have experimented with eliminating leaders and management. Governance in the "bossless" work environment is achieved through accountability to coworkers, who determine team composition and sometimes even pay.[127] Organizational characteristics such as explicit formalized goals, rigid rules and procedures, and cohesive workgroups can replace formal leadership, while indifference to organizational rewards can neutralize its effects. **Neutralizers** make it impossible for leader behavior to make any difference to follower outcomes (see Exhibit 12-8).

neutralizers Attributes that make it impossible for leader behavior to make any difference to follower outcomes.

Exhibit 12-8	Substitutes for and Neutralizers of Leadership	
Defining Characteristics	**Relationship-Oriented Leadership**	**Task-Oriented Leadership**
Individual		
Experience/training	No effect on	Substitutes for
Professionalism	Substitutes for	Substitutes for
Indifference to rewards	Neutralizes	Neutralizes
Job		
Highly structured task	No effect on	Substitutes for
Provides its own feedback	No effect on	Substitutes for
Intrinsically satisfying	Substitutes for	No effect on
Organization		
Explicit formalized goals	No effect on	Substitutes for
Rigid rules and procedures	No effect on	Substitutes for
Cohesive work groups	Substitutes for	Substitutes for

Source: K. B. Lowe and W. L. Gardner, "Ten Years of the Leadership Quarterly: Contributions and Challenges for the Future," *Leadership Quarterly* 11, no. 4 (2000): 459–514.

Sometimes the difference between substitutes and neutralizers is fuzzy. If I'm working on a task that's intrinsically enjoyable, theory predicts leadership will be less important because the task provides motivation. But does that mean intrinsically enjoyable tasks neutralize leadership effects, or substitute for them, or both? Another problem is that while substitutes for leadership (such as employee characteristics, the nature of the task, etc.) matter to performance, that doesn't necessarily mean leadership doesn't matter.[128] It's simplistic to think employees are guided to goal accomplishments solely by the actions of their leaders. We've introduced a number of variables—such as attitudes, personality, ability, and group norms—that affect employee performance and satisfaction. Leadership is simply another independent variable in our overall OB model.

Online Leadership

How do you lead people who are physically separated from you with whom you communicate electronically? This question needs attention from OB researchers.[129] Today's managers and employees are increasingly linked by networks rather than geographic proximity.

We propose that online leaders have to think carefully about what actions they want their digital messages to initiate. They confront unique challenges, the greatest of which appears to be developing and maintaining trust. **Identification-based trust**, based on a mutual understanding of each other's intentions and appreciation of the other's wants and desires, is particularly difficult to achieve without face-to-face interaction.[130] Online negotiations can also be hindered because parties tend to express lower levels of trust.[131]

We believe good leadership skills will soon include the ability to communicate support, trust, and inspiration through electronic communication and to accurately read emotions in others' messages. In electronic communication, writing skills are likely to become an extension of interpersonal skills in ways that are not yet defined.

identification-based trust Trust based on a mutual understanding of each other's intentions and appreciation of each other's wants and desires.

Selecting Leaders

The process organizations go through to fill management positions is an exercise in the identification of effective leaders. You might begin by reviewing the knowledge, skills, and abilities needed to do the job effectively. Personality tests can identify traits associated with leadership—extraversion, conscientiousness, and openness to experience. High self-monitors (see Chapter 5) are better at reading situations and adjusting their behavior accordingly. Candidates with high emotional intelligence should have an advantage, especially in situations requiring transformational leadership.[132] General experience is a poor predictor of leader effectiveness, but situation-specific experience is relevant.

Because nothing lasts forever, the most important event an organization needs to plan for is a change in leadership. JCPenney hired a CEO with no department store experience who promptly changed its overall strategy, a maneuver so disastrous that Penney's stock fell 69 percent in the roughly one year he lasted (after which Penney rehired the old CEO it had forced out, and he stayed until the company returned to a better standing). After that debacle, JCPenney seemed to learn its lesson by hiring Marvin Ellison, an executive from Home Depot who also had 15 years of experience at Target. The company's press release repeatedly described Ellison as "a highly accomplished retail executive [with] an extensive knowledge of store operations."[133]

In general, organizations seem to spend no time on leadership succession and are surprised when their picks turn out poorly. HP is on its fourth CEO in under 10 years, including one who lasted a matter of months, causing observers to

Situation-specific experience played a key role in selecting Satya Nadella (center) as Microsoft's new CEO. To strengthen its position in the growing cloud domain, Microsoft chose Nadella, who formerly led Microsoft's Cloud and Enterprise Group and was instrumental in transforming Microsoft's technology culture from client services to cloud infrastructure and services.

Source: PRNewsFoto/Microsoft Corp/AP Images

wonder whether its boards of directors had done their homework in leadership succession. Their choice of Meg Whitman, the current CEO, was based on her role as CEO of eBay, during which she was praised as a top-performing leader. She was also heavily invested in politics, having run for governor of California. It's difficult to know if Whitman will be able to turn around HP or if she will choose to run for office again, but it was not long ago she was named the "Most Underachieving CEO" for her leadership of HP.[134]

Training Leaders

Organizations spend billions of dollars on leadership training and development.[135] These efforts take many forms, from $50,000 executive leadership programs offered by universities such as Harvard to sailing trips with the Outward Bound program. Goldman Sachs is well known for developing leaders; at one point, *BusinessWeek* called it the "Leadership Factory."[136] Business schools are placing renewed emphasis on leadership development too.

How can managers get the most from their leadership-training budgets? First, leadership training is likely to be more successful with high self-monitors. Such individuals have the flexibility to change their behavior. Second, organizations can teach implementation skills. Third, we can teach skills such as trust building and mentoring. Leaders can be taught situational-analysis skills. They can learn how to evaluate situations, modify them to better fit their style, and assess which leader behaviors might be most effective in given situations. BHP Billiton, Best Buy, Nokia, and Adobe have hired coaches to help top executives to improve their interpersonal skills and act less autocratically.[137]

Fourth, behavioral training through modeling exercises can increase an individual's ability to exhibit charismatic leadership qualities. Research also indicates leaders should engage in regularly reviewing their leadership after key organizational events as part of their development. These after-event reviews are especially effective for leaders who are high in conscientiousness and openness to experience, and who are emotionally stable (low in neuroticism).[138] Finally, leaders can be trained in transformational leadership skills that have bottom-line results.

Summary

Leadership plays a central part in understanding group behavior because it's the leader who usually directs us toward our goals. Knowing what makes a good leader should thus be valuable toward improving group performance. The Big Five personality framework shows strong and consistent relationships between personality and leadership. The behavioral approach's major contribution was narrowing leadership into task-oriented (initiating structure) and people-oriented (consideration) styles. By considering the situation in which the leader operates, contingency theories promised to improve on the behavioral approach. Contemporary theories have made major contributions to our understanding of leadership effectiveness, and studies of ethics and positive leadership offer exciting promise.

Implications for Managers

- For maximum leadership effectiveness, ensure that your preferences on the initiating structure and consideration dimensions are a match for your work dynamics and culture.
- Hire candidates who exhibit transformational leadership qualities and who have demonstrated success in working through others to meet a long-term vision. Personality tests can reveal candidates higher in extraversion, conscientiousness, and openness, which may indicate leadership readiness.
- Hire candidates whom you believe are ethical and trustworthy for management roles and train current managers in your organization's ethical standards in order to increase leadership effectiveness.
- Seek to develop trusting relationships with followers because, as organizations have become less stable and predictable, strong bonds of trust are replacing bureaucratic rules in defining expectations and relationships.
- Consider investing in leadership training such as formal courses, workshops, and mentoring.

CEOs Start Early

POINT   **COUNTERPOINT**

If you really get down to specifics, you can see that CEOs start in leadership roles early in life. They have similar backgrounds, childhood challenges, and coping strategies. In fact, it's easy to see a CEO-in-the-making at your neighborhood lemonade stand.

What's the profile of burgeoning CEOs? It starts with their parents, who are almost all successful through industriousness. For example, the father of Linda Zecher, CEO of publisher Houghton Mifflin Harcourt, founded a number of businesses. Brent Frei, CEO of software company Smartsheet.com, grew up on an 800-acre farm his father owned and ran. Aspera CEO Michelle Munson's mother was a professor and her father was the fifth-generation leader of her farm.

Second, future CEOs are raised with responsibilities. Susan Story, CEO of utility company American Water, learned as a child that "no matter how bad things get, it's about working hard and taking personal responsibility, because nobody owes you anything." Frei "had an opportunity to do big things early on. When I was 6 years old, my dad…put me in the pickup, put it in first gear, and I drove it home with my 5-year-old sister in the passenger seat." A number of CEOs grow up working on family farms or taking care of their siblings.

Third, burgeoning CEOs are successful leaders when they're young. Ruth Rathblott, CEO of Harlem Educational Activities Fund, was president of her 7th grade class, then president of the middle school; Brad Jefferson, CEO of video slide show service Animoto, was the high school quarterback, captain of the football team, and senior class president; and Hannah Paramore, founder of digital agency Paramore, "was always the one in charge. I was always captain of this and captain of that."

Clearly, CEOs start early.

CEOs who start early have good stories to tell when they become successful, but that doesn't necessarily mean they represent the majority. Let's look at a few other aspects of the tender years of CEOs.

First, we know that much of our personality is attributable to genetics, but it's incorrect to infer that we can (a) map the genetic trail for a personality trait from ancestors to CEO, or (b) tell where a young person's traits will lead. Likewise, we can't say that if the parents are successful through industriousness, their children will be. Story's parents worked in a cotton mill and a wastewater plant, and they "didn't have a lot of money." Frei's family farm "was a little bit below the threshold for break-even." Mitch Rothschild, CEO of website Vitals, observed, "Parents influence you either because you want to be like them or because you want to not be like them."

Second, what child is raised without responsibilities? None, even if all they have to do is go to school. There are plenty of CEOs who had a lot of responsibilities growing up, and others who did not. Munson's parents "emphasized two things. One was education, and the other was participating in 4-H." Zecher "had a paper route. I was a girl scout, and I was involved in a lot of clubs and sports in high school."

Third, it would be a mistake to conclude that CEOs start as young leaders. The ones who don't simply don't talk about it. Ron Kaplan, CEO of manufacturer Trex, was a marksmanship competitor. Zecher didn't have a plan or a leadership role until after college.

The stories of CEOs who start early make for good press reports, but CEOs do not by definition start early. What we can say, though, is that genetics and experiences both shape young people, and that the relationship between those factors and CEO success is complex.

Sources: A. Bryant, "A Good Excuse Doesn't Fix a Problem," *The New York Times,* December 28, 2014, 2; A. Bryant, "Always Respect the Opportunity," *The New York Times,* October 19, 2014, 2; A. Bryant, "Don't Let Your Strengths Run Amok," *The New York Times,* May 18, 2014, 2; A. Bryant, "Knowing Your Company's Heartbeat," *The New York Times,* May 30, 2014, B2; A. Bryant, "The Danger of 'One Size Fits All,'" *The New York Times,* March 29, 2015, 2; A. Bryant, "The Job Description Is Just the Start," *The New York Times,* September 14, 2014, 2; A. Bryant, "Making Judgments, Instead of Decisions," *The New York Times,* May 4, 2014, 2; A. Bryant, "Pushing Beyond Comfort Zones," *The New York Times,* January 25, 2015, 2; A. Bryant, "Tell Me What's Behind Your Title," *The New York Times,* April 11, 2014, B2; and C. Crossland, J. Zyung, N. J. Hiller, and D. C. Hambrick, "CEO Career Variety: Effects on Firm-Level Strategic and Social Novelty," *Academy of Management Journal* 57, no. 3 (2014): 652–74.

CHAPTER REVIEW

MyManagementLab

Go to **mymanagementlab.com** to complete the problems marked with this icon. ✪

QUESTIONS FOR REVIEW

12-1 What are the conclusions of trait theories of leadership?

12-2 What are the central tenets and main limitations of behavioral theories of leadership?

12-3 What are the contingency theories of leadership?

12-4 How do the contemporary theories of leadership relate to earlier foundational theories?

12-5 In what ways can leaders create ethical organizations?

12-6 How can leaders have a positive impact on their organizations through building trust and mentoring?

12-7 What are the challenges to our understanding of leadership?

EXPERIENTIAL EXERCISE   What Is Leadership?

Break the class into six groups: GROUP A: Government Leaders (president, senator, governor, representative, assemblyperson); GROUP B: Business Leaders (CEO, president, leader in business); GROUP C: School Leaders (class president, informal leader); GROUP D: Sports Leaders (team captain, informal team leader, coach); GROUPS E and F: Effective Managers (manager who demonstrates competence/effectiveness in position).

12-8. Each group identifies the defining characteristics for the assigned role, not simply by

brainstorming, but by deciding upon descriptors that most of the group agrees are defining characteristics.

12-9. Reconvene the class. Draw six columns for each group and list the characteristics for each group. What similarities do you see between the lists? From the results of this exercise, does it appear that what it takes to be a good leader is different depending on the classification? Does it seem that the characteristics for leaders differ greatly from those needed for good managers?

ETHICAL DILEMMA   Smoking Success

"I've been high since I'm 13," Justin Hartfield observed, admitting that his résumé includes a stint as a high-school marijuana distributor and a member of a group of website hackers. Now in his 30s, Hartfield is a successful entrepreneur and investor. So what if he's dealing in the same venues of his childhood passions—marijuana and websites? He says, "Marijuana is not going to be profitable to make in the long term, it's going to be a dollar a gram. And so someone...needs to step in and make it profitable to grow. I'm the best guy to do it." Hartfield envisions himself as the top leader of a newly legalized industry.

Obviously, he has no issue with the ethics of marijuana consumption or distribution. He created Weedmaps.com,

the largest directory for California medical-marijuana users to find accessible doctors and dispensaries, and charges subscribers $295+ per month; his other business through Ghost Group invests in start-up marijuana operations. "I'm doing everything I can in this industry legally that isn't going to throw me in jail," he said.

So far, the government has kept Hartfield in check. Federally, marijuana is a controlled Schedule 1 narcotic (sharing the class with cocaine and heroin), so he has concentrated on the 20 states (and the District of Columbia) that allow medical marijuana use and, of course, Colorado and Washington where the drug is legal for recreational use. Hartfield hopes recreational marijuana use is legalized everywhere soon. "I care about the least amount of people suffering under prohibition," he said, "and secondarily the more money I can make."

Questions

12-10. Hartfield is a leader in his industry, and he hopes to sell the most marijuana possible. Meanwhile, a study published by the National Academy of Sciences indicated that New Zealand teenagers who were heavy marijuana smokers lost up to 8 IQ points. Do you think that as a leader Hartfield has a responsibility for the health of his customers?

12-11. How do you think the ethical responsibilities of leaders in this industry compare to those of leaders in, say, the tobacco and alcohol industries?

12-12. Would you take a leadership role in an organization if you had an ethical issue with its product or service? Why or why not?

Sources: Justin Ross Hartfield website, www.justinhartfield.me; B. Weiss, "Thank You for Smoking— Marijuana," *The Wall Street Journal*, March 15–16, 2014, A11; and K. Wagner, "Weedmaps CEO Justin Hartfield May Soon Be America's Weed Guy," *Mashable*, May 16, 2014, www.mashable .com/2014/05/16/weedmaps-ceo-justin-hartfield/.

CASE INCIDENT 1   My Holiday the Virgin Way

One day, Virgin Group founder Richard Branson received an excited e-mail from his daughter. She had read a newspaper article talking about a new vacation policy that seemed like just the thing for Virgin. According to this policy, all salaried staff are permitted to take leave whenever they want and for as long as they want. Employees need no prior approval and absolutely no one is keeping track of their holidays. If they feel like taking time off for a day, a week, or even a month, it is up to them to decide— on one condition. They need to be 100 percent sure their absence does not harm their company in any way. As a consequence, they have to be certain that they and their team are up-to-date on every project.

Modern technology has radically changed the world and that includes our working day. Since the arrival of smart phones, laptops and tablets, we actually carry the office around in our briefcases and pockets. We receive job-related e-mails and text messages anytime and anywhere, often expecting and indeed getting a prompt response. Although people might not realize it very much, their work has overtaken their free time and private lives. Thus, it is hard to tell precisely when people do or do not work. With companies no longer able to accurately track people's time on the job, why track people's time off the job? It was this point exactly that convinced Richard Branson to introduce the new vacation policy within the Virgin businesses, from entertainment and airline companies to hotels and banking. Other businesses that did the same experienced a boost in productivity, creativity, and morale. Adjusting to new developments and challenging situations seems the right thing to do for leaders who strive to successfully launch their organizations into the future.

Questions

12-13. Do you expect Virgin's new vacation policy to work within all organizations? Why or why not?

12-14. Path-goal theory suggests that leaders adjust their behavior to people's locus of control. Considering Branson's new policy, which locus of control does he expect his employees to have? Why?

12-15. Some people might consider Virgin's policy to be a sign of laissez-faire leadership. Do you agree? Why or why not?

Sources: R. Branson, *The Virgin Way: How to Listen, Learn, Laugh and Lead* (Virgin Books, 2014); P. Hersey and K.H. Blanchard, So You Want to Know Your Leadership Style? *Training and Development Journal* 28, no. 2 (1974): 22–37; J. Mesu, K. Sanders, and M. Van Riemsdijk, "Transformational Leadership and Organisational Commitment in Manufacturing and Service Small to Medium-Sized Enterprises: The Moderating Effects of Directive and Participative Leadership," *Personnel Review* 44, no. 6 (2015): 970–90; R.J. House, "A Path-Goal Theory of Leader Effectiveness," *Administrative Science Quarterly* 16, no. 3 (1971): 321–39; R.J. House, "Path-Goal Theory of Leadership: Lessons, Legacy, and a Reformulated Theory," *Leadership Quarterly* (Fall 1996): 353; B.M. Bass and R.E. Riggio, *Transformational Leadership*. Mahwah (New Jersey: Lawrence Erlbaum Associates, 2006).

CASE INCIDENT 2   Leadership Traits

Researchers have been interested in leadership traits for over a century. Hundreds of studies have been conducted, resulting in a basic consensus on leadership traits or characteristics that separate leaders from non-leaders. Today, among the key traits we often attribute to leaders, determination is one that can be seen in many who are influential and successful.

The 19th century German philosopher Frederick Nietzsche's maxim "That which does not kill us, makes us stronger" can be applied to leaders of organizations today. British Prime Minister Winston Churchill offered slightly different advice to the students in his commencement speech at the Harrow School on October 29, 1941, when he said, "Never give in, never, never, never, never—in nothing, great or small, large or petty—never give in except to convictions of honor and good sense. Never yield to force; never yield to the apparently overwhelming might of the enemy." Antonio Horta-Osorio, the Portuguese banker who became CEO of Santander UK in 2006 and assumed the helm of Lloyds Banking Group in March, 2011, demonstrates the kind of attitude that Churchill's speech describes. Horta-Osorio encountered serious personal problems that led the board to grant him a sabbatical from his leadership position at the bank. An avid tennis player, a scuba diver who routinely encountered sharks, and a 12-hour-a-day banker, Horta-Osorio had been in his position at Lloyds for just eight months when he was granted a medical leave of absence to recover from insomnia and exhaustion, which were symptoms of stress. Confidential sources speculated that he was unable to meet the demands of the position—turning around a bank in trouble—and his inexperience in leading a large complex bank brought about his medical problems. Some financial pundits believed that he would never recover sufficiently to resume his leadership at the bank. However, on January 9, 2012, some two months later, Horta-Osorio proved them wrong. By his account, during his recovery process, he reflected on the experience and learned that all people are human with strengths and weaknesses. Furthermore, since his return to the bank, he has managed to strengthen the bank's position in the industry showing as a top performer among major British banks.

Horta-Osorio's persistence, in combination with other leadership traits, enabled him to succeed where non-leaders may not have. After getting a "reality check" on his personal and mental health, he persevered, developed his strategy, remained focused and spirited, and called on others for support, rather than succumb to the negativism of naysayers.

Questions

✪12-16. What leadership traits does Antonio Hotra-Osorio demonstrate as a result of his ability to resume his role at Lloyds Bank after such a personal issue?

✪12-17. Are there other examples of leaders who have been able to overcome such adversity? Who are they? Did they approach the problem as Hotra-Osorio did?

12-18. To what degree is it possible to develop leadership traits? Are they innate? What are some ways one can develop persistence?

Sources: Stuart Taylor, "How to Build a Sustainable High-Performance Organization," Inside HR, http://www.insidehr.com.au/how-to-build-a-sustainable-high-performance-organisation/; Andrea Ovans, "What Resilience Means, and Why It Matters," Harvard Business Review, January 05, 2015, https://hbr.org/2015/01/what-resilience-means-and-why-it-matters; "Horta-Osório Steps Back at Lloyds," FT.com, November 4, 2015, http://www.ft.com/intl/cms/s/0/98e28be2-0709-11e1-90de-00144feabdc0.html#axzz3niXjZBHC; Patrick Jenkins, "Tennis with the FT: António Horta-Osório," FT.com, July 27, 2012, http://www.ft.com/intl/cms/s/2/f3a0c8e8-d6b9-11e1-ba60-00144feabdc0.html; James Quinn, "Antonio Horta-Osorio Is Leading Lloyds Back to Health with Aplomb," The Telegraph, February 27, 2015, http://www.telegraph.co.uk/finance/newsbysector/banksandfinance/11441430/Antonio-Horta-Osorio-is-leading-Lloyds-back-to-health-with-aplomb.html; "Antonio Horta-Osorio Profile: The Banker Who Swims with Sharks and Had a Good Recession," The Telegraph, November 10, 2011, http://www.telegraph.co.uk/finance/newsbysector/banksandfinance/8107440/Antonio-Horta-Osorio-profile-the-banker-who-swims-with-sharks-and-had-a-good-recession.html; Jill Treanor, "Lloyds Boss Defends His Record as Four Years of 'Doing the Right Thing'," The Guardian, March 28, 2015, http://www.theguardian.com/business/2015/mar/28/lloyds-boss-antonio-horta-osorio-defends-record; Dan Milmo, "Lloyds Bank Boss Horta-Osório Returning to Work after Sick Leave," The Guardian, December 14, 2011, http://www.theguardian.com/business/2011/dec/14/lloyds-bank-antonio-horta-osorio-returns; Julia Werdigier and Landon Thomas Jr., "At Lloyds, a Bank and Its Boss on the Rebound," DealBook, December 27, 2013, http://dealbook.nytimes.com/2013/12/27/at-lloyds-a-bank-and-its-boss-on-the-rebound/; Julia Werdigier, "Lloyds Chief, after Medical Leave, Turns Down Bonus," DealBook, January 13, 2012, http://dealbook.nytimes.com/2012/01/13/lloyds-chief-turns-down-bonus/.

MyManagementLab

Go to **mymanagementlab.com** for the following Assisted-graded writing questions:

12-19. Considering the chapter and Case Incident 2, why would a personalized leadership development program be preferable to a best-practices teaching program?

12-20. Do you think leaders are more ethical now than ever before? Why or why not?

12-21. MyManagementLab Only – comprehensive writing assignment for this chapter.

ENDNOTES

[1] See T. A. Judge, J. E. Bono, R. Ilies, and M. W. Gerhardt, "Personality and Leadership: A Qualitative and Quantitative Review," *Journal of Applied Psychology* (August 2002): 765–80.

[2] D. R. Ames and F. J. Flynn, "What Breaks a Leader: The Curvilinear Relation between Assertiveness and Leadership," *Journal of Personality and Social Psychology* 92, no. 2 (2007): 307–24.

[3] A. E. Colbert, M. R. Barrick, and B. H. Bradley, "Personality and Leadership Composition in Top Management Teams: Implications for Organizational Effectiveness," *Personnel Psychology* 67 (2014): 351-87.

[4] K.-Y. Ng, S. Ang, and K. Chan, "Personality and Leader Effectiveness: A Moderated Mediation Model of Leadership Self-Efficacy, Job Demands, and Job Autonomy," *Journal of Applied Psychology* 93, no. 4 (2008): 733–43.

[5] R. B. Kaiser, J. M. LeBreton, and J. Hogan, "The Dark Side of Personality and Extreme Leader Behavior," *Applied Psychology: An International Review* 64, no. 1 (2015): 55-92.

[6] B. H. Gaddis and J. L. Foster, "Meta-Analysis of Dark Side Personality Characteristics and Critical Work Behaviors among Leaders across the Globe: Findings and Implications for Leadership Development and Executive Coaching," *Applied Psychology: An International Review* 64, no. 1 (2015): 25-54.

[7] R. H. Humphrey, J. M. Pollack, and T. H. Hawver, "Leading with Emotional Labor," *Journal of Managerial Psychology* 23 (2008): 151–68.

[8] F. Walter, M. S. Cole, and R. H. Humphrey, "Emotional Intelligence: Sine Qua Non of Leadership or Folderol?" *Academy of Management Perspectives*, February 2011, 45–59.

[9] S. Côté, P. N. Lopez, P. Salovey, and C. T. H. Miners, "Emotional Intelligence and Leadership Emergence in Small Groups," *Leadership Quarterly* 21 (2010): 496–508.

[10] N. Ensari, R. E. Riggio, J. Christian, and G. Carslaw, "Who Emerges as a Leader? Meta-Analyses of Individual Differences as Predictors of Leadership Emergence," *Personality and Individual Differences*, September 2011, 532–36.

[11] This research is updated in T. A. Judge, R. F. Piccolo, and R. Ilies, "The Forgotten Ones? The Validity of Consideration and Initiating Structure in Leadership Research," *Journal of Applied Psychology*, February 2004, 36–51.

[12] D. Akst, "The Rewards of Recognizing a Job Well Done," *The Wall Street Journal*, January 31, 2007, D9.

[13] M. Javidan, P. W. Dorfman, M. S. de Luque, and R. J. House, "In the Eye of the Beholder: Cross Cultural Lessons in Leadership from Project GLOBE," *Academy of Management Perspectives*, February 2006, 67–90.

[14] For more current discussion on the model, see S. Altmaee, K. Tuerk, and O.-S. Toomet, "Thomas-Kilmann's Conflict Management Modes and Their Relationship to Fiedler's Leadership Styles (Basing on Estonian Organizations)," *Baltic Journal of Management* 8, no. 1 (2013): 45–65.

[15] See, for instance, G. Thompson and R. P. Vecchio, "Situational Leadership Theory: A Test of Three Versions," *Leadership Quarterly* 20, no. 5 (2009): 837–48; and R. P. Vecchio, C. R. Bullis, and D. M. Brazil, "The Utility of Situational Leadership Theory—A Replication in a Military Setting," *Small Group Research* 37, no. 5 (2006): 407–24.

[16] R. Fehr, K. C. Yam, and C. Dang, "Moralized Leadership: The Construction and Consequences of Ethical Leader Perceptions," *Academy of Management Review* 40, no. 2 (2015): 182–209; and M. Hernandez, C. P. Long, and S. B. Sitkin, "Cultivating Follower Trust: Are All Leader Behaviors Equally Influential?" *Organization Studies* 35, no. 12 (2014): 1867–92.

[17] S. J. Perry, L. A. Witt, L. M. Penney, and L. Atwater, "The Downside of Goal-Focused Leadership: The Role of Personality in Subordinate Exhaustion," *Journal of Applied Psychology* 95, no. 6 (2010): 1145–53.

[18] S. H. Malik, H. Sikandar, H. Hassan, and S. Aziz, "Path Goal Theory: A Study of Job Satisfaction in Telecom Sector," in C. Dan (ed.), *Management and Service Science* 8 (2001): 127–34; and R. R. Vecchio, J. E. Justin, and C. L. Pearce, "The Utility of Transactional and Transformational Leadership for Predicting Performance and Satisfaction within a Path-Goal Theory Framework," *Journal of Occupational and Organizational Psychology* 81 (2008): 71–82.

[19] V. H. Vroom and A. G. Jago, "The Role of the Situation in Leadership," *American Psychologist*, January 2007, 17–24.

[20] W. Bennis, "The Challenges of Leadership in the Modern World," *American Psychologist*, January 2007, 2–5.

[21] X. Zhou and C. A. Schriesheim, "Supervisor–Subordinate Convergence in Descriptions of Leader–Member Exchange (LMX) Quality: Review and Testable Propositions," *Leadership Quarterly* 20, no. 6 (2009): 920–32.

[22] B. Erdogan and T. N. Bauer, "Differentiated Leader–Member Exchanges: The Buffering Role of Justice Climate," *Journal of Applied Psychology* 95, no. 6 (2010): 1104–20; S. J. Wayne, L. M. Shore, W. H. Bommer, and L. E. Tetrick, "The Role of Fair Treatment and Rewards in Perceptions of Organizational Support and Leader–Member Exchange," *Journal of Applied Psychology* 87, no. 3 (June 2002): 590–98; and S. S. Masterson, K. Lewis, and B. M. Goldman, "Integrating Justice and Social Exchange: The Differing Effects of Fair Procedures and Treatment on Work Relationships," *Academy of Management Journal* 43, no. 4 (August 2000): 738–48.

[23] M. Uhl-Bien, "Relationship Development as a Key Ingredient for Leadership Development," in S. E. Murphy and R. E. Riggio (eds.), *Future of Leadership Development* (Mahwah, NJ: Lawrence Erlbaum, 2003), 129–47.

[24] R. Vecchio and D. M. Brazil, "Leadership and Sex-Similarity: A Comparison in a Military Setting," *Personnel Psychology* 60 (2007): 303–35.

[25] See, for instance, R. Ilies, J. D. Nahrgang, and F. P. Morgeson, "Leader–Member Exchange and Citizenship Behaviors: A Meta-Analysis," *Journal of Applied Psychology* 92, no. 1 (2007): 269–77; and Z. Chen, W. Lam, and J. A. Zhong, "Leader–Member Exchange and Member Performance: A New Look at Individual-Level Negative Feedback-Seeking Behavior and Team-Level Empowerment Culture," *Journal of Applied Psychology* 92, no. 1 (2007): 202–12.

[26]R. Eisenberger, G. Karagonlar, F. Stinglhamber, P. Neves, T. E. Becker, M. G. Gonzalez-Morales, and M. Steiger-Mueller, "Leader-Member Exchange and Affective Organizational Commitment: The Contribution of Supervisor's Organizational Embodiment," *Journal of Applied Psychology* 95, no. 6 (2010): 1085–103.

[27]J. Bagger and A. Li, "How Does Supervisory Family Support Influence Employees' Attitudes and Behaviors? A Social Exchange Perspective," *Journal of Management* 40, no. 4 (2014): 1123–50.

[28]B. Erdogan and T. N. Bauer, "Differentiated Leader-Member Exchanges: The Buffering Role of Justice Climate," *Journal of Applied Psychology* 95, no. 6 (2010): 1104–20.

[29]D. Liu, M. Hernandez, and L. Wang, "The Role of Leadership and Trust in Creating Structural Patterns of Team Procedural Justice: A Social Network Investigation," *Personnel Psychology* 67 (2014): 801–45.

[30]A. N. Li and H. Liao, "How Do Leader-Member Exchange Quality and Differentiation Affect Performance in Teams? An Integrated Multilevel Dual Process Model," *Journal of Applied Psychology* 99, no. 5 (2014): 847–66.

[31]J. Hu and R. C. Liden, "Relative Leader-Member Exchange within Team Contexts: How and When Social Comparison Impacts Individual Effectiveness," *Personnel Psychology* 66 (2013): 127–72.

[32]M. Weber, *The Theory of Social and Economic Organization,* A. M. Henderson and T. Parsons (trans.), (Eastford, CT: Martino Fine Books, 2012).

[33]V. Seyranian and M. C. Bligh, "Presidential Charismatic Leadership: Exploring the Rhetoric of Social Change," *Leadership Quarterly* 19, no. 1 (2008): 54–76.

[34]Ibid.

[35]A. Xenikou, "The Cognitive and Affective Components of Organisational Identification: The Role of Perceived Support Values and Charismatic Leadership," *Applied Psychology: An International Review* 63, no. 4 (2014): 567–88.

[36]P. A. Vlachos, N. G. Panagopoulos, and A. A. Rapp, "Feeling Good by Doing Good: Employee CSR-Induced Attributions, Job Satisfaction, and the Role of Charismatic Leadership," *Journal of Business Ethics* 118, no. 3 (2013): 577–88.

[37]D. N. Den Hartog and P. L. Koopman, "Leadership in Organizations," in N. Anderson and D. S. Ones (eds.), *Handbook of Industrial, Work and Organizational Psychology,* vol. 2 (Thousand Oaks, CA: Sage, 2002), 166–87.

[38]P. Balkundi, M. Kilduff, and D. A. Harrison, "Centrality and Charisma: Comparing How Leader Networks and Attributions Affect Team Performance," *Journal of Applied Psychology* 96 (2012): 1209–22.

[39]A. Erez, V. F. Misangyi, D. E. Johnson, M. A. LePine, and K. C. Halverson, "Stirring the Hearts of Followers: Charismatic Leadership as the Transferal of Affect," *Journal of Applied Psychology* 93, no. 3 (2008): 602–15. For reviews on the role of vision in leadership, see S. J. Zaccaro, "Visionary and Inspirational Models of Executive Leadership: Empirical Review and Evaluation," in S. J. Zaccaro (ed.), *The Nature of Executive Leadership: A Conceptual and Empirical Analysis of Success* (Washington, DC: American Psychological Association, 2001), 259–78; and M. Hauser and R. J. House, "Lead Through Vision and Values," in E. A. Locke (ed.), *Handbook of Principles of Organizational Behavior* (Malden, MA: Blackwell, 2004), 257–73.

[40]D. N. Den Hartog, A. H. B. De Hoogh, and A. E. Keegan, "The Interactive Effects of Belongingness and Charisma on Helping and Compliance," *Journal of Applied Psychology* 92, no. 4 (2007): 1131–39.

[41]J. C. Pastor, M. Mayo, and B. Shamir, "Adding Fuel to Fire: The Impact of Followers' Arousal on Ratings of Charisma," *Journal of Applied Psychology* 92, no. 6 (2007): 1584–96.

[42]A. H. B. De Hoogh and D. N. Den Hartog, "Neuroticism and Locus of Control as Moderators of the Relationships of Charismatic and Autocratic Leadership with Burnout," *Journal of Applied Psychology* 94, no. 4 (2009): 1058–67.

[43]F. Cohen, S. Solomon, M. Maxfield, T. Pyszczynski, and J. Greenberg, "Fatal Attraction: The Effects of Mortality Salience on Evaluations of Charismatic, Task-Oriented, and Relationship-Oriented Leaders," *Psychological Sciences,* December 2004, 846–51; and M. G. Ehrhart and K. J. Klein, "Predicting Followers' Preferences for Charismatic Leadership: The Influence of Follower Values and Personality," *Leadership Quarterly,* Summer 2001, 153–79.

[44]See, for instance, R. Khurana, *Searching for a Corporate Savior: The Irrational Quest for Charismatic CEOs* (Princeton, NJ: Princeton University Press, 2002); and J. A. Raelin, "The Myth of Charismatic Leaders," *Training & Development,* March 2003, 47–54.

[45]B. M. Galvin, D. A. Waldman, and P. Balthazard, "Visionary Communication Qualities as Mediators of the Relationship between Narcissism and Attributions of Leader Charisma," *Personnel Psychology* 63, no. 3 (2010): 509–37.

[46]See, for instance, D. Deichmann and D. Stam, "Leveraging Transformational and Transactional Leadership to Cultivate the Generation of Organization-Focused Ideas," *Leadership Quarterly* 26, no. 2 (2015): 204–19; H.-J. Wolfram and L. Gratton, "Gender Role Self-Concept, Categorical Gender, and Transactional-Transformational Leadership: Implications for Perceived Workgroup Performance," *Journal of Leadership & Organizational Studies* 21, no. 4 (2014): 338–53; and T. A. Judge and R. F. Piccolo, "Transformational and Transactional Leadership: A Meta-Analytic Test of Their Relative Validity," *Journal of Applied Psychology,* October 2004, 755–68.

[47]A. E. Colbert, M. R. Barrick, and B. H. Bradley, "Personality and Leadership Composition in Top Management Teams: Implications for Organizational Effectiveness," *Personnel Psychology* 67 (2014): 351–87.

[48]A. M. Grant, "Leading with Meaning: Beneficiary Contact, Prosocial Impact, and the Performance Effects of Transformational Leadership," *Academy of Management Journal* 55 (2012): 458–76.

[49]D. Deichmann and D. Stam, "Leveraging Transformational and Transactional Leadership to Cultivate the Generation of Organization-Focused Ideas"; and H.-J. Wolfram and L. Gratton, "Gender Role Self-Concept, Categorical Gender, and Transactional-Transformational Leadership: Implications for Perceived Workgroup Performance."

[50]T. R. Hinkin and C. A. Schriesheim, "An Examination of 'Nonleadership': From Laissez-Faire Leadership to Leader Reward Omission and Punishment Omission," *Journal of Applied Psychology* 93, no. 6 (2008): 1234–48.

[51]Y. Ling, Z. Simsek, M. H. Lubatkin, and J. F. Veiga, "Transformational Leadership's Role in Promoting Corporate Entrepreneurship: Examining the CEO-TMT Interface," *Academy of Management Journal* 51, no. 3 (2008): 557–76.

[52]X. Zhang and K. M. Bartol, "Linking Empowering Leadership and Employee Creativity: The Influence of Psychological Empowerment, Intrinsic Motivation, and Creative Process Engagement," *Academy of Management Journal* 53, no. 1 (2010): 107–28.

[53]S. A. Eisenbeiß and S. Boerner, "A Double-Edged Sword: Transformational Leadership and Individual Creativity," *British Journal of Management* 24 (2013): 54–68.

[54]A. E. Colbert, A. E. Kristof-Brown, B. H. Bradley, and M. R. Barrick, "CEO Transformational Leadership: The Role of Goal Importance Congruence in Top Management Teams," *Academy of Management Journal* 51, no. 1 (2008): 81–96.

[55]D. Zohar and O. Tenne-Gazit, "Transformational Leadership and Group Interaction as Climate Antecedents: A Social Network Analysis," *Journal of Applied Psychology* 93, no. 4 (2008): 744–57.

[56]R. T. Keller, "Transformational Leadership, Initiating Structure, and Substitutes for Leadership: A Longitudinal Study of Research and Development Project Team Performance," *Journal of Applied Psychology* 91, no. 1 (2006): 202–10.

[57]G. Wang, I. Oh, S. H. Courtright, and A. E. Colbert, "Transformational Leadership

and Performance across Criteria and Levels: A Meta-Analytic Review of 25 Years of Research," *Group and Organization Management* 36, no. 2 (2011): 223–70.

[58]Y. Ling, Z. Simsek, M. H. Lubatkin, and J. F. Veiga, "The Impact of Transformational CEOs on the Performance of Small- to Medium-Sized Firms: Does Organizational Context Matter?" *Journal of Applied Psychology* 93, no. 4 (2008): 923–34.

[59]X. Wang and J. M. Howell, "Exploring the Dual-Level Effects of Transformational Leadership on Followers," *Journal of Applied Psychology* 95, no. 6 (2010): 1134–44.

[60]N. Li, D. S. Chiaburu, B. L. Kirkman, and Z. Xie, "Spotlight on the Followers: An Examination of Moderators of Relationships between Transformational Leadership and Subordinates' Citizenship and Taking Charge," *Personnel Psychology* 66 (2013): 225–60.

[61]R. J. House, M. Javidan, P. Hanges, and P. Dorfman, "Understanding Cultures and Implicit Leadership Theories across the Globe: An Introduction to Project GLOBE," *Journal of World Business,* Spring 2002, 3–10.

[62]D. E. Carl and M. Javidan, "Universality of Charismatic Leadership: A Multi-Nation Study," paper presented at the National Academy of Management Conference, Washington, DC, August 2001, 29.

[63]J. Schaubroeck, S. S. K. Lam, and S. E. Cha, "Embracing Transformational Leadership: Team Values and the Impact of Leader Behavior on Team Performance," *Journal of Applied Psychology* 92, no. 4 (2007): 1020–30.

[64]J. Liu, O. Siu, and K. Shi, "Transformational Leadership and Employee Well-Being: The Mediating Role of Trust in the Leader and Self-Efficacy," *Applied Psychology: An International Review* 59, no. 3 (2010): 454–79.

[65]S. J. Shin and J. Zhou, "Transformational Leadership, Conservation, and Creativity: Evidence from Korea," *Academy of Management Journal,* December 2003, 703–14; V. J. García-Morales, F. J. Lloréns-Montes, and A. J. Verdú-Jover, "The Effects of Transformational Leadership on Organizational Performance through Knowledge and Innovation," *British Journal of Management* 19, no. 4 (2008): 299–313; and S. A. Eisenbeiss, D. van Knippenberg, and S. Boerner, "Transformational Leadership and Team Innovation: Integrating Team Climate Principles," *Journal of Applied Psychology* 93, no. 6 (2008): 1438–46.

[66]F. O. Walumbwa, B. J. Avolio, and W. Zhu, "How Transformational Leadership Weaves Its Influence on Individual Job Performance: The Role of Identification and Efficacy Beliefs," *Personnel Psychology* 61, no. 4 (2008): 793–825.

[67]Y. Gong, J. Huang, and J. Farh, "Employee Learning Orientation, Transformational Leadership, and Employee Creativity: The Mediating Role of Employee Creative Self-Efficacy," *Academy of Management Journal* 52, no. 4 (2009): 765–78.

[68]J. E. Bono and T. A. Judge, "Self-Concordance at Work: Toward Understanding the Motivational Effects of Transformational Leaders," *Academy of Management Journal,* October 2003, 554–71; Y. Berson and B. J. Avolio, "Transformational Leadership and the Dissemination of Organizational Goals: A Case Study of a Telecommunication Firm," *Leadership Quarterly,* October 2004, 625–46; and Schaubroeck, S. S. K. Lam, and S. E. Cha, "Embracing Transformational Leadership: Team Values and the Impact of Leader Behavior on Team Performance."

[69]M. Birasnav, "Knowledge Management and Organizational Performance in the Service Industry: The Role of Transformational Leadership Beyond the Effects of Transactional Leadership," *Journal of Business Research* 67, no. 8 (2014): 1622–29; H. Hetland, G. M. Sandal, and T. B. Johnsen, "Burnout in the Information Technology Sector: Does Leadership Matter?" *European Journal of Work and Organizational Psychology* 16, no. 1 (2007): 58–75; and A. K. Tyssen, A. Wald, and S. Heidenreich, "Leadership in the Context of Temporary Organizations: A Study on the Effects of Transactional and Transformational Leadership on Followers' Commitment in Projects," *Journal of Leadership & Organizational Studies* 21, no. 4 (2014): 376–93.

[70]C. Tan, "CEO Pinching Penney in a Slowing Economy," *The Wall Street Journal,* January 31, 2008, 1–2; and A. Carter, "Lighting a Fire Under Campbell," *BusinessWeek,* December 4, 2006, 96–101.

[71]B. P. Owens and D. R. Hekman, "Modeling How to Grow: An Inductive Examination of Humble Leader Behaviors, Contingencies, and Outcomes," *Academy of Management Journal* 55 (2012): 787–818.

[72]K. M. Hmieleski, M. S. Cole, and R. A. Baron, "Shared Authentic Leadership and New Venture Performance," *Journal of Management,* September 2012, 1476–99.

[73]R. Ilies, F. P. Morgeson, and J. D. Nahrgang, "Authentic Leadership and Eudaemonic Well-Being: Understanding Leader-Follower Outcomes," *Leadership Quarterly* 16 (2005): 373–94; B. Levin, "Raj Rajaratnam Did Not Appreciate Rajat Gupta's Attempt to Leave the Goldman Board, Join 'The Billionaire circle,'" *NetNet with John Carney,* March 14, 2011, downloaded July 26, 2011, from www.cnbc.com/.

[74]J. Stouten, M. van Dijke, and D. De Cremer, "Ethical Leadership: An Overview and Future Perspectives," *Journal of Personnel Psychology* 11 (2012): 1–6.

[75]J. M. Schaubroeck, S. T. Hannah, B. J. Avolio, S. W. J. Kozlowski, et al., "Embedding Ethical Leadership within and across Organization Levels," *Academy of Management Journal* 55 (2012): 1053–78.

[76]K. M. Kacmar, D. G. Bachrach, K. J. Harris, and S. Zivnuska, "Fostering Good Citizenship through Ethical Leadership: Exploring the Moderating Role of Gender and Organizational Politics," *Journal of Applied Psychology,* 96, no. 3 (May 2011): 633–42; and F. O. Walumbwa and J. Schaubroeck, "Leader Personality Traits and Employee Voice Behavior: Mediating Roles of Ethical Leadership and Work Group Psychological Safety," *Journal of Applied Psychology* 94, no. 5 (2009): 1275–86.

[77]D. M. Mayer, K. Aquino, R. L. Greenbaum, and M. Kuenzi, "Who Displays Ethical Leadership, and Why Does It Matter? An Examination of Antecedents and Consequences of Ethical Leadership," *Academy of Management Journal* 55 (2012): 151–71.

[78]D. van Knippenberg, D. De Cremer, and B. van Knippenberg, "Leadership and Fairness: The State of the Art," *European Journal of Work and Organizational Psychology* 16, no. 2 (2007): 113–40.

[79]M. E. Brown and L. K. Treviño, "Socialized Charismatic Leadership, Values Congruence, and Deviance in Work Groups," *Journal of Applied Psychology* 91, no. 4 (2006): 954–62.

[80]M. E. Brown and L. K. Treviño, "Leader-Follower Values Congruence: Are Socialized Charismatic Leaders Better Able to Achieve It?" *Journal of Applied Psychology* 94, no. 2 (2009): 478–90.

[81]S. A. Eisenbeiss and S. R. Giessner, "The Emergence and Maintenance of Ethical Leadership in Organizations," *Journal of Personnel Psychology* 11 (2012): 7–19.

[82]J. Antonakis, M. Fenley, and S. Liechti, "Learning Charisma," *Harvard Business Review,* June 2012, 127–30.

[83]D. van Dierendonck, "Servant Leadership: A Review and Synthesis," *Journal of Management* 37, no. 4 (2011): 1228–61.

[84]S. J. Peterson, F. M. Galvin, and D. Lange, "CEO Servant Leadership: Exploring Executive Characteristics and Firm Performance," *Personnel Psychology* 65 (2012): 565–96.

[85]F. Walumbwa, C. A. Hartnell, and A. Oke, "Servant Leadership, Procedural Justice Climate, Service Climate, Employee Attitudes, and Organizational Citizenship Behavior: A Cross-Level Investigation," *Journal of Applied Psychology* 95, no. 3 (2010): 517–29.

[86]D. De Cremer, D. M. Mayer, M. van Dijke, B. C. Schouten, and M. Bardes, "When Does Self-Sacrificial Leadership Motivate Prosocial Behavior? It Depends on Followers' Prevention Focus," *Journal of Applied Psychology* 2009, no. 4 (2009): 887–99.

[87]J. Hu and R. C. Liden, "Antecedents of Team Potency and Team Effectiveness: An Examination of Goal and Process Clarity and

Servant Leadership," *Journal of Applied Psychology*, 96, no. 4 (July 2011): 851–62.

[88]M. J. Neubert, K. M. Kacmar, D. S. Carlson, L. B. Chonko, and J. A. Roberts, "Regulatory Focus as a Mediator of the Influence of Initiating Structure and Servant Leadership on Employee Behavior," *Journal of Applied Psychology* 93, no. 6 (2008): 1220–33.

[89]R. C. Liden, S. J. Wayne, C. Liao, and J. D. Meuser, "Servant Leadership and Serving Culture: Influence on Individual and Unit Performance," *Academy of Management Journal* 57, no. 5 (2014): 1434–52.

[90]T. Menon, J. Sim, J. Ho-Ying Fu, C. Chiu, and Y. Hong, "Blazing the Trail versus Trailing the Group: Culture and Perceptions of the Leader's Position," *Organizational Behavior and Human Decision Processes* 113, no. 1 (2010): 51–61.

[91]D. M. Rousseau, S. B. Sitkin, R. S. Burt, and C. Camerer, "Not So Different after All: A Cross-Discipline View of Trust," *Academy of Management Review*, July 1998, 393–404; and J. A. Simpson, "Psychological Foundations of Trust," *Current Directions in Psychological Science* 16, no. 5 (2007): 264–68.

[92]See, for instance, K. T. Dirks and D. L. Ferrin, "Trust in Leadership: Meta-Analytic Findings and Implications for Research and Practice," *Journal of Applied Psychology* 87, no. 4, (2002): 611–28; D. I. Jung and B. J. Avolio, "Opening the Black Box: An Experimental Investigation of the Mediating Effects of Trust and Value Congruence on Transformational and Transactional Leadership," *Journal of Organizational Behavior*, December 2000, 949–64; and A. Zacharatos, J. Barling, and R. D. Iverson, "High-Performance Work Systems and Occupational Safety," *Journal of Applied Psychology*, January 2005, 77–93.

[93]F. D. Schoorman, R. C. Mayer, and J. H. Davis, "An Integrative Model of Organizational Trust: Past, Present, and Future," *Academy of Management Review* 32, no. 2 (2007): 344–54.

[94]J. Schaubroeck, S. S. K. Lam, and A. C. Peng, "Cognition-Based and Affect-Based Trust as Mediators of Leader Behavior Influences on Team Performance," *Journal of Applied Psychology*, 96, no. 4 (July 2011): 863–71.

[95]J. R. Detert and E. R. Burris, "Leadership Behavior and Employee Voice: Is the Door Really Open?" *Academy of Management Journal* 50, no. 4 (2007): 869–84.

[96]J. A. Colquitt, B. A. Scott, and J. A. LePine, "Trust, Trustworthiness, and Trust Propensity: A Meta-Analytic Test of Their Unique Relationships with Risk Taking and Job Performance," *Journal of Applied Psychology* 92, no. 4 (2007): 909–27.

[97]J. A. Colquitt, B. A. Scott, and J. A. LePine, "Trust, Trustworthiness, and Trust Propensity: A Meta-Analytic Test of Their Unique Relationships with Risk Taking and Job Performance;" and F. D. Schoorman, R. C. Mayer, and J. H. Davis, "An Integrative Model of Organizational Trust: Past, Present, and Future."

[98]Cited in D. Jones, "Do You Trust Your CEO?" *USA Today*, February 12, 2003, 7B.

[99]M. J. Ashleigh, M. Higgs, and V. Dulewicz, "A New Propensity to Trust Scale and Its Relationship with Individual Well-Being: Implications for HRM Policies and Practices," *Human Resource Management Journal*, 2012, 360–76; R. C. Mayer and M. B. Gavin, "Trust in Management and Performance: Who Minds the Shop While the Employees Watch the Boss?" *Academy of Management Journal* 38 (2005): 874–88; and C. F. Peralta and M. F. Saldanha, "Knowledge-Centered Culture and Knowledge Sharing: The Moderator Role of Trust Propensity," *Journal of Knowledge Management* 18, no. 3 (2014): 538–50.

[100]J. A. Simpson, "Foundations of Interpersonal Trust," in A. W. Kruglanski and E. T. Higgins (eds.), *Social Psychology: Handbook of Basic Principles*, 2nd ed. (New York: Guilford, 2007), 587–607.

[101]X.-P. Chen, M. B. Eberly, T.-J. Chiang, J.-L. Farh, and B.-Shiuan Cheng, "Affective Trust in Chinese Leaders: Linking Paternalistic Leadership to Employee Performance," *Journal of Management* 40, no. 3 (2014): 796–819.

[102]J. A. Simpson, "Foundations of Interpersonal Trust."

[103]B. Groysberg and M. Slind, "Leadership Is a Conversation," *Harvard Business Review*, June 2012, 76–84.

[104]H. Zhao, S. J. Wayne, B. C. Glibkowski, and J. Bravo, "The Impact of Psychological Contract Breach on Work-Related Outcomes: A Meta-Analysis," *Personnel Psychology* 60 (2007): 647–80.

[105]D. L. Shapiro, A. D. Boss, S. Salas, S. Tangirala, and M. A. Von Glinow, "When Are Transgressing *Leaders* Punitively Judged? An Empirical Test," *Journal of Applied Psychology* 96, no. 2 (2011): 412–22.

[106]D. L. Ferrin, P. H. Kim, C. D. Cooper, and K. T. Dirks, "Silence Speaks Volumes: The Effectiveness of Reticence in Comparison to Apology and Denial for Responding to Integrity- and Competence-Based Trust Violations," *Journal of Applied Psychology* 92, no. 4 (2007): 893–908.

[107]M. E. Schweitzer, J. C. Hershey, and E. T. Bradlow, "Promises and Lies: Restoring Violated Trust," *Organizational Behavior and Human Decision Processes* 101, no. 1 (2006): 1–19.

[108]See, for example, L. Eby, M. Buits, and A. Lockwood, "Protégés' Negative Mentoring Experiences: Construct Development and Nomological Validation," *Personnel Psychology*, Summer 2004, 411–47.

[109]C. R. Wanberg, E. T. Welsh, and S. A. Hezlett, "Mentoring Research: A Review and Dynamic Process Model," in G. R. Ferris and J. J. Martocchio (eds.), *Research in Personnel and Human Resources Management*, vol. 22 (Greenwich, CT: Elsevier Science, 2003), 39–124; and T. D. Allen, "Protégé Selection by Mentors: Contributing Individual and Organizational Factors," *Journal of Vocational Behavior* 65, no. 3 (2004): 469–83.

[110]See, for example, D. B. Turban, T. W. Dougherty, and F. K. Lee, "Gender, Race, and Perceived Similarity Effects in Developmental Relationships: The Moderating Role of Relationship Duration," *Journal of Vocational Behavior*, October 2002, 240–62.

[111]J. U. Chun, J. J. Sosik, and N. Y. Yun, "A Longitudinal Study of Mentor and Protégé Outcomes in Formal Mentoring Relationships," *Journal of Organizational Behavior*, November 12, 2012, 35–49.

[112]Ragins and Cotton, "Mentor Functions and Outcomes"; and C. M. Underhill, "The Effectiveness of Mentoring Programs in Corporate Settings: A Meta-Analytical Review of the Literature," *Journal of Vocational Behavior* 68, no. 2 (2006): 292–307.

[113]T. D. Allen, E. T. Eby, and E. Lentz, "The Relationship between Formal Mentoring Program Characteristics and Perceived Program Effectiveness," *Personnel Psychology* 59 (2006): 125–53; T. D. Allen, L. T. Eby, and E. Lentz, "Mentorship Behaviors and Mentorship Quality Associated with Formal Mentoring Programs: Closing the Gap between Research and Practice," *Journal of Applied Psychology* 91, no. 3 (2006): 567–78; and M. R. Parise and M. L. Forret, "Formal Mentoring Programs: The Relationship of Program Design and Support to Mentors' Perceptions of Benefits and Costs," *Journal of Vocational Behavior* 72, no. 2 (2008): 225–40.

[114]L. T. Eby and A. Lockwood, "Protégés' and Mentors' Reactions to Participating in Formal Mentoring Programs: A Qualitative Investigation," *Journal of Vocational Behavior* 67, no. 3 (2005): 441–58; G. T. Chao, "Formal Mentoring: Lessons Learned from Past Practice," *Professional Psychology: Research and Practice* 40, no. 3 (2009): 314–20; and C. R. Wanberg, J. D. Kammeyer-Mueller, and M. Marchese, "Mentor and Protégé Predictors and Outcomes of Mentoring in a Formal Mentoring Program," *Journal of Vocational Behavior* 69 (2006): 410–23.

[115]M. K. Feeney and B. Bozeman, "Mentoring and Network Ties," *Human Relations* 61, no. 12 (2008): 1651–76; N. Bozionelos, "Intra-Organizational Network Resources: How They Relate to Career Success and Organizational Commitment," *Personnel Review* 37, no. 3 (2008): 249–63; and S. A. Hezlett and S. K. Gibson, "Linking Mentoring and Social Capital: Implications for Career and Organization Development," *Advances in Developing Human Resources* 9, no. 3 (2007): 384–412.

[116]Comment by Jim Collins, cited in J. Useem, "Conquering Vertical Limits," *Fortune,* February 19, 2001, 94.

[117]See, for instance, B. Schyns, J. Felfe, and H. Blank, "Is Charisma Hyper-Romanticism? Empirical Evidence from New Data and a Meta-Analysis," *Applied Psychology: An International Review* 56, no. 4 (2007): 505–27.

[118]M. J. Martinko, P. Harvey, D. Sikora, and S. C. Douglas, "Perceptions of Abusive Supervision: The Role of Subordinates' Attribution Styles," *Leadership Quarterly,* August 2011, 751–64.

[119]M. C. Bligh, J. C. Kohles, C. L. Pearce, J. E. Justin, and J. F. Stovall, "When the Romance Is Over: Follower Perspectives of Aversive Leadership," *Applied Psychology: An International Review* 56, no. 4 (2007): 528–57.

[120]B. R. Agle, N. J. Nagarajan, J. A. Sonnenfeld, and D. Srinivasan, "Does CEO Charisma Matter?" *Academy of Management Journal* 49, no. 1 (2006): 161–74.

[121]Bligh, Kohles, Pearce, Justin, and Stovall, "When the Romance Is Over."

[122]Schyns, Felfe, and Blank, "Is Charisma Hyper-Romanticism?"

[123]A. S. Rosette, G. J. Leonardelli, and K. W. Phillips, "The White Standard: Racial Bias in Leader Categorization," *Journal of Applied Psychology* 93, no. 4 (2008): 758–77.

[124]A. M. Koenig, A. H. Eagly, A. A. Mitchell, and T. Ristikari, "Are Leader Stereotypes Masculine? A Meta-Analysis of Three Research Paradigms," *Psychological Bulletin* 137, no. 4 (2011): 616–42.

[125]M. Van Vugt and B. R. Spisak, "Sex Differences in the Emergence of Leadership During Competitions within and between Groups," *Psychological Science* 19, no. 9 (2008): 854–58.

[126]Ibid.

[127]R. E. Silverman, "Who's the Boss? There Isn't One," *The Wall Street Journal,* June 20, 2012, B 1, B8.

[128]S. D. Dionne, F. J. Yammarino, L. E. Atwater, and L. R. James, "Neutralizing Substitutes for Leadership Theory: Leadership Effects and Common-Source Bias," *Journal of Applied Psychology,* 87 (2002): 454–64; and J. R. Villa, J. P. Howell, P. W. Dorfman, and D. L. Daniel, "Problems with Detecting Moderators in Leadership Research Using Moderated Multiple Regression," *Leadership Quarterly* 14 (2002): 3–23.

[129]L. A. Hambley, T. A. O'Neill, and T. J. B. Kline, "Virtual Team Leadership: The Effects of Leadership Style and Communication Medium on Team Interaction Styles and Outcomes," *Organizational Behavior and Human Decision Processes* 103 (2007): 1–20; and B. J. Avolio and S. S. Kahai, "Adding the 'E' to E-Leadership: How It May Impact Your Leadership," *Organizational Dynamics* 31, no. 4 (2003): 325–38.

[130]S. J. Zaccaro and P. Bader, "E-Leadership and the Challenges of Leading E-Teams: Minimizing the Bad and Maximizing the Good," *Organizational Dynamics* 31, no. 4 (2003): 381–85.

[131]C. E. Naquin and G. D. Paulson, "Online Bargaining and Interpersonal Trust," *Journal of Applied Psychology,* February 2003, 113–20.

[132]B. M. Bass, "Cognitive, Social, and Emotional Intelligence of Transformational Leaders," in R. E. Riggio, S. E. Murphy, and F. J. Pirozzolo (eds.), *Multiple Intelligences and Leadership* (Mahwah, NJ: Lawrence Erlbaum, 2002), 113–14.

[133]"JCPenney Names Marvin Ellison President and CEO-Designee," JCPenney Press Release August 1, 2015, http://ir.jcpenney.com/phoenix.zhtml?c=70528&p=irol-newsArticle&ID=1976923.

[134]"Most Underachieving: CEOs," *Bloomberg,* 2013, http://www.bloomberg.com/visual-data/best-and-worst//most-underachieving-ceos.

[135]See, for instance, P. Dvorak, "M.B.A. Programs Hone 'Soft Skills,'" *The Wall Street Journal,* February 12, 2007, B3.

[136]J. Weber, "The Leadership Factor," *BusinessWeek,* June 12, 2006, 60–64.

[137]D. Brady, "The Rising Star of CEO Consulting," *Bloomberg Businessweek,* November 24, 2010, www.businessweek.com.

[138]D. S. DeRue, J. D. Nahrgang, J. R. Hollenbeck, and K. Workman, "A Quasi-Experimental Study of After-Event Reviews and Leadership Development," *Journal of Applied Psychology* 97 (2012): 997–1015.

13 Power and Politics

LEARNING OBJECTIVES

After studying this chapter, you should be able to:

13-1 Contrast leadership and power.

13-2 Explain the three bases of formal power and the two bases of personal power.

13-3 Explain the role of dependence in power relationships.

13-4 Identify power or influence tactics and their contingencies.

13-5 Identify the causes and consequences of abuse of power.

13-6 Describe how politics work in organizations.

13-7 Identify the causes, consequences, and ethics of political behavior.

MyManagementLab®
⭐ **Chapter Warm Up**   If your professor has chosen to assign this, go to the Assignments section of **mymanagementlab.com** to complete the chapter warm up.

POWER IN COLLEGE SPORTS

Anyone who follows sports knows the huge media presence college football and basketball have. With all this attention comes big money: Estimates put direct revenues for college sports at $16 billion for the 2014–2015 academic year alone, with forecasts for subsequent increases. Revenues from successful sports are often sufficient to provide many scholarships and fund nearly all other athletic programs. TV coverage also draws massive media attention for the top-performing schools, enhancing their reputations and attracting donors. The resulting combination of large sums of money, complex power dynamics, and loose regulation systems creates a perfect environment for power struggles. It seems the lure of money and the pressure to compete at the stratospheric level are sometimes so great that college officials may become willing to subvert the rules and use political tactics to secure financial advantages for their institutions.

In this paradigm, coaches are often more powerful and highly paid than university presidents. Many observers worry that student athletes, who are not paid at all, might be the casualties of the intense politics. Their compensation is a good university education, which sometimes just doesn't happen. These students aren't always academically qualified when they are recruited for their sports abilities, and are often not given the extra help needed to catch up. As researcher Richard Southall notes, "We pretend that it's feasible to recruit high school graduates with minimal academic qualifications, giving them a full-time job as a football or basketball player at a Division I NCAA school, and somehow have them get up to college-level reading and writing skills at the same time that they're enrolled in college-level classes."

The National Collegiate Athletic Association (NCAA), the governing body, requires that student athletes maintain certain grade point averages (GPAs) and graduation rates, but these metrics sometimes put university administrators, coaches, and professors in a power struggle. Administrators, alumni, and others who can influence the university's reputation or revenue stream can use their power to influence coaches and officials. Professors and tutors, feeling political pressure from coaches and students to pass student athletes, sometimes follow the path of least resistance, developing fictional classes with few requirements and top grades.

Few people in the chain are able to ignore the power players. In many cases, resisters and whistle-blowers even face retaliation. Athlete mentor from the University of Georgia Billy Hawkins asks, regarding students who have been pushed through the system, "Have they learned anything? Are they productive citizens now? That's a thing I worry about. To get a degree is one thing, to be functional with that degree is totally different."

The need to develop a workable solution for the power struggle in college sports is clear. Scandals like "paper classes" and/or falsified grading at Florida State University (2009), the University of Michigan (2008), Auburn University (2006), and the University of Georgia (2003) shed light on the problem. Media exposure and organizational politics can, if managed correctly, become part of the solution. Internal pressures from those who put a strong value on academic performance, as well as the desire of universities and the NCAA to preserve a positive face to external constituents, are creating much of the pressure to ensure student athletes truly receive the type of education that has been claimed.

Sources: P. M. Barrett, "The Insurgents Who Could Bring Down the NCAA," *Bloomberg Business,* August 21, 2014, http://www.bloomberg.com/bw/articles/2014-08-21/paying-ncaa-college-athletes-inside-the-legal-battle; P. M. Barrett, "In Fake Classes Scandal, UNC Fails Its Athletes—And Whistle Blower," *Bloomberg Business,* March 3, 2014, http://www.bloomberg.com/bw/articles/2014-02-27/in-fake-classes-scandal-unc-fails-its-athletes-whistle-blower; S. Ganim, "Some College Athletes Play Like Adults, Read Like 5th Graders," CNN, January 8, 2014, http://www.cnn.com/2014/01/07/us/ncaa-athletes-reading-scores/; and B. Wolverton, "NCAA Says It's Investigating Academic Fraud at 20 Colleges," *The Chronicle,* January 21, 2015, http://chronicle.com/article/NCAA-Says-It-s-Investigating/151315/.

As we can see in the opening story, politics can wreak havoc on an essentially good system—in this case, ensuring student athletes get a high-quality education. In both practice and research, *power* and *politics* have been described as dirty words. In fact, it is easier for most of us to talk about sex or money than about power or political behavior. People who have power deny it, people who want it try not to look like they're seeking it, and those who are good at getting it are secretive about how they do so.[1]

In this chapter, we show that power determines what goals people pursue, discuss how power works in organizations, and reveal the effects of political behavior. We begin by exploring our natural association of power with leadership.

> ☀ **WATCH IT!**
>
> If your professor has assigned this, go to the Assignments section of **mymanagementlab.com** to complete the video exercise titled *Power and Political Behavior*.

Power and Leadership

13-1 Contrast leadership and power.

power A capacity that *A* has to influence the behavior of *B* so that *B* acts in accordance with *A*'s wishes.

dependence *B*'s relationship to *A* when *A* possesses something that *B* requires.

In organizational behavior (OB), **power** refers to a capacity that *A* has to influence the behavior of *B* so *B* acts in accordance with *A*'s wishes.[2] Someone can thus have power but not use it; it is a capacity or potential. Probably the most important aspect of power is that it is a function of **dependence**. The greater *B*'s dependence on *A*, the greater *A*'s power in the relationship. Dependence, in turn, is based on alternatives that *B* perceives and the importance *B* places on the alternative(s) *A* controls. A person can have power over you only if he or she controls something you desire. If you want a college degree and have to pass a certain course to get it, and your current instructor is the only faculty member in the college who teaches that course, she has power over you because your alternatives are highly limited and you place a high degree of importance on the outcome. Similarly, if you're attending college on funds provided by your parents, you probably recognize the power they hold over you. But once you're out of school, have a job, and are making a good income, your parents' power is reduced significantly.

Money is a powerful variable for dependence. Who among us has not heard of a rich relative who controls family members merely through the implicit or explicit threat of "writing them out of the will"? Another example is found on Wall Street, where portfolio manager Ping Jiang allegedly was able to coerce his subordinate, analyst Andrew Tong, into taking female hormones and wearing lipstick and makeup. Why such power? Jiang controlled Tong's access to day trading and thus his livelihood.[3]

A careful comparison of our description of power with our description of leadership in Chapter 12 reveals the concepts are closely intertwined. *Leaders* use *power* as a means of attaining group goals. How are the two terms different? Power does not require goal compatibility, just dependence. Leadership, on the other hand, requires some congruence between the goals of the leader and those being led. A second difference relates to the direction of influence. Leadership research focuses on the downward influence on followers. It minimizes the importance of lateral and upward influence patterns. Power research takes all factors into consideration. For a third difference, leadership research often emphasizes style. It seeks answers to questions such as: How supportive should a leader be? How much decision making should be shared with followers? In contrast, the research on power focuses on tactics for gaining compliance. Lastly, leadership concentrates on the individual leader's influence, while the study of power acknowledges that groups as well as individuals can use power to control other individuals or groups.

You may have noted that for a power situation to exist, one person or group needs to have control over resources the other person or group values. This is usually the case in established leadership situations. However, power relationships are possible in all areas of life, and power can be obtained in many ways. Let's explore the various sources of power next.

Bases of Power

13-2 Explain the three bases of formal power and the two bases of personal power.

Where does power come from? What gives an individual or a group influence over others? We answer by dividing the bases or sources of power into two general groupings—formal and personal—and breaking each of these down into more specific categories.[4]

Formal Power

Formal power is based on an individual's position in an organization. It can come from the ability to coerce or reward, or from formal authority.

coercive power A power base that is dependent on fear of the negative results from failing to comply.

Coercive Power The **coercive power** base depends on the target's fear of negative results from failing to comply. On the physical level, coercive power rests on the application, or the threat of application, of bodily distress through the infliction of pain, the restriction of movement, or the withholding of basic physiological or safety needs.

At the organizational level, *A* has coercive power over *B* if *A* can dismiss, suspend, or demote *B*, assuming *B* values her job. If *A* can assign *B* work activities *B* finds unpleasant, or treat *B* in a manner *B* finds embarrassing, *A* possesses coercive power over *B*. Coercive power comes also from withholding key information. People in an organization who have data or knowledge others need can make others dependent on them.

reward power Compliance achieved based on the ability to distribute rewards that others view as valuable.

Reward Power The opposite of coercive power is **reward power**, with which people comply because it produces positive benefits; someone who can distribute rewards others view as valuable will have power over them. These rewards can be financial—such as controlling pay rates, raises, and bonuses—or nonfinancial, including recognition, promotions, interesting work assignments, friendly colleagues, and preferred work shifts or sales territories.[5]

legitimate power The power a person receives as a result of his or her position in the formal hierarchy of an organization.

Legitimate Power In formal groups and organizations, probably the most common access to one or more of the power bases is through **legitimate power**. It represents the formal authority to control and use organizational resources based on the person's structural position in the organization.

Legitimate power is broader than the power to coerce and reward. Specifically, it includes members' acceptance of the authority of a hierarchical position. We associate power so closely with the concept of hierarchy that just drawing longer lines in an organization chart leads people to infer the leaders are especially powerful.[6] In general, when school principals, bank presidents, or army captains speak, teachers, tellers, and first lieutenants usually comply.

Personal Power

Many of the most competent and productive chip designers at Intel have power, but they aren't managers and they have no formal power. What they have is

Internet entrepreneur Mark Zuckerberg, co-founder and CEO of Facebook, has expert power. Shown here talking with employees, Zuckerberg earned the title "software guy" during college because of his expertise in computer programming. Today, Facebook depends on his expertise to achieve company goals.
Source: Tony Avelar/AP Images

personal power, which comes from an individual's unique characteristics. There are two bases of personal power: expertise and the respect and admiration of others. Personal power is not mutually exclusive from formal power, but it can be independent.

expert power Influence based on special skills or knowledge.

Expert Power   **Expert power** is influence wielded as a result of expertise, special skills, or knowledge. As jobs become more specialized, we become dependent on experts to achieve goals. It is generally acknowledged that physicians have expertise and hence expert power: Most of us follow our doctor's advice. Computer specialists, tax accountants, economists, industrial psychologists, and other specialists wield power as a result of their expertise.

referent power Influence based on identification with a person who has desirable resources or personal traits.

Referent Power   **Referent power** is based on identification with a person who has desirable resources or personal traits. If I like, respect, and admire you, you can exercise power over me because I want to please you.

Referent power develops out of admiration of another and a desire to be like that person. It helps explain, for instance, why celebrities are paid millions of dollars to endorse products in commercials. Marketing research shows people such as LeBron James and Tom Brady have the power to influence your choice of athletic shoes and credit cards. With a little practice, you and I could probably deliver as smooth a sales pitch as these celebrities, but the buying public doesn't identify with us. Some people who are not in formal leadership positions have referent power and exert influence over others because of their charismatic dynamism, likability, and emotional appeal.

Which Bases of Power Are Most Effective?

Of the three bases of formal power (coercive, reward, legitimate) and two bases of personal power (expert, referent), which are most important? Research suggests the personal sources of power are most effective. Both expert and referent power are positively related to employees' satisfaction with supervision, their organizational commitment, and their performance, whereas reward and legitimate power seem to be unrelated to these outcomes. One source of formal power—coercive power—can be damaging.

Referent power can be a powerful motivator. Consider Steve Stoute's company, Translation, which matches pop-star spokespersons with corporations that want to promote their brands. Stoute has paired Justin Timberlake with McDonald's, Beyoncé with Tommy Hilfiger, and Jay-Z with Reebok. Stoute's business seems to be all about referent power. His firm aims to use the credibility of artists and performers to reach youth culture.[7] The success of these well-known companies attests to Stoute's expectation that the buying public identifies with and emulates his spokespersons and therefore thinks highly of the represented brands.

Dependence: The Key to Power

13-3 Explain the role of dependence in power relationships.

The most important aspect of power is that it is a function of dependence. In this section, we show how understanding dependence helps us understand the degrees of power.

The General Dependence Postulate

Let's begin with a general postulate: *The greater* B's *dependence on* A, *the more power* A *has over* B. When you possess anything others require that you alone control, you make them dependent on you, and therefore you gain power over them.[8] As the old saying goes, "In the land of the blind, the one-eyed man is king!" But if something is plentiful, possessing it will not increase your power. Therefore, the more you can expand your own options, the less power you place in the hands of others. This explains why most organizations develop multiple suppliers rather than give their business to only one. It also explains why so many people aspire to financial independence. Independence reduces the power others can wield to limit our access to opportunities and resources.

What Creates Dependence?

Dependence increases when the resource you control is important, scarce, and nonsubstitutable.[9]

Importance If nobody wants what you have, it's not going to create dependence. However, note that there are many degrees of importance, from needing the resource for survival to wanting a resource that is in fashion or adds to convenience.

Scarcity Ferruccio Lamborghini, who created the exotic supercars that still carry his name, understood the importance of scarcity and used it to his advantage during World War II. When Lamborghini was in Rhodes with the Italian army, his superiors were impressed with his mechanical skills because he demonstrated an almost uncanny ability to repair tanks and cars no one else could fix. After the war, he admitted his ability was largely due to his having been the first person on the island to receive the repair manuals, which he memorized and then destroyed so as to make himself indispensable.[10]

We see the scarcity–dependence relationship in the power situation of employment. Where the supply of labor is low relative to demand, workers can negotiate compensation and benefits packages far more attractive than those in occupations with an abundance of candidates. For example, college administrators have no problem today finding English instructors since there is a high supply and low demand. The market for network systems analysts, in contrast, is comparatively tight, with demand high and supply limited. The resulting

Scientist Maria Kovalenko is in a position of power at Gilead Sciences, a research-based biopharmaceutical firm. Scientists are in a powerful occupational group at Gilead because they discover and develop medicines that improve the lives of patients and contribute to Gilead's growth and success.
Source: David Paul Morris/Bloomberg/Getty Images

bargaining power of computer-engineering faculty allows them to negotiate higher salaries, lighter teaching loads, and other benefits.

Nonsubstitutability   The fewer viable substitutes for a resource, the more power a person controlling that resource has. At universities that value faculty publishing, for example, the more recognition the faculty member receives through publication, the more control that person has because other universities want faculty who are highly published and visible.

Social Network Analysis: A Tool for Assessing Resources

One tool to assess the exchange of resources and dependencies within an organization is *social network analysis.*[11] This method examines patterns of communication among organizational members to identify how information flows between them. Within a social network, or connections between people who share professional interests, each individual or group is called a node, and the links between nodes are called ties. When nodes communicate or exchange resources frequently, they are said to have very strong ties. Other nodes that are not engaged in direct communication with one another achieve resource flows through intermediary nodes. In other words, some nodes act as brokers between otherwise unconnected nodes. A graphical illustration of the associations among individuals in a social network is called a *sociogram* and functions like an informal version of an organization chart. The difference is that a formal organization chart shows how authority is supposed to flow, whereas a sociogram shows how resources *really* flow in an organization. An example of a sociogram is in Exhibit 13-1.

Networks can create substantial power dynamics. Those in the position of brokers tend to have more power because they can leverage the unique resources they can acquire from different groups. In other words, many people are dependent upon brokers, which gives the brokers more power. For example, organizational culture changes such as corporate social responsibility (CSR) awareness will often begin in a single connected group of individuals, grow in strength, and then slowly move to other connected groups through brokers

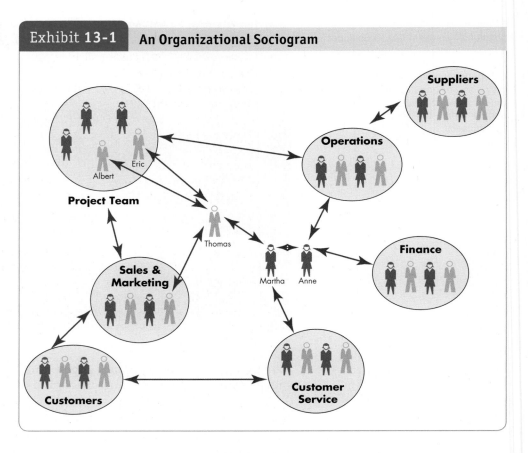

Exhibit 13-1   An Organizational Sociogram

over time.[12] Data from the United Kingdom's National Health Service show that change agents—people entrusted with helping an organization to make a significant change—have more success if they are information brokers.[13] These functions are not without cost, however. One study found that people identified as central to advice networks were more likely to quit their jobs, possibly because they did a great deal of extra work without reward.[14]

There are many ways to implement a social network analysis in an organization.[15] Some organizations keep track of the flow of e-mail communications or document sharing across departments. These big-data tools are an easy way to gather objective information about how individuals exchange information. Other organizations look at data from human resources (HR) information systems, analyzing how supervisors and subordinates interact with one another. These data sources can produce sociograms showing how resources and power flow. Leaders can then identify powerful brokers who exert the strongest influence on many groups, and address these key individuals.

Power Tactics

13-4   Identify power or influence tactics and their contingencies.

power tactics   Ways in which individuals translate power bases into specific actions.

What **power tactics** do people use to translate power bases into specific action? What options do they have for influencing their bosses, coworkers, or employees? Research has identified nine distinct influence tactics:[16]

- *Legitimacy.*   Relying on your authority position or saying a request accords with organizational policies or rules.
- *Rational persuasion.*   Presenting logical arguments and factual evidence to demonstrate a request is reasonable.

- *Inspirational appeals.*   Developing emotional commitment by appealing to a target's values, needs, hopes, and aspirations.
- *Consultation.*   Increasing support by involving the target in deciding how to accomplish your plan.
- *Exchange.*   Rewarding the target with benefits or favors in exchange for acceding to a request.
- *Personal appeals.*   Asking for compliance based on friendship or loyalty.
- *Ingratiation.*   Using flattery, praise, or friendly behavior prior to making a request.
- *Pressure.*   Using warnings, repeated demands, and threats.
- *Coalitions.*   Enlisting the aid or support of others to persuade the target to agree.

Using Power Tactics

Some tactics are more effective than others. Rational persuasion, inspirational appeals, and consultation tend to be the most effective, especially when the audience is highly interested in the outcomes of a decision process. The pressure tactic tends to backfire and is typically the least effective of the nine.[17] You can increase your chance of success by using two or more tactics together or sequentially, as long as your choices are compatible.[18] Using ingratiation and legitimacy together can lessen negative reactions, but only when the audience does not really care about the outcome of a decision process or the policy is routine.[19]

Let's consider the most effective way of getting a raise. You can start with a rational approach—figure out how your pay compares to that of your organizational peers, land a competing job offer, gather data that testify to your performance, or use salary calculators like Salary.com to compare your pay with others in your occupation—then share your findings with your manager. The results can be impressive. Kitty Dunning, a vice president at Don Jagoda Associates, landed a 16 percent raise when she e-mailed her boss numbers showing she had increased sales.[20]

While rational persuasion may work in this situation, the effectiveness of some influence tactics depends on the direction of influence,[21] and of course on the audience. As Exhibit 13-2 shows, rational persuasion is the only tactic effective across organizational levels. Inspirational appeals work best as a downward-influencing tactic with subordinates. When pressure works, it's generally downward only. Personal appeals and coalitions are most effective as lateral influence. Other factors relating to the effectiveness of influence include the sequencing of tactics, a person's skill in using the tactic, and the organizational culture.

In general, you're more likely to be effective if you begin with "softer" tactics that rely on personal power, such as personal and inspirational appeals, rational persuasion, and consultation. If these fail, you can move to "harder" tactics,

Exhibit 13-2	Preferred Power Tactics by Influence Direction	
Upward Influence	**Downward Influence**	**Lateral Influence**
Rational persuasion	Rational persuasion	Rational persuasion
	Inspirational appeals	Consultation
	Pressure	Ingratiation
	Consultation	Exchange
	Ingratiation	Legitimacy
	Exchange	Personal appeals
	Legitimacy	Coalitions

such as exchange, coalitions, and pressure, which emphasize formal power and incur greater costs and risks.[22] A single soft tactic is more effective than a single hard tactic, and combining two soft tactics or a soft tactic and rational persuasion is more effective than any single tactic or combination of hard tactics.[23]

As we mentioned, the effectiveness of tactics depends on the audience.[24] People especially likely to comply with soft power tactics tend to be more reflective and intrinsically motivated; they have high self-esteem and a greater desire for control. Those likely to comply with hard power tactics are more action-oriented and extrinsically motivated, and more focused on getting along with others than on getting their own way.

Cultural Preferences for Power Tactics

Preference for power tactics varies across cultures.[25] Those from individualist countries tend to see power in personalized terms and as a legitimate means of advancing their personal ends, whereas those in collectivist countries see power in social terms and as a legitimate means of helping others.[26] A study comparing managers in the United States and China found U.S. managers preferred rational appeal, whereas Chinese managers preferred coalition tactics.[27] Reason-based tactics are consistent with the U.S. preference for direct confrontation and rational persuasion to influence others and resolve differences, while coalition tactics align with the Chinese preference for meeting difficult or controversial requests with indirect approaches.

Applying Power Tactics

political skill The ability to influence others in such a way as to enhance one's objectives.

People differ in their **political skill**, or their ability to influence others to enhance their own objectives. The politically skilled are more effective users of all the influence tactics. Political skill is also more effective when the stakes are high, such as when the individual is accountable for important organizational outcomes. Finally, the politically skilled are able to exert their influence without others detecting it, a key element in effectiveness (it's damaging to be labeled political).[28] These individuals are able to use their political skills in environments with low levels of procedural and distributive justice. When an organization has fairly applied rules, free of favoritism or biases, political skill is actually negatively related to job performance ratings.[29]

Lastly, we know cultures within organizations differ markedly—some are warm, relaxed, and supportive; others are formal and conservative. Some encourage participation and consultation, some encourage reason, and still others rely on pressure. People who fit the culture of the organization tend to obtain more influence.[30] Specifically, extraverts tend to be more influential in team-oriented organizations, and highly conscientious people are more influential in organizations that value working alone on technical tasks. People who fit the culture are influential because they can perform especially well in the domains deemed most important for success. Thus, the organization itself will influence which subset of power tactics is viewed as acceptable for use.

How Power Affects People

13-5 Identify the causes and consequences of abuse of power.

To this point, we've discussed what power is and how it is acquired. But we've not yet answered one important question: Does power corrupt?

There is certainly evidence that there are corrupting aspects of power. Power leads people to place their own interests ahead of others' needs or goals. Why does this happen? Interestingly, power not only leads people to focus on their self-interests because they can, it liberates them to focus inward and thus come to place greater weight on their own aims and interests. Power also appears to lead individuals to "objectify" others (to see them as tools to obtain their instrumental goals) and to see relationships as more peripheral.[31]

That's not all. Powerful people react—especially negatively—to any threats to their competence. People in positions of power hold on to it when they can, and individuals who face threats to their power are exceptionally willing to take actions to retain it whether their actions harm others or not. Those given power are more likely to make self-interested decisions when faced with a moral hazard (such as when hedge fund managers take more risks with other people's money because they're rewarded for gains but less often punished for losses). People in power are more willing to denigrate others. Power also leads to overconfident decision making.[32]

Frank Lloyd Wright, perhaps the greatest U.S. architect, is a good example of power's corrupting effects. Early in his career, Wright worked for and was mentored by a renowned architect, Louis Sullivan (sometimes known as "the father of the skyscraper"). Before Wright achieved greatness, he was generous in his praise for Sullivan. Later in his career, that praise faded, and Wright even took credit for one of Sullivan's noted designs. Wright was never a benevolent man, but as his power accumulated, so did his potential to behave in a "monstrous" way toward others.[33]

Power Variables

As we've discussed, power does appear to have some important disturbing effects on us. But that is hardly the whole story—power is more complicated than that. It doesn't affect everyone in the same way, and there are even positive effects of power. Let's consider each of these in turn.

First, the toxic effects of power depend on the wielder's personality. Research suggests that if we have an anxious personality, power does not corrupt us because we are less likely to think that using power benefits us.[34] Second, the corrosive effect of power can be contained by organizational systems. One study found, for example, that while power made people behave in a self-serving manner, when accountability for this behavior was initiated, the self-serving behavior stopped. Third, we have the means to blunt the negative effects of power. One study showed that simply expressing gratitude toward powerful others makes them less likely to act aggressively against us. Finally, remember the saying that those with little power abuse what little they have? There seems to be some truth to this in that the people most likely to abuse power are those who start low in status and gain power. Why is this the case? It appears having low status is threatening, and the fear this creates is used in negative ways if power is later given.[35]

As you can see, some factors can moderate the negative effects of power. But there can be general positive effects. Power energizes and increases motivation to achieve goals. It also can enhance our motivation to help others. One study found, for example, that a desire to help others translated into actual work behavior when people felt a sense of power.[36]

This study points to an important insight about power. It is not so much that power corrupts as it *reveals what we value*. Supporting this line of reasoning, another study found that power led to self-interested behavior only in those with a weak moral identity (the degree to which morals are core to someone's identity). In those with a strong moral identity, power enhanced their moral awareness and willingness to act.[37]

Sexual Harassment: Unequal Power in the Workplace

sexual harassment   Any unwanted activity of a sexual nature that affects an individual's employment and creates a hostile work environment.

Sexual harassment is defined as any unwanted activity of a sexual nature that affects an individual's employment or creates a hostile work environment. According to the U.S. Equal Employment Opportunity Commission (EEOC), sexual harassment happens when a person encounters "unwelcome sexual advances, requests for sexual favors, and other verbal or physical conduct of a sexual nature" on the job that disrupts work performance or that creates an "intimidating, hostile, or offensive" work environment.[38] Although the definition changes from country to country, most nations have at least some policies to protect workers. Whether the policies or laws are followed is another question, however. Equal employment opportunity legislation is established in Pakistan, Bangladesh, and Oman, for example, but studies suggest it might not be well implemented.[39]

Generally, sexual harassment is more prevalent in male-dominated societies. For example, a study in Pakistan found that up to 93 percent of female workers were sexually harassed.[40] In Singapore, up to 54 percent of workers (women and men) reported they were sexually harassed.[41] The percentages in the United States and some other countries are generally much lower but still troubling. Surveys indicate about one-quarter of U.S. women and 10 percent of men have been sexually harassed.[42] Data from the EEOC suggest that sexual harassment is decreasing: Sexual harassment claims now make up 10 percent of all discrimination claims, compared with 20 percent in the mid-1990s. Of this percentage, though, claims from men have increased from 11 percent of total claims in 1997 to 17.5 percent today.[43] Sexual harassment is disproportionately prevalent for women in certain types of jobs. In the restaurant industry, for instance, 80 percent of female wait staff reported having been sexually harassed by coworkers or customers, compared to 70 percent of male wait staff.[44]

Most studies confirm that power is central to understanding sexual harassment.[45] This seems true whether the harassment comes from a supervisor, coworker, or employee. And sexual harassment is more likely to occur when

A federal jury awarded this woman a $95 million judgment in a sexual harassment lawsuit against her employer for harassment from her supervisor that included unwanted physical contact. The jury found the supervisor guilty of assault and battery and the company liable for negligent supervision and sexual harassment.
Source: Bill Greenblatt/UPI/Newscom

there are large power differentials. The supervisor–employee dyad best characterizes an unequal power relationship, where formal power gives the supervisor the capacity to reward and coerce. Because employees want favorable performance reviews, salary increases, and the like, supervisors control resources most employees consider important and scarce. When there aren't effective controls to detect and prevent sexual harassment, abusers are more likely to act. For example, male respondents in one study in Switzerland who were high in hostile sexism reported higher intentions to sexually harass in organizations that had low levels of justice, suggesting that failure to have consistent policies and procedures for all employees might increase levels of sexual harassment.[46]

Sexual harassment can detrimentally impact individuals and the organization, but it can be avoided. The manager's role is critical:

1. *Make sure an active policy defines what constitutes sexual harassment, informs employees they can be fired for inappropriate behavior, and establishes procedures for making complaints.*
2. *Reassure employees they will not encounter retaliation if they file a complaint.*
3. *Investigate every complaint, and inform the legal and HR departments.*
4. *Make sure offenders are disciplined or terminated.*
5. *Set up in-house seminars to raise employee awareness of sexual harassment issues.*

The bottom line is that managers have a responsibility to protect their employees from a hostile work environment. They may easily be unaware that one of their employees is being sexually harassed, but being unaware does not protect them or their organization. If investigators believe a manager could have known about the harassment, both the manager and the company can be held liable.

Politics: Power in Action

13-6 Describe how politics work in organizations.

Whenever people get together in groups, power will be exerted. People in organizations want to carve out a niche to exert influence, earn rewards, and advance their careers. If they convert their power into action, we describe them as being engaged in *politics*. Those with good political skills have the ability to use their bases of power effectively.[47] Politics are not only inevitable; they might be essential, too (see OB Poll).

Definition of Organizational Politics

There is no shortage of definitions of *organizational politics*. Essentially, this type of politics focuses on the use of power to affect decision making in an organization, sometimes for self-serving and organizationally unsanctioned behaviors.[48] For our purposes, **political behavior** in organizations consists of activities that are not required as part of an individual's formal role but that influence, or attempt to influence, the distribution of advantages and disadvantages within the organization.[49]

This definition encompasses what most people mean when they talk about organizational politics. Political behavior is outside specified job requirements. It requires some attempt to use power bases. It includes efforts to influence the goals, criteria, or processes used for decision making. Our definition is broad enough to include varied political behaviors such as withholding key information from decision makers, joining a coalition, whistle-blowing, spreading rumors, leaking confidential information to the media, exchanging favors with

political behavior Activities that are not required as part of a person's formal role in the organization but that influence, or attempt to influence, the distribution of advantages and disadvantages within the organization.

OB POLL

Importance of Organizational Politics

How do employees get ahead in your organization?

- Creativity: 4%
- Initiative: 18%
- Hard work: 27%
- Politics: 51%

Source: D. Crampton, "Is How Americans Feel about Their Jobs Changing?" (September 28, 2012), http://corevalues.com/employee-motivation/is-how-americans-feel-about-their-jobs-changing.

others for mutual benefit, and lobbying on behalf of or against a particular individual or decision alternative. In this way, political behavior is often negative, but not always.

The Reality of Politics

Interviews with experienced managers show most believe political behavior is a major part of organizational life.[50] Many managers report some use of political behavior is ethical, as long as it doesn't directly harm anyone else.

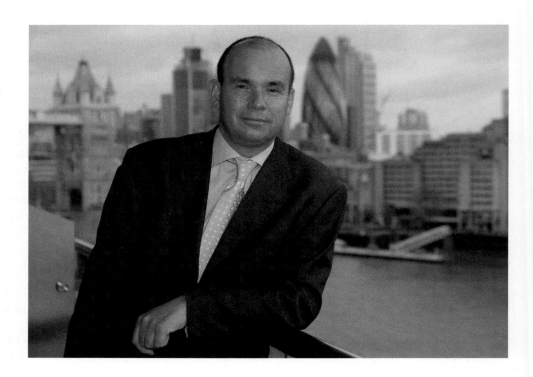

Whistle-blower Michael Woodford was fired from his position as CEO of Japanese camera-maker Olympus after informing company officials about accounting irregularities. Although not part of his job, Woodford uncovered a 13-year accounting fraud by some company executives.
Source: Luke McGregor/Reuters

They describe politics as necessary and believe someone who never uses political behavior will have a hard time getting things done. Most also indicate they have never been trained to use political behavior effectively. But why, you may wonder, must politics exist? Isn't it possible for an organization to be politics-free? It's *possible*—but unlikely.

Organizations have individuals and groups with different values, goals, and interests.[51] This sets up the potential for conflict over the allocation of limited resources, such as budgets, work space, and salary and bonus pools. If resources were abundant, all constituencies within an organization could satisfy their goals. But because they are limited, not everyone's interests can be satisfied. Furthermore, gains by one individual or group are often *perceived* as coming at the expense of others within the organization (whether they are or not). These forces create competition among members for the organization's limited resources.

Maybe the most important factor leading to politics within organizations is the realization that most of the "facts" used to allocate limited resources are open to interpretation. When allocating pay based on performance, for instance, what is *good* performance? What's an *adequate* improvement? What constitutes an *unsatisfactory* job? The manager of any major league baseball team knows a .400 hitter is a high performer and a .125 hitter is a poor performer. You don't need to be a baseball genius to know you should play your .400 hitter and send the .125 hitter back to the minors. But what if you have to choose between players who hit .280 and .290? Then less objective factors come into play: fielding expertise, attitude, potential, ability to perform in a clutch, loyalty to the team, and so on. More managerial decisions resemble the choice between a .280 and a .290 hitter than between a .125 hitter and a .400 hitter. It is in this large and ambiguous middle ground of organizational life—where the facts don't speak for themselves—that politics flourish.

Finally, because most decisions have to be made in a climate of ambiguity—where facts are rarely objective and thus open to interpretation—people within organizations will use whatever influence they can support their goals and interests. That, of course, creates the activities we call *politicking*. One person's "selfless effort to benefit the organization" is seen by another as a "blatant attempt to further his or her interest." [52]

Therefore, to answer the question of whether it is possible for an organization to be politics-free, we can say "yes"—if all members of that organization hold the same goals and interests, if organizational resources are not scarce, and if performance outcomes are completely clear and objective. But that doesn't describe the organizational world in which most of us live.

Causes and Consequences of Political Behavior

13-7 Identify the causes, consequences, and ethics of political behavior.

Now that we've discussed the constant presence of politicking in organizations, let's discuss the causes and consequences of these behaviors.

Factors Contributing to Political Behavior

Not all groups or organizations are equally political. In some organizations, politicking is overt and rampant, while in others politics plays a small role in influencing outcomes. Why this variation? Research and observation have identified a number of factors that appear to encourage political behavior. Some are individual characteristics, derived from the qualities of the people

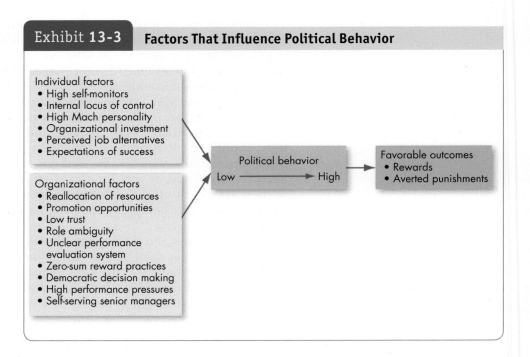

Exhibit 13-3   Factors That Influence Political Behavior

Individual factors
- High self-monitors
- Internal locus of control
- High Mach personality
- Organizational investment
- Perceived job alternatives
- Expectations of success

Organizational factors
- Reallocation of resources
- Promotion opportunities
- Low trust
- Role ambiguity
- Unclear performance evaluation system
- Zero-sum reward practices
- Democratic decision making
- High performance pressures
- Self-serving senior managers

Political behavior
Low ———→ High

Favorable outcomes
- Rewards
- Averted punishments

the organization employs; others are a result of the organization's culture or internal environment. Exhibit 13-3 illustrates how both individual and organizational factors can increase political behavior and provide favorable outcomes (increased rewards and averted punishments) for individuals and groups in the organization.

Individual Factors   At the individual level, researchers have identified certain personality traits, needs, and other factors likely to be related to political behavior. In terms of traits, we find that employees who are high self-monitors, possess an internal locus of control, and have a high need for power are more likely to engage in political behavior. The high self-monitor is more sensitive to social cues, exhibits higher levels of social conformity, and is more likely to be skilled in political behavior than the low self-monitor. Because they believe they can control their environment, individuals with an internal locus of control are more prone to take a proactive stance and attempt to manipulate situations in their favor. Not surprisingly, the Machiavellian personality—characterized by the will to manipulate and the desire for power—is consistent with using politics as a means to further personal interests.

An individual's investment in the organization and perceived alternatives influence the degree to which he or she will pursue illegitimate means of political action.[53] The more a person expects increased future benefits from the organization, and the more that person has to lose if forced out, the less likely he or she is to use illegitimate means. Conversely, the more alternate job opportunities an individual has—due to a favorable job market, possession of scarce skills or knowledge, prominent reputation, or influential contacts outside the organization—the more likely the person is to employ politics.

An individual with low expectations of success from political means is unlikely to use them. High expectations from such measures are most likely to be the province of both experienced and powerful individuals with polished political skills, and inexperienced and naïve employees who misjudge their chances.

Finally, some individuals engage in more political behavior because they simply are better at it. Such individuals read interpersonal interactions well, fit their behavior to situational needs, and excel at networking.[54] These people are often indirectly rewarded for their political efforts. For example, a study of a construction firm in southern China found that politically skilled subordinates were more likely to receive recommendations for rewards from their supervisors, and that politically oriented supervisors were especially likely to respond positively to politically skilled subordinates.[55] Other studies from countries around the world have similarly shown that higher levels of political skill are associated with higher levels of perceived job performance.[56]

Organizational Factors Although we acknowledge the role individual differences can play, the evidence more strongly suggests that certain situations and cultures promote politics. Specifically, when an organization's resources are declining, when the existing pattern of resources is changing, and when there

---

Career OBjectives

Should I become political?

My office is so political! Everyone is just looking for ways to get ahead by plotting and scheming rather than doing the job. Should I just go along with it and develop my own political strategy?
— *Julia*

Dear Julia:

There's definitely a temptation to join in when other people are behaving politically. If you want to advance your career, you need to think about social relationships and how to work with other people in a smart and diplomatic way. But that doesn't mean you have to give in to pressure to engage in organizational politics.

Of course, in many workplaces, hard work and achievement aren't recognized, which heightens politicking and lowers performance. But politics aren't just potentially bad for the company. People who are seen as political can be gradually excluded from social networks and informal communication. Coworkers can sabotage a person with a reputation for dishonesty or manipulation so they don't have to deal with him or her. It's also likely that a political person will be the direct target of

revenge from those who feel they've been wronged.

If you want to provide a positive alternative to political behavior in your workplace, there are a few steps you can take:

- *Document your work efforts, and find data to back up your accomplishments.* Political behavior thrives in an ambiguous environment where standards for success are subjective and open to manipulation. The best way to shortcut politics is to move the focus toward clear, objective markers of work performance.
- *Call out political behavior when you see it.* Political behavior is, by its very nature, secretive and underhanded. By bringing politics to light, you limit this capacity to manipulate people against one another.
- *Try to develop a network with only those individuals who are interested in performing well together.* This makes it hard for a very political person to get a lot done. On the other hand, trustworthy and cooperative

people will be able to find many allies who are genuinely supportive. These support networks will result in performance levels that a lone political person simply cannot match.

Remember, in the long run a good reputation can be your greatest asset!

Based on: A. Lavoie "How to Get Rid of Toxic Office Politics," *Fast Company,* April 10, 2014, http://www.fastcompany.com/3028856/work-smart/how-to-make-office-politicking-a-lame-duck; C. Conner, "Office Politics: Must You Play?" *Forbes,* April 14, 2013, http://www.forbes.com/sites/cherylsnappconner/2013/04/14/office-politics-must-you-play-a-handbook-for-survivalsuccess/; and J. A. Colquitt and J. B. Rodell "Justice, Trust, and Trustworthiness: A Longitudinal Analysis Integrating Three Theoretical Perspectives," *Academy of Management Journal* 54 (2011): 1183–206.

The opinions provided here are of the managers and authors only and do not necessarily reflect those of their organizations. The authors or managers are not responsible for any errors or omissions, or for the results obtained from the use of this information. In no event will the authors or managers, or their related partnerships or corporations thereof, be liable to you or anyone else for any decision made or action taken in reliance on the opinions provided here.

Organizations foster politicking when they reduce resources. By announcing plans to downsize its global workforce of 100,000 employees to increase its competitiveness, French pharmaceutical firm Sanofi stimulated political activity among employees who organized protests against the job cuts.
Source: Robert Pratta/Reuters

zero-sum approach   An approach that treats the reward "pie" as fixed, such that any gains by one individual are at the expense of another.

is opportunity for promotions, politicking is more likely to surface.[57] When resources are reduced, people may engage in political actions to safeguard what they have. Also, *any* changes, especially those implying significant reallocation of resources within the organization, are likely to stimulate conflict and increase politicking.

Cultures characterized by low trust, role ambiguity, unclear performance evaluation systems, zero-sum (win-lose) reward allocation practices, democratic decision making, high pressure for performance, and self-serving senior managers will also create breeding grounds for politicking.[58] Because political activities are not required as part of the employee's formal role, the greater the role ambiguity, the more employees can engage in unnoticed political activity. Role ambiguity means the prescribed employee behaviors are not clear. There are, therefore, fewer limits to the scope and functions of the employee's political actions.

The more an organizational culture emphasizes the zero-sum or win–lose approach to reward allocations, the more employees will be motivated to engage in politicking. The **zero-sum approach** treats the reward "pie" as fixed, so any gain one person or group achieves comes at the expense of another person or group. For example, if $15,000 is distributed among five employees for raises, any employee who gets more than $3,000 takes money away from one or more of the others. Such a practice encourages making others look bad and increasing the visibility of what you do.

There are also political forces at work in the relationships *between* organizations, where politics work differently depending on the organizational cultures.[59] One study showed when two organizations with very political environments interacted with one another, the political interactions between them hurt performance in collaborative projects. On the other hand, when companies with less internal political behavior interacted with one another, even political disputes

Myth or Science?

Powerful Leaders Keep Their (Fr)Enemies Close

This statement appears to be true. We all have heard the term "frenemies" to describe friends who are also rivals or people who act like friends but secretly dislike each other. Some observers have argued that frenemies are increasing at work due to the "abundance of very close, intertwined relationships that bridge people's professional and personal lives."

Keeping enemies close may be one reason Barack Obama appointed Hillary Clinton secretary of state after their bitter battle for the U.S. presidency. Or, in the business world, why one entrepreneur decided not to sue a former college classmate who, after working for her startup as a consultant, took that

knowledge and started his own, competing company.

Is it really wise to keep your enemies close? And, if so, why?

New research suggests answers to these questions. Three experimental studies found individuals chose to work in the same room as their rival even when informed they would probably perform better apart; sit closer to rivals when working together; and express an explicit preference to be closer to the rival. The researchers further found the primary reason for the "being closer" effect was the desire to monitor the rival's behavior and performance.

The researchers also found the "keeping enemies closer" effect was

strong under certain conditions—when the individual was socially dominant, when the individual felt more competition from the team member, and when rewards and the ability to serve as leader were dependent on performance.

These results suggest the concept of frenemies is very real and that we choose to keep our rivals close so we can keep an eye on the competition they bring.

Sources: M. Thompson, "How to Work with Your Startup Frenemies," *VentureBeat,* December 22, 2012, http://venturebeat .com/2012/12/22/frenemies/; and N. L. Mead and J. K. Maner, "On Keeping Your Enemies Close: Powerful Leaders Seek Proximity to Ingroup Power Threats," *Journal of Personality and Social Psychology* 102 (2012): 576–91.

between them did not lead to lower performance in collaborative projects. This study shows companies should be wary of forming alliances with companies that have high levels of internal political behavior.

How Do People Respond to Organizational Politics?

Trish loves her job as a writer on a weekly U.S. television comedy series but hates the internal politics. "A couple of the writers here spend more time kissing up to the executive producer than doing any work. And our head writer clearly has his favorites. While they pay me a lot and I get to really use my creativity, I'm sick of having to be on alert for backstabbers and constantly having to self-promote my contributions. I'm tired of doing most of the work and getting little of the credit." We all know friends or relatives like Trish who regularly complain about the politics at their jobs. But how do people in general react to organizational politics? Let's look at the evidence.

For most people who have modest political skills or are unwilling to play the politics game, outcomes tend to be predominantly negative. See Exhibit 13-4 for a diagram of this. However, very strong evidence indicates perceptions of organizational politics are negatively related to job satisfaction.[60] Politics may lead to self-reported declines in employee performance, perhaps because employees perceive political environments to be unfair, which demotivates them.[61] Not surprisingly, when politicking becomes too much to handle, it can lead employees to quit.[62] When employees of two agencies in a study in Nigeria viewed their work environments as political, they reported higher levels of job distress and were less likely to help their coworkers. Thus, although developing countries such as Nigeria present perhaps more ambiguous and therefore more political environments in which to work, the negative consequences of politics appear to be the same as in the United States.[63]

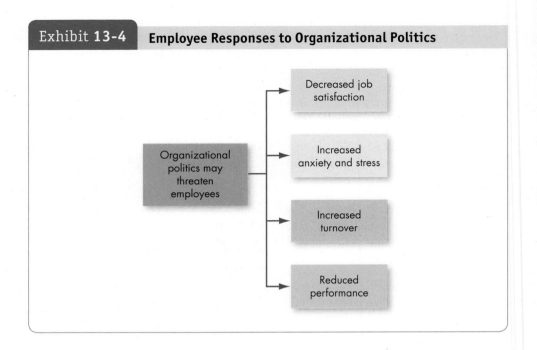

Exhibit 13-4   **Employee Responses to Organizational Politics**

Organizational politics may threaten employees

→ Decreased job satisfaction

→ Increased anxiety and stress

→ Increased turnover

→ Reduced performance

There are some qualifiers. First, the politics–performance relationship appears to be moderated by an individual's understanding of the "hows" and "whys" of organizational politics. Researchers noted, "An individual who has a clear understanding of who is responsible for making decisions and why they were selected to be the decision makers would have a better understanding of how and why things happen the way they do than someone who does not understand the decision-making process in the organization."[64] When both politics and understanding are high, performance is likely to increase because these individuals see political activity as an opportunity. This is consistent with what you might expect for individuals with well-honed political skills. But when understanding is low, individuals are more likely to see politics as a threat, which can have a negative effect on job performance.[65]

Second, political behavior at work moderates the effects of ethical leadership.[66] One study found male employees were more responsive to ethical leadership and showed the most citizenship behavior when levels of both politics and ethical leadership were high. Women, on the other hand, appeared most likely to engage in citizenship behavior when the environment was consistently ethical and *apolitical*.

Third, when employees see politics as a threat, they often respond with **defensive behaviors**—reactive and protective behaviors to avoid action, blame, or change.[67] (Exhibit 13-5 provides some examples.) In the short run, employees may find that defensiveness protects their self-interest, but in the long run it wears them down. People who consistently rely on defensiveness find that eventually it is the only way they know how to behave. At that point, they lose the trust and support of their peers, bosses, employees, and clients.

defensive behaviors   Reactive and protective behaviors to avoid action, blame, or change.

Impression Management

We know people have an ongoing interest in how others perceive and evaluate them. For example, North Americans spend billions of dollars on diets, health club memberships, cosmetics, and plastic surgery—all intended to make them more attractive to others. Being perceived positively by others has benefits in an organizational setting. It might, for instance, help us initially to get the jobs we

Exhibit 13-5	Defensive Behaviors

Avoiding Action

Overconforming. Strictly interpreting your responsibility by saying things like "The rules clearly state..."or "This is the way we've always done it."

Buck passing. Transferring responsibility for the execution of a task or decision to someone else.

Playing dumb. Avoiding an unwanted task by falsely pleading ignorance or inability

Stretching. Prolonging a task so that one person appears to be occupied—for example, turning a two-week task into a 4-month job.

Stalling. Appearing to be more or less supportive publicly while doing little or nothing privately.

Avoiding Blame

Bluffing. Rigorously documenting activity to project an image of competence and thoroughness, known as "covering your rear."

Playing safe. Evading situations that may reflect unfavorably. It includes taking on only projects with a high probability of success, having risky decisions approved by superiors, qualifying expressions of judgment, and taking neutral positions in conflicts.

Justifying. Developing explanations that lessen one's responsibility for a negative outcome and/or apologizing to demonstrate remorse, or both.

Scapegoating. Placing the blame for a negative outcome on external factors that are not entirely blameworthy.

Misrepresenting. Manipulation of information by distortion, embellishment, deception, selective presentation, or obfuscation.

Avoiding Change

Prevention. Trying to prevent a threatening change from occurring.

Self-protection. Acting in ways to protect one's self-interest during change by guarding information or other resources.

---

impression management (IM) The process by which individuals attempt to control the impression others form of them.

want in an organization and, once hired, to get favorable evaluations, superior salary increases, and more rapid promotions. The process by which individuals attempt to control the impression others form of them is called **impression management (IM)**.[68]

Who might we predict will engage in IM? No surprise here. It's our old friend, the high self-monitor.[69] Low self-monitors tend to present images of themselves that are consistent with their personalities, regardless of the beneficial or detrimental effects for them. In contrast, high self-monitors are good at reading situations and molding their appearances and behavior to fit each situation. If you want to control the impression others form of you, what IM techniques can you use? Exhibit 13-6 summarizes some of the most popular with examples.

Keep in mind when people engage in IM, they are sending a false message that might be true under other circumstances.[70] Excuses, for instance, may be offered with sincerity. Referring to the example in Exhibit 13-6, you can *actually* believe that ads contribute little to sales in your region. But misrepresentation can have a high cost. If you "cry wolf" once too often, no one is likely to believe you when the wolf really comes. So the impression manager must be cautious not to be perceived as insincere or manipulative.[71]

One study found that when managers attributed an employee's citizenship behaviors to impression management, they actually felt angry (probably because they felt manipulated) and gave subordinates lower performance ratings. When managers attributed the same behaviors to prosocial values and concern about the organization, they felt happy and gave higher performance ratings.[72] In sum,

Exhibit 13-6   Impression Management (IM) Techniques

Conformity

Agreeing with someone else's opinion to gain his or her approval is a *form of ingratiation.*

Example: A manager tells his boss, "You're absolutely right on your reorganization plan for the western regional office. I couldn' t agree with you more."

Favors

Doing something nice for someone to gain that person' s approval is a *form of ingratiation.*

Example: A salesperson says to a prospective client, "I've got two tickets to the theater tonight that I can't use. Take them. Consider it a thank-you for taking the time to talk with me."

Excuses

Explaining a predicament-creating event aimed at minimizing the apparent severity of the predicament is a *defensive IM technique.*

Example: A sales manager says to her boss, "We failed to get the ad in the paper on time, but no one responds to those ads anyway."

Apologies

Admitting responsibility for an undesirable event and simultaneously seeking to get a pardon for the action is a *defensive IM technique.*

Example: An employee says to his boss, "I'm sorry I made a mistake on the report. Please forgive me."

Self-Promotion

Highlighting your best qualities, downplaying your deficits, and calling attention to your achievements is a *self-focused IM technique.*

Example: A salesperson tells his boss, "Matt worked unsuccessfully for three years to try to get that account. I sewed it up in six weeks. I'm the best closer this company has."

Enhancement

Claiming that something you did is more valuable than most other members of the organizations would think is a *self-focused IM technique.*

Example: A journalist tells his editor, "My work on this celebrity divorce story was really a major boost to our sales" (even though the story only made it to page 3 in the entertainment section).

Flattery

Complimenting others about their virtues in an effort to make yourself appear perceptive and likeable is an *assertive IM technique.*

Example: A new sales trainee says to her peer, "You handled that client's complaint so tactfully! I could never have handled that as well as you did."

Exemplification

Doing more than you need to in an effort to show how dedicated and hard working you are is an *assertive IM technique.*

Example: An employee sends e-mails from his work computer when he works late so that his supervisor will know how long he's been working.

Sources: M. C. Bolino, K. M. Kacmar, W. H. Turnley, and J. B. Gilstrap, "A Multi-Level Review of Impression Management Motives and Behaviors," *Journal of Management* 34, no. 6 (2008): 1080–109.

people don't like to feel others are manipulating them through impression management, so such tactics should be employed with caution. Not all impression management consists of talking yourself up, either. Recent research suggests modesty, in the form of generously providing credit to others and understating your own contributions to success, may create a more positive impression on others.[73]

How Much Should You Manage Interviewer Impressions?

Almost everyone agrees that dressing professionally, highlighting previous accomplishments, and expressing interest in the job are reasonable impression management tactics to improve your presentation in an interview. Strategies like flattering the interviewer and using positive nonverbal cues like smiling and nodding are also often advised.

Is there an upside to such impression management? Research generally shows there is. The more effort applicants put into highlighting their skills, motivation, and admiration for the organization, the more likely they are to be hired. A recent study in Taiwan examined this relationship, finding that interviewers saw applicants who talked confidently about their qualifications as a better fit for the job, and applicants who said positive things about the organization as a better fit for the organization. Positive nonverbal cues improved interviewer moods, which also improved the applicant's ratings.

Despite evidence that making an effort to impress an interviewer can pay off, you can go too far. Evidence that a person misrepresented qualifications in the hiring process is usually grounds for immediate termination. Even "white lies" are a problem if they create unfounded expectations. For example, if you noted you managed budgets in the past when all you were doing was tracking expenditures, you lack skills your boss will expect you to have. When you fail to deliver, it will look very bad for you. However, if you describe your experience more accurately but note your desire to learn, the company will know you need additional training and that you'll need a bit of extra time.

So what does an ethical, effective interview strategy entail? The key is to find a positive but truthful way to manage impressions. Don't be afraid to let an employer know about your skills and accomplishments, and be sure to show your enthusiasm for the job. At the same time, keep your statements as accurate as possible, and be careful not to overstate your abilities. In the long run, you're much more likely to be happy and successful in a job where both you and the interviewer can assess fit honestly.

Sources: C. Chen and M. Lin, "The Effect of Applicant Impression Management Tactics on Hiring Recommendations: Cognitive and Affective Processes," *Applied Psychology: An International Review* 63, no. 4, (2014): 698–724; J. Levashina, C. J. Hartwell, F. P. Morgeson, and M. A. Campion "The Structured Employment Interview: Narrative and Quantitative Review of the Research Literature," *Personnel Psychology,* Spring 2014, 241–93; and M. Nemko, "The Effective, Ethical, and Less Stressful Job Interview," *Psychology Today,* March 25, 2014, https://www.psychologytoday.com/blog/how-do-life/201503/the-effective-ethical-and-less-stressful-job-interview.

Most of the studies to test the effectiveness of IM techniques have related IM to two criteria: interview success and performance evaluations. Let's consider each of these.

Interviews and IM   The evidence indicates most job applicants use IM techniques in interviews and that it works.[74] To develop a sense of how effective different IM techniques are in interviews, one study grouped data from thousands of recruiting and selection interviews into appearance-oriented efforts (like looking professional), explicit tactics (like flattering the interviewer or talking up your own accomplishments), and verbal cues (like using positive terms and showing general enthusiasm).[75] Across all the dimensions, it was quite clear that IM was a powerful predictor of how well people did. However, there was a twist. When interviews were highly structured, meaning the interviewer's questions were written out in advance and focused on applicant qualifications, the effects of IM were substantially weaker. Manipulative behaviors like IM are more likely to have an effect in ambiguous and unstructured interviews.

Performance Evaluations and IM   In terms of performance evaluations, the picture is quite different. Ingratiation is positively related to performance ratings, meaning those who ingratiate with their supervisors get higher performance evaluations. However, self-promotion appears to backfire: Those who self-promote actually may receive *lower* performance ratings.[76] There is an important qualifier to these general findings. It appears that individuals high in political skill are able to translate IM into higher performance appraisals, whereas those lower in political skill are more likely to be hurt by their IM attempts.[77] Another study of 760 boards of directors found that individuals who ingratiated themselves to current board members (expressed agreement with the director, pointed out shared attitudes and opinions, complimented the director) increased their chances of landing on a board.[78] Finally, interns who attempted to use ingratiation with their supervisors in one study were usually disliked—unless they had high levels of political skill. For those who had this ability, ingratiation led to higher levels of liking from supervisors, and higher performance ratings.[79]

What explains these consistent results across multiple studies and contexts? If you think about them, they make sense. Ingratiating always works because everyone—both interviewers and supervisors—likes to be treated nicely. However, self-promotion may work only in interviews and backfire on the job because, whereas the interviewer has little idea whether you're blowing smoke about your accomplishments, the supervisor knows because it's his or her job to observe you.

Are our conclusions about responses to politics globally valid? Should we expect employees in Israel, for instance, to respond the same way to workplace politics that employees in the United States do? Almost all our conclusions on employee reactions to organizational politics are based on studies conducted in North America. The few studies that have included other countries suggest some minor modifications.[80] One study of managers in U.S. culture and three Chinese cultures (People's Republic of China, Hong Kong, and Taiwan) found U.S. managers evaluated "gentle persuasion" tactics such as consultation and inspirational appeal as more effective than did their Chinese counterparts.[81] Other research suggests effective U.S. leaders achieve influence by focusing on the personal goals of group members and the tasks at hand (an analytical approach), whereas influential East Asian leaders focus on relationships among group members and meeting the demands of people around them (a holistic approach).[82]

The Ethics of Behaving Politically

Although there are no clear-cut ways to differentiate ethical from unethical politicking, there are some questions you should consider. For example, what is the utility of engaging in politicking? Sometimes we do it for little good reason. Major League Baseball player Al Martin claimed he played football at USC when in fact he never did. As a baseball player, he had little to gain by pretending to have played football! Outright lies like this may be a rather rare and extreme example of impression management, but many of us have at least distorted information to make a favorable impression. One thing to keep in mind is whether it's worth the risk. Another question is this: How does the utility of engaging in the political behavior balance out harm (or potential harm) it will do to others? Complimenting a supervisor on her appearance in order to curry favor is probably much less harmful than grabbing credit for a project that others deserve.

Finally, does the political activity conform to standards of equity and justice? Sometimes it is difficult to weigh the costs and benefits of a political action, but its ethicality is clear. The department head who inflates the performance evaluation of a favored employee and deflates the evaluation of a disfavored employee—and then uses these evaluations to justify giving the former a big raise and the latter nothing—has treated the disfavored employee unfairly.

Unfortunately, powerful people can become very good at explaining self-serving behaviors in terms of the organization's best interests. They can persuasively argue that unfair actions are really fair and just. Those who are powerful, articulate, and persuasive are most vulnerable to ethical lapses because they are more likely to get away with them. When faced with an ethical dilemma regarding organizational politics, try to consider whether playing politics is worth the risk and whether others might be harmed in the process. If you have a strong power base, recognize the ability of power to corrupt. Remember it's a lot easier for the powerless to act ethically, if for no other reason than they typically have very little political discretion to exploit.

✪ PERSONAL INVENTORY ASSESSMENTS

Gaining Power and Influence

Do you like power and influence? Take this PIA to learn more about gaining both.

Mapping Your Political Career

As we have seen, politics is not just for politicians. You can use the concepts presented in this chapter in some very tangible ways we have outlined in your organization. However, they also have another application: You.

One of the most useful ways to think about power and politics is in terms of your own career. What are your ambitions? Who has the power to help you achieve them? What is your relationship to these people? The best way to answer these questions is with a political map, which can help you sketch out your relationships with the people upon whom your career depends. Exhibit 13-7 contains such a political map.[83] Let's walk through it.

Assume your future promotion depends on five people, including Jamie, your immediate supervisor. As you can see in the exhibit, you have a close relationship with Jamie (you would be in real trouble otherwise). You also have a close relationship with Zack in finance. However, with the others you have either a loose relationship (Lane) or none at all (Jia, Marty). One obvious implication of this map is the need to formulate a plan to gain more influence over, and a closer relationship with, these people. How might you do that?

The map also provides for a useful way to think about the power network. Assume the five individuals all have their own networks. In this case, though, assume these aren't so much power networks like yours as they are influence networks of the people who influence the individuals in power positions.

One of the best ways to influence people is indirectly. What if you played in a tennis league with Mark, Jamie's former coworker who you know remains friends with Jamie? To influence Mark, in many cases, may also be to influence Marty. Why not post an entry on CJ's blog? You can complete a similar analysis for the other four decision-makers and their networks.

Of course, this map doesn't show you everything you need to know—no map does. For example, rarely would all five people have the same amount of power. Moreover, maps are harder to construct in the era of large social networks. Try to keep this basic, limited to the people who *really* matter to your career.

All of this may seem a bit Machiavellian to you. However, remember, only one person gets the promotion, and your competition may have a map of his or her own. As we noted in the early part of the chapter, power and politics are a part of organizational life. To decide not to play is deciding not to be effective. Better to be explicit with a political map than to proceed as if power and politics didn't matter.

| Exhibit 13-7 | Drawing Your Political Map |

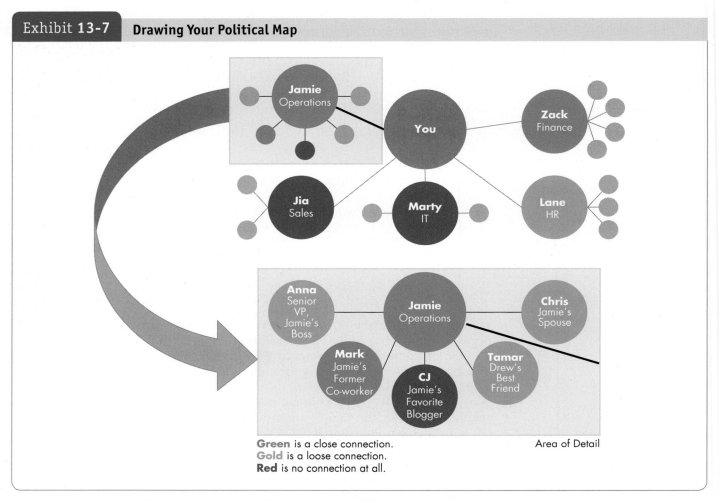

Green is a close connection.
Gold is a loose connection.
Red is no connection at all.

Area of Detail

Source: Based on Clark, "A Campaign Strategy for Your Career," *Harvard Business Review,* November 2012, 131–34.

Summary

Few employees relish being powerless in their jobs and organizations. People respond differently to the various power bases. Expert and referent power are derived from an individual's personal qualities. In contrast, coercion, reward, and legitimate power are essentially organizationally granted. Competence especially appears to offer wide appeal, and its use as a power base results in high performance by group members.

An effective manager accepts the political nature of organizations. Some people are more politically astute than others, meaning they are aware of the underlying politics and can manage impressions. Those who are good at playing politics can be expected to get higher performance evaluations and, hence, larger salary increases and more promotions than the politically naïve or inept. The politically astute are also likely to exhibit higher job satisfaction and be better able to neutralize job stressors.

Implications for Managers

- To maximize your power, increase others' dependence on you. For instance, increase your power in relation to your boss by developing a needed knowledge or skill for which there is no ready substitute.
- You will not be alone in attempting to build your power bases. Others, particularly employees and peers, will be seeking to increase your dependence on them, while you are trying to minimize it and increase their dependence on you.
- Try to avoid putting others in a position where they feel they have no power.
- By assessing behavior in a political framework, you can better predict the actions of others and use that information to formulate political strategies that will gain advantages for you and your work unit.
- Consider that employees who have poor political skills or are unwilling to play the politics game generally relate perceived organizational politics to lower job satisfaction and self-reported performance, increased anxiety, and higher turnover. Therefore, if you are adept at organizational politics, help others understand the importance of becoming politically savvy.

Everyone Wants Power

POINT

COUNTERPOINT

We don't admit to everything we want. For instance, one psychologist found people would seldom admit to wanting money, but they thought everyone else wanted it. They were half right—everyone wants money. And everyone wants power.

Harvard psychologist David McClelland was justifiably famous for his study of underlying motives. McClelland measured people's motivation for power based on how they described pictures (this method is called the Thematic Apperception Test, or TAT). Why didn't he simply ask people how much they wanted power? Because he believed that many more people really wanted power than would admit or even consciously realize. And that's exactly what he found.

Why do we want power? Because it is good for us. It gives us more control over our own lives. It gives us more freedom to do as we wish. There are few things worse in life than feeling helpless, and few better than feeling in charge of your destiny. Research shows people with power and status command more respect from others, have higher self-esteem (no surprise there), and enjoy better health than those of less stature.

Take Steve Cohen, founder of SAC Capital Advisors and one of the most powerful men on Wall Street. Worth $11.1 billion, Cohen buys Picassos, lives in a mansion, has white-gloved butlers, and travels the world first class. People will do almost anything to please him—or to even get near him. One writer notes, "Inside his offices, vast fortunes are won and lost. Careers are made and unmade. Type-A egos are inflated and crushed, sometimes in the space of hours." All this is bad for Steve Cohen how?

Usually, people who tell you power doesn't matter are those who have no hope of getting it. Wanting power, like being jealous, can be one of those secrets people just won't admit to.

Of course it's true that some people desire power—and often behave ruthlessly to get it. For most of us, however, power is not high in priority, and for some, it's actually undesirable.

Research shows most individuals feel uncomfortable when placed in powerful positions. One study asked individuals, before they began work in a four-person team, to "rank, from 1 [highest] to 4 [lowest], in terms of status and influence within the group, what rank you would like to achieve." Only about one-third (34 percent) of participants chose the highest rank. In a second study, researchers focused on employees participating in Amazon's Mechanical Turk online service. They found that the main reason people wanted power was to earn respect. If they could get respect without gaining power, that was preferred. In a third study, researchers found individuals desired power only when they had high ability—in other words, when their influence helped their groups.

These studies suggest that we often confuse the desire for power with other things—like the desire to be respected and to help our groups and organizations succeed. In these cases, power is something most of us seek for more benevolent ends—and only when we think it does good.

Another study confirmed that most people want respect from their peers, not power. Cameron Anderson, the author of this research, sums it up nicely: "You don't have to be rich to be happy, but instead be a valuable contributing member to your groups. What makes a person high in status in a group is being engaged, generous with others, and making self sacrifices for the greater good."

Oh, and about Steve Cohen...you realize he pleaded guilty and paid a $1.2 billion fine for failing to prevent insider trading and then had to shut down SAC, right?

Sources: B. Burrough and B. McLean, "The Hunt for Steve Cohen," *Vanity Fair,* June 2013, http://www.vanityfair.com/news/business/2013/06/steve-cohen-insider-trading-case; C. Anderson, R. Willer, G. J. Kilduff, and C. E. Brown, "The Origins of Deference: When Do People Prefer Lower Status?" *Journal of Personality and Social Psychology* 102 (2012): 1077–88; C. Anderson, M. W Kraus, A. D. Galinsky, and D. Keltner, "The Local-Ladder Effect: Social Status and Subjective Well-Being," *Psychological Science 23*(7) (2012): 764–71; S. Kennelly, "Happiness Is about Respect, Not Riches," *Greater Good,* July 13, 2012, http://greatergood.berkeley.edu/article/item/happiness_is_about_respect_not_riches; and P. Lattman and B. Protess, "$1.2 Billion Fine for Hedge Fund SAC Capital in Insider Case," *The New York Times Dealbook,* November 4, 2013, http://dealbook.nytimes.com/2013/11/04/sac-capital-agrees-to-plead-guilty-to-insider-trading/?_r=0.

CHAPTER REVIEW

MyManagementLab

Go to **mymanagementlab.com** to complete the problems marked with this icon. ★

QUESTIONS FOR REVIEW

13-1 How is leadership different from power?

13-2 What are the similarities and differences among the five bases of power?

13-3 What is the role of dependence in power relationships?

13-4 What are the most often identified power or influence tactics and their contingencies?

13-5 What are the causes and consequences of abuse of power?

13-6 How do politics work in organizations?

13-7 What are the causes, consequences, and ethics of political behavior?

EXPERIENTIAL EXERCISE Comparing Influence Tactics

Students working in groups of three are each assigned to a role. One person is the influencer, one will be influenced, and one is the observer. These roles can be randomly determined.

To begin, students create a deck of cards for the seven *tactics* to be used in the exercise. These are legitimacy, rational persuasion, inspirational appeals, consultation, exchange, ingratiation, and pressure (defined in the chapter). Only the influencer draws cards from the set, and no one else may see what has been drawn.

The influencer draws a card and quickly formulates and acts out a strategy to use this tactic on the party being influenced. The person being influenced reacts realistically in a back-and-forth exchange over a brief period and states whether or not the tactic was effective. The observer attempts to determine which tactic is being used and which

power base (coercive, reward, legitimate, expert, or referent) would reinforce this tactic. The influencer confirms or denies the approach used.

Change the roles and cards throughout the rounds. Afterward, the class discusses:

13-8. Based on your observations, which influence situation would probably have resulted in the best outcome for the person doing the influencing?

13-9. Was there a good match between the tactics drawn and the specific role each person took? In other words, was the tactic useful for the influencer given his or her base of power relative to the person being influenced?

13-10. What lessons about power and influence does this exercise teach us?

ETHICAL DILEMMA How Much Should You Defer to Those in Power?

Though it is not always easy to admit to ourselves, often we adapt our behavior to suit those in power. To some degree, it is important for organizational success that we do so. After all, people are in positions of authority for a reason, and if no one paid attention to the rules these people put in place, chaos would rule. But is it always ethical for us to defer to the powerful?

More often than we acknowledge, powerful individuals in organizations push our actions into ethical gray areas, or worse. For example, managers of restaurants and stores (including McDonald's, Applebee's, Taco Bell, Winn Dixie, and others) were persuaded to strip-search customers or employees when an individual impersonating a police officer phoned in and instructed them to do so.

What would you do if you thought a police officer, definitely a symbol of power, ordered you to do something you'd never choose to do as manager?

Outright abuses aside, power is wielded over us in more prosaic ways. For example, many stock analysts report pressure from their bosses to promote funds from which the organization profits most (a fact that is not disclosed to their clients). These might be good funds that the analysts would promote anyway. But maybe they're not. Should the analyst ever promote the funds without discussing the conflict of interest with the client?

Few of us might think we would perform strip-searches. But examples of power taken to the limit highlight the disturbing tendency of many of us to conform to the wishes of those in power. For all of us, knowing that blindly deferring to those in power might cause us to cross ethical lines is enough to keep us thinking.

Questions

13-11. Do you think people tailor their behavior to suit those in power more than they admit? Is that something you do?

13-12. One writer commented that bending behavior to suit those in power reminds "anyone who is under pressure to carry out orders from 'above' to constantly question the validity and prudence of what they're being asked to do." Why don't we question this more often?

13-13. What factors influence how we respond to those with power?

Sources: J. Sancton, "Milgram at McDonald's," *Bloomberg Businessweek*, September 2, 2012, 74–75; and A. Wolfson, "Compliance' Re-Creates McDonald's Strip-Search Ordeal," *USA Today*, September 1, 2012, http://usatoday30.usatoday.com/news/nation/story/2012-09-01/Compliance-strip-search-hoax/57509182/1).

CASE INCIDENT 1 Reshaping the Dubai Model

In early 2013, analysts were warning that Dubai was suffering from the global downturn. Managers and employees across all sectors were worrying about their jobs. Property owners were seeing spectacular falls in the value of their investments. Dubai had been renowned for its extravagant projects and schemes. What had been seen as a glowing example of growth and prosperity was now being cited as an example of a country in crisis management. Dubai's debt burden had reached US $100 billion.

Dubai has always been a magnet for investors. It went tax-free at the beginning of the twentieth century, but by the 1960s, oil revenue funded huge infrastructure projects. Dubai does not have significant oil reserves, so the focus has been on commerce, tourism, and aviation. To some extent it has embraced western lifestyles and courted multi-nationals. While the UAE as a whole, with its rich reserves of oil, had the capacity to ride out the global downturn, Dubai itself would need a radical rethink.

The rethink would come in the shape of new leadership. Out went the ambition to be the regional hub for 2 billion people. Just nine years before, Dubai had been able to confidently state that investors in Dubai would see greater returns on their capital (then around 18 per cent) than leaving their funds in the bank. Dubai could boast that no one who had invested in the city had ever gone bankrupt.

Key decision makers like Sultan bin Sulayem, Chairman of Dubai World; Mohammed al-Gergawi, Chairman of Dubai Holdings; and Mohammed Alabbar, Chairman of Emaar Properties, all lost influence. New, more conservative decision-makers were on the rise, such as Mohammed al-Shaibani, Ahmed al-Tayer, and Abdulrahman al-Saleh. The new decision-makers already had a reputation for careful mergers and acquisitions, cost-cutting exercises and dealing with financial problems.

The "new" men are a combination of close advisers to the ruler, Sheikh Mohammed bin Rashid al-Maktoum, members of old merchant families and, above all, more conservative in their financial approach.

Questions

13-14. How would you prioritize and delegate the tasks of the new key decisions-makers in Dubai?

13-15. Control of decision-making and financial expenditure was the root cause of the debt situation in Dubai. Sheikh Mohammed bin Rashid Al Maktoum has delegated to people who can make decisions on his behalf. Would a more "hands on" approach be more effective, or would this hinder progress?

13-16. Abu Dhabi provides much of the funding for the UAE central bank. They have bankrolled Dubai at cost in terms of political and economic freedom. To what extent do you think Dubai is losing its ability to make its own decisions?

Sources: Roula Khalaf, Simeon Kerr, and Andrew England, "Reinventing Dubai," *Business Spectator*, http://www.businessspectator.com.au/article/2013/2/22/global-financial-crisis/reinventing-dubai, accessed January 23, 2014.

CASE INCIDENT 2 Barry's Peer Becomes His Boss

As Barry looked out the window of his office in Toronto, the gloomy October skies obscured his usual view of CN Tower. "That figures," Barry thought to himself—his mood was just as gloomy.

Five months earlier, Barry's company, CTM, a relatively small but growing technology firm, reorganized itself. Although such reorganizations often imperil careers, Barry felt the change only improved his position. His coworker, Raphael, was promoted out of the department, which made sense because Raphael had been with the company for a few more years and had worked with the CEO on a successful project. Because Raphael was promoted and their past work roles were similar, Barry thought his own promotion was soon to come.

However, 6 weeks ago, Barry's boss left. Raphael was transferred back to the department and became Barry's boss. Although Barry felt a bit overlooked, he knew he was still relatively junior in the company and felt his good past relationship with Raphael would bode well for his future prospects.

The new arrangement, however, brought nothing but disappointment. Although Raphael often told Barry he was doing a great job, Barry felt that opinion was not being shared with the higher-ups. Worse, a couple of Barry's friends in the company showed Barry e-mails in which Raphael had failed to make Berry look good.

"Raphael is not the person I thought he was," thought Barry.

What was his future in the company if no one understood his contributions? He thought about looking for another job, but that prospect only darkened his mood further. He liked the company. He felt he did good work there.

As Barry looked out his window again, a light rain began to fall. The CN Tower was no more visible than before. He just didn't know what to do.

Questions

13-17. Should Barry complain about his treatment? To whom? If he does complain, what power tactics should Barry use?

★13-18. Studies have shown those prone to complaining or "whining" tend to have less power in an organization. Do you think whining leads to diminished power and influence, or the other way around? How can Barry avoid appearing to be a "whiner"?

13-19. Do you think Barry should look for another job? Why or why not?

Sources: Based on M. G. McIntyre, "Disgruntlement Won't Advance Your Career," *Pittsburgh Post-Gazette,* September 23, 2012, http://www.post-gazette.com/business/employment/2012/09/23/ Office-Coach-Disgruntlement-won-t-advance-career/stories/201209230192); and S. Shellenbarger, "What to Do with a Workplace Whiner," *The Wall Street Journal,* September 12, 2012, D1, D3.

MyManagementLab

Go to **mymanagementlab.com** for the following Assisted-graded writing questions:

13-20. In Case Incident 1, how would you expect employees who have to sign over their rights to their creative projects react in the short term? In the long term?

13-21. After reading the chapter and Case Incident 2, what impression management techniques would you say Raphael is using?

13-22. **MyManagementLab Only** – comprehensive writing assignment for this chapter.

ENDNOTES

[1] D. A. Buchanan, "You Stab My Back, I'll Stab Yours: Management Experience and Perceptions of Organization Political Behavior," *British Journal of Management* 19, no. 1 (2008): 49–64.

[2] B. Oc, M. R. Bashshur, and C. Moore, "Speaking Truth to Power: The Effect of Candid Feedback on How Individuals with Power Allocate Resources," *Journal of Applied Psychology* 100, no. 2 (2015): 450–63.

[3] M. Gongloff, "Steve Cohen, Super-Rich and Secretive Trader, Faces Possible SEC Investigation," *Huffington Post*, November 28, 2012, http://www.huffingtonpost.com/2012/11/28/steven-cohen-sac-capital_n_2205544.html.

[4] E. Landells and S. L. Albrecht, "Organizational Political Climate: Shared Perceptions about the Building and Use of Power Bases," *Human Resource Management Review* 23, no. 4 (2013): 357–65; P. Rylander, "Coaches' Bases of Power: Developing Some Initial Knowledge of Athletes' Compliance with Coaches in Team Sports," *Journal of Applied Sport Psychology* 27, no. 1 (2015): 110–21; and G. Yukl, "Use Power Effectively," in E. A. Locke (ed.), *Handbook of Principles of Organizational Behavior* (Malden, MA: Blackwell, 2004): 242–47.

[5] E. A. Ward, "Social Power Bases of Managers: Emergence of a New Factor," *Journal of Social Psychology*, February 2001, 144–47.

[6] S. R. Giessner and T. W. Schubert, "High in the Hierarchy: How Vertical Location and Judgments of Leaders' Power Are Interrelated," *Organizational Behavior and Human Decision Processes* 104, no. 1 (2007): 30–44.

[7] S. Perman, "Translation Advertising: Where Shop Meets Hip Hop," *Time*, August 30, 2010, http://content.time.com/time/magazine/article/0,9171,2011574,00.html.

[8] R. E. Sturm and J. Antonakis, "Interpersonal Power: A Review, Critique, and Research Agenda," *Journal of Management* 41, no. 1 (2015): 136–63.

[9] M. C. J. Caniels and A. Roeleveld, "Power and Dependence Perpsectives on Outsourcing Decisions," *European Management Journal* 27, no. 6 (2009): 402–17; and R.-J. Bryan, D. Kim, and R. S. Sinkovics, "Drivers and Performance Outcomes of Supplier Innovation Generation in Customer-Supplier Relationships: The Role of Power-Dependence," *Decision Sciences*, 2012, 1003–38.

[10] N. Foulkes, "Tractor Boy," *High Life*, October 2002, 90.

[11] R.S. Burt, M. Kilduff, and S. Tasselli, "Social Network Analysis: Foundations and Frontiers on Advantage," *Annual Review of Psychology* 64 (2013): 527–47; M. A. Carpenter, M. Li, and H. Jiang, "Social Network Research in Organizational Contexts: A Systematic Review of Methodological Issues and Choices," *Journal of Management*, July 1, 2012, 1328–61; and M. Kilduff and D. J. Brass, "Organizational Social Network Research: Core Ideas and Key Debates." *Academy of Management Annals*, January 1, 2010, 317–57.

[12] J. Gehman, L. K. Treviño, and R. Garud, "Values Work: A Process Study of the Emergence and Performance of Organizational Values Practices," *Academy of Management Journal*, February 1, 2013, 84–112.

[13] J. Battilana and T. Casciaro, "Change Agents, Networks, and Institutions: A Contingency Theory of Organizational Change," *Academy of Management Journal*, April 1, 2012, 381–98.

[14] S. M. Soltis, F. Agneessens, Z. Sasovova, and G. Labianca, "A Social Network Perspective on Turnover Intentions: The Role of Distributive Justice and Social Support," *Human Resource Management*, July 1, 2013, 561–84.

[15] R. Kaše, Z. King, and D. Minbaeva, "Using Social Network Research in HRM: Scratching the Surface of a Fundamental Basis of HRM," *Human Resource Management*, July 1, 2013, 473–83; R. Cross and L. Prusak, "The People Who Make Organizations Go—Or Stop," *Harvard Business Review*, June 2002, https://hbr.org/2002/06/the-people-who-make-organizations-go-or-stop.

[16] See, for example, D. M. Cable and T. A. Judge, "Managers' Upward Influence Tactic Strategies: The Roll of Manager Personality and Supervisor Leadership Style," *Journal of Organizational Behavior* 24, no. 2 (2003): 197–214; M. P. M. Chong, "Influence Behaviors and Organizational Commitment: A Comparative Study," *Leadership and Organization Development Journal* 35, no. 1 (2014): 54–78; and G. Blickle, "Influence Tactics Used by Subordinates: An Empirical Analysis of the Kipnis and Schmidt Subscales," *Psychological Reports*, February 2000, 143–54.

[17] G. R. Ferris, W. A. Hochwarter, C. Douglas, F. R. Blass, R. W. Kolodinksy, and D. C. Treadway, "Social Influence Processes in Organizations and Human Resource Systems," in G. R. Ferris and J. J. Martocchio (eds.), *Research in Personnel and Human Resources Management*, vol. 21 (Oxford, UK: JAI Press/Elsevier, 2003), 65–127; C. A. Higgins, T. A. Judge, and G. R. Ferris, "Influence Tactics and Work Outcomes: A Meta-Analysis," *Journal of Organizational Behavior*, March 2003, 89–106; and M. Uhl-Bien, R. E. Riggio, K. B. Lowe, and M. K. Carsten. "Followership Theory: A Review and Research Agenda," *The Leadership Quarterly*, February 2014, 83–104.

[18] M. P. M. Chong, "Influence Behaviors and Organizational Commitment: A Comparative Study."

[19] R. E. Petty and P. Briñol, "Persuasion: From Single to Multiple to Metacognitive Processes," *Perspectives on Psychological Science* 3, no. 2 (2008): 137–47.

[20] J. Badal, "Getting a Raise from the Boss," *The Wall Street Journal*, July 8, 2006, B1, B5.

[21] M. P. M. Chong, "Influence Behaviors and Organizational Commitment: A Comparative Study."

[22] Ibid.

[23] O. Epitropaki and R. Martin, "Transformational-Transactional Leadership and Upward Influence: The Role of Relative Leader-Member Exchanges (RLMX) and Perceived Organizational Support (POS), *Leadership Quarterly* 24, no. 2 (2013): 299–315.

[24] A. W. Kruglanski, A. Pierro, and E. T. Higgins, "Regulatory Mode and Preferred Leadership Styles: How Fit Increases Job Satisfaction," *Basic and Applied Social Psychology* 29, no. 2 (2007): 137–49; and A. Pierro, L. Cicero, and B. H. Raven, "Motivated Compliance with Bases of Social Power," *Journal of Applied Social Psychology* 38, no. 7 (2008): 1921–44.

[25] P. P. Fu and G. Yukl, "Perceived Effectiveness of Influence Tactics in the United States and China," *Leadership Quarterly*, Summer 2000, 251–66; O. Branzei, "Cultural Explanations of Individual Preferences for Influence Tactics in Cross-Cultural Encounters," *International Journal of Cross Cultural Management*, August 2002, 203–18; G. Yukl, P. P. Fu, and R. McDonald, "Cross-Cultural Differences in Perceived Effectiveness of Influence Tactics for Initiating or Resisting Change," *Applied Psychology: An International Review*, January 2003, 66–82; and P. P. Fu, T. K. Peng, J. C. Kennedy, and G. Yukl, "Examining the Preferences of Influence Tactics in Chinese Societies: A Comparison of Chinese Managers in Hong Kong, Taiwan, and Mainland China," *Organizational Dynamics* 33, no. 1 (2004): 32–46.

[26]C. J. Torelli and S. Shavitt, "Culture and Concepts of Power," *Journal of Personality and Social Psychology* 99, no. 4 (2010): 703–23.

[27]Fu and Yukl, "Perceived Effectiveness of Influence Tactics in the United States and China."

[28]G. R. Ferris, D. C. Treadway, P. L. Perrewé, R. L. Brouer, C. Douglas, and S. Lux, "Political Skill in Organizations," *Journal of Management,* June 2007, 290–320; K. J. Harris, K. M. Kacmar, S. Zivnuska, and J. D. Shaw, "The Impact of Political Skill on Impression Management Effectiveness," *Journal of Applied Psychology* 92, no. 1 (2007): 278–85; W. A. Hochwarter, G. R. Ferris, M. B. Gavin, P. L. Perrewé, A. T. Hall, and D. D. Frink, "Political Skill as Neutralizer of Felt Accountability–Job Tension Effects on Job Performance Ratings: A Longitudinal Investigation," *Organizational Behavior and Human Decision Processes* 102 (2007): 226–39; and D. C. Treadway, G. R. Ferris, A. B. Duke, G. L. Adams, and J. B. Tatcher, "The Moderating Role of Subordinate Political Skill on Supervisors' Impressions of Subordinate Ingratiation and Ratings of Subordinate Interpersonal Facilitation," *Journal of Applied Psychology* 92, no. 3 (2007): 848–55.

[29]M. C. Andrews, K. M. Kacmar, and K. J. Harris, "Got Political Skill? The Impact of Justice on the Importance of Political Skills for Job Performance," *Journal of Applied Psychology* 94, no. 6 (2009): 1427–37.

[30]C. Anderson, S. E. Spataro, and F. J. Flynn, "Personality and Organizational Culture as Determinants of Influence," *Journal of Applied Psychology* 93, no. 3 (2008): 702–10.

[31]Y. Cho and N. J. Fast, "Power, Defensive Denigration, and the Assuaging Effect of Gratitude Expression," *Journal of Experimental Social Psychology* 48 (2012): 778–82.

[32]M. Pitesa and S. Thau, "Masters of the Universe: How Power and Accountability Influence Self-Serving Decisions under Moral Hazard," *Journal of Applied Psychology* 98 (2013): 550–58; N. J. Fast, N. Sivanathan, D. D. Mayer, and A. D. Galinsky, "Power and Overconfident Decision-Making," *Organizational Behavior and Human Decision Processes* 117 (2012): 249–60; M. J. Williams, "Serving the Self from the Seat of Power: Goals and Threats Predict Leaders' Self-Interested Behavior," *Journal of Management* 40 (2014): 1365–95.

[33]A. Grant, "Yes, Power Corrupts, but Power Also Reveals," *Government Executive,* May 23, 2013, http://www.huffingtonpost.com/adam-grant/yes-power-corrupts-but-po_b_3085291.html.

[34]J. K. Maner, M. T. Gaillot, A. J. Menzel, and J. W. Kunstman, "Dispositional Anxiety Blocks the Psychological Effects of Power," *Personality and Social Psychology Bulletin* 38 (2012): 1383–95.

[35]N. J. Fast, N. Halevy, and A. D. Galinsky, "The Destructive Nature of Power without Status," *Journal of Experimental Social Psychology* 48 (2012): 391–94.

[36]T. Seppälä, J. Lipponen, A. Bardi, and A. Pirttilä-Backman, Change-Oriented Organizational Citizenship Behaviour: An Interactive Product of Openness to Change Values, Work Unit Identification, and Sense of Power," *Journal of Occupational and Organizational Psychology* 85 (2012): 136–55.

[37]K. A. DeCelles, D. S. DeRue, J. D. Margolis, and T. L. Ceranic, "Does Power Corrupt or Enable? When and Why Power Facilitates Self-Interested Behavior," *Journal of Applied Psychology* 97 (2012): 681–89.

[38]"Facts about Sexual Harassment," The U.S. Equal Employment Opportunity Commission, www.eeoc.gov/facts/fs-sex.html, accessed June 19, 2015.

[39]F. Ali and R. Kramar, "An Exploratory Study of Sexual Harassment in Pakistani Organizations," *Asia Pacific Journal of Management* 32, no. 1 (2014): 229–49.

[40]Ibid.

[41]Workplace Sexual Harassment Statistics, Association of Women for Action and Research, 2015, http://www.aware.org.sg/ati/wsh-site/14-statistics/.

[42]R. Ilies, N. Hauserman, S. Schwochau, and J. Stibal, "Reported Incidence Rates of Work-Related Sexual Harassment in the United States: Using Meta-Analysis to Explain Reported Rate Disparities," *Personnel Psychology,* Fall 2003, 607–31; and G. Langer, "One in Four U.S. Women Reports Workplace Harassment," *ABC News,* November 16, 2011, http://abcnews.go.com/blogs/politics/2011/11/one-in-four-u-s-women-reports-workplace-harassment/.

[43]"Sexual Harassment Charges," Equal Employment Opportunity Commission, from www.eeoc.gov/eeoc/statistics/, accessed August 20, 2015.

[44]B. Popken, "Report: 80% of Waitresses Report Being Sexually Harassed," *USA Today,* October 7, 2014, http://www.today.com/money/report-80-waitresses-report-being-sexually-harassed-2D80199724.

[45]L. M. Cortina and S. A. Wasti, "Profiles in Coping: Responses to Sexual Harassment across Persons, Organizations, and Cultures," *Journal of Applied Psychology,* February 2005, 182–92; K. Jiang, Y. Hong, P. F. McKay, D. R. Avery, D. C. Wilson, and S. D. Volpone, "Retaining Employees through Anti-Sexual Harassment Practices: Exploring the Mediating Role of Psychological Distress and Employee Engagement," *Human Resource Management* 54, no. 1 (2015): 1–21; and J. W. Kunstman, "Sexual Overperception: Power, Mating Motives, and Biases in Social Judgment," *Journal of Personality and Social Psychology* 100, no. 2 (2011): 282–94.

[46]F. Krings and S. Facchin, "Organizational Justice and Men's Likelihood to Sexually Harass: The Moderating Role of Sexism and Personality," *Journal of Applied Psychology* 94, no. 2 (2009): 501–10.

[47]G. R. Ferris, D. C. Treadway, R. W. Kolokinsky, W. A. Hochwarter, C. J. Kacmar, and D. D. Frink, "Development and Validation of the Political Skill Inventory," *Journal of Management,* February 2005, 126–52.

[48]A. Pullen and C. Rhodes, "Corporeal Ethics and the Politics of Resistance in Organizations," *Organization* 21, no. 6 (2014): 782–96.

[49]G. R. Ferris and W. A. Hochwarter, "Organizational Politics," in S. Zedeck (ed.), *APA Handbook of Industrial and Organizational Psychology,* vol. 3 (Washington, DC: American Psychological Association, 2011), 435–59.

[50]D. A. Buchanan, "You Stab My Back, I'll Stab Yours: Management Experience and Perceptions of Organization Political Behavior," *British Journal of Management* 19, no. 1 (2008): 49–64.

[51]J. Pfeffer, *Power: Why Some People Have It—And Others Don't* (New York: Harper Collins, 2010).

[52]S. M. Rioux and L. A. Penner, "The Causes of Organizational Citizenship Behavior: A Motivational Analysis," *Journal of Applied Psychology,* December 2001, 1306–14; M. A. Finkelstein and L. A. Penner, "Predicting Organizational Citizenship Behavior: Integrating the Functional and Role Identity Approaches," *Social Behavior & Personality* 32, no. 4 (2004): 383–98; and J. Schwarzwald, M. Koslowsky, and M. Allouf, "Group Membership, Status, and Social Power Preference," *Journal of Applied Social Psychology* 35, no. 3 (2005): 644–65.

[53]See, for example, J. Walter, F. W. Kellermans, and C. Lechner, "Decision Making within and between Organizations: Rationality, Politics, and Alliance Performance," *Journal of Management* 38, no. 5 (2012): 1582–610.

[54]G. R. Ferris, D. C. Treadway, P. L. Perrewe, R. L. Grouer, C. Douglas, and S. Lux, "Political Skill in Organizations," *Journal of Management* 33 (2007): 290–320.

[55]J. Shi, R. E. Johnson, Y. Liu, and M. Wang, "Linking Subordinate Political Skill to Supervisor Dependence and Reward Recommendations: A Moderated Mediation Model," *Journal of Applied Psychology* 98 (2013): 374–84.

[56]W. A. Gentry, D. C. Gimore, M. L. Shuffler, and J. B. Leslie, "Political Skill as an Indicator of Promotability among Multiple Rater Sources," *Journal of Organizational Behavior* 33 (2012): 89–104; I. Kapoutsis, A. Paplexandris, A. Nikolopoulous, W. A. Hochwarter, and G. R. Ferris, "Politics Perceptions as a Moderator of the Political Skill-Job Performance Relationship: A Two-Study, Cross-National, Constructive Replication," *Journal of Vocational Behavior* 78 (2011): 123–35.

[57]M. Abbas, U. Raja, W. Darr, and D. Bouckenooghe, "Combined Effects of Perceived Politics and Psychological Capital on Job Satisfaction, Turnover Intentions, and Performance," *Journal of Management* 40, no. 7 (2014): 1813–30; and C. C. Rosen, D. L. Ferris, D. J. Brown, and W.-W. Yen, "Relationships among Perceptions of Organizational Politics (POPs), Work Motivation, and Salesperson Performance," *Journal of Management and Organization* 21, no. 2 (2015): 203–16.

[58]See, for example, M. D. Laird, P. Harvey, and J. Lancaster, "Accountability, Entitlement, Tenure, and Satisfaction in Generation Y," *Journal of Managerial Psychology* 30, no. 1 (2015): 87–100; J. M. L. Poon, "Situational Antecedents and Outcomes of Organizational Politics Perceptions," *Journal of Managerial Psychology* 18, no. 2 (2003): 138–55; and K. L. Zellars, W. A. Hochwarter, S. E. Lanivich, P. L. Perrewe, and G. R. Ferris, "Accountability for Others, Perceived Resources, and Well Being: Convergent Restricted Non-Linear Results in Two Samples," *Journal of Occupational and Organizational Psychology* 84, no. 1 (2011): 95–115.

[59]J. Walter, F. W. Kellermanns, and C. Lechner, "Decision Making within and between Organizations: Rationality, Politics, and Alliance Performance," *Journal of Management* 38 (2012): 1582–610.

[60]W. A. Hochwarter, C. Kiewitz, S. L. Castro, P. L. Perrewe, and G. R. Ferris, "Positive Affectivity and Collective Efficacy as Moderators of the Relationship between Perceived Politics and Job Satisfaction," *Journal of Applied Social Psychology*, May 2003, 1009–35; and C. C. Rosen, P. E. Levy, and R. J. Hall, "Placing Perceptions of Politics in the Context of Feedback Environment, Employee Attitudes, and Job Performance," *Journal of Applied Psychology* 91, no. 1 (2006): 211–30.

[61]S. Aryee, Z. Chen, and P. S. Budhwar, "Exchange Fairness and Employee Performance: An Examination of the Relationship between Organizational Politics and Procedural Justice," *Organizational Behavior & Human Decision Processes*, May 2004, 1–14.

[62]C. Kiewitz, W. A. Hochwarter, G. R. Ferris, and S. L. Castro, "The Role of Psychological Climate in Neutralizing the Effects of Organizational Politics on Work Outcomes," *Journal of Applied Social Psychology*, June 2002, 1189–207; and M. C. Andrews, L. A. Witt, and K. M. Kacmar, "The Interactive Effects of Organizational Politics and Exchange Ideology on Manager Ratings of Retention," *Journal of Vocational Behavior*, April 2003, 357–69.

[63]O. J. Labedo, "Perceptions of Organisational Politics: Examination of the Situational Antecedent and Consequences among Nigeria's Extension Personnel," *Applied Psychology: An International Review* 55, no. 2 (2006): 255–81.

[64]K. M. Kacmar, M. C. Andrews, K. J. Harris, and B. Tepper, "Ethical Leadership and Subordinate Outcomes: The Mediating Role of Organizational Politics and the Moderating Role of Political Skill," *Journal of Business Ethics* 115, no. 1 (2013): 33–44.

[65]Ibid.

[66]K. M. Kacmar, D. G. Bachrach, K. J. Harris, and S. Zivnuska, "Fostering Good Citizenship through Ethical Leadership: Exploring the Moderating Role of Gender and Organizational Politics," *Journal of Applied Psychology* 96 (2011): 633–42.

[67]C. Homburg and A. Fuerst, "See No Evil, Hear No Evil, Speak No Evil: A Study of Defensive Organizational Behavior towards Customer Complaints," *Journal of the Academy of Marketing Science* 35, no. 4 (2007): 523–36.

[68]See, for instance, M. C. Bolino and W. H. Turnley, "More Than One Way to Make an Impression: Exploring Profiles of Impression Management," *Journal of Management* 29, no. 2 (2003): 141–60; S. Zivnuska, K. M. Kacmar, L. A. Witt, D. S. Carlson, and V. K. Bratton, "Interactive Effects of Impression Management and Organizational Politics on Job Performance," *Journal of Organizational Behavior*, August 2004, 627–40; and M. C. Bolino, K. M. Kacmar, W. H. Turnley, and J. B. Gilstrap, "A Multi-Level Review of Impression Management Motives and Behaviors," *Journal of Management* 34, no. 6 (2008): 1080–109.

[69]D. J. Howard and R. A. Kerin, "Individual Differences in the Name Similarity Effect: The Role of Self-Monitoring," *Journal of Individual Differences* 35, no. 2 (2014): 111–18.

[70]D. H. M. Chng, M. S. Rodgers, E. Shih, and X.-B. Song, "Leaders' Impression Management During Organizational Decline: The Roles of Publicity, Image Concerns, and Incentive Compensation," *The Leadership Quarterly* 26, no. 2 (2015): 270–85; and L. Uziel, "Life Seems Different with You around: Differential Shifts in Cognitive Appraisal in the Mere Presence of Others for Neuroticism and Impression Management," *Personality and Individual Differences* 73 (2015): 39–43.

[71]J. Ham and R. Vonk, "Impressions of Impression Management: Evidence of Spontaneous Suspicion of Ulterior Motivation," *Journal of Experimental Social Psychology* 47, no. 2 (2011): 466–71; and W. M. Bowler, J. R. B. Halbesleben, and J. R. B. Paul, "If You're Close with the Leader, You Must Be a Brownnose: The Role of Leader–Member Relationships in Follower, Leader, and Coworker Attributions of Organizational Citizenship Behavior Motives," *Human Resource Management Review* 20, no. 4 (2010): 309–16.

[72]J. R. B. Halbesleben, W. M. Bowler, M. C. Bolino, and W. H Turnley, "Organizational Concern, Prosocial Values, or Impression Management? How Supervisors Attribute Motives to Organizational Citizenship Behavior," *Journal of Applied Social Psychology* 40, no. 6 (2010): 1450–89.

[73]G. Blickle, C. Diekmann, P. B. Schneider, Y. Kalthöfer, and J. K. Summers, "When Modesty Wins: Impression Management through Modesty, Political Skill, and Career Success—A Two-Study Investigation," *European Journal of Work and Organizational Psychology*, December 1, 2012, 899–922.

[74]L. A. McFarland, A. M. Ryan, and S. D. Kriska, "Impression Management Use and Effectiveness across Assessment Methods," *Journal of Management* 29, no. 5 (2003): 641–61; C. A. Higgins and T. A. Judge, "The Effect of Applicant Influence Tactics on Recruiter Perceptions of Fit and Hiring Recommendations: A Field Study," *Journal of Applied Psychology* 89, no. 4 (2004): 622–32; and W. C. Tsai, C.-C. Chen, and S. F. Chiu, "Exploring Boundaries of the Effects of Applicant Impression Management Tactics in Job Interviews," *Journal of Management*, February 2005, 108–25.

[75]M. R. Barrick, J. A. Shaffer, and S. W. DeGrassi. "What You See May Not Be What You Get: Relationships among Self-Presentation

Tactics and Ratings of Interview and Job Performance," *Journal of Applied Psychology,* 94, no. 6 (2009): 1394–411.

[76]E. Molleman, B. Emans, and N. Turusbekova, "How to Control Self-Promotion among Performance-Oriented Employees: The Roles of Task Clarity and Personalized Responsibility," *Personnel Review* 41 (2012): 88–105.

[77]K. J. Harris, K. M. Kacmar, S. Zivnuska, and J. D. Shaw, "The Impact of Political Skill on Impression Management Effectiveness," *Journal of Applied Psychology* 92, no. 1 (2007): 278–85; and D. C. Treadway, G. R. Ferris, A. B. Duke, G. L. Adams, and J. B. Thatcher, "The Moderating Role of Subordinate Political Skill on Supervisors' Impressions of Subordinate Ingratiation and Ratings of Subordinate Interpersonal Facilitation,"

Journal of Applied Psychology 92, no. 3 (2007): 848–55.

[78]J. D. Westphal and I. Stern, "Flattery Will Get You Everywhere (Especially if You Are a Male Caucasian): How Ingratiation, Boardroom Behavior, and Demographic Minority Status Affect Additional Board Appointments of U.S. Companies," *Academy of Management Journal* 50, no. 2 (2007): 267–88.

[79]Y. Liu, G. R. Ferris, J. Xu, B. A. Weitz, and P. L. Perrewé, "When Ingratiation Backfires: The Role of Political Skill in the Ingratiation-Internship Performance Relationship," *Academy of Management Learning and Education* 13 (2014): 569–86.

[80]See, for example, E. Vigoda, "Reactions to Organizational Politics: A Cross-Cultural Examination in Israel and Britain," Human

Relations, November 2001, 1483–1518; and Y. Zhu and D. Li, "Negative Spillover Impact of Perceptions of Organizational Politics on Work-Family Conflict in China," Social Behavior and Personality 43, no. 5 (2015): 705–14.

[81]J. L. T. Leong, M. H. Bond, and P. P. Fu, "Perceived Effectiveness of Influence Strategies in the United States and Three Chinese Societies," *International Journal of Cross Cultural Management,* May 2006, 101–20.

[82]Y. Miyamoto and B. Wilken, "Culturally Contingent Situated Cognition: Influencing Other People Fosters Analytic Perception in the United States but Not in Japan," *Psychological Science* 21, no. 11 (2010): 1616–22.

[83]D. Clark, "A Campaign Strategy for Your Career," *Harvard Business Review,* November 2012, 131–34.

14 Conflict and Negotiation

14-1 Describe the three types of conflict and the three loci of conflict.

14-2 Outline the conflict process.

14-3 Contrast distributive and integrative bargaining.

14-4 Apply the five steps of the negotiation process.

14-5 Show how individual differences influence negotiations.

14-6 Assess the roles and functions of third-party negotiations.

MyManagementLab®
⭐ **Chapter Warm Up**

If your professor has chosen to assign this, go to the Assignments section of **mymanagementlab.com** to complete the chapter warm up.

A CHANGE OF TUNE

While most of us are accustomed to instant access to nearly any music we want over the Internet, digital music distribution is actually a relatively new and volatile market. As recently as 2005, almost all music sales came from physical media like compact discs. By 2015, however, digital downloads overtook CDs in revenue and legal streaming services comprised nearly a third of the overall music market. In Sweden and South Korea, as an extreme example, streaming music services provided 90 percent of recorded music revenues. This rapid shift for the industry in a short period of time has created ongoing high-stakes negotiations.

When Daniel Ek (pictured here) started Spotify in 2006, now one of the most successful streaming services, the music producers were suspicious that his service would lower their revenues. Ek claimed his intention was not to cheat the system, but to beat music pirates at their own game by offering a service that made legally listening to tracks easier and more pleasant than illegal downloads. He noted, "It's not like people want to be pirates. They just want a great experience. So we started sketching what that would look like." Through many conflicts and negotiations, Ek maintained that Spotify offered greater profits for everyone in the music industry, and eventually the industry's players agreed.

The basic terms between record companies and Spotify are simple—Spotify acquires the right to distribute music to fans by paying royalties to the copyright holders. In turn, Spotify can make money from either running advertisements or charging users. To maintain legal access to the music, Ek must continually negotiate with all the recording companies that administer copyrights. Spotify remains completely responsible for ensuring adherence to copyright laws.

This seemingly straightforward negotiation process of exchanging rights for revenues is actually quite complex in practice, especially since pricing models are still being worked out by the players in the industry. Spotify also needs to demonstrate to recording companies that cooperating with streaming services creates better value for them than different music distribution methods, even as prices change. The possibilities for lucrative negotiations are high—but so are the possibilities for conflict.

A number of factors have strengthened Spotify's bargaining position. For one, any record label that walks away from a deal with Spotify risks losing access to many listeners who rely exclusively on streaming services for their music. For another, it's better for record labels to make money through an agreement with Spotify than to make nothing from pirated copies of their music.

At the same time, the major labels have their own bargaining resources. First and foremost, if media companies won't deal with Spotify, the service will quickly lose its appeal. Second and related to this, if Spotify cannot obtain music rights for popular artists, disappointed listeners may easily turn to other services and threaten its existence. The highest-profile defector so far is Taylor Swift, who moved from Spotify to another streaming service that offered her a higher rate of return on plays. The impact of the music star's defection isn't completely known but may be costly since the decision was very public in the media.

The stakes of these negotiations are high. One thing is for sure: in such a turbulent market, there will surely be a lot of time spent at the bargaining table in the years to come.

Sources: J. Seabrook, "Revenue Streams," *The New Yorker,* November 24, 2014, http://www .newyorker.com/magazine/2014/11/24/revenue-streams; S. Dredge, "Ministry of Sound Boss Attacks Major Labels for Streaming 'Short Termism,'" *The Guardian,* May 15, 2015, http://www.theguardian.com/technology/2015/may/15/ministry-of-sound-major-labels-music-streaming-spotify; and N. Prins "Spotify Racks Up a Streaming Milestone: Artists Settle in for the Fight," *Forbes,* May 14, 2015, http://www.forbes.com/sites/nomiprins/2015/05/14/spotify-racks-up-a-streaming-milestone-artists-settle-in-for-the-fight/.

As the music industry example demonstrates, forms of conflict and negotiation are often complex—and controversial—interpersonal processes. While we generally see conflict as a negative topic and negotiation as a positive one, what we deem positive or negative often depends on our perspective.

Conflict can turn personal. It can create chaotic conditions that make it nearly impossible for employees to work as a team. However, conflict also has a less well-known positive side. We'll explain the difference between negative and positive conflicts in this chapter and provide a guide to help you understand how conflicts develop. We'll also present the specifics about the topic closely akin to conflict: negotiation.

A Definition of Conflict

14-1 Describe the three types of conflict and the three loci of conflict.

conflict A process that begins when one party perceives that another party has negatively affected, or is about to negatively affect, something that the first party cares about.

There has been no shortage of definitions of *conflict*,[1] but common to most is the idea that conflict is a perception. If no one is aware of a conflict, then it is generally agreed no conflict exists. Also needed to begin the conflict process are opposition or incompatibility, and interaction.

We define **conflict** broadly as a process that begins when one party perceives another party has affected or is about to negatively affect something the first party cares about. Conflict describes the point in ongoing activity when interaction becomes disagreement. People experience a wide range of conflicts in organizations over an incompatibility of goals, differences in interpretations of facts, disagreements over behavioral expectations, and the like. Our definition covers the full range of conflict levels, from overt and violent acts to subtle forms of disagreement.

There is no consensus over the role of conflict in groups and organizations. In the past, researchers tended to argue about whether conflict was uniformly good or bad. Such simplistic views eventually gave way to approaches recognizing that not all conflicts are the same and that different types of conflict have different effects.

functional conflict Conflict that supports the goals of the group and improves its performance.

dysfunctional conflict Conflict that hinders group performance.

Contemporary perspectives differentiate types of conflict based on their effects. **Functional conflict** supports the goals of the group, improves its performance, and is thus a constructive form of conflict. For example, a debate among members of a work team about the most efficient way to improve production can be functional if unique points of view are discussed and compared openly. Conflict that hinders group performance is destructive or **dysfunctional conflict**. A highly personal struggle for control in a team that distracts from the task at hand is dysfunctional. Exhibit 14-1 provides an overview depicting the effect of levels of conflict. To understand different types of conflict, we will discuss next the *types* of conflict and the *loci* of conflict.

Types of Conflict

task conflict Conflict over content and goals of the work.

relationship conflict Conflict based on interpersonal relationships.

process conflict Conflict over how work gets done.

One means of understanding conflict is to identify the *type* of disagreement, or what the conflict is about. Is it a disagreement about goals? Is it about people who just rub one another the wrong way? Or is it about the best way to get things done? Although each conflict is unique, researchers have classified conflicts into three categories: task, relationship, or process. **Task conflict** relates to the content and goals of the work. **Relationship conflict** focuses on interpersonal relationships. **Process conflict** is about how the work gets done.

Studies demonstrate that relationship conflicts, at least in work settings, are almost always dysfunctional.[2] Why? It appears that the friction and interpersonal hostilities inherent in relationship conflicts increase personality clashes and decrease mutual understanding, which hinders the completion of organizational tasks. Of the three types, relationship conflicts also appear to be the most psychologically exhausting to individuals.[3] Because they tend to revolve around personalities, you can see how relationship conflicts can become destructive. After all, we can't expect to change our coworkers' personalities,

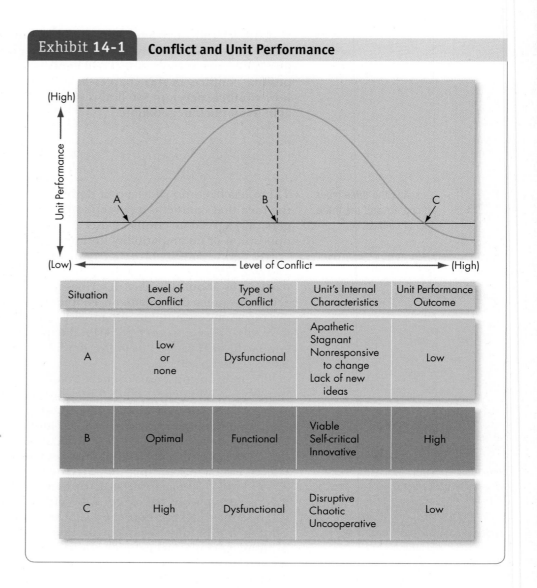

Exhibit 14-1   Conflict and Unit Performance

Situation	Level of Conflict	Type of Conflict	Unit's Internal Characteristics	Unit Performance Outcome
A	Low or none	Dysfunctional	Apathetic Stagnant Nonresponsive to change Lack of new ideas	Low
B	Optimal	Functional	Viable Self-critical Innovative	High
C	High	Dysfunctional	Disruptive Chaotic Uncooperative	Low

and we would generally take offense at criticisms directed at who we *are* as opposed to how we behave.

While scholars agree that relationship conflict is dysfunctional, there is considerably less agreement about whether task and process conflicts are functional. Early research suggested that task conflict within groups correlated to higher group performance, but a review of 116 studies found that generalized task conflict was essentially unrelated to group performance. However, there were factors of the conflict that could create a relationship between conflict and performance.[4]

One such factor was whether the conflict included top management or occurred lower in the organization. Task conflict among top management teams was positively associated with performance, whereas conflict lower in the organization was negatively associated with group performance, perhaps because people in top positions may not feel as threatened in their organizational roles by conflict. This review also found that it mattered whether other types of conflict were occurring at the same time. If task and relationship conflict occurred together, task conflict was more likely negative, whereas if task conflict occurred by itself, it more likely was positive. Also, some scholars have argued that the strength of conflict is important—if task conflict is very low, people aren't really engaged or addressing the important issues. If task conflict is too high, however, infighting will quickly degenerate into relationship conflict. Moderate levels of task conflict may thus be optimal. Supporting this argument, one study in China found that moderate levels of task conflict in the early development stage increased creativity in groups, but high levels decreased team performance.[5]

Finally, the personalities of the teams appear to matter. One study demonstrated that teams of individuals who are, on average, high in openness and emotional stability are better able to turn task conflict into increased group performance.[6] The reason may be that open and emotionally stable teams can put task conflict in perspective and focus on how the variance in ideas can help solve the problem, rather than letting it degenerate into relationship conflicts.

What about process conflict? Researchers found that process conflicts are about delegation and roles. Conflicts over delegation often revolve around the perception of some members as shirking, and conflicts over roles can leave some group members feeling marginalized. Thus, process conflicts often become highly personalized and quickly devolve into relationship conflicts. It's also true, of course, that arguing about how to do something takes time away from actually doing it. We've all been part of groups in which the arguments and debates about roles and responsibilities seem to go nowhere.

Loci of Conflict

dyadic conflict Conflict that occurs between two people.

intragroup conflict Conflict that occurs within a group or team.

intergroup conflict Conflict between different groups or teams.

Another way to understand conflict is to consider its *locus*, or the framework within which the conflict occurs. Here, too, there are three basic types. **Dyadic conflict** is conflict between two people. **Intragroup conflict** occurs *within* a group or team. **Intergroup conflict** is conflict *between* groups or teams.

Nearly all the literature on task, relationship, and process conflict considers intragroup conflict (within the group). That makes sense given that groups and teams often exist only to perform a particular task. However, it doesn't necessarily tell us all we need to know about the context and outcomes of conflict. For example, research has found that for intragroup task conflict to positively

Under the leadership of George Zimmer as the founder and CEO of Men's Warehouse and its advertising spokesman, the retailer grew into a multi-million-dollar firm with 1,143 stores. After retiring as CEO, Zimmer served as executive chairman of MW's board until an intragroup conflict between him and other members resulted in his removal from the board.
Source: Patrick Fallon/Bloomberg/Getty Images

influence performance within the team, it is important that the team has a supportive climate in which mistakes aren't penalized and every team member "[has] the other's back."[7] But is this concept applicable to the effects of intergroup conflict? Think about, say, NFL football. As we said, for a team to adapt and improve, perhaps a certain amount of intragroup conflict (but not too much) is good for team performance, especially when the team members support one another. But would we care whether members from one team supported members from another team? Probably not. In fact, if groups are competing with one another so that only one team can "win," interteam conflict seems almost inevitable. Still, it must be managed. Intense intergroup conflict can be quite stressful to group members and might well affect the way they interact. One study found, for example, that high levels of conflict between teams caused individuals to focus on complying with norms within their teams.[8]

It may surprise you that individuals become most important in intergroup conflicts. One study that focused on intergroup conflict found an interplay between an individual's position within a group and the way that individual managed conflict between groups. Group members who were relatively peripheral in their own group were better at resolving conflicts between their group and another one. But this happened only when those peripheral members were still accountable to their group.[9] Thus, being at the core of your workgroup does not necessarily make you the best person to manage conflict with other groups.

Another intriguing question about loci is whether conflicts interact with or buffer one another. Assume, for example, that Jia and Marcus are on the same team. What happens if they don't get along interpersonally (dyadic conflict) *and* their team also has high task conflict? Progress might be halted. What happens to their team if two other team members, Shawna and Justin, do get along well? The team might still be dysfunctional, or the positive relationship might prevail.

Thus, understanding functional and dysfunctional conflict requires not only that we identify the type of conflict; we also need to know where it occurs. It's possible that while the concepts of task, relationship, and process conflict are useful in understanding intragroup or even dyadic conflict, they are less useful in explaining the effects of intergroup conflict. But how do we make conflict as productive as possible? A better understanding of the conflict process, discussed next, will provide insight about potential controllable variables.

The Conflict Process

14-2 Outline the conflict process.

conflict process A process that has five stages: potential opposition or incompatibility, cognition and personalization, intentions, behavior, and outcomes.

The **conflict process** has five stages: potential opposition or incompatibility, cognition and personalization, intentions, behavior, and outcomes (see Exhibit 14-2).

Stage I: Potential Opposition or Incompatibility

The first stage of conflict is the appearance of conditions—causes or sources—that create opportunities for it to arise. These conditions *need not* lead directly to conflict, but one of them is necessary if it is to surface. We group the conditions into three general categories: communication, structure, and personal variables.

Communication Susan had worked in supply chain management at Bristol-Myers Squibb for three years. She enjoyed her work largely because her manager, Harry, was a great boss. Then Harry was promoted and Chuck took his place. Six months later, Susan says her job is frustrating. "Harry and I were

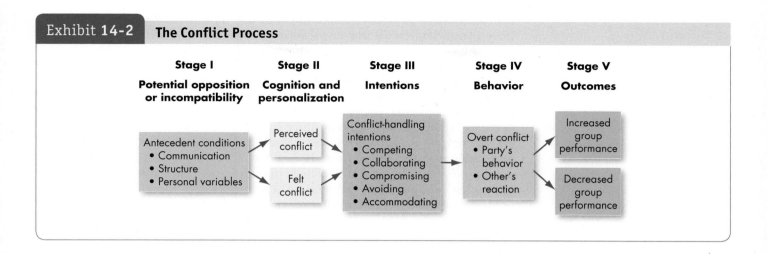

Exhibit 14-2   The Conflict Process

Stage I	Stage II	Stage III	Stage IV	Stage V
Potential opposition or incompatibility	**Cognition and personalization**	**Intentions**	**Behavior**	**Outcomes**

Antecedent conditions
• Communication
• Structure
• Personal variables

Perceived conflict

Felt conflict

Conflict-handling intentions
• Competing
• Collaborating
• Compromising
• Avoiding
• Accommodating

Overt conflict
• Party's behavior
• Other's reaction

Increased group performance

Decreased group performance

on the same wavelength. It's not that way with Chuck. He tells me something, and I do it. Then he tells me I did it wrong. I think he means one thing but says something else. It's been like this since the day he arrived. I don't think a day goes by when he isn't yelling at me for something. You know, there are some people you just find it easy to communicate with. Well, Chuck isn't one of those!"

Susan's comments illustrate that communication can be a source of conflict.[10] Her experience represents the opposing forces that arise from semantic difficulties, misunderstandings, and "noise" in the communication channel (see Chapter 11). These factors, along with jargon and insufficient information, can be barriers to communication and potential antecedent conditions to conflict. The potential for conflict has also been found to increase with too little or *too much* communication. Communication is functional up to a point, after which it is possible to overcommunicate, increasing the potential for conflict.

Structure   Charlotte is a salesperson and Mercedes is the company credit manager at Portland Furniture Mart, a large discount furniture retailer. The women have known each other for years and have much in common: They live two blocks apart, and their oldest daughters attend the same middle school and are best friends. If Charlotte and Mercedes had different jobs, they might be friends, but at work they constantly disagree. Charlotte's job is to sell furniture, and she does it well. Most of her sales are made on credit. Because Mercedes's job is to minimize credit losses, she regularly has to turn down the credit applications of Charlotte's customers. It's nothing personal between the women; the requirements of their jobs just bring them into conflict.

The conflicts between Charlotte and Mercedes are structural in nature. The term *structure* in this context includes variables such as size of group, degree of specialization in tasks assigned to group members, jurisdictional clarity, member–goal compatibility, leadership styles, reward systems, and degree of dependence between groups. The larger the group and the more specialized its activities, the greater the likelihood of conflict. Tenure and conflict are inversely related, meaning that the longer a person stays with an organization, the less likely conflict becomes. Therefore, the potential for conflict is greatest when group members are younger and when turnover is high.

Personal Variables   Have you ever met someone you immediately disliked? Perhaps you disagreed with most of his opinions. Even insignificant characteristics—his voice, facial expressions, or word choice—may have annoyed you. Sometimes our impressions are negative. When you have to work with people you don't like, the potential for conflict arises.

Our last category of potential sources of conflict is personal variables, which include personality, emotions, and values. People high in the personality traits of disagreeableness, neuroticism, or self-monitoring (see Chapter 5) are prone to tangle with other people more often—and to react poorly when conflicts occur.[11] Emotions can cause conflict even when they are not directed at others. An employee who shows up to work irate from her hectic morning commute may carry that anger into her workday, which can result in a tension-filled meeting.[12] Furthermore, differences in preferences and values can generate higher levels of conflict. For example, a study in Korea found that when group members didn't agree about their desired achievement levels, there was more task conflict; when group members didn't agree about their desired interpersonal closeness, there was more relationship conflict; and when group members didn't have similar desires for power, there was more conflict over status.[13]

Stage II: Cognition and Personalization

If the conditions cited in Stage I negatively affect something one party cares about, then the potential for opposition or incompatibility becomes actualized in the second stage.

As we noted in our definition of conflict, one or more of the parties must be aware that antecedent conditions exist. However, just because a disagreement is a **perceived conflict** does not mean it is personalized. It is at the **felt conflict** level, when individuals become emotionally involved, that they experience anxiety, tension, frustration, or hostility.

Stage II is important because it's where conflict issues tend to be defined, where the parties decide what the conflict is about.[14] The definition of conflict is important because it delineates the set of possible settlements. Most evidence suggests that people tend to default to cooperative strategies in interpersonal interactions unless there is a clear signal that they are faced with a competitive person. However, if our salary disagreement is a zero-sum situation (the increase in pay you want means there will be that much less in the raise pool for me), I am going to be far less willing to compromise than if I can frame the conflict as a potential win–win situation (the dollars in the salary pool might be increased so both of us could get the added pay we want).

Second, emotions play a major role in shaping perceptions.[15] Negative emotions allow us to oversimplify issues, lose trust, and put negative interpretations on the other party's behavior.[16] In contrast, positive feelings increase our tendency to see potential relationships among elements of a problem, take a broader view of the situation, and develop innovative solutions.[17]

Stage III: Intentions

Intentions intervene between people's perceptions and emotions, and their overt behavior. They are decisions to act in a given way.[18]

Intentions are a distinct stage because we have to infer the other's intent to know how to respond to behavior. Many conflicts escalate simply because one party attributes the wrong intentions to the other. There is slippage between intentions and behavior, so behavior does not always accurately reflect a person's intentions.

Exhibit 14-3 represents one way to identify the primary conflict-handling intentions. Using two dimensions—*assertiveness* (the degree to which one party attempts to satisfy his or her own concerns) and *cooperativeness* (the degree to

perceived conflict   Awareness by one or more parties of the existence of conditions that create opportunities for conflict to arise.

felt conflict   Emotional involvement in a conflict that creates anxiety, tenseness, frustration, or hostility.

intentions   Decisions to act in a given way.

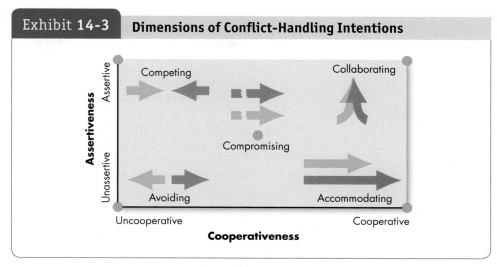

| Exhibit **14-3** | **Dimensions of Conflict-Handling Intentions** |

Source: Figure from "Conflict and Negotiation Processes in Organizations" by K. Thomas in M. D. Dunnette and L. M. Hough (eds.), *Handbook of Industrial and Organizational Psychology*, 2/e, vol. 3 (Palo Alto, CA: Consulting Psychologists Press, 1992), 668. Used with permission.

which one party attempts to satisfy the other party's concerns)—we can identify five conflict-handling intentions: *competing* (assertive and uncooperative), *collaborating* (assertive and cooperative), *avoiding* (unassertive and uncooperative), *accommodating* (unassertive and cooperative), and *compromising* (midrange on both assertiveness and cooperativeness).[19]

Competing   When one person seeks to satisfy his or her own interests regardless of the impact on the other parties in the conflict, that person is **competing**. We are more apt to compete when resources are scarce.

competing   A desire to satisfy one's interests, regardless of the impact on the other party to the conflict.

Collaborating   When parties in conflict each desire to fully satisfy the concerns of all parties, there is cooperation and a search for a mutually beneficial outcome. In **collaborating**, parties intend to solve a problem by clarifying differences rather than by accommodating various points of view. If you attempt to find a win–win solution that allows both parties' goals to be completely achieved, that's collaborating.

collaborating   A situation in which the parties to a conflict each desire to satisfy fully the concerns of all parties.

Avoiding   A person may recognize a conflict exists and want to withdraw from or suppress it. Examples of **avoiding** include trying to ignore a conflict and keeping away from others with whom you disagree.

avoiding   The desire to withdraw from or suppress a conflict.

Accommodating   A party who seeks to appease an opponent may be willing to place the opponent's interests above his or her own, sacrificing to maintain the relationship. We refer to this intention as **accommodating**. Supporting someone else's opinion despite your reservations about it, for example, is accommodating.

accommodating   The willingness of one party in a conflict to place the opponent's interests above his or her own.

Compromising   In **compromising**, there is no winner or loser. Rather, there is a willingness to ration the object of the conflict and accept a solution with incomplete satisfaction of both parties' concerns. The distinguishing characteristic of compromising, therefore, is that each party intends to give up something.

compromising   A situation in which each party to a conflict is willing to give up something.

Stage IV: Behavior

When most people think of conflict, they tend to focus on Stage IV because this is where conflicts become visible. The behavior stage includes statements, actions, and reactions made by conflicting parties, usually as overt attempts to implement their own intentions. As a result of miscalculations or unskilled enactments, overt behaviors sometimes deviate from original intentions.[20]

Stage IV is a dynamic process of interaction. For example, you make a demand on me, I respond by arguing, you threaten me, I threaten you back, and so on. Exhibit 14-4 provides a way of visualizing conflict behavior. All conflicts exist somewhere along this continuum. At the lower end are conflicts characterized by subtle, indirect, and highly controlled forms of tension, such as a student challenging a point the instructor has made. Conflict intensities escalate as they move upward along the continuum until they become highly destructive. Strikes, riots, and wars clearly fall in this upper range. Conflicts that reach the upper ranges of the continuum are almost always dysfunctional. Functional conflicts are typically confined to the lower range of the continuum.

Intentions that are brought into a conflict are eventually translated into behaviors. *Competing* brings out active attempts to contend with team members, and more individual effort to achieve ends without working together. *Collaborating* creates investigation of multiple solutions with other members of the team and trying to find a solution that satisfies all parties as much as possible. *Avoidance* is seen in behavior like refusals to discuss issues and reductions in effort toward group goals. People who *accommodate* put their relationships ahead of the issues in the conflict, deferring to others' opinions and sometimes acting as a subgroup with them. Finally, when people *compromise*, they both expect to (and do) sacrifice parts of their interests, hoping that if everyone does the same, an agreement will sift out.

A review that examined the effects of the four sets of behaviors across multiple studies found that openness and collaborating were both associated with superior group performance, whereas avoiding and competing strategies were associated with significantly worse group performance.[21] These effects were nearly as large as the effects of relationship conflict. This further demonstrates that it is not just the existence of conflict or even the type of conflict that creates problems, but rather the ways people respond to conflict and manage the process once conflicts arise.

If a conflict is dysfunctional, what can the parties do to de-escalate it? Or, conversely, what options exist if conflict is too low to be functional and

Exhibit 14-4	Conflict-Intensity Continuum

Annihilatory conflict — Overt efforts to destroy the other party

Aggressive physical attacks

Threats and ultimatums

Assertive verbal attacks

Overt questioning or challenging of others

Minor disagreements or misunderstandings

No conflict

Sources: Based on S. P. Robbins, *Managing Organizational Conflict: A Nontraditional Approach* (Upper Saddle River, NJ: Prentice Hall, 1974), 93–97; and F. Glasl, "The Process of Conflict Escalation and the Roles of Third Parties," in G. B. J. Bomers and R. Peterson (eds.), *Conflict Management and Industrial Relations* (Boston: Kluwer-Nijhoff, 1982), 119–40.

Exhibit 14-5	Conflict Management Techniques

Conflict-Resolution Techniques

Problem solving	Meeting face to face for the purpose of identifying the problem and resolving it through open discussion.
Superordinate goals	Creating a shared goal that cannot be attained without the cooperation of each of the conflicting parties.
Expansion of resources	Expanding the supply of a scarce resource (for example, money, promotion, opportunities, office space).
Avoidance	Withdrawing from or suppressing the conflict.
Smoothing	Playing down differences while emphasizing common interests between the conflicting parties.
Compromise	Having each party to the conflict give up something of value.
Authoritative command	Letting management use its formal authority to resolve the conflict and then communicating its desires to the parties involved.
Altering the human variable	Using behavioral change techniques such as human relations training to alter attitudes and behaviors that cause conflict.
Altering the structural variables	Changing the formal organization structure and the interaction patterns of conflicting parties through job redesign, transfers, creation of coordinating positions, and the like.

Conflict-Stimulation Techniques

Communication	Using ambiguous or threatening messages to increase conflict levels.
Bringing in outsiders	Adding employees to a group whose backgrounds, values, attitudes, or managerial styles differ from those of present members.
Restructuring the organization	Realigning work groups, altering rules and regulations, increasing interdependence, and making similar structural changes to disrupt the status quo.
Appointing a devil's advocate	Designating a critic to purposely argue against the majority positions held by the group.

Source: Based on S. P. Robbins, *Managing Organizational Conflict: A Nontraditional Approach* (Upper Saddle River, NJ: Prentice Hall, 1974), 59–89.

conflict management The use of resolution and stimulation techniques to achieve the desired level of conflict.

needs to be increased? This brings us to techniques of **conflict management**. Exhibit 14-5 lists the major resolution and stimulation techniques that allow managers to control conflict levels. We have already described several as conflict-handling intentions. Under ideal conditions, a person's intentions should translate into comparable behaviors.

Stage V: Outcomes

The action–reaction interplay between conflicting parties creates consequences. As our model demonstrates (see Exhibit 14-1), these outcomes may be functional if the conflict improves the group's performance, or dysfunctional if it hinders performance.

Functional Outcomes   How might conflict act as a force to increase group performance? It is hard to visualize a situation in which open or violent aggression could be functional. But it's possible to see how low or moderate levels of conflict could improve group effectiveness. Note that all our examples focus on task and process conflicts and exclude the relationship variety.

Conflict is constructive when it improves the quality of decisions, stimulates creativity and innovation, encourages interest and curiosity among group members, provides the medium for problems to be aired and tensions released, and fosters self-evaluation and change. Mild conflicts also may generate energizing emotions so members of groups become more active, energized, and engaged in their work.[22]

IBM encourages employees to engage in functional conflict that results in innovations, such as the Watson supercomputer designed to learn through the same process human brains use. For innovation to flourish, IBM relies on the creative tension from employees' different ideas and skills and provides a work environment that promotes risk taking and outside-the-box thinking.
Source: Jon Simon/Feature Photo Service/Newscom

Dysfunctional Outcomes The destructive consequences of conflict on the performance of a group or an organization are generally well known: Uncontrolled opposition breeds discontent, which acts to dissolve common ties and eventually leads to the destruction of the group. And, of course, a substantial body of literature documents how dysfunctional conflicts can reduce group effectiveness.[23] Among the undesirable consequences are poor communication, reductions in group cohesiveness, and subordination of group goals to the primacy of infighting among members. All forms of conflict—even the functional varieties—appear to reduce group member satisfaction and trust.[24] When active discussions turn into open conflicts between members, information sharing between members decreases significantly.[25] At the extreme, conflict can bring group functioning to a halt and threaten the group's survival.

Managing Functional Conflict If managers recognize that in some situations conflict can be beneficial, what can they do to manage conflict effectively in their organizations? In addition to knowing the principles of conflict motivation we just discussed, there are some practical guidelines for managers.

First, one of the keys to minimizing counterproductive conflicts is recognizing when there really is a disagreement. Many apparent conflicts are due to people using different verbiage to discuss the same general course of action. For example, someone in marketing might focus on "distribution problems," while someone from operations will talk about "supply chain management" to describe essentially the same issue. Successful conflict management recognizes these different approaches and attempts to resolve them by encouraging open, frank discussion focused on interests rather than issues. Another approach is to have opposing groups pick parts of the solution that are most important to them and then focus on how each side can get its top needs satisfied. Neither side may get exactly what it wants, but each side will achieve the most important parts of its agenda.[26]

Third, groups that resolve conflicts successfully discuss differences of opinion openly and are prepared to manage conflict when it arises.[27] The most disruptive conflicts are those that are never addressed directly. An open discussion makes it much easier to develop a shared perception of the problems at hand; it also allows groups to work toward a mutually acceptable solution. Fourth, managers need to emphasize shared interests in resolving conflicts, so groups that disagree with one another don't become too entrenched in their points of view and start to take the conflicts personally. Groups with cooperative conflict styles and a strong underlying identification with the overall group goals are more effective than groups with a competitive style.[28]

Differences across countries in conflict resolution strategies may be based on collectivistic tendencies and motives.[29] Collectivist cultures see people as deeply embedded in social situations, whereas individualist cultures see them as autonomous. As a result, collectivists are more likely to seek to preserve relationships and promote the good of the group as a whole. They will avoid the direct expression of conflict, preferring indirect methods for resolving differences of opinion. Collectivists may also be more interested in demonstrations of concern and working through third parties to resolve disputes, whereas individualists will be more likely to confront differences of opinion directly and openly.

Some research supports this theory. Compared to collectivist Japanese negotiators, their more individualist U.S. counterparts are more likely to see offers as unfair and to reject them. Another study revealed that whereas U.S. managers were more likely to use competing tactics in the face of conflicts, compromising and avoiding were the most preferred methods of conflict management in China.[30] Interview data, however, suggest that top management teams in Chinese high-technology firms prefer collaboration even more than compromising and avoiding.[31]

Cross-cultural negotiations can also create issues of trust.[32] One study of Indian and U.S. negotiators found that respondents reported having less trust in their cross-culture negotiation counterparts. The lower level of trust was associated with less discovery of common interests between parties, which occurred because cross-culture negotiators were less willing to disclose and solicit information. Another study found that both U.S. and Chinese negotiators tended to have an ingroup bias, which led them to favor negotiating partners from their own cultures. For Chinese negotiators, this was particularly true when accountability requirements were high.

Having considered conflict—its nature, causes, and consequences—we now turn to negotiation, which often resolves conflict.

✪ WATCH IT!

If your professor has assigned this, go to the Assignments section of **mymanagementlab.com** to complete the video exercise titled *Gordon Law Group: Conflict and Negotiation*.

Negotiation

14-3 Contrast distributive and integrative bargaining.

Negotiation permeates the interactions of almost everyone in groups and organizations. There's the obvious: Labor bargains with management. There's the not-so-obvious: Managers negotiate with employees, peers, and bosses;

salespeople negotiate with customers; purchasing agents negotiate with suppliers. And there's the subtle: An employee agrees to cover for a colleague for a few minutes in exchange for a future benefit. In today's loosely structured organizations, in which members work with colleagues over whom they have no direct authority and with whom they may not even share a common boss, negotiation skills are critical.

We can define **negotiation** as a process that occurs when two or more parties decide how to allocate scarce resources.[33] Although we commonly think of the outcomes of negotiation in one-shot economic terms, like negotiating over the price of a car, every negotiation in organizations also affects the relationship between negotiators and the way negotiators feel about themselves.[34] Depending on how much the parties are going to interact with one another, sometimes maintaining the social relationship and behaving ethically will be just as important as achieving an immediate outcome of bargaining. Note that we use the terms *negotiation* and *bargaining* interchangeably.

negotiation   A process in which two or more parties exchange goods or services and attempt to agree on the exchange rate for them.

Bargaining Strategies

There are two general approaches to negotiation—*distributive bargaining* and *integrative bargaining*.[35] As Exhibit 14-6 shows, they differ in their goal and motivation, focus, interests, information sharing, and duration of relationship. Let's define each and illustrate the differences.

Distributive Bargaining   You see a used car advertised for sale online that looks great. You go see the car. It's perfect, and you want it. The owner tells you the asking price. You don't want to pay that much. The two of you negotiate. The negotiating strategy you're engaging in is called **distributive bargaining**. Its identifying feature is that it operates under zero-sum conditions—that is, any gain I make is at your expense, and vice versa. Every dollar you can get the seller to cut from the car's price is a dollar you save, and every dollar the seller can get from you comes at your expense. The essence of distributive bargaining is negotiating over who gets what share of a fixed pie. By **fixed pie**, we mean a set amount of goods or services to be divvied up. When the pie is fixed, or the parties believe it is, they tend to bargain distributively.

distributive bargaining   Negotiation that seeks to divide up a fixed amount of resources; a win-lose situation.

fixed pie   The belief that there is only a set amount of goods or services to be divvied up between the parties.

Exhibit 14-6	Distributive versus Integrative Bargaining	
Bargaining Characteristic	**Distributive Bargaining**	**Integrative Bargaining**
Goal	Get as much of the pie as possible	Expand the pie so that both parties are satisfied
Motivation	Win–lose	Win–win
Focus	Positions ("I can't go beyond this point on this issue.")	Interests ("Can you explain why this issue is so important to you?")
Interests	Opposed	Congruent
Information sharing	Low (Sharing information will only allow other party to take advantage)	High (Sharing information will allow each party to find ways to satisfy interests of each party)
Duration of relationship	Short term	Long term

Exhibit 14-7 **Staking Out the Bargaining Zone**

The essence of distributive bargaining is depicted in Exhibit 14-7. Parties *A* and *B* represent two negotiators. Each has a *target point* that defines what he or she would like to achieve. Each also has a *resistance point,* which marks the lowest acceptable outcome—the point beyond which the party would break off negotiations rather than accept a less favorable settlement. The area between these two points makes up each party's *aspiration range.* As long as there is some overlap between *A*'s and *B*'s aspiration ranges, there exists a settlement range in which each one's aspirations can be met.

When you are engaged in distributive bargaining, one of the best things you can do is make the first offer, and make it an aggressive one. Making the first offer shows power; individuals in power are much more likely to make initial offers, speak first at meetings, and thereby gain the advantage. Another reason this is a good strategy is the anchoring bias, mentioned in Chapter 6. People tend to fixate on initial information. Once that anchoring point has been set, they fail to adequately adjust it based on subsequent information. A savvy negotiator sets an anchor with the initial offer, and scores of negotiation studies show that such anchors greatly favor the person who sets them.[36]

Say you have a job offer, and your prospective employer asks you what sort of starting salary you want. You've just been given a gift—you have a chance to set the anchor, meaning you should ask for the highest salary you think the employer could reasonably offer. Asking for a million dollars is only going to make most of us look ridiculous, which is why we suggest being on the high end of what you think is *reasonable.* Too often, we err on the side of caution, afraid of scaring off the employer and thus settling for far too little. It *is* possible to scare off an employer, and it's true employers don't like candidates to be assertive in salary negotiations, but liking isn't the same as doing what it takes to hire or retain someone.[37] What happens much more often is that we ask for less than we could have obtained.

Integrative Bargaining   Jake was a Chicago luxury boutique owned by Jim Wetzel and Lance Lawson. In the early days of the business, Wetzel and Lawson moved millions of dollars of merchandise from many up-and-coming designers. They developed such a good rapport that many designers would send allotments to Jake without requiring advance payment. When the economy soured in 2008, Jake had trouble selling inventory, and designers were not being paid for what they had shipped to the store. Despite the fact that many designers were willing to work with the store on a delayed payment plan, Wetzel and Lawson stopped returning their calls. Lamented one designer, Doo-Ri Chung, "You kind of feel this familiarity with people who supported you for so long. When they have cash-flow issues, you want to make sure you

Officials of General Motors and United Auto Workers participate in the ceremonial handshake that opens new contract negotiations. They are committed to integrative bargaining and work toward negotiating win–win settlements that boost GM's competitiveness. From left are GM CEO Mary Barra, UAW president Dennis Williams, GM VP Cathy Clegg, and UAW VP Cindy Estrada.
Source: Paul Sancya/AP Images

integrative bargaining   Negotiation that seeks one or more settlements that can create a win–win solution.

are there for them as well."[38] Chung's attitude shows the promise of **integrative bargaining**. In contrast to distributive bargaining, integrative bargaining assumes that one or more of the possible settlements can create a win–win solution. Of course, as the Jake example shows, both parties must be engaged for integrative bargaining to work.

In terms of intraorganizational behavior, integrative bargaining is preferable to distributive bargaining because the former builds long-term relationships. Integrative bargaining bonds negotiators and allows them to leave the bargaining table feeling they have achieved a victory. Distributive bargaining, however, leaves one party a loser. It tends to build animosity and deepen divisions when people have to work together on an ongoing basis. Research shows that over repeated bargaining episodes, a losing party who feels positively about the negotiation outcome is much more likely to bargain cooperatively in subsequent negotiations.

Why, then, don't we see more integrative bargaining in organizations? The answer lies in the conditions necessary for it to succeed. These include opposing parties who are open with information and candid about concerns, are sensitive to the other's needs and trust, and maintain flexibility.[39] Because these conditions seldom exist in organizations, negotiations often take a win-at-any-cost dynamic.

Compromise may be your worst enemy in negotiating a win–win agreement. Compromising reduces the pressure to bargain integratively. After all, if you or your opponent caves in easily, no one needs to be creative to reach a settlement. People then settle for less than they could have obtained if they had been forced to consider the other party's interests, trade off issues, and be creative.[40] Consider a classic example in which two siblings are arguing over who gets an orange. Unknown to them, one sibling wants the orange to drink the juice, whereas the other wants the orange peel to bake a cake. If one capitulates and gives the other the orange, they will not be forced to explore their reasons for wanting the orange, and thus they will never find the win–win solution: They could *each* have the orange because they want different parts.

Teams Negotiate Better Than Individuals in Collectivistic Cultures

According to a recent study, this statement appears to be false.

In general, the literature has suggested that teams negotiate more effectively than individuals negotiating alone. Some evidence indicates that team negotiations create more ambitious goals, and that teams communicate more with each other than individual negotiators do.

Common sense suggests that if this is indeed the case, it is especially true in collectivistic cultures, where individuals are more likely to think of collective goals and be more comfortable working in teams. A study of the negotiation of teams in the United States and in Taiwan, however, suggests that this common sense is wrong. The researchers conducted two studies compar-

ing two-person teams with individual negotiators. They defined negotiating effectiveness as the degree to which the negotiation produced an optimal outcome for both sides. U.S. teams did better than solo individuals in both studies. In Taiwan, solo individuals did better than teams.

Why did this happen? The researchers determined that in Taiwan norms respecting harmony already exist, and negotiating in teams only amplifies that tendency. This poses a problem because when norms for cooperation are exceptionally high, teams "satisfice" (settle for a satisfactory, but less than optimal, solution) to avoid conflict. When Taiwanese individuals negotiate solo, at least they can clearly represent their own interests. In contrast, because the United States

is individualistic, solo negotiators may focus on their own interests, which makes reaching integrative solutions more difficult. When Americans negotiate in teams, they become less inclined to focus on individual interests and therefore can reach solutions.

Overall, these findings suggest that negotiating individually works best in collectivistic cultures, and negotiating in teams works best in individualistic cultures.

Sources: Based on M. J. Gelfand et al., "Toward a Culture-by-Context Perspective on Negotiation: Negotiating Teams in the United States and Taiwan," *Journal of Applied Psychology* 98 (2013): 504–13; and A. Graf, S. T. Koeszegi, and E.-M. Pesendorfer, "Electronic Negotiations in Intercultural Interfirm Relationships," *Journal of Managerial Psychology* 25 (2010): 495–512.

The Negotiation Process

14-4 Apply the five steps of the negotiation process.

Exhibit 14-8 provides a simplified model of the negotiation process. It views negotiation as made up of five steps: (1) preparation and planning, (2) definition of ground rules, (3) clarification and justification, (4) bargaining and problem solving, and (5) closure and implementation.[41]

Preparation and Planning   Before you start negotiating, do your homework. What's the nature of the conflict? What's the history leading up to this negotiation? Who's involved and what are their perceptions of the conflict? What do you want from the negotiation? What are *your* goals? If you're a supply manager at Dell Computer, for instance, and your goal is to get a significant cost reduction from your keyboard supplier, make sure this goal stays paramount in discussions and doesn't get overshadowed by other issues. It helps to put your goals in writing and develop a range of outcomes—from "most hopeful" to "minimally acceptable"—to keep your attention focused.

You should also assess what you think are the other party's goals. What are they likely to ask? How entrenched is their position likely to be? What intangible or hidden interests may be important to them? On what might they be willing to settle? When you can anticipate your opponent's position, you are better equipped to counter arguments with facts and figures that support your position.

Relationships change as a result of negotiation, so take that into consideration. If you could "win" a negotiation but push the other side into resentment

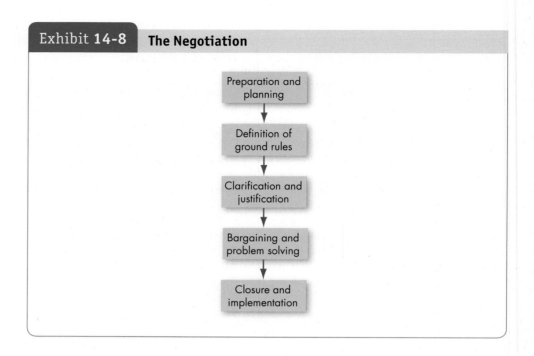

Exhibit 14-8   The Negotiation

- Preparation and planning
- Definition of ground rules
- Clarification and justification
- Bargaining and problem solving
- Closure and implementation

or animosity, it might be wiser to pursue a more compromising style. If preserving the relationship will make you seem easily exploited, you may consider a more aggressive style. As an example of how the tone of a relationship in negotiations matters, people who feel good about the *process* of a job offer negotiation are more satisfied with their jobs and less likely to turn over a year later regardless of their actual *outcomes* from these negotiations.[42]

Once you've gathered your information, develop a strategy. You should determine your and the other side's **b**est **a**lternative **t**o a **n**egotiated **a**greement, or **BATNA**. Your BATNA determines the lowest value acceptable to you for a negotiated agreement. Any offer you receive that is higher than your BATNA is better than an impasse.

In nearly all cases, the party with superior alternatives will do better in a negotiation, so experts advise negotiators to solidify their BATNA prior to any interaction.[43] There is an interesting exception to this general rule—negotiators with absolutely no alternative to a negotiated agreement sometimes "go for broke" since they don't even consider what would happen if the negotiation falls through.[44] Think carefully about what the other side is willing to give up. People who underestimate their opponent's willingness to give on key issues before the negotiation even starts end up with lower outcomes.[45] Conversely, you shouldn't expect success in your negotiation effort unless you're able to make the other side an offer it finds more attractive than its BATNA.

BATNA   The **b**est **a**lternative **t**o a **n**egotiated **a**greement; the least the individual should accept.

Definition of Ground Rules   Once you've done your planning and developed a strategy, you're ready to define with the other party the ground rules and procedures of the negotiation itself. Who will do the negotiating? Where will it take place? What time constraints, if any, will apply? To what issues will negotiation be limited? Will you follow a specific procedure if an impasse is reached? During this phase, the parties will exchange their initial proposals or demands.

Clarification and Justification   When you have exchanged initial positions, you and the other party will explain, amplify, clarify, bolster, and justify your original demands. This step needn't be confrontational. Rather, it's an opportunity for educating each other on the issues, why they are important, and how you arrived at your initial demands. Provide the other party with any documentation that supports your position.

Bargaining and Problem Solving   The essence of the negotiation process is the actual give-and-take in trying to hash out an agreement. This is where both parties need to make concessions.

Closure and Implementation   The final step in the negotiation process is formalizing your agreement and developing procedures necessary for implementing and monitoring it. For major negotiations—from labor–management negotiations to bargaining over lease terms—this requires hammering out the specifics in a formal contract. For other cases, closure of the negotiation process is nothing more formal than a handshake.

Individual Differences in Negotiation Effectiveness

14-5 Show how individual differences influence negotiations.

Are some people better negotiators than others? The answer is complex. Four factors influence how effectively individuals negotiate: personality, mood/emotions, culture, and gender.

Personality Traits in Negotiations   Can you predict an opponent's negotiating tactics if you know something about his or her personality? Because personality and negotiation outcomes are related but only weakly, the answer is, at best, "sort of."[46] Most research has focused on the Big Five trait of agreeableness, for obvious reasons—agreeable individuals are cooperative, compliant, kind, and conflict-averse. We might think such characteristics make agreeable individuals easy prey in negotiations, especially distributive ones. The evidence suggests, however, that overall agreeableness is weakly related to negotiation outcomes. Why is this the case?

It appears that the degree to which agreeableness, and personality more generally, affects negotiation outcomes depends on the situation. The importance of being extraverted in negotiations, for example, will very much depend on how the other party reacts to someone who is assertive and enthusiastic. One complicating factor for agreeableness is that it has two facets: The tendency to be cooperative and compliant is one, but so is the tendency to be warm and empathetic.[47] It may be that while the former is a hindrance to negotiating favorable outcomes, the latter helps. Empathy, after all, is the ability to take the perspective of another person and gain insight/understanding of him or her. We know perspective-taking benefits integrative negotiations, so perhaps the null effect for agreeableness is due to the two tendencies pulling against one another. If this is the case, then the best negotiator is a competitive but empathetic one, and the worst is a gentle but empathetic one.

The type of negotiations may matter as well. In one study, agreeable individuals reacted more positively and felt less stress (measured by their cortisol levels) in integrative negotiations than in distributive ones. Low levels of stress, in turn, made for more effective negotiation outcomes.[48] Similarly, in "hard-edged" distributive negotiations, where giving away information leads to a disadvantage, extraverted negotiators do less well because they tend to share more information than they should.[49]

How can I get a better job?

I feel like my career is at a standstill, and I want to talk to my boss about getting a more developmental assignment. How can I negotiate effectively for a better job position?

— Wei

Dear Wei:

You're certainly starting out on the right foot. A lot of people focus on a salary as a way to achieve success and negotiate for the best short-run offer. There's obviously an advantage to this strategy in the short run, but sustained career growth has better payoffs in the long run. Developing skills can help put you on track for multiple salary increases. A strong skill set from developmental assignments will also give you a better position for future negotiations because you will have more career options.

Long-term career negotiations based on developmental assignments also often are easier to bring up with a supervisor. That's because salary negotiations are often a zero-sum situation, but career development negotiations can bring positive outcomes to both sides. When negotiating for a developmental assignment, make sure you emphasize a few points with your supervisor:

- *When it comes to salary negotiations, either you get the money, or the company keeps the money.* Given that, your interests and the interests of your managers are directly opposed. On the other hand, negotiating for developmental assignments usually means finding ways to improve not just your skills, but also your contribution to the company's bottom line. You can, in complete honesty, frame the discussion around these mutual benefits.
- *Let your supervisor know that you are interested in getting better at your job, and that you are motivated to improve through a developmental assignment.* Asking your supervisor for opportunities to grow is a clear sign that you are an employee worth investing in.
- *Be open to creative solutions.* It's possible that there are some idiosyncratic solutions (also called "I-deals") for enhancing both your interests and those of your supervisor. One of the best things about an integrative bargaining situation like this is that you and your negotiation partner can find novel solutions that neither would have imagined separately.

Think strategically about your career, and you'll likely find you can negotiate not just for a better paycheck tomorrow, but for a paycheck that keeps increasing in the years to come.

Sources: Y. Rofcanin, T. Kiefer, and K. Strauss, "How I-Deals Build Resources to Facilitate Reciprocation: Mediating Role of Positive Affective States," *Academy of Management Proceedings,* August, 2014, DOI: 10.5465/AMBPP.2014.16096abstract; C. Liao, S. J. Wayne, and D. M. Rousseau, "Idiosyncratic Deals in Contemporary Organizations: A Qualitative and Meta-Analytical Review," *Journal of Organizational Behavior,* October 16, 2014, DOI: 10.1002/job.1959; and V. Brenninkmeijer and M. Hekkert-Koning, "To Craft or Not to Craft," *Career Development International* 20 (2015): 147–62.

Self-efficacy is one individual-difference variable that consistently seems to relate to negotiation outcomes.[50] This is a fairly intuitive finding—it isn't too surprising to hear that those who believe they will be more successful in negotiation situations tend to perform more effectively. It may be that individuals who are more confident stake out stronger claims, are less likely to back down from their positions, and exhibit confidence that intimidates others. Although the exact mechanism is not yet clear, it does seem that negotiators may benefit from trying to get a boost in confidence before going to the bargaining table.

Research suggests intelligence predicts negotiation effectiveness, but, as with personality, the effects aren't especially strong.[51] In a sense, these weak links mean you're not severely disadvantaged, even if you're an agreeable extravert, when it's time to negotiate. We all can learn to be better negotiators.[52]

Moods/Emotions in Negotiations   Do moods and emotions influence negotiation? They do, but the way they work depends on the emotion as well as the

An Ethical Choice

Using Empathy to Negotiate More Ethically

You may have noticed that much of our advice for negotiating effectively depends on understanding the perspective and goals of the person with whom you are negotiating. Preparing checklists of your negotiation partner's interests, likely tactics, and BATNA have all been shown to improve negotiation outcomes. Can these steps make you a more ethical negotiator as well? Studies suggest that they might.

Researchers asked respondents to indicate how much they tended to think about other people's feelings and emotions and to describe the types of tactics they engaged in during a negotiation exercise. More empathetic individuals consistently engaged in fewer unethical negotiation behaviors like making false promises and manipulating information and emotions.

When considering how to improve your ethical negotiation behavior, follow these guidelines:

1. **Try to understand your negotiation partner's perspective.** This isn't just by understanding cognitively what the other person wants, but by empathizing with the emotional reaction he or she will likely have to the possible outcomes.

2. **Be aware of your own emotions, because many moral reactions are fundamentally emotional.** One study found that engaging in unethical negotiation strategies increased feelings of guilt, so by extension, feeling guilty in a negotiation may mean you are engaging in behavior you'll regret later.

3. **Beware of empathizing so much that you work against your own interests.** Just because you try to understand the motives and emotional reactions of the other side does not mean you have to assume the other person is going to be honest and fair in return. So be on guard.

Sources: Based on T. R. Cohen, "Moral Emotions and Unethical Bargaining: The Differential Effects of Empathy and Perspective Taking in Deterring Deceitful Negotiation," *Journal of Business Ethics* 94, no. 4 (2010): 569–79; and R. Volkema, D. Fleck, and A. Hofmeister, "Predicting Competitive-Unethical Negotiating Behavior and Its Consequences," *Negotiation Journal* 26, no. 3 (2010): 263–86.

context. A negotiator who shows anger can induce concessions, for instance, because the other negotiator believes no further concessions from the angry party are possible. One factor that governs this outcome, however, is power—you should show anger in negotiations only if you have at least as much power as your counterpart. If you have less, showing anger actually seems to provoke "hardball" reactions from the other side.[53]

Another factor is how genuine your anger is—"faked" anger, or anger produced from surface acting (see Chapter 4), is not effective, but showing anger that is genuine (deep acting) is.[54] It also appears that having a history of showing anger, rather than sowing the seeds of revenge, actually induces more concessions because the other party perceives the negotiator as "tough."[55] Finally, culture seems to matter. For instance, one study found that when East Asian participants showed anger, it induced more concessions than when the negotiator expressing anger was from the United States or Europe, perhaps because of the stereotype of East Asians as refusing to show anger.[56]

Another relevant emotion is disappointment. Generally, a negotiator who perceives disappointment from his or her counterpart concedes more. In one study, Dutch students were given 100 chips to bargain over. Negotiators who expressed disappointment were offered 14 more chips than those who didn't. In a second study, showing disappointment yielded an average concession of 12 chips. Unlike a show of anger, the relative power of the negotiators made no difference in either study.[57]

Anxiety also appears to have an impact on negotiation. For example, one study found that individuals who experienced more anxiety about a negotiation used more deceptions in dealing with others.[58] Another study found that anxious negotiators expect lower outcomes, respond to offers more quickly, and exit the bargaining process more quickly, leading them to obtain worse outcomes.[59]

People generally negotiate more effectively within cultures than between them. Politeness and positivity characterize the typical conflict-avoidant negotiations in Japan, such as with labor union leader Hidekazu Kitagawa (right), shown here presenting wage and benefits demands to Ikuo Mori, president of Fuji Heavy Industries, which makes Subaru vehicles.

Source: Kyodo/Newscom

As you can see, emotions—especially negative ones—matter to negotiation. Even emotional unpredictability affects outcomes; researchers have found that negotiators who express positive and negative emotions in an unpredictable way extract more concessions because this behavior makes the other party feel less in control.[60] As one negotiator put it, "Out of the blue, you may have to react to something you have been working on in one way, and then something entirely new is introduced, and you have to veer off and refocus."[61]

Culture in Negotiations   Do people from different cultures negotiate differently? The simple answer is the obvious one: Yes, they do. However, there are many nuances in the way this works. It isn't as simple as "these negotiators are the best"; indeed, success in negotiations depends on the context.

So what can we say about culture and negotiations? First, it appears that people generally negotiate more effectively within cultures than between them. For example, a Colombian is apt to do better negotiating with a Colombian than with a Sri Lankan. Second, it appears that in cross-cultural negotiations, it is especially important that the negotiators be high in openness. This suggests a good strategy is to choose cross-cultural negotiators who are high on openness to experience, and to avoid factors such as time pressure that tend to inhibit learning about the other party.[62]

Finally, because emotions are culturally sensitive, negotiators need to be especially aware of the emotional dynamics in cross-cultural negotiation. One study, for example, explicitly compared how U.S. and Chinese negotiators reacted to an angry counterpart. Chinese negotiators increased their use of distributive negotiating tactics, whereas U.S. negotiators decreased their use of these tactics. That is, Chinese negotiators began to drive a harder bargain once they saw that their negotiation partner was becoming angry, whereas U.S. negotiators capitulated somewhat in the face of angry demands. Why the difference? It may be that individuals from East Asian cultures feel that using anger to get their way in a negotiation is not a legitimate tactic, so they refuse to cooperate when their opponents become upset.[63]

Gender Differences in Negotiations   There are many areas of organizational behavior (OB) in which men and women are not that different. Negotiation

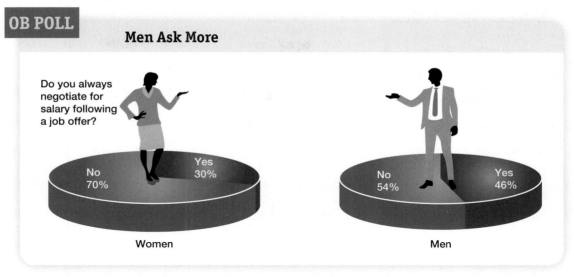

OB POLL

Men Ask More

Do you always negotiate for salary following a job offer?

Women
No 70%   Yes 30%

Men
No 54%   Yes 46%

Source: A. Gouveia, "Why Americans Are Too Scared to Negotiate Salary," *San Francisco Chronicle*, April 3, 2013, downloaded May 30, 2013 from http://www.sfgate.com/jobs/.

is not one of them. It seems fairly clear that men and women negotiate differently, men and women are treated differently by negotiation partners, and these differences affect outcomes (see OB Poll).

A popular stereotype is that women are more cooperative and pleasant in negotiations than men. Though this is controversial, there is some merit to it. Men tend to place a higher value on status, power, and recognition, whereas women tend to place a higher value on compassion and altruism. Moreover, women do tend to value relationship outcomes more than men, and men tend to value economic outcomes more than women.[64]

These differences affect both negotiation behavior and negotiation outcomes. Compared to men, women tend to behave in a less assertive, less self-interested, and more accommodating manner. As one review concluded, women "are more reluctant to initiate negotiations, and when they do initiate negotiations, they ask for less, are more willing to accept [the] offer, and make more generous offers to their negotiation partners than men do."[65] A study of MBA students at Carnegie-Mellon University found that the male students took the step of negotiating their first offer 57 percent of the time, compared to 4 percent for the female students. The net result? A $4,000 difference in starting salaries.[66]

One comprehensive literature review suggests that the tendency for men to receive better negotiation outcomes in some situations does not cover *all* situations.[67] Indeed, evidence suggested women and men bargained more equally in certain situations, women sometimes outperformed men, and men and women obtained more nearly equal outcomes when negotiating on behalf of someone else. In other words, everyone was better at advocating for others than they were at advocating for themselves.

Factors that increased the predictability of negotiations also tended to reduce gender differences. When the range of negotiation settlements was well defined, men and women were more equal in outcomes. When more experienced negotiators were at the table, men and women were also more nearly equivalent. The study authors proposed that when situations are more ambiguous, with less well-defined terms and less experienced negotiators, stereotypes may have stronger effects, leading to larger gender differences in outcomes.

So what can be done to change this troublesome state of affairs? First, organizational culture plays a role. If an organization, even unwittingly, reinforces gender-stereotypic behaviors (men negotiating competitively, women negotiating cooperatively), it will negatively affect negotiations when anyone goes against stereotype. Men and women need to know that it is acceptable for each to show a full range of negotiating behaviors. Thus, a female negotiator who behaves competitively and a male negotiator who behaves cooperatively need to know that they are not violating expectations. Making sure negotiations are designed to focus on well-defined and work-related terms also has promise for reducing gender differences by minimizing the ambiguous space for stereotypes to operate. This focus on structure and work relevance also obviously helps focus negotiations on factors that will improve the organization's performance.

Research is less clear on whether women can improve their outcomes by showing some gender-stereotypic behaviors. Researchers Laura Kray and colleagues suggested that female negotiators who were instructed to behave with "feminine charm" (be animated in body movements, make frequent eye contact with their partners, smile, laugh, be playful, and frequently compliment their partners) did better in negotiations than women not so instructed. These behaviors didn't work for men.[68]

Other researchers disagree and argue that what can best benefit women is to break down gender stereotypes for the individuals who hold them.[69] It's possible this is a short-term/long-term situation: In the short term, women can gain an advantage in negotiation by being both assertive and charming, but in the long term, their interests are best served by eliminating these sorts of sex role stereotypes.

Evidence suggests women's own attitudes and behaviors hurt them in negotiations. Managerial women demonstrate less confidence than men in anticipation of negotiating and are less satisfied with their performance afterward, even when their performance and the outcomes they achieve are similar to those for men.[70] Women are also less likely to see an ambiguous situation as an opportunity for negotiation. Women may unduly penalize themselves by failing to engage in negotiations that would be in their best interests. Some research suggests that women are less aggressive in negotiations because they are worried about backlash from others.

Negotiating in a Social Context

14-6 Assess the roles and functions of third-party negotiations.

We have mostly been discussing negotiations that occur among parties that meet only once, and in isolation from other individuals. However, in organizations, many negotiations are open-ended and public. When you are trying to figure out who in a work group should do a tedious task, negotiating with your boss to get a chance to travel internationally, or asking for more money for a project, there's a social component to the negotiation. You are probably negotiating with someone you already know and will work with again, and the negotiation and its outcome are likely to be topics people will talk about. To really understand negotiations in practice, then, we must consider the social factors of reputation and relationships.

Reputation   Your reputation is the way other people think and talk about you. When it comes to negotiation, having a reputation for being trustworthy matters. In short, trust in a negotiation process opens the door to many forms of integrative negotiation strategies that benefit both parties.[71] The most effective way to build trust is to behave in an honest way across repeated interactions. Then, others feel more comfortable making open-ended offers with many different outcomes. This helps to achieve win-win outcomes, since both parties can work to achieve what is most important to themselves while still benefitting the other party.

Sometimes we either trust or distrust people based on word-of-mouth about a person's characteristics. What type of characteristics help a person develop a trustworthy reputation? A combination of competence and integrity.[72] Negotiators higher in self-confidence and cognitive ability are seen as more competent by negotiation partners.[73] They are also considered better able to accurately describe a situation and their own resources, and more credible when they make suggestions for creative solutions to impasses. Individuals who have a reputation for integrity can also be more effective in negotiations.[74] They are seen as more likely to keep their promises and present information accurately, so others are more willing to accept their promises as part of a bargain. This opens many options for the negotiator that wouldn't be available to someone who is not seen as trustworthy. Finally, individuals who have higher reputations are better liked and have more friends and allies—in other words, they have more social resources, which may give them more understood power in negotiations.

Relationships   There is more to repeated negotiations than just reputation. The social, interpersonal component of relationships with repeated negotiations means that individuals go beyond valuing what is simply good for themselves and instead start to think about what is best for the other party and the relationship as a whole.[75] Repeated negotiations built on a foundation of trust also broaden the range of options, since a favor or concession today can be offered in return for some repayment further down the road.[76] Repeated negotiations also facilitate integrative problem solving. This occurs partly because people begin to see their negotiation partners in a more personal way over time and come to share emotional bonds.[77] Repeated negotiations also make integrative approaches more workable because a sense of trust and reliability has been built up.[78]

In sum, it's clear that an effective negotiator needs to think about more than just the outcomes of a single interaction. Negotiators who consistently act in a way that demonstrates competence, honesty, and integrity will usually have better outcomes in the long run.

Third-Party Negotiations

To this point, we've discussed bargaining in terms of direct negotiations. Occasionally, however, individuals or group representatives reach a stalemate and are unable to resolve their differences through direct negotiations. In such cases, they may turn to a third party to help them find a solution. There are three basic third-party roles: mediator, arbitrator, and conciliator.

A **mediator** is a neutral third party who facilitates a negotiated solution by using reasoning and persuasion, suggesting alternatives, and the like. Mediators are widely used in labor–management negotiations and in civil court disputes. Their overall effectiveness is fairly impressive. For example, the Equal Employment Opportunity Commission (EEOC) reported a settlement rate through mediation at 72.1 percent.[79] But the situation is the key to whether mediation will succeed; the conflicting parties must be motivated to bargain and resolve their conflict. In addition, conflict intensity can't be too high; mediation is most effective under moderate levels of conflict. Finally, perceptions of the mediator are important; to be effective, the mediator must be perceived as neutral and noncoercive.

An **arbitrator** is a third party with the authority to dictate an agreement. Arbitration can be voluntary (requested by the parties) or compulsory (forced on the parties by law or contract). The big plus of arbitration over mediation is that it always results in a settlement. Whether there is a downside depends on how heavy-handed the arbitrator appears. If one party is left feeling overwhelmingly defeated, that party is certain to be dissatisfied and the conflict may resurface at a later time.

mediator   A neutral third party who facilitates a negotiated solution by using reasoning, persuasion, and suggestions for alternatives.

arbitrator   A third party to a negotiation who has the authority to dictate an agreement.

conciliator A trusted third party who provides an informal communication link between the negotiator and the opponent.

A **conciliator** is a trusted third party who provides an informal communication link between the negotiator and the opponent. This role was made famous by Robert Duval in the first *Godfather* film. As Don Corleone's adopted son and a lawyer by training, Duval acted as an intermediary between the Corleones and the other Mafioso families. Comparing conciliation to mediation in terms of effectiveness has proven difficult because the two overlap a great deal. In practice, conciliators typically act as more than mere communication conduits. They also engage in fact-finding, interpret messages, and persuade disputants to develop agreements.

Summary

While many people assume conflict lowers group and organizational performance, this assumption is frequently incorrect. Conflict can be either constructive or destructive to the functioning of a group or unit. Levels of conflict can be either too high or too low to be constructive. Either extreme hinders performance. An optimal level is one that prevents stagnation, stimulates creativity, allows tensions to be released, and initiates the seeds of change without being disruptive or preventing the coordination of activities.

Implications for Managers

- Choose an authoritarian management style in emergencies, when unpopular actions need to be implemented (such as cost cutting, enforcement of unpopular rules, discipline), and when the issue is vital to the organization's welfare. Be certain to communicate your logic when possible to make certain others remain engaged and productive.
- Seek integrative solutions when your objective is to learn, when you want to merge insights from people with different perspectives, when you need to gain commitment by incorporating concerns into a consensus, and when you need to work through feelings that have interfered with a relationship.
- You can build trust by accommodating others when you find you're wrong, when you need to demonstrate reasonableness, when other positions need to be heard, when issues are more important to others than to yourself, when you want to satisfy others and maintain cooperation, when you can build social credits for later issues, to minimize loss when you are outmatched and losing, and when others should learn from their own mistakes.
- Consider compromising when goals are important but not worth potential disruption, when opponents with equal power are committed to mutually exclusive goals, and when you need temporary settlements to complex issues.
- Distributive bargaining can resolve disputes, but it often reduces the satisfaction of one or more negotiators because it is confrontational and focused on the short term. Integrative bargaining, in contrast, tends to provide outcomes that satisfy all parties and build lasting relationships.

★ **PERSONAL INVENTORY ASSESSMENTS**

Strategies for Handling Conflict

We all handle conflict, but few of us may have actual strategies in place. Take this PIA to further explore ways to handle conflict.

Pro Sports Strikes Are Caused by Greedy Owners

POINT

I'm as sick as anyone of the constant strikes, lockouts, and back-and-forth negotiations between sports teams and the players' unions. Of the major pro sports leagues, Major League Baseball (MLB) is the only one without a strike since 1995—and it had eight in its history. You've got to wonder why this keeps happening. Here's why: Owners' greed knows no limit.

In nearly every recent strike or lockout, the main issue was money and how to divide it. When the National Hockey League (NHL) locked out the players during the 2012-2013 season, the owners were the instigators. They wanted to reduce the players' share of hockey revenues. They wanted to eliminate salary arbitration. They wanted to introduce term limits to contracts. They wanted to change free-agency rules and eliminate signing bonuses. On a philosophical level, some of these proposals are interesting because they reveal that owners want to restrict competition when it suits them and increase it when it benefits them.

While the owners were whining about the unfairness of long-term contracts, the Minnesota Wild's owner Craig Leipold, a noted negotiations hawk, signed Zach Parise and Ryan Suter to identical 13-year, $98 million contracts. Contracts like these suggest that owners want the players' union to save them from themselves.

Perhaps some of this behavior would make sense if the owners were losing money hand over fist, but that is hardly the case. The NHL has three teams worth over $1 billion each, and few are worth less than $200 million. The owners aren't hurting, either. Most are millionaires many times over. Los Angeles Kings owner Philip Anschutz is reported to have a net worth of $12 billion.

Forbes reports the average NFL team is now worth more than $1.43 billion and the Dallas Cowboys are worth $3.2 billion; even low-earning and poorly run teams make money. Take the Jacksonville Jaguars. Wayne Weaver paid $208 million for the team in 1993. It has never made it to the Super Bowl and is almost always an also-ran in its division. Did the team's ineffectiveness really cost Weaver? He sold the club for $770 million in 2012.

In essence, what we have are rich owners trying to negotiate rules that keep them from competing with one another for players. It's a bald-faced and hypocritical attempt to use their own kind of union to negotiate favorable agreements, all the while criticizing the players' unions.

COUNTERPOINT

Major league owners are an easy target. But they have the most to lose from work stoppages. It's the players and their unions who push the envelope.

It's true that most major league players are well rewarded for their exceptional talents and the risks they take. It's also true that owners who are able to invest in teams are wealthy—investors usually are. But the fault for disputes lies with spoiled players—and the union leaders who burnish their credentials and garner the limelight by fanning the flames of discontent.

On this latter point, give all the credit in the world to the union negotiators (paid millions themselves), who do nothing if not hawk publicity and use hardball negotiating tactics. Take the NHL players' union boss Donald Fehr. For a "negotiation" set to begin at 10 A.M., he arrived at 11:15. At exactly 12:00, he announced he had a lunch meeting uptown and left.

As for the players, pro athletes are entitled almost by definition. For example, one retired NFL player and union representative, Chester Pitts, was commenting about how he had to settle for an $85,000 Mercedes instead of a $250,000 car. Well, we all have to make sacrifices. One rookie, Jets' quarterback Geno Smith, fired his agent after signing "only" a four-year contract for roughly $4.99 million. Smith called the contract "hard to stomach." I see a future in the players' union for this guy.

Do we really need labor unions for workers whose average salaries are $2 million (NFL), $2.58 million (NHL), $3.82 million (MLB), and $4.9 million (NBA)? NHL clubs spent 76 percent of their gross revenues on players' salaries and collectively lost $273 million the year before the most recent lockout. It's not much better in the NBA, where many teams lose money. Take the Dallas Mavericks, who have rarely made money since 2002, despite playing in the fourth-most populous metro area and winning the NBA title in 2011.

It's easy to argue that major league sports have an unusual number of labor disputes, but that's not necessarily accurate. Did you hear about the 2015 largest strike of oil refinery workers in decades or the ongoing worldwide strikes by low-paid workers in the fast-food industry? Somehow these strikes don't always make the news or our collective consciousness as much as sports strikes. Sports strikes interest us, but we shouldn't fall into the trap of blaming these on the owners.

Sources: #104 Philip Anschutz, *Forbes* real time net worth, http://www.forbes.com/profile/philip-anschutz/, downloaded June 9, 2015; T. Cary, "The 3 NHL Teams That Are Worth a Billion Dollars," *Sports Cheat Sheet,* June 6, 2015; K. Badenhausen, "Average MLB Player Salary Nearly Double NFL's, but Still Trails NBA's," *Forbes,* January 23, 2015, http://www.forbes.com/sites/kurtbadenhausen/2015/01/23/average-mlb-salary-nearly-double-nfls-but-trails-nba-players/; J. Feinstein, "In the NHL Lockout, the Owners Have It All Wrong," *Washington Post,* December 25, 2012, downloaded May 29, 2013, from http://articles.washingtonpost.com/; R. Cimini, "Geno Smith's Maturity Questioned," ESPN, May 3, 2013, downloaded May 3, 2013, from http://espn.go.com/; K. Campbell, "Thanks to Donald Fehr, NHL Negotiating against Itself ... and Losing," *The Hockey News,* December 29, 2012, downloaded May 29, 2013, from http://sports.yahoo.com/; B. Murphy, "20 Years of Peace and Prosperity Have Followed MLB's Last Strike," *Twin Cities,* July 5, 2014, http://www.twincities.com/sports/ci_26095630/peace-that-lasts-since-1994-season-ending-strike; and E. Seba, "Oil Refinery Strike Widens to Largest U.S. Plant," *Huffington Post,* February 21, 2015, http://www.huffingtonpost.com/2015/02/21/us-refinery-strike-wide_n_6727736.html.

CHAPTER REVIEW

MyManagementLab

Go to **mymanagementlab.com** to complete the problems marked with this icon.

QUESTIONS FOR REVIEW

14-1 What are the three types of conflict and the three loci of conflict?

14-2 What are the steps in the conflict process?

14-3 What are the differences between distributive and integrative bargaining?

14-4 What are the five steps in the negotiation process?

14-5 How do individual differences influence negotiations?

14-6 What are the roles and functions of third-party negotiations?

EXPERIENTIAL EXERCISE   A Negotiation Role-Play

There are two scenarios to consider for this case; one is more distributive, the other more integrative. Within your group of two, one of you takes the role of the engineering director, while the other takes the role of the marketing director. Read only your own side's specific information for the two negotiation processes. The overall situation is the same for both scenarios, but the priorities and outlook for the parties change depending on whether the group is doing the "contested resources" scenario or the "combined future" scenario.

The Case

Cytrix develops integrated bicycle and running performance systems. Runners and bikers wear the Cytrix watch, which uses GPS signals to identify their location and the distance they've covered. This information can then be uploaded to Cytrix Challenge website, where users record their performance over time. Social media tools also allow them to compare their performance relative to that of friends. The majority of users are either amateur student athletes or committed adult hobbyists like marathon runners.

The organization needs to determine how to allocate a fixed pool of resources for future development between the marketing and engineering groups. Rather than making an executive decision about resource allocation, the top management team has asked the respective teams to allocate $30 million dollars for planned future development and decide who will run different parts of the project.

Marketing Group Specific Information (only the marketing manager should read this)

The marketing group has been tracking the major areas of sales and has come to the conclusion that Cytrix has saturated the market. New sources of customers will need to be considered for future growth, especially general consumers who are interested in health but are not committed athletes. Research into sales of competitive products and areas where competitors are failing to meet consumer demands is needed. The marketing group's primary goal is to allocate sufficient resources to finance the research. The group also wants to retain control over which new products will be developed. Marketing would prefer to see engineering act in a consulting role, determining how best to manufacture the devices that fit the needs identified above.

Engineering Group Specific Information (only the engineering manager should read this)

The engineering group has recently been tracking the development of new hardware that will improve the accuracy of distance and speed estimates in remote areas. Several other companies are already experimenting with similar designs. To fully realize this improvement, engineering believes it will be necessary to further develop the technology so it is both lightweight and inexpensive to produce. The engineering group's primary goal is to allocate sufficient resources to develop these new technologies. The engineers would prefer to see marketing act in a consulting role, determining how best to advertise and deliver the new devices.

Contested Resources Scenario

The marketing and engineering departments are locked in a struggle for power. Your side (either marketing or engineering) should try to direct the largest possible proportion of both money and authority toward your proposed program. You still need to come up with a solution in which the other side ultimately agrees to assist you in implementing the program. If you can't reach an agreement for shared resources, the CEO will appoint new directors for both groups.

Combined Future Scenario

The marketing and engineering departments are eager to find a positive solution. Both sides should endeavor to see that the company's future needs are met. You know that to achieve success everyone needs to work together, so you'd like to find a way to divide the money and resources that benefits both marketing and engineering. Plans can incorporate multiple techniques for sharing and collaborating with resources.

The Negotiation

At the start of the negotiation, the instructor randomly assigns half the groups to the contested resources scenario, and the other half to the combined future scenario. Begin the process by outlining the goals and resources for your side of the negotiation. Then negotiate over the terms described in your scenario, attempting to advocate for a solution that matches your perspective.

Debriefing

Afterward, get the class together to discuss the processes used. Especially consider the differences in outcomes between the contested resources and combined future scenarios. Either scenario could arise in a real work environment, so think about how different negotiation situations give rise to different strategies, tactics, and outcomes.

ETHICAL DILEMMA The Lowball Applicant

Consider this first-person account:

> I am a human resource manager, so I interview people every day. Sometimes the managers in my company ask me to prescreen candidates, which I do after discussing the job at length with the manager. I usually start the candidate screening with a few personality–job fit tests; then conduct an interview, following a list of job-specific questions the manager has given me; and finally discuss the job requirements, our company, and the pay/benefits. By that time in the process, the candidate usually has a good idea of the job and is eager to suggest a level of pay at the top of the advertised bracket or, often, above the pay bracket. However, this isn't always the case. One time in particular, an excellent candidate with outstanding qualifications surprised me by saying that since she wanted flextime, she would accept a rate below the pay bracket. Confused, I asked her whether she wanted a reduction in hours below full-time. She said no, she expected to work full-time and only wanted to come in a little late and would leave a little late to make up the time. I guess she figured this was a concession worth slashing her salary for, but our company has flextime. In fact, she could have asked for 5 fewer hours per week, still have been considered full-time by our company policies, and negotiated for salary above the advertised pay grade.

> I knew the manager would be highly interested in this candidate and that he could probably get her to work the longer full-time hours at a lower rate of pay. That outcome might be best for the company, or it might not. The candidate obviously didn't fully understand the company policies in her favor, and she was unsophisticated about her worth in the marketplace. What should I have done?

Questions

14-7. If the human resource manager coached the applicant to request a higher salary, did the coaching work against the interests of the organization? Was the responsibility of the human resource (HR) manager to put the organization's financial interests first?

14-8. What do you see as the potential downside of the HR manager's abstaining from discussing the pay issue further with the candidate?

14-9. If the candidate were hired at the reduced rate she proposed, how might the situation play out over the next year when she gets to know the organization and its pay standards better?

CASE INCIDENT 1 Disorderly Conduct

The sound of Matt and Peter's arguing is familiar to everyone in the office by now. In an effort to make the best use of space and ensure a free flow of discussion and ideas, the founder of Markay Design had decided to convert the one-floor office of the company to an open plan with no walls between workers. The goal of such a layout is to eliminate boundaries and enhance creativity. But for Matt and Peter, the new arrangement creates a growing sense of tension.

The argument boils down to the question of workspace order and organization. Peter prefers to keep his desk completely clean and clear, and he keeps a stack of cleaning wipes in a drawer to eliminate any dust or dirt. Matt, on the other hand, likes to keep all his work visible on his desk, so sketches, plans, magazines, and photos are scattered everywhere, alongside boxes of crackers and coffee cups. Peter finds it hard to concentrate when he sees Matt's piles of materials everywhere, while Matt feels he can be more creative and free flowing when he's not forced to clean and organize constantly. Many of Matt and Peter's coworkers wish they'd just let the issue drop. The men enjoyed a good working relationship in the past, with Peter's attention to detail and thorough planning serving to rein in some of Matt's wild inspirations. But of late, their collaborations have been derailed in disputes.

Everyone knows it's not productive to engage in conflicts over every small irritant in the workplace. However, completely avoiding conflict can be equally negative. An emerging body of research has examined "conflict cultures" in organizations. The findings suggest having a culture that actively avoids and suppresses conflicts is associated with lower levels of creativity. Moreover, cultures that push conflict underground but do not succeed in reducing the underlying tensions can become passive-aggressive, marked by underhanded behavior against other coworkers.

Ultimately, finding a way through the clutter dispute is probably going to be an ongoing process to find a balance between perspectives. Both Matt and Peter worry that if they can't find a solution, their usually positive work relationship will be too contentious to bear. And that would be a real mess.

Questions

14-10. What could Peter and Matt's manager do to help them resolving their conflict?

14-11. The case suggests that there is research to support the notion that avoiding conflict stifles creativity. Is there such research, and do you agree?

14-12. How can Matt and Peter develop an active problem-solving discussion to resolve this conflict? What could effectively be changed, and what is probably going to just remain a problem?

Sources: S. Shellenbarger, "Clashing over Office Clutter," *Wall Street Journal,* March 19, 2014, http://www.wsj.com/articles/SB10001424052702304747404579447331212245004; S. Shellenbarger, "To Fight or Not to Fight? When to Pick Workplace Battles," *Wall Street Journal,* December 17, 2014, http://www.wsj.com/articles/picking-your-workplace-battles-1418772621; and M. J. Gelfand, J. R. Harrington, and L. M. Leslie, "Conflict Cultures: A New Frontier for Conflict Management Research and Practice," in N. M. Ashkanasy, O. B. Ayoko, and K. A. Jehn (eds.), *Handbook of Conflict Management Research,* 2014, 109–35.

CASE INCIDENT 2   Is More Cash Worth the Clash?

With 3,700 hotels located in 92 countries, Accor's revenues total more than $6 billion. About 180,000 people currently work for Accor's internationally renowned brands, including Sofitel, Novotel, and Ibis in Europe, the Middle-East, and Africa, and Huazhu, Grand Mercure (through domestic brands Mei Jue, Maha Cipta, and Manee Pura), and Sebel in Asia, Australia, and Latin America. Because Accor is opening one hotel every two days, it will employ even more people over the next few years directly and via subcontracting temporary work agencies. Not only does it mean negotiating an increasing number of employment contracts with individuals, but it also involves local negotiations with subcontractors. Work conditions and pay are often at the core of most of these negotiations.

In European hotels, labor costs represent almost 50% of revenues. Thus, human capital is either a competitive advantage you might invest in or a resource you may save money on. There is often a clash between shareholders, whose goal is to increase profit by lowering costs and generating more cash, and employees, who expect a higher pay from their company's growth.

In France, over the last five years, there have been hundreds of room attendants working for Accor hotels who publicly went on strike, complaining in the media about their pay and work conditions. These room attendants were not directly employed by Accor, but by subcontractors who paid them less than the industry minima and imposed higher production-rates on them (for example, to clean four rooms an hour) than room attendants directly employed by Accor, whose unions negotiated work conditions (three rooms an hour is the key-performance indicator used in Ibis hotels). Although the conflict occurred between temporary workers and their employing agencies, Accor had to play a role, because room attendants on strike could not be replaced on the spot and remaining employees could not accept more supplementary hours.

To foster its engagement in CSR and to solve the conflict, Accor signed a protocol with its subcontractors and the room attendants went back to work.

Unions may play a role in such labor-management conflicts. While it has excellent relationships with French unions, Accor was actually warned by the French Organisation for Economic Co-operation and Development (OECD) national contact point (NCP) in 2012 after a complaint about the violation of international guidelines was brought against it in 2010 by the International Union of Food, Agricultural, Hotel, Restaurant, Catering, Tobacco and Allied Workers' Associations (IUF), which represents over 12 million workers. The IUF stated that Accor Group Accor Group had denied the right of its employees to join collective negotiation in one hotel in Benin and to establish trade unions in three hotels in Canada. Because local unions and hotels' managers were unable to come to any agreement for years, the social conflict reached a global level with the IUF. In 2014, the French OECD NCP eventually thanked Accor for their involvement in resolving the conflicts with the IUF, and in deploying training plans to nurture hotels' franchisees and managers' sense of CSR.

Yet such conflicts should have been avoided, for Accor is strongly committed to developing compensation systems and work conditions that exceed the requirements of local legislation. In 2014, Accor signed non-discretionary profit-sharing agreements in countries like Mexico, Russia, Turkey, and the United Arab Emirates. Gender-neutral compensation and equal opportunity programs are also vital to Accor, which created a Women at Accor Generation (WAAG) network designed to help women to evolve within the group. A Singaporean general counsel states that she had to face cultural pressures that compelled her to focus on family commitments rather than to work, but WAAG assisted her in solving work–life conflicts and advancing within Accor. In Dubai, where hotel managerial positions are usually held by men, the director of two hotels spoke of how WAAG helped her with training courses and Webinars, which also covered gender-related challenges, to assume her responsibilities as a female manager.

Questions

14-13. Labor–management negotiations might be characterized as more distributive than integrative. Do you agree? Why do you think this is the case? What, if anything, would you do about it?

14-14. Be they dyadic, intragroup, or intergroup ones, labor–management conflicts are too often considered as dysfunctional while neglecting the role of third-parties that could make them more functional. Do you agree? Why?

14-15. If you were advising union and management representatives about how to solve their conflicts, drawing from the artefacts in the UIF-Accor case and the concepts in this chapter, what would you tell them?

14-16. What kind of conflicts do the Accor employees involved in WAAG networks face? Imagine, describe, and analyze both the conflict process and the negotiation process that one of them might have experienced.

Sources: P. Rosenzweig, "Accor: Global Excellence through People," *International Institute for Management Development Case,* 1999; F. Rivaud, "Comment Bazin veut faire d'Accor le meilleur groupe hôtelier du monde," *Challenges,* December 2014; Accor & Autorité des Marchés Financiers, "Enhancing Your Hotel Experience," *2014 Registration Document and Annual Financial Report,* March 2015; Direction de la Communication et des Relations Extérieures Accor, "Nous réinventons votre séjour," *Rapport d'activité 2014,* 2015; S. Stabile, "Women's Words," *Women at Accor Generation WAAG,* February 2015; European Trade Union Institute for Research, "European Trade Unions and Sustainable Development," 2008; accorhotels-group.com; oecd.org; tresor.economie.gouv.fr; uif.org; cfdt-accor.org; hrinasia.com; hotelmagazine.com; e-hotelier.com; "Hotel Industry in Benin and Canada," OECD Guidelines for Multinational Enterprises, https://mneguidelines.oecd.org/database/instances/fr0013.htm; http://www.tresor.economie.gouv.fr/File/411552.

MyManagementLab

Go to **mymanagementlab.com** for the following Assisted-graded writing questions:

14-16. In regard to Case Incident 1, how do you think modern, open workspaces contribute to or inhibit employee conflicts?

14-17. From your reading of Case Incident 2 and the text, how do you think unions have changed organizational negotiation practices?

14-18. MyManagementLab Only – comprehensive writing assignment for this chapter.

ENDNOTES

1. See, for instance, D. Tjosvold, A. S. H. Wong, and N. Y. F. Chen, "Constructively Managing Conflicts in Organizations," *Annual Review of Organizational Psychology and Organizational Behavior* 1 (March 2014): 545–68; and M. A. Korsgaard, S. S. Jeong, D. M. Mahony, and A. H. Pitariu, "A Multilevel View of Intragroup Conflict," *Journal of Management* 34, no. 6 (2008): 1222–52.

2. F. R. C. de Wit, L. L. Greer, and K. A. Jehn, "The Paradox of Intragroup Conflict: A Meta-Analysis," *Journal of Applied Psychology* 97, no. 2 (2012): 360–90; and N. Gamero, V. González-Romá, and J. M. Peiró, "The Influence of Intra-Team Conflict on Work Teams' Affective Climate: A Longitudinal Study," *Journal of Occupational and Organizational Psychology* 81, no. 1 (2008): 47–69.

3. N. Halevy, E. Y. Chou, and A. D. Galinsky, "Exhausting or Exhilarating? Conflict as Threat to Interests, Relationships and Identities," *Journal of Experimental Social Psychology* 48 (2012): 530–37.

4. F. R. C. de Wit, L. L. Greer, and K. A. Jehn, "The Paradox of Intragroup Conflict: A Meta-Analysis," *Journal of Applied Psychology* 97 (2012): 360–90.

5. J. Farh, C. Lee, and C. I. C. Farh, "Task Conflict and Team Creativity: A Question of How Much and When," *Journal of Applied Psychology* 95, no. 6 (2010): 1173–80.

6. B. H. Bradley, A. C. Klotz, B. F. Postlethwaite, and K. G. Brown, "Ready to Rumble: How Team Personality Composition and Task Conflict Interact to Improve Performance," *Journal of Applied Psychology* 98 (2013): 385–92.

7. B. H. Bradley, B. F. Postlethwaite, A. C. Klotz, M. R. Hamdani, and K. G. Brown, "Reaping the Benefits of Task Conflict in Teams: The Critical Role of Team Psychological Safety Climate," *Journal of Applied Psychology* 97 (2012), 151–58.

8. S. Benard, "Cohesion from Conflict: Does Intergroup Conflict Motivate Intragroup Norm Enforcement and Support for Centralized Leadership?" *Social Psychology Quarterly* 75 (2012): 107–30.

9. G. A. Van Kleef, W. Steinel, and A. C. Homan, "On Being Peripheral and Paying Attention: Prototypicality and Information Processing in Intergroup Conflict," *Journal of Applied Psychology* 98 (2013): 63–79.

10. R. S. Peterson and K. J. Behfar, "The Dynamic Relationship between Performance Feedback, Trust, and Conflict in Groups: A Longitudinal Study," *Organizational Behavior & Human Decision Processes*, September–November 2003, 102–12.

11. T. M. Glomb and H. Liao, "Interpersonal Aggression in Work Groups: Social Influence, Reciprocal, and Individual Effects," *Academy of Management Journal* 46, no. 4 (2003): 486–96; and V. Venkataramani and R. S. Dalal, "Who Helps and Harms Whom? Relational Aspects of Interpersonal Helping and Harming in Organizations," *Journal of Applied Psychology* 92, no. 4 (2007): 952–66.

12. R. Friedman, C. Anderson, J. Brett, M. Olekalns, N. Goates, and C. C. Lisco, "The Positive and Negative Effects of Anger on Dispute Resolution: Evidence from Electronically Mediated Disputes," *Journal of Applied Psychology*, April 2004, 369–76.

13. J. S. Chun, and J. N. Choi, "Members' Needs, Intragroup Conflict, and Group Performance," *Journal of Applied Psychology* 99 (2014): 437–50.

14. See, for instance, J. R. Curhan, "What Do People Value When They Negotiate? Mapping the Domain of Subjective Value in Negotiation," *Journal of Personality and Social Psychology*, September 2006, 117–26; N. Halevy, E. Chou, and J. K. Murnighan, "Mind Games: The Mental Representation of Conflict," *Journal of Personality and Social Psychology* 102 (2012): 132–48.

15. A. M. Isen, A. A. Labroo, and P. Durlach, "An Influence of Product and Brand Name on Positive Affect: Implicit and Explicit Measures," *Motivation & Emotion*, March 2004, 43–63.

16. Ibid.

17. C. Montes, D. Rodriguez, and G. Serrano, "Affective Choice of Conflict Management Styles," *International Journal of Conflict Management* 23 (2012): 6–18.

18. M. A. Rahim, *Managing Conflict in Organizations*, 4th ed. (New Brunswick, NJ: Transaction Publishers, 2011).

19. Ibid.

20. Ibid.

21. L. A. DeChurch, J. R. Mesmer-Magnus, and D. Doty, "Moving beyond Relationship and Task Conflict: Toward a Process-State Perspective," *Journal of Applied Psychology* 98 (2013): 559–78.

22. G. Todorova, J. B. Bear, and L. R. Weingart, "Can Conflict Be Energizing? A Study of Task Conflict, Positive Emotions, and Job Satisfaction," *Journal of Applied Psychology* 99 (2014): 451–67.

23. P. J. Hinds and D. E. Bailey, "Out of Sight, Out of Sync: Understanding Conflict in Distributed Teams," *Organization Science*, November–December 2003, 615–32.

24. K. A. Jehn, L. Greer, S. Levine, and G. Szulanski, "The Effects of Conflict Types, Dimensions, and Emergent States on Group Outcomes," *Group Decision and Negotiation* 17, no. 6 (2005): 777–96.

25. Zellmer-Bruhn, Maloney, Bhappu, and Salvador, "When and How Do Differences Matter?"

26. J. Fried, "I Know You Are, but What Am I?" *Inc.*, July/August 2010, 39–40.

27. K. J. Behfar, R. S. Peterson, E. A. Mannix, and W. M. K. Trochim, "The Critical Role of Conflict Resolution in Teams: A Close Look at the Links between Conflict Type, Conflict Management Strategies, and Team Outcomes," *Journal of Applied Psychology* 93, no. 1 (2008):. 170–88; A. G. Tekleab, N. R. Quigley, and P. E. Tesluk, "A Longitudinal Study of Team Conflict, Conflict Management, Cohesion, and Team Effectiveness," *Group and Organization Management* 34, no. 2 (2009): 170–205.

28. A. Somech, H. S. Desivilya, and H. Lidogoster, "Team Conflict Management and Team Effectiveness: The Effects of Task Interdependence and Team Identification," *Journal of Organizational Behavior* 30, no. 3 (2009): 359–78.

29. H. Ren and B. Gray, "Repairing Relationship Conflict: How Violation Types and Culture Influence the Effectiveness of Restoration Rituals," *Academy of Management Review* 34, no. 1 (2009): 105–26.

30. M. J. Gelfand, M. Higgins, L. H. Nishii, J. L. Raver, A. Dominguez, F. Murakami, S. Yamaguchi, and M. Toyama, "Culture and Egocentric Perceptions of Fairness in Conflict and Negotiation," *Journal of Applied Psychology*, October 2002, 833–45; and Z. Ma, "Chinese Conflict Management Styles and Negotiation Behaviours: An Empirical Test," *International Journal of Cross Cultural Management*, April 2007, 101–19.

31. P. P. Fu, X. H. Yan, Y. Li, E. Wang, and S. Peng, "Examining Conflict-Handling Approaches by Chinese Top Management Teams in IT Firms," *International Journal of Conflict Management* 19, no. 3 (2008): 188–209.

32. W. Liu, R. Friedman, and Y. Hong, "Culture and Accountability in Negotiation: Recognizing the Importance of In-Group Relations," *Organizational Behavior and Human Decision Processes* 117 (2012): 221–34; and B. C. Gunia, J. M. Brett, A. K. Nandkeolyar, and D. Kamdar, "Paying a Price: Culture, Trust, and Negotiation Consequences," *Journal of Applied Psychology* 96, no. 4 (2010): 774–89

33. M. H. Bazerman, J. R. Curhan, D. A. Moore, and K. L. Valley, "Negotiation," *Annual Review of Psychology* 51 (2000): 279–314.

34. See, for example, D. R. Ames, "Assertiveness Expectancies: How Hard People Push Depends on the Consequences They Predict," *Journal of Personality and Social Psychology* 95, no. 6 (2008): 1541–57; and J. R. Curhan, H. A. Elfenbein, and H. Xu, "What Do People Value When They Negotiate? Mapping the Domain of Subjective Value in Negotiation," *Journal of Personality and Social Psychology* 91, no. 3 (2006): 493–512.

35. R. Lewicki, D. Saunders, and B. Barry, *Negotiation*, 6th ed. (New York: McGraw-Hill/Irwin, 2009).

36. J. C. Magee, A. D. Galinsky, and D. H. Gruenfeld, "Power, Propensity to Negotiate, and Moving First in Competitive Interactions," *Personality and Social Psychology Bulletin*, February 2007, 200–12.

37. H. R. Bowles, L. Babcock, and L. Lei, "Social Incentives for Gender Differences in the Propensity to Initiative Negotiations: Sometimes It Does Hurt to Ask," *Organizational Behavior and Human Decision Processes* 103 (2007): 84–103.

38. E. Wilson, "The Trouble with Jake," *The New York Times*, July 15, 2009, www.nytimes.com.

39. Rahim, *Managing Conflict in Organizations*.

40. C. K. W. De Dreu, L. R. Weingart, and S. Kwon, "Influence of Social Motives on Integrative Negotiation: A Meta-Analytic Review

and Test of Two Theories," *Journal of Personality & Social Psychology*, May 2000, 889–905.

[41] This model is based on R. J. Lewicki, D. Saunders, and B. Barry, *Negotiation*, 7th ed. (New York: McGraw Hill, 2014).

[42] J. R. Curhan, H. A. Elfenbein, and G. J. Kilduff, "Getting off on the Right Foot: Subjective Value versus Economic Value in Predicting Longitudinal Job Outcomes from Job Offer Negotiations," *Journal of Applied Psychology* 94, no. 2 (2009): 524–34.

[43] L. L. Thompson, J. Wang, and B. C. Gunia. "Negotiation," *Annual Review of Psychology* 61, (2010): 491–515.

[44] Michael Schaerer, Roderick I. Swaab, and Adam D. Galinsky, "Anchors Weigh More Than Power: Why Absolute Powerlessness Liberates Negotiators to Achieve Better Outcomes," *Psychological Science*, December, 2014, doi:10.1177/0956797614558718.

[45] R. P. Larrick and G. Wu, "Claiming a Large Slice of a Small Pie: Asymmetric Disconfirmation in Negotiation," *Journal of Personality and Social Psychology* 93, no. 2 (2007): 212–33.

[46] H. A. Elfenbein, "Individual Difference in Negotiation: A Nearly Abandoned Pursuit Revived," *Current Directions in Psychological Science* 24 (2015): 131–36.

[47] T. A. Judge, B. A. Livingston, and C. Hurst, "Do Nice Guys—and Gals—Really Finish Last? The Joint Effects of Sex and Agreeableness on Income," *Journal of Personality and Social Psychology* 102 (2012): 390–407.

[48] N. Dimotakis, D. E. Conlon, and R. Ilies, "The Mind and Heart (Literally) of the Negotiator: Personality and Contextual Determinants of Experiential Reactions and Economic Outcomes in Negotiation," *Journal of Applied Psychology* 97 (2012): 183–93.

[49] E. T. Amanatullah, M. W. Morris, and J. R. Curhan, "Negotiators Who Give Too Much: Unmitigated Communion, Relational Anxieties, and Economic Costs in Distributive and Integrative Bargaining," *Journal of Personality and Social Psychology* 95, no. 3 (2008): 723–38; and D. S. DeRue, D. E. Conlon, H. Moon, and H. W. Willaby, "When Is Straightforwardness a Liability in Negotiations? The Role of Integrative Potential and Structural Power," *Journal of Applied Psychology* 94, no. 4 (2009): 1032–47.

[50] S. Sharma, W. Bottom, and H. A. Elfenbein, "On the Role of Personality, Cognitive Ability, and Emotional Intelligence in Predicting Negotiation Outcomes: A Meta-Analysis," *Organizational Psychology Review* 3 (2013): 293–336.

[51] H. A. Elfenbein, J. R. Curhan, N. Eisenkraft, A. Shirako, and L. Baccaro, "Are Some Negotiators Better Than Others? Individual Differences in Bargaining Outcomes," *Journal of Research in Personality*, December 2008, 1463–75.

[52] A. Zerres, J. Hüffmeier, P. A. Freund, K. Backhaus, and G. Hertel, "Does It Take Two to Tango? Longitudinal Effects of Unilateral and Bilateral Integrative Negotiation Training," *Journal of Applied Psychology* 98 (2013): 478–91.

[53] G. Lelieveld, E. Van Dijk, I. Van Beest, and G. A. Van Kleef, "Why Anger and Disappointment Affect Other's Bargaining Behavior Differently: The Moderating Role of Power and the Mediating Role of Reciprocal Complementary Emotions," *Personality and Social Psychology Bulletin* 38 (2012): 1209–21.

[54] S. Côté, I. Hideg, and G. A. van Kleef, "The Consequences of Faking Anger in Negotiations," *Journal of Experimental Social Psychology* 49 (2013): 453–63.

[55] G. A. Van Kleef and C. K. W. De Dreu, "Longer-Term Consequences of Anger Expression in Negotiation: Retaliation or Spillover?" *Journal of Experimental Social Psychology* 46, no. 5 (2010): 753–60.

[56] H. Adam and A. Shirako, "Not All Anger Is Created Equal: The Impact of the Expresser's Culture on the Social Effects of Anger in Negotiations," *Journal of Applied Psychology*, 2013.

[57] Lelieveld, Van Dijk, Van Beest, and Van Kleef, "Why Anger and Disappointment Affect Other's Bargaining Behavior Differently."

[58] M. Olekalns and P. L Smith, "Mutually Dependent: Power, Trust, Affect, and the Use of Deception in Negotiation," *Journal of Business Ethics* 85, no. 3 (2009): 347–65.

[59] A. W. Brooks and M. E. Schweitzer, "Can Nervous Nellie Negotiate? How Anxiety Causes Negotiators to Make Low First Offers, Exit Early, and Earn Less Profit," *Organizational Behavior and Human Decision Processes* 115, no. 1 (2011): 43–54.

[60] M. Sinaceur, H. Adam, G. A. Van Kleef, and A. D. Galinsky, "The Advantages of Being Unpredictable: How Emotional Inconsistency Extracts Concessions in Negotiation," *Journal of Experimental Social Psychology* 49 (2013): 498–508.

[61] K. Leary, J. Pillemer, and M. Wheeler, "Negotiating with Emotion," *Harvard Business Review*, January–February 2013, 96–103.

[62] L. A. Liu, R. Friedman, B. Barry, M. J. Gelfand, and Z. Zhang, "The Dynamics of Consensus Building in Intracultural and Intercultural Negotiations," *Administrative Science Quarterly* 57 (2012): 269–304.

[63] M. Liu, "The Intrapersonal and Interpersonal Effects of Anger on Negotiation Strategies: A Cross-Cultural Investigation," *Human Communication Research* 35, no. 1 (2009): 148–69; and H. Adam, A. Shirako, and W. W. Maddux, "Cultural Variance in the Interpersonal Effects of Anger in Negotiations," *Psychological Science* 21, no. 6 (2010): 882–89.

[64] P. D. Trapnell and D. L. Paulhus, "Agentic and Communal Values: Their Scope and Measurement," *Journal of Personality Assessment* 94 (2012): 39–52.

[65] C. T. Kulik and M. Olekalns, "Negotiating the Gender Divide: Lessons from the Negotiation and Organizational Behavior Literatures," *Journal of Management* 38 (2012): 1387–415.

[66] C. Suddath, "The Art of Haggling," *Bloomberg Businessweek*, November 26, 2012, 98.

[67] J. Mazei, J. Hüffmeier, P. A. Freund, A. F. Stuhlmacher, L. Bilke, and G. Hertel, "A Meta-Analysis on Gender Differences in Negotiation Outcomes and Their Moderators," *Psychological Bulletin* 141 (2015): 85–104.

[68] L. J. Kray, C. C. Locke, and A B. Van Zant, "Feminine Charm: An Experimental Analysis of its Costs and Benefits in Negotiations," *Personality and Social Psychology Bulletin* 38 (2012): 1343–57.

[69] S. de Lemus, R. Spears, M. Bukowski, M. Moya, and J. Lupiáñez, "Reversing Implicit Gender Stereotype Activation as a Function of Exposure to Traditional Gender Roles," *Social Psychology* 44 (2013): 109–16.

[70] D. A. Small, M. Gelfand, L. Babcock, and H. Gettman, "Who Goes to the Bargaining Table? The Influence of Gender and Framing on the Initiation of Negotiation," *Journal of Personality and Social Psychology* 93, no. 4 (2007): 600–13.

[71] D. T. Kong, K. T. Dirks, and D. L. Ferrin, "Interpersonal Trust within Negotiations: Meta-Analytic Evidence, Critical Contingencies, and Directions for Future Research," *Academy of Management Journal* 57 (2014): 1235–55.

[72] G. R. Ferris, J. N. Harris, Z. A. Russell, B. P. Ellen, A. D. Martinez, and F. R. Blass, "The Role of Reputation in the Organizational Sciences: A Multilevel Review, Construct Assessment, and Research Directions," *Research in Personnel and Human Resources Management* 32 (2014): 241–303.

[73] R. Zinko, G. R. Ferris, S. E. Humphrey, C. J. Meyer, and F. Aime, "Personal Reputation in Organizations: Two-Study Constructive Replication and Extension of Antecedents and Consequences," *Journal of Occupational and Organizational Psychology* 85 (2012): 156–80.

[74] A. Hinshaw, P. Reilly, and A. Kupfer Schneider, "Attorneys and Negotiation Ethics: A Material Misunderstanding?" *Negotiation Journal* 29 (2013): 265–87; N. A. Welsh, "The Reputational Advantages of Demonstrating Trustworthiness: Using the Reputation Index with Law Students," *Negotiation Journal* 28 (2012): 117–45.

[75] J. R. Curhan, H. A. Elfenbein, and X. Heng, "What Do People Value When They Negotiate? Mapping the Domain of Subjective Value in Negotiation," *Journal of Personality and Social Psychology* 91 (2006): 493–512.

[76] W. E. Baker and N. Bulkley, "Paying It Forward vs. Rewarding Reputation: Mechanisms of Generalized Reciprocity," *Organization Science* 25 (June 17, 2014): 1493–510.

[77] G. A. Van Kleef, C. K. W. De Dreu, and A. S. R. Manstead, "An Interpersonal Approach to Emotion in Social Decision Making: The Emotions as Social Information Model," *Advances in Experimental Social Psychology* 42 (2010): 45–96.

[78] F. Lumineau and J. E. Henderson, "The Influence of Relational Experience and Contractual Governance on the Negotiation Strategy in Buyer–supplier Disputes," *Journal of Operations Management* 30 (2012): 382–95.

[79] U.S. Equal Employment Opportunity Commission, http://www.eeoc.gov/eeoc/mediation/qanda.cfm, accessed June 9, 2015.

15 Foundations of Organization Structure

15-1 Identify seven elements of an organization's structure.

15-2 Identify the characteristics of the functional structure, the divisional structure, and the matrix structure.

15-3 Identify the characteristics of the virtual structure, the team structure, and the circular structure.

15-4 Describe the effects of downsizing on organizational structures and employees.

15-5 Contrast the reasons for mechanistic and organic structural models.

15-6 Analyze the behavioral implications of different organizational designs.

MyManagementLab®
⭐ **Chapter Warm Up**

If your professor has chosen to assign this, go to the Assignments section of **mymanagementlab.com** to complete the chapter warm up.

IN THE FLAT FIELD

Startups often struggle to move from executing small, collaborative, local projects to becoming complex, organized, global organizations. Their leaders sometimes believe a hierarchy would create a bloated class of middle managers whose work would change into recording and administrating, rather than imagining and creating. As Craig Silverstein, Google's first hire, says, entrepreneurs often ask, "Who needs managers? They never add any value."

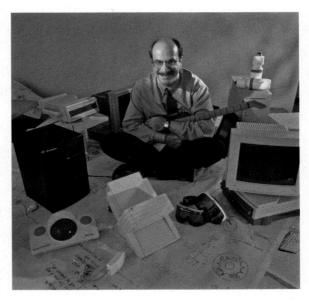

Remaining a perpetually entrepreneurial organization with an organic, flat structure may be appealing, but it's not easy to achieve. Management's core functions are to provide direction, resolve conflicts, and realize product potential in the market. Even if everyone gets along, good ideas may never be fully realized without some form of coordinating structure and a strategic business framework.

Large organizations can always restructure their units, but growing creates an orchestra of processes that need to be brought together. Each growth strategy exponentially increases the complexity of managing workers and information flow. Innovative organizations try to strike a balance between achieving the positive coordinating functions of management and avoiding a tight bureaucratic structure.

One way to stay entrepreneurial in an organizational structure is demonstrated at the video game company Valve. The company's handbook notes, "We don't have any management, and nobody 'reports to' anybody else." This suggests that Valve's organizational structure is completely flat, with everyone equal in the organization. Still, team leaders are assigned to positions of authority over specific projects. The key feature appears to be that this leadership role is temporary.

From the time of its founding by David Kelley in 1993, shown in the photo, the design firm IDEO has minimized a formal organizational structure by having employees focus on different levels of project accountability. Coordination of multiple projects is done at the "portfolio" level, whereas coordination of projects across the entire organization is done at the "enterprise" level. There is no formal hierarchy, again suggesting a flat organizational structure. Responsibility for decision making remains with the individual and his or her area of concentration.

Another approach is the use of virtual management that completely separates administration from core work tasks. For example, small biotech companies outsource lab work, financial management, and marketing so the scientist-entrepreneur can focus on what he or she does best. Some very small biotech firms share office space, allowing scientists working on very different projects to swap ideas while another set of individuals takes care of the management side of the business. Although multiple functions are being fulfilled, the formal organizational chart might just consist of one or two individuals at the top, and a loose, rather undefined network of collaborators who are accountable for the scope of work they are assigned to complete, but are self-managing.

The approaches successful companies have taken to structuring themselves during growth provide two major lessons. First, a vision is needed of how the increasingly complex organization can coordinate people around a common strategy. Second, management must ensure that organizational structures and reporting relationships don't become so restrictive that they undermine the creative passions that made the company successful in the first place. As you can see, organizational structures set up a company for future success.

Sources: M. Hutson, "Espousing Equality, but Embracing a Hierarchy," *New York Times,* June 22, 2014, http://www.nytimes.com/2014/06/22/business/espousing-equality-but-embracing-a-hierarchy.html?_r=0; J. Whalen, "Virtual Biotechs: No Lab Space, Few Employees," *Wall Street Journal,* June 4, 2014, http://www.wsj.com/articles/virtual-biotechs-no-lab-space-few-employees-1401816867; and C. Huston, "He Failed on 'Shark Tank'—But So What?" *Wall Street Journal*, March 10, 2014, http://www.wsj.com/articles/SB1000142405270230394 24045793610402247777748.

E ven for a startup with only a few employees, choosing an organizational structure requires far more than simply deciding who's the boss and how many employees are needed. The organization's structure will determine what relationships form, the formality of those relationships, and many work outcomes. The structure may also change as organizations grow and shrink, as management trends dictate, and as research uncovers better ways of maximizing productivity.

Structural decisions are arguably the most fundamental ones a leader has to make toward sustaining organizational growth.[1] In this chapter, we'll explore how structure affects employee behavior and the organization as a whole.

What Is Organizational Structure?

15-1 Identify seven elements of an organization's structure.

organizational structure The way in which job tasks are formally divided, grouped, and coordinated.

An **organizational structure** defines how job tasks are formally divided, grouped, and coordinated. Managers should address seven key elements when they design their organization's structure: work specialization, departmentalization, chain of command, span of control, centralization and decentralization, formalization, and boundary spanning.[2] Exhibit 15-1 presents each element as the answer to an important structural question, and the following sections describe them.

Work Specialization

work specialization The degree to which tasks in an organization are subdivided into separate jobs.

Early in the twentieth century, Henry Ford became rich by building automobiles on an assembly line. Every worker was assigned a specific, repetitive task such as putting on the right front wheel or installing the right front door. By dividing jobs into small standardized tasks that could be performed over and over, Ford was able to produce a car every 10 seconds, using employees with relatively limited skills. **Work specialization**, or *division of labor,* describes the degree to which activities in the organization are divided into separate jobs. The essence of work specialization is to divide a job into a number of steps, each completed by a separate individual. Individuals specialize in doing part of an activity rather

Exhibit 15-1	Key Design Questions and Answers for Designing the Proper Organizational Structure
The Key Question	**The Answer Is Provided by**
1. To what degree are activities subdivided into separate jobs?	Work specialization
2. On what basis will jobs be grouped together?	Departmentalization
3. To whom do individuals and groups report?	Chain of command
4. How many individuals can a manager efficiently and effectively direct?	Span of control
5. Where does decision-making authority lie?	Centralization and decentralization
6. To what degree will there be rules and regulations to direct employees and managers?	Formalization
7. Do individuals from different areas need to regularly interact?	Boundary spanning

than the entirety. Specialization is a means of making the most efficient use of employees' skills and even successfully improving them through repetition. Less time is spent changing tasks, putting away tools and equipment from a prior step, and getting ready for another.

By the 1960s, it increasingly seemed that the good news of specialization could be carried too far. Human diseconomies began to surface in the form of boredom, fatigue, stress, low productivity, poor quality, increased absentee-ism, and high turnover, which more than offset the economic advantages (see Exhibit 15-2). Managers could increase productivity now by enlarging, rather than narrowing, the scope of job activities. Giving employees a variety of activi-ties to do, allowing them to do a whole and complete job, and putting them into teams with interchangeable skills often achieved significantly higher out-put, with increased employee satisfaction.

Ford demonstrated work can be performed more efficiently if employees are allowed to specialize, and the practice still has applications in many industries. For example, could you build a car by yourself? Not likely! Equally important, it's easier and less costly to find and train workers to do specific tasks, especially in highly sophisticated and complex operations. Finally, work specialization increases efficiency and productivity by encouraging the creation of customized inventions and machinery.

Most managers today recognize the economies specialization provides in certain jobs and the problems when it's carried too far. High work specialization helps McDonald's make and sell hamburgers and fries efficiently and aids medical specialists in most health maintenance orga-nizations. Wherever job roles can be broken down into specific tasks or projects, specialization is possible. Specialization may still confer advan-tages outside manufacturing, particularly where job sharing and part-time work are prevalent.[3] Amazon's Mechanical Turk program, TopCoder, and others like it have facilitated a new trend in microspecialization in which extremely small pieces of programming, data processing, or evaluation tasks are delegated to a global network of individuals by a program manager who then assembles the results.[4]

This opens the way for employers to use online platforms to assign multiple workers to tasks in a broader functional role like marketing.[5] Thus, whereas spe-cialization of yesteryear focused on breaking manufacturing tasks into specific duties within the same plant, today's specialization judiciously breaks complex tasks into specific elements by technology, expertise, and region. Yet the core principle is the same.

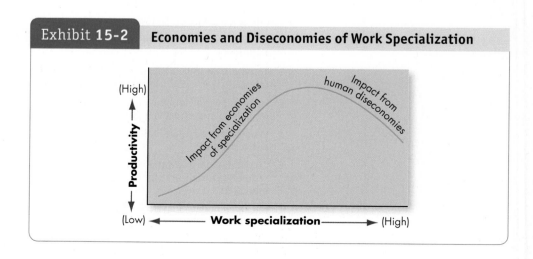

Exhibit 15-2   Economies and Diseconomies of Work Specialization

Departmentalization

Once jobs have been divided through work specialization, they must be grouped so common tasks can be coordinated. The basis by which jobs are grouped is called **departmentalization**.

departmentalization The basis by which jobs in an organization are grouped together.

One of the most popular ways to group activities is by the *functions* performed. A manufacturing manager might organize a plant into engineering, accounting, manufacturing, human resources (HR), and supply chain departments. A hospital might have departments for research, surgery, intensive care, accounting, and so forth. A professional football franchise might have departments for player personnel, ticket sales, and travel and accommodations. The major advantage of this type of functional departmentalization is efficiencies gained from putting like specialists together.

We can also departmentalize jobs by the type of *product* or *service* the organization produces. Procter & Gamble places each major product—such as Tide, Pampers, Charmin, and Pringles—under an executive who has complete global responsibility for it. The major advantage here is increased accountability for performance because all activities related to a specific product or service are under the direction of a single manager.

When a firm is departmentalized on the basis of *geography*, or territory, the sales function, for instance, may have western, southern, midwestern, and eastern regions each, in effect, a department organized around geography. This form is valuable when an organization's customers are scattered over a large geographic area and have similar needs within their locations. For this reason, Toyota changed its management structure into geographic regions "so that they may develop and deliver ever better products," said CEO Akio Toyoda.[6]

Process departmentalization works for processing customers as well as products. If you've ever been to a state motor vehicle office to get a driver's license, you probably went through several departments before receiving your license. In one typical state, applicants go through three steps, each handled by a separate department: (1) validation by the motor vehicles division, (2) processing

A global firm that operates on a local scale in more than 200 countries, The Coca-Cola Company is organized into six geographic segments: North America, Latin America, Europe, Eurasia, Africa, and Asia Pacific. The structure enables it to tailor its strategy to markets in different stages of economic development and with differing consumer tastes and buying behavior.
Source: Kim Kyung-Hoon/Reuters

by the licensing department, and (3) payment collection by the treasury department. A final category of departmentalization uses the particular type of *customer* the organization seeks to reach.

Interestingly, organizations do not always stay with the basis of departmentalization they first adopt. Microsoft, for instance, used customer departmentalization for years, organizing around its customer bases: consumers, large corporations, software developers, and small businesses. However, in a June 2013 letter from CEO Steve Ballmer to all employees, he announced a restructuring to functional departmentalization, citing a need to foster continuing innovation. The new departments grouped jobs by traditional functions including engineering, marketing, business development, strategy and research, finance, HR, and legal.[7]

Ballmer expected the change in Microsoft's organizational structure would "reshape how we interact with our customers, developers, and key innovation partners, delivering a more coherent message and family of product offerings."[8] As we see throughout this text, whenever changes are deliberately made in organizations to align practices with organizational goals, particularly the goals of strong leaders, a good execution of the changes creates a much higher probability for improvement. In Microsoft's case, the results are not yet determined—Ballmer, who is a strong leader, announced his retirement 2 months later (he officially left Microsoft in 2014), and further changes ensued. Microsoft continued to struggle with the reorganization, announcing further changes in its leadership personnel and team structure less than a year later.[9]

Chain of Command

While the chain of command was once a basic cornerstone in the design of organizations, it has far less importance today. But managers should still consider its implications, particularly in industries that deal with potential life-or-death situations when people need to quickly rely on decision makers. The **chain of command** is an unbroken line of authority that extends from the top of the organization to the lowest echelon and clarifies who reports to whom.

We can't discuss the chain of command without also discussing *authority* and *unity of command*. **Authority** refers to the rights inherent in a managerial position to give orders and expect them to be obeyed. To facilitate coordination, each managerial position is given a place in the chain of command, and each manager is given a degree of authority in order to meet his or her responsibilities. The principle of **unity of command** helps preserve the concept of an unbroken line of authority. It says a person should have one and only one superior to whom he or she is directly responsible. If the unity of command is broken, an employee might have to cope with conflicting demands or priorities from several superiors, as is often the case in organization charts' dotted-line reporting relationships depicting an employee's accountability to multiple managers.

Times change, however, and so do the basic tenets of organizational design. A low-level employee today can access information in seconds that was available only to top managers a generation ago, and many employees are empowered to make decisions previously reserved for management. Add the popularity of self-managed and cross-functional teams as well as structural designs that include multiple bosses, and you can see why authority and unity of command may appear to hold less relevance. Yet many organizations still find they can be most productive by enforcing the chain of command. Indeed, one survey of more than 1,000 managers found that 59 percent agreed with the statement, "There is an imaginary line in my company's organizational

chain of command The unbroken line of authority that extends from the top of the organization to the lowest echelon and clarifies who reports to whom.

authority The rights inherent in a managerial position to give orders and to expect the orders to be obeyed.

unity of command The idea that a subordinate should have only one superior to whom he or she is directly responsible.

chart. Strategy is created by people above this line, while strategy is executed by people below the line."[10] However, this same survey found that lower-level employees' buy-in (agreement and active support) to the organization's overall, big picture strategy was inhibited by their reliance on the hierarchy for decision making.

Span of Control

span of control The number of subordinates a manager can efficiently and effectively direct.

How many employees can a manager efficiently and effectively direct? The **span of control** describes the number of levels and managers an organization has. All things being equal, the wider or larger the span, the fewer levels, the more employees at each level, and the more efficient the organization.

Assume two organizations each have about 4,100 operative-level employees. One has a uniform span of 4 and the other a span of 8. As Exhibit 15-3 illustrates, the wider span of 8 will have two fewer levels and approximately 800 fewer managers. If the average manager makes $50,000 a year, the wider span will save $40 million a year in management salaries! Obviously, wider spans are more efficient in terms of cost. However, at some point when supervisors no longer have time to provide subordinates with the necessary leadership and support, effectiveness declines and employee performance suffers.

Narrow or small spans have their advocates. By keeping the span of control to five or six employees, a manager can maintain close control.[11] But narrow spans have three major drawbacks. First, they're expensive because they add levels of management. Second, they make vertical communication in the organization more complex. The added levels of hierarchy slow down decision making and can isolate upper management. Third, narrow spans encourage overly tight supervision and discourage employee autonomy.

The trend in recent years has been toward wider spans of control. They're consistent with firms' efforts to reduce costs, cut overhead, speed decision making, increase flexibility, get closer to customers, and empower employees. However, to ensure performance doesn't suffer because of these wider spans, organizations have been investing heavily in employee training. Managers recognize they can handle a wider span best when employees know their jobs inside and out or can turn to coworkers with questions.

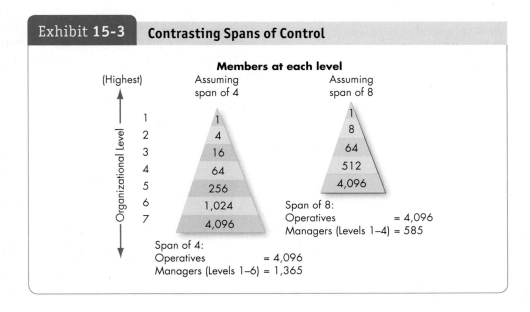

Exhibit **15-3**   **Contrasting Spans of Control**

Centralization and Decentralization

Centralization refers to the degree to which decision making is concentrated at a single point in the organization. In *centralized* organizations, top managers make all the decisions, and lower-level managers merely carry out their directives. In organizations at the other extreme, *decentralized* decision making is pushed down to the managers closest to the action or to workgroups. The concept of centralization includes only formal authority—that is, the rights inherent to a position.

An organization characterized by centralization is different structurally from one that's decentralized. A decentralized organization can act more quickly to solve problems, more people provide input into decisions, and employees are less likely to feel alienated from those who make decisions that affect their work lives. The effects of centralization and decentralization can be predicted: Centralized organizations are better for avoiding commission errors (bad choices), while decentralized organizations are better for avoiding omission errors (lost opportunities).[12]

Management efforts to make organizations more flexible and responsive have produced a trend toward decentralized decision making by lower-level managers, who are closer to the action and typically have more detailed knowledge about problems than top managers. Sears and JCPenney have given their store managers considerably more discretion in choosing what merchandise to stock in individual stores. This allows the stores to compete more effectively against local merchants. Similarly, when Procter & Gamble empowered small groups of employees to make decisions about new-product development independent of the usual hierarchy, it was able to rapidly increase the proportion of new products ready for market.[13] Concerning creativity, research investigating a large number of Finnish organizations demonstrated that companies with decentralized research and development (R&D) offices in multiple locations were better at producing innovation than companies that centralized all R&D in a single office.[14]

Decentralization is often necessary for companies with offshore sites because localized decision making is needed to respond to each region's profit

With more than 7,000 neighborhood and airport locations throughout North America and Europe, Enterprise Rent-A-Car empowers employees at the local level to make decisions that affect their work. Decentralization gives Enterprise a competitive advantage by enabling employees to provide personalized service that results in high customer satisfaction.
Source: David Carson/MCT/Landov

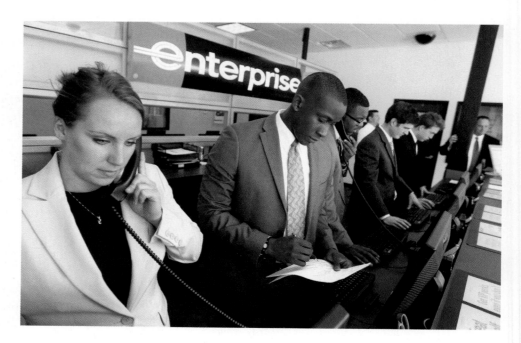

opportunities, client base, and specific laws, while centralized oversight is needed to hold regional managers accountable. Failure to successfully balance these priorities can harm not only the organization, but also its relationships with foreign governments.[15]

Formalization

formalization The degree to which jobs within an organization are standardized.

Formalization refers to the degree to which jobs within the organization are standardized. If a job is highly formalized, the employee has a minimal amount of discretion over what to do and when and how to do it, resulting in consistent and uniform output. There are explicit job descriptions, lots of organizational rules, and clearly defined procedures covering work processes. Formalization not only eliminates the possibility of employees engaging in alternative behaviors; it removes the need for them to consider alternatives. Conversely, where formalization is low, job behaviors are relatively unprogrammed and employees have a great deal of freedom to exercise discretion in their work.

The degree of formalization can vary widely between and within organizations. In general, research from 94 high-technology Chinese firms indicated that formalization is a detriment to team flexibility in decentralized organization structures, suggesting that formalization does not work as well where duties are inherently interactive, or where there is a need to be flexible and innovative.[16] For example, publishing representatives who call on college professors to inform them of their company's new publications have a great deal of freedom in their jobs. They have only a general sales pitch, which they tailor as needed, and rules and procedures governing their behavior may be little more than suggestions on what to emphasize about forthcoming titles and the requirement to submit a weekly sales report. At the other extreme, clerical and editorial employees in the same publishing houses may need to be at their desks by 8:00 a.m. and follow a set of precise procedures dictated by management.

Boundary Spanning

We've described ways that organizations create well-defined task structures and chains of authority. These systems facilitate control and coordination for specific tasks, but if there is too much division within an organization, attempts to coordinate across groups can be disastrous. One way to overcome compartmentalization and retain the positive elements of structure is to encourage or create boundary-spanning roles.

boundary spanning When individuals form relationships outside their formally assigned groups.

Within a single organization, **boundary spanning** occurs when individuals form relationships with people outside their formally assigned groups. An HR executive who frequently engages with the IT group is engaged in boundary spanning, as is a member of an R&D team who implements ideas from a production team. These activities help prevent formal structures from becoming too rigid and, not surprisingly, enhance organization and team creativity.[17]

Boundary-spanning activities occur not only within but also between organizations. Gathering information from external knowledge sources is especially advantageous in highly innovative industries where keeping up with the competition is challenging. Positive results are especially strong in organizations that encourage extensive internal communication; in other words, external boundary spanning is most effective when it is followed up with internal boundary spanning.[18]

Organizations can use formal mechanisms to facilitate boundary-spanning activities through their structures. One method is to assign formal liaison roles or develop committees of individuals from different areas of the organization.

BMW encourages all employees, including this production worker at its plant in Jakarta, Indonesia, to build relationships throughout the global company. Boundary spanning at BMW links R&D, design, production, and marketing individuals to speed problem solving and innovation and to adapt to market fluctuations.
Source: Dadang Tri/Bloomberg/Getty Images

Development activities can also facilitate boundary spanning. Employees with experience in multiple functions, such as accounting and marketing, are more likely to engage in boundary spanning.[19] Many organizations try to set the stage for these sorts of positive relationships by creating job rotation programs so new hires get a better sense of different areas of the organization. A final method to encourage boundary spanning is to bring attention to overall organizational goals and shared identity concepts.

You probably have personal experience with at least some of the results of decisions leaders have made in your school or workplace that related to the elements of organizational structure. The organizational framework, which can be depicted by a drawing of an organizational chart, can help you clarify leadership intentions. We'll discuss them next.

Common Organizational Frameworks and Structures

15-2 Identify the characteristics of the functional structure, the divisional structure, and the matrix structure.

Organizational designs are known by many names and are constantly evolving in response to changes in the way work is done. We will start with three of the more common organizational frameworks: the *simple structure*, the *bureaucracy*, and the *matrix structure*.

The Simple Structure

What do a small retail store, an electronics firm run by a hard-driving entrepreneur, and an airline's "war room" in the midst of a pilot's strike have in common? They probably all use the **simple structure**.

The simple structure has a low degree of departmentalization, wide spans of control, authority centralized in a single person, and little formalization. It is a flat organization; it usually has only two or three vertical levels, a loose body of employees, and one individual with decision-making authority. Most companies

simple structure   An organizational structure characterized by a low degree of departmentalization, wide spans of control, authority centralized in a single person, and little formalization.

Exhibit 15-4   A Simple Structure (Jack Gold's Men's Store)

start as a simple structure, and many innovative technology-based firms with short lifespans, like cell phone app development firms, remain compact by design.[20]

Exhibit 15-4 is an organization chart for a retail men's store owned and managed by Jack Gold. Jack employs five full-time salespeople, a cashier, and extra workers for weekends and holidays, but he runs the show. Though this is typical for a small business, in times of crisis large companies often simplify their structures (though not to this degree) as a means of focusing their resources.

The strength of the simple structure lies in its simplicity. It's fast, flexible, and inexpensive to operate, and accountability is clear. One major weakness is that it becomes increasingly inadequate as an organization grows because its low formalization and high centralization tend to create information overload at the top. Decision making typically becomes slower as the single executive tries to continue doing it all. This proves the undoing of many small businesses. If the structure isn't changed and made more elaborate, the firm often loses momentum and can eventually fail. The simple structure's other weakness is that it's risky—everything depends on one person. An illness at the top can literally halt the organization's information and decision-making capabilities.

The Bureaucracy

Standardization! That's the key concept that underlies all bureaucracies. Consider the bank where you keep your checking account, the store where you buy clothes, or the government offices that collect your taxes, enforce health regulations, or provide local fire protection. They all rely on standardized work processes for coordination and control.

bureaucracy An organizational structure with highly routine operating tasks achieved through specialization, very formalized rules and regulations, tasks that are grouped into functional departments, centralized authority, narrow spans of control, and decision making that follows the chain of command.

The **bureaucracy** is characterized by highly routine operating tasks achieved through specialization, strictly formalized rules and regulations, tasks grouped into units, centralized authority, narrow spans of control, and decision making that follows the chain of command. Bureaucracy incorporates all the strongest degrees of departmentalization described earlier.

Bureaucracy is a dirty word in many people's minds. However, it does have advantages, primarily the ability to perform standardized activities in a highly efficient manner. Putting like specialties together in units results in economies of scale, minimum duplication of people and equipment, and a common language employees all share. Bureaucracies can get by with less talented—and hence less costly—middle- and lower-level managers because rules and regulations substitute for managerial discretion. There is little need for innovative and experienced decision makers below the level of senior executives.

Listen in on a dialogue among four executives in one company: "You know, nothing happens in this place until we *produce* something," said the production executive. "Wrong," commented the R&D manager, "Nothing happens until we *design* something!" "What are you talking about?" asked the marketing executive,

Hospitals benefit from standardized work processes and procedures common to a bureaucratic structure because they help employees perform their jobs efficiently. At Christchurch Women's Hospital in New Zealand, registered nurse Megan Coleman (right) and midwife Sally Strathdee follow formal rules and regulations in caring for mothers and newborns.
Source: Greg Wood/AFP/Getty Images

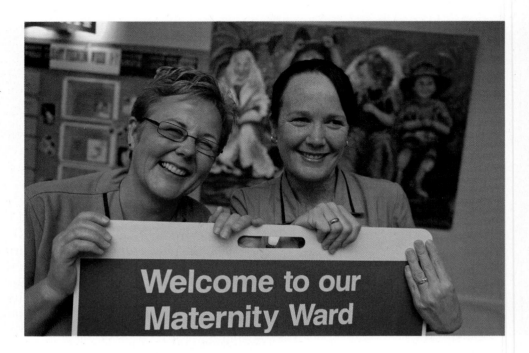

"Nothing happens until we *sell* something!" The exasperated accounting manager responded, "It doesn't matter what you produce, design, or sell. No one knows what happens until we *tally up the results!*" This conversation highlights that bureaucratic specialization can create conflicts in which the unit perspectives override the overall goals of the organization.

The other major weakness of a bureaucracy is something we've all witnessed: obsessive concern with following the rules. When cases don't precisely fit the rules, there is no room for modification. The bureaucracy is efficient only as long as employees confront familiar problems with programmed decision rules. There are two aspects of bureaucracies we should explore: functional and divisional structures.

The Functional Structure   The **functional structure** groups employees by their similar specialties, roles, or tasks.[21] An organization organized into production, marketing, HR and accounting departments is an example. Many large organizations utilize this structure, although this is evolving to allow for quick changes in response to business opportunities. Still, there are advantages, including that the functional structure allows specialists to become experts more easily than if they worked in diversified units. Employees can also be motivated by a clear career path to the top of the organization chart specific to their specialties.

The functional structure works well if the organization is focused on one product or service. Unfortunately it creates rigid, formal communications because the hierarchy dictates the communication protocol. Coordination among many units is a problem, and infighting in units and between units can lead to reduced motivation.

functional structure   An organizational structure that groups employees by their similar specialties, roles, or tasks.

The Divisional Structure   The **divisional structure** groups employees into units by product, service, customer, or geographical market area.[22] It is highly departmentalized. Sometimes this structure is known by the type of division structure it uses: *product/service organizational structure* (like units for cat food, dog food, and bird food that report to an animal food producer), *customer organizational*

divisional structure   An organizational structure that groups employees into units by product, service, customer, or geographical market area.

structure (like units for outpatient care, inpatient care, and pharmacy that report to hospital administration), or *geographic organizational structure* (like units for Europe, Asia, and South America that report to corporate headquarters).[23]

The divisional structure has the opposite benefits and disadvantages of the functional structure. It facilitates coordination in units to achieve on-time completion, budget targets, and development and introduction of new products to market, while addressing the specific concerns of each unit. It provides clear responsibility for all activities related to a product, but with duplication of functions and costs. Sometimes this is helpful, say when the organization has a unit in Spain and another in China, very different markets, and a marketing strategy is needed for a new product. Marketing experts in both places can incorporate the appropriate cultural perspectives into their region's marketing campaign. However, the organization's marketing function employees in two places may represent an increased cost, in doing basically the same task in two different countries.

The Matrix Structure

matrix structure An organizational structure that creates dual lines of authority and combines functional and product departmentalization.

The **matrix structure** combines the functional and product structures, and we find it in advertising agencies, aerospace firms, R&D laboratories, construction companies, hospitals, government agencies, universities, management consulting firms, and entertainment companies.[24] Companies that use matrix-like structures include ABB, Boeing, BMW, IBM, and P&G.

The most obvious structural characteristic of the matrix is that it breaks the unity-of-command concept. Employees in the matrix have two bosses: their functional department managers and their product managers. Exhibit 15-5 shows the matrix for a college of business administration. The academic departments of accounting, decision and information systems, marketing, and so forth are functional units. Overlaid on them are specific programs (that is, products). Thus, members in a matrix structure have a dual chain of command: to their functional department and to their product groups. A professor of accounting teaching an undergraduate course may report to the director of undergraduate programs as well as to the chairperson of the accounting department.

The strength of the matrix is its ability to facilitate coordination when the organization has a number of complex and interdependent activities. Direct and frequent contacts between different specialties in the matrix can let information permeate the organization and more quickly reach the people who

Exhibit 15-5	Matrix Structure for a College of Business Administration

Academic Departments \ Programs	Undergraduate	Master's	Ph.D.	Research	Executive Development	Community Service
Accounting						
Finance						
Decision and Information Systems						
Management						
Marketing						

need it. The matrix reduces "bureaupathologies"—its dual lines of authority limit people's tendency to protect their territories at the expense of the organization's goals.[25] A matrix also achieves economies of scale and facilitates the allocation of specialists by both providing the best resources and ensuring they are efficiently used.

The major disadvantages of the matrix lie in the confusion it creates, its tendency to foster power struggles, and the stress it places on individuals.[26] For individuals who desire security and absence from ambiguity, this work climate can be stressful. Reporting to more than one boss introduces role conflict, and unclear expectations introduce role ambiguity. Without the unity-of-command concept, ambiguity about who reports to whom is significantly increased and often leads to conflict and power struggles between functional and product managers.

Alternate Design Options

15-3 Identify the characteristics of the virtual structure, the team structure, and the circular structure.

In the ever-increasing trend toward flatter structures, many organizations have been developing new options with fewer layers of hierarchy and more emphasis on opening the boundaries of the organization.[27] In this section, we describe three such designs: the *virtual structure*, the *team structure*, and the *circular structure*.

The Virtual Structure

virtual structure   A small, core organization that outsources major business functions.

Why own when you can rent? That question captures the essence of the **virtual structure** (also sometimes called the *network*, or *modular*, structure), typically a small, core organization that outsources its major business functions.[28] The virtual structure is highly centralized, with little or no departmentalization.

The prototype of the virtual structure is today's film-making organization. In Hollywood's golden era, movies were made by huge, vertically integrated corporations. Studios such as MGM, Warner Brothers, and 20th Century Fox owned large movie lots and employed thousands of full-time specialists—set designers, camera people, film editors, directors, and even actors. Today, most movies are made by a collection of individuals and small companies who come together and make films project by project. This structural form allows each project to be staffed with the talent best suited to its demands, rather than just with the people employed by the studio. It minimizes bureaucratic overhead because there is no lasting organization to maintain. And it lessens long-term risks and their costs because there *is* no long term—a team is assembled for a finite period and then disbanded.

Exhibit 15-6 shows a virtual structure in which management outsources all the primary functions of the business. The core of the organization is a small group of executives whose job is to oversee directly any activities done in-house and to coordinate relationships with organizations that manufacture, distribute, and perform other crucial functions. The dotted lines represent the relationships typically maintained under contracts. In essence, managers in virtual structures spend most of their time coordinating and controlling external relations.

The major advantage of the virtual structure is its flexibility, which allows individuals with an innovative idea and little money to successfully compete against larger, more established organizations. The structure also saves a great deal of money by eliminating permanent offices and hierarchical roles.[29]

The drawbacks have become increasingly clear as popularity has grown.[30] Virtual organizations are in a state of perpetual flux and reorganization, which means roles, goals, and responsibilities are unclear, setting the stage for

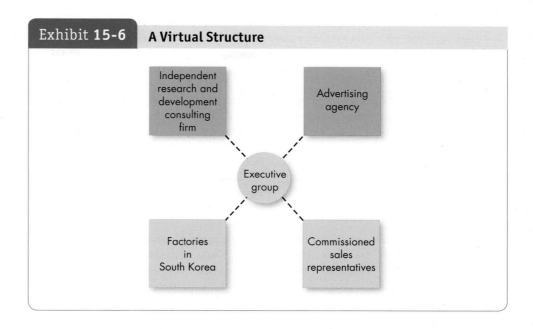

Exhibit 15-6   A Virtual Structure

political behavior. Cultural alignment and shared goals can be lost because of the low degree of interaction among members. Team members who are geographically dispersed and communicate infrequently find it difficult to share information and knowledge, which can limit innovation and slow response time. Sometimes—as with Lululemon's shipments of unintentionally see-through yoga pants, where the deficiencies weren't noticed until many had been sold—the consequences of having geographically remote managers can be embarrassing and even financially harmful to the company.[31] Ironically, some virtual organizations are less adaptable and innovative than those with well-established communication and collaboration networks. A leadership presence that reinforces the organization's purpose and facilitates communication is thus especially valuable.

The Team Structure

team structure An organizational structure that replaces departments with empowered teams, and which eliminates horizontal boundaries and external barriers between customers and suppliers.

The **team structure** seeks to eliminate the chain of command and replace departments with empowered teams.[32] This structure removes vertical and horizontal boundaries in addition to breaking down external barriers between the company and its customers and suppliers.

By removing vertical boundaries, management flattens the hierarchy and minimizes status and rank. Cross-hierarchical teams (which include top executives, middle managers, supervisors, and operative employees), participative decision-making practices, and the use of 360-degree performance appraisals (in which peers and others evaluate performance) can be used. For example, at the Danish firm Oticon A/S, the world's largest hearing aid manufacturer, all traces of hierarchy have disappeared. Everyone works at uniform mobile workstations, and project teams, not functions or departments, coordinate work.

As previously discussed, functional departments create horizontal boundaries between functions, product lines, and units. The way to reduce them is to replace functional departments with cross-functional teams and organize activities around processes. Xerox, for instance, develops new products through multidisciplinary teams that work on a single process instead of on narrow functional tasks.

What structure should I choose?

I'm running a small but growing business and need help figuring out how to keep positions flexible as we expand. What advice can you give me about designing job structures that will help combine my success today with growth for tomorrow?

　　　　　　　　　　　　　　　— Anika

Dear Anika:

A surprising number of small businesses fail right at the point where they begin to grow. There are many reasons, including financing deficits and competitors that copy their good ideas. However, a common problem is that the structure the company began with is simply not right for a larger firm.

　　There are ways to meet the challenge. Start by looking at individual jobs and their responsibilities. Make a list for each job. When job roles and responsibilities aren't defined, you do pick up a great deal of flexibility, assigning employees to tasks exactly when needed. Unfortunately, this flexibility also means it's hard to determine which skills are available, or to identify gaps between planned strategy and available human resources.

Second, you may want to now define roles based on broad sets of competencies that span multiple levels of organizational functioning. In this *strategic competency model*, job roles and incentives are defined based on a clear structure. Here are the steps:

- *Look at the top level and think about the future.* In the competency model, you should use the mission statement and overall organizational strategies to evaluate your organization's future needs.
- *Once you've identified the organization's future needs, figure out a smart way to assign responsibilities to individuals.* You'll obviously need some specialization, but at the same time, consider general skills that will be useful for both growth and long-term sustainability.
- *As your business grows, identify applicants with the potential to meet future needs, and develop employee incentives to encourage broad skills profiles.* You'll want to structure your plan so employees increase in

competency as they move up the organization chart.

　　The most important thing to remember is that you aren't creating a job structure just for today—make sure it's ready to grow and change with your business.

　　Grow well!

Sources: G. W. Stevens, "A Critical Review of the Science and Practice of Competency Modeling," *Human Resource Development Review* 12 (March 2013): 86–107; P. Capelli and J. R. Keller, "Talent Management: Conceptual Approaches and Practical Challenges," *Annual Review of Organizational Psychology and Organizational Behavior* 1 (March 2014): 305–31; and C. Fernández-Aráoz, "21st Century Talent Spotting," *Harvard Business Review,* June 2014, https://hbr.org/2014/06/21st-century-talent-spotting.

When fully operational, the team structure may break down geographic barriers. Today, most large U.S. companies see themselves as team-oriented global corporations; many, like Coca-Cola and McDonald's, do as much business overseas as in the United States, and some struggle to incorporate geographic regions into their structure. In other cases, the team approach is need-based. Such is the case with Chinese companies, which made 93 acquisitions in the oil and gas industry in five years—incorporating each acquisition as a new team unit—to meet forecasted demand their resources in China could not meet.[33] The team structure provides a solution because it considers geography as more of a tactical, logistical issue than a structural one. In short, the goal may be to break down cultural barriers and open opportunities.

Some organizations create teams incorporating their employees and their customers or suppliers. For example, to ensure important product parts are reliably made to exacting specifications by its suppliers, Honeywell International partners some of its engineers with managers at those suppliers.

Flexible Structures, Deskless Workplaces

Once upon a time, students fresh from business schools couldn't wait for that first cubicle to call home, mid-level managers aspired to an office of their own, and executives coveted the corner office. These days, the walls are coming down. As organizational structures change, so do their physical environments. Many organizations have been trying to make the physical environment reflect the organizational structures they adopt.

At online retailer Zappos, not even the CEO wants an office, and all 1,500 employees are welcome throughout the open spaces. Firms like Google have workplace designs of public rooms with lounge areas and large, multiperson tables. According to Edward Danyo, manager of workplace strategy at pharmaceuticals firm GlaxoSmithKline, shared environments create great work gains, including what he estimates is a 45 percent increase in the speed of decision making. But there are ethical concerns for the dismantling of the physical and mental organizational structure:

- *Where will confidential discussions take place?* In some contemporary workplace designs, ad hoc conference rooms address the need for separate gatherings. This may not be optimal if the walls are made of glass, if employees will feel stigmatized when called into a meeting room, or if they become reluctant to approach human resources staff with issues because of privacy concerns.
- *How can differences in personality traits be overcome?* Employees high in extraversion will be more comfortable building collaborative relationships without assigned workspaces, while introverted individuals may be uncomfortable without an established office structure where they can get to know others over time.
- *How can personal privacy be maintained?* Zappos gives employees personal lockers, asks employees to angle laptop screens away from neighbors, and tries to make open spaces more private by encouraging ear buds to create a sound barrier between working employees.

- *How can you assure your clients of confidentiality?* Even walled, soundproof rooms for virtual or live meetings may not provide the desired level of security for clients who need to know their business will stay on a need-to-know basis.
- *How will expectations and accountabilities be enforced?* In an environment without offices and sometimes without job titles, there is an even greater need for clearly assigned goals, roles, and expectations. Otherwise, open, collaborative structures may foster diffusion of responsibility and confusion.

Sources: S. Henn, "'Serendipitous Interaction' Key to Tech Firm's Workplace Design," NPR, March 13, 2013, www.npr.org/blogs/alltech considered/2013/03/13/174195695/serendipitous-interaction-key-to-tech-firms-workplace-design; H. El Nasser, "What Office? Laptops Are Workspace," *USA Today,* June 6, 2012, 1B–2B; R. W. Huppke, "Thinking Outside the Cubicle," *Chicago Tribune,* October 29, 2012, 2-1, 2-3; "Inside the New Deskless Office," *Forbes,* July 16, 2012, 34; and E. Maltby, "My Space Is Our Space," *The Wall Street Journal,* May 21, 2012, R9.

The Circular Structure

circular structure   An organizational structure in which executives are at the center, spreading their vision outward in rings grouped by function (managers, then specialists, then workers).

Picture the concentric rings of an archery target. In the center are the executives, and radiating outward in rings grouped by function are the managers, then the specialists, then the workers. This is the **circular structure**.[34] Does it seem like organizational anarchy? Actually, there is still a hierarchy, but top management is at the very heart of the organization, with its vision spreading outward.

The circular structure has intuitive appeal for creative entrepreneurs, and some small innovative firms have claimed it. However, as in many of the current hybrid approaches, employees are apt to be unclear about whom they report to and who is running the show. We are still likely to see the popularity of the circular structure spread. The concept may have intuitive appeal for spreading a vision of corporate social responsibility (CSR), for instance.

★ PERSONAL INVENTORY ASSESSMENTS

Organizational Structure Assessment

To learn more about how organizations are structured, complete this PIA.

The Leaner Organization: Downsizing

15-4
Describe the effects of downsizing on organizational structures and employees.

The goal of some organizational structures we've described is to improve agility by creating a lean, focused, and flexible organization. *Downsizing* is a systematic effort to make an organization leaner by closing locations, reducing staff, or selling off business units that don't add value. Downsizing doesn't necessarily mean physically shrinking the size of your office, although that's been happening, too (see OB Poll).

The radical shrinking of Motorola Mobility in 2012 and 2013 is a case of downsizing to survive after its 2011 $12.5 billion acquisition by Google. In response to declining demand for its smartphones, Motorola cut its workforce by 20 percent in August 2012. When the company posted a $350 million fourth-quarter loss in 2012, with a 40 percent revenue decline, it cut the workforce again, by 10 percent. Google called this "rightsizing."[35] Motorola Mobility was then sold to China's Lenovo in 2014 for $2.91 billion.

Other firms downsize to direct all their efforts toward their core competencies. American Express claims to have been doing this in a series of layoffs over more than a decade: 7,700 jobs in 2001; 6,500 jobs in 2002; 7,000 jobs (10 percent of its workforce) in 2008; 4,000 jobs in 2009. The 2013 cut of 5,400 jobs (8.5 percent of the remaining workforce) represented "its biggest retrenchment in a decade." An additional layoff of 4,000 jobs was slated for 2015. Each layoff has been accompanied by a restructuring to reflect changing customer preferences, away from personal customer service and toward online customer service. According to CEO Ken Chennault, "Our business and industry continue to become transformed by technology. As a result of these changes, we have the need and the opportunity to evolve our organization and cost structure."[36]

Some companies focus on lean management techniques to reduce bureaucracy and speed decision making. Starbucks adopted lean initiatives in 2009, which encompassed all levels of management and also focused on faster barista techniques and manufacturing processes. Customers generally applauded the shortened wait times and improved product consistency. Starbucks continues to reap returns from its lean initiatives, posting notable revenue gains each quarter.[37]

OB POLL

The Incredible Shrinking Office

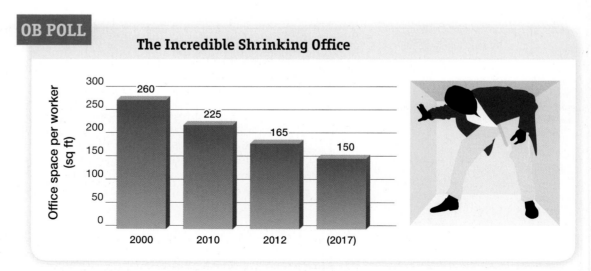

Office space per worker (sq ft)

Year	sq ft
2000	260
2010	225
2012	165
(2017)	150

Source: Based on February 28, 2012, press release "Office Space per Worker Will Drop to 100 Square Feet or Below." http://www.corenetglobal.org/files/home/info_center/global_press_releases/pdf/pr120227_officespace.pdf.

Despite the advantages of being a lean organization, the impact of downsizing on organizational performance is not without controversy. Reducing the size of the workforce has an immediately positive outcome in the form of lower wage costs, and companies downsizing to improve strategic focus often see positive effects on stock prices after the announcement. An example is Russia's Gorky Automobile Factory (GAZ), which realized a profit for the first time in many years after President Bo Andersson fired 50,000 workers, half the workforce.[38] On the other hand, among companies that only cut employees but don't restructure, profits and stock prices usually decline. Part of the problem is the effect of downsizing on employee attitudes. Employees who remain often feel worried about future layoffs and may be less committed to the organization. Stress reactions can lead to increased sickness absences, lower concentration on the job, and lower creativity. Downsizing can also lead to more voluntary turnover, so vital human capital is lost. The result is a company that is more anemic than lean.

Companies can reduce negative impacts by preparing in advance, thus alleviating some employee stress and strengthening support for the new direction. Here are some effective strategies for downsizing:

- *Invest.* Companies that downsize to focus on core competencies are more effective when they invest in high-involvement work practices afterward.
- *Communicate.* When employers make efforts to discuss downsizing with employees early, employees are less worried about the outcomes and feel the company is taking their perspective into account.
- *Participate.* Employees worry less if they can participate in the process in some way. Voluntary early-retirement programs or severance packages can help achieve leanness without layoffs.
- *Assist.* Severance, extended health care benefits, and job search assistance demonstrate a company cares about its employees and honors their contributions.

In short, companies that make themselves lean can be more agile, efficient, and productive—but only if they make cuts carefully and help employees through the process.

Why Do Structures Differ?

15-5 Contrast the reasons for mechanistic and organic structural models.

mechanistic model A structure characterized by extensive departmentalization, high formalization, a limited information network, and centralization.

organic model A structure that is flat, uses cross-hierarchical and cross-functional teams, has low formalization, possesses a comprehensive information network, and relies on participative decision making.

We've described many organization design options. Exhibit 15-7 recaps our discussions by presenting two extreme models of organizational design. One we'll call the **mechanistic model**. It's generally synonymous with the bureaucracy in that it has highly standardized processes for work, high formalization, and more managerial hierarchy. The other extreme is the **organic model**. It's flat, has fewer formal procedures for making decisions, has multiple decision makers, and favors flexible practices.[39]

With these two models in mind, let's ask a few questions: Why are some organizations structured along more mechanistic lines whereas others follow organic characteristics? What forces influence the choice of design? In this section, we present major causes or determinants of an organization's structure.[40]

Organizational Strategies

Because structure is a means to achieve objectives, and objectives derive from the organization's overall strategy, it's only logical that structure should follow strategy. If management significantly changes the organization's strategy or its values, the structure must change to accommodate. For example, recent

Exhibit 15-7   Mechanistic versus Organic Models

The Mechanistic Model

- High specialization
- Rigid departmentalization
- Clear chain of command
- Narrow spans of control
- Centralization
- High formalization

The Organic Model

- Cross-functional teams
- Cross-hierarchical teams
- Free flow of information
- Wide spans of control
- Decentralization
- Low formalization

innovation strategy   A strategy that emphasizes the introduction of major new products and services.

cost-minimization strategy   A strategy that emphasizes tight cost controls, avoidance of unnecessary innovation or marketing expenses, and price cutting.

imitation strategy   A strategy that seeks to move into new products or new markets only after their viability has already been proven.

research indicates that aspects of organizational culture may influence the success of corporate social responsibility (CSR) initiatives.[41] If the culture is supported by the structure, the initiatives are more likely to have clear paths toward application. Most current strategy frameworks focus on three strategy dimensions—innovation, cost minimization, and imitation—and the structural design that works best with each.[42]

To what degree does an organization introduce major new products or services? An **innovation strategy** strives to achieve meaningful and unique innovations. Obviously, not all firms pursue innovation. Apple and 3M do, but conservative retailer Marks & Spencer doesn't. Innovative firms use competitive pay and benefits to attract top candidates and motivate employees to take risks. Some degree of the mechanistic structure can actually benefit innovation. Well-developed communication channels, policies for enhancing long-term commitment, and clear channels of authority all may make it easier for rapid changes to occur smoothly.

An organization pursuing a **cost-minimization strategy** tightly controls costs, refrains from incurring unnecessary expenses, and cuts prices in selling a basic product. This describes the strategy pursued by Walmart and the makers of generic or store-label grocery products. Cost-minimizing organizations usually pursue fewer policies meant to develop commitment among their workforce.

Organizations following an **imitation strategy** try to both minimize risk and maximize opportunity for profit, moving new products or entering new markets only after innovators have proven their viability. Mass-market fashion manufacturers that copy designer styles follow this strategy, as do firms such as Hewlett-Packard and Caterpillar. They follow smaller and more innovative competitors with superior products, but only after competitors have demonstrated the market is there. Italy's Moleskine SpA, a small maker of fashionable notebooks, is another example of imitation strategy but in a different way: looking to open more retail shops around the world, it imitates the expansion strategies of larger, successful fashion companies Salvatore Ferragamo SpA and Brunello Cucinelli.[43]

Imitating the successful growth strategy of several large fashion firms, Italian retailer Moleskine plans to increase sales of its popular line of notebooks and travel accessories by opening about 20 new stores each year throughout the world. The expansion plan focuses on store openings in metropolitan and business hubs such as New York City, London, and Beijing.

Source: Alessandro Garofalo/Reuters /Landov

Exhibit 15-8 describes the structural option that best matches each strategy. Innovators need the flexibility of the organic structure (although, as we noted, they may use some elements of the mechanistic structure as well), whereas cost minimizers seek the efficiency and stability of the mechanistic structure. Imitators combine the two structures. They use a mechanistic structure to maintain tight controls and low costs in their current activities but create organic subunits in which to pursue new undertakings.

Organization Size

An organization's size significantly affects its structure. Organizations that employ 2,000 or more people tend to have more specialization, more departmentalization, more vertical levels, and more rules and regulations than do small organizations. However, size becomes less important as an organization expands. Why? At around 2,000 employees, an organization is already fairly mechanistic; 500 more employees won't have much impact. But adding 500 employees to an organization of only 300 is likely to significantly shift it toward a more mechanistic structure.

Exhibit 15-8	The Strategy–Structure Relationship
Strategy	**Structural Option**
Innovation	**Organic:** A loose structure; low specialization, low formalization, decentralized
Cost minimization	**Mechanistic:** Tight control; extensive work specialization, high formalization, high centralization
Imitation	**Mechanistic and organic:** Mix of loose with tight properties; tight controls over current activities and looser controls for new undertakings

technology The way in which an organization transfers its inputs into outputs.

environment Forces outside an organization that potentially affect the organization's structure.

Technology

Technology describes the way an organization transfers inputs into outputs. Every organization has at least one technology for converting financial, human, and physical resources into products or services. For example, the Chinese consumer electronics company Haier uses an assembly-line process for mass-produced products, which is complemented by more flexible and innovative structures to respond to customers and design new products.[44] Also, colleges may use a number of instructional technologies—the ever-popular lecture, case analysis, experiential exercise, programmed learning, online instruction, and distance learning. Regardless, organizational structures adapt to their technology.

Environment

An organization's **environment** includes outside institutions or forces that can affect its structure, such as suppliers, customers, competitors, and public pressure groups. Dynamic environments create significantly more uncertainty for managers than do static ones. To minimize uncertainty in key market arenas, managers may broaden their structure to sense and respond to threats. Most companies, for example Pepsi and Southwest Airlines, have added social networking departments to counter negative information posted on blogs. Or companies may form strategic alliances.

Any organization's environment has three dimensions: capacity, volatility, and complexity.[45] *Capacity* refers to the degree to which the environment can support growth. Rich and growing environments generate excess resources, which can buffer the organization in times of relative scarcity.

Volatility describes the degree of instability in the environment. A dynamic environment with a high degree of unpredictable change makes it difficult for management to make accurate predictions. Because information technology changes at such a rapid place, more organizations' environments are becoming volatile.

Finally, *complexity* is the degree of heterogeneity and concentration among environmental elements. Simple environments—like the tobacco industry where the methods of production, competitive and regulatory pressures, and the like haven't changed in quite some time—are homogeneous and concentrated. Environments characterized by heterogeneity and dispersion—like the broadband industry—are complex and diverse, with numerous competitors.

Exhibit 15-9 summarizes our definition of the environment along its three dimensions. The arrows indicate movement toward higher uncertainty. Thus,

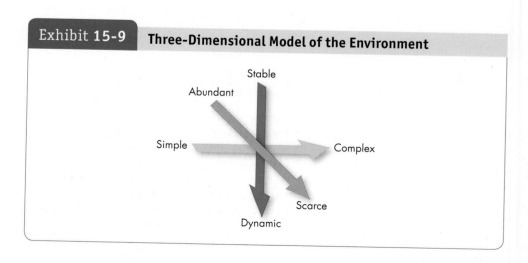

Exhibit 15-9 **Three-Dimensional Model of the Environment**

organizations that operate in environments characterized as scarce, dynamic, and complex face the greatest degree of uncertainty because they have high unpredictability, little room for error, and a diverse set of elements in the environment to monitor constantly.

Given this three-dimensional definition of *environment,* we can offer some general conclusions about environmental uncertainty and structural arrangements. The more scarce, dynamic, and complex the environment, the more organic a structure should be. The more abundant, stable, and simple the environment, the more the mechanistic structure will be preferred.

Institutions

institutions Cultural factors that lead many organizations to have similar structures, especially those factors that might not lead to adaptive consequences.

Another factor that shapes organizational structure is **institutions**. These are cultural factors that act as guidelines for appropriate behavior.[46] Institutional theory describes some of the forces that lead many organizations to have similar structures and, unlike the theories we've described so far, focuses on pressures that aren't necessarily adaptive. In fact, many institutional theorists try to highlight the ways corporate behaviors sometimes *seem* to be performance oriented but are actually guided by unquestioned social norms and conformity.

The most obvious institutional factors come from regulatory pressures; certain industries under government contracts, for instance, must have clear reporting relationships and strict information controls. Sometimes simple inertia determines an organizational form—companies can be structured in a particular way just because that's the way things have always been done. Organizations in countries with high power distance might have a structural form with strict authority relationships because it's seen as more legitimate in that culture. Some have attributed problems in adaptability in Japanese organizations to the institutional pressure to maintain authority relationships.

Sometimes organizations start to have a particular structure because of fads or trends. Organizations can try to copy other successful companies just to look good to investors, and not because they need that structure to perform better. Many companies have recently tried to copy the organic form of a company like Google only to find that such structures are a very poor fit with their operating environment. Institutional pressures are often difficult to see specifically because we take them for granted, but that doesn't mean they aren't powerful.

✪ TRY IT!

If your professor has assigned this, go to the Assignments section of **mymanagementlab.com** to complete the **Simulation: *Organizational Structure.***

Organizational Designs and Employee Behavior

15-6 Analyze the behavioral implications of different organizational designs.

We opened this chapter by implying an organization's structure can have significant effects on its members. What might those effects be?

A review of the evidence leads to a pretty clear conclusion: You can't generalize! Not everyone prefers the freedom and flexibility of organic structures. Different factors stand out in different structures as well. In highly formalized, heavily structured, mechanistic organizations, the level of fairness in formal policies and procedures (organizational justice) is a very important predictor of satisfaction. In more personal, individually adaptive organic organizations,

Employees Can Work Just as Well from Home

This statement is true, but not unequivocally. Employees who work from home even part of the time report they are happier, and as we saw in Chapter 3, happier employees are likely to be more productive than dissatisfied counterparts. From an organization's perspective, companies are realizing gains of 5 to 7 extra work hours a week for each employee working from home. There are also cost savings, from reduced overhead for office space and utilities to elimination of unproductive social time. Employers of a home-based workforce can establish work teams and organizational reporting relationships with little attention to office politics, making it possible to more objectively assign roles and responsibilities. These may be some of the reasons organizations have increasingly endorsed the concept of telecommuting, to the point where 3.1 million U.S. payrolled employees work from home.

Although we can all think of jobs that may never be conducive to working from home (such as many in the service industry), not all positions that *could* be based from home *should* be. Research indicates the success of a work-from-home position depends on the job's structure even more than on its tasks. The amount of interdependence needed between employees within a team or in a reporting relationship sometimes requires *epistemic interdependence*, which is each employee's ability to predict what other employees will do. Organization consultants pay attention to how employee roles relate in the *architecture* of the organization chart, realizing that intentional relationship building is key. Thus, while an employee may complete the tasks of a job well by working alone from home, the benefits of teamwork can be lost. We don't yet fully understand the impact of working at a

physical distance without sharing time or space with others, but it is perhaps the reason that Yahoo!, Best Buy, and other corporations have brought their employees back into the office.

The success of a work-from-home program depends on the individual, job, and culture of the organization. Work from home can be satisfying for employees and efficient for organizations, but we are learning that there are limits.

Sources: M. Mercer, "Shirk Work? Working at Home Can Mean Longer Hours," *TriCities.com,* March 4, 2013, www.tricities.com/news/opinion_columns/article_d04355b8-83cb-11e2-bc31-0019bb30f31a.html; P. Puranam, M. Raveendran, and T. Knudsen, "Organization Design: The Epistemic Interdependence Perspective," *Academy of Management Review* 37, no. 3 (2012): 419–40; N. Shah, "More Americans Working Remotely," *The Wall Street Journal,* March 6, 2013, A3; and R. E. Silverman and Q. Fottrell, "The Home Office in the Spotlight," *The Wall Street Journal,* February 27, 2013, B6.

employees value interpersonal justice more.[47] Some people are most productive and satisfied when work tasks are standardized and ambiguity is minimized—that is, in mechanistic structures. So, any discussion of the effect of organizational design on employee behavior has to address individual differences. To do so, let's consider employee preferences for work specialization, span of control, and centralization.[48]

The evidence generally indicates that *work specialization* contributes to higher employee productivity—but at the price of job satisfaction. However, work specialization is not an unending source of higher productivity. Problems start to surface, and productivity begins to suffer, when the human diseconomies of doing repetitive and narrow tasks overtake the economies of specialization. As the workforce has become more highly educated and desirous of jobs that are intrinsically rewarding, we seem to reach the point at which productivity begins to decline as a function of specialization more quickly than in the past. While decreased productivity often prompts companies to add oversight and inspection roles, the better answer may be to reorganize work functions and accountability.[49]

There is still a segment of the workforce that prefers the routine and repetitiveness of highly specialized jobs. Some individuals want work that makes minimal intellectual demands and provides the security of routine; for them, high work specialization is a source of job satisfaction. The question is whether they represent 2 percent of the workforce or 52 percent. Given that some self-selection operates in the choice of careers, we might conclude that negative behavioral outcomes from high specialization are most likely to surface in professional jobs occupied by individuals with high needs for personal growth and diversity.

It is probably safe to say no evidence supports a relationship between *span of control* and employee satisfaction or performance. Although it is intuitively attractive that large spans might lead to higher employee performance because they provide more distant supervision and more opportunity for personal initiative, research fails to support this notion. Some people like to be left alone; others prefer the security of a boss who is quickly available at all times. Consistent with several of the contingency theories of leadership discussed in Chapter 12, we would expect factors such as employees' experiences and abilities, and the degree of structure in their tasks, to explain when wide or narrow spans of control are likely to contribute to performance and job satisfaction. However, some evidence indicates that a *manager's* job satisfaction increases as the number of employees supervised increases.

We find fairly strong evidence linking *centralization* and job satisfaction. In general, less centralized organizations have a greater amount of autonomy. And autonomy appears positively related to job satisfaction. But, again, while one employee may value freedom, another may find autonomous environments frustratingly ambiguous.

We can draw one obvious insight: people don't select employers randomly. They are attracted to, are selected by, and stay with organizations that suit their personal characteristics.[50] Job candidates who prefer predictability are likely to seek out and take employment in mechanistic structures, and those who want autonomy are more likely to end up in organic structures. Thus, the effect of structure on employee behavior is undoubtedly reduced when the selection process facilitates proper matching of individual characteristics with organizational characteristics. Furthermore, companies should strive to establish, promote, and maintain the unique identity of their structures since skilled employees may quit as a result of dramatic changes.[51]

Research suggests national culture influences the preference for structure.[52] Organizations that operate with people from high power-distance cultures, such as Greece, France, and most of Latin America, often find their employees are much more accepting of mechanistic structures than are employees from low power-distance countries. So consider cultural differences along with individual differences when predicting how structure will affect employee performance and satisfaction.

Finally, the changing landscape of organizational structure designs has implications for the individual progressing on a career path. Research with managers in Japan, the United Kingdom, and the United States indicated that employees who weathered downsizing and resulting hybrid organizational structures considered their future career prospects diminished. While this may or may not have been correct, their thinking shows that organizational structure does affect the employee and thus must be carefully designed.[53]

✪ WATCH IT!

If your professor has assigned this, go to the Assignments section of **mymanagementlab.com** to complete the video exercise titled *ZipCar: Organizational Structure*.

Exhibit 15-10 **Organizational Structure: Its Determinants and Outcomes**

Summary

The theme of this chapter is that an organization's internal structure contributes to explaining and predicting behavior. That is, in addition to individual and group factors, the structural relationships in which people work have a bearing on employee attitudes and behavior. What's the basis for this argument? To the degree that an organization's structure reduces ambiguity for employees and clarifies concerns such as "What am I supposed to do?", "How am I supposed to do it?", "To whom do I report?", and "To whom do I go if I have a problem?" it shapes their attitudes and facilitates and motivates them to higher levels of performance. Exhibit 15-10 summarizes what we've discussed.

Implications for Managers

- Specialization can make operations more efficient, but remember that excessive specialization can create dissatisfaction and reduced motivation.
- Avoid designing rigid hierarchies that overly limit employees' empowerment and autonomy.
- Balance the advantages of remote work against the potential pitfalls before adding flexible workplace options into the organization's structure.
- Downsize your organization to realize major cost savings, and focus the company around core competencies—but only if necessary, because downsizing can have a significant negative impact on employee affect.
- Consider the scarcity, dynamism, and complexity of the environment, and balance organic and mechanistic elements when designing an organizational structure.

The End of Management

POINT   **COUNTERPOINT**

anagement—at least as we know it—is dying. Formal organizational structures are giving way to flatter, less bureaucratic, less formal structures. And that's a good thing. Innovative companies like Apple, Google, Facebook, Twitter, and Groupon were born and now thrive thanks not to a multilayered bureaucracy, but to an innovative idea that was creatively executed by a flexible group of people freely collaborating. Management in those companies exists to facilitate, rather than control.

The scope of what managers do has broadened to include typing, taking notes, and managing their own files/schedules, while the scope of what administrative assistants do has broadened to include making social media posts and assuming technical duties. The most innovative firms have questioned whether they need job titles at all, instead emphasizing collaboration throughout the organization.

The best companies have eliminated offices altogether and encourage employees to mingle and form teams according to their project interests. This suits younger workers who aspire to *work with* the top players rather than *report to* them, and who value flexible hours and work-from-home options. Job titles are gone, roles are ambiguous, and reporting relationships morph by project.

"There's a struggle right now between the old and the new," noted Adam Leitman Bailey, a New York real estate lawyer. "We don't know what works. In the end, it's what's going to be best for the talent we hire." The talent is ready for the elimination of management as we know it. The successful corporation of the future will have a flatter organizational structure and accountability based on performance.

here is no "right size fits all" approach to organizational structure. How flat, informal, and collaborative an organization should be depends on many factors, but no matter what, management structure is needed. Let's consider two cases.

People lauded how loosely and informally Warren Buffett structured his investment firm, Berkshire Hathaway, until it was discovered his CFO and heir apparent David Sokol was on the take. Wouldn't Buffett have known Sokol was compromised if he supervised more closely or had structures in place to check such "freedom"? It's hard to argue with Berkshire Hathaway's past successes, but they don't prove the company is ideally structured.

At Honeywell International, CEO David Cote seems relaxed and fun-loving (he rides a Harley and wears a leather bomber jacket to work), but his hard-hitting work ethic and firm hand on the reins are legendary. Cote's control focus doesn't end at the executive suite. At the factories, job titles are painted literally on the *floor* to indicate who needs to be present—and standing—at organizational meetings limited to 15 minutes by the clock. Is Cote a control freak? Maybe, but he successfully merged three disparate company cultures and more than 250 factories—the new Honeywell has climbed the Fortune 500 ranks and pulls in over $40 billion in annual sales. Profits have increased even faster than sales, in part due to Cote's insistence on freezing raises and hiring only two to three employees for every four to five who exit.

Berkshire Hathaway and Honeywell illustrate the strong need for management structure in an ever-changing, diverse, worldwide marketplace.

Sources: A. Bryant, "Structure? The Flatter the Better," *The New York Times,* January 17, 2010, BU2; "Honeywell International: From Bitter to Sweet," *The Economist,* April 14, 2012, www.economist.com/node/21552631; A. Efrati and S. Morrison, "Chief Seeks More Agile Google," *The Wall Street Journal,* January 22, 2011, B1, B4; H. El Nasser, "What Office? Laptops Are Workspace," *USA Today,* June 6, 2012; *Fortune* 500 rankings, http://money.cnn.com/magazines/fortune/fortune500/2012/full_list/; "Honeywell | Company Structure Information from ICIS," *ICIS.com,* www.icis.com/v2/companies/9145292/honeywell/structure.html; K. Linebaugh, "Honeywell's Hiring Is Bleak," *The Wall Street Journal,* March 6, 2013, B3; A. Murray, "The End of Management," *The Wall Street Journal,* August 21, 2010, W3; A. R. Sorkin, "Delegator in Chief," *The New York Times,* April 24, 2011, B4; and S. Tully, "How Dave Cote Got Honeywell's Groove Back," *CNN Money,* May 14, 2012, http://management.fortune.cnn.com/2012/05/14/500-honeywell-cote/.

CHAPTER REVIEW

MyManagementLab

Go to **mymanagementlab.com** to complete the problems marked with this icon. ⊛

QUESTIONS FOR REVIEW

15-1 What are seven key elements to define an organization's structure?

15-2 What are the characteristics of the functional, divisional, and matrix structures?

15-3 What are the characteristics of the virtual structure, the team structure, and the circular structure?

15-4 How might downsizing affect organizational structures and employees?

15-5 How are mechanistic and organic structural models similar and different?

15-6 What are the behavioral implications of different organizational designs?

EXPERIENTIAL EXERCISE   The Sandwich Shop

Divide the class into groups of at least four individuals.

As background: The managers of a new chain of sandwich shops will need to determine what types of sandwiches consumers want and find recipes and ingredients. Ingredient sources, prices, and other logistical requirements (like refrigeration) will need to be determined, purchasing decisions will be ongoing, and supplier relationships will need to be managed. Financing must also be arranged at this early phase. With this groundwork, the company will move to the next stage of marketing, including pricing and the development of advertising materials. Finally, selecting and training workers will occur.

Each group creates the following:

A Simple Structure

Determine what a simple structure would look like for this organization. Recall that a simple structure is one in which there is little hierarchy, wide spans of control, and centralized decision making. To whom would the various tasks described above be assigned? What sort of delegation might take place? Who would coordinate the multiple operations? About how many people would be acting in an administrative role, and what sort of spans of control would they have? What challenges will the organization face as it grows?

A Bureaucracy

Determine what a bureaucratic structure would look like for this organization. Bureaucracies are marked by more hierarchy, small spans of control, and specialized decision making. Again, you will want to establish task assignments, delegation, coordination, and the number of individuals required. Also consider possibilities for future growth with a bureaucratic system.

A Virtual Structure

Determine what a virtual structure would look like for this organization if many of the aspects of the business are outsourced. Consider which tasks can be adequately performed by individuals who do not work within the restaurant chain, and which should be kept in house.

Debriefing

After all groups have developed different structural options, convene for class discussion for groups to describe how they created responsibilities for different individuals. Then the class should talk about which system of organization seems most beneficial for this business.

ETHICAL DILEMMA   Post-Millennium Tensions in the Flexible Organization

The message from the business press has been consistent: don't count on long-term employment. For years, job seekers have been told they should expect to be responsible for their own careers and prepare for the possibility that they will be changing jobs frequently. A simple look at employment trends also confirms that highly routine and well-defined jobs have been decreasing in number.

The shift has often been described in fairly positive terms. Managers work to create organizations that have laudable characteristics like adaptability, flexibility, and creativity. Author Micha Kaufman notes that doing well in contemporary business environments means "having the flexibility to let go of the ideas of the past, the courage to constantly reevaluate plans for the future, and the presence of mind to adapt to life, as it is, in the moment." There is a lot of appeal in creating your own future at work.

At the same time, many workers land in precarious positions. Researchers find that individuals who feel insecure or uncertain about future employment experience higher levels of psychological strain and worry. Insecure workers also get sick more frequently. Contrary to the positive image of the freelance worker with boundless energy and creativity, evidence shows that for many individuals, a lack of job security can result in exhaustion and an apprehensive approach to work problems.

Corporate leaders ask themselves what their role in creating job security should be. Some note that companies built around stability and security are less likely to compete successfully and may go out of business. Many organizations try to maintain flexibility *and* a certain level of security. For example, Scripps Health has maintained a pool of internal transfer opportunities and training assignments for individuals whose job functions are no longer needed. As a result, even within the highly volatile health care industry, it has been able to avoid layoffs. However, systems that provide job security do not come cheaply, nor are they feasible for all companies.

Questions

15-7. Do you think that stability is good or bad for employees?

15-8. Do employers have an ethical responsibility to provide security for employees or just a warning about a lack of security?

15-9. If long-term employment security isn't feasible, what alternatives might employers provide to help employees make smoother transitions?

Sources: M. Kaufman, "The Wisdom of Job Insecurity," *Forbes*, October 3, 2014, http://www.forbes.com/sites/michakaufman/2014/10/03/the-wisdom-of-job-insecurity-dont-be-lulled-by-falling-unemployment/; C. Van Gorder, "A No-Layoffs Policy Can Work, Even in an Unpredictable Economy," *Harvard Business Review*, January 26, 2015, https://hbr.org/2015/01/a-no-layoffs-policy-can-work-even-in-an-unpredictable-economy; J. Zumbrun, "Is Your Job 'Routine'? If So, It's Probably Disappearing," *Wall Street Journal*, April 8, 2015, http://blogs.wsj.com/economics/2015/04/08/is-your-job-routine-if-so-its-probably-disappearing/; U. Kinnunen, A. Mäkikangas, S. Mauno, N. De Cuyper, and H. De Witte, "Development of Perceived Job Insecurity across Two Years: Associations with Antecedents and Employee Outcomes," *Journal of Occupational Health Psychology* 19 (2014): 243–58.

CASE INCIDENT 1   Kuuki: Reading the Atmosphere

Most Japanese businesses have very complex vertically structured organizations. Each of the key departments of the organization has its own vertical structure and operates rather like individual businesses. There is very little inter-relationship between departments. Each department has very clearly defined roles.

When the business interacts with customers, it is the sales and marketing departments that handle negotiations. Even when the customer needs technical information and support, sales and marketing are often involved as an intermediary between the company engineers and the customer. It is common for sales specialists to take on the role of negotiators on behalf of the manufacturing department or research and development. Inter-departmental communications are not common.

One of the problems is that salespeople rarely have technical expertise. The majority of salespeople would not have studied science and technology and are more likely to be qualified in the arts. They are chosen for the sales role due to their social skills. The perception is that engineers and technical specialists are not as sociable and are therefore not good sellers.

In their offices, larger Japanese companies tend to have open plan spaces. This allows the departmental head to learn what other people do and to ensure that they share information. In smaller Japanese businesses it is common for the business owner to also be based in an open plan environment.

The key to success is "reading the air" or reading the kuuki. Keeping alert to what is being said and what is being done means that Japanese managers have instant access to up-to-date information. It means that they know what individual employees know. Individuals in a department are comfortable with this situation; informal information sharing is seen as an effective and vital process.

Questions

15-10. Complex vertical organizational structures are very hierarchical in nature. They are very rigid, with each department having clearly defined roles. Is such an organization capable of being agile and responsive or is it a disadvantage?

15-11. What are the problems in having such strictly defined roles?

15-12. Is reading the air just eavesdropping and spying on others? Would most employees be comfortable with this situation?

Source: John Spacey, "Why You Need to Read the Air in Japan," *Japan Talk,* http://www.japan-talk .com/jt/new/kuuki-yomenai (accessed January 24, 2014)

CASE INCIDENT 2   Boeing Dreamliner: Engineering Nightmare or Organizational Disaster?

As a flight of imagination, Boeing's 787 Dreamliner was an excellent idea: made of composite materials, the plane would be lightweight enough to significantly reduce fuel costs while maintaining a passenger load up to 290 seats. Airline carriers chose options from a long list of unprecedented luxuries to entice the flying public and placed their orders well ahead of the expected completion dates. And then the problems started.

An airplane like the 787 has a design about as complex as that of a nuclear power plant, and Boeing's equally complex offshore organizational structure didn't help the execution. Boeing outsources 67 percent of its manufacturing and many of its engineering functions. While the official assembly site is in Everett, Washington, parts were manufactured at 100 supplier sites in countries across the globe, and some of those suppliers subcontracted piecework to other firms. Because the outsourcing plan allowed vendors to develop their own blueprints, language barriers became a problem back in Washington as workers struggled to understand multilingual assembly instructions. When components didn't fit together properly, the fixes needed along the supply chain and with engineering were almost impossible to implement. The first aircraft left the runway on a test flight in 2009, but Boeing had to buy one of the suppliers a year later (cost: $1 billion) to help make the planes. The first customer delivery was still years away.

If Boeing and industry watchers thought its troubles were over when the first order was delivered to All Nippon Airways (ANA) in 2011, 3 years behind schedule and after at least seven manufacturing delays, they were wrong. Besides the continuing woes of remaining behind schedule, Boeing's Dreamliner suffered numerous mechanical problems. After the plane's technologically advanced lithium-ion batteries started a fire on one aircraft and forced another into an emergency landing in January 2013, ANA and Japan Airlines grounded their fleets. The FAA followed suit, grounding all 787s in the United States. The remaining 50 flying Dreamliners worldwide were then confined to the tarmac until a solution could be found.

This looked like an organizational structure problem, both at corporate headquarters and abroad. However, there have been so many management changes during the 787's history that it would be difficult for anyone to identify responsibility for errors in order to make changes in the team or the organizational structure. For the work done abroad, restructuring reporting relationships in favor of smaller spans of control to heighten management accountability and tie suppliers to the organizational structure of corporate Boeing could be considered. Or "reshoring" to bring manufacturing physically close to the final assembly site and under Boeing's control while centralizing the organizational structure could be an option.

Questions

15-13. Do you think this is a case of the difficulty of launching new technology (there are "bugs" in any system), or one of an unsuccessful launch?

15-14. What type of executive management structure do you think would be most conducive to getting the Dreamliner past a component failure and back in flight? Is this a different structure than you would

suggest for fixing the ongoing manufacturing problems? Sketch out the potential design.

✪ **15-15.** What organizational structure would you suggest to effectively tie in Boeing's managers and suppliers abroad? Sketch your ideas. (Goals for managers might include facilitating teams, coordinating efforts, maintaining organizational transparency, and creating conversations.)

Sources: S. Denning, "The Boeing Debacle: Seven Lessons Every CEO Must Learn," *Forbes,* January 17, 2013, www.forbes.com/sites/stevedenning/2013/01/17/the-boeing-debacle-seven-lessons-every-ceo-must-learn/; E. Frauenheim, "Homeward Bound," *Workforce Management,* February 2013, 26–31; C. Hymowitz, "Boeing CEO's Task: Get the Dreamliner Airborne Again," *Bloomberg Businessweek,* January 24, 2013, www.businessweek.com/articles/2013-01-24/boeing-ceos-task-get-the-dreamliner-airborne-again/; D. Nosowitz, "Why Is Boeing's 787 Dreamliner Such a Piece of Crap?" *Popsci,* January 17, 2013, www.popsci.com/technology/article/2013-01/why-boeings-787-dreamliner-such-piece-crap; J. Ostrower and A. Pasztor, "Boeing Plays Down 787 Woes; Net Falls 30%," *The Wall Street Journal,* January 31, 2013, B3; and D. Terdiman, "Boeing's Dreamliner Struggles Despite Tech Superiority," *C/Net,* February 24, 2012, http://news.cnet.com/8301-13772_3-57385001-52/boeings-dreamliner-struggles-despite-tech-superiority/.

MyManagementLab

Go to **mymanagementlab.com** for the following Assisted-graded writing questions:

15-16. Considering Case Incident 2, how would you have envisioned the best organizational structure for Boeing during its development of the Dreamliner? How might you change the structure during the production phase of the airplane?

15-17. Based on what you've discovered about your personality traits on the Big Five Model through your organizational behavior studies in Chapter 5, in which organizational structures might you work best?

15-18. MyManagementLab Only – comprehensive writing assignment for this chapter.

ENDNOTES

[1]L. Garicano and Y. Wu, "Knowledge, Communication, and Organizational Capabilities," *Organization Science,* September–October 2012, 1382–97.

[2]See, for instance, R. L. Daft, *Organization Theory and Design,* 10th ed. (Cincinnati, OH: South-Western Publishing, 2010).

[3]J. G. Miller, "The Real Women's Issue: Time," *The Wall Street Journal,* March 9–10, 2013, C3.

[4]T. W. Malone, R. J. Laubacher, and T. Johns, "The Age of Hyperspecialization," *Harvard Business Review,* July–August 2011, 56–65.

[5]J. Schramm, "A Cloud of Workers," *HR Magazine,* March 2013, 80.

[6]C. Woodyard, "Toyota Brass Shakeup Aims to Give Regions More Control," *USA Today,* March 6, 2013, www.usatoday.com/story/money/cars/2013/03/06/toyota-shakeup/1966489/.

[7]S. Ballmer, "One Microsoft: Company Realigns to Enable Innovation at Greater Speed, Efficiency," Microsoft, July 11, 2013, http://blogs.microsoft.com/firehose/2013/07/11/one-microsoft-company-realigns-to-enable-innovation-at-greater-speed-efficiency/.

[8]Ibid.

[9]A. Wilhelm, "Microsoft Shakes Up Its Leadership and Internal Structure as Its Fiscal Year Comes to a Close," *TechCrunch,* June 17, 2015, http://techcrunch.com/2015/06/17/microsoft-shakes-up-its-leadership-and-internal-structure-as-its-fiscal-year-comes-to-a-close/#.mcn4eo:OnA3.

[10]See, for instance, "How Hierarchy Can Hurt Strategy Execution," *Harvard Business Review,* July–August 2010, 74–75.

[11]See, for instance, J. H. Gittell, "Supervisory Span, Relational Coordination, and Flight Departure Performance: A Reassessment of Postbureaucracy Theory," *Organization Science,* July–August 2001, 468–83.

[12]F. A. Csascar, "Organizational Structure as a Determinant of Performance: Evidence from Mutual Funds," *Strategic Management Journal,* June 2013, 611–32.

[13]B. Brown and S. D. Anthony, "How P&G Tripled Its Innovation Success Rate," *Harvard Business Review,* June 2011, 64–72.

[14]A. Leiponen and C. E. Helfat, "Location, Decentralization, and Knowledge Sources for Innovation," *Organization Science* 22, no. 3 (2011): 641–58.

[15]K. Parks, "HSBC Unit Charged in Argentine Tax Case," *The Wall Street Journal,* March 19, 2013, C2.

[16]P. Hempel, Z.-X. Zhang, and Y. Han, "Team Empowerment and the Organizational Context: Decentralization and the Contrasting Effects of Formalization," *Journal of Management,* March 2012, 475–501.

[17]J. E. Perry-Smith and C. E. Shalley, "A Social Composition View of Team Creativity: The Role of Member Nationality-Heterogeneous Ties Outside of the Team," *Organization Science* 25 (2014): 1434–52; J. Han, J. H., and D. J. Brass, "Human Capital Diversity in the Creation of Social Capital for Team Creativity," *Journal of Organizational Behavior* 35 (2014): 54–71; N. Sivasubramaniam, S. J. Liebowitz, and C. L. Lackman, "Determinants of New Product Development Team Performance: A Meta-Analytic Review," *Journal of Product Innovation Management* 29 (2012): 803–20.

[18]N. J. Foss, K. Laursen, and T. Pedersen, "Linking Customer Interaction and Innovation: The Mediating Role of New Organizational Practices," *Organization Science* 22 (2011): 980–99; N. J. Foss, J. Lyngsie, and S. A. Zahra, "The Role of External Knowledge Sources and Organizational Design in the Process of Opportunity Exploitation," *Strategic Management Journal* 34 (2013): 1453–71; A. Salter, P. Crisuolo, and A. L. J. Ter Wal, "Coping with Open Innovation: Responding to the Challenges of External Engagement in R&D," *California Management Review* 56 (Winter 2014): 77–94.

[19]T. A de Vries, F. Walter, G. S. Van der Vegt, and P. J. M. D. Essens, "Antecedents of Individuals' Interteam Coordination: Broad Functional Experiences as a Mixed Blessing," *Academy of Management Journal* 57 (2014): 1334–59.

[20]A. Murray, "Built Not to Last," *The Wall Street Journal,* March 18, 2013, A11.

[21]For a quick overview, see J. Davoren, "Functional Structure Organization Strength and Weakness," *Small Business Chronicle,* http://smallbusiness.chron.com/functional-structure-organization-strength-weakness-60111.html, accessed June 25, 2015.

[22]See, for instance, A. Writing, "Different Types of Organizational Structure," *Small Business Chronicle,* http://smallbusiness.chron.com/different-types-organizational-structure-723.html, accessed June 25, 2015.

[23]For a quick overview, see "Types of Business Organizational Structures," Pingboard, July 24, 2013, https://pingboard.com/blog/types-business-organizational-structures/, accessed June 25, 2015.

[24]J. R. Galbraith, *Designing Matrix Organizations That Actually Work: How IBM, Procter & Gamble, and Others Design for Success* (San Francisco: Jossey Bass, 2009); and E. Krell, "Managing the Matrix," *HRMagazine,* April 2011, 69–71.

[25]See, for instance, M. Bidwell, "Politics and Firm Boundaries: How Organizational Structure, Group Interests, and Resources Affect Outsourcing," *Organization Science,* November–December 2012, 1622–42.

[26]See, for instance, T. Sy and L. S. D'Annunzio, "Challenges and Strategies of Matrix Organizations: Top-Level and Mid-Level Managers' Perspectives," *Human Resource Planning* 28, no. 1 (2005): 39–48; and T. Sy and S. Cote, "Emotional Intelligence: A Key Ability to Succeed in the Matrix Organization," *Journal of Management Development* 23, no. 5 (2004): 437–55.

[27]N. Anand and R. L. Daft, "What Is the Right Organization Design?" *Organizational Dynamics* 36, no. 4 (2007): 329–44.

[28]See, for instance, N. S. Contractor, S. Wasserman, and K. Faust, "Testing Multitheoretical, Multilevel Hypotheses about Organizational Networks: An Analytic Framework and Empirical Example," *Academy of Management Review* 31, no. 3 (2006): 681–703; and Y. Shin, "A Person-Environment Fit Model for Virtual Organizations," *Journal of Management,* October 2004, 725–43.

[29]J. Schramm, "At Work in a Virtual World," *HR Magazine,* June 2010, 152.

[30]C. B. Gibson and J. L. Gibbs, "Unpacking the Concept of Virtuality: The Effects of Geographic Dispersion, Electronic Dependence, Dynamic Structure, and National Diversity on Team Innovation," *Administrative Science Quarterly* 51, no. 3 (2006): 451–95; H. M. Latapie and V. N. Tran, "Subculture Formation, Evolution, and Conflict between Regional Teams in Virtual Organizations," *The Business Review,* Summer 2007, 189–93; and S. Davenport and U. Daellenbach, "'Belonging' to a Virtual Research Center: Exploring the Influence of Social Capital Formation Processes on Member Identification in a Virtual Organization," *British Journal of Management* 22, no. 1 (2011): 54–76.

[31]A. Poon and K. Tally, "Yoga-Pants Supplier Says Lululemon Stretches Truth," *The Wall Street Journal,* March 20, 2013, B1.

[32]See, for instance, E. Devaney, "The Pros & Cons of 7 Popular Organizational Structures," http://blog.hubspot.com/marketing/team-structure-diagrams, accessed June 25, 2015.

[33]J. Scheck, L. Moloney, and A. Flynn, "Eni, CNPC Link Up in Mozambique," *The Wall Street Journal,* March 15, 2013, B3.

[34]E. Devaney, "The Pros & Cons of 7 Popular Organizational Structures."

[35]S. Ghosh, "Google's Motorola Mobility Layoffs: Sweeping Changes Axe 4,000 Jobs," *Reuters,* August 13, 2012, http://www.huffingtonpost.com/2012/08/13/google-motorola-mobility-layoffs-cuts-employees_n_1771692.html.

[36]L. Gensler, "American Express to Slash 4,000 Jobs on Heels of Strong Quarter," *Forbes,* January 21, 2015, http://www.forbes.com/sites/laurengensler/2015/01/21/american-express-earnings-rise-11-on-increased-cardholder-spending/.

[37]C. Giammona, "Starbucks First-Quarter Profit Surges 82% as Food Sales Gain," *Bloomberg Business,* January 22, 2015, http://www.bloomberg.com/news/articles/2015-01-22/

starbucks-first-quarter-profit-surges-82-as-food-sales-increase.

[38]L. I Alpert, "Can Imported CEO Fix Russian Cars?" *The Wall Street Journal*, March 20, 2013, http://www.wsj.com/articles/SB10001424127 887323639604578370121394214736.

[39]K. Walker, N. Ni, and B. Dyck, "Recipes for Successful Sustainability: Empirical Organizational Configurations for Strong Corporate Environmental Performance," *Business Strategy and the Environment* 24, no. 1 (2015): 40–57.

[40]See, for instance, J. R. Hollenbeck, H. Moon, A. P. J. Ellis, B. J. West, D. R. Ilgen, L. Sheppard, C. O. L. H. Porter, and J. A. Wagner III, "Structural Contingency Theory and Individual Differences: Examination of External and Internal Person-Team Fit," *Journal of Applied Psychology*, June 2002, 599–606; and A. Drach-Zahavy and A. Freund, "Team Effectiveness Under Stress: A Structural Contingency Approach," *Journal of Organizational Behavior* 28, no. 4 (2007): 423–50.

[41]K. Walker, N. Ni, and B. Dyck, "Recipes for Successful Sustainability: Empirical Organizational Configurations for Strong Corporate Environmental Performance."

[42]See, for instance, S. M. Toh, F. P. Morgeson, and M. A. Campion, "Human Resource Configurations: Investigating Fit with the Organizational Context," *Journal of Applied Psychology* 93, no. 4 (2008): 864–82.

[43]M. Mesco, "Moleskine Tests Appetite for IPOs," *The Wall Street Journal*, March 19, 2013, B8.

[44]J. Backaler, "Haier: A Chinese Company that Innovates," *Forbes*, June 17, 2010, http://www.forbes.com/sites/china/2010/06/17/haier-a-chinese-company-that-innovates/.

[45]See, for instance, J. A. Cogin and I. O. Williamson, "Standardize or Customize: The Interactive Effects of HRM and Environment Uncertainty on MNC Subsidiary Performance," *Human Resource Management* 53, no. 5 (2014): 701–21; G. Kim and M.-G. Huh, "Exploration and Organizational Longevity: The Moderating Role of Strategy and Environment," *Asia Pacific Journal of Management* 32, no. 2 (2015): 389–414.

[46]R. Greenwood, C. R. Hinings, and D. Whetten, "Rethinking Institutions and Organizations," *Journal of Management Studies*, 51 (2014): 1206–20; D. Chandler and H. Hwang, "Learning from Learning Theory: A Model of Organizational Adoption Strategies at the Microfoundations of Institutional Theory," *Journal of Management* 41 (2015): 1446–76.

[47]C. S. Spell and T. J. Arnold, "A Multi-Level Analysis of Organizational Justice and Climate, Structure, and Employee Mental Health," *Journal of Management* 33, no. 5 (2007): 724–51; and M. L. Ambrose and M. Schminke, "Organization Structure as a Moderator of the Relationship between Procedural Justice, Interactional Justice, Perceived Organizational Support, and Supervisory Trust," *Journal of Applied Psychology* 88, no. 2 (2003): 295–305.

[48]See, for instance, Spell and Arnold, "A Multi-Level Analysis of Organizational Justice Climate, Structure, and Employee Mental Health"; J. D. Shaw and N. Gupta, "Job Complexity, Performance, and Well-Being: When Does Supplies-Values Fit Matter? *Personnel Psychology* 57, no. 4 (2004): 847–79; and C. Anderson and C. E. Brown, "The Functions and Dysfunctions of Hierarchy," *Research in Organizational Behavior* 30 (2010): 55–89.

[49]T. Martin, "Pharmacies Feel More Heat," *The Wall Street Journal*, March 16–17, 2013, A3.

[50]See, for instance, R. E. Ployhart, J. A. Weekley, and K. Baughman, "The Structure and Function of Human Capital Emergence: A Multilevel Examination of the Attraction-Selection-Attrition Model," *Academy of Management Journal* 49, no. 4 (2006): 661–77.

[51]J. B. Stewart, "A Place to Play for Google Staff," *The New York Times*, March 16, 2013, B1.

[52]See, for instance, B. K. Park, J. A. Choi, M. Koo, et al., "Culture, Self, and Preference Structure: Transitivity and Context Independence Are Violated More by Interdependent People," *Social Cognition*, February 2013, 106–18.

[53]J. Hassard, J. Morris, and L. McCann, "'My Brilliant Career?' New Organizational Forms and Changing Managerial Careers in Japan, the UK, and USA," *Journal of Management Studies*, May 2012, 571–99.

16 Organizational Culture

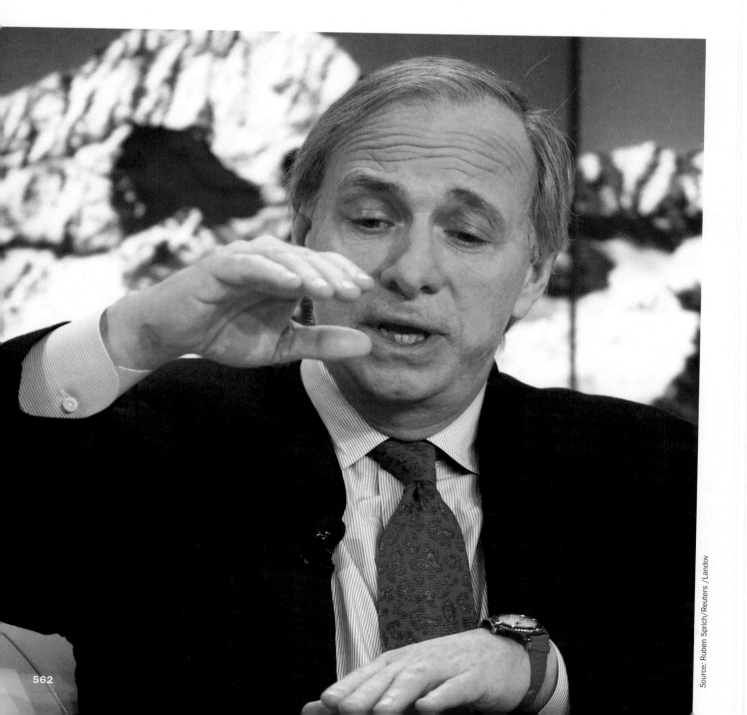

16-1 Describe the common characteristics of organizational culture.

16-2 Compare the functional and dysfunctional effects of organizational culture on people and the organization.

16-3 Identify the factors that create and sustain an organization's culture.

16-4 Show how culture is transmitted to employees.

16-5 Describe the similarities and differences in creating an ethical culture, a positive culture, and a spiritual culture.

16-6 Show how national culture can affect the way organizational culture is transported to another country.

MyManagementLab®
⭐ **Chapter Warm Up**

If your professor has chosen to assign this, go to the Assignments section of **mymanagementlab.com** to complete the chapter warm up.

WELCOME TO THE MACHINE

During the Second World War, a quiet revolution was launched in an unassuming barn in Bletchley Park that would permanently transform the culture of British military intelligence. The Allies, Great Britain in particular, regularly intercepted German communications but couldn't decode them. The traditional British code-breaking operation was notoriously inefficient, guided by individual cryptographers looking for patterns in secret communications. Finally, the innovative ideas of Alan Turing and Gordon Welchman resulted in an early computer that combed thousands of encrypted German messages to crack the code. Once its effectiveness had been demonstrated, the old bureaucratic British intelligence management system was rapidly reconfigured. A new culture now needed to embrace the role of big data while recognizing that human perceivers could still best decide how to use the decoded findings to outwit the enemy.

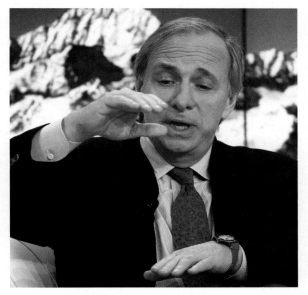

It might seem that adding an automated process for decision making is a matter of practicality and has little to do with culture. In practice, though, we encounter many cultural issues on the road to adopting electronic decision aids. The founder of massive hedge fund Bridgewater Associates, Ray Dalio (pictured here), notes that the transition to his organization's data-oriented culture isn't always easy for new hires. He said, "There's a period—usually about 18 months—of sort of adaptation to this. And some make it and some don't make it." People sometimes resist a culture in which decisions are guided by well-defined, mechanized rules for evaluating information. But over time, managers in organizations where everyone buys into these systems see clear benefits. As former Aetna CEO Ron Williams noted, "When you have a pre-agreed set of numbers presented in a uniform way, you can train the company how to think about problems."

Automated decision making requires a sophisticated organizational culture for successful implementation. Computer decision-making expert S. Barry Cooper notes that computerized decision systems do very well if they have enough data and a strict set of rules to guide them. But for fundamental decisions like figuring out how to motivate a team to work together, determining what new product is going to appeal to consumers, or responding to a competitor's attempt to enter a market, human decision makers are still far ahead of machines.

In dysfunctional cultures, managers often use data selectively to support their point of view, and conveniently ignore it when it doesn't. Rather than generating a sense of fairness and objectivity, picking and choosing only supportive data leads followers to feel distrust and cynicism. It also misses out on all the advantages of supporting decisions led by data. On the other hand, a culture that over-relies on data and does not constantly question and evaluate the system's underlying assumptions leads to equally bad decision making. The message from experienced managers is clear—big data is an effective decision aid only when it's paired with a consistent and thoughtful culture, one that acknowledges the need for human decision making and individual judgments.

Sources: C. Mims, "Why We Needn't Fear the Machines," *Wall Street Journal,* November 30, 2014, http://www.wsj.com/articles/why-we-neednt-fear-the-machines-1417394021; J. Freeman, "The Soul of a Hedge Fund 'Machine,'" *Wall Street Journal,* June 6, 2014, http://www.wsj.com/articles/james-freeman-the-soul-of-a-hedge-fund-machine-1402094722; and J. W. Ross, C. M. Beath, and A. Quaadgras, "You May Not Need Big Data after All," *Harvard Business Review,* December 2013, https://hbr.org/2013/12/you-may-not-need-big-data-after-all.

Just as tribal cultures have totems and taboos that dictate how each member should act toward fellow members and outsiders, organizations have rules and norms that govern how members behave. We call these expectations the *organizational culture.* Every organization has a culture that, depending on its strength, can have a significant influence on the attitudes and behaviors of organization members, even if that effect is hard to measure precisely. As the opening discussion of incorporating big data illustrates, even strong improvements to decision making in organizations challenge the organizational culture. In this chapter, we'll discuss what organizational culture is, how it affects employee attitudes and behavior, where it comes from, and whether it can be changed.

> ✪ **WATCH IT!**
> If your professor has assigned this, go to the Assignments section of **mymanagementlab.com** to complete the video exercise titled *Organizational Culture (TWZ Role Play).*

What Is Organizational Culture?

16-1 Describe the common characteristics of organizational culture.

An executive once was asked what he thought *organizational culture* meant. He gave essentially the same answer U.S. Supreme Court Justice Potter Stewart gave in defining pornography: "I can't define it, but I know it when I see it." In this section, we propose one definition and review several related ideas.

A Definition of Organizational Culture

organizational culture A system of shared meaning held by members that distinguishes the organization from other organizations.

Organizational culture refers to a system of shared meaning held by members that distinguishes the organization from other organizations.[1] Seven primary characteristics seem to capture the essence of an organization's culture:[2]

1. **Innovation and risk taking.**   The degree to which employees are encouraged to be innovative and take risks.
2. **Attention to detail.**   The degree to which employees are expected to exhibit precision, analysis, and attention to detail.
3. **Outcome orientation.**   The degree to which management focuses on results or outcomes rather than on the techniques and processes used to achieve them.
4. **People orientation.**   The degree to which management decisions take into consideration the effect of outcomes on people within the organization.
5. **Team orientation.**   The degree to which work activities are organized around teams rather than individuals.
6. **Aggressiveness.**   The degree to which people are aggressive and competitive rather than easygoing.
7. **Stability.**   The degree to which organizational activities emphasize maintaining the status quo in contrast to growth.

Each of these characteristics exists on a continuum from low to high. Appraising an organization on the strength of each provides a basis for the shared understanding members have about the organization, how things are done in it, and the way they are supposed to behave.

Let's identify where the data-oriented Bridgewater Associates culture described in the introduction may fall on each of these characteristics. The push to use data to continuously revise methods is a clear example of highly valuing innovation, coupled with strong attention to detail and precise analyses. Bridgewater's focus on intellectual rigor and independent thinking may place it somewhat lower than other organizations in terms of the people and teamwork dimensions. However, this is balanced by the company's less competitive approach, in which potentially negative outcomes are seen as opportunities for learning and development. Finally, the organization places little value on overall stability, under Ray Dalio's preference for constant innovation and change. Exhibit 16-1 contrasts two companies that are very different along these dimensions.

Culture Is a Descriptive Term

If you've ever been in an organization (certainly you've been in many!), you probably noticed a pervasive culture among the members. *Organizational culture* shows how employees perceive the characteristics of an organization, not

Exhibit 16-1   Contrasting Organizational Cultures

Organization A

This organization is a manufacturing firm. Managers are expected to fully document all decisions, and "good managers" are those who can provide detailed data to support their recommendations. Creative decisions that incur significant change or risk are not encouraged. Because managers of failed projects are openly criticized and penalized, managers try not to implement ideas that deviate much from the status quo. One lower-level manager quoted an often-used phrase in the company: "If it ain't broke, don't fix it."

There are extensive rules and regulations in this firm that employees are required to follow. Managers supervise employees closely to ensure there are no deviations. Management is concerned with high productivity, regardless of the impact on employee morale or turnover.

Work activities are designed around individuals. There are distinct departments and lines of authority, and employees are expected to minimize formal contact with other employees outside their functional area or line of command. Performance evaluations and rewards emphasize individual effort, although seniority tends to be the primary factor in the determination of pay raises and promotions.

Organization B

This organization is also a manufacturing firm. Here, however, management encourages and rewards risk taking and change. Decisions based on intuition are valued as much as those that are well rationalized. Management prides itself on its history of experimenting with new technologies and its success in regularly introducing innovative products. Managers or employees who have a good idea are encouraged to "run with it." And failures are treated as "learning experiences." The company prides itself on being market driven and rapidly responsive to the changing needs of its customers.

There are few rules and regulations for employees to follow, and supervision is loose because management believes that its employees are hardworking and trustworthy. Management is concerned with high productivity but believes that this comes through treating its people right. The company is proud of its reputation as being a good place to work.

Job activities are designed around work teams, and team members are encouraged to interact with people across functions and authority levels. Employees talk positively about the competition between teams. Individuals and teams have goals, and bonuses are based on achievement of these outcomes. Employees are given considerable autonomy in choosing the means by which the goals are attained.

---

whether they like them—that is, it's a descriptive term. Research on organizational culture has sought to measure how employees see their organization: Does it encourage teamwork? Does it reward innovation? Does it stifle initiative? In contrast, job satisfaction seeks to measure how employees feel about the organization's expectations, reward practices, and the like. Although the two terms have overlapping characteristics, keep in mind that *organizational culture* is descriptive, whereas *job satisfaction*, for example, is evaluative.

Do Organizations Have Uniform Cultures?

Organizational culture represents a perception the organization's members hold in common. Statements about organizational culture are valid only if individuals with different backgrounds or at different levels in the organization describe the culture in similar terms.[3] The purchasing department can have a subculture that includes the core values of the dominant culture, such as aggressiveness, plus additional values unique to members of that department, such as risk-taking.

The **dominant culture** expresses the **core values** a majority of members share and that give the organization its distinct personality.[4] **Subcultures** tend to develop in large organizations in response to common problems or experiences a group of members face in the same department or location. Most large organizations have a dominant culture and numerous subcultures.[5]

dominant culture   A culture that expresses the core values that are shared by a majority of the organization's members.

core values   The primary or dominant values that are accepted throughout the organization.

subcultures   Minicultures within an organization, typically defined by department designations and geographical separation.

An Organization's Culture Is Forever

This is actually not true. Although organizational culture is difficult to change and a significant change can take a long time, it can be done. Sometimes it is essential to survival. For years, Wisconsin's Wellspring system provided nursing homes in which inpatients had little input about their care and the organizational culture allowed lax standards to prevail. Then the network of 11 nursing homes launched a culture change initiative. Management focused on caregiver collaboration, education, accountability, and empowerment. The results were excellent. Wellspring realized fewer state standards infractions and higher employee retention rates at the facilities, and the results for the patients were even greater: fewer bedfast residents, less use of restraints and psychoactive medication, less incontinence, and fewer tube feedings than in other nursing homes.

The Wellspring program illustrates the significant effect positive organizational culture change can achieve. CEO Bob Flexon of Dynegy Inc., a Houston-based electric utility giant emerging from bankruptcy, is trying to save his company by changing the organizational culture. First, he ditched the cushy CEO office suite, $15,000 marble desk, and Oriental rugs for a small cubicle on a warehouse-style floor shared with all 235 headquarters employees. Next, he visited company facilities, trained "culture champions," reinstated annual performance reviews, and increased employee collaboration. He created a plaque as a reminder to "Be Here Now" instead of multitasking and banned smartphones from meetings. Flexon said, "The idea was to instill a winning spirit," and he counts on his visibility as CEO to broadcast the culture change down to the lowest levels of the widespread organization.

Positive results at Dynegy have included a reduction in turnover from 8 percent in 2011 to 5.8 percent in the turnaround of 2012. Flexon said, "People are cautiously beginning to believe that we can win again." The company continues to report massive earnings losses, but Flexon is optimistic about Dynegy's rebound. He says, "Our ongoing focus on culture is what will make the difference."

Sources: J. Bellot, "Nursing Home Culture Change: What Does It Mean to Nurses?" *Research in Gerontological Nursing,* October 2012, 264–73; J. S. Lublin, "This CEO Used to Have an Office," *The Wall Street Journal,* March 13, 2013, B1, B8; and J. Molineux, "Enabling Organizational Cultural Change Using Systemic Strategic Human Resource Management—A Longitudinal Case Study," *International Journal of Human Resource Management,* April 1, 2013, 1588–612.

If organizations were composed only of subcultures, the dominant organizational culture would be significantly less powerful. It is the "shared meaning" aspect of culture that makes it a potent device for guiding and shaping behavior. That's what allows us to say, for example, that the Zappos culture values customer care and dedication over speed and efficiency, which explains the behavior of Zappos executives and employees.[6]

Strong versus Weak Cultures

It's possible to differentiate between strong and weak cultures.[7] If most employees (responding to surveys) have the same opinions about the organization's mission and values, the culture is strong; if opinions vary widely, the culture is weak.

strong culture A culture in which the core values are intensely held and widely shared.

In a **strong culture**, the organization's core values are both intensely held and widely shared.[8] The more members who accept the core values and the greater their commitment, the stronger the culture and the greater its influence on member behavior. The reason is that a high degree of shared values and intensity create a climate of high behavioral control. Nordstrom employees know in no uncertain terms what is expected of them, for example, and these expectations go a long way toward shaping their behavior.

A strong culture should reduce employee turnover because it demonstrates high agreement about what the organization represents. Such unanimity of purpose builds cohesiveness, loyalty, and organizational commitment. These qualities, in turn, lessen employees' propensity to leave.[9]

Culture versus Formalization

We've seen in this text that high formalization creates predictability, orderliness, and consistency. A strong culture modifies behavior similarly. Therefore, we should view formalization and culture as two different roads to a common destination. The stronger an organization's culture, the less management needs to be concerned with developing formal rules and regulations to guide employee behavior. Those guides will be internalized in employees when they adopt the organization's culture.

What Do Cultures Do?

16-2 Compare the functional and dysfunctional effects of organizational culture on people and the organization.

Let's discuss the role culture performs and whether it can ever be a liability for an organization.

The Functions of Culture

Culture defines the rules of the game. First, it has a boundary-defining role: It creates distinctions between organizations. Second, it conveys a sense of identity for organization members. Third, culture facilitates commitment to something larger than individual self-interest. Fourth, it enhances the stability of the social system. Culture is the social glue that helps hold the organization together by providing standards for what employees should say and do. Finally, it is a sense-making and control mechanism that guides and shapes employees' attitudes and behavior. This last function is of particular interest to us.[10]

A strong culture supported by formal rules and regulations ensures employees will act in a relatively uniform and predictable way. Today's trend toward decentralized organizations makes culture more important than ever, but ironically it also makes establishing a strong culture more difficult. When formal authority and control systems are reduced through decentralization, culture's *shared meaning* can point everyone in the same direction. However, employees organized in teams may show greater allegiance to their team and its values than to the organization as a whole. Furthermore, in virtual organizations, the lack of frequent face-to-face contact makes establishing a common set of norms very difficult. Strong leadership that fosters a strong culture by communicating frequently about common goals and priorities is especially important for innovative organizations.[11]

Individual–organization "fit"—that is, whether the applicant's or employee's attitudes and behavior are compatible with the culture—strongly influences who gets a job offer, a favorable performance review, or a promotion. It's no coincidence that Disney theme park employees appear almost universally attractive, clean, and wholesome with bright smiles. The company selects employees who will maintain that image.

Culture Creates Climate

If you've worked with someone whose positive attitude inspired you to do your best, or with a lackluster team that drained your motivation, you've experienced the effects of climate. **Organizational climate** refers to the shared perceptions organizational members have about their organization and work environment.[12] This aspect of culture is like team spirit at the organizational level. When everyone has the same general feelings about what's important or how well things are working, the effect of these attitudes will be more than the sum of the individual parts. One meta-analysis found that across dozens of different samples, psychological climate was strongly related to individuals' level of job

organizational climate The shared perceptions organizational members have about their organization and work environment.

Employees of French videogame publisher Ubisoft Entertainment are shown working on "Just Dance 3" at the firm's creative studio near Paris. Ubisoft's 26 creative studios around the world share a climate of creative collaboration that reflects the diversity of team members.
Source: Charles Platiau/Reuters

satisfaction, involvement, commitment, and motivation.[13] A positive workplace climate has been linked to higher customer satisfaction and organizational financial performance as well.[14]

Dozens of dimensions of climate have been studied, including innovation, creativity, communication, warmth and support, involvement, safety, justice, diversity, and customer service.[15] For example, someone who encounters a diversity climate will feel more comfortable collaborating with coworkers regardless of their demographic backgrounds. Climates can interact with one another to produce behavior. For example, a climate of worker empowerment can lead to higher levels of performance in organizations that also have a climate of personal accountability.[16] Climate also influences the habits people adopt. If there is a climate of safety, everyone wears safety gear and follows safety procedures even if individually they wouldn't normally think very often about being safe—indeed, many studies have shown that a safety climate decreases the number of documented injuries on the job.[17]

The Ethical Dimension of Culture

ethical work climate (EWC)   The shared concept of right and wrong behavior in the workplace that reflects the true values of the organization and shapes the ethical decision making of its members.

Organizational cultures are not neutral in their ethical orientation, even when they are not openly pursuing ethical goals. Over time, the **ethical work climate (EWC)**, or the shared concept of right and wrong behavior, develops as part of the organizational climate. The ethical climate reflects the true values of the organization and shapes the ethical decision making of its members.

Researchers have developed *ethical climate theory (ECT)* and the *ethical climate index (ECI)* to categorize and measure the ethical dimensions of organizational cultures.[18] Of the nine identified ECT climate categories, five are most prevalent in organizations: *instrumental, caring, independence, law and code,* and *rules.* Each explains the general mindset, expectations, and values of the managers and employees in relationship to their organizations. For instance, in an *instrumental* ethical climate, managers may frame their decision making around the assumption that employees (and companies) are motivated by self-interest (egoistic). In a *caring* climate, conversely, managers may operate under the expectation that their decisions will positively affect the greatest number of stakeholders (employees, customers, suppliers) possible.

Ethical climates of *independence* rely on each individual's personal moral ideas to dictate his or her workplace behavior. *Law and code* climates require managers and employees to use an external standardized moral compass such as a professional code of conduct for norms, while *rules* climates tend to operate by internal standardized expectations from, perhaps, an organizational policy manual. Organizations often progress through different categories as they move through their business life cycle.

An organization's ethical climate powerfully influences the way its individual members feel they should behave, so much so that researchers have been able to predict organizational outcomes from the climate categories.[19] Instrumental climates are negatively associated with employee job satisfaction and organizational commitment, even though those climates appeal to self-interest (of the employee and the company). They are positively associated with turnover intentions, workplace bullying, and deviant behavior. Caring and rules climates may bring greater job satisfaction. Caring, independence, rules, and law and code climates also reduce employee turnover intentions, workplace bullying, and dysfunctional behavior. Research indicates that ethical cultures take a long-term perspective and balance the rights of multiple stakeholders including employees, stockholders, and the community. Managers are supported for taking risks and innovating, discouraged from engaging in unbridled competition, and guided to heed not just *what* goals are achieved but *how*.

Studies of ethical climates and workplace outcomes suggest that some ECT climate categories are likely to be found in certain organizations. Industries with exacting standards, such as engineering, accounting, and law, tend to have a rules or law and code climate. Industries that thrive on competitiveness, such as financial trading, often have an instrumental climate. Industries with missions of benevolence are likely to have a caring climate, even if they are for-profit as in an environmental protection firm.

Research is exploring why organizations tend to fall into certain climate ECT categories by industry, especially successful organizations. We cannot conclude that instrumental climates are bad or that caring climates are good. Instrumental climates may foster the individual-level successes their companies need to thrive, for example, and they may help underperformers to recognize their self-interest is better served elsewhere. Managers in caring climates may be thwarted in making the best decisions when only choices that serve the greatest number of employees are acceptable.[20] The ECI, first introduced in 2010, is one new way researchers are seeking to understand the context of ethical drivers in organizations. By measuring the collective levels of moral sensitivity, judgment, motivation, and character of our organizations, we may be able to determine the strength of the influence our ethical climates have on us.[21]

Although ECT was first introduced more than 25 years ago, researchers have been recently studying ethics in organizations more closely to determine not only how ethical climates behave but also how they might be fostered, even changed.[22] Eventually, we may be able to provide leaders with clear blueprints for designing effective ethical climates.

Culture and Sustainability

sustainability Organization practices that can be sustained over a long period of time because the tools or structures that support them are not damaged by the processes.

As the name implies, **sustainability** refers to practices that can be maintained over very long periods of time[23] because the tools or structures that support the practices are not damaged by the processes. One survey found that a great majority of executives saw sustainability as an important part of future success.[24] Concepts of sustainable management have their origins in the environmental

Committed to environmental sustainability, founder and CEO of Sole Technology Pierre-André Senizergues has set a goal for his action-sports footwear and apparel company to go carbon neutral by 2020. He believes that the most successful brands of the future must lead by example in working harmoniously with the environment.

Source: Amber Miller/ZUMA Press/Newscom

movement, so processes that are in harmony with the natural environment are encouraged. *Social sustainability* practices address the ways social systems are affected by an organization's actions over time, and in turn, how changing social systems may affect the organization.

For example, farmers in Australia have been working collectively to increase water use efficiency, minimize soil erosion, and implement tilling and harvesting methods that ensure long-term viability for their farm businesses.[25] In a very different context, 3M has an innovative pollution-prevention program rooted in cultural principles of conserving resources, creating products that have minimal effects on the environment, and collaborating with regulatory agencies to improve environmental effects.[26]

Sustainable management doesn't need to be purely altruistic. Systematic reviews of the research literature show a generally positive relationship between sustainability and financial performance.[27] However, there is often a strong moral and ethical component that shapes organizational culture and must be a genuine value in order for the relationship to exist.

To create a truly sustainable business, an organization must develop a long-term culture and put its values into practice.[28] In other words, there needs to be a sustainable system for creating sustainability! In one workplace study, a company seeking to reduce energy consumption found that soliciting group feedback reduced energy use significantly more than simply issuing reading materials about the importance of conservation.[29] In other words, talking about energy conservation and building the value into the organizational culture resulted in positive employee behavioral changes. Like other cultural practices we've discussed, sustainability needs time and nurturing to grow.

Culture and Innovation

The most innovative companies are often characterized by their open, unconventional, collaborative, vision-driven, accelerating cultures.[30] Startup firms often have innovative cultures by definition because they are usually small, agile, and focused on solving problems in order to survive and grow. Consider digital music leader Echo Nest, recently bought by Spotify. As a startup,

Founded in 1969, Samsung Electronics of South Korea is past the usual innovation life cycle stage, yet continues to foster a climate of creativity and idea-generation. Samsung emulates a startup culture through its Creative Labs, where employees like engineer Ki Yuhoon, shown here, take up to a year off from their regular jobs to work on innovative projects.
Source: Lee-Jin/AP Images

the organization was unconventional, flexible, and open, hosting music app "hack" days for users and fostering a music culture.[31] All these are hallmarks of Spotify's culture, too, making the fit rather seamless.[32] Because of the similar organizational cultures, Echo Nest and Spotify may be able to continue their startup level of innovation.

At the other end of the startup spectrum, consider 30-year-old Intuit, one of the World's 100 Most Innovative Companies according to *Forbes*. Intuit employees attend workshops to teach them how to think creatively...and unconventionally. Sessions have led to managers talking through puppets and holding bake sales to sell prototype apps with their cupcakes. The culture stresses open accountability. "I saw one senior guy whose idea they'd been working on for nine months get disproved in a day because someone had a better way. He got up in front of everyone and said, 'This is my bad. I should have checked my hypothesis earlier,'" said Eric Ries, author of *The Lean Startup*. As a consultant for entrepreneurs, Ries considers the older software company equally innovative to startups because of its culture.[33]

Alexion Pharmaceuticals is also one of *Forbes'* Most Innovative and, like Intuit, it has been in operation long past the usual innovation life-cycle stage. Unlike Intuit, though, this maker of life-saving medicines is not known for management shenanigans. The key to its continuing innovation is a culture of caring, which drives it to develop medicines that save victims of rare diseases, even when the patients affected are few, the cost of development is prohibitively high, and the probability of success is low.[34]

Culture as an Asset

As we have discussed, organizational culture can provide a positive ethical environment and foster innovation. Culture can also significantly contribute to an organization's bottom line in many ways.

One strong example is found in the case of ChildNet. ChildNet is a nonprofit child welfare agency in Florida whose organizational culture was described as "grim" from 2000, when one of its foster children disappeared, through 2007, when the CEO was fired amid FBI allegations of fraud and forgery. "We didn't know if we would have jobs or who would take over," employee Maggie Tilelli said. However, after intense turnaround efforts aimed at changing the organizational culture, ChildNet became Florida's top-ranked agency within four years and *Workforce Management*'s Optima award winner for General Excellence in 2012. President and CEO Emilio Benitez, who took charge in 2008, effected the transformation by changing the executive staff, employing new technology to support caseworkers in the field and new managers at headquarters, acknowledging the stress employees and managers felt by establishing an employee recognition program, and creating cross-departmental roundtables (workgroups) for creative problem solving. The roundtables have been able to find solutions to difficult client cases, resulting in better placement of foster children into permanent homes. "From a business perspective, [the new problem-solving approach] was a tremendous cost savings," Benitez said. "But at the end of the day, it's about the families we serve."[35]

While ChildNet demonstrates how an organizational culture can positively affect outcomes, Dish Network illustrates the elusiveness of matching a particular culture to an industry or organization. By every measure, Dish Network is a business success story—it is the second-largest U.S. satellite TV provider, and it has made founder Charlie Ergen one of the richest men in the world. Yet Dish was recently ranked as the worst U.S. company to work for, and employees say the fault is the micromanaging culture Ergen created and enforces. Employees describe arduous mandatory overtime, fingerprint scanners to record work hours to the minute, public berating (most notably from Ergen), management condescension and distrust, quarterly "bloodbath" layoffs, and no working from home. One employee advised another online, "You're part of a poisonous environment... go find a job where you can use your talents for good rather than evil."

At ChildNet, positive changes to the organization's performance have been clearly attributed to the transformation of its organizational culture. Dish, on the other hand, may have succeeded *despite* its culture. We can only wonder how much more successful it could be if it reformed its toxic culture. There are many more cases of business success stories due to excellent organizational cultures than there are of success stories despite bad cultures, and almost no success stories because of bad ones.

Culture as a Liability

Culture can enhance organizational commitment and increase the consistency of employee behavior, which clearly benefits an organization. Culture is valuable to employees too, because it spells out how things are done and what's important. But we shouldn't ignore the potentially dysfunctional aspects of culture, especially a strong one, on an organization's effectiveness. Hewlett-Packard, once known as a premier computer manufacturer, rapidly lost market share and profits as dysfunction in its top management team trickled down, leaving employees disengaged, uncreative, unappreciated, and polarized.[36] Let's unpack some of the major factors that signal a negative organizational culture, beginning with institutionalization.

institutionalization A condition that occurs when an organization takes on a life of its own, apart from any of its members, and acquires immortality.

Institutionalization When an organization undergoes **institutionalization**—that is, it becomes valued for itself and not for the goods or services it produces—it takes on a life of its own, apart from its founders or members.[37] Institutionalized organizations often don't go out of business even if the original goals are no longer relevant. Acceptable modes of behavior become largely self-evident to members, and although this isn't entirely negative, it does mean behaviors and habits go unquestioned, which can stifle innovation and make maintaining the organization's culture an end in itself.

Barriers to Change   Culture is a liability when shared values don't agree with those that further the organization's effectiveness. This is most likely when an organization's environment is undergoing rapid change, and its entrenched culture may no longer be appropriate.[38] Consistency of behavior, an asset in a stable environment, may then burden the organization and make it difficult to respond to changes.

Barriers to Diversity   Hiring new employees who differ from the majority in race, age, gender, disability, or other characteristics creates a paradox:[39] Management wants to demonstrate support for the differences these employees bring to the workplace, but newcomers who wish to fit in must accept the organization's core culture. Second, because diverse behaviors and unique strengths are likely to diminish as people assimilate, strong cultures can become liabilities when they effectively eliminate the advantages of diversity. Third, a strong culture that condones prejudice, supports bias, or becomes insensitive to differences can undermine formal corporate diversity policies.

Strengthening Dysfunctions   In general, we've discussed cultures that cohere around a positive set of values and attitudes. This consensus can create powerful forward momentum. However, coherence around negativity and dysfunctional management systems in a corporation can produce downward forces that are equally powerful. One study of thousands of hospitality-industry employees in hundreds of locations found that local organizational cultures marked by low or decreasing job satisfaction had higher levels of turnover.[40] As we know from this text, low job satisfaction and high turnover indicate dysfunction on the organization's part. Negative attitudes in groups add to negative outcomes, suggesting a powerful influence of culture on individuals.

Barriers to Acquisitions and Mergers   Historically, when management looked at acquisition or merger decisions, the key decision factors were potential financial advantage and product synergy. In recent years, cultural compatibility has become the primary concern.[41] All things being equal, whether the acquisition works seems to have much to do with how well the two organizations' cultures match up. When they don't mesh well, the organizational cultures of both become a liability to the whole new organization. A study conducted by Bain and Company found that 70 percent of mergers failed to increase shareholder values, and Hay Group found that more than 90 percent of mergers in Europe failed to reach financial goals.[42] Considering this dismal rate of success, Lawrence Chia from Deloitte Consulting observed, "One of the biggest failings is people. The people at Company A have a different way of doing things from Company B...you can't find commonality in goals." Culture clash was commonly argued to be one of the causes of AOL Time Warner's problems.

The $183 billion merger between America Online (AOL) and Time Warner in 2001 was the largest in U.S. corporate history. It was also a disaster. Only 2 years later, the new company saw its stock fall an astounding 90 percent, and it reported what was then the largest financial loss in U.S. history.

Creating and Sustaining Culture

16-3 Identify the factors that create and sustain an organization's culture.

An organization's culture doesn't pop out of thin air, and once established it rarely fades away. What influences the creation of a culture? What reinforces and sustains it once in place?

How a Culture Begins

An organization's customs, traditions, and general way of doing things are largely due to what it has done before and how successful it was in doing it. This leads us to the ultimate source of an organization's culture: the founders.[43] Founders have a vision of what the organization should be, and the firm's initial small size makes it easy to impose that vision on all members.

Culture creation occurs in three ways.[44] First, founders hire and keep only employees who think and feel the same way they do. Second, they indoctrinate and socialize employees to their way of thinking and feeling. And finally, the founders' own behavior encourages employees to identify with them and internalize their beliefs, values, and assumptions. When the organization succeeds, the founders' personalities become embedded in the culture. For example, the fierce, competitive style and disciplined, authoritarian nature of Hyundai, the giant Korean conglomerate, exhibits the same characteristics often used to describe founder Chung Ju-Yung. Other founders with sustaining impact on their organization's culture include Bill Gates at Microsoft, Ingvar Kamprad at IKEA, Herb Kelleher at Southwest Airlines, Fred Smith at FedEx, and Richard Branson at the Virgin Group.

Keeping a Culture Alive

Once a culture is in place, practices within the organization maintain it by giving employees a set of similar experiences.[45] The selection process, performance evaluation criteria, training and development activities, and promotion procedures (all discussed in Chapter 17) ensure those hired fit in with the culture, reward those employees who support it, and penalize (or even expel) those who challenge it. Three forces play a particularly important part in sustaining a culture: selection practices, actions of top management, and socialization methods. Let's look at each.

Selection   The explicit goal of the selection process is to identify and hire individuals with the knowledge, skills, and abilities to perform successfully. The final decision, because it is significantly influenced by the decision maker's judgment of how well candidates will fit into the organization, identifies people whose values are consistent with at least a good portion of the organization's.[46] The selection process also provides information to applicants. Those who perceive a conflict between their values and those of the organization can remove themselves from the applicant pool. Selection thus becomes a two-way street, allowing employer and applicant to avoid a mismatch and sustaining an organization's culture by removing those who might attack or undermine its core values, for better or worse.

W. L. Gore & Associates, the maker of Gore-Tex fabric used in outerwear, prides itself on its democratic culture and teamwork. There are no job titles at Gore, nor bosses or chains of command. All work is done in teams. In Gore's selection process, teams put job applicants through extensive interviews to ensure they can deal with the level of uncertainty, flexibility, and teamwork that's normal in Gore plants. Not surprisingly, W. L. Gore appears regularly on *Fortune*'s list of 100 Best Companies to Work For (number 17 in 2015) partially because of its selection process emphasis on culture fit.

Top Management   The actions of top management have a major impact on the organization's culture.[47] Through words and behavior, senior executives establish norms that filter through the organization about, for instance, whether risk-taking is desirable, how much freedom managers give employees, what is appropriate dress, and what actions earn pay raises, promotions, and other rewards.

The culture of supermarket chain Wegmans—which believes driven, happy, and loyal employees are more eager to help one another and provide exemplary customer service—is a direct result of the beliefs of the Wegman family. Their focus on fine foods separates Wegmans from other grocers—a focus maintained by the company's employees, many of whom are hired based on their interest in food. Top management at the company believes in taking care of employees to enhance satisfaction and loyalty. For example, Wegmans has paid more than $90 million in educational scholarships for more than 28,400 employees. Top management also supports above average pay for employees, which results in annual turnover for full-time employees at a mere 4 percent (the industry average is 24 percent). Wegmans regularly appears on *Fortune*'s 100 Best Companies to Work For list (number 7 in 2015),[48] in large measure because top management sustains the positive organizational culture begun by its founding members.

socialization   A process that adapts employees to the organization's culture.

Socialization   No matter how good a job the organization does in recruiting and selection, new employees need help adapting to the prevailing culture. That help is **socialization**.[49] Socialization can help alleviate the problem many employees report that their new jobs are different than expected (see OB Poll). For example, the consulting firm Booz Allen Hamilton begins its process of bringing new employees onboard even before their first day of work. New recruits go to an internal Web portal to learn about the company and understand the culture. After they start work, a social networking application links them with more established members of the firm and helps ensure that the

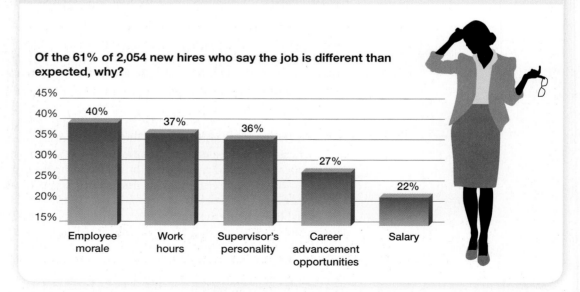

OB POLL

Job Is Not as Good as Advertised

Of the 61% of 2,054 new hires who say the job is different than expected, why?

- Employee morale: 40%
- Work hours: 37%
- Supervisor's personality: 36%
- Career advancement opportunities: 27%
- Salary: 22%

Source: S. Bates, "Majority of New Hires Say Job Is Not What They Expected," *Society for Human Resource Management*, May 28, 2012, http://www.shrm.org/hrdisciplines/employeerelations/articles/pages/newhiresfeelmisled.aspx.

Exhibit 16-2   A Socialization Model

culture is reinforced over time.[50] Clear Channel Communications, Facebook, Google, and other companies are adopting fresh onboarding (new hire acclimation) procedures, including assigning "peer coaches," holding socializing events, personalizing orientation programs, and giving out immediate work assignments. "When we can stress the personal identity of people, and let them bring more of themselves at work, they are more satisfied with their job and have better results," researcher Francesca Gino of Harvard said.[51]

We can think of socialization as a process with three stages: prearrival, encounter, and metamorphosis.[52] This process, shown in Exhibit 16-2, has an impact on the new employee's work productivity, commitment to the organization's objectives, and decision to stay with the organization.

prearrival stage The period of learning in the socialization process that occurs before a new employee joins the organization.

The **prearrival stage** recognizes that each individual arrives with a set of values, attitudes, and expectations about both the work and the organization. One major purpose of a business school, for example, is to socialize students to the attitudes and behaviors companies want. Newcomers to high-profile organizations with strong market positions have their own assumptions about what it's like to work there.[53] Most new recruits will expect Nike to be dynamic and exciting and a stock brokerage firm to be high in pressure and rewards. How accurately people judge an organization's culture before they join the organization, and how proactive their personalities are, become critical predictors of how well they adjust.[54]

encounter stage The stage in the socialization process in which a new employee sees what the organization is really like and confronts the possibility that expectations and reality may diverge.

The selection process can help inform prospective employees about the organization as a whole. Upon entry into the organization, the new member enters the **encounter stage** and confronts the possibility that expectations—about the job, coworkers, boss, and organization in general—may differ from reality. If expectations were fairly accurate, this stage merely cements earlier perceptions. However, often this is not the case. At the extreme, a new member may become disillusioned enough to resign. Proper recruiting and selection should significantly reduce this outcome, along with encouraging friendship ties in the organization—newcomers are more committed when friendly coworkers help them "learn the ropes."[55]

metamorphosis stage The stage in the socialization process in which a new employee changes and adjusts to the job, work group, and organization.

Finally, to work out any problems discovered during the encounter stage, the new member changes or goes through the **metamorphosis stage**. The options presented in Exhibit 16-3 are alternatives designed to bring about metamorphosis. Most research suggests two major "bundles" of socialization practices. The more management relies on formal, collective, fixed, and serial socialization programs while emphasizing divestiture, the more likely newcomers' differences will be stripped away and replaced by standardized predictable behaviors. These *institutional* practices are common in police departments, fire departments, and other organizations that value rule following and order. Programs that are informal, individual, variable, and random while emphasizing investiture are

---

Exhibit 16-3   Entry Socialization Options

Formal vs. Informal The more a new employee is segregated from the ongoing work setting and differentiated in some way to make explicit his or her newcomer's role, the more socialization is formal. Specific orientation and training programs are examples. Informal socialization puts the new employee directly into the job, with little or no special attention.

Individual vs. Collective New members can be socialized individually. This describes how it's done in many professional offices. They can also be grouped together and processed through an identical set of experiences, as in military boot camp.

Fixed vs. Variable This refers to the time schedule in which newcomers make the transition from outsider to insider. A fixed schedule establishes standardized stages of transition. This characterizes rotational training programs. It also includes probationary periods, such as the 8- to 10-year "associate" status used by accounting and law firms before deciding on whether or not a candidate is made a partner. Variable schedules give no advance notice of their transition timetable. Variable schedules describe the typical promotion system, in which one is not advanced to the next stage until one is "ready."

Serial vs. Random Serial socialization is characterized by the use of role models who train and encourage the newcomer. Apprenticeship and mentoring programs are examples. In random socialization, role models are deliberately withheld. New employees are left on their own to figure things out.

Investiture vs. Divestiture Investiture socialization assumes that the newcomer's qualities and qualifications are the necessary ingredients for job success, so these qualities and qualifications are confirmed and supported. Divestiture socialization tries to strip away certain characteristics of the recruit. Fraternity and sorority "pledges" go through divestiture socialization to shape them into the proper role.

---

more likely to give newcomers an innovative sense of their roles and methods of working. Creative fields such as research and development, advertising, and filmmaking rely on these *individual* practices. Most research suggests high levels of institutional practices encourage person–organization fit and high levels of commitment, whereas individual practices produce more role innovation.[56]

The three-part entry socialization process is complete when new members have internalized and accepted the norms of the organization and their work groups, are confident in their competence, and feel trusted and valued by their peers. They understand the system—not only their own tasks but the rules, procedures, and informally accepted practices as well. Finally, they know what is expected of them and what criteria will be used to measure and evaluate their work. As Exhibit 16-2 showed earlier, successful metamorphosis should have a positive impact on new employees' productivity and their commitment to the organization, and reduce their propensity to leave the organization (turnover).

Researchers examine how employee attitudes change during socialization by measuring at several points over the first few months. Several studies have now documented patterns of "honeymoons" and "hangovers" for new workers, showing that the period of initial adjustment is often marked by decreases in job satisfaction as idealized hopes come into contact with the reality of organizational life.[57] Newcomers may find that the level of social support they receive from supervisors and coworkers is gradually withdrawn over the first few weeks on the job, as everyone returns to "business as usual."[58] Role conflict and role overload may rise for newcomers over time, and workers with the largest increases in these role problems experience the largest decreases in commitment and satisfaction.[59] It may be that the initial adjustment period for newcomers presents increasing demands and difficulties, at least in the short term.

Exhibit 16-4   **How Organizational Cultures Form**

Summary: How Organizational Cultures Form

Exhibit 16-4 summarizes how an organization's culture is established and sustained. The original culture derives from the founder's philosophy and strongly influences hiring criteria as the firm grows. The success of socialization depends on the deliberateness of matching new employees' values to those of the organization in the selection process and on top management's commitment to socialization programs. Top managers' actions set the general climate, including what is acceptable behavior and what is not, and employees sustain and perpetuate the culture.

How Employees Learn Culture

16-4 Show how culture is transmitted to employees.

Culture is transmitted to employees in a number of forms, the most potent being stories, rituals, material symbols, and language.

Stories

When Henry Ford II was chairman of Ford Motor Company, you would have been hard pressed to find a manager who hadn't heard how he reminded his executives, when they got too arrogant, "It's my name that's on the building." The message was clear: Henry Ford II ran the company.

Today, a number of senior Nike executives spend much of their time serving as corporate storytellers.[60] When they tell how co-founder (and Oregon track coach) Bill Bowerman went to his workshop and poured rubber into a waffle iron to create a better running shoe, they're talking about Nike's spirit of innovation. When new hires hear tales of Oregon running star Steve Prefontaine's battles to make running a professional sport and attain better performance equipment, they learn of Nike's commitment to helping athletes.

Stories such as these circulate through many organizations, anchoring the present in the past and legitimating current practices. They typically include narratives about the organization's founders, rule breaking, rags-to-riches successes, workforce reductions, relocations of employees, reactions to past mistakes, and organizational coping.[61] Employees also create their own narratives about how they came to either fit or not fit with the organization during the process of socialization, including first days on the job, early interactions with others, and first impressions of organizational life.[62]

Rituals

Rituals are repetitive sequences of activities that express and reinforce the key values of the organization—what goals are most important, and/or which people

rituals Repetitive sequences of activities that express and reinforce the key values of the organization, which goals are most important, which people are important, and which are expendable.

are important versus which are expendable.[63] Some companies have nontraditional rituals to help support the values of their cultures. Kimpton Hotels & Restaurants, one of *Fortune*'s 100 Best Companies to Work For, maintains its customer-oriented culture with traditions like a Housekeeping Olympics that includes blindfolded bedmaking and vacuum races.[64] At marketing firm United Entertainment Group, employees work unusual hours a few times a year, arriving in the late afternoon and working until early morning. CEO Jarrod Moses does this to support a culture of creativity. He says, "You mess with somebody's internal clock, and some interesting ideas come out."[65]

Symbols

material symbols What conveys to employees who is important, the degree of egalitarianism top management desires, and the kinds of behavior that are appropriate.

The layout of corporate headquarters, the types of automobiles top executives are given, and the presence or absence of corporate aircraft are a few examples of **material symbols**. Others include the size of offices, the elegance of furnishings, perks, and attire.[66] These convey to employees who is important, the degree of egalitarianism top management desires, and the kinds of behavior that are appropriate, such as risk-taking, conservative, authoritarian, participative, individualistic, or social.

One example of the intentional use of material symbols is Texas electric company Dynegy. Dynegy's headquarters doesn't look like your typical head-office operation, as you could tell from the "Myth or Science?" box. There are few individual offices, even for senior executives. The space is essentially made up of cubicles, common areas, and meeting rooms. This informality conveys to employees that Dynegy values openness, equality, creativity, and flexibility. While some organizations provide their top executives with chauffeur-driven limousines and a corporate jet, other CEOs drive the company car themselves and travel in the economy section. At some firms, like Chicago shirtmaker Threadless, an "anything goes" atmosphere helps emphasize a creative culture. At Threadless, meetings are held in an Airstream camper parked inside the company's converted FedEx warehouse, while employees in shorts and flip-flops work in bullpens featuring disco balls and garish decorations chosen by each team.[67]

Baidu, a Chinese Web services firm, describes its culture as "simple"—meaning direct, open, and uncomplicated—and "reliable"—meaning trusting the competence of colleagues. Baidu's casual workplaces reflect this trust with lounges, gyms, yoga studios, and dome-shaped nap rooms employees may use at any time.
Source: Lou Linwei/Alamy

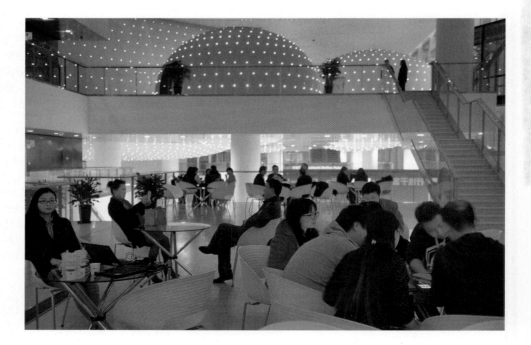

An Ethical Choice

A Culture of Compassion

In the world of banking, success and ethical culture don't necessarily go hand in hand. Leaders who desire ethical cultures in their organizations must choose to build ethics into the company's definition of success in ways that translate into ethical actions for managers and employees. Contrast two financial success stories, Goldman Sachs and Wells Fargo. Both megabanks are among the Fortune 100 (the largest U.S. companies ranked by revenue). They are also two of *Fortune*'s World's Most Admired Companies, a list that ranks the largest companies in revenue by nine criteria including social responsibility. Yet their organizational cultures appear to be vastly different. Goldman Sachs seems to struggle to achieve an ethical culture for its employees and clients, while Wells Fargo seems to emanate a culture of compassion. Consider some headlines:

- *Mefit "Mike" Mecevic was a loyal janitor for Goldman Sachs when Superstorm Sandy hit New York in 2012.* Mecevic and his coworkers rode out the storm in the company's Manhattan skyscraper and worked nonstop for days to keep floodwaters back. Then a Goldman Sachs manager threw him out without explanation. Mecevic said to him, "'I live in Staten Island, there's a state of emergency, there are no cars, no trains, no lights. The water is up to our necks.' I was begging for my life. But he said 'Leave the building.'" Mecevic left but was later fired anyway. "I worked day and night," Mecevic said. "They destroyed my life for nothing. Nothing."
- *Wells Fargo is committed to respecting its clients, even when those clients are in trouble.* For the past few years, it has held "Home Preservation Workshops" where indebted homeowners can meet with "home

retention" team members in confidential booths set up in large halls across the United States. Clients bring paperwork specific to their cases, and team members negotiate binding agreements. One client said, "It is a great feeling to not worry" about losing her home.

Organizational culture is where leaders' ethical choices demonstrate their expectations for others' decisions throughout the company. Both Goldman and Wells Fargo enjoy stellar reputations. But these examples suggest that the two cultures may make very different ethical choices.

Sources: B. Ross, A. Ng, and C. Siemaszko, "Ex-Goldman Sachs Janitor Sues for Being Forced into Post-Hurricane Sandy Destruction," *New York Daily News*, June 7, 2013, www.nydailynews.com/new-york/janitor-sues-tossed-aftermath-hurricane-sandy-article-1.1366334; M. Schifrin and H. Touryalai, "The Bank That Works," *Forbes*, February 13, 2012, 66–74.

Some cultures are known for the perks in their environments, such as Google's bocce courts, Factset Research's onsite pie/cheese/cupcake trucks, software designer Autodesk's bring-your-dog office, SAS's free health care clinic, Microsoft's organic spa, and adventure-gear specialist REI's free equipment rentals. Other companies communicate the values of their cultures through the gift of time to think creatively, either with leaders or offsite. For instance, Biotech leader Genentech and many other top companies provide paid sabbaticals. Genentech offers every employee 6 weeks' paid leave for every 6 years of service to support a culture of equitability and innovative thinking.[68]

Language

Many organizations and subunits within them use language to help members identify with the culture, attest to their acceptance of it, and help preserve it. Unique terms describe equipment, officers, key individuals, suppliers, customers, or products that relate to the business. New employees may at first be overwhelmed by acronyms and jargon that, once assimilated, act as a common denominator to unite members of a given culture or subculture.

✪ **TRY IT!**

If your professor has assigned this, go to the Assignments section of **mymanagementlab.com** to complete the **Simulation: *Organizational Culture***.

Influencing an Organizational Culture

16-5

Describe the similarities and differences in creating an ethical culture, a positive culture, and a spiritual culture.

As we discussed, the culture of an organization is set by its founders and often difficult to change afterward. It's true that the ideal scenario is a strong founder (or founders) who carefully plans the organization's culture beforehand. That's seldom the case, though; organizational culture usually grows organically over time. When we think of the development of culture as ongoing and conducted through each employee, we can see ways to increase the ethical, positive, and/ or spiritual aspects of the environment, discussed next.

An Ethical Culture

Despite differences across industries and cultures, ethical organizational cultures share some common values and processes.[69] Therefore, managers can create a more ethical culture by adhering to the following principles:[70]

- *Be a visible role model.*   Employees will look to the actions of top management as a benchmark for appropriate behavior, but everyone can be a role model to positively influence the ethical atmosphere. Send a positive message.
- *Communicate ethical expectations.*   Whenever you serve in a leadership capacity, minimize ethical ambiguities by sharing a code of ethics that states the organization's primary values and the judgment rules employees must follow.
- *Provide ethical training.*   Set up seminars, workshops, and training programs to reinforce the organization's standards of conduct, clarify what practices are permissible, and address potential ethical dilemmas.
- *Visibly reward ethical acts and punish unethical ones.*   Evaluate subordinates on how their decisions measure up against the organization's code of ethics. Review the means as well as the ends. Visibly reward those who act ethically and conspicuously punish those who don't.
- *Provide protective mechanisms.*   Seek formal mechanisms so everyone can discuss ethical dilemmas and report unethical behavior without fear of reprimand. These might include identifying ethical counselors, ombudspeople, or ethical officers for liaison roles.

A widespread positive ethical climate has to start at the top of the organization.[71] One study demonstrated that when top management emphasizes strong ethical values, supervisors are more likely to practice ethical leadership. Positive attitudes transfer down to line employees, who show lower levels of deviant behavior and higher levels of cooperation and assistance. Several other studies have come to the same general conclusion: The values of top management are a good predictor of ethical behavior among employees. One study involving auditors found perceived pressure from organizational leaders to behave unethically was associated with increased intentions to engage in unethical practices.[72] Clearly the wrong type of organizational culture can negatively influence employee ethical behavior. Finally, employees whose ethical values are similar to those of their department are more likely to be promoted, so we can think of ethical culture as flowing from the bottom up as well.[73]

A Positive Culture

At first blush, creating a positive culture may sound hopelessly naïve or like a Dilbert-style conspiracy. The one thing that makes us believe this trend is here to stay, however, are signs that management practice and OB research are

Market Technologies, a family-owned trading software developer, fosters a positive climate. The firm rewards employees in many ways, including fun events like tacky tourist days, shown here, birthday and achievement celebrations, frequent family outings, and catered breakfasts and lunches.
Source: St. Petersburg Times/ZumaPress/Newscom

positive organizational culture
A culture that emphasizes building on employee strengths, rewards more than punishes, and emphasizes individual vitality and growth.

converging. A **positive organizational culture** emphasizes building on employee strengths, rewards more than it punishes, and encourages individual vitality and growth.[74] Let's consider each of these areas.

Building on Employee Strengths   Although a positive organizational culture does not ignore problems, it does emphasize showing workers how they can capitalize on their strengths. As management guru Peter Drucker said, "Most Americans do not know what their strengths are. When you ask them, they look at you with a blank stare, or they respond in terms of subject knowledge, which is the wrong answer." Wouldn't it be better to be in an organizational culture that helped you discover your strengths and how to make the most of them?

As CEO of Auglaize Provico, an agribusiness based in Ohio, Larry Hammond used this approach in the midst of the firm's worst financial struggles. When the organization had to lay off one-quarter of its workforce, he took advantage of what was right, rather than dwelling on what went wrong. "If you really want to [excel], you have to know yourself—you have to know what you're good at, and you have to know what you're not so good at," he said. With the help of Gallup consultant Barry Conchie, Hammond focused on discovering and using employee strengths to help the company turn itself around. "You ask Larry [Hammond] what the difference is, and he'll say that it's individuals using their natural talents," says Conchie.[75]

Rewarding More Than Punishing   Although most organizations are sufficiently focused on extrinsic rewards such as pay and promotions, they often forget about the power of smaller (and cheaper) rewards such as praise. Part of creating a positive organizational culture is "catching employees doing something right." Many managers withhold praise because they're afraid employees will coast or because they think praise is not valued. Employees generally don't ask for praise, and managers usually don't realize the costs of failing to give it.

Consider El´zbieta Górska-Kolodziejczyk, a plant manager for International Paper's facility in Kwidzyn, Poland. Employees worked in a bleak windowless basement. Staffing became roughly one-third its prior level, while production tripled. These challenges had done in the previous three managers. So when she took over, at the top of her list were recognition and praise for staff. She initially found it difficult to give praise to those who weren't used to it, especially men. "They were like cement at the beginning," she said. "Like cement." Over time, however, she found they valued and even reciprocated praise. One day a department supervisor pulled her over to tell her she was doing a good job. "This I do remember, yes," she said.[76]

Encouraging Vitality and Growth   No organization will get the best from employees who see themselves as mere cogs in the machine. A positive culture recognizes the difference between a job and a career. It supports not only what the employee contributes to organizational effectiveness but how the organization can make the employee more effective—personally and professionally. Top companies recognize the value of helping people grow. Safelite AutoGlass, *Workforce Management*'s 2012 Optima award winner for Competitive Advantage, attributes its success in part to its PeopleFirst Plan talent development initiative. "The only way we can stand out is if we have the best people," says Senior Vice President Steve Miggo.[77]

It may take more creativity to encourage employee growth in some industries. From the Masterfoods headquarters in Brussels, Philippe Lescornez led a team of sales promoters including Didier Brynaert, who worked in Luxembourg, nearly 150 miles away. Lescornez decided Brynaert's role could be improved if he were seen as an expert on the unique features of the Luxembourg market. So Lescornez asked Brynaert for information he could share with the home office. "I started to communicate much more what he did to other people [within the company], because there's quite some distance between the Brussels office and the section he's working in. So I started to communicate, communicate, communicate. The more I communicated, the more he started to provide material," he said. As a result, "Now he's recognized as the specialist for Luxembourg—the guy who is able to build a strong relationship with the Luxembourg clients," says Lescornez. What's good for Brynaert was, of course, also good for Lescornez, who got credit for helping Brynaert grow and develop.[78]

Limits of Positive Culture   Is a positive culture a cure-all? Though many companies have embraced aspects of a positive organizational culture, it is a new enough idea for us to be uncertain about how and when it works best.

Not all national cultures value being positive as much as the U.S. culture does and, even within U.S. culture, there surely are limits to how far organizations should go. The limits may need to be dictated by the industry and society. For example, Admiral, a British insurance company, has established a Ministry of Fun in its call centers to organize poem writing, foosball, conkers (a British game involving chestnuts), and fancy-dress days, which may clash with an industry value of more serious cultures. When does the pursuit of a positive culture start to seem coercive? As one critic notes, "Promoting a social orthodoxy of positiveness focuses on a particular constellation of desirable states and traits but, in so doing, can stigmatize those who fail to fit the template."[79] There may be benefits to establishing a positive culture, but an organization also needs to be objective and not pursue it past the point of effectiveness.

A Spiritual Culture

What do Southwest Airlines, Hewlett-Packard, Ford, The Men's Wearhouse, Tyson Foods, Wetherill Associates, and Tom's of Maine have in common? They're among a growing number of organizations that have embraced workplace spirituality.

What Is Spirituality?   Workplace spirituality is *not* about organized religious practices. It's not about God or theology. **Workplace spirituality** recognizes that people have an inner life that nourishes and is nourished by meaningful work in the context of community.[80] Organizations that support a spiritual culture recognize that people seek to find meaning and purpose in their work and desire to connect with other human beings as part of a community. Many of the topics we have discussed—ranging from job design to corporate social responsibility (CSR)—are well matched to the concept of organizational spirituality. When a company emphasizes its commitment to paying Third World suppliers a fair (above-market) price for their products to facilitate community development—as did Starbucks—or encourages employees to share prayers or inspirational messages through e-mail—as did Interstate Batteries—it may encourage a more spiritual culture.[81]

workplace spirituality   The recognition that people have an inner life that nourishes and is nourished by meaningful work that takes place in the context of community.

Why Spirituality Now?   As noted in our discussion of emotions in Chapter 4, the myth of rationality assumed the well-run organization eliminated people's feelings. Concern about an employee's inner life had no role in the perfectly rational model. But just as we realize that the study of emotions improves our understanding of OB, an awareness of spirituality can help us better understand employee behavior.

Of course, employees have always had an inner life. So why has the search for meaning and purposefulness in work surfaced now? We summarize the reasons in Exhibit 16-5.

Characteristics of a Spiritual Organization   The concept of workplace spirituality draws on our previous discussions of values, ethics, motivation, and leadership. Although research remains preliminary, several cultural characteristics tend to be evident in spiritual organizations:[82]

- *Benevolence.*   Spiritual organizations value kindness toward others and the happiness of employees and other organizational stakeholders.
- *Strong sense of purpose.*   Spiritual organizations build their cultures around a meaningful purpose. Although profits may be important, they're not the primary value.

Exhibit 16-5   Reasons for the Growing Interest in Spirituality

- Spirituality can counterbalance the pressures and stress of a turbulent pace of life. Contemporary lifestyles—single-parent families, geographic mobility, the temporary nature of jobs, new technologies that create distance between people—underscore the lack of community many people feel and increase the need for involvement and connection.
- Formalized religion hasn't worked for many people, and they continue to look for anchors to replace lack of faith and to fill a growing feeling of emptiness.
- Job demands have made the workplace dominant in many people's lives, yet they continue to question the meaning of work.
- People want to integrate personal life values with their professional lives.
- An increasing number of people are finding that the pursuit of more material acquisitions leaves them unfulfilled.

- *Trust and respect.* Spiritual organizations are characterized by mutual trust, honesty, and openness. Employees are treated with esteem and value, consistent with the dignity of each individual.
- *Open-mindedness.* Spiritual organizations value flexible thinking and creativity among employees.

Achieving Spirituality in the Organization   Many organizations have grown interested in spirituality but have experienced difficulty putting principles into practice. Several types of practices can facilitate a spiritual workplace,[83] including those that support work–life balance. Leaders can demonstrate values, attitudes, and behaviors that trigger intrinsic motivation and a sense of fulfilling a calling through work. Second, encouraging employees to consider how their work provides a sense of purpose can help achieve a spiritual workplace; often this is done through group counseling and organizational development, a topic we take up in Chapter 18. Third, a growing number of companies, including Taco Bell and Sturdisteel, offer employees the counseling services of corporate chaplains. Many chaplains are employed by agencies, such as Marketplace Chaplains USA, while some corporations, such as R.J. Reynolds Tobacco and Tyson Foods, employ chaplains directly. The workplace presence of corporate chaplains, who are often ordained Christian ministers, is obviously controversial, although their role is not to increase spirituality but to help human resources departments serve the employees who already have Christian beliefs.[84] Similar roles for leaders of other faiths certainly must be encouraged.

Criticisms of Spirituality   Critics of the spirituality movement in organizations have focused on three issues. First is the question of scientific foundation. What really is workplace spirituality? Is it just a new management buzzword? Second, are spiritual organizations legitimate? Specifically, do organizations have the right to claim spiritual values? Third is the question of economics: Are spirituality and profits compatible?

First, as you might imagine, there is comparatively little research on workplace spirituality. Spirituality has been defined so broadly in some sources that practices from job rotation to corporate retreats at meditation centers have been identified as spiritual. Questions need to be answered before the concept gains full credibility.

Second, an emphasis on spirituality can clearly make some employees uneasy. Critics have argued that secular institutions, especially business firms, should not impose spiritual values on employees.[85] This criticism is undoubtedly valid when spirituality is defined as bringing religion and God into the workplace. However, it seems less stinging when the goal is limited to helping employees find meaning and purpose in their work lives. If the concerns listed in Exhibit 16-5 truly characterize a large segment of the workforce, then perhaps organizations can help.

Finally, whether spirituality and profits are compatible objectives is a relevant concern for managers and investors in business. The evidence, although limited, indicates they are. In one study, organizations that provided their employees with opportunities for spiritual development outperformed those that didn't.[86] Other studies reported that spirituality in organizations was positively related to creativity, employee satisfaction, job involvement, and organizational commitment.[87]

How do I learn to lead?

I'll be starting a new job in a few weeks. It's my first time working as a leader for a team, and I know I have a lot to learn. Is there any way I can be sure I'll achieve success as a leader?
— *Gordon*

Dear Gordon:

Learning about a new job is always complicated. Learning how to be a leader is doubly complicated. It's expected that you have the capacity to provide direction and purpose for employees, and that you will respect the existing culture of the group as well as the capacities of individual members. Here are a few key insights toward making your transition into leadership successful:

- *Ask questions.* New leaders are often anxious about asking questions of direct reports for fear of being seen as incompetent or weak. However, inquiring about how things have been done in the past and asking about individual goals signals that you are concerned about the team members. Familiarizing yourself with the group's culture and practices can also help you develop techniques to harness the team's strengths and overcome challenges.

- *Build relationships with other leaders.* Remember—you were put into this role for a reason, and the company wants to see you succeed, so make the most of the resources of others. Take detailed notes regarding specific activities and strategies that were successful, and schedule a check-in to discuss how these strategies have worked over time. If you can show you are truly engaged in the learning process, you'll find others are more willing to provide you with assistance and advice.

- *Start small.* Much has been written about the importance of gaining small wins early on to build your reputation. The old saying "you never get a second chance to make a first impression" definitely holds true in the workplace. Try to develop new initiatives with clear outcomes that will allow you to demonstrate your leadership traits.

The best leadership transitions include learning what the situation calls for, and setting your team up for success from the start.

Be proactive!

_____

Sources: T. B. Harris, N. Li, W. R. Boswell, X. Zhang, and Z. Xie, "Getting What's New from Newcomers: Empowering Leadership, Creativity, and Adjustment in the Socialization Context," *Personnel Psychology* 67 (2014): 567–604; Y. H. Ji, N. A. Cohen, A. Daly, K. Finnigan, and K. Klein, "The Dynamics of Voice Behavior and Leaders' Network Ties in Times of Leadership Successions," *Academy of Management Proceedings*, 2014, 16324; and B. Eckfeldt, "5 Things New CEOS Should Focus On," *Business Insider*, June 1, 2015, http://www.businessinsider.com/5-things-new-ceos-should-focus-on-2015-6.

The Global Context

16-6 Show how national culture can affect the way organizational culture is transported to another country.

We considered global cultural values (collectivism–individualism, power distance, and so on) in Chapter 5. Here our focus is a bit narrower: How is organizational culture affected by the global context? Organizational culture is so powerful that it often transcends national boundaries. But that doesn't mean organizations should, or could, ignore local culture.

Organizational cultures often reflect national culture. The culture at AirAsia, a Malaysian-based airline, emphasizes openness and friendships. The carrier has lots of parties, participative management, and no private offices, reflecting Malaysia's relatively collectivistic culture. The culture of many U.S. airlines do not reflect the same degree of informality. If a U.S. airline were to merge with AirAsia, it would need to take these cultural differences into account. Organizational culture differences are not always due to international culture differences, however. One of the chief challenges of the merger of US Airways and American Airlines was the integration of US Airway's "open-collar" culture with American's "button-down" culture.[88]

One of the primary things U.S. managers can do is to be culturally sensitive. The United States is a dominant force in business and in culture—and with that influence comes a reputation. "We are broadly seen throughout the world as arrogant people, totally self-absorbed and loud," says one U.S. executive. Some ways in which U.S. managers can be culturally sensitive include talking in a low tone of voice, speaking slowly, listening more, and avoiding discussions of religion and politics.

The management of ethical behavior is one area where national culture can rub against corporate culture.[89] U.S. managers endorse the supremacy of anonymous market forces as a moral obligation for business organizations. This worldview sees bribery, nepotism, and favoring personal contacts as highly unethical. They also value profit maximization, so any action that deviates from profit maximization may suggest inappropriate or corrupt behavior. In contrast, managers in developing economies are more likely to see ethical decisions as embedded in the social environment. That means doing special favors for family and friends is not only appropriate but possibly even an ethical responsibility. Managers in many nations view capitalism skeptically and believe the interests of workers should be put on a par with the interests of shareholders, which may limit profit maximization.

Creating a multinational organizational culture can initiate strife between employees of traditionally competing countries. When Swedish, Norwegian, Finnish, and Danish banks combined to form Nordea Bank AB, the stereotypes some employees held based on the countries' historical relationships created tensions. Finland had originally been a colony of Sweden, and Norway had been a part of Denmark and then of Sweden. The fact that none of the employees had yet been born when their countries were colonies didn't matter; complex alliances within Nordea formed along nationalistic lines. To bridge these gaps, Nordea employed storytelling to help employees identify with positive aspects of their shared geographical *region*. The organization reinforced the shared identity through press releases, corporate correspondence, equal country representation in top management, and championing of shared values. Although the organization continues to struggle with a multinational culture, the successes it has enjoyed can be attributed to careful attention to national differences.[90]

As national organizations seek to employ workers in overseas operations, management must decide whether to standardize many facets of organizational culture. For example, should organizations offer wellness plans and work–life balance initiatives from the home country to the satellite offices, or tailor the plans for the norms of each society? Either can be problematic. For instance, when U.S. company Rothenberg International introduced its alcohol abuse remediation plan to Russian employees as part of its employee assistance program (EAP), it didn't foresee that Russians resist the concept of "assistance" and prefer "support" instead. Rothenberg was able to adjust, but sometimes local laws intercede (as a help or a hindrance) when employers roll out homeland plans. Brazil has a government anti-HIV plan that employers can use, for instance, and the U.K.'s National Health Service pays for smoking cessation programs, while in Germany private insurance must pay for wellness plans.[91] At this point, there is no clear consensus on the best course of action, but the first step is for companies to be sensitive to differing standards.

Exhibit 16-6 How Organizational Cultures Have an Impact on Employee Performance and Satisfaction

Summary

Exhibit 16-6 depicts the impact of organizational culture. Employees form an overall subjective perception of the organization based on factors such as the degree of risk tolerance, team emphasis, and support of individuals. This overall perception represents, in effect, the organization's culture or personality and affects employee performance and satisfaction, with stronger cultures having greater impact.

Implications for Managers

- Realize that an organization's culture is relatively fixed in the short term. To effect change, involve top management and strategize a long-term plan.
- Hire individuals whose values align with those of the organization; these employees will tend to remain committed and satisfied. Not surprisingly, "misfits" have considerably higher turnover rates.
- Understand that employees' performance and socialization depend to a considerable degree on their knowing what to do and not do. Train your employees well and keep them informed of changes to their job roles.
- You can shape the culture of your work environment, sometimes as much as it shapes you. All managers can especially do their part to create an ethical culture and to consider spirituality and its role in creating a positive organizational culture.
- Be aware that your company's organizational culture may not be "transportable" to other countries. Understand the cultural relevance of your organization's norms before introducing new plans or initiatives overseas.

⭐ **PERSONAL INVENTORY ASSESSMENTS**   PERSONAL INVENTORY ASSESSMENT

Comfort with Change Scale

Do you like change? Hate change? Few people are neutral about their preference for change. Take this PIA to see how comfortable you are with change.

Organizations Should Strive to Create a Positive Organizational Culture

POINT

Organizations should do everything they can to establish a positive culture, because it works. Scores of studies have shown that individuals who are in positive states of mind at work and in life lead happier, more productive, and more fulfilling lives. Given the accumulating evidence, researchers are now studying ways to make that happen.

In a *Harvard Business Review* article, Adam Grant discusses an interesting concept: *outsourcing inspiration*. What does he mean by that? Grant writes: "A growing body of research shows that end users—customers, clients, patients, and others who benefit from a company's products and services—are surprisingly effective in motivating people to work harder, smarter, and more productively."

Some tangible examples of how this can work:

- Northwestern University's "buddy program" introduces Alzheimer's patients to scientists working to develop treatments for the disease.
- At a Merrill Lynch branch, weekly team meetings begin with stories about how the team has made a difference in customers' lives.
- "All Medtronic employees have a 'defining moment' in which they come face-to-face with a patient whose story deeply touches them," writes former CEO Bill George.

Of course, there are other ways of creating a positive organizational culture, including building on strengths and rewarding more than punishing.

Outsourcing inspiration is a great way for employees to feel appreciated, to experience empathy, and to see the impact of their work—all motivating outcomes that will lead organizations to be more effective and individuals more fulfilled in their work. Creating a positive organizational culture is not magic, but it tends to have extremely positive benefits for organizations that embrace it.

COUNTERPOINT

There are many unanswered questions about the merits of using positive organizational scholarship to build positive organizational cultures. Let's focus on three.

What is a positive culture? The employment relationship can be amicable and even mutually beneficial. However, glossing over natural differences in interests with the frosting of positive culture is intellectually dishonest and potentially harmful. From time to time, any organization needs to undertake unpopular actions. Can anyone terminate an employee positively (and honestly), or explain to someone why others received a raise? There's a danger in trying to sugarcoat. Positive relationships will develop—or not—on their own. We'd be better off preaching that people, and organizational cultures, should be honest and fair, rather than unabashedly positive.

Is practice ahead of science? Before we start beseeching organizations to build positive cultures, we should make sure these initiatives work as expected. Many have unintended consequences, and we simply don't have enough research to support the claims. As one reviewer noted, "Everyone wants to believe they could have greater control over their lives by simply changing the way they think. Research that supports this idea gets promoted loudly and widely." But it's not based on a mountain of evidence.

Is building a positive culture manipulative? Psychologist Lisa Aspinwall writes of "saccharine terrorism," where employees are coerced into positive mindsets by happiness coaches. You may think this an exaggeration, but companies like UBS, American Express, KPMG, FedEx, Adobe, and IBM have used happiness coaches to do exactly that. As one critic noted, "Encouraging people to maintain a happy outlook in the face of less-than-ideal conditions is a good way of keeping citizens under control in spite of severe societal problems, or keeping employees productive while keeping pay and benefits low." Rather than insisting on positive cultures, how about promoting honest cultures as an idea?

Sources: B. Azar, "Positive Psychology Advances, with Growing Pains," *Monitor on Psychology*, April 2011, 32–36; A. Grant, "How Customers Can Rally Your Troops," *Harvard Business Review*, June 2011, downloaded on July 12, 2011, from http://hbr.org/; and J. McCarthy, "5 Big Problems with Positive Thinking (And Why You Should Do It Anyway)," *Positive Psychology*, October 2010, downloaded on July 10, 2011, from http://psychologyofwellbeing.com/.

CHAPTER REVIEW

MyManagementLab

Go to **mymanagementlab.com** to complete the problems marked with this icon.

QUESTIONS FOR REVIEW

16-1 What is organizational culture, and what are its common characteristics?

16-2 What are the functional and dysfunctional effects of organizational culture?

16-3 What factors create and sustain an organization's culture?

16-4 How is culture transmitted to employees?

16-5 What are the similarities and differences in creating an ethical culture, a positive culture, and a spiritual culture?

16-6 How does national culture affect what happens when an organizational culture is transported to another country?

EXPERIENTIAL EXERCISE   Greeting Newcomers

Divide into groups of 3–4 students. Discuss these four primary issues:

- *Describe your first impressions of the university when you applied.* This is important because it helps to identify assumptions other new students may have coming in.
- *Describe some of your early experiences in the new environment, and how they either reinforced or changed your pre-entry expectations.* Include activities officially sponsored by your school, as well as unplanned experiences that told you what the culture was like.
- *Identify key issues you wish you had learned more about when you arrived.* Think of the sorts of things that caused the most trouble for you, or that were difficult for you to figure out on your own.
- *Contrast your early experiences with your current knowledge of what the culture is like.* How has long-term interaction changed your ideas about the culture of the university?

After describing your school's culture as a whole, consider the same four issues as they relate to your major field of study.

Design a Program

Use the material from the chapter to develop an "ideal" program that could be used to introduce new students to the culture. This might closely resemble what you've experienced, of it may be very different. The goal should be to reduce student anxiety and stress during the transition, and to promote a culture that helps newcomers meet their goals as efficiently and effectively as possible. Your socialization program should include pre-entry messages, like recruiting information, early orientation sessions, and long-term follow-up. You'll want to determine, at each phase, who should be sending these messages so they have the most impact on newcomers.

16-7. Based on your observations and group discussion, what seem to be the most important elements of the culture that newcomers need to adjust to?

16-8. Do you think your school doesn't communicate some aspects of the culture to newcomers? If so, why?

16-9. How is the introduction to a business organizational culture and department similar to, or different from, introduction into a university and field of study?

ETHICAL DILEMMA   Culture of Deceit

We have noted throughout this chapter, and the text overall, that honesty is generally the best policy in managing OB. But that doesn't mean honest dealing is always the rule in business.

Studies have found, in fact, that whole industries may encourage dishonesty. In one experiment, subjects were first asked either to think about their professional identities, or to complete a generic survey. They were then asked to report on a series of coin flips; they were told in advance that the more times the coin showed heads, the more money they would make. The bankers who took the generic survey were about as honest in reporting coin flips as people who worked in other fields. The bankers told to think about their professional identities, however, exaggerated how often the coin turned up heads. People in other professions didn't do so—the tie between professional identity and dishonesty was unique to those who worked in banking. These results are certainly not limited to the banking industry. Many other ways of priming people to think about financial transactions seem to generate more dishonesty. And studies have also found that many individuals feel pressured to engage in dishonest behavior to meet the bottom line. Whenever there is money under consideration, there are powerful motives.

Money motivations are strong in professional sports. For example, the number of top leaders in FIFA (world soccer's governing body) who were indicted in 2015 suggests that behaving dishonestly has been accepted within FIFA, and covering up for the dishonesty of others has been encouraged. Domenico Scala, FIFA's audit and compliance committee chair, noted, "To support the change we need a culture that censures inappropriate behavior and enforces rules vigorously, fairly, and [is] responsive." There is general consensus that to overcome corruption, those in positions of authority must demonstrate commitment to an ethical culture. As Scala noted, "It is the leaders' tone that ensures it is embedded at all levels of the organization. This must be honest and communicated with sincerity in both words and actions." There may well be a tendency to become dishonest when there's money to be made, so leaders may need to be especially vigilant and communicate clear expectations for ethical behavior.

Fortunately, evidence shows that asking people to focus on relationships and the way they spend their time can actually make them behave more honestly and helpfully. This suggests that a focus on the social consequences of our actions can indeed help to overcome corruption.

Questions

16-10. What are the negative effects of a culture that encourages dishonesty and corruption on its reputation and employees?

16-11. Why might some organizations push employees to behave in a dishonest or corrupt manner? Are there personal benefits to corruption that culture can counteract?

16-12. What actions can you take as a new employee if you are pressured to violate your own ethical standards at work? How might mid-level employees' responses to this question differ from those of more senior managers?

Sources: F. Gino, "Banking Culture Encourages Dishonesty," *Scientific American*, December 30, 2014, http://www.scientificamerican.com/article/banking-culture-encourages-dishonesty/; A. Cohn, Alain, E. Fehr, and M. A. Maréchal, "Business Culture and Dishonesty in the Banking Industry," *Nature*, 2014, doi: 10.1038/nature13977; L. Geggel, "FIFA Scandal: The Complicated Science of Corruption," *Scientific American*, May 31, 2015, http://www.scientificamerican.com/article/fifa-scandal-the-complicated-science-of-corruption/; and K. Radnedge, "Culture Change Required If FIFA Is to Eliminate Wrongdoing," *World Soccer*, May 29, 2015, http://www.worldsoccer.com/columnists/keir-radnedge/culture-change-required-if-fifa-is-to-eliminate-wrongdoing-362278.

CASE INCIDENT 1 The Place Makes the People

At Gerson Lehrman Group, you won't find an employee working in a cubicle day after day. You also won't find an employee working in a free-form open office area consistently either. The reason is that Gerson Lehrman is invested in "activity based working." In this system, employees have access to cubicle spaces for privacy, conference rooms for group meetings, café seating for working with a laptop, and full open-office environments. Where you work on a particular day is entirely up to you.

It may be hard to remember, but office allocations were a uniform signal of hierarchical status and part of organizational culture until fairly recently. As organizations have become flatter and the need for creativity and flexibility has increased, the "open office" plan has become a mainstay of the business world. The goal is to encourage free-flowing conversation and discussion, enhance creativity, and minimize hierarchy—in other words, to foster a creative and collaborative culture and remove office space from its status position.

Research on open offices, however, shows there is a downside. Open offices decrease the sense of privacy, reduce the feeling of owning your own space, and create a distracting level of background stimulation. As psychology writer Maria Konnikova noted, "When we're exposed to too many inputs at once—a computer screen, music, a colleague's conversation, the ping of an instant message—our senses become overloaded, and it requires more work to achieve a given result."

So is the activity-based hybrid described earlier a potential solution? With its constantly shifting workspace and lack of consistent locations, this may be an even less controlled environment than an open office. However, it does signal a culture that values the autonomy of individual workers to choose their own best environment at a particular time. The lack of consistency creates other problems, though. Workers cannot achieve even the modest level of personal control over any specific space that they had with the open design. Design expert Louis Lhoest notes that managers in an activity-based office "have to learn to cope with not having people within their line of sight." This is a difficult transition for many managers to make, especially if they are used to a command-and-control culture.

Whether a traditional, open, or activity-based design is best overall is obviously hard to say. Perhaps the better question is, which type will be appropriate for each organization?

Questions

16-13. The case describes activity-based working and the ways in which the office and work are organized. What are the inherent managerial concerns or problems with this approach and office design?

16-14. Can the effects of a new office design be assessed objectively? How could you go about measuring whether new office designs are improving the organizational culture?

✪16-15. What types of jobs do you think might benefit most from the various forms of office design described above?

Sources: B. Lanks, "Don't Get Too Cozy," *Bloomberg Businessweek*, October 30, 2014, http://www.businessweekme.com/Bloomberg/newsmid/190/newsid/271; M. Konnikova, "The Open-Office Trap," *New Yorker*, January 7, 2014, http://www.newyorker.com/business/currency/the-open-office-trap; N. Ashkanasy, O. B. Ayoko, and K. A. Jehn, "Understanding the Physical Environment of Work and Employee Behavior: An Affective Events Perspective," *Journal of Organizational Behavior* 35 (2014): 1169–84.

CASE INCIDENT 2   Active Cultures

Employees at many successful companies start the day by checking the economic forecast. Patagonia's Ventura, California, employees start the day by checking the surf forecast. The outdoor clothing company encourages its workforce to take time from the work day to get outside and get active. For Patagonia, linking employees with the natural environment is a major part of the culture.

New hires are introduced to this mindset very quickly. Soon after starting at Patagonia, marketing executive Joy Howard was immediately encouraged to go fly fishing, surfing, and rock climbing all around the world. She notes that all this vacationing is not just playing around—it's an important part of her job. "I needed to be familiar with the products we market," she said. Other practices support this outdoors-oriented, healthy culture. The company has an on-site organic café featuring locally grown produce. Employees at all levels are encouraged through an employee discount program to try out activewear in the field. And highly flexible hours ensure that employees feel free to take the occasional afternoon off to catch the waves or get out of town for a weekend hiking trip.

Are there bottom-line benefits to this organizational culture? Some corporate leaders think so. As Neil Blumenthal, one of the founders of Warby Parker eyewear, observes, "they've shown that you can build a profitable business while thinking about the environment and thinking about your team and community." As Patagonia CEO Rose Marcario says, "People recognize Patagonia as a company that's...looking at business through a more holistic lens other than profit." However, she is quick to add, "Profit is important; if it wasn't you wouldn't be talking to me."

Patagonia's culture obviously makes for an ideal workplace for some people—but not for others who don't share its values. People who are just not outdoor types would likely feel excluded. While the unique mission and values of Patagonia may not be for everyone, for its specific niche in the product and employment market, the culture fits like a glove.

Questions

✪ **16-16.** What do you think are the key dimensions of culture that make Patagonia successful? How does the organization help to foster this culture?

16-17. Does Patagonia use strategies to build its culture that you think could work for other companies? Is the company a useful model for others that aren't so tied to a lifestyle? Why or why not?

16-18. What are the drawbacks of Patagonia's culture? Might it sometimes be a liability, and if so, in what situations?

Sources: J. Murphy, "At Patagonia, Trying New Outdoor Adventures Is a Job Requirement," *Wall Street Journal,* March 10, 2015, http://www.wsj.com/articles/at-patagonia-trying-new-outdoor-adventures-is-a-job-requirement-1425918931; B. Schulte, "A Company That Profits as It Pampers Workers," *Washington Post,* October 25, 2014, http://www.washingtonpost.com/business/a-company-that-profits-as-it-pampers-workers/2014/10/22/d3321b34-4818-11e4-b72e-d60a9229cc10_story.html; and D. Baer, "Patagonia CEO: 'There's No Way I Should Make One Decision Based on Quarterly Results,'" *Business Insider,* November 19, 2014, http://www.businessinsider.com/patagonia-ceo-interview-2014-11.

MyManagementLab

Go to **mymanagementlab.com** for the following Assisted-graded writing questions:

16-19. From your reading of Case Incident 1, in what ways can office design shape culture?

16-20. In regard to Case Incident 2, what might Patagonia do to further reinforce its culture?

16-21. MyManagementLab Only – comprehensive writing assignment for this chapter.

ENDNOTES

[1] See, for example, B. Schneider, M. G. Ehrhart, and W. H. Macey, "Organizational Climate and Culture," *Annual Review of Psychology*, 2013, 361–88.

[2] I. Borg, P. J. F. Groenen, K. A. Jehn, W. Bilsky, and S. H. Schwartz, "Embedding the Organizational Culture Profile into Schwartz's Theory of Universals in Values," *Journal of Personnel Psychology* 10 (2011): 1–12.

[3] See, for example, C. Ostroff, A. J. Kinicki, and M. M. Tamkins, "Organizational Culture and Climate," in W. C. Borman, D. R. Ilgen, and R. J. Klimoski (eds.), *Handbook of Psychology: Industrial and Organizational Psychology*, 2003, 565–93.

[4] D. A. Hoffman and L. M. Jones, "Leadership, Collective Personality, and Performance," *Journal of Applied Psychology* 90, no. 3 (2005): 509–22.

[5] P. Lok, R. Westwood, and J. Crawford, "Perceptions of Organisational Subculture and Their Significance for Organisational Commitment," *Applied Psychology: An International Review* 54, no. 4 (2005): 490–514; B. E. Ashforth, K. M. Rogers, and K. G. Corley, "Identity in Organizations: Exploring Cross-Level Dynamics," *Organization Science* 22 (2011): 1144–56.

[6] T. Hsieh, "Zappos's CEO on Going to Extremes for Customers," *Harvard Business Review*, July/August 2010, 41–45.

[7] For discussions of how culture can be evaluated as a shared perception, see D. Chan, "Mutlilevel and Aggregation Issues in Climate and Culture Research," in B. Schneider and K. M. Barbera (eds.), *The Oxford Handbook of Organizational Climate and Culture* (New York: Oxford University Press, 2014), 484–95; J. B. Sorensen, "The Strength of Corporate Culture and the Reliability of Firm Performance," *Administrative Science Quarterly*, March 2002, 70–91.

[8] B. Schneider, A. N. Salvaggio, and M. Subirats, "Climate Strength: A New Direction for Climate Research," *Journal of Applied Psychology* 87 (2002): 220–29; L. M. Kotrba, M. A. Gillespie, A. M. Schmidt, R. E. Smerek, S. A. Ritchie, and D. R. Denison, "Do Consistent Corporate Cultures Have Better Business Performance: Exploring the Interaction Effects," *Human Relations* 65 (2012): 241–62; and M. W. Dickson, C. J. Resick, and P. J. Hanges, "When Organizational Climate Is Unambiguous, It Is also Strong," *Journal of Applied Psychology* 91 (2006): 351–64.

[9] M. Schulte, C. Ostroff, S. Shmulyian, and A. Kinicki, "Organizational Climate Configurations: Relationships to Collective Attitudes, Customer Satisfaction, and Financial Performance," *Journal of Applied Psychology* 94, no. 3 (2009): 618–34.

[10] See S. Maitlis and M. Christianson, "Sensemaking in Organizations: Taking Stock and Moving Forward," *The Academy of Management Annals* 8 (2014): 57–125; K. Weber and M. T. Dacin, "The Cultural Construction of Organizational Life," *Organization Science* 22 (2011): 287–98.

[11] Y. Ling, Z. Simsek, M. H. Lubatkin, and J. F. Veiga, "Transformational Leadership's Role in Promoting Corporate Entrepreneurship: Examining the CEO-TMT Interface," *Academy of Management Journal* 51, no. 3 (2008): 557–76; and A. Malhotra, A. Majchrzak, and B. Rosen, "Leading Virtual Teams," *Academy of Management Perspectives* 21, no. 1 (2007): 60–70.

[12] L. R. James, C. C. Choi, C. E. Ko, P. K. McNeil, M. K. Minton, M. A. Wright, and K. Kim, "Organizational and Psychological Climate: A Review of Theory and Research," *European Journal of Work and Organizational Psychology* 17, no. 1 (2008): 5–32; B. Schneider and K. M. Barbera, "Introduction and Overview," in B. Schneider and K. M. Barbera (eds.), *The Oxford Handbook of Organizational Climate and Culture*, (New York: Oxford University Press, 2014), 3–22.

[13] J. Z. Carr, A. M. Schmidt, J. K. Ford, and R. P. DeShon, "Climate Perceptions Matter: A Meta-Analytic Path Analysis Relating Molar Climate, Cognitive and Affective States, and Individual Level Work Outcomes," *Journal of Applied Psychology* 88, no. (2003): 605–19.

[14] Schulte, Ostroff, Shmulyian, and Kinicki, "Organizational Climate Configurations."

[15] S. D. Pugh, J. Dietz, A. P. Brief, and J. W. Wiley, "Looking Inside and Out: The Impact of Employee and Community Demographic Composition on Organizational Diversity Climate," *Journal of Applied Psychology* 93, no. 6 (2008): 1422–28; K. H. Ehrhart, L. A. Witt, B. Schneider, and S. J. Perry, "Service Employees Give as They Get: Internal Service as a Moderator of the Service Climate-Service Outcomes Link," *Journal of Applied Psychology* 96, no. 2 (2011): 423–31; and A. Simha and J. B. Cullen, "Ethical Climates and Their Effects on Organizational Outcomes: Implications from the Past and Prophecies for the Future," *Academy of Management Perspectives*, November 2011, 20–34.

[16] J. C. Wallace, P. D. Johnson, K. Mathe, and J. Paul, "Structural and Psychological Empowerment Climates, Performance, and the Moderating Role of Shared Felt Accountability: A Managerial Perspective," *Journal of Applied Psychology* 96, no. 3 (2011): 840–50.

[17] J. M. Beus, S. C. Payne, M. E. Bergman, and W. Arthur, "Safety Climate and Injuries: An Examination of Theoretical and Empirical Relationships," *Journal of Applied Psychology* 95, no. 4 (2010): 713–27.

[18] A. Simha and J. B. Cullen, "Ethical Climates and Their Effects on Organizational Outcomes: Implications from the Past and Prophecies for the Future," *Academy of Management*, November 2012, 20–34.

[19] Ibid.

[20] Simha and Cullen, "Ethical Climates and Their Effects on Organizational Outcomes."

[21] A. Arnaud, "Conceptualizing and Measuring Ethical Work Climate Development and Validation of the Ethical Climate Index," *Business & Society*, June 2010, 345–458.

[22] A. Arnaud and M. Schminke, "The Ethical Climate and Context of Organizations: A Comprehensive Model," *Organization Science*, November–December 2012, 1767–80.

[23] J. Howard-Greenville, S. Bertels, and B. Lahneman, "Sustainability: How It Shapes Organizational Culture and Climate," in B. Schneider and K. M. Barbera (eds.), *The Oxford Handbook of Organizational Climate and Culture* (New York: Oxford University Press, 2014), 257–75.

[24] P. Lacy, T. Cooper, R. Hayward, and L. Neuberger, "A New Era of Sustainability: UN Global Compact-Accenture CEO Study 2010," June 2010, www.uncsd2012.org/content/documents/Accenture_A_New_era_of_Sustainability_CEO_study.pdf

[25] B. Fitzgerald, "Sustainable Farming Will Be Next, 'Revolution in Agriculture,'" *Australian Broadcasting Company*, May 29, 2015, http://www.abc.net.au/news/2015-05-29/state-of-tomorrow-sustainable-farming/6504842.

[26] A. A. Marcus and A. R. Fremeth, "Green Management Matters Regardless," *Academy of Management Perspectives* 23 (2009): 17–26.

[27] H. R. Dixon-Fowler, D. J. Slater, J. L. Johnson, A. E. Ellstrand, and A. M. Romi, "Beyond 'Does It Pay to Be Green?' A Meta-Analysis of Moderators of the CEP-CFP Relationship," *Journal of Business Ethics* 112 (2013): 353–66.

[28] P. Bansal, "From Issues to Actions: The Importance of Individual Concerns and Organizational Values in Responding to Natural Environmental Issues," *Organization Science* 14 (2003): 510–27; P. Bansal, "Evolving Sustainably: A Longitudinal Study of Corporate Sustainable Development," *Strategic Management Journal* 26 (2005): 197–218; J. Howard-Grenville and A. J. Hoffman, "The Importance of Cultural Framing to the Success of Social Initiatives in Business," *Academy of Management Executive* 17 (2003): 70–84.

[29] A. R. Carrico and M. Riemer, "Motivating Energy Conservation in the Workplace: An Evaluation of the Use of Group-Level Feedback and Peer Education," *Journal of Environmental Psychology* 31 (2011): 1–13.

[30] J. P. Kotter, "Change Management: Accelerate!" *Harvard Business Review*, November 2012, 44–58.

[31]R. Walker, "Behind the Music," *Fortune*, October 29, 2012, 57–58.

[32]J. P. Titlow, "How Spotify's Music-Obsessed Culture Keeps Employees Hooked," *Fast Company*, August 20, 2014, http://www.fastcompany.com/3034617/how-spotifys-music-obsessed-culture-makes-the-company-rock.

[33]E. Ries, *The Lean Startup* (New York: Crown Business, 2011).

[34]M. Herper, "Niche Pharma," *Forbes*, September 24, 2012, 80–89.

[35]R. Pyrillis, "2012 Optimas Award Winners: ChildNet," *Workforce Management*, November 2012, 24–26.

[36]J. Bandler and D. Burke, "How HP Lost Its Way," *Fortune*, May 21, 2012, 147–64.

[37]G. F. Lanzara and G. Patriotta, "The Institutionalization of Knowledge in an Automotive Factory: Templates, Inscriptions, and the Problems of Durability," *Organization Studies* 28, no. 5 (2007): 635–60; and T. B. Lawrence, M. K. Mauws, B. Dyck, and R. F. Kleysen, "The Politics of Organizational Learning: Integrating Power into the 4I Framework," *Academy of Management Review*, January 2005, 180–91.

[38]J. B. Sorensen, "The Strength of Corporate Culture and the Reliability of Firm Performance," *Administrative Science Quarterly*, March 2002, 70–91.

[39]See D. L. Stone, E. F. Stone-Romero, and K. M. Lukaszewski, "The Impact of Cultural Values on the Acceptance and Effectiveness of Human Resource Management Policies and Practices," *Human Resource Management Review* 17, no. 2 (2007): 152–65; D. R. Avery, "Support for Diversity in Organizations: A Theoretical Exploration of Its Origins and Offshoots," *Organizational Psychology Review* 1 (2011): 239–56; A. Groggins and A. M. Ryan. "Embracing Uniqueness: The Underpinnings of a Positive Climate for Diversity," *Journal of Occupational and Organizational Psychology* 86 (2013): 264–82.

[40]D. Liu, T. R. Mitchell, T. W. Lee, B. C. Holtom, and T. R. Hinkin. "When Employees Are out of Step with Coworkers: How Job Satisfaction Trajectory and Dispersion Influence Individual-and Unit-Level Voluntary Turnover," *Academy of Management Journal* 55 (2012): 1360–80.

[41]R. A. Weber and C. F. Camerer, "Cultural Conflict and Merger Failure: An Experimental Approach," *Management Science*, April 2003, 400–12; and I. H. Gleibs, A. Mummendey, and P. Noack, "Predictors of Change in Postmerger Identification During a Merger Process: A Longitudinal Study," *Journal of Personality and Social Psychology* 95, no. 5 (2008): 1095–112; F. Bauer and K. Matzler, "Antecedents of M&A Success: The Role of Strategic Complementarity, Cultural Fit, and Degree and Speed of Integration," *Strategic Management Journal* 35 (2014): 269–91.

[42]K. Voigt, "Mergers Fail More Often Than Marriages," CNN, May 22, 2009, http://edition.cnn.com/2009/BUSINESS/05/21/merger.marriage/

[43]Y. L. Zhao, O. H. Erekson, T. Wang, and M. Song, "Pioneering Advantages and Entrepreneurs' First-Mover Decisions: An Empirical Investigation for the United States and China," *Journal of Product Innovation Management*, December 2012, 190–210.

[44]E. H. Schein, *Organizational Culture and Leadership*, Vol. 2. (New York: John Wiley & Sons, 2010).

[45]See, for example, D. E. Bowen and C. Ostroff, "The 'Strength' of the HRM System, Organizational Climate Formation, and Firm Performance," *Academy of Management Review* 29 (2004): 203–21.

[46]W. Li, Y. Wang, P. Taylor, K. Shi, and D. He, "The Influence of Organizational Culture on Work-Related Personality Requirement Ratings: A Multilevel Analysis," *International Journal of Selection and Assessment* 16, no. 4 (2008): 366–84; I. Oh, K. S. Kim, and C. H. Van Iddekinge, "Taking It to another Level: Do Personality-Based Human Capital Resources Matter to Firm Performance?" *Journal of Applied Psychology* 100 (2015): 935–47; and A. Bardi, K. E. Buchanan, R. Goodwin, L. Slabu, and M. Robinson. "Value Stability and Change during Self-Chosen Life Transitions: Self-Selection versus Socialization Effects," *Journal of Personality and Social Psychology* 106 (2014): 131–47.

[47]D. C. Hambrick, "Upper Echelons Theory: An Update," *Academy of Management Review* 32 (2007): 334–43; M. A. Carpenter, M. A. Geletkanycz, and W. G. Sanders, "Upper Echelons Research Revisited: Antecedents, Elements, and Consequences of Top Management Team Composition," *Journal of Management* 30, no. 6 (2004): 749–78, and H. Wang, A. S. Tsui, and K. R. Xin, "CEO Leadership Behaviors, Organizational Performance, and Employees' Attitudes," *The Leadership Quarterly* 22, no. 1 (2011): 92–105.

[48]"100 Best Companies to Work For," *Fortune*, 2013, http://money.cnn.com/magazines/fortune/best-companies/2013/snapshots/5.html, accessed June 28, 2013.

[49]D. M. Cable and C. K. Parsons, "Socialization Tactics and Person-Organization Fit," *Personnel Psychology*, Spring 2001, 1–23; and T. N. Bauer, T. Bodner, B. Erdogan, D. M. Truxillo, and J. S. Tucker, "Newcomer Adjustment during Organizational Socialization: A Meta-Analytic Review of Antecedents, Outcomes, and Methods," *Journal of Applied Psychology* 92, no. 3 (2007): 707–21.

[50]G. Kranz, "Training That Starts before the Job Begins," *Workforce Management Online*, July 2009, www.workforce.com.

[51]R. E. Silverman, "Companies Try to Make the First Day for New Hires More Fun," *The Wall Street Journal*, May 28, 2013, http://online.wsj.com/article/SB10001424127887323336104578501631475934850.html.

[52]D. M. Cable, F. Gino, and B. R. Staats, "Breaking Them In or Eliciting Their Best? Reframing Socialization around Newcomers' Authentic Self-Expression," *Administrative Science Quarterly* 58 (2013): 1–36; and M. Tuttle, "A Review and Critique of Van Maanen and Schein's 'Toward a Theory of Organizational Socialization' and Implications for Human Resource Development," *Human Resource Development Review* 1 (2002): 66–90.

[53]C. J. Collins, "The Interactive Effects of Recruitment Practices and Product Awareness on Job Seekers' Employer Knowledge and Application Behaviors," *Journal of Applied Psychology* 92, no. 1 (2007): 180–90.

[54]J. D. Kammeyer-Mueller and C. R. Wanberg, "Unwrapping the Organizational Entry Process: Disentangling Multiple Antecedents and Their Pathways to Adjustment," *Journal of Applied Psychology* 88 (2003): 779–94; E. W. Morrison, "Longitudinal Study of the Effects of Information Seeking on Newcomer Socialization," *Journal of Applied Psychology* 78 (2003): 173–83; and M. Wangm Y. Zhan, E. McCune, and D. Truxillo, "Understanding Newcomers' Adaptability and Work-Related Outcomes: Testing the Mediating Roles of Perceived P-E Fit Variables," *Personnel Psychology* 64, no. 1 (2011): 163–89.

[55]E. W. Morrison, "Newcomers' Relationships: The Role of Social Network Ties During Socialization," *Academy of Management Journal* 45 (2002): 1149–60.

[56]T. N. Bauer, T. Bodner, B. Erdogan, D. M. Truxillo, and J. S. Tucker, "Newcomer Adjustment during Organizational Socialization: A Meta-Analytic Review of Antecedents, Outcomes, and Methods," *Journal of Applied Psychology* 92, no. 3 (2007): 707–21.

[57]W. R. Boswell, A. J. Shipp, S. C., Payne, and S. S. Culbertson, "Changes in Newcomer Job Satisfaction over Time: Examining the Pattern of Honeymoons and Hangovers," *Journal of Applied Psychology* 94, no. 4 (2009): 844–58; W. R. Boswell, J. W. Boudreau, and J. Tichy, "The Relationship between Employee Job Change and Job Satisfaction: The Honeymoon-Hangover Effect," *Journal of Applied Psychology* 90 (2005): 882–92.

[58]J. D. Kammeyer-Mueller, C. R. Wanberg, A. L. Rubenstein, and Z. Song, "Support, Undermining, and Newcomer Socialization: Fitting in during the First 90 Days," *Academy of Management Journal* 56 (2013): 1104–24; M. Jokisaari and J. Nurmi, "Change in Newcomers' Supervisor Support and Socialization Outcomes after Organizational Entry," *Academy of Management Journal* 52 (2009): 527–44.

[59]C Vandenberghe, A. Panaccio, K. Bentein, K. Mignonac, and P. Roussel, "Assessing Longitudinal Change of and Dynamic

Relationships among Role Stressors, Job Attitudes, Turnover Intention, and Well-Being in Neophyte Newcomers," *Journal of Organizational Behavior* 32, no. 4 (2011): 652–71.

[60]E. Ransdell, "The Nike Story? Just Tell It!" *Fast Company,* January–February 2000, 44–46; and A. Muccino, "Exclusive Interview with Chuck Eichten," *Liquid Brand Summit Blog,* February 4, 2011, http://blog.liquidbrandsummit.com/.

[61]S. L. Dailey and L. Browning, "Retelling Stories in Organizations; Understanding the Functions of Narrative Repetition," *Academy of Management Review* 39 (2014): 22–43.

[62]A. J. Shipp and K. J. Jansen, "Reinterpreting Time in Fit Theory: Crafting and Recrafting Narratives of Fit in Medias Res," *Academy of Management Review* 36, no. 1 (2011): 76–101.

[63]See G. Islam and M. J. Zyphur, "Rituals in Organizations: A Review and Expansion of Current Theory," *Group and Organization Management* 34, no. 1 (2009): 114–39.

[64]M. Moskowitz and F. Levering, "The 100 Best Companies to Work For," *Fortune,* February 6, 2012, 120.

[65]A. Bryant, "Take the Bus, and Watch the Ideas Flow," *The New York Times,* September 16, 2012, 2.

[66]M. G. Pratt and A. Rafaeli "Artifacts and Organizations: Understanding Our Objective Reality," in A. Rafaeli and M. G. Pratt, *Artifacts and Organizations: Beyond Mere Symbolism* (Mahwah, NJ: Lawrence Erlbaum, 2006), 279–88.

[67]B. Gruley, "Relaxed Fit," *Bloomberg Businessweek,* September 17–23, 2012, 98–99.

[68]M. Moskowitz and R. Levering, "The 100 Best Companies to Work For," *Fortune,* February 6, 2012, 117–24.

[69]A. Ardichvilli, J. A. Mitchell, and D. Jondle, "Characteristics of Ethical Business Cultures," *Journal of Business Ethics* 85, no. 4 (2009): 445–51; D. M. Mayer, "A Review of the Literature on Ethical Climate and Culture," in B. Schneider and K. M. Barbera (eds.), *The Oxford Handbook of Organizational Climate and Culture* (New York: Oxford University Press, 2014), 415–40.

[70]J. P. Mulki, J. F. Jaramillo, and W. B. Locander, "Critical Role of Leadership on Ethical Climate and Salesperson Behaviors," *Journal of Business Ethics* 86, no. 2 (2009): 125–41; M. Schminke, M. L. Ambrose, and D. O. Neubaum, "The Effect of Leader Moral Development on Ethical Climate and Employee Attitudes," *Organizational Behavior and Human Decision Processes* 97, no. 2 (2005): 135–51; and M. E. Brown, L. K. Treviño, and D. A. Harrison, "Ethical Leadership: A Social Learning Perspective for Construct Development and

Testing," *Organizational Behavior and Human Decision Processes* 97, no. 2 (2005): 117–34.

[71]D. M. Mayer, R. Kuenzi, R. Greenbaum, M. Bardes, and S. Salvador, "How Low Does Ethical Leadership Flow? Test of a Trickle-Down Model," *Organizational Behavior and Human Decision Processes* 108, no. 1 (2009): 1–13; L. J. Christensen, A. Mackey, and D. Whetten, "Taking Responsibility for Corporate Social Responsibility: The Role of Leaders in Creating, Implementing, Sustaining, or Avoiding Socially Responsible Firm Behaviors," *Academy of Management Perspectives* 28 (2014): 164–78.

[72]B. Sweeney, D. Arnold, and B. Pierce, "The Impact of Perceived Ethical Culture of the Firm and Demographic Variables on Auditors' Ethical Evaluation and Intention to Act Decisions," *Journal of Business Ethics* 93, no. 4 (2010): 531–51.

[73]M. L. Gruys, S. M. Stewart, J. Goodstein, M. N. Bing, and A. C. Wicks, "Values Enactment in Organizations: A Multi-Level Examination," *Journal of Management* 34, no. 4 (2008): 806–43.

[74]D. L. Nelson and C. L. Cooper (eds.), *Positive Organizational Behavior* (London: Sage, 2007); K. S. Cameron, J. E. Dutton, and R. E. Quinn (eds.), *Positive Organizational Scholarship: Foundations of a New Discipline* (San Francisco: Berrett-Koehler, 2003); and F. Luthans and C. M. Youssef, "Emerging Positive Organizational Behavior," *Journal of Management,* June 2007, 321–49.

[75]J. Robison, "Great Leadership under Fire," *Gallup Leadership Journal,* March 8, 2007, 1–3.

[76]R. Wagner and J. K. Harter, *12: The Elements of Great Managing* (New York: Gallup Press, 2006).

[77]M. Mihelich, "2012 Optimas Award Winners: Safelite AutoGlass," *Workforce Management,* November 2012, 27.

[78]R. Wagner and J. K. Harter, "Performance Reviews without the Anxiety," *Gallup Leadership Journal,* July 12, 2007, 1–4; and Wagner and Harter, *12: The Elements of Great Managing.*

[79]S. Fineman, "On Being Positive: Concerns and Counterpoints," *Academy of Management Review* 31, no. 2 (2006): 270–91.

[80]E. Poole, "Organisational Spirituality: A Literature Review," *Journal of Business Ethics* 84, no. 4 (2009): 577–88.

[81]L. W. Fry and J. W. Slocum, "Managing the Triple Bottom Line through Spiritual Leadership," *Organizational Dynamics* 37, no. 1 (2008): 86–96.

[82]See, for example, C. L. Jurkiewicz and R. A. Giacalone, "A Values Framework for Measuring the Impact of Workplace Spirituality on Organizational Performance," *Journal of Business Ethics* 49, no. 2 (2004): 129–42.

[83]See, for example, B. S. Pawar, "Workplace Spirituality Facilitation: A Comprehensive Model," *Journal of Business Ethics* 90, no. 3 (2009): 375–86; and L. Lambert, *Spirituality Inc.: Religion in the American Workplace* (New York: New York University Press, 2009).

[84]M. Oppenheimer, "The Rise of the Corporate Chaplain," *Bloomberg Businessweek,* August 23, 2012, 58–61.

[85]M. Lips-Miersma, K. L. Dean, and C. J. Fornaciari, "Theorizing the Dark Side of the Workplace Spirituality Movement," *Journal of Management Inquiry* 18, no. 4 (2009): 288–300.

[86]J.-C. Garcia-Zamor, "Workplace Spirituality and Organizational Performance," *Public Administration Review,* May–June 2003, 355–63; and L. W. Fry, S. T. Hannah, M. Noel, and F. O. Walumbwa, "Impact of Spiritual Leadership on Unit Performance," *Leadership Quarterly* 22, no. 2 (2011): 259–70.

[87]A. Rego and M. Pina e Cunha, "Workplace Spirituality and Organizational Commitment: An Empirical Study," *Journal of Organizational Change Management* 21, no. 1 (2008): 53–75; R. W. Kolodinsky, R. A. Giacalone, and C. L. Jurkiewicz, "Workplace Values and Outcomes: Exploring Personal, Organizational, and Interactive Workplace Spirituality," *Journal of Business Ethics* 81, no. 2 (2008): 465–80; M. Gupta, V. Kumar, and M. Singh, "Creating Satisfied Employees through Workplace Spirituality: A Study of the Private Insurance Sector in Punjab India," *Journal of Business Ethics* 122 (2014): 79–88.

[88]J. Nicas, "American, US Airways Face Challenges in Integration," *The Wall Street Journal,* February 14, 2013, http://online.wsj.com/article/SB1000142412788732443200457830419216293154.html.

[89]D. J. McCarthy and S. M. Puffer, "Interpreting the Ethicality of Corporate Governance Decision in Russia: Utilizing Integrative Social Contracts Theory to Evaluate the Relevance of Agency Theory Norms," *Academy of Management Review* 33, no. 1 (2008): 11–31.

[90]P. Monin, N. Noorderhavin, E. Vaara, and D. Kroon, "Giving Sense to and Making Sense of Justice in Postmerger Integration," *Academy of Management Journal,* February 2013, 256–84; A. Simha and J. B. Cullen, "Ethical Climates and Their Effects on Organizational Outcomes: Implications from the Past and Prophecies for the Future," *Academy of Management Perspectives,* November 2011, 20–34; and E. Vaara and J. Tienari, "On the Narrative Construction of Multinational Corporations: An Antenarrative Analysis of Legitimation and Resistance in a Cross-Border Merger," *Organization Science,* March–April 2011, 370–90.

[91]R. Vesely, "Seven Seas Change," *Workforce Management,* September 2012, 20–21.

17 Human Resource Policies and Practices

LEARNING OBJECTIVES

After studying this chapter, you should be able to:

17-1	Describe the value of recruitment methods.	**17-4**	Compare the main types of training.
17-2	Specify initial selection methods.	**17-5**	List the methods of performance evaluation.
17-3	Identify the most useful substantive selection methods.	**17-6**	Describe the leadership role of HR in organizations.

MyManagementLab®
⭐ **Chapter Warm Up**   If your professor has chosen to assign this, go to the Assignments section of **mymanagementlab.com** to complete the chapter warm up.

SWEDISH WORK–LIFE BALANCE POLICY THRIVES IN CHINA

Work–life balance is a luxury in China. Although Chinese labor law stipulates that workers can work no more than eight hours per day and 40 hours per week, many employees in China willingly work much longer. To them, working overtime can be more like a blessing. For instance, a female worker in Chongqing chooses to work 70 to 80 hours a week so that her brother can have enough money to attend school.

In addition to the need for extra income, long working hours in China also relate to the country's culture. According to Justine Campbell, a counsellor and coach at Mindquest Group, there is a hidden rule that Chinese employees should not leave their workplace until their boss leaves. Working longer hours is considered a virtue in China.

Work–life balance is generally considered to be the daily effort to make time for family and social life in addition to the demands of the workplace. As the general income level has improved significantly in the past few years, people in China are now demanding a more balanced work life. According to a survey by Regus, Chinese workers report that they are feeling increasingly stressed out, with 75 percent saying their stress level has risen in the past year. In the rest of the world, on the other hand, only 48 percent of workers said they felt more stress.

A balanced work life cannot be pursued by employees alone. It needs to be supported by employers who institute policies and procedures that enable employees to have more balanced lives. A good example can be seen in IKEA China, a Swedish furniture company founded in 1943. It entered China in 1998, when it opened its first store in Shanghai.

Jill Burgess, a senior manager at IKEA, states that work–life balance is a priority in its own right in IKEA's business plan. IKEA's Swedish heritage is important to the company, as demonstrated by its national values of commitment to family and society, combined with concern for a healthy environment. These values acknowledge work–life balance as a means to put in place a pleasant working environment for all staff.

In IKEA China, while the mandatory working hours are closely followed, work–life balance is further enforced by the company's provision of paid leave for all staff for important occasions such as marriage leave, maternity leave, and moving-house leave. IKEA China also provides work–life balance offerings such as flexibility in work time, special shift arrangements, non-standard work weeks and special leave for a domestic crisis or community service.

Are employees satisfied now? A team leader in IKEA's Shanghai store stated in a social forum that there were strong humanistic values in IKEA, with good opportunities to develop within different units, and a friendly and relaxed environment that encouraged diversity, where people could be themselves.

Sources: Pham Ngoc Binh and Xue Hongyu, "A Case Study on Ikea in China and Their Staffs," *DiVA*, http://www.diva-portal.org/smash/get/diva2:539330/FULLTEXT01.pdf; Wei Gu, "The Struggle for Work-Life Balance in China," *The Wall Street Journal*, September 12, 2013, http://www.wsj.com/articles/SB10001424127887324549004579070411599297846; Graeme Russell and Meredith Ross, "Work-Life in China," Boston College: Center for Work & Family, https://www.bc.edu/content/dam/files/centers/cwf/pdf/BC_CWF_EBS-China.pdf; "The Work-Life Balance Dilemma in China," *Today*, September 17, 2013, http://www.todayonline.com/chinaindia/china/work-life-balance-dilemma-china; IKEA China Reviews, Glassdoor, http://www.glassdoor.com/Reviews/IKEA-China-Reviews-EI_IE3957.0,4_IL.5,10_IN48.htm; Adam Ozimek, "Why Do Some Chinese Workers Have Such Long Work Weeks?," *Forbes*, December 27, 2012, http://www.forbes.com/sites/modeledbehavior/2012/12/27/why-do-some-chinese-workers-have-such-long-work-weeks/; Susan M. Heathfield, "Work-Life Balance," About.com, January 14, 2015, http://humanresources.about.com/od/glossaryw/g/balance.htm.

The message of this chapter is that human resource (HR) policies and practices—such as employee recruitment, selection, training, and performance management—influence an organization's effectiveness.[1] Studies show that managers—even HR managers—often don't know which HR practices work and which don't, so they constantly experiment with techniques ranging from free tuition to stress-based interviews. Let's discuss both new and tried-and-true methods, and their effect on OB, beginning with the recruitment function.

Recruitment Practices

17-1 Describe the value of recruitment methods.

The first stage in any HR program is recruiting, closely followed by selection. A selection system can only be as good as the individuals who apply in the first place.[2] Strategic recruiting has become a cornerstone for many companies, in which recruiting practices are developed in alignment with long-term strategic goals. As for defining "success" in recruiting, most research suggests that the best system attracts candidates who are highly knowledgeable about the job and the organization.[3] Such candidates are likely to have a better fit between their skills and job requirements, and to be more satisfied in the jobs they take. Consistent with these findings, some of the most effective recruiting techniques include internal referrals, internship programs, and other methods that give potential applicants enough information to adequately evaluate the roles they may be occupying.

Companies are increasingly turning away from outside recruiting agencies and relying on their own executives and HR professionals for talent searches.[4] The most effective recruiters—internal or external—are well informed about the job, are efficient in communicating with potential recruits, and treat recruits with consideration and respect.[5] They also use a variety of online tools, including job boards and social media, to bring in applications. Online recruiting has yielded an exponentially increased number of applications, even as the means to identify the best online recruitment sources are still developing.[6] Social networking services have facilitated many connections. Some organizations are pioneering unique methods, such as online programming contests that masquerade as games, to identify individuals with top skill sets who may be attracted to apply for positions. These contests have been successful for recruiting applicants from all over the globe.[7]

Selection Practices

17-2 Specify initial selection methods.

One of the most important HR functions is hiring the right people. How do you figure out who the right people are from all the candidates? Identifying the top candidates is the objective of the selection process, which matches individual characteristics (ability, experience, and so on) with the requirements of the job.[8] When management fails to get a proper match, employee performance and satisfaction both suffer. With more applications than ever coming in the door, it is paramount to ensure that your organization has an effective method for identifying the most qualified applicants. Technology has come a long way in a short time, but its recruiting uses are not yet streamlined. Technology that sorts through applications to find the unique combinations of traits and experience needed for the job is not enough, you are looking for top performers. Even technology to inform applicants of their status in the hiring process is not universally operational.[9]

How the Selection Process Works

Exhibit 17-1 shows how the selection process works in most organizations. Having decided to apply for a job, applicants go through several stages—three are shown in the exhibit—during which they can be rejected at any time. In practice, often organizations forego some of these steps in the interests of saving time. (For example, a meat-packing plant may hire anyone who walks in the door since there is not a long line of people who want to "thread" a pig's intestines for a living.) But most organizations follow a process that looks something like this exhibit. Let's go into a bit more detail about each stage.

Exhibit 17-1   **Model of Selection Process in Organizations**

Applicant applies for job.

Initial Selection

Goal: Use for preliminary "rough cuts" to decide whether an applicant meets the basic qualifications for a job.

Examples: Application forms, background checks

Applicants who don't meet basic qualifications are rejected.

Applicant meets basic qualifications.

Substantive Selection

Goal: Determine the most qualified applicants from among those who meet basic qualifications.

Examples: Written tests, performance tests, interviews

Applicants who meet basic qualifications, but are less qualified than others, are rejected.

Applicant is among best qualified.

Contingent Selection

Goal: Make final check before making offer to applicants.

Examples: Drug tests, medical exams

Applicants who are among best qualified, but who fail contingent selection, are rejected.

Applicant receives job offer.

Initial Selection

Initial selection devices are used for preliminary rough cuts to decide whether the applicant meets the basic qualifications for a job. Application forms and résumés (including letters of recommendation) are initial selection devices. Background checks are either an initial selection device or a contingent selection device, depending on how the organization handles them. Some organizations prefer to look into an applicant's background right away. Others wait until the applicant is about to be hired, contingent on everything else checking out. Still others seem barely to check anything, instead hiring friends and family. This practice is controversial partly because it thwarts the workplace diversity that can increase organizational performance.[10]

Application Forms   You've no doubt submitted your fair share of applications. By itself, the information submitted on an application form is not a very useful predictor of performance. However, it can be a good initial screen. For example, there's no sense spending time interviewing an applicant for a registered nurse position if he doesn't have the proper credentials (education, certification, experience). Managers must be careful about the questions they ask on applications, though. Obviously, questions about race, gender, and nationality are disallowed. However, other questions also put companies in legal jeopardy. For example, applications should not inquire about marital status, dependents, and family obligations.

Many organizations encourage applicants to apply online. It takes them only a few minutes, and the form can easily be forwarded around to the people responsible for making the hiring decision. Most major corporations have a career page on their websites where prospective employees can search for available positions by location or job type and then apply online. These days, you are more likely to e-mail or upload your résumé than send anything by mail, and applicants sometimes create video résumés. Candidate preferences are constantly changing. Research in the Netherlands suggested that applicants from minority ethnic groups (in this case, Turkish and Moroccan) preferred the personal nature of the video résumé.[11]

Increasingly, employers are asking for photos with applicant submissions, and some are then scanning the photo with facial-recognition software to match the face to the applicant's home address, Social Security number, criminal record, and affiliations. While this seems like a good business practice, experts recommend against it, unless the business operates in a high-security environment, because applicants can claim discrimination based on their facial characteristics.[12]

When you are the candidate, be careful about what you put on your online applications. Many HR departments, faced with an overwhelming number of electronic submissions, are using software to pre-select candidates based on keyword matches between applications and the qualifications needed for the job. Their software often seeks to screen out unacceptable candidates rather than select potentially good ones. While you will want to incorporate all the keywords that accurately describe your experience, including paid and volunteer work,[13] and use whatever prompts you are given to outline the personal characteristics that qualify you, be careful not to overstate.[14]

Background Checks   More than 80 percent of employers conduct both employment and personal reference checks on applicants at some point in the hiring process. The reason is obvious: They want to know how an applicant did in past jobs and whether former employers would recommend hiring the person. The problem is that former employers rarely provide useful information. In fact, nearly two-thirds refuse to give detailed references because they are afraid of being sued for saying something bad about a former employee. Although this concern is often unfounded (employers are safe as long as they stick to documented facts, and several states have passed laws protecting truthful information provided in reference checks), in our litigious society, most employers play it safe. The result is a paradox: Most employers want reference information, but few will give it out. Employers do call personal references for a more candid idea of the applicant; however, research found that 30 percent of hiring managers regularly discovered references that were false or misleading.[15] Some organizations have turned to reference-checking software that sends 10-minute surveys to references. Research indicates this new technology may result in better (more objective) information.[16]

Letters of recommendation are another form of background check. These aren't as useful as they may seem. Applicants select references who will write good things about them, so almost all letters of recommendation are positive. In the end, readers either ignore them or read "between the lines" to try to find hidden meaning.

Many employers search for candidates online through a general Internet search or through a targeted search of social networking sites. The legality of this practice has come into question, but there is no doubt that many employers include an electronic search to see whether candidates have any history that might make them a dubious choice for employment. For some potential employees, an embarrassing or incriminating photo circulated through Facebook may make it hard to get a job. On the other hand, a study found that independent raters viewing candidate Facebook profiles were able to accurately determine candidate conscientiousness, agreeability, and intelligence that later translated into predictable job performance scores as rated by supervisors.[17]

Some employers check credit histories. A bank hiring tellers, for example, would probably want to know about a candidate's credit history, but credit checks are increasingly being used for nonbanking jobs. There is some evidence in favor of this practice. Task performance, organizational citizenship behavior (OCB), and conscientiousness (which is a predictor of job performance, see Chapter 5) were found to be positively related to credit scores.[18] However, the consistency of the links is questioned—research also found that minority status was adversely related to credit scores, while age and educational attainment were positively related.[19] Because of discrimination concerns and the invasive nature of credit checks, employers must be sure there is a need for them.

Finally, some employers conduct criminal background checks. Currently, 65 million U.S. adults (one in four) have criminal records, and for many it is difficult or impossible to find work.[20] The Equal Employment Opportunity Commission (EEOC) states that candidates cannot be denied employment based only on the findings of background checks, and experts point out that the checks are often inaccurate anyway. Also, because job candidates are seldom told why they are turned down, individuals can be hurt without having the opportunity for correction.[21] To further complicate matters, a criminal history can legally be used for rejection only if the violation relates to the job (an embezzler could be disqualified for jobs in finance, but not in, say, the medical field).[22] A civil rights movement has sought to ban employers from even asking applicants whether they have criminal convictions.

Background checks are usually but not always necessary, with interesting outcomes. Notably, some companies deliberately set out to hire applicants who wouldn't pass background checks, like those with criminal backgrounds. These organizations value "second chances" in their cultures and report that many of these workers become valuable contributors to their organizations and society. Such hires are not without risk, however, and so must be carefully managed.[23] Although it would seem best that employers refrain from conducting criminal background checks, *not* checking can carry a legal cost if an employee with a record commits a crime while on the job.

Substantive and Contingent Selection

17-3   Identify the most useful substantive selection methods.

If an applicant passes the initial screens, next are substantive selection methods. These are the heart of the selection process and include written tests, performance-simulation tests, and interviews. We will discuss these and contingent selection tests, which are usually issued to candidates who pass the substantive tests.

Written Tests

Long popular as selection devices, written employment tests—called "paper-and-pencil" tests, though most are now available online—declined in use between the late 1960s and mid-1980s, especially in the United States. They were frequently characterized as discriminatory, and many organizations had not validated them as job-related. Since then, however, there has been a resurgence,

At this Sarku Japan fast-food restaurant, employees applying for management positions must take written tests as part of the company's substantive selection process. Written tests for intelligence, integrity, personality, and interests are popular selection devices that help predict which applicants will be successful on the job.
Source: Michael S. Williamson/The Washington Post/ Getty Images

and today most organizations have at least considered using one or more tests.[24] Managers recognize that valid tests can help predict who will be successful on the job.[25] Applicants, however, tend to view written tests as less valid and fair than interviews or performance tests.[26] Typical tests include (1) intelligence or cognitive ability tests, (2) personality tests, and (3) integrity tests.

Intelligence or Cognitive Ability Tests   Tests of intellectual ability/cognitive ability/intelligence (the terms are sometimes used interchangeably), spatial and mechanical ability, perceptual accuracy, and motor ability have long proven valid predictors for the performance of many skilled, semiskilled, and unskilled operative jobs.[27] Overall, intelligence tests have proven to be particularly good predictors for jobs that include cognitively complex tasks (like learning the ever-more-complicated playbooks in the NFL).[28] Many experts say intelligence tests are the *single best* selection measure across jobs and that they are at least as valid in the European Union (EU) as in the United States.[29] While cognitive ability tests have long been considered to measure a single, unified cognitive capacity, some recent work suggests that they may be useful tests for different specific abilities depending on the requirements of a job.[30] For example, differentiating mathematical, verbal, and technical abilities in hiring processes may lead to better predictions of job performance than relying on just one overall cognitive ability score.

Personality Tests   Personality tests are inexpensive and simple to administer, and their use has grown. However, concerns about applicants faking responses remain, partly because it's fairly easy to claim to be hard-working, motivated, and dependable when asked in a job application setting even if that's not accurate, and partly because applicants aren't always aware they are faking.[31] One study of Croatian university students suggested that individuals can be partially successful in faking a desirable profile.[32] Thankfully, another study in China indicated that including warning messages for potential faking behavior with the tests may help curb the behavior.[33] Two reviews comparing self-reported personality to observer-rated personality found that observer ratings are better predictors of job performance and other behaviors.[34] Thus, employers might want to consider adding messages about the need for truthfulness in personality tests, and asking employment references about an applicant's personality, as part of the screening process.

Integrity Tests   As ethical problems in organizations have increased, integrity tests have gained popularity. These paper-and-pencil tests measure factors such as dependability, carefulness, responsibility, and honesty. They have proven to be powerful predictors of job performance (as measured as objectively as possible by supervisors) and of the potential for theft, discipline problems, and excessive absenteeism.[35] However, the many available tests do not all predict job performance outcomes equally well. Managers must be careful to choose one that measures ethical criteria matched to the job responsibilities.[36]

Performance-Simulation Tests

What better way to find out whether applicants can do a job successfully than by having them do it? That's precisely the logic of performance-simulation tests. Although they are more complicated to develop and administer than standardized tests, performance-simulation tests have higher *face validity* (the measurement of whether applicants perceive the measures to be accurate), and their popularity has increased. Predictive simulations are commonly available through work samples, assessment centers, situational judgment tests, and realistic job previews.

work sample tests   Hands-on simulations of part or all of the work that applicants for routine jobs must perform.

Work Sample Tests   **Work sample tests** are hands-on simulations of part or all the work that workers in the job routinely must perform. Each work sample element is matched with a job-performance element to measure applicants' knowledge, skills, and abilities with more specificity than written aptitude and personality tests.[37] Work samples are widely used in the hiring of skilled workers such as welders, machinists, carpenters, and electricians. Work sample tests are increasingly used for all levels of employment.

assessment centers   Off-site places where candidates are given a set of performance-simulation tests designed to evaluate their managerial potential.

Assessment Centers   A more elaborate set of performance-simulation tests, specifically designed to evaluate a candidate's managerial potential, is administered in **assessment centers**. Line executives, supervisors, and/or trained psychologists evaluate candidates as they go through one to several days of exercises that simulate real problems they would confront on the job.[38] For example, a candidate might be required to play the role of a manager who must decide how to respond to 10 memos in an in-basket within a 2-hour period.

situational judgment tests   Substantive selection tests that ask applicants how they would perform in a variety of job situations; the answers are then compared to the answers of high-performing employees.

Situational Judgment Tests   To reduce the costs of job simulations, many organizations have started to use **situational judgment tests**, which ask applicants how they would perform in a variety of job situations and then compare their answers to the answers of high-performing employees.[39] Coaching can improve scores on these tests, though, which raises questions about whether they reflect true judgment or merely good test preparation.[40] One study comparing situational judgment tests to assessment centers found the assessment center was a better predictor of job performance, although the difference was not large.[41] Ultimately, the lower cost of the situational judgment test may make it a better choice for some organizations than a more elaborate work sample or assessment center experience.

realistic job previews Substantive selection tests that are job tryouts to assess talent versus experience.

Realistic Job Previews   Employers are increasingly using work sample methods that go beyond assessment testing into the realm of actual work performed and evaluated. These are sometimes known as **realistic job previews** or job tryouts, and they are given as a way to assess talent versus experience. Experts are finding they also decrease turnover because both employers and new hires know what they are getting into ahead of time.[42] When George McAfee applied for a vice president position in the tech industry, he was required to give presentations, conduct research, and hold talks with executives about their ongoing business concerns for over a week, all unpaid. He felt the employer was taking advantage of his free labor, but he said, "You just have to accept that and not be offended."[43] HR managers may risk losing qualified candidates who object to this extensive job test and withdraw from the process. Those who identify with an organization's mission, people, or products will be less likely to withdraw, suggesting that HR managers should seek to engage candidates with the organization early in the selection process.[44]

Interviews

Of all the selection devices organizations around the globe use to differentiate candidates, the interview has always been a standard practice. It also tends to have a disproportionate amount of influence. Overreliance on interviews is problematic because extensive evidence shows that impression management techniques (see Chapter 13) like self-promotion have a strong effect on interviewer preferences even when the displayed traits are unrelated to the job.[45] Conversely, the candidate who performs poorly in the employment interview is likely to be cut from the applicant pool regardless of experience, test scores, or letters of recommendation. And unfortunately, candidates can be rated lower for something as trivial as a blemish on their faces, one study found.[46]

unstructured interviews Short, casual interviews made up of random questions.

Interviews are either structured or unstructured. The popular **unstructured interview**—short, casual, and made up of random questions—is simply not a very effective selection device,[47] and it can easily derail into nonproductive conversation (see OB Poll). The data it gathers are typically biased and often only

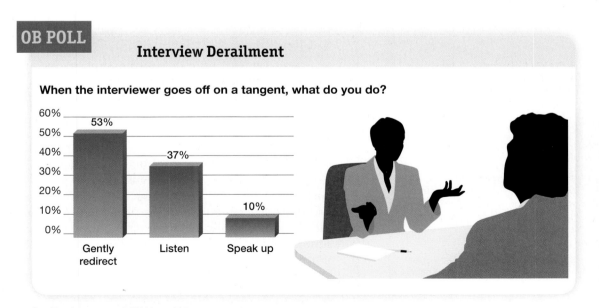

OB POLL

Interview Derailment

When the interviewer goes off on a tangent, what do you do?

- Gently redirect: 53%
- Listen: 37%
- Speak up: 10%

Note: Based on a survey of 150 job candidates.
Source: Based on J. Yang and P. Trap, *USA Today*, November 13, 2012, p. 1B.

Arcadio Cruz (left) uses a structured interview approach in gathering information from job applicants for positions at Orchard Hardware Supply store in Los Angeles. Questions asked in structured interviews are objective and standardized for all applicants and encourage open-ended responses.

Source: Patrick Fallon/Bloomberg/Getty Images

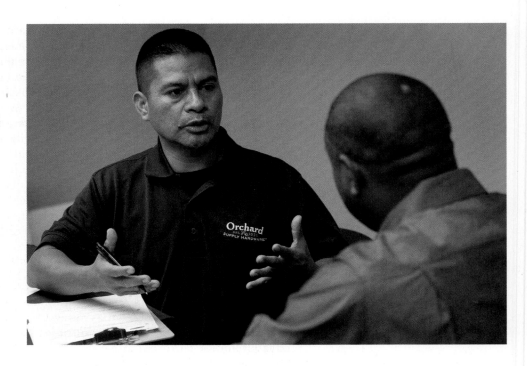

structured interviews   Planned interviews designed to gather job-related information.

modestly related to future job performance. Still, managers are reluctant to use **structured interviews**—planned interviews designed to gather job-related information—in place of their favorite questions, such as "If you could be any animal, what would you be, and why?" Structured interviews limit subjectivity as much as possible and therefore can provide more reliable responses. Harry West, CEO of innovation design firm Continuum, asks all candidates the same basic questions: "What is it you want to do? What is it that you're good at? What is it that you're not good at? Tell me about what you've done." This is an excellent start in that the questions are objective in nature, prompt open-ended responses, and are standardized for all candidates.[48]

Without structure, interviewers tend to favor applicants who share their attitudes, give undue weight to negative information, and allow the order in which applicants are interviewed to influence their evaluations.[49] Structured interviews, on the other hand, reduce the extent to which interviewers are influenced by applicant appearance and impression management tactics, like flattery and self-promotion.[50] To reduce bias and improve the validity of interviews, managers should adopt a standardized set of questions, a uniform method of recording information, and standardized ratings of applicants' qualifications. Training interviewers to focus on specific dimensions of job performance, practicing evaluation procedures of candidates, and giving *interviewers* feedback on how well they focused on job-relevant characteristics significantly improves the accuracy of their ratings.[51] Interview effectiveness also improves when employers use *behavioral structured interviews,* probably because these assessments are less influenced by interviewer biases.[52] These interviews require applicants to describe how they handled specific problems and situations in past jobs, based on the assumption that past behavior offers the best predictor of future behavior. **Panel interviews**—structured interviews conducted with a candidate and a number of panel members in a joint meeting—also minimize the influence of individual biases and have higher validity.

panel interviews   Structured interviews conducted with a candidate and a number of panel members in a joint meeting.

In practice, most organizations use interviews for a number of reasons. Companies as diverse as Southwest Airlines, Disney, Bank of America, Microsoft,

Procter & Gamble, and Harrah's Entertainment use interviews to assess applicant–organization fit. In addition to evaluating specific, job-related skills, managers look at personality characteristics and personal values to find individuals who fit the organization's culture and image. Some companies also use job interviews as a recruiting tool, trying to "sell" applicants on the value of the job and organization. This strategy may sometimes be necessary because of a tight labor market, but it may also be problematic. One study showed that interviewers who were trying to promote the organization during interviews were significantly worse at identifying applicant personality traits and selection than those who focused exclusively on assessing candidate qualifications.[53]

Contingent Selection Tests

If applicants pass the substantive selection methods, they are ready to be hired, contingent on final checks. One common contingent check is a drug test. Publix grocery stores make tentative offers to applicants contingent on their passing such a test and checking out as drug-free, as do many other organizations.

Drug testing is controversial. Many applicants think testing without reasonable suspicion is invasive or unfair and say they should be tested on job-performance factors, not lifestyle choices that may not be relevant. Employers might counter that drug use and abuse are extremely costly, not just in financial terms but also in terms of people's safety. In the United States, they have the law on their side. The Supreme Court has concluded that drug tests are "minimally invasive" selection procedures that as a rule do not violate individuals' rights.

Under the Americans with Disabilities Act (ADA), U.S. firms may not require employees to pass a medical exam before a job offer is made. However, they can conduct medical exams *after* making a contingent offer—but only to determine whether an applicant is physically or mentally able to do the job. Employers also sometimes use medical exams to find out whether and how they can accommodate employees with disabilities. For jobs requiring exposure to heavy physical or psychological demands, such as air traffic controllers or firefighters, medical exams are obviously an important indicator of the ability to perform.

Training and Development Programs

17-4 Compare the main types of training.

Competent employees don't remain competent forever. Skills deteriorate and can become obsolete, and new skills need to be learned. That's why corporations in the United States spend over $70 billion annually, and organizations worldwide spend over $130 billion annually, on training.[54]

Types of Training

Training and development programs are usually in the purview of HR departments. Training can include everything from teaching employees basic reading skills to conducting advanced courses in executive leadership. Here we discuss four general skill categories—basic skills, technical skills, problem-solving skills, and interpersonal skills—and civility and ethics training.

Basic Skills   One survey of more than 400 HR professionals found that 40 percent of employers believe high school graduates lack basic skills in reading comprehension, writing, and math.[55] As work has become more sophisticated, the need for these basic skills has grown significantly, leading to a gap between employer demands for skills and the available skills in the workforce.[56] The challenge isn't unique to the United States; it's a worldwide problem from the most developed countries to the least.[57] For many undeveloped countries, widespread illiteracy means there is almost no hope of competing in a global economy.

Organizations increasingly have to teach employees basic reading and math skills. These interventions can yield worthwhile improvements for the organization. In a classic example, a literacy audit showed that employees at gun manufacturer Smith & Wesson needed at least an eighth-grade reading level to do typical workplace tasks.[58] Yet 30 percent of the company's 676 workers with no degree scored below eighth-grade levels in either reading or math. After the first round of basic-skills classes, company-paid and on company time, 70 percent of attendees brought their skills up to the target level, allowing them to do a better job. They displayed increased abilities to use fractions and decimals; better overall communication; greater ease in writing and reading charts, graphs, and bulletin boards; and a significant increase in confidence.

Technical Skills   Most training is directed at upgrading and improving an employee's technical skills, which is increasingly important for two reasons: new technology and new structural designs in the organization.

As organizations flatten their structures, expand their use of teams, and break down traditional departmental barriers, employees need mastery of a wider variety of tasks and increased knowledge of how their organization operates. Indian companies and others have faced a dramatic increase in demand for skilled workers in areas like engineering for emerging technologies, but many recent engineering graduates lack up-to-date knowledge required to perform these technical tasks.[59] Many organizations offer technical training to bridge the gap. Companies like Tata and Wipro provide new hires with up to 3 months of training to ensure they have the knowledge to perform the technical work demanded. In addition, these organizations are attempting to form partnerships with engineering schools to ensure academic curricula meet the needs of contemporary employers.

Problem-Solving Skills   Problem-solving training for managers and other employees can include activities to sharpen their logic, reasoning, and problem-defining skills as well as their ability to assess causation, develop and analyze alternatives, and select solutions. Problem-solving training has become a part of almost every organizational effort to introduce self-managed teams or implement quality-management programs.

Interpersonal Skills   Most employees belong to a work unit, and their work performance depends on their ability to effectively interact with their coworkers and bosses. Some employees have excellent interpersonal abilities, but others require training to improve listening, communicating, and team-building skills. Although many professionals are greatly interested in interpersonal skills training, most evidence suggests that skills learned in such training do not readily transfer back to the workplace.[60]

Civility Training   As HR managers have become increasingly aware of the effects of social behavior in the workplace, they have paid more attention to the problems of incivility, bullying, and abusive supervision in organizations. Examples of incivility include being ignored, being blamed for others' mistakes and receiving no credit for your achievements, having your reputation undermined in front of others, and experiencing other situations meant to demean or disparage you or others.[61] Researchers have shown that these forms of negative behavior can

After receiving many complaints from patients about rude and insulting behavior from its nursing staff, hospital officials at a clinic in southern China hired flight attendants to give the nurses civility training. During a training intervention, nurses learned how to greet patients politely and care for them with grace, kindness, and patience.

Source: Europics/Newscom

decrease satisfaction, reduce job performance, increase perceptions of unfair treatment, increase depression, and lead to psychological withdrawal from the workplace.[62] Organizations are therefore getting involved in reducing the incidence rate to improve their workplaces and limit their liability.

Is there anything HR departments can do to minimize incivility, bullying, and abusive supervision? One possibility is training specifically targeted to building civility by holding directed conversations about it and supporting the reduction of incivility on an ongoing basis. Following one training intervention, civility, respect, job satisfaction, and trust increased, while incivility, cynicism, and absences decreased.[63] Thus, the evidence suggests that deliberate interventions to improve the workplace climate and foster positive behavior can indeed minimize the problems of incivility.

Ethics Training It is common for employees to receive ethics and values guidance incorporated in new-employee orientations, ongoing developmental programs, or as periodic reinforcements of ethical principles.[64] But the jury is still out on whether you can actually teach ethics.[65] Critics argue that ethics are based on values, and value systems are learned by example at an early age. They say that by the time employees are hired, ethical values are fixed. In support, some research suggests ethics training does not have a significant long-term effect on participants' values and even that exposure to business and law school programs *decreases* students' level of prosocial ethical values.[66]

Supporters of ethics training say values *can* be learned and changed after early childhood. And even if an individual's values can't be changed, ethics training helps employees recognize ethical dilemmas and become more aware of the ethical issues underlying their actions. It also reaffirms an organization's expectations that members will act ethically. Research has found that individuals who have greater exposure to organizational ethics codes and ethics training tend to be more satisfied and perceive their organizations as more socially responsible, so ethics training does have some positive effects.[67]

Training Methods

Historically, *training* meant "formal training," planned in advance and following a structured format. HR departments play a big role in this training. Formal training and development programs are in use, but much of the workplace learning takes place in *informal training*—unstructured, unplanned, and easily adapted for situations and individuals. In reality, most informal training is nothing other than employees helping each other out, sharing information, and solving work-related problems together. Thus, many managers are now supportive of what used to be considered "idle chatter."

Job Training   *On-the-job training* methods include job rotation, apprenticeships, understudy assignments, and formal mentoring programs. U.S. companies have been increasingly using longer-term job rotations to train managers for higher positions and foster collaboration.[68] But because on-the-job training methods often disrupt the workplace, organizations also invest in *off-the-job training*. The $130 billion figure we cited earlier for training was largely spent on the formal off-the-job variety, the most popular method being live classroom lectures. But it also encompasses public seminars, self-study programs, Internet courses, webinars, podcasts, and group activities that use role-plays and case studies. Larger organizations are increasingly building "corporate universities" to house formal training programs. The formal instruction given in the corporate university classes is often supplemented with informal online training.[69]

Computer-Based Training   The fastest-growing training medium is computer-based training, or e-training/e-learning.[70] E-learning systems emphasize learner control over the pace and content of instruction, allow e-learners to interact through online communities, and incorporate other techniques such as simulations and group discussions. Computer-based training that lets learners actively participate in exercises and quizzes can be more effective than traditional classroom instruction.[71] Employers can improve computer-based training

Off-the-job training at Chrysler's World Class Manufacturing Academy includes hands-on and classroom learning for engineers and plant employees that teaches them how to reduce waste and increase productivity and quality. Shown here is an employee using a human motion capture system in learning how to analyze the movements of assembly-line workers.
Source: Jim West/Alamy

by providing learners with regular prompts to set goals for learning, effective study strategies, and progress measurements toward the learning goals.[72] Organizations are even exploring delivering e-training through micro-lessons, on-the-spot tips, and learning games sent to mobile devices.[73]

Evaluating Effectiveness

The *effectiveness* of a training program can refer to the level of student satisfaction, the amount students learn, the extent to which they transfer the learned material to their jobs, and/or the company's financial return on investments in training.[74] These results are not always related. Some people who have a positive experience in an upbeat, fun class learn very little; some who learn a great deal have difficulty figuring out how to use their knowledge at work; and changes in employee behavior are sometimes not large enough to justify the expense of training. This means rigorous measurement of multiple training outcomes should be a part of every training effort.

The success of training also depends on the individual. If individuals are unmotivated, they will learn very little. What creates training motivation? Personality is important: Those with an internal locus of control, high conscientiousness, high cognitive ability, and high self-efficacy learn more. The climate also is important: People need to see how the training they're receiving is directly applicable to their jobs. Finally, after-training support from supervisors and coworkers has a strong influence on whether employees transfer their learning into new behavior.[75] For a training program to be effective, it must not just teach the skills, but also change the work environment to support the trainees.

Is there general evidence related to training, development practices, and organizational performance? A variety of studies show that investments in on-the-job training lead to increases in productivity of significantly greater value than the cost of providing the training.[76] Similarly, research indicated that cross-cultural training was effective in raising performance when the training was done after the person was working in a new country, but not when the training was conducted before departure to a new country.[77] The climate for employee development has also been related to business unit performance.[78] For example, one study of 260 companies in Korea found that training expenditures were positively related to corporate innovation.[79] Overall, most studies have shown that investments in training can indeed have positive effects at the aggregate level.

Performance Evaluation

17-5 List the methods of performance evaluation.

Would you study differently or exert a different level of effort for a college course graded on a pass–fail basis than for one that awarded letter grades A to F? Students typically tell us they study harder when letter grades are at stake. When they take a course on a pass–fail basis, they tend to do just enough to ensure a passing grade.

What applies in the college context also applies to employees at work. In this section, we show how the choice of a performance evaluation system and the way it's administered can influence employee behavior.

What Is Performance?

In the past, most organizations assessed only how well employees performed the tasks listed on a job description, but today's less hierarchical and more service-oriented organizations require more. Researchers now recognize three major types of behavior that constitute performance at work:

task performance The combination of effectiveness and efficiency at doing your core job tasks.

citizenship Actions that contribute to the psychological environment of the organization, such as helping others when not required.

counterproductivity Actions that actively damage the organization, including stealing, behaving aggressively toward coworkers, or being late or absent.

1. **Task performance.** Performance of the duties and responsibilities that contribute to the production of a good or service, or to administrative tasks. These include most of the tasks in a conventional job description.
2. **Citizenship.** Performance of actions that contribute to the psychological environment of the organization, such as helping others when not required, supporting organizational objectives, treating coworkers with respect, making constructive suggestions, and saying positive things about the workplace.
3. **Counterproductivity.** Behavior that actively damages the organization, including stealing, damaging company property, acting aggressively toward coworkers, and taking avoidable absences.

Most managers believe good performance means doing well on the first two dimensions and avoiding the third.[80] A person who does core job tasks very well but is rude and aggressive toward coworkers is not going to be considered a good employee in most organizations, and the most pleasant and upbeat worker who can't do the main job tasks well is not going to be a good employee either.

Purposes of Performance Evaluation

Performance evaluation serves a number of purposes.[81] One is to help management make general *human resource decisions* about promotions, transfers, and terminations. Evaluations also *identify training and development needs.* They *pinpoint employee skills and competencies* for which remedial programs can be developed. Finally, they *provide feedback to employees* on how the organization views their performance and are often the *basis for reward allocations,* including merit pay increases.

Because our interest is in OB, here we emphasize the performance evaluation as a mechanism for providing feedback and determining reward allocations.

What Do We Evaluate?

The criteria management chooses to evaluate will have a major influence on what employees do. The three most popular sets of criteria are individual task outcomes, behaviors, and traits.

Individual Task Outcomes If ends count rather than means, management should evaluate on outcomes such as quantity produced, scrap generated, and cost per unit of production for a plant manager, or on overall sales volume in the territory, dollar increase in sales, and number of new accounts established for a salesperson.

Behaviors It is difficult to attribute specific outcomes to the actions of employees in advisory or support positions whose work assignments are part of a group effort. We may readily evaluate the group's performance, but if it is hard to identify the contribution of each group member, management will often evaluate the employee's behavior. A plant manager might be evaluated on promptness in submitting monthly reports or leadership style, and a salesperson on average number of contact calls made per day or helpfulness toward other sales representatives.

Measured behaviors needn't be limited to those directly related to individual productivity. As we pointed out in discussing OCB (see Chapters 1 and 3), helping others, making suggestions for improvements, and volunteering for extra duties make work groups and organizations more effective and often are incorporated into evaluations of employee performance.

Behaviors such as helping children, assisting coworkers, and building trusting relationships with parents are important elements in evaluating the performance of employees working at this child daycare center in Leipzig, Germany. These subjective factors add to the center's reputation as a high-quality, safe, and respectful organization.

Source: Waltraud Grubitzsch/dpa picture alliance/Alamy

Traits   Having a good attitude, showing confidence, being dependable, staying busy, or possessing a wealth of experience can be desirable in the workplace, but it's important to remember they may not be highly correlated with positive task outcomes. However, we cannot ignore the reality that organizations still use such traits to assess job performance.

Who Should Do the Evaluating?

Who should evaluate an employee's performance? By tradition, the task has fallen to managers because they are held responsible for their employees' performance. But others may do the job better, particularly with the help of HR departments.

With many of today's organizations using self-managed teams, telecommuting, and other formats that distance bosses from employees, the immediate superior may not be the most reliable judge of an employee's performance. Peers and even subordinates are being asked to take part in the process, and employees are participating in their own evaluations. As you might expect, self-evaluations often suffer from overinflated assessment and self-serving bias, and they seldom agree with superiors' ratings.[82] They are probably better suited to developmental than evaluative purposes.

In most situations, it is highly advisable to use multiple sources of ratings; any individual performance rating may say as much about the rater as about the person being evaluated. By averaging across raters, we can obtain a more reliable, unbiased, and accurate performance evaluation.

Another popular approach to performance evaluation is the use of 360-degree evaluations.[83] These provide performance feedback from the employee's full circle of daily contacts, from subordinates to customers to bosses to peers (see Exhibit 17-2). The number of appraisals can be as few as 3 or 4 or as many as 25; most organizations collect 5 to 10 per employee.

What's the appeal of the 360-degree appraisal? By relying on feedback from people who know the employee well in a variety of contexts, organizations

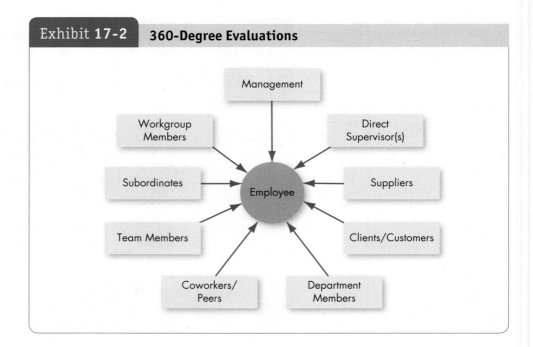

Exhibit 17-2   360-Degree Evaluations

hope to give everyone a sense of participation in the review process, increase employee accountability, and obtain more accurate readings on employee performance.

Evidence on its effectiveness is mixed.[84] The 360-degree evaluation provides employees with a wider perspective on their performance, but many organizations don't spend the time to train evaluators in giving constructive criticism. Some organizations allow employees to choose the peers and subordinates who evaluate them, which can artificially inflate feedback. There is a risk of giving too much weight to people who don't know much about the employee's actual performance. It's also difficult to reconcile disagreements between rater groups. There is clear evidence that peers tend to give much more lenient ratings than supervisors or subordinates, and also to make more errors in appraising performance. These evaluations may thus supplement an understanding of the consistency of an employee but should not supplant objective evaluations of performance.

Methods of Performance Evaluation

We've discussed *what* we evaluate and *who* should do the evaluating. Now we ask: *How* do we evaluate an employee's performance? What are the specific techniques for evaluation?

Written Essays   Probably the simplest method is to write a narrative describing an employee's strengths, weaknesses, past performance, potential, and suggestions for improvement. The written essay requires no complex forms or extensive training to complete. But a written appraisal may be determined as much by the evaluator's writing skill as by the employee's actual level of performance. It's also difficult to compare essays for different employees (or for the same employees written by different managers) because there is no standardized scoring key.

critical incidents   A way of evaluating the behaviors that are key in making the difference between executing a job effectively and executing it ineffectively.

graphic rating scales   An evaluation method in which the evaluator rates performance factors on an incremental scale.

behaviorally anchored rating scales (BARS)   Scales that combine major elements from the critical incident and graphic rating scale approaches. The appraiser rates the employees based on items along a continuum, but the points are examples of actual behavior on the given job rather than general descriptions or traits.

forced comparison   Method of performance evaluation where an employee's performance is made in explicit comparison to others (e.g., an employee may rank third out of 10 employees in her work unit).

group order ranking   An evaluation method that places employees into a particular classification, such as quartiles.

individual ranking   An evaluation method that rank-orders employees from best to worst.

Critical Incidents   **Critical incidents** focus the evaluator's attention on the difference between executing a job effectively and ineffectively. The appraiser describes what the employee did that was especially effective or ineffective in a situation, citing only specific behaviors. A list of such critical incidents provides a rich set of examples to show the employee desirable behaviors that call for improvement.

Graphic Rating Scales   One of the oldest and most popular methods of evaluation is **graphic rating scales**. The evaluator goes through a set of performance factors—such as quantity and quality of work, depth of knowledge, cooperation, attendance, and initiative—and rates each on incremental scales. The scales may specify, say, five points, where *job knowledge* might be rated 1 ("is poorly informed about work duties") to 5 ("has complete mastery of all phases of the job"). Although they don't provide the depth of information that essays or critical incidents do, graphic rating scales are less time consuming to develop and administer, and they allow for quantitative analysis and comparison.

Behaviorally Anchored Rating Scales   Behaviorally anchored rating scales (BARS) combine major elements from the critical incident and graphic rating scale approaches. The appraiser rates employees on items along a continuum, but the items are examples of actual behavior on the job rather than general descriptions or traits. To develop the BARS, participants first contribute specific illustrations of effective and ineffective behavior, which are translated into a set of performance dimensions with varying levels of quality.

Forced Comparisons   Forced comparisons evaluate one individual's performance against the performance of another or others. It is a relative rather than an absolute measuring device. The two most popular comparisons are group order ranking and individual ranking.

Group order ranking requires the evaluator to place employees into a particular classification, such as the top one-fifth or the second one-fifth. If a rater has 20 employees, only 4 can be in the top fifth, so, of course, 4 must also be relegated to the bottom fifth. This method is often used in recommending students to graduate schools.

The **individual ranking** approach rank-orders employees from best to worst. If the manager is required to appraise 30 employees, the difference between the 1st and 2nd employee is assumed to be the same as that between the 21st and 22nd. Some employees may be closely grouped, but no ties are permitted. The result is a clear ordering from the highest performer to the lowest.

One parallel to forced ranking is forced distribution of college grades. As shown in Exhibit 17-3, average GPAs have risen.[85] Although it is not clear exactly why, many attribute the rise to the popularity of student evaluations as a means of assessing professor performance (generous grades might produce higher student evaluations). It's also the case that higher grades can help students become more competitive candidates for graduate school and jobs.

In response to grade inflation, some colleges have instituted forced grade distributions, whereby professors must give a certain percentage of A's, B's, and C's. This is exactly what Princeton did; each department can give A's to no more than 35 percent of its students.

Improving Performance Evaluations

The performance evaluation process is a potential minefield. Evaluators can unconsciously inflate evaluations (positive leniency), understate performance

Exhibit 17-3   **Median Grade Point Average (GPA) by Academic Year and Degree Level**

Note: Study of GPA from 1,683 courses, 28 departments, and 3,176 instructors at a large public university.

Source: R. Todd Jewell, M. A. McPherson, and M. A. Tieslau, "Whose Fault Is It? Assigning Blame for Grade Inflation in Higher Education," *Applied Economics* 45 (2013): 1185–200.

(negative leniency), or allow the assessment of one characteristic to unduly influence the assessment of others (the halo error). Some appraisers bias their evaluations by unconsciously favoring people who have qualities and traits similar to their own (the similarity error). And some evaluators see the evaluation process as a political opportunity to overtly reward or punish employees they like or dislike. One review on performance appraisals demonstrates that many managers deliberately distort performance ratings in order to maintain a positive relationship with their subordinates or to achieve a positive image of themselves by showing that all their employees are performing well.[86] Although no protections *guarantee* accurate performance evaluations, the following suggestions can make the process more objective and fair.

Use Multiple Evaluators   As the number of evaluators increases, the probability of attaining more accurate information increases, as does the likelihood that the employee will accept the feedback as valid.[87] We often see multiple evaluators in competitions in such sports as diving and gymnastics. A set of evaluators judges a performance, the highest and lowest scores are dropped, and the final evaluation is made up of those remaining. The logic of multiple evaluators applies to organizations as well. If an employee has ten supervisors, of whom nine rated her excellent and one poor, we can safely discount the one poor evaluation. By moving employees around within the organization to gain a number of evaluations, or by using multiple assessors (as in 360-degree appraisals), we increase the probability of achieving more valid and reliable evaluations.

Evaluate Selectively   To increase agreement among evaluations, appraisers should evaluate the areas of performance for which they have working knowledge.[88] Appraisers should thus be as close as possible, in organizational level, to the individual being evaluated. The more levels that separate the evaluator from the employee, the less opportunity the evaluator has to observe the individual's behavior and, therefore, the greater the possibility for inaccuracies.

Train Evaluators   If you can't *find* good evaluators, *make* them. Training can produce more accurate raters.[89] Most rater training courses emphasize changing the raters' frame of reference by teaching them what to look for, so everyone in the organization defines *good performance* in the same way. Another effective training technique is to encourage raters to describe the employee's behavior in as much detail as possible. Asking for more detail encourages raters to remember more about the employee's performance, rather than just acting on their feelings about the employee at the moment.

Provide Employees with Due Process   The concept of *due process* can be applied to appraisals to increase the perception that employees are being treated fairly.[90] Three features characterize due process systems: (1) Individuals are provided with adequate notice of what is expected of them, (2) all evidence relevant to a proposed violation is aired in a fair hearing so the individuals affected can respond, and (3) the final decision is based on the evidence and free of bias.

One technique organizations might consider to enhance due process is posting appraisals online so employees can see their own performance scores exactly as the supervisor enters them. One company that did so found employees believed rater accountability and employee participation were higher when appraisal information was available online prior to appraisal interviews.[91] It might be that raters were more sensitive to providing accurate ratings when they knew employees would be able to see their own information directly.

Providing Performance Feedback

Few activities are more unpleasant for many managers than providing performance feedback to employees. In fact, unless pressured by organizational policies and controls, managers are likely to ignore this responsibility.

Why? First, even though almost every employee could stand to improve in some areas, managers fear confrontation when presenting negative feedback. Second, many employees do tend to become defensive when their weaknesses are pointed out. Instead of accepting the feedback as constructive and a basis for improving performance, some criticize the manager or redirect blame to someone else. Finally, employees tend to have an inflated assessment of their own performance. Statistically speaking, half of all employees must be below-average performers. But the average employee's estimate of his or her own performance level generally falls much higher. So even when managers are providing good news, employees are likely to perceive it as not good enough.

How do I fire someone?

One of the people who reports to me really isn't living up to his job responsibilities, and I'm afraid that I have to let him go. I have no idea how to approach him so the meeting will turn out okay. What's the best way to terminate him?
— *Ariana*

Dear Ariana:

Most supervisors agree that terminating a problem employee can be one of the hardest parts of management. In general, the number-one way to reduce the stress of firing is to avoid giving surprises. A problem employee needs to be told as soon as possible that there are issues with performance. Be sure to document performance problems early, and let your employee know the consequences of failing to improve. It may even be the case that identifying problems can eliminate the need for firing through initiating development strategies and providing training that may improve his performance.

If you've decided the termination needs to proceed, then begin to plan the termination meeting. Good HR guidance can be one of your best resources in this process. It's natural to be worried about how your employee is going to react, but here are some strategies that may help you end the employment relationship in a way that minimizes conflicts:

- *Ask your HR representatives what alternatives and techniques they'd recommend.* Many companies have established policies and procedures that will help you conduct this meeting in a professional manner.

- *Practice.* A chance to practice the meeting with a neutral party (*not* someone with connections to the person or your organization) will help you reduce stress and anticipate how the meeting will go.

- *Be sure to respect your employee during the process.* When possible, conduct the termination behind closed doors. Send a clear message that his employment is at an end. The last thing you want is a situation where he doesn't get the message or feels you are so indecisive that he can argue his way out of the termination. Attempts to "soften the blow" by providing positive feedback or working your way up to the bad news are often confusing and can create an opening for an extended, unpleasant, and unproductive argument.

- *Avoid going over past mistakes in detail.* At the point of termination, there is no reason to rehash old problems you've previously discussed—it's better to just make a clean statement that things aren't working out, and your documentation should have the details for later reference if needed. Going over the reasons the relationship is over will make your employee feel insulted or offended.

- *Have an after-meeting plan.* What are your organization's policies—does your employee need to be escorted immediately out of the building, for instance? What are the policies for returning business property? Demonstrate adherence to the plan to keep the termination process objective.

Of course, none of this advice can remove all the stress of terminations, but a combination of preparation, respect, and clarity can help make the situation better than it would be otherwise.

Sources: S. R. McDonnell, "10 Steps Needed to Properly Fire Someone," *Entrepreneur*, May 26, 2015, http://www.entrepreneur.com/article/246573; E Frauenheim, "Employee Crisis Communications 101," *Workforce*, November 13, 2013, http://www.workforce.com/articles/20036-employee-crisis-communications-101; and R. A. Mueller-Hanson and E. D. Pulakos, "Putting the 'Performance' Back in Performance Management," *SHRM-SIOP Science of HR White Paper Series*, 2015, http://www.shrm.org/Research/Documents/SHRM-SIOP%20Performance%20Management.pdf.

The solution to the problem is not to ignore it but to train managers to conduct constructive feedback sessions. An effective review—in which the employee perceives the appraisal as fair, the manager as sincere, and the climate as constructive—can leave the employee feeling upbeat, informed about areas needing improvement, and determined to correct them.[92] This is a perfect outcome if the evaluation is fair and thorough, but unfortunately an employee may feel this way in situations where the evaluator feels an interdependence with the employee and therefore is more lenient in the evaluation.[93]

It probably won't surprise you that employees in a bad mood are much less likely to take advice than employees in a good mood.[94] Appraisals should also be as specific as possible. People are most likely to overrate their own performance when asked about overall job performance, but they can be more objective when feedback is about a specific area.[95] It's also hard to figure out how to improve your performance globally—it's much easier to improve in specific areas. The performance review should be a counseling activity more than a judgment process, best accomplished by allowing it to evolve from the employee's self-evaluation.

International Variations in Performance Appraisal

Let's examine performance evaluation globally in the context of cultural dimensions, particularly individualism/collectivism.

Individual-oriented cultures such as the United States emphasize formal performance evaluation systems more than informal systems. They advocate written evaluations performed at regular intervals, the results of which managers share with employees and use in the determination of rewards. On the other hand, the collectivist cultures that dominate Asia and much of Latin America are characterized by more informal systems—downplaying formal feedback and disconnecting reward allocations from performance ratings. Some of these differences may be narrowing, however. In Korea, Singapore, and Japan, the use of performance evaluations has increased dramatically in the past decade, though not always smoothly or without controversy. One survey of Korean employees revealed that a majority questioned the validity of their performance evaluation results.[96]

One study focused on the banking industry found significant differences across countries in performance appraisal practices.[97] Formal performance appraisals were used more frequently in countries that were high in assertiveness, high in uncertainty avoidance, and low in in-group collectivism. In other words, assertive countries that see performance as an individual responsibility, and that desire certainty about where people stand, were more likely to use formal performance appraisals. On the other hand, in high uncertainty-avoidance cultures, performance appraisals were also used more frequently for communication and development purposes (as opposed to being used for rewards and promotion). Another study found that individuals who were high in power distance and high in collectivism tend to give more lenient performance appraisals.[98]

✪ TRY IT!

If your professor has assigned this, go to the Assignments section of **mymanagementlab.com** to complete the **Simulation: *HR*.**

The Leadership Role of HR

17-6 Describe the leadership role of HR in organizations.

We have discussed the important functions HR departments serve in recruiting, selection practices, training and development, and the performance evaluation process. Arguably, these are an organization's most important tasks in managing its most valuable asset—its people. However, HR also plays a key leadership role in nearly all facets of the workplace environment, from designing and administering benefit programs to conducting attitude surveys to drafting and enforcing employment policies. HR is on the front lines in managing adversarial employment conditions such as work–life conflicts, mediations, terminations, and layoffs. It is on the scene when an employee joins and leaves, and all along the way. HR departments uniquely represent both the employees' and the company's perspectives as needed, so we will discuss the importance of HR communication before each of the facets of HR leadership.

Companies have only recently begun to recognize the potential for HR to influence employee performance. Researchers have been examining the effects of a high-performance work system (HPWS), a group of "mutually reinforcing, overlapping, and synergistic individual human resource practices" that some organizations have been developing. A study of 163 Spanish companies suggests that an HPWS can especially increase performance when the organization has a learning culture.[99]

Communicating HR Practices

Leadership by HR begins with informing employees about HR practices and explaining the implications of decisions that might be made around these practices. It is not enough to simply have a practice in place; HR needs to let employees know about it. When a company successfully communicates how the whole system of HR practices has been developed and what function this system serves, employees feel they can control and manage what they get out of work.[100] We've noted in other chapters that knowing you can influence the outcomes of your work is highly motivational. Employees can come to see the HR philosophy and system as an employer's expression of concern, and the positive feelings that result have been shown to increase employee commitment, retention, and engagement.[101]

The evidence supporting the contribution of communication and perception to HR effectiveness is considerable. For example, one study of different business units within a large food-service organization found that employee perceptions of HR practices, rated at the workgroup level, were significant predictors of OCB, commitment, and intention to remain with the company,[102] but the HR practices led to these positive outcomes only if employees were aware they were in place. Other studies have found that HR practices have different effects depending on how employees perceive the reason for them.[103] Employees who think HR practices are established to improve performance and benefit workers reciprocate these feelings with greater commitment and performance. Employees who think these same practices are established to exploit workers do not have the same positive reactions.

The effectiveness of HR practices also depends on employee attitudes. One review found that HR practices were more likely to lead to positive outcomes when employees felt motivated.[104] Other research indicated that employees who were more knowledgeable about the purpose of a performance management system used the system more effectively to improve their efficiency and effectiveness.[105] Taken together, these results suggest that it isn't enough for employers to simply set up practices—they need to show the practices are actually attempts to make the company more successful and help employees achieve better outcomes. Leadership communication can help shape employee attitudes and perceptions about HR practices.

Practices tend to be perceived differently in various business cultures. For example, the use of educational qualifications in screening candidates seems to be a universal practice, but aside from this, different countries emphasize different selection techniques. Structured interviews are popular in some countries and nonexistent in others. Research shows that across the Netherlands, the United States, France, Spain, Portugal, and Singapore, most applicants prefer interviews and work sample tests and dislike the use of personal contacts and integrity tests.[106] There was little variation in preferences across these countries. In other words, it appears that even if there are international differences in practices, there are not as many international differences in what employees consider fair. Communication is the bridge for HR to demonstrate fairness intentions.

Designing and Administering Benefit Programs

As we've seen throughout this text, employers are more willing than ever to consider an infinite range of benefits to offer employees in efforts to recruit and retain the best talent. For every issue facing workers—health, child care, aging parents, education, workplace conditions, and others—there exists a potential benefit organizations may consider to meet the need. The responsibility for designing and administering an organization's benefit program falls to the HR department, with input from executive management.

Ideally, a benefit program should be uniquely suited to the organizational culture, reflect the values of the organization, demonstrate economic feasibility, and be sustainable in the long term. Such benefits will likely improve employees' psychological well-being and therefore increase organizational performance.[107]

Consider employees who are mothers of infant children. Benefit options HR might consider could range from support to intolerance. Should the company give paid time off for working mothers to breast-feed their babies? Should it provide a break room for mothers to breast-feed their babies at work? Should it allow mothers to pump milk at work to give to babies at home? What about mothers who are bottle-feeding? Federal laws do not require companies to provide any accommodation for breast-feeding mothers beyond an undefined "reasonable break time," and a case in Texas originally ruled against a woman who was fired for asking to use the back room to pump milk for her child.[108] While that case was settled out of court after the Court of Appeals reversed the decision, stating it was a sex discrimination case and a medical condition, the issue is not definitive.[109] An HR manager in a company that produces lactation pumps, supports La Leche League International, and employs women of child-bearing age may want to offer some benefit because the policies would agree with the company's principles. An HR manager in a company whose mission is unrelated to the issue may explore providing some benefit upon employee requests. Each manager may then perform an analysis of the costs associated with providing different levels of benefits, along with the positive organizational outcomes for each, to determine which benefit would be sustainable for the company long-term. Of course, this is just one example of possible benefits to consider, and it applies only to a segmented group of workers. Other benefits may affect a larger population of your workforce, such as health care options and vacation benefits.

Drafting and Enforcing Employment Policies

Along with benefits come responsibilities, and employees need to know what the organization expects from them. Employment policies that are informed by current laws but go beyond minimum requirements will help define a positive organizational culture. Policies differ from benefits in that they provide the guidelines for behavior, not just the working conditions. A company might provide the benefit of a special break room for mothers of young children, but a policy is needed to outline the expectation for conduct. May mothers elect to feed their babies in other places in the facility, or only in the break room? What timing is acceptable? Where can collected breast milk be stored? Establishing policies to address potential questions can help minimize confusion and awkwardness for all employees.

HIV/AIDS and the Multinational Organization

It wasn't long ago that an AIDS diagnosis was a death sentence, and the ethical choices for HR departments were about offering palliative care and death benefits. Thankfully, those days are gone, at least for most. Now the ethical choice is about the standards of care and support organizations want to provide, for which employees worldwide, and for how long. "There has been an uptick with those employed that have HIV/AIDS" as the disease has become more chronic than fatal, said Randy Vogenberg of the Institute for Integrated Healthcare. However, whether someone can continue working still depends upon drug therapy, workplace accommodations, and employee education. In most countries, standards are not specifically mandated, leaving employers to choose the level of support to offer. "It's not a question of whether a business is going to be confronted with this," labor law attorney Peter Petesch says. "It's a question of how soon."

By current estimates, more than 1.2 million people in the United States and 36.9 million people globally live with HIV. Over two-thirds of HIV infections are in sub-Saharan Africa, and 70 percent of new cases are in this region. Worldwide, there is little consistency in the approach to the problem. Few U.S. companies have specific HIV/AIDS policies, for example, and although benefit plans cover the illness, employees' out-of-pocket costs for the expensive drug therapy can range significantly. HIV/AIDS treatment is available in Europe through the national health care system. Some larger African companies run clinics where national health care or insurance is insufficient, but not all companies offer insurance. In India and China, insurers do not cover HIV/AIDS, so companies need to consider separate employee reimbursement to match their intentions for coverage.

When it comes to HIV/AIDS, an ounce of prevention is worth a pound of cure, or more literally, dramatic corporate savings. Research found that the investment companies made in preventing the disease from spreading and in treating infected employees saved money and lives. HR initiatives like providing peer educators to teach employees about prevention and accommodation, free counseling services, free voluntary testing, and well-being monitoring have been effective worldwide.

"Nobody needs to die of this disease anymore," said Jenni Gillies, head of business development for beer brewer SABMiller, which has 70,000 employees in 75 countries and is committed to helping eradicate HIV/AIDS through employee education and support. But there are costs and responsibilities associated with each decision about the level of care to support or supply, and the distance companies should go to meet this need over other employee needs will be a constant question. Some organizations may conclude that governments and other systems are responsible for the care of citizens. It's a tough call. Meanwhile, individual managers can assist in preventing discrimination and encouraging education.

Sources: "HIV/AIDS Basics Statistics," Center for Disease Control, http://www.cdc.gov/hiv/statistics/basics.html, accessed July 21, 2015; J. Mooney, "People with HIV and AIDS: Living and Working Longer," *HR Magazine,* June 2012, 41–44; SABMiller corporate website, "Inside View" page, www.insideview.com/directory/sabmiller-plc, accessed June 18, 2013; and World Health Organization, "HIV/AIDS" fact page, http://www.who.int/mediacentre/factsheets/fs360/en/, updated July 2015.

The lactation case is an example of a potential benefit and policy combination that will ensure employees recognize the benefit as an employer's aid to their well-being while understanding how and where to use it. However, any policy must have enforcement to be effective. HR managers are responsible for setting the organizational consequences of infractions and often for enforcing policies as well.

Sometimes, HR managers will need to take action even when the employee's direct manager may not agree, especially if compliance with the law is at issue. For example, many companies in the entertainment, nonprofit, publishing, and marketing industries use unpaid post-college interns, who are supposed to receive on-the-job experience as compensation. The Labor Department stipulates that interns who are unpaid must be provided a vocational education experience and that their work cannot profit the employer. Interns report getting stuck doing menial tasks an employer would need to pay someone else to do. If these companies want to continue using unpaid interns, HR managers need to set policies that clarify the assignments supervisors can give and then ensure the policies are followed. Otherwise, their organizations will face lawsuits like the one from Eric Glatt, an intern on the movie *Black Swan*, who sued for minimum wage violations.[110] A judge in the U.S. District Court ruled that he was improperly cataloged as an intern.[111] The decision cited criteria from the Labor Department wherein an unpaid internship must provide work similar to training the person would receive in a school, benefit the intern not the employer, and not displace other employees.[112] This ruling sparked similar claims against NBC Universal, Fox, Viacom, and other large organizations, often ending in out-of-court settlements. The issue is far from conclusive, however, leaving the burden on interns to litigate if they are unfairly treated. See Case Incident 1 for discussion on the role of interns from a different perspective: Yours.

Managing Work–Life Conflicts

We introduced work–life balance in Chapter 1 and discussed the blurring lines between work life and personal life. Here, we specifically focus on what organizations can do to help employees reduce conflicts.

Work–life conflicts grabbed management's attention in the 1980s, largely as a result of the increased entry into the workforce of women with dependent children. In response, most major organizations took actions to make their workplaces more family-friendly.[113] They introduced onsite child care, summer

Myth or Science?

The 24-Hour Workplace Is Harmful

This statement appears to be true in many cases. Although technology makes it possible for employees to be plugged in all the time, in constant contact around the globe, research suggests that employers who push employees to check in at all hours and stay connected may well be doing themselves (and their employees) a disservice.

A growing body of research has uncovered serious health consequences of insufficient sleep, and work practices that encourage employees to be plugged in 24 hours per day may be making the situation worse. One study examined how late-night work influenced job outcomes by having employees complete diary surveys on their sleep and engagement at work over multiple days. Those who used smartphones at night for work were less engaged in their work tasks the next day, even after accounting for other technology use.

From another angle, researchers have looked at the personal consequences of "workaholism," which is the tendency to think constantly about work off the job and to feel compelled to work excessive hours. This habit is associated with higher levels of burnout, stress, and family problems. While workaholism is partially driven by personality factors, surveys suggest that features of the workplace itself can enhance workaholic tendencies, including excessive workloads, conflicting work priorities, and time pressures. The employee may not immediately perceive these effects, since workaholics are often highly committed to their work and enjoy it in the short term, until burnout occurs.

The key to maintaining performance over time may lie in developing psychological detachment from work. Alongside studies showing the negative effects of overexposure to work demands we can place another body of work showing that short regular breaks made

up of total rest and avoidance of work responsibilities can recharge a person's energy. Unplugging from constant work demands for short periods actually makes us much more productive over the long haul. Therefore the evidence is clear: unplug to recharge yourself. HR can support this effort by presenting the research findings to managers and helping to establish practices and boundaries that benefit everyone.

Sources: K. Lanaj, R. E. Johnson, and C. M. Barnes, "Beginning the Workday Yet Already Deprived? Consequences of Late-Night Smartphone Use and Sleep," *Organizational Behavior and Human Decision Processes* 124 (May 2014): 11–23; M. A. Clark, J. S. Michel, L. Zhdanova, S. Y. Pui, and B. B. Baltes, "All Work and No Play? A Meta-Analytic Examination of the Correlates and Outcomes of Workaholism," *Journal of Management,* February 2014, doi: 10.1177/0149206314522301; S. Sonnentag and C. Fritz, "Recovery from Job Stress: The Stressor-Detachment Model as an Integrative Framework," *Journal of Organizational Behavior* 36 (2015): S72–S103.

day camps, flextime, job sharing, leaves for school functions, telecommuting, and part-time employment. But organizations quickly realized work–life conflicts were not limited to female employees with children. Heavy workloads and increased travel demands, for instance, made it increasingly hard for male workers and women without children to meet both work and personal responsibilities. A Boston College survey of nearly 1,000 fathers with professional careers showed that participants put more importance on job security and flexible, family-friendly working schedules than on high income and advancement opportunities.[114]

Organizations are modifying their workplaces with scheduling options and benefits to accommodate the varied needs of a diverse workforce. Employees at NestléPurina can bring their dogs into the office; SAS Institute has onsite child care, a health care center, and a fitness center; and other firms offer perks ranging from onsite laundry to food services to free child care.[115] Colgate-Palmolive, number one in 2015 on *Forbes'* Best Companies for Work-Life Balance list, offers emergency in-home care for dependents and professional counseling services to help employees stay on the job.[116] Exhibit 17-4 lists some other initiatives to help employees reduce work–life conflicts.

Time pressures aren't the primary problem underlying work–life conflicts.[117] The psychological incursion of work into the family domain—and vice versa—leaves people worrying about personal problems at work and thinking about work problems at home, creating conflict. This suggests organizations should spend less effort helping employees with time-management issues and more effort helping them clearly segment their lives. Keeping workloads reasonable, reducing work-related travel, and offering onsite high-quality child care are examples of practices that can help in this endeavor. Employees can also reduce interference between work and home by increasing the amount of planning they do.[118]

Not surprisingly, people differ in their preference for scheduling options and benefits.[119] Some prefer organizational initiatives that better segment work from their personal lives, as flextime, job sharing, and part-time hours do by allowing employees to schedule work hours less likely to conflict with personal responsibilities. Others prefer initiatives to integrate work and personal life, such as gym facilities and company-sponsored family picnics. On average, most people prefer an organization that provides support for work–life balance. A study found that potential employees, particularly women, are more attracted to organizations that have a reputation for supporting employee work–life balance.[120]

⊙ WATCH IT!

If your professor has assigned this, go to the Assignments section of **mymanagementlab.com** to complete the video exercise titled *Patagonia: Human Resource Management*.

Mediations, Terminations, and Layoffs

HR departments often take center stage when unpleasant events such as disputes, substandard performance, and downsizing occur. Employees need to be able to trust their HR professionals to maintain appropriate confidentiality and a balanced perspective. Managers need to be able to trust HR, too, to know the laws and represent the company's perspective. The HR

Exhibit 17-4	Work–Life Initiatives	
Time based strategies	• Flextime • Job sharing • Leave for new parents • Telecommuting • Paid time off	Management consulting firm A. T. Kearney's Success with Flex program allows for schedule adjusments, telecommuting, and "hybird" positions. At biopharmaceutical firm AbbVie, 98% of employees use a flextime schedule. Cisco provides job-sharing and videoconferencing facilities to minimize needs for travel away from family. Deloitte offers employees 3–6 months sabbatical at 40% salary, and they have 40 paid days off per year.
Information based strategies	• Work–life support • Relocation assistance • Elder care resources • Counseling services	Blue Cross Blue Shield of North Carolina provides networking opportunities to remote workers. Hallmark offers employees monthly meetings to talk about career management for women. Johnson and Johnson promotes weekends free of e-mail. Hewlett-Packard offers counselors, mentors, and $5,000 annual tuition aid.
Money-based strategies	• Insurance subsidies • Flexible benefits • Adoption assistance • Discounts for child care tuition • Direct financial assistance • Domestic partner benefits • Scholarships, tuition reimbursement	Accenture offers a $5,000 adoption assistance benefit. Carlson offers employees scholarships of up to $20,000 to attend the University of Minnesota's Carlson School of Management. Citi employees can save up to $5,000 per year in pretax dependent care accounts, with a match of up to 30% from the company. Colgate-Palmolive provides up to $10,000 per year in annual tuition aid for job-related courses. Prudential employees who are caregivers can use 100 hours of dependent backup care and six hours of geriatric care management services annually.
Direct services	• Onsite child care • Fitness center • Summer child care • Onsite conveniences • Concierge services • Free or discounted company products	Abbott provides a child-care center that serves 800 and discounts for 2,800 day care facilities. Comparies like AOL and Verizon have onsite fitness centers and discounts at gyms nationwide. Bristol-Myers Squibb offers full-time, part-time, and backup care for kids up to age 5 and summer camps for older children. Turner Broadcasting offers a caregiver concierge to arrange babysiting, dog walking, and elder companions. REI employees can participate in a program that offers large discounts on company products.
Culture-change strategies	• Establishing work–life balanced culture; training managers to help employees deal with work–life conflicts • Tie manager pay to employee satisfaction • Focus on employees' actual performance, not "face time"	At American Express, employee networks have been established to address issues directly. Investment firm Robert W. Baird's CEO Paul Purcell has one rule: "There are no a**holes here." W. L. Gore & Associates company slogan reads, "We don't manage people, we expect people to manage themselves." Pearson developed a Flexible Work Options Accountability Guide that trains managers in the use of flextime for their employees.

Sources: "2014 100 Best Companies," *Working Mother*, http://www.workingmother.com/best-company-list/156592, accessed July 21, 2015; "100 Best Companies to Work For," *CNNMoney*, www.money.cnn.com, accessed June 18, 2013.

professional should be well trained in mediation techniques and rely upon company policies to seek positive resolutions. Sometimes, HR managers are integral to the termination process, when employees are not able to resolve issues with management. Termination processes are subject to union labor contracts and laws, which can confound the situation. In Spain, for instance, labor laws have traditionally protected older workers with near-guaranteed employment.[121]

For departing employees, the HR department is often the last stop on their way out the door. HR managers are thus in charge of leaving a favorable impression with the employee and collecting helpful input from the exit interview. This is never truer than when organizations terminate employees in layoffs. Employees who think the layoff process was handled fairly are more apt to recommend the company to others and to return to work if asked.[122] Employees who survive a layoff and stay employed with the company also evaluate the fairness of the downsizing process, according to another study, particularly in individualistic countries. Downsizing organizations that are able to demonstrate fairness are therefore more likely to realize the financial gains they hoped for.[123]

In sum, the role of HR is increasing in organizations worldwide, and top management is realizing human resource leadership is needed to create the cultures and positive business outcomes top corporations need to stay competitive.

Summary

An organization's human resource (HR) policies and practices create important forces that greatly influence organizational behavior (OB) and important work outcomes. HR departments have become increasingly integral in shaping the composition of the organization's workforce. First, as more organizations have turned to internal recruitment methods, HR departments have taken the lead in creating online portals and other easy-access methods for candidates to learn about the organization and be attracted to apply. Second, HR departments are involved in all phases of selection: initial selection, substantive selection, and contingent selection. The greatest increase in the involvement of HR in selection may be in the initial selection phase, wherein HR professionals develop, monitor, and screen the great numbers of applications that are submitted. However, HR involvement has increased in all areas of selection, and HR professionals are responsible for understanding the applicable laws and guidelines to serve as an informed, up-to-date resource for managers.

In effective organizations, HR remains present throughout an employee's time with the organization. HR departments create and administer training and development programs, and they set policies and practices with top management that govern the performance evaluation system. HR serves in a leadership capacity with responsibilities including the need to regularly communicate practices to employees, design and administer benefit programs, manage work-life conflicts, and conduct mediations, terminations, and layoffs. HR should bring an awareness of ethical issues to all stages of an individual's experience with the organization. Knowledgeable HR professionals are therefore a great resource to all levels of the organization, from top management to managers to employees.

Implications for Managers

- An organization's selection practices can identify competent candidates and accurately match them to the job and the organization. Consider assessment methods that are most likely to evaluate the skills directly needed for jobs you are looking to fill.

- Use training programs for your employees to achieve direct improvement in the skills necessary to successfully complete the job. Employees who are motivated will use those skills for their greater productivity.
- Training and development programs offer ways to achieve new skill levels and thus add value to your organization. Successful training and development programs include an ethical component.
- Use performance evaluations to assess an individual's performance accurately and as a basis for allocating rewards. Make sure the performance evaluations are as fair as possible. As demonstrated in Chapter 7's discussion of equity theory, evaluations perceived as unfair can result in reduced effort, increased absenteeism, or a search for another job.
- Give your employees the opportunity to participate in their evaluations so they understand the performance criteria and engage with the improvement process.

 PERSONAL INVENTORY ASSESSMENTS

Positive Practices Survey

Take this PIA to learn more about positive practices you can use today and in the future.

Employers Should Check Applicant Criminal Backgrounds

POINT

Depending on where you live, you may have been asked about your criminal arrest record on a job application. Even if you weren't asked outright, the company may have investigated anyway by using a background check service. Surveys suggest that nearly 70 percent of companies do some sort of criminal background check on job applicants. When so many are using the same basic strategy, it's likely they have a good reason.

Companies check criminal records for many purposes. Most obviously, nothing predicts future criminal behavior like prior criminal behavior. Many employees have used the access and privileges of their jobs to commit crimes, ranging from theft to assault or even murder. A check of their criminal records may have helped screen out these individuals.

As Lucia Bone, founder of the nonprofit Sue Weaver Cause, says, "It is the employer's responsibility to protect both their business, their employees, and their customers." This is a deeply meaningful issue for Bone. The organization she founded is named after her sister, Sue Weaver, murdered by a man with a criminal record who had access to her home to clean air ducts. Many hiring managers check criminal backgrounds specifically because they do not want their own lack of diligence to lead to similarly tragic outcomes.

Besides signaling the direct risk of criminal activity on the job, criminal records may be good behavioral indicators of other deviant workplace behavior. People who are willing to violate social conventions in one area may well be likely to violate them in others. When employers screen for use of illegal drugs or shoplifting arrests, they are trying to identify people who might lie to supervisors or embezzle money. Information gathered from criminal records is likely to be more objective and accurate than a manager's gut feelings about who is going to pose a problem in the future.

COUNTERPOINT

According to sociologist Devah Pager, the high U.S. incarceration rate means employers' hiring decisions have major labor market and social implications if based on criminal records. Koch Industries has stopped asking applicants about criminal records. CEO Charles Koch notes, "If ex-offenders can't get a job, education, or housing, how can we possibly expect them to have a productive life?" Koch's concern is valid. One study linked a young-adult arrest record to lower incomes and education levels later in life, and a conviction record to even lower levels.

There are also substantial racial and ethnic group differences in arrest rates, and men are much more likely to have arrest and conviction records than women. The Equal Employment Opportunity Commission (EEOC) concludes that excluding individuals with criminal records from jobs effectively discriminates against African American men in particular.

Furthermore, criminal background checks don't necessarily give employers the information they seek. A core principle of modern criminal justice holds that we all are innocent until proven guilty. However, some screens will turn up both conviction and arrest records. This is problematic because fewer than half of arrests end in conviction. While the use of arrest records is prohibited in many localities, that is far from a universal rule. Other investigations have found that online criminal records checks are prone to false positives, reporting that someone has a criminal past who really doesn't.

Another problem is lack of relevance. While many would agree that a person convicted of assault is not a good candidate for work that requires carrying a weapon or associating with vulnerable populations, it's less clear how a petty-theft conviction might raise the same concerns. Sociologist Christopher Uggen summarizes by observing, "We haven't really figured out what a disqualifying offense should be for particular activities."

Sources: B. Appelbaum, "Out of Trouble, but Criminal Records Keep Men out of Work," *New York Times,* February 28, 2015, http://www.nytimes.com/2015/03/01/business/out-of-trouble-but-criminal-records-keep-men-out-of-work .html?_r=0; C. Zillman, "Koch Industries Stops Asking Job Candidates about Their Criminal Records," *Fortune,* April 27, 2015, http://fortune.com/2015/04/27/koch-industries-stops-asking-job-candidates-about-their-criminal-records/; and G. Fields and J. R. Emshwiller, "As Arrest Records Rise, Americans Find Consequences Can Last a Lifetime," *Wall Street Journal,* August 18, 2014, http://www.wsj.com/articles/as-arrest-records-rise-americans-find-consequences-can-last-a-lifetime-1408415402.

CHAPTER REVIEW

MyManagementLab

Go to **mymanagementlab.com** to complete the problems marked with this icon.

QUESTIONS FOR REVIEW

17-1 What is the value of various recruitment methods?

17-2 What are the methods of initial selection?

17-3 What are the most useful methods of substantive selection?

17-4 What are the similarities and differences among the main types of training?

17-5 What are the methods of performance evaluation?

17-6 What are the various roles of HR in the leadership of organizations?

EXPERIENTIAL EXERCISE Designing an Effective Structured Job Interview

Break up into groups of two or three people each. Each group collaborates to write a short interview questionnaire for evaluating a job candidate.

Step 1: Start by considering the core job tasks of a pharmaceutical sales representative who markets medicines directly to care providers (doctors' offices, nursing homes, and hospitals). Together come up with a list of the three most important things you think this person needs to do on the job. You can look up a job description online for more detail. Don't describe personal characteristics an individual should *have* ("needs to be hardworking and friendly"). Instead, focus on the three most important tasks the representative *does* on the job.

Step 2: Next, write down one core skill or ability that would help someone do each task. Think about what a person could naturally be good at (an ability or personality trait) and what the person would know through practice and instruction (knowledge and skills).

Step 3: Now develop three questions you would ask a candidate (one for each task) to assess whether he or she has the ability, personality, knowledge, or skills to do the job. Remember to ask questions that get at the very specific core skills/abilities you have described for that task. Try writing at least one question about something the person has done in the past, and at least one about something

the person would do if faced with a situation on the job. For example, you could start the question about the past with "Tell me about a time you had to…," and start the question about what the person would do with "Imagine you're in the following situation. Tell me what you'd do."

Step 4: The last part of your structured job interview is developing a scoring key to help the interviewer rate different responses. Don't just rate answers from "1 = very good" to "3 = very bad." Instead, rate answers in a way that is as objective and specific as possible.

To help you with this process, the following is a structured job interview questionnaire that relates to keeping track of inventory in a retail sales job. It illustrates each step of the process, but for just one task.

Example Step 1: Task: Greeting customers.

Example Step 2: Skill or ability required: Social skill in making others feel welcome.

Example Step 3: "Tell me about a time when you've had to get to meet a new person," or, "Imagine you're just meeting a customer. What would you do to help this person feel at ease?"

Example Step 4: The scoring key for the "tell me about a time…" question might be: 1 = describes meeting new people as uncomfortable, 2 = describes situation where a new introduction went well after a while,

3 = describes situation where meeting a new person went very well. The scoring key for the "imagine you're just meeting…" question might be: 1 = isn't sure what to do, 2 = would say hello and leave customer alone, 3 = would say hello, ask what customer wants, and try to help meet those needs.

Class discussion

After all the groups have written their questions, get together and discuss your steps. Was this an easy process? What might be the advantages of writing interview questions and scoring keys in advance like this, compared to a more informal conversational approach? Are there any disadvantages to the more structured approach? If so, what are they?

ETHICAL DILEMMA Are On-Demand Workers Really Employees?

The ascendancy of Uber and Lyft was both rapid and widespread. Over the course of a few years, these rideshare companies leveraged the ready availability of mobile technology to create a new type of service that was faster and more convenient for many passengers than calling a taxi dispatch office.

Rideshare systems link people in search of rides with people who sign up to drive their own cars. In fact, the drivers registered with rideshare firms not only use their own cars; they also pay all maintenance and insurance costs. There are no time cards, supervisors, career paths, or health insurance arrangements, because the companies have not considered the drivers as employees at all. Instead, they are independent contractors, members of the "sharing economy" that links them to online work portals for one-off interactions with customers. Other organizations, such as the delivery service Postmates, Amazon's Mechanical Turk, and Handy Cleaning Service, have adopted the same model.

A series of ongoing lawsuits asks whether these companies are actually treating contractors like employees. Legally, an employer cannot formally evaluate the performance or direct the work activities of an independent contractor. However, there are some ways in which these companies do exercise control. Uber, for example, has documented cases in which its drivers were "deactivated" because their online customer reviews were too low. Hours are only somewhat flexible because drivers have been told they will be suspended if they accept fewer than 90 percent of the rides sent to them. Evaluating work quality and hours worked both fall on the side of employment rather than independent contractor relationships.

What is at stake? Rules and regulations that cover employees go beyond protections offered to independent contractors. For example, independent contractors do not receive the workers' compensation, overtime wage premiums, health care, paid time off, or mandatory minimum wage coverage that extends to employees. Employers also bear significant tax and legal liabilities for employees that don't apply to their hiring of independent contractors. Some advocates argue that drivers may have much to gain if they can be classified as employees, because it will bring stability and predictability to their work.

The social and ethical consequences of the sharing economy are only beginning to be considered. Organizations that have been built on the sharing economy will all have to face questions about how their policies affect the willingness of the workers they rely on.

Questions

17-7. What would you advise HR departments to do about the ethical dilemma organizations like Uber and Lyft face?

17-8. How might changes in the legal employment status of drivers affect companies like Uber and Lyft? Do you think these organizations would be able to survive in relation to their competition of, say, traditional taxi companies?

17-9. To what degree do you think employers have a responsibility to these independent contractors? What changes might these organizations consider regardless of legal requirements, if you feel there is an ethical obligation that remains unfulfilled?

Sources: A. Griswold, "Are Uber Drivers Employees?" *Slate,* March 12, 2015; R. Silverman, "Uber, Lyft Cases Focus on Drivers' Legal Status," *Wall Street Journal,* March 15, 2015; and R Weiner and L. DePillis, "How Congress Can Make Life Better for Uber Drivers and Bike Messengers," *Washington Post,* June 3, 2015, http://www.washingtonpost.com/local/virginia-politics/how-congress-can-make-life-better-for-uber-drivers/2015/06/03/621d89f4-09f8-11e5-9e39-0db921c47b93_story.html.

CASE INCIDENT 1 Who Are You?

Today, we all seem to be very concerned with who we are. "Who am I?" Oprah asked herself, as she has asked others for years when interviewing. We tend to ask this question often as we compete with others 24/7. In fact, the competition seems to have grown fiercer as students try to edge their foot inside the doors of top organizations. This is definitely the case in Beirut, Lebanon, a developing country in the Middle East and North African Area (MENA), where successful companies begin with interview screening, having done an initial background check (sometimes without the applicant's consent) in order to monitor whether the candidates did well in university, were successful in the local or regional market, or had a criminal record.

Today, job applicants are aware of "impression management" and the importance of perception. How important is a candidate's appearance? For instance, the highly competitive local market in Lebanon adheres to the French tradition in terms of mannerism and dress code. Managers and employees alike adhere to a custom that favors bright, attractive, very fashionably dressed personnel. As such, before they went to be interviewed at Byblos Bank, a leading domestic multinational bank, Zeina Samaha spent a small fortune on cosmetic surgery, whereas Josiane El Khoury spent it on her briefcase, suit, shoes, and jewelry. Even though they had both graduated with distinction from university and had shown professional competence in their previous job, they understood that appearance played a crucial role in the business world. These issues also influenced Joseph Boustany, the human resource manager at a trendy clothing shop on the Jounieh shopping strip of Kaslik. Before being interviewed at Zara, the hip Spanish clothes shop at the ABC Mall in Aschrafieh, Joseph went over the company's history and the job description; then he thought through the upcoming interview and mulled over his dress code before he bought a fashionable trendy suit, tie, and jewelry.

Questions

⭐17-10. People in general spend a fortune to improve their physical image as well as their résumé. Do you think candidates eliminate competition when improving their personal image?

17-11. What is the extent of candidates' control in terms of "dressing up" their résumé and letters of recommendation? In effect, how much latitude do companies give when they assess candidates' portfolios?

⭐17-12. Is it ethical that potential employers have the right to carry out an assessment of the candidate's past?

Sources: R. Feintzeig and M. Korn, "Internships Go under the Microscope," *Wall Street Journal*, April 23, 2014, B7; L. Gellman, "Diving into the Intern Pool before Starting at B-School," *Wall Street Journal*, February 5, 2014, B7; C. Zillman, "Unpaid Interns Have Their Day in Court—Again," *Fortune*, January 29, 2015, http://fortune.com/2015/01/29/unpaid-internships-legal-battle/.

CASE INCIDENT 2 Indentured Doctors

Brazil abolished slavery in 1888, but in 2013 a new wave of workers, dubbed by many as slaves belonging to Cuba, arrived in Brazil. But these 5,400 had little in common with the estimated 4 million slaves working on plantations in Brazil when they finally won their freedom all those years ago. Under an agreement signed between Cuba and Brazil, the workers were in fact trained doctors.

The deal was worth an estimated US $225 million to Cuba in hard currency. The doctors would work for three years for the hard-pressed and undermanned Brazilian health service. The deal was in response to widespread unrest across Brazil at the poor state of the health service. In poorer regions that had no doctors, the influx of new doctors allowed many health centers to reopen.

For many years, Cuba has been providing doctors to countries that shared its ideological beliefs. Now the export of doctors is for a more prosaic reason: cash. In exchange for preferential deals in oil, Cuba has sent an estimated 30,000 health workers to Venezuela. Under the terms of the Barrio Adentro plan, Cuban workers operate in many of the shanty towns surrounding Caracas. At home, Cuban doctors can earn a maximum monthly salary of US $50. Even with the bulk of their pay going to the Cuba government, the doctors can still earn more abroad.

Despite the misgivings of many Brazilians, in most areas, the arrival of the Cuban doctors signals that the Brazilian government is actually trying to do something about the healthcare. Cuba, it seems, has plenty of doctors to spare; they have an estimated 6.7 per 1,000 people, compared to just 1.9 in Brazil.

Brazil pays the Cuban doctors US $4,300 per month. However, 80 percent of that goes to the Cuban government. The doctors receive less than half of the remaining pay (in cash in Brazil); the rest is passed on the doctor's family in Cuba. The doctors are provided with free board and lodging but are not allowed to bring their families with them to Brazil.

The deals have drawn enormous criticism from many different quarters. Many point to the fact that this form of indentured labor has more to do with Cuba's inability to pay for infrastructure and other projects than humanitarian concern for the sick in Brazil. Brazilian businesses have renovated a Cuban port at a cost of US $600 million and a further US $200 million was spent on improving Cuban airports. The export of Cuban doctors is seen as a means by which the Cuban government can pay for these investments.

Critics allege that the doctor's passports are taken from them, that Cuba maintains surveillance on them, and that a huge proportion of their pay is withheld. All of this is claimed to be in breach of the Trafficking in Persons Protocol and the International Labor Organization's Convention on the Protection of Wages.

Questions

17-13. Are these Cuban doctors little more than modern-day slaves?

17-14. In the absence of complaints from Cuban doctors, is there really a case to answer?

17-15. Why might the doctors be reluctant to return to Cuba?

Sources: "Cuban Doctors Tend to Brazil's Poor, Giving Rousseff a Boost," Reuters, http://www.reuters.com/article/2013/12/01/us-brazil-doctors-cuba-idUSBRE9B005720131201, accessed January 24, 2014; "Brazil Forging Economic Ties with Cuba, While Hiring Its Doctors," *New York Times.* http://www.nytimes.com/2013/12/30/world/americas/brazil-forging-economic-ties-with-cuba-while-hiring-its-doctors.html?_r=0, accessed January 24, 2014.

MyManagementLab

Go to **mymanagementlab.com** for the following Assisted-graded writing questions:

17-16. Based on your own experiences, how would you evaluate the effectiveness of training programs?

17-17. For an HR manager, what is the importance of an initial selection process? What are the major tasks in this process?

17-18. **MyManagementLab Only** – comprehensive writing assignment for this chapter.

ENDNOTES

[1] See C. J. Collins and K. D. Clark, "Strategic Human Resource Practices, Top Management Team Social Networks, and Firm Performance: The Role of Human Resource Practices in Creating Organizational Competitive Advantage," *Academy of Management Journal,* December 2003, 740–51; D. E. Bowen and C. Ostroff, "Understanding HRM–Firm Performance Linkages: The Role of the 'Strength' of the HRM System," *Academy of Management Review,* April 2004, 203–21; and K. Birdi, C. Clegg, M. Patterson, A. Robinson, C. B. Stride, T. D. Wall, and S. J. Wood, "The Impact of Human Resource and Operational Management Practices on Company Productivity: A Longitudinal Study," *Personnel Psychology* 61, no. 3 (2008): 467–501.

[2] J. M. Phillips and S. M. Gully. "Multilevel and Strategic Recruiting: Where Have We Been, Where Can We Go from Here?" *Journal of Management* 41 (2015): 1416–45.

[3] J. A. Breaugh, "Employee Recruitment," *Annual Review of Psychology* 64 (2013): 389–416; D. R. Earnest, D. G. Allen, and R. S. Landis. "A Meta-Analytic Path Analysis of the Mechanisms Linking Realistic Job Previews and Turnover," *Personnel Psychology* 64 (2011): 865–97; J. E. Slaughter, D. M. Cable, and D. B. Turban, "Changing Job Seekers' Image Perceptions during Recruitment Visits: The Moderating Role of Belief Confidence," *Journal of Applied Psychology* 99 (2014): 1146–58.

[4] C. Hymowitz and J. Green, "Executive Headhunters Squeezed by In-House Recruiters," *Bloomberg Businessweek,* January 17, 2013, www.businessweek.com/articles/2013-01-17/executive-headhunters-squeezed-by-in-house-recruiters.

[5] H. J. Walker, T. Bauer, M. Cole, J. Bernerth, H. Feild, and J. Short, "Is This How I Will Be Treated? Reducing Uncertainty through Recruitment Interactions," *Academy of Management Journal* 56 (2013): 1325–47.

[6] D. Zielinski, "Get to the Source," *HR Magazine,* November 2012, 67–70.

[7] G. Anders, "Solve Puzzle, Get Job," *Forbes,* May 6, 2013, 46–48; and S. Sengupta, "Waiting and Waiting for Green Cards," *The Wall Street Journal,* April 12, 2013, B1, B6.

[8] See, for instance, A. L. Kristof-Brown, R. D. Zimmerman, and E. C. Johnson, "Consequences of Individual's Fit at Work: A Meta-Analysis of Person-Job, Person-Organization, Person-Group, and Person-Supervisor Fit,"

Personnel Psychology 58, no. 2 (2005): 281–342; and D. S. DeRue and F. P. Morgeson, "Stability and Change in Person-Team and Person-Role Fit over Time: The Effects of Growth Satisfaction, Performance, and General Self-Efficacy," *Journal of Applied Psychology* 92, no. 5 (2007): 1242–53.

[9] L. Weber, "Seeking Software Fix for Job-Search Game," *The Wall Street Journal,* June 6, 2012, B8.

[10] L. Hill, "Only BFFs Need Apply," *Bloomberg Businessweek,* January 7–13, 2013, 63–65; and L. Petrecca, "Entrepreneurs Hire Close to Home: Their Moms," *USA Today,* August 20, 2012, 4B.

[11] A. M. F. Hiemstra, E. Derous, A. W. Serlie, and M. P. Born, "Fairness Perceptions of Video Résumés among Ethnically Diverse Applicants," *International Journal of Selection and Assessment,* December 2012, 423–33.

[12] K. Gray, "Facial-Recognition Technology Might Get Employers in Trouble," *HR Magazine,* April 2012, 17.

[13] C. L. Wilkin and C. E. Connelly, "Do I Look Like Someone Who Cares? Recruiters' Ratings of Applicants' Paid and Volunteer Experience," *International Journal of Selection and Assessment,* September 2012, 308–16.

[14] M. M. Breslin, "Can You Handle Rejection?" *Workforce Management,* October 2012, 32–36.

[15] C. Suddath, "Imaginary Friends," *Bloomberg Businessweek,* January 21–27, 2013, 68.

[16] M. Goodman, "Reference Checks Go Tech," *Workforce Management,* May 2012, 26–28.

[17] L. Kwoh, "Workplace Crystal Ball, Courtesy of Facebook," *The Wall Street Journal,* February 21, 2012, B8.

[18] J. B. Bernerth, S. G. Taylor, H. J. Walker, and D. S. Whitman, "An Empirical Investigation of Dispositional Antecedents and Performance-Related Outcomes of Credit Scores," *Journal of Applied Psychology* 97 (2012): 469–78.

[19] H. B. Bernerth, "Demographic Variables and Credit Scores: An Empirical Study of a Controversial Selection Tool," *International Journal of Selection and Assessment,* June 2012, 242–50.

[20] H. O'Neill, "Thinking Outside the Box," *Workforce Management,* January 2012, 24–26.

[21] L. Weber, "Didn't Get the Job? You'll Never Know Why," *The Wall Street Journal,* June 4, 2013, www.online.wsj.com/article/SB10001424127887324423904578523683173841190.html?mod=wsj_valettop_email; and

D. Meinert, "Search and Verify," *HR Magazine,* December 2012, 37–41.

[22] E. J. Hirst, "Business Risks Rise in Criminal History Discrimination," *The Chicago Tribune,* October 21, 2012, http://articles.chicagotribune.com/2012-10-21/business/ct-biz-1021-eeoc-felony-20121021_1_criminal-records-eeoc-s-chicago-district-office-court-case.

[23] H. Husock, "From Prison to a Paycheck," *The Wall Street Journal,* August 4, 2012, C3; E. Krell, "Criminal Background," *HR Magazine,* February 2012, 45–54; and M. Waldo, "Second Chances: Employing Convicted Felons," *HR Magazine,* March 2012, 36–41.

[24] E. Frauenheim, "Personality Tests Adapt to the Times," *Workforce Management,* February 2010, 4.

[25] E. Maltby, "To Find Best Hires, Firms Become Creative," *The Wall Street Journal,* November 17, 2009, B6.

[26] J. P. Hausknecht, D. V. Day, and S. C. Thomas, "Applicant Reactions to Selection Procedures: An Updated Model and Meta-Analysis," *Personnel Psychology,* September 2004, 639–83.

[27] F. L. Schmidt, "Cognitive Tests Used in Selection Can Have Content Validity as Well as Criterion Validity: A Broader Research Review and Implications for Practice," *International Journal of Selection and Assessment,* March 2012, 1–13; and N. Schmitt, "Personality and Cognitive Ability as Predictors of Effective Performance at Work," *Annual Review of Organizational Psychology and Organizational Behavior* 1 (2014): 45–65.

[28] F. L. Schmidt and J. Hunter, "General Mental Ability in the World of Work: Occupational Attainment and Job Performance," *Journal of Personality and Social Psychology* 86, no. 1 (2004): 162–73; and F. L. Schmidt, J. A. Shaffer, and I. Oh, "Increased Accuracy for Range Restriction Corrections: Implications for the Role of Personality and General Mental Ability in Job and Training Performance," *Personnel Psychology* 61, no. 4 (2008): 827–68.

[29] J. F. Salgado, N. Anderson, S. Moscoso, C. Bertua, F. de Fruyt, and J. P. Rolland, "A Meta-Analytic Study of General Mental Ability Validity for Different Occupations in the European Community," *Journal of Applied Psychology,* December 2003, 1068–81.

[30] S. Wee, D. A. Newman, and D. L. Joseph, "More Than *g*: Selection Quality and Adverse Impact Implications of Considering Second

Stratum Cognitive Abilities," *Journal of Applied Psychology* 99 (2014): 547–63; P. D. G. Steel and J. D. Kammeyer-Mueller, "Using a Meta-Analytic Perspective to Enhance Job Component Validation," *Personnel Psychology* 62 (2009): 533–52.

[31]C. J. König, A.-S. Merz, and N. Trauffer, "What Is in Applicants' Minds When They Fill Out a Personality Test? Insights from a Qualitative Study," *International Journal of Selection and Assessment,* December 2012, 442–50; R. N. Landers, P. R. Sackett, and K. A. Tuzinski, "Retesting after Initial Failure, Coaching Rumors, and Warnings against Faking in Online Personality Measures for Selection," *Journal of Applied Psychology* 96, no. 1 (2011): 202–10; and J. P. Hausknecht, "Candidate Persistence and Personality Test Practice Effects: Implications for Staffing System Management," *Personnel Psychology* 63, no. 2 (2010): 299–324.

[32]Z. Galic, Z. Jerneic, and M. P. Kovacic, "Do Applicants Fake Their Personality Questionnaire Responses and How Successful Are Their Attempts? A Case of Military Pilot Cadet Selection," *International Journal of Selection and Assessment,* June 2012, 229–41.

[33]J. Fan, D. Gao, S. A. Carroll, F. J. Lopen, T. S. Tian, and H. Meng, "Testing the Efficacy of a New Procedure for Reducing Faking on Personality Tests within Selection Contexts," *Journal of Applied Psychology* 97 (2012): 866–80.

[34]I. Oh, G. Wang, and M. K. Mount, "Validity of Observer Ratings of the Five-Factor Model of Personality Traits: A Meta-Analysis," *Journal of Applied Psychology* 96, no. 4 (2011): 762–73; and B. S. Connelly and D. S. Ones, "An Other Perspective on Personality: Meta-Analytic Integration of Observers' Accuracy and Predictive Validity," *Psychological Bulletin* 136, no. 6 (2010): 1092–122.

[35]C. M. Berry, P. R. Sackett, and S. Wiemann, "A Review of Recent Developments in Integrity Test Research," *Personnel Psychology* 60, no. 2 (2007): 271–301.

[36]C. H. Van Iddekinge, P. L. Roth, P. H. Raymark, and H. N. Odle-Dusseau, "The Criterion-Related Validity of Integrity Tests: An Updated Meta-Analysis," *Journal of Applied Psychology* 97 (2012): 499–530.

[37]P. L. Roth, P. Bobko, and L. A. McFarland, "A Meta-Analysis of Work Sample Test Validity: Updating and Integrating Some Classic Literature," *Personnel Psychology* 58, no. 4 (2005): 1009–37.

[38]See, for instance, N. R. Kuncel and P. R. Sackett. "Resolving the Assessment Center Construct Validity Problem (As We Know It)," *Journal of Applied Psychology* 99 (2014): 38–47; and J. Schettler, "Building Bench Strength," *Training,* June 2002, 55–58.

[39]F. Lievens, H. Peeters, and E. Schollaert, "Situational Judgment Tests: A Review of Recent Research," *Personnel Review* 37, no. 4 (2008): 426–41.

[40]F. Lievens, T. Buyse, P. R. Sackett, and B. S. Connelly, "The Effects of Coaching on Situational Judgment Tests in High-Stakes Selection," *International Journal of Selection and Assessment,* September 2012, 272–82.

[41]F. Lievens, and F. Patterson, "The Validity and Incremental Validity of Knowledge Tests, Low-Fidelity Simulations, and High-Fidelity Simulations for Predicting Job Performance in Advanced-Level High-Stakes Selection," *Journal of Applied Psychology,* Online First Publication, April 11, 2011, doi: 10.1037/a0023496.

[42]M. A. Tucker, "Show and Tell," *HR Magazine,* January 2012, 51–53.

[43]J. Alsever, "How to Get a Job: Show, Don't Tell," *Fortune,* March 19, 2012, 29–31.

[44]B. K. Griepentrog, C. M. Harold, B. C. Holtz, R. J. Kimoski, and S. M. Marsh, "Integrating Social Identity and the Theory of Planned Behavior: Predicting Withdrawal from an Organizational Recruitment Process," *Personnel Psychology* 65 (2012): 723–53.

[45]B. W. Swider, M. R. Barrick, T. B. Harris, and A. C. Stoverink, "Managing and Creating an Image in the Interview; The Role of Interviewee Initial Impressions," *Journal of Applied Psychology,* Online First Publication, May 30, 2011, doi: 10.1037/a0024005.

[46]J. M. Madera and M. R. Hebl, "Discrimination against Facially Stigmatized Applicants in Interviews: An Eye-Tracking and Face-to-Face Investigation," *Journal of Applied Psychology* 97 (2012): 317–30.

[47]See J. Levashina, C. J. Hartwell, F. P. Morgeson, and M. A. Campion, "The Structured Employment Interview: Narrative and Quantitative Review of the Research Literature," *Personnel Psychology* 67 (2014): 241–93.

[48]A. Bryant, "You Can't Find the Future in the Archives," *The New York Times,* January 29, 2012, 2.

[49]M. R. Barrick, B. W. Swider, and G. L. Stewart, "Initial Evaluations in the Interview: Relationships with Subsequent Interviewer Evaluations

and Employment Offers," *Journal of Applied Psychology* 95, no. 6 (2010): 1163–72.

[50]M. R. Barrick, J. A. Shaffer, and S. W. DeGrassi, "What You See May Not Be What You Get: Relationships among Self-Presentation Tactics and Ratings of Interview and Job Performance," *Journal of Applied Psychology* 94 (2009): 1394–411.

[51]K. G. Melchers, N. Lienhardt, M. von Aarburg, and M. Kleinmann, "Is More Structure Really Better? A Comparison of Frame-of-Reference Training and Descriptively Anchored Rating Scales to Improve Interviewers' Rating Quality," *Personnel Psychology* 64, no. 1 (2011): 53–87.

[52]F. L. Schmidt and R. D. Zimmerman, "A Counterintuitive Hypothesis about Employment Interview Validity and Some Supporting Evidence," *Journal of Applied Psychology* 89, no. 3 (2004): 553–61.

[53]J. C. Marr and D. M. Cable, "Do Interviewers Sell Themselves Short? The Effects of Selling Orientation on Interviewers' Judgments," *Academy of Management Journal* 57 (2014): 624–51.

[54]J. Bersin, "Spending on Corporate Training Soars: Employee Capabilities Now a Priority," *Forbes,* February 4, 2014, http://www.forbes.com/sites/joshbersin/2014/02/04/the-recovery-arrives-corporate-training-spend-skyrockets/.

[55]T. Minton-Eversole and K. Gurchiek, "New Workers Not Ready for Prime Time," *HR Magazine,* December 2006, 28–34.

[56]P. Galagan, "Bridging the Skills Gap: New Factors Compound the Growing Skills Shortage," T1D, February 2010, 44–49.

[57]M. Smulian, "England Fails on Numeracy and Literacy," *Public Finance,* February 6, 2009, 13; E. K. Sharma, "Growing a New Crop of Talent: India Inc. Is Increasingly Going Rural," *Business Today,* June 28, 2009, http://businesstoday.intoday.in/; and G. Paton, "Almost Half of Employers Forced to Teach Teenagers Basic Literacy and Numeracy Skills," *Telegraph,* May 9, 2011, www.telegraph.com.

[58]D. Baynton, "America's $60 Billion Problem," *Training,* May 2001, 52.

[59]G. Anand, "India Graduates Millions, But Few Are Fit to Hire," *The Wall Street Journal,* April 5, 2011, www.online.wsj.com.

[60]See, for example, P. J. Taylor, D. F. Russ-Eft, and H. Taylor, "Transfer of Management Training from Alternative Perspectives,"

Journal of Applied Psychology 94, no. 1 (2009): 104–21.

[61]C. Porath, "No Time to Be Nice at Work," *The New York Times,* June 19, 2015, http://www.nytimes.com/2015/06/21/opinion/sunday/is-your-boss-mean.html?_r=1.

[62]See, for example, S. Lim and A. Lee, "Work and Nonwork Outcomes of Workplace Incivility: Does Family Support Help?" *Journal of Occupational Health Psychology* 16, no. 1 (2011): 95–111; C. L. Porath and C. M. Pearson, "The Cost of Bad Behavior," *Organizational Dynamics* 39, no. 1 (2010): 64–71; and B. Estes and J. Wang, "Workplace Incivility: Impacts on Individual and Organizational Performance," *Human Resource Development Review* 7, no. 2 (2008): 218–40.

[63]M. P. Leiter, H. K. S. Laschinger, A. Day, and D. G. Oore, "The Impact of Civility Interventions on Employee Social Behavior, Distress, and Attitudes," *Journal of Applied Psychology,* advance online publication, July 11, 2011, doi: 10.1037/a0024442.

[64]M. B. Wood, *Business Ethics in Uncertain Times* (Upper Saddle River, NJ: Prentice Hall, 2004), 61.

[65]See, for example, A. Becker, "Can You Teach Ethics to MBAs?" *BNet,* October 19, 2009, www.bnet.com.

[66]W. R. Allen, P. Bacdayan, K. B. Kowalski, and M. H. Roy, "Examining the Impact of Ethics Training on Business Student Values," *Education and Training* 47, no. 3 (2005): 170–82; A. Lämsä, M. Vehkaperä, T. Puttonen, and H. Pesonen, "Effect of Business Education on Women and Men Students' Attitudes on Corporate Responsibility in Society," *Journal of Business Ethics* 82, no. 1 (2008): 45–58; and K. M. Sheldon and L. S. Krieger, "Understanding the Negative Effects of Legal Education on Law Students: A Longitudinal Test of Self-Determination Theory," *Personality and Social Psychology Bulletin* 33, no. 6 (2007): 883–97.

[67]S. Valentine and G. Fleischman, "Ethics Programs, Perceived Corporate Social Responsibility, and Job Satisfaction," *Journal of Business Ethics* 77, no. 2 (2008): 159–72.

[68]L. Weber and L. Kwoh, "Co-Workers Change Places," *The Wall Street Journal,* February 21, 2012, B8.

[69]K. Tyler, "A New U," *HR Magazine,* April 2012, 27–34.

[70]See, for instance, R. E. Derouin, B. A. Fritzsche, and E. Salas, "E-Learning in Organizations," *Journal of Management* 31, no. 3 (2005): 920–40; and K. A. Orvis, S. L. Fisher, and M. E. Wasserman, "Power to the People: Using Learner Control to Improve Trainee Reactions and Learning in Web-Based Instructional Environments," *Journal of Applied Psychology* 94, no 4 (2009): 960–71.

[71]T. Sitzmann, K. Kraiger, D. Stewart, and R. Wisher, "The Comparative Effectiveness of Web-Based and Classroom Instruction: A Meta-Analysis," *Personnel Psychology* 59, no. 3 (2006): 623–64.

[72]T. Sitzmann, B. S. Bell, K. Kraiger, and A. M. Kanar, "A Multilevel Analysis of the Effect of Prompting Self-Regulation in Technology-Delivered Instruction," *Personnel Psychology* 62, no. 4 (2009): 697–734.

[73]B. Roberts, "From E-Learning to Mobile Learning," *HR Magazine,* August 2012, 61–65.

[74]J. P. Santos, A. Caetano, and S. M. Tavares, "Is Training Leaders in Functional Leadership a Useful Tool for Improving the Performance of Leadership Functions and Team Effectiveness?" *Leadership Quarterly* 26, no. 3 (2015): 470–84; and T. Sitzmann, K. G. Brown, W. J. Casper, K. Ely, and R. D. Zimmerman, "A Review and Meta-Analysis of the Nomological Network of Trainee Reactions," *Journal of Applied Psychology* 93, no. 2 (2008): 280–95.

[75]See L. A. Burke and H. S. Hutchins, "Training Transfer: An Integrative Literature Review," *Human Resource Development Review* 6 (2007): 263–96; and D. S. Chiaburu and S. V. Marinova, "What Predicts Skill Transfer? An Exploratory Study of Goal Orientation, Training Self-Efficacy, and Organizational Supports," *International Journal of Training and Development* 9, no. 2 (2005): 110–23.

[76]Y. Kim and R. E. Ployhart, "The Effects of Staffing and Training on Firm Productivity and Profit Growth before, during, and after the Great Recession," *Journal of Applied Psychology* 99, (2014): 361–89; J. Konings and S. Vanormelingen, "The Impact of Training on Productivity and Wages: Firm-Level Evidence," *Review of Economics and Statistics* 97 (2014): 485–97; and T. Zwick, "The Impact of Training Intensity on Establishment Productivity," *Industrial Relations* 45 (2006): 26–46.

[77]O. Wurtz, "An Empirical Investigation of the Effectiveness of Pre-Departure and In-Country Cross-Cultural Training," *International Journal of Human Resource Management* 25, no. 14 (2014): 2088–101.

[78]A. Dysvik and B. Kuvaas, "Perceived Supervisor Support Climate, Perceived Investment in Employee Development Climate, and Business-Unit Performance," *Human Resource Management* 51 (2012): 651–64.

[79]S. Y. Sung and J. N. Choi, "Do Organizations Spend Wisely on Employees? Effects of Training and Development Investments on Learning and Innovation in Organizations," *Journal of Organizational Behavior* 35 (2014): 393–412.

[80]M. Rotundo and P. R. Sackett, "The Relative Importance of Task, Citizenship, and Counterproductive Performance to Global Ratings of Job Performance: A Policy Capturing Approach," *Journal of Applied Psychology* 87, no. 1 (2002): 66–80; and S. W. Whiting, P. M. Podsakoff, and J. R. Pierce, "Effects of Task Performance, Helping, Voice, and Organizational Loyalty on Performance Appraisal Ratings," *Journal of Applied Psychology* 93, no. 1 (2008): 125–39.

[81]W. F. Cascio and H. Aguinis, *Applied Psychology in Human Resource Management,* 7th ed. (Upper Saddle River, NJ: Prentice Hall, 2010).

[82]D. J. Woehr, M. K. Sheehan, and W. Bennett, "Assessing Measurement Equivalence across Rating Sources: A Multitrait-Multirater Approach," *Journal of Applied Psychology* 90, no. 3 (2005): 592–600; and H. Heidemeier and K. Moser, "Self–Other Agreement in Job Performance Ratings: A Meta-Analytic Test of a Process Model," *Journal of Applied Psychology* 94, no. 2 (March 2009): 353–70.

[83]See, for instance, F. Luthans and S. J. Peterson, "360 Degree Feedback with Systematic Coaching: Empirical Analysis Suggests a Winning Combination," *Human Resource Management,* Fall 2003, 243–56; R. Ladyshewsky and R. Taplin, "Evaluation of Curriculum and Student Learning Needs Using 360 Degree Assessment," *Assessment & Evaluation in Higher Education* 40, no. 5 (2015): 698–711; and B. I. J. M. van der Heijden and A. H. J. Nijhof, "The Value of Subjectivity: Problems and Prospects for 360-Degree Appraisal Systems," *International Journal of Human Resource Management,* May 2004, 493–511.

[84]M. K. Mount and S. E. Scullen, "Multisource Feedback Ratings: What Do They Really Measure?" in M. London (ed.), *How People Evaluate Others in Organizations* (Mahwah, NJ: Lawrence Erlbaum, 2001), 155–76; and K.-Y. Ng, C. Koh, S. Ang, J. C. Kennedy, and K. Chan, "Rating Leniency and Halo

in Multisource Feedback Ratings: Testing Cultural Assumptions of Power Distance and Individualism-Collectivism," *Journal of Applied Psychology,* Online First Publication, April 11, 2011, doi: 10.1037/a0023368.

[85]C. Rampbell, "A History of College Grade Inflation," *The New York Times,* July 14, 2011, accessed at http://-economix.blogs .nytimes.com/2011/07/14/the-history-of-college-grade-inflation/?scp51&sq5grade%20 inflation&st5cse.

[86]X. M. Wang, K. F. E. Wong, and J. Y. Y. Kwong, "The Roles of Rater Goals and Ratee Performance Levels in the Distortion of Performance Ratings," *Journal of Applied Psychology* 95, no. 3 (2010): 546–61; J. R. Spence and L. M. Keeping, "The Impact of Non-Performance Information on Ratings of Job Performance: A Policy-Capturing Approach," *Journal of Organizational Behavior* 31 (2010): 587–608; and J. R Spence and L. Keeping, "Conscious Rating Distortion in Performance Appraisal: A Review, Commentary, and Proposed Framework for Research," *Human Resource Management Review* 21, no. 2 (2011): 85–95.

[87]L. E. Atwater, J. F. Brett, and A. C. Charles, "Multisource Feedback: Lessons Learned and Implications for Practice," *Human Resource Management* 46, no. 2 (2007): 285–307; and R. Hensel, F. Meijers, R. van der Leeden, and J. Kessels, "360 Degree Feedback: How Many Raters Are Needed for Reliable Ratings on the Capacity to Develop Competences, with Personal Qualities as Developmental Goals?" *International Journal of Human Resource Management* 21, no. 15 (2010): 2813–30.

[88]I. Hussain, "Subjective Performance Evaluation in the Public Sector: Evidence from School Inspections," *Journal of Human Resources* 50, no. 1 (2015): 189–221; and G. van Helden, A Johnsen, and J. Vakkuri, "The Life-Cycle Approach to Performance Management: Implications for Public Management and Evaluation," *Evaluation* 18, no. 2 (2012): 169–75.

[89]See, for instance, K. L. Uggerslev and L. M. Sulsky, "Using Frame-of-Reference Training to Understand the Implications of Rater Idiosyncrasy for Rating Accuracy," *Journal of Applied Psychology* 93, no. 3 (2008): 711–19; and R. F. Martell and D. P. Evans, "Source-Monitoring Training: Toward Reducing Rater Expectancy Effects in Behavioral Measurement," *Journal of Applied Psychology* 90, no. 5 (2005): 956–63.

[90]B. Erdogan, "Antecedents and Consequences of Justice Perceptions in Performance Appraisals," *Human Resource Management Review* 12, no. 4 (2002): 555–78; and I. M. Jawahar, "The Mediating Role of Appraisal Feedback Reactions on the Relationship between Rater Feedback-Related Behaviors and Ratee

Performance," *Group and Organization Management* 35, no. 4 (2010): 494–526.

[91]S. C. Payne, M. T. Horner, W. R. Boswell, A. N. Schroeder, and K. J. Stine-Cheyne, "Comparison of Online and Traditional Performance Appraisal Systems," *Journal of Managerial Psychology* 24, no. 6 (2009): 526–44.

[92]P. E. Levy and J. R. Williams, "The Social Context of Performance Appraisal: A Review and Framework for the Future," *Journal of Management* 30, no. 6 (2004): 881–905.

[93]M. C. Saffie-Robertson and S. Brutus, "The Impact of Interdependence on Performance Evaluations: The Mediating Role of Discomfort with Performance Appraisal," *International Journal of Human Resource Management* 25, no. 3 (2014): 459–73.

[94]F. Gino and M. E. Schweitzer, "Blinded by Anger or Feeling the Love: How Emotions Influence Advice Taking," *Journal of Applied Psychology* 93, no. 3 (2008): 1165–73.

[95]Heidemeier and Moser, "Self–Other Agreement in Job Performance Ratings."

[96]J. Han, "Does Performance-Based Salary System Suit Korea?" *The Korea Times,* January 15, 2008, www.koreatimes.co.kr.

[97]F. F. T. Chiang and T. A. Birtch, "Appraising Performance across Borders: An Empirical Examination of the Purposes and Practices of Performance Appraisal in a Multi-Country Context," *Journal of Management Studies* 47, no. 7 (2010): 1365–93.

[98]K.-Y. Ng, C. Koh, S. Ang, J. C. Kennedy, and K. Chan, "Rating Leniency and Halo in Multisource Feedback Ratings: Testing Cultural Assumptions of Power Distance and Individualism-Collectivism," *Journal of Applied Psychology,* Online First Publication, April 11, 2011, doi: 10.1037/a0023368.

[99]J. Camps and R. Luna-Arocas, "A Matter of Learning: How Human Resources Affect Organizational Performance," *British Journal of Management* 23 (2012): 1–21.

[100]G. C. Banks and S. Kepes, "The Influence of Internal HRM Activity Fit on the Dynamics within the 'Black Box.'" *Human Resource Management Review,* 2015, in press; E. P. Piening, A. M. Baluch, and H. Ridder, "Mind the Intended-Implemented Gap: Understanding Employees' Perceptions of HRM," *Human Resource Management* 53 (2014): 545–67.

[101]D. S. Whitman, D. L. Van Rooy, and C. Viswesvaran, "Satisfaction, Citizenship Behaviors, and Performance in Work Units: A Meta-Analysis of Collective Construct Relations," *Personnel Psychology* 63 (2010): 41–81; K. W. Mossholder, H. A. Richardson, and R. P. Settoon, "Human Resource Systems and Helping in Organizations: A Relational Perspective," *Academy of Management Review* 36 (2011): 33–52.

[102]R. R. Kehoe and P. M. Wright, "The Impact of High-Performance Human Resource Practices on Employees' Attitudes and Behaviors," *Journal of Management* 39 (2013): 366–91.

[103]L. H. Nishii, D. P. Lepak, and B. Schneider, "Employee Attributions of the 'Why' of HR Practices: Their Effects on Employee Attitudes and Behaviors, and Customer Satisfaction," *Personnel psychology* 61 (2008): 503–45; K. Sanders and H. Yang, "The HRM Process Approach: The Influence of Employees' Attribution to Explain the HRM-Performance Relationship," *Human Resource Management,* 2015, in press.

[104]K. Jiang, D. P. Lepak, J. Hu, and J. C. Baer, "How Does Human Resource Management Influence Organizational Outcomes? A Meta-Analytic Investigation of Mediating Mechanisms," *Academy of Management Journal* 55 (2012): 1264–94.

[105]T. C. Bednall, K. Sanders, and P. Runhaar, "Stimulating Informal Learning Activities through Perceptions of Performance Appraisal Quality and Human Resource Management System Strength: A Two-Wave Study," *Academy of Management Learning & Education* 13 (2014): 45–61.

[106]N. Anderson and C. Witvliet, "Fairness Reactions to Personnel Selection Methods: An International Comparison between the Netherlands, the United States, France, Spain, Portugal, and Singapore," *International Journal of Selection and Assessment* 16, no. 1 (2008): 1–13.

[107]K. Van De Voorde, J. Paauwe, and M. Van Veldhoven, "Employee Well-Being and the HRM-Organizational Performance Relationship: A Review of Quantitative Studies," *International Journal of Management Reviews* 14 (2012): 391–407.

[108]M. Heller, "Title VII Protections Debated in 'Great Texas Lactation Case,'" *Workforce Management,* October 2012, 6.

[109]F. Rothschild, "The 'Great Texas Lactation' Case Settles!" *Employment Discrimination Report,* May 12, 2014, http://employmentdiscrimina tion.foxrothschild.com/2014/05/articles/ another-category/gender-discrimination/the-great-texas-lactation-case-settles/.

[110]S. Greenhouse, "With Jobs Few, Internships Lure More Graduates to Unpaid Work," *The New York Times,* May 6, 2012, 1, 4.

[111]J.-A. B. Casuga, "Judge Rules Fox Searchlight Interns Are FLSA Employees, Certifies Class Action," *Bloomberg BNA,* June 19, 2013, http://www.bna.com/judge-rules-fox-n17179874627/.

[112]N. Scheiber, "Employers Have Greater Leeway on Unpaid Internships, Court Rules," *The New York Times,* July 2, 2015, http://www.nytimes.com/2015/07/03/

business/unpaid-internships-allowed-if-they-serve-educational-purpose-court-rules.html.
[113]See, for instance, *Harvard Business Review on Work and Life Balance* (Boston: Harvard Business School Press, 2000); R. Rapoport, L. Bailyn, J. K. Fletcher, and B. H. Pruitt, *Beyond Work-Family Balance* (San Francisco: Jossey-Bass, 2002); and E. E. Kossek, S. Pichler, T. Bodner, and L. B. Hammer, "Workplace Social Support and Work-Family Conflict: A Meta-Analysis Clarifying the Influence of General and Work-Family Specific Supervisor and Organizational Support," *Personnel Psychology* 64, no. 2 (2011): 289–313.
[114]B. Harrington, F. Van Deusen, and B. Humberd, *The New Dad: Caring Committed and Conflicted* (Boston: Boston College Center for Work and Family, 2011).
[115]A. Grant, "Top 25 Companies for Work-Life Balance," *US News and World Report*, May 11, 2011, www.money.usnews.com.

[116]K. Dill, "The Best Companies for Work-Life Balance," *Forbes,* July 17, 2015, http://www.forbes.com/sites/kathryndill/2015/07/17/the-best-companies-for-work-life-balance-2/.
[117]C. P. Maertz and S. L. Boyar, "Work-Family Conflict, Enrichment, and Balance under 'Levels' and 'Episodes' Approaches," *Journal of Management* 37, no. 1 (2011): 68–98.
[118]L. M. Lapierre and T. D. Allen, "Control at Work, Control at Home, and Planning Behavior: Implications for Work-Family Conflict," *Journal of Management*, September 2012, 1500–16.
[119]J. S. Michel and M. B. Hargis, "Linking Mechanisms of Work-Family Conflict and Segmentation," *Journal of Vocational Behavior* 73, no. 3 (2008): 509–22; G. E. Kreiner, "Consequences of Work-Home Segmentation or Integration: A Person-Environment Fit Perspective," *Journal of Organizational Behavior* 27, no. 4 (2006): 485–507; and C. A. Bulger, R. A. Matthews, and M. E. Hoffman, "Work

and Personal Life Boundary Management: Boundary Strength, Work/Personal Life Balance, and the Segmentation-Integration Continuum," *Journal of Occupational Health Psychology* 12, no. 4 (2007): 365–75.
[120]D. Catanzaro, H. Moore, and T. R. Marshall, "The Impact of Organizational Culture on Attraction and Recruitment of Job Applicants," *Journal of Business and Psychology* 25 (2010): 649–62.
[121]E. O'Regan, "Spain Hampered by Rigid Labor Laws," *The Wall Street Journal,* June 11, 2012, 4A.
[122]D. Meinert, "Layoff Victims Won't Hold a Grudge If Treated Fairly," *HR Magazine,* November 2012, 24.
[123]D. van Dierendonck and G. Jacobs, "Survivors and Victims, a Meta-Analytical Review of Fairness and Organizational Commitment after Downsizing," *British Journal of Management* 23 (2012): 96–109.

18 Organizational Change and Stress Management

LEARNING OBJECTIVES

After studying this chapter, you should be able to:

18-1 Contrast the forces for change and planned change.

18-2 Describe ways to overcome resistance to change.

18-3 Compare the four main approaches to managing organizational change.

18-4 Demonstrate three ways of creating a culture for change.

18-5 Identify the potential environmental, organizational, and personal sources of stress at work and the role of individual and cultural differences.

18-6 Identify the physiological, psychological, and behavioral symptoms of stress at work.

18-7 Describe individual and organizational approaches to managing stress at work.

MyManagementLab®
⭐ **Chapter Warm Up**

If your professor has chosen to assign this, go to the Assignments section of **mymanagementlab.com** to complete the chapter warm up.

SUPPORTING CHANGE FROM THE BOTTOM UP

Moving, finishing school, and starting a new job are life-changing events that can be seen as adventures or chores, and viewed with anticipation or dread. Some changes are simple to make while others can be agonizing; yet we accept that change is a part of life. Now imagine having to make changes on a global level that will affect tens of thousands of people in dozens of countries, changes that need to honor differing laws and regulations in various cultures. Such is the task faced by leaders of global companies, who must continually evaluate how well their practices are working to reach their market and achieve their goals.

As CEO of Hyatt Hotels Corporation, Mark Hoplamazian (pictured here) was concerned with this issue. The worldwide hotel company experienced significant growth in 2013, adding hotels to its brand and entering new areas of the hospitality industry, but working with over 90,000 employees in 45 different countries presented implementation challenges. It was particularly vital for Hyatt, spread across the globe and highly decentralized, to make sure its associates understood and shared the mission of the company. To get the message across, Hoplamazian wanted to create a uniform employment experience for each employee, starting with a cohesive orientation/ onboarding program for new hires.

His path toward change began with gathering information about associates' perceptions. Known for being a hands-on leader, he went to the source—the associates (as they're known) themselves—to learn how policies and procedures played a role in the working and private lives of those in the Hyatt family. He looked at the situation from different perspectives to see where things weren't connecting and learned that employees saw orientation not as a welcome but as a time when they learned all the ways they could lose their new jobs by breaking the rules, and as a time for forms and regulations. "They didn't join the company because we have a better set of rules and regulations," he reasoned. "They joined because of culture and emotional connection." With input from all levels, the company changed its orientation process to highlight the organizational culture aspects over the legal formalities.

Keeping the Hyatt culture in mind also helped guide changes in other areas. Making meaningful and personal connections with guests was difficult when associates had to divide their attention between the guest in front of them and the computer screen providing the information necessary to help that guest. Changing to a more user-friendly interface on various hotel operating systems allowed associates to engage more directly with guests.

Commitment to the environment, one of Hyatt's global platforms, provided a different set of challenges. The principle of thinking globally while acting locally was truly put to the test. Not all locations had the same resources or needs, and cities and countries had their own mandatory regulations and policies. There couldn't be a single plan or solution that would accomplish the company's goal, yet at the same time, Hoplamazian wanted each hotel to contribute to Hyatt's corporate social responsibility (CSR) initiatives in a meaningful way. To address this, he decided to stop giving associates mapped-out plans for their decisions and instead "give them a compass and say 'You figure out how you want to bring yourself to bear.' A compass instead of a map is really one of the key concepts that we are moving towards."

Change is just as inevitable for companies as it is for individuals, and each company will have its own way of responding to current changes and strategizing future changes. Taking away the maps and switching to compasses is not something all global corporations can do, but maybe someday that will change, too.

Sources: M. Solomon, "To Transform Your Company Culture, Change Your POV: Hyatt CEO's Perspective," *Forbes,* May 11, 2015, http://www.forbes.com/sites/micahsolomon/2015/05/11/transform-your-corporate-culture-by-changing-your-pov-the-hyatt-ceo-interview/; B. Witt, "Hyatt Hotels: Making CSR Work in a Decentralized Global Company," *Hotel Business Review,* May, 2015, http://hotelexecutive.com/business_review/3098/hyatt-hotels-making-csr-work-in-a-decentralized-global-company; and S. Shankman, "How Hyatt's CEO Empowers Employees to Drive the Guest Experience," *Skift,* December 14, 2014, http://skift.com/2014/12/15/interview-how-hyatts-ceo-empowers-employees-to-drive-the-guest-experience/.

While changes can be good, such as finishing school or responding to considerable organizational growth like Hyatt has, many changes bring stress to everyone involved. This chapter is about change and stress. We describe environmental forces that require firms to change, the reasons people and organizations often resist change, and the way this resistance can be overcome. We review processes for managing organizational change. Then we move to the topic of stress and its sources and consequences. In closing, we discuss what individuals and organizations can do to better manage stress levels and realize positive outcomes for organizational behavior (OB), which after all is the purpose of this text in its entirety.

Change

18-1 Contrast the forces for change and planned change.

No company today is in a particularly stable environment. Even those with a dominant market share must change, sometimes radically. For example, the market for smartphones has been especially volatile.[1] During the fourth quarter of 2014, there were 74.8 million iPhones sold, compared with 73 million Samsung sales. Contrast this with the fourth quarter of 2013, in which considerably fewer (50.2 million) iPhones were sold, versus considerably more (83.3 million) Samsung phones. At the same time, the Chinese mobile phone company Xiaomi has been rapidly rising. A look just a few years further back shows formerly dominant players like Nokia or Research in Motion (makers of the Blackberry) shrinking dramatically in size. In this and many markets, competitors are constantly entering and exiting the field, gaining and losing ground quickly.

Forces for Change

"Change or die!" is the rallying cry among today's managers worldwide. Exhibit 18-1 summarizes six specific forces stimulating change.

In a number of places in this text, we've discussed the *changing nature of the workforce.* Almost every organization must adjust to a multicultural environment, demographic changes, immigration, and outsourcing. *Technology* is continually changing jobs and organizations. It is not difficult to imagine the idea of an office becoming an antiquated concept in the near future.

Economic shocks also have a huge impact on organizations. During the great recession of 2007 to 2009, millions of jobs were lost worldwide, home values dropped dramatically, and many large, well-known corporations like Merrill Lynch, Countrywide Financial, and Ameriquest disappeared or were acquired. Recovery has occurred in many countries, and with it, new job prospects and investments. Other countries, like Greece and Spain, struggle to regain their economic footing, limiting the economic viability of many Greek and Spanish organizations.

Competition is changing. Competitors are as likely to be across the ocean as across town. Successful organizations are fast on their feet, capable of developing new products rapidly and getting them to market quickly. In other words, they are flexible and require an equally flexible and responsive workforce.

Social trends don't remain static either. Consumers who are otherwise strangers now meet and share product information in chat rooms and blogs. Organizations must therefore continually adjust product and marketing strategies to be sensitive to changing social trends, as Liz Claiborne did when it sold off fashion brands such as Ellen Tracy, deemphasized large vendors such as Macy's, streamlined operations, and cut staff. Consumers, employees, and organizational leaders are increasingly sensitive to environmental concerns. "Green" practices are quickly becoming expected rather than optional.

Exhibit 18-1	Forces for Change

Force	Examples
Nature of the workforce	More cultural diversity
	Aging population
	Increased immigration and outsourcing
Technology	Faster, cheaper, and more mobile computers and handheld devices
	Emergence and growth of social networking sites
	Deciphering of the human genetic code
Economic shocks	Rise and fall of global housing market
	Financial sector collapse
	Global recession
Competition	Global competitors
	Mergers and consolidations
	Increased government regulation of commerce
Social trends	Increased environmental awareness
	Liberalization of attitudes toward gay, lesbian, and transgender employees
	More multitasking and connectivity
World politics	Rising health care costs
	Negative social attitudes toward business and executives
	Opening of new markets worldwide

Not even globalization's strongest proponents could have imagined the change in *world politics* in recent years. We've seen a major set of financial crises that have rocked global markets, a dramatic rise in the power and influence of China, and intense shakeups in governments across the Arab world. Throughout the industrialized world, businesses—particularly in the banking and financial sectors—have come under new scrutiny.

Planned Change

A group of housekeeping employees who work for a small hotel confronted the owner: "It's very hard for most of us to maintain 7-to-4 work hours," said their spokeswoman. "Each of us has significant family and personal responsibilities. Rigid hours don't work for us. We're going to begin looking for someplace else to work if you don't set up flexible work hours." The owner listened thoughtfully to the group's ultimatum and agreed to make changes. The next day, a flextime plan for these employees was introduced.

A major automobile manufacturer spent several billion dollars to install state-of-the-art robotics. One area that received the new equipment was quality control, where sophisticated computers significantly improved the company's ability to find and correct defects. Because the new equipment dramatically changed the jobs in the quality-control area, and because management anticipated considerable employee resistance to it, executives developed a program to help people become familiar with the change and deal with any anxieties they might be feeling.

Both of these scenarios are examples of **change**, or making things different. However, only the second scenario describes **planned change**. Many changes are like the one that occurred at the hotel: They just happen. Some organizations

change Making things different.

planned change Change activities that are intentional and goal oriented.

treat all change as an accidental occurrence. In this chapter, we address change as an intentional, goal-oriented activity.

What are the goals of planned change? First, it seeks to improve the ability of the organization to adapt to changes in its environment. Second, it seeks to change employee behavior.

Who in organizations is responsible for managing change activities? The answer is **change agents**.[2] They see a future for the organization others have not identified, and they are able to motivate, invent, and implement this vision. Change agents can be managers or nonmanagers, current or new employees, or outside consultants.

change agents Persons who act as catalysts and assume the responsibility for managing change activities.

Some change agents look to transform old industries to meet new capabilities and demands. For instance, Sandy Jen, Cameron Ring, Monica Lo, and Seth Sternberg are working together to apply social marketplace concepts to online business—a concept exemplified by rideshare company Uber and crowdfunding firm Kickstarter. The group has created an innovative service for senior care called Honor.[3] In contrast to older methods of matching seniors and their families with services through nursing facilities, Honor uses an online marketplace. Caregivers list qualifications and desired job attributes, and seniors specify the type of services they need. Then Honor facilitates meeting the needs. This new model could alter the entire field of care, based on the vision of a core group of dedicated leaders.

Finding true change agents in long-established organizations can pose unique challenges. General Motors (GM) expects its human resource (HR) managers to be change agents and its top HR executive to set the tone. Experts attributed some of the failed changes at GM to Kathleen Barclay's stint as global HR vice president. GM next hired Mary Barra, a manufacturing executive they thought could bring about better changes. Barra seemed like a change agent, but even then-CEO Dan Akerson said, "It was the worst application of talent I've ever seen." Barra was later named as GM's new CEO, displacing Akerson.[4] For the top HR spot, GM next selected Cynthia Brinkley, who supposedly had the right combination of skills to be a change agent. Yet, she had no HR background[5] and was replaced shortly afterward by John Quattrone. Quattrone has over 25 years of experience in HR (and over 40 years of tenure with GM).[6] Time will tell. Many change agents fail because organizational members resist change. In the next section, we discuss resistance to change and what managers can do about it.

Resistance to Change

18-2   Describe ways to overcome resistance to change.

Our egos are fragile, and we often see change as threatening. Even when employees are shown data that suggest they need to change, they latch onto whatever data they can find that suggest they are okay and don't need to change.[7] Employees who have negative feelings about a change cope by not thinking about it, increasing their use of sick time, or quitting. All these reactions can sap the organization of vital energy when it is most needed.[8] Resistance to change doesn't just come from lower levels of the organization. In many cases, higher-level managers will resist changes proposed by subordinates, especially if these leaders are focused on immediate performance.[9] Conversely, when leaders are more focused on mastery and exploration, they are more willing to hear and adopt subordinates' suggestions for change.

Resistance to change can be positive if it leads to open discussion and debate.[10] These responses are usually preferable to apathy or silence and can indicate that members of the organization are engaged in the process, providing change agents an opportunity to explain the change effort. Change agents can also monitor the resistance to modify the change to fit the preferences of members of the organization.

Resistance doesn't necessarily surface in standardized ways. It can be overt, implicit, immediate, or deferred. It's easiest for management to deal with overt and immediate resistance such as complaints, a work slowdown, or a strike threat. The greater challenge is managing resistance that is implicit or deferred because these responses—loss of loyalty or motivation, increased errors or absenteeism—are more subtle and more difficult to recognize for what they are. Deferred actions also cloud the link between the change and the reaction to it, sometimes surfacing weeks, months, or even years later. Or a single change of little inherent impact may be the straw that breaks the camel's back because resistance to earlier changes has been deferred and stockpiled.

Exhibit 18-2 summarizes major forces for resistance to change, categorized by their sources. Individual sources reside in human characteristics such as perceptions, personalities, and needs. Organizational sources reside in the structural makeup of organizations themselves.

It's worth noting that not all change is good. Rapid, transformational change is risky, so change agents need to carefully think through the full implications. Speed can lead to bad decisions, and sometimes those initiating change fail to realize the full magnitude of the effects or their true costs.

Exhibit 18-2   Sources of Resistance to Change

Individual Sources

Habit—To cope with life's complexities, we rely on habits or programmed responses. But when confronted with change, this tendency to respond in our accustomed ways becomes a source of resistance.

Security—People with a high need for security are likely to resist change because it threatens their feelings of safety.

Economic factors—Changes in job tasks or established work routines can arouse economic fears if people are concerned that they won't be able to perform the new tasks or routines to their previous standards, especially when pay is closely tied to productivity.

Fear of the unknown—Change substitutes ambiguity and uncertainty for the unknown.

Selective information processing—Individuals are guilty of selectively processing information in order to keep their perceptions intact. They hear what they want to hear, and they ignore information that challenges the world they've created.

Organizational Sources

Structural inertia—Organizations have built-in mechanisms—such as their selection processes and formalized regulations—to produce stability. When an organization is confronted with change, this structural inertia acts as a counterbalance to sustain stability.

Limited focus of change—Organizations consist of a number of interdependent subsystems. One can't be changed without affecting the others. So limited changes in subsystems tend to be nullified by the larger system.

Group inertia—Even if individuals want to change their behavior, group norms may act as a constraint.

Threat to expertise—Changes in organizational patterns may threaten the expertise of specialized groups.

Threat to established power relationships—Any redistribution of decision-making authority can threaten long-established power relationships within the organization.

Overcoming Resistance to Change

Eight tactics can help change agents deal with resistance to change.[11] Let's review them briefly.

Communication   Communication is more important than ever in times of change. One study of German companies revealed changes are most effective when a company communicates a rationale that balances the interests of various stakeholders (shareholders, employees, community, customers) rather than those of shareholders only.[12] Other research on a changing organization in the Philippines found that formal information sessions decreased employees' anxiety about the change, while providing high-quality information about the change increased their commitment to it.[13]

Participation   It's difficult to resist a change decision in which we've participated. Assuming participants have the expertise to make a meaningful contribution, their involvement can reduce resistance, obtain commitment, and increase the quality of the change decision. However, against these advantages are the negatives: the potential for a poor solution and a great consumption of time.

Building Support and Commitment   When managers or employees have low emotional commitment to change, they resist it and favor the status quo.[14] Employees are also more accepting of changes when they are committed to the organization as a whole.[15] So, firing up employees and emphasizing their commitment to the organization overall can help them emotionally commit to the change rather than embrace the status quo. When employees' fear and anxiety are high, counseling and therapy, new-skills training, or a short paid leave of absence may facilitate adjustment to change.

Develop Positive Relationships   People are more willing to accept changes if they trust the managers implementing them.[16] One study surveyed 235 employees from a large housing corporation in the Netherlands that was experiencing a merger. Those who had a more positive relationship with their supervisor, and who felt that the work environment supported development, were much more positive about

The Ohio Department of Natural Resources used participation as an effective tactic for overcoming resistance to change. Faced with the tough task of reducing the use of time and resources, the cash-strapped department involved employees in a continuous improvement process, shown here, to find better ways to work more efficiently.
Source: Kiichiro Sato/AP Images

the change process.[17] Underscoring the importance of social context, other work shows that even individuals who are generally resistant to change will be more willing to accept new and different ideas when they feel supported by their coworkers and believe the environment is safe for taking risks.[18] Another set of studies found that individuals who were dispositionally resistant to change felt more positive about it if they trusted the change agent.[19] This research suggests that if managers are able to facilitate positive relationships, they may be able to overcome resistance to change even among those who ordinarily don't like changes.

Implementing Changes Fairly　One way organizations can minimize negative impact is to make sure change is implemented fairly. As we saw in Chapter 7, procedural fairness is especially important when employees perceive an outcome as negative, so it's crucial that employees see the reason for the change and perceive its implementation as consistent and fair.[20]

Manipulation and Cooptation　*Manipulation* refers to covert influence attempts. Twisting facts to make them more attractive, withholding information, and creating false rumors to get employees to accept change are all examples of manipulation. If management threatens to close a manufacturing plant whose employees are resisting an across-the-board pay cut, and if the threat is actually unfounded, management is using manipulation. *Cooptation,* on the other hand, combines manipulation and participation. It seeks to buy off the leaders of a resistance group by giving them a key role, seeking their advice not to find a better solution but to get their endorsement. Both manipulation and cooptation are relatively inexpensive ways to gain the support of adversaries, but they can backfire if the targets become aware they are being tricked or used. Once that's discovered, the change agent's credibility may drop to zero.

Selecting People Who Accept Change　Research suggests the ability to easily accept and adapt to *change* is related to personality—some people simply have more positive attitudes.[21] Individuals who are open to experience, take a positive attitude toward change, are willing to take risks, and are flexible in their behavior are prime candidates. This seems to be universal. One study of managers in the United States, Europe, and Asia found those with a positive self-concept and high risk tolerance coped better with organizational change. A study of 258 police officers found those who were higher in the need for growth/development and internal work motivation, and who had an internal locus of control, held more positive attitudes about organizational change efforts.[22] Individuals higher in general mental ability are also better able to learn and adapt to changes in the workplace.[23] In sum, an impressive body of evidence shows organizations can facilitate change by selecting people predisposed to accept it.

Besides selecting individuals who are willing to accept changes, it is also possible to select teams that are more adaptable. In general, teams that are strongly motivated by learning about and mastering tasks are better able to adapt to changing environments.[24] It may thus be necessary to consider not just individual motivation, but also group motivation, when trying to implement changes.

Coercion　Last on the list of tactics is *coercion,* the application of direct threats or force on the resisters. If management is determined to close a manufacturing plant whose employees don't acquiesce to a pay cut, the company is using coercion. Other examples include threatening employees with transfers, blocked promotions, negative performance evaluations, and poor letters of recommendation. Coercion is most effective when some force or pressure is enacted on at least some resisters—for instance, if an employee is publicly refused a transfer request, the threat of blocked promotions will become a real possibility in the minds of other employees. The advantages and drawbacks of coercion are approximately the same as for manipulation and cooptation.

The Politics of Change

No discussion of resistance would be complete without a brief mention of the politics of change. Because change invariably threatens the status quo, it inherently implies political activity.

Politics suggests the impetus for change is more likely to come from outside change agents, employees new to the organization (who have less invested in the status quo), or managers slightly removed from the main power structure. Managers who have spent a long time with an organization and achieved a senior position in the hierarchy are often major impediments to change. For them, change can be a very real threat to their status and position. Yet they may be expected to implement changes to demonstrate they're not merely caretakers. By acting as change agents, they can convey to stockholders, suppliers, employees, and customers that they are addressing problems and adapting to a dynamic environment. Of course, as you might guess, when forced to introduce change, these longtime power holders tend to implement incremental changes. Radical change is often considered too threatening. This explains why boards of directors that recognize the imperative for rapid and radical change frequently turn to outside candidates for new leadership.[25]

Approaches to Managing Organizational Change

18-3   Compare the four main approaches to managing organizational change.

We now turn to several approaches to managing change: Lewin's classic three-step model of the change process, Kotter's eight-step plan, action research, and organizational development.

Lewin's Three-Step Model

Kurt Lewin argued that successful change in organizations should follow three steps: *unfreezing* the status quo, *movement* to a desired end state, and *refreezing* the new change to make it permanent[26] (see Exhibit 18-3).

By definition, status quo is an equilibrium state. To move from equilibrium—to overcome the pressures of both individual resistance and group conformity—unfreezing must happen in one of three ways (see Exhibit 18-4). For one, the **driving forces**, which direct behavior away from the status quo, can be increased. For another, the **restraining forces**, which hinder movement away from equilibrium, can be decreased. A third alternative is to combine the first two approaches. Companies that have been successful in the past are likely to encounter restraining forces because people question the need for change.[27]

driving forces   Forces that direct behavior away from the status quo (Lewin).

restraining forces   Forces that hinder movement from the existing equilibrium (Lewin).

Exhibit 18-3	Lewin's Three-Step Change Model

Unfreezing → Movement → Refreezing

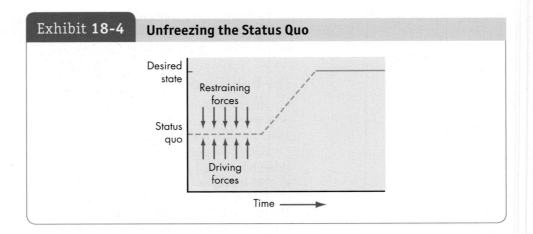

Exhibit 18-4   **Unfreezing the Status Quo**

Once the movement stage begins, it's important to keep the momentum going. Organizations that build up to change do less well than those that get to and through the movement stage quickly. When change has been implemented, the new situation must be refrozen so it can be sustained over time. Without this last step, change will likely be short-lived and employees will attempt to revert to the previous equilibrium state. The objective of refreezing, then, is to stabilize the new situation by balancing the driving and restraining forces.

Kotter's Eight-Step Plan

John Kotter of Harvard Business School built on Lewin's three-step model to create a more detailed approach for implementing change.[28] Kotter began by listing common mistakes managers make when trying to initiate change. They may fail to create a sense of urgency about the need for change, a coalition for managing the change process, a vision for change and effectively communicate it, and/or to anchor the changes into the organization's culture. They also may fail to remove obstacles that could impede the vision's achievement and/or provide short-term and achievable goals. Finally, they may declare victory too soon.

Kotter established eight sequential steps to overcome these problems. They're listed in Exhibit 18-5.

Exhibit 18-5   **Kotter's Eight-Step Plan for Implementing Change**

1. Establish a sense of urgency by creating a compelling reason for why change is needed.
2. Form a coalition with enough power to lead the change.
3. Create a new vision to direct the change and strategies for achieving the vision.
4. Communicate the vision throughout the organization.
5. Empower others to act on the vision by removing barriers to change and encouraging risk taking and creative problem solving.
6. Plan for, create, and reward short-term "wins" that move the organization toward the new vision.
7. Consolidate improvements, reassess changes, and make necessary adjustments in the new programs.
8. Reinforce the changes by demonstrating the relationship between new behaviors and organizational success.

Source: Based on M. du Plessis, "Re-implementing an Individual Performance Management System as a Change Intervention at Higher Education Institutions Overcoming Staff Resistance," *Proceedings of the 7th European Conference on Management Leadership and Governance,* 2011, 105–15.

Notice how Kotter's first four steps essentially extrapolate Lewin's "unfreezing" stage. Steps 5, 6, and 7 represent "movement," and the final step works on "refreezing." So Kotter's contribution lies in providing managers and change agents with a more detailed guide for successfully implementing change.

Action Research

action research A change process based on systematic collection of data and then selection of a change action based on what the analyzed data indicate.

Action research is a change process based on the systematic collection of data and selection of a change action based on what the analyzed data indicate.[29] Its value is in providing a scientific methodology for managing planned change. Action research consists of five steps (note how they closely parallel the scientific method): diagnosis, analysis, feedback, action, and evaluation.

The change agent, often an outside consultant in action research, begins by gathering information about problems, concerns, and needed changes from members of the organization. This *diagnosis* is analogous to the physician's search to find specifically what ails a patient. In action research, the change agent asks questions, reviews records, and interviews employees, actively listening to their concerns.

Diagnosis is followed by *analysis*. What problems do people key in on? What patterns do these problems seem to take? The change agent synthesizes this information into primary concerns, problem areas, and possible actions.

Action research requires the people who will participate in a change program to help identify the problem and determine the solution. So the third step—*feedback*—requires sharing with employees what has been found from the first and second steps. The employees, with the help of the change agent, develop action plans for bringing about needed change.

Now the *action* part of action research is set in motion. The employees and the change agent carry out the specific actions they have identified to correct the problem.

The final step, consistent with the scientific underpinnings of action research, is *evaluation* of the action plan's effectiveness, using the initial data gathered as a benchmark.

Action research provides at least two specific benefits. First, it's problem-focused. The change agent objectively looks for problems, and the type of problem determines the type of change action. This is a process that makes intuitive sense. Unfortunately, this is too often not the case in reality. Change activities can become solution-centered and therefore erroneously predetermined. The change agent has a favorite solution—for example, implementing flextime, teams, or a process reengineering program—and then seeks out problems that the solution fits.

A second benefit of action research is the lowering of resistance. Because action research engages employees so thoroughly in the process, it reduces resistance to change. Once employees have actively participated in the feedback stage, the change process typically takes on a momentum of its own.

Organizational Development

organizational development (OD) A collection of planned change interventions, built on humanistic–democratic values, that seeks to improve organizational effectiveness and employee well-being.

Organizational development (OD) is a collection of change methods that try to improve organizational effectiveness and employee well-being.[30]

OD methods value human and organizational growth, collaborative and participative processes, and a spirit of inquiry.[31] Contemporary OD borrows heavily from postmodern philosophy in placing heavy emphasis on the subjective ways people see and make sense of their work environment. The change agent may take the lead in OD, but there is a strong emphasis on collaboration.

What are some OD techniques or interventions for bringing about change? Here are six.

sensitivity training   Training groups that seek to change behavior through unstructured group interaction.

Sensitivity Training   A variety of names—**sensitivity training**, laboratory training, encounter groups, and T-groups (training groups)—all refer to an early method of changing behavior through unstructured group interaction.[32] Current organizational interventions such as diversity training, executive coaching, and team-building exercises are descendants of this early OD intervention technique.

In classic sensitivity training, members were brought together in a free and open environment in which participants discussed themselves and their interactive processes, loosely directed by a professional behavioral scientist who created the opportunity to express ideas, beliefs, and attitudes without taking any leadership role. The group was process oriented, which means individuals learned through observing and participating rather than being told. With all forms of OD, caution must be taken so the unstructured groups are not intimidating, chaotic, and damaging to work relationships.

survey feedback   The use of questionnaires to identify discrepancies among member perceptions; discussion follows, and remedies are suggested.

Survey Feedback   One tool for assessing the attitudes of organizational members, identifying discrepancies among member perceptions, and solving differences is the **survey feedback** approach.[33]

Everyone in an organization can participate in survey feedback, but of key importance is the organizational "family"—the manager of any given unit and the employees who report directly to him or her. All usually complete a questionnaire about their perceptions and attitudes on a range of topics, including decision-making practices; communication effectiveness; coordination among units; and satisfaction with the organization, job, peers, and immediate supervisor.

Data from questionnaires are tabulated along with data pertaining to an individual's specific "family" and the entire organization, and then distributed to employees. These data become the springboard for identifying problems and clarifying issues that may be creating difficulties for people. Particular attention is given to encouraging discussion and ensuring it focuses on issues and ideas, not on attacking individuals. For instance, are people listening? Are new ideas being generated? Can decision making, interpersonal relations, or job assignments be improved? Answers should lead the group to commit to various remedies for the problems.

The survey feedback approach can be helpful to keep decision makers informed about the attitudes of employees toward the organization. However, individuals are influenced by many factors when they respond to surveys, which may make some findings unreliable. Second, a high number of nonresponses may indicate organizational dysfunction or decreased job satisfaction, which the absence of data will not show. Managers who use the survey feedback approach should therefore monitor their organization's current events and employee response rates.

process consultation (PC)   A meeting in which a consultant assists a client in understanding process events with which he or she must deal and identifying processes that need improvement.

Process Consultation   Managers often sense their unit's performance can be improved but are unable to identify what to improve and how. The purpose of **process consultation (PC)** is for an outside consultant to assist a client, usually a manager, "to perceive, understand, and act upon process events" with which the manager must deal.[34] These events might include workflow, informal relationships among unit members, and formal communication channels.

PC is similar to sensitivity training in assuming we can improve organizational effectiveness by dealing with interpersonal problems and in emphasizing involvement. But PC is more task directed, and consultants do not solve the organization's problems, but rather guide or coach the client to solve his or her own problems after *jointly* diagnosing what needs improvement. The client develops the skill to analyze processes within his or her unit and can therefore use the skill long after the consultant is gone. Because the client actively participates in both the diagnosis and the development of alternatives, he or she arrives at a greater understanding of the process and the remedy, and becomes less resistant to the action plan chosen.

Team Building   We've noted throughout this text that organizations increasingly rely on teams to accomplish work tasks. **Team building** uses high-interaction group activities to increase trust and openness among team members, improve coordinative efforts, and increase team performance.[35] Here, we emphasize the intragroup level, meaning within organizational families (command groups) as well as committees, project teams, self-managed teams, and task groups.

Team building typically includes goal-setting, development of interpersonal relations among team members, role analysis to clarify each member's role and responsibilities, and team process analysis. It may emphasize or exclude certain activities, depending on the purpose of the development effort and the specific problems the team is confronting. Basically, however, team building uses high interaction among members to increase trust and openness. In these times when organizations increasingly rely on teams, team building is an important topic.

Intergroup Development   A major area of concern in OD is dysfunctional conflict among groups. **Intergroup development** seeks to change groups' attitudes, stereotypes, and perceptions about each other. Here, training sessions closely resemble diversity training, except rather than focusing on demographic differences, they focus on differences among occupations, departments, or divisions within an organization.

In one organization, for example, the engineers saw the accounting department as composed of shy and conservative types, and the HR department as having a bunch of "ultra-liberals more concerned that some protected group of employees might get their feelings hurt than with the company making a profit." Such stereotypes can have an obvious negative impact on coordination efforts among departments.

team building   High interaction among team members to increase trust and openness.

intergroup development   Organizational development (OD) efforts to change the attitudes, stereotypes, and perceptions that groups have of each other.

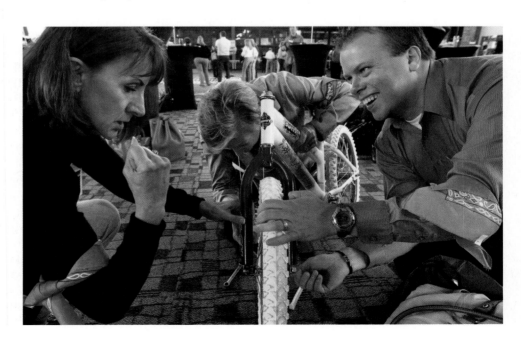

United Health Group employee volunteers participate in a team-building activity that makes bicycles for children in need. The high-interaction project increases trust and deepens respect among employees, which transfers to better communication and cooperation in the workplace.
Source: Tom Wallace/Minneapolis Star Tribune/MCT/Landov

Among several approaches for improving intergroup relations, a popular one emphasizes problem solving.[36] Each group meets independently to list its perceptions of itself and another group and how it believes the other group perceives it. The groups then share their lists, discuss similarities and differences, and look for causes of disparities. Are the groups' goals at odds? Are the perceptions distorted? On what basis were stereotypes formulated? Have some differences been caused by a misunderstanding of intentions? Have words and concepts been defined differently by each group? Answers to questions like these clarify the exact nature of the conflict.

Once they have identified the causes of discrepancies, the groups move to the integration phase—developing solutions to improve relations between them. Subgroups can be formed of members from each of the conflicting groups to conduct further diagnoses and formulate alternative solutions.

appreciative inquiry (AI) An approach that seeks to identify the unique qualities and special strengths of an organization, which can then be built on to improve performance.

Appreciative Inquiry Most OD approaches are problem-centered. They identify a problem or set of problems, then look for a solution. **Appreciative inquiry (AI)** instead accentuates the positive.[37] Rather than looking for problems to fix, it seeks to identify the unique qualities and special strengths of an organization, which members can build on to improve performance. That is, AI focuses on an organization's successes rather than its problems.

The AI process consists of four steps—discovery, dreaming, design, and destiny—often played out in a large-group meeting over 2 to 3 days and overseen by a trained change agent. *Discovery* sets out to identify what people think are the organization's strengths. Employees recount times they felt the organization worked best or when they specifically felt most satisfied with their jobs. In *dreaming*, employees use information from the discovery phase to speculate on possible futures, such as what the organization will be like in 5 years. In *design*, participants find a common vision of how the organization will look in the future and agree on its unique qualities. For the fourth step, participants seek to define the organization's *destiny* or how to fulfill their dream, and they typically write action plans and develop implementation strategies.

AI has proven an effective change strategy in organizations such as GTE, Roadway Express, and the U.S. Navy. American Express used AI to revitalize its culture during a lean economy. In workshops, employees described how they already felt proud of working at American Express and were encouraged to create a change vision by describing how it could be better in the future. The efforts led to some concrete improvements. Senior managers were able to use employees' information to better their methods of making financial forecasts, improve IT investments, and create new performance-management tools for managers. The end result was a renewed culture focused on winning attitudes and behaviors.[38]

> ✪ **TRY IT!**
>
> If your professor has assigned this, go to the Assignments section of **mymanagementlab.com** to complete the **Simulation:** *Change*.

Creating a Culture for Change

18-4 Demonstrate three ways of creating a culture for change.

We've considered how organizations can *adapt* to change. But recently, some OB scholars have focused on a more proactive approach—how organizations can *embrace* change by transforming their cultures. In this section, we review three approaches: managing paradox, stimulating an innovative culture, and creating a learning organization. We also address the issue of organizational change and stress.

Managing Paradox

In a *paradox* situation, we are required to balance tensions across various courses of action. There is a constant process of finding a balancing point, a dynamic equilibrium, among shifting priorities over time. Think of riding a bicycle: you must maintain forward momentum or you'll fall over. From this perspective, there is no such thing as a separate discipline of "change management" because all management is dealing with constant change and adaptation.

The idea of paradox sounds abstract, but more specific concepts have begun to emerge from a growing body of research.[39] Several key paradoxes have been identified. *Learning* is a paradox because it requires building on the past while rejecting it at the same time. *Organizing* is a paradox because it calls for setting direction and leading while requiring empowerment and flexibility. *Performing* is a paradox between creating organization-wide goals to concentrate effort and recognizing the diverse goals of stakeholders inside and outside the organization. And finally, *belonging* is a paradox between establishing a sense of collective identity and acknowledging our desire to be recognized and accepted as unique individuals.

paradox theory The theory that the key paradox in management is that there is no final optimal status for an organization.

Managers can learn a few lessons from **paradox theory**,[40] which states the key paradox in management is that there is no final optimal status for an organization.[41] The first lesson is that as the environment and members of the organization change, different elements take on more or less importance. For example, sometimes a company needs to acknowledge past success and learn how it worked, while at other times looking backward will only hinder progress. There is some evidence that managers who think holistically and recognize the importance of balancing paradoxical factors are more effective, especially in generating adaptive and creative behavior in those they are managing.[42]

Stimulating a Culture of Innovation

How can an organization become more innovative? An excellent model is W. L. Gore, the $2.6-billion-per-year company best known as the maker of Gore-Tex fabric.[43] Gore has developed a reputation as one of the most innovative U.S. companies by developing a stream of diverse products—including guitar strings, vacuum cleaner filters, industrial sealants, and fuel cell components.

What's the secret of Gore's success? What can other organizations do to duplicate its track record for innovation? Gore pioneered a flat, unique lattice-type organizational structure (now termed an open allocation structure)[44] run by employees (associates) working in self-organized project groups.[45] Although there is no guaranteed formula, certain characteristics surface repeatedly when researchers study innovative organizations. They are structural, cultural, and human resource characteristics. Change agents should consider introducing these characteristics into their organizations to create an innovative climate. Let's start by clarifying what we mean by innovation.

innovation A new idea applied to initiating or improving a product, process, or service.

Definition of *Innovation* We said change refers to making things different. **Innovation**, a specialized kind of change, is applied to initiating or improving a product, process, or service; a better solution.[46] So all innovations imply change, but not all changes introduce new ideas or lead to significant improvements. Innovations can range from incremental improvements, such as tablets, to radical breakthroughs, such as Nissan's electric Leaf car.

Based on its motto "Think Different," Apple has built a culture of innovation where employees share a passion for creating consumer friendly products like the Apple Watch, shown here displayed by a customer at an Apple store in Toronto, Canada. Apple's supportive culture embraces cross-fertilization of ideas, collaboration, experimentation, and risk taking.

Source: Ryan Emberley/Invision for Apple/AP Images

Sources of Innovation   *Structural variables* are one potential source of innovation.[47] A comprehensive review of the structure–innovation relationship leads to the following conclusions:[48]

1. **Organic structures positively influence innovation.**   Because they're lower in vertical differentiation, formalization, and centralization, organic organizations facilitate the flexibility, adaptation, and cross-fertilization that make the adoption of innovations easier.
2. **Long tenure in management is associated with innovation.**   Managerial tenure can provide the legitimacy and knowledge of how to accomplish tasks and obtain desired outcomes through creative methods.
3. **Innovation is nurtured when there are slack resources.**   Having an abundance of resources allows an organization to afford to purchase or develop innovations, bear the cost of instituting them, and absorb failures.
4. **Interunit communication is high in innovative organizations.**[49]   These organizations are heavy users of committees, task forces, cross-functional teams, and other mechanisms that facilitate interaction across departmental lines.

Context and Innovation   Innovative organizations tend to have similar *cultures.* They encourage experimentation and reward both successes and failures. They celebrate mistakes. Unfortunately, in too many organizations, people are rewarded for the absence of failures rather than for the presence of successes. Such cultures extinguish risk taking and innovation. People will suggest and try new ideas only when they feel such behaviors exact no penalties. Managers in innovative organizations recognize that failures are a natural by-product of venturing into the unknown.

Within the *human resources* category, innovative organizations actively promote the training and development of their members so they keep current, offer high job security so employees don't fear getting fired for making mistakes, and encourage individuals to become champions of change. These practices should be mirrored for workgroups as well. One study of 1,059 individuals on over 200 different teams in a Chinese high-tech company found that work systems emphasizing commitment to employees increased creativity in teams.[50] These effects were even greater in teams where there was cohesion among coworkers.

idea champions   Individuals who take an innovation and actively and enthusiastically promote the idea, build support, overcome resistance, and ensure that the idea is implemented.

Idea Champions and Innovation   Once a new idea has been developed, **idea champions** actively and enthusiastically promote it, build support, overcome resistance, and ensure it is implemented.[51] Champions often have similar personality characteristics: extremely high self-confidence, persistence, energy, and a tendency to take risks. They usually display traits associated with transformational leadership—they inspire and energize others with their vision of an innovation's potential and their strong personal conviction about their mission. Situations can also influence the extent to which idea champions are forces for change. For example, passion for change among entrepreneurs is greatest when work roles and the social environment encourage them to put their creative identities forward.[52] On the flip side, work roles that push creative individuals to do routine management and administration tasks will diminish both the passion for and implementation of change. Idea champions are good at gaining the commitment of others, and their jobs should provide considerable decision-making discretion. This autonomy helps them introduce and implement innovations[53] when the context is supportive.

Do successful idea champions do things differently in varied cultures? Yes.[54] Generally, people in collectivist cultures prefer appeals for cross-functional support for innovation efforts; people in high power-distance cultures prefer champions to work closely with those in authority to approve innovative activities before work is begun; and the higher the uncertainty avoidance of a society, the more champions should work within the organization's rules and procedures to develop the innovation. These findings suggest that effective managers will alter their organization's innovation strategies to reflect cultural values. So, for instance, although idea champions in Russia might succeed by ignoring budgetary limitations and working around confining procedures, champions in Austria, Denmark, Germany, or other cultures high in uncertainty avoidance will be more effective by closely following budgets and procedures.

Sergio Marcchione, CEO of Fiat-Chrysler, originally acted as an idea champion for the single objective of updating the company's product pipeline. To facilitate the change, he radically dismantled the bureaucracy, tearing up Chrysler's organization chart and introducing a flatter structure with himself at the head. As a result, the company introduced a more innovative line of vehicles and planned to redesign or substantially refresh 75 percent of its lineup in 2010 alone.[55] In 2014, Marchionne announced an ambitious plan to significantly increase the company's U.S. auto sales through innovations in the product line. The organization is struggling to make his dreams a reality by 2018, but they remain committed to his goals. "We've always had something that came out of left field and made us very, very uncomfortable," Marcchione said—the rallying cry for any idea champion.[56]

Creating a Learning Organization

Another way an organization can proactively manage change is to make continuous growth part of its culture—to become a learning organization.[57]

learning organization   An organization that has developed the continuous capacity to adapt and change.

What's a Learning Organization?   Just as individuals learn, so too do organizations. A **learning organization** has developed the continuous capacity to adapt and change. The Dimensions of the Learning Organization Questionnaire (DLOQ) has been adopted and adapted internationally to assess the degree of commitment to learning organization principles.[58]

Exhibit 18-6	Characteristics of a Learning Organization

1. There exists a shared vision that everyone agrees on.

2. People discard their old ways of thinking and the standard routines they use for solving problems or doing their jobs.

3. Members think of all organizational processes, activities, functions, and interactions with the environment as part of a system of interrelationships.

4. People openly communicate with each other (across vertical and horizontal boundaries) without fear of criticism or punishment.

5. People sublimate their personal self-interest and fragmented departmental interests to work together to achieve the organization's shared vision.

Source: Based on P. M. Senge, *The Fifth Discipline: The Art and Practice of the Learning Organization* (New York: Doubleday, 2006).

Exhibit 18-6 summarizes the five basic characteristics of a learning organization—one in which people put aside their old ways of thinking, learn to be open with each other, understand how their organization really works, form a plan or vision everyone can agree on, and work together to achieve that vision.[59]

Proponents of the learning organization envision it as a remedy for three fundamental problems of traditional organizations: fragmentation, competition, and reactiveness.[60] First, *fragmentation* based on specialization creates "walls" and "chimneys" that separate different functions into independent and often warring fiefdoms. Second, an overemphasis on *competition* often undermines collaboration. Managers compete to show who is right, knows more, or is more persuasive. Divisions compete when they ought to cooperate and share knowledge. Team leaders compete to show who the best manager is. And third, *reactiveness* misdirects management's attention to solving problems rather than creating. The problem solver tries to make something go away, while a creator tries to bring something new into being. An emphasis on reactiveness to problems pushes out innovation and continuous improvement and, in its place, encourages people to constantly run around "putting out fires."

Managing Learning   What can managers do to make their firms learning organizations? Here are some suggestions:

- *Establish a strategy.*   Management needs to make explicit its commitment to change, innovation, and continuous improvement.
- *Redesign the organization's structure.*   The formal structure can be a serious impediment to learning. Flattening the structure, eliminating or combining departments, and increasing the use of cross-functional teams reinforces interdependence and reduces boundaries.
- *Reshape the organization's culture.*   To become a learning organization, managers must demonstrate by their actions that taking risks and admitting failures are desirable. This means rewarding people who take chances and make mistakes. And management needs to encourage functional conflict.

Organizational Change and Stress

Think about the times you have felt stressed during your work life. Look past the everyday stress factors that can spill over to the workplace, like a traffic jam that makes you late for work or a broken coffee machine that keeps you from your morning java. What were your more memorable and lasting stressful times at work? For many people, these were caused by organizational change.

Researchers are increasingly studying the effects of organizational change on employees. We are interested in determining the specific causes and mitigating factors of stress to learn how to manage organizational change effectively. The overall findings are that organizational changes that incorporate OB knowledge of how people react to stressors may yield more effective results than organizational changes that are managed only objectively through goal-setting plans.[61]

Not surprisingly, we also find the role of leadership is critical. One study indicated that transformational leaders can help shape employee affect so employees stay committed to the change and do not perceive it as stressful.[62] Other research indicated that a positive orientation toward change *before* new initiatives are planned will decrease employees' stress when they go through organizational changes and increase their positive attitudes. Managers can be continually working to increase employees' self-efficacy, change-related attitudes, and perceived control over the situation to create this positive change orientation. For instance, they can use role clarification and continual rewards to increase self-efficacy, and they can enhance employees' perceived control and positive attitudes toward change by including them from the planning stages to the application of new processes.[63] Another study added the need for increasing the amount of communication to employees during change, assessing and enhancing employees' psychological resilience through offering social support, and training employees in emotional self-regulation techniques.[64] Through these methods, managers can help employees keep their stress levels low and their commitment high.

Often, organizational changes are stressful because some employees perceive aspects of the changes as threatening. These employees are more likely to quit, partially in reaction to their stress. To reduce the perception of threat, employees need to perceive the organizational changes as fair. Research indicates that those who have a positive change orientation before changes are planned are less likely to perceive of changes as unfair or threatening.

✪ WATCH IT!

If your professor has assigned this, go to the Assignments section of **mymanagementlab.com** to complete the video exercise titled *East Haven Fire Department: Managing Stress.*

Stress at Work

18-5 Identify the potential environmental, organizational, and personal sources of stress at work and the role of individual and cultural differences.

Friends say they're stressed from greater workloads and longer hours because of downsizing at their organizations. Parents worry about the lack of job stability and reminisce about a time when a job with a large corporation implied lifetime security. Employees complain about the stress of trying to balance work and family responsibilities. Harris, Rothenberg International, a leading provider of employee assistance programs (EAPs), finds that employees are having mental breakdowns and needing professional help at higher rates than ever.[65] Indeed, as Exhibit 18-7 shows, work is a major source of stress in most people's lives. What are the causes and consequences of stress, and what can individuals and organizations do to reduce it?

What Is Stress?

stress An unpleasant psychological process that occurs in response to environmental pressures.

Do you feel stressed? If so, join the crowd (see OB Poll). **Stress** is a dynamic condition in which an individual is confronted with an opportunity, demand, or resource related to what the individual desires and for which the outcome is

Exhibit 18-7	**Work Is a Top Source of Stress**

What area of your life causes you the most stress?

Area	Causes Most Stress
Financial worries	64%
Work	60%
Family responsibilities	47%
Health concerns	46%

Source: Stress in America: Paying with Our Health," American Psychological Association, February 4, 2015, http://www.apa.org/news/press/releases/stress/2014/stress-report.pdf.

perceived to be both uncertain and important.[66] This is a complicated definition. Let's look at its components more closely.

Although stress is typically discussed in a negative context, it also has a positive purpose. In response to stress, your nervous system, hypothalamus, pituitary, and adrenal glands supply you with stress hormones to cope. Your heartbeat and breathing accelerate to increase oxygen, while your muscles tense for action.[67] This is a time when stress offers potential gain. Consider, for example, the superior performance an athlete or stage performer gives in a "clutch" situation. Such individuals often use stress positively to rise to the occasion and perform at their maximum. Similarly, many professionals see the pressures of heavy workloads and deadlines as positive challenges that enhance the quality of their work and the satisfaction they get from their job. However, when the situation is negative, stress is harmful and may hinder your progress by elevating your blood pressure uncomfortably and creating an erratic heart rhythm as you struggle to speak and think logically.[68]

challenge stressors Stressors associated with workload, pressure to complete tasks, and time urgency.

Stressors   Researchers have argued that **challenge stressors**—or stressors associated with workload, pressure to complete tasks, and time urgency—

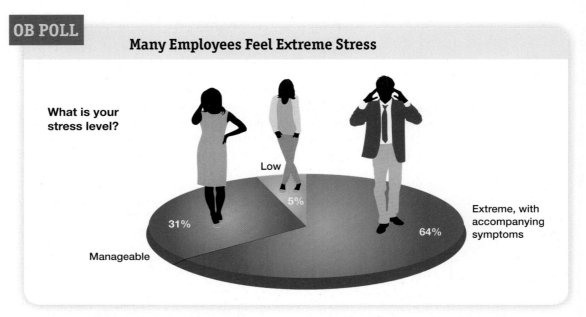

OB POLL

Many Employees Feel Extreme Stress

What is your stress level?

Low 5%

31% Manageable

Extreme, with accompanying symptoms 64%

Source: J. Hudson, "High Stress Has Employees Seeking Both Wellness and Employee Assistance Help," ComPsych Corporation press release, November 12, 2014, http://www.compsych.com/press-room/press-releases-2014/818-nov-12-2014.

hindrance stressors   Stressors that keep you from reaching your goals (for example, red tape, office politics, confusion over job responsibilities).

operate quite differently from **hindrance stressors**—or stressors that keep you from reaching your goals (for example, red tape, office politics, confusion over job responsibilities). Although research is just starting to accumulate, early evidence suggests challenge stressors produce less strain than hindrance stressors.[69]

Researchers have sought to clarify the conditions under which each type of stress exists. It appears that employees who have stronger affective commitment to their organizations can transfer psychological stress into greater focus and higher sales performance, whereas employees with low levels of commitment perform worse under stress.[70] And when challenge stress increases, those with high levels of organizational support realize higher role-based performance, but those with low levels of organizational support do not.[71]

demands   Responsibilities, pressures, obligations, and even uncertainties that individuals face in the workplace.

resources   Things within an individual's control that can be used to resolve demands.

Demands and Resources   More typically, stress is associated with **demands** and **resources**. Demands are responsibilities, pressures, obligations, and uncertainties individuals face in the workplace. Resources are things within an individual's control that he or she can use to resolve the demands. Let's discuss what this demands–resources model means.[72]

When you take a test at school or undergo your annual performance review at work, you feel stress because you confront opportunities and performance pressures. A good performance review may lead to a promotion, greater responsibilities, and a higher salary. A poor review may prevent you from getting a promotion. An extremely poor review might even result in your being fired. To the extent you can apply resources to the demands on you—such as preparing for the review, putting the review in perspective (it's not the end of the world), or obtaining social support—you will feel less stress. In fact, this last resource—social support—may be more important on an ongoing basis than anything else. According to recent research, people with emotional support may feel lower stress levels, less depressed from stress, and more likely to make lifestyle changes that may reduce stress.[73] Overall, under the demands–resources perspective, having resources to cope with stress is just as important in offsetting stress as demands are in increasing it.[74]

allostasis   Working to change behavior and attitudes to find stability.

Allostasis   All this may give you the impression that individuals are seeking a steady state in which demands perfectly match resources. While early research tended to emphasize such a *homeostatic,* or balanced equilibrium, perspective, it has now become clear that no single ideal state exists. Instead, it's more accurate to talk about *allostatic* models in which demands shift, resources shift, and systems of addressing imbalances shift.[75] By **allostasis**, we work to find stability by changing our behaviors and attitudes. It all depends on the allostatic load, or the cumulative effect of stressors on us given the resources we draw upon.[76] For example, if you're feeling especially confident in your abilities and have lots of support from others, you may increase your willingness to experience strain and be better able to mobilize coping resources. This would be a situation where the allostatic load was not too great; in other cases where the allostatic load is too great and too prolonged, we may experience psychological or physiological stress symptoms.

There are also cycles in stress preferences. You've experienced this when you sometimes just feel like relaxing and recovering, while at other times you welcome more stimulation and challenge. So, much like organizations are in a constant state of change and flux, we respond to stress processes by continually adapting to both internal and external sources, and our stability is constantly redefined.

Potential Sources of Stress at Work

What causes stress? Let's examine the model in Exhibit 18-8.

Exhibit 18-8   A Model of Stress

Potential sources

Environmental factors
- Economic uncertainty
- Political uncertainty
- Technological change

Organizational factors
- Task demands
- Role demands
- Interpersonal demands

Personal factors
- Family problems
- Economic problems

Individual differences
- Perception
- Job experience
- Social support
- Personality traits

Experienced stress

Cultural differences

Consequences

Physiological symptoms
- Immediate effects
- Illness
- Chronic health conditions

Psychological symptoms
- Anxiety
- Lower emotional well-being
- Lower job satisfaction

Behavioral symptoms
- Lower job performance
- Higher absenteeism
- Higher turnover

Environmental Factors   Just as environmental uncertainty influences the design of an organization's structure, it also influences stress levels among employees in that organization. Indeed, uncertainty is the biggest reason people have trouble coping with organizational changes.[77] There are three main types of environmental uncertainty: economic, political, and technological.

Changes in the business cycle create *economic uncertainties*. When the economy is contracting, for example, people become increasingly anxious about their job security. *Political uncertainties* don't tend to create stress among North Americans as much as they do for employees in countries such as Haiti or Venezuela. The obvious reason is that the United States and Canada have more stable political systems, in which change is typically implemented in an orderly manner. Yet political threats and changes in all countries can induce stress. Because innovations can make an employee's skills and experience obsolete in a very short time, keeping up with new computer programs, robotics, automation, and similar forms of *technological change* are a further challenge to many people at work that cause them stress.

Organizational Factors   There is no shortage of factors within an organization that can cause stress. Pressures to avoid errors or complete tasks in a limited time, work overload, a demanding and insensitive boss, and unpleasant coworkers are a few examples. We've categorized these factors around task, role, and interpersonal demands.

Task demands relate to a person's job. They include the design of the job (including its degree of autonomy, task variety, and automation), working conditions, and the physical work layout. The single factor most consistently related to stress in the workplace is the amount of work that needs to be done, followed closely by the presence of looming deadlines.[78] Working in an overcrowded room or a visible location where noise and interruptions are constant can also increase anxiety and stress.[79] As we discussed in earlier chapters, emotional labor causes stress.

Role demands relate to pressures placed on a person as a function of the particular role he or she plays in the organization. Role conflicts create expectations that may be hard to reconcile or satisfy. Role overload occurs when the employee is expected to take on too much. Role ambiguity means role expectations are not clearly understood and the employee is not sure what to do. Unfortunately, individuals who face high situational constraints by their roles (such as fixed work hours or demanding job responsibilities) are less able to engage in the proactive coping behaviors, like taking a break, that reduce stress levels.[80] When faced with hassles at work, they will not only have higher levels of distress at the time, but they'll also be less likely to take steps to eliminate stressors in the future.

Interpersonal demands are pressures created by other employees. Some pressures are expected, but a rapidly growing body of research has shown that negative coworker and supervisor behaviors, including fights, bullying, incivility, racial harassment, and sexual harassment, are especially strongly related to stress at work.[81] Interpersonal mistreatment can have effects at a physiological level, with one study finding that unfair treatment in a controlled setting triggered the release of cortisol, a hormone involved in the stress-reaction process.[82] Furthermore, individuals who believe they are experiencing a social climate of discrimination from multiple sources over time have higher levels

Career OBjectives

How can I bring my team's overall stress level down?

My coworkers and I are under a lot of pressure because we have a huge deadline coming up. We're working a lot of extra hours, and tensions are starting to ramp up to arguments. Is there any way I can get my team to chill out?

— Hakim

Dear Hakim:

It sounds like you're facing some of the core issues that produce stress at work: high demands, critical outcomes, and time pressure. There's no question tempers can start to flare under these conditions. While it may not even be desirable to get your team to relax, or chill out as you say, lowering your team's aggregate stress level will increase your group's effectiveness. Fortunately, there are some well-established ways to help lower stress in groups. Some of the most effective are directly related to getting people to recommit to the team:

· *To help minimize infighting, get the group to focus on a common*

goal. Shared objectives are one of the most effective ways to reduce conflict in times of stress, and they remind everyone that cooperation is key.

· *Review what the team has done and what steps toward the goal remain.* When the team can see how much work they have accomplished, they will naturally feel better.

· *When the team feels most tense, take a collective temporary break.* It can be difficult to step away from a project with heavy time demands, but working at a point of maximum tension and conflict is often counterproductive. A chance to stop and gain perspective will help everyone recharge and focus.

Remember that minimizing team stress shouldn't happen through lowering standards and accepting lower-quality work, but by reducing counterproductive organizational behavior. A positive work environment with high member engagement will do a lot to

move the group forward. A combination of focus, progress, and perspective will ultimately be the best approach to limiting your stress.

Sources: P. M. Poortvliet, F. Anseel, and F. Theuwis, "Mastery-Approach and Mastery-Avoidance Goals and Their Relation with Exhaustion and Engagement at Work: The Roles of Emotional and Instrumental Support," *Work & Stress* 29 (April 2015): 150–70; J. P. Trougakos, D. J. Beal, B. H. Cheng, I. Hideg, and D. Zweig, "Too Drained to Help: A Resource Depletion Perspective on Daily Interpersonal Citizenship Behaviors," *Journal of Applied Psychology* 100 (2015): 227–36; and J. P. Trougakos, I. Hideg, B. H. Cheng, and D. J. Beal, "Lunch Breaks Unpacked: The Role of Autonomy as a Moderator of Recovery during Lunch," *Academy of Management Journal* 57 (2014): 405–21.

of psychological strain, even after accounting for differing baseline levels of well-being.[83] Social exclusion, perhaps as a form of interpersonal mistreatment, can also be a significant source of psychological strain. One study found that experiences of ostracism may have even more negative effects than experiences of interpersonal conflict.[84]

Personal Factors   The typical individual may work between 40 and 50 hours a week. But the experiences and problems people encounter in the other 120-plus hours can spill over to the job. The final category of sources of stress at work includes factors of an employee's personal life: family issues and personal economic problems.

National surveys consistently show people hold family and personal relationships dear. *Family issues*, even good ones, can cause stress that significantly impacts individuals. Family issues are often closely related to work–life conflict.

Regardless of income level, some people are poor money managers or have wants that exceed their earning capacity. People who make $100,000 per year seem to have as much trouble handling their finances as those who earn $20,000, although recent research indicates that those who make under $50,000 per year do experience more stress.[85] The *personal economic problems* of overextended financial resources create stress and siphon attention away from work.

Stressors Are Additive   When we review stressors individually, it's easy to overlook that stress is an additive phenomenon—it builds up.[86] Each new and persistent stressor adds to an individual's stress level. So a single stressor may be relatively unimportant in and of itself, but if added to an already high level of stress, it can be too much. To appraise the total amount of stress an individual is under, we have to sum up all of the sources and severity levels of that person's stress. Since this cannot be easily quantified or observed, managers should remain aware of the potential stress loads from organizational factors in particular. Many employees are willing to express their perceived stress load at work to a caring manager.

Individual Differences

Some people thrive on stressful situations, while others are overwhelmed by them. What differentiates people in terms of their ability to handle stress? What individual variables moderate the relationship between *potential* stressors and *experienced* stress? At least four are relevant—perception, job experience, social support, and personality traits.

Perception   In Chapter 6, we demonstrated that employees react in response to their perception of reality, rather than to reality itself. *Perception*, therefore, will moderate the relationship between a potential stress condition and an employee's reaction to it. Layoffs may cause one person to fear losing his job, while another sees an opportunity to get a large severance allowance and start her own business. So stress potential doesn't lie in objective conditions; rather, it lies in an employee's interpretation of those conditions.

Job Experience   *Experience* on the job tends to be negatively related to work stress. Why? Two explanations have been offered.[87] First is selective withdrawal. Voluntary turnover is more probable among people who experience more stress. Therefore, people who remain with an organization longer are those with more stress-resistant traits or those more resistant to the stress characteristics of the organization. Second, people eventually develop coping mechanisms

DentalPlans.com employee Kristen Reineke celebrates after scoring a point while playing foosball in the employee lounge. In giving its employees the opportunity to form collegial relationships by playing games like foosball and Wii, DentalPlans provides them with the social support that can lessen the impact of on-the-job stress.
Source: Charles Trainor Jr/MCT/Newscom

to deal with stress. Because this takes time, senior members of the organization are more likely to be fully adapted and should experience less stress.

Social Support   *Social support*—collegial relationships with coworkers or supervisors—can buffer the impact of stress.[88] This is among the best-documented relationships in the stress literature. Social support acts as a palliative, mitigating the negative effects of even high-strain jobs.

Personality Traits   Stress symptoms expressed on the job may originate in the person's personality.[89] Perhaps the most widely studied *personality trait* in research on stress is neuroticism, which we discussed in Chapter 5. As you might expect, neurotic individuals are more prone to experience psychological strain.[90] Evidence suggests that neurotic individuals are more likely to find stressors in their work environments, so they believe their environments are more threatening. They also tend to select less adaptive coping mechanisms, relying on avoidance as a way of dealing with problems rather than attempting to resolve them.[91]

Workaholism is another personal characteristic related to stress levels. Workaholics are people obsessed with their work; they put in an enormous number of hours, think about work even when not working, and create additional work responsibilities to satisfy an inner compulsion to work more. In some ways, they might seem like ideal employees. That's probably why when most people are asked in interviews what their greatest weakness is, they reflexively say, "I just work too hard." However, there is a difference between working hard and working compulsively. Workaholics are not necessarily more productive than other employees, despite their extreme efforts. The strain of putting in such a high level of work effort eventually begins to wear on the person, leading to higher levels of work–life conflict and psychological burnout.[92]

Cultural Differences

Research suggests the job conditions that cause stress show some differences across cultures. One study revealed that whereas U.S. employees were stressed by a lack of control, Chinese employees were stressed by job evaluations and lack of training. It doesn't appear that personality effects on stress are different across cultures, however. One study of employees in Hungary, Italy, the United Kingdom, Israel, and the United States found Type A personality traits (see Chapter 5) predicted stress equally well across countries.[93] A study of 5,270 managers from 20 countries found individuals from individualistic countries such as the United States, Canada, and the United Kingdom experienced higher levels of stress due to work interfering with family than did individuals from collectivist countries in Asia and Latin America.[94] The authors proposed that this may occur because, in collectivist cultures, working extra hours is seen as a sacrifice to help the family, whereas in individualistic cultures, work is seen as a means to personal achievement that takes away from the family.

Evidence suggests that stressors are associated with perceived stress and strains among employees in different countries. In other words, stress is equally bad for employees of all cultures.[95]

Consequences of Stress at Work

18-6 Identify the physiological, psychological, and behavioral symptoms of stress at work.

Stress shows itself in a number of ways, such as high blood pressure, ulcers, irritability, difficulty making routine decisions, changes in appetite, accident proneness, and the like. Refer back to Exhibit 8-8. These symptoms fit under three general categories: physiological, psychological, and behavioral symptoms.

Physiological Symptoms   Most early concern with stress was directed at physiological symptoms because most researchers were specialists in the health and medical sciences. Their work led to the conclusion that stress could create changes in metabolism, increase heart and breathing rates and blood pressure, bring on headaches, and induce heart attacks.

Evidence now clearly suggests stress may have other harmful physiological effects. A long-term study conducted in the United Kingdom found that job strain was associated with higher levels of coronary heart disease.[96] Still another study conducted with Danish human services workers found that higher levels of psychological burnout at the work-unit level were related to significantly higher levels of sickness absence.[97] Many other studies have shown similar results linking work stress to a variety of indicators of poor health.

Psychological Symptoms   Job dissatisfaction is an obvious cause of stress. But stress shows itself in other psychological states—for instance, tension, anxiety, irritability, boredom, and procrastination. One study that tracked physiological responses of employees over time found that stress due to high workloads was related to lower emotional well-being.[98]

Jobs that make multiple and conflicting demands or that lack clarity about the incumbent's duties, authority, and responsibilities increase both stress and dissatisfaction.[99] Similarly, the less control people have over the pace of their work, the greater their stress and dissatisfaction. Jobs that provide a low level of variety, significance, autonomy, feedback, and identity appear to create stress and reduce satisfaction and involvement in the job.[100] Not everyone reacts to autonomy in the same way, however. For those with an external locus of control, increased job control increases the tendency to experience stress and exhaustion.[101]

Myth or Science?

When You're Working Hard, Sleep Is Optional

This is false. Individuals who do not get enough sleep are unable to perform well on the job. One study found that sleeplessness costs U.S. employers $63.2 billion per year, almost $2,300 per employee, partially due to decreased productivity and increased safety issues. Sleep deprivation has been cited as a contributing factor in heart disease, obesity, stroke, and cancer. It can also lead to disastrous accidents. For example, U.S. military researchers report that sleep deprivation is one of the top causes of friendly fire (when soldiers mistakenly fire on their own troops), and 20 percent of auto accidents are due to drowsy drivers. More than 160 people on Air India Flight 812 from Dubai to Mangalore were killed when pilot Zlatko Glusica awoke from a nap and, suffering from sleep inertia, overshot the runway in one of India's deadliest air crashes.

Sleeplessness is affecting the performance of millions of workers. According to research, one-third of U.S. employees in most industries, and more than one-quarter of workers in the finance and insurance industry, are sleep deprived, getting fewer than 6 hours of sleep per night (7 to 9 are recommended). More than 50 percent of U.S. adults age 19 to 29, 43 percent age 30 to 45, and 38 percent age 46 to 64 report that they rarely or never get a good nightly rest on weekdays.

Research has shown that lack of sleep impairs our ability to learn skills and find solutions, which may be part of the reason law-enforcement organizations, Super Bowl-winning football teams, and half the Fortune 500 companies employ "fatigue management specialists" as performance consultants.

Along with sleeplessness, insomnia has been a growing problem. Recent research in Norway indicated that up to 34 percent of motor vehicle deaths during their 14-year study period might have been prevented if there hadn't been insomnia symptoms of people involved in the crashes. Managers and employees increasingly take prescription sleep aids, attend sleep labs, and consume caffeine in efforts to either sleep better or reduce the effects of sleeplessness on their performance. These methods often backfire. Studies indicate that prescription sleep aids increase sleep time by only 11 minutes and cause short-term memory loss. The effects of sleep labs may not be helpful after the sessions are over. And the diminishing returns of caffeine, perhaps the most popular method of fighting sleep deprivation (74 percent of U.S. adults consume caffeine every day), require the ingestion of increasing amounts to achieve alertness, which can make users jittery before the effect wears off and leave them exhausted.

When you're working hard, it's easy to consider using sleep hours to get the job done, and to think that the stress and adrenaline from working will keep you alert. It's also easy to consider artificial methods in attempts to counteract the negative impact of sleep deprivation. However, research indicates that when it comes to maximizing performance and reducing accidents, we are not good at assessing our impaired capabilities when we are sleep deprived. In the end, there is no substitute for a solid night's sleep.

Sources: M. J. Breus, "Insomnia Could Kill You—By Accident," *The Huffington Post,* May 9, 2015, http://www.huffingtonpost.com/dr-michael-j-breus/insomnia-could-kill-you-by-accident_b_7235264.html; D. K. Randall, "Decoding the Science of Sleep," *The Wall Street Journal,* August 4–5, 2012, C1–C2; M. Sallinen, J. Onninen, K. Tirkkonen, M.-L. Haavisto, M. Harma, T. Kubo, et al., "Effects of Cumulative Sleep Restriction on Self-Perceptions While Multitasking," *Journal of Sleep Research,* June 2012, 273–81; and P. Walker, "Pilot Was Snoring before Air India Crash," *The Guardian,* November 17, 2010, www.guardian.co.uk/world/2010/nov/17/sleepy-pilot-blamed-air-india-crash.

Behavioral Symptoms   Research on behavior and stress has been conducted across several countries and over time, and the relationships appear relatively consistent. Behavior-related stress symptoms include reductions in productivity; increases in absences and turnover; and personal changes in eating habits, increased smoking or consumption of alcohol, rapid speech, fidgeting, and sleep disorders.[102]

A significant amount of research has investigated the stress–performance relationship. One proposed pattern of this relationship is the inverted U shown in Exhibit 18-9.[103] The logic underlying the figure is that low to moderate levels of stress stimulate the body and increase its ability to react. Individuals may perform tasks better, more intensely, or more rapidly. But too much stress places unattainable demands on a person, which result in lower performance. In spite of its popularity and intuitive appeal, the inverted-U model hasn't earned a lot

Exhibit **18-9**   **The Proposed Inverted-U Relationship between Stress and Job Performance**

of empirical support.[104] It may be that the model misses links between stressors and felt stress and job performance, meaning that sometimes there are reasons we could be stressed but feel fine because of positive moderating factors. We may be able to not let stress affect our job performance.[105] For example, one study indicated that individuals with high emotional intelligence (EI, discussed in Chapter 4) may be able to mitigate the effects of job stress on performance.[106] Therefore, this model may be a good, neutral starting point from which to study differences.

As we mentioned earlier, researchers have begun to differentiate challenge and hindrance stressors, showing that these two forms of stress have opposite effects on job behaviors, especially job performance. A meta-analysis of responses from more than 35,000 individuals showed role ambiguity, role conflict, role overload, job insecurity, environmental uncertainty, and situational constraints were all consistently negatively related to job performance.[107] There is also evidence that challenge stress improves job performance in a supportive work environment, whereas hindrance stress reduces job performance in all work environments.[108]

Managing Stress

18-7   Describe individual and organizational approaches to managing stress at work.

What should we do about stress? Should we do anything? Because low to moderate levels of stress can be functional and lead to higher performance, management may not be concerned when employees experience them. Employees, however, are likely to perceive even low levels of stress as undesirable. It's not unlikely, therefore, for employees and management to have different notions of what constitutes an acceptable level of stress on the job. What management may consider to be "a positive stimulus that keeps the adrenaline running" is very likely to be seen as "excessive pressure" by the employee. Keep this in mind as we discuss individual and organizational approaches toward managing stress.[109]

Individual Approaches

An employee can and should take personal responsibility for reducing stress levels. Individual strategies that have proven effective include time-management techniques, physical exercise, relaxation techniques, and social support networks.

Many people manage their time poorly. The well-organized employee, like the well-organized student, can often accomplish twice as much as the person who is poorly organized. A few of the best-known *time-management techniques* are: (1) maintaining to-do lists, (2) scheduling activities based on priorities, not what you can accomplish, (3) doing the hard tasks first, and (4) blocking out distraction-free time to accomplish tasks. These time-management skills can help minimize procrastination by focusing efforts on immediate goals and boosting motivation even in the face of tasks that are less enjoyable.[110]

Physicians have recommended noncompetitive *physical exercise*, such as aerobics, walking, jogging, swimming, and riding a bicycle, as a way to deal with excessive stress levels. These activities decrease the detrimental physiological responses to stress and allow us to recover from stress more quickly.[111]

Individuals can teach themselves to reduce tension through *relaxation techniques* such as meditation, hypnosis, and deep breathing. The objective is to reach a state of deep physical relaxation, in which you focus all your energy on the release of muscle tension.[112] Deep relaxation for 15 or 20 minutes a day releases strain and provides a pronounced sense of peacefulness, as well as significant changes in heart rate, blood pressure, and other physiological factors. A growing body of research shows that simply taking breaks from work at routine intervals can facilitate psychological recovery and reduce stress significantly and may improve job performance, and these effects are even greater if relaxation techniques are employed.[113]

As we have noted, friends, family, or work colleagues can provide an outlet when stress levels become excessive. Expanding your *social support network* provides someone to hear your problems and offer a more objective perspective on a stressful situation than your own.

Organizational Approaches

Several organizational factors that cause stress—particularly task and role demands—are controlled by management and thus can be modified or changed. Strategies to consider include improved employee selection and job placement, training, goal-setting, redesign of jobs, increased organizational communication, employee involvement, employee sabbaticals, and corporate wellness programs.

Selection and Placement, and Training   Certain jobs are more stressful than others but, as we've seen, individuals differ in their response to stressful situations. We know individuals with little experience or an external locus of control tend to be more prone to stress. *Selection and placement* decisions should take these facts into consideration. Obviously, management shouldn't hire only experienced individuals with an internal locus, but such individuals may adapt better to high-stress jobs and perform those jobs more effectively. Similarly, *training* can increase an individual's self-efficacy and thus lessen job strain.

Goal-Setting   We discussed *goal-setting* in Chapter 7. Individuals perform better when they have specific and challenging goals and receive feedback on their progress toward these goals. Goals can reduce stress as well as provide motivation.[114] Employees who are highly committed to their goals and see purpose in their jobs experience less stress because they are more likely to perceive stressors as challenges rather than hindrances. Specific goals perceived as attainable clarify performance expectations. In addition, goal feedback reduces uncertainties about actual job performance. The result is less employee frustration, role ambiguity, and stress.

Manager and Employee Stress during Organizational Change

When organizations are in a state of change, employees feel the stress. In fact, a recent study indicated that job pressures, often due to downsizing and other organizational changes, are the second-leading cause of stress. Dealing with that stress was previously in the domain of workers alone, who could turn to constructive (counselors, health professionals, support networks) or destructive (alcohol, gossip, counterproductive work behaviors) options as coping mechanisms. Employees who couldn't cope with stress suffered job burnout and headed to the unemployment line.

Beneficent employers provided employee assistance programs (EAP) through subcontracted counselors or in-house HR departments to counsel employees dealing with stress. Managers simply steered individuals toward these resources when workplace problems indicated a need for intervention. This help often arrived too late to mitigate the negative outcomes of stress such as lost productivity and burnout—and sometimes too late to save the employee's job. Research suggests that continually occurring job stressors, such as when organizations are in the midst of change, reduce employee engagement because workers are deprived of recovery periods. Employee stress thus needs to be addressed proactively at the manager level if it is to be effective, before there are negative work outcomes. Are managers ethically obligated to alleviate employee stress?

On the one hand, managers are responsible for maximizing productivity and realize that organizations increase profitability when fewer employees perform increased work. On the other hand, overwork will increase employee stress, particularly when the organization is in a state of change due to downsizing or growth. Managers who keep head count low and workloads high may realize short-term gains from lower workforce costs but long-term losses from negative stress outcomes, such as increased turnover and lowered productivity. Experts recommend that managers consider hiring the workers they need to keep employee workloads reasonable, adding reward programs to keep top employees engaged, and cutting non-workforce costs to maintain profitability. Smaller methods, such as teaching employees stress reduction techniques and creating a "greenery room" for a nature retreat from the office environment, can also be helpful. Managers must make the ethical choice between spending more money now on labor costs and stress reduction methods, versus later on the more hidden but salient costs of employee stress.

As research increasingly indicates, when employees react to stress, they and their organizations suffer the consequences. Managers must, therefore, consider their opportunity to help alleviate the stress before it's too late.

Sources: E. Frauenheim, "Stressed & Pressed," *Workforce Management,* January 2012, 18–22; J. B. Oldroyd and S. S. Morris, "Catching Falling Stars: A Human Resource Responses to Social Capital's Detrimental Effect of Information Overload on Star Employees," *Academy of Management Review* 37 (2012): 396–418; and S. Sonnentag, E. J. Mojza, E. Demerouti, and A. B. Bakker, "Reciprocal Relations between Recovery and Work Engagement: The Moderating Role of Job Stressors," *Journal of Applied Psychology* 97 (2012): 842–53.

Redesigning Jobs　*Redesigning jobs* to give employees more responsibility, more meaningful work, more autonomy, and increased feedback can reduce stress because these factors give employees greater control over work activities and lessen dependence on others. But as we noted in our discussion of work design, not all employees want enriched jobs. The right redesign for employees with a low need for growth might include less responsibility and increased specialization. If individuals prefer structure and routine, reducing skill variety should reduce uncertainties and stress levels.

Employee Involvement　Role stress is detrimental to a large extent because employees feel uncertain about goals, expectations, how they'll be evaluated, and the like. By giving these employees a voice in the decisions that directly affect their job performance, management can increase employee control and reduce role stress. Thus, managers should consider increasing *employee involvement* in decision making because evidence clearly shows that increases in employee empowerment reduce psychological strain.[115]

Organizational Communication   Increasing formal *organizational communication* with employees reduces uncertainty by lessening role ambiguity and role conflict. Given the importance that perceptions play in moderating the stress–response relationship, management can also use effective communications as a means to shape employee perceptions. Remember that what employees categorize as demands, threats, or opportunities at work is an interpretation and that interpretation can be affected by the symbols and actions communicated by management.

Employee Sabbaticals   Some employees need an occasional escape from the frenetic pace of their work. Companies including Genentech, American Express, Intel, General Mills, Microsoft, Morningstar, DreamWorks Animation, and Adobe Systems have begun to provide extended voluntary leaves.[116] These *sabbaticals*—ranging in length from a few weeks to several months—allow employees to travel, relax, or pursue personal projects that consume time beyond normal vacations. Proponents say sabbaticals can revive and rejuvenate workers who might otherwise be headed for burnout.

wellness programs Organizationally supported programs that focus on the employee's total physical and mental condition.

Wellness Programs   Our final suggestion is organizationally supported **wellness programs**. These typically provide workshops to help people quit smoking, control alcohol use, lose weight, eat better, and develop a regular exercise program; they focus on the employee's total physical and mental condition.[117] Some programs help employees improve their psychological health as well. A meta-analysis of 36 programs designed to reduce stress (including wellness programs) showed that interventions to help employees reframe stressful situations and use active coping strategies appreciably reduced stress levels.[118] Most wellness programs assume employees need to take personal responsibility for their physical and mental health and that the organization is merely a means to that end.

Corporate wellness programs can help employees manage stress. As part of its wellness and fitness initiatives, the Fowler White Boggs law firm brings in yoga instructors during employees' lunch hours to lead them in stretching and breathing exercises that help relieve stress and promote a sense of well-being.
Source: ZUMA Press, Inc/Alamy

Most firms that have introduced wellness programs have found significant benefits. Johnson & Johnson reported that their wellness program has saved the organization $250 million on health care costs in 10 years, and research indicated that effective wellness programs significantly decreased turnover rates for most organizations.[119] Other research sponsored by the U.S. Department of Labor and Department of Health and Human Services indicated that organizational wellness programs create healthier employees with fewer health risk factors.[120]

Summary

The need for change has been implied throughout this text. For instance, think about attitudes, motivation, work teams, communication, leadership, organizational structures, HR practices, and organizational cultures. Change was an integral part in our discussion of each. If environments were perfectly static, if employees' skills and abilities were always up to date and incapable of deteriorating, and if tomorrow were always exactly the same as today, organizational change would have little or no relevance to managers. But the real world is turbulent, requiring organizations and their members to undergo dynamic change if they are to perform at competitive levels. Coping with all these changes can be a source of stress, but with effective management, challenge can enhance engagement and fulfillment, leading to the high performance that, as you've discovered in this text, is one major goal of the study of organizational behavior (OB).

Implications for Managers

- Consider that, as a manager, you are a change agent in your organization. The decisions you make and your role-modeling behaviors will help shape the organization's change culture.
- Your management policies and practices will determine the degree to which the organization learns and adapts to changing environmental factors.
- Some stress is good. Increasing challenges brought by autonomy and responsibility at work will lead to some stress but also increase feelings of accomplishment and fulfillment. Hindrance stressors like bureaucracy and interpersonal conflicts, on the other hand, are entirely negative and should be eliminated.
- You can help alleviate harmful workplace stress for your employees by accurately matching workloads to employees, providing employees with stress-coping resources, and responding to their concerns.
- You can identify extreme stress in your employees when performance declines, turnover increases, health-related absenteeism increases, and engagement declines. However, by the time these symptoms are visible, it may be too late to be helpful, so stay alert for early indicators and be proactive.

✪ PERSONAL INVENTORY ASSESSMENTS

Tolerance of Ambiguity Scale

How well can you tolerate the ambiguity that change brings? Take this PIA to learn more about your tolerance level for this challenge.

Companies Should Encourage Stress Reduction

POINT

Companies make substantial investments in their employees, so the health and well-being of the workforce is a central concern. One of the most direct ways to provide assistance to employees is to engage in one of the stress-reduction interventions.

One major financial benefit of stress reduction programs is a reduction in health-related costs. Workplace stress leads to dozens of negative and expensive health-related consequences. Stress weakens the immune system, leading to increased illness and sickness absences. If employees feel extreme stress related to work, they may be more likely to come in when they are contagious, leading to sickness for many others. Over the longer run, stress levels also can contribute to conditions like heart disease that ultimately result in very expensive medical treatments. These medical treatments, in turn, increase employer health insurance expenses.

Reductions in employee stress can facilitate job performance. Employees who are overburdened have difficulty concentrating, can lose energy and motivation at work, and find it difficult to come up with new and creative ideas. Stress can also create conflicts with coworkers and lead to rude or hostile treatment of clients or customers. Ultimately, employees who are experiencing high levels of stress may leave, so all the costs attendant upon turnover are incurred.

Stress reduction programs also have an ethical component. The workplace generates a great deal of stress for many employees, so employers have a certain responsibility to offset its negative consequences. Stress reduction programs are a direct way to help employees feel better. Finally, when employers show concern for employees by helping reduce stress, employees feel more committed.

COUNTERPOINT

While employers may have a direct financial interest in certain elements of stress reduction, it's worth asking whether investing in stress reduction programs is actually a good idea. The first problem is operational. Some stress reduction interventions are expensive, requiring professional facilitators or exercise equipment. These can take a long time to show financial returns, and the up-front costs of researching, designing, and implementing them are substantial. A growing number of corporations report that the expected returns on investment in wellness programs have failed to materialize. And the time employees spend in stress reduction interventions is time they spend not working.

Another problem is that stress reduction programs are invasive. Should your boss or other individuals in the workplace tell you how you're supposed to feel? Many stress reduction programs step even further into employees' personal lives by encouraging open discussions about sources of stress. Do you really want your manager and coworkers to know why you're experiencing stress? The more that sensitive topics related to stress are discussed, the harder it is to keep work relationships professional.

A final concern is that it is too hard to draw the line between stress from work and general life stress. A company's stress reduction program may try to target problems of work overload or social conflict, but these issues often affect other areas of life. How should a stress reduction program operate when the reasons for employee stress come, say, from a sick relative or conflicts with family members?

Organizations often mean well, but it may be more important to let employees keep their private lives private.

Sources: L. Vanderkam, "The Dark Side of Corporate Wellness Programs," *Fast Company,* June 8, 2015, http://www .fastcompany.com/3047115/the-dark-side-of-corporate-wellness-programs; D. R. Stover and J. Wood, "Most Company Wellness Programs Are a Bust," *Gallup Business Journal,* February 4, 2015, http://www.gallup.com/businessjournal/ 181481/company-wellness-programs-bust.aspx; A. Frakt and A. E. Carroll, "Do Wellness Programs Work? Usually Not," *New York Times,* September 11, 2014, http://www.nytimes.com/2014/09/12/upshot/do-workplace-wellness-programs-work-usually-not.html.

CHAPTER REVIEW

MyManagementLab

Go to **mymanagementlab.com** to complete the problems marked with this icon. ⭐

QUESTIONS FOR REVIEW

18-1 What are the differences between the forces for change and planned change?

18-2 How can resistance to change be overcome?

18-3 What are the four main approaches to managing organizational change?

18-4 How can managers create a culture for change?

18-5 What are the potential environmental, organizational, and personal sources of stress at work and the role of individual and cultural differences?

18-6 What are the physiological, psychological, and behavioral symptoms of stress at work?

18-7 What are the individual and organizational approaches to managing stress?

EXPERIENTIAL EXERCISE   Mindfulness at Work

The concept of mindfulness emphasizes trying to focus your mind in the present moment, immersing yourself in what's going on around you. Core principles include suspending immediate judgment of the environment and your own thoughts, and keeping yourself open to what is around you. The benefits of mindfulness can reach beyond reducing stress to include increased creativity, longer spans of attention, reductions in procrastination, and improved performance.

The Procedure

Start this exercise individually, and then come together into groups of three to four individuals to discuss what you have found. Although full workplace mindfulness interventions can take several weeks, some basic starting exercises can be done in a relatively short period of time and give you a feeling for what a full course of mindfulness would be like. Here are three simple exercises to try. For all these, everyone needs to put everything away (especially phones, tablets, and computers!) and focus on what is going on in the immediate environment.

- *Mindful breathing:* Clear your head of everything except thoughts of your own breaths. Concentrate on

how you are inhaling and exhaling. It is sometimes helpful to count how long each breath takes. Try to maintain this mindful breathing for 3 minutes. The group will then take 3 minutes to discuss how this made them feel.

- *Mindful listening:* Now clear your head of everything except what is going on in the immediate environment. Try to hear as many sounds around you as you can, without judging or evaluating them. Try to maintain this mindful listening for 3 minutes. The group will then take 3 minutes to discuss some of the things they noticed.

- *Mindful thinking:* As with listening, clear your head of everything, but now focus just on your ideas about mindfulness and stress. Do not talk about or write down what you're thinking (yet); just focus your whole quiet attention on this exercise and what it means. Try to maintain this mindful thinking for 3 minutes. The group will then take 3 minutes to talk about what this experience was like.

As noted earlier, this is just a brief example of what mindfulness exercises are like. In a full mindfulness program, you would go through several sessions of up to an hour each. Now that you have an idea of what it feels like to do mindfulness work, consider the following questions in your groups:

18-8. Were there any aspects of the mindfulness practice sessions that you found especially pleasant or useful? Were there any aspects of the sessions that you found unpleasant or uncomfortable?

18-9. What concerns might you have about implementing a mindfulness intervention in the workplace? What are some of the obstacles you might face in trying to have employees engage in a mindfulness stress reduction program?

18-10. Bring the class together and discuss your responses.

Sources: E. Langer, "Mindfulness in the Age of Complexity," *Harvard Business Review,* March 2014, 68–73; H. J. E. M. Alberts and U. R. Hülsheger, "Applying Mindfulness in the Context of Work: Mindfulness-Based Interventions," in J. Reb and P. W. B. Atkins, *Mindfulness in Organizations* (Cambridge, UK: Cambridge University Press, 2015), 17–41; K. A. Aikens, J. Astin, K. R. Pelletier, K. Levanovich, C. M. Baase, Y. Y. Park, and C. M. Bodnar, "Mindfulness Goes to Work: Impact of an Online Workplace Intervention," *Journal of Occupational and Environmental Medicine 56* (2014): 721–31.

ETHICAL DILEMMA All Present and Accounted For

Diya looked at the records of Jose's workstation logins, and she wasn't pleased. Day after day, week after week, the record showed that Jose had consistently been at his computer, writing code and compiling data on user experiences. In the tech industry, long hours without a break are expected, but Diya knew that her friend Jose was pushing himself past the point of exhaustion. He had been suffering for weeks from an unidentified upper respiratory ailment, and she worried that without rest he'd never get better. But pressure for rapid progress from their supervisor left Jose feeling like he had little choice but to keep grinding out the long hours, sick or not.

The problem of absenteeism, not showing up for work when expected, is a classic struggle for managers. Recent attention has suggested, however, that absenteeism has an opposite with its own negative consequences—presenteeism. Presenteeism occurs when an employee continues to go to work despite illness. Unlike absenteeism, presenteeism may arise specifically because management is pushing for it.

An employee can engage in presenteeism for a variety of reasons, but as the story of Jose describes, sometimes it's a response to work pressure. Companies that put extensive resources into monitoring employee attendance also tend to experience higher levels of presenteeism. In other words, empirical evidence suggests companies are sending signals to employees that attendance is required—even when they are too ill to work.

Some companies have started to buck the trend. Microsoft, for example, has pushed its contractors to provide employees with greater access to sick-leave benefits. Pressure to come to work when sick is obviously a significant source of stress. And stress weakens the immune response. This means a culture of presenteeism will eventually lead to long-term illness. It therefore seems Diya's concerns for Jose's long-term health are well-founded. When sick employees come into work, it also increases the odds that others will be infected. Over time, this can result in systemic work delays.

A large, stable organization like Microsoft may have a comparatively easy time seeing the big-picture positive consequences of discouraging presenteeism. In a small firm that has short-term contracts with larger organizations, like the one Jose and Diya work for, it can be very tempting to push employees to come into work no matter what. A few days off the job could mean the loss of a significant business opportunity. And so employees give in to pressure and struggle through their work days, as long as they can.

Questions

18-11. How might presenteeism be an adaptive response to perceived performance pressure? How is it a response to work demand pressures?

18-12. Do employers have an ethical responsibility to discourage presenteeism? Why or why not?

18-13. How might a company work to change employee attitudes and behaviors about presenteeism? In other words, what would an effective presenteeism prevention program look like?

Sources: D. Engber, "Quit Whining about Your Sick Colleague," *New York Times,* December 29, 2014, http://www.nytimes.com/2014/12/30/opinion/quit-whining-about-your-sick-colleague.html; C. C. Miller, "From Microsoft, a Novel Way to Mandate Sick Leave," *New York Times,* March 26, 2015, http://www.nytimes.com/2015/03/26/upshot/26up-leave.html?abt=0002&abg=0; and S. Deery, J. Walsh, and C. D. Zatzick, "A Moderated Mediation Analysis of Job Demands, Presenteeism, and Absenteeism," *Journal of Occupational and Organizational Psychology,* June 2014, 352–69.

CASE INCIDENT 1   Atos: Zero Email Program

The technology that gave us the smart phone, tablet, and laptop has enabled employees to access their work from anywhere in the world. Communication has been enhanced by the use of texts, calls, instant messages, email, and social networking sites. The burden of being an anytime–anywhere worker is having a negative impact on the health of employees, family life, and productivity. Employees are experiencing unmanageable workloads, the loss of face-to-face relationships with colleagues, and the overuse of emails in managing difficult work-related issues. However, the future of work is changing from a directive approach towards collaborative frameworks that cause employees to think and act differently.

In 2011, Thierry Breton, Chairman and CEO of technology giant ATOS, launched a Zero Email program. The organization focuses on business technology and helps organizations to develop into firms of the future. Atos recognized that email is a barrier to collaborative transformation. Breton's initiative was launched to completely eliminate the use of email for internal communications and to use enterprise social initiatives instead. Eliminating email is a key pillar of the organization's internal wellbeing at work initiative, which is designed to enhance working conditions. The aim was to move towards a social, collaborative enterprise that shares knowledge and finds experts easily to respond to the needs of clients quickly and efficiently, delivering tangible business results. The culture evolved from one based on hierarchies and command-and-control to a more open environment. Leaders and employees can now engage with each other quickly and easily. This challenged established ways of working and the tools that were used, and introduced new technologies and behaviours.

The focus of the Zero Email initiative was to reduce the overall messaging load on the 76,000 business technologists who work for Atos in 52 countries. Emails that were previously used to assign employees to tasks have been replaced by discussions in online communities where employees communicate, share best practices, and develop new ideas. Collaborative operations have resulted in more efficient teamwork: 25 percent of work time previously devoted to email activities is now spent on business activities. Internal email disruption and overload has been reduced by 60 percent. In addition, Atos has introduced a certification process that has resulted in the redesign of 220 business processes to become email-free.

Greater digital connectivity goes hand-in-hand with greater worker responsibility. According to Randstad's Workmonitor Global Report in 2015, 57 percent of employees surveyed stated that their employer expects them to be available outside regular office hours. The results revealed that 89 percent of Chinese workers believed that they should be available outside of working times in contrast to 40 percent of employees in Sweden. Globally, 47 percent of the respondents said that their employer expects them to be available by phone and email during holidays.

Rather than getting rid of emails or texting, we must put them to better use. Organizations need to advise employees on the acceptable times to email, how to avoid overload of information, the overuse of email and the benefits of face-to-face communication. They must also address the need for work–life balance. Recently, the French trade union that represents employees in the technology and consultancy sectors, which includes divisions of Google, Facebook, and Deloitte, agreed to allow staff to shut off their phones and computers after 6 PM. It was agreed that organizations cannot pressure their employees or make them feel bad about not checking or responding to their email.

As employees across the world see their work days grow longer and the boundaries between their personal and work lives getting increasingly blurred, firms—like Atos—must address this challenge by implementing a cultural change supported by the adaptation of employee behavior and management styles.

Questions

18-14. Consider the sources of stress in modern organizations such as Atos. Identify individual differences that can moderate the effect of stress.

18-15. Describe the symptoms of stress that may be experienced by employees.

18-16. Recommend two further strategies that could be introduced in Atos to help employees manage the demands of the "always on" working environment.

Sources: "Collaboration and Social Media," Atos Official Website, http://atos.net/en-us/home/we-are/zero-email.html#; C. Cooper, "Work Email Is Making Us a 'Generation of Idiots'. Time to Switch Off," *The Guardian,* May 14, 2015, http://www.theguardian.com/commentisfree/2015/may/14/work-email-benefits-technology-human-interaction; Global Report Randstad Workmonitor, "Working Hours vs. Private Time: Blurred Lines Incl. Quarterly Mobility, Job Change and Job Satisfaction," Wave 2 2015, Group Communications Randstad Holding nv.; A. Kjerulf, "5 Awesome Corporate Email Policies," November 20, 2014, http://positivesharing.com/2014/11/5-awesome-corporate-email-policies/.

CASE INCIDENT 2   When Companies Fail to Change

The Triniton TV, transistor radio, Walkman, and VCR are the stuff of time capsules nowadays, but not long ago they were cutting-edge technology. Japan was at the pinnacle of the home consumer electronics industry from the 1970s to the 1990s, introducing new innovations to the world each year. Now those same Japanese firms are at the back of the pack and struggling to stay in the game. Japanese electronics production has fallen by more than 41 percent, and Japan's global market share of electronics goods and services has decreased by more than half since 2000. Sony, for example, hasn't earned a profit since 2008. What happened?

The simple answer is failure to innovate. While firms outside Japan pioneered digital technology and conquered the Internet, Japanese firms stuck to semiconductors and hardware. But the deeper issue is the refusal of Japanese managers to adapt to the global environment and change their organizations accordingly. For instance, Sony mastered the technology needed for a digital music player years before Apple introduced the iPod in 2001, but its engineers resisted the change. Sony's divisions would not cooperate with one another fast enough to compete in this market or in the new market for flat-screen TVs. Even now, Sony has not managed to change its organization to reflect current global thinking in the industry. For instance, it and other Japanese firms make a larger number of products than most of their global competitors. Former Sony executive Yoshiaki Sakito said, "Sony makes too many models, and for none of them can they say, 'This contains our best, most cutting-edge technology.' Apple, on the other hand, makes one amazing phone in just two colors and says, 'This is the one.'"

For Japanese electronics companies to survive, they must change. They were once able to structure their organizations around abundant, inexpensive labor to keep costs down and prices competitive, but that's no longer the case. One complicating factor is that Japan is an ancient country of many traditions, with a low birth rate and an aging population, so there will be an increasing shortage of workers. The country's culture will make it even more difficult to realign to globalization. It now must change to foster innovation, which may involve a cultural as much as an organizational transformation.

Questions

18-17. What made the Japanese electronics industry initially successful?

18-18. How does a corporation such as Sony fundamentally differ from one like Apple?

18-19. Where might Japanese organizations outsource production to remain competitive in today's markets?

Sources: H. Hiyama, "Sony Break-Up Call Shines Light on Electronics Industry Problems," *Japan Today,* June 7, 2013, www.japantoday.com/category/opinions/view/sony-break-up-call-shines-light-on-electronic-industry-problems; R. Katz, "How Japan Blew Its Lead in Electronics," *The Wall Street Journal,* March 23, 2012, A15; and H. Tabuchi, "How the Parade Passed Sony By," *The New York Times,* April 15, 2012, B1, B7.

MyManagementLab

Go to **mymanagementlab.com** for the following Assisted-graded writing questions:

18-20. How can employers create a favorable context for cultural innovation? What sources of innovation can the employer rely upon?

18-21. In regard to Case Incident 2, only 13 of the top 21 U.S. electronics manufacturers today were in existence in 1970 (and six were smaller than Fortune 500 firms), while there have been no new top Japanese electronics manufacturers for more than 50 years. How do you think age issues affect the ability of Japanese firms to bring about the changes they need to be competitive?

18-22. **MyManagementLab Only** – comprehensive writing assignment for this chapter.

ENDNOTES

[1] A. Chowdhry, "Apple Surpassed Samsung as Global Phone Market Leader, Says Report," *Forbes*, March 3, 2015, http://www.forbes .com/sites/amitchowdhry/2015/03/04/ apple-passes-samsung/.

[2] See, for instance, J. Birkinshaw, G. Hamel, and M. J. Mol, "Management Innovation," *Academy of Management Review* 33, no. 4 (2008): 825–45; and J. Welch and S. Welch, "What Change Agents Are Made Of," *Business-Week*, October 20, 2008, 96.

[3] M. Helft, "How the Tech Elite Plans to Reinvent Senior Care," *Forbes*, April 2, 2015, http://www.forbes.com/sites/miguelhelft/ 2015/04/02/how-the-tech-elite-plans-to-reinvent-senior-care.

[4] General Motors website, http://www.gm .com/company/corporate-officers/mary-barra, accessed July 22, 2015.

[5] R. J. Grossman, "Accelerating Change at GM," *HR Magazine*, June 2012, 58–64.

[6] General Motors website, http://www.gm .com/company/aboutGM/GM_Corporate_ Officers/John_Quattrone.html, accessed July 22, 2015.

[7] P. G. Audia and S. Brion, "Reluctant to Change: Self-Enhancing Responses to Diverging Performance Measures," *Organizational Behavior and Human Decision Processes* 102 (2007): 255–69.

[8] M. Fugate, A. J. Kinicki, and G. E. Prussia, "Employee Coping with Organizational Change: An Examination of Alternative Theoretical Perspectives and Models," *Personnel Psychology* 61, no. 1 (2008): 1–36.

[9] R. B. L. Sijbom, O. Janssen, and N. W. Van Yperen, "How to Get Radical Creative Ideas into a Leader's Mind? Leader's Achievement Goals and Subordinates' Voice of Creative Ideas," *European Journal of Work and Organizational Psychology* 24 (2015): 279–96.

[10] J. D. Ford, L. W. Ford, and A. D'Amelio, "Resistance to Change: The Rest of the Story," *Academy of Management Review* 33, no. 2 (2008): 362–77.

[11] R. K. Smollan, "The Multi-Dimensional Nature of Resistance to Change," *Journal of Management & Organization*, November 2011, 828–49.

[12] P. C. Fiss and E. J. Zajac, "The Symbolic Management of Strategic Change: Sensegiving via Framing and Decoupling," *Academy of Management Journal* 49, no. 6 (2006): 1173–93.

[13] A. E. Rafferty and S. L. D. Restubog, "The Impact of Change Process and Context on Change Reactions and Turnover During a Merger," *Journal of Management* 36, no. 5 (2010): 1309–38.

[14] Q. N. Huy, "Emotional Balancing of Organizational Continuity and Radical Change: The Contribution of Middle Managers," *Administrative Science Quarterly*, March 2002, 31–69; D. M. Herold, D. B. Fedor, and S. D. Caldwell, "Beyond Change Management: A Multilevel Investigation of Contextual and Personal Influences on Employees' Commitment to Change," *Journal of Applied Psychology* 92, no. 4 (2007): 942–51; and G. B. Cunningham, "The Relationships among Commitment to Change, Coping with Change, and Turnover Intentions," *European Journal of Work and Organizational Psychology* 15, no. 1 (2006): 29–45.

[15] R. Peccei, A. Giangreco, and A. Sebastiano, "The Role of Organizational Commitment in the Analysis of Resistance to Change: Co-predictor and Moderator Effects," *Personnel Review* 40, no. 2 (2011): 185–204.

[16] J. P. Kotter, "Leading Change: Why Transformational Efforts Fail," *Harvard Business Review* 85 (January 2007): 96–103.

[17] K. van Dam, S. Oreg, and B. Schyns, "Daily Work Contexts and Resistance to Organisational Change: The Role of Leader-Member Exchange, Development Climate, and Change Process Characteristics," *Applied Psychology: An International Review* 57, no. 2 (2008): 313–34.

[18] A. H. Y. Hon, M. Bloom, and J. M. Crant, "Overcoming Resistance to Change and Enhancing Creative Performance," *Journal of Management* 40 (2014): 919–41.

[19] S. Oreg and N. Sverdlik, "Ambivalence toward Imposed Change: The Conflict between Dispositional Resistance to Change and the Orientation toward the Change Agent," *Journal of Applied Psychology* 96, no. 2 (2011): 337–49.

[20] D. B. Fedor, S. Caldwell, and D. M. Herold, "The Effects of Organizational Changes on Employee Commitment: A Multilevel Investigation," *Personnel Psychology* 59 (2006): 1–29; and R. D. Foster, "Resistance, Justice, and Commitment to Change," *Human Resource Development Quarterly* 21, no. 1 (2010): 3–39.

[21] S. Oreg, "Personality, Context, and Resistance to Organizational Change," *European Journal of Work and Organizational Psychology* 15, no. 1 (2006): 73–101.

[22] S. M. Elias, "Employee Commitment in Times of Change: Assessing the Importance of Attitudes toward Organizational Change," *Journal of Management* 35, no. 1 (2009): 37–55.

[23] J. W. B. Lang and P. D. Bliese, "General Mental Ability and Two Types of Adaptation to Unforeseen Change: Applying Discontinuous Growth Models to the Task-Change Paradigm," *Journal of Applied Psychology* 94, no. 2 (2009): 411–28.

[24] C. O. L. H. Porter, J. W. Webb, and C. I. Gogus, "When Goal Orientations Collide: Effects of Learning and Performance Orientation on Team Adaptability in Response to Workload Imbalance," *Journal of Applied Psychology* 95, no. 5 (2010): 935–43.

[25] See, for instance, A. Karaevli, "Performance Consequences for New CEO 'Outsiderness': Moderating Effects of Pre- and Post-Succession Contexts," *Strategic Management Journal* 28, no. 7 (2007): 681–706.

[26] See, for instance, J. Manchester, D. L. Gray-Miceli, J. A. Metcalf, C. A. Paolini, A. H. Napier, C. L. Coogle, and M. G. Owens, "Facilitating Lewin's Change Model with Collaborative Evaluation in Promoting Evidence Based Practices of Health Professionals," *Evaluation and Program Planning*, December 2014, 82–90.

[27] P. G. Audia, E. A. Locke, and K. G. Smith, "The Paradox of Success: An Archival and a Laboratory Study of Strategic Persistence Following Radical Environmental Change," *Academy of Management Journal*, October 2000, 837–53; and P. G. Audia and S. Brion, "Reluctant to Change: Self-Enhancing Responses to Diverging Performance Measures," *Organizational Behavior and Human Decision Processes* 102, no. 2 (2007): 255–69.

[28] See, for instance, J. Kim, "Use of Kotter's Leading Change Model to Develop and Implement a Heart Failure Education Program for Certified Nursing Assistants in a Long-Term Care Facility," *Nursing Research* 64, no. 2 (2015): E35; and J. Pollack and R. Pollack, "Using Kotter's Eight Stage Process to Manage an Organisational Change Program: Presentation and Practice," *Systemic Practice and Action Research* 28, no. 1 (2015): 41–66.

[29] See, for example, L. S. Lüscher and M. W. Lewis, "Organizational Change and Managerial Sensemaking: Working through Paradox," *Academy of Management Journal* 51, no. 2 (2008): 221–40.

[30] For example, see R. J. Marshak and D. Grant, "Organizational Discourse and New Organization Development Practices," *British Journal of Management* 19, no. 1 (2008): S7–S19.

[31] See, for instance, R. Lines, "Influence of Participation in Strategic Change: Resistance, Organizational Commitment and Change Goal Achievement," *Journal of Change Management*, September 2004, 193–215.

[32] S. Highhouse, "A History of the T-Group and Its Early Application in Management Development," *Group Dynamics: Theory, Research, & Practice*, December 2002, 277–90.

[33] T. Fauth, K. Hattrub, K. Mueller, and B. Roberts, "Nonresponse in Employee Attitude Surveys: A Group-Level Analysis," *Journal of Business and Psychology*, March 2013, 1–16.

[34] F. J. Lambrechts, R. Bouwen, S. Grieten, J. P. Huybrechts, and E. H. Schein, "Learning to Help through Humble Inquiry and Implications for Management Research, Practice, and Education: An Interview with Edgar H. Schein," *Academy of Management Learning & Education*, March 2011, 131–48.

[35] W. W. G. Dyer, W. G. Dyer, and J. H. Dyer, *Team Building: Proven Strategies for Improving Team Performance* (Hoboken, NJ: Jossey-Bass, 2007).

[36] U. Wagner, L. Tropp, G. Finchilescu, and C. Tredoux (eds.), *Improving Intergroup Relations* (New York: Wiley-Blackwell, 2008).

[37]See, for example, B. Verleysen, F. Lambrechts, and F. Van Acker, "Building Psychological Capital with Appreciative Inquiry: Investigating the Mediating Role of Basic Psychological Need Satisfaction," *Journal of Applied Behavioral Science* 51, no. 1 (2015): 10–35.

[38]G. Giglio, S. Michalcova, and C. Yates, "Instilling a Culture of Winning at American Express," *Organization Development Journal* 25, no. 4 (2007): P33–P37.

[39]W. K. Smith and M. W. Lewis, "Toward a Theory of Paradox: A Dynamic Equilibrium Model of Organizing," *Academy of Management Review* 36 (2011): 381–403.

[40]P. Jarzabkowski, J. Lê, and A. Van de Ven, "Responding to Competing Strategic Demands: How Organizing, Belonging, and Performing Paradoxes Coevolve," *Strategic Organization* 11 (2013): 245–80; W. K. Smith, "Dynamic Decision Making: A Model of Senior Leaders Managing Strategic Paradoxes," *Academy of Management Journal* 57 (2014): 1592–623.

[41]J. Jay, "Navigating Paradox as a Mechanism of Change and Innovation in Hybrid Organizations," *Academy of Management Journal* 56 (2013): 137–59.

[42]Y. Zhang, D. A. Waldman, Y. Han, and X. Li, "Paradoxical Leader Behaviors in People Management: Antecedents and Consequences," *Academy of Management Journal* 58 (2015): 538–66.

[43]A. Harrington, "Who's Afraid of a New Product?" *Fortune*, November 10, 2003, 189–92; and C. C. Manz, F. Shipper, and G. L. Stewart, "Everyone a Team Leader: Shared Influence at W. L. Gore and Associates," *Organizational Dynamics* 38, no. 3 (2009): 239–44.

[44]"A Team-Based, Flat Lattice Organization," Gore website, http://www.gore.com/en_xx/aboutus/culture/index.html, accessed July 23, 2015.

[45]S. Caulkin, "Gore-Text Gets Made without Managers," *The Observer*, November 1, 2008, http://www.theguardian.com/business/2008/nov/02/gore-tex-textiles-terri-kelly.

[46]See, for instance, G. P. Pisano, "You Need an Innovation Strategy," *Harvard Business Review*, June 2015, 44–54.

[47]H. W. Volberda, F. A. J. Van den Bosch, and C. V. Heij, "Management Innovation: Management as Fertile Ground for Innovation," *European Management Review*, Spring 2013, 1–15.

[48]Damanpour, "Organizational Innovation," 555–90; and G. Westerman, F. W. McFarlan, and M. Iansiti, "Organization Design and Effectiveness over the Innovation Life Cycle," *Organization Science* 17, no. 2 (2006): 230–38.

[49]See P. Schepers and P. T. van den Berg, "Social Factors of Work-Environment Creativity," *Journal of Business and Psychology* 21, no. 3 (2007): 407–28.

[50]S. Chang, L. Jia, R. Takeuchi, and Y. Cai, "Do High-Commitment Work Systems Affect Creativity? A Multilevel Combinational Approach to Employee Creativity," *Journal of Applied Psychology* 99 (2014): 665–80.

[51]M. E. Mullins, S. W. J. Kozlowski, N. Schmitt, and A. W. Howell, "The Role of the Idea Champion in Innovation: The Case of the Internet in the Mid-1990s," *Computers in Human Behavior* 24, no. 2 (2008): 451–67.

[52]C. Y. Murnieks, E. Mosakowski, and M. S. Cardon, "Pathways of Passion Identity Centrality, Passion, and Behavior among Entrepreneurs," *Journal of Management* 40, (2014): 1583–606.

[53]S. C. Parker, "Intrapreneurship or Entrepreneurship?" *Journal of Business Venturing*, January 2011, 19–34.

[54]M. Cerne, M. Jaklic, and M. Skerlavaj, "Decoupling Management and Technological Innovations: Resolving the Individualism-Collectivism Controversy," *Journal of International Management*, June 2013, 103–17.

[55]A. Taylor, "Chrysler's Speed Merchant," *Fortune*, September 6, 2010, 77–82.

[56]D. Buss, "Marcchione May Risk Fiat Chrysler Morale by Pressing Consolidation," *Forbes*, May 31, 2015, http://www.forbes.com/sites/dalebuss/2015/05/31/in-pressing-for-consolidation-marchionne-may-be-risking-fiat-chrysler-morale/.

[57]See, for example, T. B. Lawrence, M. K. Mauws, B. Dyck, and R. F. Kleysen, "The Politics of Organizational Learning: Integrating Power into the 4I Framework," *Academy of Management Review*, January 2005, 180–91.

[58]J. Kim, T. Egan, and H. Tolson, "Examining the Dimensions of the Learning Organization Questionnaire: A Review and Critique of Research Utilizing the DLOQ," *Human Resource Development Review*, March 2015, 91–112.

[59]L. Berghman, P. Matthyssens, S. Streukens, and K. Vandenbempt, "Deliberate Learning Mechanisms for Stimulating Strategic Innovation Capacity," *Long Range Planning*, February–April 2013, 39–71.

[60]R. Chiva and J. Habib, "A Framework for Organizational Learning: Zero, Adaptive, and Generative Learning," *Journal of Management & Organization* 21, no. 3 (2015): 350–68; and J. Kim, T. Egan, and H. Tolson, "Examining the Dimensions of the Learning Organization Questionnaire: A Review and Critique of Research Utilizing the DLOQ," *Human Resource Development Review* 14, no. 1 (2015): 91–112.

[61]D. Meinert, "Wings of Change," *HR Magazine*, November 2012, 30–36.

[62]M.-G. Seo, M. S. Taylor, N. S. Hill, X. Zhang, P. E. Tesluk, and N. M. Lorinkova, "The Role of Affect and Leadership during Organizational Change," *Personnel Psychology* 65 (2012): 121–65.

[63]M. Fugate, G. E. Prussia, and A. J. Kinicki, "Managing Employee Withdrawal during Organizational Change: The Role of Threat Appraisal," *Journal of Management*, May 2012, 890–914.

[64]J. Shin, M. S. Taylor, and M.-G. Seo, "Resources for Change: The Relationships of Organizational Inducements and Psychological Resilience to Employees' Attitudes and Behaviors toward Organizational Change," *Academy of Management Journal* 55 (2012): 727–48.

[65]B. Mirza, "Workplace Stress Hits Three-Year High," *HR Magazine*, April 2012, 15.

[66]C. L. Cooper, P. J. Dewe, and M. P. O'Driscoll, *Organizational Stress: A Review and Critique of Theory, Research, and Applications* (Thousand Oaks, CA: Sage, 2002).

[67]S. Shellenbarger, "When Stress Is Good for You," *The Wall Street Journal*, January 24, 2012, D1, D5.

[68]Ibid.

[69]N. P. Podsakoff, J. A. LePine, and M. A. LePine, "Differential Challenge-Hindrance Stressor Relationships with Job Attitudes, Turnover Intentions, Turnover, and Withdrawal Behavior: A Meta-Analysis," *Journal of Applied Psychology* 92, no. 2 (2007): 438–54; and J. A. LePine, M. A. LePine, and C. L. Jackson, "Challenge and Hindrance Stress: Relationships with Exhaustion, Motivation to Learn, and Learning Performance," *Journal of Applied Psychology*, October 2004, 883–91.

[70]L. W. Hunter and S. M. B. Thatcher, "Feeling the Heat: Effects of Stress, Commitment, and Job Experience on Job Performance," *Academy of Management Journal* 50, no. 4 (2007): 953–68.

[71]J. C. Wallace, B. D. Edwards, T. Arnold, M. L. Frazier, and D. M. Finch, "Work Stressors, Role-Based Performance, and the Moderating Influence of Organizational Support," *Journal of Applied Psychology* 94, no. 1 (2009): 254–62.

[72]A. B. Bakker, E. Demerouti, and A. I. Sanz-Vergel, "Burnout and Work Engagement: The JD–R Approach," *Annual Review of Organizational Psychology and Organizational Behavior* 1 (2014): 389–411.

[73]"Stress in America: Paying with Our Health," *American Psychological Association*, February 4, 2015, 8.

[74]J. de Jonge and C. Dormann, "Stressors, Resources, and Strain at Work: A Longitudinal Test of the Triple-Match Principle," *Journal of Applied Psychology* 91, no. 5 (2006): 1359–74.

[75]D. C. Ganster and C. C. Rosen, "Work Stress and Employee Health: A Multidisciplinary Review," *Journal of Management* 39 (2013): 1085–122.

[76]P. Sterling, "Allostasis: A Model of Predictive Regulation," *Physiology & Behavior*, April 12, 2012, 5–15.

[77]A. E. Rafferty and M. A. Griffin, "Perceptions of Organizational Change: A Stress and Coping Perspective," *Journal of Applied Psychology* 71, no. 5 (2007): 1154–62.

[78]R. Ilies, N. Dimotakis, and I. E. De Pater, "Psychological and Physiological Reactions to High Workloads: Implications for Well-Being," *Personnel Psychology*, Summer 2010, 407–36; A. B. Bakker, E. Demerouti, and

A. I. Sanz-Vergel, "Burnout and Work Engagement: The JD–R Approach," *Annual Review of Organizational Psychology and Organizational Behavior* 1 (2014): 389–411.

[79]T. L. Smith-Jackson and K. W. Klein, "Open-Plan Offices: Task Performance and Mental Workload," *Journal of Environmental Psychology* 29, no. 2 (2009): 279–89.

[80]C. Fritz and S. Sonnentag, "Antecedents of Day-Level Proactive Behavior: A Look at Job Stressors and Positive Affect during the Workday," *Journal of Management* 35, no. 1 (2009): 94–111.

[81]S. Lim, L. M. Cortina, and V. J. Magley, "Personal and Workgroup Incivility: Impact on Work and Health Outcomes," *Journal of Applied Psychology* 93, no. 1 (2008): 95–107; N. T. Buchanan and L. F. Fitzgerald, "Effects of Racial and Sexual Harassment on Work and the Psychological Well-Being of African American Women," *Journal of Occupational Health Psychology* 13, no. 2 (2008): 137–51; C. R. Willness, P. Steel, and K. Lee, "A Meta-Analysis of the Antecedents and Consequences of Workplace Sexual Harassment," *Personnel Psychology* 60, no. 1 (2007): 127–62; and B. Moreno-Jiménez, A. Rodríguez-Muñoz, J. C. Pastor, A. I. Sanz-Vergel, and E. Garrosa, "The Moderating Effects of Psychological Detachment and Thoughts of Revenge in Workplace Bullying," *Personality and Individual Differences* 46, no. 3 (2009): 359–64.

[82]L. Yang, J. Bauer, R. E. Johnson, M. W. Groer, and K. Salomon, "Physiological Mechanisms That Underlie the Effects of Interactional Unfairness on Deviant Behavior: The Role of Cortisol Activity," *Journal of Applied Psychology* 99 (2014): 310–21.

[83]M. T. Schmitt, N. R. Branscombe, T. Postmes, and A. Garcia, "The Consequences of Perceived Discrimination for Psychological Well-Being: A Meta-Analytic Review," *Psychological Bulletin* 140 (2014): 921–48.

[84]J. O'Reilly, S. L. Robinson, J. L. Berdahl, and S. Banki, "Is Negative Attention Better Than No Attention? The Comparative Effects of Ostracism and Harassment at Work," *Organization Science* (2014): 774–93.

[85]"Stress in America: Paying with Our Health," *American Psychological Association*, February 4, 2015, http://www.apa.org/news/press/releases/stress/2014/stress-report.pdf.

[86]Q. Hu, W. B. Schaufeli, and T. W. Taris, "The Job Demands–Resources Model: An Analysis of Additive and Joint Effects of Demands and Resources," *Journal of Vocational Behavior* 79, no. 1 (2011): 181–90.

[87]E. R. Crawford, J. A. LePine, and B. L. Rich, "Linking Job Demands and Resources to Employee Engagement and Burnout: A Theoretical Extension and Meta-Analytic Test," *Journal of Applied Psychology* 95, no. 5 (2010): 834–48.

[88]See J. B. Halbesleben, "Sources of Social Support and Burnout: A Meta-Analytic Test of the Conservation of Resources Model,"

Journal of Applied Psychology 91, no. 5 (2006): 1134–45; N. Bolger and D. Amarel, "Effects of Social Support Visibility on Adjustment to Stress: Experimental Evidence," *Journal of Applied Psychology* 92, no. 3 (2007): 458–75; and C. Fernet, M. Gagné, and S. Austin, "When Does Quality of Relationships with Coworkers Predict Burnout over Time? The Moderating Role of Work Motivation," *Journal of Organizational Behavior* 31 (2010): 1163–80.

[89]J. B. Avey, F. Luthans, and S. M. Jensen, "Psychological Capital: A Positive Resource for Combating Employee Stress and Turnover," *Human Resource Management*, September–October 2009, 677–93.

[90]See, for example, C. M. Middeldorp, D. C. Cath, A. L. Beem, G. Willemsen, and D. I. Boomsma, "Life Events, Anxious Depression, and Personality: A Prospective and Genetic Study," *Psychological Medicine* 38, no. 11 (2008): 1557–65; A. A. Uliaszek, R. E. Zinbarg, S. Mineka, M. G. Craske, J. M. Sutton, J. W. Griffith, R. Rose, A. Waters, and C. Hammen, "The Role of Neuroticism and Extraversion in the Stress-Anxiety and Stress-Depression Relationships," *Anxiety, Stress, and Coping* 23, no. 4 (2010): 363–81.

[91]J. D. Kammeyer-Mueller, T. A. Judge, and B. A. Scott, "The Role of Core Self-Evaluations in the Coping Process," *Journal of Applied Psychology* 94, no. 1 (2009): 177–95.

[92]R. J. Burke, A. M. Richardson, and M. Mortinussen, "Workaholism among Norwegian Managers: Work and Well-Being Outcomes," *Journal of Organizational Change Management* 7 (2004): 459–70; and W. B. Schaufeli, T. W. Taris, and W. van Rhenen, "Workaholism, Burnout, and Work Engagement: Three of a Kind or Three Different Kinds of Employee Well-Being," *Applied Psychology: An International Review* 57, no. 2 (2008): 173–203.

[93]J. Chen, C. Silverthorne, and J. Hung, "Organization Communication, Job Stress, Organizational Commitment, and Job Performance of Accounting Professionals in Taiwan and America," *Leadership & Organization Development Journal* 27, no. 4 (2006): 242–49; and C. Liu, P. E. Spector, and L. Shi, "Cross-National Job Stress: A Quantitative and Qualitative Study," *Journal of Organizational Behavior*, February 2007, 209–39.

[94]P. E. Spector, T. D. Allen, S. A. Y. Poelmans, L. M. Lapierre, C. L. Cooper, M. O'Driscoll, et al., "Cross National Differences in Relationships of Work Demands, Job Satisfaction, and Turnover Intention with Work-Family Conflict," *Personnel Psychology* 60, no. 4 (2007): 805–35.

[95]H. M. Addae and X. Wang, "Stress at Work: Linear and Curvilinear Effects of Psychological-, Job-, and Organization-Related Factors: An Exploratory Study of Trinidad and Tobago," *International Journal of Stress Management*, November 2006, 476–93.

[96]M. Kivimäki, J. Head, J. E. Ferrie, E. Brunner, M. G. Marmot, J. Vahtera, and M. J. Shipley, "Why Is Evidence on Job Strain and Coronary Heart Disease Mixed? An Illustration of Measurement Challenges in the Whitehall II Study," *Psychosomatic Medicine* 68, no. 3 (2006): 398–401.

[97]M. Borritz, K. B. Christensen, U. Bültmann, R. Rugulies, T. Lund, I Andersen, E. Villadsen, F. Didreichsen, and T. S. Krisensen, "Impact on Burnout and Psychosocial Work Characteristics on Future Long-Term Sickness Absence, Prospective Results of the Danish PUMA Study among Human Service Workers," *Journal of Occupational and Environmental Medicine* 52, no. 10 (2010): 964–70.

[98]R. Ilies, N. Dimotakis, and I. E. DePater, "Psychological and Physiological Reactions to High Workloads: Implications for Well-Being," *Personnel Psychology* 63, no. 2 (2010): 407–63.

[99]D. Örtqvist and J. Wincent, "Prominent Consequences of Role Stress: A Meta-Analytic Review," *International Journal of Stress Management*, 13, no. 4 (2006): 399–422.

[100]J. J. Hakanen, A. B. Bakker, and M. Jokisaari, "A 35-Year Follow-Up Study on Burnout among Finnish Employees," *Journal of Occupational Health Psychology* 16, no. 3 (2011): 345–60; Crawford, LePine, and Rich, "Linking Job Demands and Resources to Employee Engagement and Burnout"; and G. A. Chung-Yan, "The Nonlinear Effects of Job Complexity and Autonomy on Job Satisfaction, Turnover, and Psychological Well-Being," *Journal of Occupational Health Psychology* 15, no. 3 (2010): 237–51.

[101]L. L. Meier, N. K. Semmer, A. Elfering, and N. Jacobshagen, "The Double Meaning of Control: Three-Way Interactions between Internal Resources, Job Control, and Stressors at Work," *Journal of Occupational Health Psychology* 13, no. 3 (2008): 244–58.

[102]E. M. de Croon, J. K. Sluiter, R. W. B. Blonk, J. P. J. Broersen, and M. H. W. Frings-Dresen, "Stressful Work, Psychological Job Strain, and Turnover: A 2-Year Prospective Cohort Study of Truck Drivers," *Journal of Applied Psychology*, June 2004, 442–54; R. Cropanzano, D. E. Rupp, and Z. S. Byrne, "The Relationship of Emotional Exhaustion to Work Attitudes, Job Performance, and Organizational Citizenship Behaviors," *Journal of Applied Psychology*, February 2003, 160–69; and S. Diestel and K. Schmidt, "Costs of Simultaneous Coping with Emotional Dissonance and Self-Control Demands at Work: Results from Two German Samples," *Journal of Applied Psychology* 96, no. 3 (2011): 643–53.

[103]See, for instance, S. Zivnuska, C. Kiewitz, W. A. Hochwarter, P. L. Perrewe, and K. L. Zellars, "What Is Too Much or Too Little? The Curvilinear Effects of Job Tension on Turnover Intent, Value Attainment, and Job Satisfaction," *Journal of Applied Social Psychology*, July 2002, 1344–60.

[104]Y.-F. Chen, "Job Stress and Performance: A Study of Police Officers in Central Taiwan," *Social Behavior and Personality* 37, no. 10 (2009): 1341–66; and L. A. Muse, S. G. Harris, and H. S. Field, "Has the Inverted-U Theory of Stress and Job Performance Had a Fair Test?" *Human Performance* 16, no. 4 (2003): 349–64.

[105]See, for example, L. W. Hunter and M. B. Thatcher, "Feeling the Heat: Effects of Stress, Commitment, and Job Experience on Job Performance," *Academy of Management Journal* 50, no. 4 (2007): 953–68; and J. C. Vischer, "The Effects of the Physical Environment on Job Performance: Towards a Theoretical Model of Workplace Stress," *Stress and Health* 23, no. 3 (2007): 175–84.

[106]Y.-C. Wu, "Job Stress and Job Performance among Employees on the Taiwanese Finance Sector: The Role of Emotional Intelligence," *Social Behavior and Personality* 39, no. 1 (2011): 21–31. This study was replicated with similar results in U. Yozgat, S. Yurtkoru, and E. Bilginoglu, "Job Stress and Job Performance among Employees in Public Sector in Istanbul: Examining the Moderating Role of Emotional Intelligence," in E. Eren (ed.), *Procedia Social and Behavioral Sciences* vol. 75 (2013): 518–24.

[107]S. Gilboa, A. Shirom, Y. Fried, and C. L. Cooper, "A Meta-Analysis of Work Demand Stressors and Job Performance: Examining Main and Moderating Effects," *Personnel Psychology* 61, no. 2 (2008): 227–71.

[108]J. C. Wallace, B. D. Edwards, T. Arnold, M. L. Frazier, and D. M. Finch, "Work Stressors, Role-Based Performance, and the Moderating Influence of Organizational Support," *Journal of Applied Psychology* 94, no. 1 (2009): 254–62.

[109]K. M. Richardson and H. R. Rothstein, "Effects of Occupational Stress Management Intervention Programs: A Meta-Analysis," *Journal of Occupational Health Psychology* 13, no. 1 (2008): 69–93.

[110]R. W. Renn, D. G. Allen, and T. M. Huning, "Empirical Examination of Individual-Level Personality-Based Theory of Self-Management Failure," *Journal of Organizational Behavior* 32, no. 1 (2011): 25–43; and P. Gröpel and P. Steel, "A Mega-Trial Investigation of Goal Setting, Interest Enhancement, and Energy on Procrastination," *Personality and Individual Differences* 45, no. 5 (2008): 406–11.

[111]S. Klaperski, B. von Dawans, M. Heinrichs, and R. Fuchs, "Does the Level of Physical Exercise Affect Physiological and Psychological Responses to Psychosocial Stress in Women?" *Psychology of Sport and Exercise* 14, no. 2 (2013): 266–74.

[112]K. M. Richardson and H. R. Rothstein, "Effects of Occupational Stress Management Intervention Programs: A Meta-Analysis," *Journal of Occupational Health Psychology* 13, no. 1 (2008): 69–93.

[113]V. C. Hahn, C. Binnewies, S. Sonnentag, and E. J. Mojza, "Learning How to Recover from Job Stress: Effects of a Recovery Training Program on Recovery, Recovery-Related Self-Efficacy, and Well-Being," *Journal of Occupational Health Psychology* 16, no. 2 (2011): 202–16; and C. Binnewies, S. Sonnentag, and E. J. Mojza, "Recovery during the Weekend and Fluctuations in Weekly Job Performance: A Week-Level Study Examining Intra-Individual Relationships," *Journal of Occupational and Organizational Psychology* 83, no. 2 (2010): 419–41.

[114]E. R. Greenglass and L. Fiksenbaum, "Proactive Coping, Positive Affect, and Well-Being: Testing for Mediation Using Path Analysis," *European Psychologist* 14, no. 1 (2009): 29–39; and P. Miquelon and R. J. Vallerand, "Goal Motives, Well-Being, and Physical Health: Happiness and Self-Realization as Psychological Resources under Challenge," *Motivation and Emotion* 30, no. 4 (2006): 259–72.

[115]M. M. Butts, R. J. Vandenberg, D. M. DeJoy, B. S. Schaffer, and M. G. Wilson, "Individual Reactions to High Involvement Work Processes: Investigating the Role of Empowerment and Perceived Organizational Support," *Journal of Occupational Health Psychology* 14, no. 2 (2009): 122–36.

[116]"100 Best Companies to Work For," *Fortune*, August 17, 2011, http://money.cnn.com/magazines/fortune.

[117]L. Blue, "Making Good Health Easy," *Time*, November 12, 2009, www.time.com; and M. Andrews, "America's Best Health Plans," *US News and World Report*, November 5, 2007, 54–60.

[118]K. M. Richardson and H. R. Rothstein, "Effects of Occupational Stress Management Intervention Programs: A Meta-Analysis," *Journal of Occupational Health Psychology* 13, no. 1 (2008): 69–93.

[119]L. L. Berry, A. M. Mirabito, and W. B. Baun, "What's the Hard Return on Employee Wellness Programs?" *Harvard Business Review*, December 2010, https://hbr.org/2010/12/whats-the-hard-return-on-employee-wellness-programs.

[120]S. Mattke, L. Hangsheng, J. P. Caloyeras, C. Y. Huan, K. R. Van Busum, D. Khodyakov, and V. Shier, *Workplace Wellness Programs Study* (Santa Monica, CA: RAND, 2013).

Appendix   Research in Organizational Behavior

A number of years ago, a friend of mine was excited because he had read about the findings from a research study that finally, once and for all, resolved the question of what it takes to make it to the top in a large corporation. I doubted there was any simple answer to this question but, not wanting to dampen his enthusiasm, I asked him to tell me of what he had read. The answer, according to my friend, was *participation in college athletics*. To say I was skeptical of his claim is a gross understatement, so I asked him to tell me more.

The study encompassed 1,700 successful senior executives at the 500 largest U.S. corporations. The researchers found that half of these executives had played varsity-level college sports.[1] My friend, who happens to be good with statistics, informed me that since fewer than 2 percent of all college students participate in intercollegiate athletics, the probability of this finding occurring by mere chance is less than 1 in 10 million! He concluded his analysis by telling me that, based on this research, I should encourage my management students to get into shape and to make one of the varsity teams.

My friend was somewhat perturbed when I suggested that his conclusions were likely to be flawed. These executives were all males who attended college in the 1940s and 1950s. Would his advice be meaningful to females in the twenty-first century? These executives also weren't your typical college students. For the most part, they had attended elite private colleges such as Princeton and Amherst, where a large proportion of the student body participates in intercollegiate sports. And these "jocks" hadn't necessarily played football or basketball; many had participated in golf, tennis, baseball, cross-country running, crew, rugby, and similar minor sports. Moreover, maybe the researchers had confused the direction of causality. That is, maybe individuals with the motivation and ability to make it to the top of a large corporation are drawn to competitive activities like college athletics.

My friend was guilty of misusing research data. Of course, he is not alone. We are all continually bombarded with reports of experiments that link certain substances to cancer in mice and surveys that show changing attitudes toward sex among college students, for example. Many of these studies are carefully designed, with great caution taken to note the implications and limitations of the findings. But some studies are poorly designed, making their conclusions at best suspect, and at worst meaningless.

Rather than attempting to make you a researcher, the purpose of this appendix is to increase your awareness as a consumer of behavioral research. A knowledge of research methods will allow you to appreciate more fully the care in data collection that underlies the information and conclusions presented in this text. Moreover, an understanding of research methods will make you a more skilled evaluator of the OB studies you will encounter in business and professional journals. So an appreciation of behavioral research is important because (1) it's the foundation on which the theories in this text are built, and (2) it will benefit you in future years when you read reports of research and attempt to assess their value.

Purposes of Research

Research is concerned with the systematic gathering of information. Its purpose is to help us in our search for the truth. Although we will never find ultimate truth—in our case, that would be to know precisely how any person or group would behave in any organizational context—ongoing research adds to our body of OB knowledge by supporting some theories, contradicting others, and suggesting new theories to replace those that fail to gain support.

Research Terminology

Researchers have their own vocabulary for communicating among themselves and with outsiders. The following briefly defines some of the more popular terms you're likely to encounter in behavioral science studies.[2]

Variable

A *variable* is any general characteristic that can be measured and that changes in amplitude, intensity, or both. Some examples of OB variables found in this textbook are job satisfaction, employee productivity, work stress, ability, personality, and group norms.

Hypothesis

A tentative explanation of the relationship between two or more variables is called a *hypothesis*. My friend's statement that participation in college athletics leads to a top executive position in a large corporation is an example of a hypothesis. Until confirmed by empirical research, a hypothesis remains only a tentative explanation.

Dependent Variable

A *dependent variable* is a response that is affected by an independent variable. In terms of the hypothesis, it is the variable that the researcher is interested in explaining. Referring back to our opening example, the dependent variable in my friend's hypothesis was executive succession. In organizational behavior research, the most popular dependent variables are productivity, absenteeism, turnover, job satisfaction, and organizational commitment.[3]

Independent Variable

An *independent variable* is the presumed cause of some change in the dependent variable. Participating in varsity athletics was the independent variable in my friend's hypothesis. Popular independent variables studied by OB researchers include intelligence, personality, job satisfaction, experience, motivation, reinforcement patterns, leadership style, reward allocations, selection methods, and organization design.

You may have noticed we said that job satisfaction is frequently used by OB researchers as both a dependent and an independent variable. This is not an error. It merely reflects that the label given to a variable depends on its place in the hypothesis. In the statement "Increases in job satisfaction lead to reduced turnover," job satisfaction is an independent variable. However, in the statement "Increases in money lead to higher job satisfaction," job satisfaction becomes a dependent variable.

Moderating Variable

A *moderating variable* abates the effect of the independent variable on the dependent variable. It might also be thought of as the contingency variable: If X (independent variable), then Y (dependent variable) will occur, but only under conditions Z (moderating variable). To translate this into a real-life example, we might say that if we increase the amount of direct supervision in the work area (X), then there will be a change in worker productivity (Y), but this effect will be moderated by the complexity of the tasks being performed (Z).

Causality

A hypothesis, by definition, implies a relationship. That is, it implies a presumed cause and effect. This direction of cause and effect is called *causality*. Changes in the independent variable are assumed to cause changes in the dependent variable. However, in behavioral research, it's possible to make an incorrect assumption of causality when relationships are found. For example, early behavioral scientists found a relationship between employee satisfaction and productivity. They concluded that a happy worker was a productive worker. Followup research has supported the relationship, but disconfirmed the direction of the arrow. The evidence more correctly suggests that high productivity leads to satisfaction rather than the other way around.

Correlation Coefficient

It's one thing to know that there is a relationship between two or more variables. It's another to know the *strength* of that relationship. The term *correlation coefficient* is used to indicate that strength, and is expressed as a number between –1.00 (a perfect negative relationship) and +1.00 (a perfect positive correlation).

When two variables vary directly with one another, the correlation will be expressed as a positive number. When they vary inversely—that is, one increases as the other decreases—the correlation will be expressed as a negative number. If the two variables vary independently of each other, we say that the correlation between them is zero.

For example, a researcher might survey a group of employees to determine the satisfaction of each with his or her job. Then, using company absenteeism reports, the researcher could correlate the job satisfaction scores against individual attendance records to determine whether employees who are more satisfied with their jobs have better attendance records than their counterparts who indicated lower job satisfaction. Let's suppose the researcher found a correlation coefficient of +0.50 between satisfaction and attendance. Would that be a strong association? There is, unfortunately, no precise numerical cutoff separating strong and weak relationships. A standard statistical test would need to be applied to determine whether the relationship was a significant one.

A final point needs to be made before we move on: A correlation coefficient measures only the strength of association between two variables. A high value does *not* imply causality. The length of women's skirts and stock market prices, for instance, have long been noted to be highly correlated, but one should be careful not to infer that a causal relationship between the two exists. In this instance, the high correlation is more happenstance than predictive.

Theory

The final term we introduce in this section is *theory*. Theory describes a set of systematically interrelated concepts or hypotheses that purports to explain and predict phenomena. In OB, theories are also frequently referred to as *models*. We use the two terms interchangeably.

There are no shortages of theories in OB. For instance, we have theories to describe what motivates people, the most effective leadership styles, the best way to resolve conflicts, and how people acquire power. In some cases, we have half a dozen or more separate theories that purport to explain and predict a given phenomenon. In such cases, is one right and the others wrong? No! They tend to reflect science at work—researchers testing previous theories, modifying them, and, when appropriate, proposing new models that may prove to have higher explanatory and predictive powers. Multiple theories attempting to explain common phenomena merely attest that OB is an active discipline, still growing and evolving.

Evaluating Research

As a potential consumer of behavioral research, you should follow the dictum of *caveat emptor*—let the buyer beware! In evaluating any research study, you need to ask three questions.[4]

Is it valid? Is the study actually measuring what it claims to be measuring? A number of psychological tests have been discarded by employers in recent years because they have not been found to be valid measures of the applicants' ability to do a given job successfully. But the validity issue is relevant to all research studies. So, if you find a study that links cohesive work teams with higher productivity, you want to know how each of these variables was measured and whether it is actually measuring what it is supposed to be measuring.

Is it reliable? Reliability refers to consistency of measurement. If you were to have your height measured every day with a wooden yardstick, you'd get highly reliable results. On the other hand, if you were measured each day by an elastic tape measure, there would probably be considerable disparity between your height measurements from one day to the next. Your height, of course, doesn't change from day to day. The variability is due to the unreliability of the measuring device. So if a company asked a group of its employees to complete a reliable job satisfaction questionnaire, and then repeat the questionnaire six months later, we'd expect the results to be very similar—provided nothing changed in the interim that might significantly affect employee satisfaction.

Is it generalizable? Are the results of the research study generalizable to groups of individuals other than those who participated in the original study? Be aware, for example, of the limitations that might exist in research that uses college students as subjects. Are the findings in

such studies generalizable to full-time employees in real jobs? Similarly, how generalizable to the overall work population are the results from a study that assesses job stress among 10 nuclear power plant engineers in the hamlet of Mahone Bay, Nova Scotia?

Research Design

Doing research is an exercise in trade-offs. Richness of information typically comes with reduced generalizability. The more a researcher seeks to control for confounding variables, the less realistic his or her results are likely to be. High precision, generalizability, and control almost always translate into higher costs. When researchers make choices about whom they'll study, where their research will be done, the methods they'll use to collect data, and so on, they must make some concessions. Good research designs are not perfect, but they do carefully reflect the questions being addressed. Keep these facts in mind as we review the strengths and weaknesses of five popular research designs: case studies, field surveys, laboratory experiments, field experiments, and aggregate quantitative reviews.

Case Study

You pick up a copy of Soichiro Honda's autobiography. In it he describes his impoverished childhood; his decisions to open a small garage, assemble motorcycles, and eventually build automobiles; and how this led to the creation of one of the largest and most successful corporations in the world. Or you're in a business class and the instructor distributes a 50-page handout covering two companies: Walmart and Kmart. The handout details the two firms' histories; describes their corporate strategies, management philosophies, and merchandising plans; and includes copies of their recent balance sheets and income statements. The instructor asks the class members to read the handout, analyze the data, and determine why Walmart has been so much more successful than Kmart in recent years.

Soichiro Honda's autobiography and the Walmart and Kmart handouts are case studies. Drawn from real-life situations, case studies present an in-depth analysis of one setting. They are thorough descriptions, rich in details about an individual, a group, or an organization. The primary source of information in case studies is obtained through observation, occasionally backed up by interviews and a review of records and documents.

Case studies have their drawbacks. They're open to the perceptual bias and subjective interpretations of the observer. The reader of a case is captive to what the observer/case writer chooses to include and exclude. Cases also trade off generalizability for depth of information and richness of detail. Because it's always dangerous to generalize from a sample of one, case studies make it difficult to prove or reject a hypothesis. On the other hand, you can't ignore the in-depth analysis that cases often provide. They are an excellent device for initial exploratory research and for evaluating real-life problems in organizations.

Field Survey

A lengthy questionnaire was created to assess the use of ethics policies, formal ethics structures, formalized activities such as ethics training, and executive involvement in ethics programs among billion-dollar corporations. The public affairs or corporate communications office of all Fortune 500 industrial firms and 500 service corporations were contacted to get the name and address of the "officer most responsible for dealing with ethics and conduct issues" in each firm. The questionnaire, with a cover letter explaining the nature of the study, was mailed to these 1,000 officers. Of the total, 254 returned a completed questionnaire, for a response rate just above 25 percent. The results of the survey found, among other things, that 77 percent had formal codes of ethics and 54 percent had a single officer specifically assigned to deal with ethics and conduct issues.[5]

The preceding study illustrates a typical field survey. A sample of respondents (in this case, 1,000 corporate officers in the largest U.S. publicly held corporations) was selected to represent a larger group that was under examination (billion-dollar U.S. business firms). The respondents were then surveyed using a questionnaire or interviewed to collect data on particular characteristics (the content and structure of ethics programs and practices) of interest to the researchers. The standardization of response items allows for data to be easily quantified, analyzed, and summarized, and for the researchers to make inferences from the representative sample about the larger population.

The field survey provides economies for doing research. It's less costly to sample a population than to obtain data from every member of that population. (There are, for instance, more than 5,000 U.S. business firms with sales in excess of a billion dollars; and since some of these are privately held and don't release financial data to the public, they are excluded from the *Fortune* list). Moreover, as the ethics study illustrates, field surveys provide an efficient way to find out how people feel about issues or how they say they behave. These data can then be easily quantified.

But the field survey has a number of potential weaknesses. First, mailed questionnaires rarely obtain 100 percent returns. Low response rates call into question whether conclusions based on respondents' answers are generalizable to nonrespondents. Second, the format is better at tapping respondents' attitudes and perceptions than behaviors. Third, responses can suffer from social desirability; that is, people saying what they think the researcher wants to hear. Fourth, since field surveys are designed to focus on specific issues, they're a relatively poor means of acquiring depth of information. Finally, the quality of the generalizations is largely a factor of the population chosen. Responses from executives at Fortune 500 firms, for instance, tell us nothing about small- or medium-sized firms or not-for-profit organizations. In summary, even a well-designed field survey trades off depth of information for breadth, generalizability, and economic efficiencies.

Laboratory Experiment

The following study is a classic example of the laboratory experiment. A researcher, Stanley Milgram, wondered how far individuals would go in following commands. If subjects were placed in the role of a teacher in a learning experiment and told by an experimenter to administer a shock to a learner each time that learner made a mistake, would the subjects follow the commands of the experimenter? Would their willingness to comply decrease as the intensity of the shock was increased?

To test these hypotheses, Milgram hired a set of subjects. Each was led to believe that the experiment was to investigate the effect of punishment on memory. Their job was to act as teachers and administer punishment whenever the learner made a mistake on the learning test.

Punishment was administered by an electric shock. The subject sat in front of a shock generator with 30 levels of shock—beginning at zero and progressing in 15-volt increments to a high of 450 volts. The demarcations of these positions ranged from "Slight Shock" at 15 volts to "Danger: Severe Shock" at 450 volts. To increase the realism of the experiment, the subjects received a sample shock of 45 volts and saw the learner—a pleasant, mild-mannered man about 50 years old—strapped into an "electric chair" in an adjacent room. Of course, the learner was an actor, and the electric shocks were phony, but the subjects didn't know this.

Taking his seat in front of the shock generator, the subject was directed to begin at the lowest shock level and to increase the shock intensity to the next level each time the learner made a mistake or failed to respond.

When the test began, the shock intensity rose rapidly because the learner made many errors. The subject got verbal feedback from the learner: At 75 volts, the learner began to grunt and moan; at 150 volts, he demanded to be released from the experiment; at 180 volts, he cried out that he could no longer stand the pain; and at 300 volts, he insisted that he be let out, yelled about his heart condition, screamed, and then failed to respond to further questions.

Most subjects protested and, fearful they might kill the learner if the increased shocks were to bring on a heart attack, insisted they could not go on with their job. Hesitations or protests by the subject were met by the experimenter's statement, "You have no choice, you must go on! Your job is to punish the learner's mistakes." Of course, the subjects did have a choice. All they had to do was stand up and walk out.

The majority of the subjects dissented. But dissension isn't synonymous with disobedience. Sixty-two percent of the subjects increased the shock level to the maximum of 450 volts. The average level of shock administered by the remaining 38 percent was nearly 370 volts.[6]

In a laboratory experiment such as that conducted by Milgram, an artificial environment is created by the researcher. Then the researcher manipulates an independent variable under controlled conditions. Finally, since all other things are held equal, the researcher is able to conclude that any change in the dependent variable is due to the manipulation or change imposed on the independent variable. Note that, because of the controlled conditions, the researcher is able to imply causation between the independent and dependent variables.

The laboratory experiment trades off realism and generalizability for precision and control. It provides a high degree of control over variables and precise measurement of those variables. But findings from laboratory studies are often difficult to generalize to the real world of work. This is because the artificial laboratory rarely duplicates the intricacies and nuances of real organizations. In addition, many laboratory experiments deal with phenomena that cannot be reproduced or applied to real-life situations.

Field Experiment

The following is an example of a field experiment. The management of a large company is interested in determining the impact that a 4-day workweek would have on employee absenteeism. To be more specific, management wants to know if employees working four 10-hour days have lower absence rates than similar employees working the traditional 5 day week of 8 hours each day. Because the company is large, it has a number of manufacturing plants that employ essentially similar workforces. Two of these are chosen for the experiment, both located in the greater Cleveland area. Obviously, it would not be appropriate to compare two similar-sized plants if one is in rural Mississippi and the other is in urban Copenhagen because factors such as national culture, transportation, and weather might be more likely to explain any differences found than changes in the number of days worked per week.

In one plant, the experiment was put into place—workers began the 4-day week. At the other plant, which became the control group, no changes were made in the employees' 5-day week. Absence data were gathered from the company's records at both locations for a period of 18 months. This extended time period lessened the possibility that any results would be distorted by the mere novelty of changes being implemented in the experimental plant. After 18 months, management found that absenteeism had dropped by 40 percent at the experimental plant, and by only 6 percent in the control plant. Because of the design of this study, management believed that the larger drop in absences at the experimental plant was due to the introduction of the compressed workweek.

The field experiment is similar to the laboratory experiment except it is conducted in a real organization. The natural setting is more realistic than the laboratory setting, and this enhances validity but hinders control. In addition, unless control groups are maintained, there can be a loss of control if extraneous forces intervene—for example, an employee strike, a major layoff, or a corporate restructuring. Maybe the greatest concern with field studies has to do with organizational selection bias. Not all organizations are going to allow outside researchers to come in and study their employees and operations. This is especially true of organizations that have serious problems. Therefore, since most published studies in OB are done by outside researchers, the selection bias might work toward the publication of studies conducted almost exclusively at successful and well-managed organizations.

Our general conclusion is that, of the four research designs we've discussed to this point, the field experiment typically provides the most valid and generalizable findings and, except for its high cost, trades off the least to get the most.[7]

Aggregate Quantitative Reviews

What's the overall effect of organizational behavior modification (OB Mod) on task performance? There have been a number of field experiments that have sought to throw light on this question. Unfortunately, the wide range of effects from these various studies makes it hard to generalize.

To try to reconcile these diverse findings, two researchers reviewed all the empirical studies they could find on the impact of OB Mod on task performance over a 20-year period.[8] After discarding reports that had inadequate information, had nonquantitative data, or didn't meet all conditions associated with principles of behavioral modification, the researchers narrowed their set to 19 studies that included data on 2,818 individuals. Using an aggregating technique called *meta-analysis,* the researchers were able to synthesize the studies quantitatively and to conclude that the average person's task performance will rise from the 50th percentile to the 67th percentile after an OB Mod intervention.

The OB Mod–task performance review done by these researchers illustrates the use of meta-analysis, a quantitative form of literature review that enables researchers to look at validity findings from a comprehensive set of individual studies, and then apply a formula to them to determine if they consistently produced similar results.[9] If results prove to be consistent, it allows researchers to conclude more confidently that validity is generalizable. Meta-analysis is a means for overcoming the potentially imprecise interpretations of qualitative reviews and to synthesize variations in quantitative studies. In addition, the technique enables researchers to identify potential moderating variables between an independent and a dependent variable.

In the past 25 years, there's been a surge in the popularity of this research method. Why? It appears to offer a more objective means for doing traditional literature reviews. Although the use of meta-analysis requires researchers to make a number of judgment calls, which can introduce a considerable amount of subjectivity into the process, there is no denying that meta-analysis reviews have now become widespread in the OB literature.

Ethics in Research

Researchers are not always tactful or candid with subjects when they do their studies. For instance, questions in field surveys may be perceived as embarrassing by respondents or as an invasion of privacy. Also, researchers in laboratory studies have been known to deceive participants about the true purpose of their experiment "because they felt deception was necessary to get honest responses."[10]

The "learning experiments" conducted by Stanley Milgram, which were conducted more than 30 years ago, have been widely criticized by psychologists on ethical grounds. He lied to subjects, telling them his study was investigating learning, when, in fact, he was concerned with obedience. The shock machine he used was a fake. Even the "learner" was an accomplice of Milgram's who had been trained to act as if he were hurt and in pain. Yet ethical lapses continue. For instance, in 2001, a professor of organizational behavior at Columbia University sent out a common letter on university letterhead to 240 New York City restaurants in which he detailed how he had eaten at this restaurant with his wife in celebration of their wedding anniversary, how he had gotten food poisoning, and that he had spent the night in his bathroom throwing up.[11] The letter closed with: "Although it is not my intention to file any reports with the Better Business Bureau or the Department of Health, I want you to understand what I went through in anticipation that you will respond accordingly. I await your response." The fictitious letter was part of the professor's study to determine how restaurants responded to complaints. But it created culinary chaos among many of the restaurant owners, managers, and chefs as they reviewed menus and produce deliveries for possibly spoiled food, and questioned kitchen workers about possible lapses. A follow-up letter of apology from the university for "an egregious error in judgment by a junior faculty member" did little to offset the distress it created for those affected.

Professional associations like the American Psychological Association, the American Sociological Association, and the Academy of Management have published formal guidelines for the conduct of research. Yet the ethical debate continues. On one side are those who argue that strict ethical controls can damage the scientific validity of an experiment and cripple future research. Deception, for example, is often necessary to avoid contaminating results. Moreover, proponents of minimizing ethical controls note that few subjects have been appreciably harmed by deceptive experiments. Even in Milgram's highly manipulative experiment, only 1.3 percent of the subjects reported negative feelings about their experience. The other side of this debate focuses on the rights of participants. Those favoring strict ethical controls argue that no procedure should ever be emotionally or physically distressing to subjects, and that, as professionals, researchers are obliged to be completely honest with their subjects and to protect the subjects' privacy at all costs.

Summary

The subject of organizational behavior is composed of a large number of theories that are research based. Research studies, when cumulatively integrated, become theories, and theories are proposed and followed by research studies designed to validate them. The concepts that make up OB, therefore, are only as valid as the research that supports them.

The topics and issues in this book are for the most part research-derived. They represent the result of systematic information gathering rather than merely hunch, intuition, or opinion. This doesn't mean, of course, that we have all the answers to OB issues. Many require far more corroborating evidence. The generalizability of others is limited by the research methods used. But new information is being created and published at an accelerated rate. To keep up with the latest findings, we strongly encourage you to regularly review the latest research in organizational behavior. More academic work can be found in journals such as the *Academy of Management*

Journal, Academy of Management Review, Administrative Science Quarterly, Human Relations, Journal of Applied Psychology, Journal of Management, Journal of Organizational behavior, and *Leadership Quarterly.* For more practical interpretations of OB research findings, you may want to read the *Academy of Management Executive, California Management Review, Harvard Business Review, Organizational Dynamics,* and the *Sloan Management Review.*

Endnotes

1. J. A. Byrne, "Executive Sweat," *Forbes* (May 20), 1985, pp. 198–200.

2. See D. P. Schwab, *Research Methods for Organizational Behavior* (Mahwah, NJ: Lawrence Erlbaum Associates, 1999); and S. G. Rogelberg (ed.), *Blackwell Handbook of Research Methods in Industrial and Organizational Psychology* (Malden, MA: Blackwell, 2002).

3. B. M. Staw and G. R. Oldham, "Reconsidering Our Dependent Variables: A Critique and Empirical Study," *Academy of Management Journal* (December 1978), pp. 539–559; and B. M. Staw, "Organizational Behavior: A Review and Reformulation of the Field's Outcome Variables," in M. R. Rosenzweig and L. W. Porter (eds.), *Annual Review of Psychology,* vol. 35 (Palo Alto, CA: Annual Reviews, 1984), pp. 627–666.

4. R. S. Blackburn, "Experimental Design in Organizational Settings," in J. W. Lorsch (ed.), *Handbook of Organizational Behavior* (Upper Saddle River, NJ: Prentice Hall, 1987), pp. 127–128; and F. L. Schmidt, C. Viswesvaran, D. S. Ones, "Reliability Is Not Validity and Validity Is Not Reliability," *Personnel Psychology* (Winter 2000), pp. 901–912.

5. G. R. Weaver, L. K. Trevino, and P. L. Cochran, "Corporate Ethics Practices in the Mid-1990's: An Empirical Study of the Fortune 1000," *Journal of Business Ethics* (February 1999), pp. 283–294.

6. S. Milgram, *Obedience to Authority* (New York: Harper & Row, 1974). For a critique of this research, see T. Blass, "Understanding Behavior in the Milgram Obedience Experiment: The Role of Personality, Situations, and Their Interactions," *Journal of Personality and Social Psychology* (March 1991), pp. 398–413.

7. See, for example, W. N. Kaghan, A. L. Strauss, S. R. Barley, M. Y. Brannen, and R. J. Thomas, "The Practice and Uses of Field Research in the 21st Century Organization," *Journal of Management Inquiry* (March 1999), pp. 67–81.

8. A. D. Stajkovic and F. Luthans, "A Meta-Analysis of the Effects of Organizational Behavior Modification on Task Performance, 1975–1995," *Academy of Management Journal* (October 1997), pp. 1122–1149.

9. See, for example, K. Zakzanis, "The Reliability of Meta Analytic Review," *Psychological Reports* (August 1998), pp. 215–222; C. Ostroff and D. A. Harrison, "Meta-Analysis, Level of Analysis, and Best Estimates of Population Correlations: Cautions for Interpreting Meta-Analytic Results in Organizational Behavior," *Journal of Applied Psychology* (April 1999), pp. 260–270; R. Rosenthal and M. R. DiMatteo, "Meta-Analysis: Recent Developments in Quantitative Methods for Literature Reviews," in S. T. Fiske, D. L. Schacter, and C. Zahn-Wacher (eds.), *Annual Review of Psychology,* vol. 52 (Palo Alto, CA: Annual Reviews, 2001), pp. 59–82; and F. L. Schmidt and J. E. Hunter, "Meta-Analysis," in N. Anderson, D. S. Ones, H. K. Sinangil, and C. Viswesvaran (eds.), *Handbook of Industrial, Work & Organizational Psychology,* vol. 1 (Thousand Oaks, CA: Sage, 2001), pp. 51–70.

10. For more on ethical issues in research, see T. L. Beauchamp, R. R. Faden, R. J. Wallace, Jr., and L. Walters (eds.), *Ethical Issues in Social Science Research* (Baltimore, MD: Johns Hopkins University Press, 1982); and J. G. Adair, "Ethics of Psychological Research: New Policies, Continuing Issues, New Concerns," *Canadian Psychology* (February 2001), pp. 25–37.

11. J. Kifner, "Scholar Sets Off Gastronomic False Alarm," *New York Times* (September 8, 2001), p. A1.

Comprehensive Cases

CASE 1

Managing Motivation in a Difficult Economy

Learning Goals

In this case, you'll have an opportunity to assess a motivational program designed to reenergize a troubled company's workforce. Acting on behalf of the company's executive board, you'll evaluate the board's current strategy based on survey data. You'll also advise board members about improving the effectiveness of this program based on what you've learned about goal-setting and motivation in organizations.

Major Topic Areas

- Changing nature of work
- Diversity and age
- Goal-setting
- Organizational downsizing
- Organizational justice

The Scenario

Morgan-Moe's drugstores are in trouble. A major regional player in the retail industry, the company has hundreds of stores in the upper Midwest. Unfortunately, a sharp decline in the region's manufacturing economy has put management in a serious financial bind. Revenues have been consistently dwindling. Customers spend less, and the stores have had to switch their focus to very low-margin commodities, such as milk and generic drugs, rather than the high-margin impulse-buy items that used to be the company's bread and butter. The firm has closed quite a few locations, reversing its expansion plans for the first time since it incorporated.

Being that this is uncharted territory for the company, Jim Claussen, vice president for human relations, had been struggling with how to address the issue with employees. As the company's fortunes worsened, he could see that employees were becoming more and more disaffected. Their insecurity about their jobs was taking a toll on attitudes. The company's downsizing was big news, and the employees didn't like what they were hearing.

Media reports of Morgan-Moe's store closings have focused on the lack of advance notice or communication from the company's corporate offices, as well as the lack of severance payments for departing employees. In the absence of official information, rumors and gossip have spread like wildfire among remaining employees. A few angry blogs developed by laid-off employees, like IHateMorganMoe.blogspot.com, have made the morale and public relations picture even worse.

Morgan-Moe is changing in other ways as well. The average age of its workforce is increasing rapidly. A couple of factors have contributed to this shift. First, fewer qualified young people are around because many families have moved away to find jobs. Second, stores have been actively encouraged to hire older workers, such as retirees looking for supplemental income. Managers are very receptive to these older workers because they are more mature, miss fewer days of work, and do not have child care responsibilities. They are also often more qualified than younger workers because they have more experience, sometimes in the managerial or executive ranks.

These older workers have been a great asset to the company in troubled times, but they are especially likely to leave if things get bad. If these older workers start to leave the company, taking their hard-earned experience with them, it seems likely that Morgan-Moe will sink deeper toward bankruptcy.

The System

Claussen wasn't sure how to respond to employees' sense of hopelessness and fear until a friend gave him a book entitled *Man's Search for Meaning*. The book was written by a psychologist named Victor Frankl, who survived the concentration camps at Auschwitz. Frankl found that those who had a clear sense of purpose, a reason to live, were more likely to persevere in the face of nearly unspeakable suffering. Something about this book, and its advocacy of finding meaning and direction as a way to triumph over adversity, really stuck with Claussen. He thought he might be able to apply its lessons to his workforce. He proposed the idea of a new direction for management to the company's executive committee, and they reluctantly agreed to try his suggestions.

Over the last 6 months, stores throughout the company have used a performance management system that, as Claussen says, "gets people to buy into the idea of performing so that they can see some real results in their stores. It's all about seeing that your work serves a broader purpose. I read about how some companies have been sharing store performance information with employees to get them to understand what their jobs really mean and participate in making changes, and I thought that was something we'd be able to do."

The HR team came up with five options for the management system. Corporate allowed individual managers to choose the option they thought would work best with their employees so that managers wouldn't feel too much like a rapid change was being forced on them. Program I is opting out of the new idea, continuing to stay the course and providing employees with little to no information or opportunities for participation. Program II tracks employee absence and sick leave data and shares that information with individual employees, giving them feedback about things they can control. Management takes no further action. Program III tracks sales and inventory replacement rates across shifts. As in Program II, information is shared with employees, but without providing employee feedback about absence and sick leave data. Program IV, the most comprehensive, tracks the same information as Programs II and III. Managers communicate it in weekly brainstorming sessions, during which employees try to determine what they can do better in the future and make suggestions for improving store performance. Program V keeps the idea of brainstorming but doesn't provide employees with information about their behavior or company profits.

Since implementing the system, Claussen has spoken with several managers about what motivated them to choose the program they did. Artie Washington, who chose Program IV, said, "I want to have my employees' input on how to keep the store running smoothly. Everybody worries about their job security in this economy. Letting them know what's going on and giving them ways to change things keeps them involved."

Betty Alvarez couldn't disagree more. She selected Program I. "I would rather have my employees doing their jobs than going to meetings to talk about doing their jobs. That's what management is for." Michael Ostremski, another proponent of Program I, added, "It's okay for the employees to feel a little uncertain—if they think we're in the clear, they'll slack off. If they think we're in trouble, they'll give up."

Cal Martins also questions the need to provide information to the whole team, but he chose Program II. "A person should know where he or she stands in the job, but they don't have to know about everyone else. It creates unnecessary tension."

This is somewhat similar to Cindy Ang's reason for picking Program V. "When we have our brainstorming meetings, I learn what they [the employees] think is most pressing, not what some spreadsheet says. It gives me a better feel for what's going on in my store. Numbers count, of course, but they don't tell you everything. I was also a little worried that employees would be upset if they saw that we aren't performing well."

Results to Date

Claussen is convinced the most elaborate procedure (Program IV) is the most effective, but not everyone in the executive committee is won over by his advocacy. Although they have supported the test implementation of the system because it appears to have relatively low costs, others on the committee want to see results. CEO Jean Masterson has asked for a complete breakdown of the performance of the various stores over the past 4 years. She's especially interested in seeing how sales figures and turnover rates have been affected by the new program.

The company has been collecting data in spreadsheets on sales and turnover rates, and it prepared the following report, which also estimates the dollar cost of staff time taken up in each method. These costs are based on the number of hours employees spend working on the program multiplied by their wage rate. Estimates of turnover, profit, and staff time are collected per store. Profit and turnover data include means and standard deviations across locations; profit is net of the monthly time cost. Turnover information refers to the percentage of employees who either quit or are terminated in a month.

To see if any patterns emerged in managers' selection of programs, the company calculated relationships between program selection and various attributes of the stores. Program I was selected most frequently by the oldest stores and those in the most economically distressed areas. Programs II and III were selected most frequently by stores in urban areas and in areas where the workforce was younger on average. Programs IV and V were selected most frequently in stores in rural areas, and especially where the workforce is older on average.

Program	Methods	Number of Stores	Average Turnover	Weekly Profit per Month	Monthly Staff Time Cost
Program I	Traditional management	83	Mean = 30% SD = 10%	Mean = $5,700 SD = $3,000	None
Program II	Share absence and sick leave	27	Mean = 23% SD = 14%	Mean = $7,000 SD = $5,800	$1,960
Program III	Share sales and inventory	35	Mean = 37% SD = 20%	Mean = $11,000 SD = $2,700	$2,440
Program IV	Share information and brainstorm	67	Mean = 17% SD = 20%	Mean = $13,000 SD = $3,400	$3,420
Program V	Brainstorm without sharing information	87	Mean = 21% SD = 12%	Mean = $14,000 SD = $2,400	$2,750

Your Assignment

Your task is to prepare a report for the company's executive committee on the effectiveness of these programs. Make certain it is in the form of a professional business document. Your audience won't necessarily know about the organizational principles you're describing, so make sure you provide detailed explanations that someone in a real business can understand.

When you write, make sure you touch on the following points:

CC-1. Consider the five management systems as variables in an experiment. Identify the independent and dependent variables, and explain how they are related to one another.

CC-2. Based on the discussion of independent and dependent variables in the textbook, is there anything else you'd like to measure as an outcome?

CC-3. Look over the data and decide which method of management appears most effective in generating revenues and reducing turnover, and why. Which methods appear least effective, and why?

CC-4. Are there any concerns you have about these data?

CC-5. Does a comparison of the number of stores using each method influence your conclusions at all?

CC-6. Does the fact that managers are selecting the specific program to use (including Program I, which continues the status quo) affect the inferences you can draw about program success?

CC-7. What are the advantages of randomly assigning different conditions to the stores instead of using this self-selection process?

CC-8. How does the changing nature of the workforce and the economy, described in your textbook and in the case, affect your conclusions about how to manage retail employees? Does the participation of a more experienced workforce help or hurt these programs? Why might these programs work differently in an economy that isn't doing so poorly?

CC-9. Claussen essentially designed the program on his own, with very little research into goal-setting and motivation. Based on your textbook, how well has he done? Which parts of the program appear to fit well with research evidence on goal-setting? What parts would you change to get more substantial improvements in employee motivation?

CC-10. Describe the feelings employees might have when these systems are implemented that could help or hinder the program's success. What advice would you give managers about how to implement the programs so they match the principles of organizational justice described in your textbook?

CASE 2

Repairing Jobs That Fail to Satisfy

Learning Goals

Companies often divide up work as a way to improve efficiency, but specialization can lead to negative consequences. DrainFlow is a company that has effectively used specialization to reduce costs relative to its competitors' costs for years, but rising customer complaints suggest the firm's strong position may be slipping. After reading the case, you will suggest some ways it can create more interesting work for employees. You'll also tackle the problem of finding people qualified and ready to perform the multiple responsibilities required in these jobs.

Major Topic Areas

- Job design
- Job satisfaction
- Personality
- Emotional labor

The Scenario

DrainFlow is a large residential and commercial plumbing maintenance firm that operates around the United States. It has been a major player in residential plumbing for decades, and its familiar rhyming motto, "When Your Drain Won't Go, Call DrainFlow," has been plastered on billboards since the 1960s.

Lee Reynaldo has been a regional manager at Drain-Flow for about 2 years. She used to work for a newer competing chain, Lightning Plumber, that has been drawing more and more customers from DrainFlow. Although her job at DrainFlow pays more, Reynaldo isn't happy with the way things are going. She's noticed the work environment just isn't as vital or energetic as the environment she saw at Lightning.

Reynaldo thinks the problem is that employees aren't motivated to provide the type of customer service Lightning Plumber employees offer. She recently sent surveys to customers to collect information about performance, and the data confirmed her fears. Although 60 percent of respondents said they were satisfied with their experience and would use DrainFlow again, 40 percent felt their experience was not good, and 30 percent said they

would use a competitor the next time they had a plumbing problem.

Reynaldo is wondering whether DrainFlow's job design might be contributing to its problems in retaining customers. DrainFlow has about 2,000 employees in four basic job categories: plumbers, plumber's assistants, order processors, and billing representatives. This structure is designed to keep costs as low as possible. Plumbers make very high wages, whereas plumber's assistants make about one-quarter of what a licensed plumber makes. Using plumber's assistants is therefore a very cost-effective strategy that has enabled DrainFlow to easily undercut the competition when it comes to price. Order processors make even less than assistants but about the same as billing processors. All work is very specialized, but employees are often dependent on another job category to perform at their most efficient level.

Like most plumbing companies, DrainFlow gets business mostly from the Yellow Pages and the Internet. Customers either call in to describe a plumbing problem or submit an online request for plumbing services, receiving a return call with information within 24 hours. In either case, DrainFlow's order processors listen to the customer's description of the problem to determine whether a plumber or a plumber's assistant should make the service call. The job is then assigned accordingly, and a service provider goes to the location. When the job has been completed, via cell phone a billing representative relays the fee to the service rep, who presents a bill to the customer for payment. Billing representatives can take customers' credit card payments by phone or e-mail an invoice for online payment.

The Problem

Although specialization does cut costs significantly, Reynaldo is worried about customer dissatisfaction. According to her survey, about 25 percent of customer contacts ended in no service call because customers were confused by the diagnostic questions the order processors asked and because the order processors did not have sufficient knowledge or skill to explain the situation. That means fully one in four people who call DrainFlow to hire a plumber are worse than dissatisfied: they aren't customers at all! The remaining 75 percent of calls that did end in a customer service encounter resulted in other problems.

The most frequent complaints Reynaldo found in the customer surveys were about response time and cost, especially when the wrong person was sent to a job. A plumber's assistant cannot complete a more technically complicated job. The appointment has to be rescheduled, and the customer's time and the staff's time have been wasted. The resulting delay often caused customers in these situations to decline further contact with DrainFlow—many of them decided to go with Lightning Plumber.

"When I arrive at a job I can't take care of," says plumber's assistant Jim Larson, "the customer gets ticked off. They thought they were getting a licensed plumber, since they were calling for a plumber. Telling them they have to have someone else come out doesn't go over well."

On the other hand, when a plumber responds to a job easily handled by a plumber's assistant, the customer is still charged at the plumber's higher pay rate. Licensed plumber Luis Berger also does not like being in the position of giving customers bad news. "If I get called out to do something like snake a drain, the customer isn't expecting a hefty bill. I'm caught between a rock and a hard place—I don't set the rates or make the appointments, but I'm the one who gets it from the customer." Plumbers also resent being sent to do such simple work.

Susie McCarty is one of DrainFlow's order processors. She's frustrated too when the wrong person is sent to a job but feels she and the other order processors are doing the best they can. "We have a survey we're supposed to follow with the calls to find out what the problem is and who needs to take the job," she explains. "The customers don't know that we have a standard form, so they think we can answer all their questions. Most of us don't know any more about plumbing than the caller. If they don't use the terms on the survey, we don't understand what they're talking about. A plumber would, but we're not plumbers; we just take the calls."

Customer service issues also involve the billing representatives. They are the ones who have to keep contacting customers about payment. "It's not my fault the wrong guy was sent," says Elizabeth Monty. "If two guys went out, that's two trips. If a plumber did the work, you pay plumber rates. Some of these customers don't get that I didn't take their first call, and so I get yelled at." The billing representatives also complain that they see only the tail end of the process, so they don't know what the original call entailed. The job is fairly impersonal, and much of the work is recording customer complaints. Remember—40 percent of customers aren't satisfied, and it's the billing representatives who take the brunt of their negative reactions on the phone.

As you can probably tell, all employees have to engage in emotional labor, as described in this textbook, and many lack the skills or personality traits to complete the customer interaction component of their jobs. They aren't trained to provide customer service, and they see their work mostly in technical, or mechanical, terms. Quite a few are actually anxious about speaking directly with customers. The office staff (order processors and billing representatives) realize customer service is part of their job, but they also find dealing with negative feedback from customers and coworkers taxing.

A couple of years ago a management consulting company was hired to survey DrainFlow worker attitudes. The results showed they were less satisfied than workers in other comparable jobs. The following table provides a breakdown of respondent satisfaction levels across a number of categories:

	DrainFlow Plumbers	DrainFlow Plumber Assistants	DrainFlow Office Workers	Average Plumber	Average Office Workers
I am satisfied with the work I am asked to do.	3.7	2.5	2.5	4.3	3.5
I am satisfied with my working conditions.	3.8	2.4	3.7	4.1	4.2
I am satisfied with my interactions with coworkers.	3.5	3.2	2.7	3.8	3.9
I am satisfied with my interactions with my supervisor.	2.5	2.3	2.2	3.5	3.4

The information about average plumbers and average office workers is taken from the management consulting company's records of other companies. They aren't exactly surprising, given some of the complaints DrainFlow employees have made. Top management is worried about these results, but they haven't been able to formulate a solution. The traditional DrainFlow culture has been focused on cost containment, and the "soft stuff" like employee satisfaction hasn't been a major issue.

The Proposed Solution

The company is in trouble, and as revenues shrink and the cost savings that were supposed to be achieved by dividing up work fail to materialize, a change seems to be in order.

Reynaldo is proposing using cash rewards to improve performance among employees. She thinks if employees were paid based on work outcomes, they'd work harder to satisfy customers. Because it's not easy to measure how satisfied people are with the initial call-in, Reynaldo would like to give the order processors a small reward for every 20 calls successfully completed. For the hands-on work, she'd like to have each billing representative collect information about customer satisfaction for each completed call. If no complaints are made and the job is handled promptly, a moderate cash reward would be given to the plumber or plumber's assistant. If the customer indicates real satisfaction with the service, a larger cash reward would be provided.

Reynaldo also wants to find people who are a better fit with the company's new goals. Current hiring procedure relies on unstructured interviews with each location's general manager, and little consistency is found in the way these managers choose employees. Most lack training in customer service and organizational behavior. Reynaldo thinks it would be better if hiring methods were standardized across all branches in her region to help managers identify recruits who can actually succeed in the job.

Your Assignment

Your task is to prepare a report for Reynaldo on the potential effectiveness of her cash reward and structured-interview programs. Make certain it is in the form of a professional business document that you'd actually give to an experienced manager at this level of a fairly large corporation. Reynaldo is very smart when it comes to managing finances and running a plumbing business, but she won't necessarily know about the organizational behavior principles you're describing. Because any new proposals must be passed through top management, you should also address their concerns about cost containment. You'll need to make a strong evidence-based financial case that changing the management style will benefit the company.

When you write, make sure you touch on the following points:

CC-11. Although it's clear employees are not especially satisfied with their work, do you think this is a reason for concern? Does research suggest satisfied workers are actually better at their jobs? Are any other behavioral outcomes associated with job satisfaction?

CC-12. Using job characteristics theory, explain why the present system of job design may be contributing to employee dissatisfaction. Describe some ways you could help employees feel more satisfied with their work by redesigning their jobs.

CC-13. Reynaldo has a somewhat vague idea about how to implement the cash rewards system. Describe some of the specific ways you would make the reward system work better, based on the case.

CC-14. Explain the advantages and disadvantages of using financial incentives in a program of this nature. What, if any, potential problems might arise if people are given money for achieving customer satisfaction goals? What other types of incentives might be considered?

CC-15. Create a specific plan to assess whether the reward system is working. What are the dependent variables that should change if the system works? How will you go about measuring success?

CC-16. What types of hiring recommendations would you make to find people better suited for these jobs? Which Big Five personality traits would be useful for the customer service responsibilities and emotional labor?

Learning Goals

Many of the most important organizational behavior challenges require coordinating plans and goals among groups. This case describes a multiorganizational effort, but the same principles of accommodation and compromise also apply when trying to work with multiple divisions within a single organization. You'll create a blueprint for managing a complex development team's progress, steering team members away from negative conflicts and toward productive discussion. You'll also be asked to help create a new message for executives so they can lead effectively.

Major Topic Areas

- Group dynamics
- Maximizing team performance
- Organizational culture
- Integrative bargaining

The Scenario

The Woodson Foundation, a large nonprofit social service agency, is teaming up with the public school system in Washington, D.C., to improve student outcomes. There's ample room for improvement. The schools have problems with truancy, low student performance, and crime. New staff quickly burn out as their initial enthusiasm for helping students is blunted by the harsh realities they encounter in the classroom. Turnover among new teachers is very high, and many of the best and brightest are the most likely to leave for schools that aren't as troubled.

The plan is to create an experimental after-school program that will combine the Woodson Foundation's skill in raising private money and coordinating community leaders with the educational expertise of school staff. Ideally, the system will be financially self-sufficient, which is important because less money is available for schools than in the past. After several months of negotiation, the leaders of the Woodson Foundation and the school system have agreed that the best course is to develop a new agency that will draw on resources from both organizations. The Woodson foundation will provide logistical support and program development

and measurement staff; the school system will provide classrooms and teaching staff.

The first stage in bringing this new plan to fruition is the formation of an executive development team. This team will span multiple functional areas and establish the operating plan for improving school performance. Its cross-organizational nature means representatives from both the Woodson Foundation and the school district must participate. The National Coalition for Parental Involvement in Education (NCPIE) is also going to be a major partner in the program, acting as a representative for parents on behalf of the PTA.

Conflict and Agreement in the Development Team

While it would be perfect if all the groups could work together easily to improve student outcomes, there is little doubt some substantive conflicts will arise. Each group has its own interests, and in some cases these are directly opposed to one another.

School district representatives want to ensure the new jobs will be unionized and will operate in a way consistent with current school board policies. They are very concerned that if Woodson assumes too dominant a role, the school board won't be able to control the operations of the new system. The complexity of the school system has led to the development of a highly complex bureaucratic structure over time, and administrators want to make sure their policies and procedures will still hold for teachers in these programs even outside the regular school day. They also worry that jobs going into the new system will take funding from other school district jobs.

Woodson, founded by entrepreneur Theodore Woodson around 1910, still bears the hallmarks of its founder's way of doing business. Woodson emphasized efficiency and experimentation in everything he did. Many of the foundation's charities have won awards for minimizing costs while still providing excellent services. Their focus on using hard data to measure performance for all their initiatives is not consistent with the school district culture.

Finally, the NCPIE is driven by a mission to increase parental control. The organization believes that when communities are able to drive their own educational methods, students and parents are better able to achieve success together. The organization is strongly committed to celebrating diversity along racial, gender, ethnic, and disability status categories. Its members are most interested in the process by which changes are made, ensuring everyone has the ability to weigh in.

Some demographic diversity issues complicate the team's situation. Most of the students served by the Washington, D.C., school district are African American, along with large populations of Caucasians and Hispanics. The NCPIE makeup generally matches the demographic diversity of the areas served by the public schools. The Woodson foundation, based in northern Virginia, is predominantly staffed by Caucasian professionals. There is some concern with the idea that a new group that does not understand the demographic concerns of the community will be so involved in a major change in educational administration. The leadership of the new program will have to be able to present an effective message for generating enthusiasm for the program across diverse stakeholder groups.

Although the groups differ in important ways, it's also worth considering what they have in common. All are interested in meeting the needs of students. All would like to increase student learning. The school system does benefit from anything that increases student test scores. And the Woodson Foundation and NCPIE are united in their desire to see more parents engaged in the system.

Candidates for the Development Team

The development team will consist of three individuals—HR representatives from the Woodson Foundation, the schools, and the NCPIE—who have prepared the following list of potential candidates for consideration.

Victoria Adams is the superintendent of schools for Washington, D.C. She spearheaded the initial communication with the Woodson Foundation and has been building support among teachers and principals. She thinks the schools and the foundation need to have larger roles than the parents and communities. "Of course we want their involvement and support, but as the professionals, we should have more say when it comes to making decisions and implementing programs. We don't want to shut anyone out, but we have to be realistic about what the parents can do."

Duane Hardy has been a principal in the Washington area for more than 15 years. He also thinks the schools should have the most power. "We're the ones who work with these kids every day. I've watched class sizes get bigger, and scores and graduation rates go down. Yes, we need to fix this, but these outside groups can't understand the limitations we're dealing with. We have the community, the politicians, the taxpayers—everyone watching what we're doing, everyone thinking they know what's

best. The parents, at least, have more of a stake in this."

"The most important thing is the kids," says second-year teacher Ari Kaufman. He is well liked by his students but doesn't get along well with other faculty members. He's seen as a "squeaky wheel." "The schools need change so badly. And how did they get this way? From too little outside involvement."

Community organizer Mason Dupree doesn't like the level of bureaucracy either. He worries that the school's answer to its problems is to throw more money at them. "I know these kids. I grew up in these neighborhoods. My parents knew every single teacher I had. The schools wanted our involvement then. Now all they want is our money. And I wouldn't mind giving it to them if I thought it would be used responsibly, not spent on raises for people who haven't shown they can get the job done."

Meredith Watson, with the Woodson Foundation, agrees the schools have become less focused on the families. A former teacher, she left the field of education after being in the classroom for 6 years. "There is so much waste in the system," she complains. "Jobs are unnecessarily duplicated, change processes are needlessly convoluted. Unless you're an insider already, you can't get anything done. These parents want to be involved. They know their kids best."

Unlike her NCPIE colleagues, Candace Sharpe thinks the schools are doing the best they can. She is a county social worker, relatively new to the D.C. area. "Parents say they want to be involved but then don't follow through. *We* need to step it up, *we* need to lead the way. Lasting change doesn't come from the outside, it comes from the home."

Victor Martinez has been at the Woodson Foundation for 10 years, starting as an intern straight out of college. "It's sometimes hard to see a situation when you're in the thick of it," he explains. "Nobody likes to be told they're doing something wrong, but sometimes it has to be said. We all know there are flaws in the system. We can't keep the status quo. It just isn't cutting it."

Strategies for the Program Team

Once the basic membership and principles for the development team have been established, the program team would also like to develop a handbook for those who will be running the new program. Ideally, this set of principles can help train new leaders to create an inspirational message that will facilitate success. The actual content of the program and the nature of the message will be hammered out by the development team, but it is still possible to generate some overriding principles for the program team in advance of these decisions.

Your Assignment

The Woodson Foundation, the NCPIE, and the schools have asked you to provide some information about how to form teams effectively. They would like your response to explain what should be done at each step of the way, from the selection of appropriate team members to setting group priorities and goals, setting deadlines, and describing effective methods for resolving conflicts that arise. After this, they'd like you to prepare a brief set of principles for leaders of the newly established program. That means you will have two audiences: the development team, which will receive one report on how it can effectively design the program, and the program team, which will receive one report on how it can effectively lead the new program.

The following points should help you form a comprehensive message for the development team:

CC-17. The development team will be more effective if members have some idea about how groups and teams typically operate. Review the dominant perspectives on team formation and performance from the chapters in the book for the committee so it can know what to expect.

CC-18. Given the profiles of candidates for the development team, provide suggestions for who would likely be a good group member and who might be less effective in this situation. Be sure you are using the research on groups and teams in the textbook to defend your choices.

CC-19. Using principles from the chapters on groups and teams, describe how you will advise the team to manage conflict effectively.

CC-20. Describe how integrative negotiation strategies might achieve joint goals for the development team.

The following points should help you form a message for the program team:

CC-21. Leaders of the new combined organization should have a good idea of the culture of the school district, the NCPIE, and the Woodson Foundation because they will need to manage relationships with all three groups on an ongoing basis. How would you describe the culture of these various stakeholder organizations? Use concepts from the chapter on organizational culture to describe how they differ and how they are similar.

CC-22. Consider how leaders of the new program can generate a transformational message and encourage employee and parent trust. Using material from the chapter on leadership, describe how you would advise leaders to accomplish these ends.

CC-23. Given the potential for demographic fault lines in negotiating these changes, what would you advise as a strategy for managing diversity issues for program leaders?

CASE 4 Boundaryless Organizations

Learning Goals

The multinational organization is an increasingly common and important part of the economy. This case takes you into the world of a cutting-edge music software business seeking success across three very different national and organizational cultures. Its managers need to make important decisions about how to structure work processes so employees can be satisfied and productive doing very different tasks.

Major Topic Areas

- Organizational structure and boundaryless organizations
- Organizational culture
- Human resources
- Organizational socialization

The Scenario

Newskool Grooves is a transnational company developing music software. The software is used to compose music, play recordings in clubs, and produce albums. Founder and CEO Gerd Finger is, understandably, the company's biggest fan. "I started this company from nothing, from just me, my ideas, and my computer. I love music—love playing music, love writing programs for making music, love listening to music—and the money is nice, too." Finger says he never wanted to work for someone else, to give away his ideas and let someone else profit from them. He wanted to keep control over them, and their image. "Newskool Grooves is always ahead of the pack. In this business, if you can't keep up, you're out. And we are the company everyone else must keep up with. Everyone knows when they get something from us, they're getting only the best and the newest."

The company headquarters are in Berlin, the nerve center for the organization, where new products are developed and the organizational strategy is established. Newskool outsources a great deal of its coding work to programmers in Kiev, Ukraine. Its marketing efforts are increasingly based in its Los Angeles offices. This division of labor is at least partially based on technical expertise and cost issues. The German team excels at design and production tasks. Because most of Newskool's customers are English speakers, the Los Angeles office has been the best group to write ads and market products. The Kiev offices are filled with outstanding programmers who don't require the very high rates of compensation you'd find in German or U.S. offices. The combination of high-tech software, rapid reorganization, and outsourcing makes Newskool the very definition of a boundaryless organization.

Finger also makes the final decision on hiring every employee for the company and places a heavy emphasis on independent work styles. "Why would I want to put my company in the hands of people I can't count on?" he asks with a laugh. "They have to believe in what we're doing here, really understand our direction and be able to go with it. I'm not the babysitter, I'm not the school master handing out homework. School time is over. This is the real world."

The Work Culture

Employees want to work at this company because it's cutting edge. Newskool's software is used by a number of dance musicians and DJs, who have been the firm's core market, seeing it as a relatively expensive but very high-quality and innovative brand. Whenever the rest of the market for music software goes in one direction, it seems like Newskool heads in a completely different direction in an effort to keep itself separate from the pack. This strategy has tended to pay off. While competitors develop similar products and therefore need to continually lower their prices to compete with one another, Newskool has kept revenues high by creating completely new types of products that don't face this type of price competition.

Unfortunately, computer piracy has eroded Newskool's ability to make money with just software-based music tools, and it has had to move into the production of hardware, such as drum machines and amplifiers that incorporate its computer technology. Making this massive market change might be challenging for some companies, but for an organization that reinvents itself every 2 or 3 years like Newskool does, the bigger fight is a constant war against stagnation and rigidity.

The organization has a very decentralized culture. With only 115 employees, the original management philosophy of allowing all employees to participate in decision making and innovation is still the lifeblood of the company's culture. One developer notes, "At Newskool, they want you to be part of the process. If you are a person who wants to do what you're told at work, you're in trouble. Most times, they can't tell you what they want you to do next—they don't even know what comes next! That's why they hire employees who are creative, people who can try to make the next thing happen. It's challenging, but a lot of us think it's very much an exciting environment."

The Boundaryless Environment

Because so much of the work can be performed on computers, Finger decided early to allow employees to work outside the office. The senior management in Berlin and Los Angeles are both quite happy with this arrangement. Because some marketing work does require face-to-face contact, the Los Angeles office has weekly in-person meetings. Employees who like Newskool are happiest when they can work through the night and sleep most of the day, firing up their computers to get work done at the drop of a hat. Project discussions often happen via social networking on the company's intranet.

The Kiev offices have been less eager to work with the boundaryless model. Managers say their computer programmers find working with so little structure rather uncomfortable. They are more used to the idea of a strong leadership structure and well-defined work processes.

"When I started," says one manager, "Gerd said getting in touch with him would be no problem, getting in touch with L.A. would be no problem. We're small, we're family, he said. Well, it is a problem. When I call L.A., they say to wait until their meeting day. I can't always wait until they decide to get together. I call Gerd—he says, 'Figure it out.' Then when I do, he says it isn't right and we have to start again. If he just told me in the first place, we would have done it."

Some recent events have also shaken up the company's usual way of doing business. Developers in the corporate offices had a major communications breakdown about their hardware DJ controller, which required many hours of discussion to resolve. It seems that people who seldom met face to face had all made progress—but had moved in opposite directions. To test and design the company's hardware products, employees apparently need to do more than send each other code; sometimes they need to collaborate face to face. Some spirited disagreements have been voiced within the organization about how to move forward in this new environment.

The offices are experiencing additional difficulties. Since the shift to newer products, Sandra Pelham in the Los Angeles office has been more critical of the company. "With the software, we were more limited in the kinds of advertising media we could access. So now, with the hardware—real instruments—we finally thought, 'All right, this is something we can work with!' We had a whole slate of musicians and DJs and producers to contact for endorsements, but Gerd said, 'No way.' He didn't want customers who only cared that a celebrity liked us. He scrapped the whole campaign. He says we're all about creativity and doing our own thing—until we don't want to do things his way."

Although the organization is not without problems, there is little question Newskool has been a standout success in the computer music software industry. While many are shuttering their operations, Newskool is using its market power to push forward the next generation of electronic music-making tools. As Gerd Finger puts it, "Once the rest of the industry has gotten together and figured out how they're all going to cope with change, they'll look around and see that we're already three miles ahead of them down the road to the future."

Your Assignment

Finger has asked for your advice on how to keep his organization successful. He wants to have some sort of benchmark for how other boundaryless organizations in the tech sector stay competitive despite the challenges of so many workers heading in so many different directions. You will need to prepare a report for the company's executive committee. Your report should read like a proposal to a corporate executive who has a great deal of knowledge about the technical aspects of his company but might not have much knowledge of organizational behavior.

When you write, make sure you touch on the following points:

CC-24. Identify some of the problems likely to occur in a boundaryless organization like Newskool Grooves. What are the advantages of boundaryless organizations?

CC-25. Consider some of the cultural issues that will affect a company operating in such different parts of the world and whose employees may not be representative of the national cultures of each country. Are the conflicts you observe a function of the different types of work people have to perform?

CC-26. Based on what you know about motivation and personality, what types of people are likely to be satisfied in each area of the company? Use concepts from job characteristics theory and the emerging social relationships perspective on work to describe what might need to change to increase employee satisfaction in all areas.

CC-27. What types of human resources practices need to be implemented in this sort of organization? What principles of selection and hiring are likely to be effective? Which Big Five traits and abilities might Newskool supervisors want to use for selection?

CC-28. What kind of performance measures might you want to see for each office?

CC-29. How can the company establish a socialization program that will maximize employee creativity and independence? Do employees in all its locations need equal levels of creativity?

The Stress of Caring

Learning Goals

One of the most consistent changes in the structure of work over the past few decades has been a shift from a manufacturing economy to a service economy. More workers are now engaged in jobs that include providing care and assistance, especially in education and medicine. This work is satisfying for some people, but it can also be highly stressful. In the following scenario, consider how a company in the nursing care industry is responding to the challenges of the new environment.

Major Topic Areas

- Stress
- Organizational change
- Emotions
- Leadership

The Scenario

Parkway Nursing Care is an organization facing a massive change. The company was founded in 1972 with just two nursing homes in Phoenix, Arizona. The company was very successful, and throughout the 1980s it continued to turn a consistent profit while slowly acquiring or building 30 more units. This low-profile approach changed forever in 1993 when venture capitalist Robert Quine decided to make a major investment in expanding Parkway in return for a portion of its profits over the coming years. The number of nursing homes exploded, and Parkway was operating 180 homes by the year 2000.

The company now has 220 facilities in the southwestern United States, with an average of 115 beds per facility and a total of nearly 30,000 employees. In addition to health care facilities, it also provides skilled in-home nursing care. Parkway is seen as one of the best care facilities in the region, and it has won numerous awards for its achievements in the field.

As members of the Baby Boom generation become senior citizens, the need for skilled care will only increase. Parkway wants to make sure it is in a good position to meet this growing need. This means the company must continue expanding rapidly.

The pressure for growth is one significant challenge, but it's not the only one. The nursing home industry has come under increasing government scrutiny following investigations that turned up widespread patient abuse and billing fraud. Parkway has always had outstanding patient care, and no substantiated claim of abuse or neglect in any of its homes has ever been made, but the need for increased documentation will still affect the company. As the federal government tries to trim Medicare expenses, Parkway may face a reduction in funding.

The Problem

As growth has continued, Parkway has remained committed to providing dignity and health to all residents in its facilities. The board of directors wants to see renewed commitment to the firm's mission and core values, not a diffusion of its culture. Its members are worried there might be problems to address. Interviews with employees suggest there's plenty to worry about.

Shift leader Maxine Vernon has been with Parkway for 15 years. "Now that the government keeps a closer eye on our staffing levels, I've seen management do what it can to keep positions filled, and I don't always agree with who is hired. Some of the basic job skills can be taught, sure, but how to *care* for our patients—a lot of these new kids just don't pick up on that."

"The problem isn't with staff—it's with Parkway's focus on filling the beds," says nurse's aide Bobby Reed. "When I started here, Parkway's reputation was still about the service. Now it's about numbers. No one is intentionally negligent—there just are too many patients to see."

A recent college graduate with a B.A. in psychology, Dalton Manetti is more stressed than he expected he would be. "These aren't the sweet grannies you see in the movies. Our patients are demanding. They complain about everything, even about being called patients, probably because most of them think they shouldn't be here in the first place. A lot of times, their gripes amount to nothing, but we have to log them in anyway."

Carmen Frank has been with Parkway almost a year and is already considering finding a new job. "I knew there were going to be physical parts to this job, and I thought I'd be able to handle that. It's not like I was looking for a desk job, you know? I go home after every shift with aches all over—my back, my arms, my legs. I've never had to take so much time off from a job because I hurt. And then when I come back, I feel like the rest of the staff thinks I'm weak."

Year	Patients	Injuries per Staff Member	Incidents per Patient	Certified Absences per Staff	Other Absences per Staff	Turnover Rate
2000	21,200	3.32	4.98	4.55	3.14	0.31
2001	22,300	3.97	5.37	5.09	3.31	0.29
2002	22,600	4.87	5.92	4.71	3.47	0.28
2003	23,100	4.10	6.36	5.11	3.61	0.35
2004	23,300	4.21	6.87	5.66	4.03	0.31
2005	23,450	5.03	7.36	5.33	3.45	0.28
2006	23,600	5.84	7.88	5.28	4.24	0.36
2007	24,500	5.62	8.35	5.86	4.06	0.33
2008	24,100	7.12	8.84	5.63	3.89	0.35
2009	25,300	6.95	9.34	6.11	4.28	0.35

"I started working here right out of high school because it was the best-paid of the jobs I could get," says Niecey Wilson. "I had no idea what I was getting myself into. Now I really like my job. Next year I'm going to start taking some night classes so I can move into another position. But some of the staff just think of this as any other job. They don't see the patients as people, more like inventory. If they want to work with inventory, they should get a job in retail."

Last month, the company's human resources department pulled the above information from its records at the request of the board of directors. The numbers provide some quantitative support for the concerns voiced by staff.

Injuries to staff occur mostly because of back strain from lifting patients. Patient incidents reflect injuries due to slips, falls, medication errors, or other accidents. Certified absences are days off from work due to medically verified illnesses or injuries. Other absences are days missed that are not due to injuries or illnesses; these are excused absences (unexcused absences are grounds for immediate firing).

Using Organizational Development to Combat Stress and Improve Performance

The company wants to use such organizational development methods as appreciative inquiry (AI) to create change and reenergize its sense of mission. As the chapter on organizational change explains, AI procedures systematically collect employee input and then use this information to create a change message everyone can support. The human resources department conducted focus groups, asking employees to describe some of their concerns and suggestions for the future. The focus groups highlighted a number of suggestions, although they don't all suggest movement in the same direction.

Many suggestions concerned schedule flexibility. One representative comment was this: "Most of the stress on this job comes because we can't take time off when we need it. The LPNs [licensed practical nurses, who do much of the care] and orderlies can't take time off when they need to, but a lot of them are single parents or primary caregivers for their own children. When they have to leave for child care responsibilities, the work suffers and there's no contingency plan to help smooth things over. Then everyone who is left has to work extra hard. The person who takes time off feels guilty, and there can be fights over taking time off. If we had some way of covering these emergency absences, we'd all be a lot happier, and I think the care would be a lot better."

Other suggestions proposed a better method for communicating information across shifts. Most of the documentation for shift work is done in large spiral notebooks. When a new shift begins, staff members say they don't have much time to check on what happened in the previous shift. Some younger caregivers would like to have a method that lets them document patient outcomes electronically because they type faster than they can write. The older caregivers are more committed to the paper-based process, in part because they think switching systems would require a lot of work. (Government regulations on health care reporting require that any documentation be made in a form that cannot be altered after the fact, to prevent covering up abuse, so specialized software systems must be used for electronic documentation.)

Finally, the nursing care staff believes its perspectives on patient care are seldom given an appropriate hearing. "We're the ones who are with the patients most of the time, but when it comes to doing this the right way, our point of view gets lost. We really could save a lot of money by eliminating some of these unnecessary routines and programs, but it's something management always just says it will consider." Staff members seem to want some way to provide suggestions for improvement, but it isn't clear what method they would prefer.

Your Assignment

Parkway has taken some initial steps toward a new direction, but clearly it has a lot of work left to do. You've been brought in as a change management consultant to help the company change its culture and respond to the stress that employees experience. Remember to create your report as if for the leadership of a major corporation.

When you write your recommendations, make sure you touch on the following points:

CC-30. What do the data on employee injuries, incidents, absences, and turnover suggest to you? Is there reason for concern about the company's direction?

CC-31. The company is going to be making some significant changes based on the AI process, and most change efforts are associated with resistance. What are the most common forms of resistance, and which would you expect to see at Parkway?

CC-32. Given the board of directors' desire to reenergize the workforce, what advice would you provide for creating a leadership strategy? What leader behaviors should nursing home directors and nurse supervisors demonstrate?

CC-33. What are the major sources of job stress at Parkway? What does the research on employee stress suggest you should do to help minimize the experience of psychological strain for employees? Create a plan for how to reduce stress among employees.

CC-34. Based on the information collected in the focus groups, design a survey to hand out to employees. What sort of data should the survey gather? What types of data analysis methods would you like to employ for these data?

Glossary

ability An individual's capacity to perform the various tasks in a job.

accommodating The willingness of one party in a conflict to place the opponent's interests above his or her own.

action research A change process based on systematic collection of data and then selection of a change action based on what the analyzed data indicate.

affect A broad range of feelings that people experience.

affect intensity Individual differences in the strength with which individuals experience their emotions.

affective component The emotional or feeling segment of an attitude.

affective events theory (AET) A model that suggests that workplace events cause emotional reactions on the part of employees, which then influence workplace attitudes and behaviors.

agreeableness A personality dimension that describes someone who is good natured, cooperative, and trusting.

allostasis Working to change behavior and attitudes to find stability.

anchoring bias A tendency to fixate on initial information, from which one then fails to adequately adjust for subsequent information.

anthropology The study of societies to learn about human beings and their activities.

appreciative inquiry (AI) An approach that seeks to identify the unique qualities and special strengths of an organization, which can then be built on to improve performance.

arbitrator A third party to a negotiation who has the authority to dictate an agreement.

assessment centers A set of performance-simulation tests designed to evaluate a candidate's managerial potential.

attitudes Evaluations employees make about objects, people, or events.

attribution theory An attempt to determine whether an individual's behavior is internally or externally caused.

attribution theory of leadership A leadership theory that says that leadership is merely an attribution that people make about other individuals.

authentic leaders Leaders who know who they are, know what they believe in and value, and act on those values and beliefs openly and candidly. Their followers would consider them to be ethical people.

authority The rights inherent in a managerial position to give orders and to expect the orders to be obeyed.

automatic processing A relatively superficial consideration of evidence and information making use of heuristics.

autonomy The degree to which a job provides substantial freedom and discretion to the individual in scheduling the work and in determining the procedures to be used in carrying it out.

availability bias The tendency for people to base their judgments on information that is readily available to them.

avoiding The desire to withdraw from or suppress a conflict.

BATNA The best alternative to a negotiated agreement; the least the individual should accept.

behavioral component An intention to behave in a certain way toward someone or something.

behavioral ethics Analyzing how people actually behave when confronted with ethical dilemmas.

behavioral theories of leadership Theories proposing that specific behaviors differentiate leaders from nonleaders.

behaviorally anchored rating scales (BARS) Scales that combine major elements from the critical incident and graphic rating scale approaches. The appraiser rates the employees based on items along a continuum, but the points are examples of actual behavior on the given job rather than general descriptions or traits.

behaviorism A theory that argues that behavior follows stimuli in a relatively unthinking manner.

Big Five Model A personality assessment model that taps five basic dimensions.

biographical characteristics Personal characteristics—such as age, gender, race, and length of tenure—that are objective and easily obtained from personnel records. These characteristics are representative of surface-level diversity.

bonus A pay plan that rewards employees for recent performance rather than historical performance.

boundary spanning When individuals form relationships outside their formally-assigned groups.

bounded rationality A process of making decisions by constructing simplified models that extract the essential features from problems without capturing all their complexity.

brainstorming An idea-generation process that specifically encourages any and all alternatives while withholding any criticism of those alternatives.

bureaucracy An organization structure with highly routine operating tasks achieved through specialization, very formalized rules and regulations, tasks that are grouped into functional departments, centralized authority, narrow spans of control, and decision making that follows the chain of command.

centralization The degree to which decision making is concentrated at a single point in an organization.

chain of command The unbroken line of authority that extends from the top of the organization to the lowest echelon and clarifies who reports to whom.

challenge stressors Stressors associated with workload, pressure to complete tasks, and time urgency.

change Making things different.

change agents Persons who act as catalysts and assume the responsibility for managing change activities.

channel richness The amount of information that can be transmitted during a communication episode.

charismatic leadership theory A leadership theory that states that followers make attributions of heroic or extraordinary leadership abilities when they observe certain behaviors.

circular structure   An organizational structure in which executives are at the center, spreading their vision outward in rings grouped by function (managers, then specialists, then workers).

citizenship   Actions that contribute to the psychological environment of the organization, such as helping others when not required.

coercive power   A power base that is dependent on fear of the negative results from failing to comply.

cognitive component   The opinion or belief segment of an attitude.

cognitive dissonance   Any incompatibility between two or more attitudes or between behavior and attitudes.

cognitive evaluation theory   A version of self-determination theory which holds that allocating extrinsic rewards for behavior that had been previously intrinsically rewarding tends to decrease the overall level of motivation if the rewards are seen as controlling.

cohesiveness   The degree to which group members are attracted to each other and are motivated to stay in the group.

collaborating   A situation in which the parties to a conflict each desire to satisfy fully the concerns of all parties.

collectivism   A national culture attribute that describes a tight social framework in which people expect others in groups of which they are a part to look after them and protect them.

communication   The transfer and the understanding of meaning.

communication apprehension   Undue tension and anxiety about oral communication, written communication, or both.

communication process   The steps between a source and a receiver that result in the transfer and understanding of meaning.

competing   A desire to satisfy one's interests, regardless of the impact on the other party to the conflict.

compromising   A situation in which each party to a conflict is willing to give up something.

conceptual skills   The mental ability to analyze and diagnose complex situations.

conciliator   A trusted third party who provides an informal communication link between the negotiator and the opponent.

confirmation bias   The tendency to seek out information that reaffirms past choices and to discount information that contradicts past judgments.

conflict   A process that begins when one party perceives that another party has negatively affected, or is about to negatively affect, something that the first party cares about.

conflict management   The use of resolution and stimulation techniques to achieve the desired level of conflict.

conflict process   A process that has five stages: potential opposition or incompatibility, cognition and personalization, intentions, behavior, and outcomes.

conformity   The adjustment of one's behavior to align with the norms of the group.

conscientiousness   A personality dimension that describes someone who is responsible, dependable, persistent, and organized.

consideration   The extent to which a leader is likely to have job relationships characterized by mutual trust, respect for subordinates' ideas, and regard for their feelings.

contingency variables   Situational factors: variables that moderate the relationship between two or more variables.

contrast effect   Evaluation of a person's characteristics that is affected by comparisons with other people recently encountered who rank higher or lower on the same characteristics.

controlled processing   A detailed consideration of evidence and information relying on facts, figures, and logic.

controlling   Monitoring activities to ensure they are being accomplished as planned and correcting any significant deviations.

core self-evaluation (CSE)   Bottom-line conclusions individuals have about their capabilities, competence, and worth as a person.

core values   The primary or dominant values that are accepted throughout the organization.

corporate social responsibility (CSR)   An organization's self-regulated actions to benefit society or the environment beyond what is required by law.

cost-minimization strategy   A strategy that emphasizes tight cost controls, avoidance of unnecessary innovation or marketing expenses, and price cutting.

counterproductive work behavior (CWB)   Intentional employee behavior that is contrary to the interests of the organization, also termed deviant behavior in the workplace or employee withdrawal.

counterproductivity   Actions that actively damage the organization, including stealing, behaving aggressively toward coworkers, or being late or absent.

creativity   The ability to produce novel and useful ideas.

critical incidents   A way of evaluating the behaviors that are key in making the difference between executing a job effectively and executing it ineffectively.

cross-functional teams   Employees from about the same hierarchical level, but from different work areas, who come together to accomplish a task.

Dark Triad   A constellation of negative personality traits consisting of Machiavellianism, narcissism, and psychopathy.

decisions   Choices made from among two or more alternatives.

deep acting   Trying to modify one's true inner feelings based on display rules.

deep-level diversity   Differences in values, personality, and work preferences that become progressively more important for determining similarity as people get to know one another better.

defensive behaviors   Reactive and protective behaviors to avoid action, blame, or change.

demands   Responsibilities, pressures, obligations, and even uncertainties that individuals face in the workplace.

departmentalization   The basis by which jobs in an organization are grouped together.

dependence   B's relationship to A when A possesses something that B requires.

deviant workplace behavior   Voluntary behavior that violates significant organizational norms and, in so doing, threatens the well-being of the organization or its members. Also called antisocial behavior or workplace incivility. Referred to often in relation to counterproductive work behavior (CWB).

discrimination Noting of a difference between things; often we refer to unfair discrimination, which means making judgments about individuals based on stereotypes regarding their demographic group.

displayed emotions Emotions that are organizationally required and considered appropriate in a given job.

distributive bargaining Negotiation that seeks to divide up a fixed amount of resources; a win–lose situation.

distributive justice Perceived fairness of the amount and allocation of rewards among individuals.

diversity The extent to which members of a group are similar to, or different from, one another.

diversity management The process and programs by which managers make everyone more aware of and sensitive to the needs and differences of others.

divisional structure An organizational structure that groups employees into units by product, service, customer, or geographical market area.

dominant culture A culture that expresses the core values that are shared by a majority of the organization's members.

driving forces Forces that direct behavior away from the status quo (Lewin).

dyadic conflict Conflict that occurs between two people.

dysfunctional conflict Conflict that hinders group performance.

effectiveness The degree to which an organization meets the needs of its clientele or customers.

efficiency The degree to which an organization can achieve its ends at a low cost.

emotional contagion The process by which peoples' emotions are caused by the emotions of others.

emotional dissonance Inconsistencies between the emotions people feel and the emotions they project.

emotional intelligence (EI) The ability to detect and to manage emotional cues and information.

emotional labor A situation in which an employee expresses organizationally desired emotions during interpersonal transactions at work.

emotional stability A personality dimension that characterizes someone as calm, self-confident, secure (positive) versus nervous, depressed, and insecure (negative).

emotions Intense feelings that are directed at someone or something.

employee engagement An individual's involvement with, satisfaction with, and enthusiasm for the work he or she does.

employee involvement and participation (EIP) A participative process that uses the input of employees and is intended to increase employee commitment to organizational success.

employee recognition program An organizational plan to encourage specific behaviors by formally appreciating specific employee contributions.

employee stock ownership plan (ESOP) A company-established benefits plan in which employees acquire stock, often at below-market prices, as part of their benefits.

encounter stage The stage in the socialization process in which a new employee sees what the organization is really like and confronts the possibility that expectations and reality may diverge.

environment Institutions or forces outside an organization that potentially affect the organization's performance.

equity theory A theory that says that individuals compare their job inputs and outcomes with those of others and then respond to eliminate any inequities.

escalation of commitment An increased commitment to a previous decision in spite of negative information.

ethical dilemmas and ethical choices Situations in which individuals are required to define right and wrong conduct.

ethical work climate (EWC) The shared concept of right and wrong behavior in the workplace that reflects the true values of the organization and shapes the ethical decision making of its members.

evidence-based management (EBM) The basing of managerial decisions on the best available scientific evidence.

exit response Dissatisfaction expressed through behavior directed toward leaving the organization.

expectancy theory A theory that says that the strength of a tendency to act in a certain way depends on the strength of an expectation that the act will be followed by a given outcome and on the attractiveness of that outcome to the individual.

expert power Influence based on special skills or knowledge.

extraversion A personality dimension describing someone who is sociable, gregarious, and assertive.

faultlines The perceived divisions that split groups into two or more subgroups based on individual differences such as sex, race, age, work experience, and education.

feedback The degree to which carrying out the work activities required by a job results in the individual obtaining direct and clear information about the effectiveness of his or her performance.

felt conflict Emotional involvement in a conflict that creates anxiety, tenseness, frustration, or hostility.

felt emotions An individual's actual emotions.

femininity A national culture attribute that indicates little differentiation between male and female roles; a high rating indicates that women are treated as the equals of men in all aspects of the society.

Fiedler contingency model The theory that effective groups depend on a proper match between a leader's style of interacting with subordinates and the degree to which the situation gives control and influence to the leader.

filtering A sender's manipulation of information so that it will be seen more favorably by the receiver.

fixed pie The belief that there is only a set amount of goods or services to be divvied up between the parties.

flexible benefits A benefits plan that allows each employee to put together a benefits package individually tailored to his or her own needs and situation.

flextime Flexible work hours and a core of expected work hours.

forced comparison Method of performance evaluation where an employee's performance is made in explicit comparison to others (e.g., an employee may rank third out of 10 employees in her work unit).

formal channels   Communication channels established by an organization to transmit messages related to the professional activities of members.

formal group   A designated work group defined by an organization's structure.

formalization   The degree to which jobs within an organization are standardized.

full range of leadership model   A model that depicts seven management styles on a continuum: laissez-faire, management by exception, contingent reward leadership, individualized consideration, intellectual stimulation, inspirational motivation, and idealized influence.

functional conflict   Conflict that supports the goals of the group and improves its performance.

functional structure   An organization structure that groups employees by their similar specialties, roles, or tasks.

fundamental attribution error   The tendency to underestimate the influence of external factors and overestimate the influence of internal factors when making judgments about the behavior of others.

general mental ability (GMA)   An overall factor of intelligence, as suggested by the positive correlations among specific intellectual ability dimensions.

goal-setting theory   A theory that says that specific and difficult goals, with feedback, lead to higher performance.

grapevine   An organization's informal communication network.

graphic rating scales   An evaluation method in which the evaluator rates performance factors on an incremental scale.

group   Two or more individuals, interacting and interdependent, who have come together to achieve particular objectives.

group cohesion   The extent to which members of a group support and validate one another while at work.

group functioning   The quantity and quality of a work group's output.

group order ranking   An evaluation method that places employees into a particular classification, such as quartiles.

groupshift   A change between a group's decision and an individual decision that a member within the group would make; the shift can be toward either conservatism or greater risk but it generally is toward a more extreme version of the group's original position.

groupthink   A phenomenon in which the norm for consensus overrides the realistic appraisal of alternative courses of action.

halo effect   The tendency to draw a general impression about an individual on the basis of a single characteristic.

heredity   Factors determined at conception; one's biological, physiological, and inherent psychological makeup.

hierarchy of needs   Abraham Maslow's hierarchy of five needs—physiological, safety, social, esteem, and self-actualization—in which, as each need is substantially satisfied, the next need becomes dominant.

high-context cultures   Cultures that rely heavily on nonverbal and subtle situational cues in communication.

hindrance stressors   Stressors that keep you from reaching your goals (for example, red tape, office politics, confusion over job responsibilities).

hindsight bias   The tendency to believe falsely, after an outcome of an event is actually known, that one would have accurately predicted that outcome.

human skills   The ability to work with, understand, and motivate other people, both individually and in groups.

idea champions   Individuals who take an innovation and actively and enthusiastically promote the idea, build support, overcome resistance, and ensure that the idea is implemented.

idea evaluation   The process of creative behavior involving the evaluation of potential solutions to problems to identify the best one.

idea generation   The process of creative behavior that involves developing possible solutions to a problem from relevant information and knowledge.

identification-based trust   Trust based on a mutual understanding of each other's intentions and appreciation of each other's wants and desires.

illusory correlation   The tendency of people to associate two events when in reality there is no connection.

imitation strategy   A strategy that seeks to move into new products or new markets only after their viability has already been proven.

impression management (IM)   The process by which individuals attempt to control the impression others form of them.

individualism   A national culture attribute that describes the degree to which people prefer to act as individuals rather than as members of groups.

individual ranking   An evaluation method that rank-orders employees from best to worst.

informal channels   Communication channels that are created spontaneously and that emerge as responses to individual choice.

informal group   A group that is neither formally structured nor organizationally determined; such a group appears in response to the need for social contact.

informational justice   The degree to which employees are provided truthful explanations for decisions.

information gathering   The stage of creative behavior when possible solutions to a problem incubate in an individual's mind.

ingroup favoritism   Perspective in which we see members of our ingroup as better than other people, and people not in our group as all the same.

initiating structure   The extent to which a leader is likely to define and structure his or her role and those of subordinates in the search for goal attainment.

innovation   A new idea applied to initiating or improving a product, process, or service.

innovation strategy   A strategy that emphasizes the introduction of major new products and services.

input   Variables that lead to processes.

institutions   Cultural factors that lead many organizations to have similar structures, especially those factors that might not lead to adaptive consequences.

instrumental values   Preferable modes of behavior or means of achieving one's terminal values.

integrative bargaining   Negotiation that seeks one or more settlements that can create a win–win solution.

intellectual abilities   The capacity to do mental activities—thinking, reasoning, and problem solving.

intentions   Decisions to act in a given way.

interacting groups   Typical groups in which members interact with each other face to face.

intergroup conflict   Conflict between different groups or teams.

intergroup development   Organizational development (OD) efforts to change the attitudes, stereotypes, and perceptions that groups have of each other.

interpersonal justice   The degree to which employees are treated with dignity and respect.

interrole conflict   A situation in which the expectations of an individual's different, separate groups are in opposition.

intragroup conflict   Conflict that occurs within a group or team.

intuition   A gut feeling not necessarily supported by research.

intuitive decision making   An unconscious process created out of distilled experience.

job characteristics model (JCM)   A model that proposes that any job can be described in terms of five core job dimensions: skill variety, task identity, task significance, autonomy, and feedback.

job design   The way the elements in a job are organized.

job engagement   The investment of an employee's physical, cognitive, and emotional energies into job performance.

job involvement   The degree to which a person identifies with a job, actively participates in it, and considers performance important to self-worth.

job rotation   The periodic shifting of an employee from one task to another with similar skill requirements at the same organizational level.

job satisfaction   A positive feeling about one's job resulting from an evaluation of its characteristics.

job sharing   An arrangement that allows two or more individuals to split a traditional full-time job.

leader–member exchange (LMX) theory   A theory that supports leaders' creation of ingroups and outgroups; subordinates with ingroup status will have higher performance ratings, less turnover, and greater job satisfaction.

leader–member relations   The degree of confidence, trust, and respect subordinates have in their leader.

leader-participation model   A leadership theory that provides a set of rules to determine the form and amount of participative decision making in different situations.

leadership   The ability to influence a group toward the achievement of a vision or set of goals.

leading   A function that includes motivating employees, directing others, selecting the most effective communication channels, and resolving conflicts.

learning organization   An organization that has developed the continuous capacity to adapt and change.

least preferred co-worker (LPC) questionnaire   An instrument that purports to measure whether a person is task or relationship oriented.

legitimate power   The power a person receives as a result of his or her position in the formal hierarchy of an organization.

long-term orientation   A national culture attribute that emphasizes the future, thrift, and persistence.

low-context cultures   Cultures that rely heavily on words to convey meaning in communication.

loyalty response   Dissatisfaction expressed by passively waiting for conditions to improve.

Machiavellianism   The degree to which an individual is pragmatic, maintains emotional distance, and believes that ends can justify means.

management by objectives (MBO)   A program that encompasses specific goals, participatively set, for an explicit time period, with feedback on goal progress.

manager   An individual who achieves goals through other people.

masculinity   A national culture attribute that describes the extent to which the culture favors traditional masculine work roles of achievement, power, and control. Societal values are characterized by assertiveness and materialism.

material symbols   What conveys to employees who is important, the degree of egalitarianism top management desires, and the kinds of behavior that are appropriate.

matrix structure   An organization structure that creates dual lines of authority and combines functional and product departmentalization.

McClelland's theory of needs   A theory that states achievement, power, and affiliation are three important needs that help explain motivation.

mechanistic model   A structure characterized by extensive departmentalization, high formalization, a limited information network, and centralization.

mediator   A neutral third party who facilitates a negotiated solution by using reasoning, persuasion, and suggestions for alternatives.

mental models   Team members' knowledge and beliefs about how the work gets done by the team.

mentor   A senior employee who sponsors and supports a less-experienced employee, called a protégé.

merit-based pay plan   A pay plan based on performance appraisal ratings.

metamorphosis stage   The stage in the socialization process in which a new employee changes and adjusts to the job, work group, and organization.

mindfulness   Objectively and deliberately evaluating one's own emotional situation in the moment.

model   An abstraction of reality. A simplified representation of some real-world phenomenon.

moods   Feelings that tend to be less intense than emotions and that lack a contextual stimulus.

moral emotions   Emotions that have moral implications.

motivating potential score (MPS)   A predictive index that suggests the motivating potential in a job.

motivation   The processes that account for an individual's intensity, direction, and persistence of effort toward attaining a goal.

multiteam system   A collection of two or more interdependent teams that share a superordinate goal; a team of teams.

Myers-Briggs Type Indicator (MBTI)   A personality test that taps four characteristics and classifies people into 1 of 16 personality types.

narcissism   The tendency to be arrogant, have a grandiose sense of self-importance, require excessive admiration, and have a sense of entitlement.

need for achievement (nAch)   The drive to excel, to achieve in relationship to a set of standards, and to strive to succeed.

need for affiliation (nAff)   The desire for friendly and close interpersonal relationships.

need for cognition   A personality trait of individuals depicting the ongoing desire to think and learn

need for power (nPow)   The need to make others behave in a way in which they would not have behaved otherwise.

negative affect   A mood dimension that consists of emotions such as nervousness, stress, and anxiety at the high end.

neglect response   Dissatisfaction expressed through allowing conditions to worsen.

negotiation   A process in which two or more parties exchange goods or services and attempt to agree on the exchange rate for them.

neutralizers   Attributes that make it impossible for leader behavior to make any difference to follower outcomes.

nominal group technique   A group decision-making method in which individual members meet face to face to pool their judgments in a systematic but independent fashion.

norms   Acceptable standards of behavior within a group that are shared by the group's members.

openness to experience   A personality dimension that characterizes someone in terms of imagination, sensitivity, and curiosity.

organic model   A structure that is flat, uses cross-hierarchical and cross-functional teams, has low formalization, possesses a comprehensive information network, and relies on participative decision making.

organization   A consciously coordinated social unit, composed of two or more people, that functions on a relatively continuous basis to achieve a common goal or set of goals.

organizational behavior (OB)   A field of study that investigates the impact that individuals, groups, and structure have on behavior within organizations, for the purpose of applying such knowledge toward improving an organization's effectiveness.

organizational citizenship behavior (OCB)   Discretionary behavior that is not part of an employee's formal job requirements, and that contributes to the psychological and social environment of the workplace.

organizational climate   The shared perceptions organizational members have about their organization and work environment.

organizational commitment   The degree to which an employee identifies with a particular organization and its goals and wishes to maintain membership in the organization.

organizational culture   A system of shared meaning held by members that distinguishes the organization from other organizations.

organizational demography   The degree to which members of a work unit share a common demographic attribute, such as age, sex, race, educational level, or length of service in an organization.

organizational development (OD)   A collection of planned change interventions, built on humanistic–democratic values, that seeks to improve organizational effectiveness and employee well-being.

organizational justice   An overall perception of what is fair in the workplace, composed of distributive, procedural, informational, and interpersonal justice.

organizational structure   The way in which job tasks are formally divided, grouped, and coordinated.

organizational survival   The degree to which an organization is able to exist and grow over the long term.

organizing   Determining what tasks are to be done, who is to do them, how the tasks are to be grouped, who reports to whom, and where decisions are to be made.

outcomes   Key factors that are affected by some other variables.

outgroup   The inverse of an ingroup, which can mean everyone outside the group, but more usually an identified other group.

panel interviews   Structured interviews conducted with a candidate and a number of panel members in a joint meeting.

paradox theory   The theory that the key paradox in management is that there is no final optimal status for an organization.

participative management   A process in which subordinates share a significant degree of decision-making power with their immediate superiors.

path–goal theory   A theory that states that it is the leader's job to assist followers in attaining their goals and to provide the necessary direction and/or support to ensure that their goals are compatible with the overall objectives of the group or organization.

perceived conflict   Awareness by one or more parties of the existence of conditions that create opportunities for conflict to arise.

perceived organizational support (POS)   The degree to which employees believe an organization values their contribution and cares about their well-being.

perception   A process by which individuals organize and interpret their sensory impressions in order to give meaning to their environment.

personality   The sum total of ways in which an individual reacts to and interacts with others.

personality–job fit theory   A theory that identifies six personality types and proposes that the fit between personality type and occupational environment determines satisfaction and turnover.

personality traits   Enduring characteristics that describe an individual's behavior.

person–organization fit   The concept that people are attracted to and selected by organizations that match their values and leave organizations that are not compatible with their personalities.

physical abilities   The capacity to do tasks that demand stamina, dexterity, strength, and similar characteristics.

piece-rate pay plan   A pay plan in which workers are paid a fixed sum for each unit of production completed.

planned change   Change activities that are intentional and goal oriented.

planning   A process that includes defining goals, establishing strategy, and developing plans to coordinate activities.

political behavior Activities that are not required as part of a person's formal role in the organization but that influence, or attempt to influence, the distribution of advantages and disadvantages within the organization.

political skill The ability to influence others in such a way as to enhance one's objectives.

position power Influence derived from one's formal structural position in the organization; includes power to hire, fire, discipline, promote, and give salary increases.

positive affect A mood dimension that consists of specific positive emotions such as excitement, enthusiasm, and elation at the high end.

positive diversity climate An environment of inclusiveness and acceptance of diversity in an organization.

positive organizational culture A culture that emphasizes building on employee strengths, rewards more than punishes, and emphasizes individual vitality and growth.

positive organizational scholarship An area of OB research that concerns how organizations develop human strengths, foster vitality and resilience, and unlock potential.

positivity offset The tendency of most individuals to experience a mildly positive mood at zero input (when nothing in particular is going on).

power A capacity that **A** has to influence the behavior of **B** so that **B** acts in accordance with **A**'s wishes.

power distance A national culture attribute that describes the extent to which a society accepts that power in institutions and organizations is distributed unequally.

power tactics Ways in which individuals translate power bases into specific actions.

prearrival stage The period of learning in the socialization process that occurs before a new employee joins the organization.

prevention focus A self-regulation strategy that involves striving for goals by fulfilling duties and obligations and avoiding conditions that pull them away from desired goals.

proactive personality People who identify opportunities, show initiative, take action, and persevere until meaningful change occurs.

problem A discrepancy between the current state of affairs and some desired state.

problem formulation The stage of creative behavior that involves identifying a problem or opportunity requiring a solution that is as yet unknown.

problem-solving teams Groups of employees from the same department who meet for a few hours each week to discuss ways of improving quality, efficiency, and the work environment.

procedural justice The perceived fairness of the process used to determine the distribution of rewards.

process conflict Conflict over how work gets done.

process consultation (PC) A meeting in which a consultant assists a client in understanding process events with which he or she must deal and identifying processes that need improvement.

processes Actions that individuals, groups, and organizations engage in as a result of inputs and that lead to certain outcomes.

productivity The combination of the effectiveness and efficiency of an organization.

profit-sharing plan An organization-wide program that distributes compensation based on some established formula designed around a company's profitability.

promotion focus A self-regulation strategy that involves striving for goals through advancement and accomplishment.

psychological contract An unwritten agreement that sets out what management expects from an employee and vice versa.

psychological empowerment Employees' belief in the degree to which they affect their work environment, their competence, the meaningfulness of their job, and their perceived autonomy in their work.

psychology The science that seeks to measure, explain, and sometimes change the behavior of humans and other animals.

psychopathy The tendency for a lack of concern for others and a lack of guilt or remorse when their actions cause harm.

punctuated-equilibrium model A set of phases that temporary groups go through that involves transitions between inertia and activity.

randomness error The tendency of individuals to believe that they can predict the outcome of random events.

rational Characterized by making consistent, value-maximizing choices within specified constraints.

rational decision-making model A decision-making model that describes how individuals should behave in order to maximize some outcome.

realistic job previews Substantive selection tests that are job tryouts to assess talent versus experience.

reference groups Important groups to which individuals belong or hope to belong and with whose norms individuals are likely to conform.

referent power Influence based on identification with a person who has desirable resources or personal traits.

reflexivity A team characteristic of reflecting on and adjusting the master plan when necessary.

reinforcement theory A theory that says that behavior is a function of its consequences.

relational job design Motivation through attention to the end beneficiaries of an employee's work.

relationship conflict Conflict based on interpersonal relationships.

representative participation A system in which workers participate in organizational decision making through a small group of representative employees.

resources Things within an individual's control that can be used to resolve demands.

restraining forces Forces that hinder movement from the existing equilibrium (Lewin).

reward power Compliance achieved based on the ability to distribute rewards that others view as valuable.

risk aversion The tendency to prefer a sure gain of a moderate amount over a riskier outcome, even if the riskier outcome might have a higher expected payoff.

rituals Repetitive sequences of activities that express and reinforce the key values of the organization, which goals are most important, which people are important, and which are expendable.

role A set of expected behavior patterns attributed to someone occupying a given position in a social unit.

role conflict A situation in which an individual is confronted by divergent role expectations.

role expectations How others believe a person should act in a given situation.

role perception An individual's view of how he or she is supposed to act in a given situation.

selective perception The tendency to selectively interpret what one sees on the basis of one's interests, background, experience, and attitudes.

self-concordance The degree to which peoples' reasons for pursuing goals are consistent with their interests and core values.

self-determination theory A theory of motivation that is concerned with the beneficial effects of intrinsic motivation and the harmful effects of extrinsic motivation.

self-efficacy theory An individual's belief that he or she is capable of performing a task.

self-fulfilling prophecy A situation in which a person inaccurately perceives a second person, and the resulting expectations cause the second person to behave in ways consistent with the original perception.

self-managed work teams Groups of 10 to 15 people who form highly-related or interdependent jobs.

self-monitoring A personality trait that measures an individual's ability to adjust his or her behavior to external, situational factors.

self-serving bias The tendency for individuals to attribute their own successes to internal factors and put the blame for failures on external factors.

sensitivity training Training groups that seek to change behavior through unstructured group interaction.

servant leadership A leadership style marked by going beyond the leader's own self-interest and instead focusing on opportunities to help followers grow and develop.

sexual harassment Any unwanted activity of a sexual nature that affects an individual's employment and creates a hostile work environment.

short-term orientation A national culture attribute that emphasizes the present and accepts change.

simple structure An organization structure characterized by a low degree of departmentalization, wide spans of control, authority centralized in a single person, and little formalization.

situational judgment tests Substantive selection tests that ask applicants how they would perform in a variety of job situations; the answers are then compared to the answers of high-performing employees.

situational leadership theory (SLT) A contingency theory that focuses on followers' readiness.

situation-strength theory A theory indicating that the way personality translates into behavior depends on the strength of the situation.

skill variety The degree to which a job requires a variety of different activities using specialized skills and talents.

social identity theory The tendency to personally invest in the accomplishments of a group.

social-learning theory The view that we can learn through both observation and direct experience.

socialization A process that adapts employees to the organization's culture.

socialized charismatic leadership A leadership concept that states that leaders convey values that are other-centered versus self-centered and who role-model ethical conduct.

social loafing The tendency for individuals to expend less effort when working collectively than when working individually.

social psychology An area of psychology that blends concepts from psychology and sociology and that focuses on the influence of people on one another.

sociology The study of people in relation to their social environment or culture.

span of control The number of subordinates a manager can efficiently and effectively direct.

status A socially defined position or rank given to groups or group members by others.

status characteristics theory A theory that states that differences in status characteristics create status hierarchies within groups.

stereotype threat The degree to which people internally agree with the generally negative stereotyped perceptions of their groups.

stereotyping Judging someone on the basis of one's perception of the group to which that person belongs.

stress An unpleasant psychological process that occurs in response to environmental pressures.

strong culture A culture in which the core values are intensely held and widely shared.

structured interviews Planned interviews designed to gather job-related information.

subcultures Minicultures within an organization, typically defined by department designations and geographical separation.

substitutes Attributes, such as experience and training, that can replace the need for a leader's support or ability to create structure.

surface acting Hiding one's inner feelings and forgoing emotional expressions in response to display rules.

surface-level diversity Differences in easily perceived characteristics, such as gender, race, ethnicity, age, or disability, that do not necessarily reflect the ways people think or feel but that may activate certain stereotypes.

survey feedback The use of questionnaires to identify discrepancies among member perceptions; discussion follows, and remedies are suggested.

sustainability Organization practices that can be sustained over a long period of time because the tools or structures that support them are not damaged by the processes.

systematic study Looking at relationships, attempting to attribute causes and effects, and drawing conclusions based on scientific evidence.

task conflict   Conflict over content and goals of the work.

task identity   The degree to which a job requires completion of a whole and identifiable piece of work.

task performance   The combination of effectiveness and efficiency at doing your core job tasks.

task significance   The degree to which a job has a substantial impact on the lives or work of other people.

task structure   The degree to which job assignments are procedurized.

team building   High interaction among team members to increase trust and openness.

team cohesion   A situation when members are emotionally attached to one another and motivated toward the team because of their attachment.

team efficacy   A team's collective belief that they can succeed at their tasks.

team identity   A team member's affinity for and sense of belongingness to his or her team.

team structure   An organization structure that replaces departments with empowered teams, and which eliminates horizontal boundaries and external barriers between customers and suppliers.

technical skills   The ability to apply specialized knowledge or expertise.

technology   The way in which an organization transfers its inputs into outputs.

telecommuting   Working from home or elsewhere at least 2 days a week on a computer that is linked to the employer's office.

terminal values   Desirable end-states of existence; the goals a person would like to achieve during his or her lifetime.

three-stage model of creativity   The proposition that creativity involves three stages: causes (creative potential and creative environment), creative behavior, and creative outcomes (innovation).

trait activation theory (TAT)   A theory that predicts that some situations, events, or interventions "activate" a trait more than others.

trait theories of leadership   Theories that consider personal qualities and characteristics that differentiate leaders from nonleaders.

transactional leaders   Leaders who guide or motivate their followers in the direction of established goals by clarifying role and task requirements.

transformational leaders   Leaders who inspire followers to transcend their own self-interests and who are capable of having a profound and extraordinary effect on followers.

trust   A positive expectation that another will not act opportunistically.

trust propensity   How likely an employee is to trust a leader.

two-factor theory   A theory that relates intrinsic factors to job satisfaction and associates extrinsic factors with dissatisfaction. Also called motivation-hygiene theory.

uncertainty avoidance   A national culture attribute that describes the extent to which a society feels threatened by uncertain and ambiguous situations and tries to avoid them.

unity of command   The idea that a subordinate should have only one superior to whom he or she is directly responsible.

unstructured interviews   Short, casual interviews made up of random questions.

utilitarianism   A system in which decisions are made to provide the greatest good for the greatest number.

values   Basic convictions that a specific mode of conduct or end-state of existence is personally or socially preferable to an opposite or converse mode of conduct or end-state of existence.

value system   A hierarchy based on a ranking of an individual's values in terms of their intensity.

variable-pay program   A pay plan that bases a portion of an employee's pay on some individual and/or organizational measure of performance.

virtual structure   A small, core organization that outsources major business functions.

virtual teams   Teams that use computer technology to tie together physically dispersed members in order to achieve a common goal.

vision   A long-term strategy for attaining a goal or goals.

vision statement   A formal articulation of an organization's vision or mission.

voice response   Dissatisfaction expressed through active and constructive attempts to improve conditions.

wellness programs   Organizationally supported programs that focus on the employee's total physical and mental condition.

whistle-blowers   Individuals who report unethical practices by their employer to outsiders.

withdrawal behavior   The set of actions employee take to separate themselves from the organization.

workforce diversity   The concept that organizations are becoming more heterogeneous in terms of gender, age, race, ethnicity, sexual orientation, and inclusion of other diverse groups.

workgroup   A group that interacts primarily to share information and to make decisions to help each group member perform within his or her area of responsibility.

workplace spirituality   The recognition that people have an inner life that nourishes and is nourished by meaningful work that takes place in the context of community.

work sample tests   Hands-on simulations of part or all of the work that applicants for routine jobs must perform.

work specialization   The degree to which tasks in an organization are subdivided into separate jobs.

work team   A group whose individual efforts result in performance that is greater than the sum of the individual inputs.

zero-sum approach   An approach that treats the reward "pie" as fixed, such that any gains by one individual are at the expense of another.

Name Index

A

Abosch, Ken, 299
Acohido, B., 413
Aikens, K. A., 675
Akdere, M., 131
Akerson, Dan, 645
Alatorre, Shari, 289
Alberts, J. E. M., 675
Alderman, L., 292
Aldrick, R. J., 395
Allen, Herbert A., 382
Allenmeier, K., 80
Ambady, N., 216
Anderson, C., 486
Anderson, J. R., 55
Andersson, Bo, 547
Andreessen, Marc, 87
Angermeier, I., 63
Angolia, Tad, 246
Annabi, H., 413
Anschutz, Philip, 521
Anseel, F., 663
Ante, S. E., 412
Anthony, Carmelo, 368
Applebaum, B., 630
Appleman, Jack, 398
Aquino, K., 321
Arglye, M., 201
Ariely, Dan, 229, 252
Arkani, S., 131
Asch, Solomon, 322, 323, 335
Ashkanasy, N. M., 521, 593
Asimov, Isaac, 382
Asimov, Janet, 382
Aspinwall, Lisa, 590
Astin, J., 675
Atkins, P. W. B., 675
Austin, E., 155
Avugos, S., 360
Ayoko, O. B., 521, 593
Azar, B., 590

B

Baase, C. M., 675
Back, M. D., 186
Badenhausen, K., 521
Baer, D., 87, 594
Bailey, Adam Leitman, 555
Bailey, F. Lee, 382
Bakker, A. B., 134, 412, 670
Baldridge, D. C., 83
Ballmer, Steve, 534
Baltes, B. B., 625
Balthazard, Michel, 131
Bandura, Albert, 258–259
Barboza, David, 42

Barclay, Kathleen, 645
Bar-Eli, M., 360
Barnes, C. M., 625
Barra, Mary, 510, 645
Barrett, P. M., 460
Barrick, M. R., 423
Bass, B. M., 451
Bauer, Billy, 115
Baumann, A., 112
Bazerman, M. H., 229
Beal, D. J., 663
Beasley, M. A., 216
Beath, C. M., 564
Beer, A., 186
Belkin, L., 134
Bellot, J., 567
Belojevic, G., 201
Benioff, Marc, 116
Benitez, Emilio, 573
Bennett, John, 230
Berg, J. M., 134
Bergeron, D. M., 254
Bergsieker, H. B., 235
Bernard, T. S., 292
Bernerth, J. B., 201
Bernstein, E., 167, 374
Berrien, Jacqueline, 80
Bezos, Jeff, 87, 362, 389
Bialosiewicz, S., 126
Billingsley, Traci, 306–307
Bing, M. N., 176
Binh, Pham Ngoc, 600
Biron, M., 63
Birtel, M. D., 94
Blackman, A., 286
Blakely, Sara, 238
Blanchard, K. H., 451
Blankenship, Mark, 129
Blankfein, Lloyd, 87
Bloodgood, J. M., 191
Blumenthal, Neil, 594
Blythe, J., 112
Bodie, Graham, 389
Bodnar, C. M., 675
Bolino, M. C., 55
Bone, Lucia, 630
Boos, L., 112
Borre, Karen, 164
Borrough, B., 486
Boss, R. W., 63
Boswell, W. R., 587
Bowels, P., 246
Bowerman, Bill, 579
Bradford, E. E. F., 375
Bradley, B. H., 423
Bradsher, K., 74

Braken, K., 80
Branson, Richard, 139–140, 177, 245, 395, 433, 451, 575
Braverman, Amy, 74
Brenninkmeijer, V., 514
Breton, Thierry, 676
Breus, M. J., 667
Bridoux, F., 305
Brinkema, Leonie, 282
Brinkley, Cynthia, 645
Brooke, Beth, 94
Broomfield, J., 94
Brower, H. H., 335
Brown, C. E., 486
Brown, D. J., 167
Browne, John, 93
Brunaert, Didier, 584
Bryant, A., 174, 449, 555
Bryant, Jerald, 82
Buckelew, Alan, 385
Budescu, D. V., 375
Buffett, Warren, 219, 555
Bulkeley, W. M., 85
Burdette, Heather, 112
Burgess, Jill, 599
Burgert, Natasha, 399
Bush, George W., 382

C

Cain, S., 201, 339
Campbell, Justine, 599
Campbell, K., 521
Campbell, W. K., 198
Campion, M. A., 105, 481
Canavan, K., 229
Canino, Robert, 80
Carbee, Marshall, 230
Cardwell, D., 307
Carey, B., 164
Carmichael, M., 191
Carpenter, J., 201
Carr, Evan, 142
Carroll, A. E., 673
Carstensen, Laura, 88
Casmir, Fred, 408
Castro, Fidel, 382
Cavens, Darrell, 307
Chabris, C., 375
Chen, Bocco, 132–133
Chen, B. X., 74
Chen, C., 481
Chen, Y.-P., 55
Cheng, B. H., 663
Chennault, Ken, 546
Cheryan, S., 216
Cheung, R. Y., 164

Organization Index

Subject Index